ANNUAL REVIEW OF PSYCHOLOGY

ANNUAL REVIEW OF PSYCHOLOGY

VOLUME 52, 2001

SUSAN T. FISKE, *Editor*
Princeton University

DANIEL L. SCHACTER, *Associate Editor*
Harvard University

CAROLYN ZAHN-WAXLER, *Associate Editor*
National Institute of Mental Health

www.AnnualReviews.org   science@AnnualReviews.org   650-493-4400

ANNUAL REVIEWS
4139 El Camino Way • P.O. BOX 10139 • Palo Alto, California 94303-0139

ANNUAL REVIEWS
Palo Alto, California, USA

International Standard Serial Number: 0066-4308
International Standard Book Number: 0-8243-0252-4
Library of Congress Catalog Card Number: 50-13143

TYPESET BY TECHBOOKS, FAIRFAX, VA
PRINTED AND BOUND IN THE UNITED STATES OF AMERICA

PREFACE

We shall cope with the information explosion, in the long run, only if some scientists are prepared to commit themselves to the job of sifting, reviewing, and synthesizing information; i.e., to handling information with sophistication and meaning, not merely mechanically. Such scientists must create new science, not just shuffle documents: their activities of reviewing, writing books, criticizing, and synthesizing are as much a part of science as is traditional research. We urge the technical community to accord such individuals that esteem that matches the importance of their job and reward them for their efforts.

(Science, Government, and Information: The Responsibilities of the Technical Community and the Government in the Transfer of Information. A Report of the President's Science Advisory Committee, January 10, 1963.)

Invitations to write an *Annual Review* chapter typically elicit some mix of thrill, dread, pleasure, indecision, burden, intimidation, and challenge—not unlike commencing one's PhD or undertaking a skydive. The free fall is cushioned by a parachute of the scientist's own invention, and that structure prevents the whole domain from rushing by too fast. As noted in the apt opening quotation, passed along by Annual Reviews Editor-in-Chief Sam Gubins, the skilled scholarly reviewer sifts, synthesizes, and criticizes, thereby creating new science. That new psychological science rewards author, editors, colleagues, and other readers. Consequently, the thrill, pleasure, and challenge trump the dread, indecision, burden, and intimidation. Most invitees commit themselves to the job, and the science benefits.

What our authors do for science changes over time. Reviewers search the literature electronically, send drafts by e-mail, and submit final copy as attachments. Most significantly, *Annual Review* chapters are now available on-line, with the mere click of a mouse, doubtless increasing the readership of the reviews. We are grateful to Annual Reviews for keeping up with the latest forms of publishing.

But it would be nothing without authors who handle information with sophistication and meaning, not merely mechanically. Thanks to the authors, the editorial committee who selected them, and our Production Editor who piloted all of us.

Susan T. Fiske, Princeton
Daniel L. Schacter, Cambridge
Carolyn Zahn-Waxler, Bethesda

CONTENTS

RELATED ARTICLES

NOTICE TO READERS

It appears likely that Figure 1 which appears without attribution on page 653 of the *Annual Review of Psychology*, Volume 48, 1997, in "Central Cholinergic Systems and Cognition" by B. J. Everitt and T. W. Robbins, was prepared by an artist who relied in large part on a prior illustration by N. J. Woolf. Dr. Woolf's illustration appeared in several articles which she authored or co-authored and in her 1983 UCLA doctoral thesis, "Projections of the Cholinergic Basal Forebrain and the Cholinergic Pontine Tegmentum." Drs. Everitt and Robbins acknowledge this error of omission and state that it was inadvertent. They apologize to Dr. Woolf.

BOARD OF DIRECTORS
ANNUAL REVIEWS

Albert Bandura

Annu. Rev. Psychol. 2001. 52:1–26

SOCIAL COGNITIVE THEORY: An Agentic Perspective

Albert Bandura

*Department of Psychology, Stanford University, Stanford, California 94305-2131;
e-mail: bandura@psych.stanford.edu*

Key Words biosocial coevolution, collective efficacy, emergent properties, human agency, self-efficacy

■ **Abstract** The capacity to exercise control over the nature and quality of one's life is the essence of humanness. Human agency is characterized by a number of core features that operate through phenomenal and functional consciousness. These include the temporal extension of agency through intentionality and forethought, self-regulation by self-reactive influence, and self-reflectiveness about one's capabilities, quality of functioning, and the meaning and purpose of one's life pursuits. Personal agency operates within a broad network of sociostructural influences. In these agentic transactions, people are producers as well as products of social systems. Social cognitive theory distinguishes among three modes of agency: direct personal agency, proxy agency that relies on others to act on one's behest to secure desired outcomes, and collective agency exercised through socially coordinative and interdependent effort. Growing transnational embeddedness and interdependence are placing a premium on collective efficacy to exercise control over personal destinies and national life.

CONTENTS

INTRODUCTION

To be an agent is to intentionally make things happen by one's actions. Agency embodies the endowments, belief systems, self-regulatory capabilities and distributed structures and functions through which personal influence exercised, rather than residing as a discrete entity in a particular place. The core features of agency enable people to play a part in their self-development, adaptation, and self-renewal with changing times. Before presenting the agentic perspective of social cognitive theory, the paradigm shifts that the field of psychology has undergone in its short history warrant a brief discussion. In these theoretical transformations, the core metaphors have changed but for the most part, the theories grant humans little, if any, agentic capabilities.

PARADIGM SHIFTS IN PSYCHOLOGICAL THEORIZING

Much of the early psychological theorizing was founded on behavioristic principles that embraced an input-output model linked by an internal conduit that makes behavior possible but exerts no influence of its own on behavior. In this view, human behavior was shaped and controlled automatically and mechanically by environmental stimuli. This line of theorizing was eventually put out of vogue by the advent of the computer, which likened the mind to a biological calculator. This model filled the internal conduit with a lot of representational and computational operations created by smart and inventive thinkers.

If computers can perform cognitive operations that solve problems, regulative thought could no longer be denied to humans. The input-output model was supplanted by an input-linear throughput-output model. The mind as digital computer became the conceptual model for the times. Although the mindless organism became a more cognitive one, it was still devoid of consciousness and agentic capabilities. For decades, the reigning computer metaphor of human functioning was a linear computational system in which information is fed through a central processor that cranks out solutions according to preordained rules. The architecture of the linear computer at the time dictated the conceptual model of human functioning.

The linear model was, in turn, supplanted by more dynamically organized computational models that perform multiple operations simultaneously and interactively to mimic better how the human brain works. In this model, environmental input activates a multifaceted dynamic throughput that produces the output. These dynamic models include multilevel neural networks with intentional functions lodged in a subpersonal executive network operating without any consciousness via lower subsystems. Sensory organs deliver up information to a neural network acting as the mental machinery that does the construing, planning, motivating, and regulating nonconsciously. Harré (1983) notes in his analysis of computationalism that it is not people but their componentized subpersonal parts that are orchestrating the courses of action. The personal level involves phenomenal consciousness and the purposive use of information and self-regulative means to make desired things happen.

Consciousness is the very substance of mental life that not only makes life personally manageable but worth living. A functional consciousness involves purposive accessing and deliberative processing of information for selecting, constructing, regulating, and evaluating courses of action. This is achieved through intentional mobilization and productive use of semantic and pragmatic representations of activities, goals, and other future events. In his discerning book on experienced cognition, Carlson (1997) underscores the central role that consciousness plays in the cognitive regulation of action and the flow of mental events. There have been some attempts to reduce consciousness to an epiphenomenal by-product of activities at the subpersonal level, to an executive subsystem in the information processing machinery, or to an attentional aspect of information processing. Like the legendary ponderous elephant that goes unnoticed, in these subpersonal accounts of consciousness there is no experiencing person conceiving of ends and acting purposefully to attain them. However, these reductive accounts remain conceptually problematic because they omit prime features of humanness such as subjectivity, deliberative self-guidance, and reflective self-reactiveness. For reasons to be given shortly, consciousness cannot be reduced to a nonfunctional by-product of the output of a mental process realized mechanically at nonconscious lower levels. Why would an epiphenomenal consciousness that can do nothing evolve and endure as a reigning psychic environment in people's lives? Without a phenomenal and functional consciousness people are essentially higher-level automatons undergoing actions devoid of any subjectivity or conscious control. Nor do such beings possess a meaningful phenomenal life or a continuing self-identity derived from how they live their life and reflect upon it.

Green & Vervaeke (1996) observed that originally many connectionists and computationalists regarded their conceptual models as approximations of cognitive activities. More recently, however, some have become eliminative materialists, likening cognitive factors to the phlogiston of yesteryear. In this view, people do not act on beliefs, goals, aspirations, and expectations. Rather, activation of their network structure at a subpersonal level makes them do things. In a critique of eliminativism, Greenwood (1992) notes that cognitions are contentful psychological factors whose meaning does not depend on the explanatory propositions in which they figure. Phlogiston neither had any evidential basis nor explanatory or predictive value. In contrast, cognitive factors do quite well in predicting human behavior and guiding effective interventions. To make their way successfully through a complex world full of challenges and hazards, people have to make good judgments about their capabilities, anticipate the probable effects of different events and courses of action, size up sociostructural opportunities and constraints, and regulate their behavior accordingly. These belief systems are a working model of the world that enables people to achieve desired outcomes and avoid untoward ones. Forethoughtful, generative, and reflective capabilities are, therefore, vital for survival and human progress. Agentic factors that are explanatory, predictive, and of demonstrated functional value may be translatable and modeled in another theoretical language but not eliminatable (Rottschaefer 1985, 1991).

PHYSICALISTIC THEORY OF HUMAN AGENCY

As has already been noted, people are not just onlooking hosts of internal mechanisms orchestrated by environmental events. They are agents of experiences rather than simply undergoers of experiences. The sensory, motor, and cerebral systems are tools people use to accomplish the tasks and goals that give meaning, direction, and satisfaction to their lives (Bandura 1997, Harré & Gillet 1994).

Research on brain development underscores the influential role that agentic action plays in shaping the neuronal and functional structure of the brain (Diamond 1988, Kolb & Whishaw 1998). It is not just exposure to stimulation, but agentic action in exploring, manipulating, and influencing the environment that counts. By regulating their motivation and activities, people produce the experiences that form the functional neurobiological substrate of symbolic, social, psychomotor, and other skills. The nature of these experiences is, of course, heavily dependent on the types of social and physical environments people select and construct. An agentic perspective fosters lines of research that provide new insights into the social construction of the functional structure of the human brain (Eisenberg 1995). This is a realm of inquiry in which psychology can make fundamental unique contributions to the biopsychosocial understanding of human development, adaptation, and change.

Social cognitive theory subscribes to a model of emergent interactive agency (Bandura 1986, 1999a). Thoughts are not disembodied, immaterial entities that exist apart from neural events. Cognitive processes are emergent brain activities that exert determinative influence. Emergent properties differ qualitatively from their constituent elements and therefore are not reducible to them. To use Bunge's (1977) analogy, the unique emergent properties of water, such as fluidity, viscosity, and transparency are not simply the aggregate properties of its microcomponents of oxygen and hydrogen. Through their interactive effects they are transformed into new phenomena.

One must distinguish between the physical basis of thought and its deliberative construction and functional use. The human mind is generative, creative, proactive, and reflective, not just reactive. The dignified burial of the dualistic Descartes forces us to address the formidable explanatory challenge for a physicalistic theory of human agency and a nondualistic cognitivism. How do people operate as thinkers of the thoughts that exert determinative influence on their actions? What are the functional circuitries of forethought, planful proaction, aspiration, self-appraisal, and self-reflection? Even more important, how are they intentionally recruited?

Cognitive agents regulate their actions by cognitive downward causation as well as undergo upward activation by sensory stimulation (Sperry 1993). People can designedly conceive unique events and different novel courses of action and choose to execute one of them. Under the indefinite prompt to concoct something new, for example, one can deliberatively construct a whimsically novel scenario of a graceful hippopotamus attired in a chartreuse tuxedo hang gliding over lunar craters while singing the mad scene from the opera *Lucia di Lammermoor*. Intentionality and agency raise the fundamental question of how people bring about activities over which they command personal control that activate the subpersonal neurophysiological events for realizing particular intentions and aspirations. Thus, in acting on the well-grounded belief that exercise enhances health, individuals get themselves to perform physical activities that produce health promotive biological events without observing or knowing how the activated events work at the subpersonal level. The health outcome is the product of both agent causality and event causality, operating at different phases of the sequence.

Our psychological discipline is proceeding down two major divergent routes. One line of theorizing seeks to clarify the basic mechanisms governing human functioning. This line of inquiry centers heavily on microanalyses of the inner workings of the mind in processing, representing, retrieving, and using the coded information to manage various task demands, and locating where the brain activity for these events occurs. These cognitive processes are generally studied disembodied from interpersonal life, purposeful pursuits, and self-reflectiveness. People are sentient, purposive beings. Faced with prescribed task demands, they act mindfully to make desired things happen rather than simply undergo happenings in which situational forces activate their subpersonal structures that generate solutions. In experimental situations, participants try to figure out what is wanted of them; they construct hypotheses and reflectively test their adequacy by evaluating the results of their actions; they set personal goals and otherwise motivate themselves to perform in ways that please or impress others or bring self-satisfaction; when they run into trouble they engage in self-enabling or self-debilitating self-talk; if they construe their failures as presenting surmountable challenges they redouble their efforts, but they drive themselves to despondency if they read their failures as indicants of personal deficiencies; if they believe they are being exploited, coerced, disrespected, or manipulated, they respond apathetically, oppositionally, or hostilely. These motivational and other self-regulative factors that govern the manner and level of personal engagement in prescribed activities are simply taken for granted in cognitive science rather than included in causal structures (Carlson 1997).

The second line of theorizing centers on the macroanalytic workings of socially situated factors in human development, adaptation, and change. Within this theoretical framework, human functioning is analyzed as socially interdependent, richly contextualized, and conditionally orchestrated within the dynamics of various societal subsystems and their complex interplay. The mechanisms linking sociostructural factors to action in this macroanalytic approach are left largely unexplained, however. A comprehensive theory must merge the analytic dualism by integrating personal and social foci of causation within a unified causal structure.

In the paths of influence, sociostructural influences operate through psychological mechanisms to produce behavioral effects. We shall return later to this issue and to the bidirectionality of influence between social structure and personal agency.

CORE FEATURES OF HUMAN AGENCY

The core features of personal agency address the issue of what it means to be human. The main agentic features are discussed in the sections that follow.

Intentionality

Agency refers to acts done intentionally. For example, a person who smashed a vase in an antique shop upon being tripped by another shopper would not be considered the agent of the event. Human transactions, of course, involve situational inducements, but they do not operate as determinate forces. Individuals can choose to behave accommodatively or, through the exercise of self-influence, to behave otherwise. An intention is a representation of a future course of action to be performed. It is not simply an expectation or prediction of future actions but a proactive commitment to bringing them about. Intentions and actions are different aspects of a functional relation separated in time. It is, therefore, meaningful to speak of intentions grounded in self-motivators affecting the likelihood of actions at a future point in time.

Planning agency can be used to produce different outcomes. Outcomes are not the characteristics of agentive acts; they are the consequences of them. As Davidson (1971) explains, actions intended to serve a certain purpose can cause quite different things to happen. He cites the example of the melancholic Hamlet, who intentionally stabbed the man behind a tapestry believing it to be the king, only to discover, much to his horror, that he had killed Polonius. The killing of the hidden person was intentional, but the wrong victim was done in. Some of the actions performed in the belief that they will bring desired outcomes actually produce outcomes that were neither intended nor wanted. For example, it is not uncommon for individuals to contribute to their own misery through intentional transgressive acts spawned by gross miscalculation of consequences. Some social policies and practices originally designed with well-meaning intent turn out bad because their harmful effects were unforeseen. In short, the power to originate actions for given purposes is the key feature of personal agency. Whether the exercise of that agency has beneficial or detrimental effects, or produces unintended consequences, is another matter.

Intentions center on plans of action. Future-directed plans are rarely specified in full detail at the outset. It would require omniscience to anticipate every situational detail. Moreover, turning visualized futurities into reality requires proximal or present-directed intentions that guide and keep one moving ahead (Bandura 1991b). In the functionalist approach to intentional agency enunciated by Bratman (1999), initial partial intentions are filled in and adjusted, revised, refined or even reconsidered in the face of new information during execution of an intention. We shall see shortly, however, that realization of forward looking plans requires more than an intentional state because it is not causally sufficient by itself. Other self-regulatory aspects of agency enter into the successful implementation of intentions. To add a further functional dimension to intention, most human pursuits involve other participating agents. Such joint activities require commitment to a shared intention and coordination of interdependent plans of action. The challenge in collaborative activities is to meld diverse self-interests in the service of common goals and intentions collectively pursued in concert.

Forethought

The temporal extension of agency goes beyond forward-directed planning. The future time perspective manifests itself in many different ways. People set goals for themselves, anticipate the likely consequences of prospective actions, and select and create courses of action likely to produce desired outcomes and avoid detrimental ones (Bandura 1991b, Feather 1982, Locke & Latham 1990). Through the exercise of forethought, people motivate themselves and guide their actions in anticipation of future events. When projected over a long time course on matters of value, a forethoughtful perspective provides direction, coherence, and meaning to one's life. As people progress in their life course they continue to plan ahead, reorder their priorities, and structure their lives accordingly.

Future events cannot, of course, be causes of current motivation and action because they have no actual existence. However, by being represented cognitively in the present, foreseeable future events are converted into current motivators and regulators of behavior. In this form of anticipatory self-guidance, behavior is motivated and directed by projected goals and anticipated outcomes rather than being pulled by an unrealized future state.

People construct outcome expectations from observed conditional relations between environmental events in the world around them, and the outcomes given actions produce (Bandura 1986). The ability to bring anticipated outcomes to bear on current activities promotes foresightful behavior. It enables people to transcend the dictates of their immediate environment and to shape and regulate the present to fit a desired future. In regulating their behavior by outcome expectations, people adopt courses of action that are likely to produce positive outcomes and generally discard those that bring unrewarding or punishing outcomes. However, anticipated material and social outcomes are not the only kind of incentives that influence human behavior, as a crude functionalism would suggest. If actions were performed only on behalf of anticipated external rewards and punishments, people would behave like weather vanes, constantly shifting direction to conform to whatever influence happened to impinge upon them at the moment. In actuality, people display considerable self-direction in the face of competing influences. After they adopt personal standards, people regulate their behavior by self-evaluative outcomes, which may augment or override the influence of external outcomes.

Self-Reactiveness

An agent has to be not only a planner and forethinker, but a motivator and self-regulator as well. Having adopted an intention and an action plan, one cannot simply sit back and wait for the appropriate performances to appear. Agency thus involves not only the deliberative ability to make choices and action plans, but the ability to give shape to appropriate courses of action and to motivate and regulate their execution. This multifaceted self-directedness operates through self-regulatory processes that link thought to action. The self-regulation of motivation, affect, and action is governed by a set of self-referent subfunctions. These include self-monitoring, performance self-guidance via personal standards, and corrective self-reactions (Bandura 1986, 1991b).

Monitoring one's pattern of behavior and the cognitive and environmental conditions under which it occurs is the first step toward doing something to affect it. Actions give rise to self-reactive influence through performance comparison with personal goals and standards. Goals, rooted in a value system and a sense of personal identity, invest activities with meaning and purpose. Goals motivate by enlisting self-evaluative engagement in activities rather than directly. By making self-evaluation conditional on matching personal standards, people give direction to their pursuits and create self-incentives to sustain their efforts for goal attainment. They do things that give them self-satisfaction and a sense of pride and self-worth, and refrain from behaving in ways that give rise to self-dissatisfaction, self-devaluation, and self-censure.

Goals do not automatically activate the self-influences that govern motivation and action. Evaluative self-engagement through goal setting is affected by the characteristics of goals, namely, their specificity, level of challenge and temporal proximity. General goals are too indefinite and noncommitting to serve as guides and incentives. Strong interest and engrossment in activities is sparked by challenging goals. The self-regulative effectiveness of goals depends greatly on how far into the future they are projected. Proximal subgoals mobilize self-influences and direct what one does in the here and now. Distal goals alone set the general course of pursuits but are too far removed in time to provide effective incentives and guides for present action, given inviting competing activities at hand. Progress toward valued futures is best achieved by hierarchically structured goal systems combining distal aspirations with proximal self-guidance. Goals embodying self-engaging properties serve as powerful motivators of action (Bandura 1991b, Locke & Latham 1990).

Moral agency forms an important part of self-directedness. Psychological theories of morality focus heavily on moral reasoning to the neglect of moral conduct. A complete theory of moral agency must link moral knowledge and reasoning to moral conduct. This requires an agentic theory of morality rather than one confined mainly to cognitions about morality. Moral reasoning is translated into actions through self-regulatory mechanisms, which include moral judgment of the rightness or wrongness of conduct evaluated against personal standards and situational circumstances, and self-sanctions by which moral agency is exercised (Bandura 1991a).

In competency development and aspirational pursuits, the personal standards of merit are progressively raised as knowledge and competencies are expanded and challenges are met. In social and moral conduct, the self-regulatory standards are more stable. People do not change from week to week what they regard as right or wrong or good or bad. After people adopt a standard of morality, their negative self-sanctions for actions that violate their personal standards, and their positive self-sanctions for conduct faithful to their moral standards serve as the regulatory influences (Bandura 1991b). The capacity for self-sanctions gives meaning to moral agency. The anticipatory evaluative self-reactions provide the motivational as well as the cognitive regulators of moral conduct. Self-sanctions keep conduct in line with personal standards. Individuals with a strong communal ethic will act to further the welfare of others even at costs to their self-interest. In the face of situational pressures to behave inhumanely, people can choose to behave otherwise by exerting counteracting self-influence. It is not uncommon for individuals to invest their self-worth so strongly in certain convictions that they will submit to harsh and punitive treatment rather than cede to what they regard as unjust or immoral.

The exercise of moral agency has dual aspects—inhibitive and proactive (Bandura 1999b). The inhibitive form is manifested in the power to refrain from behaving inhumanely. The proactive form of morality is expressed in the power to behave humanely.

Moral standards do not function as fixed internal regulators of conduct, however. Self-regulatory mechanisms do not operate unless they are enlisted in given activities. There are many psychosocial maneuvers by which moral self-reactions can be selectively disengaged from inhumane conduct (Bandura 1991b). Several of these mechanisms of moral disengagement center on the cognitive reconstrual of the conduct itself. This is achieved by making harmful conduct personally and socially acceptable by portraying it as serving socially worthy or moral purposes, masking it in sanitizing euphemistic language, and creating exonerating comparison with worse inhumanities. Other mechanisms reduce the sense of personal agency for harmful conduct through diffusion and displacement of responsibility. Moral self-sanctions are also weakened or disengaged at the outcome locus of the control process by ignoring, minimizing, or disputing the injurious effects of one's conduct. The final set of practices disengage restraining self-sanctions by dehumanizing the victims, attributing bestial qualities to them, and blaming them for bringing the suffering on themselves. High moral disengagers experience low guilt over harmful conduct, are less prosocial, and are more prone to vengeful rumination (Bandura et al 1996b). Through selective disengagement of moral agency, people who otherwise behave righteously and considerately perpetrate transgressions and inhumanities in other spheres of their lives (Bandura 1999b, Zimbardo 1995).

Self-Reflectiveness

People are not only agents of action but self-examiners of their own functioning. The metacognitive capability to reflect upon oneself and the adequacy of one's thoughts and actions is another distinctly core human feature of agency. Through reflective self-consciousness, people evaluate their motivation, values, and the meaning of their life pursuits. It is at this higher level of self-reflectiveness that individuals address conflicts in motivational inducements and choose to act in favor of one over another. Verification of the soundness of one's thinking also relies heavily on self-reflective means (Bandura 1986). In this metacognitive activity, people judge the correctness of their predictive and operative thinking against the outcomes of their actions, the effects that other people's actions produce, what others believe, deductions from established knowledge and what necessarily follows from it.

Among the mechanisms of personal agency, none is more central or pervasive than people's beliefs in their capability to exercise some measure of control over their own functioning and over environmental events (Bandura 1997). Efficacy beliefs are the foundation of human agency. Unless people believe they can produce desired results and forestall detrimental ones by their actions, they have little incentive to act or to persevere in the face of difficulties. Whatever other factors may operate as guides and motivators, they are rooted in the core belief that one has the power to produce effects by one's actions. Meta-analyses attest to the influential role played by efficacy beliefs in human functioning (Holden 1991, Holden et al 1990, Multon et al 1991, Stajkovic & Luthans 1998).

Perceived self-efficacy occupies a pivotal role in the causal structure of social cognitive theory because efficacy beliefs affect adaptation and change not only in their own right, but through their impact on other determinants (Bandura 1997, Maddux 1995; Schwarzer 1992). Such beliefs influence whether people think pessimistically or optimistically and in ways that are self-enhancing or self-hindering. Efficacy beliefs play a central role in the self-regulation of motivation through goal challenges and outcome expectations. It is partly on the basis of efficacy beliefs that people choose what challenges to undertake, how much effort to expend in the endeavor, how long to persevere in the face of obstacles and failures, and whether failures are motivating or demoralizing. The likelihood that people will act on the outcomes they expect prospective performances to produce depends on their beliefs about whether or not they can produce those performances. A strong sense of coping efficacy reduces vulnerability to stress and depression in taxing situations and strengthens resiliency to adversity.

Efficacy beliefs also play a key role in shaping the courses lives take by influencing the types of activities and environments people choose to get into. Any factor that influences choice behavior can profoundly affect the direction of personal development. This is because the social influences operating in selected environments continue to promote certain competencies, values, and interests long after the decisional determinant has rendered its inaugurating effect. Thus, by choosing and shaping their environments, people can have a hand in what they become.

The rapid pace of informational, social, and technological change is placing a premium on personal efficacy for self-development and self-renewal throughout the life course. In the past, students' educational development was largely determined by the schools to which they were assigned. Nowadays, the Internet provides vast opportunities for students to control their own learning. They now have the best libraries, museums, laboratories, and instructors at their fingertips, unrestricted by time and place. Good self-regulators expand their knowledge and cognitive competencies; poor self-regulators fall behind (Zimmerman 1990).

Self-regulation is also becoming a key factor in occupational life. In the past, employees learned a given trade and performed it much the same way and in the same organization throughout their lifetime. With the fast pace of change, knowledge and technical skills are quickly outmoded unless they are updated to fit the new technologies. In the modern workplace, workers have to take charge of their self-development for a variety of positions and careers over the full course of their worklife. They have to cultivate multiple competencies to meet the ever-changing occupational demands and roles. Collective agentic adaptability applies at the organizational level as well as the workforce level. Organizations have to be fast learners and continuously innovative to survive and prosper under rapidly changing technologies and global marketplaces. They face the paradox of preparing for change at the height of success. Slow changers become big losers.

Health illustrates self-regulation in another important sphere of life. In recent years, there has been a major change in the conception of health from a disease model to a health model. Human health is heavily influenced by lifestyle habits and environmental conditions. This enables people to exercise some measure of control over their health status. Indeed, through self-management of health habits people reduce major health risks and live healthier and more productive lives (Bandura 1997). If the huge health benefits of these few lifestyle habits were put into a pill, it would be declared a spectacular breakthrough in the field of medicine.

AGENTIC MANAGEMENT OF FORTUITY

There is much that people do designedly to exercise some measure of control over their self-development and life circumstances, but there is also a lot of fortuity in the courses lives take. Indeed, some of the most important determinants of life paths occur through the most trivial of circumstances. People are often inaugurated into new developmental trajectories, marital partnerships, occupational careers, or untoward life paths through fortuitous circumstances. Consider the influence of fortuitous events in the formation of marital partnerships. A flight delayed by an unexpected storm creates a fortuitous encounter by two people who find themselves seated next to each other at the airport waiting for the weather to clear. This chance happening eventuates in a marriage, geographic relocation, and a shift in career trajectories, none of which would have occurred if the original flight had not been grounded by a sudden storm (Krantz 1998). A book editor enters a lecture hall as it was rapidly filling up, for a talk on the "Psychology of Chance Encounters and Life Paths." He seizes an empty chair near the entrance. Some months later, he marries the woman he happened to sit next to. With only a momentary change in entry, seating constellations would have altered, and their lives would have taken quite different courses. A marital partnership was formed fortuitously at a talk devoted to fortuitous determinants of life paths (Bandura 1982)!

A fortuitous event in socially mediated happenstances is defined as an unintended meeting of persons unfamiliar with each other. Although the separate chains of events in a chance encounter have their own determinants, their intersection occurs fortuitously rather than by design (Nagel 1961). It is not that a fortuitous event is uncaused but, rather, there is a lot of randomness to the determining conditions of its intersection. Of the myriad fortuitous elements encountered in everyday life, many of them touch people only lightly, others leave more lasting effects, and still others thrust people into new life trajectories. The power of most fortuitous influences lies not so much in the properties of the events themselves, but in the constellation of transactional influences they set in motion (Bandura 1982, 1998). On the personal side, people's attributes, belief systems, interests, and competencies influence whether or not a given chance encounter gets converted into a lasting relationship. On the social side, the impact of fortuitous encounters partly depends on the holding and molding power of the social milieus into which people are fortuitously inaugurated.

Fortuity does not mean uncontrollability of its effects. There are ways people can capitalize on the fortuitous character of life. They can make chance happen by pursuing an active life that increases the level and type of fortuitous encounters they will experience. Chance favors the inquisitive and venturesome who go places, do things, and explore new activities (Austin 1978). People also make chance work for them by cultivating their interests, enabling self-beliefs and competencies. These personal resources enable them to make the most of opportunities that arise unexpectedly from time to time. Pasteur (1854) put it well when he noted that "chance favors only the prepared mind." Self-development gives people a greater hand in shaping their destiny in the life paths they travel. These various proactive activities illustrate the agentic management of fortuity.

Fortuitous factors receive little notice in causal analyses of developmental trajectories, but they figure prominently in prescriptions for realizing valued futures and safeguarding against detrimental ones (Bandura 1995, 1997; Hamburg 1992; Masten et al 1990; Rutter 1990). On the self-development side, the efforts center on cultivating personal resources that enable individuals to exploit promising fortuities. On the safeguarding side, individuals are helped to expand the self-regulative capabilities that enable them to resist fortuitous social traps leading down detrimental paths, and to extricate themselves from such predicaments should they become enmeshed in them.

MODES OF HUMAN AGENCY

Theorizing and research on human agency has been essentially confined to personal agency exercised individually. However, this is not the only way in which people bring their influence to bear on events that affect how they live their lives. Social cognitive theory distinguishes among three different modes of human agency: personal, proxy, and collective.

The preceding analyses centered on the nature of direct personal agency and the cognitive, motivational, affective, and choice processes through which it is exercised to produce given effects. In many spheres of functioning, people do not have direct control over the social conditions and institutional practices that affect their everyday lives. Under these circumstances, they seek their well-being, security, and valued outcomes through the exercise of proxy agency. In this socially mediated mode of agency, people try by one means or another to get those who have access to resources or expertise or who wield influence and power to act at their behest to secure the outcomes they desire. No one has the time, energy, and resources to master every realm of everyday life. Successful functioning necessarily involves a blend of reliance on proxy agency in some areas of functioning to free time and effort to manage directly other aspects of one's life (Baltes 1996, Brandtstädter 1992). For example, children turn to parents, marital partners to spouses, and citizens to their legislative representatives to act for them. Proxy agency relies heavily on perceived social efficacy for enlisting the mediative efforts of others.

People also turn to proxy control in areas in which they can exert direct influence when they have not developed the means to do so, they believe others can do it better, or they do not want to saddle themselves with the burdensome aspects that direct control entails. Personal control is neither an inherent drive nor universally desired, as is commonly claimed. There is an onerous side to direct personal control that can dull the appetite for it. The exercise of effective control requires mastery of knowledge and skills attainable only through long hours of arduous work. Moreover, maintaining proficiency under the ever-changing conditions of life demands continued investment of time, effort, and resources in self-renewal.

In addition to the hard work of continual self-development, the exercise of personal control often carries heavy responsibilities, stressors, and risks. People are not especially eager to shoulder the burdens of responsibility. All too often, they surrender control to intermediaries in activities over which they can command direct influence. They do so to free themselves of the performance demands and onerous responsibilities that personal control entails. Proxy agency can be used in ways that promote self-development or impede the cultivation of personal competencies. In the latter case, part of the price of proxy agency is a vulnerable security that rests on the competence, power, and favors of others.

People do not live their lives in isolation. Many of the things they seek are achievable only through socially interdependent effort. Hence, they have to work in coordination with others to secure what they cannot accomplish on their own.

Social cognitive theory extends the conception of human agency to collective agency (Bandura 1997). People's shared belief in their collective power to produce desired results is a key ingredient of collective agency. Group attainments are the product not only of the shared intentions, knowledge, and skills of its members, but also of the interactive, coordinated, and synergistic dynamics of their transactions. Because the collective performance of a social system involves transactional dynamics, perceived collective efficacy is an emergent group-level property, not simply the sum of the efficacy beliefs of individual members. However, there is no emergent entity that operates independently of the beliefs and actions of the individuals who make up a social system. It is people acting conjointly on a shared belief, not a disembodied group mind that is doing the cognizing, aspiring, motivating, and regulating. Beliefs of collective efficacy serve functions similar to those of personal efficacy beliefs and operate through similar processes (Bandura 1997).

Evidence from diverse lines of research attests to the impact of perceived collective efficacy on group functioning (Bandura 2000). Some of these studies have assessed the effects of perceived collective efficacy instilled experimentally to differential levels. Other studies have examined the effects of naturally developed beliefs of collective efficacy on the functioning of diverse social systems, including educational systems, business organizations, athletic teams, combat teams, urban neighborhoods, and political action groups. The findings taken as a whole show that the stronger the perceived collective efficacy, the higher the groups' aspirations and motivational investment in their undertakings, the stronger their staying power in the face of impediments and setbacks, the higher their morale and resilience to stressors, and the greater their performance accomplishments.

Theorizing about human agency and collectivities is replete with contentious dualisms that social cognitive theory rejects. These dualities include personal agency versus social structure, self-centered agency versus communality, and individualism verses collectivism. The agency-sociostructural duality pits psychological theories and sociostructural theories as rival conceptions of human behavior or as representing different levels and temporal proximity of causation. Human functioning is rooted in social systems. Therefore, personal agency operates within a broad network of sociostructural influences. For the most part, social structures represent authorized systems of rules, social practices, and sanctions designed to regulate human affairs. These sociostructural functions are carried out by human beings occupying authorized roles (Giddens 1984).

Within the rule structures of social systems, there is a lot of personal variation in their interpretation, enforcement, adoption, circumvention, and even active opposition (Burns & Dietz 2000). These transactions do not involve a duality between a reified social structure disembodied from people and personal agency, but a dynamic interplay between individuals and those who preside over the institutionalized operations of social systems. Social cognitive theory explains human functioning in terms of triadic reciprocal causation (Bandura 1986). In this model of reciprocal causality, internal personal factors in the form of cognitive, affective, and biological events, behavioral patterns, and environmental influences all operate as interacting determinants that influence one another bidirectionally. The environment is not a monolithic entity. Social cognitive theory distinguishes between three types of environmental structures (Bandura 1997). They include the imposed environment, selected environment, and constructed environment. These different environmental structures represent gradations of changeability requiring the exercise of differing scope and focus of personal agency.

In social cognitive theory, sociostructural factors operate through psychological mechanisms of the self system to produce behavioral effects. Thus, for example, economic conditions, socioeconomic status, and educational and family structures affect behavior largely through their impact on people's aspirations, sense of efficacy, personal standards, affective states, and other self-regulatory influences, rather than directly (Baldwin et al 1989; Bandura 1993; Bandura et al 1996a, 2000a; Elder & Ardelt 1992). Nor can sociostructural and psychological determinants be dichotomized neatly into remote and proximate influences. Poverty, indexed as low socioeconomic status, is not a matter of multilayered or distal causation. Lacking the money to provide for the subsistence of one's family impinges pervasively on everyday life in a very proximal way. Multicausality involves codetermination of behavior by different sources of influence, not causal dependencies between levels.

The self system is not merely a conduit for sociostructural influences. Although the self is socially constituted, by exercising self-influence human agents operate generatively and proactively, not just reactively, to shape the character of their social systems. In these agentic transactions, people are producers as well as products of social systems. Personal agency and social structure operate interdependently. Social structures are created by human activity, and sociostructural practices, in turn, impose constraints and provide enabling resources and opportunity structures for personal development and functioning.

Another disputable duality inappropriately equates self-efficacy with self-centered individualism feeding selfishness, and then pits it against communal attachments and civic responsibility. A sense of efficacy does not necessarily exalt the self or spawn an individualistic lifestyle, identity, or morality that slights collective welfare. Through unwavering exercise of commanding self-efficacy, Gandhi mobilized a massive collective force that brought about major sociopolitical changes. He lived ascetically, not self-indulgently. If belief in the power to produce results is put in the service of relational goals and beneficial social purposes, it fosters a communal life rather than eroding it. Indeed, developmental studies show that a high sense of efficacy promotes a prosocial orientation characterized by cooperativeness, helpfulness, and sharing, with a vested interest in each other's welfare (Bandura et al 1996a, Bandura et al 1999, 2000b).

Another dualistic antithesis inappropriately equates self-efficacy with individualism and pits it against collectivism at a cultural level (Schooler 1990). Cultures are not static monolithic entities, as the stereotypic portrayals would lead one to believe. These global cultural classifications mask intracultural diversity as well as the many commonalities among people of different cultural backgrounds. Both individualistic and collectivistic sociocultural systems come in a variety of forms (Kim et al 1994). There is substantial generational and socioeconomic heterogeneity in communality among individuals in different cultural systems, and even greater intraindividual variation across social relationships with family members, friends, and colleagues (Matsumoto et al 1996). Moreover, people express their cultural orientations conditionally rather than invariantly, behaving communally under some incentive structures and individualistically under others (Yamagishi 1988). Bicultural contrasts, in which individuals from a single collectivistic locale are compared on global indices to individuals from a single individualistic one, can spawn a lot of misleading generalizations.

If people are to pool their resources and work together successfully, the members of a group have to perform their roles and coordinated activities with a high sense of efficacy. One cannot achieve an efficacious collectivity with members who approach life consumed by nagging self-doubts about their ability to succeed and their staying power in the face of difficulties. Personal efficacy is valued, not because of reverence for individualism, but because a strong sense of efficacy is vital for successful functioning regardless of whether it is achieved individually or by group members working together. Indeed, a strong sense of personal efficacy to manage one's life circumstances and to have a hand in effecting societal changes contributes substantially to perceived collective efficacy (Fernández-Ballesteros et al 2000).

Cross-cultural research attests to the general functional value of efficacy beliefs. Perceived personal efficacy contributes to productive functioning by members of collectivistic cultures just as it does to functioning by people raised in individualistic cultures (Earley 1993, 1994). However, cultural embeddedness shapes the ways in which efficacy beliefs are developed, the purposes to which they are put, and the sociostructural arrangements through which they are best exercised. People from individualistic cultures feel most efficacious and perform best under an individually oriented system, whereas those from collectivistic cultures judge themselves most efficacious and work most productively under a group-oriented system. A low sense of coping efficacy is as stressful in collectivisitic cultures as in individualistic ones (Matsui & Onglatco 1991).

There are collectivists in individualistic cultures and individualists in collectivistic cultures. Regardless of cultural background, people achieve the greatest personal efficacy and productivity when their psychological orientation is congruent with the structure of the social system (Earley 1994). Both at the societal and individual level of analysis, a strong perceived efficacy fosters high group effort and performance attainments.

Cultures are no longer insular. Transnational interdependencies and global economic forces are weakening social and cultural normative systems, restructuring national economies and shaping the political and social life of societies (Keohane 1993, Keohane & Nye 1977). Social bonds and communal commitments that lack marketability are especially vulnerable to erosion by global market forces unfettered by social obligation. Because of extensive global interconnectedness, what happens economically and politically in one part of the world can affect the welfare of vast populations elsewhere. Moreover, advanced telecommunications technologies are disseminating ideas, values and styles of behavior transnationally at an unprecedented rate. The symbolic environment feeding off communication satellites is altering national cultures and homogenizing collective consciousness. With further development of the cyberworld, people will be even more heavily embedded in global symbolic environments. In addition, mass migrations of people are changing cultural landscapes. This growing ethnic diversity accords functional value to bicultural efficacy to navigate the demands of both one's ethnic subculture and that of the larger society.

These new realities call for broadening the scope of cross-cultural analyses beyond the focus on the social forces operating within the boundaries of given societies to the forces impinging upon them from abroad. With growing international embeddedness and interdependence of societies, and enmeshment in the Internet symbolic culture, the issues of interest center on how national and global forces interact to shape the nature of cultural life. As globalization reaches ever deeper into people's lives, a strong sense of collective efficacy to make transnational systems work for them becomes critical to furthering their common interests.

UNDERMINERS OF COLLECTIVE EFFICACY
IN CHANGING SOCIETIES

The revolutionary advances in electronic technologies have transformed the nature, reach, and loci of human influence. These new social realities provide vast opportunities for people to bring their influence to bear on their personal development and to shape their social future. However, many of the contemporary conditions of life undermine the development and maintenance of collective efficacy. Distal transnational influences have wide-ranging consequential local effects on people's lives. These transnational forces are hard to disentangle, let alone control. They challenge the efficacy of governmental systems to exert a determining influence on their own economic and national life. As the need for efficacious collective civic action grows, so does the sense of collective powerlessness. Under the new realities of growing transnational control, nation states increase their controlling leverage by merging into larger regional units such as the European Union. However, these regional marriages do not come without a price. Paradoxically, to gain international control, nations have to negotiate reciprocal pacts that require some loss of national autonomy and changes in traditional ways of life (Keohane 1993).

Everyday life is increasingly regulated by complex technologies that most people neither understand nor believe they can do much to influence. The very technologies they create to control their life environment paradoxically can become a constraining force that, in turn, controls how they think and behave. The social machinery of society is no less challenging. The beneficiaries of existing sociostructural practices wield their influence to maintain their vested interests. Long delays between action and noticeable results further discourage efforts at socially significant changes. In the metaphoric words of John Gardner, "Getting things done socially is no sport for the short-winded."

Social efforts to change lives for the better require merging diverse self-interests in support of common core values and goals. Recent years have witnessed growing social fragmentation into separate interest groups, each flexing its own factional efficacy. Pluralism is taking the form of militant factionalism. As a result, people are exercising greater factional influence but achieving less collectively because of mutual immobilization. In addition, mass migration can further contribute to social fragmentation. Societies are thus becoming more diverse and harder to unite around a national vision and purpose.

The magnitude of human problems also undermines perceived efficacy to find effective solutions for them. Worldwide problems of growing magnitude instill a sense of paralysis that there is little people can do to reduce such problems. Global effects are the products of local actions. The strategy of "Think globally, act locally" is an effort to restore in people a sense of efficacy that they can make a difference. Macrosocial applications of sociocognitive principles via the electronic media illustrate how small collective efforts can have substantial impact on such urgent global problems as soaring population growth (Bandura 1997, Singhal & Rogers 1999).

EMERGING PRIMACY OF HUMAN AGENCY IN BIOSOCIAL COEVOLUTION

There is growing unease about progressive divestiture of different aspects of psychology to biology. Biological determinants of human behavior are being widely heralded, and psychosocial dynamics are being downgraded for neurodynamics. It is feared that as we give away more and more psychology to disciplines lower down on the food chain, there will be no core psychological discipline left. Disciplinary fragmentation, dispersion, and absorption in neuroscience, we are told, may be our discipline's destiny. Contrary to the proclamations of the divestitive oracles, psychology is the one discipline that uniquely encompasses the complex interplay between intrapersonal, biological, interpersonal, and sociostructural determinants of human functioning. Psychology is, therefore, best suited to advance understanding of the integrated biopsychosocial nature of humans and how they manage and shape the everyday world around them. It is ironic that an integrative core discipline, which deals with the whole person acting in and on environments, should consider fractionating and farming out subpersonal parts to other disciplines. The field of psychology should be articulating a broad vision of human beings, not a reductive fragmentary one.

The divestitive line of thinking is fueled by conceptual reductionism, nature-nurture analytic dualism, and one-sided evolutionism. As previously noted, mental events are brain activities, but physicality does not imply reduction of psychology to biology. Knowing how the biological machinery works tells one little about how to orchestrate that machinery for diverse purposes. To use an analogy, the "psychosocial software" is not reducible to the "biological hardware." Each is governed by its own set of principles that must be studied in their own right.

Much of psychology is concerned with discovering principles about how to structure environments to promote given psychosocial changes and levels of functioning. This exogenous subject matter does not have a counterpart in neurobiological theory and, hence, psychological laws are not derivable from it. For example, knowledge of the locality and brain circuitry subserving learning can say little about how best to devise conditions of learning in terms of level of abstractness, novelty, and challenge; how to provide incentives to get people to attend to, process, and organize relevant information; in what modes to present information; and whether learning is better achieved independently, cooperatively, or competitively. The optimal conditions must be specified by psychological principles.

Mapping the activation of the neuronal circuitry subserving Martin Luther King's "I Have a Dream" speech would tell us little about its powerful socially inspirational nature, the agentic deliberative effort that went into its creation, and the civic-minded passion that energized its origination and public declaration. Nor will analyses at the molecular, cellular, and biochemical levels explain these agentic activities. There is little at the neuronal level that can tell us how to develop efficacious parents, teachers, executives, or social reformers.

Psychological principles cannot violate the neurophysiological capabilities of the systems that subserve them. However, the psychological principles need to be pursued in their own right. Were one to embark on the slippery slope of reductionism, the journey would traverse biology and chemistry and eventually end in atomic subparticles. Because of emergent properties across levels of complexity, neither the intermediate locales nor the final stop in atomic subparticles supply the psychological laws of human behavior.

The biologizing of psychology, which lately has become highly fashionable, is also being promoted by uncritical adoption of one-sided evolutionism. Not to be outdone, the geneticization of human behavior is being promoted more fervently by psychological evolutionists than by biological evolutionists (Buss & Schmitt 1993, Bussey & Bandura 1999). In these analyses, human behavior is readily attributed to determinative ancestral programming and universalized traits. Biological evolutionists underscore the diversifying selection pressures for adaptiveness of different types of ecological milieus (Dobzhansky 1972, Fausto-Sterling 1992, Gould 1987). Socially constructed milieus differ markedly so no single mode of social adaptation fits all situations.

Ancestral origin of bodily structures and biological potentialities and the determinants governing contemporary behavior and social practices are quite different matters. Because evolved potentialities can serve diverse purposes, ancestral origin dictates neither current social function nor a singular sociostructural arrangement. All too often, the multicausality of human behavior is misleadingly framed in terms of partitioning behavioral variance into percent nature and percent nurture. This analytic dualism is mistaken for several reasons: It disregards the intricate interdependence of nature and nurture. Moreover, socially constructed nurture has a hand in shaping human nature.

Social cognitive theory acknowledges the influential role of evolved factors in human adaptation and change, but it rejects one-sided evolutionism in which evolved biology shapes behavior but the selection pressures of social and technological innovations on biological evolution get ignored. In the bidirectional view of evolutionary processes, environmental pressures fostered changes in biological structures and upright posture conducive to the development and use of tools. These endowments enabled an organism to manipulate, alter, and construct new environmental conditions. Environmental innovations of increasing complexity, in turn, created new selection pressures for the evolution of cognitive capacities and specialized biological systems for functional consciousness, thought, language, and symbolic communication.

Human evolution provides bodily structures and biological potentialities, not behavioral dictates. Psychosocial influences operate through these biological resources to fashion adaptive forms of behavior. Having evolved, the advanced biological capacities can be used to create diverse cultures—aggressive, pacific, egalitarian, or autocratic. Gould (1987) builds a strong case that biology sets constraints that vary in nature, degree, and strength in different activity domains, but in most spheres of human functioning biology permits a broad range of cultural possibilities. He argues cogently that evidence favors a potentialist view over a determinist view. In this insightful analysis, the major explanatory battle is not between nature and nurture as commonly framed, but whether nature operates as a determinist or as a potentialist. For example, tall individuals have the potential to become successful basketball players. But tallness does not ordain basketball pursuits. I seriously doubt that the genetic make-up of the Nazi Germans who committed unprecedented barbarity is really different from the genetic make-up of peaceful Swiss residing in the German canton of Switzerland. People possess the biological potential for aggression, but the answer to the cultural variation in aggressiveness lies more in ideology than in biology.

Gould makes the further interesting point that biological determinism is often clothed in the language of interactionism to make it more palatable. The bidirectional biology-culture coevolution is acknowledged, but then evolved biology is portrayed as the ruling force. The cultural side of this two-way causation, in which genetic make-up is shaped by the adaptational pressures of socially constructed environments, receives little notice. Biological determinism is also often clothed in the language of changeability: The malleability of evolved dispositions is acknowledged, but determinative potency is then ascribed to them with caution against efforts to change existing sociostructural arrangements and practices allegedly ruled by the evolved dispositions. Such efforts are regarded as not only doomed to failure but socially harmful because they go against the rule of nature (Wilson 1998).

In Gould's view (1987), biology has culture on a "loose leash," whereas Wilson argues that, biology has culture on a "tight leash." How human nature is construed determines the extent to which obstructions to sociostructural changes are sought in genetic mismatch or in the counterforce of entrenched vested interests. Biological determinists favor the rule of nature, whereas biological potentialists, who regard human nature as permitting a range of possibilities, give greater weight to the rule of distributed opportunities, privileges, and power. Thus, a biological determinist view highlights inherent constraints and limitations. A biological potentialist view of human nature emphasizes human possibilities.

There is much genetic homogeneity across cultures but vast diversity in belief systems and conduct. Given this variability, genetic coding that characterizes humans underscores the power of the environment orchestrated through agentic action. Aggression, which is allegedly genetically programmed as a biological universal, is a good case in point. Wide intercultural diversity challenges the view that people are inherently aggressive. There are fighting cultures that breed aggression by modeling it pervasively, attaching prestige to it and according it functional value for gaining social status, material benefits, and social control. There are also pacific cultures in which interpersonal aggression is a rarity because it is devalued, rarely modeled, and has no functional value (Alland 1972; Bandura 1973, Sanday 1981).

Intracultural diversity also calls into question aggression as an innate human nature. The United States is a relatively violent society, but American Quakers, who are fully immersed in the culture, adopt pacifism as a way of life. The third form of variability involves rapid transformation of warring societies into peaceful ones. The Swiss used to be the main suppliers of mercenary fighters in Europe, but as they transformed into a pacific society their militaristic vestige is evident only in the plumage of the Vatican guards. For ages the Vikings plundered other nations. After a prolonged war with Russia that exhausted Sweden's resources, the populous rose up and forced a constitutional change that prohibited kings from starting wars (Moerk 1995). This political act promptly transformed a fighting society into a peaceable one that has served as a mediator for peace among warring nations. This rapid cultural metamorphosis underscores the power of nurture. In cross-cultural comparisons, Sweden ranks at the very bottom of all forms of violence.

A biologically deterministic view has even thornier problems with the rapid pace of social change. People have changed little genetically over recent decades, but they have changed markedly through rapid cultural and technological evolution in their beliefs, mores, social roles, and styles of behavior. Social systems and lifestyles are being altered by social means rather than by reliance on the slow, protracted process of biological selection. As Dobzhansky (1972) puts it succinctly, the human species has been selected for learnability and plasticity of behavior adaptive to remarkably diverse habitats, not for behavioral fixedness. The pace of social change gives testimony that biology, indeed, permits a range of possibilities.

To say that a hallmark of humans is their endowed plasticity is not to say that they have no nature (Midgley 1978), or that they come structureless and biologically limitless. The plasticity, which is intrinsic to the nature of humans, depends upon specialized neurophysiological structures and mechanisms that have evolved over time. These advanced neural systems are specialized for channeling attention, detecting the causal structure of the outside world, transforming that information into abstract representations, and integrating and using them for adaptive purposes. These evolved information processing systems provide the capacity for the very agentic characteristics that are distinctly human—generative symbolization, forethought, evaluative self-regulation, reflective self-consciousness, and symbolic communication.

Neurophysiological systems have been shaped by evolutionary pressures, but people are not just reactive products of selection pressures. Other species are heavily innately programmed for stereotypic survival in a particular habitat. In contrast, human lifestyles are, in large part, experientially fashioned within biological limits rather than come ready made. The exercise of agentic capabilities is a prime player in the human coevolution process. People are not only reactors to selection pressures, but they are producers of new ones at an increasingly dizzying pace.

Through agentic action, people devise ways of adapting flexibly to remarkably diverse geographic, climatic and social environments; they figure out ways to circumvent physical and environmental constraints, redesign and construct environments to their liking, create styles of behavior that enable them to realize desired outcomes, and pass on the effective ones to others by social modeling and other experiential modes of influence. By these inventive means, people improve their odds in the fitness survival game. Growth of knowledge is increasingly enhancing human power to control, transform, and create environments of increasing complexity and consequence. We build physical technologies that drastically alter how we live our daily lives. We create mechanical devices that compensate immensely for our sensory and physical limitations. We develop medical and psychological methods that enable us to exert some measure of control over our physical and psychosocial lives. Through contraceptive ingenuity that disjoined sex from procreation, humans have outwitted and taken control over their evolved reproductive system. Carl Djerassi, who begot the birth control pill, predicts that further developments in reproductive technologies will separate sex from fertilization by storing eggs and injecting sperm in vitro for uteral reinsertion and childbearing at a time of one's choosing (Levy 2000).

Humans have created biotechnologies for replacing defective genes with modified ones and for changing the genetic make-up of plants and animals by implanting genes from different sources. In a budding biotechnology that is forging ahead in ways that bypass evolutionary genetic processes, we are now cloning clones and exploring methods that could alter the genetic codes of humans. As people devise ever more powerful technologies that enable them to fashion some aspects of their nature, the psychosocial side of coevolution is gaining ascendancy. Thus, through agentic genetic engineering, humans are becoming major agents of their own evolution, for better or for worse.

With further development of biotechnology, we face the prospect that more direct social construction of human nature through genetic design of human beings for desired properties will increasingly command our attention and ethical concerns.

What is technologically possible eventually gets applied. As previously noted, the genetic factors provide only potentialities, not the finished psychosocial attributes. However, there is no shortage of individuals with the resources and belief in genetic determinism to underwrite attempts at genetic engineering of human nature. The values to which we subscribe and the social systems we devise to oversee the uses to which our powerful technologies are put will play a vital role in what we become and how we shape our destiny.

ACKNOWLEDGMENTS

Preparation of this chapter and some of the cited research was supported by grants from the Grant Foundation, the Spencer Foundation, and the Jacobs Foundation. Some sections of this chapter include revised, updated and expanded material from the books, *Social Foundations or Thought and Action: A Social Cognitive Theory*, Prentice-Hall 1986, *Self-Efficacy: The Exercise of Control*, Freeman 1997; and "A Social Cognitive Theory of Personality" in *Handbook of Personality*, ed. L Pervin, O John (2nd ed.), Guilford.

Visit the Annual Reviews home page at www.AnnualReviews.org

LITERATURE CITED

Alland A Jr. 1972. *The Human Imperative*. New York: Columbia Univ. Press

Austin JH. 1978. *Chase, Chance, and Creativity: The Lucky Art of Novelty*. New York: Columbia Univ. Press

Baldwin C, Baldwin A, Sameroff A, Seifer R. 1989. *The role of family interaction in the prediction of adolescent competence*. Presented at Bienn. Meet. Soc. Res. Child Dev., Kansas City, MO

Baltes MM. 1996. *The Many Faces of Dependency in Old Age*. New York: Cambridge Univ. Press

Bandura A. 1973. *Aggression: A Social Learning Analysis*. Englewood Cliffs, NJ: Prentice-Hall

Bandura A. 1982. The psychology of chance encounters and life paths. *Am. Psychol.* 37:747–55

Bandura A. 1986. *Social Foundations of Thought and Action: A Social Cognitive Theory*. Englewood Cliffs, NJ: Prentice-Hall

Bandura A. 1991a. Social cognitive theory of moral thought and action. In *Handbook of Moral Behavior and Development*, ed. WM Kurtines, JL Gewirtz, 1:45–103. Hillsdale, NJ: Erlbaum

Bandura A. 1991b. Self-regulation of motivation through anticipatory and self-reactive mechanisms. In *Perspectives on Motivation: Nebraska Symposium on Motivation*, ed. RA Dienstbier, 38:69–164. Lincoln: Univ. Nebraska Press

Bandura A. 1993. Perceived self-efficacy in cognitive development and functioning. *Educ. Psychol.* 28:117–48

Bandura A, ed. 1995. *Self-Efficacy in Changing Societies*. New York: Cambridge Univ. Press

Bandura A. 1997. *Self-Efficacy: The Exercise of Control.* New York: Freeman

Bandura A. 1998. Exploration of fortuitous determinants of life paths. *Psychol. Inq.* 9:95–99

Bandura A. 1999a. A social cognitive theory of personality. In *Handbook of Personality,* ed. L Pervin, O John, pp. 154–96. New York: Guilford. 2nd ed.

Bandura A. 1999b. Moral disengagement in the perpetration of inhumanities. *Pers. Soc. Psychol. Rev. (Special issue on Evil and Violence)* 3:193–209

Bandura A. 2000. Exercise of human agency through collective efficacy. *Curr. Dir. Psychol. Sci.* 9:75–78

Bandura A, Barbaranelli C, Caprara GV, Pastorelli C. 1996a. Multifaceted impact of self-efficacy beliefs on academic functioning. *Child Dev.* 67:1206–22

Bandura A, Barbaranelli C, Caprara GV, Pastorelli C. 1996b. Mechanisms of moral disengagement in the exercise of moral agency. *J. Pers. Soc. Psychol.* 71:364–74

Bandura A, Barbaranelli C, Caprara GV, Pastorelli C. 2000a. Self-efficacy beliefs as shapers of children's aspirations and career trajectories. *Child Dev.* In press

Bandura A, Barbaranelli C, Caprara GV, Pastorelli C, Regalia C. 2000b. Sociocognitive Self-Regulatory Mechanisms Governing Transgressive Behavior. *J. Pers. Soc. Psychol.* In press

Bandura A, Pastorelli C, Barbaranelli C, Caprara GV. 1999. Self-efficacy pathways to childhood depression. *J. Pers. Soc. Psychol.* 76:258–69

Brandtstädter J. 1992. Personal control over development: implications of self-efficacy. In *Self-Efficacy: Thought Control of Action,* ed. R Schwarzer, pp. 127–45. Washington, DC: Hemisphere

Bratman ME. 1999. *Faces of Intention: Selected Essays on Intention and Agency.* New York: Cambridge Univ. Press

Bunge M. 1977. Emergence and the mind. *Neuroscience* 2:501–9

Burns TR, Dietz T. 2000. Human agency and evolutionary processes: institutional dynamics and social revolution. In *Agency in Social Theory,* ed. B Wittrock. Thousand Oaks, CA: Sage. In press

Buss DM, Schmitt DP. 1993. Sexual strategies theory: an evolutionary perspective on human mating. *Psychol. Rev.* 100:204–32

Bussey K, Bandura A. 1999. Social cognitive theory of gender development and differentiation. *Psychol. Rev.* 106:676–713

Carlson RA. 1997. *Experienced Cognition.* Mahwah, NJ: Erlbaum

Davidson D. 1971. Agency. In *Agent, Action, and Reason,* ed. R Binkley, R Bronaugh, A Marras, pp. 3–37. Univ. Toronto Press

Diamond MC. 1988. *Enriching Heredity.* New York: Free Press

Dobzhansky T. 1972. Genetics and the diversity of behavior. *Am. Psychol.* 27:523–30

Earley PC. 1993. East meets West meets Mideast: Further explorations of collectivistic and individualistic work groups. *Acad. Manage. J.* 36:319–48

Earley PC. 1994. Self or group? Cultural effects of training on self-efficacy and performance. *Admin. Sci. Q.* 39:89–117

Eisenberg L. 1995. The social construction of the human brain. *Am. J. Psychiatry* 152:1563–75

Elder GH, Ardelt M. 1992. *Families Adapting to Economic Pressure: Some Consequences for Parents and Adolescents.* Presented at Soc. Res. Adolesc., Washington, DC

Fausto-Sterling A. 1992. *Myths of Gender: Biological Theories About Women and Men.* New York: Basic Books. 2nd ed.

Feather NT, ed. 1982. *Expectations and Actions: Expectancy-Value Models in Psychology.* Hillsdale, NJ: Erlbaum

Fernández-Ballesteros R, Díez-Nicolás J, Caprara GV, Barbaranelli C, Bandura A. 2000. *Structural Relation of Perceived Personal Efficacy to Perceived Collective Efficacy.* Submitted for publication

Giddens A. 1984. *The Constitution of Society: Outline of the Theory of Structuration.*

Cambridge: Polity/Berkeley: Univ. Calif. Press

Gould SJ. 1987. *An Urchin in the Storm.* New York: Norton

Green CD, Vervaeke J. 1996. What kind of explanation, if any, is a connectionist net? In *Problems of Theoretical Psychology*, ed. CW Tolman, F Cherry, R van Hezewijk, I Lubek, pp. 201–8. North York, Ont.: Captus

Greenwood JD. 1992. Against eliminative materialism: from folk psychology to völkerpsychologie. *Philos. Psychol.* 5:349–67

Hamburg DA. 1992. *Today's Children: Creating a Future for a Generation in Crisis.* New York: Times Books

Harré R. 1983. *Personal Being: A Theory for Individual Psychology.* Oxford: Blackwell

Harré R, Gillet G. 1994. *The Discursive Mind.* Thousand Oaks, CA: Sage

Holden G. 1991. The relationship of self-efficacy appraisals to subsequent health-related outcomes: a meta-analysis. *Soc. Work. Health Care* 16:53–93

Holden G, Moncher MS, Schinke SP, Barker KM. 1990. Self-efficacy of children and adolescents: a meta-analysis. *Psychol. Rep.* 66:1044–46

Keohane RO. 1993. Sovereignty, interdependence and international institutions. In *Ideas and Ideals: Essays on Politics in Honor of Stanley Hoffman*, ed. L Miller, M Smith, pp. 91–107. Boulder, CO: Westview

Keohane RO, Nye JS. 1977. *Power and Interdependence: World Politics in Transition.* Boston: Little, Brown

Kim U, Triandis HC, Kâğitçibasi C, Choi S, Yoon G, eds. 1994. *Individualism and Collectivism: Theory, Method, and Applications.* Thousand Oaks, CA: Sage

Kolb B, Whishaw IQ. 1998. Brain plasticity and behavior. *Annu. Rev. Psychol.* 49:43–64

Krantz DL. 1998. Taming chance: social science and everyday narratives. *Psychol. Inq.* 9:87–94

Levy D. 2000. *Djerassi sees shift in reproductive roles.* Stanford Rep. 32:1

Locke EA, Latham GP. 1990. *A Theory of Goal Setting and Task Performance.* Englewood Cliffs, NJ: Prentice-Hall

Maddux JE. 1995. *Self-efficacy, adaptation, and adjustment: Theory, research, and application.* New York: Plenum

Masten AS, Best KM, Garmezy N. 1990. Resilience and development: contributions from the study of children who overcome adversity. *Dev. Psychopathol.* 2:425–44

Matsui T, Onglatco ML. 1991. Instrumentality, expressiveness, and self-efficacy in career activities among Japanese working women. *J. Vocat. Behav.* 41:79–88

Matsumoto D, Kudoh T, Takeuchi S. 1996. Changing patterns of individualism and collectivism in the United States and Japan. *Cult. Psychol.* 2:77–107

Midgley M. 1978. *Beast and Man: The Roots of Human Nature.* Ithaca, NY: Cornell Univ. Press

Moerk EL. 1995. Acquisition and transmission of pacifist mentalities in Sweden. *Peace Confl.: J. Peace Psychol.* 1:291–307

Multon KD, Brown SD, Lent RW. 1991. Relation of self-efficacy beliefs to academic outcomes: a meta-analytic investigation. *J. Couns. Psychol.* 38:30–38

Nagel E. 1961. *The Structure of Science.* New York: Harcourt, Brace and World

Pasteur L. 1854. *Inaugural lecture.* University of Lille, France

Rottschaefer WA. 1985. Evading conceptual self-annihilation: some implications of Albert Bandura's theory of the self-system for the status of psychology. *New Ideas Psychol.* 2:223–30

Rottschaefer WA. 1991. Some philosophical implications of Bandura's social cognitive theory of human agency. *Am. Psychol.* 46:153–55

Rutter M. 1990. Psychosocial resilience and protective mechanisms. In *Risk and Protective Factors in the Development of Psychopathology*, ed. J Rolf, AS Masten, D Cicchetti, KH Neuchterlein, S Weintraub, pp. 181–214. New York: Cambridge Univ. Press

Sanday PR. 1981. The socio-cultural context of rape: a cross-cultural study. *J. Soc. Issues* 37:5–27

Schooler C. 1990. Individualism and the historical and social-structural determinants of people's concerns over self-directedness and efficacy. In *Self-Directedness: Cause and Effects Throughout the Life Course*, ed. J Rodin, C Schooler, KW Schaie, pp. 19–58. Hillsdale, NJ: Erlbaum

Schwarzer R, ed. 1992. *Self-Efficacy: Thought Control of Action*. Washington, DC: Hemisphere

Singhal A, Rogers EM. 1999. *Entertainment-Education: A Communication Strategy for Social Change*. Mahwah, NJ: Erlbaum

Sperry RW. 1993. The impact and promise of the cognitive revolution. *Am. Psychol.* 48:878–85

Stajkovic AD, Luthans F. 1998. Self-efficacy and work-related performance: a meta-analysis. *Psychol. Bull.* 124:240–61

Wilson EO. 1998. *Consilience: The Unity of Knowledge*. New York: Knopf

Yamagishi T. 1988. The provision of a sanctioning system in the United States and Japan. *Soc. Psychol. Q.* 51:265–71

Zimbardo PG. 1995. The psychology of evil: a situationist perspective on recruiting good people to engage in anti-social acts. *Res. Soc. Psychol. (Japn. J.)* 11:125–33

Zimmerman BJ. 1990. Self-regulating academic learning and achievement: the emergence of a social cognitive perspective. *Educ. Psychol. Rev.* 2:173–201

Annu. Rev. Psychol. 2001. 52:27–58

NATURE AND OPERATION OF ATTITUDES

Icek Ajzen

Department of Psychology, University of Massachusetts, Amherst, Massachusetts 01003;
e-mail: aizen@psych.umass.edu

Key Words   belief, evaluation, attitude strength, accessibility,
attitude-behavior relation

■ **Abstract**   This survey of attitude theory and research published between 1996 and 1999 covers the conceptualization of attitude, attitude formation and activation, attitude structure and function, and the attitude-behavior relation. Research regarding the expectancy-value model of attitude is considered, as are the roles of accessible beliefs and affective versus cognitive processes in the formation of attitudes. The survey reviews research on attitude strength and its antecedents and consequences, and covers progress made on the assessment of attitudinal ambivalence and its effects. Also considered is research on automatic attitude activation, attitude functions, and the relation of attitudes to broader values. A large number of studies dealt with the relation between attitudes and behavior. Research revealing additional moderators of this relation is reviewed, as are theory and research on the link between intentions and actions. Most work in this context was devoted to issues raised by the theories of reasoned action and planned behavior. The present review highlights the nature of perceived behavioral control, the relative importance of attitudes and subjective norms, the utility of adding more predictors, and the roles of prior behavior and habit.

CONTENTS

0066-4308/01/0201-0027$14.00

INTRODUCTION

The attitude construct continues to be a major focus of theory and research in the social and behavioral sciences, as evidenced by the proliferation of articles, chapters, and books on attitude-related topics published between 1996 and 1999, the period covered in this review. To the relief of authors, the *Annual Review of Psychology* now divides this burgeoning field into two separate chapters, one surveying attitude change, persuasion, and social influence (Wood 2000), and this chapter, intended to deal with most of the remaining topics: conceptualization of attitudes, attitude formation and activation, attitude structure and function, and the attitude-behavior relation. Space limitations confine this review to basic, theory-oriented research, and to topics not covered in other *Annual Review* chapters, such as biases in judgment and decision making (Mellers et al 1998, Johnson-Laird 1999), social cognition and social perception (Fiske 1993), mood and emotion (Cacioppo & Gardner 1999), the self and self esteem (Demo 1989, Banaji & Prentice 1994), and stereotypes and prejudice (Hilton & von Hippel 1996), as well as intra- and inter-group attitudes (Levine & Moreland 1990, Pettigrew 1998). A new collection of attitude scales in the political domain (Robinson et al 1999) provides a useful discussion of available instruments.

CONCEPTUALIZATION OF ATTITUDE

There is general agreement that attitude represents a summary evaluation of a psychological object captured in such attribute dimensions as good-bad, harmful-beneficial, pleasant-unpleasant, and likable-dislikable (Ajzen & Fishbein 2000, Eagly & Chaiken 1993, Petty et al 1997; an in-depth discussion of issues related to evaluation can be found in Tesser & Martin 1996; see also Brendl & Higgins 1996). Recent neurological evidence suggests that evaluative judgments differ in important ways from nonevaluative judgments. Crites & Cacioppo (1996; see also Cacioppo et al 1996) asked respondents to categorize food items either as positive versus nonpositive or as vegetable versus nonvegetable. Compared with the late positive brain potential evoked by nonevaluative categorizations, evaluative categorizations were found to evoke a potential that was relatively larger over wide areas of the right than the left scalp regions. So fundamental and ubiquitous are evaluative reactions to psychological objects that investigators have posited a need to evaluate (Jarvis & Petty 1996, Petty & Jarvis 1996). Individuals are said to differ in their chronic tendency to engage in evaluative responding. Jarvis & Petty

(1996) developed a 16-item scale to measure this tendency, a scale shown to have high internal consistency, a single-factor structure, high test-retest reliability, and convergent and discriminant validity. Compared to respondents with low scores, respondents high in the need to evaluate were found to be more likely to hold attitudes toward various social and political issues and to list more evaluative thoughts about unfamiliar paintings and about a typical day in their lives.

Attitude Objects

The idea that attitudes are dispositions to evaluate psychological objects would seem to imply that we hold one, and only one, attitude toward any given object or issue. Recent work, however, suggests that this may be too simplistic a conception. Thus, when attitudes change, the new attitude overrides but may not replace the old attitude (Wilson et al 2000). According to this model of dual attitudes, people can simultaneously hold two different attitudes toward a given object in the same context, one attitude implicit or habitual, the other explicit. Motivation and capacity are assumed to be required to retrieve the explicit attitude in favor of the implicit evaluative response.

Depending on perspective, different evaluations of the same object in different contexts can be considered evidence for multiple attitudes toward the same object, or attitudes toward different psychological objects. One mechanism for the development of different context-dependent attitudes has been found in the presence of illusory correlations between a target's behavior and the context in which the behavior is observed (McConnell et al 1997). These investigators suggest that some apparent discrepancies between attitudes and behavior may reflect the presence of multiple context–dependent attitudes toward social targets. In a similar vein, respondents have been found to hold different attitudes with respect to high and low relevance versions of the same attitudinal issue (Liberman & Chaiken 1996).

Evaluation Versus Affect

Reflected in Thurstone's (1931) well-known definition of attitude as affect for or against a psychological object, early theorists used the term affect in the sense in which we now use the term attitude, i.e. to denote overall degree of favorability. The current preference is to reserve the term affect for general moods (happiness, sadness) and specific emotions (fear, anger, envy), states that contain degrees of valence as well as arousal (Ajzen & Fishbein 2000, Giner-Sorolla 1999, Schwarz & Clore 1996, Tesser & Martin 1996).

Bipolarity of Affect   Somewhat beyond the scope of this review, an emerging resolution of the controversy regarding bipolarity of affect is worth noting. Findings reported in the 1960s (e.g. Nowlis 1965) suggested that, contrary to intuition and theory, positive moods and emotions may be orthogonal to their negative counterparts, and many investigators subsequently accepted the relative independence and separability of positive and negative affect (e.g. Cacioppo & Berntson 1994, Ito et al 1998a). In a persuasive reconceptualization and series of experiments, Feldman Barrett & Russell (1998) and Russell & Carroll (1999) posed a serious challenge to this view (see also Watson & Tellegen 1999). The apparent independence of positive and negative affect is shown to be largely an artifact of the methodology used in empirical investigations. When items are selected to be semantic bipolar opposites of affective experience, to represent the full domain of positive and negative terms, and to separate high and low levels of activation inherent in the experience, strong negative correlations between positive and negative affect are obtained.

ATTITUDE FORMATION AND ACTIVATION

The Expectancy-Value Model

Evaluation is known to be a fundamental aspect of any concept's connotative meaning (Osgood et al 1957). According to the most popular conceptualization of attitude, the expectancy-value model (see Feather 1982, Fishbein 1963, Fishbein & Ajzen 1975), this evaluative meaning arises spontaneously and inevitably as we form beliefs about the object (see Ajzen & Fishbein 2000). Each belief associates the object with a certain attribute, and a person's overall attitude toward an object is determined by the subjective values of the object's attributes in interaction with the strength of the associations. Although people can form many different beliefs about an object, it is assumed that only beliefs that are readily accessible in memory influence attitude at any given moment. A belief's chronic accessibility tends to increase as a function of the frequency with which the expectancy is activated and the recency of its activation, as well as the belief's importance (Higgins 1996, Olson et al 1996). The expectancy-value model will serve as a conceptual framework for the remaining sections of this review.

Critical Issues   Despite, or perhaps because of, its popularity, the expectancy-value model continues to draw critical attention. In a provocative article, Fishbein & Middlestadt (1995) presented evidence that overall evaluations or attitudes are indeed based on beliefs and their associated evaluations, and argued that when noncognitive factors are sometimes found to have a direct effect on attitudes, this is due to methodological artifacts. A torrent of replies has challenged this conclusion, reaffirming the idea that beliefs are only one possible influence on attitudes (Haugtvedt 1997, Miniard & Barone 1997, Priester & Fleming 1997, Schwarz 1997; but see Fishbein & Middlestadt 1997 for a rejoinder).

A recurrent issue regarding the expectancy-value model has to do with the relative importance of different beliefs as determinants of attitude. Assuming that importance affects accessibility (see Higgins 1996), and hence that only important beliefs are likely to be activated spontaneously, the expectancy-value model assigns equal weights to all belief-value products. Following up on a study by Budd (1986), van der Pligt & de Vries (1998; see also van der Pligt et al 2000) examined the role of belief importance in smoking attitudes and behavior. Student smokers and nonsmokers expressed their attitudes toward smoking, rated the likelihood and value of each of 15 potential consequences of smoking, and selected the 3 consequences they considered most important. In comparison to an expectancy-value index based on the 12 low-importance beliefs, an index based on only the 3 most important beliefs correlated better with the direct semantic differential measure of attitude toward smoking and with reported smoking behavior. However, the 15 consequences of smoking included in the survey were selected by the investigators and did not necessarily represent accessible beliefs. Consistent with this reasoning, the authors noted that their measure of perceived importance may have served primarily to identify the beliefs that were accessible for smokers and nonsmokers. Indeed, follow-up research (van Harreveld et al 2000) showed that beliefs judged to be important are more accessible in memory, as indicated by lower response latencies.

Another concern regarding the expectancy-value model is that the assumed belief × evaluation interaction may misrepresent the cognitive processes involved in attitude formation. Thus, it has been proposed that beliefs and values may relate independently to overall attitudes in a process termed double denial (Sjoeberg & Montgomery 1999). To illustrate, a person with a strong negative attitude toward drinking alcohol may deny (rate as highly unlikely) that drinking makes you happy, yet at the same time assign a negative evaluation to "being happy." When multiplied in accordance with the expectancy-value model, the product term implies a relatively favorable attitude toward drinking alcohol, or at least a less negative attitude than if the likelihood rating had been high. Sjoeberg & Montgomery (1999) obtained data in support of this phenomenon, in an apparent contradiction of the expectancy-value model. However, according to the expectancy-value model, when attributes come to be linked to an object in the process of belief formation, the pre-existing attribute evaluations are associated with the object, producing an overall positive or negative attitude. It is thus important to assess attribute evaluations independent of their link to the attitude object. In the above example, a person who rates "being happy" as negative most likely does so in the context of drinking alcohol, i.e. the person asserts that being happy as a result of drinking alcohol is undesirable, not that being happy is bad in general.

Although not dealing directly with attitudes, an interesting perspective on the interaction between expectancies and values has arisen out of theorizing on regulatory focus (Higgins 1987). Shah & Higgins (1997) either measured or manipulated promotion and prevention focus, and predicted task performance or decisions from expectancies and values associated with potential outcomes of goal attainment. Positive expectancies and values generally had the anticipated effects, increasing goal commitment. However, after entering the expectancy and value measures as main effects, the added contribution of the interaction varied as a function of regulatory focus: The interaction term had a significant positive coefficient for participants with a promotion focus, but a negative coefficient for participants with a prevention focus.

Automatic Attitude Activation

As noted earlier, the expectancy-value model assumes that an object's evaluative meaning arises spontaneously, without conscious effort. Evidence indicating that evaluative reactions tend to be immediate and fast, and can occur outside of awareness, has been accumulating rapidly. Much of this research relies on the sequential evaluative priming paradigm in which stimuli with known positive or negative valence, usually words, serve as priming events. Presented at subliminal exposure times, these primes are found to influence the speed at which subsequent target stimuli, usually adjectives, are judged to be good or bad. Judgments are faster when the valence of the target adjective matches the valence of the prime (see, however, Glaser & Banaji 1999 for a reversal of this effect in the case of evaluatively extreme primes).

Initial research tried to demonstrate that attitudes can be automatically activated, and—more importantly—to establish the conditions necessary for automatic attitude activation. Thus, it was first proposed that attitudes are activated automatically only by stimuli that elicit a quick, conscious evaluative response (Fazio et al 1986). Low-conscious evaluation latencies were assumed to indicate the presence of a strong, chronically accessible attitude amenable to automatic activation. Subsequent research, however, showed that preconscious automatic attitude activation is independent of attitude strength, i.e. of the speed at which conscious evaluations occur (Bargh et al 1992). In fact, it is now clear that automatic attitude activation occurs even in the absence of an explicit goal to make evaluative judgments (Bargh et al 1996, Bargh & Chartrand 1999). In the first of three experiments, explicit evaluation of the target adjectives was removed by asking participants to simply pronounce the target stimuli as quickly as possible. Although nonevaluative, these responses were found to be faster when prime and target valences were congruent rather than incongruent. In the remaining two experiments, the need to obtain an initial evaluation of the priming stimuli was obviated by using normative data from previous research. Shorter pronunciation latencies for target adjectives with prime-congruent valences again confirmed the automatic attitude activation effect. Moreover, the experiments demonstrated automatic attitude activation not only for primes with strongly positive and negative valences, but also for primes with mildly positive and negative valences. Similarly, using drawings of animate and inanimate objects instead of words as primes, Giner-Sorolla et al (1999) again extended the generality of the automatic evaluation effect to moderately valenced priming stimuli, and to situations that do not pose evaluation as an explicit processing goal.

If automatic attitude activation seems to be unaffected by degree of accessibility, a recent series of experiments suggests that it may be moderated by familiarity with the attitude object (Ottati et al, submitted for publication). Using a variation of the sequential priming paradigm, it was shown that automatic attitude activation is produced by primes representing well-known positive or negative person types (e.g. genius, bully) but not by primes representing newly acquired attitude objects (fictitious persons who performed positive or negative behaviors).

The finding that attitudes are activated automatically has led investigators to propose that response latencies be used to obtain measures of attitude that are free of reactive effects, especially when trying to assess racial attitudes or attitudes toward other socially sensitive issues. Ingenious methods have been developed to take advantage of reaction times to relevant stimuli, and evidence for the validity of these methods is becoming available (see Fazio et al 1995, Greenwald & Banaji 1995, Greenwald et al 1998).

Affect Versus Cognition as Antecedents of Evaluation

Inherent in the expectancy-value model of attitude is the assumption that evaluative judgments are the result of cognitive processes: associations between the attitude object and valued attributes. Some theorists have challenged this assumption, proposing that evaluations may also be controlled by affective processes. In fact, the affective primacy hypothesis (Zajonc 1980) assigns precedence to affect over cognition.

Affective Primacy   It is well established that repeated exposure to novel stimuli tends to increase linking for those stimuli even—and especially—when participants are unaware of having been exposed (see Bornstein 1989 for a review). A recent attempt to validate the affective basis of evaluative judgments pitted the affective primacy hypothesis against Schwarz & Clore's (1983) feelings-as-information model (Winkielman et al 1997). Participants evaluated Chinese ideographs following subliminal exposure to positive, negative, or neutral affect primes. Happy and angry faces served as positive and negative primes, respectively, whereas polygons or neutral faces served as neutral primes. The feelings-as-information model assumes that positive or negative feelings elicited by the primes are misattributed to the neutral ideographs, thus producing an affective priming effect. However, participants were also explicitly induced to expect feeling positively or negatively (or were given no such expectation) by either telling them of the subliminal primes (in one experiment) or by playing new-age background music (in a second experiment). This affective expectation manipulation was intended to give participants a situational cue to which they could misattribute their positive or negative feelings. The results were incompatible with the feelings-as-information model. Although subliminal exposure to happy or angry faces produced the usual affective priming effect on evaluations, this effect was not moderated by the affective expectation. Affective priming thus seems to be unaffected by, and independent of, such higher-order cognitive processes as attributional judgments. Of course, this does not rule out the operation of lower-level cognitive processes that may have preceded the evaluative judgments. In fact, the question as to whether evaluation is preceded by low-level affective processes, low-level cognitive processes, or both may not be amenable to resolution by currently available means.

Joint Effects of Affect and Cognition   An alternative and by far more popular position is based on the multi-component view of attitude and assumes that evaluations are influenced by cognition as well as affect (see Eagly & Chaiken 1993, van der Pligt et al 1998). Recent research suggests that the affective and cognitive components of attitude may differ in accessibility (Verplanken et al 1998b). Participants were asked to indicate, on a set of evaluative semantic differential scales, how they thought versus how they felt about attitude objects in two different domains: brand names and countries. Response times were significantly shorter for affective judgments, suggesting that the affective aspects underlying attitudes are more easily accessible in memory.

Consistent with this finding, when beliefs and feelings regarding an object are of opposite valence, feelings tend to predominate (Lavine et al 1998b). Using national survey data, the investigators measured the feelings (e.g. proud, angry) engendered by candidates in four recent U.S. presidential elections as well as their beliefs about the candidates' personal characteristics (e.g. knowledgeable, dishonest). The participants were then divided into those whose affect and cognition scores were evaluatively consistent (univalent) and those who reported oppositely valenced beliefs and feelings (ambivalent). A univalent pattern of affect and cognition permitted better prediction of overall attitudes toward the candidates and of reported voting choice. Of greater interest, when affect and cognition were consistent with each other, both contributed strongly and about equally to the prediction. However, among the ambivalent respondents, feelings toward the candidates were found to be the primary determinants of attitudes and voting behavior. In a related study (Simons & Carey 1998), experience with drug and alcohol use was found to influence the relative importance of the cognitive and affective bases of attitudes: The importance of affect as a predictor of attitudes increased with experience.

In a chapter describing their recent research program, Haddock & Zanna (2000) summarized the results of several studies that provide support for the joint effects of beliefs and feelings on evaluations. Of more interest, they also show that individuals differ in their tendency to base their attitudes on cognition or affect. After developing a measure to capture individual differences in the tendency to rely on thoughts or feelings, the investigators administered the instrument together with a survey of beliefs, feelings, and attitudes with respect to several social issues (Haddock & Zanna 1998). Regression analyses showed the expected results: The attitudes of individuals identified as "thinkers" were predicted by their beliefs about the attitude objects, but not by their feelings, and the reverse was true for individuals identified as "feelers."

In a parallel manner, attitudes toward some objects rely more on affect than cognition, whereas attitudes toward other objects rely more on cognition than affect (Kempf 1999). Participants in this study were asked to try one of two computer software products, a computer game or a grammar checking program, and to report their feelings and beliefs with respect to the product. Evaluation of the trial experience with the hedonic product (the computer game) was found to be based largely on feelings, whereas for the functional product (grammar checking program) the evaluation was determined primarily by beliefs about brand attributes.

In sum, it has been found that individuals differ in their reliance on cognition versus affect as determinants of attitude, and that the two components also take on different degrees of importance for different attitude objects.

Negativity Bias   Whether cognitive or affective in nature, it is well known that negative information tends to have a greater impact on overall evaluations than comparably extreme positive information. The negativity bias was again demonstrated by research regarding the effects of positive and negative information on evaluations of political candidates (Klein 1996) and sponsors of political advertising (Matthews & Dietz-Uhler 1998), and by research showing greater cognitive activity and better memory for negative as compared to positive stimulus words (Ohira et al 1998). Research that assessed event-related brain potentials while participants viewed positive, negative, and neutral pictures (Ito et al 1998b) has shown that this negativity bias occurs very early in the processing of information, as the information is being categorized into positive or negative valence classes.

Accessibility of Beliefs

According to the expectancy-value model, chronically accessible beliefs provide the foundation for our current, relatively stable attitudes, but various contextual factors can temporarily make certain beliefs more readily accessible. Depending on the valence of these beliefs, the prevailing attitude could shift in either a positive or negative direction (Ajzen & Sexton 1999). A systematic approach to the relation between accessibility of beliefs and its effects on attitudes is provided by attitude representation theory (Lord & Lepper 1999; see also Sia et al 1999), which makes a strong case for the dependence of evaluation on the subjective representation of the attitude object. An experimental test of the theory showed that measured attitudes toward such social categories as politicians, homosexuals, and rock musicians remain relatively stable over time to the extent that the same representations (exemplars) of the category are accessed on different occasions (Sia et al 1997). In a somewhat related approach, the goal compatibility framework (Markman & Brendl 2000) suggests that people evaluate objects in relation to currently active goals.

Perhaps the simplest way to influence people's accessible beliefs in a positive or negative direction is to ask them to think about positive or negative aspects of the attitude object, a directed thinking task that can at least temporarily impact even such a fundamental aspect of personality as self-esteem (McGuire & McGuire 1996). College students asked to list desirable characteristics they possess or undesirable characteristics they do not possess expressed more favorable attitudes toward themselves than did students who were asked to list undesirable characteristics they possess or desirable characteristics they do not possess. A related experiment (Ratcliff et al 1999) showed that directed thinking about the actions people could take to make studying enjoyable increased intentions to spend time studying, but directed thinking about reasons why people should find studying enjoyable did not. Other research (Levine et al 1996) also supported the proposition that thinking about the reasons for holding an attitude can distort attitudinal judgments and disrupt the attitude-behavior relation.

A study by Waenke et al (1996) similarly illustrated that activation of beliefs can have paradoxical effects on attitudes. Participants generated either three or seven arguments in favor of or opposed to the use of public transportation, and then expressed their attitudes toward this issue. The elicitation of pro versus con beliefs produced a corresponding difference in attitudes when three beliefs were generated (easy task) but no significant difference when seven beliefs were generated (difficult task). Readers of the same arguments, however, displayed the intuitively expected pattern: Their attitudes were affected more by seven than by three arguments. It appears that the attitudes expressed by participants who generated the arguments took account of the subjective difficulty of the task.

According to temporal construal theory (Liberman & Trope 1998), a goal's desirability is represented at an abstract level, whereas the likelihood that the goal will be attained is construed at a more concrete level. Furthermore, the value of the abstract aspects of the goal, i.e. the goal's desirability, increases with temporal distance from the goal, whereas the value of the concrete aspects, i.e. its probability, decreases with temporal distance. In a series of experiments, Liberman and Trope found that people give weight to a goal's positive aspects (its desirability) when making decisions for the long term, and to the goal's negative aspects (i.e. its difficulty) when making decisions for the short term. These findings imply that positive beliefs about the goal are more readily accessible in long-term decisions, whereas negative beliefs predominate in short-term decisions.

Studying impression formation, Wojciszke et al (1998) distinguished between morality- and competence-related beliefs. Personality traits related to morality (e.g. sincere, generous) were found to be more chronically accessible than traits related to competence (e.g. intelligent, foresighted): Many more morality than competence traits were emitted spontaneously as being important in others. Consistent with this finding, global impressions of real persons were better predicted from beliefs about morality-related traits than from beliefs about competence-related traits, and attitudes toward fictitious persons were based more on the morality than on the competence of their behaviors.

An interesting finding regarding the accessibility of beliefs comes from research on the effects of alcohol on behavioral decisions. According to the alcohol myopia hypothesis (Steele & Josephs 1990), alcohol consumption decreases cognitive capacity so that intoxicated individuals are likely to attend to the most salient cues in a situation. In laboratory and field experiments (MacDonald et al 1996), intoxicated participants indicated a greater likelihood of engaging in unprotected sex than did sober participants and, in support of the alcohol myopia hypothesis, they were more likely to endorse beliefs that provide justifications for unprotected sex.

In short, personal and contextual factors combine to increase or decrease the accessibility of different kinds of beliefs, with potentially important ramifications for evaluative judgments and behavioral decisions.

ATTITUDE STRENGTH

Strong attitudes are thought to have a number of interesting qualities. They are said to be relatively stable over time, to be resistant to persuasion, and to predict manifest behavior. Visser & Krosnick (1998) documented changes in attitude strength over the life cycle. Contrary to the common belief that cognitive flexibility and readiness to change one's attitudes decline with age, the results of several studies demonstrated that susceptibility to attitude change declines from early to middle adulthood and then increases again in late adulthood. Similarly, rated importance of attitudinal issues, certainty, and perceived quantity of attitude-relevant knowledge were greater in middle adulthood than during early or late adulthood. However, these various indexes of attitude strength were found to correlate differentially with education, gender, and race, challenging the notion that attitude strength is a unitary construct.

High personal relevance of information on which an attitude is based has been found to increase its strength (Kokkinaki & Lunt 1999), as measured by response times, i.e. accessibility. College students were exposed to an advertisement for an unfamiliar product under high and low personal relevance conditions, and subsequently their brand attitudes, as well as the response latencies of these attitudes, were assessed. In line with dual-mode processing models, high personal relevance, or involvement, was expected to increase information processing and, consistent with predictions, attitudes formed under conditions of high involvement were found to be significantly more accessible compared to those formed under low levels of involvement.

Consequences of Attitude Strength

Using a sequential priming paradigm, Bassili & Roy (1998) examined the effects of attitude strength on the representation of attitudes in memory. Participants either first evaluated a policy and then thought of one of its consequences, or they first thought of a possible consequence and then evaluated the policy. In general, it took participants longer to think of a consequence of a policy than to evaluate it, suggesting that evaluations are relatively automatic, whereas belief emission requires some cognitive effort. Results further showed that thinking of a consequence of a policy speeded up its subsequent evaluation, regardless of whether the participant held a strong or weak attitude about the policy. Evaluating the policy speeded up thinking of one of its consequences for strong attitudes but not for weak ones.

Strong attitudes are, among other things, expected to be relatively resistant to change. Drawing a distinction between meta-attitudinal and operative indexes of attitude strength, Bassili (1996) reported the results of two studies concerning resistance to attitude change with respect to three social issues: employment quotas for women, laws regulating pornography, and laws prohibiting hateful expressions. Meta-attitudinal measures of strength were of a subjective nature, asking participants in the first study to judge the certainty, importance, and strength of their attitudes, as well as their knowledge, attention, and frequency of thought concerning the issues. The operative, and relatively more objective, indexes were measures of attitude extremity, ambivalence, and response latency. In the second study, participants were also asked to provide subjective judgments of these operative aspects of their attitudes. Resistance to change was, in both studies, assessed by observing reactions to a counter argument, and in the second study also by stability over a two-week period. The results of multiple regression analyses showed that resistance to change was affected only by the operative measures of attitude strength; the meta-attitudinal measures did not account for unique variance.

A possible clue to the inferiority of the subjective or meta-attitudinal measures of attitude strength can be found in a study by Haddock et al (1996), who showed that the subjective experience of attitude strength is quite malleable. After expressing their attitudes toward doctor-assisted suicide, college students were asked to list either three or seven arguments pro or counter their own positions. This was followed by several questions designed to assess subjective attitude strength. As might be expected, participants found it easier to generate three as compared to seven arguments. They then apparently used the ease of argument generation to infer the strength of their attitudes. Attitude importance, intensity, and certainty were judged greater when generation of arguments in favor of one's position was relatively easy (three pro arguments) and when generation of arguments opposed to one's position was relatively difficult (seven con arguments). Interestingly, these findings were obtained only when subjective attitude strength was assessed in terms of importance, intensity, and certainty, not when attitude strength was measured in terms of frequency of thinking or knowledge concerning the issue. Furthermore, in a subsequent experiment, ease of argument retrieval was found to have no effect on subjective certainty for individuals with relatively extreme attitudes (Haddock et al 1999). These findings again support the relative independence of different aspects of attitude strength.

A similar conclusion emerged in another series of studies concerning the effects of attitude strength on temporal stability (Prislin 1996). Undergraduates expressed their attitudes toward affirmative action, euthanasia, and legalized abortion on two occasions. Different dimensions of attitude strength were found to predict the stability of these different attitudes. Generalized attitude strength (judged certainty, importance, vested interest, frequency of thought, experience, knowledge) moderated the stability of attitudes toward affirmative action, with strong attitudes being more stable than weak attitudes; internal consistency of the attitude (evaluative-cognitive and evaluative-affective consistencies) moderated stability of attitudes toward euthanasia; and attitude extremity affected the stability of attitudes toward legalized abortion.

Lavine et al (1998a) showed that attitude strength moderates the susceptibility of attitudes to item context effects in surveys, with relatively weak attitudes being more susceptible to context effects than relatively strong attitudes. However, this finding was obtained only with a multi-item aggregate measure of attitude strength (containing measures of importance, certainty, extremity, frequency of thought, intensity, and ambivalence), not when a single item was used to assess attitude strength.

The strength of evaluative reactions has proven to be an important characteristic of attitudes, but its multidimensional nature is proving to be a serious obstacle to progress. Attitude strength has been operationalized in different ways, including importance of the issue, extremity of the attitude, its stability over time, certainty in one's position, vested interest, involvement, affective-cognitive consistency, knowledge about the issue, frequency of thinking about it, and—consistent with Fazio's (Fazio et al 1986, Fazio & Towles-Schwen 1999) theorizing—latency of conscious, deliberate responses to attitudinal inquiries (see Krosnick et al 1993, Petty & Krosnick 1995). Yet, research continues to reveal only weak relations among these dimensions of attitude strength, and different measures tend to produce conflicting research findings.

ATTITUDINAL AMBIVALENCE

Generally speaking, ambivalence reflects the co-existence of positive and negative dispositions toward an attitude object. This ambivalence can result from simultaneously accessible conflicting beliefs within the cognitive component (McGregor et al 1999), or from a conflict between cognition and affect (for discussions, see Eagly & Chaiken 1993, Maio et al 2000, McGregor et al 1999). Recent attempts to quantify this property of attitudes have focused on ambivalence within the cognitive component. By differentially weighting the strength of conflicting beliefs, it is possible to derive varying formulas for the computation of ambivalence. Building on earlier work (Thompson et al 1995), Priester & Petty (1996) reviewed and then evaluated the relative merits of different operational definitions by comparing their ability to predict the subjective experience of ambivalence. Following a sophisticated analysis, they presented data to support the superiority of a gradual threshold model. According to this model, ambivalence increases as a negatively accelerating function of the number of conflicting beliefs, and decreases with the number of dominant reactions (i.e. the more frequent reactions, whether positive or negative) up to a threshold defined by a certain level of conflicting reactions. Despite its unique features, however, the proposed formulation was found to correlate quite highly with other quantifications of ambivalence, and although it was superior to other indices in some respects, the proposed measure accounted for only a moderate amount of variance in the subjective ambivalence criterion.

Consequences of Ambivalence

Holding ambivalent attitudes has been shown to affect judgments and behavior in profound ways. Thus, although equal in stability over time, relatively nonambivalent attitudes toward eating a low-fat diet were found to be more predictive of subsequent intentions and behavior than ambivalent attitudes, and they were also more resistant to a persuasive communication (Armitage & Conner 2000b; see also Conner et al 1998b). However, this may hold only for attitudes toward familiar objects or issues. Arguing that ambivalence decreases people's confidence in their attitudes toward behaviors involving the attitude object, Jonas et al (1997) postulated that ambivalent attitudes are associated with more systematic information processing and hence, predict intentions better than nonambivalent attitudes. Two experiments confirmed these expectations: Attitudes of participants provided with evaluatively inconsistent information about fictional shampoos predicted buying intentions better than did attitudes based on evaluatively consistent information. Similarly, people with ambivalent attitudes toward a minority group were found to be more likely to systematically process information about the group (Maio et al 1996) and, in comparison to individuals with less ambivalent attitudes, their reactions toward the group reflected more readily a mood-induced priming of positive and negative feelings (Bell & Esses 1997).

Ambivalence is a dominant theme in theorizing about racial, ethnic, and gender-related prejudice (Fiske & Glick 1995, Gaertner & Dovidio 1986). Drawing on this work, MacDonald & Zanna (1998) reported that men who exhibit ambivalent attitudes toward feminists tend to rate them positively on the dimension of admiration but negatively on the dimension of affection. Priming respondents with related positive (agentic) or negative interpersonal qualities had little impact on nonambivalent respondents but it had a significant effect on the attitudes and hiring preferences of ambivalent respondents. After reading a résumé of a feminist applicant, ambivalent participants who were positively primed expressed more liking for the applicant and greater intentions to hire her than did negatively primed ambivalent participants.

Attitudinal ambivalence is emerging as a promising area of research with the potential to throw light on attitude structure—within as well as between attitude components—on the processing of attitude-relevant information, on attitude change, and on the effect of attitudes on behavior.

FUNCTIONS OF ATTITUDES

In the broadest sense of functionality, attitudes facilitate adaptation to the environment (Eagly & Chaiken 1998). Researchers continue their attempts to identify the functions served by attitudes and to investigate their role in the formation and consequences of attitudes (see Maio & Olson 1999 for a collection of chapters on this topic). Among the functions recognized by most theorists are the value-expressive function of attitudes, the knowledge function, the ego-defensive function, the social-adjustive function, and the utilitarian function (see e.g. Murray et al 1996). The operation of some of these functions has been investigated in recent studies.

In a laboratory experiment, Chen & Bargh (1999) demonstrated that positive and negative evaluations serve to orient people toward approach and avoidance, respectively. Participants exposed to positive words responded faster when instructed to pull a lever toward them than to push it away, whereas the reverse pattern was observed for participants exposed to negative words.

Attitudinal function can be associated with positions on social issues (cf. Reeder & Pryor 1999). Studying the functions of attitudes toward lifting the ban on homosexuals in the military, Wyman & Snyder (1997) examined ego-defensive beliefs (e.g. "Admitting gays to the military would create many more problems of unwelcome sexual advances") and value-expressive beliefs (e.g. "Homosexuality is wrong and this policy would be condoning it"). Respondents who approved of lifting the ban rejected ego-defensive reasons for keeping it and they endorsed value-expressive reasons to lift it. Conversely, respondents opposed to lifting the ban endorsed ego-defensive and value-expressive reasons for keeping the ban and rejected value-expressive reasons to lift it. Approaching this issue in the context of the expectancy-value model, Demski & McGlynn (1999) showed that attitudes toward parolees were based primarily on beliefs related to the instrumental or utilitarian function (i.e. practical concerns) rather than to beliefs related to the value-expressive function (i.e. moral or symbolic concerns).

An attitude's functional basis has been shown to influence the extent to which people process function-consistent and function-inconsistent information (Petty & Wegener 1998). College students preselected to be high or low in self monitoring tendency were exposed to a message that matched or mismatched the functional basis of their attitudes toward common products: an image appeal for high self-monitors and a quality appeal for low self-monitors, or vice versa. To examine depth of information processing, the message contained either strong or weak arguments. The strength of the arguments had a greater impact on attitudes toward the products when they matched rather than mismatched the functional basis of the attitude and, in a second study, this difference was especially pronounced for individuals low in need for cognition.

Biasing Effects of Attitudes   If attitudes serve a variety of functions for the individual, they are likely to bias judgments and memory. It is generally hypothesized that attitudes bias information processing and memory in favor of attitude-consistent material. Thus, participants judged research consistent with their attitudes toward homosexuality as more convincing than they judged research inconsistent with their attitudes (Munro & Ditto 1997), and they classified multiply categorizable objects in line with their most accessible attitudes (Smith et al 1996). A meta-analysis of research on the attitude congeniality hypothesis (Eagly et al 1999; see also Eagly 1998), however, failed to provide clear support.

Results across studies were inconsistent, and the overall effect was weak. Attitude structure and motivation to process attitude-relevant information were found to be of possible significance in understanding the inconsistent findings. In line with this suggestion, amount of prior knowledge combined with high fear of AIDS was found to bias processing of information relevant to risk estimates, enabling respondents to defend their existing views regarding the risk of contracting AIDS (Biek et al 1996).

Attitudes and Values   Favorable valences associated with such abstract concepts as freedom and equality are known as values. Interest in the measurement and function of values continues (see Seligman et al 1996). It has been suggested that global values reflect cultural truisms, i.e. widely shared and rarely questioned beliefs supported by a very limited cognitive foundation (Maio & Olson 1998). Consistent with this assumption, asking participants to analyze their reasons for holding such values as altruism and equality caused them to change their ratings of these values. Moreover, this change was observed only when participants were not provided with cognitive support for their values.

General values, once activated, are assumed to influence evaluations of specific objects and events (Feather 1996). Indeed, broad values, as assessed by Schwartz's (1992) survey instrument, have been found to be related to food preferences in different contexts (Feather et al 1998). Similarly, the values of security through order, humanistic and expressive concerns, and religiosity and personal restraint are related to liberal versus conservative attitudes (Braithwaite 1998; see also Braithwaite 1997), and values of communalism and the work ethic predict attitudes toward welfare (P Kulesa & AH Eagly, unpublished). On a somewhat narrower scale, attitudes toward fat people were found to be linked to strong value placed on responsibility for one's actions in the United States, but not in Mexico (Crandall & Martinez 1996).

The functional approach to attitudes has so far held out more promise than it has been able to deliver. Attempts to link the functional basis of attitudes to processing of function-relevant information may help to integrate work on attitudinal functions with other theory and research on attitude formation and change.

PREDICTION OF BEHAVIOR

The ability of attitudes to predict behavioral intentions and overt behavior continues to be a major focus of theory and research. By far the greatest number of publications on a single topic were concerned with this issue.

Moderators of Attitude-Behavior Consistency

Several studies continued to explore the role of moderating variables. Operationalizing attitude embeddedness as the number of free associations respondents produced in relation to an issue, Prislin & Ouellette (1996) found that highly embedded attitudes toward preservation of the environment were more strongly related to an aggregate measure of behavioral intentions than were low-embedded attitudes. Also dealing with environmental issues, Schultz & Oskamp (1996) determined that the relation between concern about the environment and recycling behavior increased, as expected, to the extent that the behavior required effort on the part of the participant. Others have investigated the effects on the attitude-behavior relation of prior experience and thought (Millar & Millar 1998), cognitive load and positive mood (Blessum et al 1998), direct and indirect experience (Millar & Millar 1996), and the accessibility of alternative actions (Posavac et al 1997).

Returning to a theme of the 1970s, several studies dealt with the moderating effect of involvement. In one experiment (Kokkinaki & Lunt 1997), involvement as well as response latency (accessibility) were found to increase the impact of attitudes on product choices. Involvement also took central stage in an exchange about the role of vested interest in political behavior (Crano 1997a,b; Sears 1997). Contrary to earlier research that reported limited impact of vested interest on political attitudes and actions, Crano (1997b) presented data to show that vested interest—although uncorrelated with attitude valence—does affect the strength of the relation between attitudes and behavior. In response, Sears (1997) contended that the moderating effects of vested interest tend to be relatively small and restricted largely to the daily lives of college students. According to Sears, symbolic aspects of an attitude (ideology and values evoked by the attitude object) take on greater significance in the public arena where they overshadow the impact of narrow self-interest.

Theories of Reasoned Action and Planned Behavior

Most studies concerned with the prediction of behavior from attitudinal variables were conducted in the framework of the theory of planned behavior (Ajzen 1991) and, to a lesser extent, its predecessor, the theory of reasoned action (Ajzen & Fishbein 1980). According to the theory of planned behavior, people act in accordance with their intentions and perceptions of control over the behavior, while intentions in turn are influenced by attitudes toward the behavior, subjective norms, and perceptions of behavioral control. The cognitive foundations of these factors are consistent with an expectancy-value formulation. Support for the theory in general is summarized in a meta-analysis (Armitage & Conner 2000a) and a review of the literature (Sutton 1998), and another review summarizes its applications to health-related behavior (Conner & Sparks 1996).

Several studies have compared the predictive power of the theory of planned behavior with that of other models, including the information-motivation-behavioral-skills model (de Witt et al 2000), the health belief model (Quine et al 1998), and the integrated waste management model (Taylor & Todd 1997). Although designed for application in specific domains, the alternative models were found to perform not much better, and sometimes worse, than the general, content-free theory of planned behavior.

Applications   Many investigators continue to demonstrate the applicability of the theory in various content domains, including condom use (e.g. Albarracin et al 1998, de Witt et al 2000, Jamner et al 1998, Reinecke et al 1996; see Sheeran & Taylor 1999 for a meta-analysis) and other safe-sex behaviors (Boldero et al 1999, de Vroome et al 2000), smoking (e.g. Norman et al 1999, Morrison et al 1996), getting hormone replacement therapy (Quine & Rubin 1997), adhering to a medication regimen (Conner et al 1998a), drinking alcohol (Morrison et al 1996, Trafimow 1996), using illegal substances (Conner et al 1998b, Conner & McMillan 1999), eating low-fat food (e.g. Armitage & Conner 1999a, Paisley & Sparks 1998), engaging in physical activity (e.g. Courneya et al 1999b, Trafimow & Trafimow 1998), choosing a career (Vincent et al 1998), playing basketball (Arnscheid & Schomers 1996), wearing a safety helmet (Quine et al 1998), using dental floss (Rise et al 1998), exposing oneself to sunlight (Hillhouse et al 1997), and composting (Kaiser et al 1999). By and large, these studies have found support for the theory, and little can be gained at this point by further demonstrations of the theory's applicability to particular domains.

Perceived Behavioral Control   Going beyond the demonstration of applicability, several studies have pursued a distinction between perceived controllability (whether people believe that they have volitional control over performance of a behavior) and self-efficacy, conceptualized as the degree of anticipated difficulty in performing a behavior (see Bandura 1997 for a comprehensive discussion of self-efficacy). Factor analyses of items designed to tap these two constructs revealed the expected factors in the domains of eating behavior (Armitage & Conner 1999a,b; Sparks et al 1997) and academic achievement (Manstead & van Eekelen 1998), but only perceived difficulty—not perceived controllability—added significantly to the prediction of intentions and behavior (Armitage & Conner 1999b, Manstead & van Eekelen 1998, Sparks et al 1997). In a somewhat related study, Trafimow & Duran (1998) validated the distinction between attitude and perceived behavioral control.

Attitudes Versus Norms   Another issue has to do with the relative contributions of attitudes and subjective norms to the prediction of intentions. Relying on within-subjects analyses across 30 different behaviors, Trafimow & Finlay (1996; see also Finlay et al 1997, 1999) confirmed that individuals differ in the relative weights they place on attitudes and subjective norms, and that the weights of these predictors also vary across behaviors. At the group level, workers' turnover intentions were, as might be expected, more under the influence of subjective norms in a collectivist culture (Japan) than in an individualistic culture (Britain) (Abrams et al 1998). Similarly, the intentions of general medical practitioners to refer Asian patients to mental health services were more under control of subjective norms, whereas their intentions to refer non-Asian patients were more under the control of attitudinal considerations (Conner & Heywood-Everett 1998). In an experimental analogue, Ybarra & Trafimow (1998) primed the accessibility of either the private or the collective self. Intentions to use condoms during sexual intercourse were more under the control of attitudes in the former condition and more under control of subjective norms in the latter. Similarly, intentions to avoid exposure to the sun were influenced by the perceived norms of a reference group among respondents who strongly identified with the group, whereas among low identifiers, personal attitudes were a better predictor (Terry & Hogg 1996).

In a study on the effects of mood (Armitage et al 1999) it was found that attitudes influenced intentions to use condoms and to eat low-fat foods after induction of a negative mood, whereas subjective norms influenced these behaviors in a positive mood condition. Intentions to eat sweets showed a consistent pattern of gender differences: women's intentions were under the influence of both attitudes and subjective norms, whereas only attitudes significantly predicted the intentions of men (Grogan et al 1997). Finally, the readiness of managers to undertake benchmarking in their organization was influenced by their attitudes toward this behavior, but only if they had past experience with it. Inexperienced managers were influenced by their normative beliefs concerning the expectations of others in the organization (Hill et al 1996).

Past research has often reported strong correlations between attitudes and subjective norms. The differential patterns of impact on intentions and behavior documented in recent investigations tend to validate the conceptual distinction between attitudinal and normative considerations.

Sufficiency   Many studies challenge the assumption that the predictors in the theory of planned behavior are sufficient to account for intentions and behavior. This is done by including measures of additional variables in the prediction equation and showing significant improvement in the prediction of intentions or behavior (see Conner & Armitage 1998 for a review). Thus, several investigations showed that the inclusion of a measure of self-identity can account for additional variance in adherence to a low-fat diet (Armitage & Conner 1999a,b; Sparks & Guthrie 1998) and in marijuana use (Conner & McMillan 1999). Other studies demonstrated improved prediction of environmentally relevant behavior with the addition of personal or moral norms (Harland et al 1999; see also Kristiansen & Hotte 1996 and Manstead 2000 for a general discussion) and improved prediction of playing the lottery and of precautionary sexual behavior with the addition of anticipated regret (Richard et al 1998, Sheeran & Orbell 1999a; see also van der Pligt et al 1998). Measures of personality traits also improved prediction (Courneya et al 1999a), but the addition of various demographic variables did not (Albarracin et al 1997). In general, however, even when improvements were found, for the most part the improvements in prediction of intentions or behavior were relatively minor, and their generalizability to other behavioral domains has yet to be demonstrated.

Past Behavior   Related to the question of sufficiency is the role of past behavior. Based on the assumption that frequent performance of a behavior leads to the formation of a habit, and that habits can influence behavior independent of attitudes and intentions, theorists have proposed that frequency of past behavior be added to our predictive models (e.g. Bentler & Speckart 1979, Triandis 1977; see also Ouellette & Wood 1998). Several investigators have tested this idea by including a measure of past conduct in the theory of planned behavior and have shown that doing so can help account for a substantial portion of additional variance in intentions or actual behavior (e.g. Conner et al 1999, O'Callaghan et al 1999). For example, in a study of travel mode choice, prediction of car use from intentions and perceptions of behavioral control was significantly improved by the addition of past car use (Verplanken et al 1998a). More importantly, this study revealed a significant interaction between intention and past behavior. When the relation between intention and behavior was examined separately for respondents with high, moderate, and low levels of past car use, it was significant only at the lowest use level (see also Verplanken et al 1997). This finding suggests that intentions may become largely irrelevant when a behavior has been performed many times, i.e. when it has become habitual.

The prediction of studying intentions and behavior among college students was also shown to benefit from the inclusion of a measure of past behavior (Leone et al 1999). This study found, however, that the contribution of past behavior declined when perceived behavioral control was included in the prediction equation. Consistent with this finding, perceived behavioral control was shown to mediate the impact of similar past behaviors on acceptance of hormone replacement therapy (Quine & Rubin 1997).

In short, the frequency with which a behavior has been performed in the past tends to correlate well with later actions. Although there is some indication that this relation may be mediated in part by perceived behavioral control, neither this variable nor intentions completely explain the link between prior and later behavior. Some investigators have interpreted these findings to mean that behavior has come at least in part under the control of automatic processes or habits (e.g. Aarts & Dijksterhuis 2000, Aarts et al 1998, Ouellette & Wood 1998). However, this is not the only possible interpretation. Frequency of past behavioral performance may capture and reflect a number of psychological processes or variables other than habituation (see Ajzen & Fishbein 2000 for a discussion).

From Intentions to Actions

As in research on the attitude-behavior relation, investigators continued their search for moderators of the intention-behavior relation. Studies showed that, as might be expected, the temporal stability of intentions (Conner et al 2000, Sheeran et al 1999b) and of perceived behavioral control (Conner et al 2000) influence predictive validity: Relatively stable intentions and perceptions of behavioral control were better predictors of subsequent behavior. In a meta-analysis of research on intended and actual condom use, shorter time intervals, older samples, and condom use with steady versus casual partners were each found to be associated with stronger correlations (Sheeran & Orbell 1998). Similarly, participants who had developed a schema relevant for dieting were found to exhibit stronger relations between dieting intentions and behavior than did aschematic participants (Kendzierski & Whitaker 1997); easily accessible voting intentions were better predictors of voting choice than intentions with longer response latencies (Bassili 1995); and intentions based on attitudes tended to predict performance of everyday behaviors better than did intentions based on subjective norms (Sheeran et al 1999a).

Implementation Intentions   In an impressive program of research, Gollwitzer (1996, 1999) and his associates (Gollwitzer & Brandstaetter 1997, Gollwitzer & Schaal 1998) have explored the cognitive processes that mediate the relation between intentions and behavior. A fundamental assumption in this work is that the initiation of goal-directed responses becomes automatized following formation of implementation intentions, i.e. intentions to perform a goal-directed behavior when a specific context is encountered (see Gollwitzer & Schaal 1998). Specific plans of this kind are assumed to serve as powerful self-regulatory tools and to facilitate implementation of intended behavior. In an empirical investigation (Gollwitzer & Brandstaetter 1997) implementation intentions were found to facilitate the immediate initiation of goal-directed action when the intended opportunity was encountered, and intentions to attain difficult goals were more likely to be carried out when participants had formed implementation intentions. Similarly, participants asked to formulate plans in the form of implementation intentions were found to be better able to carry out their intentions to go on a healthier diet (Verplanken & Faes 1999) and to take a vitamin C pill each day (Sheeran & Orbell 1999b). Clearly, intentions play an important role in guiding human action, but recent research also reveals the complexities involved in translating intentions into actual behavior.

CONCLUSIONS

Examination of the last four years of basic research on the nature and operation of attitudes reveals continued interest in the major themes of the past. We can see definite progress in some areas, but—as might be expected—no groundbreaking developments in such a short period of time. The ubiquity and importance of evaluative reactions were reaffirmed, with increased emphasis being placed on automatic processes in attitude formation and activation. Evaluative reactions have been shown to occur without awareness, even in the absence of conscious intent to evaluate a stimulus object. The expectancy-value model of attitudes has continued to provide a useful framework for research on attitude formation and organization, but the debate over the cognitive versus affective basis of attitudes has yet to be completely resolved. The research reviewed found that the contributions of affect and cognition to overall evaluation vary with the attitude object and as a function of individual differences. Research has continued to explore the role of attitude strength, revealing again the problematic, multidimensional nature of this aspect of attitudes. Nevertheless, some interesting conclusions emerged: It was reported that the strength of attitudes varies over the life cycle, with greatest strength being displayed in mid-life. Strong attitudes were found to be associated with more accessible beliefs and, when attitude strength was assessed by relatively objective means, to be more resistant to change. New attempts to operationalize attitudinal ambiguity and explore its implications were also reported.

The largest number of studies on any single topic had to do with the attitude-behavior relation. Although it is now generally recognized that attitudes are relevant for understanding and predicting social behavior, many questions remain. Investigators continued to identify factors that moderate the effects of attitudes and intentions on overt actions. Many other investigations applied or tested the theories of reasoned action and planned behavior. There is now little doubt that these theories can be usefully employed in various domains, but specific aspects continue to draw critical attention. Research has shown that a distinction can be drawn between perceived controllability and perceived difficulty of performing a behavior (self-efficacy) and that the latter may be a more important antecedent of intentions and actions; that the relative contributions of attitudes and subjective norms vary across behaviors and subject populations; that other predictors may have to be added to the theory; and that behavior may contain automatic, habitual aspects not accounted for in models of reasoned action.

ACKNOWLEDGMENT

I would like to thank Jim Averill for his helpful comments on an earlier draft.

Visit the Annual Reviews home page at www.AnnualReviews.org

LITERATURE CITED

Aarts H, Dijksterhuis A. 2000. Habits as knowledge structures: automaticity in goal-directed behavior. *J. Pers. Soc. Psychol.* 78:53–63

Aarts H, Verplanken B, van Knippenberg A. 1998. Predicting behavior from actions in the past: repeated decision making or a matter of habit? *J. Appl. Soc. Psychol.* 28:1355–74

Abrams D, Ando K, Hinkle S. 1998. Psychological attachment to the group: cross-cultural differences in organizational identification and subjective norms as predictors of workers' turnover intentions. *Pers. Soc. Psychol. Bull.* 24:1027–39

Ajzen I. 1991. The theory of planned behavior.

Org. Behav. Hum. Decis. Process. 50:179–211

Ajzen I, Fishbein M. 1980. *Understanding Attitudes and Predicting Social Behavior.* Englewood-Cliffs, NJ: Prentice-Hall

Ajzen I, Fishbein M. 2000. Attitudes and the attitude-behavior relation: reasoned and automatic processes. In *European Review of Social Psychology*, ed. W Stroebe, M Hewstone. Chichester, England: Wiley. In press

Ajzen I, Sexton J. 1999. Depth of processing, belief congruence, and attitude-behavior correspondence. In *Dual-Process Theories in Social Psychology*, ed. S Chaiken, Y Trope, pp. 117–38. New York: Guilford

Albarracin D, Fishbein M, Goldestein de

Muchinik E. 1997. Seeking social support in old age as reasoned action: structural and volitional determinants in a middle-aged sample of Argentinean women. *J. Appl. Soc. Psychol.* 27:463–76

Albarracin D, Fishbein M, Middlestadt S. 1998. Generalizing behavioral findings across times, samples, and measures: a study of condom use. *J. Appl. Soc. Psychol.* 28:657–74

Armitage CJ, Conner M. 1999a. Distinguishing perceptions of control from self-efficacy: predicting consumption of a low-fat diet using the theory of planned behavior. *J. Appl. Soc. Psychol.* 29:72–90

Armitage CJ, Conner M. 1999b. The theory of planned behaviour: assessment of predictive validity and 'perceived control'. *Br. J. Soc. Psychol.* 38:35–54

Armitage CJ, Conner M. 2000. Efficacy of the theory of planned behavior: a meta-analytic review. *Br. J. Soc. Psychol.* In press

Armitage CJ, Conner M. 2000. Attitudinal ambivalence: a test of three key hypotheses. *Pers. Soc. Psychol. Bull.* In press

Armitage CJ, Conner M, Norman P. 1999. Differential effects of mood on information processing: evidence from the theories of reasoned action and planned behaviour. *Eur. J. Soc. Psychol.* 29:419–33

Arnscheid R, Schomers P. 1996. Attitude and performance in groups: a test of the theory of planned behavior on basketball players. *Z. Sozialpsychol.* 27:61–69

Banaji MR, Prentice DA. 1994. The self in social context. *Annu. Rev. Psychol.* 45:297–332

Bandura A. 1997. *Self-Efficacy: The Exercise of Control.* New York: Freeman

Bargh JA, Chaiken S, Govender R, Pratto F. 1992. The generality of the automatic attitude activation effect. *J. Pers. Soc. Psychol.* 62:893–912

Bargh JA, Chaiken S, Raymond P, Hymes C. 1996. The automatic evaluation effect: unconditional automatic attitude activation with a pronunciation task. *J. Exp. Soc. Psychol.* 32:104–28

Bargh JA, Chartrand TL. 1999. The unbearable automaticity of being. *Am. Psychol.* 54:462–79

Bassili JN. 1995. Response latency and the accessibility of voting intentions: what contributes to accessibility and how it affects vote choice. *Pers. Soc. Psychol. Bull.* 21:686–95

Bassili JN. 1996. Meta-judgmental versus operative indexes of psychological attributes: the case of measures of attitude strength. *J. Pers. Soc. Psychol.* 71:637–53

Bassili JN, Roy J-P. 1998. On the representation of strong and weak attitudes about policy in memory. *Polit. Psychol.* 19:669–81

Bell DW, Esses VM. 1997. Ambivalence and response amplification toward native peoples. *J. Appl. Soc. Psychol.* 27:1063–84

Bentler PM, Speckart G. 1979. Models of attitude behavior relations. *Psychol. Rev.* 86:452–64

Biek M, Wood W, Chaiken S. 1996. Working knowledge, cognitive processing, and attitudes: on the determinants of bias. *Pers. Soc. Psychol. Bull.* 22:547–56

Blessum KA, Lord CG, Sia TL. 1998. Cognitive load and positive mood reduce typicality effects in attitude-behavior consistency. *Pers. Soc. Psychol. Bull.* 24:496–504

Boldero J, Sanitioso R, Brain B. 1999. Gay Asian Australians' safer-sex behavior and behavioral skills: the predictive utility of the theory of planned behavior and cultural factors. *J. Appl. Soc. Psychol.* 29:2143–63

Bornstein RF. 1989. Exposure and affect: overview and meta-analysis of research, 1968–1987. *Psychol. Bull.* 106:265–89

Braithwaite V. 1997. Harmony and security value orientations in political evaluation. *Pers. Soc. Psychol. Bull.* 23:401–14

Braithwaite V. 1998. The value orientations underlying liberalism-conservatism. *Pers. Individ. Differ.* 25:575–89

Brendl CM, Higgins ET. 1996. Principles of judging valence: What makes events positive or negative? In *Advances in Experimental*

Social Psychology, ed. MP Zanna, 28:95–160. San Diego, CA: Academic

Budd RJ. 1986. Predicting cigarette use: the need to incorporate measures of salience in the theory of reasoned action. J. Appl. Soc. Psychol. 16:663–85

Cacioppo JT, Berntson GG. 1994. Relationship between attitudes and evaluative space: a critical review, with emphasis on the separability of positive and negative substrates. Psychol. Bull. 115:401–23

Cacioppo JT, Crites SL Jr, Gardner WL. 1996. Attitudes to the right: evaluative processing is associated with lateralized late positive event-related brain potentials. Pers. Soc. Psychol. Bull. 22:1205–19

Cacioppo JT, Gardner WL. 1999. Emotion. Annu. Rev. Psychol. 50:191–214

Chen M, Bargh JA. 1999. Consequences of automatic evaluation: immediate behavioral predispositions to approach or avoid the stimulus. Pers. Soc. Psychol. Bull. 25:215–24

Conner M, Armitage CJ. 1998. Extending the theory of planned behavior: a review and avenues for further research. J. Appl. Soc. Psychol. 28:1429–64

Conner M, Black K, Stratton P. 1998a. Understanding drug compliance in a psychiatric population: an application of the Theory of Planned Behaviour. Psychol. Health Med. 3:337–44

Conner M, Heywood-Everett S. 1998. Addressing mental health problems with the Theory of Planned Behaviour. Psychol. Health Med. 3:87–95

Conner M, McMillan B. 1999. Interaction effects in the theory of planned behavior: studying cannabis use. Br. J. Soc. Psychol. 38:195–222

Conner M, Sheeran P, Norman P, Armitage CJ. 2000. Temporal stability as a moderator of the relationships in the theory of planned behavior. Br. J. Soc. Psychol. In press

Conner M, Sherlock K, Orbell S. 1998b. Psychosocial determinants of ecstasy use in young people in the UK. Br. J. Health Psychol. 3:295–317

Conner M, Sparks P. 1996. The theory of planned behaviour and health behaviours. In Predicting Health Behaviour: Research and Practice with Social Cognition Models, ed. M Conner, P Norman, pp. 121–62. Buckingham, England: Open Univ. Press

Conner M, Warren R, Close S, Sparks P. 1999. Alcohol consumption and theory of planned behavior: an examination of the cognitive mediation of past behavior. J. Appl. Soc. Psychol. 29:1676–704

Courneya KS, Bobick TM, Schinke RJ. 1999a. Does the theory of planned behavior mediate the relation between personality and exercise behavior? Basic Appl. Soc. Psychol. 21:317–24

Courneya KS, Friedenreich CM, Arthur K, Bobick TM. 1999b. Understanding exercise motivation in colorectal cancer patients: a prospective study using the theory of planned behavior. Rehabil. Psychol. 44:68–84

Crandall CS, Martinez R. 1996. Culture, ideology, and antifat attitudes. Pers. Soc. Psychol. Bull. 22:1165–76

Crano WD. 1997a. Vested interest and symbolic politics—observations and recommendations: reply to Sears (1997). J. Pers. Soc. Psychol. 72:497–500

Crano WD. 1997b. Vested interest, symbolic politics, and attitude-behavior consistency. J. Pers. Soc. Psychol. 72:485–91

Crites SL Jr, Cacioppo JT. 1996. Electrocortical differentiation of evaluative and nonevaluative categorizations. Psychol. Sci. 7:318–21

de Vroome EMM, Stroebe W, Sandfort TGM, de Witt JBF, van Griensven GJP. 2000. Safe sex in social context: individualistic and relational determinants of AIDS preventive behavior among gay men. J. Appl. Soc. Psychol. In press

de Witt JBF, Stroebe W, de Vroome EMM, Sandfort TGM, van Griensven GJP. 2000. Understanding AIDS preventive behavior in homosexual men: the theory of planned behavior and the information-motivation-behavioral-skills model prospectively compared. Psychol. Health. In press

Demo DH. 1989. The self-concept over time: research issues and directions. *Annu. Rev. Sociol.* 18:23–52

Demski RM, McGlynn RP. 1999. Fear or moral indignation? Predicting attitudes toward parolees. *J. Appl. Soc. Psychol.* 29:2024–58

Eagly AH. 1998. Attitudes and the processing of attitude-relevant information. In *Advances in Psychological Science*, Vol. 1. *Social, Personal, and Cultural Aspects*, ed. JG Adair, D Belanger, pp. 185–201. Hove, UK: Psychol. Press/Erlbaum (UK) Taylor & Francis

Eagly AH, Chaiken S. 1993. *The Psychology of Attitudes*. Fort Worth, TX: Harcourt Brace

Eagly AH, Chaiken S. 1998. Attitude structure and function. In *The Handbook of Social Psychology*, ed. DT Gilbert, ST Fiske, 2:269–322. Boston: McGraw-Hill. 4th ed.

Eagly AH, Chen S, Chaiken S, Shaw-Barnes K. 1999. The impact of attitudes on memory: an affair to remember. *Psychol. Bull.* 125:64–89

Fazio RH, Jackson JR, Dunton BC, Williams CJ. 1995. Variability in automatic activation as an unobstrusive measure of racial attitudes: a bona fide pipeline? *J. Pers. Soc. Psychol.* 69:1013–27

Fazio RH, Sanbonmatsu DM, Powell MC, Kardes FR. 1986. On the automatic activation of attitudes. *J. Pers. Soc. Psychol.* 50:229–38

Fazio RH, Towles-Schwen T. 1999. The MODE model of attitude-behavior processes. In *Dual-Process Theories in Social Psychology*, ed. S Chaiken, Y Trope, pp. 97–116. New York: Guilford

Feather NT, ed. 1982. *Expectations and Actions: Expectancy-Value Models in Psychology*. Hillsdale, NJ: Erlbaum

Feather NT. 1996. Values, deservingness, and attitudes toward high achievers: research on tall poppies. See Seligman et al 1996, pp. 215–51

Feather NT, Norman MA, Worsley A. 1998. Values and valences: variables relating to the attractiveness and choice of food in different contexts. *J. Appl. Soc. Psychol.* 28:639–56

Feldman Barrett L, Russell JA. 1998. Independence and bipolarity in the structure of current affect. *J. Pers. Soc. Psychol.* 74:967–84

Finlay KA, Trafimow D, Jones D. 1997. Predicting health behaviors from attitudes and subjective norms: between-subjects and within-subjects analyses. *J. Appl. Soc. Psychol.* 27:2015–31

Finlay KA, Trafimow D, Moroi E. 1999. The importance of subjective norms on intentions to perform health behaviors. *J. Appl. Soc. Psychol.* 29:2381–93

Fishbein M. 1963. An investigation of the relationships between beliefs about an object and the attitude toward that object. *Hum. Relat.* 16:233–40

Fishbein M, Ajzen I. 1975. *Belief, Attitude, Intention, and Behavior: An Introduction to Theory and Research*. Reading, MA: Addison-Wesley

Fishbein M, Middlestadt S. 1995. Noncognitive effects on attitude formation and change: fact or artifact? *J. Consum. Psychol.* 4:181–202

Fishbein M, Middlestadt SE. 1997. A striking lack of evidence for nonbelief-based attitude formation and change: a response to five commentaries. *J. Consum. Psychol.* 6:107–15

Fiske ST. 1993. Social cognition and social perception. *Annu. Rev. Psychol.* 44:155–94

Fiske ST, Glick P. 1995. Ambivalence and stereotypes cause sexual harassment: a theory with implications for organizational change. *J. Soc. Issues* 51:97–115

Gaertner SL, Dovidio JF. 1986. The aversive form of racism. In *Prejudice, Discrimination, and Racism*, ed. JF Dovidio, SL Gaertner, pp. 61–89. Orlando, FL: Academic

Giner-Sorolla R. 1999. Affect in attitude: immediate and deliberative perspectives. In *Dual-Process Theories in Social Psychology*, ed. S Chaiken, Y Trope, pp. 441–61. New York: Guilford

Giner-Sorolla R, Garcia MT, Bargh JA. 1999. The automatic evaluation of pictures. *Soc. Cogn.* 17:76–96

Glaser J, Banaji MR. 1999. When fair is foul and foul is fair: reverse priming in automatic evaluation. *J. Pers. Soc. Psychol.* 77:669–87

Gollwitzer PM. 1996. The volitional benefits of planning. In *The Psychology of Action: Linking Cognition and Motivation to Behavior*, ed. PM Gollwitzer, JA Bargh, pp. 287–312. New York: Guilford

Gollwitzer PM. 1999. Implementation intentions: strong effects of simple plans. *Am. Psychol.* 54:493–503

Gollwitzer PM, Brandstaetter V. 1997. Implementation intentions and effective goal pursuit. *J. Pers. Soc. Psychol.* 73:186–99

Gollwitzer PM, Schaal B. 1998. Metacognition in action: the importance of implementation intentions. *Pers. Soc. Psychol. Rev.* 2:124–36

Greenwald AG, Banaji MR. 1995. Implicit social cognition: attitudes, self-esteem, and stereotypes. *Psychol. Rev.* 102:4–27

Greenwald AG, McGhee DE, Schwartz JLK. 1998. Measuring individual differences in implicit cognition: the implicit association test. *J. Pers. Soc. Psychol.* 74:1464–80

Grogan SC, Bell R, Conner M. 1997. Eating sweet snacks: gender differences in attitudes and behaviour. *Appetite* 28:19–31

Haddock G, Rothman AJ, Reber R, Schwarz N. 1999. Forming judgments of attitude certainty, intensity, and importance: the role of subjective experience. *Pers. Soc. Psychol. Bull.* 25:771–82

Haddock G, Rothman AJ, Schwarz N. 1996. Are (some) reports of attitude strength context dependent? *Can. J. Behav. Sci.* 28:313–16

Haddock G, Zanna MP. 1998. Assessing the impact of affective and cognitive information in predicting attitudes toward capital punishment. *Law Hum. Behav.* 22:325–39

Haddock G, Zanna MP. 2000. Cognition, affect, and the prediction of social attitudes. In *European Review of Social Psychology*, Vol. 10, ed. W Stroebe, M Hewstone. Chichester, UK: Wiley. In press

Harland P, Staats H, Wilke HAM. 1999. Explaining proenvironmental intention and behavior by personal norms and the theory of planned behavior. *J. Appl. Soc. Psychol.* 29:2505–28

Haugtvedt CP. 1997. Beyond fact or artifact: an assessment of Fishbein and Middlestadt's perspectives on attitude change processes. *J. Consum. Psychol.* 6:99–106

Higgins ET. 1987. Self-discrepancies: a theory relating self and affect. *Psychol. Rev.* 94:319–40

Higgins ET. 1996. Knowledge activation: accessibility, applicability, and salience. In *Social Psychology: Handbook of Basic Principles*, ed. ET Higgins, AW Kruglanski, pp. 133–68. New York: Guilford

Hill M, Mann L, Wearing AJ. 1996. The effects of attitude, subjective norm and self-efficacy on intention to benchmark: a comparison between managers with experience and no experience in benchmarking. *J. Organ. Behav.* 17:313–27

Hillhouse JJ, Adler CM, Drinnon J, Turrisi R. 1997. Application of Ajzen's theory of planned behavior to predict sunbathing, tanning salon use, and sunscreen use intentions and behaviors. *J. Behav. Med.* 20:365–78

Hilton JL, von Hippel W. 1996. Stereotypes. *Annu. Rev. Psychol.* 47:237–71

Ito TA, Cacioppo JT, Lang PJ. 1998a. Eliciting affect using the International Affective Picture System: trajectories through evaluative space. *Pers. Soc. Psychol. Bull.* 24:855–79

Ito TA, Larsen JT, Smith NK, Cacioppo JT. 1998b. Negative information weighs more heavily on the brain: the negativity bias in evaluative categorizations. *J. Pers. Soc. Psychol.* 75:887–900

Jamner MS, Wolitski RJ, Corby NH, Fishbein M. 1998. Using the theory of planned behavior to predict intention to use condoms among female sex workers. *Psychol. Health* 13:187–205

Jarvis WBG, Petty RE. 1996. The need to evaluate. *J. Pers. Soc. Psychol.* 70:172–94

Johnson-Laird PN. 1999. Deductive reasoning. *Annu. Rev. Psychol.* 50:109–35

Jonas K, Diehl M, Bromer P. 1997. Effects of attitudinal ambivalence on information processing and attitude-intention consistency. *J. Exp. Soc. Psychol.* 33:190–210

Kaiser FG, Woelfing S, Fuhrer U. 1999. Environmental attitude and ecological behaviour. *J. Environ. Psychol.* 19:1–19

Kempf DS. 1999. Attitude formation from product trial: distinct roles of cognition and affect for hedonic and functional products. *Psychol. Mark.* 16:35–50

Kendzierski D, Whitaker DJ. 1997. The role of self-schema in linking intentions with behavior. *Pers. Soc. Psychol. Bull.* 23:139–47

Klein JG. 1996. Negativity in impressions of presidential candidates revisited: the 1992 election. *Pers. Soc. Psychol. Bull.* 22:288–95

Kokkinaki F, Lunt P. 1997. The relationship between involvement, attitude accessibility and attitude-behaviour consistency. *Br. J. Soc. Psychol.* 36,497–509

Kokkinaki F, Lunt P. 1999. The effect of advertising message involvement on brand attitude accessibility. *J. Econ. Psychol.* 20:41–51

Kristiansen CM, Hotte AM. 1996. Morality and the self: implications for the when and how of value-attitude-behavior relations. See Seligman et al 1996, pp. 77–105

Krosnick JA, Boninger DS, Chuang YC, Berent MK, et al. 1993. Attitude strength: one construct or many related constructs? *J. Pers. Soc. Psychol.* 65:1132–51

Lavine H, Huff JW, Wagner SH, Sweeney D. 1998a. The moderating influence of attitude strength on the susceptibility to context effects in attitude surveys. *J. Pers. Soc. Psychol.* 75:359–73

Lavine H, Thomsen CJ, Zanna MP, Borgida E. 1998b. On the primacy of affect in the determination of attitudes and behavior: the moderating role of affective-cognitive ambivalence. *J. Exp. Soc. Psychol.* 34:398–421

Leone L, Perugini M, Ercolani AP. 1999. A comparison of three models of attitude-behavior relationships in the studying behavior domain. *Eur. J. Soc. Psychol.* 29:161–89

Levine GM, Halberstadt JB, Goldstone RL. 1996. Reasoning and the weighting of attributes in attitude judgments. *J. Pers. Soc. Psychol.* 70:230–40

Levine JM, Moreland RL. 1990. Progress in small group research. *Annu. Rev. Psychol.* 41:585–634

Liberman A, Chaiken S. 1996. The direct effect of personal relevance on attitudes. *Pers. Soc. Psychol. Bull.* 22:269–79

Liberman N, Trope Y. 1998. The role of feasibility and desirability considerations in near and distant future decisions: a test of temporal construal theory. *J. Pers. Soc. Psychol.* 75:5–18

Lord CG, Lepper MR. 1999. Attitude representation theory. In *Advances in Experimental Social Psychology*, ed. MP Zanna, 31:265–343. San Diego, CA: Academic

MacDonald TK, Zanna MP. 1998. Cross-dimension ambivalence toward social groups: can ambivalence affect intentions to hire feminists? *Pers. Soc. Psychol. Bull.* 24:427–41

MacDonald TK, Zanna MP, Fong GT. 1996. Why common sense goes out the window: effects of alcohol on intentions to use condoms. *Pers. Soc. Psychol. Bull.* 22:763–75

Maio GR, Bell DW, Esses VM. 1996. Ambivalence and persuasion: the processing of messages about immigrant groups. *J. Exp. Soc. Psychol.* 32:513–36

Maio GR, Fincham FD, Lycett EJ. 2000. Attitudinal ambivalence toward parents and attachment style. *Pers. Soc. Psychol. Bull.* In press

Maio GR, Olson JM. 1998. Values as truisms: evidence and implications. *J. Pers. Soc. Psychol.* 74:294–311

Maio GR, Olson JM, eds. 1999. *Why We Evaluate: Functions of Attitudes.* Mahwah, NJ: Erlbaum

Manstead ASR. 2000. The role of moral norm in the attitude-behavior relationship. In *Attitudes, Behavior, and Social Context: The Role of Norms and Group Membership*, ed. DJ Terry, MA Hogg. Mahwah, NJ: Erlbaum. In press

Manstead ASR, van Eekelen SAM. 1998.

Distinguishing between perceived behavioral control and self-efficacy in the domain of academic intentions and behaviors. *J. Appl. Soc. Psychol.* 28:1375–92

Markman AB, Brendl CM. 2000. The influence of goals on value and choice. In *The Psychology of Learning and Motivation,* Vol. 39, ed. DL Medin. San Diego, CA: Academic. In press

Matthews D, Dietz-Uhler B. 1998. The black-sheep effect: how positive and negative advertisements affect voter's perceptions of the sponsor of the advertisement. *J. Appl. Soc. Psychol.* 28:1903–15

McConnell AR, Leibold JM, Sherman SJ. 1997. Within-target illusory correlations and the formation of context-dependent attitudes. *J. Pers. Soc. Psychol.* 73:675–86

McGregor I, Newby-Clark IR, Zanna MP. 1999. "Remembering" dissonance: simultaneous accessibility of inconsistent cognitive elements moderates epistemic discomfort. In *Cognitive Dissonance: Progress on a Pivotal Theory in Social Psychology. Science Conference Series,* ed. E Harmon-Jones, J Mills, pp. 325–53. Washington, DC: Am. Psychol. Assoc.

McGuire WJ, McGuire CV. 1996. Enhancing self-esteem by directed-thinking tasks: cognitive and affective positivity asymmetries. *J. Pers. Soc. Psychol.* 70:1117–25

Mellers BA, Schwartz A, Cooke ADJ. 1998. Judgment and decision making. *Annu. Rev. Psychol.* 49:447–77

Millar MG, Millar KU. 1996. The effects of direct and indirect experience on affective and cognitive responses and the attitude-behavior relation. *J. Exp. Soc. Psychol.* 32:561–79

Millar MG, Millar KU. 1998. The effects of prior experience and thought on the attitude-behavior relation. *Soc. Behav. Pers.* 26:105–14

Miniard PW, Barone MJ. 1997. The case for noncognitive determinants of attitude: a critique of Fishbein and Middlestadt. *J. Consum. Psychol.* 6:77–91

Morrison DM, Gillmore MR, Simpson EE,

Wells EA. 1996. Children's decisions about substance use: an application and extension of the theory of reasoned action. *J. Appl. Soc. Psychol.* 26:1658–79

Munro GD, Ditto PH. 1997. Biased assimilation, attitude polarization, and affect in reactions to stereotyped-relevant scientific information. *Pers. Soc. Psychol. Bull.* 23:636–53

Murray SL, Haddock G, Zanna MP. 1996. On creating value-expressive attitudes: an experimental approach. See Seligman et al 1996, pp. 107–33

Norman P, Conner M, Bell R. 1999. The theory of planned behavior and smoking cessation. *Health Psychol.* 18:89–94

Nowlis V. 1965. Research with the Mood Adjective Checklist. In *Affect, Cognition, and Personality,* ed. SS Tomkin, CE Izard, pp. 352–89. New York: Springer

O'Callaghan FV, Callan VJ, Baglioni A. 1999. Cigarette use by adolescents: attitude-behavior relationships. *Subst. Use Misuse* 34:455–68

Ohira H, Winton WM, Oyama M. 1998. Effects of stimulus valence on recognition memory and endogenous eyeblinks: further evidence for positive-negative asymmetry. *Pers. Soc. Psychol. Bull.* 24:986–93

Olson JM, Roese NJ, Zanna MP. 1996. Expectancies. In *Social Psychology: Handbook of Basic Principles,* ed. ET Higgins, AW Kruglanski, pp. 211–38. New York: Guilford

Osgood CE, Suci GJ, Tannenbaum PH. 1957. *The Measurement of Meaning.* Urbana, IL: Univ. Illinois Press

Ouellette JA, Wood W. 1998. Habit and intention in everyday life: the multiple processes by which past behavior predicts future behavior. *Psychol. Bull.* 124:54–74

Paisley CM, Sparks P. 1998. Expectations of reducing fat intake: the role of perceived need within the theory of planned behavior. *Psychol. Health* 13:341–53

Pettigrew TF. 1998. Intergroup contact theory. *Annu. Rev. Psychol.* 49:65–85

Petty RE, Jarvis WBG. 1996. An individual

differences perspective on assessing cognitive processes. In *Answering Questions: Methodology for Determining Cognitive and Communicative Processes in Survey Research*, ed. N Schwarz, S Sudman, pp. 221–57. San Francisco: Jossey-Bass

Petty RE, Krosnick JA, eds. 1995. *Attitude Strength: Antecedents and Consequences*, Vol. 4. Ohio State Univ. Series on attitudes and persuasion. Mahwah, NJ: Erlbaum

Petty RE, Wegener DT. 1998. Matching versus mismatching attitude functions: implications for scrutiny of persuasive messages. *Pers. Soc. Psychol. Bull.* 24:227–40

Petty RE, Wegener DT, Fabrigar LR. 1997. Attitudes and attitude change. *Annu. Rev. Psychol.* 48:609–47

Posavac SS, Sanbonmatsu DM, Fazio RH. 1997. Considering the best choice: effects of the salience and accessibility of alternatives on attitude-decision consistency. *J. Pers. Soc. Psychol.* 72:253–61

Priester JR, Fleming MA. 1997. Artifact or meaningful theoretical constructs?: examining evidence for nonbelief- and belief-based attitude change processes. *J. Consum. Psychol.* 6:67–76

Priester JR, Petty RE. 1996. The gradual threshold model of ambivalence: relating the positive and negative bases of attitudes to subjective ambivalence. *J. Pers. Soc. Psychol.* 71:431–49

Prislin R. 1996. Attitude stability and attitude strength: One is enough to make it stable. *Eur. J. Soc. Psychol.* 26:447–77

Prislin R, Ouellette J. 1996. When it is embedded, it is potent: effects of general attitude embeddedness on formation of specific attitudes and behavioral intentions. *Pers. Soc. Psychol. Bull.* 22:845–61

Quine L, Rubin R. 1997. Attitude, subjective norm and perceived behavioural control as predictors of women's intentions to take hormone replacement therapy. *Br. J. Health Psychol.* 2:199–216

Quine L, Rutter DR, Arnold L. 1998. Predicting and understanding safety helmet use among

schoolboy cyclists: a comparison of the theory of planned behavior and the health belief model. *Psychol. Health* 13:251–69

Ratcliff CD, Czuchry M, Scarberry NC, Thomas JC, Dansereau DF, Lord CG. 1999. Effects of directed thinking on intentions to engage in beneficial activities: actions versus reasons. *J. Appl. Soc. Psychol.* 29:994–1009

Reeder GD, Pryor JB. 1999. Attitudes toward persons with HIV/AIDS: linking a functional approach with underlying process. In *Why We Evaluate: Functions of Attitudes*, ed. G Maio, J Olson, pp. 295–323. Mahwah, NJ: Erlbaum

Reinecke J, Schmidt P, Ajzen I. 1996. Application of the theory of planned behavior to adolescents' condom use: a panel study. *J. Appl. Soc. Psychol.* 26:749–72

Richard R, de Vries NK, van der Pligt J. 1998. Anticipated regret and precautionary sexual behavior. *J. Appl. Soc. Psychol.* 28:1411–28

Rise J, Astrom AN, Sutton S. 1998. Predicting intentions and use of dental floss among adolescents: an application of the theory of planned behavior. *Psychol. Health* 13:223–36

Robinson JP, Shaver PR, Wrightsman LS, eds. 1999. *Measures of Political Attitudes. Measures of Social Psychological Attitudes*, Vol. 2. San Diego, CA: Academic

Russell JA, Carroll JM. 1999. On the bipolarity of positive and negative affect. *Psychol. Bull.* 125:3–30

Schultz PW, Oskamp S. 1996. Effort as a moderator of the attitude-behavior relationship: general environmental concern and recycling. *Soc. Psychol. Q.* 59:375–83

Schwartz SH. 1992. Universals in the content and structure of values: theoretical advances and empirical tests in 20 countries. In *Advances in Experimental Social Psychology*, ed. MP Zanna, 25:1–65. San Diego, CA: Academic

Schwarz N. 1997. Moods and attitude judgments: a comment on Fishbein and Middlestadt. *J. Consum. Psychol.* 6:93–98

Schwarz N, Clore GL. 1983. Mood, misattribution, and judgments of well-being: informative and directive functions of affective states. *J. Pers. Soc. Psychol.* 45:513–23

Schwarz N, Clore GL. 1996. Feelings and phenomenal experiences. In *Social Psychology: Handbook of Basic Principles*, ed. ET Higgins, AW Kruglanski, pp. 433–65. New York: Guilford

Sears DO. 1997. The impact of self-interest on attitudes—a symbolic politics perspective on differences between survey and experimental findings: comment on Crano (1997). *J. Pers. Soc. Psychol.* 72:492–96

Seligman C, Olson JM, Zanna MP, eds. 1996. *The Psychology of Values: The Ontario Symposium*, Vol. 8. *The Ontario Symposium on Personality and Social Psychology*. Mahwah, NJ: Erlbaum

Shah J, Higgins ET. 1997. Expectancy × value effects: regulatory focus as determinant of magnitude and direction. *J. Pers. Soc. Psychol.* 73:447–58

Sheeran P, Norman P, Orbell S. 1999a. Evidence that intentions based on attitudes better predict behaviour than intentions based on subjective norms. *Eur. J. Soc. Psychol.* 29:403–6

Sheeran P, Orbell S. 1998. Do intentions predict condom use? Meta-analysis and examination of six moderator variables. *Br. J. Soc. Psychol.* 37:231–50

Sheeran P, Orbell S. 1999a. Augmenting the theory of planned behavior: roles for anticipated regret and descriptive norms. *J. Appl. Soc. Psychol.* 29:2107–42

Sheeran P, Orbell S. 1999b. Implementation intentions and repeated behaviour: augmenting the predictive validity of the theory of planned behaviour. *Eur. J. Soc. Psychol.* 29:349–69

Sheeran P, Orbell S, Trafimow D. 1999b. Does the temporal stability of behavioral intentions moderate intention-behavior and past behavior-future behavior relations? *Pers. Soc. Psychol. Bull.* 25:721–30

Sheeran P, Taylor S. 1999. Predicting intentions to use condoms: a meta-analysis and comparison of the theories of reasoned action and planned behavior. *J. Appl. Soc. Psychol.* 29:1624–75

Sia TL, Lord CG, Blessum KA, Ratcliff CD, Lepper MR. 1997. Is a rose always a rose? The role of social category exemplar change in attitude stability and attitude-behavior consistency. *J. Pers. Soc. Psychol.* 72:501–14

Sia TL, Lord CG, Blessum KA, Thomas JC, Lepper MR. 1999. Activation of exemplars in the process of assessing social category attitudes. *J. Pers. Soc. Psychol.* 76:517–32

Simons J, Carey KB. 1998. A structural analysis of attitudes toward alcohol and marijuana use. *Pers. Soc. Psychol. Bull.* 24:727–35

Sjoeberg L, Montgomery H. 1999. Double denial in attitude formation. *J. Appl. Soc. Psychol.* 29:606–21

Smith ER, Fazio RH, Cejka MA. 1996. Accessible attitudes influence categorization of multiply categorizable objects. *J. Pers. Soc. Psychol.* 71:888–98

Sparks P, Guthrie CA. 1998. Self-identity and the theory of planned behavior: a useful addition or an unhelpful artifice? *J. Appl. Soc. Psychol.* 28:1393–410

Sparks P, Guthrie CA, Shepherd R. 1997. The dimensional structure of the perceived behavioral control construct. *J. Appl. Soc. Psychol.* 27:418–38

Steele CM, Josephs RA. 1990. Alcohol myopia: its prized and dangerous effects. *Am. Psychol.* 45:921–33

Sutton S. 1998. Predicting and explaining intentions and behavior: How well are we doing? *J. Appl. Soc. Psychol.* 28:1317–38

Taylor S, Todd P. 1997. Understanding the determinants of consumer composting behavior. *J. Appl. Soc. Psychol.* 27:602–28

Terry DJ, Hogg MA. 1996. Group norms and the attitude-behavior relationship: a role for group identification. *Pers. Soc. Psychol. Bull.* 22:776–93

Tesser A, Martin L. 1996. The psychology of evaluation. In *Social Psychology: Handbook of Basic Principles*, ed. ET Higgins, AW Kruglanski, pp. 400–32. New York: Guilford

Thompson MM, Zanna MP, Griffin DW. 1995. Let's not be indifferent about (attitudinal) ambivalence. In *Attitude Strength: Antecedents and Consequences. Ohio State University Series on Attitudes and Persuasion*, ed. RE Petty, JA Krosnick, 4:361–86. Mahwah, NJ: Erlbaum

Thurstone LL. 1931. The measurement of social attitudes. *J. Abnorm. Soc. Psychol.* 26:249–69

Trafimow D. 1996. The importance of attitudes in the prediction of college students' intentions to drink. *J. Appl. Soc. Psychol.* 26:2167–88

Trafimow D, Duran A. 1998. Some tests of the distinction between attitude and perceived behavioural control. *Br. J. Soc. Psychol.* 37:1–14

Trafimow D, Finlay KA. 1996. The importance of subjective norms for a minority of people: between-subjects and within-subjects analyses. *Pers. Soc. Psychol. Bull.* 22:820–28

Trafimow D, Trafimow JH. 1998. Predicting back pain sufferers' intentions to exercise. *J. Psychol.* 132:581–92

Triandis HC. 1977. *Interpersonal Behavior*. Monterey, CA: Brooks/Cole

van der Pligt J, de Vries NK. 1998. Belief importance in expectancy-value models of attitudes. *J. Appl. Soc. Psychol.* 28:1339–54

van der Pligt J, de Vries NK, Manstead ASR, van Harreveld F. 2000. The importance of being selective: weighing the role of attribute importance in attitudinal judgment. In *Advances in Experimental Social Psychology*, Vol. 32, ed. MP Zanna. New York: Academic. In press

van der Pligt J, Zeelenberg M, van Dijk WW, de Vries NK, Richard R. 1998. Affect, attitudes and decisions: Let's be more specific. In *European Review of Social Psychology*, ed. W Stroebe, M Hewstone, 8:33–66. Chichester, UK: Wiley

van Harreveld F, van der Pligt J, de Vries NK, Andreas S. 2000. The structure of attitudes: attribute importance, accessibility, and judgment. *Br. J. Soc. Psychol.* In press

Verplanken B, Aarts H, van Knippenberg A, Moonen A. 1998a. Habit versus planned behavior: a field experiment. *Br. J. Soc. Psychol.* 37:111–28

Verplanken B, Aarts H, van Knippenberg A. 1997. Habit, information acquisition, and the process of making travel mode choices. *Eur. J. Soc. Psychol.* 27:539–60

Verplanken B, Faes S. 1999. Good intentions, bad habits, and effects of forming implementation intentions on healthy eating. *Eur. J. Soc. Psychol.* 29:591–604

Verplanken B, Hofstee G, Janssen HJW. 1998b. Accessibility of affective versus cognitive components of attitudes. *Eur. J. Soc. Psychol.* 28:23–35

Vincent PC, Peplau LA, Hill CT. 1998. A longitudinal application of the theory of reasoned action to women's career behavior. *J. Appl. Soc. Psychol.* 28:761–78

Visser PS, Krosnick JA. 1998. Development of attitude strength over the life cycle: surge and decline. *J. Pers. Soc. Psychol.* 75:1389–410

Waenke M, Bless H, Biller B. 1996. Subjective experience versus content of information in the construction of attitude judgments. *Pers. Soc. Psychol. Bull.* 22:1105–13

Watson D, Tellegen A. 1999. Issues in the dimensional structure of affect—effects of descriptors, measurement error, and response format: comment on Russell and Carroll (1999). *Psychol. Bull.* 125:601–10

Wilson TD, Lindsey S, Schooler TY. 2000. A model of dual attitudes. *Psychol. Rev.* 107:101–26

Winkielman P, Zajonc RB, Schwarz N. 1997. Subliminal affective priming resists attributional interventions. *Cogn. Emot.* 11:433–65

Wojciszke B, Bazinska R, Jaworski M. 1998. On the dominance of moral categories in impression formation. *Pers. Soc. Psychol. Bull.* 24:1251–63

Wood W. 2000. Attitude change: Persuasion and social influence. *Annu. Rev. Psychol.* 51:539–70

Wyman MA, Snyder M. 1997. Attitudes toward "gays in the military": a functional perspective. *J. Appl. Soc. Psychol.* 27:306–29

Ybarra O, Trafimow D. 1998. How priming the private self or collective self affects the relative weights of attitudes and subjective norms. *Pers. Soc. Psychol. Bull.* 24:362–70

Zajonc RB. 1980. Feeling and thinking: preferences need no inferences. *Am. Psychol.* 35:117–23

Annu. Rev. Psychol. 2001. 52:59–82

META-ANALYSIS: Recent Developments in Quantitative Methods for Literature Reviews

R. Rosenthal and M. R. DiMatteo
Department of Psychology, University of California, Riverside, Riverside, California 92521

Key Words   effect size, graphic displays, contrast analysis, moderator analysis, heterogeneity analysis

■ **Abstract**   We describe the history and current status of the meta-analytic enterprise. The advantages and historical criticisms of meta-analysis are described, as are the basic steps in a meta-analysis and the role of effect sizes as chief coins of the meta-analytic realm. Advantages of the meta-analytic procedures include seeing the "landscape" of a research domain, keeping statistical significance in perspective, minimizing wasted data, becoming intimate with the data summarized, asking focused research questions, and finding moderator variables. Much of the criticism of meta-analysis has been based on simple misunderstanding of how meta-analyses are actually carried out. Criticisms of meta-analysis that are applicable are equally applicable to traditional, nonquantitative, narrative reviews of the literature. Much of the remainder of the chapter deals with the processes of effect size estimation, the understanding of the heterogeneity of the obtained effect sizes, and the practical and scientific importance of the effect sizes obtained.

CONTENTS

0066-4308/01/0201-0059$14.00

59

INTRODUCTION

As the twenty-first century unfolds, and scientific research in nearly every field is growing almost explosively, new findings daily "overthrow" old ones, and a "relentless cross fire" (Hunt 1997:1) sometimes occurs as researchers and the public try to make sense of the stories that our scientific data are trying to tell us. Findings are often confusing and conflicting about central issues of theory and practice, not only in psychology more narrowly defined, but in the related domains of education, medicine, and other biopsychological and sociopsychological disciplines. Do vitamins prevent cancer and does exercise extend life span? Does yo-yo dieting pose significant health problems? Does exposure to electromagnetic fields increase the risk of brain cancer and leukemia? Does noncompliance with medical treatment regimens affect outcomes? Does the Head Start program work? What is the relationship between gender and various kinds of social behavior, such as helping, nonverbal communication, and conforming to group values? These, and many other topics, have been addressed by myriad studies that have varying outcomes—some show effects in one direction and some in the opposite, and some show effects that are close to zero.

A resolution of conflicting evidence regarding these outcomes is often necessary for further advance of a field and for any practical application. Further, social and health policy sometimes demands accurate estimation of certain descriptive statistics that, in the available research, show such variability that making intervention decisions based on them is both challenging and precarious. For example, as Hunt (1997) notes, estimates of the occurrence of mental health problems in the homeless range from 1% to 70%, and estimates of drug problems range from 2% to 90%. Patient noncompliance with medical treatment regimens is estimated to range between 20% and 70% (DiMatteo & DiNicola 1982).

ENTER META-ANALYSIS

The quantitative procedures of meta-analysis help to address some of the challenges introduced by the existence of multiple answers to a given research question. Meta-analysis allows the combining of numerical results from a few or many studies, the accurate estimate of descriptive statistics (Hedges 1987, Rosenthal 1978) and the explanation of inconsistencies as well as the discovery of moderators and mediators in bodies of research findings.

Meta-analysis allows researchers to arrive at conclusions that are more accurate and more credible than can be presented in any one primary study or in a nonquantitative, narrative review.

Meta-analysis began with a medical problem. This is perhaps appropriate because inquiries in the field of biomedicine often demand immediate answers to complex and multifaceted questions in which existing data may be quite variable and clinical steps depend upon reconciliation of disparate findings. In the case of the first meta-analysis, the year was 1904 and Karl Pearson collected correlation coefficients to determine the extent to which inoculation against smallpox was related to survival (Pearson 1904). The unweighted mean of the correlations between inoculation and survival was 0.63, the weighted mean r was 0.64, and the median was 0.61—a truly huge effect with massive clinical significance. Pearson's process of combining of research results across many studies was an unusual approach in 1904. Had his technique continued to be regularly employed throughout the first three-quarters of the twentieth century, cumulative research may have been brought to bear on some frustrating dilemmas in clinical treatment (Hunt 1997: Ch. 4, Robin 1984). Instead, it was not until the latter two decades of the twentieth century that meta-analysis became popular in fields such as biomedicine, the behavioral sciences, the interface of the two (the fields of health psychology, medical psychology, and behavioral medicine), and others. This popularity has come about partly because these disciplines generate too much information to manage easily, and methods are needed to synthesize that information. In medicine, for example, over two million medical articles are published every year. When different researchers, or even the same researchers, try to study a phenomenon more than once, they are bound to find different results from study to study, making it difficult to make sense of a body of research using narrative methods of synthesis. As Hall and Rosenthal (1995) have noted, there has been a shift in perspective recently such that a broader and more objective view of research is emerging and the "landscape" or distribution of results has become of greater interest than the results of individual studies.

Reviews of research have been valuable to many fields, but when presented and described only qualitatively, the results of conflicting studies can be confusing.

Qualitative or narrative methods approach controversy by listing and describing conflicting findings, and sometimes by trying to group or otherwise configure those that have various types of results or outcomes. Yet, it may be all too tempting for authors of narrative reviews consciously or unconsciously to select and describe studies to support their own understanding of the literature and/or their own established theoretical positions.

In an effort to avoid such influence—specifically preconceptions about the effectiveness of psychotherapy—Gene Glass and Mary Lee Smith conducted an extensive, systematic review of the entire literature on its outcomes, including every empirical article that provided an effect size (or the data to compute it) estimating the magnitude of the relationship between psychotherapy and an outcome (Smith & Glass 1977, Smith et al 1980). This research marks the beginning of the meta-analytic movement in psychology; the term meta-analysis was first used by Gene Glass in his 1976 presidential address to the American Educational Research Association. In this work, it became clear that meta-analysis is more than a statistical technique; it is a methodology for systematically examining a body of research, carefully formulating hypotheses, conducting an exhaustive search and establishing inclusion/exclusion criteria for articles, recording and statistically synthesizing and combining data and effect sizes from these studies, searching for moderator and mediator variables to explain effects of interest, and reporting results. Writing in the *Annual Review of Psychology*, Green & Hall (1984:52) foretold the future of this versatile and useful approach to scientific research: "...careful quantitative reviews are likely to play a larger role in further advances in psychology." Their prediction was accurate. That year, PsychLit catalogued 89 English-language entries with the key word "meta-analysis;" in 1999, that number was 262. In the medical literature database, Medline, only 34 English-language citations with the key word: "meta-analysis" were catalogued in 1984; in 1999, there were 823 entries.

By virtue of its ability to extract fairly clear answers from the research literature, meta-analysis has likely made a big difference in the lives of patients of medicine and psychotherapy by providing answers to clinical questions about their care—answers that might not be available from a morass of conflicting research findings. For example, from a meta-analysis of the effects on mortality rates of bypass surgery versus medical therapy for ischemic heart disease, it was found that mortality owing to bypass was 10.2%, whereas for medical management mortality was 15.8% (Yusuf et al 1994). In another meta-analysis, this one on the use of antibiotics prior to colon surgery, effects combined across 26 clinical trials showed that antibiotic therapy reduced infection from 36% to 22%, and reduced death rates from 11.2% to 4.5% (Baum et al 1981). Finally, a meta-analysis of more than 200 studies on the effects of viewing violent TV demonstrated a greater tendency toward aggressive/antisocial acts after viewing TV violence against another person (Paik & Comstock 1994). The above three research domains had been burdened with controversy because the studies yielded such varying results that an overall message from the data seemed impossible—that is, until meta-analysis.

THE ADVANTAGES OF META-ANALYSIS

Seeing the Landscape of a Research Enterprise

Meta-analysis has come to occupy a major place in contemporary scientific research partly because, as demonstrated in the above examples, it helps overcome much of the equivocation about research findings in the social sciences and medicine by providing a method for combining research results. Meta-analysis is valuable for several other reasons as well. The methodology requires us to be extremely thorough in our search for relevant research reports and requires careful review and analysis of all of the published, and often the unpublished, data available on a specific research question. Thus, meta-analysis keeps us from relying on the results of a single study or a narrative, nonquantitative review in attempting to understand a phenomenon. A cumulative view of psychology and other sciences provides the opportunity to view the whole picture in a research enterprise, and meta-analysis helps us see the similarities and differences among the methodologies and the results of many studies.

Keeping Statistical Significance In Perspective

In the literature of psychology and medicine, among other fields, researchers often refer to the statistical significance of a finding; significance is considered good, and nonsignificance is considered bad. Yet, the significance of any given effect size will be determined by the size of the sample studied. The simple equation, in prose, is:

$$\text{Significance Test} = \text{Effect Size} \times \text{Study Size}.$$

The implications of this equation for understanding a body of research are considerable. For example, two studies with exactly the same effect sizes can vary greatly in their significance level depending simply upon the number of participants or other sampling units employed. A focus on significance has often misled us in traditional narrative reviews of the literature, whereas in quantitative reviews, we typically focus on effect sizes. Meta-analysis prevents our reliance on the significance test of any one finding as a measure of its value and helps us realize that repeated results in the same direction across several studies, even if not one is significant, are much more powerful evidence than a single significant result. For example, two results at $p = .06$ are much stronger evidence ($p = 0.014$) against the null hypothesis than is one 0.05 result; and ten results at $p = 0.10$ are stronger evidence ($p = 0.000025$) against the null than are five at $p = 0.05$ ($p = 0.00012$). Meta-analysis thus provides the opportunity for even small and nonsignificant effects to contribute to the overall picture of the results of a research enterprise. As has been demonstrated elsewhere, in biomedical research in particular, the clinical application of what is learned from the cumulation of even very small effects can save many lives (Rosenthal 1995a).

Toward Wasting No Data

Data collection/acquisition in psychology, and many other fields of science, can range from difficult to intensely frustrating, and from modestly to exceedingly expensive in terms of finances, time, trouble, and opportunity costs. It is fair to suggest that no appropriately collected data from a well-designed study should ever be wasted. In practice, however, data are wasted all the time—such as when researchers fail to write-up results that were not significant, and when journals reject articles with nonsignificant findings. Meta-analysis allows the combination of results from studies with samples so small that they never achieve statistical significance. Approaching the analysis of pilot studies with cumulative techniques of meta-analysis allows researchers to further a field in which the nature of the research precludes large studies. In *Science*, for example, Cohen (1993) reported on two pilot studies in which experimental monkeys were vaccinated with simian immunodeficiency virus (SIV; akin to HIV). Control monkeys were not vaccinated. Because of the complexity of such research and limits on availability of experimental animals, Study One had only three experimental and three control monkeys. The experimental animals had better health outcomes (two of three improved) than did the control animals (none improved). In the second pilot, experimental animals also did better (two of five improved) than controls (zero of six improved). Neither of these pilot studies showed results even close to traditional levels of significance. Meta-analytic combining of these results, however, showed p noticeably smaller and r dramatically large.

Intimacy with the Data

The process of summarizing a research domain in a quantitative fashion forces a meta-analyst to be complete in finding all the research articles in the literature, and to be precise in extracting the necessary data from them. A meta-analyst cannot read just the abstracts and discussion sections of articles, as interesting and even as accurate as they might be, to obtain what is needed to summarize a research realm. Whereas in a narrative review, one might accumulate conclusions, in doing meta-analysis a researcher must accumulate data by gathering research articles, scrutinizing their methods for inclusion/exclusion criteria and comparison to other studies, and attending carefully to measures and operationalizations of the independent and dependent variables. To extract the information needed to calculate effect sizes, a meta-analyst must become quite familiar with precisely what any given study actually found. These findings might be in the form of means and standard deviations, or tables of counts (that sometimes need to be constructed from textual material), or test statistics such as t, F, χ^2, or Z; or their associated p levels. Thus, meta-analysts are forced to develop a certain intimacy with existing published (and often unpublished) data in a research area. Reading a research paper is quite a thorough enterprise when conducting a meta-analysis.

Focused Research Hypotheses

Conducting a meta-analysis is also an exercise in research precision. Diffuse hypotheses tested with more than one degree of freedom in the numerator of an F test or in a χ^2, although common in the literature, are problematic theoretically as well as statistically. Suppose, for example, a study is done in the area of patient adherence to (or compliance with) antibiotic treatment. The researcher wishes to determine the effect on a patient health outcome (say, eradication of the infection) of "perfect" versus "less than perfect" compliance with a doctor's recommendation to take four pills a day (referred to as QID, or roughly every six hours). Suppose further that the researcher randomly divides patients into four treatment groups, which respectively actually take one, two, three, or four pills a day. The outcome, appropriately, is the extent to which the patients get better (i.e, are cured of their infections). An analysis of variance "omnibus F-test" with 3 df in the numerator might show no significant differences among the four groups, and it could be erroneously concluded that the number of pills a patient actually takes of a QID antibiotic regimen does not matter at all in affecting whether or not an infection clears up. Besides making little intuitive sense, this conclusion can be massively incorrect statistically, and could lead to some serious erroneous clinical choices. A focused research question is essential. One or more contrasts from these three possibilities might be chosen: (a) a contrast between the group taking the prescribed number of pills each day (four) and the average of the other three groups (those taking three, two, or one); (b) a linear contrast, looking at the outcome as a function of increasing numbers of pills taken per day; or (c) a contrast of the average of the groups taking three or four pills per day versus the average of the groups taking one or two pills a day. In all of these cases, the test is a one df F-test, or a t-test, and it focuses on the real research questions: Is there a better result if one complies with the doctors' recommended treatment than if one does not? The question that is asked needs to be as scientifically precise as possible, especially given the potentially serious implications of failing to follow treatment advice. Because meta-analysis demands focused one-degree-of-freedom contrasts, it trains researchers to be attentive to the precise formulation of the questions they ask and meticulous in the answers they extract (Rosenthal & Rosnow 1985, Rosenthal et al 2000).

Identifying Moderator Variables

In virtually every research area, there is bound to be variation in the effect sizes discovered in a meta-analytic review. Sometimes there is wide variation, and the questions that are asked seem to be inadequate to deal with it.

For example, meta-analysis of the effects of a particular drug on depression might yield varying estimates, some strongly positive, some close to zero, and even some that are strongly negative. The issue of concern might then appropriately shift, such that the pattern of findings can be examined in relationship to moderating variables of interest. Perhaps, for example, the drug works well for middle adult patients, but negative effect sizes obtain in geriatric populations. Or the drug works well at low doses, but not at higher ones, or in the first few months of the illness but not later, or the effect is moderated by the extent of patient compliance. The search for important patterns in the quantitative reviews is facilitated by an inquisitive approach, emphasizing exploration instead of confirmation—an approach that allows examination and reconciliation of differences among studies. Correlations between moderator variables and effect sizes sometimes point to associations that are very helpful to understand. Meta-analysis allows us to formulate potential causal influences and to try to understand why various results occurred. Examination of moderator variables (e.g. year of publication, race/ethnicity of subject group, and sex of researcher) adds to theory development and increases the richness of empirical work.

CRITICISMS OF META-ANALYSIS

Bias in Sampling the Findings

Every meta-analysis has some inherent bias by virtue of the inclusion/exclusion criteria and the methods chosen to review the literature. Not every computer-assisted search will be complete, and not every journal article identified. Ideally one would obtain every piece of data ever collected on the topic of concern, but some data are not published, particularly if they yield results that do not achieve statistical significance. These limitations apply, of course, to qualitative and narrative, as well as to quantitative reviews, and concerns about publication bias in favor of significant results can be addressed with a statistical procedure addressing the file drawer problem, i.e. the problem that significant results are published while nonsignificant results are relegated to file drawers (Rosenthal 1979). Other biases are not so straightforward. For example, some researchers provide enough information to compute an effect size, whereas others do not. This difference may reflect a more serious bias in research sophistication.

Garbage In and Garbage Out

A meta-analysis usually includes studies that vary considerably in their sampling units, methods of measuring and operationalizing independent and dependent variables, data-analytic approaches, and statistical findings. Such variation can increase the generalizability of results when the findings are clear, but when they are not, varying theoretical and methodological approaches and an unsuccessful search for moderators can be confusing and can obscure a full understanding of the story the data are trying to tell. In the midst of this method variation is variation in quality: Meta-analysis is sometimes criticized for mixing together good and bad studies. This criticism, known as the "garbage in and garbage out" issue (Hunt 1997:42), can be dealt with using a weighting technique that takes into account and quantifies the methodological strength of each study in the analysis. Rosenthal (1991) has argued for "quality weighting" of studies, suggesting four-point scales as practical and valuable, and up to nine points as useful in some circumstances. Further, studies can also be blocked according to their type of methodology (randomized clinical trials versus observational; studies with and without control groups) and type of operationalization of dependent and independent variables (see DiMatteo et al 1996).

Singularity and Nonindependence of Effects

This criticism is easy to deal with if meta-analysts remember that effect sizes that are not independent of one another may need to be combined differently from effect sizes that are independent of each other—i.e. from different studies with nonoverlapping samples. If a study has more than one effect size, these can be used individually in analyses of subgroups or in examination of moderating variables, or they can be combined either by conservative averaging or by using less conservative techniques recommended by Rosenthal & Rubin (1986). Nonindependence may be a problem if the same research lab contributes a number of studies and this fact is ignored. It is possible and often valuable to block by laboratory or researcher and examine this as a moderator variable.

An Overemphasis on Individual Effects

Meta-analysis systematically assesses only individual effects, e.g. differences between means (effect size d) or zero-order correlations (effect size r) between independent and dependent variables—without necessarily viewing the big picture. It is true that meta-analytic techniques systematically assess only individual relationships between independent and dependent variables. In most research domains, however, this simple, systematic approach is essential. Consider the example of research on adherence to medical regimens. Many hundreds of empirical articles have been published on social-psychological variables that correlate with whether or not patients follow the recommendations that their health professionals have given them. A multifactorial model is indeed necessary, but before building that model, the individual correlates of adherence need to be taken into account (DiMatteo 2000). Before examining the combination and interaction of these components, meta-analysis is essential for achieving a clear picture of the straightforward operation of each individual component. Then informed studies using multifactorial, longitudinal designs can be built based on what meta-analysis has told us is important to examine. Whereas there is admittedly some loss of information when one concentrates on single effects in meta-analysis, a singular focus helps to target specific questions and to distill the essential elements of a phenomenon under study.

Combining Apples and Oranges

Another evocative image in the list of criticisms of meta-analysis is the apples and oranges argument (Hunt 1997:61). Meta-analysis is sometimes criticized because it involves summarizing results from studies that vary notably in their operationalization and measurement of independent and dependent variables and that employ very different types of sampling units to achieve answers to questions that are similar, though often not identical. It is argued, therefore, that meta-analysis is analogous to taking apples and oranges and averaging such measures as their weights, sizes, flavors, and shelf lives (Hunt 1997). The figures arrived at might be meaningless. It is true that in all reviews of the literature, qualitative and quantitative, we encounter replications that are rarely precisely the same. It can be argued, however, that it is a good thing to mix apples and oranges, particularly if one wants to generalize about fruit, and that studies that are exactly the same in all respects are actually limited in generalizability. Further, when studies vary methodologically, well-done meta-analyses take these differences into account by treating them as moderator variables. Hall and others (Hall et al 1994) do note, of course, that synthesis of very disparate studies requires sensitivity to issues of inference in trying to aggregate very diverse approaches to sampling and operationalization, and awareness of the existence of interesting and relevant moderator variables.

DOING META-ANALYSIS

As Hall & Rosenthal (1995) have noted, there is no single correct way to perform a meta-analysis. There are certain goals that should be addressed, however, and some methods better serve these goals than others. They offer three interrelated basic principles to guide meta-analysis: accuracy, simplicity, and clarity. The simpler a meta-analysis, the more likely it is to be accurate; it is not possible to present one that is too simple. The best quality scientific exploration is often one that poses unadorned, straightforward questions and uses simple statistical techniques for analysis. Alternatively, it is possible to do a meta-analysis, or any statistical analysis for that matter, that suffers from "high-tech statistication." Such analyses lend an impressive air of sophistication but may be massively inappropriate. Staying simple and staying close to the data helps to avoid serious misconceptions about it (Rosenthal 1995b). This point is underscored in the report of the APA Science Directorate's Task Force on Statistical Inference (Wilkinson et al 1999), which notes that scientific inquiry should remain logical and straightforward, understanding clearly the differences between correlation and causality, adopting an exploratory orientation, posing clear and straightforward scientific questions, analyzing them with straightforward and well-understood statistical tests, and avoiding the temptation to stuff data into the computer and hope for a sophisticated answer. Statistical analyses, complicated or not, must be used to aid thought about scientific research, not obscure it with mechanical approaches.

Despite developments in methodological and statistical techniques, meta-analysis remains at heart as simple now as it was in 1904. The level of quantitative skill and training required to do meta-analysis is very modest, and researchers who can analyze their own data can learn (easily) the few rather simple calculations needed to carry out a high-quality meta-analysis.

At this point in the extensive proliferation of research in psychology, health, and health psychology, among other fields, anyone who is considering a review of the literature has little justification for not doing it quantitatively. All the valuable aspects of narrative reviews can be preserved in meta-analysis, and quantitative features can be added. In approaching meta-analysis, researchers would do well to carefully examine the following basic bookshelf: Chalmers & Altman (1995), Cook et al (1992), Cooper (1989), Cooper & Hedges (1994), Glass et al (1981), Hedges & Olkin (1985), Hunt (1997), Hunter & Schmidt (1990), Light & Pillemer (1984), Rosenthal (1991), Wachter & Straf (1990). Some of the more complex procedures are described by Hedges & Olkin (1985) and by Hunter & Schmidt (1990); those that are quantitatively less demanding are by Cooper (1989), Hunt (1997), Light & Pillemer (1984), and Rosenthal (1991).

In the remaining pages of this chapter, we review some of the recent developments in the use of meta-analysis as a set of quantitative procedures.

Basic Steps

The basic steps in a meta-analysis follow.

1. Define the independent and dependent variables of interest, e.g. the effects of patient depression on patient adherence to medical treatment (DiMatteo et al 2000).

2. Collect the studies in a systematic way, attempting to find all the published (and often the unpublished) research available. Read each article's method and results very carefully, assessing how independent and dependent variables were operationalized and measured. Hope the researchers have reported effect sizes and *ns*, and if they have not, scour the articles for the information necessary to calculate these.

3. Examine the variability among the obtained effect sizes informally with graphs and charts. Most approaches to meta-analysis operationalize heterogeneity as a chi-square test of significance. It must be kept in mind, however, that the significance of this chi-square test depends upon sample size and can yield highly significant results even when there is little variation in the effect sizes; the standard deviation is a straightforward measure of the variability in effect sizes that is not dependent upon sample sizes. Variability among effect sizes points to the likelihood that a moderator variable might account for the variability in the effect sizes, and possibilities should be explored.

4. Combine the effects using several measures of their central tendency, i.e. medians and both weighted and unweighted means. When several approaches to central tendency yield different results, the reasons for such differences need to be explored.

5. Examine the significance level of the indices of central tendency. It is almost always useful to employ confidence intervals around the unweighted mean effect size based on a random effects model (i.e. using studies as the unit of analysis) and it is sometimes useful to employ confidence intervals around the weighted mean effect size based on a fixed effects model. The latter fixed effects model employs subjects nested within studies as the units of analysis, and yields a more powerful test of an overall null hypothesis, a null that is probably always false in any case (Cohen 1994). The disadvantage of the fixed effect model is that it does not permit generalization to studies other than those already in the sample. The random effects approach, though less powerful, does permit generalization to studies not yet in the sample, and if only one approach were to be used it would be the one we prefer. A new statistical procedure called the counternull value of the effect size is often helpful in meta-analytic work as well as in the analysis of individual studies. The counternull gives that value of the effect size that is greater than the one obtained and has exactly the same probability level as does the null value. For example, if we obtain $r = 0.10$, not significant at e.g. $p = 0.05$, before we decide r must, therefore, really be 0.00, the counternull tells us that the true value of r could as easily be 0.20 as it could be 0.00 (Rosenthal & Rubin 1994).

6. Using an examination of the binomial effect size display (see below), evaluate the importance of the obtained effect size.

EFFECT SIZES: Chief Coins of the Meta-Analytic Realm

There are two main families of effect sizes, the r family and the d family.

The r family of product moment correlations includes Pearson r when both variables are continuous, *phi* when both variables are dichotomous, point biserial r when one variable is continuous and one is dichotomous, and *rho* when both variables are in ranked form, as well as Z_r, the Fisher transformation of r.

This family also includes the various squared indices of r and related quantities, such as r^2, *omega* squared, *epsilon* squared, and *eta* squared. Squared indices are problematic, however, because they lose their directionality (although this can be retrieved through careful analysis of the findings), and the practical magnitude of these indices is often misinterpreted. In an example regarding the latter problem, it may be concluded that one percent of the variance in a dependent variable owing to the independent variable is too little to matter. However, if the independent variable is a very inexpensive and safe intervention, and the dependent variable involves saving lives [as was the case in research on prevention of heart attacks with low-dose aspirin (Rosenthal & Rosnow 1991)], the percentage of variance explained may be very small, but its implications might be quite substantial.

The three main members of the d family of effect sizes are Cohen's d, Hedges' g, and Glass's delta. All three employ the same numerator (comparing the difference between two means). The square root of the pooled variance (σ^2) of the two groups is used as the denominator in d, the square root of the pooled variance (S^2) is used in g, and the denominator of delta is the square root of the control group variance (S^2) only. The equations are:

$$\text{Cohen's } d = \frac{M_1 - M_2}{\sigma_{pooled}}$$

$$\text{Hedges's } g = \frac{M_1 - M_2}{S_{pooled}}$$

$$\text{Glass's } \Delta = \frac{M_1 - M_2}{S_{control\ group}}$$

The Advantages of r

Studies in the psychological literature vary considerably in their reporting of r or d effect sizes, and any review of a substantial amount of the literature is bound to reveal data presented with both types of effect sizes (not to mention no effect sizes at all). Both r and d estimates can be readily converted to one another, and eventually meta-analytic researchers need to decide to which index they should convert all effect size estimates obtained. Two examples of such conversions are:

$$r = \sqrt{\frac{d^2}{d^2 + 4}}$$

$$d = \frac{2r}{\sqrt{1 - r^2}}$$

The effect size r has several advantages over d. First, converting d's to r's makes sense because r in its point biserial form represents the relationship between two levels of the independent variable and scores on the dependent variable, but converting the continuous Pearson r to the dichotomous d loses information. Furthermore, using 1 df contrasts (see below), r allows for the analysis of trends across more than two groups, whereas d is limited to two. The r index requires no computational adjustment in going from cases of t-tests of two or more samples, to t-tests of only a single sample. Also, r is more simply interpreted in terms of practical importance than are d or g (see below for more about practical importance.)

Getting to "r"

Obtaining an effect size r from a given study may be easy or it may be a daunting challenge, depending upon the information the author has presented. Ideally, a researcher publishes a measure of the relationship between the independent and dependent variable in terms of a Pearson r, a point biserial r, a Spearman *rho*, or a *phi* coefficient, depending upon the nature of the independent and dependent variables as continuous variables, as ranks, or as dichotomous variables. The effect size r can be easily computed from t statistics, and from F statistics with 1 df in the numerator using the following:

$$r = \sqrt{\frac{t^2}{t^2 + df}}$$

$$r = \sqrt{\frac{F}{F + df_{error}}}$$

Effect size r's can also be computed from chi square and from the standard normal deviate Z.

$$r = \sqrt{\frac{\chi^2(1)}{N}}$$

$$r = \frac{Z}{\sqrt{N}}$$

If an article contains nothing but p values, we can proceed as follows: Convert p to its associated one-tailed standard normal deviate Z and use the equation above. Often, however, a range is given, and the following can be used: For $p < 0.05$, $Z = 1.645$; for $p < 0.01$, $Z = 2.326$; and for $p < 0.001$, $Z = 3.090$. Sometimes the meta-analyst must search a paper to find out what happened in the data and may turn up nothing more specific than the following: "The independent variable had no significant effect on the dependent variable." In this case the meta-analyst is forced to assign a Z of zero, with a corresponding r of zero, an approach that usually represents a loss of information and an underestimate of the size of the effect. The standardized *beta* from a multiple regression, as well as a partial correlation, can be used as effect size estimates, but it must be remembered that these represent the relationship between the independent and the dependent variable controlling for other factors (and the meta-analyst might want separately to combine r's and partial r's/standardized *betas*). It should be noted that an r effect size cannot be computed from kappa, percent agreement, relative risk, risk difference, or the odds ratio unless all the raw data are available, so the meta-analyst can compute the proper index. Also, when meta-analyzing reliabilities, one should always report whether they have been corrected using the Spearman-Brown equations (Rosenthal 1987). Raters' reliabilities should be reported Spearman-Brown "upped" (the reliability of the set of k raters) as well as Spearman-Brown "downed" (the reliability of a single rater).

The Four r's

In our discussion of the effect size estimate r we have, up until now, been referring to a specific r called $r_{contrast}$. It is the most generally useful r in meta-analytic work, but it is not the only r. Indeed, there is a set of four effect size correlations, all of which provide quite different information, and all of which should ideally be computed in meta-analytic work. The details are given elsewhere (Rosenthal et al 2000) and here we give only an overview.

1. $r_{alerting}$: the correlation between the means and their contrast coefficients or weights[1] (which may be constructed from authors' written hypotheses in the text or even from the meta-analyst's own). $r_{alerting}$ ignores within group noise.

2. $r_{effect size}$: the correlation between an individual's score on the dependent variable and the contrast weight assigned to the condition to which the individual belongs.

3. $r_{contrast}$: a special case of $r_{effect size}$ in which noncontrast between group variation is partialed out. $r_{contrast}$ tends to be larger than $r_{effect size}$ because the variation associated with other between groups effects is removed from the error term.

4. r_{BESD}: a more conservative effect size r, but one that permits generalization not only to other subjects in the same conditions but also to other levels of the same independent variable.

The four r's can be computed as follows:

$$r_{alerting} = \sqrt{\frac{F_{contrast}}{F_{contrast} + F_{noncontrast}(df_{noncontrast})}}$$

$$r_{effect\ size} = \sqrt{\frac{F_{contrast}}{F_{contrast} + F_{noncontrast}(df_{noncontrast}) + df_{within}}}$$

$$r_{contrast} = \sqrt{\frac{F_{contrast}}{F_{contrast} + df_{within}}}$$

$$r_{BESD}^{2} = \sqrt{\frac{F_{contrast}}{F + F_{noncontrast}(df_{noncontrast} + df_{within})}}$$

---

[1] Contrast weights (or λs) are the predicted results of a study (using, e.g. predictions ranging from 0 to 100) with the restriction that the sum of the weights $= 0$. Subtracting the mean of the predicted values from each prediction achieves this requirement.

[2] When $F_{noncontrast}$ is less than 1.00, it is entered here as equal to 1.00. $F_{noncontrast}$ is computed as $\frac{F_{between}\ (df_{between}) - F_{contrast}}{df_{between} - 1}$.

Contrasts with Categorical Data

If categorical data are presented in a simple 2×2 table, the *phi* coefficient provides a useful r effect size index; if there are more than two rows and/or columns, however, the following equation can be used for a contrast:

$$Z = \frac{\sum P\lambda}{\sqrt{\sum S_p^2 \lambda^2}},$$

where P is the proportion of each column meeting some criterion (e.g. above average performance), λ is the contrast weight, and, $S_P^2 = \frac{P(1-P)}{N}$, where N is the total column count (Rosenthal & Rosnow 1985, 1991).

Combining r's

Combining r effect sizes is a straightforward enterprise. First, each r is transformed into the Fisher Z transformation of r in order to normalize the distribution. The unweighted mean of these Fisher Z transformed r's may then be calculated, as well as the mean of the Fisher Z transformed r's weighted by the N-3 of each study. These weighted and unweighted average Fisher Z transformed r's are then converted back to r, and the weighted and unweighted mean r's reported. Confidence intervals around these estimates reveal the degree to which they differ significantly from zero (i.e. do not cross zero). For the unweighted mean r, the random effects confidence interval is usually preferred, yielding wider confidence intervals but allowing generalization to studies other than those in the collected sample. The equation for the 95% confidence interval around the unweighted mean employs the Z_r transformation of the correlations:

$$\overline{Z_r} \pm t_{(.05)} S / \sqrt{k},$$

where $\overline{Z_r}$ is the unweighted mean of the Z-transformed r's, $t_{(0.05)}$ is the value of t required for the two-tailed p value of 0.05 for k-1 df, k is the number of studies yielding Zrs, and S is the standard deviation of the k Zrs.

Dealing with Heterogeneity

As noted earlier, it is important to examine the variability of effect sizes. The least useful and least appropriate way is simply to compute a significance test of heterogeneity and give up on combining the effects if the test is significant. This is inappropriate because the significance level depends so heavily on the size of the studies being examined. It is more valuable to examine the standard deviation of the effect sizes, plot them, look for outliers and naturally occurring groupings, and focus on finding blocking variables or moderators that explain the data. The simplest way to examine moderators is to compare average effect sizes in the different subgroups that form the levels of the moderator. Examining moderators in meta-analyses allows for further testing of details of theory, and a better understanding of the research literature. It is not necessary to show that a sample of effect sizes is significantly heterogeneous in order to look for moderators (Hall & Rosenthal 1991). Just as in analysis of variance, an overall F with more than 1 df in the numerator can be nonsignificant, whereas a planned contrast can be highly significant; a distribution of effect sizes that is not significantly heterogeneous can contain one or more contrasts that are both substantial in magnitude and statistically significant. Effect sizes and significance levels can be readily computed for moderator variables by means of the following equation:

$$Z = \frac{\sum (Z_r \lambda)}{\sqrt{\sum \left(\frac{\lambda^2}{N-3}\right)}},$$

where Z_r is the Z transformed effect size r, λ is the contrast weight associated with each of the k studies, and N is the number of subjects or other sampling units on which each Z_r is based.

Of course, in practice it is sometimes the case that no moderator can be found in a group of highly variable effects. For example, in a meta-analysis by DiMatteo et al (2000), across 13 studies, anxiety had an exceptionally variable relationship to patient adherence to treatment: The effect sizes range from -0.64 to 0.39 with great diversity in between (S $= 0.08$, $\chi^2(12) = 27.58$, $p = 0.0063$). Although the average of these effects was close to zero, it would not have been useful to state that there was no effect of anxiety on patient adherence; one summary statistic simply does not do justice to the apparent complexity of the literature. The authors were, however, unable to find any moderator to account for this variation. This difficulty is partly conceptual. Anxiety itself can be quite heterogeneous and range from panic, which may have no direct effect on adherence, to obsessive-compulsive disorder and generalized anxiety about health, which may improve compliance activities, to anxiety with a depressive overlay, which may reduce adherence considerably (Mineka et al 1998). There were simply not enough studies available yet that had assessed these moderator variables to conduct a thorough analysis; however, future studies may permit the emergence of trends.

Where to Go From r?: Graphics and the Binomial Effect Size Display

Light et al (1994) present a number of useful methods for displaying data graphically. In one method, the sample size is plotted on the X axis and the effect size on the Y axis, with the data points being those from the studies included in the meta-analysis. In another, odds ratios are graphed in increasing magnitudes along with their 95% confidence intervals. Stem and leaf displays and schematic plots from Tukey's (1977) exploratory data analysis are recommended as well, and are particularly useful to display the effect of moderator variables in side-by-side schematic plots. In another graphical display, effect size is plotted on the Y axis and levels of a monotonically increasing independent variable are plotted on the X axis. Side-by-side scatterplots for several different dependent variables can also be used. Whatever graphical displays are used, meta-analysis should clearly convey the distribution of the effect sizes in some informative way.

The binomial effect size display (BESD) is a useful and informative technique for examining the practical importance of any effect indexed by r. The correlation coefficient is shown to be the simple difference in outcome rates of two groups (e.g. experimental/control, female/male) in a standard table with column and row totals of 100 each (Rosenthal & Rubin 1982). We obtain the BESD from any obtained effect size r by computing the treatment condition success rate as 0.50 plus $r/2$, and the control condition success rate as 0.50 minus $r/2$. Thus, an r of 0.20 yields treatment success rates and a BESD as follows (with cell entries multiplied by 100):

Outcome

		Live	Die	Σ
Independent Variable	Treatment	60	40	100
	Control	40	60	100
	Σ	100	100	200

The correlation r of 0.20 is simply the difference between the success rates of the experimental versus the control group (0.60 − 0.40). In general, BESD involves a 2×2 table with the cell counts labeled A, B, C, D as follows, and with column and row totals of 100:

Outcome

		Live	Die	Σ
Independent Variable	Treatment	A	B	A+B
	Control	C	D	C+D
	Σ	A+C	B+D	

There are three other indices of effect size that are often useful (and commonplace in biomedical contexts). These are relative risk, odds ratio, and risk difference. In an effort to better capture the implications of the data for the population as a whole, it has been suggested that before computing relative risks, odds ratios, and risk differences, we compute r, display it as a BESD, and then compute "standardized" relative risks, odds ratios, and risk differences (Rosenthal et al 2000). Relative risk is defined as the ratio of the proportion of control patients at risk, divided by the proportion of treated patients at risk for the bad outcome. Relative risk $= [A/(A+B)]/[C/(C+D)]$; in the BESD where $A = D$ and $B = C$, standardized relative risk $= A/C$. Suppose a treatment is so important that a possible outcome of noncompliance is death; in fact, renal dialysis is such an example. Suppose that the correlation between noncompliance and death is 0.60, so that the BESD entries are

Outcome

Independent Variable		Live	Die	Σ
	Compliant	80	20	100
	Noncompliant	20	80	100
	Σ	100	100	200

Then, the relative risk of death if one is noncompliant is $80/20 = 4$; there is a 4 times greater likelihood that one will die if noncompliant than if compliant. The odds ratio is an index that is very common in biomedical research. It is defined as the ratio of bad outcomes to good outcomes in the control (noncompliant) group, divided by the ratio of bad outcomes to good outcomes in the treated (compliant) group. In the case above, this would be the ratio of the odds of dying if noncompliant (ratio of dying to living, if noncompliant, $80/20$) to the odds of dying if compliant (ratio of dying to living, if compliant, $20/80$). The odds ratio, then, is $80/20$ divided by $20/80$, which is 16. Thus, the odds of dying if noncompliant are 16 times greater than the odds of dying if compliant.

A third index is the risk difference, and that is simply the difference (0.60) between the proportion of control or untreated (noncompliant) patients who have a poor outcome ($80/100$) and the proportion of treated (compliant) patients who have a poor outcome ($20/100$). The standardized risk difference is equal to the value of r.

THE EFFECT SIZE r IN THE LARGER CONTEXT

Interpreting the Size of r

Is r ever too small to matter? Answering this question is an important exercise in scientific inquiry and in developing an understanding of a body of research in a broad context. The importance of an effect size is determined both statistically and theoretically within a given field, and in comparison across fields. Consider, for example, the aspirin trial in the Physicians' Health Study (Steering Comm. Physicians' Health Study Res. Group 1988).

Here, the effect size of taking low-dose aspirin in preventing a heart attack was $r = 0.034$ and $r^2 = 0.0012$, indicating that less than 1/8 of 1% of the variance in heart attack was accounted for by using aspirin. Under some circumstances, an effect size r of 0.034 might be seen as unimportant, but examination of the BESD, and a clear understanding of the issues at hand, presents a different picture. According to the BESD, with an effect size r of 0.034 and among persons similar to those represented in the study with comparable risk factors, 34 out of every 1000 would be saved from a heart attack if they used low dose aspirin on a regular basis. Given the ease, safety, and low cost of low dose aspirin therapy, and the high prevalence as well as high cost and potential threat to life and well-being of heart attacks, this finding is, in fact, very important and translates into substantial reductions in morbidity and mortality.

Elsewhere, Rosenthal has compared known effect sizes (Rosenthal 1995a). For example, Smith et al (1980) report the average effect of psychotherapy on improvement to be equivalent to an r of 0.39. Table 1 presents some additional average r effect sizes from 24 meta-analyses in the fields of medicine, behavioral medicine, organizational psychology, and social psychology based on from 5 to 76 studies each. Very few are larger than the effects of psychotherapy.

CONCLUSION

In this chapter, we have explored some of the issues of concern regarding the advantages and criticisms of meta-analysis, and reviewed some of the more recent developments in the statistical procedures of meta-analysis. In concluding, we want to call attention to the role of meta-analyses in drawing causal inferences. If the meta-analysis is based on randomized experiments, strong causal inferences are often warranted. If the meta-analysis is based on observational studies, causal inferences are as risky as they are in the case of individual observational studies. If the meta-analysis includes some randomized experiments and some observational studies, we can meta-analyze them separately and combine their results if they are quite similar, borrowing strength for the randomized experiments from the similar results of the nonrandomized studies. Finally, results of moderator analyses rarely permit strong causal inferences but often suggest fresh studies permitting such inferences.

EPILOGUE

Good researchers who can analyze their own data can conduct meta-analyses. Meta-analysis is not inherently different from primary data analysis; it requires the same basic tools, thought processes, and cautions. Meta-analytic procedures are straightforward enough to carry out with a statistical calculator, with extensive

TABLE 1 Average effect size estimates from 24 meta-analyses conducted in three domains of research

Reference	Effects of:	Effects on:	N of studies	r effect size
Medicine and Behavioral Medicine				
Devine, 1996	Psycho-educational care	Adult asthmatics' adherence to treatment	7	0.36
Devine & Reifschneider, 1995	Psycho-educational care	Adult hypertensives' medication compliance	17	0.34
Devine & Pearcy, 1996	Psycho-educational care	Functioning of adult patients with chronic obstructive pulmonary disease (COPD)	8	0.30
Devine & Reifschneider, 1995	Psycho-educational care	Adult hypertensives' blood pressure	76	0.28
Brown, 1990	Educational interventions for diabetics	Dietary compliance	15	0.27
Devine, 1996	Psycho-educational care	Adult asthmatics' reduction in asthma attacks	11	0.27
Devine & Pearcy, 1996	Psycho-educational care	VO_2 (volume oxygen) levels in adult COPD patients	5	0.27
Mullen, et al. 1992	Cardiac patient education	Blood pressure	5	0.25
Brown, 1990	Educational interventions for diabetics	Glycosolated hemoglobin	27	0.20
DiFabio, 1995	Comprehensive rehabilitation program and back school	Efficacy in pain reduction, increased spinal mobility, increased strength	19	0.14
Mullen, et al. 1992	Cardiac patient education	Diet	9	0.09
Mullen, et al. 1992	Cardiac patient education	Exercise	12	0.09
Social and Clinical Psychology				
Durlak, et al. 1991	Cognitive-behavior therapy for dysfunctional children	Expert rating	8	0.44
Shoham-Salomon & Rosenthal, 1987	Paradoxical intervention in psychotherapy	Psychotherapy outcome	12	0.42
Ambady & Rosenthal, 1992	Ratings of brief segments of nonverbal behavior	External, objective behavioral criterion	38	0.39
Eagly, et al. 1991	Physical attractiveness	Attributions of social competence	35	0.32
Durlak, et al. 1991	Cognitive-behavior therapy for dysfunctional children	Behavioral observation	58	0.27
Eagly, et al. 1991	Physical attractiveness	Attributions of intellectual competence	38	0.22
Organizational Psychology				
Harris & Schaubroeck, 1988	Source of job performance ratings (peer, supervisor, self)	Correlation between sources of assessment: peer-supervisor	23	0.62
Conway & Huffcutt, 1997	Source of job performance ratings (subordinate, supervisor, peers)	Mean reliability of job performance ratings: supervisors	69	0.50
Conway & Huffcutt, 1997	Source of job performance ratings (subordinate, supervisor, peers)	Mean reliablity of job performance ratings: peers	26	0.37
Harris & Schaubroeck, 1988	Source of job performance ratings (peer, supervisor, self)	Correlation between sources of assessment: self-peer	11	0.36
Harris & Schaubroeck, 1988	Source of job performance ratings (peer, supervisor, self)	Correlation between sources of assessment: self-supervisor	36	0.35
Conway & Huffcutt, 1997	Source of job performance ratings (subordinate, supervisor, peers)	Mean reliablity of job performance ratings: subordinates	28	0.30

tables of Z and *t*. A desire to impose order on chaos may be helpful given the challenges of certain research fields, and patience with the limitations of some research write-ups will certainly help. Intimate communing with the data, particularly within the context of the theory guiding the work, is an essential and rewarding requirement.

Visit the Annual Reviews home page at www.AnnualReviews.org

LITERATURE CITED

Ambady N, Rosenthal R. 1992. Thin slices of expressive behavior as predictors of interpersonal consequences: a meta-analysis. *Psychol. Bull.* 111:256–74

Baum ML, Anish DS, Chalmers TC, Sacks HS, Smith H Jr, et al. 1981. A survey of clinical trials of antibiotic prophylaxis in colon surgery: evidence against further use of no-treatment controls. *N. Engl. J. Med.* 305(14):795–99

Brown SA. 1990. Studies of educational interventions and outcomes in diabetic adults: a meta-analysis revisited. *Patient Educ. Couns.* 16:189–215

Chalmers I, Altman DG. 1995. *Systematic Reviews.* London: BJM

Cohen J. 1993. A new goal: preventing disease, not infection. *Science* 262:1820–21

Cohen J. 1994. The earth is round (*p* < .05). *Am. Psychol.* 49:997–1003

Conway JM, Huffcutt AI. 1997. Psychometric properties of multisource performance ratings: a meta-analysis of subordinate, supervisor, peer, and self-ratings. *Hum. Perform.* 10(4):331–60

Cook TD, Cooper H, Cordray DS, Hartmann H, Hedges LV, et al. 1992. *Meta-Analysis for Explanation: A Casebook.* New York: Russell Sage Found.

Cooper H, Hedges LV, eds. 1994. *Handbook of Research Synthesis.* New York: Russell Sage Found.

Cooper HM. 1989. *Integrating Research: A Guide to Literature Reviews.* Newbury Park, CA: Sage. 2nd ed.

Devine EC. 1996. Meta-analysis of the effects of psychoeducational care in adults with asthma. *Res. Nurs. Health.* 19:367–76

Devine EC, Pearcy J. 1996. Meta-analysis of the effects of psychoeducational care in adults with chronic obstructive pulmonary disease. *Patient Educ. Couns.* 29:167–78

Devine EC, Reifschneider E. 1995. A meta-analysis of the effects of psychoeducational care in adults with hypertension. *Nurs. Res.* 44:237–45

DiFabio RP. 1995. Efficacy of comprehensive rehabilitation programs and back school for patients with low back pain: a meta-analysis. *Phys. Ther.* 75:865–78

DiMatteo MR. 2000. Practitioner-family-patient communication in pediatric adherence: implications for research and clinical practice. In *Promoting Adherence to Medical Treatment in Childhood Chronic Illness: Concepts, Methods and Interventions*, ed. D Drotar. Mahweh, NJ: Erlbaum. In press

DiMatteo MR, DiNicola DD. 1982. *Achieving Patient Compliance: The Psychology of the Medical Practitioner's Role.* New York: Pergamon

DiMatteo MR, Morton S, Lepper HS, Damush T, Carney M, et al. 1996. Cesarean childbirth and psychosocial outcomes: a meta-analysis. *Health Psychol.* 15(3):230–41

DiMatteo MR, Lepper HS, Croghan TW. 2000. Depression is a risk factor for noncompliance with medical treatment: a meta-analysis of the effects of anxiety and depression on patient adherence. *Arch. Intern. Med.* 160: 2101–7

Durlak JA, Fuhrman T, Lampman C. 1991. Effectiveness of cognitive behavior therapy for maladapting children: a meta-analysis. *Psychol. Bull.* 110:204–14

Eagly AH, Ashmore RD, Makhijani MG, Longo LC. 1991. What is beautiful is good, but...: a meta-analysis review of research on the physical attractiveness stereotype. *Psychol. Bull.* 110:109–28

Glass GV, McGaw B, Smith ML. 1981. *Meta-Analysis in Social Research*. Beverly Hills, CA: Sage

Green BF, Hall JA. 1984. Quantitative methods for literature reviews. *Annu. Rev. Psychol.* 35:37–53

Hall JA, Rosenthal R. 1991. Testing for moderator variables in meta-analysis: issues and methods. *Commun. Monogr.* 58:437–48

Hall JA, Rosenthal R. 1995. Interpreting and evaluating meta-analysis. *Eval. Health Prof.* 18:393–407

Hall JA, Rosenthal R, Tickle-Degnen L, Mosteller F. 1994. Hypotheses and problems in research synthesis. See Cooper & Hedges 1994, pp. 17–28

Harris MM, Schaubroeck J. 1988. A meta-analysis of self-supervisor, self-peer, and peer-supervisor ratings. *Personnel Psychol.* 41:43–61

Hedges LV. 1987. How hard is hard science, how soft is soft science? *Am. Psychol.* 42:443–55

Hedges LV, Olkin I. 1985. *Statistical Methods for Meta-Analysis*. New York: Academic

Hunt M. 1997. *How Science Takes Stock*. New York: Russell Sage Found.

Hunter JE, Schmidt FL. 1990. *Methods of Meta-Analysis: Correcting Error and Bias in Research Findings*. Newbury Park, CA: Sage

Light RJ, Pillemer DB. 1984. *Summing Up: The Science of Reviewing Research*. Cambridge, MA: Harvard Univ. Press

Light RJ, Singer JD, Willett JB. 1994. The visual presentation and interpretation of meta-analyses. See Cooper & Hedges 1994, pp. 439–53

Mineka S, Watson D, Clark LA. 1998. Comorbidity of anxiety and unipolar mood disorders. *Annu. Rev. Psychol.* 49:377–412

Mullen PD, Mains DA, Velez R. 1992. A meta-analysis of controlled trials of cardiac patient education. *Patient Educ. Couns.* 19:143–62

Paik H, Comstock G. 1994. The effects of television violence on antisocial behavior: a meta-analysis. *Commun. Res.* 21:516–46

Pearson K. 1904. Report on certain enteric fever inoculation statistics. *Br. Med. J. Nov.* 5:1243–46

Robin ED. 1984. *Matters of Life and Death: Risks vs. Benefits of Medical Care*. New York: Freeman

Rosenthal R. 1978. How often are our numbers wrong? *Am. Psychol.* 33:1005–8

Rosenthal R. 1979. The "file drawer problem" and tolerance for null results. *Psychol. Bull.* 86:638–41

Rosenthal R. 1987. *Judgment Studies: Design, Analysis, and Meta-Analysis*. New York: Cambridge Univ. Press

Rosenthal R. 1991. Quality-weighting of studies in meta-analysis research. *Psychother. Res.* 1:25–28

Rosenthal R. 1991. *Meta-Analytic Procedures for Social Research*. Newbury Park, CA: Sage. Rev. ed.

Rosenthal R. 1995a. Progress in clinical psychology: Is there any? *Clin. Psychol.: Sci. Pract.* 2:133–50

Rosenthal R. 1995b. Writing meta-analytic reviews. *Psychol. Bull.* 118:183–92

Rosenthal R, Rosnow RL. 1985. *Contrast Analysis: Focused Comparisons in the Analysis of Variance*. Cambridge, UK: Cambridge Univ. Press

Rosenthal R, Rosnow RL. 1991. *Essentials of Behavioral Research*. New York: McGraw-Hill. 2nd ed.

Rosenthal R, Rosnow RL, Rubin DB. 2000. *Contrasts and Effect Sizes in Behavioral Research: A Correlational Approach*. New York: Cambridge Univ. Press

Rosenthal R, Rubin DB. 1982. A simple, general purpose display of magnitude of experimental effect. *J. Educ. Psychol.* 74:166–69

Rosenthal R, Rubin DB. 1986. Meta-analytic procedures for combining studies with multiple effect sizes. *Psychol. Bull.* 99:400–6

Rosenthal R, Rubin DB. 1994. The counternull value of an effect size: a new statistic. *Psychol. Sci.* 5:329–34

Shoham-Salomon V, Rosenthal R. 1987. Paradoxical interventions: a meta-analysis. *J. Consult. Clin. Psychol.* 55:22–28

Smith ML, Glass GV. 1977. Meta-analysis of psychotherapy outcome studies. *Am. Psychol.* 32:752–60

Smith ML, Glass GV, Miller TI. 1980. *The Benefits of Psychotherapy*. Baltimore, MD: Johns Hopkins Univ. Press

Steering Comm. Physicians' Health Study Res. Group. 1988. Preliminary report: findings from the aspirin component of the ongoing physicians' health study. *N. Engl. J. Med.* 318:262–64

Tukey JW. 1977. *Exploratory Data Analysis.* Reading, MA: Addison-Wesley

Wachter KW, Straf ML, eds. 1990. *The Future of Meta-Analysis*. New York: Russell Sage Found.

Wilkinson L, Task Force Stat. Inference, APA Board Sci. Aff. 1999. Statistical methods in psychology journals. *Am. Psychol.* 54:594–604

Yusuf S, Zucker D, Peduzzi P, Fisher LD, Takaro T, et al. 1994. Effect of coronary artery bypass graft surgery on survival: overview of 10-year results from randomised trials by the Coronary Artery Bypass Graft Surgery Trialists Collaboration. *Lancet* 344:563–70

Annu. Rev. Psychol. 2001. 52:83–110

ADOLESCENT DEVELOPMENT

Laurence Steinberg

*Department of Psychology, Temple University, Philadelphia, Pennsylvania 19122;
e-mail: lds@astro.temple.edu*

Amanda Sheffield Morris

Department of Psychology, Arizona State University, Tempe, Arizona 85287

Key Words   adolescence, problem behavior, parenting, context, puberty

■ **Abstract**   This chapter identifies the most robust conclusions and ideas about adolescent development and psychological functioning that have emerged since Petersen's 1988 review. We begin with a discussion of topics that have dominated recent research, including adolescent problem behavior, parent-adolescent relations, puberty, the development of the self, and peer relations. We then identify and examine what seem to us to be the most important new directions that have come to the fore in the last decade, including research on diverse populations, contextual influences on development, behavioral genetics, and siblings. We conclude with a series of recommendations for future research on adolescence.

CONTENTS

INTRODUCTION

Research on growth and development during adolescence expanded at a remarkable rate during the past 13 years, since the last time a comprehensive review of the literature on adolescent development appeared in this series (Petersen

1988). [Although two other contributions to the *Annual Review of Psychology* published during the last decade focused on adolescence (Compas et al 1995, Lerner & Galambos 1998), neither of these were intended to provide a broad overview of the literature.] The flood of interest in adolescence during the past decade sparked the appearance of numerous new journals devoted to the publication of theoretical and empirical articles on this age period (e.g. the *Journal of Research on Adolescence*), as well as a substantial increase in the number of pages devoted to adolescence in established outlets within the subfield of developmental psychology (e.g. *Child Development, Developmental Psychology*) and within psychology as a whole (e.g. *American Psychologist, Psychological Bulletin*). The Society for Research on Adolescence, the major association of social and behavioral scientists interested in adolescent development, which met for the first time in 1986, grew from a fledgling organization of a few hundred individuals to an association with some 1000 members. In view of the fact that the empirical study of adolescence barely existed as recently as 25 years ago, the remarkable rise of interest in the second decade of life merits some explanation.

Four broad trends were likely responsible for the growth of this interest area. First, the increased influence of the "ecological perspective on human development" (Bronfenbrenner 1979) during the late 1980s and early 1990s within the field of developmental psychology drew researchers' attention toward periods of the lifespan characterized by dramatic changes in the context, and not simply the content, of development, making adolescence a natural magnet for researchers interested in contextual variations and their impact. Second, methodological improvements in the study of puberty enabled researchers interested in "biosocial" models of development to test these models within a developmental period characterized by wide, but easily documented, variation in both biology and context. Third, the shift in research funding priorities toward more applied areas of study, and toward the study of social problems in particular, encouraged many scholars to turn their attention to such issues as antisocial behavior, drug use, nonmarital pregnancy, and depression—problems that typically emerge for the first time during adolescence. Finally, many of the important longitudinal studies of development launched during the 1980s shifted their focus toward adolescence as the study samples matured into preadolescence and beyond.

These general trends are reflected in the specific topic areas that have dominated the adolescence literature over the past decade or so. Our informal content analysis of several journals (*Child Development, Developmental Psychology*, and the *Journal of Research on Adolescence*) revealed that the most popular areas of inquiry were adolescent development in the family context, problem behavior, and, to a lesser extent, puberty and its impact. Although other topics did receive concerted, if not sustained, attention during this same period of time—the study of changes in self-image and of adolescents' peer relations were well-represented— the family-puberty-problem behavior triumvirate accounted for about two-thirds of the published articles on adolescence during the past decade. Indeed, if a visitor from another planet were to peruse the recent literature, he or she would likely conclude that teenagers' lives revolve around three things: parents, problems, and hormones. We suspect that this characterization is only partially true.

NEW RESEARCH ON OLD TOPICS

The Causes and Correlates of Problem Behavior

From its beginnings at the turn of the century, the scientific study of adolescent development has always had as part of its implicit and explicit agendas the goal of describing, explaining, predicting, and ameliorating problematic behavior. Despite oft-repeated pleas to "de-dramatize" adolescence (e.g. Dornbusch et al 1991), frequent reminders that adolescence is not a period of "normative disturbance," and accumulating evidence that the majority of teenagers weather the challenges of the period without developing significant social, emotional, or behavioral difficulties (Steinberg 1999), the study of problem behavior continued to dominate the literature on adolescent development during the 1980s and 1990s. Indeed, one recent article (Arnett 1999) suggested that scholars might reconsider the fashionable assertion that the "storm and stress" view is incorrect and acknowledge that the early writers on the subject may have been onto something.

The notions that adolescence is inherently a period of difficulty, that during this phase of the life-cycle problematic development is more interesting than normative development, and that healthy adolescent development is more about the avoidance of problems than about the growth of competencies have persisted virtually unabated since the publication of Hall's treatise on the topic, nearly a century ago (Hall 1904). Thus, whereas there continue to exist overarching frameworks to explain dysfunction and maladaptation in adolescence (Jessor's "Problem Behavior Theory," perhaps the most influential of these, continued to dominate research during the past decade), no attempt to develop a general theory of normative adolescent development has met with widespread acceptance, and theories of normative adolescent development that had once been popular have declined considerably in their influence. Erikson's (1968) theory of adolescent identity development, for example, once a dominant force in adolescence research, endures in undergraduate textbooks but has all but disappeared from the empirical landscape. Piaget's theory of formal operations, the chief organizing framework for adolescence research during the 1970s and early 1980s, was more or less abandoned, as the study of cognitive development became more and more dominated by information-processing and computational models, and as empirical studies cast increasing doubt on many of Piaget's fundamental propositions about cognitive development during adolescence (Keating 1990).

Although one may bemoan the relative lack of attention paid to normative adolescent development in recent decades, the field's concerted focus on adolescent problem behavior has paid off with a wealth of information based on solid research.

In addition, much of what we learn about atypical development in adolescence informs our understanding of normal adolescent development. The influence of the discipline of developmental psychopathology on the study of dysfunction in adolescence has been especially important, as have the many longitudinal studies that have been carried out within this framework (e.g. Farrington 1995, Henry et al 1993, Rutter 1989). As a consequence, a number of general conclusions about adolescent problem behavior have begun to emerge, and they have shaped, and will continue to shape, research on the topic.

First, one needs to distinguish between occasional experimentation and enduring patterns of dangerous or troublesome behavior. Many prevalence studies indicate that rates of occasional, usually harmless, experimentation far exceed rates of enduring problems (Johnston et al 1997). For example, the majority of adolescents experiment with alcohol sometime before high school graduation, and the majority will have been drunk at least once; but relatively few teenagers will develop drinking problems or will permit alcohol to adversely affect their school or personal relationships (Hughs et al 1992, Johnston et al 1997). Similarly, although the vast majority of teenagers do something during adolescence that is against the law, very few young people develop criminal careers (Farrington 1995).

Second, one must distinguish between problems that have their origins and onset during adolescence and those that have their roots in earlier periods. It is true, for example, that some teenagers fall into patterns of criminal or delinquent behavior during adolescence, and for this reason we tend to associate delinquency with the adolescent years. However, most teenagers who have recurrent problems with the law had problems at home and at school from an early age; in some samples of delinquents, the problems were evident as early as preschool (Moffitt 1993). Likewise, longitudinal studies indicate that many individuals who develop depression and other sorts of internalizing problems during adolescence suffered from one or another form of psychological distress, such as excessive anxiety, as children (Zahn-Waxler et al 2000, Rubin et al 1995). We now understand that simply because a problem may be displayed during adolescence does not mean that it is a problem of adolescence.

Third, many of the problems experienced by adolescents are relatively transitory in nature and are resolved by the beginning of adulthood, with few long-term repercussions. Substance abuse, unemployment, and delinquency are three examples: Rates of drug and alcohol use, unemployment, and delinquency are all higher within the adolescent and youth population than among adults, but most individuals who have abused drugs and alcohol, been unemployed, or committed delinquent acts as teenagers grow up to be sober, employed, law-abiding adults (Steinberg 1999). Unfortunately, little is known about the mechanisms through which individuals "age out" of certain types of problems, although it has been suggested that much of this phenomenon is due to the settling-down effects of marriage and full-time work (e.g. Sampson & Laub 1995). Nevertheless, many researchers have begun to search for ways of distinguishing, during adolescence, between so-called "adolescence-limited" problems and those that are "life-course persistent" (Moffitt 1993). Ironically, the predictors that discriminate between adolescents who persist versus those who do not are best assessed prior to, not during, adolescence (e.g. attention deficit disorder, neurological insult, conduct problems in preschool). This finding reminds us that development during adolescence cannot be understood without considering development prior to adolescence.

Far less is known about the developmental course of internalizing problems than externalizing problems, but it appears that the inverted U-shaped developmental curve of externalizing in adolescence, with prevalence rates peaking during the middle adolescent years and then declining, does not characterize age changes in internalizing problems. The prevalence of depression, for example, increases during early adolescence and continues to increase, albeit less dramatically, during adulthood (Avenevoli & Steinberg 2000). Perhaps more interestingly, the widely-reported gender difference in rates of adult depression, with women far more likely than men to suffer from this disorder, does not emerge until adolescence (Nolen-Hoeksema & Girgus 1994). Indeed, at least one analysis indicates that the gender difference in rates of adult depression can be accounted for entirely by gender differences in adolescent-onset depression; gender differences in rates of adult-onset depression are not significant (Kessler et al 1993).

Although the spike in prevalence rates of depression at adolescence and the emergence of gender differences in depression in adolescence are both well-established, surprisingly little is known about the underlying mechanisms for either phenomenon; interesting theories abound, but definitive data that differentiate among alternative hypotheses are surprisingly scarce. Among the most frequently offered explanations are those that point to developmental and gender differences in (a) hormonal changes at puberty (e.g. Cyranowski & Frank 2000), (b) the prevalence and nature of stressful life events (e.g. Petersen et al 1991), and (c) the emergence of certain types of cognitive abilities and coping mechanisms (e.g. Nolen-Hoeksema et al 1991). The disappointing truth, though, is that we do not know why depression increases in early adolescence or why adolescent girls are more likely to manifest the disorder than adolescent boys.

Parent-Adolescent Relationships

Of the many contexts in which adolescents develop, none has received as much concerted attention as the family. Research on family relationships has focused predominantly on the parent-adolescent relationship, although there is a small but growing literature on adolescents and their siblings (see section on siblings, below).

Studies of changes in family relations during adolescence continued to focus on parent-adolescent conflict (e.g. Smetana 1995), although a number of investigations examined changes in closeness and companionship as well (e.g. Mayseless et al 1998; for a recent review, see Grotevant 1998) Much of this work continued to build on theoretical models articulated in the early and mid 1980s, which framed transformations in family relations in terms of the adolescent's need to individuate within the context of close and harmonious parent-adolescent relations (Cooper et al 1983, Hauser et al 1984).

Several broad conclusions have emerged from this research. First, there is a genuine increase in bickering and squabbling between parents and teenagers during the early adolescent years, although there is no clear consensus as to why this occurs when it does; psychoanalytic (Holmbeck 1996), cognitive (Smetana et al 1991), social-psychological (Laursen 1995), and evolutionary (Steinberg 1988) explanations all have been offered. Second, this increase in mild conflict is accompanied by a decline in reported closeness, and especially, in the amount of time adolescents and parents spend together (Larson & Richards 1991). Third, the transformations that take place in parent-adolescent relationships have implications for the mental health of parents as well as for the psychological development of teenagers, with a substantial number of parents reporting difficulties adjusting to the adolescent's individuation and autonomy-striving (Silverberg & Steinberg 1990). Finally, the process of disequilibration in early adolescence is typically followed by the establishment of a parent-adolescent relationship that is less contentious, more egalitarian, and less volatile (Steinberg 1990).

The study of adolescent socialization in the family context was an exceptionally popular topic of inquiry during the past decade or so (Darling & Steinberg 1993). Most of the work in this area derived in one form or another from Baumrind's (1978) seminal studies of parental influences on the development of competence in childhood, which demonstrated that children whose parents were "authoritative"—warm and firm—showed higher levels of competence and psychosocial maturity than their peers who had been raised by parents who were permissive, authoritarian, or indifferent. Dozens of studies of adolescents and their parents conducted during the last 12 years, using different methods, measures, and samples, have reached the same conclusion—namely, that authoritative parenting is associated with a wide range of psychological and social advantages in adolescence, just as it is in early and middle childhood. Although various researchers have labeled and operationalized authoritativeness in different ways (e.g. "effective parenting," "positive parenting"), the combination of parental responsiveness and demandingness is consistently related to adolescent adjustment, school performance, and psychosocial maturity (Steinberg 2000).

The notion that authoritativeness influences, rather than merely accompanies, or perhaps even follows from, adolescent adjustment was challenged on several fronts during the 1990s, however. Some writers argued that the link between parental authoritativeness and adolescent adjustment was due to the genetic transmission of certain traits from parents to children (see Behavioral Genetics, below). Others argued that parents' influence on adolescent behavior and development was insignificant and far less important than the influence of peers and the mass media (Harris 1995). These claims were countered by researchers who pointed to conceptual problems in the behavioral genetics analyses that led to the overestimation of shared genetic variance, the success of experimental interventions designed to enhance parental effectiveness and children's adjustment, and longitudinal studies indicating that parental influence during childhood affects adolescents' choices of peers (Collins et al 2000). It seems safe to say that adolescent development is affected by an interplay of genetic, familial, and nonfamilial influences, and that efforts to partition the variability in adolescent adjustment into genetic and various environmental components fail to capture the complexity of socialization processes.

The generally consistent pattern of results concerning parenting and adolescent adjustment prompted many researchers to investigate how factors external to the parent-child relationship moderate the link between parental authoritativeness and adolescent adjustment. These studies have examined the moderating roles of ethnicity (Steinberg et al 1991), interparental consistency (Fletcher et al 1999), social networks (Fletcher et al 1995), neighborhood influences (Furstenberg et al 1999), family structure (Hetherington et al 1992), and peer groups (Steinberg et al 1992). Whereas the general relation between authoritativeness and adjustment is found across a variety of contextual conditions, the strength of the relation between authoritativeness and adolescent adjustment varies across samples, contexts, and the specific outcome measures in question (Steinberg 2000).

Puberty and Its Impact

Advances in methodological techniques for assessing pubertal maturation sparked an increase in the amount of research devoted to this topic during the past two decades. Much of this research has focused on the ways in which puberty affects adolescents' relationships with their parents. Studies indicate that pubertal maturation leads to a more egalitarian relationship between adolescents and their parents, with adolescents having more autonomy and influence in family decision-making. There is also evidence that conflict between adolescents and parents, especially mothers, increases around the onset of puberty. It was once believed that this conflict subsided as adolescents matured; however, there is now less certainty that parent-child conflict declines in later adolescence (Laursen et al 1998, Sagrestano et al 1999). Although negativity may increase between parents and adolescents during puberty, positive affect and emotional closeness likely remain unchanged (e.g. Holmbeck & Hill 1991, Montemayor et al 1993).

One interesting controversy to emerge in the recent study of puberty concerns the causal direction of the link between pubertal development and relational transformation in the family (Steinberg 1988). Several studies have indicated that the quality of family relationships may affect the timing and course of puberty, with earlier and faster maturation observed among adolescents raised in homes characterized by less closeness and more conflict (Graber et al 1995, Kim & Smith 1998) and among girls from homes in which their biological father is not present (Surbey 1990). Although the underlying mechanism for this is not understood, the general observation that reproductive development in adolescence can be influenced by close relationships has been documented in studies of menstrual synchrony (e.g. McClintock 1980) and is well established in studies of nonhuman primates and other mammals (see Steinberg 1988).

Recent studies of early versus late maturation have confirmed earlier findings, indicating that the impact of pubertal timing differs between boys and girls. Late-maturing boys have relatively lower self-esteem and stronger feelings of inadequacy, whereas early-maturing boys are more popular and have a more positive self-image (Petersen 1985). At the same time, however, early-maturing boys are at greater risk for delinquency and are more likely than their peers to engage in antisocial behaviors, including drug and alcohol use, truancy, and precocious sexual activity (e.g. Williams & Dunlop 1999). This increase in risky behavior is likely due to early-maturers' friendships with older peers (Silbereisen et al 1989).

Recent research on the timing of puberty among females also has corroborated earlier studies indicating that early-maturing girls have more emotional problems, a lower self-image, and higher rates of depression, anxiety, and disordered eating than their peers (e.g. Ge et al 1996b). These effects are particularly strong in Western countries where cultural beliefs about attractiveness emphasize thinness, consistent with other research indicating that the effects of early or late maturation vary across social contexts. Interestingly, girls' perceptions of their maturational timing relative to peers may be more influential than their actual physical maturation (Dubas et al 1991). Like early-maturing boys, early-maturing girls are more popular, but they are also more likely to become involved in delinquent activities, use drugs and alcohol, have problems in school, and experience early sexual intercourse (e.g. Flannery et al 1993), although there is some suggestion that early maturation may be associated with an increase in problem behavior only among girls who have had a history of difficulties prior to adolescence (Caspi & Moffitt 1991). It also has been found that early-maturing females spend more time with older adolescents, particularly older boys, and that these relations have a negative influence on their adjustment (Silbereisen et al 1989). Indeed, early-maturing girls are more vulnerable to psychological difficulties and problem behavior when they have more opposite sex friendships, and when they attend co-educational, rather than single-sex, schools (Caspi et al 1993).

Another area of recent study concerns the effects of puberty on adolescent moodiness, and the role of hormonal changes in emotional development more generally. On the whole, evidence for hormonally driven moodiness in adolescence is weaker than popular stereotypes would suggest, although few studies have examined moodiness per se (as opposed to negative affect) (Buchanan et al 1992). Richards & Larson (1993) found no association of average mood or mood variability with puberty among girls, and among boys they found that more advanced pubertal status was associated with positive, not negative, feelings. Also, whereas moodiness may be more characteristic of adolescence than adulthood, it is no more characteristic of adolescence than childhood (Buchanan et al 1992).

There was a surge of research in the late 1980s and early 1990s on the direct and indirect effects of hormones on psychosocial functioning in adolescence. Studies indicate that puberty is not characterized by "raging" hormones, and that the turmoil once associated with puberty was exaggerated (Brooks-Gunn & Reiter 1990, Petersen 1985). When studies do find a connection between hormones and mood it is typically in early adolescence, where fluctuations in hormones are associated with greater irritability and aggression among males and depression among females (Buchanan et al 1992). Nevertheless, variation in hormone levels account for only a tiny percentage of the variance in adolescents' negative affect, and social influences account for considerably more (Brooks-Gunn et al 1994).

Although there is little evidence that psychological difficulties stem directly from hormonal changes at puberty, it is likely that the bodily changes of adolescence play a role in the development of depression and disordered eating among girls (Wichstrom 1999). As body mass increases during puberty, adolescent females may develop a more negative body image and, in turn, disordered eating and depression (Archibald et al 1999, Keel et al 1997). This phenomenon may be accentuated among girls who are especially interested in dating. There is evidence that the combination of puberty and involvement in romantic relationships may place girls at special risk for the development of eating problems (Cauffman & Steinberg 1996).

The Development of the Self

Adolescence has long been characterized as a time when individuals begin to explore and examine psychological characteristics of the self in order to discover who they really are, and how they fit in the social world in which they live. Especially since Erkison's (1968) theory of the adolescent identity crisis was introduced, scholars have viewed adolescence as a time of self-exploration. In general, research has supported Erikson's model, with one important exception: the timetable. It now appears that, at least in contemporary society, the bulk of identity "work" occurs late in adolescence, and perhaps not even until young adulthood. As a consequence, research on adolescent identity development came to focus less on identity development in the Eriksonian sense (for exceptions, see Meeus et al 1999), and more on the development of self-conceptions.

In the transition from childhood to adolescence, individuals begin to develop more abstract characterizations of themselves, and self-concepts become more differentiated and better organized. Adolescents begin to view themselves in terms of personal beliefs and standards, and less in terms of social comparisons (Harter 1998). Middle adolescence is marked by individuals describing themselves in ways that are occasionally discrepant (e.g. shy with friends, outgoing at home), but these discrepancies tend to decline in later years, with adolescents forming a more consonant view of themselves (Harter & Monsour 1992). We also know that adolescents evaluate themselves both globally and along several distinct dimensions—academics, athletics, appearance, social relations, and moral conduct (Masten et al 1995)—and that the link between specific dimensions of the self-concept and global self-worth varies across domains. For example, appearance is most important for overall self-esteem, especially so among females (Usmiani & Daniluk 1997). There is also evidence that adolescents' self-conceptions differ across contexts, and that teenagers see themselves differently when they are with peers compared with parents and teachers (Harter et al 1998). Research has shown that adolescents often engage in false self behavior (acting in ways that are not the true self), particularly when among classmates and in romantic relationships. The impact of false self behavior on adolescents' mental health depends on the reasons for it: Adolescents who engage in false self behavior because they devalue their true self suffer from depression and hopelessness; adolescents who engage in false self behavior to please others or just for experimentation do not (Harter et al 1996).

In general, global self-esteem is stable during adolescence and increases slightly over the period (Harter 1998). Early adolescents report more daily fluctuations in self-esteem than younger or older individuals, but self-esteem becomes stable with age (Alasker & Olweus 1992). Research also indicates that some adolescents show high levels of stability in self-esteem, whereas others do not (e.g. Deihl et al 1997), and that self-esteem varies according to ethnicity and gender. For example, recent meta-analyses have indicated that Black adolescents have higher self-esteem than whites (Gray-Little & Hafdahl 2000) and that males have slightly higher self-esteem than females (Kling et al 1999). Across all groups, however, high self-esteem is related to parental approval, peer support, adjustment, and success in school (e.g. DuBois et al 1998, Luster & McAdoo 1995).

During the 1990s, many researchers studied the development of ethnic identity. In general, a strong ethnic identity is associated with higher self-esteem and self-efficacy among minority adolescents (e.g. Phinney et al 1997). Most studies on ethnic identity have focused on Black adolescents (e.g. Marshall 1995), although recently there have been a number of studies examining ethnic identity among Latino, Native American, and Asian youth (e.g. Lysne & Levy 1997, Spencer & Markstrom-Adams 1990). There may be different pathways in the process of ethnic identity development as a function of recency of immigration, differences in parents' ethnic identities and ethnic socialization, and the ethnic make-up of the school the adolescent attends (Quintana et al 1999, Rumbaut 1996).

Phinney and colleagues (e.g. Phinney & Alipuria 1990) suggest that minority adolescents' associations with mainstream culture can take on a variety of forms. Adolescents can assimilate into the majority culture by rejecting their own culture, can live in the majority culture but feel estranged, can reject the majority culture, or can maintain ties to both majority and minority cultures. Research suggests that maintaining ties to both cultures, or biculturalism, is associated with better psychological adjustment (e.g. DeBerry et al 1996, Phinney & Devich-Navarro 1997).

Adolescents and Their Peers

Popular images of adolescence have long emphasized an adolescent peer culture characterized as a separate society whose values are opposed to those of adults. In reality, there are many peer cultures, and little evidence exists to support the existence of a substantial "generation gap" between parents and adolescents (Brown 1990). During the transition into adolescence, however, adolescents spend increasing amounts of time alone and with friends, and there is a dramatic drop in time adolescents spend with their parents (Larson & Richards 1991). Despite these changes in time allocation, research indicates that adolescents' relationships with their parents influence their interactions with peers (e.g. Brown et al 1993). Indeed, adolescents bring many qualities to their peer relationships that develop early in life as a result of socialization experiences in the family. Studies find that adolescents from warm, supportive families are more socially competent and report more positive friendships (e.g. Lieberman et al 1999). Further, there is evidence that authoritative parenting lessens the effects of negative peer influences (Bogenschneider et al 1998, Mounts & Steinberg 1995). Research also suggests that adolescents without close friends are more influenced by families than peers, and that adolescents in less cohesive and less adaptive families are more influenced by peers than parents (Gauze et al 1996).

In examining the ways in which peers influence adolescent development, there are several important findings from recent work to consider. First, peers influence adolescents in both positive and negative ways. Peers influence academic achievement and prosocial behaviors (Mounts & Steinberg 1995, Wentzel & Caldwell 1997), as well as problem behaviors such as drug and alcohol use, cigarette smoking, and delinquency (Urberg et al 1997). Second, peers do not influence one another during adolescence through coercive pressures; most adolescents are influenced by peers because they admire them and respect their opinions (Susman et al 1994). Third, adolescents and their friends are often similar, but not simply because they influence each other (Hartup 1996). Adolescents choose friends with similar behaviors, attitudes, and identities (Akers et al 1998, Hogue & Steinberg 1995). Finally, susceptibility to peer influence is not uniform among adolescents. Factors such as adolescents' age, personality, socialization history, and perceptions of peers are all important to consider. Adolescents are most influenced by peers in middle adolescence, compared to early and late adolescence (Brown 1990). Research also suggests that peer contact may only predict problem behavior among adolescents who have a history of externalizing problems (Pettit et al 1999).

Prior to Brown's seminal work on adolescent peer groups (Brown et al 1994), most researchers assumed that the key distinction between peer crowds and cliques was in their size. Brown pointed out, however, that crowds and cliques are different from each other in structure and function. Crowds emerge during early adolescence and are large collections of peers defined by reputations and stereotypes (e.g. jocks, nerds, brains, populars, druggies). Crowds place adolescents in a social network and contribute to identity development by influencing the ways in which adolescents view themselves and others. They influence adolescents' behavior by establishing norms for their members (Susman et al 1994). Crowds affect adolescents' self-esteem as well, and adolescents feel better about themselves when they are a member of a crowd with higher status (Brown & Lohr 1987). There is some evidence that crowds divide across ethnic lines (Brown &

Mounts 1989), and that the meaning of crowd membership may differ across ethnic groups (Fordham & Ogbu 1986). Despite these cultural differences, however, for most adolescents crowds become less important, less hierarchical, and more permeable between middle and late adolescence (e.g. Gavin & Furman 1989).

Cliques are much smaller groups of peers that are based on friendship and shared activities. Members of a clique tend to be similar in terms of age, race, socioeconomic status, behaviors, and attitudes. Clique memberships seems to be somewhat stable over time in terms of the defining characteristics of the group (Hogue & Steinberg 1995), but there is evidence that actual membership is more fluid than was once believed, and that many adolescents are not members of a clique or may interact with more than one clique (Cairns et al 1995, Ennett & Bauman 1996, Urberg et al 1995). During middle adolescence, cliques change from being single-sexed to mixed-sexed, and in late adolescence cliques are often transformed into groups of dating couples (Brown 1990).

Little has changed over the past two decades in researchers' descriptions of popular and rejected adolescents. Popular adolescents have close friendships and tend to be friendly, humorous, and intelligent (e.g. Wentzel & Erdley 1993). In contrast, rejected adolescents are often aggressive, irritable, withdrawn, anxious, and socially awkward (e.g. Pope & Bierman 1999). It is important to distinguish among unpopular adolescents who are aggressive, withdrawn, or both aggressive and withdrawn, because the causes, correlates, and consequences of rejection differ across these groups. Aggressive adolescents are typically part of antisocial peer groups and are at risk for conduct problems (e.g. Underwood et al 1996). In contrast, rejected adolescents who are withdrawn tend to be lonely, have low self-esteem, and suffer from depression (e.g. Rubin et al 1995); aggressive-withdrawn teens display a range of psychological problems (e.g. Parkhurst & Asher 1992). Research also indicates that there are some adolescents who are aggressive and also popular, who are described by their peers as aggressive but "cool," and who are often athletic leaders (Rodkin et al 2000).

Some adolescents are not only unpopular, but are also victimized by their peers. Not surprisingly, peer victimization leads to the development of poor self-conceptions as well as internalizing and externalizing problems (Egan & Perry 1998, Graham & Juvonen 1998). Although adolescents who are victimized tend to have few friends (Hodges et al 1997), having a best friend or a friend who is strong and protective weakens the effects of victimization (Hodges et al 1999).

Despite the harmful effects of peer rejection and victimization, there is evidence that unpopular adolescents in middle school can become more popular and accepted in later adolescence, as adolescents become less rigid in their expectations for "normal" behavior and more tolerant of individual differences among their peers (Kinney 1993). Further, interventions designed to improve social competence and social skills have been found to improve adolescents' abilities to get along with peers (e.g. Kelly & de Arma 1989).

As children move into adolescence, friendships evolve into more intimate, supportive, communicative relationships (Buhrmester 1990, Levitt et al 1993). Close friendships begin typically within same sex pairs, but as adolescents mature, many become intimate friends with members of the opposite sex, usually around the time that they start dating (Richards et al 1998). Social competencies such as initiating interactions, self-disclosure, and provision of support increase as preadolescents mature into early adolescents, and are related to quality of friendship (Buhrmester 1996). In general, during early adolescence friends begin to value loyalty and intimacy more, becoming more trusting and self-disclosing. There is some evidence that among girls, friendship intimacy is fostered by conversation, whereas among boys it is gained through shared activities (McNelles & Connolly 1999). Research also indicates that the tolerance of individuality between close friends increases with age, whereas friends' emphasis on control and conformity decreases (Shulman et al 1997).

One final note about the study of adolescents and their peers: Researchers interested in adolescent development have paid shockingly little attention to the nature and function of teenagers' romantic relationships, despite the well-documented fact that, by middle adolescence, most adolescents have had a boyfriend or girlfriend, and despite the well-founded suspicion that concerns over the presence, absence, and quality of romance in one's life are paramount during this age period (Steinberg 1999). There has been a modest increase recently in theoretical and conceptual writings on adolescent romance (e.g. Furman et al 1999), but this has not been matched by a comparable increase in systematic empirical research. When studies of romance during the second decade of life are to be found, they tend to focus on college undergraduates (e.g. Feldman & Cauffman 1999); seldom do they examine individuals at the beginning stages of experimentation with intimate, sexual relationships. We know virtually nothing about the ways in which romantic relationships change over the course of adolescence, about the antecedents of individual differences in romantic relationships in adolescence, or about the impact of romantic involvement on adolescents' mental health and well-being. This is an area much in need of empirical attention.

NEW DIRECTIONS DURING THE PAST DECADE

A decade ago, Dornbusch, Hetherington, and Petersen—at the time the incoming, current, and outgoing Presidents of the Society for Research on Adolescence, respectively—published an article that described the state of the scientific literature on adolescence and suggested some future directions for the field (1991). In retrospect, this article was either remarkably influential or remarkably prescient, because much of what these three scholars recommended, in fact, came to be. Two of their suggestions, in particular, were dominant themes in the study of adolescence during the 1990s: an increased focus on diverse populations of adolescents (and especially on ethnic diversity within North America) and an increased concern for the context in which contemporary adolescents come of age. Additional foci that reflected new, or at least substantially enhanced, interest were studies of behavior genetics in populations of adolescents and studies of adolescents and their siblings.

Increasing Focus on Diverse Populations

Calls for the research community to expand its focus beyond population of white, middle-class, and suburban teenagers were heeded by many during the past decade. Although there is certainly a long distance to travel before we can say that our knowledge about nonwhite and poor youth is as well-developed as our knowledge about their white and affluent counterparts, there is no question that the field made significant progress in closing this knowledge gap.

Despite broad agreement among social scientists that the field can no longer ignore the ethnic and socioeconomic diversity of the adolescent population, however, many issues remain unresolved about how best to incorporate these factors into empirical research (see McLoyd & Steinberg 1998). First, much of the focus in research on ethnic-minority and poor youth continues to overemphasize problematic aspects of adolescence (e.g. drug use, delinquency, nonmarital pregnancy, school failure, unemployment) and underemphasize the study of normative development within these populations. Whereas it is true that a disproportionate share of many social problems touch the lives of poor and nonwhite youth, the majority of adolescents from these backgrounds develop in psychologically healthy ways, and it makes little sense to focus the study of these youth on adolescent malady.

Second, there is little agreement about the guiding principles or theoretical frameworks that would best advance the knowledge base about the development of ethnic-minority and poor youth (McLoyd & Steinberg 1998). Among the issues that have been discussed are the use and misuse of comparative models; whether constructs and measures are equivalent across different study samples; the relative importance of qualitative versus quantitative methods in studies of different subgroups of youth; and the difficulties one encounters in disentangling the effects of race, ethnicity, immigration status, and social class. Furthermore, much of the work that incorporates diversity into its research designs is not developmental in nature.

Third, the growth of interest in the study of diversity has been disproportionately focused on studies of Black adolescents. Far less is known about normative and atypical development among Hispanic and Asian youth, and virtually nothing is known about Native American adolescents. Moreover, researchers have tended to blur important distinctions within the broad categories of ethnicity typically used in research on adolescents, ignoring differences among, for example, Korean, Vietnamese, and Indian youth (all typically classified as Asian), among Mexican, Puerto Rican, and Cuban youth (all typically classified as Hispanic), or among adolescents who are recent immigrants versus their peers who are not (but see, for example, Feldman et al 1992 and Fuligni 1997 for research on adolescents from immigrant families; and Greenberger & Chen 1996 for more nuanced approaches to the study of ethnic differences among Asian and Asian-American youth). This is all by way of saying that, whereas the 1990s marked a very good beginning in the study of diversity and adolescent development, there remain many important unstudied and understudied issues that warrant concerted research attention.

Understanding Adolescent Development in Context

Accompanying the move toward incorporating diversity into research on adolescents has been an increased interest in studying adolescent development in context. Whereas most research on adolescent development prior to the mid 1980s focused on describing individual development and functioning (e.g. logical thinking, identity development, moral reasoning, self-esteem, sexual attitudes and values, psychosocial maturity), there was a pronounced shift toward studying the contexts in which these developments take place, including the family and peer group, but also schools (e.g. Eccles & Midgely 1993) and the workplace (e.g. Mortimer et al 1996, Steinberg et al 1993). It is beyond the scope of this review to summarize the major substantive findings to emerge within such a vast literature as adolescent development in context. Rather, we point to several broad trends that deserve comment.

The first was a move away from a global conceptualization of context toward a perspective that attempts to draw finer distinctions within settings and identify the specific dimensions of context that are most important. Many scholars began to abandon the social address model of context, in which individuals are sorted into groups defined by structural variables, such as household composition (e.g. married versus divorced), peer crowd (e.g. jocks versus brains), school organization (e.g. middle school versus junior high school), and employment status (working versus not working). Instead, researchers began to identify the most important me diating processes and variables that accounted for differences between structurally-defined groups, e.g. parent-adolescent conflict in intact versus divorced homes (Hetherington & Stanley-Hagan 1995), differences in peer crowds' values regarding academic achievement (Brown 1990), the developmental appropriateness of different school organizations (Eccles & Barber 1999), and hours per week of employment (Steinberg et al 1993).

A second important development was the expansion of contextual research to include studies of neighborhoods and communities. Several large-scale research programs were launched in this area, many stimulated by the work of Coleman on functional communities (Coleman & Hoffer 1987). Generally speaking, three types of questions were asked by community researchers. First, are there direct effects of community variables on adolescent development—that is, effects of neighborhoods that are over and above those of families, schools, or peer groups (e.g. Sampson 1997)? Second, are there indirect effects of communities on adolescent development—effects that are mediated through the impact of communities on families, schools, and peer groups (e.g. Furstenberg et al 1999)? Finally, do communities moderate the impact of other settings on adolescents' development—for example, do certain parenting practices affect adolescents differently in different sorts of neighborhoods (e.g. Darling & Steinberg 1997)? Although more research is needed, it appears that the answers to these questions vary considerably as a function of the outcome variable assessed and the way in which "neighborhood" is operationalized.

A third noteworthy trend was the broadening of studies of single contexts examined independently to studies of the interplay between multiple settings. Thus, a growing number of studies appeared that examined the family-peer group nexus (e.g. Brown et al 1993, Fuligni & Eccles 1993); links between the home and school environments (e.g. Eccles & Flanagan 1996) or between school and work (Steinberg et al 1993); the interplay between peer groups and schools (e.g. Fordham & Ogbu 1986); and interconnections among home, peer group, school, and community (Steinberg et al 1992). Several studies also looked at the interplay among hierarchically-ordered (e.g. "nested") settings, in an effort to examine how variations in a larger context (e.g. the community) moderate the influence of a smaller context contained within its sphere (e.g. the family) (e.g. Furstenberg et al 1999).

Behavioral Genetics

Growing interest in understanding the joint influence of biology and environment on adolescent development led to an increase in behavioral genetics research in recent years focused specifically on adolescents and their families. Most of this work has employed an additive statistical model, where the variance of a psychological or interpersonal characteristic is partitioned among three components: genetic influences, shared environmental influences (i.e. facets of the environment that family members, such as siblings, share in common), and nonshared environmental influences (i.e. facets of the environment that family members do not share in common; Plomin & Daniels 1987). Research over that past decade indicates that both genetic and nonshared environmental influences, such as parental differential treatment, peer relations, and school experiences, are particularly strong in adolescence. Shared environmental factors, such as socioeconomic status, neighborhood quality, and parental psychopathology, are less influential (e.g. McGue et al 1996, Pike et al 1996).

Genetic factors strongly influence aggression, antisocial behavior, and delinquency. Evidence suggests that aggressive behavior is more biologically driven than other behaviors, although shared and nonshared influences on adolescents' externalizing behaviors, including aggression, also have been found (Deater-Deckard & Plomin 1999, Jacobson & Rowe 1999). Genetic factors also have been linked to internalizing problems in adolescence, such as risk for suicide and depressed mood (Blumenthal & Kupfer 1988, Jacobson & Rowe 1999). Interestingly, sex differences in heritability estimates for adolescent adjustment indicate that female adolescents may be more influenced by genetic factors compared with male adolescents, with respect to both internalizing and externalizing problems. Rowe and colleagues (1992), for example, found no nonshared environmental influences on adolescent delinquency among sister-sister or sister-brother pairs. However, they found that, among pairs of brothers, delinquent behaviors are significantly influenced by nonshared environmental factors.

Research also has found strong genetic influences on adolescent competence, self-image, and intelligence. Adolescents' self-perceptions of scholastic competence, athletic competence, physical appearance, social competence, and general self-worth are highly heritable, with little evidence for shared environmental influences (McGuire et al 1994, 1999). Intelligence in adolescence (as indexed by IQ) is also under strong genetic control, with genetic influences compounding over time and becoming more influential than the family environment (Loehlin et al 1989). Parental education moderates the heritability of IQ, however, with genetic influences being stronger in families with highly-educated parents, consistent with the general notion that heritablities are generally higher in more favorable environments (Rowe et al 1999).

One of the most important findings to emerge in recent years is that assessments of the adolescent's family environment via adolescent or parent reports—measures previously presumed to assess the environment—may also reflect features of the adolescent's and parents' genetic make-up (which affect the ways in which individuals perceive and describe their family situations) (Plomin et al 1994). Actual and reported levels of conflict, support, and involvement in the family are significantly influenced by adolescents' genetic make-up (Neiderhiser et al 1999), in part because adolescents who display hostile and antisocial behaviors are more likely than adolescents not prone to these problems to illicit negative behaviors from their parents (Ge et al 1996a). Genetic influences on family relations become even more pronounced as adolescents mature, perhaps because older adolescents have more influence in family relationships (Elkins et al 1997).

There is also growing evidence that some of the impact of parenting on adolescent adjustment, depression, and antisocial behavior can be explained to a large extent by genetic transmission (Neiderhiser et al 1999). It is important to note, however, that a good deal of research indicates that most psychological traits and behaviors in adolescence are influenced by both nature and nurture and that, within the domain of environmental influence, it is the nonshared component of the environment that is most influential (Plomin & Daniels 1987); on average, features of the family environment that siblings share explain only 5%–10% of the variance in psychological behaviors and attitudes (Collins et al 2000). However, research also indicates that variance in the family climate (as opposed to the adolescent behavior or personality) across sibling and parent-adolescent relationships is explained more by shared than nonshared influences (Bussell et al 1999).

As noted earlier, however, many scholars find fault with some of the research methods involved in behavior genetics for several reasons (for more extensive reviews of problems with behavior genetics research designs see Collins et al 2000, Stoolmiller 1999, Turkheimer & Waldron 2000). First, behavior genetics research is nondevelopmental and does not address individual development or malleability (Gottlieb 1995). Second, studies examining behavior genetics typically allow for main effects only and ignore the possibility that genes may function differently in different environments, or that genetic and environmental influences are typically correlated (Collins et al 2000). Third, the largest effects for environmental influences on development are found in studies that employ observational methods, yet most research on behavior genetics in adolescence relies on parental and adolescent self-report (Collins et al 2000). Finally, estimates of nonshared environmental influences may be inflated because objectively shared events may have different effects on siblings, resulting in a shared event contributing to nonshared variance (Turkheimer & Waldron 2000).

Adolescents and Their Siblings

During the past 10 years, research on adolescence and the family moved beyond its traditional focus on the parent-adolescent relationship to also include studies of the family system (Rueter & Conger 1995), the extended family (e.g. Clingempeel et al 1992, Spieker & Bensley 1994), and siblings. Of these areas of study, there was a particular surge of interest in sibling relationships and the ways in which siblings influence adolescent development.

The sibling relationship in adolescence is an emotionally charged one, marked by conflict and rivalry, but also nurturance and social support (Lempers & Clark-Lempers 1992). As children mature from childhood to early adolescence, sibling conflict increases (Brody et al 1994), with adolescents reporting more negativity in their sibling relationships compared to their relationships with peers (Buhrmester & Furman 1990). High levels of conflict in early adolescence gradually diminish as adolescents move into middle and late adolescence. As siblings mature, relations become more egalitarian and supportive, and as with the parent-adolescent relationship, siblings become less influential as adolescents expand their relations outside the family (Hetherington et al 1999).

Several researchers have uncovered important interconnections among parent-child, sibling, and peer relationships in adolescence. A considerable amount of research indicates that the quality of the parent-adolescent relationship influences the quality of relations among adolescent brothers and sisters (e.g. Brody et al 1994). Harmony and cohesiveness in the parent-adolescent relationship are associated with less sibling conflict and a more positive sibling relationship (e.g. Jodl et al 1999). In contrast, adolescents who experience maternal rejection and negativity are more likely to display aggression with both siblings and peers (MacKinnon-Lewis et al 1997). By the same token, children and adolescents learn much about social relationships from sibling interactions, and they bring this knowledge and experience to friendships outside the family. The end result of these interconnections is that adolescents' relations with siblings are similar to their relations with parents and peers.

The quality of the sibling relationship affects not only adolescents' peer relations, but their adjustment in general (Seginer 1998). Positive sibling relationships contribute to adolescent school competence, sociability, autonomy, and self-worth (e.g. Jodl et al 1999). At the same time, siblings can influence the development of problem behavior (Conger et al 1997). For example, younger sisters of childbearing adolescents are more likely to engage in early sexual activity and to become pregnant during adolescence (e.g. East 1996). Siblings also influence each other's drug use and antisocial behavior (e.g. Rowe et al 1989).

Another important area of research on adolescent siblings in recent years has focused on parents' differential treatment of their children. Parents treat siblings differently because of differences in siblings' ages, personalities, and temperament. Unequal treatment from mothers or fathers can create more conflict among siblings (Brody et al 1987) and is linked to problem behaviors, such as depression and antisocial behavior (Reiss et al 1995). Differential parental closeness and warmth is also associated with psychological adjustment in adolescence (Anderson et al 1994). Despite this evidence for differential treatment and its influence on adolescent development, adolescents report that 75% of parental treatment is not differential, and when treatment is differential it is usually perceived by adolescents as fair and justified, either because of the situation, or because of the other sibling's age or personality (Kowal & Kramer 1997).

CONCLUSIONS AND FUTURE DIRECTIONS

Knowledge about psychological development and functioning during adolescence continued to expand during the past decade at a rapid pace. Although many of the foci of recent research have been familiar ones—problem behavior, puberty, parent-adolescent relations, the development of the self, and peer relations—new themes and guiding frameworks transformed the research landscape. Compared with studies conducted prior to the mid 1980s, recent research was more contextual, inclusive, and cognizant of the interplay between genetic and environmental influences on development.

Although we commend these shifts in perspective, it is reasonable to ask what happened to research on the psychological development of the individual adolescent amidst all of this focus on context, diversity, and biology. The study of psychosocial development—the study of identity, autonomy, intimacy, and so forth—once a central focus of research on adolescence, waned considerably, as researchers turned their attention to contextual influences on behavior and functioning and to the study of individual differences. The study of cognitive development in adolescence has been moribund for some time now, replaced by studies of adolescent decision-making and judgment (e.g. Cauffman & Steinberg 2000, Fischhoff 1988). The study of physical development has progressed little beyond tracking youngsters through Tanner's well-worn stages of the development of secondary sex characteristics. No comprehensive theories of normative adolescent development have emerged to fill the voids created by the declining influence of Freud, Erikson, and Piaget. Instead, the study of adolescence has come to be organized around a collection of "mini-theories"—frameworks designed to explain only small pieces of the larger puzzle. As a consequence, although the field of adolescence research is certainly much bigger now than before, it is less coherent and, in a sense, less developmental than it had been in the past.

Shifts in emphasis and changes in perspective are both natural and healthy for a field. But there is now a need for new, longitudinal research on normative psychosocial, cognitive, and biological development during the second decade of life that builds on recent findings on the context of adolescence, charts new territory, and takes advantage of methodological and technological innovations in the study of brain, biology, and behavior. The application of recent advances in our understanding and assessment of neuropsychological functioning, brain growth and development, neuroendocrine functioning, and the biological bases of emotion, cognition, and social relationships (e.g. Damasio 1999, Nelson & Bloom 1997) has yet to occur in the study of adolescence. Such a foundation holds great promise for the development of a comprehensive theory of normative and atypical adolescent development that takes advantage of the period's remarkable potential as an arena for research that integrates biology, context, and psychological development. In our view, it this sort of integrative, interdisciplinary work that should be the focus of the next decade of research on development during adolescence.

ACKNOWLEDGMENTS

The authors' work on this chapter was supported by the John D. and Catherine T. MacArthur Foundation Research Network on Psychopathology and Development.

Visit the Annual Reviews home page at www.AnnualReviews.org

LITERATURE CITED

Akers JF, Jones RM, Coyl DD. 1998. Adolescent friendship pairs: similarities in identity status development, behaviors, attitudes, and intentions. *J. Adolesc. Res.* 13:178–201

Alasker F, Olweus D. 1992. Stability of global self-evaluations in early adolescence: a cohort longitudinal study. *J. Res. Adolesc.* 1:123–45

Anderson ER, Hetherington EM, Reiss D, Howe G. 1994. Parents' nonshared treatment of siblings and the development of social competence during adolescence. *J. Fam. Psychol.* 8:303–20

Archibald AB, Graber JA, Brooks-Gunn J. 1999. Associations among parent-adolescent relationships, pubertal growth, dieting, and body image in young adolescent girls. *J. Res. Adolesc.* 9:395–416

Arnett JJ. 1999. Adolescent storm and stress, reconsidered. *Am. Psychol.* 54:317–26

Avenevoli S, Steinberg L. 2000. The continuity of depression across the adolescent transition. In *Advances in Child Development and Behavior*, ed. H Reese, R Kail. In press

Baumrind D. 1978. Parental disciplinary patterns and social competence in children. *Youth Soc.* 9:239–76

Blumenthal SJ, Kupfer DJ. 1988. Overview of early detection and treatment strategies for suicidal behavior in young people. *J. Youth Adolesc.* 17:1–23

Bogenschneider K, Wu M, Raffaelli M, Tsay JC. 1998. Parent influences on adolescent peer orientation and substance use: the interface of parenting practices and values. *Child Dev.* 69:1672–88

Brody GH, Stoneman Z, Burke M. 1987. Child temperaments, maternal differential treatment, and sibling relationships. *Dev. Psychol.* 23:354–62

Brody GH, Stoneman Z, McCoy JK. 1994. Forecasting sibling relationships in early adolescence from child temperaments and family processes in middle childhood. *Child Dev.* 65:771–84

Bronfenbrenner U. 1979. *The Ecology of Human Development.* Cambridge, MA: Harvard Univ. Press

Brooks-Gunn J, Graber JA, Paikoff RL. 1994. Studying links between hormones and negative affect: models and measures. *J. Res. Adolesc.* 4:469–86

Brooks-Gunn J, Reiter EO. 1990. The role of pubertal processes. See Feldman & Elliot 1990, pp. 17–53

Brown BB. 1990. Peer groups and peer cultures. See Feldman & Elliott 1990, pp. 171–96

Brown BB, Lohr MJ. 1987. Peer group affiliation and adolescent self-esteem: an integration of ego-identity and symbolic interaction theories. *J. Pers. Soc. Psychol.* 52:47–55

Brown BB, Mory M, Kinney D. 1994. Casting crowds in a relational perspective: caricature, channel, and context. In *Advances in Adolescent Development, Personal Relationships During Adolescence*, ed. R Montemayor, G Adams, T Gullotta, 5:123–67. Newbury Park, CA: Sage

Brown BB, Mounts N. 1989. *Peer group structures in single versus multiethnic high schools.* Presented at Biennial Meeting of Soc. Res. Child Dev., Kansas City

Brown BB, Mounts N, Lamborn SD, Steinberg L. 1993. Parenting practices and peer group affiliation in adolescence. *Child Dev.* 64:467–82

Buchanan CM, Eccles JS, Becker JB. 1992. Are adolescents victims of raging hormones: evidence for activational effects of hormones on moods and behavior at adolescence. *Psychol. Bull.* 111:62–107

Buhrmester D. 1990. Intimacy of friendship, interpersonal competence, and adjustment during preadolescence and adolescence. *Child Dev.* 61:1101–11

Buhrmester D. 1996. Need fulfillment, interpersonal competence, and the developmental contexts of early adolescent friendship. In *The Company They Keep*, ed. W Bukowski, A Newcomb, W Hartup, pp. 158–85. New York: Cambridge Univ. Press

Buhrmester D, Furman W. 1990. Perceptions of sibling relationships during middle childhood and adolescence. *Child Dev.* 61:1387–98

Bussell DA, Neiderhiser JM, Pike A, Plomin R, Simmens S, et al. 1999. Adolescents' relationships to siblings and mothers: a multivariate genetic analysis. *Dev. Psychol.* 35:1248–59

Cairns RB, Leung MC, Buchanan L, Cairns BD. 1995. Friendships and social networks in childhood and adolescence: fluidity, reliability, and interrelations. *Child Dev.* 66:1330–45

Caspi A, Lynam D, Moffitt TE, Silva PA. 1993. Unraveling girls' delinquency: biological, dispositional, and contextual contributions to adolescent misbehavior. *Dev. Psychol.* 29:19–30

Caspi A, Moffitt T. 1991. Individual differences and personal transitions: the sample case of girls at puberty. *J. Pers. Soc. Psychol.* 61:157–68

Cauffman E, Steinberg L. 1996. Interactive effects of menarcheal status and dating on dieting and disordered eating among adolescent girls. *Dev. Psychol.* 32:631–35

Cauffman E, Steinberg L. 2000. (Im)maturity of judgement in adolescence. *Behav. Sci. Law.* In press

Clingempeel WG, Colyar JJ, Brand E, Hetherington EM. 1992. Children's relationships with maternal grandparents: a longitudinal study of family structure and pubertal status effects. *Child Dev.* 63:1404–22

Coleman J, Hoffer T. 1987. *Public and Private High Schools: The Impact of Communities.* New York: Basic Books

Collins WA, Maccoby EE, Steinberg L, Hetherington ME, Bornstein MH. 2000. The case for nature and nurture. *Am. Psychol.* 55:218–32

Compas BE, Hinden BR, Gerhardt CA. 1995. Adolescent development: pathways and processes of risk and resilience. *Annu. Rev. Psychol.* 46:265–93

Conger KJ, Conger RD, Scaramella LV. 1997. Parents, siblings, psychological control, and adolescent adjustment. *J. Adolesc. Res.* 12:113–38

Cooper C, Grotevant H, Condon S. 1983. Individuality and connectedness in the family as a context for adolescent identity formation and role taking-skill. In *Adolescent Development in the Family*, ed. H Grotevant, C Cooper, pp. 43–60. San Francisco: Jossey-Bass

Cyranowski J, Frank E. 2000. Adolescent onset of the gender difference in lifetime rates of major depression. *Arch. Gen. Psychiatry* 57: 21–27

Damasio A. 1999. *The Feeling of What Happens*. New York: Harcourt Brace

Darling N, Steinberg A. 1993. Parenting style as context: an integrative model. *Psychol. Bull.* 113:487–96

Darling N, Steinberg L. 1997. Community influences on adolescent achievement and deviance. In *Neighborhood Poverty: Context and Consequences for Children*, Vol. 2. *Conceptual, Methodological, and Policy Approaches to Studying Neighborhoods*, ed. J Brooks-Gunn, G Duncan, L Aber, pp. 120–31. New York: Russell Sage Found.

Deater-Deckard K, Plomin R. 1999. An adoption study of etiology of teacher and parent reports of externalizing behavior problems in middle childhood. *Child Dev.* 70:144–54

DeBerry KM, Scarr S, Weinberg R. 1996. Family racial socialization and ecological competence: longitudinal assessments of African-American transracial adoptees. *Child Dev.* 67:2375–99

Deihl LM, Vicary JR, Deike RC. 1997. Longitudinal trajectories of self-esteem from early to middle adolescence and related psychosocial variables among rural adolescents. *J. Res. Adolesc.* 7:393–411

Dornbusch SM, Petersen AC, Hetherington EM. 1991. Projecting the future of research on adolescence. *J. Res. Adolesc.* 1:7–17

Dubas JS, Graber JA, Petersen AC. 1991. A longitudinal investigation of adolescents' changing perceptions of pubertal timing. *Dev. Psychol.* 27:580–86

DuBois DL, Bull CA, Sherman MD, Roberts M. 1998. Self-esteem and adjustment in early adolescence: a social-contextual perspective. *J. Youth Adolesc.* 27:557–83

East PL. 1996. The younger sisters of childbearing adolescents: their attitudes, expectations, and behaviors. *Child Dev.* 67:267–82

Eccles JS, Barber BL. 1999. Student council, volunteering, basketball, or marching band: What kind of extracurricular involvement matters? *J. Adolesc. Res.* 14:10–43

Eccles JS, Flanagan C. 1996. Schools, families, and early adolescents: What are we doing wrong and what can we do instead? *J. Dev. Behav. Pediatr.* 17:267–76

Eccles JS, Midgely C. 1993. Development during adolescence: the impact of stage-environment fit on young adolescents' experiences in schools and in families. *Am. Psychol.* 48:90–101

Egan SK, Perry DG. 1998. Does low self-regard invite victimization? *Dev. Psychol.* 34:299–309

Eisenberg N, ed. 1998. *Handbook of Child Psychology*, Vol. 3. *Social, Emotional, and Personality Development*. Series ed. W Damon. New York: Wiley. 5th ed.

Elkins IJ, McGue M, Iacono WG. 1997. Genetic and environmental influences on parent-son relationships: evidence for increasing genetic influence during adolescence. *Dev. Psychol.* 33:351–63

Ennett ST, Bauman KE. 1996. Adolescent social networks: school, demographic and longitudinal considerations. *J. Adolesc. Res.* 11:194–215

Erikson E. 1968. *Identity, Youth, and Crisis*. New York: Norton

Farrington D. 1995. The development of offending and antisocial behaviour from childhood: key findings from the Cambridge

Study in Delinquent Youth. *J. Child Psychol. Psychiatry* 36:1–35

Feldman SS, Cauffman E. 1999. Your cheatin' heart: attitudes, behaviors, and correlates of sexual betrayal in late adolescents. *J. Res. Adolesc.* 9:227–52

Feldman SS, Elliott GR, eds. 1990. *At the Threshold: The Developing Adolescent.* Cambridge, MA: Harvard Univ. Press

Feldman SS, Mont-Reynaud R, Rosenthal DA. 1992. When East moves West: the acculturation of values of Chinese adolescents in the U.S. and Australia. *J. Res. Adolesc.* 2:147–73

Fischhoff B. 1988. Judgement and decision making. In *The Psychology of Human Thought*, ed. R Sternberg, E Smith, pp. 153–87. New York: Cambridge Univ. Press

Flannery DJ, Rowe DC, Gulley BL. 1993. Impact of pubertal status, timing, and age on adolescent sexual experience and delinquency. *J. Adolesc. Res.* 8:21–40

Fletcher A, Darling N, Steinberg L, Dornbusch S. 1995. The company they keep: relation of adolescents' adjustment and behavior to their friends' perceptions of authoritative parenting in the social network. *Dev. Psychol.* 31:300–10

Fletcher A, Steinberg L, Sellers E. 1999. Adolescents' well-being as a function of perceived inter-parental consistency. *J. Marriage Fam.* 61:599–610

Fordham C, Ogbu J. 1986. Black students' success: coping with the burden of "acting white." *Urban Rev.* 18:176–206

Fuligni AJ. 1997. The academic achievement of adolescents from immigrant families: the roles of family background, attitudes, and behavior. *Child Dev.* 68:351–63

Fuligni AJ, Eccles JS. 1993. Perceived parent-child relationships and early adolescents' orientation toward peers. *Dev. Psychol.* 29:622–32

Furman W, Brown B, Feiring C, eds. 1999. *Contemporary Perspectives on Adolescent Romantic Relationships.* New York: Cambridge Univ. Press

Furstenberg F Jr, Cook TD, Eccles JS, Elder GH, Sameroff A. 1999. *Managing to Make It: Urban Families and Adolescent Success.* Chicago: Univ. Chicago Press

Gauze C, Bukowski WM, Aquan-Assee J, Sippola LK. 1996. Interactions between family environment and friendship and associations with self-perceived well-being during adolescence. *Child Dev.* 67:2201–16

Gavin LA, Furman W. 1989. Age differences in adolescents' perceptions of their peer groups. *Dev. Psychol.* 25:827–34

Ge X, Conger RD, Cadoret RJ, Neiderhiser JM, Yates W, et al. 1996a. The developmental interface between nature and nurture: a mutual influence model of child antisocial behavior and parent behaviors. *Dev. Psychol.* 32:574–89

Ge X, Conger RD, Elder GH Jr. 1996b. Coming of age too early: pubertal influences on girls' vulnerability to psychological distress. *Child Dev.* 67:3386–400

Gottlieb G. 1995. Some conceptual deficiencies in 'developmental' behavior genetics. *Hum. Dev.* 58:131–41

Graber JA, Brooks-Gunn J, Warren MP. 1995. The antecedents of menarcheal age: heredity, family environment, and stressful life events. *Child Dev.* 66:346–59

Graham S, Juvonen J. 1998. Self-blame and peer victimization in middle school: an attributional analysis. *Dev. Psychol.* 34:587–38

Gray-Little B, Hafdahl AR. 2000. Factors influencing racial comparisons of self-esteem: a quantitative review. *Psychol. Bull.* 126:26–54

Greenberger E, Chen C. 1996. Perceived family relationships and depressed mood in early and late adolescence: a comparison of European and Asian Americans. *Dev. Psychol.* 32:707–16

Grotevant H. 1998. Adolescent development in family contexts. See Eisenberg 1998, pp. 1097–149

Hall GS. 1904. *Adolescence.* New York: Appleton

Harris JR. 1995. Where is the children's environment? A group socialization theory of development. *Psychol. Rev.* 102:458–89

Harter S. 1998. The development of self-representations. See Eisenberg 1998, pp. 553–618

Harter S, Marold DB, Whitesell NR, Cobbs G. 1996. A model of the effects of perceived parent and peer support on adolescent false self behavior. *Child Dev.* 67:360–74

Harter S, Monsour A. 1992. Development analysis of conflict caused by opposing attributes in the adolescent self-portrait. *Dev. Psychol.* 28:251–60

Harter S, Waters P, Whitesell NR. 1998. Relational self-worth: differences in perceived worth as a person across interpersonal contexts among adolescents. *Child Dev.* 69:756–66

Hartup WW. 1996. The company they keep: friendships and their developmental significance. *Child Dev.* 67:1–13

Hauser ST, Powers S, Jacobson A, Noam G, Weiss B, Follansbee D. 1984. Family contexts of adolescent ego development. *Child Dev.* 55:195–213

Henry B, Moffitt TE, Robins LN, Earls F, Silva PA. 1993. Early family predictors of child and adolescent antisocial behavior: Who are the mothers of delinquents? *Crim. Behav. Ment. Health* 3:97–118

Hetherington EM, Clingempeel W, Anderson E, Deal J, Hagan M, et al. 1992. Coping with marital transitions: a family systems perspective. *Monogr. Soc. Res. Child Dev.* Vol. 57, Serial No. 227

Hetherington EM, Henderson SH, Reiss D. 1999. Adolescent siblings in stepfamilies: family functioning and adolescent adjustment. *Monogr. Soc. Res. Child Dev.* Vol. 64, Serial No. 259

Hetherington EM, Stanley-Hagan M. 1995. Parenting in divorced and remarried families. In *Handbook of Parenting*, Vol. 3. *Status and Social Conditions of Parenting*, ed. M Bornstein, pp. 233–54. Mahwah, NJ: Erlbaum

Hodges EVE, Boivin M, Vitaro F, Bukowski WM. 1999. The power of friendship: protection against an escalating cycle of peer victimization. *Dev. Psychol.* 35:94–101

Hodges EVE, Malone MJ, Perry DG. 1997. Individual risk and social risk as interacting determinants of victimization in the peer group. *Dev. Psychol.* 33:1032–39

Hogue A, Steinberg L. 1995. Homophily of internalized distress in adolescent peer groups. *Dev. Psychol.* 31:897–906

Holmbeck GN. 1996. A model of family relational transformations during the transition to adolescence: parent-adolescent conflict. In *Transitions Through Adolescence: Interpersonal Domains and Contexts*, ed. J Graber, J Brooks-Gunn, A Peterson, pp. 167–99. Mahwah, NJ: Erlbaum

Holmbeck GN, Hill JP. 1991. Conflictive engagement, positive affect, and menarche in families with seventh-grade girls. *Child Dev.* 62:1030–48

Hughs S, Power T, Francis D. 1992. Defining patterns of drinking in adolescence: a cluster analytic approach. *J. Stud. Alcohol* 53:40–47

Jacobson KC, Rowe DC. 1999. Genetic and environmental influences on the relationships between family connectedness, school connectedness, and adolescent depressed mood: sex differences. *Dev. Psychol.* 35:926–39

Jodl KM, Bridges M, Kim JE, Mitchell AS, Chan RW. 1999. Relations among relationships: a family systems perspective. See Hetherington et al 1999, pp. 150–83

Johnston L, Bachman J, O'Malley P. 1997. *Monitoring the Future.* Ann Arbor, MI: Inst. Soc. Res.

Keating DP. 1990. Adolescent thinking. See Feldman & Elliott 1990, pp. 54–89

Keel PK, Fulkerson JA, Leon GR. 1997. Disordered eating precursors in pre- and early adolescent girls and boys. *J. Youth Adolesc.* 26:203–16

Kelly J, de Arma A. 1989. Social relationships in adolescence: skill development and training. In *The Adolescent as Decision-Maker*, ed. J Worell, F Danner. San Diego: Academic

Kessler RC, McGonagle KA, Swartz M, Blazer DG, Nelson CB. 1993. Sex and depression in the National Comorbidity Survey: I. Lifetime prevalence, chronicity and recurrence. *J. Affect. Disord.* 29:85–96

Kim K, Smith PK. 1998. Childhood stress, behavioural symptoms and mother-daughter pubertal development. *J. Adolesc.* 21:231–40

Kinney D. 1993. From nerds to normals: the recovery of identity among adolescents from middle school to high school. *Sociol. Educ.* 66:21–40

Kling KC, Hyde JS, Showers CJ, Buswell BN. 1999. Gender differences in self-esteem: a meta-analysis. *Psychol. Bull.* 125:470–500

Kowal A, Kramer L. 1997. Children's understanding of parental differential treatment. *Child Dev.* 68:113–26

Larson R, Richards MH. 1991. Daily companionship in late childhood and early adolescence: changing developmental contexts. *Child Dev.* 62:284–300

Laursen B. 1995. Conflict and social interaction in adolescent relationships. *J. Res. Adolesc.* 5:55–70

Laursen B, Coy KC, Collins WA. 1998. Reconsidering changes in parent-child conflict across adolescence: a meta-analysis. *Child Dev.* 69:817–32

Lempers JD, Clark-Lempers DS. 1992. Young, middle, and late adolescents' comparisons of the functional importance of five significant relationships. *J. Youth Adolesc.* 21:53–96

Lerner RM, Galambos NL. 1998. Adolescent development: challenges and opportunities for research, programs, and policics. *Annu. Rev. Psychol.* 49:413–46

Levitt MJ, Guacci-Franco N, Levitt JL. 1993. Convoys of social support in childhood and early adolescence: structure and function. *Dev. Psychol.* 29:811–18

Lieberman M, Doyle AB, Markiewicz D. 1999. Developmental patterns in security of attachment to mother and father in late childhood and early adolescence: associations with peer relations. *Child Dev.* 70:202–13

Loehlin JC, Horn JM, Willerman L. 1989. Modeling IQ change: evidence from the Texas Adoption Project. *Child Dev.* 60:993–1004

Luster T, McAdoo HP. 1995. Factors re-lated to self-esteem among African American youths: a secondary analysis of the High/Scope Perry Preschool data. *J. Res. Adolesc.* 5:451–67

Lysne M, Levy GD. 1997. Differences in ethnic identity in Native American adolescents as a function of school context. *J. Adolesc. Res.* 12:372–88

MacKinnon-Lewis C, Starnes R, Volling B, Johnson S. 1997. Perceptions of parenting as predictors of boys' sibling and peer relations. *Dev. Psychol.* 33:1024–31

Marshall S. 1995. Ethnic socialization of African American children: implications for parenting, identity development, and academic achievement. *J. Youth Adolesc.* 24:377–96

Masten A, Coatsworth J, Neemann J, Gest S, Tellegen A, Garmezy N. 1995. The structure and coherence of competence from childhood through adolescence. *Child Dev.* 66:1635–59

Mayseless O, Wiseman H, Hai I. 1998. Adolescents' relationships with father, mother, and same-gender friend. *J. Adolesc. Res.* 13:101–23

McClintock M. 1980. Major gaps in menstrual cycle research: behavioral and physiological controls in a biological context. In *The Menstrual Cycle*, ed. M Komenich, J McSweeney, J Noack, N Elder, 2:7–23. New York: Springer

McGue M, Sharma A, Benson P. 1996. The effect of common rearing on adolescent adjustment: evidence from a U.S. adoption cohort. *Dev. Psychol.* 32:604–13

McGuire S, Manke B, Saudino KJ, Reiss D, Hetherington EM, Plomin R. 1999. Perceived competence and self-worth during adolescence: a longitudinal behavioral genetic study. *Child Dev.* 70:1283–96

McGuire S, Neiderhiser JM, Reiss D, Hetherington EM, et al. 1994. Genetic and environmental influences on perceptions of self-worth and competence in adolescence: a study of twins, full siblings, and step-siblings. *Child Dev.* 65:785–99

McLoyd V, Steinberg L, ed. 1998. *Studying Minority Adolescents: Conceptual, Methodological, and Theoretical Issues.* Mahwah, NJ: Erlbaum

McNelles LR, Connolly JA. 1999. Intimacy between adolescent friends: age and gender differences in intimate affect and intimate behaviors. *J. Res. Adolesc.* 9:143–59

Meeus W, Iedema J, Helsen M, Vollebergh W. 1999. Patterns of identity development: review of literature and longitudinal analysis. *Dev. Rev.* 19:419–61

Moffitt TE. 1993. Adolescence-limited and life-course-persistent antisocial behavior: a developmental taxonomy. *Psychol. Rev.* 100:674–701

Montemayor R, Eberly M, Flannery DJ. 1993. Effects of pubertal status and conversation topic on parent and adolescent affective expression. *J. Early Adolesc.* 13:431–47

Mortimer JT, Finch MD, Ryu S, Shanahan MJ, et al. 1996. The effects of work intensity on adolescent mental health, achievement, and behavioral adjustment: new evidence from a prospective study. *Child Dev.* 67:1243–61

Mounts NS, Steinberg L. 1995. An ecological analysis of peer influence on adolescent grade point average and drug use. *Dev. Psychol.* 31:915–22

Neiderhiser JM, Reiss D, Hetherington EM, Plomin R. 1999. Relationships between parenting and adolescent adjustment over time: genetic and environmental contributions. *Dev. Psychol.* 35:680–92

Nelson CA, Bloom FE. 1997. Child development and neuroscience. *Child Dev.* 68:970–87

Nolen-Hoeksema S, Girgus J. 1994. The emergence of gender differences in depression during adolescence. *Psychol. Bull.* 115:424–43

Nolen-Hoeksema S, Girgus JS, Seligman ME. 1991. Sex differences in depression and explanatory style in children. *J. Youth Adolesc.* 20:233–45

Parkhurst JT, Asher SR. 1992. Peer rejection in middle school: subgroup differences in behavior, loneliness, and interpersonal concerns. *Dev. Psychol.* 28:231–41

Petersen AC. 1985. Pubertal development as a cause of disturbance: myths, realities, and unanswered questions. *Genet. Soc. Gen. Psychol. Monogr.* 111:205–32

Petersen AC. 1988. Adolescent development. *Annu. Rev. Psychol.* 39:583–607

Petersen AC, Sarigiani PA, Kennedy RE. 1991. Adolescent depression: Why more girls? *J. Youth Adolesc.* 20:247–71

Pettit GS, Bates JE, Dodge KA, Meece DW. 1999. The impact of after-school peer contact on early adolescent externalizing problems is moderated by parental monitoring, perceived neighborhood safety, and prior adjustment. *Child Dev.* 70:768–78

Phinney JS, Alipuria LL. 1990. Ethnic identity in college students from four ethnic groups. *J. Adolesc.* 13:171–83

Phinney JS, Cantu CL, Kurtz DA. 1997. Ethnic and American identity as predictors of self-esteem among African American, Latino, and White adolescents. *J. Youth Adolesc.* 26:165–85

Phinney JS, Devich-Navarro M. 1997. Variations in bicultural identification among African American and Mexican American adolescents. *J. Res. Adolesc.* 7:3–32

Pike A, McGuire S, Hetherington EM, Reiss D, Plomin R. 1996. Family environment and adolescent depressive symptoms and antisocial behavior: a multivariate genetic analysis. *Dev. Psychol.* 32:590–604

Plomin R, Daniels D. 1987. Why are children in the same family so different from one another? *Behav. Brain Sci.* 10:1–60

Plomin R, Reiss D, Hetherington EM, Howe GW. 1994. Nature and nurture: genetic contributions to measures of the family environment. *Dev. Psychol.* 30:32–43

Pope AW, Bierman KL. 1999. Predicting adolescent peer problems and antisocial activities: the relative roles of aggression and dysregulation. *Dev. Psychol.* 35:335–46

Quintana SM, Castaneda-English P, Ybarra VC. 1999. Role of perspective-taking abilities and ethnic socialization in development of adolescent ethnic identity. *J. Res. Adolesc.* 9:161–84

Reiss D, Hetherington EM, Plomin R, Howe GW, Simmens SJ, et al. 1995. Genetic questions for environmental studies. *Arch Gen. Psychiatry* 52:925–36

Richards MH, Crowe PA, Larson R, Swarr A. 1998. Developmental patterns and gender differences in the experience of peer companionship during adolescence. *Child Dev.* 69:154–63

Richards MH, Larson R. 1993. Pubertal development and the daily subjective states of young adolescents. *J. Res. Adolesc.* 3:145–69

Rodkin PC, Farmer TW, Pearl R, Van Acker R. 2000. Heterogeneity of popular boys: antisocial and prosocial configurations. *Dev. Psychol.* 36:14–24

Rowe DC, Jacobson KC, Van den Oord EJCG. 1999. Genetic and environmental influences on vocabulary IQ: parental education level as moderator. *Child Dev.* 70:1151–62

Rowe DC, Rodgers JL, Meseck-Bushey S. 1992. Sibling delinquency and the family environment: shared and unshared influences. *Child Dev.* 63:59–67

Rowe DC, Rodgers JL, Meseck-Bushey S, St. John C. 1989. Sexual behavior and nonsexual deviance: a sibling study of their relationship. *Dev. Psychol.* 25:61–69

Rubin KH, Xinyin C, McDougall P, Bowker A, McKinnon J. 1995. The Waterloo Longitudinal Project: predicting internalizing and externalizing problems in adolescence. *Dev. Psychopathol.* 7:751–64

Rueter MA, Conger RD. 1995. Interaction style, problem-solving behavior, and family problem-solving effectiveness. *Child Dev.* 66:98–115

Rumbaut R. 1996. The crucible within: ethnic identity, self-esteem, and segmented assimilation among children of immigrants. *Int. Migr. Rev.* 28:748–94

Rutter M. 1989. Pathways from childhood to adult life. *J. Child Psychol. Psychiatry* 30:23–51

Sagrestano LM, McCormick SH, Paikoff RL, Holmbeck GN. 1999. Pubertal development and parent-child conflict in low-income, urban, African American adolescents. *J. Res. Adolesc.* 9:85–107

Sampson RJ. 1997. Collective regulation of adolescent misbehavior: validation results from eighty Chicago neighborhoods. *J. Adolesc. Res.* 12:227–44

Sampson RJ, Laub JH. 1995. Understanding variability in lives through time: contributions of life-course criminology. *Stud. Crime Crime Prev.* 4:143–58

Seginer R. 1998. Adolescents' perceptions of relationships with older siblings in the context of other close relationships. *J. Res. Adolesc.* 8:287–308

Shulman S, Laursen B, Kalman Z, Karpovsky S. 1997. Adolescent intimacy revisited. *J. Youth Adolesc.* 26:597–617

Silbereisen RK, Petersen AC, Albrecht HT, Kracke B. 1989. Maturational timing and the development of problem behavior: longitudinal studies in adolescence. *J. Early Adolesc.* 9:247–68

Silverberg SB, Steinberg L. 1990. Psychological well-being of parents with early adolescent children. *Dev. Psychol.* 26:658–66

Smetana JG. 1995. Parenting styles and conceptions of parental authority during adolescence. *Child Dev.* 66:299–316

Smetana JG, Yau J, Hanson S. 1991. Conflict resolution in families with adolescents. *J. Res. Adolesc.* 1:189–206

Spencer MB, Markstrom-Adams C. 1990. Identity processes among racial and ethnic minority children in America. *Child Dev.* 61:290–310

Spieker SJ, Bensley L. 1994. Roles of living arrangements and grandmother social support in adolescent mothering and infant attachment. *Dev. Psychol.* 30:102–11

Steinberg L. 1988. Reciprocal relation between parent-child distance and pubertal maturation. *Dev. Psychol.* 24:122–28

Steinberg L. 1990. Autonomy, conflict, and

harmony in the family relationship. See Feldman & Elliot 1990, pp. 54–89

Steinberg L. 1999. *Adolescence.* Boston: McGraw-Hill. 5th ed.

Steinberg L. 2000. We know some things: parent-adolescent relations in retrospect and prospect. *J. Res. Adolesc.* In press

Steinberg L, Dornbusch SM, Brown BB. 1992. Ethnic differences in adolescent achievement: an ecological perspective. *Am. Psychol.* 47:723–29

Steinberg L, Fegley S, Dornbusch SM. 1993. Negative impact of part-time work on adolescent adjustment: evidence from a longitudinal study. *Dev. Psychol.* 29:171–80

Steinberg L, Mounts NS, Lamborn SD, Dornbusch SM. 1991. Authoritative parenting and adolescent adjustment across varied ecological niches. *J. Res. Adolesc.* 1:19–36

Stoolmiller M. 1999. Implications of the restricted range of family environments for estimates of heritability and nonshared environment in behavior-genetic adoption studies. *Psychol. Bull.* 125:392–409

Surbey M. 1990. Family composition, stress, and human menarche. In *The Socioendocrinology of Primate Reproduction*, ed. F Bercovitch, T Zeigler, pp. 1–25. New York: Liss

Susman S, Dent C, McAdams L, Stacy A, Burton D, Flay B. 1994. Group self-identification and adolescent cigarette smoking: a 1-year prospective study. *J. Abnorm. Psychol.* 103:576–80

Turkheimer E, Waldron M. 2000. Nonshared environment: a theoretical, methodological, and quantitative review. *Psychol. Bull.* 126:78–108

Underwood MK, Kupersmidt JB, Coie JD. 1996. Childhood peer sociometric status and aggression as predictors of adolescent childbearing. *J. Res. Adolesc.* 6:201–23

Urberg KA, Degirmencioglu SM, Pilgrim C. 1997. Close friend and group influence on adolescent cigarette smoking and alcohol use. *Dev. Psychol.* 33:834–44

Urberg KA, Degirmencioglu SM, Tolson JM, Halliday-Scher K. 1995. The structure of adolescent peer networks. *Dev. Psychol.* 31:540–47

Usmiani S, Daniluk J. 1997. Mothers and their adolescent daughters: relationship between self-esteem, gender role identity, and body image. *J. Youth Adolesc.* 26:45–62

Wentzel KR, Caldwell K. 1997. Friendships, peer acceptance, and group membership: relations to academic achievement in middle school. *Child Dev.* 68:1198–209

Wentzel KR, Erdley CA. 1993. Strategies for making friends: relations to social behavior and peer acceptance in early adolescence. *Dev. Psychol.* 29:819–26

Wichstrom L. 1999. The emergence of gender difference in depressed mood during adolescence: the role of intensified gender socialization. *Dev. Psychol.* 35:232–45

Williams JM, Dunlop LC. 1999. Pubertal timing and self-reported delinquency among male adolescents. *J. Adolesc.* 22:157–71

Zahn-Waxler C, Klimes-Dougan B, Slattery M. 2000. Internalizing problems of childhood and adolescence: Prospects, pitfalls, and progress in understanding the development of anxiety and depression. *Dev. Psychopathol.* In press

Annu. Rev. Psychol. 2001. 52:111–39

THEORIES OF ASSOCIATIVE LEARNING IN ANIMALS

John M. Pearce
School of Psychology, Cardiff University, Cardiff CF1 3YG, United Kingdom;
e-mail: pearcejm@cardiff.ac.uk

Mark E. Bouton
Department of Psychology, University of Vermont, Burlington, Vermont 05405-0134;
e-mail: mbouton@zoo.uvm.edu

Key Words   conditioning, occasion setting, causal judgment, attention, context

■ **Abstract**   Theories of associative learning are concerned with the factors that govern association formation when two stimuli are presented together. In this article we review the relative merits of the currently influential theories of associative learning. Some theories focus on the role of attention in association formation, but differ in the rules they propose for determining whether or not attention is paid to a stimulus. Other theories focus on the nature of the association that is formed, but differ as to whether this association is regarded as elemental, configural, or hierarchical. Recent developments involve modifications to existing theories in order to account for associative learning between two stimuli, A and B, when A is accompanied, not by B, but by a stimulus that has been paired with B. The implications of the theories for understanding how humans derive causal judgments and solve categorization problems is considered.

CONTENTS

INTRODUCTION

The first theory of associative learning in animals was proposed more than a century ago by Thorndike (1898). Thorndike argued that learning consists of the formation of connections between stimuli and responses and that these connections are formed whenever a response is followed by reward. Thorndike's proposals formed the basis of a number of subsequent theories of associative learning, all of which shared the assumption that learning is based on the growth of stimulus-response connections (e.g. Hull 1943). Although stimulus-response connections are still believed to play a role in learning and behavior (Dickinson 1994, Rescorla 1991a), theories of associative learning since 1970 have focused more on stimulus-stimulus than stimulus-response connections. One reason for this change is purely practical. Thorndike based his theorizing on studies of instrumental conditioning in which a response, such as pressing a lever, resulted in the delivery of a reward, such as food. The problem with this design is that the animal, not the experimenter, determines when reward will be delivered and it is difficult to control when each learning episode occurs. Researchers accordingly turned their attention to Pavlovian conditioning, in which a neutral stimulus, such as a tone, signals the delivery of a biologically significant event, such as food. Evidence of learning in this task, where each training episode is entirely under the control of the experimenter, is found when the neutral stimulus (the conditioned stimulus, CS) elicits a response such as salivation (the conditioned response, CR), which is appropriate to the imminent delivery of the biologically significant event (the unconditioned stimulus, US).

Because Pavlovian conditioning involves the presentation two stimuli paired together, it became natural to assume that learning about this relationship depends upon the growth of stimulus-stimulus connections. In keeping with this assumption, experiments revealed that the CS is indeed able to activate a representation, or memory, of the US with which it has been paired (Rescorla 1973).

Pavlovian conditioning merits study for two important reasons. First, as a behavioral phenomenon it plays a fundamental role in both animal and human behavior. For example, it is a mechanism that allows animals to adapt to imminent biologically significant events (Hollis 1982, 1997), and in humans it is further involved in abnormal behavior such as drug abuse (Siegel 1989) and anxiety disorders (e.g. Bouton et al 2000). Second, classical conditioning provides a valuable method for studying how animals and humans learn to associate two events. The most influential theory of associative learning was proposed by Rescorla & Wagner (1972, Wagner & Rescorla 1972). Although more than 25 years have elapsed since it was published, there is no sign of a decline in the influence of this theory. According to the Social Science Citation Index, between 1981 and 1985 it was cited on more than 330 occasions, whereas between 1995 and 1999 it was cited on more than 480 occasions. The Rescorla-Wagner model has not gone un-challenged. A variety of experimental findings have been reported that are difficult for the theory to explain (see Miller et al 1995), and some of these findings have prompted alternative theories of associative learning. The purpose of this article is to review these theories. We do not consider each theory in detail. Instead, we focus on the extent to which the various theories overcome shortcomings of the Rescorla-Wagner theory. By doing so, we hope to convey an accurate impression of the issues that are of current theoretical concern in the study of associative learning in animals, why they are of concern, and how close they are to being resolved.

THE RESCORLA-WAGNER THEORY

According to contemporary thinking, the strength of a Pavlovian CR depends upon the strength of the connection between internal representations of the CS and the US or, as it is frequently referred to, the associative strength of the CS. Equation 1 was proposed by Rescorla & Wagner (1972) to account for the change in associative strength of stimulus A, ΔV_A, on a conditioning trial.

$$\Delta V_A = \alpha\beta(\lambda - V_T) \tag{1}$$

The change in associative strength is directly related to the discrepancy between an asymptotic value set by the magnitude of the US, λ, and the sum of the associative strengths of all the stimuli present on the trial, V_T. The extent of this change is modified by two learning-rate parameters with values between 0 and 1. The value of α is determined by the salience of the CS, and that of β by characteristics of the reinforcer. By far the most important feature of the Rescorla-Wagner (1972) theory is the assumption that the change in associative strength of a stimulus on any trial is determined by the discrepancy between λ and the sum of the associative strengths of all the stimuli present on the trial in question. In previous theories, the degree of learning about a stimulus was determined by the discrepancy between the asymptote for conditioning and the associative strength of the stimulus by itself (e.g. Bush & Mosteller 1955). As a consequence of this difference, the Rescorla-Wagner (1972) theory is able to explain a far wider range of experimental findings than its predecessors. One such finding is blocking. Kamin (1969) demonstrated that if rats receive foot shock after one stimulus, A, and then A is paired with another stimulus, B, and the AB compound is paired with the same shock, then very little is learned about the relationship between B and shock. According to Equation 1, when B is introduced for conditioning, the increment in its associative strength will be given by the discrepancy between λ and the combined associative strengths of A and B. The pretraining with A will mean this discrepancy is close to zero, and B will gain little associative strength.

Other findings that are well accounted for by the theory concern the effects of nonreinforcement. Suppose stimulus A is paired with a US and the compound AB is followed by nothing. The model assumes that λ will be zero on nonreinforced trials and B will therefore acquire negative associative strength. As a consequence, conditioning with B is predicted to progress slowly if it should be paired with the same US that was paired with A; the presence of B is also predicted to suppress responding in the presence of any CS that has been paired with the US. That is, the discrimination training with B is correctly predicted to result in B functioning as a conditioned inhibitor. A great deal of the popularity of the Rescorla-Wagner model can be attributed to the successful predictions it made concerning such stimulus selection effects as blocking, and to the account it offered for inhibitory conditioning. Furthermore, despite the shortcomings of the theory enumerated below, most contemporary theories of conditioning adopt an error-correction principle similar to that advocated by Rescorla and Wagner to account for such effects as blocking and conditioned inhibition.

THE ASSOCIABILITY OF A STIMULUS DOES NOT REMAIN CONSTANT

In terms of Equation 1, the ease with which the associative strength of a CS can change is determined by the value of the parameter, α, which reflects the conditionability, or associability of a stimulus. Wagner & Rescorla (1972) proposed that the value of α was determined by the intensity of the CS. They also acknowledged that the value of α could change through exposure to a stimulus, but they did not state formally how this change might take place. Latent inhibition provides one example of how exposure to a stimulus might influence its associability. The first demonstration of latent inhibition was provided by Lubow & Moore (1959), who found that repeatedly presenting a CS by itself significantly retarded subsequent conditioning when the CS was paired with a US. That is, simple exposure to a stimulus was sufficient to reduce its associability. We now consider three different accounts for the way in which the associability of a stimulus can be altered (for an explanation of latent inhibition that does not depend upon associability changes see Bouton 1993).

Wagner

Although the Rescorla-Wagner (1972) model can be interpreted as a rule describing the growth of associations between internal representations of the CS and US, it does not explain how these representations are formed, what they consist of, and how they influence performance. Wagner (1981; see also Brandon & Wagner 1998, Wagner & Brandon 1989) has addressed some of these issues in a theory of standard operating procedures (SOP) in memory. Any stimulus is assumed to excite a node that consists of a set of elements. Normally the elements are in an inactive state, but they may occasionally be in one of two states of activation, A1 and A2. An A1 state of activation can be likened to the stimulus being at the focus of attention, or in a state of rehearsal; the A2 state can be likened to the stimulus being at the margin of attention. The only route by which elements in a node may enter the A1 state is by presenting the stimulus itself, but there are two routes by which elements may enter the A2 state. One route is through decay from the A1 state. The other route depends upon previously formed associations. If a CS has been paired with a US, subsequent presentations of the CS will excite US elements directly to the A2 state. Once elements are in the A2 state they can move only into the inactive state, even if the stimulus to which they are related should be presented.

The distinction between A1 and A2 states of activation is important because Wagner (1981) argued that the associative strength of a CS can be changed only when its elements are in the A1 state. To explain latent inhibition he suggested that repeatedly presenting a stimulus in a given context will encourage the growth of associations between the context and the stimulus. These associations will then allow the context to activate an A2 representation of the preexposed stimulus and thus prevent the CS, when it is presented for conditioning, from activating an A1 representation that is essential if learning is to take place. One prediction that follows from this account is that latent inhibition will be context specific. If preexposure is conducted in one context, and the CS is presented in a different context for conditioning, the new context will be less likely than the old context to excite a representation of the CS into the A2 state. As a consequence, the CS should now be able to excite its representation into the A1 state and enter readily into an association with the US. Experiments have confirmed the context-specific nature of latent inhibition with a variety of methods (Channell & Hall 1983, Hall & Channell 1985, Hall & Minor 1984, Lovibond et al 1984, Rosas & Bouton 1997). According to Wagner's (1981) theory, it should also be possible to reduce latent inhibition by exposing animals to the context after preexposure, but before conditioning, and thereby extinguish the context-stimulus associations. Westbrook et al (1981) cite evidence in support of this prediction, but both Baker & Mercier (1982) and Hall & Minor (1984) found no effect of extensive exposure to the context on latent inhibition. These findings are difficult to interpret, however, because we do not know if sufficient exposure to the context was given in order for the context-CS associations to be extinguished.

The analysis of latent inhibition in terms of SOP has implications for habituation, the decrease in unconditioned responding to a repeatedly presented stimulus. If we assume that the response evoked by the stimulus depends on it being in the A1 state, then habituation may result (in part) from the context entering into an association with the stimulus and retrieving it into A2 instead of A1. This associative perspective on habituation predicts that habituation (like latent inhibition) will be context specific. Although experiments have failed to confirm this prediction (Marlin & Miller 1981), the role for context may depend on the response system investigated (Jordan et al 2000). For example, habituation of responding to drug stimuli (tolerance) often appears to be context specific (Baker & Tiffany 1985, Siegel 1989).

A further prediction of the SOP theory is that it should be possible to disrupt conditioning by presenting a CS shortly before a trial in which the same CS is paired with a US. The initial presentation will put the representation of the CS into the A1 state, which will decay to the A2 state. If the CS should be presented while its representation is in the A2 state, it will be unable to activate its A1 representation and conditioning will not be effective. Evidence in support of this analysis comes from studies in which the adverse consequences of pairing a flavor with illness have been mitigated by allowing rats brief access to the flavor 3.5 h before the conditioning episode (Best & Gemberling 1977; see also Westbrook et al 1981). Best & Gemberling (1977) further demonstrated that this effect is not apparent when the interval between the two presentations of the flavor is increased to 23.5 h. At this longer interval, the states of activation engendered by the first exposure to the CS will have had time to decay to the inactive state, thus permitting the CS on its second exposure to activate its A1 representation and for conditioning to progress as normal. Best et al (1979) also demonstrated that interposing a distracting event between the first and second presentation of the CS reduced the disruptive influence of the first CS presentation on subsequent conditioning. Such a result is consistent with Wagner's (1981) proposal that a limited number of stimuli can be in the A2 state at any one time.

The idea that latent inhibition results from the development of associations between the preexposed stimulus and the context can also be found in the theory of McLaren et al (1989), which has been used to explain why preexposure to two stimuli, or two stimulus compounds, can facilitate a discrimination between them: perceptual learning. Suppose two compounds, AX and BX, are repeatedly presented. These compounds have both unique elements (A and B) and a common element (X). According to McLaren et al, one consequence of this treatment is that it will allow the components of the compounds to enter into associations with each other and with the experimental context. As these associations gain in strength, the associability of the stimuli will eventually decline. Because the common element, X, is presented more often than the unique features, A and B, it follows that the associability of X will decline more rapidly than that of A and B. If the two compounds should be used for a discrimination after they have been preexposed, the relatively low associability of the common feature will ensure that the discrimination will be acquired more readily than when the compounds are novel and the associability of the common feature is high. Evidence in support of these ideas has been reported by Mackintosh et al (1991) and Symonds & Hall (1995).

Mackintosh

Mackintosh (1975) proposed that the associability of a stimulus is determined by how accurately it predicts reinforcement. If the CS is the best available predictor of a US, its associability will be high. However, if the stimulus is a poor predictor of reinforcement, its associability will be low. Stimulus A is regarded as a good predictor of the US if the discrepancy between its current associative strength and the asymptote for conditioning $(\lambda - V_A)$, is less than $(\lambda - V_X)$, where V_X is given by the sum of the associative strengths of all the stimuli apart from A that accompany A. Stimulus A is regarded as a poor predictor of the US if $(\lambda - V_A)$ is greater than or equal to $(\lambda - V_X)$. In these conditions the associability of A is predicted to decrease. To explain latent inhibition, Mackintosh (1975) proposed that during stimulus preexposure, the event that follows a CS—nothing—is predicted equally well by the stimuli accompanying the CS as by the CS itself. On these occasions, therefore, the expression $(\lambda - V_A)$ will be equal to the value of $(\lambda - V_X)$ and there will be a loss in the associability of A.

Equation 2 shows how the associability of Stimulus A, α_A, determined as above, influences the rate of conditioning with this stimulus. This equation differs in one important respect from the Rescorla-Wagner (1972) equation. On any trial, the change in associative strength of a stimulus is determined by the discrepancy $(\lambda - V_A)$ rather than $(\lambda - V_T)$. An important implication of this difference is that stimulus selection effects are not attributed to stimuli competing for a limited amount of associative strength, as the Rescorla-Wagner model implies. Instead, effects such as blocking occur because animals will pay little attention to, and hence learn rather little about, stimuli that are relatively poor predictors of the US. Although there is evidence to suggest that attentional processes akin to those envisaged by Mackintosh (1975) play a role in blocking (Dickinson et al 1976), there is also evidence that supports the analysis offered by Rescorla & Wagner (1972) for this effect (Balaz et al 1982). Blocking and related stimulus selection effects are thus likely to be multiply determined (Holland 1988).

$$\Delta V_A = \alpha_A \beta (\lambda - V_A) \qquad (2)$$

A major problem for Mackintosh's theory (1975) rests with the prediction that attention to a stimulus will increase if it is the best available predictor of reinforcement. The fairest conclusion to draw from the many experiments that have been designed to test this prediction is that their findings are contradictory. Support for this prediction comes from studies that have compared the effects of intradimensional (ID) and extradimensional (ED) shifts on the acquisition of a discrimination (George & Pearce 1999, Mackintosh & Little 1969, Shepp & Eimas 1964). In these experiments animals are required to discriminate between patterns composed of elements from two dimensions. For example, they may be exposed to four patterns: red horizontal lines, red vertical lines, blue horizontal lines, and blue vertical lines. Initially, reward may be signaled by the two red patterns, but not the two blue patterns, thus making color the relevant dimension and orientation the irrelevant dimension. A new discrimination is then given for the test stage, based on four new patterns composed of new colors and new line orientations. For an ID shift, the new elements from the previously relevant dimension will signal reward, and for an ED shift the new elements from the previously irrelevant dimension will signal reward. In the experiments cited above, the new discrimination was acquired more rapidly when it involved the ID rather than the ED shift, which can be most readily explained by assuming that the training in the first stage encouraged animals to pay more attention to the relevant than the irrelevant dimension. Such a conclusion is clearly in keeping with the principles advocated by Mackintosh (1975).

Evidence less in keeping with the theory of Mackintosh (1975) is provided by Hall & Pearce (1979), who used a CS to signal a weak shock for 60 trials. The CS was then paired with a stronger shock, and they found that conditioning progressed more slowly than for a group that received the strong shock signaled by a novel CS. That is, pairing the CS with a weak shock resulted in latent inhibition (see also Hall & Pearce 1982). According to Mackintosh's theory (1975), the training with the weak shock should have enhanced the associability of the CS and resulted in rapid rather than slow conditioning during the second phase of the experiment. At present it is not clear how the findings described by Hall & Pearce (1979) can be reconciled with successful demonstrations of an ID-ED effect.

Pearce and Hall

Pearce & Hall (1980) proposed that attention to a stimulus is necessary while subjects are learning about its significance, but once learning has reached a stable asymptote no further attention to the stimulus is required. Obviously, the animal will need to detect the stimulus in order to respond appropriately in its presence, but Pearce and Hall regarded this as a rather different form of attention than the one necessary for learning. They therefore proposed that attention to a CS, and hence its associability, will be governed by Equation 3. The associability of Stimulus A on trial n, is determined by the absolute value of the discrepancy $\cdot \lambda - V_T \cdot$ for the previous occasion on which A was presented (where V_T is determined in the same way as for the Rescorla-Wagner theory).

$$\alpha_{An} = |\lambda - V_T|_{n-1} \qquad (3)$$

The associability of a stimulus will be high when it has been followed by a US that is unexpected (when $\cdot \lambda - V_T \cdot$ is high), but its associability will be low when it has been followed by a US that is expected (when $\cdot \lambda - V_T \cdot$ is low). The outcome of the experiment by Hall & Pearce (1979) that has just been mentioned is consistent with these proposals. The large number of pairings between the CS and the weak shock in the first stage of the experiment would reduce the associability of the CS by ensuring that it was an accurate predictor of the shock. The low associability of the CS would then be responsible for the slow conditioning observed during the second stage when the weak shock was replaced with a stronger shock. Wagner's theory (1981) can also explain the findings by Hall & Pearce (1979). During conditioning with the weak shock, the CS will enter into an association with the context, and the consequent loss of associability will disrupt conditioning with the large shock (Swartzentruber & Bouton 1986). However, experiments that have shown that the associability of a stimulus is higher when it is an inaccurate than an accurate predictor of the events that follow it lend unique support to the Pearce-Hall (1980) theory (Hall & Pearce 1982, Swan & Pearce 1988, Wilson et al 1992).

There is, therefore, evidence in support of each of the three theories considered in this section. Given the diverse nature of these theories, it is likely that there is more than one mechanism for altering stimulus associability, and that the different mechanisms are governed by different principles.

CONFIGURAL OR ELEMENTAL ASSOCIATIONS

The theories considered thus far all share the assumption that when two or more stimuli are presented at the same time for conditioning, each element may enter into an association with the reinforcer. In general, such elemental theories further assume that responding in the presence of the compound is determined by the sum of the associative strengths of its constituents. As an alternative, configural theories are based on the assumption that conditioning with a compound results in a unitary representation of the compound entering into a single association with the reinforcer (Friedman & Gelfand 1964; Gulliksen & Wolfle 1938; Pearce 1987, 1994). Responding in the presence of the compound is then determined by its own associative strength, together with any associative strength that generalizes to it from similar compounds that have also taken part in conditioning.

Before reviewing the evidence that relates to these contrasting theoretical positions, we should clarify that a strictly elemental theory needs to be elaborated if it is to explain the solution of certain discriminations. Wagner & Rescorla (1972) acknowledged the need for such an elaboration in order to explain the ability of animals to solve discriminations such as negative patterning. For this discrimination a US is presented after each of two stimuli when they are presented alone, but not when they are presented together ($A + B + AB_o$). As the theory has been described thus far, it predicts that the associative properties of A and B will summate so that responding during the nonreinforced trials with AB will be consistently stronger, rather than weaker, than during either A or B alone. To avoid making this incorrect prediction, Wagner & Rescorla (1972) proposed that compounds create unique, configural cues that function in the same way as normal stimuli. Hence, for negative patterning, the cue created by the compound AB will acquire negative associative strength and eventually result in little or no responding during the compound. Even though a theory might assume the existence of such cues, it must still be regarded as an elemental theory because each element of the compound (including the configural cue) has the potential for entering into a separate association with the reinforcer.

According to Pearce (1987, 1994), conditioning with a pattern of stimulation, P, will result in the development of a single association with the US. The strength of this association will be referred to as E_P. Should a new pattern, P', be presented on a subsequent trial, then it will not itself possess any associative strength. However, if P' is similar to P it will elicit a response through stimulus generalization. The strength of the response will be determined by the similarity of P to P', $_PS_{P'}$, multiplied by the associative strength of P, that is, $_PS_{P'}{}^*E_P$. The similarity of P and P' (which can vary between 0 and 1) is a function of the proportion of common elements they share. Formally, $_PS_{P'}$ is given by the expression $N_C^2/(N_P{}^*N_{P'})$, where the number of stimulus elements in P and P' determine N_P and $N_{P'}$, and N_C is the number of elements common to both patterns. Equation 4, which can be viewed as a variation on the Rescorla-Wagner (1972) learning rule (Equation 1), shows that the change in associative strength of P is determined by the difference between λ and P's own associative strength plus that which generalizes to it from similar patterns. As before, β is related to properties of the US. Equation 4 does not contain a parameter that reflects stimulus salience because this property of the CS exerts its influence by contributing to the degree of generalization from one pattern to another. [Pearce et al (1998) discuss how these ideas can be developed to take account of changes in stimulus associability.]

$$\Delta E_P = \beta(\lambda - (E_P + {}_P S_{P'}{}^* E_{P'})) \tag{4}$$

In contrast to elemental theories, no special assumptions are necessary for configural theory to explain the successful solution of negative patterning discriminations. If trials are given in which a US is presented after A and B alone, but not after the compound, the theory predicts that representations of A and B will enter into excitatory (positive) associations and a representation of AB will enter into an inhibitory (negative) association. Thus, whenever AB is presented, generalized excitation from A and B will encourage responding, but this will be counteracted by the inhibition associated with AB.

Elemental and configural theories of associative learning differ in the predictions they make concerning an effect known as one-trial overshadowing. Mackintosh (1971; James & Wagner 1980) has shown that the presence of one stimulus will overshadow or restrict conditioning with another stimulus if they are presented together for a single compound conditioning trial. According to Rescorla & Wagner (1972), overshadowing should not occur in these circumstances because for the first trial with a compound CS, each component will gain as much associative strength as if it were conditioned in isolation. In contrast, configural theory correctly predicts that overshadowing will be seen after a single compound trial because of the generalization decrement incurred by the transition from training with a compound to testing with an element.

A further difference between elemental and configural theories rests with the predictions they make concerning retroactive interference. In keeping with a number of connectionist networks that represent patterns of stimulation in a distributed fashion, elemental theories predict that retroactive interference can be catastrophic (McCloskey & Cohen 1989, Page 2000). In contrast, configural theories make less dramatic predictions about some forms of retroactive interference. An experiment by Pearce & Wilson (1991) highlights this difference between the two classes of theory. Rats first received a feature negative discrimination (A+/ABo) with food presented after A, but not after AB. Stimulus B was then paired with food, before subjects were tested with the original discrimination. An elemental solution to the original discrimination requires that B develop negative associative strength, which will be transformed to positive associative strength by pairing B with food. Upon the reintroduction of the discrimination, the combination of the associative strengths of A and B is then predicted to reverse the original discrimination and produce stronger responding during AB than A. The test trials revealed no support for this prediction, although there was some recovery of responding during AB. This outcome is consistent with configural theory, which predicts that the training in Stages 1 and 2 will result, first, in AB entering into an inhibitory association and, second, B entering into an excitatory association. When AB is then presented for testing, its original inhibitory properties will be reduced by excitatory generalization from B, but this generalization will be incomplete, and AB will continue to elicit a weaker response than A. It should be noted that configural and many elemental theories still predict catastrophic interference in some simple tasks, for instance conditioning followed by extinction. Effects such as spontaneous recovery indicate that extinction does not necessarily erase the effects of conditioning.

Configural and elemental theories of associative learning also differ in the predictions they make concerning the influence of similarity on discrimination learning. A general prediction of configural theory is that a discrimination between two patterns of stimulation will be more difficult when they are similar than when they are different. Elemental theories do not always make this prediction. Redhead & Pearce (1995a) trained a group of pigeons with an A | BC | ABCo discrimination, in which food was presented after stimulus A, after compound BC, but not after the triple-element compound, ABC. According to the principles outlined above, ABC is more similar to BC than to A, and configural theory therefore predicts that the discrimination between BC and ABC will be more difficult than between A and ABC. The results confirmed this prediction.

Surprisingly, elemental theories of associative learning predict the opposite outcome. According to Equation 1, for instance, the trials with BC will allow both B and C to gain excitatory strength. The summation of these strengths will then lead to responding during BC being consistently stronger than during A. Because responding is reduced on the nonreinforced trials with ABC, it follows that the discrimination between BC and ABC will be more marked than between A and ABC, but this was not the case (for related confirmations of configural theory, see Pearce & Redhead 1998, Redhead & Pearce 1995b).

Another method for choosing between configural and elemental theories of associative learning is to use a variety of elements and compounds to signal a US, and then to conduct a test trial with a novel combination of stimuli. Elemental theories assume that responding to the test compound will be determined by the sum of the associative strengths of its components, whereas configural theory assumes that responding will be determined by generalization from the various training patterns to the test compound. Unfortunately, attempts to evaluate these different theoretical accounts have led to conflicting results. A number of studies, have lent more support to configural than elemental theories (Aydin & Pearce 1997, Nakajima 1997, Nakajima & Urushihara 1999), whereas other studies have lent more support to elemental than configural theories (Rescorla 1997, 1999).

There are, therefore, good reasons for believing that associations based on the entire pattern of stimulation that signals a US are acquired during conditioning.

However, it is too early to say whether these associations underlie all aspects of associative learning, or whether conditioned responding is a consequence of the influence of such configural associations in some circumstances and elemental associations in others (Fanselow 1999, Williams et al 1994). If the latter should be the case, then one important goal for future research is to identify when animals will rely on one sort of association rather than the other. It will also be important to develop a theory that explicates how these different types of association interact with each other.

CONDITIONAL ASSOCIATIONS

Learning, as implied by Rescorla & Wagner (1972), consists of a change in the strength of an association between the CS and the US. During the early 1980s the results from a variety of experiments indicated that a CS may alternatively control responding in a manner that is independent of its direct association with the US. This type of effect is now known as occasion setting because one CS appears to "set the occasion for" responding to a second CS without entering into a direct association with the US (Holland 1985).

Occasion setting is most readily studied using either a feature-negative (A+/ABo) or a feature positive (Ao/AB+) discrimination in both of which responding during one stimulus, A, is controlled by the presence or absence of another stimulus, B. A successful solution of these discriminations is easily explained by all the theories discussed so far. For example, according to elemental theories, these discriminations will result in B gaining either positive or negative associative strength. However, when B (the so-called feature stimulus) either precedes or is considerably weaker in salience than A (the so-called target stimulus), B appears to become an occasion setter instead of a simple inhibitor or excitor (Holland 1985, 1989c).

At least three kinds of evidence suggest that occasion setters do not operate through direct excitatory or inhibitory associations with the US. First, several feature positive (Ao/AB+) experiments have used features and targets that evoke qualitatively different CRs (Rescorla 1985, Ross & Holland 1981). For example, in a study by Ross & Holland (1981) rats received the sequence light(B)-tone(A)-food, or the tone by itself without food. The normal CR to the light is rearing and to the tone it is head jerking. Even though the tone by itself eventually elicited little head jerking, this activity was enhanced considerably during the tone when it was preceded by the light. Thus, animals behaved as if the light enabled or activated the association between the tone and food. Second, occasion setters have unusual properties when they are tested with excitors that have been conditioned separately. An occasion setter may not influence responding to a conventional CS (Holland 1986, 1989a), but it will influence responding to a stimulus that has been the target in another occasion-setting discrimination (Holland 1989d, Lamarre & Holland 1987, Rescorla 1985) or has been conditioned and then extinguished (Rescorla

1985, Swartzentruber & Rescorla 1994, but see Bonardi & Hall 1994, Holland 1989b). Third, occasion setters can be less affected than conventional CSs by a change in their relationship with the US. When B is a positive occasion setter, it does not lose its ability to enable responding to A even after it has been extinguished through separate presentation without food (Holland 1989b). Similarly, when B is a negative occasion setter, separate reinforcement of it has less impact than when it is a simple inhibitor (Holland 1984). Rescorla (1991b) has even shown that separate reinforcement of a negative occasion setter can actually facilitate the learning of an A+/ABo discrimination. Other evidence besides the three classic lines just described has also appeared. For example, rats generalize more between features that signal the same target-US relations than features that signal the same target and US in different combinations (Honey & Watt 1998). This sort of result suggests that animals may connect a feature with a particular target-US relation over and above the individual events themselves.

These findings all suggest that occasion setting discriminations are not necessarily controlled by simple B-US associations. They are thus generally viewed as being inconsistent with simple elemental theories of associative learning. In contrast, configural theories have fared better. For example, we have already shown that a configural model correctly predicts that reinforcing B after A+/ABo training will have little impact on the discrimination (Pearce & Wilson 1991), and a similar argument would explain the lack of effect of nonreinforcing B after Ao/AB+ training. However, without elaboration, configural models are less able to deal with the fact that a transfer target's reinforcement history appears so important in determining whether an occasion setter will influence responding to it. Other findings that are also inconsistent with the Pearce model (Bouton & Nelson 1994, 1998; Holland 1989a; Honey & Watt 1998) seem more consistent with the idea that the animal often encodes the feature and target as separable elements in the compound.

Most theorists assume that occasion setting depends upon the feature modulating the target's association with the US in a hierarchical manner (but see Brandon & Wagner 1998). Holland (1983a, 1985) was perhaps the first to make this proposal by suggesting that the occasion setter excited or inhibited the association between the target and US. As it stands, this account predicts that the influence of an occasion setter should be confined to the CS with which it was originally trained but, as noted above, occasion setters can influence responding to targets from another occasion-setting discrimination. As an alternative explanation, Rescorla (1985) suggested that occasion setters are effective by either raising (negative occasion setter) or lowering (positive occasion setter) the threshold for activation of the US representation and thus alter the ease with which the target can elicit a response. Although this proposal explains how an occasion setter can influence responding to a stimulus with which it has never before been paired, it is unable to explain why the effects of an occasion setter can be specific to the target used during training (Holland 1985).

A third explanation for occasion setting is based on findings that suggest that conventional extinction results in a loss of responding through the development of inhibitory associations, and that these associations are more affected by changes in context than the original excitatory associations (Bouton 1993, see below). Bouton & Nelson (1994, 1998; Nelson & Bouton 1997) suggested (*a*) that reinforcing and nonreinforcing the target during an occasion-setting discrimination will allow it to enter into excitatory and inhibitory associations with the US and (*b*) that the effects of the latter are more context specific than the former. The role of the occasion setter is either to activate or inhibit the target's inhibitory association with the US. A similar idea was independently derived in a connectionist treatment of occasion-setting phenomena (Schmajuk et al 1998). In that scheme, the target enters into an excitatory association with the US and also an inhibitory association that is mediated by a hidden unit. The occasion setter excites or inhibits the hidden unit, and thus the inhibitory target-US association. The occasion setter will "transfer" and influence responding to a new target as long as the new target has acquired this inhibitory association, either because the target has participated in an occasion-setting discrimination or because it has been conditioned and extinguished in a salient context (Lamoureux et al 1998). Interestingly, this mechanism was described as a "configural" one. One might say that the trend in research on conditional associations has been toward progressively refining the meaning of configural conditioning.

A SPECIAL ROLE FOR CONTEXT

One of the earliest triumphs of the Rescorla-Wagner (1972) model was the analysis that it offered for Rescorla's (1968) work showing the importance of the CS-US contingency for conditioning. Rescorla (1968) varied the probability with which a US could occur during both the presence and the absence of a CS. Conditioning was effective when the CS signaled an increase in the probability of the US, but conditioning was not effective when the probability of the US was the same in both the presence and absence of the CS. The model can explain this result by allowing the experimental context to be associated with the US like any other CS. When shock was presented frequently in the absence of the CS, the opportunity would arise for the growth of a strong context-US association that would then block conditioning with the CS.

The foregoing analysis encourages the view that a role for context may be important in many conditioning experiments. If the context functions as another CS, as the model assumes, then responding to a CS in a given context will always be affected by the strength of the association between the context and the US. Although the context does turn out to be important, its associative strength often is not. Consider extinction, which is particularly sensitive to a change of context. If conditioning takes place in one context, and extinction in a second context, then returning the animal to the original context typically results in some recovery from the effects of extinction (Bouton & King 1983, Bouton & Peck 1989). This renewal effect also occurs when the CS is tested in a third context (Bouton & Bolles 1979, Bouton & Brooks 1993), and when testing takes place in a second context after conditioning and extinction have both occurred in the first context (Bouton & Ricker 1994). The last result implies that simple excitatory conditioning may be less affected than extinction by a context switch. That is, although extinction performance is usually disrupted by a context switch, conditioning performance is often not (Bouton & King 1983, Bouton & Peck 1989, Hall & Honey 1989, Kaye & Mackintosh 1990, Lovibond et al 1984).

Unfortunately, these findings are not easy to explain if it is assumed that a context functions in the same way as a normal CS. For example, it might be supposed that the renewal effect is a consequence of the context in which extinction takes place acquiring negative associative strength that protects the CS from extinction (Chorozyna 1962). However, there is no evidence that the extinction context acquires negative strength during the extinction phase (Bouton & King 1983, Bouton & Swartzentruber 1986). Alternatively, it might be assumed that the context in which conditioning is conducted acquires positive associative strength, which through summation, would boost responding to the CS at the time of the renewal test. Once again, however, there is little evidence to support the operation of this mechanism in typical procedures (Bouton & King 1983, Bouton & Swartzentruber 1986). The renewal effect is also difficult to explain by configural models emphasizing generalization decrement. The fact that there is little or no decrement in responding when the CS is first presented in the new context for extinction suggests that there should be an equally small decrement in the effects of extinction when the CS is returned to the original context for the renewal test.

In addition to these difficulties, other research has shown that contextual associative strength is neither necessary nor sufficient for a context to control responding to a CS. Thus, contexts may influence responding to a CS when independent tests have failed to reveal any evidence of a context-US associations (Bouton & King 1983, Bouton & Swartzentruber 1986). Conversely, responding to a CS can be unaffected by demonstrable context-US associations (Bouton 1984, Bouton & King 1986). Interestingly, context-US associations created after extinction do augment responding to an extinguished CS, but not a CS for which responding has not been extinguished (Bouton 1984, Bouton & King 1986). Rather than function as conventional CSs, contexts thus appear to have much in common with occasion setters. They modulate responding to a CS that is under the influence of inhibition or extinction, and this influence is independent of their direct associations with a US. In support of this conclusion, experimental tests for the interaction between contexts and occasion setters suggest that they act through a common mechanism (Honey & Watt 1999, Swartzentruber 1991).

In effect, research on contextual control and research on occasion setting has converged on the idea that CS-US associations may be hierarchically controlled by other cues. If this is correct, a further implication of the research on context is that this hierarchical function may be ubiquitous. Perhaps, for example, any association acquired after a CS has already entered into an association may involve hierarchical control by the context (Nelson 1997, Swartzentruber & Bouton 1992; cf. Harris et al 2000). Moreover, this control may be exerted by a variety of contextual cues, including interoceptive states created by drugs, moods, or even the passage of time (Bouton 1993, Bouton et al 1999, Spear 1978). Spontaneous recovery after extinction, the fundamental phenomenon known since Pavlov (1927) but ignored by all current models of associative learning, can now be understood as the renewal effect that occurs with a change of temporal context (Bouton 1993, Brooks & Bouton 1993). These proposals are also of relevance to the catastrophic interference problem noted earlier (McCloskey & Cohen 1989). By the end of Phase 2, the original CS-US association may not be destroyed, but inhibited by a second association whose activation depends on the current context, whether it is provided by exteroceptive cues, interoceptive cues, or time.

We opened this section by showing how it is possible to explain the influence of the CS-US contingency on conditioning, by assuming that the context functions in the same way as any other stimulus. There are, however, alternative explanations for the contingency effect that postulate yet another role for the context (Gallistel & Gibbon 2000, Gibbon & Balsam 1981, Miller & Matzel 1988). Associations involving the context and a CS are assumed to progress independently of each other, and performance to the CS is determined by a comparison between the strength of the two. When the associative strength of the context is high, responding to the CS is commensurately weakened. A finding that is consistent with this comparator view is that nonreinforced exposure to the context after conditioning can increase responding to the CS (Matzel et al 1987). However, increasing the value of the context has no corresponding effect (Miller et al 1990), and comparator theory's account of related competition phenomena has also been challenged (Holland 1999; Rauhut et al 1999, 2000). Nonetheless, comparator theory has generated some new predictions that have been tentatively confirmed (e.g. Blaisdell et al 1998). Although comparator theory gives the context a novel role, this role is not unique to contexts and can be played by any CS.

In the end, although the Rescorla-Wagner model was correct in pointing toward the role of contextual cues in many learning paradigms, it is unlikely that contexts work solely through simple associations with the US. Like parallel research on occasion setting, research on contextual control suggests that a more complex associative structure may often be acquired in associative learning.

LEARNING ABOUT ABSENT STIMULI

The Rescorla-Wagner (1972) theory has been used principally to account for the associative changes that occur when the CS and US are physically present for conditioning. Several studies have shown, however, that it is not essential for a stimulus to be present for it to participate in associative learning. In a study of mediated conditioning, Holland (1981) used a tone to signal the delivery of distinctively flavored food pellets to rats. The tone was then presented by itself and followed by the injection of a toxin. Subsequent tests revealed that the attractiveness of the food pellets was reduced by this treatment. Such a finding implies

TABLE 1   The predictions made by different theories for conditioning with a
CS and a US when they are either physically present (A1), or when a stimulus is
present that has been paired with the CS or US (A2)

CS	US	Wagner	Holland	Dickinson & Burke
A1	A1	Excitatory	Excitatory	Excitatory
A1	A2	Inhibitory	Inhibitory	Inhibitory
A2	A1	No change	Excitatory	Inhibitory
A2	A2	No change	Inhibitory	Excitatory

that presenting the tone by itself activated a representation of food, which then
entered into an association with the effects of the toxin (see also Ward-Robinson
& Hall 1996). Holland (1983b) offered an explanation for this result in terms of
a modified version of Wagner's (1981) theory, SOP. Recall that Wagner proposed
that a representation of a stimulus can be in two states of activation: A1 or A2. If
the representations of a CS and US are both in the A1 state, which will occur if the
stimuli have just been presented, excitatory conditioning will take place. If one
representation is in the A1 state and the other is in the A2 state, inhibitory conditioning will take place. If both representations are in the A2 state, no learning will
occur. These principles, which are summarized in Table 1, are unable to explain
mediated conditioning (Holland 1981). According to SOP, when the tone is presented by itself, the representation of food should be activated to the A2 state and
the development of an excitatory association between food and illness should not be
possible. Holland (1983b) therefore proposed that when the representations of the
CS and US are, respectively, in the A2 and A1 states excitatory conditioning will
occur in the same way as when both representations are in the A1 state (see Table 1).
   A study of mediated extinction led Holland (1983b) to propose a further modification to Wagner's theory. Holland & Forbes (1982) gave rats a distinctively
flavored food in the presence of a tone, prior to conditioned taste aversion training
with the food. The aversion to food was then extinguished by repeatedly presenting the tone by itself. According to the original version of SOP, the tone by itself
will activate a representation of food to the A2 state, which in turn, will activate
the representation of illness to the A2 state. As Table 1 shows, the properties of
food are predicted to be unaffected by this training. To explain his finding to the
contrary, Holland (1983b) suggested that if representations of two stimuli are both
in the A2 state then an inhibitory association will develop between them.
   More recent findings indicate that the modification proposed by Holland (1983b)
to Wagner's theory may apply in only restricted circumstances. Dwyer et al (1998;
see also Harris & Westbrook 1998) studied mediated conditioning by capitalizing
on the fact that animals will acquire a preference for a particular flavor if it has
been paired with a sweet substance such as sucrose. Rats were allowed to drink a
peppermint flavored solution in one context, and a mixture of almond and sucrose

in a different context. They were then allowed to drink almond in the first context. It was hoped that simultaneous exposure to the original context and to almond would activate representations of the events previously associated with them—peppermint and sucrose—and permit the development of an association between them. That is, this treatment was intended to enhance the preference for peppermint even though neither peppermint nor sucrose was presented. Subsequent test trials confirmed this prediction. In this experiment, therefore, allowing rats to drink almond in the original context can be assumed to activate A2 representations of both peppermint and sucrose, which according to the proposals of Holland (1983b), should have resulted in inhibitory rather than excitatory associations.

Dwyer et al (1998) explained their findings by referring to yet another modification to Wagner's theory (1981), which was originally proposed by Dickinson & Burke (1996). They proposed that excitatory associations will develop between representations in the same state (either both in A1 or both in A2) and that inhibitory associations will develop between representations in different states (one in A1 and the other in A2; see Table 1). These proposals can explain the findings of Dwyer et al (1998), but they are unable to explain the findings reported by Holland (1981) and Holland & Forbes (1982).

Additional support for the Dickinson & Burke (1996) version of SOP is provided by studies of retrospective revaluation. In these experiments, an experience in the presence of a CS, which changes its associative properties, has the opposite effect on the properties of a stimulus that was paired with the CS in a prior conditioning task. For example, Kaufman & Bolles (1981) used a simultaneous noise-light compound to signal shock before the light was repeatedly presented without shock. Later test trials then revealed that the extinction treatment with the light enhanced conditioned responding to the noise (see also Miller et al 1992). According to Dickinson & Burke's proposals (1996), the extinction trials with the light will activate into the A2 state representations of the stimuli with which it was paired—shock and noise—and thus strengthen the excitatory connection between them.

For the moment, it is very difficult to draw any clear theoretical conclusions from the experiments considered in this section. Wagner's theoretical proposals (1981) provide an important step towards enhancing our understanding of the factors that govern the associability of stimuli, and of the associations that will be formed when a CS is actually present. However, it is not obvious how the theory can account for changes in the associative properties of a stimulus brought about through manipulations conducted in its absence. The results from different experiments are consistent with one or the other of two contradictory modifications to Wagner's theory, and the conditions that determine whether or not certain experimental manipulations will be effective remain to be specified. To complicate matters further, it is important to note that retrospective revaluation is not always found with animals (Rescorla & Cunningham 1978, Speers et al 1980, Holland 1999, Rauhut et al 2000), and there are explanations for the phenomenon that do not appeal to any version of SOP (Miller & Matzel 1988). The theoretical analysis of learning about absent stimuli is thus likely to progress slowly until the factors are identified that determine both the nature of this learning and whether or not it will take place. For a discussion of one factor, biological significance, that may influence this type of learning see Miller & Matute (1996).

APPLICATION OF THEORIES OF ANIMAL LEARNING TO HUMAN LEARNING

An important reason for studying associative learning in animals is the hope that once a set of theoretical principles has been identified, they will extend to learning in humans. There are two relatively recent areas of research in which theories of associative learning in animals are relevant to human learning: the judgment of causality, and categorization.

The Judgment of Causality

In a causal judgment task, participants are given hypothetical information about the relationship between a number of different possible causes and effects, often on a trial-by-trial basis. They may, for example, be told that an allergic reaction results from eating some food compounds, but not others (Van Hamme & Wasserman 1994). Participants are then asked to judge the degree to which a particular food causes the allergic reaction. According to contingency-based theories, people make this judgment on the basis of a statistical computation. They might calculate a value, Δp, which is the estimated probability of the outcome given the cause, minus the estimated probability of the outcome in the absence of the cause (Allan 1980). Alternative contingency-based methods for deriving causal judgments have been proposed by Cheng & Novick (1990) and Cheng (1997).

A different way of explaining how causal judgments are derived was proposed by Dickinson et al (1984), who suggested they develop on a trial-by-trial basis according to principles embodied in theories of associative learning. That is, causes are believed to be associated with effects in the same way as CSs become associated with USs. One justification for this belief is that effects such as blocking and conditioned inhibition can be reliably obtained in causal judgment tasks with humans (Baker et al 1993, Chapman & Robbins 1990, Dickinson et al 1984). A further justification is that when the effects of training have reached asymptote, the predictions made by the Rescorla-Wagner (1972) theory concerning a predictive cue are the same as those that can be derived by calculating Δp (Chapman & Robbins 1990).

At least four different lines of research have derived from the application of theories of associative learning in animals to causal judgment by humans. First, there have been studies that have examined whether these theories do indeed provide an acceptable account of causal judgment by humans. Some researchers have claimed that fairly simple empirical phenomena are inconsistent with associative theory.

Cheng (1997), for instance, has cited a number of findings that she believes are more readily explained by a contingency-based account of causal judgment than an associative account—the Rescorla-Wagner (1972) theory. Interestingly, Lober & Shanks (2000) have pointed out that many of Cheng's (1997) arguments are valid only if it is assumed that the learning rate parameter, β, has the same value for reinforced and nonreinforced trials. Other researchers have reported findings that are more consistent with an associative- than a contingency-based account of causal judgment (e.g. López et al 1998, Vallée-Tourangeau et al 1998b). Another criticism of associative theory is that causal judgments are based on an understanding of how causes actually operate: Whereas two causes of an effect may compete with one another, two effects of one cause may not (Waldmann 2000, Waldmann & Holyoak 1992; but see Shanks & López 1996), yet associative theory has no way of distinguishing these cases because it treats them as identical associative learning problems.

Second, there have been studies that have evaluated the predictions made by different theories of associative learning in the context of human causal judgment. Thus, attempts have been made to compare predictions made by an elemental or a configural theory of associative learning. On some occasions these have lent clear support for configural theory (López et al 1998, Vallée-Tourangeau et al 1998a); on others, neither type of theory has provided a satisfactory explanation for the data. For example, Shanks et al (1998b) used a task that was similar in design to the study by Pearce & Wilson (1991) mentioned earlier. They found that presenting B+ trials after an A+/ABo discrimination had no effect on subsequent test trials with the AB compound. This demonstration of an immunity to the effects of retroactive interference contradicts predictions from both elemental and configural theories of associative learning. On a related issue, there have been attempts to explore whether prior training can encourage participants to adopt either an elemental or a configural strategy when they are confronted with a causal judgment task. Experiments by Williams (1995), Williams & Braker (1999), and Williams et al (1994) have lent considerable support to this proposal (but see Shanks et al 1998a).

Third, experiments have been directed at evaluating the relative contribution made by the acquisition of associations and rules to causal judgments. Thus, Shanks & Darby (1998) presented participants with trials in which individual stimuli, A or B, signaled nothing, and a compound CD signaled an outcome. These trials were intermixed among discriminations involving negative (E+/F+/EFo) or positive (Go/Ho/GH+) patterning. On testing, the participants indicated that they thought it more likely that AB than either C or D would be followed by the outcome. According to associative theories of learning, the opposite pattern of results should have been found. As a consequence, Shanks & Darby (1998) concluded that during the training stage subjects learned the rule "a compound and its elements predict opposite outcomes." Not only would the use of this rule facilitate the acquisition of the discriminations, but it would also account for the results of the test trials (Lachnit & Kimmel 1993).

Finally, causal judgment experiments have been used to study retrospective revaluation (see previous section) in humans (Chapman 1991, Dickinson & Burke 1996, Shanks 1985, Wasserman & Berglan 1998). Participants may be first told that a meal of two different foods, AB, is followed by an allergic reaction. Subsequently being told that B alone produces the same reaction is then generally found to reduce the degree to which A is seen a cause of the allergic reaction. Such retrospective revaluation of A is hard to explain with many associative theories (e.g. Rescorla & Wagner 1972), but it is easy to explain by contingency-based theories of causal judgment because they do not take account of the order in which trials are presented. Although it might therefore seem that retrospective revaluation is more consistent with contingency-based than associative theories of causal judgment, recent theoretical developments caution against such a conclusion. Retrospective revaluation can be explained by Miller & Matzel's (1988) theory, as well as by the modifications to the Rescorla-Wagner (1972) theory proposed by Van Hamme & Wasserman (1994) and to SOP proposed by Dickinson & Burke (1996). Indeed, Aitken et al (2000) argue that the modifications to SOP provide a better account of causal judgment than contingency based theories.

Categorization

Theories of associative learning in animals have had relatively little impact on the study of categorization in humans (but see Gluck & Bower 1988). Nonetheless, there is a close correspondence between some of these theories and certain theories of categorization in humans. The basic idea is that features of exemplars become associated with categories in the same way that CSs are associated with USs. Thus, the Rescorla-Wagner (1972) theory is formally equivalent to the model of categorization proposed by Gluck & Bower (1988). Furthermore, because the delta rule, which lies at the heart of a number of connectionist theories of learning and categorization (Rumelhart et al 1988), is similar to the error-correction rule used by Rescorla & Wagner (1972), it can be shown that the Rescorla-Wagner theory is closely related to these theories (Sutton & Barto 1981). There are also close links between the configural theory of conditioning proposed by Pearce (1987, 1994) and the exemplar-based theory of categorization proposed by Kruschke (1992). Although the relative merits of these different classes of theories of human learning are still under scrutiny, the fact that they correspond closely to theories of learning in animals strongly encourages the belief that there is much in common between the fundamental mechanisms of associative learning in animals and humans.

CONCLUDING COMMENTS

Theories of associative learning provide parsimonious, formal explanations for findings from both Pavlovian and instrumental conditioning. They have made steady progress over the years. However, we may note at least two gaps that still remain in our current understanding. First, although the theories now provide a reasonably sophisticated understanding of the processes involved in association formation, they say relatively little about how the association is manifested in the performance of behaving animals. We must therefore look to other theories to understand the behavioral output of the processes reviewed here (Domjan 1998, Fanselow 1994, Timberlake & Silva 1995). Second, recent research has been increasingly directed at understanding the role of timing in conditioning (Denniston et al 1998, Gallistel 1990, Gibbon 1977). Gallistel & Gibbon (2000) have argued that timing plays a fundamental role in conditioning by determining not only when an animal responds, but also whether or not it responds during both acquisition and extinction. They further argue that an adequate account of timing in conditioning lies beyond the scope of associative learning theory. Instead they favor a radically different theory that assumes that the duration and rate of events, rather than the conditioning trial, is the psychological "primitive" from which all conditioning phenomena are ultimately derived. Associative learning theory is likely to rise to this, and other, challenges by finding new, hopefully elegant, ways of accommodating problematic phenomena within existing theoretical frameworks.

ACKNOWLEDGMENTS

We are grateful to Anthony Dickinson and David Shanks for their valuable suggestions concerning this article and to the UK and Biological Sciences Research Council and the Medical Research Council of the UK for helping support the research of JMP and to the US National Science Foundation for helping support the research of MEB.

Visit the Annual Reviews home page at www.AnnualReviews.org

LITERATURE CITED

Aitken MRF, Larkin MJW, Dickinson A. 2000. Super-learning of causal judgements. *Q. J. Exp. Psychol. B* 53:59–81

Allan LG. 1980. A note on measurement of contingency between two binary variables in a judgement task. *Bull. Psychon. Soc.* 15:147–49

Aydin A, Pearce JM. 1997. Some determinants of response summation. *Anim. Learn. Behav.* 25:108–21

Baker A, Mercier P, Vallée-Tourangeau F, Frank R, Pan M. 1993. Selective associations and causality judgements: Presence of a strong causal factor may reduce judgements of

weaker ones. *J. Exp. Psychol.: Learn. Mem. Cogn.* 19:414–32

Baker AG, Mercier P. 1982. Extinction of the context and latent inhibition. *Learn. Motiv.* 13:391–416

Baker TB, Tiffany ST. 1985. Morphine tolerance as habituation. *Psychol. Rev.* 92:78–108

Balaz MA, Kasprow WJ, Miller RR. 1982. Blocking with a single compound trial. *Anim. Learn. Behav.* 10:271–76

Best MR, Gemberling GA. 1977. Role of short-term processes in the conditioned stimulus preexposure effect and the delay of reinforcement gradient in long-delay taste-aversion learning. *J. Exp. Psychol.: Anim. Behav. Process.* 3:253–63

Best MR, Gemberling GA, Johnson PE. 1979. Disrupting the conditioned stimulus pre-exposure effect in flavor-aversion learning: effects of interoceptive distractor manipulations. *J. Exp. Psychol.: Anim. Behav. Process.* 5:321–34

Blaisdell AP, Bristol AS, Gunther LM, Miller RR. 1998. Overshadowing and latent inhibition counteract each other: support for the comparator hypothesis. *J. Exp. Psychol.: Anim. Behav. Process.* 24:335–51

Bonardi C, Hall G. 1994. Occasion-setting training renders stimuli more similar: acquired equivalence between targets of feature-positive and feature-negative discriminations. *Q. J. Exp. Psychol. B* 47:63–81

Bouton ME. 1984. Differential control by context in the inflation and reinstatement paradigms. *J. Exp. Psychol.: Anim. Behav. Process.* 10:56–74

Bouton ME. 1993. Context, time, and memory retrieval in the interference paradigms of Pavlovian learning. *Psychol. Bull.* 114:80–99

Bouton ME, Bolles RC. 1979. Contextual control of the extinction of conditioned fear. *Learn. Motiv.* 10:445–66

Bouton ME, Brooks DC. 1993. Time and physical context effects in Pavlovian discrimination reversal. *J. Exp. Psychol.: Anim. Behav. Process.* 19:165–79

Bouton ME, King DA. 1983. Contextual control of the extinction of conditioned fear: tests for the associative value of the context. *J. Exp. Psychol.: Anim. Behav. Process.* 9:248–65

Bouton ME, King DA. 1986. Effects of performance to conditioned stimuli with mixed histories of reinforcement and nonreinforcement. *J. Exp. Psychol.: Anim. Behav. Process.* 12:4–15

Bouton ME, Mineka S, Barlow DH. 2000. A modern learning theory perspective on the etiology of panic. *Psychol. Rev.* In press

Bouton ME, Nelson JB. 1994. Context-specificity of target versus feature inhibition in a feature negative discrimination. *J. Exp.*

Psychol.: Anim. Behav. Process. 20:51–65

Bouton ME, Nelson JB. 1998. Mechanisms of feature-positive and feature-negative discrimination learning in an appetitive conditioning paradigm. See Schmajuk & Holland 1998, pp. 69–112

Bouton ME, Nelson JB, Rosas JM. 1999. Stimulus generalization, context change, and forgetting. *Psychol. Bull.* 125:171–86

Bouton ME, Peck CA. 1989. Context effects on conditioning, extinction, and reinstatement in an appetitive conditioning preparation. *Anim. Learn. Behav.* 17:188–98

Bouton ME, Ricker ST. 1994. Renewal of extinguished responding in a second context. *Anim. Learn. Behav.* 22:317–24

Bouton ME, Swartzentruber D. 1986. Analysis of the associative and occasion-setting properties of contexts participating in a Pavlovian discrimination. *J. Exp. Psychol.: Anim. Behav. Process.* 12:333–50

Brandon SE, Wagner AR. 1998. Occasion setting: influences of conditional emotional responses and configural cues. See Schmajuk & Holland 1998, pp. 343–82

Brooks DC, Bouton ME. 1993. A retrieval cue for extinction attenuates spontaneous recovery. *J. Exp. Psychol.: Anim. Behav. Process.* 19:77–89

Bush RR, Mosteller F. 1955. *Stochastic Models for Learning.* New York: Wiley

Channell S, Hall G. 1983. Contextual effects in latent inhibition with an appetitive conditioning procedure. *Anim. Learn. Behav.* 11:67–74

Chapman GB. 1991. Trial order affects cue interaction in contingency judgement. *J. Exp. Psychol.: Learn. Mem. Cogn.* 17:837–54

Chapman GB, Robbins SJ. 1990. Cue interaction in human contingency judgement. *Mem. Cogn.* 18:537–45

Cheng PW. 1997. From covariation to causation: a causal power theory. *Psychol. Rev.* 104:367–405

Cheng PW, Novick LR. 1990. A probabilistic contrast model of causal induction. *J. Pers. Soc. Psychol.* 58:545–67

Chorozyna H. 1962. Some properties of conditioned inhibition. *Acta Biol. Exp.* 22:5–13

Denniston JC, Cole RP, Miller RR. 1998. The role of temporal relationships in the transfer of conditioned inhibition. *J. Exp. Psychol.: Anim. Behav. Process.* 24:20–14

Dickinson A. 1994. Instrumental conditioning. In *Animal Learning and Cognition*, ed. NJ Mackintosh, pp. 45–79. San Diego, CA: Academic

Dickinson A, Burke J. 1996. Within-compound associations mediate the retrospective revaluation of causality judgements. *Q. J. Exp. Psychol. B* 49:60–80

Dickinson A, Hall G, Mackintosh NJ. 1976. Surprise and the attenuation of blocking. *J. Exp. Psychol.: Anim. Behav. Process.* 2:313–22

Dickinson A, Shanks DR, Evenden JL. 1984. Judgement of act-outcome contingency: the role of selective attribution. *Q. J. Exp. Psychol. A* 36:29–50

Domjan M. 1998. Going wild in the laboratory: learning about species typical cues. In *The Psychology of Learning and Motivation*, ed. DL Medin, 38:155–86. San Diego, CA: Academic

Dwyer DM, Mackintosh NJ, Boakes RA. 1998. Simultaneous activation of representations of absent cues results in the formation of an excitatory association between them. *J. Exp. Psychol.: Anim. Behav. Process.* 24:163–71

Fanselow MS. 1994. Neural organization of the defensive behavior system responsible for fear. *Psychol. Bull. Rev.* 1:429–38

Fanselow MS. 1999. Learning theory and neuropsychology: configuring their disparate elements in the hippocampus. *J. Exp. Psychol.: Anim. Behav. Process.* 25:275–83

Friedman MP, Gelfand H. 1964. Transfer effects in discrimination learning. *J. Math. Psychol.* 1:204–14

Gallistel CR. 1990. *The Organization of Learning*. Cambridge, MA: MIT Press

Gallistel CR. Gibbon J. 2000. Time rate and conditioning. *Psychol. Rev.* 107:289–344

George DN, Pearce JM. 1999. Acquired distinctiveness is controlled by stimulus relevance not correlation with reward. *J. Exp. Psychol.: Anim. Behav. Process.* 25:363–73

Gibbon J. 1977. Scalar expectancy theory and Weber's law in animal timing. *Psychol. Rev.* 84:279–325

Gibbon J, Balsam P. 1981. Spreading associations in time. In *Autoshaping and Conditioning Theory*, ed. CM Locurto, HS Terrace, J Gibbon, pp. 219–53. New York: Academic

Gluck MA, Bower GH. 1988. From conditioning to category learning: an adaptive network model *J. Exp. Psychol.: Gen.* 117:225–44

Gulliksen H, Wolfle DL. 1938. A theory of learning and transfer: I. *Psychometrika* 3:127–49

Hall G, Channell S. 1985. Differential effects of contextual change on latent inhibition and on the habituation of an orienting response. *J. Exp. Psychol.: Anim. Behav. Process.* 11:470–81

Hall G, Honey RC. 1989. Contextual effects in conditioning, latent inhibition, and habituation: associative and retrieval functions of contextual cues. *J. Exp. Psychol.: Anim. Behav. Process.* 15:232–41

Hall G, Minor H. 1984. A search for context-stimulus associations in latent inhibition. *Q. J. Exp. Psychol. B* 36:145–69

Hall G, Pearce JM. 1979. Latent inhibition of a CS during CS-US pairings. *J. Exp. Psychol.: Anim. Behav. Process.* 5:31–42

Hall G, Pearce JM. 1982. Restoring the associability of a preexposed CS by a surprising event. *Q. J. Exp. Psychol. B* 34:127–40

Harris JA, Jones ML, Bailey GK, Westbrook RF. 2000. Contextual control over conditioned responding in an extinction paradigm. *J. Exp. Psychol.: Anim. Behav. Process.* 26:174–85

Harris JA, Westbrook RF. 1998. Retroactive revaluation of an odor-taste association. *Anim. Learn. Behav.* 26:326–35

Holland PC. 1981. Acquisition of representation-mediated conditioned food aversions. *Learn. Motiv.* 12:1–18

Holland PC. 1983a. Occasion setting in Pavlovian feature positive discriminations. In *Quantitative Analyses of Behavior*, ed. ML Commons, RJ Herrnstein, AR Wagner, 4:183–206. New York: Ballinger

Holland PC. 1983b. Representation-mediated overshadowing and potentiation of conditioned aversions. *J. Exp. Psychol.: Anim. Behav. Process.* 9:1–13

Holland PC. 1984. Differential effects of reinforcement of an inhibitory feature after serial and simultaneous feature negative discrimination training. *J. Exp. Psychol.: Anim. Behav. Process.* 10:461–75

Holland PC. 1985. The nature of conditioned inhibition in serial and simultaneous feature negative discriminations. See Miller & Spear 1985, pp. 267–97

Holland PC. 1986. Transfer after serial feature positive discrimination training. *Learn. Motiv.* 17:243–68

Holland PC. 1988. Excitation and inhibition in unblocking. *J. Exp. Psychol.: Anim. Behav. Process.* 14.261–79

Holland PC. 1989a. Acquisition and transfer of conditioned discrimination performance. *J. Exp. Psychol.: Anim. Behav. Process.* 15:154–65

Holland PC. 1989b. Feature extinction enhances transfer of occasion setting. *Anim. Learn. Behav.* 17:269–79

Holland PC. 1989c. Occasion setting with simultaneous compounds in rats. *J. Exp. Psychol.: Anim. Behav. Process.* 15:183–93

Holland PC. 1989d. Transfer of negative occasion setting and conditioned inhibitors across conditioned and unconditioned stimuli. *J. Exp. Psychol.: Anim. Behav. Process.* 15:183–93

Holland PC. 1999. Overshadowing and blocking as acquisition deficits: no recovery after extinction of overshadowing or blocking cues. *Q. J. Exp. Psychol. B* 52:307–33

Holland PC, Forbes DT. 1982. Representation-mediated extinction of conditioned flavor aversions. *Learn. Motiv.* 13:454–71

Hollis KL. 1982. Pavlovian conditioning of signal-centered action patterns and autonomic behaviour: a biological analysis of function. *Adv. Study Behav.* 12:1–64

Hollis KL. 1997. Contemporary research on Pavlovian conditioning: a "new" functional analysis. *Am. Psychol.* 52:956–65

Honey RC, Watt A. 1998. Acquired relational equivalence: implications for the nature of associative structures. *J. Exp. Psychol.: Anim. Behav. Process.* 24:325–34

Honey RC, Watt A. 1999. Acquired relational equivalence between contexts and features. *J. Exp. Psychol.: Anim. Behav. Process.* 25:324–33

Hull CL. 1943. *Principles of Behavior.* New York: Appleton-Century-Crofts

James JH, Wagner AR. 1980. One trial overshadowing: evidence of distributive processing. *J. Exp. Psychol.: Anim. Behav. Process.* 6:188–205

Jordan WP, Strasser H, McHale L. 2000. Contextual control of long-term habituation in the rat. *J. Exp. Psychol.: Anim. Behav. Process.* 26. In press

Kamin LJ. 1969. Selective association and conditioning. In *Fundamental Issues in Associative Learning*, ed. NJ Mackintosh, WK Honig, pp. 42–64. Halifax, Nova Scotia: Dalhousie Univ. Press

Kaufman MA, Bolles RC. 1981. A nonassociative aspect of overshadowing. *Bull. Psychon. Soc.* 18:318–20

Kaye H, Mackintosh NJ. 1990. A change of context can enhance performance of an aversive but not an appetitive conditioned response. *Q. J. Exp. Psychol.* 42:113–34

Kruschke JK. 1992. ALCOVE: an exemplar-based connectionist model of category learning. *Psychol. Rev.* 99:22–44

Lachnit H, Kimmel HD. 1993. Positive and negative patterning in human classical skin conductance response conditioning. *Anim. Learn. Behav.* 21:314–26

Lamarre J, Holland PC. 1987. Transfer of inhibition after serial feature negative discrimination training. *Learn. Motiv.* 18:319–42

Lamoureux JA, Buhusi CV, Schmajuk NA.

1998. A real-time theory of Pavlovian conditioning: simple stimuli and occasion setters. See Schmajuk & Holland 1998, pp. 383–424

Lober K, Shanks DR. 2000. Is causal induction based on causal power? Critique of Cheng 1997. *Psychol. Rev.* 107:195–212

López FJ, Shanks DR, Almarez J, Fernandez P. 1998. Effects of trial order on contingency judgments: a comparison of associative and probabilistic contrast accounts. *J. Exp. Psychol.: Learn. Mem. Cogn.* 24:672–94

Lovibond PF, Preston GC, Mackintosh NJ. 1984. Context specificity of conditioning and latent inhibition. *J. Exp. Psychol.: Anim. Behav. Process.* 10:360–75

Lubow RE, Moore AU. 1959. Latent inhibition: the effect of nonreinforced preexposure to the conditional stimulus. *J. Comp. Physiol. Psychol.* 52:415–19

Mackintosh NJ. 1971. An analysis of overshadowing and blocking. *Q. J. Exp. Psychol.* 23:118–25

Mackintosh NJ. 1975. A theory of attention: variations in the associability of stimuli with reinforcement *Psychol. Rev.* 82:276–98

Mackintosh NJ, Kaye H, Bennett CH. 1991. Perceptual learning in flavour aversion conditioning. *Q. J. Exp. Psychol. B* 43:297–322

Mackintosh NJ, Little L. 1969. Intradimensional and extradimensional shift learning by pigeons. *Psychon. Sci.* 15:5–6

Marlin NA, Miller RR. 1981. Associations to contextual stimuli as a determinant of longterm habituation. *J. Exp. Psychol.: Anim. Behav. Process.* 7:313–33

Matzel LD, Brown AM, Miller RR. 1987. Associative effects of US preexposure: modulation of conditioned responding by an excitatory training context. *J. Exp. Psychol.: Anim. Behav. Process.* 13:65–72

McCloskey M, Cohen NJ. 1989. Catastrophic interference in connectionist networks: the sequential learning problem. In *The Psychology of Learning and Motivation*, ed. G Bower 24:109–65. San Diego, CA: Academic

McLaren IPL, Kaye H, Mackintosh NJ. 1989.

An associative theory of the representation of stimuli: applications to perceptual learning and latent inhibition. In *Parallel Distributed Processing: Implications for Psychology and Neurobiology*, ed. RGM Morris, pp. 102–30. Oxford: Clarendon

Miller RR, Barnet RC, Graham NJ. 1992. Responding to a conditioned stimulus depends on the current associative status of other cues present during training of that specific stimulus. *J. Exp. Psychol.: Anim. Behav. Process.* 18:251–64

Miller RR, Barnet RC, Grahame NJ. 1995. Assessment of the Rescorla-Wagner model. *Psychol. Bull.* 117:363–86

Miller RR, Hallam SC, Grahame NJ. 1990. Inflation of comparator stimuli following CS training. *Anim. Learn. Behav.* 18:434–43

Miller RR, Matute H. 1996. Biological significance in forward and backward blocking: resolution of a discrepancy between animal conditioning and human causal judgement. *J. Exp. Psychol.: Gen.* 125:370–86

Miller RR, Matzel LD. 1988. The comparator hypothesis: a response rule for the expression of associations. In *The Psychology of Learning and Motivation*, ed. DL Medin, 22:1–92. San Diego, CA: Academic

Miller RR, Spear NE, eds. 1985. *Information Processing in Animals: Conditioned Inhibition.* Hillsdale, NJ: Erlbaum

Nakajima S. 1997. Failure of inhibition by B over C afer A+, AB−, ABC+ training. *J. Exp. Psychol.: Anim. Behav. Process.* 23:482–90

Nakajima S, Urushihara K. 1999. Inhibition and facilitation by B over C after A+, AB−, and ABC+ training with multimodality stimulus combinations. *J. Exp. Psychol.: Anim. Behav. Process.* 25:68–81

Nelson JB. 1997. *The context specificity of second learned information.* PhD thesis. Univ. Vermont, Burlington

Nelson JB, Bouton ME. 1997. The effects of a context switch following serial and simultaneous feature negative discriminations. *Learn. Motiv.* 28:56–84

Page M. 2000. Connectionist modelling in psychology: a localist manifesto. *Behav. Brain Sci.* In press

Pavlov IP. 1927. *Conditioned Reflexes.* London: Oxford Univ. Press

Pearce JM. 1987. A model of stimulus generalization for Pavlovian conditioning. *Psychol. Rev.* 94:61–73

Pearce JM. 1994. Similarity and discrimination: a selective review and a connectionist model. *Psychol. Rev.* 101:587–607

Pearce JM, George DN, Redhead ES. 1998. The role of attention in the solution of conditional discriminations. See Schmajuk & Holland 1998, pp. 249–75

Pearce JM, Hall G. 1980. A model for Pavlovian learning: variations in the effectiveness of conditioned but not unconditioned stimuli. *Psychol. Rev.* 87:532–52

Pearce JM, Redhead ES. 1998. Some factors that determine the influence of a stimulus that is irrelevant to a discrimination. *J. Exp. Psychol.: Anim. Behav. Process.* 24:123–35

Pearce JM, Wilson PN. 1991. Failure of excitatory conditioning to extinguish the influence of a conditioned inhibitor. *J. Exp. Psychol.: Anim. Behav. Process.* 17:519–29

Rauhut AS, McPhee JE, Ayres JJB. 1999. Blocked and overshadowed stimuli are weakened in their ability to serve as blockers and second-order reinforcers in Pavlovian conditioning. *J. Exp. Psychol.: Anim. Behav. Process.* 25:45–67

Rauhut AS, McPhee JE, DiPietro NT, Ayres JJB. 2000. Conditioned inhibition training of the competing cue after compound conditioning does not reduce cue competition. *Anim. Learn. Behav.* 28:92–108

Redhead ES, Pearce JM. 1995a. Similarity and discrimination learning. *Q. J. Exp. Psychol.* 48B:46–66

Redhead ES, Pearce JM. 1995b. Stimulus salience and negative patterning. *Q. J. Exp. Psychol. B* 48:67–83

Rescorla RA. 1968. Probability of shock in the presence and absence of CS in fear conditioning. *J. Comp. Physiol. Psychol.* 67:504–9

Rescorla RA. 1973. Effect of US habituation following conditioning. *J. Comp. Physiol. Psychol.* 82:137–43

Rescorla RA. 1985. Conditioned inhibition and facilitation. See Miller & Spear 1985, pp. 299–326

Rescorla RA. 1991a. Associative relations in instrumental learning: the eighteenth Bartlett memorial lecture. *Q. J. Exp. Psychol. B* 43:1–23

Rescorla RA. 1991b. Separate reinforcement can enhance the effectiveness of modulators. *J. Exp. Psychol.: Anim. Behav. Process.* 17:259–69

Rescorla RA. 1997. Summation: test of a configural theory. *Anim. Learn. Behav.* 25:200–9

Rescorla RA. 1999. Associative changes in elements and compounds when the other is reinforced. *J. Exp. Psychol.: Anim. Behav. Process.* 25:247–55

Rescorla RA, Cunningham CL. 1978. Within-compound flavor associations. *J. Exp. Psychol.: Anim. Behav. Process.* 4:267–75

Rescorla RA, Wagner AR. 1972. A theory of Pavlovian conditioning: variations in the effectiveness of reinforcement and nonreinforcement. In *Classical Conditioning II: Current Research and Theory,* ed. AH Black, WF Prokasy, pp. 64–99. New York: Appleton-Century-Crofts

Rosas JM, Bouton ME. 1997. Additivity of the effects of retention interval and context change on latent inhibition: toward resolution of the context forgetting paradox. *J. Exp. Psychol.: Anim. Behav. Process.* 23:283–94

Ross RT, Holland PC. 1981. Conditioning of simultaneous and serial feature-positive discriminations. *Anim. Learn. Behav.* 9:293–303

Rumelhart DE, Hinton GE, Williams RJ. 1988. Learning internal representations by error propagation. In *Parallel Distributed Processing,* ed. DE Rumelhart, JL McClelland, 1:318–62. Cambridge, MA: MIT Press

Schmajuk NA, Holland PC, eds. 1998. *Occasion Setting: Associative Learning and*

Cognition in Animals. Washington, DC: Am. Psychol. Assoc.

Schmajuk NA, Lamoureux JA, Holland PC. 1998. Occasion setting: a neural network approach. *Psychol. Rev.* 105:3–32

Shanks DR. 1985. Forward and backward blocking in human contingency judgement. *Q. J. Exp. Psychol. B* 37:1–21

Shanks DR, Charles D, Darby RJ, Azmi A. 1998a. Configural processes in human associative learning. *J. Exp. Psychol.: Learn. Mem. Cogn.* 24:1353–78

Shanks DR, Darby RJ. 1998. Feature- and rule-based generalization in human associative learning. *J. Exp. Psychol.: Anim. Behav. Process.* 24:405–15

Shanks DR, Darby RJ, Charles D. 1998b. Resistance to interference in human associative learning: evidence of configural processing. *J. Exp. Psychol.: Anim. Behav. Process.* 24:136–50

Shanks DR, López FJ. 1996. Causal order does not affect cue selection in human associative learning. *Mem. Cogn.* 24:511–22

Shepp BE, Eimas PD. 1964. Intradimensional and extradimensional shifts in the rat. *J. Comp. Physiol. Psychol.* 57:357–64

Siegel S. 1989. Pharmacological conditioning and drug effects. In *Psychoactive Drugs*, ed. AJ Goudie, M Emmett-Oglesby, pp. 115–80. Clifton, NJ: Human Press

Spear NE. 1978. *The Processing of Memories: Forgetting and Retention.* Hillsdale, NJ: Lawrence Erlbaum

Speers MA, Gillan DJ, Rescorla RA. 1980. Within-compound associations in a variety of conditioning procedures. *Learn. Motiv.* 11:135–49

Sutton RS, Barto AG. 1981. Toward a modern theory of adaptive networks: expectation and prediction. *Psychol. Rev.* 88:135–70

Swan JA, Pearce JM. 1988. The orienting response as an index of stimulus associability in rats. *J. Exp. Psychol.: Anim. Behav. Process.* 4:292–301

Swartzentruber D. 1991. Blocking between occasion setters and contextual stimuli. *J. Exp.*

Psychol.: Anim. Behav. Process. 17:163–73

Swartzentruber D, Bouton ME. 1986. Contextual control of negative transfer produced by prior CS-US pairings. *Learn. Motiv.* 17:366–85

Swartzentruber D, Bouton ME. 1992. Context sensitivity of conditioned suppression following preexposure to the conditioned stimulus. *Anim. Learn. Behav.* 20:97–103

Swartzentruber D, Rescorla RA. 1994. Modulation of trained and extinguished stimuli by facilitators and inhibitors. *Anim. Learn. Behav.* 22:309–16

Symonds M, Hall G. 1995. Perceptual learning in flavor aversion conditioning: roles of stimulus comparison and latent inhibition of common stimulus elements. *Learn. Motiv.* 26:203–19

Thorndike EL. 1898. Animal intelligence: an experimental study of the associative processes in animals. *Psychol. Monogr.* 24(8): entire issue

Timberlake W, Silva KM. 1995. Appetitive behavior in ethology, psychology, and behavior systems. In *Perspectives in Ethology: Behavioral Design*, ed. NS Thompson, 11:211–53. New York: Plenum

Vallée-Tourangeau F, Murphy RA, Baker AG. 1998a. Causal induction in the presence of a perfect negative cue: contrasting predictions from associative and statistical models. *Q. J. Exp. Psychol. B* 51:173–90

Vallée-Tourangeau F, Murphy RA, Drew S, Baker AG. 1998b. Judging the importance of constant and variable candidate causes: a test of the power PC theory. *Q. J. Exp. Psychol. A* 51:65–84

Van Hamme LJ, Wasserman EA. 1994. Cue competition in causality judgements: the role of nonpresentation of compound stimulus elements. *Learn. Motiv.* 25:127–51

Wagner AR. 1981. SOP: a model of automatic memory processing in animal behavior. In *Information Processing in Animals: Memory Mechanisms*, ed. NE Spear, RR Miller, pp. 5-47. Hillsdale, NJ: Erlbaum

Wagner AR, Brandon SE. 1989. Evolution of a structured connectionist model of Pavlovian conditioning AESOP. In *Contemporary Learning Theories: Pavlovian Conditioning and the Status of Traditional Learning Theory*, ed. SB Klein, RR Mowrer, pp. 149–89. Hillsdale, NJ: Erlbaum

Wagner AR, Rescorla RA. 1972. Inhibition in Pavlovian conditioning: application of a theory. In *Inhibition and Learning*, ed. RA Boakes, MS Halliday, pp. 301–36. New York: Academic

Waldmann MR. 2000. Competition among causes but not effects in predictive and diagnostic learning. *J. Exp. Psychol.: Learn. Mem. Cogn.* 26:53–76

Waldmann MR, Holyoak KJ. 1992. Predictive and diagnostic learning within causal models: asymmetries in cue competition. *J. Exp. Psychol.: Gen.* 121:222–36

Ward-Robinson J, Hall G. 1996. Backward sensory preconditioning. *J. Exp. Psychol.: Anim. Behav. Process.* 22:395–404

Wasserman EA, Berglan LR. 1998. Backward blocking and recovery from overshadowing in human causal judgment: the role of within-compound associations. *Q. J. Exp. Psychol. B* 51:121–38

Westbrook RF, Bond NW, Feyer AM. 1981. Short- and long-term decrements in toxicosis-induced odor-aversion learning: the role of duration of exposure to an odor. *J. Exp. Psychol.: Anim. Behav. Process.* 7:362–81

Williams DA. 1995. Forms of inhibition in animal and human learning. *J. Exp. Psychol.: Anim. Behav. Process.* 21:129–42

Williams DA, Braker DS. 1999. Influence of past experience on the coding of compound stimuli. *J. Exp. Psychol.: Anim. Behav. Process.* 25:461–74

Williams DA, Sagness KE, McPhee JE. 1994. Configural and elemental strategies in predictive learning. *J. Exp. Psychol.: Learn. Mem. Cogn.* 20:694–709

Wilson PN, Boumphrey P, Pearce JM. 1992. Restoration of the orienting response to a light by a change in its predictive accuracy. *Q. J. Exp. Psychol. B* 44:17–36

Annu. Rev. Psychol. 2001. 52:141–66

ON HAPPINESS AND HUMAN POTENTIALS: A Review of Research on Hedonic and Eudaimonic Well-Being

Richard M. Ryan and Edward L. Deci

Department of Clinical and Social Sciences in Psychology, University of Rochester, Rochester, NY 14627; e-mail: ryan@psych.rochester.edu, deci@psych.rochester.edu

Key Words subjective well-being, psychological well-being, eudaimonia, happiness, wellness

■ **Abstract** Well-being is a complex construct that concerns optimal experience and functioning. Current research on well-being has been derived from two general perspectives: the hedonic approach, which focuses on happiness and defines well-being in terms of pleasure attainment and pain avoidance; and the eudaimonic approach, which focuses on meaning and self-realization and defines well-being in terms of the degree to which a person is fully functioning. These two views have given rise to different research foci and a body of knowledge that is in some areas divergent and in others complementary. New methodological developments concerning multilevel modeling and construct comparisons are also allowing researchers to formulate new questions for the field. This review considers research from both perspectives concerning the nature of well-being, its antecedents, and its stability across time and culture.

CONTENTS

0066-4308/01/0201-0141$14.00

141

INTRODUCTION

The concept of well-being refers to optimal psychological functioning and experience. It is the focus not only of everyday interpersonal inquiries (e.g. "How are you?") but also of intense scientific scrutiny. Although the question, "How are you?" may seem simple enough, theorists have found the issue of well-being to be complex and controversial. Indeed, from the beginnings of intellectual history, there has been considerable debate about what defines optimal experience and what constitutes "the good life." Obviously, this debate has enormous theoretical and practical implications. How we define well-being influences our practices of government, teaching, therapy, parenting, and preaching, as all such endeavors aim to change humans for the better, and thus require some vision of what "the better" is.

Well-being research seems especially prominent in current empirical psychology. In part this reflects the increasing awareness that, just as positive affect is not the opposite of negative affect (Cacioppo & Berntson 1999), well-being is not the absence of mental illness. For much of the last century, psychology's focus on the amelioration of psychopathology overshadowed the promotion of well-being and personal growth. But beginning in the 1960s with a shift in focus toward prevention, and continuing to the present, a few researchers have been studying growth (Deci 1975), well-being (Diener 1984), and the promotion of wellness (Cowen 1991).

Still, it is interesting that there seem to have been two periods when the American public, as well as the community of scientific psychologists, evidenced a particularly strong interest in issues of psychological growth and health, namely, the 1960s when the human potential movement swept this country, and currently when considerable attention is being given to positive psychology (Seligman & Csikszentmihalyi 2000). It may be no accident that these two periods represent times of relative affluence, when the economically advantaged have found that material security and luxury do not, in themselves, secure happiness. In this sense, the bursts of interest in well-being may have been prompted by a culture of surplus.

For whatever reasons, the field is burgeoning. A Psychinfo search using the terms well-being and mental health brought forth 28,612 and 12,009 citations, respectively, for the past 5 years. When the search was broadened to include terms such as health, happiness, quality of life, and other related topics, the numbers swelled even further. Clearly, this important area of psychology cannot be thoroughly reviewed in a short survey. Nonetheless, recent years have seen a crystallization of themes within the field of well-being that both organize this voluminous literature and provide directions for future research.

First and foremost, the field has witnessed the formation of two relatively distinct, yet overlapping, perspectives and paradigms for empirical inquiry into well-being that revolve around two distinct philosophies. The first of these can be broadly labeled hedonism (Kahneman et al 1999) and reflects the view that well-being consists of pleasure or happiness. The second view, both as ancient and as current as the hedonic view, is that well-being consists of more than just happiness. It lies instead in the actualization of human potentials. This view has been called eudaimonism (Waterman 1993), conveying the belief that well-being consists of fulfilling or realizing one's daimon or true nature. The two traditions—hedonism and eudaimonism—are founded on distinct views of human nature and of what constitutes a good society. Accordingly, they ask different questions concerning how developmental and social processes relate to well-being, and they implicitly or explicitly prescribe different approaches to the enterprise of living. As we shall see, the findings from the two intersect, but they also diverge at critical junctures.

Second, methodological and theoretical advances have enabled researchers to ask more sophisticated questions about well-being. The advent of multilevel modeling [e.g. hierarchial linear modeling (HLM)] has allowed researchers to go beyond the between-person or individual-difference focus that dominated the field. Instead of merely asking why person A has higher well-being than person B, researchers can now also examine the largely independent question of why person A is better off today than he or she was yesterday (Gable & Reis 1999). Complementing this advance, expansion of research methods to include ideographic assessments of goals, values, and aspirations has allowed an examination of how people's experiences of well-being are shaped by attributes of their personal goals and their motives for pursuing them (Emmons 1986, Little 1989, Sheldon & Kasser 1995). Similarly, new statistical methods for examining the cross-cultural equivalence of psychological constructs (Little 1997) have allowed more exacting research on the relation of culture to well-being. This is especially crucial because formulations from evolutionary psychology have challenged the "standard social science model" of humans as infinitely malleable (Tooby & Cosmides 1992), lending relevance to the search for the invariant as well as variant features of human functioning. Together, such advances have made well-being research a field in transition.

In this chapter, we begin by reviewing the two principal approaches to defining well-being, namely, the hedonic and eudaimonic approaches, considering their meta-theoretical, theoretical, and methodological aspects. We then proceed to a topical review of the literature, taking note, when appropriate, of the relation of the topics to the two general perspectives.

TWO TRADITIONS IN THE STUDY OF WELL-BEING

The Hedonic View

Equating well-being with hedonic pleasure or happiness has a long history. Aristippus, a Greek philosopher from the fourth century B.C., taught that the goal of life is to experience the maximum amount of pleasure, and that happiness is the totality of one's hedonic moments. His early philosophical hedonism has been followed by many others. Hobbes argued that happiness lies in the successful pursuit of our human appetites, and DeSade believed that pursuit of sensation and pleasure is the ultimate goal of life. Utilitarian philosophers such as Bentham argued that it is through individuals' attempting to maximize pleasure and self-interest that the good society is built. Hedonism, as a view of well-being, has thus been expressed in many forms and has varied from a relatively narrow focus on bodily pleasures to a broad focus on appetites and self-interests.

Psychologists who have adopted the hedonic view have tended to focus on a broad conception of hedonism that includes the preferences and pleasures of the mind as well as the body (Kubovy 1999). Indeed, the predominant view among hedonic psychologists is that well-being consists of subjective happiness and concerns the experience of pleasure versus displeasure broadly construed to include all judgments about the good/bad elements of life. Happiness is thus not reducible to physical hedonism, for it can be derived from attainment of goals or valued outcomes in varied realms (Diener et al 1998).

In a volume that announced "the existence of a new field of psychology," Kahneman et al (1999) defined hedonic psychology as the study of "what makes experiences and life pleasant and unpleasant" (p. ix). Its title, *Well-being: The Foundations of Hedonic Psychology*, clearly suggests that, within this paradigm, the terms well-being and hedonism are essentially equivalent. By defining well-being in terms of pleasure versus pain, hedonic psychology poses for itself a clear and unambiguous target of research and intervention, namely maximizing human happiness. Accordingly, the volume is replete with evidence about how people calculate utilities, maximize the density of reward, and optimize inputs associated with pleasure versus displeasure.

Although there are many ways to evaluate the pleasure/pain continuum in human experience, most research within the new hedonic psychology has used assessment of subjective well-being (SWB) (Diener & Lucas 1999). SWB consists of three components: life satisfaction, the presence of positive mood, and the absence of negative mood, together often summarized as happiness.

Just as there have been philosophical arguments about equating hedonic pleasure with well-being, there has been considerable debate about the degree to which measures of SWB adequately define psychological wellness (e.g. Ryff & Singer 1998). Accordingly, there are two important issues concerning the hedonic position in research on well-being. One concerns the validity of SWB and related measures as operational definitions of (*a*) hedonism and/or (*b*) well-being. The other concerns the types of social activities, goals, and attainments theorized to promote well-being, however it is assessed. As such, there are three defensible positions that could result from a consideration of these questions. First, one could accept both the hedonic view and SWB as its indicator. Second, one could accept the use of SWB as an operational definition of well-being but endorse a eudaimonic view of what fosters SWB. And third, one could both reject the measure of SWB as an indicator of well-being and argue against hedonic principles as the vehicle to produce well-being. Regardless of what is said about this debate, SWB has reigned as the primary index of well-being during the past decade and a half, and much of the research reviewed herein employs SWB as a major outcome variable.

Although there are various theoretical perspectives associated with hedonic psychology, some of its most prominent proponents have eschewed theory, arguing for a bottom-up empirical approach. Specifically, some have argued that we need to know more "elementary facts before a large theory is created" (Diener et al 1998, p. 35). Nevertheless, one can characterize the dominant work in hedonic psychology in theoretical terms, even if they remain implicit. Overall, the theories, whether implicit or explicit, tend to fit within what Tooby & Cosmides (1992) refer to as the standard social science model, which is built on the assumption of an enormous amount of malleability to human nature. With this meta-theoretical starting point, much of the work fits with the expectancy-value approach (e.g. Oishi et al 1999), which in its simplest form suggests that well-being is a function of expecting to attain (and ultimately attaining) the outcomes one values, whatever those might be. The focus of hedonic psychology on pleasure versus pain also readily links it with behavioral theories of reward and punishment (e.g. Shizgal 1999) and theories focused on cognitive expectations about such outcomes (e.g. Peterson 1999). Furthermore, the claim of hedonic psychologists and expectancy-value theorists that the goals through which well-being is enhanced can be highly idiosyncratic and culturally specific would also seem to fit well within a relativistic, postmodern view. Thus, although explicit theory is often not endorsed by hedonic researchers, implicit theoretical themes are identifiable.

The Eudaimonic View

Despite the currency of the hedonic view, many philosophers, religious masters, and visionaries, from both the East and West, have denigrated happiness per se as a principal criterion of well-being. Aristotle, for example, considered hedonic happiness to be a vulgar ideal, making humans slavish followers of desires. He posited, instead, that true happiness is found in the expression of virtue—that is, in doing what is worth doing. Fromm (1981), drawing on this Aristotelian view, argued that optimal well-being (vivere bene) requires distinguishing

> between those needs (desires) that are only subjectively felt and whose satisfaction leads to momentary pleasure, and those needs that are rooted in human nature and whose realization is conducive to human growth and produces eudaimonia, i.e. "well-being." In other words... the distinction between purely subjectively felt needs and objectively valid needs—part of the former being harmful to human growth and the latter being in accordance with the requirements of human nature (p. xxvi).

The term eudaimonia is valuable because it refers to well-being as distinct from happiness per se. Eudaimonic theories maintain that not all desires—not all outcomes that a person might value—would yield well-being when achieved. Even though they are pleasure producing, some outcomes are not good for people and would not promote wellness. Thus, from the eudaimonic perspective, subjective happiness cannot be equated with well-being.

Waterman (1993) stated that, whereas happiness is hedonically defined, the eudaimonic conception of well-being calls upon people to live in accordance with their daimon, or true self. He suggested that eudaimonia occurs when people's life activities are most congruent or meshing with deeply held values and are holistically or fully engaged. Under such circumstances people would feel intensely alive and authentic, existing as who they really are—a state Waterman labeled personal expressiveness (PE). Empirically, Waterman showed that measures of hedonic enjoyment and PE were strongly correlated, but were nonetheless indicative of distinct types of experience. For example, whereas both PE and hedonic measures were associated with drive fulfillments, PE was more strongly related to activities that afforded personal growth and development. Furthermore, PE was more associated with being challenged and exerting effort, whereas hedonic enjoyment was more related to being relaxed, away from problems, and happy.

Ryff & Singer (1998, 2000) have explored the question of well-being in the context of developing a lifespan theory of human flourishing. Also drawing from Aristotle, they describe well-being not simply as the attaining of pleasure, but as "the striving for perfection that represents the realization of one's true potential" (Ryff 1995, p. 100). Ryff & Keyes (1995) thus spoke of psychological well-being (PWB) as distinct from SWB and presented a multidimensional approach to the measurement of PWB that taps six distinct aspects of human actualization: autonomy, personal growth, self-acceptance, life purpose, mastery, and positive relatedness. These six constructs define PWB both theoretically and operationally and they specify what promotes emotional and physical health (Ryff & Singer 1998). They have presented evidence, for example, that eudaimonic living, as represented by PWB, can influence specific physiological systems relating to immunological functioning and health promotion.

In an engaging and instructive debate, Ryff & Singer (1998) challenged SWB models of well-being as being of limited scope where positive functioning is concerned, and specifically that SWB is often a fallible indicator of healthy living. In turn, Diener et al (1998) retorted that Ryff & Singer's eudaimonic criteria lets experts define well-being, whereas SWB research allows people to tell researchers what makes their life good. What is most clear from this clash of paradigms is that these differing definitions of wellness have led to quite different types of inquiry concerning the causes, consequences, and dynamics of well-being.

Self-determination theory (SDT) (Ryan & Deci 2000) is another perspective that has both embraced the concept of eudaimonia, or self-realization, as a central definitional aspect of well-being and attempted to specify both what it means to actualize the self and how that can be accomplished. Specifically, SDT posits three basic psychological needs—autonomy, competence, and relatedness—and theorizes that fulfillment of these needs is essential for psychological growth (e.g. intrinsic motivation), integrity (e.g. internalization and assimilation of cultural practices), and well-being (e.g. life satisfaction and psychological health), as well as the experiences of vitality (Ryan & Frederick 1997) and self-congruence (Sheldon & Elliot 1999). Need fulfillment is thus viewed as a natural aim of human life that delineates many of the meanings and purposes underlying human actions (Deci & Ryan 2000).

Specification of basic needs defines not only the minimum requirements of psychological health but also delineates prescriptively the nutriments that the social environment must supply for people to thrive and grow psychologically. Thus, SDT describes the conditions that facilitate versus undermine well-being within varied developmental periods and specific social contexts such as schools, workplaces, and friendships. SDT does not, however, suggest that the basic needs are equally valued in all families, social groups, or cultures, but it does maintain that thwarting of these needs will result in negative psychological consequences in all social or cultural contexts. As such, contextual and cultural, as well as developmental, factors continually influence the modes of expression, the means of satisfaction, and the ambient supports for these needs, and it is because of their effects on need satisfaction that they, in turn, influence growth, integrity, and well-being at both between-person and within-person levels of analysis.

SDT has both important similarities and differences with Ryff & Singer's (1998) eudaimonic approach. We wholly concur that well-being consists in what Rogers (1963) referred to as being fully functioning, rather than as simply attaining desires. We also are largely in agreement concerning the content of being eudaimonic— e.g. being autonomous, competent, and related. However, our approach theorizes that these contents are the principal factors that foster well-being, whereas Ryff and Singer's approach uses them to define well-being.

SDT posits that satisfaction of the basic psychological needs typically fosters SWB as well as eudaimonic well-being. This results from our belief that being satisfied with one's life and feeling both relatively more positive affect and less negative affect (the typical measures of SWB) do frequently point to psychological wellness, for, as Rogers (1963) suggested, emotional states are indicative of organismic valuation processes. That is, the assessment of positive and negative affect is useful insofar as emotions are, in part, appraisals of the relevance and valence of events and conditions of life with respect to the self. Thus, in SDT research, we have typically used SWB as one of several indicators of well-being. However, we have at the same time maintained that there are different types of positive experience and that some conditions that foster SWB do not promote eudaimonic well-being. For example, research by Nix et al (1999) showed that succeeding at an activity while feeling pressured to do so resulted in happiness (a positive affect closely linked to SWB), but it did not result in vitality (a positive affect more closely aligned with eudaimonic well-being). On the other hand, as predicted by SDT, succeeding at an activity while feeling autonomous resulted in both happiness and vitality. Thus, because conditions that promote SWB may not necessarily yield eudaimonic well-being, SDT research has typically supplemented SWB measures with assessments of self-actualization, vitality, and mental health in an effort to assess well-being conceived of as healthy, congruent, and vital functioning.

Applying the Two Viewpoints

The debate between hedonic and eudaimonic theorists is, as we have said, both ancient and contemporary and has often been quite heated. It will not be resolved herein. Rather, we have highlighted these two positions because of their theoretical and practical importance and because these approaches have generated distinct, but interfacing, research literatures in topical areas that we review.

Evidence from a number of investigators has indicated that well-being is probably best conceived as a multidimensional phenomenon that includes aspects of both the hedonic and eudaimonic conceptions of well-being. For example, Compton et al (1996) investigated the relation among 18 indicators of well-being and mental health, identifying two factors, one that seemed to reflect SWB and the other, personal growth. These two factors were themselves moderately correlated. The results of this study thus suggested that the hedonic and eudaimonic foci are both overlapping and distinct and that an understanding of well-being may be enhanced by measuring it in differentiated ways. King & Napa (1998) asked lay people to rate features of the good life and found that both happiness and meaning were implicated. McGregor & Little (1998) analyzed a diverse set of mental health indicators and also found two factors, one reflecting happiness and the other, meaningfulness. These researchers showed that, when pursuing personal goals, doing well and feeling happy may be disconnected from finding meaning and acting with integrity. Thus, in spite of the significant overlap, the most interesting results may be those that highlight the factors leading to divergence rather than just convergence in the hedonic and eudaimonic indicators of well-being.

RESEARCH TOPICS IN THE PSYCHOLOGY OF WELL-BEING

In what follows we briefly survey a number of research topics concerning well-being, focusing especially on those with a lively presence in contemporary research. The topics are quite diverse. Some grapple with the psychological meaning of well-being. For example, to what extent is well-being an individual difference? What is the role of emotions in well-being? and To what extent is physical health intertwined with well-being? Other topics search for antecedents of well-being at the between-person and within-person levels. Such factors as wealth, satisfying relationships, and goal attainment have been addressed. Still other topics concern whether well-being is different across time or place, for example, in different developmental periods and in different cultures. As we shall see, in many of these topical areas researchers with hedonic versus eudaimonic interests have tended to ask different kinds of questions and approach the answers by different routes.

Personality, Individual Differences, and Well-Being

Two closely related and frequently asked question are, What type of people are likely to be well or happy? and Are there people who can be characterized as being happy or well? In other words, are there personality factors that consistently relate to well-being, and can well-being itself be thought of as a personality variable?

These questions have been actively researched with regard to SWB. DeNeve (1999) suggested that SWB is determined to a substantial degree by genetic factors and argued that SWB is relatively stable across the life span. In fact, DeNeve & Cooper (1998) did a meta-analysis involving 197 samples with more than 40,000 adults, in which SWB was a criterion variable related to various personality traits. Many personality traits were significantly associated with SWB, suggesting a correspondence between chronic personality styles and individual differences in SWB. For instance, of the "big five" traits (Costa & McCrae 1992), DeNeve & Cooper reported that extraversion and agreeableness were consistently positively associated with SWB, whereas neuroticism was consistently negatively associated with it.

Diener & Lucas (1999) suggested that these big five findings should come as no surprise because extraversion is characterized by positive affect and neuroticism is virtually defined by negative affect. For instance, they cited evidence that, controlling for measurement error, the correlation between extraversion and positive mood was 0.80, and that neuroticism and trait negative affect were indistinguishable. That is, the negative relation between SWB and neuroticism, which concerns the tendency to experience negative affect, is somewhat tautological. In line with Seidlitz (1993), Diener & Lucas further suggest that conscientiousness, agreeableness, and openness to experience are less strongly and consistently linked to SWB because these traits have their sources in "rewards in the environment" (p. 320). In other words, as individual differences, these three are more a function of environmental influences, whereas extraversion and neuroticism may be more a function of genetic factors.

Because of the trait-like features of SWB, some studies have focused on contrasts between chronically happy and unhappy people. Lyubomirsky & Tucker (1998), for example, demonstrated that characteristically happy people tend to construe the same life events and encounters more favorably than unhappy people. Further, Lyubomirsky & Ross (1999) showed that individuals high, relative to low, in SWB tended to cast events and situations in a more positive light, to be less responsive to negative feedback, and to more strongly denigrate opportunities that are not available to them. Thus, people high in SWB may have attributional styles that are more self-enhancing and, perhaps, more enabling, which in turn could contribute to the relative stability of their happiness.

Ryff and colleagues have examined the relation of the big five traits to their multiple dimensions of psychological well-being. Schmutte & Ryff (1997) found that extraversion, conscientiousness, and low neuroticism were linked with the eudaimonic dimensions of self-acceptance, mastery, and life purpose; openness to experience was linked to personal growth; agreeableness and extraversion were linked to positive relationships; and low neuroticism was linked to autonomy.

Sheldon et al (1997) examined relations between the big five and well-being, but these researchers explored whether the degree of variability in a person's ratings on each trait across life roles (e.g. student, child, friend, etc), rather than the person's characteristic level on each trait, would relate to well-being, regardless of the specific trait being considered. In line with work by Roberts & Donahue (1994), Sheldon et al showed that greater variability in individuals' endorsements of traits across roles was associated with lower general well-being. Further, as predicted by SDT, Sheldon et al postulated and found that people were most likely to depart from their general trait characteristics in life roles in which they were least authentic, that is, where they felt least able to express their true self. In a similar vein, AW Paradise & MH Kernis (unpublished manuscript) found that greater variability in self-esteem scores over time, even among people whose average self-esteem was high, was associated with poorer well-being assessed with Ryff's (1989a) measure.

Emotions and Well-Being

The relation of emotions to well-being, like that of traits to well-being, deals to some extent with the meaning of well-being itself. As such, the hedonic and eudaimonic perspectives have quite different views and have engaged in diverse types of research.

Research on emotions and SWB has found that: (a) people ongoingly experience affect; (b) affect is valenced and easily judged as positive or negative; and (c) most people report having positive affect most of the time (Diener & Lucas 2000). Thus, because having more positive emotion and less negative emotion is SWB, the studies imply that people, in general, have fairly high SWB. Some researchers have focused on how to maintain positive affect and ameliorate negative affect, and others have focused on daily fluctuations in affect and on how ongoing experiences of affect relate to global SWB. Considerable research has addressed how people estimate mood over time, including the weight they give to various events (Kahneman 1999), as well as how response styles and the order of questions can affect global estimates (Schwarz & Strack 1991). For example, Diener et al (1991) found global judgments of subjective well-being to be based more in the frequency than intensity of positive experiences. In fact, it seems that intense positive emotions are often attended by increased unpleasant affect (Larsen & Diener 1987).

There is some indication that SWB is affected by positive and negative life events (Headey & Wearing 1989), but Suh et al (1996) found that the impact of events on SWB was brief. Further, because SWB is to some extent traitlike and people high, relative to low, in SWB are likely to construe the same event more positively, it is still unclear how much effect actual life events have on well-being.

The eudaimonic position, in contrast to the hedonic view, suggests that the important issue concerning emotions is not feeling positive per se (see Parrott 1993), but rather is the extent to which a person is fully functioning (Rogers 1963). Thus, under some conditions (e.g. the death of a loved one) a person would be considered to be more fully functioning, and, ultimately, to have greater well-being, if he or she experienced rather than avoided the negative feeling of sadness. From a eudaimonic view, such issues as the repression, disclosure, compartmentalization, and overcontrol versus undercontrol of emotions are highly pertinent to what defines wellness. For instance, work reviewed by King & Pennebaker (1998) suggests that suppressing or withholding emotions has clear costs for psychological and physical health, and DeNeve & Cooper (1998) found that people high in repressive tendencies tend to have lower SWB. Conversely, there seem to be well-being benefits to emotional disclosure (Butzel & Ryan 1997). Such findings fit the claims of eudaimonic theorists that emotional access and congruence are important for well-being.

Another line of eudaimonic research on emotions suggests that, because emotional positivity is not part of the definition of well-being, affect can be studied as an outcome of eudaimonic processes. Thus, although more positive affect is not considered an end in itself, it would be expected, under many circumstances, to be a byproduct of eudaimonic living. Ryff & Singer (1998), for example, reported moderate correlations between their eudaimonic assessment of well-being and SWB. They emphasize some dimensions over others in these relations—in particular, positive relations were found to be particularly strongly related to positive emotional experiences. More generally, these researchers viewed emotions as a catalyst to health states, and they focused on the capacity of deep emotional experience to mobilize antistress and disease resistant functions.

A final strand of research on emotions using a eudaimonic perspective has examined psychological conditions that promote positive emotions, including happiness and vitality. This work, which has been done at both the between persons and within-person levels, has considered the relation of basic need satisfaction to these emotional indices of well-being. In one study, Sheldon et al (1996) examined daily fluctuations in satisfaction of autonomy and competence over 2 weeks. Using HLM, they found that at the between-persons level feelings of autonomy and competence predicted happiness and vitality, but also that at the within-person level fluctuations in experiences of fulfillment of the two needs significantly predicted fluctuations in the affects. Subsequently, Reis et al (2000) showed that within-person fluctuations in all three of SDT's basic needs predicted the positive affects. Specifically, daily experiences of autonomy, competence, and relatedness each contributed unique variance to the prediction of happiness and vitality.

Physical Health and Its Relations to Well-Being

That there ought to be an association between health status and well-being seems intuitively clear. Sickness is often associated with displeasure or pain, so the presence of illness might directly increase negative affect. Further, illness often presents functional limitations, which can detract from opportunities for positive affect and life satisfaction.

Empirical results have supported these speculations. Specifically, an early meta-analysis by Okun et al (1984) relating self-reported physical health to SWB found an average correlation of 0.32. However, the relation seems to be more complex than one might expect. Some people with objectively poor health have high SWB, whereas, conversely, some people with low well-being have no signs of somatic illness. Befitting these observations, Okun et al found that when health was rated by others (e.g. doctors) the correlation dropped noticeably to 0.16. This suggests that the meaning and construal of health states may be a major factor in SWB. SWB is, after all, subjective, so one would expect it to be affected by personality and by interpretive and reporting styles.

Ryan & Frederick (1997) assessed subjective vitality, a positive and phenomenologically accessible state of having energy available to the self, and used it as an indicator of eudaimonic well-being. They found that subjective vitality not only correlated with psychological factors such as personal autonomy and relatedness, but that it also covaried with physical symptoms. That is, more physical symptoms in a day predicted decreased energy and aliveness for that day, as did poor health habits such as smoking and fatty diets. They argued that vitality is a phenomenally salient variable that is affected by both somatic and psychological factors.

Ryff & Singer (2000) used both empirical and case study evidence to underscore how various dimensions of eudaimonic living yield salubrious effects on health more generally, including lower allostatic load and better autoimmune functioning. Their work indicated that the PWB dimension of positive relationships with others was particularly critical to the promotion of health-related processes.

RESEARCH ON ANTECEDENTS OF WELL-BEING

Considerable research has examined antecedent conditions likely to facilitate well-being. We review some of that work, organized in terms of wealth, relationships, and goal pursuits. Because the literature is voluminous, the review is necessarily, and perhaps arbitrarily, selective.

Social Class and Wealth as Predictors of Well-Being

A question of widespread interest among researchers and laypeople alike concerns the relation of wealth to happiness and well-being. Relations of both attained wealth and wealth-related goals and aspirations have been addressed from both hedonic and eudaimonic perspectives.

Does money make people happy? Long traditions in folklore and lay wisdom suggest answers in both directions. From the view of hedonic psychology, which has no a priori basis for speculating on this matter, the question is empirical, and thus far the answer has been mixed.

In a recent review, E Diener & R Biswas-Diener (unpublished) summarized research on wealth and SWB as follows: (*a*) people in richer nations are happier than people in poorer nations; (*b*) increases in national wealth within developed nations have not, over recent decades, been associated with increases in SWB; (*c*) within-nation differences in wealth show only small positive correlations with happiness; (*d*) increases in personal wealth do not typically result in increased happiness; and (*e*) people who strongly desire wealth and money are more unhappy than those who do not. Although they reviewed different theoretical accounts of these findings, they concluded that there remain too many unknowns to supply an integrated model. However, they stated that avoiding poverty, living in a rich country, and focusing on goals other than material wealth are associated with attaining happiness.

Diener & Diener (1995) examined the strength of the relations between satisfaction with specific domains (family, friends, finances) and life satisfaction in college students from 31 nations. They found that, among the differential relations, financial status was more correlated with life satisfaction in poorer nations than wealthier nations.

Why might wealth be more important for increasing life satisfaction among people in poorer nations? Although there is not yet a clear answer, one key issue concerns the functional freedoms that accompany national wealth for all cultural members. A poor infrastructure within a nation constrains opportunities for stable relationships, personal expressiveness, and productivity. Thus, not only can national poverty interfere with satisfaction of physical needs, such as food and shelter, but it can also block access to exercising competencies, pursuing interests, and maintaining relationships, which would provide psychological need satisfaction. Thus, within poorer nations, the value of money for satisfying needs may be more critical than it is within a nation where most citizens have access to some basic resources for pursuing their goals.

Although the hedonic viewpoint would have little reason to view money as a problematic goal, a long tradition of eudaimonic and organismic theorists have questioned wealth and materialism as life goals. Drawing from the eudaimonic view and from SDT, Kasser & Ryan (1993, 1996) related money and materialism to well-being. They predicted that people who place a strong value on wealth relative to goals such as close relationships, personal growth, and community generativity, which are more closely related to basic psychological need fulfillment, should show lower well-being. From a eudaimonic view, placing too much priority on material goods (as well as goals such as fame and image), which in themselves do not satisfy basic psychological needs, can at best only partially satisfy the needs, and at worst can distract from foci that would yield need fulfillment. Further, because achieving money, fame, and image is often contingent on engaging in nonautonomous activities, emphasizing such goals may detract from a sense of authenticity and result in lower well-being. Beyond the relations of relative values to well-being, this view further suggests that once a person is beyond poverty level (and thus has sustenance and security) the attainment of more wealth should add little to well-being, whereas attaining fulfillment of goals more deeply connected with the basic psychological needs should directly enhance well-being.

Several studies have supported this overall model, showing that the more people focus on financial and materialistic goals, the lower their well-being. This result has been confirmed both in developed countries such as the United States and Germany

(Kasser & Ryan 1996, Schmuck et al 2000) and in less economically developed nations such as Russia and India (e.g. Ryan et al 1999). Furthermore, both cross sectional (Ryan et al 1999) and longitudinal (Sheldon & Kasser 1998) studies suggest that, whereas progress toward intrinsic goals enhances well-being, progress toward extrinsic goals such as money either does not enhance well-being or does so to a lesser extent. Finally, as Carver & Baird (1998) found, the relation between money and well-being is in part a function of the loss of autonomy associated with this life goal.

Ryff et al (1999) examined the impact of impoverishment on eudaimonic outcomes. Using the PWB measure, they found that socio-economic status was linked to the dimensions of self-acceptance, purpose, mastery, and growth. Many of the negative effects of lower socio-economic status on these dimensions appeared to result from social comparison processes, in which poorer individuals compared themselves unfavorably with others and felt unable to gain resources that could adjust perceived inequalities.

In sum, work in both the hedonic and eudaimonic traditions converges on the point that money does not appear to be a reliable route to either happiness or well-being. The relation of wealth to well-being is at best a low positive one, although it is clear that material supports can enhance access to resources that are important for happiness and self-realization. There appear to be many risks to poverty but few benefits to wealth when it comes to well-being. Furthermore, studies show specifiable eudaimonic hazards for those who overly value wealth and material goods.

Attachment, Relatedness, and Well-Being

There has been increasing appreciation within psychology of the fundamental importance of warm, trusting, and supportive interpersonal relationships for well-being. So important is relatedness that some theorists have defined relatedness as a basic human need that is essential for well-being (Baumeister & Leary 1995, Deci & Ryan 1991), and others have suggested that having stable, satisfying relationships is a general resilience factor across the lifespan (Mikulincer & Florian 1998). Insofar as there is validity to this view, one would expect a strong, universal association between the quality of relationships and well-being outcomes.

Evidence supporting the link of relatedness to SWB is manifold. Studies suggest that, of all factors that influence happiness, relatedness is at or very near the top of the list (Argyle 1987, Myers 1999). Furthermore, as DeNeve (1999) noted, affiliation and relationship-enhancing traits are among the most strongly related with SWB. Furthermore, loneliness is consistently negatively related to positive affect and life satisfaction (Lee & Ishii-Kuntz 1987). Still, the topic of relationships is complex, and even close relationships are multifaceted, so specificity is warranted concerning what aspects of relationships engender wellness. Two concepts–attachment and intimacy–are especially relevant (Reis & Patrick 1996).

The construct of attachment derives from the work of Bowlby (1969), who argued that early relationships with caregivers can be characterized in terms of differing degrees of felt security and support. Attachment studies were initially done with relationships during infancy (Ainsworth et al 1978) and more recently during adolescence and adulthood (Hazan & Shaver 1987). The main idea is that individuals have a predominant working model that varies in the degree to which it represents secure versus insecure attachment to others. Many studies have confirmed a relation between attachment security and well-being broadly construed, and some theorists have argued that secure attachments themselves are an indicator of well-being (e.g. Simpson 1990).

Although security of attachment has typically been viewed as a stable individual difference, recent work suggests that there is considerable within-person variation in attachment security with different relational partners. Baldwin et al (1996) showed descriptively that most people exhibit different attachment styles with different figures in their lives. La Guardia et al (2000) found that this within-person variability in security of attachment was predicted by the degree to which an individual experiences need satisfaction with particular partners; those with whom one experiences security are those who facilitate feelings of autonomy, competence, and relatedness. The researchers further showed that, to a considerable degree, the positive effects of attachment security on well-being were mediated by need satisfaction. Thus, it appears that secure attachments foster well being in large part because they represent relationships within which a person satisfies needs for autonomy, competence, and relatedness.

Research on intimacy also highlights the importance of relatedness for well-being and underscores that it is the quality of relatedness which engenders well being. For example, Nezlek (2000) reviewed a number of studies showing that, whereas quantity of interactions does not predict well-being, quality of relatedness does. Carstensen's (1998) Social Selectivity Theory, as well as work in SDT (e.g. V. Kasser & Ryan 1999) points to the same conclusion.

This work on the quality of relationships examining between-person relations has found that individuals who in general have more intimate or higher-quality relationships tend to demonstrate greater well-being. Work by Reis et al (2000) showed further that within-person, day-to-day variations in feelings of relatedness over a two-week period predicted daily indicators of well-being, including positive affect and vitality. Data were also gathered concerning the type of interactions that fostered relatedness and, in turn, well-being. In support of both intimacy theory and SDT, it was found that people experienced greater relatedness when they felt understood, engaged in meaningful dialog, or had fun with others.

Recall that, in the work of Ryff and colleagues, positive relations with others is a dimension of well-being. Thus, whereas much of the work reviewed herein treats relationships as a source of well-being, Ryff & Singer (2000) treat it as a defining element of PWB, viewing positive relations with others as an essential element in human flourishing. In relating this variable to others, Ryff et al (2001) reviewed evidence that positive relations predicted physiological functioning and health outcomes, including the secretion of oxytocin, which is associated with positive mood and stress relief. Their view is also supported by Uchino et al (1999), who showed that social support influences mortality via changes in cardiovascular, endocrine, and autoimmune systems.

Goal Pursuit and Well-Being: The Ups and Downs of Trying

Another active area of research has been the relations of goals and goal progress to well-being. It fits with many theories in psychology that feelings of competence or efficacy with regard to life goals should be associated with greater positive affect and well-being. More controversial is the issue of whether goal pursuits must be autonomous or integrated to the self in order to yield greater wellness. Whereas hedonic theory has typically adhered to an expectancy value model where autonomy has had no role, issues related to the autonomy, authenticity, and congruence of goal pursuits have been a concern of eudaimonic researchers.

Perceived Competence and Self-Efficacy   A large body of research points clearly to the fact that feeling competent and confident with respect to valued goals is associated with enhanced well-being (Carver & Scheier 1999, McGregor & Little 1998). Furthermore, it is clear that goal progress, on average, predicts enhanced well-being, particularly goals that are rated as important (e.g. Brunstein 1993). However, these general findings can be unpacked into various processes that contribute to the relation.

One issue concerns the level of challenge posed by one's goals. When life goals are nonoptimally challenging—either too easy or too difficult—positive affect is lower (Csikszentmihalyi & Csikszentmihalyi 1988). Low expectations of success have also been associated with high negative affect (Emmons 1986), and as noted, Waterman (1993) found an association between eudaimonic outcomes (PE) and growth-related, effortful challenge.

Another concern is whether one's goal activities are characterized by approach or avoidance motivational systems. Elliot & Sheldon (1997), for example, classified goals as approach or avoidance and then examined the effects of goal progress over a short-term period. Pursuit of avoidance goals was associated with both poorer goal progress and with lower well-being. Elliot et al (1997) similarly showed that people whose personal goals contained a higher proportion of avoidance had lower SWB. They also demonstrated the association between neuroticism and avoidance goals, but showed that the impact of avoidance regulation was evident even when controlling for neuroticism. Carver & Scheier (1999) also presented research linking approach goals (positively) and avoidance goals (negatively) to well-being outcomes.

Other work points to the importance of goals and motives being aligned for well-being effects to accrue. For example, Brunstein et al (1998) found that motive-goal congruence accounted for the effects of goal progress on SWB. Furthermore, they showed that commitment to motive-incongruent goals can even result in well-being declines. Such evidence suggests that how goals are anchored within the self bears on their influence on well-being.

Autonomy and Integration of Goals   Another actively researched issue concerns how autonomous one is in pursuing goals. SDT in particular has taken a strong stand on this by proposing that only self-endorsed goals will enhance well-being, so pursuit of heteronomous goals, even when done efficaciously, will not. The relative autonomy of personal goals has, accordingly, been shown repeatedly to be predictive of well-being outcomes controlling for goal efficacy at both between-person and within-person levels of analysis (Ryan & Deci 2000). Interestingly this pattern of findings has been supported in cross-cultural research, suggesting that the relative autonomy of one's pursuits matters whether one is collectivistic or individualistic, male or female (e.g. V Chirkov & RM Ryan 2001; Hayamizu 1997, Vallerand 1997).

Sheldon & Elliot (1999) developed a self-concordance model of how autonomy relates to well-being. Self-concordant goals are those that fulfill basic needs and are aligned with one's true self. These goals are well-internalized and therefore autonomous, and they emanate from intrinsic or identified motivations. Goals that are not self-concordant encompass external or introjected motivation, and are either unrelated or indirectly related to need fulfillment. Sheldon & Elliot found that, although goal attainment in itself was associated with greater well-being, this effect was significantly weaker when the attained goals were not self-concordant. People who attained more self-concordant goals had more need-satisfying experiences, and this greater need satisfaction was predictive of greater SWB. Similarly, Sheldon & Kasser (1998) studied progress toward goals in a longitudinal design, finding that goal progress was associated with enhanced SWB and lower symptoms of depression. However, the impact of goal progress was again moderated by goal concordance. Goals that were poorly integrated to the self, whose focus was not related to basic psychological needs, conveyed less SWB benefits, even when achieved.

Finally, the previously mentioned Nix et al (1999) study showed that whereas successful goal pursuits led to happiness, it was only when the pursuits were autonomous that success yielded vitality. McGregor & Little (1998) suggested that the meaningfulness of goals is a separate issue from that of goal efficacy, and in a study of personal projects they found that, whereas perceived efficacy was linked to happiness, the relative integrity of goals was linked to meaningfulness.

From the perspective of SDT, psychological well-being results in large part from satisfaction of the basic psychological needs for autonomy, competence, and relatedness, so it makes sense that autonomy as well as efficacy would be important for eudaimonic well-being, just as relatedness or attachment contribute considerably to well-being (Reis et al 2000).

RESEARCH ON DIFFERENCES IN WELL-BEING ACROSS TIME AND PLACE

Lifespan Perspectives on Well-Being

The past decade has witnessed tremendous advances in lifespan psychology, and some of the most intriguing findings concern well-being. Indeed, seemingly anomalous findings in lifespan studies have generated many new understandings of the dynamics of well-being. Perhaps the most salient of these is the so-called paradox of aging. It has been found that in old age not only does subjective well-being not decline, but it typically increases, despite evidence that with age comes many challenges and losses (Carstensen 1998, Mroczek & Kolarz 1998). Thus, lifespan studies offer a window into the dynamics of SWB and eudaimonic well-being, as resources, capacities, and support systems change systematically with age.

Because Ryff defines well-being in a multidimensional way, her work especially lends itself to the descriptive study of lifespan changes in well-being. She and coworkers have investigated, first, whether people's conceptions of well-being change with age and, second, whether different components of well-being vary with age. The answer to both questions is yes. Regarding people's conceptions of well-being, Ryff (1989b) found that, although diverse age groups endorse good relationships and the pursuit of enjoyable activities as important for well-being, there were age differences on other dimensions, with younger adults focused more on self-knowledge, competence, and self-acceptance, and older adults focused more on positive coping with change. These findings accord well with those of Carstensen (1998), who suggested that the functions of relationships change with age. Younger adults are more interested in novelty, knowledge, and experience expansion, and older adults are more interested in depth and poignancy. With regard to variation in the components of well-being, Ryff (1991) compared groups of young, middle-aged, and older adults, identifying age trends on a number of dimensions. Older adults experienced less personal growth than younger groups; middle-aged adults experienced more autonomy than younger or older groups; and middle and older groups experienced more mastery than the younger group. There were no age trends for positive relations with others or for self-acceptance.

Ryan & La Guardia (2000) discussed the relations of need fulfillment to motivation and well-being across the lifespan. They reviewed evidence for the critical role of relatedness, competence, and autonomy in fostering well-being at all ages, suggesting that basic psychological needs influence well-being across life. However, the manner in which these needs are expressed and satisfied varies with age and with the life tasks, challenges, and affordances that change with age. They focused particularly on the role of age-related social contexts such as school and work in affecting well-being and on the adequacy of cultural scaffolds in supporting eudaimonia.

Work on SWB and aging also reveals that earlier theories of declines in well-being were not accurate. Diener & Lucas (2000) pointed out that pleasant affect tends to decline with age, but life satisfaction and negative affect do not change with age. They said that many measures of positive affect focus on aroused, excited states and this focus may account for the observed decline, whereas measures more focused on less activated states might not indicate a decline.

Cultural Influences: Universality versus Relativism and Well-Being

At the outset of this review we commented that the definition of well-being is controversial and unresolved. The meaning of well-being and the factors that facilitate it are particularly at issue in cross-cultural studies in which a principal quest is the search for systematic variants versus invariants in well-being dynamics across widely discrepant social arrangements. Christopher (1999) instructively argued that definitions of well-being are inherently culturally rooted and further, that there can be no such thing as a value-free assessment of well-being. According to Christopher, all understandings of well-being are essentially moral visions, based on individuals' judgments about what it means to be well.

Because the very definition of well-being raises cultural questions about the meaning and equivalence of constructs, quantitatively oriented researchers have often been bereft of answers to criticisms of cultural bias. Although such concerns should continue, at least some strategies have emerged that allow statistical assessments of the cultural equivalence of psychological constructs. Illustrative is the means and covariance structure analyses, which assess the degree to which the psychometric properties of a construct can be comparably modeled across diverse populations (Little 1997). Cross-cultural researchers in this area will need to employ such methods as a requisite for interpretive confidence in their findings. However, because of the newness of these techniques, few studies have employed them.

Diener and colleagues have reported a number of cross-cultural factors associated with SWB. Their analyses have included both mean level differences between nations on SWB and differential correlates of well-being across nations. For example, Diener & Diener (1995) found that across nations, self-esteem was associated with well-being, but that relation was stronger in countries characterized by individualism. The strength of association of SWB to satisfaction with wealth, friends, and family also varied by nation.

Suh et al (1998) studied the relations of emotions and norms (social approval) to life satisfaction in 61 nations. They found that whereas emotions were a stronger predictor of life satisfaction in nations classified as individualist, norms and emotions were equally predictive within collectivist nations. Oishi et al (1999) tested hypotheses based on Maslow's (1971) need theory and their own expectancy valence position, finding some support for each. They found that in poorer nations satisfaction with wealth was a stronger predictor of life satisfaction, whereas satisfaction with home life was more predictive in wealthier nations, suggesting to them a hierarchy of needs. They also found evidence that satisfaction with freedom was less predictive of SWB in collectivistic nations than in individualistic ones. They used this finding to dispute SDT's claims about the importance of volition to well-being, although their discussion reveals misconceptions about the meaning of autonomy and about SDT's position on needs. Still, the findings reveal that deeply held values play a role in well-being, a position with which SDT concurs.

A major conceptual issue in research on autonomy and well-being concerns the constant confusion in the literature between independence (nonreliance) and autonomy (volition). Cross-cultural psychologists such as Markus et al (1996) equate autonomy with independence in their conceptions of East-West differences and thus do not examine the separate effects of these dimensions. Diener & Lucas (2000) similarly cast autonomy as something one has "from" other people, indicating their definition of autonomy as separateness or independence rather than self-endorsement or volition. This melding of constructs persists despite research showing that, if anything, trusting interdependencies support the development of more autonomous regulation (e.g. Ryan & Lynch 1989). From an SDT perspective, cultural styles associated with independence should, of course, detract from relatedness satisfaction and well-being, but this is a separate issue from the relation to well-being of the relative autonomy of one's goals, life tasks, and values.

Indeed, evidence of the importance of autonomy is evident even in collectivist nations. Studies in Japan reveal that SDT-based assessments of autonomy predict the motivation and adjustment of students (e.g. Hayamizu 1997). Deci et al (2001) examined the relation of well-being to the satisfaction of autonomy, competence, and relatedness needs both in Bulgarian workers in state-owned, collectivistically managed companies and in a sample of US workers. They found that the measures of need satisfaction stood up to stringent cross-cultural meaning-equivalence criteria, suggesting the generalizability of these constructs; they found further that satisfaction of these needs in the workplace significantly predicted the workers' general well-being in each country, despite the highly differing cultural contexts. Even more intriguing, mean levels of autonomy at work were higher in Bulgaria, for reasons made clear by ethnographic observations. Ryan et al (1999) studied goals in Russian and US college students and found support for the model that lower well-being is predicted by overvaluing of extrinsic goals. Furthermore, Chirkov & Ryan (2001), also using means and covariance structure analyses, showed that Russian adolescents predictably viewed their parents and teachers as less autonomy supportive than did their US counterparts; however, despite its cultural normativeness, less perceived autonomy support was associated with lower well-being, including SWB, in Russia, as well as in the United States.

Sen (1999), a Nobel laureate in economics, has gone so far as to argue that freedom is a more rational goal for national development than is gross national product per se. His analysis shows that in cultures where relative freedoms have been expanded, both quality of life and economic growth are enhanced. Similarly, Frey & Stutzer (1999) showed on a large sample of Swiss citizens that, whereas economic wealth was poorly predictive of well-being, citizens who were active in their democratic participation experienced higher well-being. Thus, without denying either cultural variation in values or the importance of values in giving goals their potency, we maintain that the positions that fail to recognize the importance of autonomy for well-being may be inadvertently condoning the denial of human freedom to a significant portion of the inhabitants of the globe. Surely, this issue will receive further study.

SUMMARY

Cowen (1991) suggested that wellness should be defined not simply as the absence of psychopathology, but instead as an array of positive aspects of functioning that are promoted by attainment of strong attachment relationships, acquisition of age-appropriate cognitive, interpersonal, and coping skills, and exposure to environments that empower the person. This survey of recent work on well-being indicates clearly that study of the meaning of well-being, the conditions that engender it, and how it differs across place or time is yielding a rich and varied body of knowledge on human wellness.

Interestingly, research on well-being had tended to fall into two general groups, based on what is meant by well-being. The hedonic viewpoint focuses on subjective well-being, which is frequently equated with happiness and is formally defined as more positive affect, less negative affect, and greater life satisfaction (e.g. Diener & Lucas 1999). In contrast, the eudaimonic viewpoint focuses on psychological well-being, which is defined more broadly in terms of the fully functioning person and has been operationalized either as a set of six dimensions (Ryff 1989a), as happiness plus meaningfulness (McGregor & Little 1998), or as a set of wellness variables such as self-actualization and vitality (Ryan & Deci 2000). Interestingly, despite divisions over definitional and philosophical issues, the two research literatures, although to some degree overlapping, have tended to ask different questions and thus complement each other, providing an extensive picture of myriad person, context, and cultural factors that relate to the nature and promotion of wellness. Exciting findings have challenged old theories, raised new questions, and supplied nutriment for structured interventions to better the lives of people.

One also finds that researchers within the field of well-being are grappling with an issue that cross-cuts all social sciences, namely that concerning cultural relativism versus universals in human nature. This issue will no doubt continue to receive empirical attention, and it will likely be addressed by use of multilevel analytic strategies. That is, research will continue to uncover the relatively independent sources of variance in well-being owing to cultures and more proximal social contexts, as well as to between-person and within-person influences.

Perhaps the concern of greatest importance, not only for psychological theorists, but also for humanity, is the study of the relations between personal well-being and the broader issues of the collective wellness of humanity and the wellness of the planet. It is clear that, as individuals pursue aims they find satisfying or pleasurable, they may create conditions that make more formidable the attainment of well-being by others. An important issue, therefore, concerns the extent to which factors that foster individual well-being can be aligned or made congruent with factors that facilitate wellness at collective or global levels. Such research will, one would hope, point the way toward means through which individuals can seek hedonic or eudaimonic outcomes in ways that are sustainable in the context of the four billion others who also aspire to be fully functioning and satisfied in this earthly life.

ACKNOWLEDGMENTS

Preparation of this chapter was supported in part by grant MH-53385 from the National Institute of Mental Health.

Visit the Annual Reviews home page at www.AnnualReviews.org

LITERATURE CITED

Ainsworth MDS, Blehar MC, Waters E, Wall S. 1978. *Patterns of Attachment.* Hillsdale, NJ: Erlbaum

Argyle M. 1987. *The Psychology of Happiness.* London: Methuen

Baldwin MW, Keelan JPR, Fehr B, Enns V, Koh-Rangarajoo E. 1996. Social-cognitive conceptualization of attachment working models: availability and accessibility effect. *J. Pers. Soc. Psychol.* 71:94–109

Baumeister R, Leary MR. 1995. The need to belong: desire for interpersonal attachments as a fundamental human motivation. *Psychol. Bull.* 117:497–529

Bowlby J. 1969. *Attachment.* New York: Basic

Brunstein JC. 1993. Personal goals and subjective well-being: a longitudinal study. *J. Pers. Soc. Psychol.* 65:1061–70

Brunstein JC, Schultheiss OC, Grässman R. 1998. Personal goals and emotional well-being: the moderating role of motive dispositions. *J. Pers. Soc. Psychol.* 75:494–508

Butzel JS, Ryan RM. 1997. The dynamics of volitional reliance: a motivational perspective on dependence, independence, and social support. In *Sourcebook of Social Support and Personality,* ed. GR Pierce, B Lakey, IG Sarason, BR Sarason, pp. 49–67. New York: Plenum

Cacioppo JT, Berntson GG. 1999. The affect system: architecture and operating characteristics. *Curr. Dir. Psychol. Sci.* 8:133–37

Carstensen LL. 1998. A life-span approach to social motivation. In *Motivation and Self-Regulation Across the Life Span,* ed. J Heckhausen, CS Dweck, pp. 341–64. New York: Cambridge Univ. Press

Carver CS, Baird E. 1998. The American dream revisited: Is it what you want or why you want it that matters? *Psychol. Sci.* 9:289–92

Carver CS, Scheier MF. 1999. Themes and issues in the self-regulation of behavior. In *Perspectives on Behavioral Self-Regulation: Advances in Social Cognition,* ed. RS Wyer Jr, XII:1–105. Mahwah, NJ: Erlbaum

Chirkov V, Ryan RM. 2001. Control versus autonomy support in Russia and the U.S.: effects on well-being and academic motivation. *J. Cross-Cultural Psychol.* In press

Christopher JC. 1999. Situating psychological well-being: exploring the cultural roots of its theory and research. *J. Couns. Dev.* 77:141–52

Compton WC, Smith ML, Cornish KA, Qualls DL. 1996. Factor structure of mental health measures. *J. Pers. Soc. Psychol.* 71:406–13

Costa PT, McCrae RR. 1992. The five-factor model of personality and its relevance to personality disorders. *J. Pers. Disord.* 6:343–59

Cowen EL. 1991. In pursuit of wellness. *Am. Psychol.* 46:404–8

Csikszentmihalyi M, Csikszentmihalyi IS. 1988. *Optimal Experience: Psychological Studies of Flow in Consciousness.* New York: Cambridge Univ. Press

Deci EL. 1975. *Intrinsic Motivation.* New York: Plenum

Deci EL, Ryan RM. 1991. A motivational approach to self: integration in personality. In *Nebraska Symposium on Motivation: Perspectives on Motivation* ed. R Dienstbier, 38:237–88. Lincoln: Univ. Nebr. Press

Deci EL, Ryan RM. 2000. The "what" and "why" of goal pursuits: human needs and the self-determination of behavior. *Psychol. Inq.* 11:227–68

Deci EL, Ryan RM, Gagné M, Leone DR, Usunov J, Kornazheva BP. 2001. Need satisfaction, motivation, and well-being in the work organizations of a former Eastern Bloc country: a cross-cultural study of self-determination. *Pers. Soc. Psychol. Bull.* In press

DeNeve KM. 1999. Happy as an extraverted clam? The role of personality for subjective well-being. *Curr. Dir. Psychol. Sci.* 8:141–44

DeNeve KM, Cooper H. 1998. The happy personality: a meta-analysis of 137 personality traits and subjective well-being. *Psychol. Bull.* 124:197–229

Diener E. 1984. Subjective well-being. *Psychol. Bull.* 95:542–75

Diener E, Diener M. 1995. Cross-cultural correlates of life satisfaction and self-esteem. *J. Pers. Soc. Psychol.* 68:653–63

Diener E, Lucas RE. 1999. Personality and subjective well-being. See Kahneman et al 1999, pp. 213–29

Diener E, Lucas RE. 2000. Subjective emotional well-being. In *Handbook of Emotions*, ed. M Lewis, JM Haviland, pp. 325–37. New York: Guilford. 2nd ed.

Diener E, Sandvik E, Pavot W. 1991. Happiness is the frequency, not the intensity, of positive versus negative affect. In *Subjective Well-Being: An Interdisciplinary Perspective*, ed. F Strack, M Argyle, N Schwarz, pp. 119–39. New York: Pergamon

Diener E, Sapyta JJ, Suh E. 1998. Subjective well-being is essential to well-being. *Psychol. Inq.* 9:33–37

Elliot AJ, Sheldon KM. 1997. Avoidance achievement motivation: a personal goals analysis. *J. Pers. Soc. Psychol.* 73:171–85

Elliot AJ, Sheldon KM, Church MA. 1997. Avoidance personal goals and subjective well-being. *Pers. Soc. Psychol. Bull.* 23:915–27

Emmons RA. 1986. Personal strivings: an approach to personality and subjective well-being. *J. Pers. Soc. Psychol.* 51:1058–68

Frey BS, Stutzer A. 1999. Measuring preferences by subjective well-being. *J. Inst. Theor. Econ.* 155:755–78

Fromm E. 1981. Primary and secondary process in waking and in altered states of consciousness. *Acad. Psychol. Bull.* 3:29–45

Gable SL, Reis HT. 1999. Now and then, them and us, this and that: studying relationships across time, partner, context, and person. *Pers. Relat.* 6:415–32

Hayamizu T. 1997. Between intrinsic and extrinsic motivation: examination of reasons for academic study based on the theory of internalization. *Jpn. Psychol. Res.* 39:98–108

Hazan C, Shaver P. 1987. Romantic love conceptualized as an attachment process. *J. Pers. Soc. Psychol.* 52:511–24

Headey B, Wearing A. 1989. Personality, life events, and subjective well-being: toward a dynamic equilibrium model. *J. Pers. Soc. Psychol.* 57:731–39

Higgins ET, Kruglanski AW, eds. 1996. *Social Psychology: Handbook of Basic Principles.* New York: Guilford

Kahneman D. 1999. Objective happiness. See Kahneman et al 1999, pp. 3–25

Kahneman D, Diener E, Schwarz N, eds. 1999. *Well-Being: The Foundations of Hedonic Psychology.* New York: Russell Sage Found.

Kasser T, Ryan RM. 1993. A dark side of the American dream: correlates of financial success as a central life aspiration. *J. Pers. Soc. Psychol.* 65:410–22

Kasser T, Ryan RM. 1996. Further examining the American dream: differential correlates of intrinsic and extrinsic goals. *Pers. Soc. Psychol. Bull.* 22:280–87

Kasser VM, Ryan RM. 1999. The relation of psychological needs for autonomy and relatedness to health, vitality, well-being and mortality in a nursing home. *J. Appl. Soc. Psychol.* 29:935–54

King LA, Napa CK. 1998. What makes life good? *J. Pers. Soc. Psychol.* 75:156–65

King LA, Pennebaker JW. 1998. What's so great about feeling good? *Psychol. Inq.* 9:53–56

Kubovy M. 1999. On the pleasures of the mind. See Kahneman et al 1999, pp. 134–54

La Guardia JG, Ryan RM, Couchman C, Deci EL. 2000. Within-person variation in security of attachment: a self-determination theory perspective on attachment, need fulfillment, and well-being. *J. Pers. Soc. Psychol.* 79:367–84

Larsen RJ, Diener E. 1987. Affect intensity as an individual difference characteristic: a review. *J. Res. Pers.* 21:1–39

Lee GR, Ishii-Kuntz M. 1987. Social interaction, loneliness, and emotional well-being among the elderly. *Res. Aging* 9:459–82

Little BR. 1989. Personal projects analysis: trivial pursuits and magnificent obsessions, and the search for coherence. In *Personality Psychology: Recent Trends and Emerging Directions*, ed. D Buss, N Cantor, pp. 15–31. New York: Springer-Verlag

Little TD. 1997. Mean and covariance structures (MACS) analyses of cross-cultural data: practical and theoretical issues. *Multiv. Behav. Res.* 32:53–76

Lyubomirsky S, Ross L. 1999. Changes in attractiveness of elected, rejected, and precluded alternatives: a comparison of happy and unhappy individuals. *J. Pers. Soc. Psychol.* 76:988–1007

Lyubomirsky S, Tucker KL. 1998. Implications of individual differences in subjective happiness for perceiving, interpreting, and thinking about life events. *Motiv. Emot.* 22:155–86

Markus HR, Kitayama S, Heiman RJ. 1996. Culture and basic psychological principles. See Higgins & Kruglanski 1996, pp. 857–913

Maslow AH. 1971. *The Farther Reaches of Human Nature.* New York: Viking

McGregor I, Little BR. 1998. Personal projects, happiness, and meaning: on doing well and being yourself. *J. Pers. Soc. Psychol.* 74:494–512

Mikulincer M, Florian V. 1998. The relationship between adult attachment styles and emotional and cognitive reactions to stressful events. In *Attachment Theory and Close Relationships*, ed. JA Simpson, WS Rholes, pp. 143–65. New York: Guilford

Mroczek DK, Kolarz CM. 1998. The effect of age on positive and negative affect: a developmental perspective on happiness. *J. Pers. Soc. Psychol.* 75:1333–49

Myers DG. 1999. Close relationships and quality of life. See Kahneman et al 1999, pp. 374–91

Nezlek JB. 2000. The motivational and cognitive dynamics of day-to-day social life. In *The Social Mind: Cognitive and Motivational Aspects of Interpersonal Behaviour*, ed. JP Forgas, K Williams, L Wheeler, pp. 92–111. New York: Cambridge Univ. Press

Nix G, Ryan RM, Manly JB, Deci EL. 1999. Revitalization through self-regulation: the effects of autonomous versus controlled motivation on happiness and vitality. *J. Exp. Soc. Psychol.* 35:266–84

Oishi S, Diener E, Lucas RE, Suh E. 1999. Cross-cultural variations in predictors of life satisfaction: perspectives from needs and values. *Pers. Soc. Psychol. Bull.* 25:980–90

Okun MA, Stock WA, Haring MJ, Witter RA. 1984. The social activity/subjective well-being relation: a quantitative synthesis. *Res. Aging* 6:45–65

Parrott WG. 1993. Beyond hedonism: motives for inhibiting good moods and for maintaining bad moods. In *Handbook of Mental Control*, ed. DM Wegner, JW Pennebaker, pp. 278–305. Englewood Cliffs, NJ: Prentice-Hall

Peterson C. 1999. Personal control and well-being. See Kahneman et al 1999, pp. 288–301

Reis HT, Patrick BC. 1996. Attachment and intimacy: component process. See Higgins & Kruglanski 1996, pp. 523–63

Reis HT, Sheldon KM, Gable SL, Roscoe J, Ryan RM. 2000. Daily well-being: the role of autonomy, competence, and relatedness. *Pers. Soc. Psychol. Bull.* 26:419–35

Roberts BW, Donahue EM. 1994. One personality, multiple selves: integrating personality and social roles. *J. Pers.* 62:199–218

Rogers C. 1963. The actualizing tendency in relation to "motives" and to consciousness. In *Nebraska Symposium on Motivation*, ed. MR

Jones, 11:1–24. Lincoln: Univ. Nebr. Press

Ryan RM, Chirkov VI, Little TD, Sheldon KM, Timoshina E, Deci EL. 1999. The American dream in Russia: extrinsic aspirations in two cultures. *Pers. Soc. Psychol. Bull.* 25:1509–24

Ryan RM, Deci EL. 2000. Self-determination theory and the facilitation of intrinsic motivation, social development, and well-being. *Am. Psychol.* 55:68–78

Ryan RM, Frederick CM. 1997. On energy, personality and health: subjective vitality as a dynamic reflection of well-being. *J. Pers.* 65:529–65

Ryan RM, La Guardia JG. 2000. What is being optimized over development? A self-determination theory perspective on basic psychological needs across the life span. In *Psychology and the Aging Revolution*, ed. SH Qualls, N Abeles, pp. 145–72. Washington, DC: APA Books. In press

Ryan RM, Lynch J. 1989. Emotional autonomy versus detachment: revisiting the vicissitudes of adolescence and young adulthood. *Child Dev.* 60:340–56

Ryff CD. 1989a. Happiness is everything, or is it? Explorations on the meaning of psychological well-being. *J. Pers. Soc. Psychol.* 57:1069–81

Ryff CD. 1989b. In the eye of the beholder: views of psychological well-being among middle-aged and older adults. *Psychol. Aging* 4:195–210

Ryff CD. 1991. Possible selves in adulthood and old age: a tale of shifting horizons. *Psychol. Aging* 6:286–95

Ryff CD. 1995. Psychological well-being in adult life. *Curr. Dir. Psychol. Sci.* 4:99–104

Ryff CD, Keyes CLM. 1995. The structure of psychological well-being revisited. *J. Pers. Soc. Psychol.* 69:719–27

Ryff CD, Magee WJ, Kling KC, Wing EH. 1999. Forging macro-micro linkages in the study of psychological well-being. In *The Self and Society in Aging Processes*, ed. CD Ryff, VW Marshall, pp. 247–78. New York: Springer

Ryff CD, Singer B. 1998. The contours of positive human health. *Psychol. Inq.* 9:1–28

Ryff CD, Singer B. 2000. Interpersonal flourishing: a positive health agenda for the new millennium. *Pers. Soc. Psychol. Rev.* 4:30–44

Ryff CD, Singer BH, Wing E, Love GD. 2001. Elective affinities and uninvited agonies: mapping emotion with significant others onto health. In *Emotion, Social Relationships, and Health: Third Annual Wisconsin Symposium on Emotion*, ed. CD Ryff, BH Singer. New York: Oxford Univ. Press. In press

Schmuck P, Kasser T, Ryan RM. 2000. The relationship of well-being to intrinsic and extrinsic goals in Germany and the U.S. *Soc. Indic. Res.* 50:225–41

Schmutte PS, Ryff CD. 1997. Personality and well-being: reexamining methods and meanings. *J. Pers. Soc. Psychol.* 73:549–59

Schwarz N, Strack F. 1991. Evaluating one's life: a judgment model of subjective well-being. In *Subjective Well-Being: An Interdisciplinary Perspective*, ed. F Strack, M Argyle, pp. 27–47. Oxford, UK: Pergamon

Seidlitz L. 1993. *Agreeableness, conscientiousness, and openness as related to subjective well-being*. Presented at 6th Meet. Int. Soc. Study Individ. Differ., Baltimore, MD

Seligman M, Csikszentmihalyi M. 2000. Positive psychology: an introduction. *Am. Psychol.* 55:5–14

Sen A. 1999. *Development as Freedom*. New York: Knopf

Sheldon KM, Elliot AJ. 1999. Goal striving, need satisfaction, and longitudinal well-being: the self-concordance model. *J. Pers. Soc. Psychol.* 76:482–97

Sheldon KM, Kasser T. 1995. Coherence and congruence: two aspects of personality integration. *J. Pers. Soc. Psychol.* 68:531–43

Sheldon KM, Kasser T. 1998. Pursuing personal goals: Skills enable progress, but not all progress is beneficial. *Pers. Soc. Psychol. Bull.* 24:1319–31

Sheldon KM, Ryan RM, Rawsthorne LJ, Ilardi B. 1997. "Trait" self and "true" self:

cross-role variation in the big five personality traits and its relations with psychological authenticity and subjective well-being. *J. Pers. Soc. Psychol.* 73:1380–93

Sheldon KM, Ryan RM, Reis HT. 1996. What makes for a good day? Competence and autonomy in the day and in the person. *Pers. Soc. Psychol. Bull.* 22:1270–79

Shizgal P. 1999. On the neural computation of utility: See Kahneman et al 1999, pp. 500–24

Simpson JA. 1990. Influence of attachment styles on romantic relationships. *J. Pers. Soc. Psychol.* 59:971–80

Suh E, Diener E, Fujita F. 1996. Events and subjective well-being: Only recent events matter. *J. Pers. Soc. Psychol.* 70:1091–102

Suh E, Diener E, Oishi S, Triandis HC. 1998. The shifting basis of life satisfaction judgements across cultures: emotions versus norms. *J. Pers. Soc. Psychol.* 74:482–93

Tooby J, Cosmides L. 1992. The psychological foundations of culture. In *The Adapted Mind: Evolutionary Psychology and the Generation of Culture*, ed. JH Barkow, L Cosmides, J Tooby, pp. 19–136. New York: Oxford Univ. Press

Uchino BN, Uno D, Holt-Lunstad J. 1999. Social support, physiological processes, and health. *Curr. Dir. Psychol. Sci.* 8:145–48

Vallerand RJ. 1997. Toward a hierarchical model of intrinsic and extrinsic motivation. In *Advances in Experimental Social Psychology*, ed. MP Zanna, 29:271–360. San Diego, CA: Academic

Waterman AS. 1993. Two conceptions of happiness: contrasts of personal expressiveness (eudaimonia) and hedonic enjoyment. *J. Pers. Soc. Psychol.* 64:678–91

Annu. Rev. Psychol. 2001. 52:167–96

SENTENCE AND TEXT COMPREHENSION: Roles of Linguistic Structure

Charles Clifton, Jr. and Susan A. Duffy

Department of Psychology, University of Massachusetts, Amherst, Massachusetts 01003;
e-mail: cec@psych.umass.edu, duffy@psych.umass.edu

Key Words psycholinguistics, parsing, grammar, anaphora, discourse

■ **Abstract** Readers and listeners use linguistic structure in comprehending sentences and texts. We review research, mostly published in the past five years, that addresses the question of how they use it. We consider effects of syntactic, lexical, prosodic, morphological, semantic, and discourse structure, as well as reviewing research on how discourse context and frequency of experience, the contents of long-term memory, and the mental models being constructed by a reader or listener affect sentence and text comprehension. We point out areas of theoretical debate including depth-first versus breadth-first models of parsing and memory-based versus constructionist models of discourse comprehension, attempt to show how the empirical effects we review bear on such theoretical questions, and discuss how new lines of research, including research on languages other than English, may enrich the discussion of these questions.

CONTENTS

0066-4308/01/0201-0167$14.00

BACKGROUND: The Rises and Falls of Structural Analysis

Since the beginning of the cognitive revolution, psycholinguists have recognized that knowledge of linguistic structure allows us to construct and comprehend sentences (Miller 1962). However, they have continually argued about what role this knowledge might play in language comprehension.

The first modern psycholinguists reveled in their discovery of grammar and strove to demonstrate that linguistic structure does play a role in understanding sentences and texts (Fodor et al 1974). Although they were successful in demonstrating the relevance of linguistic structure, they were not successful in formulating coherent theories of how a processing mechanism could use the grammar to parse a sentence or to interpret it semantically. Interest shifted from asking how linguistic structure is used to asking how a reader or listener could make use of the myriad cues that language provided, resulting in the "detective theory" of sentence comprehension (Fodor et al 1974), which views language comprehension as a largely unconstrained exercise in problem solving.

In the mid-1970s, the pendulum swung back toward an emphasis on how linguistic structure is used in comprehension. The impetus was a series of theoretical proposals from linguists and computer scientists (Frazier 1979, Frazier & Fodor 1978, Kimball 1973, Marcus 1980) describing how the algorithmic use of phrase structure rules and other grammatical devices could account for a range of sentence comprehension phenomena. A similar interest in how a limited range of information constrains and guides comprehension process grew in the field of discourse processing, fueled by the development of story grammars (Mandler & Johnson 1977, Rumelhart 1975) and analyses of how readers use anaphoric reference and related reference principles to connect sentences in discourse (Haviland & Clark 1974, Kintsch & van Dijk 1978, McKoon & Ratcliff 1980).

The pendulum has since swung back. Beginning in the mid-1980s, sentence processing researchers provided myriad demonstrations that factors other than the structural geometry of sentences could influence how they are comprehended. Interactive connectionist theories of sentence comprehension became dominant, describing how a uniform processing system resolves constraints arising from frequency of use, lexical structure, plausibility, context, and the like (MacDonald et al 1994, Tanenhaus & Trueswell 1995). The current models can be seen as more explicit and principled versions of the old detective models of the 1970s. In the realm of discourse comprehension, models have also tended to lose their focus on purely linguistic structure. Some models emphasize how comprehension processes can be driven by linguistically unsophisticated processes of memory retrieval (McKoon & Ratcliff 1992, Myers & O'Brien 1998). Others focus on the end-product of the comprehension process, postulating "situation models" that incorporate nonlinguistic as well as linguistic information (Graesser et al 1994, Zwaan 1996).

Much has been gained from these repeated shifts in fashion. We now know a great deal about what factors influence sentence and discourse comprehension. We also know that any adequate theory of sentence comprehension must address how linguistic knowledge is used to create syntactic structure and that any adequate theory of discourse comprehension must address the interplay between structural constraints and memory processes. Current theories face the challenge of having to explain how syntactic structures are created, how a reader or listener selects and interprets a single structure, and how these interpreted structures are integrated into mental models of discourse. No current theory is fully adequate. For instance, the most explicit versions of current connectionist models of parsing (McRae et al 1998, Tanenhaus et al 2000) do not address the question of where structural alternatives come from; they are simply models of choice between existing alternatives. Similarly, structurally based models are schematic at best in how they characterize interaction among different information types (see the following discussion of reanalysis processes for some relevant theoretical suggestions). In the hope of stimulating the development of more adequate theories, we concentrate on reviewing recent empirical evidence about how linguistic structure influences the comprehension of sentences and discourses, including how linguistic structure interacts with nonlinguistic knowledge. We conclude with a section that reviews current models of the use of knowledge in discourse comprehension.

SYNTACTIC STRUCTURE

Much recent research on sentence comprehension was provoked by a simple claim that a reader or listener initially constructs a single representation of a sentence based solely on grammatical principles, semantically interpreting this representation in a nearly word-by-word fashion and revising as needed (Frazier 1979, Frazier & Rayner 1982). This serial, depth-first, "garden-path" theory claimed specifically that a reader or listener parses a sentence by attaching each new word into a single syntactic structure in the quickest possible way, guided by knowledge of the phrase structure rules of the language (which are essentially templates for possible local structural configurations of words) (Frazier 1989). This "first analysis" process results in the construction of the simplest syntactic structure, measured in terms of the number of syntactic nodes (or phrase structure rule applications) needed to attach each new word into the structure (see Frazier 1987 for description of this "minimal attachment" principle). In case two or more structural analyses are equally simple, the one that attaches the new word into the more recently processed phrase will generally be preferred because this phrase will be the most active and will thus be available for attachment most quickly.

Garden-path theory makes predictions about the relative difficulty of comprehending a wide range of structurally different sentences. A sentence that requires revision of the initial, structurally simplest analysis will generally take longer to comprehend than a sentence that does not require such revision. Many experiments have supported these predictions, showing longer reading times, longer eye fixations, and more regressive eye movements in the forms that are predicted to be difficult (see Frazier & Clifton 1996 for a review).

Several principles of garden-path theory have come under sharp attack in recent years. Some lines of criticism retain the garden-path theory's emphasis on grammatical structure but propose different decision principles. To take one example, consider the widely recognized preference to link a new phrase in parsing to the most recently processed phrase. Phillips & Gibson (1997) argued that such a recency preference is the most dominant preference in parsing. They presented evidence that sentences like 1a below are (under some experimental conditions) read more quickly than sentences like 1b. Apart from recency, all the parsing principles Phillips & Gibson consider (including structural simplicity) favor attaching the temporarily ambiguous phrase beginning "I made" as the start of the main clause of (1a) and (1b). Only recency favors attaching it as a relative clause modifying "the recipe," but this seems to be the favored analysis.

1. a. Because Rose praised the recipe I made for her birthday it was worth all the effort.
    b. Because Rose praised the recipe I made it for her birthday as a surprise.

Gibson et al (1996a) provided additional arguments for the importance of recency (cf also Stevenson 1994). They used an incremental grammaticality judgment task to show that both Spanish and English readers faced with complex noun phrases (NPs) containing a sequence like the "lamps near the paintings of the house" followed by a relative clause, prefer to have the relative clause modify the most recent NP, with progressively lesser preference for modification of the first and then the middle NP. Gibson et al claimed these data reflect competing preferences for recent attachment and for modification of a phrase that is structurally near the head of a predicate phrase (the presumed verb in a sentence containing the complex NP).

Other criticisms of garden-path theory de-emphasize its use of grammatical knowledge in creating a single structure to be interpreted, claiming instead that multiple analyses compete on the basis of a wide range of grammatical and extragrammatical information. Some influential versions of these criticisms will be considered in the next section (MacDonald et al 1994, Tanenhaus & Trueswell 1995). These attacks have not forced garden-path theorists to discard their models. Rayner et al (1983) sketched one response, that factors other than structural simplicity affect a process of reanalyzing the initially created structure, not building the initial structural analysis itself. The only legitimate way to defend such a response is to develop a serious account of reanalysis. Such development is an active focus of current research (Fodor & Ferreira 1998; cf Sturt et al 2000 for discussion of the relevance of reanalysis to models other than serial models).

Much research on reanalysis has been influenced by Fodor & Inoue's (1994) proposal that reanalysis consists in revising or repairing an already-constructed analysis rather than starting over again. Fodor & Inoue (2000) generalized the principle underlying garden-path theory to apply to reanalysis as well, terming the principle minimal everything. All choices of either initial analysis or reanalysis are made following a very general least effort principle, in which a preference for recency or local attachment weighs heavily. However, other factors may operate as well in reanalysis. For instance, Bader (1998) presented evidence from German suggesting that requiring a revision in the prosody presumably assigned to a sentence during silent reading slows reanalysis. In another approach, Sturt & Crocker (1998) developed a description theory parser in which initial structural analyses are underspecified (e.g. a new phrase is analyzed as being dominated by some existing node, rather than being immediately dominated by that node; thus, new intervening nodes can be added without revising the initial structure). In reanalysis, the parser preferentially only makes changes that require additions to the initial structure, not deletions or other changes.

Case Structure

Until quite recently, most research on syntactic structure in parsing has focused on the role of word order in English. Syntactic structure is more than word order. Current syntactic theories place substantial emphasis on morphosyntactic features, including case, number, gender, tense, and aspect. Some psycholinguistic researchers have begun to study the processing of such features (see Cairns & Teller 2000). Consider case, which is explicitly marked in many languages. The case of a noun (traditionally nominative, accusative, dative, etc) is related to its role in sentence structure (subject, object of verb, etc) and to the role it plays in the argument structure of a verb. One can ask what role case and explicit casemarking may play in parsing.

English exhibits a case system in its pronouns (where "he, she" is nominative, "her" accusative or genitive or dative, etc). Traxler & Pickering (1996) showed that this casemarking is used in parsing English. In an eyetracking study of sentences like 2, they found longer reading times on the case-disambiguated "she" than on the case-ambiguous "you," suggesting that the nominative casemarking on she forced the readers to avoid or quickly give up the normally preferred direct object interpretation of the NP after the initial verb. The following verb phrase ("would leave") was read faster following a casemarked than a noncasemarked pronoun, also suggesting that the casemarked pronoun blocked the normal garden path.

2.   a. I knew you and your mother would leave the party early.

b. I knew she and her mother would leave the party early.

The contributions that casemarking makes to parsing have been studied most intensively in German (cf Kim 1999 for research on Korean case and Yamashita 1997 for Japanese). German determiners are marked for nominative, accusative, dative, and genitive case, but only some are unambiguously marked. Further, German permits "scrambling." The order of German NPs within a clause is quite flexible. Whereas the canonical German sentence has subject before object, other orders are possible, depending in part on pragmatic factors such as focus (Hemforth & Konieczny 2000b).

These facts, together with the fact that German clauses are generally verb-final, permit researchers to examine whether case is assigned even before a case-assigning verb. Numerous authors (see Hemforth & Konieczny 2000a) have observed a preference for subject-before-object word order (nominative before accusative case). Bader & Meng (1999) demonstrated such a preference in several different constructions, including the scrambling constructions of Sentence 3, in which the article "*die*" in the embedded clause is ambiguous between nominative and accusative. This casemarking ambiguity was resolved by the number of the final auxiliary verb. Speeded grammaticality judgments were more accurate when the sentence was singular, indicating that the NP "*die neue Lehrerin*" had initially been assigned nominative case (cf Friederici & Mecklinger 1996 for a similar conclusion based on measuring electrical potentials in the brain):

3.   a. *Die Direktorin hat ersählt, dass die neue Lehrerin einige der Kollegen angerufen hat.* The director has said, that the new teacher some the colleagues phoned has. (The director said that the new teacher phoned some of the colleagues.)

      b. *Die Direktorin hat ersählt, dass die neue Lehrerin einige der Kollegen angerufen haben.* The director has said, that the new teacher some the colleagues phoned have. (The director said that some of the colleagues phoned the new teacher.)

Various accounts of the subject-before-object preference exist, including appeals to simplicity (Gorrell 2000), memory load (Schlesewsky et al 2000), and thematic role ordering preferences (Scheepers et al 2000; note that these authors conclude that thematic ordering preference only plays a secondary role). Bader et al (2000) also examined the dative case, a lexical case needing a specific lexical licenser (as opposed to nominative and accusative, generally considered structural cases). They argued that structural case is preferred over lexical case in resolving an ambiguity, and claimed that a substantial amount of syntactic structure is built before reaching the lexical head of a sentence (see the discussion of lexical projection of structure, above).

Memory Limitation and Frequency Effects

Phrase structure, word order, and casemarking do not exhaust the possible factors that might influence parsing. One factor that has long been recognized is memory limitation. The difficulty of multiply self-embedded sentences such as, "The patient who the nurse who the clinic had hired admitted met Jack" has generally been attributed to their exceeding some memory capacity (e.g. Lewis 1996, 2000; Miller

& Isard 1964). Gibson (1998) developed a version of this claim that accounts for a range of sentence complexity effects in a variety of languages, including English, Spanish, Dutch, and Japanese. The basic claim of his syntactic prediction locality theory is that there is a processing cost to predicting, holding, and integrating obligatory syntactic requirements (e.g. a subject-predicate relation) when new discourse entities are introduced, and that the maximum local cost affects comprehension difficulty and choice among ambiguous alternatives.

A final factor in some structural theories is the frequency with which structures are encountered. The most thorough exploration of frequency appears in Jurafsky 1996. Jurafsky assumed a construction grammar framework, one in which syntactic structures and lexical items are all listed (and mentally represented) in the same way, as grammatical constructions. He described a parallel-parsing algorithm that determines both access and choice of constructions in a Bayesian fashion, computing the conditional probability of each construction, given the evidence. The model eliminates relatively unlikely candidates from further consideration (accounting for garden-path effects when the unlikely candidate is required) and is biased toward favoring the more frequent candidates. Jurafsky demonstrated that his model can account for a wide variety of parsing phenomena. Although he did not provide any new evidence specifically testing predictions of his model, research on lexical category ambiguity reported by Corley & Crocker (2000, Crocker & Corley 2000) support an approach whose statistical basis is close to Jurafsky's.

However, just to illustrate the fluidity of theory development in the field of parsing, we will close this section by noting that Crocker is coauthor of a theory that explicitly denies both frequency and structural simplicity as bases of parsing decisions. Instead, Pickering et al (2000; cf also Chater et al 1998) suggested that the preferred alternative is the most informative alternative, the choice that is most easily and quickly falsified. This turns out often (possibly always) to be the structurally simplest one, not the most frequent or probable one.

LEXICAL STRUCTURE

Argument Structure, Frequency, and Plausibility Effects

The linguistic theory that guided the parsing models of the 1970s emphasized structural regularities that could be expressed by rules (e.g. phrase structure rules). Since that time, linguistic theory has moved toward formulating very general principles governing possible sentence structures and encoding much of the detailed information about sentence structure with individual lexical items. This "lexicalist" movement stimulated a new round of psycholinguistic theories emphasizing contributions individual lexical items make to parsing (e.g. MacDonald et al 1994, Tanenhaus & Trueswell 1995; cf Ford et al 1982 for an important precursor, cf MacDonald 1997 for a brief survey).

Tanenhaus and his students and colleagues (e.g. Carlson & Tanenhaus 1988; Tanenhaus et al 1990, 1993) have studied how different types of lexical information combine to guide how a sentence is understood. Their early focus was on the use of thematic roles (the semantic roles that can be played by the complements or arguments of verbs and other words) (Tanenhaus et al 1989). For instance, Boland et al (1995) used a "stops making sense" judgment task to show processing difficulty at the word "them" in sentences like 4a compared with 4b:

4.   a. Which child did Mark remind them to watch ....
      b. Which movie did Mark remind them to watch ....

The "filler," "which child," is presumably assigned a thematic role like "recipient" of "remind" in 4a, in which case the pronoun "them" must trigger revision. However, no such revision is needed in the case of "which movie," which is an inappropriate recipient; further, no disruption was observed at "remind" in this case because the verb contains other possible complements that could provide a thematic role for "which movie."

Although the task used by Boland et al (1995) could be criticized for slowing reading and possibly permitting unusual judgment processes to operate, the same is not true for Trueswell et al (1994). These authors used eyetracking measures to demonstrate substantial disruption in the disambiguating region of temporarily ambiguous reduced relative clause sentences like 5a compared with unambiguous controls, and the essential absence of disruption in sentences like 5b:

5.   a. The defendant examined by the lawyer turned out to be unreliable.
      b. The evidence examined by the lawyer turned out to be unreliable.

Trueswell et al (1994) proposed that the appropriateness of the initial NP as theme versus agent guided initial parsing. Their proposal conflicted with results presented by Ferreira & Clifton (1986), but they argued that not all of the Ferreira & Clifton materials had strong enough thematic biases.

Another line of evidence is found in Spivey-Knowlton & Sedivy (1995), who measured the phrase-by-phrase self-paced reading time of sentences like (6):

6.   a. The salesman glanced at a/the customer with suspicion and then walked away.
      b. The salesman glanced at a/the customer with ripped jeans and then walked away.

These sentences have a temporary ambiguity in terms of where the prepositional phrase (PP) "with suspicion"/"ripped jeans" will attach. The minimal attachment principle of garden-path theory claims that the preferred attachment is to the verb "glance *at*" and thus predicts that Sentence 6b will show slower reading time at or after the noun phrase NP that ends the PP than Sentence 6a. Spivey-Knowlton & Sedivy obtained this result when the main verb of the sentence was an action verb such as smash down. However, when the main verb was a "psych" or perception verb such as glance at or hope for, and when the NP direct object of this verb is indefinite (with "a" rather than "the"), precisely the opposite result held: Reading time was slowed during the PP in Sentence 6a compared to Sentence 6b.

One result of the investigations made by the Tanenhaus group is the formulation of the most explicit and precise models to date of how lexical (and contextual) information guides the choice between alternative syntactic analyses (McRae et al 1998, Spivey & Tanenhaus 1998, Tanenhaus et al 2000). The McRae et al and Spivey & Tanenhaus models are simple networks for choosing between pairs of analyses (e.g. relative clause versus main clause, as in Sentence 5) that permit a theorist to unambiguously compute the consequences of the assumptions he or she chooses to make. They do a good job of fitting reading time measures of sentences that are resolved in favor of the normally unpreferred analysis (e.g. the reduced relative clause analysis. However, some evidence suggests that they may not adequately fit reading time of sentences that are resolved in favor of the normally preferred (main clause) analysis (Binder et al 2000; cf Frazier 1995, Clifton 2000).

In addition to claiming that the argument structures of verbs and other words guide parsing, many interactive lexicalist theories claim that the relative frequency of these structures also affect parsing. The underlying connectionist metaphor holds that a given lexical item passes more activation to its more frequently used structures, and that frequent structures should therefore be preferred and more easily processed. Numerous demonstrations of the importance of frequency exist. Some assess frequency of usage directly, through corpus counts; others assess frequency of usage indirectly, through empirical production norms. Merlo (1994) discusses the relative merits of these procedures. MacDonald (1994) demonstrated easier comprehension of temporarily ambiguous, reduced relative clause sentences such as 7 when the ambiguous verb was more frequently used (in production norms) as a transitive verb ("pushed" in Sentence 7a) than when its more frequent use was as an intransitive ("moved" in Sentence 7b).

7. a. The rancher could see that the nervous cattle pushed into the crowded pen were afraid of the cowboys.
    b. The rancher could see that the nervous cattle moved into the crowded pen were afraid of the cowboys.

Trueswell (1996) also showed that the ease of understanding sentences like these is affected by the relative frequency with which the verb is used as a passive participle versus a simple past tense.

Examining a different structure, illustrated in Sentence 8, Trueswell et al (1993) compared verbs whose most frequent usage (in production norms) was with a direct object complement (e.g. "confirm") versus with a sentence complement (e.g. "insist").

8. a. The waiter confirmed (that) the reservation was made yesterday.
    b. The waiter insisted (that) the reservation was made yesterday.

Contrary to Ferreira & Henderson (1990), whose experiment they were following up, Trueswell et al found faster reading for sentences like 8b, where the more frequent usage matched the actual use in the sentence, than for sentences like 8a, where it did not.

MacDonald et al (1994) provide a variety of reasons why frequency should play a major role in parsing. Others have provided arguments against its centrality. One argument is that the effect of frequency is not always obtained. Kennison (2000) failed to observe any sign of a frequency effect in an experiment similar to that of Trueswell et al 1993, using materials that were very tightly controlled for plausibility. A second argument is that preferences for some constructions flatly go against frequency considerations, as shown by Gibson et al (1996b) and Gibson & Schütze (1999) for conjoined NPs. A third argument against a pure frequency account is that no existing frequency account has given a motivated reason for the level at which frequency is counted (cf Mitchell et al 1995). Gibson et al (1996b) examined a range of "grain sizes" for the NP conjunction construction they studied and demonstrated that none showed that frequency determined parsing preferences.

Finally, some research exists that strongly suggests readers initially analyze ambiguous phrases in a manner that ignores frequency of usage, even though frequency may play a role in recovering from the initial misanalysis. Pickering & Traxler (1998) used eyetracking measures to demonstrate disruption essentially immediately upon reading "magazine" in sentences like "As the woman sailed the magazine about fishing amused all the reporters." They suggested that this means that "the magazine" is initially analyzed as the direct object of "sailed" and that its implausibility as a direct object slows reading. Pickering et al (2000) observed the same effect in sentences with verbs like "hinted" that are much more frequently used with sentence complements than with direct objects. They argued that this showed that the direct object analysis was constructed in spite of its low frequency (cf Garnsey et al 1997).

If sheer frequency, however measured, is incomplete as the basis of a full theory of parsing, results like those of MacDonald (1994) and Trueswell (1996) still suggest that it plays some role. Furthermore, any shortcomings of a simple frequency account do not invalidate the more general lexicalist position. Some researchers have advocated a position in which the existence but not the frequency of lexical structures guides parsing. Ferreira & McClure (1997) show that the disruption of reading normally observed when a postverbal NP turns out to be the subject of a complement sentence is essentially eliminated when the verb is a reciprocal verb such as "kissed" and the matrix subject is plural, as in Sentence 9a (compared with nonreciprocal verbs such as in Sentence 9b and other controls):

9.   a. After Jose and the bride kissed the party began in earnest.
       b. After Jose and the bride signaled the party began in earnest.

Ferreira & McClure argue that a reader avoids taking "the party" as object of "kissed" not because kiss is infrequently used as a transitive verb (it is not), but because its plural subject has already saturated its argument structure.

Is Sentence Structure Projected from Lexical Heads?

Some parsing theories that emphasize lexical guidance propose that all sentence structure is projected from the lexical heads of phrases (e.g. MacDonald et al 1994, Pritchett 1992). This claim is not a necessary part of a lexicalist model, so long as the grammatical principles in the model go beyond projection from lexical heads (see Crocker 1995 for a model that permits projection from functional as well as lexical heads). Furthermore, the claim must be wrong. It would make readers and listeners of all the languages in the world where a head comes at the very end of a phrase (about half of existing languages) have to wait until the end of a sentence before beginning to understand it (see Bader & Lasser 1994, and Frazier 1995 for further discussion).

Experimental evidence exists that points the way toward a lexicalist model that is not limited to creating structure by head projection. Konieczny et al (1997) presented eyetracking data for German sentences that they argue support a "parameterized head attachment principle." They showed that whereas PPs are preferentially taken to modify a verb as opposed to a noun in sentences with subject-verb-object-PP order, they preferentially modify the noun in verb-final constructions (subject-object-PP-verb). They argued that this finding contradicts the predictions of minimal attachment and supports a principle according to which a new constituent is attached to a phrase whose head (preferably a verbal head) has already been encountered, if possible. However, the (serial, depth-first) architecture of the model Konieczny et al (1997) proposed permits parsing to proceed without waiting for a head; it simply favors attachment to a head if one exists.

The Konieczny et al experiment is an instance of a refreshing new wave of sentence comprehension research done on languages other than English. This research exploits properties of these languages to test theories and to explore possible new information sources that can influence parsing. German is a language in which verbs must generally appear in the final position of a clause (except in root clauses with simple tense), allowing a researcher to ask what structure is created before the head of the sentence (the verb) is read or heard. Hemforth & Konieczny (2000a) provide a collection of investigations of German sentence processing, including (but not limited to) experimental studies of head-final constructions. Additional evidence from strongly head-final languages, including Korean and Japanese (plus other East Asian languages), appears in Mazuka & Nagai (1995) and in Chen & Zhou (1999). Much of this research (e.g. Kamide & Mitchell 1999, Koh 1997) strongly suggests that readers analyze NPs as arguments of a sentence well before they read the verb that ends the sentence.

PROSODIC STRUCTURE

The reader will have noted that most research discussed to this point examined reading, not listening. This reflects a characteristic of the field that is regrettable, given that any specialized language faculties people may have surely were shaped by the need to comprehend spoken language, and given that the prosody (the rhythm and melody) of spoken language carries information that could potentially guide parsing (Cutler & Clifton 2000).

Fortunately, the situation is changing, and more and more research is being conducted on auditory sentence comprehension (see Warren 1996, Nicol 1996). Current research has gone beyond demonstrating that prosody can disambiguate ambiguous sentences (Lehiste 1973) and examines the roles that prosody plays in parsing. Linguistic analyses of prosody and the prosody-syntax interface (e.g. Selkirk 1984, 1995) indicate that prosody has a structure of its own, constrained, but not determined by, syntactic structure. Psycholinguistic research asks how this prosodic structure is identified (cf Beckman 1996) and how it constrains the parsing and interpretation of sentences.

In contrast to earlier research, most of which focused on what types of ambiguities can be resolved prosodically (e.g. Nespor & Vogel 1986), Kjelgaard & Speer (1999) asked whether appropriate prosody can overcome the effects of structural or lexical biases and block garden paths (see Marslen-Wilson et al 1992, for a precursor). Kjelgaard & Speer examined temporary late-closure ambiguities like those in Sentence 10:

10.   a. When Madonna sings the song is a hit.
        b. When Madonna sings the song it's a hit.

In the written language, the phrase "the song" is taken as the direct object of "sings," leading to disruption in reading the end of Sentence 10a. Kjelgaard & Speer recorded sentences like these in two disambiguating prosodies (one with the boundary of an intonational phrase after the verb "sings," appropriate for early closure, and one with the boundary of an intonational phrase after the NP "the song," appropriate for late closure). They showed that an appropriate prosody eliminated comprehension difficulty and that an inappropriate (cross-spliced) prosody increased it, relative to a baseline condition with prosody appropriate to either interpretation. The results indicated that prosody can eliminate structural garden-pathing, leading Kjelgaard & Speer to argue that prosody is used at a very early stage in parsing.

Not all researchers hold this position. For instance, Pynte & Prieur (1996) suggested that the effect of prosody may simply be to speed recovery from a garden path. However, others claim that prosody determines the initial structuring of an auditory sentence (e.g. Schafer 1997, Schafer & Speer 1997). Schafer (1997) proposed a "prosodic visibility hypothesis" that suggested that listeners may form a "prosodic package" of material within a single prosodic phrase. Material within a prosodic package is more visible than material outside it, making attachment to the current phrase easy. She predicted that attaching the PP "with a mean look" to the NP "the rider" in Sentence 11 would be preferred in Sentence 11b relative to the other conditions because in Sentence 11b only the NP-attachment site is inside the current prosodic package (brackets indicate phonological phrases):

11.   a. [The bus driver angered the rider] [with a mean look].
        b. [The bus driver angered] [the rider with a mean look].
        c. [The bus driver angered the rider with a mean look].
        d. [The bus driver] [angered] [the rider] [with a mean look].

Schafer also predicted that Sentence 11d would be intermediate between Sentences 11b and 11a,c because the rider should be more visible than angered in Sentence 11d but not in the others. Data from a listening study confirmed these predictions.

Schafer et al (2000) showed that these types of prosodic effects could be seen in spontaneously produced speech. They devised a board game in which two people communicate using a constrained set of sentence forms (including ones like those in Sentence 11). The players proved to use prosodies that effectively disambiguated their utterances and that had phonological properties similar to those manipulated in Schafer's earlier work.

Schafer argued against a "local cue" analysis of prosody, and argued that the interpretation of a prosodic boundary depends on the global prosodic representation of the sentence. In order for this to be a substantive claim, it is necessary to propose a specific scheme for representing prosody. Fortunately, a promising scheme, called "ToBI" (for tones and break indices), has developed out of the work of J Pierrehumbert (see Beckman 1996 or Shattuck-Huffnagel & Turk 1996 for tutorial introductions). Just as the formal descriptions of syntax devised in the 1950s and 1960s permitted the development of a psycholinguistics that seriously investigated the use of syntactic structure, the existence of a formal description of prosody will allow researchers to describe their auditory language materials and should stimulate new hypotheses about the role prosody might play in parsing.

SEMANTIC STRUCTURE

Most research on parsing has focused on the creation or recovery of syntactic structure. It is a truism that building syntactic structure is not the final goal of parsing, comprehension is. Logically, a process of semantic interpretation must bridge the gap between a syntactic form and a proposition that can become part of a discourse representation. Some recent research examines aspects of this process, including the processing of causality, tense, aspect, and quantifiers.

One example of such research is that done by Stevenson & Merlo (1997), who reopened the old question of why sentences like "The horse raced past the barn fell" are so terribly hard to understand. They suggest that it is not enough to note, as MacDonald (1994) did, that the transitivity preference of a verb affects difficulty. They proposed instead that the verbs (particularly manner of motion verbs) that lead to major garden-path effects are the ones that acquire a complex causal structure when they are used transitively: not only must an unexpressed causal agent be posited, but also the superficial subject "the horse" (the underlying object of "race") is assigned a role as agent. Verbs like "melt," which do not have this two-agent complication when they are taken to be transitive, do not lead to nearly as much garden-pathing (cf "The butter melted in the microwave was lumpy").

Another instance of research at the syntax/semantic interface is that done by Piñango et al (1999). These researchers presented a visual lexical decision task immediately after the word "time" while a listener was hearing sentences like (12a) and (12b) (this probe position is marked by ^). They found evidence of slower reaction times, indicating greater processing load, in Sentence (12a) than in Sentence (12b).

12.   a. The man kicked the little bundle of fur for a long time ^ to see if it
          was alive.
       b. The man examined the little bundle of fur for a long time ^ to see if it
          was alive.

The verb "examine" denotes a temporally unbounded activity, compatible with for *a* "long time." The verb "kick" on the other hand is telic, with an intrinsic beginning and end, and must be aspectually coerced (or typeshifted) to a verb that refers to a repeated activity. Presumably, the action of aspectual coercion is forced by the need to comprehend "for a long time," and requires processing capacity.

A third instance of research at the syntax/semantics interface was done by Frazier (1999). Among other topics, Frazier discussed the scope ambiguity of Sentence 13 (from Kurtzman & MacDonald 1993):

13.   a. Every kid climbed a tree.
       b. A kid climbed every tree.

Although Sentence 13a could have either one or multiple trees (and Sentence 13b one or multiple kids), readers seem to prefer interpretations where the first quantifier takes logical scope over the second (e.g. in Sentence 13a, every kid could have his or her own tree). Frazier argued that this reflects a deeper fact, namely that scope interpretation takes place at Logical Form, where the quantifiers could appear in either order (giving rise to the ambiguity). She proposed a "minimal lowering hypothesis" to the effect that the language comprehension system moves phrases from their (high) position in the surface structure to other (lower) positions in Logical Form only if necessary. Frazier demonstrated how this principle accounts for a variety of observations, including the apparent fact that in the discourse, "Five ships appeared on the horizon. Three ships sank," the three ships are most often taken to be three of the five original ones, not three different ships.

EFFECTS OF CONTEXT ON SENTENCE PROCESSING

Meaning and syntax can interface in a different way. The situational or discourse context in which a sentence appears must affect how it is interpreted and may affect how it is parsed. The research examining how discourse affects parsing has largely been limited to one type of possible contextual influence, how the existence of one versus more than one possible discourse antecedent for a simple noun affects the analysis of a phrase that might modify the noun (Altmann 1988, Altmann & Steedman 1988, Altmann et al 1994).

The motivation for this research came from Crain & Steedman (1985), who proposed that garden paths arise because of semantic selection principles. A reader or listener's syntactic knowledge makes available, in parallel, the possible interpretations of a phrase or sentence, and semantic principles guide the selection of one of these interpretations. Crain & Steedman assumed that analyzing a phrase as a modifier of a definite NP presupposes the existence of contrasting potential referents, and claimed that in isolation a modifier interpretation is semantically unpreferred because the reader/listener lacks the presupposed referents. If context provided these referents, then normal garden path preferences would disappear (see Clifton & Ferreira 1989, Steedman & Altmann 1989 for discussion).

Existing data do allow some fairly solid conclusions (Altmann 1988, Altmann & Steedman 1988, Altmann et al 1994, Britt 1994, Ferreira & Clifton 1986, Mitchell & Corley 1994, Murray & Liversedge 1994; see Mitchell 1994 for a summary). First, if a discourse contains two possible antecedents for an unmodified definite NP, the failure of the NP to refer will disrupt processing. Interpretation in this case seems to be nearly immediate. Second, if the out-of-context preference for the nonmodifier resolution of an ambiguity is weak (e.g. for a PP that is an optional argument of a verb), a context that supports the modifier resolution can greatly reduce or eliminate evidence for a garden path when the normally unpreferred analysis is selected. This may mean that context guided the initial analysis, but could simply reflect a much-facilitated revision. Third, while referential context can substantially reduce strong garden-path effects (involving, e.g. obligatory arguments of verbs, reduced relative clauses, or adverbs that could modify recent versus distant verbs), it cannot eliminate them.

It appears that garden paths do not simply result from a failure to satisfy semantic presuppositions. Structural factors are involved, perhaps in interaction with contextual factors, perhaps in a separate and modular fashion. A few studies of sentence processing in contexts other than one versus two antecedent referential contexts show some promise of shedding light on the relation between structural and semantic processing. Altmann et al (1998) used direct or indirect questions in discourse to vary the appropriateness of NP modification. Their contexts queried (e.g.) "When will Fiona implement the plan she proposed?" and then answered it with "She'll implement the plan she proposed last week." This answer is infelicitous; "last week" should have been the answer to the when question, which focused a modifier of the matrix verb implement. However, it is forced by its tense to modify the most recent verb, "proposed." Under certain conditions, Altmann et al observed that this infelicity eliminated the normal "late closure" preference for the adverb to modify the most recent verb, and in conjunction with other factors even seemed to reverse it.

Another apparently successful attempt to use context to eliminate a normally strong garden path is found in Trueswell & Tanenhaus (1991, 1992). They found that contexts that described a future event (e.g. "...tomorrow...a proctor will notice one of the students cheating") largely eliminated the normal main clause preference for a following reduced relative clause like "The student spotted by the proctor..."

A promising new line of research creates a nonlinguistic context and sees how its contents influence the comprehension of words and sentences about it. Tanenhaus and his colleagues (e.g. Allopenna et al 1998, Eberhard et al 1995, Sedivy et al 1999, Tanenhaus et al 1995) extended a technique introduced by Cooper (1974) to study a person's eye movements while following verbal instructions about an array of objects. The speed of word identification seems to be affected by the set of possible referents; thus, the speed with which a person's eyes move to the candle when told to pick up the candle, is slowed by the presence of another object whose name begins with /kaen/. The contrasts that exist in an array affect the interpretation of adjectival modifiers; thus, fixation on a tall glass given an instruction to "touch the tall glass" is speeded when the array contains a contrasting short glass. The existence of two same-named referents in the array (e.g. two cups) that contrast in some attribute apparently facilitates interpretation of a PP as a postnominal modifier (e.g. the cup "on the napkin"), eliminating the out-of-context preference for the PP to be taken as the argument of a verb.

Only a few published examples of this research exist, and it may turn out that some of the apparently most interesting effects depend on as-yet-unexplored details of the procedure used (e.g. the possibility that the participant can use the properties of the array to anticipate the linguistic form that will be used). However, interesting extensions of the work are already appearing. For instance, Altmann & Kamide (1999) used it to examine how quickly referential interpretation takes place. Their subjects observed a scene on a video display and judged whether an auditory sentence could apply to the scene. Eye movements to a relevant target item were speeded when the verb in the sentence was stereotypically appropriate to the target item (e.g. participants looked more quickly at a picture of a cake when the sentence was "The boy will eat the cake" than when it was "The boy will move the cake"). Keysar et al (2000) used the technique to see whether listeners respect mutual knowledge in comprehending a speaker's utterances. Do they tend to look at a possible referent that they as listener can see although they know the speaker can't see it and wouldn't say anything about it? Keysar et al's answer is basically yes, mutual knowledge does not fully override other sentence comprehension preferences (cf Hanna et al 1997).

ANAPHORA AND LOCAL COHERENCE

The extent to which a sentence is coherent in its local context affects how it is processed. A major source of local coherence is co-reference relations between an anaphoric phrase in the current sentence and its antecedent in a preceding sentence. Research on anaphoric reference has focused on three general questions: how the form of the anaphoric phrase influences processing, what factors influence the availability of various entities as antecedents, and what factors determine the ease of matching anaphor to antecedent.

Form of Anaphoric Phrase

Gordon, Grosz, and colleagues (Gordon et al 1993, Grosz et al 1995) have addressed these questions through centering theory. Under the assumptions of the theory, each noninitial utterance of a discourse has two kinds of centers, a backward-looking center (Cb) by which it is linked to the previous utterance and one or more forward–looking centers (Cfs), one of which will become the Cb for the next utterance. One critical prediction of centering theory is that a Cb must appear as a pronoun in order to signal its role in creating coherence.

The repeated-name penalty supports this claim. Reading times for sentences in discourse are longer when the Cb in the current utterance appears as a repeated name rather than as a pronoun (Gordon et al 1993). Structural factors influence interpretation of an entity in the current sentence as the Cb. For example, by varying the voice of the verb (passive versus active), Gordon & Chan (1995) found a repeated name penalty for entities appearing in subject position, regardless of whether they were also the agent of the verb, suggesting that grammatical structure of the current utterance rather than thematic structure governs identification of Cb.

Almor (1999) reinterpreted the repeated name penalty within a broader view of various types of anaphoric phrases including nonrepeated names. He claimed that anaphoric phrases can be characterized along a continuum of "informational load," which reflects how much information the anaphor conveys about its antecedent. In general, when an antecedent is relatively unavailable, a high informational load anaphor like a repeated name is required for successful coreference. In contrast, when an antecedent is relatively available (e.g. in focus in the preceding sentence), a high informational load anaphor is inappropriate and slows processing, producing a repeated name penalty.

Availability of Potential Antecedents

Several factors influence the relative availability of the entities mentioned in the preceding sentence as antecedents. Consistent with centering theory, structural factors such as syntactic role and serial position in the sentence influence anaphor availability (availability of the Cfs). Gordon and his colleagues (Gordon et al 1993, Gordon & Scearce 1995) found that pronouns are comprehended more quickly when their antecedents are the grammatical subject or the first-mentioned entity of the preceding sentence. These structural factors played a role in comprehension even in sentences where preceding semantic information disambiguated the pronoun (Gordon & Scearce 1995).

In contrast to the focus on structural factors, Stevenson et al (1994) found an influence of thematic role on the availability of antecedents from the preceding sentence. In a sentence continuation task, participants tended to continue with the goal in goal-source sentences, with the patient in agent-patient sentences, and with the stimulus in experience-stimulus sentences. For example, in source-goal sentences like Sentence 14 participants tended to begin

14.   a. John took the book from Phil.
        b. Phil gave the book to John.

with John (the goal) in their continuation regardless of whether John was mentioned first or second in the sentence. Stevenson et al claimed that the preferred continuation entities are represented as part of the consequences of the preceding event and consequences are in focus. Whereas grammatical position of the entity had no effect on the content of continuations, grammatical position did influence the form of the anaphoric phrase used. When the antecedent was the subject of the sentence, a pronoun was used as the anaphor; when the antecedent was not the first-mentioned entity in the sentence, the tendency was to use a repeated name. This suggests that thematic role in the mental model influences which entities are initially in focus and available as antecedents, and structural constraints influence the actual form of the anaphor.

Sanford et al (1996) and Paterson et al (1998) investigated the effect of quantifiers on focus. A positive quantifier ("a few" in Sentence 15a) seemed to create a focus on the set of items being referred to in the quantified phrase, facilitating a subsequent anaphoric reference to that reference set. In contrast, a negative quantifier ("few" in Sentence 15b) permitted the MPs who did not attend to be in focus.

15.   a. A few of the MPs attended the meeting.
        b. Few of the MPs attended the meeting.

Matching Antecedent to Anaphor

Chambers & Smyth (1998) found that structural parallelism plays a role in coherence relations between sentences. Their readers tended to interpret a pronoun in a sentence as co-referential with an entity in a parallel structural position in the preceding sentence. In contrast to the predictions of centering theory, a pronoun in direct object position is most readily interpreted as coreferential with the entity in direct object position in the preceding sentence. Furthermore, they found a repeated name penalty for an entity that was coreferential with an entity in a parallel position in the preceding sentence. Critically, this occurred for entities in nonsubject position as well as subject position and occurred even when a pronoun in subject position provided the standard Cb predicted by centering theory. This research suggests that other structural constraints are operating in the ranking of Cfs and that a sentence may have more than one Cb when it has multiple entities, each of which is coreferential with entities in parallel position in the preceding sentence.

A number of recent studies investigated the effect of another purely structural characteristic of pronouns, grammatical gender independent of meaning, by using languages other than English. Garnham et al (1995) looked at reading times for sentences in both Spanish and French containing a target pronoun with grammatical gender (e.g. *lo* versus *la* in Spanish and *il* versus *elle* in French). The advantage of using these languages is that these pronouns are appropriately used to refer to entities with grammatical gender but no semantic gender (e.g. the feminine pronoun *la* can refer to a table, which is grammatically feminine but has no semantic gender). Garnham et al (1995) found effects of grammatical gender on the comprehension of pronouns whose antecedents had no semantic gender. Cacciari et al (1997) found similar effects in Italian using epicenes, a class of words whose grammatical gender does not always match the semantic gender of their referents (e.g. in Italian *la vittima* (the victim) is grammatically female, but it can refer to a male individual).

MEMORY AND KNOWLEDGE IN DISCOURSE COMPREHENSION

Early models of discourse comprehension focused on the process of establishing links between sentences that were relatively close in the discourse (Haviland & Clark 1974, Kintsch & van Dijk 1978). It was assumed that information in long-term memory (LTM) (either world knowledge or the portion of the text representation that resides in LTM) was retrieved through an effortful and time-consuming search only when there was a local coherence break in which no local connection could be established. More recent work, however, has established that some critical LTM information is retrieved in the absence of local coherence breaks and seems to be retrieved effortlessly. Two current models, the memory based models and constructionist models, address the question of how to characterize this process.

Memory-Based Models

During the 1980s researchers in sentence processing developed the concept of modularity, in which fast, highly-specialized processors did the initial work in activating word meaning and determining syntactic structure for a sentence. These processors were fast because they were "dumb." They took as input only a small set of the data available to them and ignored other potentially useful information. For example, the lexical access processor ignored prior context and the syntactic processor ignored meaning.

A similar approach has recently been taken in the memory-based models of discourse processing. In these models, beginning with Kintsch's (1988) construction-integration model and McKoon & Ratcliff's (1992) minimalist model, and extending to current memory-based models (McKoon et al 1996, Myers & O'Brien 1998), activation of related information from LTM is assumed to be a passive, automatic process that occurs continually during comprehension. All concepts currently in short-term memory serve as cues that broadcast a signal in parallel to the contents of LTM. Information in LTM is activated through a passive resonance process, with level of activation for a given item determined by overlap in semantic features and strength (but not type) of association between activated item and cue.

This model is able to account for a number of findings in the literature where lengthened reading times are observed for sentences that are locally coherent but that conflict with information presented in a distant sentence earlier in the text. For example, Albrecht & O'Brien (1993) asked participants to read long passages in which the main character Mary was introduced as a strict vegetarian. After 6 filler sentences, the reader encountered the target sentence in which Mary ordered a cheeseburger and fries. This sentence was locally coherent with the preceding sentence, but reading times for this sentence were longer than in a neutral version of the paragraph that gave no preliminary information about Mary's eating habits. A memory-based model accounts for this result by claiming that the concept of vegetarian was re-activated through a resonance process initiated by the word "cheeseburger." This allowed the reader to detect the inconsistency in the text.

Evidence that this resonance process has the dumb characteristic of earlier modular processors was provided in follow-up studies (O'Brien et al 1998), in which similar results were obtained even when the concept of vegetarian was linked to Mary through a statement that made it clear that she was not a vegetarian (e.g. participants read that Mary had once been a vegetarian but wasn't any more). Findings such as these support the claim that the initial resonance process is a dumb process that is insensitive to the precise nature of the syntactic and semantic relationships among the relevant concepts.

Memory-based processing has also been used to account for readers' ability to comprehend "unheralded pronouns" whose antecedents do not appear in the immediately preceding discourse context (Greene et al 1994, McKoon et al 1996). For example, in one paragraph, Jane and Gloria discuss Jane's invitation to dinner at her cousin's (the target individual). While Jane goes off to her cousin's, the text remains with Gloria at home. Finally, a reunion sentence brings Gloria and Jane back together, and Gloria asks Jane, "Did she play you old disco records?" The pronoun "she" (referring to the cousin, who has not been mentioned since the introduction) is unheralded. Results from a probe recognition task indicated that the concept "cousin" increased in availability immediately after the reunion sentence (before the pronoun referring to the cousin was encountered). This result can be accounted for by a resonance process in which "cousin" is re-activated by the reunion sentence. Thus, it is not the unheralded pronoun itself that does the work of retrieving its distant antecedent. Rather, it is the reunion sentence that does the work through memory-based processing.

Constructionist Models

An alternative to the memory-based view is the constructionist view of text comprehension (Graesser et al 1994). According to this view, text comprehension involves a more active and intelligent "search after meaning." Comprehension of narrative text is assumed to involve building a representation of the causal relations among events in the text, where events are classified by types (e.g. goals, reactions, actions) reminiscent of the categories proposed in the original story grammars. Within this representation a character's goals have special status because an as-yet-unsatisfied goal can provide a causal antecedent for many events in the narrative, including events quite distant from the initial goal statement. Evidence for the critical status of unsatisfied goals was established by Suh & Trabasso (1993). In their texts, a character's initial goal was either immediately satisfied or was not. For example, Jimmy wanted a new bicycle (goal). In the goal-satisfied version, Jimmy's mother immediately bought him a bicycle; in the goal-unsatisfied version, she did not. Several sentences later Jimmy has earned a large amount of money and heads for a department store where, in the case of the goal-unsatisfied version of the story, one might infer that he was intending to buy a bicycle (finally satisfying his distant goal). Suh & Trabasso provided evidence that this is indeed what readers inferred. In particular, they found that the bicycle goal was much more available after the sentence in which Jimmy headed for the department store in the goal-unsatisfied version of the text than in the goal-satisfied version.

This kind of result would seem to be evidence against a dumb memory-based process like the resonance process. In both the goal-satisfied and goal-unsatisfied version of the stories there is the same featural overlap and distance between the original goal sentence ("Jimmy wanted to have a new bike") and the critical sentence ("He went to a department store"). In this analysis, the resonance process operating at the critical sentence should activate the goal equally in the goal-satisfied versus goal-unsatisfied version. However, Lutz & Radvansky (1997) observed that in the goal unsatisfied version of the story, the goal is more likely to be linked to later sentences in the text than in the goal-satisfied version. Because it is more interconnected with other concepts in the text that the target sentence may activate, the unsatisfied goal is more likely to be activated by the target sentence than the satisfied goal.

Albrecht & Myers (1995) illustrated the importance of this interconnectivity. In one example paragraph Mary had to make an airline reservation by midnight (goal). The target sentence occurs later in the text: "She was tired and decided to go to bed." Albrecht & Myers found that this sentence was not sufficient to reactivate the unsatisfied goal when it was distant in the text. In a modification of the text, the authors introduced a critical concept that provided the interconnection. After the initial goal statement, Mary sits down on her leather couch to look up the phone number in the telephone book (in the unsatisfied goal version, she is interrupted before she calls the airline). Mentioning the leather couch again immediately before Mary decides to go to bed was sufficient to reactivate the goal even when the goal was distant. Notice that the leather couch is arbitrarily associated with the airline reservation goal rather than being related through the kind of causal connection that is important in constructionist models. The fact that this arbitrary connection was sufficient to trigger activation of an unsatisfied goal lends support to claims of memory-based models that the resonance process is insensitive to type of connection.

Although these models are frequently seen as being in opposition to each other, it is not clear that they have to be. Myers & O'Brien (1998) presented the resonance process as the first stage of the comprehension process. A later stage of processing (unspecified in their theory) makes use of the information activated in the resonance stage. This later stage might be sensitive to the type of propositions activated (e.g. unsatisfied versus satisfied goals) and to the relations among the critical concepts (e.g. Mary is or is not a vegetarian). Indeed, Rizzella & O'Brien (1996) suggested that the resonance process might be conceptualized as the first stage in a constructionist model.

Mental Models

Another traditional focus has been on characterizing the mental representation that is created through the comprehension process. During the "local coherence" phase of research on discourse processing, the focus was on the construction of a textbase that preserved the propositions of the individual sentences with their connections (through argument overlap) with other propositions in the text. As processing research has come to focus on the creation of links between distant sentences in the text, research on discourse representation has come to focus on a new representation, variously labeled a situation model (van Dijk & Kintsch 1983) or a mental model (Johnson-Laird 1983). In contrast to a propositional textbase, a mental model is a representation of what the text is about rather than of the text itself. This representation includes information relevant to the constructionist model of comprehension (i.e. causal relations among events, protagonists' goals) as well as spatial and temporal information relevant to the text. Although it has a constructionist flavor, the mental model view has supporters on both sides of the memory-based versus constructionist model debate (e.g. O'Brien & Albrecht 1992, Zwaan et al 1995a).

Much of the research that initially motivated the constructionist model of comprehension provided evidence that readers represent causal relations among events. In addition, several studies provided evidence for the preservation of spatial information. In an early study, Glenberg, Meyer and Lindem (1987) found that a target concept (e.g. a sweatshirt) that remained physically close to the protagonist (the protagonist put on the sweatshirt and then jogged around the track) remained more available during comprehension than the same concept when it was physically distant from the protagonist (the protagonist took off the sweatshirt and then jogged around the track). Furthermore, O'Brien & Albrecht (1992) found that readers keep track of the spatial location of protagonists in narrative, taking longer to comprehend a sentence that conflicted with an earlier sentence about protagonist location.

Recently, Zwaan (1996) investigated the claim that temporal relationships among events are reflected in the reader's mental model. Drawing upon work of Dowty (1986), he outlined the "strong iconicity assumption," in which readers assume that (*a*) events took place in the order in which they are mentioned in a text and (*b*) successively mentioned events are contiguous in time. Time adverbials can overturn these default assumptions, but the cost is processing time. Evidence for the first iconicity assumption already existed; Mandler (1986) and Ohtsuka & Brewer (1992) found that reading time for sentences increased when the chronological order of events in the sentences does not match the order of their occurrence. So Zwaan (1996) focused on testing the contiguity assumption, creating texts in which a second target event did or did not occur immediately after a first target event (see also Anderson et al 1983). For example, in a text about the opening of Maurice's new art gallery, Maurice is shaking hands and beaming, and in the next sentence he turned very pale. However, this second event is introduced by one of three time adverbials: "a moment later" or "an hour later" or "a day later". The first adverbial preserves the contiguity assumption and the other two violate it. Zwaan demonstrated that reading times for the second event were longer when the two events were not contiguous in time, supporting the contiguity assumption.

Zwaan et al (1995a) have proposed the event-indexing model, a specific version of a mental or situation model. Under the assumptions of this model the reader keeps track of the current situation or state of the textual world at each sentence. Five indices of the current situation are coded: spatial location, time, protagonist, cause, and goals. If an incoming event differs from the preceding event on one or more of these indices (e.g. it conveys a change in time or location or an event that is causally unrelated to the immediately preceding events), then the current situation model must be updated to reflect this change. This leads to two predictions. First, a sentence that elicits this updating will take longer to read than a sentence that does not. Second, the distance between events in the mental model will be determined by number of shared situational indices. Zwaan et al (1995b) provided evidence for the first prediction in a study in which they found that reading times for sentences in naturalistic texts were positively correlated with the number of indices that needed updating for the sentence. Zwaan et al (1995a) provided evidence for the second claim by demonstrating that in a verb-clustering task, readers' judgments of which verbs from a text "belonged together" reflected the number of shared situational indices among the verbs.

The event-indexing model provides a new answer to an old question. One of the insights in the original Kintsch and van Dijk (1978) model was that the critical linking processes in discourse comprehension are carried out on the contents of working memory. This raised the question of what already-comprehended information would have the privilege of being held in working memory as the reader went on to read the next sentence. A variety of answers to this question have been proposed over the years. Zwaan et al (1995a) continue this tradition by proposing a new answer: what is held over is the current situation (who, where, when, cause, and goal).

A FINAL WORD

One must go beyond linguistic structure to understand fully how sentences and texts are understood. Still, our examination of the recent literature on sentence and text comprehension convinces us that there is much to be learned by continuing to study the various roles that linguistic structure play in the process. We have had to overlook a great many interesting topics, including the use of evoked brain potentials to study sentence processing, immediacy in language comprehension, the comprehension of sentences with long-distance dependencies, and the role of discourse context in word recognition, to name only a few. We can only hope that our presentation of the material we were able to discuss has convinced the reader that our belief in the value of studying structural factors in comprehension is not misplaced.

ACKNOWLEDGMENTS

We thank our colleagues Rachel Clifton, Lyn Frazier, and Keith Rayner for helpful readings of an earlier version of this paper. Preparation of the chapter was supported in part by grant HD-18708 to the University of Massachusetts.

Visit the Annual Reviews home page at www.AnnualReviews.org

LITERATURE CITED

Albrecht JE, Myers JL. 1995. Role of context in accessing distant information during reading. *J. Exp. Psychol: Learn. Mem. Cogn.* 21:1459–68

Albrecht JE, O'Brien EJ. 1993. Updating a mental model: maintaining both local and global coherence. *J. Exp. Psychol: Learn. Mem. Cogn.* 19:1061–70

Allopenna PD, Magnuson JS, Tanenhaus MK. 1998. Tracking the time course of spoken word recognition using eye movements: evidence for continuous mapping models. *J. Mem. Lang.* 38:419–39

Almor A. 1999. Noun-phrase anaphora and focus: the informational load hypothesis. *Psychol. Rev.* 106:748–65

Altmann GTM. 1988. Ambiguity, parsing strategies, and computational models. *Lang. Cogn. Process.* 3:73–98

Altmann GTM, Steedman M. 1988. Interaction with context during human sentence processing. *Cognition* 30:191–238

Altmann GTM, Garnham A, Henstra JA. 1994. Effects of syntax in human sentence parsing: evidence against a structure-based parsing mechanism. *J. Exp. Psychol: Learn. Mem. Cogn.* 20:209–16

Altmann GTM, Kamide Y. 1999. Incremental interpretation at verbs: restricting the domain of subsequent reference. *Cognition* 73:247–64

Altmann GTM, van Nice KY, Garnham A, Henstra J-A. 1998. Late closure in context. *J. Mem. Lang.* 38:459–84

Anderson A, Garrod SC, Sanford AJ. 1983. The accessibility of pronominal antecedents as a function of episode shifts in narrative texts. *Q. J. Exp. Psychol: Hum. Exp. Psychol. A* 35:427–40

Bader M. 1998. Prosodic influences on reading syntactically ambiguous sentences. In *Reanalysis in Sentence Processing*, ed. J Fodor,

F Ferreira, pp. 1–46. Dordrecht, The Netherlands: Kluwer

Bader M, Lasser I. 1994. German verb-final clauses and sentence processing: evidence for immediate attachment. In *Perspectives on Sentence Processing*, ed. C Fliftion, L Frazier, K Rayner, pp. 225–42. Hillsdale, NJ: L Erlbaum

Bader M, Meng M. 1999. Subject-object ambiguities in German embedded clauses: an across-the-board comparison. *J. Psycholinguist. Res.* 28:121–44

Bader M, Meng M, Bayer J. 2000. Case and reanalysis. *J. Psycholinguist. Res.* 29:37–52

Beckman M. 1996. The parsing of prosody. *Lang. Cogn. Process.* 11:17–67

Binder K, Duffy S, Rayner K. 2000. The effects of thematic fit and discourse context on syntactic ambiguity resolution. *J. Mem. Lang.* In press

Boland JE, Tanenhaus MK, Garnsey SM, Carlson GN. 1995. Verb argument structure in parsing and interpretation: Evidence from wh-questions. *J. Mem. Lang.* 34:774–806

Britt MA. 1994. The interaction of referential ambiguity and argument structure in the parsing of prepositional phrases. *J. Mem. Lang.* 33:251–83

Cacciari C, Carreiras M, Cionini CB. 1997. When words have two genders: anaphor resolution for Italian functionally ambiguous words. *J. Mem. Lang.* 37:517–32

Cairns HS, Teller V, eds. 2000. *J. Psycholinguist. Res.: Spec. Issue Role Syntactic Features in Sentence Process.* 29(1):1–106.

Carlson GN, Tanenhaus MK. 1988. Thematic roles and language comprehension. In *Syntax and Semantics: Thematic Relations*, ed. W Wilkins, pp. 263–300. New York: Academic

Chambers CG, Smyth R. 1998. Structural parallelism and discourse coherence: a test of centering theory. *J. Mem. Lang.* 39:593–608

Chater N, Crocker MJ, Pickering MJ. 1998. The rational analysis of inquiry: the case of parsing. In *Rational Models of Cognition*, ed. M Oaksford, N Chater, pp. 441–69. Oxford, UK Oxford Univ. Press

Chen H-C, Zhou X, eds. 1999. *Lang. Cogn. Process.: Spec. Issue Process. East Asian Lang.* 14:(5/6)

Clifton C Jr. 2000. Evaluating models of sentence processing. See Crocker et al 2000, pp. 31–55

Clifton C Jr, Ferreira F. 1989. Ambiguity in context. *Lang. Cogn. Process.* 4:SI77–104

Cooper RM. 1974. The control of eye fixation by the meaning of spoken language: a new methodology for the real-time investigation of speech perception, memory, and language processing. *Cogn. Psychol.* 6:61–83

Corley S, Crocker MW. 2000. The modular statistical hypothesis: exploring lexical category ambiguity. See Crocker et al 2000 pp. 135–60

Crain S, Steedman M. 1985. On not being led up the garden path: the use of context by the psychological parser. In *Natural Language Parsing*, ed. D Dowty, L Kartunnen, A Zwicky, pp. 320–58. Cambridge, UK: Cambridge Univ. Press

Crocker M. 1995. *Computational Psycholinguistics: An Interdisciplinary Approach to the Study of Language*. Dordrecht, The Netherlands: Kluwer

Crocker MW, Corley S. 2000. Modular architectures and statistical mechanism: the case from lexical category disambiguation. In *The Lexical Basis of Sentence Processing*, ed. P Merlo, S Stevenson. Amsterdam: Benjamins. In press

Crocker MW, Pickering M, Clifton C Jr, eds. 2000. *Architectures and Mechanisms for Language Processing*. Cambridge, UK: Cambridge Univ. Press

Cutler A, Clifton C Jr. 2000. Blueprint of the listener. In *Neurocognition of Language Processing*, ed. P Hagoort, C Brown, pp. 123–66. Oxford, UK: Oxford Univ. Press

Dowty DR. 1986. The effects of aspectual class on the temporal structure of discourse: semantics or pragmatics? *Linguist. Philos.* 9: 37–61

Eberhard KM, Spivey-Knowlton MJ, Sedivy JC, Tanenhaus MK. 1995. Eye movements as a window into real-time spoken language comprehension in natural contexts. *J. Psycholinguist. Res.* 24:409–36

Ferreira F, Clifton C Jr. 1986. The independence of syntactic processing. *J. Mem. Lang.* 25:348–68

Ferreira F, Henderson J. 1990. The use of verb information in syntactic parsing: evidence from eye movements and word-by-word self-paced reading. *J. Exp. Psychol: Learn. Mem. Cogn.* 16:555–68

Ferreira F, McClure KK. 1997. Parsing of garden-path sentences with reciprocal verbs. *Lang. Cogn. Process.* 12:273–306

Fodor JA, Bever TG, Garrett M. 1974. *The Psychology of Language: An Introduction to Psycholinguistics and Generative Grammar.* New York: McGraw-Hill

Fodor JD, Ferreira F, eds. 1998. *Sentence Reanalysis.* Dordrecht, The Netherlands: Kluwer

Fodor JD, Inoue A. 1994. The diagnosis and cure of garden paths. *J. Psycholinguist. Res.* 23:407–34

Fodor JD, Inoue A. 2000. Garden path reanalysis: attach (anyway) and revision as last resort. In *Cross-Linguistic Perspectives in Language Processing*, ed. M DiVincenzi, V Lombardo, pp. 21–61. Dordrecht, The Netherlands: Kluwer

Ford M, Bresnan J, Kaplan R. 1982. A competence-based theory of syntactic closure. In *The Mental Representation of Grammatical Relations*, ed. J Bresnan pp. 727–96. Cambridge, MA: MIT Press

Frazier L. 1979. *On Comprehending Sentences: Syntactic Parsing Strategies.* Bloomington: Indiana Univ. Linguist. Club

Frazier L. 1987. Sentence processing: a tutorial review. In *Attention and Performance XII*, ed. M Coltheart, pp. 559–86. Hillsdale, NJ: Erlbaum

Frazier L. 1989. Against lexical generation of syntax. In *Lexical Representation and Process*, ed. W Marslen-Wilson, pp. 505–28. Cambridge, MA: MIT Press

Frazier L. 1995. Constraint satisfaction as a theory of sentence processing. *J. Psycholinguist. Res.* 24:437–68

Frazier L. 1999. *On Sentence Interpretation.* Dordrecht, The Netherlands: Kluwer

Frazier L, Clifton C Jr. 1996. *Construal.* Cambridge, MA: MIT Press

Frazier L, Fodor JD. 1978. The sausage machine: a new two-stage parsing model. *Cognition* 6:291–326

Frazier L, Rayner K. 1982. Making and correcting errors during sentence comprehension: eye movements in the analysis of structurally ambiguous sentences. *Cogn. Psychol.* 14:178–210

Friederici A, Mecklinger A. 1996. Syntactic parsing as revealed by brain responses: first-pass and second-pass parsing processes. *J. Psycholinguist. Res.* 25:157–76

Garnham A, Oakhill J, Ehrlich M-F, Carreiras M. 1995. Representations and processes in the interpretation of pronouns: new evidence from Spanish and French. *J. Mem. Lang.* 34:41–62

Garnsey SM, Pearlmutter NJ, Myers E, Lotocky MA. 1997. The contributions of verb bias and plausibility to the comprehension of temporarily ambiguous sentences. *J. Mem. Lang.* 37:58–93

Gibson E. 1998. Linguistic complexity: locality of syntactic dependencies. *Cognition* 68:1–76

Gibson E, Pearlmutter N, Canseco-Gonzalez E, Hickok G. 1996a. Recency preference in the human sentence processing mechanism. *Cognition* 59:23–59

Gibson E, Schütze CT. 1999. Disambiguation preferences in noun phrase conjunction do not mirror corpus frequency. *J. Mem. Lang.* 40:263–79

Gibson E, Schütze CT, Salomon A. 1996b. The relationship between the frequency and the processing complexity of linguistic structure. *J. Psycholinguist. Res.* 25:59–92

Glenberg AM, Meyer M, Lindem K. 1987.

Mental models contribute to foregrounding during text comprehension. *J. Mem. Lang.* 26:69–83

Gordon PC, Chan D. 1995. Pronouns, passives, and discourse coherence. *J. Mem. Lang.* 34:216–31

Gordon PC, Grosz BJ, Gilliom LA. 1993. Pronouns, names, and the centering of attention in discourse. *Cogn. Sci.* 17:311–47

Gordon PC, Scearce KA. 1995. Pronominalization and discourse coherence, discourse structure and pronoun interpretation. *Mem. Cogn.* 23:313–23

Gorrell P. 2000. The subject-before-object preference in German clauses. See Hemforth & Konieczny 2000a, pp. 25–64

Graesser AC, Singer M, Trabasso T. 1994. Constructing inferences during narrative text comprehension. *Psychol. Rev.* 101:371–95

Greene SB, Gerrig RJ, McKoon G, Ratcliff R. 1994. Unheralded pronouns and management by common ground. *J. Mem. Lang.* 33:511–26

Grosz BJ, Joshi AK, Weinstein A. 1995. Centering: a framework for modeling the local coherence of discourse. *Comput. Linguist.* 21:203–25

Hanna JE, Trueswell JC, Tanenhaus MK, Novick JM. 1997. *Common ground as a probabilistic constraint on reference.* Presented at 38th Annu. Psychon. Soc., Philadelphia, PA

Haviland S, Clark HH. 1974. What's new? Acquiring new information as a process in comprehension. *J. Verbal Learn. Verbal Behav.* 13:512–21

Hemforth B, Konieczny L. 2000a. *German Sentence Processing.* Dordrecht, The Netherlands: Kluwer

Hemforth B, Konieczny L. 2000b. Cognitive parsing in German: an introduction. See Hemforth & Konieczny 2000a, pp. 1–24

Jurafsky D. 1996. A probabilistic model of lexical and syntactic access and disambiguation. *Cogn. Sci.* 20:137–94

Johnson-Laird PN. 1983. *Mental Models.* Cambridge, UK: Cambridge Univ. Press

Kamide Y, Mitchell DC. 1999. Incremental pre-head attachment in Japanese parsing. *Lang. Cogn. Process.* 14:631–63

Kennison SM. 2000. Limitations on the use of verb information during sentence comprehension. *Psychon. Bull. Rev.* In press

Keysar B, Barr DJ, Balin JA, Brauner JS. 2000. Taking perspective in conversation: the role of mutual knowledge in comprehension. *Psychol. Sci.* 11:32–38

Kim Y. 1999. The effects of case marking information on Korean sentence processing. *Lang. Cogn. Process.* 14:687–714

Kimball J. 1973. Seven principles of surface structure parsing in natural language. *Cognition* 2:15 47

Kintsch W. 1988. The role of knowledge in discourse comprehension: a construction-integration model. *Psychol. Rev.* 95:163–82

Kintsch W, van Dijk TA. 1978. Toward a model of text comprehension and production. *Psychol. Rev.* 85:363–94

Kjelgaard MM, Speer SR. 1999. Prosodic facilitation and interference in the resolution of temporary syntactic closure ambiguity. *J. Mem. Lang.* 40:153–94

Koh S. 1997. The resolution of the dative NP ambiguity in Korean. *J. Psycholinguist. Res.* 26:265–73

Konieczny L, Hemforth B, Scheepers C, Strube G. 1997. The role of lexical heads in parsing: evidence from German. *Lang. Cogn. Process.* 12:307–48

Kurtzman HS, MacDonald MC. 1993. Resolution of quantifier scope ambiguities. *Cognition* 48:243–79

Lehiste I. 1973. Phonetic disambiguation of syntactic ambiguity. *Glossa* 7:107–22

Lewis RL. 1996. A theory of grammatical but unacceptable embeddings. *J. Psycholinguist. Res.* 25:93–116

Lewis RL. 2000. Specifying architectures for language processing: process, control, and memory in parsing and interpretation. See Crocker et al. 2000, pp. 56–89

Lutz MF, Radvansky G. 1997. The fate of completed goal information in narrative comprehension. *J. Mem. Lang.* 36:293–310

MacDonald M. 1997. Lexical representations and sentence processing: an introduction. *Lang. Cogn. Processes* 12:121–36

MacDonald MC. 1994. Probabilistic constraints and syntactic ambiguity resolution. *Lang. Cogn. Processes* 9:157–201

MacDonald MC, Pearlmutter NJ, Seidenberg MS. 1994. Lexical nature of syntactic ambiguity resolution. *Pyschological Review* 101:676–703

Mandler JM. 1986. On the comprehension of temporal order. *Lang. Cogn. Processes* 1:309–320

Mandler JM, Johnson NS. 1977. Remembrance of things parsed: story structure and recall. *Cogn. Psychol.* 9:111–51

Marcus M. 1980. *A Theory of Syntactic Recognition for Natural Language.* Cambridge, MA: MIT Press

Marslen-Wilson WD, Tyler LK, Warren P, Grenier P, Lee CS. 1992. Prosodic effects in minimal attachment. *Q. J. Exp. Psychol. A* 45:73–87

Mazuka R, Nagai N. 1995. *Japanese Sentence Processing.* Hillsdale, NJ: Erlbaum

McKoon G, Gerrig RJ, Greene SB. 1996. Pronoun resolution without pronouns: some consequences of memory-based text processing. *J. Exp. Psychol: Learn. Mem. Cogn.* 22: 919–32

McKoon G, Ratcliff R. 1980. The comprehension processes and memory structures involved in anaphoric reference. *J. Verbal Learn. Verbal Behav.* 19:668–82

McKoon G, Ratcliff R. 1992. Inference during reading. *Psychol. Rev.* 99:440–66

McRae K, Spivey-Knowlton MJ, Tanenhaus MK. 1998. Modeling the influence of thematic fit (and other constraints) in on-line sentence comprehension. *J. Mem. Lang.* 38:283–312

Merlo P. 1994. A corpus-based analysis of verb continuation frequencies for syntactic processing. *J. Psycholinguist. Res.* 23:435–57

Miller GA. 1962. Some psychological studies of grammar. *Am. Psychol.* 17:748–62

Miller GA, Isard S. 1964. Free recall of self-embedded English sentences. *Inf. Control* 4:292–303

Mitchell DC. 1994. Sentence parsing. In *Handbook of Psycholinguistics,* ed. MA Gernsbacher, pp. 375–410. New York: Academic

Mitchell DC, Corley MMB. 1994. Immediate biases in parsing: discourse effects or experimental artifacts? *J. Exp. Psychol: Learn. Mem. Cogn.* 20:217–22

Mitchell DC, Cuetos F, Corley MMB, Brysbaert M. 1995. Exposure-based models of human parsing: evidence for the use of coarse-grained (non-lexical) statistical records. *J. Psycholinguist. Res.* 24:469–88

Murray WS, Liversedge SP. 1994. Referential context effects on syntactic processing. In *Perspectives on Sentence Processing,* ed. C Clifton, L Frazier, K Rayner, pp. 359–88. Hillsdale, NJ: Erlbaum

Myers JL, O'Brien EJ. 1998. Accessing discourse representation during reading. *Discourse Process.* 26:131–57

Nespor M, Vogel I. 1986. *Prosodic Phonology.* Dordrecht, The Netherlands: Foris

Nicol J, ed. 1996. *J. Psycholinguist. Res.: Spec. Issue: Sentence Process.* 25:Number 2

O'Brien EJ, Albrecht JE. 1992. Comprehension strategies in the development of a mental model. *J. Exp. Psychol: Learn. Mem. Cogn.* 18:777–84

O'Brien EJ, Rizzella ML, Albrecht JE, Halleran JG. 1998. Updating a situation model: a memory-based text processing view. *J. Exp. Psychol: Learn. Mem. Cogn.* 24:1200–10

Ohtsuka K, Brewer WF. 1992. Discourse organization in the comprehension of temporal order in narrative texts. *Discourse Process.* 15:317–36

Paterson KB, Sanford AJ, Moxey LM, Dawydiak E. 1998. Quantifier polarity and referential focus during reading. *J. Mem. Lang.* 39:290–306

Phillips C, Gibson E. 1997. On the strength of

the local attachment preference. *J. Psycholin-guist. Res.* 26:323–46

Pickering M, Traxler M. 1998. Plausibility and the recovery from garden paths: an eyetrack-ing study. *J. Exp. Psychol: Learn. Mem. Cogn.* 24:940–61

Pickering MJ, Traxler MJ, Crocker MW. 2000. Ambiguity resolution in sentence processing: evidence against likelihood. *J. Mem. Lang.* In press

Piñango MM, Zurif E, Jackendoff R. 1999. Real-time processing implications of en-riched composition at the syntax-semantics interface. *J. Psycholinguist. Res.* 28:395–414

Pritchett BL. 1992. *Grammatical Competence and Parsing Performance.* Chicago: Univ. Chicago Press

Pynte J, Prieur B. 1996. Prosodic breaks and attachment decisions in sentence processing. *Lang. Cogn. Process.* 11:165–92

Rayner K, Carlson M, Frazier L. 1983. The interaction of syntax and semantics during sentence processing: eye movements in the analysis of semantically biased sentences. *J. Verbal Learn. Verbal Behav.* 22:358–74

Rizzella ML, O'Brien EJ. 1996. Accessing global causes during reading. *J. Exp. Psy-chol.: Learn., Mem., Cogn.* 22:1208–18

Rumelhart DE. 1975. Notes on a schema for stories. In *Representations and Understand-ing: Studies in Cognitive Science,* ed. DG Bobrow, AM Collins, pp. 211–36. New York: Academic

Sanford AJ, Moxey LM, Paterson KB. 1996. Attentional focusing with quantifiers in pro-duction and comprehension. *Mem. Cogn.* 24:144–55

Schafer A. 1997. *Prosodic parsing: the role of prosody in sentence comprehension.* PhD thesis. Univ. Mass. Amherst

Schafer AJ, Speer SR. 1997. *The role of prosodic phrasing in sentence comprehen-sion.* Presented at CUNY Conf. Human Sen-tence Process., Santa Monica, CA, March, 1997

Schafer AJ, Speer SR, Warren P, White SD. 2000. Intonational disambiguation in sen-tence production and comprehension. *J. Psy-cholinguist. Res.* 29:169–82

Scheepers C, Hemforth B, Konieczny L. 2000. Linking syntactic functions with thematic roles: psych-verbs and the resolution of subject-object ambiguity. See Hemforth & Konieczny 2000, pp. 95–136

Schlesewsky M, Fanselow G, Kliegl R, Krems J. 2000. The subject preference in the pro-cessing of locally ambiguous wh-questions in German. See Hemforth & Konieczny 2000, pp. 65–95

Sedivy JC, Tanenhaus MK, Chambers CG, Carlson GN. 1999. Achieving incremental semantic interpretation through contextual representation. *Cognition* 71:109–47

Selkirk EO. 1984. *Phonology and Syntax: The Relation Between Sound and Structure.* Cam-bridge, MA: MIT Press

Selkirk EO. 1995. Sentence prosody: intona-tion, stress, and phasing. In *Handbook of Phonological Theory,* ed. J Goldsmith, pp. 550–69. Oxford, UK: Blackwell

Shattuck-Hufnagel S, Turk AE. 1996. A prosody tutorial for investigators of auditory sentence processing. *J. Psycholinguist. Res.* 25:193–248

Spivey MJ, Tanenhaus MK. 1998. Syntactic ambiguity resolution in discourse: model-ing the effects of referential context and lexi-cal frequency. *J. Exp. Psychol: Learn. Mem. Cogn.* 24:1521–43

Spivey-Knowlton M, Sedivy JC. 1995. Re-solving attachment ambiguities with multiple constraints. *Cognition* 55:227–67

Steedman MJ, Altmann GTM. 1989. Ambigu-ity in context: a reply. *Lang. Cogn. Process.* 4:S177–105

Stevenson R, Crawley RJ, Kleinman D. 1994. Thematic roles, focus, and the representation of events. *Lang. Cogn. Process.* 9:519–48

Stevenson S. 1994. Competition and recency in a hybrid network model of syntactic depen-dencies. *J. Psycholinguist. Res.* 23:295–322

Stevenson S, Merlo P. 1997. Lexical structure and parsing complexity. *Lang. Cogn. Pro-cess.* 12:349–99

Sturt P, Crocker M. 1998. Generalized mono-tonicity for reanalysis models. In *Reanalysis in Sentence Comprehension*, ed. JD Fodor, F Ferreira, pp. 365–400. Dordrecht, The Netherlands: Kluwer

Sturt P, Pickering MJ, Crocker MW. 2000. Search strategies in syntactic reanalysis. *J. Psycholinguist. Res.* 29:183–92

Suh S, Trabasso T. 1993. Inferences during reading: converging evidence from discourse analysis, talk-aloud protocols, and recognition priming. *J. Mem. Lang.* 32:279–300

Tanenhaus M, Carlson G, Trueswell JC. 1989. The role of thematic structures in interpretation and parsing. *Lang. Cogn. Process.* 4:SI211–34

Tanenhaus M, Garnsey S, Boland J. 1990. Combinatory lexical information and language comprehension. In *Cognitive Models of Speech Processing*, ed. G Altmann, pp. 383–408. Cambridge, MA: MIT Press

Tanenhaus MK, Boland JE, Mauner G, Carlson GN. 1993. More on combinatory lexical information: thematic structure in parsing and interpretation. In *Cognitive Models of Speech Processing: The Second Sperlonga Meeting*, ed. G Altmann, R Shillcock, pp. 297–319. Hillsdale, NJ: Erlbaum

Tanenhaus MK, Spivey-Knowlton MJ, Eberhard KM, Sedivy JC. 1995. Integration of visual and linguistic information in spoken language comprehension. *Science* 268:1632-34

Tanenhaus MK, Spivey-Knowlton MJ, Hanna JE. 2000. Modeling thematic and discourse context effects within a multiple constraints framework: implications for the architecture of the language comprehension system. See Crocker et al 2000, pp. 90–118

Tanenhaus MK, Trueswell JC. 1995. Sentence comprehension. In *Handbook of Perception and Cognition: Speech, Language, and Communication*, ed. J Miller, P Eimas, 11:217–62. San Diego, CA: Academic. 2nd ed.

Traxler MJ, Pickering MJ. 1996. Case-marking in the parsing of complement sentences: evidence from eye movements. *Q. J. Exp. Psychol. A* 49:991–1004

Trueswell JC. 1996. The role of lexical frequency in syntactic ambiguity resolution. *J. Mem. Lang.* 35:566–85

Trueswell JC, Tanenhaus M. 1991. Tense, temporal context and syntactic ambiguity resolution. Presented at 14th Annu. Conf. Cogn. Sci. Soc., Bloomington, IN. *Lang. Cogn. Process.* 6:303–38

Trueswell JC, Tanenhaus MK. 1992. *Consulting temporal context during sentence comprehension: evidence from the monitoring of eye movements in reading*. Presented at 14th Annu. Conf. Cogn. Sci. Soc.

Trueswell JC, Tanenhaus MK, Garnsey SM. 1994. Semantic influences on parsing: use of thematic role information in syntactic disambiguation. *J. Mem. Lang.* 33:285–318

Trueswell JC, Tanenhaus MK, Kello C. 1993. Verb-specific constraints in sentence processing: separating effects of lexical preference from garden-paths. *J. Exp. Psychol: Learn. Mem. Cogn.* 19:528–53

van Dijk T, Kintsch W. 1983. *Strategies of Discourse Comprehension*. San Diego, CA: Academic

Warren P, ed. 1996. *Lang. Cogn. Process.: Spec. Issue: Prosody Parsing.* 11(1–2)

Yamashita H. 1997. The effects of word-order and case marking information on the processing of Japanese. *J. Psycholinguist. Res.* 26:163–88

Zwaan RA. 1996. Processing narrative time shifts. *J. Exp. Psychol: Learn. Mem. Cogn.* 22:1196–207

Zwaan RA, Langston MC, Graesser AC. 1995a. The construction of situation models in narrative comprehension. *Psychol. Sci.* 6:292–97

Zwaan RA, Magliano JP, Graesser AC. 1995b. Dimensions of situation model construction in narrative comprehension. *J. Exp. Psychol: Learn. Mem. Cogn.* 21:386–97

Annu. Rev. Psychol. 2001. 52:197–221

PERSONALITY

David C. Funder

Department of Psychology, University of California, Riverside, California, 92521;
e-mail: Funder@citrus.ucr.edu

Key Words   traits, social-cognitive processes, individual differences,
institutional issues, evolutionary psychology, biological psychology

■ **Abstract**   Personality psychology is as active today as at any point in its history. The classic psychoanalytic and trait paradigms are active areas of research, the
behaviorist paradigm has evolved into a new social-cognitive paradigm, and the humanistic paradigm is a basis of current work on cross-cultural psychology. Biology
and evolutionary theory have also attained the status of new paradigms for personality.
Three challenges for the next generation of research are to integrate these disparate
approaches to personality (particularly the trait and social-cognitive paradigms), to
remedy the imbalance in the person-situation-behavior triad by conceptualizing the
basic properties of situations and behaviors, and to add to personality psychology's
thin inventory of basic facts concerning the relations between personality and behavior.

CONTENTS

0066-4308/01/0201-0197$14.00

INTRODUCTION

The mission of personality psychology is theoretical, empirical, and institutional. The theoretical mission is to account for individuals' characteristic patterns of thought, emotion, and behavior together with the psychological mechanisms—hidden or not—behind those patterns (Funder 2001). The empirical mission in service of this theoretical goal is to gather and analyze data that reveal how persons, situations, and behaviors are inter-related, and to develop psychometric tools to clarify the nature of these relations. The institutional mission, perhaps the most important one, is to provide an integrative force in an era of scientific specialization and fragmentation. Personality psychology seeks to bring together the contributions of developmental, social, cognitive and biological psychology into an understanding of whole persons and the dimensions of difference that allow them to be psychologically distinguished from one another.

Personality psychology is extraordinarily active at present, perhaps more so than at any time in its history. The past decade has seen a dramatic upsurge in research activity, conference presentations, journal submissions, and student interest. For example, the *Journal of Research in Personality* (currently edited by the author of this review) has seen an increase in submissions every year since 1996. A particularly interesting trend is that many of these submissions come from psychologists who are not affiliated with formal programs in personality psychology, and may not even think of themselves as personality psychologists. A further indication of the vitality of the field is the founding of a new Association for Research in Personality (D Watson, personal communication).

Some current activity concerns perennial issues such as the status of the classic paradigms and controversies concerning appropriate units and levels of analysis. Old empirical issues such as the person-situation debate (Kenrick & Funder 1988) and even the response set controversy (Rorer 1965, Paulhus 1991) continue to simmer and generate an occasional new report. However, the most genuinely exciting activity in personality research consists of the efforts to generate new conceptual and empirical ties to other historically isolated parts of psychology. Each of these intersections is the site of important progress, and together they offer the prospect of personality psychology eventually fulfilling its institutional mission of being the place where the rest of psychology comes together.

STATUS OF THE CLASSIC PARADIGMS

Personality is unique in psychology by being historically based upon several different widely encompassing paradigms: psychoanalytic, trait, behaviorist, and humanistic. Each has sought to subsume not just all of personality, but all of psychology, as befits personality psychology's integrative mission. In recent years, all four of these paradigms have expanded their scope, two of them to the degree that they have spun off independent new paradigms.

Psychoanalytic

Amid much resistance, the psychoanalytic paradigm has begun to evolve beyond armchair speculation into a field of empirical research, as witnessed by a special issue of the *Journal of Personality* on defense mechanisms (Baumeister et al 1998, Cramer & Davidson 1998, Norem 1998), and a major review of recent, relevant research published in *Psychological Bulletin* (Westen 1998). Sigmund Freud's psychoanalytic theorizing is also beginning to receive some belated credit—deserved or not—for having anticipated the current parallel distributed processing models of cognition, which conceptualize behavior and consciousness as the result of an ongoing compromise among numerous independently operating mental subsystems (Rumelhart et al 1986). Finally, and least edifying, the personal life of Sigmund Freud, deceased these 60 years and more, continues to generate controversy (Crews 1998, Swales 1988).

Trait

The End of the Debate   The person-situation debate, concerning whether consistencies in individuals' behavior are pervasive or broad enough to be meaningfully described in terms of personality traits (Mischel 1968, Kenrick & Funder 1988), can at last be declared about 98% over. Two hard-won empirical recognitions have been particularly important in the resolution.

The first recognition is that the behavior of a sample of individuals observed in one situation correlates with their behavior in a second situation with a magnitude that routinely reaches $r = .40$ or greater (Funder & Colvin 1991). Even protagonists of the situationist side of the debate grant this figure (Nisbett 1980), though interpretations of its meaning still differ. Some writers calculate that this .40 reveals that only 16% of variance in behavior is accounted for by individual differences (Mischel 1968, Pervin 1994). In response, other writers have noted that (a) the figure refers only to the prediction of single behaviors and not aggregate trends (Epstein 1979, Hogan 1998), (b) the practice of squaring correlations to interpret their size is misleading (Ozer 1985), (c) a .40 correlation represents 70% accuracy in predicting a dichotomous criterion (Rosenthal & Rubin 1982), and (d) this correlation represents the approximate size of some of the most important situational effects in social psychology (Funder & Ozer 1983).

The second recognition, more slow to be widely appreciated, is that behavioral consistency and change are orthogonal phenomena (Funder & Colvin 1991). Findings that seemingly small alterations in an experimental situation can lead to large mean differences in behavior have been interpreted as implying that cross-situational consistency and the influence of personality on behavior are low (Mischel 1984). However, the magnitude of the mean difference in behavior between two situations has no implications (barring ceiling or floor effects) for the magnitude of the correlation that indexes the consistency of individual differences across them (Ozer 1986). Observations that children can wait twice as long for a preferred treat when a small change is made in the stimulus situation therefore are not in the least inconsistent with the common finding that a child who can wait longer than other children in one situation is probably able to do so in other situations as well (Funder & Harris 1986). The long-standing and controversy-generating dichotomy between the effect of the situation versus the effect of the person on behavior, therefore, is and always was a false dichotomy.

Even in the darkest days of the person-situation debate, personality trait constructs found an appreciative audience and useful application in industrial and organizational settings (Hogan et al 1996). Today, well-trained personality psychologists find themselves eminently employable in the private sector (M Schmitt, personal communication). In the academic realm, journals give the impression of a field newly unshackled, as trait constructs are used to understand outcomes such as violence, alcohol abuse, unsafe sex, dangerous driving (Krueger et al 2000), job performance (Ones et al 1993), management (Chatman et al 1999, Roberts & Hogan 2001), and marriage (Caughlin et al 2000).

The Big Five   The "big five" organization of personality trait constructs seems almost ubiquitous in the current literature, despite some persistent opposition (McAdams 1992; Block 1995, 2001). Extraversion, neuroticism, conscientiousness, agreeableness, and openness to experience (or culture) have been correlated with many other personality traits and some behavioral and social outcomes (McCrae & Costa 1999). Personality psychology has been long beset by a chaotic plethora of personality constructs that sometimes differ in label while measuring nearly the same thing, and sometimes have the same label while measuring very different things. The use of five broad traits as a common currency for personality psychology has been an important counterforce to this Tower of Babel. A previous *Annual Review of Psychology* chapter aptly characterized the big five as the "latitude and longitude" along which any new personality construct should be routinely mapped (Ozer & Reise 1994, p. 361; also Goldberg 1993).

For all the popularity and evident orienting usefulness of the big five, two issues remain problematic. The first concerns whether the five traits are independent of each other. They were derived in the first place using orthogonal rotations, so at the factor level the big five may be considered independent (Goldberg 1990). However, the personality scales used to measure them in practice typically are intercorrelated (e.g. Saucier 1994), although some measurement refinements (e.g. ipsatizing the data) make the intercorrelations smaller. When neuroticism is reflected (as it sometimes is) and renamed emotional stability, then all five of the basic factors are positively correlated, probably because all of them (in American culture) are socially desirable (Digman 1997).

A second and more important issue concerns whether the big five subsume all there is to say about personality. The answer is almost certainly no: Whereas almost any personality construct can be mapped onto the big five, you cannot derive every personality construct from the big five. For example, whereas an individual high on self-monitoring (Snyder 1987) might be described as high on extraversion, high on agreeableness, and low on conscientiousness, a description of someone in terms of these three elements would not capture the essence of self-monitoring. By the same token, an authoritarian personality (Adorno et al 1950) would be high on conscientiousness and low on agreeableness and openness to experience, but again much would be lost if we tried to reduce our understanding of authoritarianism to these three dimensions. There are also particular reasons to doubt that the big five are sufficient to account for personality disorders (Clark 1993). This lack of comprehensiveness becomes a problem when researchers, seduced by convenience and seeming consensus, act as if they can obtain a complete portrait of personality by grabbing five quick ratings.

Other Approaches to Individual Differences   Beyond the study of single personality traits and the big five, several other themes are becoming increasingly prominent within the study of individual differences in personality. One theme concerns the study of whole lives using narrative methods (McAdams 1999) and, increasingly often, longitudinal data (Caspi & Siva 1995, Kremen & Block 1998, Roberts & Helson 1997).

A second theme concerns an apparent mini-revival of the typological approach to personality. Despite the field's history of disrespect for the concept of personality types (Mendelsohn et al 1982), Caspi (1998) recently marshaled impressive evidence from several independent research programs converging on the conclusion that many individuals can be classified as well-adjusted, maladjusted overcontrolled, or maladjusted undercontrolled.

Finally, research on the biology of personality has exploded over the past few years. Two very different methodologies, behavioral genetics and physiology/anatomy, converge on the inescapable conclusion that stable individual differences in personality are to a large extent biologically based. This realization has led the trait approach to generate and spin off a new paradigm, the biological approach to personality (see below).

Behaviorist

The behaviorist approach to personality has undergone an interesting and even ironic evolution in recent years. Behaviorism began with the ambition of its founders—John Watson (1925) and BF Skinner (1938, 1971)—to excise from psychology all that is subjective and unobservable. This led to a research approach in which behavior was viewed exclusively as a function of environmentally imposed reinforcement contingencies. Unobservable mediators such as perceptions, memories, thoughts, and traits were banished from the analysis.

Although a small number of psychologists remained true to this creed, to others it became clear that this restriction was unsustainable. The behaviorist analysis omits important phenomena such as vicarious learning, and the "social learning" theorists pointed out that for a human—if not for a rat—it is one's beliefs about potential reinforcements, not the reinforcements themselves, that determine behavior

(Rotter 1954, 1982; Bandura 1977). Social learning theory itself evolved from Rotter's emphasis on expectancies concerning reinforcement probabilities to Bandura's emphasis on self-efficacy, which concerns beliefs about one's capacities. Bandura increasingly turned his attention to the "self system" (Bandura 1978), and eventually renamed his approach "social cognitive theory" (Bandura 1999, p. 185). At the same time, another social learning theorist, Walter Mischel, developed a "cognitive-affective personality system" (CAPS) influenced by current research on parallel distributed processing models of cognition (Mischel 1999).

The irony in this evolution is that a paradigm that began with the goal of banishing cognitive concepts from psychology evolved into an approach that places such concepts front and center. A further irony is that although individual difference constructs were anathema to the classic behaviorists, such constructs (e.g. optimism, pessimism, goal orientation, and the degree to which one is schematic) play an important role in the new cognitive approach to personality (see below).

Humanistic

The humanistic approach to personality has a proud history and is the route through which influences as diverse as European existentialism and Asian Zen Buddhism entered mainstream psychological thought through the writings of Carl Rogers (1951), Abraham Maslow (1987), George Kelly (1955), and others. The approach has fallen on hard times in recent years, however. Some of its subjectivist interpretation of personality had an indirect influence on the social-cognitive approach (Mischel was a student of Kelly), but the remaining self-proclaimed humanists fell to squabbling among themselves when they were not excoriating mainstream psychology for its narrow-minded, scientific values (e.g. Mair 1979). Joseph Rychlak (1988) made a vigorous attempt to revive a scientifically respectable brand of humanistic psychology, with a degree of success that is not evident so far.

Cross-Cultural Issues   A revival of humanistic concerns can be discerned, however, within the growing emphasis on cross-cultural issues in psychology. A hallmark of the humanistic perspective has been its insistence that the only way to understand another human being is phenomenologically, that is, by understanding his or her distinctive experience of reality (Rogers 1951, Kelly 1955). This concern comes to the fore when psychologists begin to consider the degree to which their analyses, developed for the most part within North American and European culture, might apply to members of different cultures with perhaps fundamentally different views of reality. These cultures might be from diverse geographic locations such as India, China, and Japan, or be subcultures such as inner city, ethnic, or immigrant populations.

This phenomenological, cross-cultural concern has led researchers in two directions. One direction is to conclude that precisely because our own cultural background is the unavoidable basis of everything we do and think, any analysis of another culture must be hopelessly distorted. In particular, psychological comparisons between cultures are impossible because there is no common set of terms on which different cultures can be meaningfully compared (Shweder & Sullivan 1993). The other direction is to try to distinguish between the psychological elements that are shared by all cultures (etics) and those that are distinctive to particular cultures (emics) (Triandis 1997). The big five have been offered as possible etics; a vigorous research effort is attempting to demonstrate their cross-cultural applicability (e.g. McCrae et al 1998, Yang et al 1999).

NEW PARADIGMS

In the past few years, three new basic paradigms for the study of personality have joined the four classics just considered. Two of these—the social-cognitive and biological approaches—grew out of the behaviorist and trait paradigms, respectively. The third—evolutionary psychology—deserves to be considered a new paradigm (for personality psychology) in its own right.

Social Cognitive

As befits a relatively new approach, the social-cognitive paradigm for the study of personality is difficult to define with any precision. The research forms a fuzzy set characterized by a focus on cognitive processes of the individual, especially perception and memory, a use of terms borrowed from cognitive psychology ("schema" being a particular favorite), and—in an apparent holdover from its behaviorist roots—an aversion to construing its individual difference constructs as generalizable beyond a narrow range of contexts.

Examples of Current Research   Much of the research that marches behind this banner—see the recent collection assembled by Cervone & Shoda (1999)—is interrelated in this loose sense. A few recent examples are described in this section.

Higgins (1999) continues to advance his theory of self-comparison that focuses on the way people compare who they believe they are with who they ought to be and who they hope to be. A perceived failure to be who you should be leads to anxiety, Higgins theorizes, whereas a failure to be who you wish to be leads to depression. The relative mix of these two discrepancies, within an individual, appears to affect emotional reactivity, memory retrieval, and even reaction time (Higgins 1999).

Baldwin (1999) described recent research on "relational schemas," which are self-images evoked by interactions with specific other people. These schemas affect information processing and behavior and are theorized to control the distinctive way in which an individual might act with different other people. A self-image as a "teacher" might be evoked by encountering someone associated with an other-schema for a "learner"; the self-schema of a "rebellious, put-upon teenager" might be evoked by the activation of the complementary schema of the "overbearing parent" (Baldwin 1999, p. 129; Markus & Kunda 1986). In principle, one could have as many relational self-schemas as there are different people with whom one interacts.

This fragmentation of the self-concept has generated some opposition. The social-cognitive theorist Albert Bandura writes that

> Social cognitive theory ... rejects the fractionation of human agency into multiple selves. A theory of personality cast in terms of multiple selves plunges one into deep philosophical waters. It requires a regress of selves to a presiding overseer self that selects and manages the collection of selves... Actually, there is only one self that can visualize different futures and select courses of action (Bandura 1999, p. 194).

A third and final example of current social-cognitive research on personality comes from the influential program by Carol Dweck (Dweck 1997, Grant & Dweck 1999). Dweck's elegant theory ties a person's fundamental worldview (incremental versus entity) to a goal orientation (learning versus performance) to a behavioral pattern in response to failure (mastery versus helplessness). The theory is backed by an impressive array of data and is directly applicable to real-life issues concerning people who fail to achieve to their potential.

Prospects for an Integrated Social-Cognitive Approach   A wide variety of research programs of the sort just mentioned could be cited, which indicates the current vitality of the social-cognitive paradigm. At the same time, the plethora of topics reveals a degree of disorganization and even immaturity. Much like the trait paradigm before the advent of the big five, the social-cognitive paradigm seems to comprise a vast range of diverse mini-topics pursued largely independently of each other, and no overall theme (beyond the sort of fuzzy set identification mentioned above) has yet tied them all together.

The two leading candidates for potential integrators of this diverse approach are two of its founders. Bandura's (2001) social cognitive theory of personality updates his well-known version of social learning theory with a particular emphasis on self-regulation. Bandura described the development of a self-system as the result of the interaction of the person and his or her environment, which allows self-control through self-reward and self-punishment—a possible basis of moral behavior. Mischel's CAPS theory integrates cognitive social learning variables (e.g. encoding processes, subjective stimulus values) into a model that includes previously neglected influences such as culture and society and even genetic background (see Mischel 1999, p. 49). The most notable aspect of CAPS is its reconceptualization of personality dispositions in terms of "behavioral signatures" or *if ... then* behavioral profiles, which for each individual specify what he or she will do in each situational context he or she encounters.

Much remains to be done before the CAPS approach will achieve its full potential. One unfulfilled task is the classification of situations that will allow *if ... then* profiles to become less complex than the phenomena they are intended to explain. When psychology achieves a well-accepted, thorough system for identifying classes of situations, *if... then* profiles might be economically used to predict what a person will do in certain kinds of situations. So far, however, the task of psychologically classifying situations has barely begun (see below).

Prospects for Integration with the Trait Approach   Another challenge for CAPS, and the whole social-cognitive approach to personality, is to identify areas of distinctiveness and overlap with the trait approach. It would be possible, for example, to view sets of *if... then* profiles as specific instantiations of personality traits: *If* a friendly person finds himself with a stranger, *then* he will walk up and introduce himself. *If* a dominant person joins a meeting, *then* she will quickly assume a leadership role, and so on. Rather than being merely old wine in new bottles (Johnson 1999), such constructs could prove to be a useful way to help trait constructs become more specific. For example, how does the *if... then* profile differ between, say, someone high on extraversion and someone high on agreeableness?

For its part, the assessment technology developed by the trait approach could provide a methodological contribution to cognitively oriented research. It can be astonishing to review major studies within the social-cognitive paradigm and to find, again and again, that all rests upon an independent variable that is an individual difference construct measured with a short self-report scale. Sometimes, the scale may be only three or four items long, change its content in large or small ways from one study to the next, and have unknown (and unexamined) reliability and factorial structure.

Moreover, investigators seldom administer other measures at the same time that would allow assessment of the degree to which social-cognitive constructs might be related and perhaps even identical to widely studied trait constructs. If this were done more often, the results might be surprising. In one study, scores on the Sociability and Responsibility scales of the California Psychological Inventory successfully predicted self-descriptive reaction time and other indicators of having a "self-schema" introduced by Markus (1977, Fuhrman & Funder 1995). This finding suggests that the constructs tapped by new measures of self-schemas and traditional personality assessment instruments such as the California Psychological Inventory may not be fundamentally different. A finding like this could be viewed cynically, but is more productively regarded as suggesting an opportunity for integrating the theoretical, empirical, and methodological achievements of the social-cognitive and trait paradigms into an exciting new hybrid for personality study.

It appears that such integration will not be easily achieved. A major obstacle is the almost dispositional reluctance of some investigators within the social-cognitive paradigm to grant the very existence of general patterns to behavior that their theories are well suited to explain. Perhaps as a holdover from the paradigm's behavioristic legacy, theorists such as Bandura choose to emphasize how "one and the same person" will behave "differently for different purposes, in different activity domains, and in different social contexts" (Bandura 1999, p. 194), rather than the cross-situational consistencies in behavior that a unitary self system could help account for. Similarly, Grant & Dweck (1999) emphasize how being an "incremental theorist" in a social domain has no implications for one's view of the academic domain (and vice versa). Also, none of these investigators has compared his or her cognitive individual difference construct with the big five or any other widely used trait measure.

The implicit resistance to integration with the trait approach is on occasion made more than amply explicit. Cervone & Shoda (1999) set social-cognitive theory in direct opposition to personality trait models, and argue that any integration of the two approaches is "conceptually problematic and empirically unnecessary" (Cervone 1999, p. 329). Although a "merger of trait and social-cognitive theories is appealing at first," they comment, "this merger is generally not accepted by social-cognitive theorists" (Cervone & Shoda 1999, p. 10).

On a more hopeful note, one of the original social-cognitive theorists, Walter Mischel, observes,

> Personality psychology has been committed since its beginnings to characterizing individuals in terms of their stable and distinctive qualities. Other personality theorists and researchers have focused instead on the processes that underlie these coherences and that influence how people function. These two goals ... have been pursued in two increasingly separated (and warring) subdisciplines with different agendas that seem to be in conflict with each other ... [but] both goals may be pursued in concert with no necessary conflict or incompatibility because ... dispositions and processing dynamics are two complementary facets of the same phenomena and the same unitary personality system (Mischel 1999, pp. 55–56).

Biological

Anatomy and Physiology   The search for associations between personality traits and the structure and function of the nervous system has recently produced some dramatic gains. Just a few years ago, it was possible to regard research in neuroanatomy and physiology as relevant to personality in principle, but as having very little to contribute in fact. Such an attitude is no longer tenable. Anatomical sites within the brain have been located that are important for personality traits; for example, the frontal lobes for foresight and anticipation (Damasio 1994) and the amygdala for aggression and certain types of emotionality (Buck 1999). Even more impressive have been the contributions of physiology that show how, for example, the hormone testosterone is important for sociability and positive affectivity as well as aggressiveness and sexuality (Dabbs et al 1997, 1998), and the neurotransmitter serotonin is important for affect regulation (Knutson et al 1998, Zuckerman 1998).

A potential danger now is that some observers seem ready to jump from these achievements to simplistic, one-cause → one-effect conclusions such as that testosterone causes aggression or depression is just a matter of insufficient serotonin. The truth is always more complex, in part because neuroanatomy and physiology are complicated, but equally because (a point sometimes forgotten) behavioral patterns such as aggression and depression are every bit as complicated, if not more so (Bandura 2001).

Behavioral Genetics   Another, very different, kind of biological investigation also has permanently changed personality psychology. Behavioral genetics has documented, without a shadow of a remaining doubt, that personality is to some degree genetically influenced: Identical twins reared apart have similar traits (Plomin et al 1990a). The *tabula rasa* view of personality as a blank slate at birth that is written upon by experience, for many years a basic assumption of theories of all stripes, is wrong.

In the aftermath of this stunning revelation, a few limitations of behavioral genetics research have become apparent. One limitation is that almost the entire field is based upon calculations of the similarities and differences among closer and more distant relatives in scores on self-report personality inventories. Behavior is rarely observed directly, and the field would have been more accurately named trait genetics—though it is interesting to speculate whether it would have achieved its current ascendancy under that label. A second limitation of the approach has been its sometime obsession with establishing the exact magnitude of heritability coefficients. As Turkheimer (1998) observed, once it is established that a trait has a nonzero heritability—and nearly every trait does—the psychologically interesting questions lie elsewhere than in making the heritability estimate more precise.

A third limitation is that the field sometimes seems in danger of making claims that go beyond the data (Maccoby 2000). The most widely advertised finding of behavioral genetics—beyond the ubiquitous influence of genetic factors itself—is that the shared family environment is unimportant for children's personality-related outcomes (Rowe 1997, Scarr 1992). Two children raised in the same family turn out to be little more similar to each other than if they had been raised in different families, according to standard behavioral genetic analyses, leading at least one writer (Harris 1995) to take things a step further and argue that the family itself is psychologically unimportant.

However, this conclusion is based on a complex analytic technique, and its data consist almost entirely of self-report questionnaires—when behavioral measures are used the shared family environment appears more important (Turkheimer 1998). It can also be observed that the families in behavioral genetics data bases are not as different from each other as families at large, leading the impact of the differences between families to be underestimated (Stoolmiller 1999). Recent studies of behavioral genetics are beginning to report important effects of shared environmental effects (e.g. Bussell et al 1999). Perhaps most importantly, any conclusion that the family does not matter flies in the face of decades of research in developmental psychology documenting effects of early experience on later life outcomes and even experimental studies showing that when parents change their child-rearing strategies the outcomes for their children change (Eisenberg et al 1999, Collins et al 2000). The calm confidence of some behavioral geneticists that their method trumps these considerations should perhaps be considered a limitation, rather than a virtue, of their approach.

The fourth and most significant limitation of behavioral genetics research also presents its biggest opportunity. The approach addresses distal rather than proximal causes of behavior—it jumps immediately from degree of genetic relatedness to similarity of behavioral outcome. This jump creates problems when substantial heritabilities are found for outcomes such as divorce (Jocklin et al 1996) and television watching (Plomin et al 1990b), seemingly inviting a search for the DNA code of the "divorce gene" or even the "Fox TV gene." In reference to the TV finding, Plomin et al (1990b) remarked a few years ago that "it is likely to be difficult to find specific mechanisms of genetic influence on television viewing because genetic mechanisms have not as yet been uncovered for any complex behavioral trait, including cognitive abilities and personality" (p. 376). The situation is not much different today (Turkheimer 1998).

The challenge for the next phase of behavioral genetics research is to turn its attention toward the development of process models that describe how a gene creates a neural structure that creates a disposition to respond that, in interaction with the environment, creates a personality trait that, in some cultural contexts, might make a person more likely to watch TV or even become divorced. Bem (1996) offered a speculative example of how such a process might lead to a heterosexual or homosexual orientation, and his theory provides a model of how a comprehensive psychological analysis can include genetic, cultural, environmental and cognitive processes. Many more firmly grounded efforts of this sort are needed in relation to many more outcomes.

Evolutionary

A third new paradigm also has biological roots. However, it is so different from the biological approaches just discussed that it is best considered separately. Neuroanatomic, physiological and genetic approaches to personality all focus on the biological substrate of individual differences in behavioral patterns. The evolutionary approach to personality, by contrast, focuses on the possibility that behavioral patterns common to all people—human nature itself—has a biological foundation that can be illuminated by considering the evolutionary history of the human species.

Evolutionary ideas became an important part of biology beginning with Darwin (1859). Whereas Darwin himself offered some theorizing about the roots of behavior, the modern field of evolutionary psychology can be said to have begun with the "sociobiology" of the entomologist Wilson (1975), and current major advocates include Buss (1999), Kenrick (2000), and Simpson and Gangestad (Simpson et al 1999). Their work shares the key idea that during the "environment of evolutionary adaptation" humans with certain behavioral propensities were particularly likely to survive and leave descendants. For example, humans who defended territory, nurtured children, and strove for domination were more likely to successfully reproduce than humans who did not do these things, with the result that their ultimate descendants—members of the present generation—generally have all of these behavioral tendencies.

Although no serious scientist doubts the theory of evolution, the evolutionary approach to psychology has been questioned on several grounds. One ground is that evolutionary theorists seem quick to assume that quite specific behavioral patterns—for example, the tendency of women to seek mates who have large amounts of money (Buss 1989), or of men to kill wives suspected of infidelity (Wilson & Daly 1996)—are directly determined by biological mechanisms. Yet no such mechanism that would allow genetic or physiological determination of human behavior to such a precise degree has ever been specifically identified. It might seem more plausible to posit that to the degree that behavioral patterns are biologically hard-wired, the wiring produces general capacities and propensities. Evolutionary theorists, in response, point to examples such as bird songs and spider web–spinning to show that specific behaviors can be built into an organism. Still, proximal biological or even psychological mechanisms in humans are almost totally missing from evolutionary theorizing. As one writer has observed,

> It would be refreshing to hear evolutionary psychologists directly
> acknowledge the importance of empirically evaluating whether those
> human social preferences posited to be adaptations are indeed genetically
> specified. Skeptical ... psychologists might be more receptive to evolutionary
> accounts ... if these critical and controversial points were put forth as
> hypotheses that need to be tested rather than as forgone conclusions.
> (Berry 2000, p. 325)

A second source of controversy—perhaps intentionally stirred—is the specific focus of many current theorists on sexual behavior. A large proportion of both theorizing and empirical research within evolutionary personality psychology has focused on such topics as sexual attraction, sexual jealousy, mating strategies, rape, and even uxoricide (spousal murder).

On the one hand, reproduction is a natural place for evolutionary theorizing to focus because of the obvious relevance to the basic mechanism of evolution, and this focus has yielded the secondary gain of drawing large amounts of attention, including from the popular press, on evolutionary theorizing. On the other hand, the traditional division of labor, resources, and power between the sexes is a fundamental aspect of many cultures, leaving many if not most of the phenomena addressed by evolutionary theorists susceptible to cultural explanation (Eagly & Wood 1999).

Perhaps just as consequentially, some of the evolutionary theorizing concerning sexuality has aroused the ire of feminists and others who believe it seeks to justify older men's obsessions with younger women, young women's obsessions with older men's money, the unequal distribution of material resources and power between the sexes, and even rape. Readers who find distasteful accounts of how rape is a naturally evolved reproductive strategy that is adaptive for males who can obtain mates no other way (Thornhill & Palmer 2000) are likely to develop, perhaps unfairly, a negative view of evolutionary theorizing in general. To the degree that evolutionary psychology begins to balance its emphasis across other behavioral patterns with adaptive implications, these controversies will become less of a distraction, and the approach may be better evaluated on its scientific merits rather than on political grounds.

The third source of difficulty for evolutionary psychology is a by-product of its greatest strength. Its greatest strength is its ability to account for a wide range of behaviors, from preferences for salty foods to strivings to achieve dominance, that otherwise would have to be accepted as having become part of human nature for no particular reason. Pinker's (1997) ambitious survey vividly demonstrates how evolutionary theorizing can organize a broad sweep of behavioral phenomena. This very breadth, however, makes the theory difficult to test in any convincing way. The ability of evolutionary psychology to explain nearly everything is not an absolute virtue.

BASIC RESEARCH ISSUES

Imbalance in the Personality Triad

The empirical study of personality properly encompasses three elements: the person, the situation, and behavior. Ideally, knowledge about any two of these should lead to an understanding of the third. If we know everything about a person, and everything about his or her situation, we should be able to predict what he or she will do. By the same token, a knowledge of a person and his or her behavior should lead us to understand the situation, and a knowledge of a situation and a behavior should lead us to understand the person.

The traditional psychology of personality traits has used descriptions of persons to predict their behavior in implicitly specified classes of situations (e.g. sociability predicts behavior only in social situations) (Johnson 1997). In a parallel manner, Bem & Funder (1978) conceptualized situations in terms of "template-behavior pairs" that described how certain kinds of people would be predicted to behave in them. More recently, Mischel's (1999) CAPS theory of personality described *if... then* profiles in which persons are described in terms of how they behave in specified situations.

Despite these starts, the personality triad is unbalanced because two out of three of its elements have received only a small amount of attention in theory and research. The person element is well studied and almost all personality theory and assessment focuses on the variables that characterize a person's psychology so as to make him or her different from other people. Particular effort has gone into attempts to discern which of these variables are the most critical, such as investigations of the big five, personality typologies, and *if... then* profiles. These attempts to identify the fundamental aspects of persons may not have achieved consensus, but no one can argue that the issue has been ignored.

The case is very different for situations and behaviors. For all the arguments that the situation is all-important (Ross & Nisbett 1991), little is empirically known or even theorized about how situations influence behavior, or what the basic kinds of situations are (or, alternatively, what variables are useful for comparing one situation with another). Evidence for the importance of situations is typically obtained by subtraction; that is, if a personality variable is found to correlate with a behavior with an $r = .40$, the remaining 84% of the variance is assigned to the situation by default. Yet this is clearly an illegitimate practice. It would be just as plausible to assign the remaining variance to other personality variables that were not measured (Ahadi & Diener 1989) as it is to assign it to situational variables that were also not measured. Moreover, the assigning of behavioral variance to a situation by subtraction provides no information about how the situation's influence came about or what aspects of the situation were crucial. In the words of one writer, "...situations turn out to be 'powerful' in the same sense as Scud missiles [the erratic weapons used by Iraq during the Persian Gulf war] are powerful: They may have huge effects, or no effects, and such effects may occur virtually anywhere, all over the map" (Goldberg 1992, p. 90).

A conceptualization of the key variables for characterizing the psychologically effective aspects of situations is sorely needed, as is a method for assessing these variables. A few starts towards this goal have been offered over the years (Bem & Funder 1978, Moos 1973, Frederiksen 1972, Van Mechelen & De Raad 1999), but the enterprise can still be considered only barely begun.

If little is known about situations, even less is known about behaviors. Behaviorism, the approach that judging by its label one might think would address this issue, historically has treated behaviors as functionally interchangeable. A bar press is much the same as a linguistic utterance from the perspective of behavioral theory (Skinner 1957). Other research programs have zeroed in on particular behaviors seen as intrinsically important (e.g. criminal behavior, obedience, altruism) or on behaviors that serve as convenient dependent variables for investigations of theoretical interest (e.g. reaction times, written responses on attitude questionnaires). Techniques for measuring behavior typically are similarly ad hoc.

At a broader level, only the most tentative efforts can be reported. Bakeman & Gottman (1997) provided general guidelines for the coding of observed behaviors at a low and specific level of analysis. Buss & Craik (1983) offered an "act frequency" approach that raised a possibility of someday reconceptualizing traits in terms of frequencies of classes of relevant behaviors. Funder and colleagues (Funder et al 2000) presented a "behavioral Q-sort" that provides 64 general descriptors to characterize an individual's behavior in a particular observed context. Funder & Colvin (1991) demonstrated properties of these behaviors that differentiated the ones that manifest more and less consistency. However, none of these efforts achieved the goal of identifying the fundamentally important variables for the classification of behavior. Indeed, very little progress has even been made towards the task of counting behaviors. The reader might verify the difficulty of the latter issue by asking himself or herself: How many behaviors have you performed so far today?

Need for Descriptive Data

The typical research strategy in personality (as well as social) psychology is based upon explicit or implicit hypothesis testing, and data are gathered for the purpose of supporting or disconfirming a theoretical idea. This is a time-honored and proven strategy for scientific progress, but some commentators have begun to note its downside (Greenwald 1999, Hogan 1998). When data are gathered only for the purpose of hypothesis testing, basic descriptive data rarely enter the literature.

For personality psychology, this omission has become critical, as after three-quarters of a century of research on traits the catalog of basic facts concerning the relationships between personality and behavior remains thin. If, for example, one were to go to the literature and look for a list of contextualized behaviors that had been shown to be robustly associated with, say, extraversion, one would find surprisingly little. There would be no shortage of hypotheses tested concerning extraversion (e.g. do extraverts respond less intensely than introverts to lemon juice on the tongue), and an outright surplus of data concerning the correlations among extraversion questionnaires and other similar measures, but as for what extraverts have been observed to actually do, beyond some indication that they speak loudly (Scherer 1978), little would be found. Even less information is available about the behavioral correlates of other personality traits.

When Mischel (1968) challenged trait psychology for concrete examples of where a trait measure directly predicted behavior, or where one behavior predicted another, the trait psychologists were caught flat-footed. They had gathered very little such data, and both sides returned repeatedly (even embarrassingly often) to a summer camp study published by Hartshorne & May in 1928. Some new behavioral data relevant to personality have been reported in the intervening years (e.g. Block & Block 1980, Mischel & Peake 1982, Funder & Colvin 1991), but less than one might expect, given their fundamental importance.

The reasons for this lack are twofold. First, relative to other sciences, psychology devalues descriptive data (Greenwald 1999). A researcher willing to incur the effort to map out the behaviors that are associated with one or more important personality traits would find grant reviewers and journal editors typically unsympathetic. The counter-intuitive hypothesis will almost always win out over basic data gathering. Second, as mentioned above, even to the degree that the institutional obstacles could be overcome, a would-be data gatherer might be daunted by the lack of consensus concerning what behaviors to measure and which situational contexts to measure them in.

These reasons for neglect are of course not justifications. Personality psychology will make an important step towards fulfilling its potential when it begins to assemble a comprehensive inventory of facts concerning the associations between personality and behavior, directly observed in a wide range of situations.

Need for a Broader Range of Data

As the preceding discussion implies, the facts important to personality psychology go beyond those that can be gathered by questionnaires. The construction and intercorrelation of self-report measures of personality is an economical and fruitful research method utilized both by trait psychologists and their social-cognitive brethren (e.g. Cervone & Shoda 1999). The method is limited, however, because people are imperfectly trustworthy when it comes to describing themselves, because correlations among questionnaires can reflect method variance (and even item overlap) as much as substantive relationships, and most fundamentally, because questionnaire responses are not what psychologists wish ultimately to know about. Psychologists want and need to know what people actually do, think, and feel in the various contexts of their lives.

Several related schemes for classifying data beyond questionnaires have been offered (Block & Block 1980, Cattell 1950, Funder 2001, Moffitt 1991). The other types include life outcome data (such as health outcomes, job performance, criminal record), peers' reports (reputation), interviews, diary and beeper reports of daily experience, and—most difficult of all—direct behavioral observation (Funder et al 2000). All of these other kinds of data are much more difficult and expensive to gather than questionnaire data, which probably helps to explain why they are employed relatively rarely. Personality psychology will become a more relevant and firmly rooted discipline to the extent that, in coming years, this imbalance begins to be remedied.

INSTITUTIONAL ISSUES

Programs and Training

Someday a comprehensive history will be written of the permanent damage to the infrastructure of personality psychology wreaked by the person-situation debate of the 1970s and 1980s. Even as enthusiasm for the substance of personality research has revived, the institutional consequences continue. Indeed, one reason for the trend, noted above, for so much personality research being done by investigators not affiliated with formal programs in personality may be that there are so few formal programs to be affiliated with. The graduate programs in personality psychology that were shrunken beyond recognition or even abolished during the 1970s and 1980s have not been revived.

As already noted, interest in the substance of personality psychology continues unabated and may even be increasing, but two side effects of the field's institutional depletion present causes for concern. First, the intellectual continuity of personality psychology is threatened as few graduate students learn about the field in an environment where the field is well understood or, sometimes, even respected. Second, some of the hard-won, basic methodological knowledge of personality psychology is not being transmitted to new generations (Aiken et al 1990). Consider the surprising number of studies within the social-cognitive approach that utilize brief self-report scales of unknown and unexamined reliability and construct validity. This widespread casual attitude toward measurement is not malicious; very likely, the investigators simply never learned the basic technology of personality assessment because they were never taught how it was relevant.

Ironically, at the same time that basic psychometric training is becoming rare, psychometric technology continues to develop apace into daunting techniques that make full use of the increased availability of computer power. These techniques, however, do not always shed unique new light on the substantive phenomena to which they are applied (Wilkinson and the Task Force on Statistical Inference, 1999). The advance of knowledge in the coming decades will be enhanced to the extent that some attention can be redirected from esoteric new technologies back to basic psychometric instruction. Even more so, psychological research will be improved to the degree that faculty in all its subdisciplines become aware that basic training in psychometrics—the essentials of measurement, reliability, and validity—is a crucial part of the preparation of any PhD in psychology.

Relations with Other Subfields

Personality psychology has close conceptual ties to three other subfields.

Clinical Psychology   First, it has a long historical, as well as conceptual, association with clinical psychology; many of the classic personality theorists were and some theorists still are clinical practitioners. A basic issue in this relationship concerns the degree to which psychopathological syndromes are qualitatively distinct phenomena, or extremes on dimensions of normal personality (Krueger et al 2001). The continuity position seems to be winning (Clark et al 1997, Frances 1993).

A particularly persuasive demonstration comes from analyses of a longitudinal sample in New Zealand, which found a close relationship between several aspects of personality and the development of psychopathologies (Krueger et al 2001). In another study, variations in well-being measured by a tool for assessment of clinical depression had important implications for behavior and well-being even in a population where no one was clinically depressed (Furr & Funder 1998). Another piece of evidence comes from a recent study that found the antidepressant paroxetine [related to fluoxetine (Prozac)] reduced levels of negative affect in nondepressed persons who did not have a history of mental disorder either in themselves or their first-degree relatives (Knutson et al 1998). This finding suggests that some treatments aimed at specific disorders such as depression might exert their influence by affecting underlying personality variables (Krueger et al 2001), which may in turn help explain why "antidepressants" like paraoxetine and fluoxetine are helpful in the treatment of so many putatively different affective and anxiety disorders (Dunner 1998). They may affect a trait or traits that underlie a wide range of psychopathology.

Developmental Psychology   Developmental psychology is the second related subfield. The personality of preverbal children is called temperament, but otherwise the difference between temperament and personality is slight (Caspi & Siva 1995). To the extent that research in developmental and personality psychology can become integrated, the benefits could be substantial for both sides. It would be useful to better understand how adult personality is related to its temperamental precursors (Clark & Watson 1999, Rothbart et al 2000). Also, personality psychology might do well to learn some of developmental psychology's ingenious methods for assessing personality in small persons who will not fill out trait questionnaires.

Social Psychology   Relations with a third related subfield, social psychology, historically have been problematic. Important topics such as the accuracy of personality judgment require research that draws upon both fields (e.g. Funder 1999). Yet many social psychologists still seem to think that an important part of their mission is to teach the world that only situations, and not personality, have an important effect on behavior (Conner 2000). Moreover, it appears as if part of the professional identity of some social psychologists is tied up in an insistence on not using trait measures or any part of conventional psychometric technology, even when their research topics (e.g. individual differences in emotion, self-evaluation, or goal orientation) fall squarely in the personality domain.

There is reason to expect that this attitudinal obstacle to integrating the two fields will be overcome as new generations of psychologists take charge, leaving the debates of their forebears in the unlamented past. In the long run, a hybrid field of personality and social psychology may be in the offing. The advantages and disadvantages of such an outcome depend upon what is gained and lost by each side in the merger. Will schemas become recognized as traits, or will traits be reconceptualized as schemas? Will conventional psychometrics be forgotten by the merged field, only to have to be reinvented by a subsequent generation? Will social psychologists move away from their ingenious simulated microcosms of social situations and creative choices for behavioral dependent variables, towards the seductively convenient administration of questionnaires? Or will both social and personality psychologists add valuable methodological tools to their repertoire, and finally appreciate that concepts from both fields can be fruitfully applied to questions concerning persons, situations, and behaviors?

CONCLUSION

It is not really possible to doubt that personality psychology has an active and productive future. It may revive as an independent field with a separate identity, institutional memory, and research and educational infrastructure, or it may be absorbed into a hybrid of social psychology, or it may continue on in some other form that cannot presently be anticipated. Under whatever disciplinary flag, however, someone will always ask how individuals are different from each other, how behavior changes, how people perceive, think, and plan, how people experience reality, and even what might be going on in the regions of the mind usually hidden from view (Funder 1998). The basic questions of personality psychology will simply not go away.

ACKNOWLEDGMENTS

Preparation of this chapter was aided by grant R01-MH42427 from the National Institute of Mental Health. Valuable advice was provided by LA Clark, LR Goldberg, R Hogan, and DJ Ozer, none of whom are responsible for the chapter's errors and omissions.

Visit the Annual Reviews home page at www.AnnualReviews.org

LITERATURE CITED

Adorno TW, Frenkel-Brunswik E, Levinson D, Sanford N. 1950. *The Authoritarian Personality.* New York: Harper

Ahadi S, Diener E. 1989. Multiple determinants and effect size. *J. Pers. Soc. Psychol.* 56:398–406

Aiken LS, West SG, Sechrest L, Reno RR. 1990. Graduate training in statistics, methodology and measurement in psychology: a survey of PhD programs in North America. *Am. Psychol.* 45:721–34

Bakeman R, Gottman JM. 1997. *Observing Interaction: An Introduction to Sequential Analysis.* New York: Cambridge Univ. Press. 2nd ed.

Baldwin MW. 1999. Relational schemas: research into social-cognitive aspects of interpersonal experience. See Cervone & Shoda 1999, pp. 127–54

Bandura A. 1977. *Social Learning Theory.* Englewood Cliffs, NJ: Prentice-Hall

Bandura A. 1978. The self system in reciprocal determinism. *Am. Psychol.* 33:344–58

Bandura A. 1999. Social cognitive theory of personality. See Cervone & Shoda 1999, pp. 185–241

Bandura A. 2001. Social cognitive theory: an agentic perspective. *Annu. Rev. Psychol.* 52:1–26

Baumeister RF, Dale K, Sommer KL. 1998. Freudian defense mechanisms and empirical findings in modern social psychology: reaction formation, projection, displacement, undoing, isolation, sublimation, and denial. *J. Pers.* 66:1081–124

Bem DJ. 1996. Exotic becomes erotic: a developmental theory of sexual orientiation. *Psychol. Rev.* 103:320–35

Bem DJ, Funder DC. 1978. Predicting more of the people more of the time: assessing the personality of situations. *Psychol. Rev.* 85:485–501

Berry DS. 2000. Attractiveness, attraction, and sexual selection: evolutionary perspectives on the form and function of physical attractiveness. *Adv. Exp. Soc. Psychol.* 32:273–342

Block J. 1995. A contrarian view of the five-factor approach to personality description. *Psychol. Bull.* 117:187–215

Block J. 2001. Millenial contrarianism: The five factor approach to personality description five years later. *J. Res. Pers.* In press

Block JH, Block J. 1980. The role of ego-control and ego-resiliency in the organization of behavior. In *Development of Cognition, Affect and Social Relations: The Minnesota Symposia on Child Psychology*, ed. WA Collins, 13:40–101. Hillsdale, NJ: Erlbaum

Buck R. 1999. The biological affects: a typology. *Psychol. Rev.* 106:301–36

Buss DM. 1989. Sex differences in human mate preferences: evolutionary hypotheses tested in 37 cultures. *Behav. Brain. Sci.* 12:1–49

Buss DM. 1999. *Evolutionary Psychology: The New Science of the Mind*. Boston: Allyn & Bacon

Buss DM, Craik KH. 1983. The act frequency approach to personality. *Psychol. Rev.* 90:105–26

Bussell DA, Neiderhiser JM, Pike A, Plomin R, Simmens S, et al. 1999. Adolescents' relationships to siblings and mothers: a multivariate genetic analysis. *Dev. Psychol.* 35:1248–59

Caspi A. 1998. Personality development across the life course. In *Handbook of Child Psychology*, ed. N Eisenberg, pp. 311–88. New York: Wiley

Caspi A, Siva PA. 1995. Temperamental qualities at age 3 predict personality traits in young adulthood: longitudinal evidence from a birth cohort. *Child Dev.* 66:486–98

Cattell RB. 1950. *Personality: A Systematic, Theoretical and Factual Study*. New York: McGraw-Hill

Caughlin JP, Huston TL, Houts RM. 2000. How does personality matter in marriage? Anxiety, interpersonal negativity and marital satisfaction. *J. Pers. Soc. Psychol.* 78:326–36

Cervone D. 1999. Bottom-up explanation in personality psychology: the case of cross-situational coherence. See Cervone & Shoda 1999, pp. 303–41

Cervone D, Shoda Y, eds. 1999. *The Coherence of Personality: Social-Cognitive Bases of Consistency, Variability, and Organization*. New York: Guilford

Chatman JA, Caldwell DF, O'Reilly CA. 1999. Managerial personality and performance: a semi-idiographic approach. *J. Res. Pers.* 33:514–45

Clark LA. 1993. Personality disorder diagnosis: limitations of the five-factor model. *Psychol. Inq.* 4:100–4

Clark LA, Livesley WJ, Morey L. 1997. Personality disorder assessment: the challenge of construct validity. *J. Pers. Disord.* 11:205–31

Clark LA, Watson D. 1999. Temperament: a new paradigm for trait psychology. See Pervin & John 1999, pp. 399–423

Collins WA, Maccoby EE, Steinberg L, Hetherington EM, Bornstein MH. 2000. Contemporary research on parenting: the case for nature and nurture. *Am. Psychol.* 55:218–32

Conner A. 2000. The 'shocking' truth about classic experiments in social psychology. *APS Observ.* 13:1–35

Cramer P, Davidson K, eds. 1998. Defense mechanisms in contemporary personality research (special issue). *J. Pers.* 66:879–1157

Crews FC, ed. 1998. *Unauthorized Freud: Doubters Confront a Legend*. New York: Viking Penguin

Dabbs JM Jr, Alford EC, Fielden JA. 1998. Trial lawyers and testosterone: blue-collar talent in a white-collar world. *J. Appl. Psychol.* 28:84–94

Dabbs JM Jr, Strong R, Milun R. 1997. Exploring the mind of testosterone: a beeper study. *J. Res. Pers.* 31:577–87

Damasio AR. 1994. *Descartes' Error: Emotion, Reason, and the Human Brain*. New York: Avon

Digman JM. 1997. Higher-order factors of the Big Five. *J. Pers. Soc. Psychol.* 73:1246–56

Dunner DL. 1998. The issue of comorbidity in the treament of panic. *Int. Clin. Psychopharmacol.* 13:S19–24

Dwek CS. 1997. Capturing the dynamic nature of personality. *J. Res. Pers.* 30:348–62

Eagly AH, Wood W. 1999. The origins of sex differences in human behavior: evolved dispositions versus social roles. *Am. Psychol.* 54:408–23

Eisenberg N, Spinrad TL, Cumberland A. 1999.

The socialization of emotion: reply to commentaries. *Psychol. Inq.* 9:317–33

Epstein S. 1979. The stability of behavior: I. On predicting most of the people much of the time. *J. Pers. Soc. Psychol.* 37:1097–126

Frances A. 1993. Dimensional diagnosis of personality—not whether, but when and which. *Psychol. Inq.* 4:110–11

Frederiksen N. 1972. Toward a taxonomy of situations. *Am. Psychol.* 27:114–23

Fuhrman RW, Funder DC. 1995. Convergence between self and peer in the response-time processing of trait-relevant information. *J. Pers. Soc. Psychol.* 69:961–74

Funder DC. 1998. Why does personality psychology exist? *Psychol. Inq.* 9:150–52

Funder DC. 1999. *Personality Judgment: A Realistic Approach to Person Perception.* San Diego: Academic

Funder DC. 2001. *The Personality Puzzle.* New York: Norton. 2nd ed.

Funder DC, Colvin CR. 1991. Explorations in behavioral consistency: properties of persons, situations, and behaviors. *J. Pers. Soc. Psychol.* 60:773–94

Funder DC, Furr RM, Colvin CR. 2000. The Riverside Behavioral Q-sort: a tool for the description of social behavior. *J. Pers.* 68:450–89

Funder DC, Harris MJ. 1986. Experimental effects and person effects in delay of gratification. *Am. Psychol.* 41:476–77

Funder DC, Ozer DJ. 1983. Behavior as a function of the situation. *J. Pers. Soc. Psychol.* 44:107–12

Furr RM, Funder DC. 1998. A multimodal analysis of personal negativity. *J. Pers. Soc. Psychol.* 74:1580–91

Goldberg LR. 1990. An alternative "description of personality": the Big-Five factor structure. *J. Pers. Soc. Psychol.* 59:1216–29

Goldberg LR. 1992. The social psychology of personality. *Psychol. Inq.* 3:89–94

Goldberg LR. 1993. The structure of phenotypic personality traits. *Am. Psychol.* 48:26–34

Grant H, Dwek CS. 1999. A goal analysis of personality and personality coherence. See Cervone & Shoda 1999, pp. 345–71

Greenwald AG. 1999. *Avoiding wasted effort in illusory competition among theories.* Presented at Annu. Meet. Soc. Exp. Soc. Psychol., St. Louis

Harris JR. 1995. Where is the child's environment? A group socialization theory of development. *Psychol. Rev.* 102:458–89

Hartshorne H, May A. 1928. *Studies in the Nature of Character.* Vol. 1. *Studies in Deceit.* New York: Macmillan

Higgins ET. 1999. Persons and situations: unique explanatory principles or variability in general principles? See Cervone & Shoda 1999, pp. 61–93

Hogan R, Johnson JA, Briggs S, eds. 1997. *Handbook of Personality Psychology.* San Diego, CA: Academic

Hogan R. 1998. Reinventing personality. *J. Soc. Clin. Psychol.* 17:1–10

Hogan R, Hogan J, Roberts BW. 1996. Personality measurement and employment decisions: questions and answers. *Am. Psychol.* 51:469–77

Jocklin V, McGue M, Lykken DT. 1996. Personality and divorce: a genetic analysis. *J. Pers. Soc. Psychol.* 71:288–99

Johnson JA. 1997. Units of analysis for description and explanation in psychology. See Hogan et al 1997, pp. 73–93

Johnson JA. 1999. Persons in situations: distinguishing new wine from old wine in new bottles. *Eur. J. Pers. Psychol.* 13:443–54

Kelly GA. 1955. *The Psychology of Personal Contructs.* New York: Norton

Kenrick DT. 2000. Evolutionary psychology, cognitive science, and dynamical systems: building an integrative paradigm. *Curr. Dir. Psychol. Sci.* In press

Kenrick DT, Funder DC. 1988. Profiting from controversy: lessons from the person-situation debate. *Am. Psychol.* 43:23–34

Knutson B, Wolkowitz OM, Cole SW, Chan T, Moore EA, et al. 1998. Selective alteration of personality and social behavior by serotonergic intervention. *Am. J. Psychiatry* 155:373–79

Kremen AM, Block J. 1998. The roots of ego-control in young adulthood: links with parenting in early childhood. *J. Pers. Soc. Psychol.* 75:1062–75

Krueger RF, Caspi A, Moffitt TE. 2001. Epidemiological personality: the unifying role of personality in population-based research on problem behaviors. *J. Pers.* In press

Maccoby E. 2000. Parenting and its effects on children: on reading and misreading behavioral genetics. *Annu. Rev. Psychol.* 51:1–27

Mair M. 1979. The person venture. In *Constructs of Personality and Individuality*, ed. P Stringer, D Bannister, pp. 35–48. London: Academic

Markus H. 1977. Self-schemata and processing information about the self. *J. Pers. Soc. Psychol.* 35:63–78

Markus H, Kunda Z. 1986. Stability and malleability of the self-concept. *J. Pers. Soc. Psychol.* 51:858–66

Maslow AH. 1987. *Motivation and Personality.* New York: Harper. 3rd ed.

McAdams DP. 1992. The five factor model of personality: a critical appraisal. *J. Pers.* 60:329–61

McAdams DP. 1999. Personal narratives and the life story. See Pervin & John 1999, pp. 478–500

McCrae RR, Costa PT Jr. 1999. A five-factor theory of personality. See Pervin & John 1999, pp. 139–53

McCrae RR, Costa PT Jr, Del Pilar GH, Rolland JP, Parker WD. 1998. Cross-cultural assessment of the five-factor model: the Revised NEO Personality Inventory. *J. Cross-Cult. Psychol.* 29:171–88

Mendelsohn GA, Weiss DS, Feimer NR. 1982. Conceptual and empirical analysis of the typological implications of patterns of socialization and femininity. *J. Pers. Soc. Psychol.* 42:1157–70

Mischel W. 1968. *Personality and Assessment.* New York: Wiley

Mischel W. 1984. Convergences and challenges in the search for consistency. *Am. Psychol.* 39:351–64

Mischel W. 1999. Personality coherence and dispositions in a cognitive-affective personality system (CAPS) approach. See Cervone & Shoda 1999, pp. 37–60

Mischel W, Peake PK. 1982. Beyond déjà vu in the search for cross-situational consistency. *Psychol. Rev.* 89:730–55

Moffitt TE. 1991. *An Approach to Organizing the Task of Selecting Measures for Longitudinal Research.* Tech. Rep., Univ. Wisconsin, Madison

Moos RH. 1973. Conceptualizations of human environments. *Am. Psychol.* 28:652–65

Nisbett RE. 1980. The trait construct in lay and professional psychology. In *Retrospections on Social Psychology*, ed. L Festinger, pp. 109–30. New York: Oxford Univ. Press

Norem JK. 1998. Why should we lower our defenses about defense mechanisms? *J. Pers.* 66:895–917

Ones DS, Viswesvaran C, Schmidt FL. 1993. Comprehensive meta-analysis of integrity test validities: findings and implications for personnel selection and theories of job performance. *J. Appl. Psychol.* 78:679–703

Ozer DJ. 1985. Correlation and the coefficient of determination. *Psychol. Bull.* 97:307–15

Ozer DJ. 1986. *Consistency in Personality: A Methodological Framework.* Berlin/New York: Springer-Verlag

Ozer DJ, Reise SP. 1994. Personality assessment. *Annu. Rev. Psychol.* 45:357–88

Paulhus DL. 1991. Measurement and control of response bias. In *Measures of Personality and Social Psychological Attitudes*, ed. JP Robinson, PR Shaver, pp. 17–59. San Diego, CA: Academic

Pervin LA, John OP, eds. 1999. *Handbook of Personality: Theory and Research.* New York: Guilford. 2nd ed.

Pervin LA. 1994. A critical analysis of current trait theory. *Psychol. Inq.* 5:103–13

Pinker S. 1997. *How the Mind Works.* New York: Norton

Plomin R, Chipuer HM, Loehlin JC. 1990a. Behavioral genetics and personality. In *Handbook of Personality: Theory and Research*, ed. L. Pervin, pp. 225–243. New York: Guilford

Plomin R, Corley R, DeFries JC, Fulker DW. 1990b. Individual differences in television-viewing in early childhood: Nature as well as nurture. *Psychol. Sci.* 1:371–77

Roberts BW, Helson R. 1997. Changes in culture, changes in personality: the influence of individualism in a longitudinal study of women. *J. Pers. Soc. Psychol.* 72:641–51

Roberts BW, Hogan R. 2001. *Applied Personality Psychology: The Intersection of Personality and I/O Psychology*. Washington, DC: Am. Psychol. Assoc.

Rogers CR. 1951. *Client-Centered Therapy: Its Current Practice, Implications, and Theory*. Boston: Houghton-Mifflin

Rorer LG. 1965. The great response-style myth. *Psychol. Bull.* 129–56

Rosenthal R, Rubin DB. 1982. A simple, general purpose display of magnitude of experimental effect. *J. Educ. Psychol.* 74:166–69

Ross L, Nisbett RE. 1991. *The Person and the Situation: Perspectives of Social Psychology*. New York: McGraw-Hill

Rothbart MK, Ahadi SA, Evans DE. 2000. Temperament and personality: origins and outcomes. *J. Pers. Soc. Psychol.* 78:122–35

Rotter JB. 1954. *Social Learning and Clinical Psychology*. Englewood Cliffs, NJ: Prentice-Hall

Rotter JB. 1982. *The Development and Applications of Social Learning Theory: Selected Papers*. New York: Praeger

Rowe DC. 1997. Genetics, temperament and personality. See Hogan et al 1997, pp. 367–86

Rumelhart DE, McClelland JL, PDP Research Group, eds. 1986. *Parallel Distributed Processing: Explorations in the Microstructure of Cognition*. Vol. 1. *Foundations*. Cambridge, MA: MIT Press

Rychlak JF. 1988. *The Psychology of Rigorous Humanism*. New York: New York Univ. Press. 2nd ed.

Saucier G. 1994. Mini-markers: a brief version of Goldberg's unipolar Big-Five markers. *J. Pers. Assess.* 63:506–16

Scarr S. 1992. Developmental theories for the 1990s: development and individual differences. *Child Dev.* 63:1–19

Scherer KR, Klaus R. 1978. Personality inference from voice quality: the loud voice of extroversion. *Eur. J. Soc. Psychol.* 8:467–87

Shweder RA, Sullivan MA. 1993. Cultural psychology: Who needs it? *Annu. Rev. Psychol.* 44:497–523

Simpson JA, Gangestad SW, Christensen P, Niels P, Leck K. 1999. Fluctuating asymmetry, sociosexuality, and intrasexual competitive tactics. *J. Pers. Soc. Psychol.* 76:159–72

Skinner BF. 1938. *The Behavior of Organisms: An Experimental Analysis*. New York: Macmillan

Skinner BF. 1971. *Beyond Freedom and Dignity*. New York: Knopf

Skinner BF. 1957. *Verbal Behavior*. New York: Appleton-Century-Crofts

Snyder M. 1987. *Public Appearances, Private Realities: The Psychology of Self-Monitoring*. New York: Freeman

Stoolmiller M. 1999. Implications of the restricted range of family environments for estimates of heritability and nonshared environment in behavior-genetic adoption studies. *Psychol. Bull.* 125:392–409

Swales PJ. 1988. Freud, Katharina and the first "wild analysis." In *Freud: Appraisals and Reappraisals*, ed. PE Stepansky, pp. 80–164. Hillsdale, NJ: Erlbaum

Thornhill R, Palmer C. 2000. *A Natural History of Rape: Biological Bases of Sexual Coercion*. Cambridge, MA: MIT Press

Triandis HC. 1997. Cross-cultural perspectives on personality. See Hogan et al 1997, pp. 440–64

Turkheimer E. 1998. Heritability and biological explanation. *Psychol. Rev.* 105:782–91

Van Mechelen I, De Raad B, eds. 1999. Personality and situations (special issue). *Eur. J. Pers.* 13:333–461

Watson JB. 1925. *Behaviorism.* New York: Norton

Westen D. 1998. The scientific legacy of Sigmund Freud: toward a psychodynamically informed psychological science. *Psychol. Bull.* 124:333–71

Wilkinson L, Task Force on Statistical Inference. 1999. Statistical methods in psychology journals: guidelines and explanations. *Am. Psychol.* 54:594–604

Wilson EO. 1975. *Sociobiology: The New Synthesis.* Cambridge, MA: Harvard University Press

Wilson MI, Daly M. 1996. Male sexual proprietariness and violence against wives. *Curr. Dir. Psychol. Sci.* 5:2–7

Yang J, McCrae RR, Costa PT Jr, Dai X, Yao S, et al. 1999. Cross-cultural personality assessment in psychiatric populations: the NEO-PI-R in the People's Republic of China. *Psychol. Assess.* 11:359–68

Zuckerman M. 1998. Psychobiological theories of personality. In *Advanced Personality*, ed. DF Barone, M Herson, VB Van Hasselt, pp. 123–54. New York: Plenum

Annu. Rev. Psychol. 2001. 52:223–47

THINKING

Arthur B. Markman

Department of Psychology, University of Texas, Austin, Texas 78712;
e-mail: markman@psy.utexas.edu

Dedre Gentner

Department of Psychology, Northwestern University, Evanston, Illinois 60208;
e-mail: gentner@nwu.edu

Key Words   reasoning, analogy, domain-specific processes, mental models, learning

■ **Abstract** Reasoning processes allow the human cognitive system to go beyond the information readily available in the environment. This review focuses on the processes of human thinking, including deductive reasoning, induction, mental simulation, and analogy. We survey recent trends across several areas, including categorization, mental models, cognitive development, and decision making. Our chief organizing principle is the contrast between traditional approaches that focus on abstract logical reasoning and a number of current approaches that posit domain-specific, knowledge-intensive cognition. We suggest that some instances of domain-specific cognition result from domain-general processes operating on domain-specific representations. Another theme is the link between reasoning and learning. We suggest that learning typically occurs as a byproduct of reasoning, rather than as an end in itself.

CONTENTS

0066-4308/01/0201-0223$14.00

INTRODUCTION

We have called this chapter "Thinking" rather than using the more traditional title "Reasoning" because we think it important to go beyond the traditional deductive logic focus of the term reasoning and include other ways of arriving at new conclusions, including induction and analogy. In this paper we survey recent trends in the field across several areas, including categorization, mental models, cognitive development, and decision making. A theme that emerges frequently in recent research is an interest in going beyond lab-oriented paradigms to investigations of real-life cognitive activities. A related theme is the relation between abstract logical reasoning and concrete domain-specific reasoning—or to put it another way, between abstract and knowledge-based approaches to reasoning. The idea of reasoning is often equated with the notion of purely logical processes that operate independent of content. In popular imagery, icons such as Mr. Spock and HAL draw their intellectual power from pure logic. Likewise, within psychology the study of reasoning has focused largely on the use of content-independent logical rules (e.g. Johnson-Laird & Byrne 1991, Rips 1994). However, other research shows that the content being reasoned about influences people's reasoning ability, even for tasks to which logical rules are applicable (e.g. Cheng & Holyoak 1985, Cosmides 1989, Wason & Johnson-Laird 1972). Partly because of these findings, there has been considerable recent interest in how people learn and use rich domain representations such as theories and mental models.

As an example of the kinds of phenomena that need explanation, Bassok et al (1998) asked college undergraduates to write addition and division word problems. Presumably, college students are experts at addition and division; it should be straightforward for them to think abstractly about simple arithmetic. However, the content of the problem influenced the form of the word problem written. When asked to write a problem involving two members of the same category (e.g. apples and pears), the students found it easier to write an addition problem than a division problem. In contrast, when given members of thematically related categories (e.g. apples and baskets), they found it easier to write a division problem than an addition problem. Thus, even in the seemingly abstract domain of mathematics, cognitive performance is affected by domain content.

Such effects have led some researchers to suggest that content and context are fundamental to reasoning (Newell & Simon 1972). Some theorists assert that human learning is conservative, with representations that are tied to the initial learning situation (Gentner 1989, Medin & Ross 1989). Indeed, some have taken the extreme opposite of the logicist view, arguing that there is no utility to a general notion of representation or process. One such view is the situated cognition approach that assumes all thinking is fundamentally context-governed (Suchman 1987). A related position is the embodied cognition view, according to which cognitive processes are optimized to mesh with particular sensorimotor activities (Glenberg 1997, Pfeifer & Scheier 1999). For example, Glenberg reviewed evidence that some spatial reasoning tasks are facilitated by specific motor movements consistent with route-following.

Another approach to domain-specific reasoning is modularity theory, which assumes that human learning and development requires innate modules for certain domains such as physical causality or psychology (e.g. Hirschfeld & Gelman 1994). Finally, another approach that postulates domain-specific reasoning is evolutionary psychology, which posits domain-specific modules selected by evolution to solve complex reasoning tasks (Tooby & Cosmides 1989).

These views have had the salutary effect of pointing to phenomena neglected by traditional approaches to cognition. However, in the extreme, the focus on domain-specific modules can lead to abandoning the search for general processes in favor of particularistic descriptions. Our reading of the findings supports a more moderate conclusion. We suggest that both domain-general and domain-specific reasoning have a place in psychology and suggest three lines of reconciliation. First, we invoke a distinction proposed by Newell & Simon (1972) between strong and weak methods of reasoning. Weak methods are general strategies that can operate without special knowledge of a domain, such as means-ends analysis or logical inference rules like modus ponens. Strong methods make intensive use of represented knowledge, as in reasoning by example. Weak methods are valuable because of their generality; they provide a means of operating on novel or knowledge-poor domains. However, Newell and Simon asserted that strong methods are typically superior when the appropriate knowledge is present. Many recent systems have focused on architectures that permit both general and specific knowledge to be used. For example, Sloman (1996) reviewed evidence that people apply specific knowledge to problems in order to answer them quickly, and that this knowledge can even compete with rule-based processes.

The second point of contact is that many instances of domain-specific cognition result from domain-general processes operating on domain-specific representations. Domain specificity can thus be captured without abandoning the idea of domain-general cognitive processes. For example, in cognitive architectures like Anderson's ACT system (Anderson 1993, Anderson & Lebiere 1998), it is assumed that the structure of semantic memory can strongly influence the performance of the model. A third point of connection is that the distinction between abstract and concrete cognition often behaves as a continuum rather than as a dichotomy. Furthermore, the continuum is learning related. As discussed in the next section, alignment and abstraction processes can result in a natural transition from domain-specific to domain-general reasoning (Cheng and Holyoak 1985, Gentner & Medina 1998). This last trend is an instance of another basic theme that emerges from our survey: In many natural contexts, learning occurs as a byproduct of reasoning, rather than as an end in itself. For example, Ross (1997) showed that people's representations of categories are influenced by the way they use the categories in problem solving.

The plan of this chapter is as follows. We first lay out structure mapping, a general process that can capture many domain-specific effects. We then cover research in mental models and theories, traditionally an arena of rich domain-specific cognition. Finally, we survey research in categorization and category-based induction as a case study of the ways domain-general and domain-specific information interact in cognitive processing.

STRUCTURAL ALIGNMENT AND MAPPING

As noted above, we need accounts of reasoning processes that can deal with rich domain-specific knowledge. In each of these cases, we need to find a way to allow information about the new situation to be related to background knowledge.

Comparison is a domain-general process that allows the detection of commonalities and differences in a pair of situations or domains. Many models of similarity have been proposed (e.g. Shepard 1964, Tversky 1977). We focus on recent accounts of similarity that are structurally sensitive, and that allow for complex mental representations and hierarchical relational structures (Falkenhainer et al 1989, Gentner & Markman 1997, Goldstone 1994, Holyoak & Thagard 1989, Hummel & Holyoak 1997, Medin et al 1993). In particular, structure-mapping theory (Gentner 1983) has been used to model analogy, similarity, and metaphor in perceptual and conceptual tasks (Gentner & Markman 1994, 1997; Markman & Gentner 1993a,b, 1996, 1997).

Structure mapping involves two processes: structural alignment and inference projection. The idea behind structural alignment is that comparing structured representations requires a process that is sensitive to similarities, not only between the elements but also between the connections between elements. The structural alignment process matches semantically similar relations, but beyond this it seeks maximal structurally consistent systems of matches. Structural consistency involves two constraints: parallel connectivity and one-to-one correspondence. Parallel connectivity requires that if a pair of predicates is placed in correspondence, then their arguments must also be placed in correspondence, and one-to-one correspondence requires that an element in one representation can match to at most one element in the other representation.

For example, consider the following analogy:

(1) Fred loves Mary,
so Fred bought Mary cookies.

(2) Joyce loves Fred,
so Joyce bought Fred candy.

Fred let Joyce drive his car.

A process that was not sensitive to relational structure would arrive at the correspondences Fred(1)_Fred(2), cookies_candy, and so on. Structural alignment invites the arguments of matching relations to be placed in correspondence. Thus, once the relational correspondence loves(1)_loves(2) is found, Fred(1) is mapped to Joyce and Mary is mapped to Fred(2). Further, by one-to-one correspondence, once the correspondence Fred(1)_Joyce is determined, Fred(1) cannot also match with Fred(2).

A further tenet of structure-mapping is the systematicity principle (Gentner 1983, 1989), which posits that matches between systems of relations connected by higher-order constraining relations are preferred to matches between isolated relations. Such relations include causality or means-end relations in conceptual domains and symmetry or monotonicity in perceptual arenas. This claim is supported by studies that have demonstrated that pairs are seen as more similar when they share systematic relational matches than when they do not (e.g. Gentner et al 1993, Lassaline 1996, Markman & Gentner 1993b) and that matches are seen as more central to an analogy when they are connected to other matching assertions than when they are not (Clement & Gentner 1991).

Systematicity is manifest not only in which commonalities emerge from a comparison but also in which differences are noticed (Markman & Gentner 1993a). In particular, alignable differences tend to be highly salient in similarity comparisons. These are differences that result when nonidentical elements are placed in correspondence by virtue of their connections to the common structure. For example, in the example analogy, cookies and candy will be placed in correspondence, because they fill the same role. Thus, they are an alignable difference. In contrast, Fred's car, which has no correspondence in the first set, is a nonalignable difference—a difference not connected to the common system that has no correspondence in the other domain.

Commonalities are more important in judgments of similarity than are differences (Sjöberg 1972, Tversky 1977). Structural alignment extends this observation to alignable differences, assuming that alignable differences are more prominent than nonalignable differences in similarity tasks. As evidence for this supposition, it has been shown that alignable differences influence similarity comparisons more than do nonalignable differences (Markman & Gentner 1996), are more likely to be listed than nonalignable difference in difference-listing tasks (Markman & Gentner 1993a), are more fluently produced in speeded tasks (Gentner & Markman 1994), and serve as better recall cues for information presented in a comparison than do nonalignable differences (Markman & Gentner 1997).

Systematicity also influences which new inferences are drawn from a comparison (Bowdle & Gentner 1997, Clement & Gentner 1991, Markman 1997, Spellman & Holyoak 1996), thus providing a means of constraining possible inferences. Information that is connected via higher-order constraining relations, such as causality, to the common system is more likely to be projected to the target than is other knowledge about the base. These candidate inferences serve as informed guesses.

Recent research has begun to investigate the real-time processes of comparison. There is evidence for an initial alignment process that is symmetric between base and target, followed by a directional inference process (Falkenhainer et al 1989, Wolff & Gentner 2000). The alignment between two representations is computed via a local-to-global process that begins with individual element matches and then imposes global consistency constraints (Goldstone & Medin 1994).

To summarize, comparison can be viewed as the alignment of structured representations. This process begins with local matches and gradually arrives at the maximal structurally consistent system of correspondences. The comparison process can generate new conclusions in at least four ways: (*a*) it promotes a focus on common connected relational systems that can serve as useful abstractions; (*b*) it highlights alignable differences of a pair, which are likely to be relevant; (*c*) it invites candidate inferences; and (*d*) it sometimes leads to re-representations of one or both domains to increase their similarity (Gentner & Wolff 2000). These processes contribute to learning as well as to online reasoning.

Learning and Reasoning: The Shift from Active Processing to Storage

It is often easier to retrieve something from memory than to derive it by reasoning processes. This idea is evident in many theories of automaticity. For example, Logan (1988, 1996) suggested that in the initial stages of learning a skill, people obtain solutions by carrying out an algorithm. For example, they might learn to add two numbers by starting with the larger one and counting on to add the other. With sufficient practice, they come to be able to retrieve previously stored answers. Siegler & Shipley (1995) observed this progression in children learning to do arithmetic, who shifted from overtly counting on their fingers to retrieving answers from memory.

A similar process of shifting from active computation to memory retrieval can be seen in metaphor comprehension (Bowdle & Gentner 1999; Gentner & Wolff 1997, 2000). When a novel metaphor is presented (e.g. that lawyer is a boa constrictor), an interpretation (e.g. the lawyer is inexorable) is actively computed via alignment processes. However, if the metaphor base is repeatedly used in the same nonliteral way, its metaphorical interpretation may be stored as an alternate word sense. Such stock metaphors can behave like conventional categories (Glucksberg et al 1997) and do not need to be recomputed.

People's propensity to cache frequently encountered solutions can be used to predict their future behavior. In consumer psychology, the single best predictor of a person's purchases in a category is "brand loyalty"—the prior probability distribution of purchases of products in that category (e.g. Guidagni & Little 1983). People tend to buy again what they bought in the past. Our pattern of storing the results of frequently experienced processes is a form of cognitive economy, but it sometimes works against us. In the classic *Einstellung* or "set" effect noted by the Gestaltists, people's continued use of a past successful solution hampers their ability to see a better solution to a problem.

MENTAL MODELS

A mental model is a representation of some domain or situation that supports understanding, reasoning, and prediction. There are two main approaches to the study of mental models. One approach seeks to characterize the knowledge and processes that support understanding and reasoning in knowledge-rich domains. The other approach focuses on mental models as working-memory constructs that support logical reasoning (Johnson-Laird 1983, Johnson-Laird & Byrne 1991). Although we are primarily interested in causal mental models, we first briefly discuss logical mental models.

Logical Mental Models

There is considerable research on how people perform logical reasoning tasks (Evans & Over 1996; Johnson-Laird 1983, 1999; Rips 1994). One prominent explanation for the way people perform logical reasoning is that they form a mental model of the situation (Johnson-Laird 1983). In this view, when faced with a logic problem, the solver imagines a set of tokens organized so as to capture the relevant aspects of the premises. For example, given the premise "all archers are bakers," the solver might imagine a group of people. All those with arrows would also have cakes, but there would be others with cakes and no arrows. With each additional premise, the model is adjusted, and if more than one model is consistent with the premises, then alternate models are constructed. After all the premises have been presented, the resulting model(s) are summarized to give the conclusion. The difficulty of a given problem is determined by the number of different mental models that have to be constructed. This approach has been applied to a variety of logical reasoning situations, including classical syllogisms, multiply quantified statements, and inductive arguments (Johnson-Laird 1983, 1999; Johnson-Laird & Byrne 1991). However, some researchers have argued that logical mental models fail to capture aspects of human processing that are captured in propositional models (Rips 1986, 1994), or that mental models are actually isomorphic to other forms of diagrammatic reasoning in logic (Stenning & Oberlander 1995).

Causal Mental Models

Causal mental models are mental representations that are used in reasoning and that are based on long-term domain knowledge or theories (Gentner & Stevens 1983). They are used to explain reasoning about physical systems and mechanisms (Hegarty & Just 1993, McCloskey 1983) such as spatial representation (Tversky 1991), human-computer interaction (Norman 1988), ecology (Kempton et al 1994), and the development of astronomical knowledge (Vosniadou & Brewer 1992).

Causal mental models differ from logical mental models in two further ways besides their domain of application. First, the elements in a logical mental model are tokens rather like algebraic symbols, whereas the tokens in a causal mental model correspond to elements of causal systems. Second, logical mental models are created on the spot and involve only information currently active in working memory, whereas causal mental models, even those currently active in working memory, are assumed to draw on long-term memory structures.

Causal mental models (hereafter called mental models) are related to several other kinds of representational structures (Markman 1999). Schemas (or schemata) are general belief structures. Scripts are schemas summarizing event sequences and are characterized by a chiefly linear temporal order with limited inferential flexibility. Naive theories or folk theories are global systems of belief, typically encompassing larger domains such as biology. The terms mental models and naive or intuitive theories overlap in their application, though mental models are typically more specific in their application than are theories.

The Use of Mental Models   One way people employ their mental models is to perform mental simulations—to imagine the future trajectory of a system given a set of initial conditions. These predictions involve qualitative estimates and often neglect some of the information relevant to the behavior of a system. For example, Gilden & Proffitt (1989) showed people collisions between a moving ball and a stationary ball and asked them which ball was heavier. Making this judgment requires attending both to the velocity of the balls and their trajectories prior to and following the collision. The results showed that people tended to use simple heuristics such as "the ball moving faster after the collision is lighter," or "the ball that ricochets is lighter." Whereas these heuristics are often correct, they do not reflect an integration of the information necessary to answer the question correctly on all trials. A similar analysis of people's predictions about the behavior of rolling wheels suggests that people understand the physics of forward (i.e. translational) motion of rolling wheels, but not the physics of rotational motion (Proffitt et al 1990).

An important aspect of these mental simulations is that they are qualitative (Forbus 1984, Kuipers 1994). That is, people reason about relative properties of physical systems such as direction of motion, relative speed, and relative mass. People do not estimate values of specific quantities, nor do they carry out mathematical simulations of the behavior of a system. These strategies are quite powerful, and have been used as the basis of computational simulations of complex physical systems (e.g. Forbus et al 1991), but they do not require the significant computational machinery that would be necessary to carry out detailed quantitative simulations.

Mental simulation often involves the use of imagery. Schwartz & Black (1996) asked people to solve gear problems such as, "Imagine a pegboard with seven gears on it arranged in a circle so that each gear meshes with one next to it on each side. If you rotate one gear clockwise, in which direction will the gear next to it move?" To answer such questions people often mentally simulate the gears' motions, sometimes with accompanying hand gestures (Hegarty & Just 1993, Metz 1985, Schwartz & J. Black 1996, Schwartz & T. Black 1999). Over time, people gradually learn the parity rule—that every other gear in a sequence turns in the same direction, whereas adjacent gears turn in the opposite direction—and shift from using imagery to solving the problems by rule. (Use of the parity rule reveals that the above problem is a trick. Circuits consisting of an odd number of gears will lock, because two adjacent gears will attempt to move in the same direction.)

Mental simulations may also have a motor component. In one set of studies, Schwartz & Black (1999) showed people a partially filled glass and asked them to predict how far it would have to be tilted in order for the liquid to pour out. People performed poorly, consistent with the Piagetian finding that people have difficulty predicting the level of water in a tilted glass (e.g. Howard 1978). However, when those same people were asked to hold a glass with a line drawn on it at the water level, and to tilt it until the glass would pour (with their eyes closed), they were significantly more accurate than in the explicit prediction task. Thus, it appears that some aspects of mental simulations involve representations that are strongly coupled with motor movements.

To summarize, recent research in mental models suggests that people can use mental simulations to reason about physical events. These simulations incorporate a small number of variables about the event and are often qualitative. Because the simulation process is effortful, with increasing experience people shift to using learned rules or cached results. More generally, this research reveals that people typically possess multiple models of complex systems, some highly context-bound and others more abstract.

Relating Mental Models to Theories

As noted above, there is a close relationship between mental models and intuitive theories. Many researchers have suggested that people's knowledge can be characterized as a theory about the world (Carey 1985, Gopnik & Meltzoff 1997, Keil 1989, Murphy & Medin 1985). The word theory has been used in a number of different ways to describe knowledge. In its loosest form, the term theory is used for the causal knowledge that people use to infer nonobvious properties and to explain observed patterns in the world.

Gopnik & Meltzoff (1997) have explored the possibility that children's knowledge can be characterized in the same terms as scientific theories: as theoretical knowledge that is abstract and coherent, that has explicit causal knowledge, and that makes specific commitments about the ontology of objects. They suggest that children create and use theories much as scientists do to predict and interpret events in the world. This does not, of course, mean that children's understanding is as deep as that of scientists (or even as adults). Preschool children often focus on object properties in their categorizations and explanations and fail to perceive functional or relational commonalities (Gentner & Medina 1998, Halford 1992).

There are some points in favor of the claim that scientific reasoning provides a good model for reasoning in children and adults. First, as Nersessian (1999) notes, scientific reasoning encompasses processes that go beyond hypothesis testing, such as mental simulation and analogy, that are also found in commonsense reasoning. Second, both scientists and nonscientists appear more willing to accept evidence that supports their beliefs than evidence against them. Kuhn (1997) showed this pattern in nonscientists. She first ascertained their views as to which factors matter in a situation and then showed them counterevidence. For example, people who believed that humor increases TV show ratings were shown pairs that differed only in humor, but received identical ratings. People did not change their belief in the importance of humor, but instead constructed other explanations for the finding.

Koehler (1993) found a similar pattern among scientists. Even though scientists state that their prior beliefs should not influence their evaluation of new evidence, they often set a more stringent acceptance criterion for contrary evidence than for consistent evidence. Thus, both scientists and nonscientists appear to resist negative evidence, although possibly to different degrees. Interestingly, there is some divergence of opinion as to the best policy on inconsistencies. Koehler suggests that on Bayesian grounds it is reasonable for scientists to be skeptical of evidence that contradicts their beliefs. However, Dunbar (1995) carried out long-term observations of working microbiology laboratories and concluded that attention to inconsistent findings is a major predictor of success in a laboratory.

There are also differences between scientists and nonscientists. First, scientists possess deeper causal theories than novices. Chi et al (1981) showed that expert physicists sorted physics problems into principle-based categories such as "momentum" and "conservation of energy," whereas novices sorted them into categories with similar diagrams. Second, scientists' knowledge in the domain of expertise is likely to be more explicit than that of novices. This greater degree of explicitness may arise in part from the need for scientists to communicate with other members of the scientific community, and from the specific feedback that scientists get about their ideas. Consistent with this proposal, Chi & VanLehn (1991) found that students learning science benefit significantly from generating explicit explanations for themselves as they study.

Third, although both scientists and nonscientists show resistance to data that are inconsistent with their prior beliefs, scientists are trained to seek such data: e.g. to include in their studies conditions that could disconfirm the hypotheses. In contrast, nonscientists have a strong confirmation bias when testing hypotheses (Evans & Over 1996, Klayman & Ha 1987). The Wason 246 task is a classic demonstration of this confirmation bias. People are told that the sequence 2–4–6 was generated using a rule, and asked to determine the rule by producing further elements. The typical strategy is to guess the rule (such as "increasing by 2") and then test only sequences that satisfy the rule, thereby collecting confirmatory evidence. Most people fail to discover the correct rule ("any increasing sequence"), because they do not test sequences that would disconfirm their hypothesized rule.

In summary, there are commonalities in reasoning styles between scientists and nonscientists, and the differences are often of degree, not kind. However, the combined force of these differences—such as greater explicitness of knowledge and greater commitment to seeking disconfirming evidence—may lead to a substantial overall difference in practice.

The Development of Theories and Mental Models

One route to understanding domain-specific reasoning is to study its development. Developmentalists have explored the way in which domain knowledge is acquired and structured in key domains such as mathematics, physics, and biology. Much of this research is motivated by the question of whether infants are born with domain-specific modular capacities for learning and reasoning. Just as linguistic development has been posited to be the result of an innate language acquisition device, so too might other conceptual abilities reflect an innate endowment for particular domains such as naive physics or a naive biology. For example, Leslie (1991) has proposed a specific theory of mind module and posited that autism is the result of a defective theory of mind module. Some theorists propose a combination of domain-specific and domain-general attentional capacities and learning processes (Baillargeon 1994, Carey 1985). At the other extreme, some theorists argue that purely general learning principles can account for the development of domain-specific modules (Elman et al 1996, Thelen & Smith 1993). According to these theorists, modules are the result of learning. At present, the issue is not resolved. Regardless of the outcome of the debate between nativists and empiricists, however, this body of work is of immense value for understanding how domain knowledge is acquired.

The development of biological knowledge is an arena of intense current interest. Carey (1985) probed children's understanding of the properties of animals (e.g. dogs or worms), plants, and inanimate objects. She asked about biological properties (bones and a heart), biological behaviors (eating, sleeping, and having babies) and psychological properties (thinking). The youngest children (4-year-olds) seemed to take a "man is the measure of all things" approach. They determined the likelihood that an entity had a property based on its similarity to humans. For example, they attributed biological properties to a mechanical monkey—but not to other inanimate objects—over half the time. With increasing age, children came to differentiate based on biological categories—e.g. between mammals and nonmammals. By the age of 10, children correctly treated the mechanical monkey as an inanimate object. Inagaki & Hatano (1987) suggested that the early "personification" responses represent children's productive use of analogy to reason from a well-understood base domain—human beings—to other less familiar species.

Carey's findings suggest that young children's biological theories may not differentiate among animals, or even between animals and plants. Carey further suggested that children's naive biology develops from their naive psychology, which is initially used to predict the actions of the people around them. Other researchers maintain that a naive theory of biology appears early in development. For example, Coley (1995) found that kindergarteners attributed biological properties (e.g. "has blood") according to taxonomic category membership, but attributed psychological properties (e.g. "thinks") according to whether the animal was domesticated. Coley concluded that a distinction between biological and psychological properties is present in young children and becomes more pronounced over development.

Young children reason about animate and inanimate objects in very different ways. Rosengren et al (1991) showed children pictures of animals labeled as "baby animals." When the children were shown new pictures and asked to choose which picture showed the baby as an adult, even preschool children consistently selected the larger animal. They would even accept a shape transformation (e.g. from a caterpillar to a butterfly) rather than choose a smaller "adult." Thus, children expect that animals will get larger, and would rather assume that an animal changed shape than that it got smaller. In contrast, when children were presented with artifacts, they expected them to stay the same size (though possibly to become chipped and broken). Hatano & Inagaki (1999) extended this method to plants and found that children expected both plants and animals to grow rather than to stay the same size. These findings suggest that young children distinguish between living and nonliving things.

However, children's initial understanding of the living-nonliving distinction may not go very deep. Simons & Keil (1995) showed children pairs of pictures of animals or machines with cutaways showing the "insides"—either organs or machinery (e.g. gears and chains)—and asked them to select the right insides for each whole. Only half of the 3- and 4-year-olds associated organs with the insides of animals and machinery with the insides of artifacts. Other children could choose correctly for artifacts but not for animals. Not until 8 years of age could children all select correctly. Simons & Keil suggest a developmental shift from abstract comprehension to specific causal knowledge: Preschool children distinguish between animate and artifact categories, but lack deep causal understanding of these domains. Although this claim that children possess abstract domain theories but lack causal understanding may seem rather tenuous, Keil and his colleagues suggest that adults' mental models of physical systems are similarly incomplete (Wilson & Keil 1998). They find that college students often believe that they know how complex artifacts like car starters and toilets work, but are unable to explain when probed for details. They argue that people are generally unaware of their lack of specific causal information about how common objects work, and call this effect the shallowness of explanation.

Finally, there has been research on how biological information is organized in the brain. Some neuropsychological patients appear to have category-specific impairments for animals; they can name pictures of artifacts but have trouble naming animals (e.g. Caramazza & Shelton 1998, Warrington & Shallice 1984). On the basis of these findings, Caramazza & Shelton (1998) suggest that evolution might have selected for specific mechanisms that facilitate the representation of animate and inanimate objects, and that the observed deficits reflect the breakdown of these systems. Regardless of the resolution of this issue, these findings add weight to the animate/inanimate distinction as an organizing principle for category information.

To summarize, studies of biological knowledge suggest that preschool children can make core distinctions such as the animate/inanimate distinction, but that their understanding deepens with development. Both children and adults have significant gaps in their models and may be unaware of the extent of the missing information. Much remains to be understood. For example, do the various facets of the animate/inanimate distinction—living/nonliving, self-moving/nonself-moving, and so on—reflect unified categories from the start, or are they acquired piecemeal? Is naive biology acquired through general learning processes or through domain-specific processes?

CATEGORIZATION

Categorization research includes both how people classify things into categories and how people draw inferences from known categories. Most research on categorization has focused on domain-general issues such as the role of similarity or the perception of feature centrality. We begin with these approaches and then describe some domain-specific approaches.

Similarity and Categorization

Intuitively, similarity and categorization seem tightly linked. It is not surprising, then, that many studies of categorization have focused on the kinds of similarity relationships between a new exemplar and a stored category representation that allow the new item to be classified as a member of a known category. Prototype models assume that the stored category representation is a summary of the most typical feature values for members of a category, and that new exemplars are classified on the basis of their similarity to these prototypes (e.g. Hampton 1995, Reed 1972, Rosch & Mervis 1975). Exemplar models assume that people store away specific exemplars of the category and classify new items on the basis of their similarity to the stored exemplars (e.g. Kruschke 1992, Medin & Schaffer 1978, Nosofsky 1986).

Most models of similarity are domain general: They assume that some measure of proximity can be calculated for any pair of representations. Two classic influential approaches are the spatial view and the featural view. Spatial models of similarity (e.g. Nosofsky 1986; Shepard 1962, 1964) model individual concepts as points in a multidimensional space and assume that the similarity of a pair of objects is inversely related to the distance between them. Feature-based models of similarity (e.g. Tversky 1977) assume that objects are represented by sets of features, and that the commonalities of a pair are the features in the intersection of the sets representing each object, whereas the differences are just the features not in the intersection. These models have been criticized because they typically assume that a fixed set of dimensions or properties applies to a category (Schank et al 1986), ignoring the role of feature learning during categorization (Schyns et al 1998). Reflecting this perspective, classification experiments typically utilize a fixed set of dimensions, each with a small number of values. Similarity-based models of categorization have also been faulted for ignoring the role of theory in determining the relevance of features to categories (Goldstone 1994, Murphy & Medin 1985).

Current approaches to similarity like the structure-mapping approach described above may better meet some of these requirements. As Goldstone (1994) points out, structural alignment provides constraints on which commonalities among items are relevant for categorizing them. In particular, systematic relational structures are likely to be important for categorization. This point helps to bridge the gap between theory-based and similarity-based categorization. If similarity is computed by a structural alignment process rather than a feature-matching process, then common relational systems will be included in the similarity computation (and even favored, by the systematicity principle); thus, common causal systems will naturally be part of the category representation (Gentner & Medina 1998).

Structural alignment may also influence the way category representations are learned (Lassaline & Murphy 1998). Markman & Wisniewski (1997) asked people to list commonalities and differences of pairs of object categories at different levels of abstraction. People could more easily list commonalities and alignable differences for pairs of categories within a superordinate (e.g. pairs of vehicles or pairs of weapons) than for pairs from different superordinates (e.g. a vehicle and a weapon). This result suggests that object categories are organized around taxonomic clusters whose numbers are readily comparable with other members of the cluster, but not with members of different clusters.

These clusters may develop through reminding-based category learning (Ross et al 1990, Spalding & Ross 1994). In this view, when a new item is presented, it is given an initial representation that serves as a retrieval cue for items in memory. The concepts retrieved serve as a template for constructing the representation of the new item. This process helps create clusters of categories whose members are all comparable. There is some evidence for this reminding-based process. Zhang & Markman (1998) had people learn about a sequence of new brands of microwave popcorn. People first saw a description of the first brand; in a second session, they saw a description of the first brand again followed by descriptions of two more brands whose properties overlapped with those of the first brand. People learned properties of the later brands better if they were alignable differences with the first brand than if they were nonalignable differences, suggesting that they learned the later brands by aligning them to the initial one. These findings suggest that structural alignment influences the representations of new categories.

The studies just described are part of a larger movement that explores the influence of reasoning with categories on what is learned about categories—an instance of the "learning as a byproduct of reasoning" theme mentioned at the beginning of this paper (see Brooks 1978). Ross (1997, 1999) has demonstrated that when features are relevant to a secondary task (either problem solving or a secondary classification) their salience is increased in a primary classification task. Yamauchi & Markman (1998) found that when categories are learned in the process of making feature predictions, their representations focus more on relationships among features than do those of categories learned by classifying new instances.

Finally, the issue of whether language influences category structures has returned to the research foreground. Recent work is exploring whether and how possessing specific semantic categories affects conceptual processing (e.g. Cabrera & Billman 1996, Gentner & Loewenstein 2000, Gumperz & Levinson 1996, Malt et al 1999), as well as how the act of communication affects people's learning and reasoning (Clark 1996, Garrod & Anderson 1987, Markman & Makin 1998).

Inference from Categories

Once categories are established, people can use them to infer features of a new situation. This kind of reasoning is studied using the category-based induction task. In these tasks, people are told that one or more categories has some property and asked how likely it is that some other category has the same property. For example, people might be told that robins have property X and that bluebirds have property X, and asked how likely it is that all birds have property X. The strength of this argument can be compared to that of another argument, such as: "Robins have X, Ostriches have X, how likely are all Birds to have X?"

Many of the central phenomena in category-based induction were mapped out by Osherson et al (1990). According to their similarity-coverage model, the perceived strength of a conclusion increases with the similarity between the premises and the conclusion category. Thus, "robins have X, therefore bluebirds have X" is judged to be a stronger argument than "ostriches have X, therefore bluebirds have X." The similarity-coverage model also predicts a diversity effect in reasoning. Premises from diverse categories lead to stronger arguments than premises that are highly similar to each other. For example, college undergraduates find the argument "robins have X, ostriches have X, therefore all birds have X" to be stronger than the argument "robins have X, bluebirds have X, therefore all birds have X." A related model of induction based on feature overlap was developed by Sloman (1993).

These views of category-based induction rely on overall similarity or feature overlap as a predictor of argument strength. However, recent research suggests that the comparisons involved here may be sensitive to causal alignments. For example, Heit & Rubinstein (1994) showed people arguments in which the properties to be inferred were either behaviors or anatomical properties. People based their judgments of argument strength not on overall similarity, but on similarity with respect to the particular dimension: Thus, whales were considered likely to share a new behavioral property of fish, but a new anatomical property of cattle. Furthermore, it appears that the subjective strength of the induction depends on the causal alignment between premises and conclusion categories (Lassaline 1996).

Category-based induction is also influenced by expertise in a domain. Medin, Atran, and their colleagues (Coley et al 1999, Medin et al 1997) have undertaken a cross-cultural study of biological reasoning. They contrasted category-based induction performance of college undergraduates with that of Itzaj Mayans from Guatemala (who have extensive experience with their native flora), with scientific taxonomists (who study classification of trees), landscape workers (who decide where to plant trees in residential settings), and park maintenance workers (who take care of trees in local parks). One striking difference among these groups arises with diversity-based reasoning. As discussed above, college students consider that a diverse set of premise categories increases the strength of an argument. The taxonomists and landscape workers also preferred diverse arguments. However, both Itzaj Mayans and park maintenance workers showed the opposite effect, preferring arguments with similar categories in the premises to arguments with dissimilar categories in the premises. An analysis of the justifications suggests that the Mayans and landscape workers based their judgments on ecological factors. For example, landscape workers thought that a disease affecting white birches and river birches would affect more trees than a disease affecting white pines and weeping willows (Coley et al 1999). Although the second pair is more diverse than the first, maintenance workers argued that the first pair (the birches) were more likely to cause diseases of all trees, because this pair of trees is more widely planted and more susceptible to disease than pine and willow. Thus, differences in expertise influenced how people evaluated inductive arguments.

To summarize, recent research in category-based induction explores both general processes and specific knowledge structures. People align specific causal systems between the premises and conclusions to guide their inductions. With increasing expertise, people are able to form more elaborate causal explanations.

Feature Centrality

A related area in which domain-general approaches have been applied to categorization is in the determination of the centrality of a feature in a category. The notion of centrality is that some properties of a category are more important than others. For example, for a robin, the property of having wings seems to be more central than the property of having a red breast. It is easier to imagine a robin without a red breast than one without wings. A related point is that some categories seem more cohesive than others. Research has focused on structural properties that may determine cohesiveness and feature centrality.

Gentner (1981) explored the differences between nouns and verbs and suggested that nouns differ from verbs in the relational density of their representations. That is, the semantic components of noun meanings are more strongly interconnected than those of verbs. One consequence of this difference is that the meanings of nouns seem less mutable than the meanings of verbs. For example, people asked to paraphrase a sentence like "the lizard worshipped" are more likely to change the verb's meaning (e.g. "the small gray reptile lay on a hot rock and stared at the sun") than the noun's meaning (e.g. "a man with scaly skin prayed"). In this view, the ease of altering a property of a concept is influenced by the degree to which that property is interconnected with others.

This interconnectivity idea was explored at the level of individual properties by Sloman, Love, and Ahn (Love & Sloman 1995, Sloman et al 1998). They found that the perceived mutability of a feature—that is, how willing people were to accept changes in those features for members of the category—was influenced by its interconnectivity with other features of the category. Features with few interconnections were more mutable than features with many interconnections.

More specifically, there is evidence that an important determinant of feature centrality is whether a property participates in a higher-order constraining structure such as causality. This is consistent with the systematicity principle discussed above. For example, Ahn and colleagues have demonstrated the importance of causally relevant properties (Ahn 1999, Ahn et al 2000). Using sorting tasks, Ahn (1999) demonstrated that people prefer to create categories based on items with a common cause or a common effect, suggesting that they align causal structures across items, and focus on the alignable information. Likewise, Rehder & Hastie (1998) found that common causal relations led items to be placed in the same category. Ramscar & Pain (1996) asked subjects to categorize a set of stories that varied systematically in their similarity relations. Subjects classified the stories by common causal structure rather than by common object features.

Ahn et al (2000) further suggested that causes may be more important than effects. They found that when people categorize new items with missing features, they are more likely to classify an item into a given category when the cause is present and the effect is missing than when the reverse is true (provided the causal relation is plausible). This suggests that the position of a property within a relational structure (as the cause rather than as the effect) influences the importance of that feature in a category.

Similar findings have been shown with temporal relations (Sloman et al 1998). However, we would not expect that just any relation (e.g. taller or darker) or even any relation between relations (e.g. conjunctions) would contribute to centrality. The systematicity effect depends on higher-order constraining relations: relations that bind their relational arguments in informative ways. Future work will have to investigate the effects of content and structure further.

Domain-Specific Approaches to Categorization

Although categorization has traditionally been modeled using domain-general processes, recent research has focused on domain-specific aspects of categorization. First, research in the interface between psychology and anthropology has used cross-cultural similarities and differences in categorization to study the relative contributions of the objective structure of the world and the constraints of the cognitive system to human conceptual structure. Second, as discussed above, research in cognitive development has traced the development knowledge structures that characterize specific domains. One major focus in this work is naive biology: e.g. the distinction between animate and inanimate entities in category acquisition.

Malt (1995) reviewed studies exploring folk biological categories across cultures to examine whether category structure is more strongly influenced by the objective information available in the world or by the structure of the cognitive system. One way to approach this is to compare folk systems with scientific taxonomies, which presumably are designed to capture objective facts about the world. Perhaps unsurprisingly, the evidence that bears on these questions shows a mixture of influences. In general, folk biological (and folk botanical) categories often do bear a strong resemblance to scientific categories, particularly at the genus level (roughly similar to the basic level). This suggests that there are clusters of features in the world, and that people are sensitive to these clusters (Atran 1990, Berlin 1972). However, there are also clear influences of cultural factors on these categories. For example, the folk botanical category "tree" does not pick out a distinct class of plants, and many objects labeled as trees are more closely related in scientific taxonomies to plants we would call bushes than they are to other trees. Instead, categories like tree carry with them certain functional properties such as providing shade.

A second way in which domain-specific information influences categorization is that, as noted above, domain theories can affect the set of features people use to classify an item. This phenomenon can be seen in children as their domain theories develop. Many researchers have found that when children hear a new noun applied to an object, they tend to generalize the word to other objects with the same shape (e.g. Baldwin 1989, Landau et al 1988), but that with increasing knowledge there is a shape-to-taxonomic shift (Imai et al 1994). Children come to use taxonomic information to generalize word meanings (Markman 1989, Waxman 1990).

Consistent with our earlier discussion of the development of domain theories, children appear to consider animacy important in categorization. There is evidence that children are less likely to generalize a new label according to shape when they believe that the object is animate. Jones et al (1991) found that preschool children given labels for a set of novel objects generalized according to shape unless the objects had eyes, in which case they also took into account the texture of the objects. Another early dimension may be whether something is an artifact. Bloom (1998) found that young children pay more attention to the intended function of an item if they are told it is an artifact.

People's knowledge of the functions of categories can also constrain the features they focus on (Heit 1997, Murphy & Allopenna 1994, Spalding & Murphy 1996, Wisniewski & Medin 1994). Wisniewski (1995) had people learn about novel functional categories whose features varied in frequency of association and in functional relevance. For example, if the function of a particular category was to kill bugs, then a functionally relevant feature might be "contains poison," and an irrelevant feature might be "manufactured in Florida." People who were told the functions of the categories prior to learning focused strongly on functionally relevant features, even when these features occurred more rarely than functionally irrelevant features.

These examples illustrate both the importance of specific content and the way in which content interacts with higher-level beliefs. For example, in the developmental studies described here, the importance of a given feature is influenced by children's domain understanding. In cross-cultural research, the content of categories is explored in order to ask fundamental questions about how perceptual experience and cultural conventions interact in cognitive structure.

SUMMARY AND CONCLUSIONS

Human reasoning is characterized by a mix of domain-general and domain-specific aspects. Domain-general processes such as logical deduction operate on the structure of representations, independent of content. Their value is in their wide applicability across domains. At the other extreme are reasoning processes that are specific to particular modalities or content areas. Analogy—structural alignment and mapping—operates at an intermediate level. It has a domain-specific aspect in that it is sensitive to domain content. However, the constraints on these processes (e.g. structural consistency and systematicity) are domain general. Our review suggests that many domain-specific effects can be captured using alignment and mapping processes.

The research reviewed here opens up a number of important avenues for future research. One particularly important area is cross-cultural work. In the section on categorization, we briefly touched on some research with specialized populations including Itzaj Mayans, and groups of American tree experts. This work is part of a growing trend in psychology to move beyond the college undergraduates who typically participate in studies to examine how cultural difference and knowledge difference influence behavior. For example, members of collectivist cultures (like many Asian cultures) may be more willing to take risks than members of individualistic cultures (like the one in the United States), because of a belief that the cultural influences are likely to become an important part of research on reasoning processes.

The role of domain-specific knowledge in reasoning is also central to evolutionary psychology. Cosmides and Tooby (1994) point out that the interests in domain-specific modules in development that we discussed above intersects with work by evolutionary psychologists on mechanisms for solving domain-specific problems. Evolutionary psychology argues that these domain-specific modules evolved to solve problems that were prominent in the environment of early hominids. While it is too early to evaluate the evolutionary perspective, the parallels between this work and research in cognitive development bear further scrutiny.

Domain-specificity has also been explored in cognitive neuroscience. Earlier, we mentioned the proposal by Caramazza and Shelton that there may be specific brain mechanisms to process animate and inanimate objects. There is continued exploration of the way the brain processes information about animate and inanimate objects (as well as faces) in both lesion studies (e.g. Tranel et al 1997) and imaging studies (e.g. Perani et al 1999). At present it is difficult to draw firm conclusions from this work, but significant new research is likely to be done in this area as techniques for brain imaging improve.

The rise of research on imaging heightens the importance of behavioral research on thinking that was the focus of this paper. Current brain imaging techniques are only able to explore tasks that take place in a few seconds. Long complex tasks are difficult to give to patients who may have significant cognitive impairments. Further, complex tasks that take place over a period of minutes or even hours are inappropriate for imaging techniques. However, a better understanding of reasoning behavior will lead to task decompositions that may be more amenable to techniques from cognitive neuroscience.

We are entering an exciting period of research on reasoning. Significant progress have been made on both domain-general and domain-specific processes. This work has opened up new avenues for exploration. The next step in this progression of research will require the development of models that combine domain-general and domain-specific approaches into unified models of reasoning in cognition.

ACKNOWLEDGMENTS

This research was supported by ONR grant N00014-92-J-1098 and NSF-LIS grant SBR-9511757 to DG and by NSF grant SBR-9905013 given to ABM. This chapter was partially prepared while DG was a Fellow at the Center for Advanced Study in the Behavioral Sciences. We are grateful for the financial support provided by the William T. Grant Foundation, award #95167795

Visit the Annual Reviews home page at www.AnnualReviews.org

LITERATURE CITED

Ahn WK. 1999. Effect of causal structure on category construction. *Mem. Cogn.* 27:1008–23

Ahn WK, Kim NS, Lassaline ME, Dennis MJ. 2000. Causal status as a determinant of feature centrality. *Cogn. Psychol.* In press

Anderson JR. 1993. *Rules of the Mind.* Hillsdale, NJ: Erlbaum

Anderson JR, Lebiere C, eds. 1998. *The Atomic Components of Thought.* Mahwah, NJ: Erlbaum

Atran S. 1990. *Cognitive Foundations of Natural History: Towards an Anthropology of Science.* New York: Cambridge Univ. Press

Baillargeon R. 1994. How do infants learn about the physical world? *Curr. Dir. Psychol. Sci.* 3(5):133–40

Baldwin DA. 1989. Priorities in children's expectations about object label reference: form over color. *Child Dev.* 60:1289–306

Bassok M, Chase VM, Martin SA. 1998. Adding apples and oranges: semantic constraints on application of formal rules. *Cogn. Psychol.* 35:99–134

Berlin B. 1972. Speculations on the growth of ethnobotanical nomenclature. *Lang. Soc.* 1:51–86

Bloom P. 1998. Theories of artifact categorization. *Cognition* 66:87–93

Bowdle B, Gentner D. 1997. Informativity and asymmetry in comparisons. *Cogn. Psychol.* 34(3):244–86

Bowdle B, Gentner D. 1999. Metaphor comprehension: from comparison to categorization. In *Proc. 21st Annu. Conf. Cogn. Sci. Soc.,* pp. 90–95. Vancouver, BC: Erlbaum

Brooks LR. 1978. Non analytic concept formation and memory for instances. In *Cognition and Categorization,* ed. E Rosch, BB Lloyd, pp. 169–211. Hillsdale, NJ: Erlbaum

Cabrera A, Billman D. 1996. Language-driven concept learning: deciphering Jabberwocky. *J. Exp. Psychol.: Learn. Mem. Cogn.* 22(2): 539–55

Caramazza A, Shelton JR. 1998. Domain-specific knowledge systems in the brain: the animate-inanimate distinction. *J. Cogn. Neurosci.* 10:1–34

Carey S. 1985. *Conceptual Change in Childhood.* Cambridge, MA: MIT Press

Cheng PW, Holyoak KJ. 1985. Pragmatic reasoning schemas. *Cogn. Psychol.* 17:391–416

Chi MTH, Feltovich PJ, Glaser R. 1981. Categorization and representation of physics problems by experts and novices. *Cogn. Sci.* 5:121–52

Chi MTH, VanLehn KA. 1991. The content of physics self-explanations. *J. Learn. Sci.* 1:69 105

Clark HH. 1996. *Using Language.* London: Cambridge Univ. Press

Clement CA, Gentner D. 1991. Systematicity as a selection constraint in analogical mapping. *Cogn. Sci.* 15:89–132

Coley JD. 1995. Emerging differentiation of folkbiology and folkpsychology: attributions of biological and psychological properties to living things. *Child Dev.* 66:1856–74

Coley JD, Medin DL, Proffitt JB, Lynch E, Atran S. 1999. Inductive reasoning in folkbiological thought. See Medin & Atran 1999, pp. 205–32

Cosmides L. 1989. The logic of social exchange: Has natural selection shaped how humans reason? Studies with the Wason selection task. *Cognition* 31:187–276

Cosmides L, Tooby J. 1994. Origins of domain specificity: the evolution of functional organization. In *Mapping the Mind*, ed. LA Hirschfeld, SA Gelman, pp. 85–116. New York: Cambridge Univ. Press

Dunbar K. 1995. How scientists really reason: scientific reasoning in real-world laboratories. In *The Nature of Insight*, ed. RJ Sternberg, JE Davidson, pp. 365–95. Cambridge, MA: MIT Press

Elman JL, Bates EA, Johnson MH, Karmiloff-Smith A, Parisi D, Plunkett K. 1996. *Rethinking Innateness: A Connectionist Perspective on Development.* Cambridge, MA: MIT Press

Evans JS, Over DE. 1996. *Rationality and Reasoning.* East Sussex, UK: Psychology Press

Falkenhainer B, Forbus KD, Gentner D. 1989. The structure-mapping engine: algorithm and examples. *Artif. Intell.* 41:1–63

Forbus KD. 1984. Qualitative process theory. *Artif. Intell.* 24:85–168

Forbus KD, Nielsen P, Faltings B. 1991. Qualitative spatial reasoning: The CLOCK project. *Artif. Intell.* 52:417–72

Garrod S, Anderson A. 1987. Saying what you mean in dialogue: a study in conceptual and semantic co-ordination. *Cognition* 27:181–218

Gentner D. 1981. Some interesting differences between nouns and verbs. *Cogn. Brain Theory* 4:161–78

Gentner D. 1983. Structure-mapping: a theoretical framework for analogy. *Cogn. Sci.* 7:155–70

Gentner D. 1989. The mechanism of analogical learning. In *Similarity and Analogical Reasoning*, ed. S Vosniadou, A Ortony, pp. 199–241. New York: Cambridge Univ. Press

Gentner D, Loewenstein J. 2000. Relational language and relational thought. In *Language, Literacy, and Cognitive Development*, ed. J Byrnes, E Amsel. Hillsdale, NJ: Erlbaum. In press

Gentner D, Markman AB. 1994. Structural alignment in comparison: no difference without similarity. *Psychol. Sci.* 5:152–58

Gentner D, Markman AB. 1997. Structural alignment in analogy and similarity. *Am. Psychol.* 52:45–56

Gentner D, Medina J. 1998. Similarity and the development of rules. *Cognition* 65:263–97

Gentner D, Rattermann MJ, Forbus KD. 1993. The roles of similarity in transfer: separating retrievability from inferential soundness. *Cogn. Psychol.* 25:524–75

Gentner D, Stevens AL, eds. 1983. *Mental Models*. Hillsdale, NJ: Erlbaum

Gentner D, Wolff P. 1997. Alignment in the processing of metaphor. *J. Mem. Lang.* 37:331–55

Gentner D, Wolff P. 2000. Metaphor and knowledge change. In *Cognitive Dynamics*, ed. E Dietrich, AB Markman, pp. 295–342. Mahwah, NJ: Erlbaum

Gilden DL, Proffitt DR. 1989. Understanding collision dynamics. *J. Exp. Psychol.: Hum. Percep. Perform.* 15:372–83

Glenberg AM. 1997. What memory is for. *Behav. Brain Sci.* 20(1):1–55

Glucksberg S, McGlone MS, Manfredi D. 1997. Property attribution in metaphor comprehension. *J. Mem. Lang.* 36:50–67

Goldstone RL. 1994. The role of similarity in categorization: providing a groundwork. *Cognition* 52:125–57

Goldstone RL, Medin DL. 1994. The time course of comparison. *J. Exp. Psychol.: Learn. Mem. Cogn.* 20:29–50

Gopnik A, Meltzoff AN. 1997. *Words, Thoughts and Theories*. Cambridge, MA: MIT Press

Guidagni PM, Little JDC. 1983. A logit model of brand choice calibrated on scanner data. *Mark. Sci.* 2:203–38

Gumperz JJ, Levinson SC. 1996. Introduction: linguistic relativity re-examined. In *Rethinking Linguistic Relativity*, ed. JJ Gumperz, SC Levinson, pp. 1–18. Cambridge, MA: Cambridge Univ. Press

Halford GS. 1992. Analogical reasoning and conceptual complexity in cognitive development. *Hum. Dev.* 35(4):193–218

Hampton JA. 1995. Testing the prototype theory of concepts. *J. Mem. Lang.* 34:686–708

Hatano G, Inagaki K. 1999. A developmental perspective on informal biology. See Medin & Atran 1999, pp. 321–54

Hegarty M, Just MA. 1993. Constructing mental models of machines from text and diagrams. *J. Mem. Lang.* 32: 717–42

Heit E. 1997. Knowledge and concept learning. In *Knowledge, Concepts, and Categories*, ed. K Lamberts, D Shanks, pp. 7–41. Cambridge, MA: MIT Press

Heit E, Rubinstein J. 1994. Similarity and property effects in inductive reasoning. *J. Exp. Psychol.: Learn. Mem. Cogn.* 20:411–22

Hirschfeld LA, Gelman SA, eds. 1994. *Mapping the Mind: Domain Specificity in Cognition and Culture*. New York: Cambridge Univ. Press

Holyoak KJ, Thagard P. 1989. Analogical mapping by constraint satisfaction. *Cogn. Sci.* 13:295–355

Howard IP. 1978. Recognition and knowledge of the water-level principle. *Perception* 7:151–60

Hummel JE, Holyoak KJ. 1997. Distributed representations of structure: a theory of analogical access and mapping. *Psychol. Rev.* 104:427–66

Imai M, Gentner D, Uchida N. 1994. Children's theories of word meaning: the role of shape similarity in early acquisition. *Cogn. Dev.* 9:45–75

Inagaki K, Hatano G. 1987. Young children's spontaneous personification as analogy. *Child Dev.* 58:1013–20

Johnson-Laird PN. 1983. *Mental Models*. Cambridge, MA: Harvard Univ. Press

Johnson-Laird PN. 1999. Deductive reasoning. *Annu. Rev. Psychol.* 50:109–35

Johnson-Laird PN, Byrne RMJ. 1991. *Deduction*. Hillsdale, NJ: Erlbaum

Jones SS, Smith LB, Landau B. 1991. Object properties and knowledge in early lexical learning. *Child Dev.* 62:499–516

Keil FC. 1989. *Concepts, Kinds and Cognitive Development*. Cambridge, MA: MIT Press

Kempton W, Boster JS, Hartley J. 1994. *Environmental Values in American Culture*. Cambridge, MA: MIT Press

Klayman J, Ha Y. 1987. Confirmation, disconfirmation and information in hypothesis testing. *Psychol. Rev.* 94:211–28

Koehler JJ. 1993. The influence of prior beliefs on scientific judgments of evidence quality. *Organ. Behav. Hum. Decis. Process.* 56:28–55

Kruschke JK. 1992. ALCOVE: an exemplar-based connectionist model of category learning. *Psychol. Rev.* 99:22–44

Kuhn D. 1997. Is good thinking scientific thinking? In *Modes of Thought: Explorations in Culture and Cognition*, ed. DR Olson, N Torrance, pp. 261–81. New York: Cambridge Univ. Press

Kuipers B. 1994. *Qualitative Reasoning: Modeling and Simulation with Incomplete Knowledge*. Cambridge, MA: MIT Press

Landau B, Smith LB, Jones SS. 1988. The importance of shape in early lexical learning. *Cogn. Dev.* 3:299–321

Lassaline ME. 1996. Structural alignment in induction and similarity. *J. Exp. Psychol.: Learn. Mem. Cogn.* 22:754–70

Lassaline ME, Murphy GL. 1998. Alignment and category learning. *J. Exp. Psychol.: Learn. Mem. Cogn.* 24:144–60

Leslie AM. 1991. The theory of mind impairment in autism: evidence for a modular mechanism of development? In *Natural Theories of Mind: Evolution, Development and Simulation of Everyday Mindreading*, ed. A Whiten. Oxford/Cambridge, MA: Blackwell

Logan GD. 1988. Toward an instance theory of automaticity. *Psychol. Rev.* 95:492–527

Logan GD. 1996. The CODE theory of visual attention: an integration of space-based and object-based attention. *Psychol. Rev.* 103:603–49

Love BC, Sloman SA. 1995. Mutability and the determinants of conceptual transformability. In *Proc. 17th Annu. Conf. Cogn. Sci. Soc.*, pp. 65–59. Pittsburgh, PA: Erlbaum

Malt BC. 1995. Category coherence in cross-cultural perspective. *Cogn. Psychol.* 29:85–148

Malt BC, Sloman SA, Gennari S, Shi M, Wang Y. 1999. Knowing versus naming: similarity and the linguistic categorization of artifacts. *J. Mem. Lang.* 40:230–62

Markman AB. 1997. Constraints on analogical inference. *Cogn. Sci.* 21:373–418

Markman AB. 1999. *Knowledge Representation*. Mahwah, NJ: Erlbaum

Markman AB, Gentner D. 1993a. Splitting the differences: a structural alignment view of similarity. *J. Mem. Lang.* 32:517–35

Markman AB, Gentner D. 1993b. Structural alignment during similarity comparisons. *Cogn. Psychol.* 25:431–67

Markman AB, Gentner D. 1996. Commonalities and differences in similarity comparisons. *Mem. Cogn.* 24:235–49

Markman AB, Gentner D. 1997. The effects of alignability on memory. *Psychol. Sci.* 8:363–67

Markman AB, Makin VS. 1998. Referential communication and category acquisition. *J. Exp. Psychol.: Gen.* 127(4):331–54

Markman AB, Wisniewski EJ. 1997. Similar and different: the differentiation of basic level categories. *J. Exp. Psychol.: Learn. Mem. Cogn.* 23:54–70

Markman EM. 1989. *Categorization and Naming in Children*. Cambridge, MA: MIT Press

McCloskey M. 1983. Naive theories of motion. See Gentner & Stevens 1983, pp. 299–324

Medin DL, Atran S, eds. 1999. *Folkbiology*. Cambridge, MA: MIT Press

Medin DL, Goldstone RL, Gentner D. 1993. Respects for similarity. *Psychol. Rev.* 100(2):254–78

Medin DL, Lynch EB, Coley JD, Atran S. 1997. Categorization and reasoning among tree experts: Do all roads lead to Rome? *Cogn. Psychol.* 32:49–96

Medin DL, Ross BH. 1989. The specific character of abstract thought: categorization, problem solving and induction. In *Advances in the Psychology of Human Intelligence*, ed. RS Sternberg, 5:189–223. Hillsdale, NJ: Erlbaum

Medin DL, Schaffer MM. 1978. Context theory of classification. *Psychol. Rev.* 85:207–38

Metz KE. 1985. The development of children's problem solving in a gears task: a problem space perspective. *Cogn. Sci.* 9:431–71

Murphy GL, Allopenna PD. 1994. The locus of knowledge effects in concept learning. *J. Exp. Psychol.: Learn. Mem. Cogn.* 20:904–19

Murphy GL, Medin DL. 1985. The role of theories in conceptual coherence. *Psychol. Rev.* 92:289–315

Nersessian N. 1999. Model-based reasoning in conceptual change. In *Model-Based Reasoning in Scientific Discovery*, ed. L Magroni, N Nersessian, P Thagard, pp. 5–22. Dordrecht, The Netherlands: Kluwer

Newell A, Simon HA. 1972. *Human Problem Solving*. Englewood Cliffs, NJ: Prentice-Hall

Norman DA. 1988. *The Psychology of Everyday Things*. New York: Basic Books

Nosofsky RM. 1986. Attention, similarity and the identification-categorization relationship. *J. Exp. Psychol.: Gen.* 115:39–57

Osherson DN, Smith EE, Wilkie O, Lopez A, Shafir E. 1990. Category based induction. *Psychol. Rev.* 97:185–200

Perani D, Schnur T, Tettamanti M, Gorno-Tempini M, Cappa S, Fazio F. 1999. Word and picture matching: a PET study of semantic category effects. *Neuropsychologia* 37:293–306

Pfeifer R, Scheier C. 1999. *Understanding Intelligence*. Cambridge, MA: MIT Press

Proffitt DR, Kaiser MK, Whelan SM. 1990. Understanding wheel dynamics. *Cogn. Psychol.* 22:342–73

Ramscar M, Pain H. 1996. Can a real distinction be made between cognitive theories of analogy and categorisation? *Proc. 18th Annu. Conf. Cogn. Sci. Soc.*, pp. 346–51. Hillsdale, NJ: Erlbaum

Reed SK. 1972. Pattern recognition and categorization. *Cogn. Psychol.* 3:382–407

Rehder B, Hastie R. 1998. The differential effects of causes on categorization and similarity. *Proc. 20th Annu. Conf. Cogn. Sci. Soc.*, pp. 893–98. Hillsdale, NJ: Erlbaum

Rips LJ. 1986. Mental muddles. In *The Representation of Knowledge and Belief*, ed. H Brand, RM Harnish. Tucson: Univ. Ariz. Press

Rips LJ. 1994. *The Psychology of Proof: Deductive Reasoning in Human Thinking*. Cambridge, MA: MIT Press

Rosch E, Mervis CB. 1975. Family resemblances: studies in the internal structure of categories. *Cogn. Psychol.* 7:573–605

Rosengren KS, Gelman SA, Kalish CW, McCormick M. 1991. As time goes by: children's early understanding of growth in animals. *Child Dev.* 62:1302–20

Ross BH. 1997. The use of categories affects classification. *J. Mem. Lang.* 37(2):240–67

Ross BH. 1999. Postclassification category use: the effects of learning to use categories after learning to classify. *J. Exp. Psychol.: Learn. Mem. Cogn.* 25(3):743–57

Ross BH, Perkins SJ, Tenpenny PL. 1990. Reminding-based category learning. *Cogn. Psychol.* 22:460–92

Schank RC, Collins GC, Hunter LE. 1986. Transcending inductive category formation in learning. *Behav. Brain Sci.* 9:639–86

Schwartz DL, Black JB. 1996. Shuttling between depictive models and abstract rules: induction and fallback. *Cogn. Sci.* 20:457–98

Schwartz DL, Black T. 1999. Inferences through imagined actions: knowing by simulated doing. *J. Exp. Psychol.: Learn. Mem. Cogn.* 25:116–36

Schyns PG, Goldstone RL, Thibaut JP. 1998. The development of features in object concepts. *Behav. Brain Sci.* 21:1–54

Shepard RN. 1962. The analysis of proximities: multidimensional scaling with an unknown distance function. I. *Psychometrika* 27:125–40

Shepard RN. 1964. Attention and the metric structure of the stimulus space. *J. Math. Psychol.* 1:54–87

Siegler RS, Shipley C. 1995. Variation, selection, and cognitive change. In *Developing Cognitive Competence: New Approaches to Process Modeling*, ed. TJ Simon, GS Halford, pp. 31–76. Hillsdale, NJ: Erlbaum

Simons DJ, Keil FC. 1995. An abstract to concrete shift in the development of biological thought: the insides story. *Cognition* 56:129–63

Sjöberg L. 1972. A cognitive theory of similarity. *Göteborg Psychol. Rep.* 2 (monograph)

Sloman SA. 1993. Feature-based induction. *Cogn. Psychol.* 25:231–80

Sloman SA. 1996. The empirical case for two systems of reasoning. *Psychol. Bull.* 119:3–22

Sloman SA, Love BC, Ahn WK. 1998. Feature centrality and conceptual coherence. *Cogn. Sci.* 22:189–228

Spalding TL, Murphy GL. 1996. Effects of background knowledge on category construction. *J. Exp. Psychol.: Learn. Mem. Cogn.* 22:525–38

Spalding TL, Ross BH. 1994. Comparison-based learning: effects of comparing instances during category learning. *J. Exp. Psychol.: Learn. Mem. Cogn.* 20:1251–63

Spellman BA, Holyoak KJ. 1996. Pragmatics in analogical mapping. *Cogn. Psychol.* 31:307–46

Stenning K, Oberlander J. 1995. A cognitive theory of graphical and linguistic reasoning: logic and implementation. *Cogn. Sci.* 19:97–140

Suchman LA. 1987. *Plans and Situated Actions: The Problem of Human-Machine Communication.* Cambridge, UK: Cambridge Univ. Press

Thelen E, Smith LB. 1993. *A Dynamic Systems Approach to the Development of Cognition and Action.* Cambridge, MA: MIT Press

Tooby J, Cosmides L. 1989. Evolutionary psychology and the generation of culture: 1. Theoretical considerations. *Ethol. Sociobiol.* 10(1–3):29–49

Tranel D, Damasio H, Damasio AR. 1997. A neural basis for the retrieval of conceptual knowledge. *Neuropsychologia* 35:1319–27

Tversky A. 1977. Features of similarity. *Psychol. Rev.* 84:327–52

Tversky B. 1991. Distortions in memory for visual displays. In *Spatial Instruments and Spatial Displays*, ed. SR Ellis, M Kaiser, A Grunewald, pp. 61–75. Hillsdale, NJ: Erlbaum

Vosniadou S, Brewer WF. 1992. Mental models of the earth: a study of conceptual change in childhood. *Cogn. Psychol.* 24:535–85

Warrington EK, Shallice T. 1984. Category specific semantic impairments. *Brain* 107:829–54

Wason PC, Johnson-Laird PN. 1972. *Psychology of Reasoning Structure and Content.* London: Routledge

Waxman SR. 1990. Linguistic biases and the establishment of conceptual hierarchies: evidence from preschool children. *Cogn. Dev.* 5:123–50

Wilson RA, Keil F. 1998. The shadows and shallows of explanation. *Minds Mach.* 8:137–59

Wisniewski EJ. 1995. Prior knowledge and functionally relevant features in concept learning. *J. Exp. Psychol.: Learn. Mem. Cogn.* 21:449–68

Wisniewski EJ, Medin DL. 1994. On the interaction of theory and data in concept learning. *Cogn. Sci.* 18:221–82

Wolff P, Gentner D. 2000. Evidence for role-neutral initial processing of metaphors. *J. Exp. Psychol.: Learn. Mem. Cogn.* 26:512–28

Yamauchi T, Markman AB. 1998. Category learning by inference and classification. *J. Mem. Lang.* 39:124–48

Zhang S, Markman AB. 1998. Overcoming the early entrant advantage: the role of alignable and nonalignable differences. *J. Mark. Res.* 35:413–26

Annu. Rev. Psychol. 2001. 52:249–75

CONSUMER RESEARCH: In Search of Identity

Itamar Simonson,[1] Ziv Carmon,[2] Ravi Dhar,[3]
Aimee Drolet,[4] and Stephen M. Nowlis[5]

[1]Graduate School of Business, Stanford University, Stanford, California 94305-5015;
e-mail: simonson_itamar@gsb.stanford.edu
[2]INSEAD, 77305 Fountainbleau Cedex, France; e-mail: ziv.carmon@insead.fr
[3]School of Management, Yale University, New Haven, Connecticut 06520;
e-mail: ravi.dhar@yale.edu
[4]Anderson School of Management, University of California at Los Angeles,
Los Angeles, California 90048; e-mail: aimee.drolet@anderson.ucla.edu
[5]College of Business, Arizona State University, Tempe, Arizona 85287;
e-mail: stephen.nowlis@asu.edu

Key Words buyer behavior, disciplinary influence, theory testing,
substantive phenomena

■ **Abstract** Although the consumer research field has made great progress over the past 30 years with respect to the scope, quality, and quantity of research, there are still significant disagreements about what consumer research is, what its objectives are, and how it should differ from related disciplines. As a result, the field appears to be rather fragmented and even divided on some fundamental issues. In this review we first examine the original vision for the field and its limitations. In the second section we explore the consequences of the ambiguity about the domain and identity of consumer research and the multidisciplinary influences on the field. In particular, we review key trends and "camps" in consumer research, which represent complementary and, in some cases, conflicting views regarding the main topics of investigation and how research is conducted. This review is based in part on systematic analyses of articles that have been published in the leading consumer research journals over the past 30 years. Finally, in the third section we revisit the question of what might differentiate the field from related disciplines, as well as the role of theory testing, studies of substantive phenomena, and relevance in consumer research.

CONTENTS

0066-4308/01/0201-0249$14.00

INTRODUCTION

The first chapter on "Consumer Analysis" to appear in the *Annual Review of Psychology* (Guest 1962) focused on survey techniques and other methodological aspects of consumer research, with a brief review of the hot topics of the 1950s—motivation research and subliminal advertising. The field of consumer research has made great progress since then, with a significant expansion of the range of topics studied and of the academic community of consumer researchers (for reviews, see e.g. Bettman 1986, Cohen & Chakravarti 1990, Jacoby 1976, Kassarjian 1982, Tybout & Artz 1994). The Association for Consumer Research (ACR) was founded in 1969, and the first consumer behavior textbooks and courses appeared in the late 1960s (e.g. Engel et al 1968, Kassarjian & Robertson 1968). Today, consumer researchers account for close to half of all (business school) marketing faculty, and the study of consumption is also a growing area in other disciplines, such as sociology, communication, and anthropology (e.g. Miller 1995). However, despite the rapid development of the field, there are still significant disagreements about what consumer research is, what its objectives are, and how it should differ from related disciplines. As a result, the field appears to be rather fragmented and even divided on some fundamental issues.

In this chapter, instead of following the format of providing a review of articles published in the previous 4 years, we take a broader perspective and examine the developments, the main influences, and the current state of consumer research. We also explore some of the ongoing debates regarding the identity and objectives of consumer research. Although we try to represent the different subfields and points of view, our own bias undoubtedly affects our interpretation of the developments and the alternative approaches to consumer research.

This review consists of three main sections. In the first we examine the original vision regarding the objectives of consumer research and the subjects of investigation, as well as the limitations of that research agenda. In the second section we explore the consequences of the ambiguity about the domain and identity of consumer research and the multidisciplinary influences on the field. In particular, we review the key trends and "camps" in consumer research, which represent complementary and, in some cases, conflicting views regarding the main topics of investigation and how research is conducted. This review is based, in part, on systematic analyses we conducted of articles that have been published in the leading consumer research journals over the past 30 years.[1] Finally, in the third section we revisit the question of what might differentiate the consumer research field from related fields, as well as the role of theory testing, studies of substantive phenomena, and relevance in consumer research.

IN THE BEGINNING: Domain-Specific Topics and Grand Theories of Consumer Behavior

Ronald Frank, the first editor of the *Journal of Consumer Research* (*JCR*), expected research to be published in the journal to encompass such topics as family planning behavior, occupational choices, mobility, determinants of fertility rates, attitudes towards and use of social services, and determinants of educational attainment (Frank 1974, p. i). Although this is not representative of the types of consumer research conducted at that time (see e.g. Bettman 1971, Jacoby et al 1974, Monroe 1973, Wright 1973), one is struck by the emphasis on topics that are specific to particular consumption categories, such as occupations and social services, and the omission of more general issues, such as persuasion and choice. An apparent assumption underlying this vision for *JCR* was that consumer researchers and researchers from related disciplines would primarily adapt, apply, and possibly extend theories developed in the basic disciplines, such as psychology, sociology, economics, and communication, to specific consumption categories.

It is noteworthy that the most influential frameworks in the early days of the consumer research field were comprehensive models of buyer behavior (e.g. Engel et al 1968, Howard & Sheth 1969, Nicosia 1966). The implicit assumption was that buyer behavior can be captured in one comprehensive model or "grand theory." The emphasis on comprehensive models of buyer behavior declined significantly during the 1980s, which appears to be a natural progression for the field. First, consumer behavior is too complex to be meaningfully captured in a single model. After all, consumer psychology involves most of the elements of human psychology, which cannot be meaningfully represented in any single model or theory. Second, although comprehensive models of buyer behavior served a purpose in integrating various components and, in some ways, defining the field, they could not be effectively tested, and the significance of the actual insights they provided may be debatable.

These models, as well as Frank's (1974) vision for *JCR*, did not resolve the question of what differentiates the consumer research field. In particular, whereas studying topics such as attitudes towards educational services and contraceptives might be relevant and useful for those interested in these subjects, many researchers

---

[1] Given space limitations, we report only the main findings from these analyses. Additional information regarding the method of analysis and findings can be obtained from the authors.

are likely to perceive as more important and interesting, more general issues, such as how attitudes are formed and choices made. However, focusing on more generic questions raises other "problems" relating to the unique identity and role of consumer research. As described in the next section, owing to this ambiguity and the overlap with more established fields, consumer research has been shaped to a large degree by developments and sometimes conflicting criteria and methods of related disciplines.

MULTIDISCIPLINARY INFLUENCES ON TRENDS AND CAMPS IN CONSUMER RESEARCH

In this section we examine the current state of consumer research, focusing on the multidisciplinary influences on the field with respect to both topics of investigation and research methods. In particular:

1. Because most key aspects of buyer behavior are also central research topics in other disciplines, especially psychology, one would expect developments in consumer research to reflect approaches and developments in the related disciplines. In this review we examine the trends in consumer research with respect to (*a*) the share of "social" versus "cognitive" topics and (*b*) the share of research on "cold" (e.g. attitudes, multi-attribute models, decision rules) versus "hot" (e.g. emotions, arousal, conflict) aspects of consumer behavior.

2. Although psychology has had the greatest impact on consumer research, other fields, such as economics and anthropology, have also had significant influences. Many consumer researchers have tended to be associated with particular other disciplines, representing alternative approaches to research. Consequently, consumer research camps have correspondingly differed in their views regarding important research questions and acceptable research methods. In this review we examine two distinctions within the consumer research field that can be traced to multidisciplinary influences: (*a*) behavioral decision theory (BDT) compared with social cognition consumer research and (*b*) postmodern (or interpretive) compared to positivist consumer research (including both social cognition and BDT research).

3. To further explore the changes in disciplinary impact on consumer research, we analyze the trend in the share of articles representing applications of theories developed in other fields compared with work involving original theory development and/or identification of new phenomena and explanations.

The Correspondence Between Trends in Psychology and Consumer Research: Social Versus Cognitive and "Hot" Versus "Cold" Topics

Social Versus Cognitive Consumer Research   Unlike researchers in psychology, consumer researchers are not identified as social or cognitive, and many researchers in the field have examined issues in both domains. However, following the common distinction in psychology between the social and cognitive domains and the increasing importance and sophistication of research on cognition, it is of interest to study whether there has been a corresponding increase in the share of cognitive relative to social topics studied by consumer researchers. To explore this question, two independent judges (doctoral students working in the area of consumer behavior) classified all consumer behavior articles that have appeared in the leading consumer research journals (*JCR* 1974–1999, *Journal of Marketing Research* 1969–1999, and *Journal of Consumer Psychology* 1990–1999) based on whether they dealt with issues that fall in the domain of social or cognitive psychology.

The exact results of this analysis depend on the manner in which articles in the general area of social cognition (e.g. attitude, persuasion, information processing), which is central to consumer research, are classified. However, regardless of whether social cognition topics are classified as social or cognitive, the qualitative conclusion made from this analysis is that the proportion of social topics has declined significantly, whereas the proportion of cognitive topics has correspondingly increased. Social areas of consumer research that have declined in importance include such topics as family and social influences, reference groups, attribution, and self-perception (e.g. Bearden & Etzel 1982; Folkes 1984, Scott & Yalch 1980). Some of the cognitive topics that have increased in importance include behavioral decision making (see Bettman et al 1998 for a review), memory and knowledge (e.g. Alba & Hutchinson 1987), language (e.g. Schmitt & Zhang 1998), variety seeking (e.g. McAlister 1982, Ratner et al 1999, Simonson 1990), and preconscious processing (e.g. Janiszewski 1988). It is noteworthy that some social topics have become more central, such as cross-cultural and ethnic influences on buyer behavior (e.g. Deshpande & Stayman 1994), the development of children as consumers (e.g. Gregan-Paxton & Roedder-John 1997), and gender differences (e.g. Meyers-Levy & Maheswaran 1991).

A major change has been the decline of attitudes as the central topic of research. In particular, the Fishbein & Ajzen (1975) multi-attribute attitude model and theory of reasoned action received a great deal of attention from consumer researchers in the 1970s and early 1980s, examining such questions as whether intentions mediate the effect of attitudes on behavior and the role of the normative component in the formation of attitudes (e.g. Lutz 1977, Miniard & Cohen 1983, Shimp & Kavas 1984; see also Bagozzi et al 1992).

Since the early 1980s, the elaboration likelihood model of Petty and Cacioppo (e.g. Petty et al 1983) and related dual process models (Chaiken 1980, Fiske &

Pavelchek 1986) have been accepted by most consumer researchers as the approach that can best account for the diverse findings on the formation of attitudes, persuasion, and related information processing issues (e.g. Aaker & Maheswaran 1997, Sujan 1985). In addition, consumer researchers have started to examine persuasion processes that relate specifically to marketing and were not derived from existing psychological theories, such as the persuasion knowledge model (Friestad & Wright 1994).

Another important development, which likely contributed to the decrease in the proportion of attitude and persuasion research, has been the growing interest in consumer decision making and the rise of BDT consumer research. In particular, Bettman's (1979) influential book, *An Information Processing Theory of Consumer Choice*, inspired by the work of Newell & Simon (1972), Payne (1976), and other decision-making researchers, presented a framework that describes how information inputs are processed to achieve a decision. It emphasized the role of short- and long-term memory, decision rules and heuristics, and other issues that have subsequently received much attention from consumer researchers.

Finally, memory and cognitive elaboration is another cognitive area that has received growing attention from consumer researchers, including the use of principles of memory operation to explain persuasive communication effects (e.g. Johar & Pham 1999, Keller 1987). For example, according to the resource-matching hypothesis (Norman & Borrow 1975; see Anand & Sternthal 1990 for a review), persuasion is enhanced or hindered depending on the match between the level of cognitive resources available for message processing and the level of cognitive resources that the message requires (e.g. Meyers-Levy & Tybout 1997, Unnava et al 1996).

Research on "Hot" Versus "Cold" Aspects of Consumer Behavior   A great deal of attitude and decision-making research has examined what might be considered "cold" aspects of consumer behavior. "Cold" aspects include such topics as the role of beliefs in attitude formation, attention, perception, information acquisition, learning, expertise, attribution, and decision rules. Conversely, "hot" aspects include such topics as the role of affect and mood, arousal, regret, low-involvement peripheral persuasion, hedonic aspects of consumption, conflict, and self-expressive motives for brand preference. In psychology there has been growing emphasis on the role of emotions and other "hot" aspects of cognition (see, e.g. Zajonc 1998).

We examined the proportion over time of "cold" and "hot" topics in consumer research based on a classification of articles that have been published in the leading consumer research journals (*JCR* 1974–1999, *Journal of Marketing Research* 1969–1999, and *Journal of Consumer Psychology* 1990–1999). Counting only articles that the judges coded as "cold" or "hot" (excluding the "other" category), there has been a decline in the relative proportion of "cold" topic articles from about 85% in the 1970s, to 75% in the 1980s, and 64% in the 1990s. For example, until recently decision-making research was clearly a "cold" domain, perhaps reflecting the cold economic benchmark often used by decision researchers. However, BDT consumer researchers have recently started to study the role of emotions in decision making (e.g. Bettman 1993). For example, Luce (1998) examined the effect of emotional tradeoff difficulty on the type and amount of information processing (see also Pham 1998, Shiv & Fedorikhin 1999). Other "hot" topics include, for example, affective responses to advertising (e.g. Baumgartner et al 1997, Edell & Chapman-Burke 1987), consumers' fun and fantasies (Holbrook & Hirschman 1982), and measures of consumption emotions (Richins 1997).

In summary, a review of articles published in the leading consumer research journals reveals two trends, both reflecting similar trends in psychology. There has been a decline in the proportion of classic social topics and an increase in the proportion of cognitive topics. Further, the proportion of "hot" topics has increased relative to "cold" topics, though the latter category still accounts for the majority of consumer research articles.

Disciplinary Influence and Alternative Orientations in Consumer Research: Behavioral Decision Theory Versus Social Cognition and Positivist Versus Postmodern

As indicated, consumer researchers who have been influenced by particular fields have tended to work on different topics and employ different research methods. In this section we explore two contrasts: (*a*) BDT versus social cognition consumer research and (*b*) positivist versus postmodern consumer research.

The Behavioral Decision Theory and Social-Cognition Approaches to Consumer Research   Whereas the distinction between social and cognitive research does not play nearly as significant a role in consumer research as it does in psychology, the somewhat loose distinction between social cognition–based research and so-called BDT is more prominent in consumer research. In psychology, BDT accounts for a relatively small segment of the literature, although leading BDT researchers such as Daniel Kahneman and Amos Tversky have had great impact on both the cognitive and social psychological literatures. In the consumer behavior literature, research that follows the BDT research paradigm has accounted for a large and growing proportion of all nonpostmodern articles published in the leading journals. Indeed, the central BDT issues of judgment and choice are directly relevant to the most researched area in marketing and consumer behavior, namely, influences on purchase decisions. Furthermore, BDT research serves as a bridge between the "behavioral" and "quantitative" sides of marketing because both BDT and quantitative research share the link to economics and the focus on consumer choice. Conversely, quantitative research in marketing tends to have less in common with social cognition consumer research (and even less with postmodern research).

First, it should be emphasized that social cognition and BDT researchers in marketing share many of the same research values and methods. For example, in the debate between the positivist and postmodern approaches to research, both social cognition and BDT researchers, by and large, are on the same (positivist) side. Furthermore, there are differences in emphasis among researchers within the consumer BDT and social cognition subfields, making it difficult to generalize regarding differences between the two camps. In particular, much BDT consumer research has investigated the processes underlying judgments and decisions (e.g. Coupey 1994, Dhar & Nowlis 1999, Sen & Johnson 1997). Conversely, other BDT research has focused more on judgment and decision-making phenomena, such as the manner in which consumers integrate the opinions of multiple critics (e.g. West & Broniarczyk 1998) or the impact of anticipating regret (e.g. Simonson 1992), where process measures are either not used at all or provide additional insights but are not the focus of the research. Similarly, there are large differences among social cognition consumer researchers with respect to both research methods and topics (see, e.g. Kisielius & Sternthal 1984 and Tybout et al 1983, compared with Alba et al 1999 and Lynch et al 1988).

With the caveat that there are exceptions to each of the following generalizations, there are several key differences between BDT and social cognition consumer research:

1. One obvious difference relates to the primary influences on each area. Social cognition consumer research has been influenced primarily by social cognition research in psychology (e.g. Chaiken 1980, Fiske & Taylor 1984). Conversely, the primary influence on BDT consumer research has been the BDT literature, including the work of Kahneman & Tversky (e.g. 1979), Thaler (1985), and other researchers. Furthermore, similar to BDT research published in nonmarketing journals, BDT consumer research has tended to use the normative benchmark of value maximization and time-consistent preferences for evaluating the significance of research findings. Thus, findings that demonstrate violations of the classical economic assumptions regarding buyer behavior have typically been regarded as interesting and important. For example, BDT consumer researchers have demonstrated that, (a) the framing of product attributes (e.g. ground beef that is "80% lean" or has "20% fat") influences product evaluation even after actual experience ("80% lean beef" tasted better than "20% fat beef;" Gaeth & Levin 1988); (b) when costs significantly precede benefits, the sunk cost effect is greatly diminished (Gourville & Soman 1998); (c) the interaction between the pleasure of consumption and the pain of paying has predictable impact on consumer behavior and hedonics (Prelec & Loewenstein 1998); and (d) preference elicitation tasks involving comparison of options (e.g. choice), judgments of individual options (e.g. ratings), and matching of two options varying in price and quality, produce systematically different preferences (e.g. Carmon & Simonson 1998, Hsee & Leclerc 1998, Nowlis & Simonson 1997). In recent years, the focus has shifted from demonstrations of value maximization violations

to studies that are designed to gain a better understanding of the factors that influence the construction of preferences (e.g. Drolet et al 2000; for a review, see Bettman et al 1998).

2. Social cognition and BDT consumer research have tended to build on different underlying models of buyer behavior and the communication process. One often referenced response hierarchy model (e.g. McGuire 1969), which has its origin in the communications area, includes the following stages: exposure/attention → reception/encoding → cognitive response → attitude → intention → behavior. The other model, which focuses on consumer decision making (or buying process), includes the following stages (e.g. Peter & Olson 1993): problem recognition → information search → evaluation of alternatives → purchase decision/choice → postpurchase evaluation. Although these two models highlight somewhat different elements in the consumer response and decision-making process (e.g. attention and intention versus search and evaluation) and employ different terminology, the essential components are quite similar. Thus, for example, most studies that examine influences on attitudes and attitude change also effectively investigate the formation of preferences and alternative evaluation, and vice versa (e.g. Morwitz et al 1993). However, whereas social cognition consumer research has focused on the stages in the communications (or hierarchy of-effects) model and on how judgments and attitudes are formed, BDT consumer research has tended to examine the decision-making model and particularly the determinants of choice.

3. Related to item 2, whereas BDT consumer researchers have studied primarily stimulus-based phenomena (e.g. Dhar 1997, Kahn & Louie 1990), social cognition research has focused more on memory-based tasks (e.g. Alba et al 1991; Biehal & Chakravarti 1982, 1983). For example, building on the influential accessibility-diagnosticity model of Feldman & Lynch (1988), Lynch et al (1988) proposed that decisions arise from a process whereby inputs are sequentially retrieved from memory, with the consumer updating the implications of already considered evidence with each new input retrieved. The order of retrieval is a function of the accessibility of each input, but accessible information can be actively disregarded if it is perceived to be nondiagnostic.

4. Although there are certainly exceptions to this generalization, BDT research has tended to focus more on substantive phenomena, which are explained based on existing theories or lead to theoretical extensions. Conversely, a greater share of social cognition consumer research has involved theory testing and extensions that have implications for the consumer environment (e.g. Ratneshwar & Chaiken 1991).

5. There are also differences in the process measures that social cognition and BDT consumer researchers tend to use. Social cognition researchers often

employ measures such as cognitive response (e.g. Sternthal et al 1978) and recall to gain insights into cognitive processes. In the BDT area, researchers who have used process measures tended to rely primarily on measures of information acquisition, verbal protocols, and response time (e.g. Bettman & Park 1980, Brucks 1988, Johnson 1984, Sen & Johnson 1997). There is no obvious explanation for the different process measures employed. Finally, the use of mediation and path analysis is more common in social cognition than in BDT consumer research.

Despite the differences between the social cognition and BDT approaches to consumer research, the main topics of investigation are closely related and the research methods, by and large, are similar. Thus, decreasing the division between the two areas and increasing communication and collaboration can advance the consumer research field. Consider, for example, the currently dominant view of consumer persuasion based on the elaboration likelihood model (e.g. Petty et al 1983). Briefly, evaluation of arguments presented in an ad is a frequent example of processing through the central route, whereas the impact of background music represents an example of persuasion through the peripheral route. However, depending on the motivation and ability to process the information, the same cue (e.g. the product endorser) might influence persuasion through either the central or peripheral route (e.g. Petty et al 1991).

In the BDT literature researchers have made a related distinction between compensatory and heuristic-based decision rules (see, e.g. Bettman 1979). This distinction, however, refers typically to the manner in which consumers process attribute information, as opposed to different types of information. Interestingly, BDT researchers have not paid much attention to the manner in which typical peripheral cues, such as source characteristics and background music, impact consumer preferences. On the other hand, BDT consumer researchers have studied extensively the impact of various contextual factors, such as task characteristics (e.g. Fischer et al 1999) and the configuration of the option set under consideration (e.g. Huber et al 1982, Huber & Puto 1983, Wernerfelt 1995), on consumer preferences. These contextual moderators have not received much attention in social cognition research on attitude and persuasion, even though such factors appear quite relevant to our understanding of attitude and persuasion.

Another area that could potentially benefit from increased integration of BDT and social cognition research involves the BDT notion of construction of preferences and the related concepts in social cognition of attitude accessibility and diagnosticity (e.g. Fazio et al 1989, Feldman & Lynch 1988), as well as the notions of attitude strength and ambivalence (e.g. Priester & Petty 1996). For example, Krosnick & Shuman (1988) showed that, contrary to common assumptions, measured attitudes of individuals whose attitudes are intense, important, and held with certainty, are just as susceptible to response order effects as other respondents'. A related finding from BDT consumer research is that expertise and involvement (e.g. owing to accountability) often do not diminish and, in some cases, enhance the susceptibility of consumers to judgment and decision errors such as overconfidence and the attraction effect (e.g. Mahajan 1992, Simonson 1989; but see Coupey et al 1998). Thus, by integrating findings from the social cognition and BDT areas, we are likely to gain a better understanding of the moderators of consumer susceptibility to various biases.

Another example of a finding in social cognition research that might have significant BDT implications is the observation that stronger, more accessible attitudes diminish sensitivity to changes in the attitude object (Fazio et al 2000). In particular, it suggests that, although well-formed, stable preferences might represent the ideal sovereign consumer, it might actually reduce consumer welfare and choice effectiveness. Finally, social cognition research on the measurement and construction of attitudes (e.g. Menon et al 1995; for a review, see Schwarz & Bohner 2000) can have significant implications for decision research, and vice versa. In sum, despite the differences in research traditions, issues, and methods, we believe there is a need and opportunity for greater interaction and collaboration between social cognition and BDT consumer researchers.

Postmodern and Positivist Consumer Research   So-called postmodern consumer research emerged in the 1980s (see also Levy 1959) and offered an alternative perspective to the purpose of consumer research, the important topics of investigation, and the research methods. An analysis of articles published between 1980 and 1999 in the major journal in the field, *JCR*, reveals that the proportion of postmodern research increased during the 1980s and represented approximately 20% of the published articles since 1990 (with the majority of the remaining articles representing positivist research). Briefly, whereas positivist research attempts to uncover cause-and-effect relationships and focuses on explanations, the postmodern approach focuses more on interpretation than causation and believes in a more subjective view of data interpretation (for a contrast of the two approaches, see Hudson & Ozanne 1988).

Postmodern researchers have also emphasized the need to distinguish consumer research from other fields and to avoid using managerial relevance as a criterion for evaluating research. For example, Belk (1986, p. 423) writes, "My own vision is one of consumer behavior as a discipline unto itself, with a variety of constituent groups, but with no overriding loyalty to any existing discipline or interest group. That is, consumer behavior should not be a subdiscipline of marketing, advertising, psychology, sociology, or anthropology, nor the handmaiden of business, government, or consumers. It should instead be a viable field of study, just as these other disciplines are, with some potential relevance to each of these constituent groups." Holbrook (1987, p. 128) proposes that consumer research refers to the "study of consummation in all its many aspects." Indeed, whereas most positivist research has focused on issues related to purchase decisions, a main emphasis in postmodern consumer research has been on specific consumption experiences and aspects of consumer behavior that had not previously been considered important areas for consumer research. For example, Belk & Costa (1998) recently published a paper regarding the mountain man myth, Thompson (1996) studied the juggling lifestyles of mothers, Arnould & Price (1993) studied the experience of river rafting, and Holbrook & Grayson (1986) provided a semiotic perspective of the movie *Out of Africa*. Also, in his 1998 presidential address to the Association of Consumer Research, John Sherry argued that traditional prose articles might be insufficient vessels for our understanding of consumer behavior and that other vehicles, such as poetry, can more effectively capture the subjective experience of inquiries about consumer behavior.

It should be noted that, in addition to what many positivist researchers regard as unusual topics, some postmodern consumer researchers have examined mainstream topics, such as customer satisfaction (Fournier & Mick 1999). However, by and large, postmodern researchers have introduced both new methods and new kinds of topics, inspired by research in anthropology, literature, and other fields that had previously had limited impact on consumer research. Similar to postmodern researchers in other disciplines such as anthropology, postmodern consumer researchers have employed different methodologies, including existential phenomenology (e.g. O'Guinn & Faber 1989, Thompson et al 1989), hermeneutics (Arnould & Fischer 1994), participant observation (Schouten & McAlexander 1995), in-depth interviews (Hirschman 1994), ethnography (Arnould & Wallendorf 1994), critical theory (Murray & Ozanne 1991), literary criticism (Stern 1989), and introspection (Gould 1991; but see Wallendorf & Brucks 1993).

The combination of what was perceived as a different kind of science, which deviates from traditional methods of analyzing and interpreting data, with what was perceived as unusual topics, has evoked strong opposition from many positivist researchers. For example, Cohen (1989) criticizes Belk's research on the role of consumer possessions (1988), arguing that it lacks meaning, empirical identification, and explanatory power. On the other hand, Firat & Venkatesh (1995, p. 260) appeal to positivist researchers to be more receptive to alternative paradigms, stating, "We therefore ask the consumer researchers who are steeped in the methods of cognitive psychology to come out of their protective shells, to set themselves free from unidimensional conceptions. ...It means that we must opt for multiple theories of consumer behavior rather than a single theory that silences all other theories."

At this stage, after the positions of proponents of the two convictions have been expressed in different forums, there is rather limited ongoing communication between them. Looking ahead, it is reasonable to expect that the intensity of the postmodern-positivist debate will diminish. Furthermore, because current marketing doctoral students in some schools are exposed to both positivist and postmodern professors, they are likely to be more receptive to both approaches. Most importantly, despite the current differences in methodology and topics, there are significant opportunities for collaboration. McQuarrie & Mick (1992) provided a fine example of the virtues of combining semiotics analysis and experiments in their research on advertising resonance. Indeed, with more openness and tolerance on both sides, there is significant room for collaboration and combining the advantages of both approaches. Although many positivist researchers are unlikely to change their views regarding data collection and analysis, the limitations of the traditional experimental methodologies and measures may enhance their willingness to combine quantitative data with less structured, more qualitative methods. Also, although positivist and postmodern consumer researchers have so far focused on different kinds of topics, as indicated, the methods employed by postmodern researchers could also be applied to more traditional topics, such as decision making, persuasion, regret, and affect.

Types of Consumer Research: Theory Development Versus Theory Application

Consumer research can be classified along a continuum from basic research, involving new theories, concepts, and explanations, to applications and minor extensions of existing theories and concepts. One might expect that in the early development of a new applied field such as consumer research there would be greater emphasis on applications of existing theories and borrowing from other, more established fields. However, over time, consumer researchers may seek to go beyond mere applications and minor theoretical extensions and introduce significant theoretical extensions and concepts, and in some cases, new theories relating to buyer behavior.

To examine this question more systematically, two independent judges (doctoral students specializing in consumer behavior) coded consumer research articles (not including postmodern articles) that have appeared in the August issues of the *Journal of Marketing Research* between 1969 and 1999 and articles that appeared in the September issues of the *JCR* between 1974 (the journal's first year) and 1999. Specifically, the judges coded articles dealing with consumer behavior on 1–4 scale, where 1 represents applications or minor extensions of established theories and phenomena (e.g. an investigation of a particular moderator or boundary condition, or ruling out an alternative explanation), and 4 represents articles introducing new constructs, theories, and/or phenomena.

The results show a significant time trend (correlation = 0.15), with the linear regression model yielding a significant coefficient for year as a predictor (p < 0.005). Specifically, looking at 5-year periods from 1969 through 1998, the proportion of articles coded as applications of existing theories and minor extensions (i.e. articles coded 1 or 2 on the 1–4 scale) declined continuously, from 94 % in 1969–1973 to 66% in 1994–1998. This trend is consistent with the notion that, as the field has evolved, the appreciation for research that merely applies theories developed elsewhere has declined. Although the consumer environment places some interesting constraints, and demonstrations that certain theories have implications for consumers and marketers can be important, such research is increasingly regarded as making limited (conceptual) contributions and not worthy of publication in the leading journals. Indeed, to the extent that the consumer environment is just another instance of the relevant constructs, there is no conceptual reason to expect the theories not to apply.

We also examined whether there has been a trend with respect to research topics that examine issues that are specific to and relevant primarily to consumer research and marketing as opposed to topics of general interest that might have been published in psychology and other basic discipline journals. For example, whereas the topic of brand equity and extension is central to marketing (e.g. Aaker 1997, Aaker & Keller 1990, Broniarczyk & Alba 1994, Fournier 1998, Keller 1993, Gardner & Levy 1955, Park et al 1991), it has limited significance to other fields. Excluding postmodern articles from the analysis, there has not been a significant change on that dimension; during 1969–1973, 67% of the articles were classified as consumer/marketing specific (1 or 2 on the 1–4 scale), and since 1973 the two topic categories (consumer-specific versus general) have accounted for approximately the same share of consumer research articles.

In summary, our review of the state of consumer research and developments in the field over the past 30 years points to several key trends. First, research topics continue to be influenced by trends in other disciplines, especially psychology. Second, related to the multidisciplinary impact, the consumer research field is characterized by significant divisions between subareas, which not only tend to study different topics, but also differ in terms of their research orientation and methods. Finally, our analysis points to a growing emphasis on original topics and theories compared with applications of existing theories adopted from other fields.

IN SEARCH OF IDENTITY: The Role of Relevance, Theory Testing, and Substantive Phenomena

As the preceding review of developments in consumer research and multidisciplinary influence on the field suggests, despite the progress in terms of the quality and quantity of published articles, some of the fundamental debates regarding the objectives and the appropriate topics and methods have not been resolved. The view that consumer research "seeks to produce knowledge about consumer behavior" (Calder & Tybout 1987, p. 136) implies that the important consumer research topics are also main topics in other disciplines, creating ambiguity as to what distinguishes consumer research (other than being a "one-stop shop" for studies of relevance to consumer behavior). Another "constraint" that significantly affects the priorities of many consumer researchers is the fact that most of them are marketing professors in schools of business and might have (explicit and/or implicit) incentives to focus on research topics that are potentially relevant to managers and, to a lesser degree, other constituencies. In this concluding section we examine the different perspectives on the role of relevance and the emphasis on theory-testing versus substantive phenomena-driven research (which leads to theory development), as well as the implications of these approaches for the purpose and identity of the consumer research field.

The Objectives and (Ir)Relevance of Consumer Research   One would expect any research field or discipline to have a unique identity and purpose that separate it from other fields. Earlier we cited the vision of the first editor of the *JCR*, Ronald Frank (1974), regarding the domain-specific aspects of consumer behavior that he expected researchers from multiple disciplines to examine. At about the same time, the Association for Consumer Research (ACR) was founded with the goal of providing "a forum for exchange of ideas among those interested in consumer behavior research in academic disciplines, in government at all levels from local through national, in private business, and in other sectors such as non-profit organizations and foundations" (Pratt 1974, p. 4). In 1993, Wells argued that the original vision for the consumer research field has faded and the discipline "faces inward, toward a narrower range of issues, and away from the real world."

Whether or not one shares this assessment of the state of the field, it appears that the original vision regarding the direction and objectives of the ACR and *JCR* has not materialized. With relatively few exceptions, *JCR* and the ACR have not become forums in which researchers from multiple fields exchange ideas about consumer behavior. Also, although some articles published in *JCR* and other journals have examined specific consumer issues, such as food and energy consumption and the provision of nutrition information (e.g. Reilly & Wallendorf 1987, Ritchie et al 1981, Russo et al 1986), most articles published in the leading journals have examined more generic topics such as choice and attitudes. Thus, it is sometimes unclear what differentiates consumer research from other disciplines, except for the experimental stimuli used (e.g. choice between cars versus choice between bets) and the research positioning.

It is also noteworthy that consumer research has not differed significantly from psychology with respect to the proportion of laboratory studies and the use of student subjects. Specifically, our analysis of articles published in the leading consumer research journals[2] indicates that (*a*) the proportion of laboratory studies (defined as studies in which participants were aware that they were participating in a study) climbed from about 80% to around 90% in the mid-1970s and has stayed at that level ever since and (*b*) whereas the proportion of studies using student subjects was only about 30% until the early 1980s, the use of student subjects has increased steadily since then, representing approximately 75% of (positivist) studies published during the 1995–1999 period (see McGrath & Brinberg 1983, Calder et al 1981, and Lynch 1982 for a discussion of the virtues of using homogeneous subject populations such as students).

A related question regarding the role and identity of consumer research is the issue of relevance (see Shimp 1994 for a comprehensive and insightful discussion of this question). Should consumer research be relevant and useful in a concrete way to particular constituencies, or should consumer research produce general knowledge about consumer behavior that could potentially be relevant to various constituencies? Shimp argues that, although consumer research may not be directly relevant to managers and other particular constituencies (other than fellow academics), the knowledge produced by consumer researchers is eventually diffused through teaching, books, consulting, and other channels.

---

[2]This analysis is based on an examination of consumer behavior articles published in the August issues of the *Journal of Marketing Research* between 1969 and 1999, and articles published in the September issues of the *JCR* from 1974 till 1999.

The (ir)relevance of consumer research to managers has received particular attention, and as business schools become more sensitive and responsive to criticism of companies, students, and the popular media, this issue has gained prominence. Although there is continuing disagreement among consumer researchers regarding the virtues of being relevant to managers (e.g. Holbrook 1985), there appears to be general consensus that (academic) consumer research has had rather limited actual impact on managerial practice [(e.g. Lutz 1991, Wells 1993; an exception to this generalization is some of the studies dealing with new research methodologies [e.g. Green & Srinivasan 1978])]. Interestingly, consumer research articles increasingly emphasize the managerial implications of the findings, and in some journals, having specific managerial implications is one of the conditions for publication. Yet, few managers (or consumers) read consumer research articles that are published in the major journals, and the issues investigated are typically not at a level that is of much use for them.

Also, the proportion of articles published in the major marketing journals that have public policy implications declined in the 1990s compared with the 1970s and 1980s (though this trend might be explained in part by the introduction of the *Journal of Public Policy & Marketing*). Our analysis[3] indicates that, during the second half of the 1970s through the 1980s, approximately 20% of the consumer research articles published in major consumer research journals included public policy implications (e.g. Andreasen 1985, Beales et al 1981), but the proportion of public policy–relevant articles declined to approximately 3% in the 1990s (e.g. Block & Anand-Keller 1995, Pechmann & Ratneshwar 1994).

This situation, whereby a field of research has limited concrete relevance or immediate impact on particular constituencies, is certainly not unique to consumer research. Furthermore, it is easy to identify reasons for the limited relevance of consumer research, including (*a*) the emphasis on theoretical contribution, rigor, and statistical (rather than practical) significance tends to limit the practical relevance; (*b*) the research, review, and publication process typically takes several years; (*c*) unlike researchers in other departments (e.g. medical researchers), who depend on external funding, many consumer researchers require limited funds, and these funds are typically provided by the business schools; (*d*) the gatekeepers of the leading consumer research journals are almost exclusively academics (for example, in 1999, 88 of the 90 members of the *JCR* Editorial Board were university professors); and (*e*) many consumer researchers have limited institutional knowledge and may be removed from the concerns and problems faced by managers, public policy makers, and even consumers (e.g. Armstrong 1991, Hoch 1988).

---

[3]Two independent coders rated each consumer research article published in August issues of the *Journal of Marketing Research* (since 1969), September issues of the *JCR* (since 1974), and Summer issues of the *Journal of Consumer Psychology* (since 1991) in terms of the relevance of its findings and conclusions to public policy makers. The coders used a 0–3 scale where 0 = not at all relevant and 3 = very relevant.

Theory-Testing Versus Substantive Phenomena-Driven Consumer Research
Calder & Tybout (1999; see also Calder et al 1981) distinguish between
(*a*) theory testing, which involves testing of explanations and relations among
underlying constructs as well as "intervention testing" (i.e. theory applications)
and (*b*) effect applications, in which the research question is whether previously
observed effects derived from a particular theory extend to specific other settings.
In the former a study is designed to provide the strongest test of the theory, with
an emphasis on internal rather than external validity, whereas the latter requires
that the experimental design represents most accurately the settings of interest.
Importantly, both types of research are driven by existing theories—either theory
testing or applications and extensions of theories to particular settings. The argument for emphasizing research that is designed to test and apply theories is that it
generates universal principles that "explain any real-world situation within their
domain" (Calder et al 1981). From that perspective, theoretical explanations are
the most important product of research, whereas generalized empirical phenomena
have a lower status and are primarily designed to test and potentially falsify the
theory. However, the starting point and motivation for a research project might
be either theory testing or a study of a particular substantive (or methodological)
domain that yields a set of observations (see discussion of the validity network
schema [McGrath & Brinberg 1983, Brinberg & McGrath 1985]). Such empirical
observations are typically interpreted based on existing theories, and they often
suggest extensions or modifications of existing theories.

Although both theory tests and research that begins with substantive issues
and phenomena can contribute to theory building, there are important differences
between them. First, with the latter approach, the substantive phenomena investigated are considered interesting in their own right, as opposed to being merely
arenas for theory testing. For example, understanding whether and under what
conditions consumers discount missing attribute values (e.g. Meyer 1981), draw
spontaneous inferences when processing ads (e.g. Kardes 1988), tend to confirm
hypotheses generated by ads (e.g. Deighton 1984, Hoch & Ha 1986), prefer pioneering brands (e.g. Carpenter & Nakamoto 1989, Kardes et al 1993), and prefer
to co-consume items (e.g. a tasty, unhealthy appetizer and a healthier, less tasty en-
tree) that "balance" each other (e.g. Dhar & Simonson 1999) are research-worthy
questions in their own right. The findings of such investigations, in turn, often
contribute to theory development.

A second implication of substantive issue-driven research is that identifying
generalized empirical phenomena is an important step in the research process.
For example, Huber et al (1982) made an interesting observation whereby the
addition of an asymmetrically dominated option to a two-option set increases the
(absolute) choice share of the dominating option, in violation of the economic
assumption of value maximization. Although Huber et al offered several possible
explanations, there was no clear theoretical account for this phenomenon when
the article was published. However, this finding generated a great deal of interest,
leading subsequently to the development of theoretical accounts for such "context

effects" (e.g. Ariely & Wallsten 1995, Simonson & Tversky 1992). In that respect, consumer researchers can learn from the "quantitative" researchers in marketing, who often begin with an examination of relevant empirical phenomena, leading to empirical generalizations and theory building (Bass & Wind 1995).[4]

Relatedly, Alba (1999) suggested that less emphasis on theory tests and greater emphasis on obtaining data points would help advance the consumer research field. He writes, "Despite its multidisciplinary positioning, consumer research has been influenced by a narrow set of scientific traditions. A characteristic trait of these traditions is an emphasis on 'theory,' which is loosely conceived but frequently embodied in structural models or process explanations of empirical phenomena. ...The irony for consumer research, however, is that it places premium on theory when in reality it is starved for reliable data points." This point of view is consistent with the approach employed, for example, in medical research, where robust effects are regarded as interesting and important in and of themselves, with the theory often developed at a later time.

This does not mean that theory testing is not an important priority for consumer researchers (e.g. Petty & Cacioppo 1996). Indeed, theories such as the elaboration likelihood model (e.g. Petty et al 1983) and prospect theory (Kahneman & Tversky 1979) have had tremendous impact on the field. However, a question that arises is whether the dominant emphasis on theory-tests as opposed to substantive domain-driven consumer research has indeed enhanced the contribution and the impact of consumer research on its various constituencies. Lutz (1991) argued that the likelihood that theory-tests will yield insights into substantive phenomena of interest is quite remote and that the most likely yield is with respect to the theory being tested. He further proposed that one way to ensure better representation of the substantive domain is to conduct research in naturally occurring consumer purchase, consumption, and communications situations (see also Winer 1999). This argument is related to the debate in the consumer research literature regarding the proper role and significance of external validity in theory tests (e.g. Calder et al 1981, Lynch 1982). Consistent with Lutz's position, if in addition to theory testing, the goal of a research program is to gain a better understanding of particular substantive phenomena and the boundaries of relevant theories, then inclusion of field studies, even if they require some compromise with respect to internal validity, becomes important. As Taylor argued (1998, p. 84), "... to the extent that any program of research must ultimately address both what can happen and what does happen, making use of laboratory experiments to the exclusion of parallel field studies is unwise. Moreover, field studies ... provide valuable insights into the

---

[4]A possible limitation of substantive domain-driven research is that there are no clear criteria for determining which questions are interesting and worthy of research, whereas theory tests might offer clearer guidelines. However, the research community, in general, and journal reviewers, in particular, can help educate researchers as to the types of substantive issues considered interesting.

natural contexts in which phenomena occur; they provide information about the strength of the phenomena, given correlated environmental circumstances; they may be helpful in elucidating mediation; and they are extremely important for identifying variables both internal to the person and the environmental nature that moderate the phenomenon."

Similarly, Shimp (1994; see also Lehmann 1996) proposed that consumer research needs to put far greater emphasis on "consumer behavior that occurs within the milieu of actual marketplace phenomena." He suggested that theories taken from other disciplines should be used as instruments rather than as the primary objectives of empirical inquiry. The ultimate goal, he argues, is "the development of theory about actual consumer behavior that may serve the needs of all markets interested in consumer research: academics, students, businesspeople, public policy officials, and society at large"(p. 5).

CONCLUSION

We have examined the current state of consumer research, the multidisciplinary influences on the field and their consquences, as well as the question of what differentiates it from other fields. Multiple influences on an applied area and an identity problem are probably not unique to consumer research (see, e.g. Tetlock's 1998 discussion of the "reductionist syllogism"in his review of research on world politics). However, because consumer behavior is such a broad area in which the central topics are shared with other fields and disciplines, it is particularly susceptible to division and disagreement regarding the key research topics and how research should be conducted. In this review we have explored the differences between three particular subfields—social cognition, BDT, and postmodern consumer research—and highlighted the opportunities for greater collaboration.

Importantly, although multiple and, in some cases, incompatible influences tend to generate disagreements, the exposure to multidisciplinary influences and the different approaches represented in consumer research are also a significant strength that contributes to the quality and diversity of scholarly work. Thus, some studies conducted by consumer researchers represent basic research, dealing with the same fundamental issues that researchers in the related disciplines investigate. In fact, in certain basic research areas that are particularly relevant to businesses and consumers, such as decision making, business schools, including consumer researchers, appear to have taken the lead from the relevant disciplines (e.g. psychology). In addition to basic research, consumer researchers will also continue to apply, test, and extend theories developed in other disciplines. Such research can have significant impact on the field and often contributes to theory development. In particular, the consumer environment imposes relevant constraints and the stimuli used are often richer and more complex than those employed by researchers in psychology. This, in turn, forces the researcher to evaluate the boundaries of the theory, which can lead to theoretical extensions and improve our understanding of the moderating factors and the conditions under which the theory is applicable.

A third type of consumer research, which we believe deserves greater emphasis, focuses on substantive phenomena of interest and often leads to theory development (e.g. Alba 1999, Lutz 1991, Shimp 1994; see also Cialdini 1980). Because such research tends to be motivated by phenomena rather than by theory-testing, it is sometimes viewed as atheoretical and of lower status. However, rigorous studies of substantive phenomena build on the relative advantages and incentives of consumer researchers (and business school faculty more generally), and in many cases make significant contributions to theory development. Furthermore, compared to researchers in the basic disciplines, consumer researchers often have greater exposure to "real world" problems (e.g. of organizations and consumers) and easier access to data relating to substantive phenomena.

The saying that "there is nothing more practical than a good theory" not withstanding, another advantage of substantive phenomena-driven research is that it is usually more relevant, particularly to the phenomena being investigated. Whether or not researchers believe it is good for consumer research (e.g. Holbrook 1985), the pressure on business school faculty to be relevant and the incentives to conduct research that is relevant in a reasonably concrete way to managers and/or other constituencies continue to play a significant role that many researchers are unlikely to ignore. Although ulterior motives have some negative associations, an emphasis on relevance should not come at the expense of rigor and, ultimately, theoretical contribution. Furthermore, in addition to tightly controlled lab studies that allow unconfounded tests of cause and effect, substantive domain-focused investigations will benefit from the inclusion of studies in more naturalistic settings, even if such tests involve a certain compromise in terms of internal validity. Also, when conducting lab studies, consumer research will benefit from greater attention to using stimuli and tasks that include the essential characteristics of the relevant substantive domains.

Consider, for example, a study of buyer behavior in online auctions, which examines various factors that influence bidding behavior and the willingness to pay for items being auctioned. In addition to improving our understanding of online auctions, such research might have significant theoretical implications regarding escalation, competitive behavior, inference making, perceived value, and other conceptually important issues. A researcher embarking on such a project may begin the investigation by observing actual online auctions, which might offer some tentative hypotheses regarding relevant influences. However, in all likelihood, the presence of confounding factors will limit the researcher's ability to establish unambiguously the generality of the observed phenomena and their causes. Accordingly, the researcher may conduct lab studies using simulated auctions, possibly providing incentives to participants, such as indicating that one or more of the auctions will actually be applied. This lab research, in turn, may lead to additional field experiments that might provide further insights.

In summary, the relative emphasis on theory-testing versus substantive domain-driven research and on external validity is relevant also to the question of the identity of the consumer research field. A greater emphasis on substantive phenomena and the combination of tightly controlled lab studies with investigations in more naturalistic settings, we believe, will differentiate the field and enhance its impact on both theory and practice. Indeed, buyer behavior offers an exceptionally rich domain for studying a wide range of real world phenomena that have potentially important theoretical implications. Furthermore, with the advancement of new technologies and the rise of the Internet, consumer researchers are in a much better position today to conduct investigations that deal with marketplace phenomena while maintaining experimental control. Finally, a greater emphasis on rigorous, systematic, substantive phenomena-driven research has the potential to produce major contributions to theory, precisely because the starting point is not an existing theory. Thus, such research can significantly enhance the impact of the consumer research field on researchers in the consumer and related fields, industry, and public policy makers.

ACKNOWLEDGMENTS

This chapter has benefited greatly from the suggestions of many leading consumer researchers; special thanks to James Bettman, Richard Lutz, and Terry Shimp for their helpful comments.

Visit the Annual Reviews home page at www.AnnualReviews.org

LITERATURE CITED

Aaker D, Keller K. 1990. Consumer evaluations of brand extensions. *J. Mark.* 54:27–41

Aaker JL. 1997. Dimensions of brand personality. *J. Mark. Res.* 34:347–56

Aaker JL, Maheswaran D. 1997. The effect of cultural orientation on persuasion. *J. Consum. Res.* 24:315–28

Alba J. 1999. President's column: loose ends. *Assoc. Consum. Res. Newsl.*, Dec., p. 2

Alba J, Hutchinson W. 1987. Dimensions of consumer expertise. *J. Consum. Res.* 13:411–45

Alba J, Hutchinson W, Lynch J. 1991. Memory and decision making. See Robertson & Kassarjian 1991, pp. 1–49

Alba JW, Mela CF, Shimp TA, Urbany JE. 1999. The effect of discount frequency and depth on consumer price judgments. *J. Consum. Res.* 26:99–114

Anand P, Sternthal B. 1990. Ease of message processing as a moderator of repetition effects in advertising. *J. Mark. Res.* 27:345–53

Andreasen AR. 1985. Consumer responses to dissatisfaction in loose monopolies. *J. Consum. Res.* 12:135–41

Ariely D, Wallsten TS. 1995. Seeking subjective dominance in multidimensional space: an explanation of the asymmetric dominance effect. *Organ. Behav. Hum. Decis. Process.* 63(3):223–32

Armstrong JS. 1991. Prediction of consumer behavior by experts and novices. *J. Consum. Res.* 18(2):251–56

Arnould E, Wallendorf M. 1994. Market-oriented ethnography: interpretation building and marketing strategy formulation. *J. Mark. Res.* 31(4):484–504

Arnould EJ, Fischer E. 1994. Hermeneutics and consumer research. *J. Consum. Res.* 21(1):55–70

Arnould EJ, Price LL. 1993. River magic: extraordinary experience and the extended service encounter. *J. Consum. Res.* 20(1):24–45

Bagozzi RP, Baumgartner H, Yi Y. 1992. State versus action orientation and the theory of reasoned action: an application to coupon usage. *J. Consum. Res.* 18:505–18

Bass FM, Wind J. 1995. Introduction to the special issue: empirical generalizations in marketing, *Mark. Sci.* 14(3) Part 2:G6–19

Baumgartner H, Sujan M, Padgett D. 1997. Patterns of affective reactions to advertisements: the integration of moment-to-moment responses into overall judgments. *J. Mark. Res.* 34:219–32

Beales H, Mazis MB, Salop SC, Staelin R. 1981. Consumer search and public policy. *J. Consum. Res.* 8:11–22

Bearden WO, Etzel MJ. 1982. Reference group influence on product and brand purchase decisions. *J. Consum. Res.* 9:183–94

Belk RW. 1986. Generational differences in the meaning of things. *Advert. Consum. Psychol.* 3:199–213

Belk RW. 1988. Possessions and the extended self. *J. Consum. Res.* 15(2):139–68

Belk RW, Costa JA. 1998. The mountain man myth: a contemporary consuming fantasy. *J. Consum. Res.* 218–40

Bettman J, Luce MF, Payne JW. 1998. Constructive consumer choice processes. *J. Consum. Res.* 25:187–217

Bettman JR. 1971. The structure of consumer choice processes. *J. Mark. Res.* 8:465–71

Bettman JR. 1979. *An Information Processing Theory of Consumer Choice.* Reading, MA: Addison Wesley

Bettman JR. 1986. Consumer psychology. *Annu. Rev. Psychol.* 37:257–89

Bettman JR. 1993. The decision maker who came in from the cold. In *Advances in Consumer Research*, ed. L McAlister, M Rothschild, 20:7–11. Provo, UT: Assoc. for Consum. Res.

Bettman JR, Park CW. 1980. Effects of prior knowledge and experience and phase of the choice process: a protocol analysis. *J. Consum. Res.* 7:234–48

Biehal G, Chakravarti D. 1982. Information presentation format and learning goals as determinants of consumers' memory retrieval and choice processes. *J. Consum. Res.* 8:431–41

Biehal G, Chakravarti D. 1983. Information accessibility as a moderator of consumer choice. *J. Consum. Res.* 10:1–14

Block LG, Anand Keller P. 1995. When to accentuate the negative: the effects of perceived efficacy and message framing on intentions to perform health-related behavior. *J. Mark. Res.* 32:192–203

Brinberg D, McGrath J. 1985. *Validity and the Research Process.* Beverly Hills, CA: Sage

Broniarczyk SM, Alba J. 1994. The importance of the brand in brand extension. *J. Mark. Res.* 31:214–28

Brucks M. 1988. Search monitor: an approach for computer controlled experiments involving consumer information search. *J. Consum. Res.* 15:117–21

Calder BJ, Phillips LW, Tybout AM. 1981. Designing research for applications. *J. Consum. Res.* 8:197–207

Calder BJ, Tybout AM. 1987. What consumer research is. *J. Consum. Res.* 14(1):136–40

Calder B, Tybout AM. 1999. A vision of theory, research, and the future of business schools. *J. Acad. Mark. Sci.* 27(3):359–66

Carmon Z, Simonson I. 1998. Price-quality tradeoffs in choice vs. matching: new insights into the prominence effect. *J. Consum. Psychol.* 7:323–43

Carpenter GS, Nakamoto K. 1989. Consumer preference formation and pioneering advantage. *J. Mark. Res.* 26:285–98

Chaiken S. 1980. Heuristic versus systematic information processing and the use of source versus message cues in persuasion. *J. Pers. Soc. Psychol.* 39:752–66

Cialdini RB. 1980. Full cycle social psychology. In *Applied Social Psychology Annual*, ed. L Bickman, 1:21–47. Beverly Hills, CA: Sage

Cohen JB, Chakravarti D. 1990. Consumer psychology. *Annu. Rev. Psychol.* 41:243–88

Cohen JB. 1989. An overextended self? *J. Consum. Res.* 16:125–28

Coupey E. 1994. Restructuring: constructive processing of information displays in consumer choice. *J. Consum. Res.* 21:83–99

Coupey E, Irwin JR, Payne JW. 1998. Product category familiarity and preference construction. *J. Consum. Res.* 24:459–68

Deighton J. 1984. The interaction of advertising and evidence. *J. Consum. Res.* 11:763–70

Deshpande R, Stayman DM. 1994. A tale of two cities: distinctiveness theory and advertising effectiveness. *J. Mark. Res.* 31:57–64

Dhar R. 1997. Consumer preference for a no-choice option. *J. Consum. Res.* 24:215–31

Dhar R, Nowlis SM. 1999. The effect of time pressure on consumer choice deferral. *J. Consum. Res.* 25:369–84

Dhar R, Simonson I. 1999. Making complementary choices in consumption episodes: highlighting versus balancing. *J. Mark. Res.* 36:29–44

Drolet A, Simonson I, Tversky A. 2000. Indifference curves that travel with the choice set. *Mark. Lett.* 11:199–209

Edell JA, Chapman Burke M. 1987. The power of feelings in understanding advertising effects. *J. Consum. Res.* 14:421–33

Engel J, Kollat D, Blackwell R. 1968. *Consumer Behavior.* New York: Holt, Rinehart & Winston

Fazio RH, Ledbetter JE, Towles-Schwen T. 2000. On the cost of accessible attitudes: detecting that the attitude object has changed. *J. Pers. Soc. Psychol.* 78:197–210

Fazio RH, Powell MC, Williams CJ. 1989. The role of attitude accessibility in the attitude-to-behavior process. *J. Consum. Res.* 16:280–88

Feldman JM, Lynch JG Jr. 1988. Self generated validity and other effects of measurement on belief, attitude, intention and behavior. *J. Appl. Psychol.* 73:421–35

Firat AF, Venkatesh A. 1995. Liberatory postmodernism and the reenchantment of consumption. *J. Consum. Res.* 22:239–67

Fischer G, Carmon Z, Ariely D, Zauberman G. 1999. Goal-based construction of preference: task goals & the prominence effect. *Manage. Sci.* 45:1057–75

Fishbein M, Ajzen I. 1975. *Belief, Attitude, Intention and Behavior: An Introduction to Theory and Research.* Reading, MA: Addison-Wesley

Fiske ST, Taylor SE. 1984. *Social Cognition.* New York: McGraw-Hill

Fiske ST, Pavelchek MA. 1986. Category-based versus piecemeal-based affective responses: development in schema-triggered affect. In *Handbook of Motivation and Cognition: Foundations of Social Behavior*, ed. RM Sorrentino, ET Higgins, pp. 167–203. New York: Guilford

Folkes VS. 1984. Consumer reactions to product failure: an attributional approach. *J. Consum. Res.* 10:398–409

Fournier S. 1998. Consumers and their brands: developing relationship theory in consumer research. *J. Consum. Res.* 24:343–73

Fournier S, Mick DG. 1999. Rediscovering satisfaction. *J. Mark.* 63:5–23

Frank R. 1974. Letter from the editor. *J. Consum. Res.* 1:i

Friestad M, Wright P. 1994. The Persuasion Knowledge Model: how people cope with persuasion attempts. *J. Consum. Res.* 21:1–31

Gaeth G, Levin I. 1988. How consumers are affected by the framing of attribute information before and after consuming the product. *J. Consum. Res.* 15:374–78

Gardner BB, Levy SL. 1955. The product and the brand. *Harv. Bus. Rev.* Mar–Apr:33–38

Gilbert D, Fiske ST, Lindzey G. 1998. *The Handbook of Social Psychology*, Vol. 1. New York: McGraw-Hill. 4th ed.

Gould SJ. 1991. The self manipulation of my pervasive, perceived vital energy through product use: an introspective-Praxis perspective. *J. Consum. Res.* 18:194–207

Gourville JT, Soman D. 1998. Payment depreciation: the behavioral effects of temporally separating payments from consumption. *J. Consum. Res.* 25:160–74

Green PE, Srinivasan V. 1978. Conjoint analysis in consumer research: issues and outlook. *J. Consum. Res.* 5:103–23

Gregan-Paxton J, Roedder-John D. 1997. The emergence of adaptive decision making in children. *J. Consum. Res.* 24:43–56

Guest L. 1962. Consumer analysis. *Annu. Rev. Psychol.* 13:315–344

Hirschman EC. 1994. Consumers and their animal companions. *J. Consum. Res.* 20:616–32

Hoch SJ. 1988. Who do we know: predicting the interests and opinions of the American consumer. *J. Consum. Res.* 15:315–24

Hoch SJ, Ha Y. 1986. Consumer learning: advertising and the ambiguity of product experience. *J. Consum. Res.* 13:221–33

Holbrook MB. 1985. Why business is bad for consumer research: the three bears revisited. *Adv. Consum. Res.* 12:145–56

Holbrook MB. 1987. What is consumer research? *J. Consum. Res.* 14:128–32

Holbrook MB, Grayson MW. 1986. The semiology of cinematic consumption: symbolic consumer behavior in *Out of Africa. J. Consum. Res.* 13:374–81

Holbrook MB, Hirschman E. 1982. The experiential aspects of consumption: consumer fantasies, feelings, and fun. *J. Consum. Res.* 9:132–40

Howard JA, Sheth JN. 1969. *The Theory of Buyer Behavior.* New York: Wiley

Hsee CK, Leclerc F. 1998. Will products look more attractive when presented separately or together? *J. Consum. Res.* 25:175–86

Huber J, Payne J, Puto C. 1982. Adding asymmetrically dominated alternatives: violations of regularity and the similarity hypothesis. *J. Consum. Res.* 9:90–98

Huber J, Puto C. 1983. Market boundaries and product choice: illustrating attraction and substitution effects. *J. Consum. Res.* 10:31–44

Hudson LA, Ozanne JL. 1988. Alternative ways of seeking knowledge in consumer research. *J. Consum. Res.* 14:508–21

Jacoby J, Speller DE, Berning CK. 1974. Brand choice behavior as a function of information load. *J. Consum. Res.* 1:33–42

Jacoby J. 1976. Consumer psychology: an octennium. *Annu. Rev. Psychol.* 27:331–58

Janiszewski C. 1988. Preconscious processing effects: the independence of attitude formation and conscious thought. *J. Consum. Res.* 15:199–209

Johar G, Pham MT. 1999. Relatedness, prominence, and constructive sponsor identification. *J. Mark. Res.* 26:299–312

Johnson MD. 1984. Consumer choice strategies for comparing noncomparable alternatives. *J. Consum. Res.* 11:741–53

Kahn BE, Louie TA. 1990. Effects of retraction of price promotions on brand choice behavior for variety-seeking and last-purchase-loyal consumers. *J. Mark. Res.* 27:279–89

Kahneman D, Tversky 1979. Prospect theory: an analysis of decision under risk. *Econometrica* 47:263–91

Kardes FR. 1988. Spontaneous inference processes in advertising: the effects of conclusion omission and involvement on persuasion. *J. Consum. Res.* 15:225–33

Kardes FR, Kalyanaram G, Chandrashekaran M, Dornof RJ. 1993. Brand retrieval, consideration set composition, consumer choice, and the pioneering advantage. *J. Consum. Res.* 20:62–75

Kassarjian H. 1982. Consumer psychology. *Annu. Rev. Psychol.* 33:619–49

Kassarjian H, Robertson T. 1968. *Perspectives in Consumer Behavior.* Englewood Cliffs, NJ: Prentice Hall

Keller KL. 1987. Memory factors in advertising: the effect of advertising retrieval cues on brand evaluations. *J. Consum. Res.* 14:316–33

Keller KL. 1993. Conceptualizing, measuring,

and managing customer-based brand equity. *J. Mark.* 57:1–22

Kisielius J, Sternthal B. 1984. Detecting and explaining vividness effects in attitudinal judgments. *J. Mark. Res.* 21:54–64

Krosnick JA, Shuman H. 1988. Attitude intensity, importance, and certainty and susceptibility to response effects. *J. Pers. Soc. Psychol.* 54:940–52

Lehmann DR. 1996. Presidential address: knowledge generalization and the conventions of consumer research: a study in inconsistency. In *Advances in Consumer Research*, ed. KP Corfman, JG Lynch Jr, 23:1–5. Provo, UT: Assoc. Consum. Res.

Levy SL. 1959. Symbols for sale. *Harv. Bus. Rev.* Jul–Aug:117–24

Luce MF. 1998. Choosing to avoid: coping with negatively emotion-laden consumer decisions. *J. Consum. Res.* 24:409–22

Lutz RJ. 1977. An experimental investigation of causal relations among cognitions, affect, and behavioral intention. *J. Consum. Res.* 3:197–208

Lutz RJ. 1991. Editorial. *J. Consum. Res.* 17:i–v

Lynch JG Jr. 1982. On the external validity of experiments in consumer research. *J. Consum. Res.* 9:225–39

Lynch JG Jr, Marmorstein H, Weigold MF. 1988. Choices from sets including remembered brands: use of recalled attributes and prior overall evaluations. *J. Consum. Res.* 15:169–84

Mahajan J. 1992. The overconfidence effect in marketing management predictions. *J. Mark. Res.* 29:329–42

McAlister L. 1982. A dynamic attribute satiation model of variety seeking behavior. *J. Consum. Res.* 9:141–50

McGrath JE, Brinberg D. 1983. External validity and the research process: a comment on the Calder/Lynch dialogue. *J. Consum. Res.* 10(1):115–24

McGuire WG. 1969. The nature of attitudes and attitude change. In *Handbook of Social Psychology*, ed. G Lindzey, E Aronson, 3:136–314. 2nd ed.

McQuarrie EF, Mick DG. 1992. On resonance: a critical pluralistic inquiry into advertising rhetoric. *J. Consum. Res.* 17:180–97

Menon G, Raghubir P, Schwarz N. 1995. Behavioral frequency judgments: an accessibility-diagnosticity framework. *J. Consum. Res.* 22:212–28

Meyer RJ. 1981. A model of multiattribute judgments under attribute uncertainty and informational constraint. *J. Mark. Res.* 18:428–41

Meyers-Levy J, Maheswaran D. 1991. Exploring differences in males' and females' processing strategies. *J. Consum. Res.* 18:63–70

Meyers-Levy J, Tybout AM. 1997. Context effects at encoding and judgment in consumption settings: the role of cognitive resources. *J. Consum. Res.* 24:1–14

Miller D. 1995. Consumption and commodities. *Annu. Rev. Anthropol.* 24:141–61

Miniard PW, Cohen J. 1983. Modeling personal and normative influences on behavior. *J. Consum. Res.* 10:169–80

Monroe KB. 1973. Buyer's subjective perceptions of price. *J. Mark. Res.* 10:70–80

Morwitz VG, Johnson E, Schmittlein D. 1993. Does measuring intent change behavior? *J. Consum. Res.* 20:46–61

Murray JB, Ozanne JL. 1991. The critical imagination: emancipatory interests in consumer research. *J. Consum. Res.* 18:129–44

Newell A, Simon HA. 1972. *Human Problem Solving*. Englewood Cliffs, NJ: Prentice-Hall

Nicosia F. 1966. *Consumer Decision Processes*. Englewood Cliffs, NJ: Prentice-Hall

Norman DA, Borrow DG. 1975. On data-limited and resource-limited processes. *Cogn. Psychol.* 7:44–64

Nowlis S, Simonson I. 1997. Attribute-task compatibility as a determinant of consumer preference reversals. *J. Mark. Res.* 34:205–18

O'Guinn TC, Faber R. 1989. Compulsive buying: a phenomenological exploration. *J. Consum. Res.* 16:147–57

Park CW, Milberg S, Lawson R. 1991. Evaluation of brand extensions: the role of product feature similarity and brand concept consistency. *J. Consum. Res.* 18:185–93

Payne J. 1976. Task complexity and contingent processing in decision making: an information search and protocol analysis. *Organ. Behav. Hum. Perform.* 16:366–87

Pechmann C, Ratneshwar S. 1994. The effects of antismoking and cigarette advertising on young adolescents' perceptions of peers who smoke. *J. Consum. Res.* 21:236–51

Peter JP, Olson JC. 1993. *Consumer Behavior and Marketing Strategy.* Homewood, IL: Richard D. Irwin, Inc. 3rd ed.

Petty RE, Cacioppo JT. 1996. Addressing disturbing and disturbed consumer behavior: Is it necessary to change the way we conduct behavioral science? *J. Mark. Res.* 33:1–8

Petty RE, Cacioppo JT, Schumann D. 1983. Central and peripheral routes to advertising effectiveness: the moderating role of involvement. *J. Consum. Res.* 10:134–48

Petty RE, Unnava R, Strathman AJ. 1991. Theories of attitude change. See Robertson & Kassarjian 1991, pp. 241–80

Pham MT. 1998. Representativeness, relevance, and the use of feelings in decision making. *J. Consum. Res.* 25:144–59

Pratt RW. 1974. ACR: a perspective. In *Advances in Consumer Research*, ed. S Ward, P Wright, 1:1–8. Urbana, IL: Assoc. Consum. Res.

Prelec D, Loewenstein GF. 1998. The red and the black: mental accounting of savings and debt. *Mark. Sci.* 17:4–28

Priester JR, Petty RE. 1996. The gradual threshold model of ambivalence: relating the positive and negative bases of attitudes to subjective ambivalence. *J. Pers. Soc. Psychol.* 71:431–49

Ratner RK, Kahn BE, Kahneman D. 1999. Choosing less-preferred experiences for the sake of variety. *J. Consum. Res.* 26:1–15

Ratneshwar S, Chaiken S. 1991. Comprehension's role in persuasion: the case of its moderating effect on the persuasive impact of source cues. *J. Consum. Res.* 18:52–62

Reilly MD, Wallendorf M. 1987. A comparison of group differences in food consumption using household refuse. *J. Consum. Res.* 14:289–94

Richins M. 1997. Measuring emotions in the consumption experience. *J. Consum. Res.* 24:127–46

Ritchie JRB, McDougall GHG, Claxton JD. 1981. Complexities of household energy consumption and conservation. *J. Consum. Res.* 8:233–42

Robertson TS, Kassarjian HH, eds. 1991. *Handbook of Consumer Behavior.* Englewood Cliffs, NJ: Prentice-Hall

Russo JE, Staelin R, Nolan CA, Russell GJ, Metcalf BL. 1986. Nutrition information in the supermarket. *J. Consum. Res.* 13:48–70

Schmitt BH, Zhang S. 1998. Language structure and categorizatin: a study of classifiers in consumer cognition, judgment, and choice. *J. Consum. Res.* 25:108–22

Schwarz N, Bohner G. 2000. The construction of attitudes. In *Blackwell Handbook of Social Psychology: Intrapersonal Processes*, ed. A Tesser, N Schwarz. Oxford: Blackwell. In press

Schouten JW, McAlexander JH. 1995. Subcultures of consumption: an ethnography of the new bikers. *J. Consum. Res.* 22:43–61

Scott CA, Yalch RF. 1980. Consumer response to initial product trial: Bayesian analysis. *J. Consum. Res.* 7:32–41

Sen S, Johnson EJ. 1997. Mere-possession effects without possession in consumer choice. *J. Consum. Res.* 24:105–17

Shimp T. 1994. Presidential address: academic Appalachia and the discipline of consumer research. *Adv. Consum. Res.* 21:1–7

Shimp TA, Kavas A. 1984. The theory of reasoned action applied to coupon usage. *J. Consum. Res.* 11:795–809

Shiv B, Fedorikhin A. 1999. Heart and mind in conflict: the interplay of affect and cognition in consumer decision making. *J. Consum. Res.* 26:278–92

Simonson I. 1989. Choice based on reasons: the case of attraction and compromise effects. *J. Consum. Res.* 16:158–74

Simonson I. 1990. The effect of purchase quantity and timing on variety seeking behavior. *J. Mark. Res.* 27:150–62

Simonson I. 1992. The influence of anticipating regret and responsibility on purchase decisions. *J. Mark. Res.* 19:105–18

Simonson I, Tversky A. 1992. Choice in context: tradeoff contrast and extremeness aversion. *J. Mark. Res.* 29:281–95

Stern BB. 1989. Literary criticism and consumer research: overview and illustrative analysis. *J. Consum. Res.* 16:322–34

Sternthal B, Dholakia R, Leavitt C. 1978. The persuasive effect of source credibility: tests of cognitive response. *J. Consum. Res.* 4:252–60

Sujan M. 1985. Consumer knowledge: effects on evaluation strategies mediating consumer judgments. *J. Consum. Res.* 12:31–46

Taylor SE. 1998. The social being in social psychology. See Gilbert et al 1998, pp. 58–95

Tetlock P. 1998. Social psychology and world politics. In *The Handbook of Social Psychology*, ed. D Gilbert, S Fiske, G Lindzey, 2:868–912. New York: McGraw-Hill. 4th ed.

Thaler R. 1985. Mental accounting and consumer choice. *Mark. Sci.* 4:199–214

Thompson CJW. 1996. Caring consumers: gendered consumption meanings and the juggling lifestyle. *J. Consum. Res.* 22:388–407

Thompson CJW, Locander WB, Pollio HR.

1989. Putting consumer experience back into consumer research: the philosophy and method of existential-phenomenology. *J. Consum. Res.* 16:133–46

Tybout A, Artz N. 1994. Consumer psychology. *Annu. Rev. Psychol.* 45:131–69

Tybout A, Sternthal B, Calder B. 1983. Information availability as a determinant of multiple request effectiveness. *J. Mark. Res.* 20:280–90

Unnava R, Agarwal S, Haugtvedt C. 1996. Interactive effects of presentation modality and message-generated imagery on recall of advertising information. *J. Consum. Res.* 23:81–93

Wallendorf M, Brucks M. 1993. Introspecting in consumer research: implementation and implications. *J. Consum. Res.* 20:339–59

Wells WD. 1993. Discovery oriented consumer research. *J. Consum. Res.* 21:319–31

Wernerfelt B. 1995. A rational reconstruction of the compromise effect: using market data to infer utilities. *J. Consum. Res.* 21:627–33

West PM, Broniarczyk SM. 1998. Integrating multiple opinions: the role of aspiration level on consumer response to critic consensus. *J. Consum. Res.* 25:38–51

Winer RS. 1999. Experimentation in the 21st century: the importance of external validity. *J. Acad. Mark. Sci.* 27:349–58

Wright P. 1973. The cognitive processes mediating acceptance of advertising. *J. Mark. Res.* 10:53–62

Zajonc R. 1998. Emotions. See Gilbert et al 1998, pp. 591–632

Annu. Rev. Psychol. 2001. 52:277–303

SLEEP-WAKE AS A BIOLOGICAL RHYTHM

P. Lavie

Sleep Laboratory, Faculty of Medicine, Technion-Israel Institute of Technology, Haifa, Israel; e-mail: plavie@tx.technion.ac.il

Key Words   sleep-wake rhythms, free-running rhythms, light, melatonin

■ **Abstract**   Evidence that the sleep-wake rhythm is generated endogenously has been provided by studies employing a variety of experimental paradigms such as sleep deprivation, sleep displacement, isolating subjects in environments free of time cues, or imposing on subjects sleep-wake schedules widely deviating from 24 hours. The initial observations obtained in isolated subjects revealed that the period of the endogenous circadian pacemaker regulating sleep is of approximately 25 hours. More recent studies, however, in which a more rigorous control of subjects' behavior was exerted, particularly over lighting conditions, have shown that the true periodicity of the endogenous pacemaker deviates from 24 hours by a few minutes only. Besides sleep propensity, the circadian pacemaker has been shown to regulate sleep consolidation, sleep stage structure, and electroencephalographic activities. The pattern of light exposure throughout the 24 hours appears to participate in the entrainment of the circadian pacemaker to the geophysical day-night cycle. Melatonin, the pineal hormone produced during the dark hours, participates in communicating both between the environmental light-dark cycle and the circadian pacemaker, and between the circadian pacemaker and the sleep-wake-generating mechanism. In contrast to prevailing views that have placed great emphasis on homeostatic sleep drive, recent data have revealed a potent circadian cycle in the drive for wakefulness, which is generated by the suprachiasmatic nucleus. This drive reaches a peak during the evening hours just before habitual bedtime.

CONTENTS

0066-4308/01/0201-0277$14.00

FROM PASSIVE TO ACTIVE THEORIES OF SLEEP-WAKE RHYTHMS—AN INTRODUCTION

In spite of the ubiquitous periodic nature of sleep and wakefulness, recognition of the sleep-wake cycle as a biological rhythm controlled by brain oscillators has been slow to come. Until the 1960s, sleep was mostly conceptualized within the framework of homeostatic principles. During sleep, energy or essential brain or bodily ingredients, depleted during waking, were thought to be restored. A complementary view posited the accumulation of toxic substances during wakefulness that are detoxified or removed from circulation during sleep. The immediate cause of sleep was sought in the production of these hypnotoxins that inhibit brain activities. Other mechanisms such as physical detachment of nerve cells, excess or diminution of blood supply to the brain, or periodic depletion of brain cells' oxygen supply, had also been envisioned (for brain isolation theories of sleep see Moruzzi 1964). The turn-of-the-century experiments of Piéron (1913), demonstrating that injecting cerebral spinal fluid from a sleep-deprived dog into the fourth ventricle of a wide-awake dog, induced sleep in the latter within 2–6 h, greatly enhanced the attraction of the hypnotoxins' theory. Constantin von Economo, renowned for the 1917 discovery of encephalitis lethargica, enlarged upon the hypnotoxin's sleep theory to also explain sleep-wake periodicity (see Lavie 1993 for more about von Economo's sleep theory). Accepting the idea that hypnotoxins accumulated during wakefulness induced sleep, von Economo posited that during sleep a process of detoxification occurred, by which the hypnotoxins were removed from the blood stream. Sleep ended with the completion of this process. The process of toxins' accumulation and removal was the basis for the sleep-wake cycle. In our time, the influential two-process theory of sleep regulation adopted this argument (Daan et al 1984). Von Economo further refined his hypothesis concerning sleep-wake periodicity by assuming that a brain center located between the diencephalon and the midbrain functioned as a "sleep center" by being more sensitive than the rest of the brain to the activity of the hypnotoxins. Its activation induced sleep in other parts of the brain by Pavlovian inhibition, thus preventing widespread brain intoxication. Because everyday experience showed that accumulated fatigue was not obligatory to sleep induction, and that sleep could be interrupted at any time, even before complete detoxification of the hypnotoxins was possibly achieved, he suggested that habit and suggestion also played a role in sleep behavior.

Another impediment to the recognition of the sleep-wake cycle as an endogenous biological rhythm was Nathaniel Kleitman's firm conviction that bodily rhythms were extrinsic in nature (Kleitman 1963). Kleitman believed that to satisfy the definition of a rhythm, a periodic "regularly recurring" change in a biological process should be "extrinsic in origin, depending upon a regular change in the environment, such as light or temperature," and that "when fully established, it must persist for some time, even when the environmental changes are absent" (p. 131). Thus, Kleitman considered biological rhythms to be conditioned responses. This explained, in his opinion, their continuation for some time after the extrinsic influences ceased. Kleitman, considered by many to be the most influential figure in modern sleep research, summarized his observation on the sleep-wakefulness rhythm by saying, "The development and maintenance of 24-hour sleep wakefulness and body-temperature rhythms stems from being born into, and living in, a family and community run according to alterations of light and darkness, resulting from the period of rotation of the earth around its axis" (p. 147).

The discovery of rapid eye movement (REM) sleep in 1953 by Aserinsky & Kleitman marks the beginning of the scientific era of sleep research that resulted in an entirely new outlook on sleep and its regulation. However, during the first years succeeding the discovery of REM sleep, most research was focused on the infrastructure of sleep and on the newly opened opportunities to study dreaming scientifically. The question as to the causes of the regular alternations of sleep and wakefulness attracted little attention prior to the 1980s.

ENDOGENOUS ORIGIN OF THE SLEEP-WAKE RHYTHM: Early Studies

The Emerging Concept of Endogenous Rhythms

A relatively large number of publications appeared in the 1960s and early 1970s, including several influential books that dealt with circadian rhythms, i.e. rhythms of approximately 24-h periodicity [from *circa*, (about) and *dies* (day)]. They described rhythms in diverse biological systems ranging from single cell activities to complex human behaviors (e.g. Bünning 1964, Sollberger 1965, Halberg 1969, Conroy & Mills 1970, Colquoun 1971a, Mills 1973). Although covering a wide spectrum of biological rhythms, none of these publications dealt directly with the sleep-wake rhythm. Importantly, however, in many the newly formalized concept of endogenous rhythms, i.e. rhythms that are not imposed by the environment but generated from within the organism, were discussed at length for the very first time.

Endogenous rhythms must satisfy the following criteria: (*a*) persisting in the absence of all known external periodic influences, (*b*) retaining nearly 24-h periodicity when a different periodicity is adopted by the environment, (*c*) changing their phase slowly after an abrupt change in the environment, (d) not reverting immediately after having been entrained to a new phase or periodicity, and (e) drifting away from 24 h after all known synchronizers are removed (Conroy & Mills 1970). In the following chapters, I review the evidence that led to the conclusion that sleep-wake rhythms are endogenously driven in a more or less chronological order, with an emphasis on the diverse experimental paradigms used to investigate sleep-wake rhythms. As is shown, these paradigms had a profound influence on the evolving views of sleep-wake regulation.

Sleep Deprivation

The initial experimental results that point in the direction that the sleep-wake rhythm is not passively controlled by the environment, nor solely responding to accumulated wake time, came from studies in which sleep was completely eliminated. Keeping subjects awake for prolonged periods of time revealed that although sleep pressure monotonically increased throughout the deprivation period, it also exhibited pronounced, nearly 24-h rhythms with peak alertness during the afternoon and peak sleepiness during the night (Fröberg 1977, Thayer 1970, Åkerstedt et al 1979). Likewise, when sleep-deprived subjects were repeatedly tested with psychomotor and cognitive tests, there were similar rhythms in mental performance that paralleled those in sleep pressure (Moses et al 1978, Fröberg 1977, Bjerner et al 1955, Folkard 1975). In some of these studies it was apparent that sleep propensity had a bimodal distribution, having a major nighttime peak and a secondary, minor mid-day peak (Blake 1967, Colquoun 1971b). Enforcing constant posture on sleep-deprived subjects, in addition to uniform and well-controlled lighting and feeding schedules, a procedure termed the constant routine, did not eliminate the sleepiness cycle (Mills et al 1978). Regardless of the specific procedure used in association with the sleep deprivation paradigm to quantify sleepiness, i.e. subjective assessment of alertness using a variety of scales, continuous or intermittent EEG monitoring, counting inadvertent sleep episodes, etc, they all showed that the most profound increase in sleepiness coincided with the early morning hours, whereas the nadir in sleepiness occurred during the early evening period. This cyclic pattern in sleep propensity was superimposed on an increasing trend of sleepiness throughout the deprivation period, representing the homeostatic sleep drive.

Sleep Displacement

Early studies that investigated the effect of sleep displacement were practically oriented to examine the effects of rotating shift work schedules and jet traveling on sleep structure (Endo et al 1978, Evans et al 1972, Kripke et al 1971, Globus et al 1972, Klein et al 1970, Åkerstedt 1977). Studies differed with respect to the amount of control over the environmental synchronizers that could potentially affect the sleep-wake cycles. This varied from no control at all, such as in field studies investigating sleep-wake cycles of shift workers, to conditions in which all conflicting environmental synchronizers were altered simultaneously, such as after long-haul flights. The first sleep laboratory study investigating the effects of displacement on sleep was conducted by Weitzman et al (1970). They inverted subjects' sleep-wake cycle by 180 degrees by displacing sleep from 2200–0600 to 1000–1800. Generally, subjects were confined to the laboratory during the scheduled wake periods, although they could "leave the ward for several hours during their waking time." The most prominent effect of sleep inversion was a significant increase in wakefulness, particularly toward the end of sleep. This effect, which persisted throughout the experiment, was at the expense of REM sleep, which was shifted toward an earlier time in the sleep period. A year later, a similar study was conducted by Webb et al (1971), who displaced sleep from 2300–0700 to 0800–1600 for 4 days. Similarly, Webb et al found an increase in wake time after sleep onset during the reversal sleep, accompanied by an increase in the amount of REM during the first half of the sleep period, and a decrease in first REM latency. Inducing more moderate phase shifts of 6–8 h in the advance or delay directions also revealed a gradual adaptation of the sleep-wake cycle to the abrupt phase shift (Hume 1980, Monk et al 1988).

Field studies of shift workers and jet travelers have reached similar conclusions. Displacing sleep from its normal timing has been generally associated with transient insomnia, for at least a few days after the shift. This was particularly evident in phase shifts associated with transmeridian flights. Here, in spite of the rapid and homogenous change in all geophysical and social time cues that should potentially facilitate rapid adaptation of the sleep-wake rhythm to the new time zone, jet travelers experience sleep disturbances, which may last between 4–10 days. Sleep disturbances together with complaints of fatigue and performance deterioration, and sometimes even psychosomatic symptoms, constitute the jet-lag syndrome (see review in Nicholson et al 1986). Generally, jet lag is more severe after eastward than westward flights (Monk et al 1995). Likewise, sleep displacement to daytime hours in rotating shift workers results in sleep disruption. Day sleep in shift workers is characterized by being shorter than night sleep, by being more fragmented, and by having a different sleep stage structure, particularly with respect to REM sleep (Åkerstedt 1988). Although some of these findings may be explained by physical sleep conditions such as effects of noise in the bedroom environment and inability to completely darken the bedroom during the day, there is a general agreement that the major underlying cause of the disruption of sleep is its displacement to daytime hours during which the circadian rhythm in sleep pressure is at its minimum.

SLEEP-WAKE RHYTHMS IN ISOLATION

The 25-h Sleep-Wake Rhythm

Modern research of circadian sleep-wake rhythms began with the first studies in which sleep-wake rhythms were investigated in subjects isolated from all possible time cues that could potentially affect their rhythmic behavior. This environment was termed time-free environment. Juergen Aschoff and Rütger Wever, working in Ehrling Andechs in Germany, pioneered the studies of sleep-wake rhythms in a time-free environment (Aschoff 1965; Aschoff et al 1967, 1971). They isolated subjects in two units of an underground building, specially constructed for such experiments. The units were isolated from all environmental noises, and one was also shielded from electric and magnetic fields. The variables that were initially recorded were rectal temperature and subjects' motility. Only in later studies was sleep monitored by electrophysiological means that have become the conventional methods of investigating sleep. Thus, in actuality, the initial studies in Andechs investigated rest-activity rhythms rather than sleep-wake rhythms. In the first reported study of rest-activity rhythms of isolated subjects (Aschoff & Wever 1962), during the 10 days of isolation there was an increase in the period of the rest-activity rhythm to 25.1 h. A similar increase was found in rectal temperature. The term Aschoff & Wever used to describe the circadian rhythms that deviated slightly from 24 h was free-running rhythms. A total of 150 subjects were investigated under isolation conditions in Andechs until 1976 (Wever 1979). The average length of the isolation period was 29 days, with a range of 10–89 days. In the vast majority of them, rest-activity rhythms and, as was found later, also their sleep-wake rhythms, lengthened to approximately 25 h, although there was a large between-subjects variability (Wever 1979). The lengthening of the free-running sleep-wake rhythms was independent of the intensity of activity during the isolation experiment (Aschoff 1990). Furthermore, subjects with a scheduled workload during isolation showed free-running rest-activity rhythms similar to subjects who were sedentary throughout the experiment. Identical results were reported by Webb & Agnew (1974). However, some aspects of the experimental conditions could affect the length of the cycle. Allowing subjects to switch on the light as they woke up and to switch it off when they decided to go to sleep, resulted in longer rest-activity cycles compared with the condition in which subjects were isolated under constant illumination. The reason for this phenomenon became apparent only after the decisive role of light stimulus on the circadian sleep-wake cycle, even at room light intensities, was discovered (Boivin et al 1994).

It is a matter of curiosity that free-running rhythms were also observed in people isolated in caves for extended periods. Long periods of isolation in natural caves were generally considered as a test of human endurance. Sleep diaries, however, kept by these volunteers spending periods ranging from 15–205 days in isolation, provided clear evidence of a lengthening of the sleep-wake cycle to 25 h and even considerably longer (Siffre 1963, Mills 1964). Likewise, free-running rhythms were reported in subjects living in isolation in the natural environment of the high arctic region under constant daylight lighting conditions (Steel et al 1995).

Internal Desynchronization

Lengthening of the sleep-wake periodicity was not the only change noted in sleep-wake rhythms in the time-free environment. Of no less importance was the change observed in the phase relationship between temperature and other rhythms, and sleep-wake rhythms. When the sleep-wake rhythm is synchronized with the 24-h geophysical light-dark cycle, the peak rectal temperature occurs in the late afternoon/early evening period, and the nadir, in the second half of the sleep period. In the time-free environment, after several days, the temperature peak advanced to the first half of the activity period, and the nadir to the first half of the sleep period. Under these new phase relationships, which remained stable in some subjects until the end of the experimental period, sleep tended to be initiated close to the temperature minimum, and wake-ups clustered on the rising limb of the temperature cycle. These preferred zones for falling asleep and for waking up had a profound effect on sleep duration, which minimized the effects of prior wakefulness on subsequent sleep (Wever 1979). Thus, counterintuitively to what could be expected under the assumption that sleep is regulated homeostatically, in time-free environments the duration of prior wakefulness was negatively correlated with the length of subsequent sleep.

In many subjects, however, the synchronization between temperature and sleep-wake rhythms under the new phase relationships lasted for a few days only. After that the cycles were spontaneously dissociated from each other, each assuming a different period. Of the 150 subjects investigated by Aschoff & Wever, 38 showed this spontaneous dissociation, which was termed internal desynchronization. In all, the temperature rhythm assumed a period closer to 25 h (mean of 24.9 h), and the rest-activity rhythms lengthened to the range of 30–40 h or shortened to periods of 15–20 h. Because the internally desynchronized circadian rhythms assumed different periods, there were continuous variations in the phase relationship between them throughout the isolation period. Thus, in one cycle a subject initiated sleep at the peak of his temperature rhythm, whereas some cycles later sleep was initiated at the temperature nadir. Therefore, in experiments lasting for several weeks, internally desynchronized subjects initiated sleep at multiple phases of the temperature rhythm. This allowed an intensive investigation of the mutual interaction between the two rhythms, which demonstrated for the first time the decisive role played by the circadian regulating system on sleep initiation and on waking up from sleep, and consequently on the sleep-wake cycle.

The first analysis of sleep-wake cycles of internally desynchronized subjects was reported by Zulley & Schulz in the Fourth European Congress of Sleep Research in 1978 (Zulley & Schulz 1980). Later, it was published by Zulley et al (1981). They reported that the circadian phase of the temperature cycle not only influenced the duration of subsequent sleep but also the probability of falling asleep. When internally synchronized, subjects opted to go to sleep about 1.5 h before the temperature minimum, and woke up approximately 7 h after the minimum, thus sleeping for about 8.5 h. In contrast, when internally desynchronized, there were 2 distinct peaks of sleep initiation, either 1.3 or 6.3 h before the temperature minimum, whereas the end of sleep still clustered at one time, on the rising limb of the temperature rhythm, some 5 h after the minimum (Figure 1). Thus, sleep was longest when subjects decided to go to sleep at the earlier of the two preferred

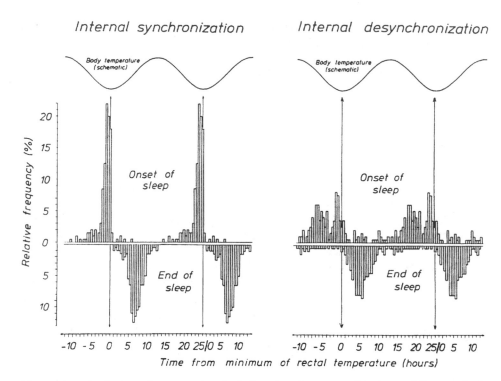

Figure 1   Distribution of onset and end of sleep in reference to the phase of the core body temperature rhythm. Data from isolated free-running subjects who remained synchronized (205 sleep episodes) or showed internal desynchronization (206 sleep episodes) are depicted in a double plot format. Note the single preferred zone for sleep and for wake-up in the synchronized condition, and the two preferrred zones for sleep onset in the desynchronized condition (reproduced by permission from Zulley et al 1981).

zones for sleep, 6 h before the temperature minimum, and became shorter when sleep onset occurred at the second preferred zone, about 1 h before the minimum.

The observations of the Andech's group on the profound influence of the phase of the temperature cycle on sleep behavior were confirmed and further elaborated by Czeisler et al. In his doctoral dissertation (Czeisler 1978), which was the basis for a paper in *Science* 2 years later (Czeisler et al 1980a), it was confirmed that the duration of polysomnographically recorded sleep episodes was dependent on the circadian phase of the temperature rhythm at which sleep was initiated, and not on the length of prior wakefulness. When subjects' chosen bedtimes were near the temperature nadir, subsequent sleep duration was approximately 8 h. When bedtimes were around the temperature peak, i.e. approximately 6–8 h before the minimum, sleep length almost doubled, averaging 14.4 h.

A closer observation of the sleep-wake behavior of free-running subjects who were internally desynchronized with reference to the core body temperature, revealed that there were not only two well-defined zones of high probability to go to sleep, but also two zones of distinctly low probability to do so (Strogatz 1986, Strogatz et al 1987). All subjects avoided bedtimes at about 8 h before and 5 h after the temperature minimum. Both zones were 2–3 h wide. Assuming that in normally entrained individuals, temperature nadir occurs at around 0500–0600, these findings led to what appeared to be a paradoxical conclusion, that it should be most difficult to fall asleep a few hours before what in most individuals would be their regular bedtime. As will be detailed shortly, the occurrence of a 'wake maintenance' zone, as it was termed by Strogatz et al (1987), during the evening hours, which has been consistently observed in studies investigating sleep propensity, has necessitated revision in the prevailing concepts of sleep regulation.

What About Napping?

The research methodology employed in studies conducted in time-free environments has been focused on monophasic sleep-wake cycles, i.e. the alternation of a single major sleep episode with a single prolonged wake episode: Conscious efforts were made to avoid the occurrence of naps, i.e. short sleep episodes of 1–3 h duration, during the isolation period. This was done by explicitly instructing the subjects to avoid napping and to go to sleep only when they were convinced they would be retiring for a nocturnal sleep (Campbell & Zulley 1989). Furthermore, sleep episodes shorter than a predetermined duration were eliminated from data analysis. Was this justified? Evidence of daytime periods of increased tendency to fall asleep, particularly at midday, has been provided by studies demonstrating poor psychomotor and cognition performance at that time (Blake 1967, Colquoun 1971b, Monk et al 1996), by a variety of studies investigating cross-cultural sleep habits (Webb & Dinges 1989), and as will be discussed later, in studies utilizing short and ultrashort sleep-wake cycles (e.g. Lavie 1986). In an attempt to investigate whether napping is part of the sleep-wake regulating system, Zulley & Campbell (1985) reanalyzed data of internally desynchronized subjects who, contrary to instructions, took multiple naps during the isolation period. They reported that naps were clustered at two circadian phases, at the temperature nadir and halfway between successive temperature nadirs. Naps initiated during the temperature nadir, although shorter than the major sleep episodes (6.3 h versus 9 h) were longer than those initiated halfway between successive nadirs (2.4 h). This led them to suggest that whereas the longer naps were major sleep episodes misjudged by subjects to be naps, the naps appearing halfway between successive nadirs could be explained by the existence of a secondary preferred circadian sleep position that under normally entrained conditions corresponds to the midafternoon period. Aschoff (1994), reanalyzing data of the free-running subjects from the Andechs studies, also came to the conclusion that naps are an integral feature of the circadian rhythm. He viewed naps as an integral part of wake time, the duration of which remains relatively unaffected by the presence of naps. Earlier, Broughton (1975) speculated that our endogenous rhythm of sleep tendency is bimodal, and hence the afternoon nap is biologically based. Recently, a further elaboration of his early suggestion, now based on the wealth of data that has accumulated since his earlier proposal, was published (Broughton 1998).

THE FORCED DESYNCHRONY PROTOCOL

Sleep Propensity

Although isolation experiments provided convincing evidence that the endogenous core temperature and sleep-wake rhythms were about an hour longer than 24 h, there were some hints that the lighting conditions in the isolation chamber could influence the length of the cycle, and thereby bias the results. This led to the adoption of the forced desynchrony protocol, which allowed more stringent control over the experimental conditions. When subjects are isolated from all environmental time cues, the length of the day can be experimentally controlled, and day lengths shorter or longer than 24 h can be imperceptibly enforced on the subjects. This technique, first used by Kleitman (1939), then by the Andechs group, followed by Hume and Mills (1977), was initially utilized to investigate the limits of entrainment of circadian cycles to different day lengths. Recently it was used to provide a more controlled environment to investigate the properties of the circadian pacemaker (Dijk & Czeisler 1995, Czeisler et al 1999, Wyatt et al 1999).

Kleitman (1939) attempted to adopt a 48-h sleep-wake cycle, with 8 h sleep and 39–40 h wake, for 30 days, and investigated the effects of the imposed day length on the temperature rhythm. In spite of successfully adapting to the 48-h sleep-wake rhythm, there was no change in the body temperature rhythm that remained close to 24 h. Similarly, imposing a 12-h sleep-wake rhythm also failed to modify the temperature rhythm. Only adopting 21-h and 28-h cycles, which, in Kleitman's words, were "not too far removed from 24 h to make one sleepy, or not sleepy enough, at the scheduled bedtime" (p. 255), successfully modified the temperature rhythm to the sleep-wake rhythm in 2 out of 4 subjects. Similar results were later reported by the Andechs group. Thirty-four subjects were exposed to light-dark cycles ranging from 20 to 32 h for at least a 1-week period. None of the subjects exposed to a 20-, 28-, 30- and 32-h "day" was entrained with his rectal temperature rhythm to the new periods. In most of these cases, the rhythm in rectal temperature free-ran in spite of the fact that subjects successfully adhered to the newly imposed rest-activity cycle. Partial or complete success was achieved when the imposed light-dark cycle was closer to 24 h, either 25.3 or 22.7 hours (Aschoff & Wever 1976). The fact that under enforced day length, which is beyond the range of entrainment, the body temperature rhythm free-ran with its intrinsic periodicity, made the forced desynchrony an alternative paradigm to the isolation experiments (Dijk & Czeisler 1995, Czeisler et al 1999, Wyatt et al 1999). Furthermore, because under forced desynchronized conditions the duration of wakefulness between successive sleep episodes remains constant while sleep occurs at different circadian phases, this enables separating the circadian-dependent and sleep-dependent effects on sleep processes. To assess the period of the circadian pacemaker, the phase of the circadian temperature rhythm was twice assessed by a constant routine paradigm (see Figure 2).

The period of the circadian pacemaker as determined by the forced desynchrony protocol was unaffected by the length of the imposed sleep-wake schedule. Imposing a 28-h day, with 9-h, 20-min sleep and 18-h, 40-min awake, which caused subjects to delay their bedtimes and waketimes in each rest/activity cycle, or imposing a 20 h day with 6-h, 40-min scheduled sleep and 13-h, 20-min awake, which caused subjects to advance their bedtimes and waketimes, provided remarkably similar estimates of the period of the circadian pacemaker. Unlike the results obtained under the classical isolation protocols, according to which the endogenous circadian pacemaker has an approximately 25-h periodicity, the period of the circadian pacemaker in both the "short day" and the "long day" protocols was much shorter and considerably less variable. Its average period was 24 h, 10 min ±7 min in the 28-h day and 24 h, 10 min ± 9 min in the 20-h day. This periodicity was observed for a group of young adults as well as for elderly subjects aged 64–74 yr, putting to rest a prolonged controversy as to whether the period of the circadian pacemaker is altered with age (Czeisler et al 1999). Furthermore, identical period lengths were found for the circadian rhythms in cortisol and melatonin secretions, pointing to the possibility that a single circadian pacemaker was driving all of these variables.

What was the reason for the almost 1 h disparity between the isolation experiments and the forced desynchrony protocol? Czeisler et al (1999) suggested that the uneven distribution of the sleep episodes across the circadian phases in the isolation studies could exert a feedback effect on the pacemaker, and thus artificially lengthen the cycle. Thus, if isolated subjects were preferentially awake and selected room light exposure before their circadian temperature minimum, they could induce systematic phase delays of the circadian pacemaker, which would lead to overestimation of the circadian free-running rhythm (see later notes on the effects of light).

The forced desynchrony paradigm provided compelling evidence that not only sleep propensity but also sleep consolidation, sleep termination, sleep structure, and the dynamics of EEG activity during sleep are all under the influence of a single circadian pacemaker that interacts with sleep- and wake-dependent processes. Sleep pressure, indexed by the latency to fall asleep, is maximal near the nadir of core body temperature, close to the habitual time of waking up, and reaches a nadir during the evening hours, near the temperature maximum close to the habitual sleep time. The change from the evening low levels of sleep pressure to the high levels occurs rather rapidly. A similar picture emerged when sleep pressure was assessed by the propensity to terminate sleep. This was lowest around the temperature minimum and highest around the temperature maximum.

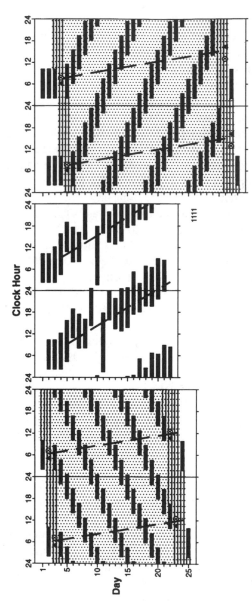

Figure 2   Experimental results of a 22-year old subject who was investigated in the time-free environment 3 times: twice with the forced desynchrony paradigm when on a 20 h day (*left panel*), and 28 h day (*right panel*), and then with the classical free-running paradigm (*center panel*). The sleep-rest activity cycle is plotted in a double raster format, with successive days plotted both next to and beneath each other, and clock hour indicated on the abscissa. There were 3 baseline sleep episodes in the 28-h day and the free-running conditions and one baseline night in the 20-h day, which were scheduled at the subject's habitual sleep times. During the wake episodes, light intensity was 15 Lux in the 20- and 28-h protocols, and 150 Lux in the free-running protocol. The *open bars* in the forced desynchrony protocols indicate the circadian nadir of body temperature and the maximum of melatonin secretion. These were conducted before and after the forced desynchrony protocol. The phase of the temperature cycle (*dashed line*) was estimated by nonorthogonal spectral analysis. The estimated periods of the temperature cycle are nearly equivalent under 20-h and 28-h day protocols (24.29 and 24.28 h, respectively), and much shorter than the estimated period in the free-running protocol (25.07 h) (reproduced by permission from Czeisler et al 1999).

Sleep Structure and EEG Activity

Studies utilizing polysomnographic recordings of subjects isolated in time-free environments have revealed that not only the timing of sleep and its length are regulated by the circadian pacemaker, but also its structure. Under normal entrained conditions, sleep is characterized by regular alternations between REM and non-REM sleep. In young adults the length of the REM-non-REM cycle is about 90 min and the first REM period appears after 90 min of non-REM sleep. Across the sleep period there is a gradual increase in the length of REM episodes, resulting in the largest accumulation of REM sleep during the last third of the sleep period. In contrast to REM sleep, slow wave sleep dominates during the first third of the sleep period and declines thereafter. It should be noted that some of these characteristics of the REM-non-REM cycle are age-dependent. As described above, the first evidence that the infrastructure of sleep may be also under circadian influences was provided by studies in which sleep was displaced from the night to daytime hours (Weitzman et al 1970, Webb et al 1971). This resulted in an increase in the amount of REM sleep during the first third of the sleep period. Both shortening of the latency to the first REM period and an increase in its duration contributed to this accumulation. Changes in REM sleep were also the hallmark of the modification of sleep structure found in free-running subjects and in the forced desynchrony protocol (Hume & Mills 1977, Zulley 1980, Czeisler et al 1980b, Dijk & Czeisler 1995, Wyatt et al 1999). Zulley (1980), analyzing the polysomnographic recordings of subjects isolated in Andechs under time-free conditions, reported that there was a higher amount of REM sleep during the first third of the sleep period in comparison with the entrained condition. As was found in the displaced sleep paradigm, the increased REM resulted from both shortening of the latency to the first REM period and from the increased duration of the first REM episode. Zulley speculated that the observed change in the timing of REM sleep was caused by the change in the phase relationship between body temperature and sleep in the time-free environment. These results were confirmed and extended by Czeisler et al (1980b). They showed that REM propensity in free-running subjects peaked 1–2 h after the nadir in core body temperature rhythm. In contrast with the prominent circadian rhythm in REM sleep, the distribution of sleep stage 3-4 ("deep," slow wave sleep), showed change neither in isolation studies nor in the forced desynchrony protocols (Weitzman et al 1980, Dijk & Czeisler 1995). In the forced desynchrony paradigm with the 28-h day, however, combining stages 2, and 3-4 into a single non-REM sleep, revealed a low amplitude circadian modulation with a crest coinciding with the peak of core body temperature. In addition to the circadian rhythms in sleep stages, the forced desynchrony protocol revealed prominent circadian rhythms in spindles' activity. The spindle is a phasic EEG activity with a frequency of 12–15 Hz, which appears during sleep stage 2 (light sleep). Low frequency sleep spindles (12.25–13 Hz) activity peaked during the phase of high sleep propensity, whereas high frequency sleep spindles activity (14.25–15.5 Hz) peaked at the opposite phase of low sleep propensity (Dijk et al 1997).

FRAGMENTED SLEEP-WAKE CYCLES

Short Sleep-Wake Cycles

An alternative way to investigate the relationship between sleep-dependent and circadian-dependent components of sleep-wake regulation is to allow sleep to occur for short periods at different times across the 24 hours. This has provided important information concerning the existence of circadian rhythms in the propensity to fall asleep. Various investigators have used short sleep-wake cycles. Their studies differed in the duration of allocated sleep time, the frequency of the sleep episodes, and the length of the testing periods. The first to investigate circadian rhythmicity in sleepiness using such a "multiple naps" strategy were Weitzman et al (1974), Carskadon & Dement (1977), and Moses et al (1975). Weitzman et al (1974) investigated 7 subjects under a 3 h sleep-wake schedule, for 10 24-h periods. Thus, in each 24-h period, subjects were allowed 8 1-h sleep periods. The authors reported on a striking persistence of the circadian pattern of total sleep time throughout the 240-h study period. The time of maximum sleep in the 3-h "day" schedule occurred at 0500–0700, and the minimum at 2100–2200. Although the authors noted that the times of maximum and minimum sleep occurred later than expected, they did not further elaborate on these phase delays. Moses et al (1975), after one baseline night, put subjects on a schedule of 60-min sleep/160-min wake for 40 h. Their results also indicated that fragmenting the sleep-wake cycle into hourly episodes, spaced 3 h apart, did not affect the circadian rhythmicity in sleep time. Total sleep during the naps peaked during the morning hours at about 0500–0900, and showed a nadir at approximately 1900. Moses et al did not discuss the delay in the time of maximum and minimum sleep time. Carskadon & Dement (1977) placed 10 subjects on a 90-min sleep-wake schedule for 5.5 or 6 days. Subjects were permitted to sleep for 30-min periods, separated by 60 min of enforced wakefulness. Similar to the two earlier studies, here too, a clear-cut 24-h rhythm of total sleep was evident. Maximum sleep occurred in the late morning and minimum sleep in the evening, at around 2200. Carskadon & Dement also noted the shift in the distribution of total sleep time, for which they had no explanation. However, the finding of the late peak in alertness was not specifically addressed.

The Multiple Sleep Latency Test (MSLT), devised to assess pathological daytime sleepiness, is a variant of the short sleep-wake cycle paradigm (Richardson et al 1978, Carskadon & Dement 1982). The MSLT measures the speed of falling asleep in a standard setting at different times of the day, but without allowing any sleep accumulation. The first test is usually conducted 2 h after waking up from sleep and then at 2-h intervals throughout the day. In agreement with the results of the short sleep-wake cycles, Carskadon & Dement found that sleep latencies were lowest in the evening, although a morning nadir in sleepiness was also evident. Clodoré et al (1990), who investigated 55 young subjects with the MSLT, confirmed Richardson et al's and Carskadon & Dement's findings, but also reported on an increased midday sleep propensity at around 1400.

Thus, studies utilizing short sleep-wake cycles, although having different sleep/wake ratios, and being conducted for different lengths of time, have demonstrated the persistence of a circadian rhythm in the occurrence of total sleep. In each of them, the peak of sleep time was delayed to the morning hours, whereas the nadir was delayed to the late evening hours. Perhaps because the investigators were more interested in the influence of sleep fragmentation on the infrastructure of sleep than in circadian regulation of sleep, this unique pattern of sleep propensity and in particular the late nadir in sleepiness, failed to attract their attention.

Ultrashort Sleep-Wake Cycles

The ultrashort sleep-wake cycle further fragmented the sleep-wake cycle to even shorter sleep and wake episodes. It was first used to describe short-term variations in the ability to fall asleep across the 24-hour day (Lavie & Scherson 1981). Generally, in these experiments (Lavie 1986, Lavie & Segal 1989, Tzischinsky et al 1993, Lack & Lushington 1996, Liu et al 2000), subjects came to the laboratory on the evening before the study, spent the night asleep or awake, under supervision, in the laboratory, and in the morning began a schedule of 7 min asleep/13 min awake for at least 24 h. At the end of each 7-min sleep attempt, whether asleep or awake, subjects were taken outside the bedroom for 13 minutes. Since the speed of falling asleep was the major determinant of total sleep time during the 7-min allowed sleep periods, the total amount of sleep during each trial was used as representing sleep propensity at that particular time. Studies varied from each other by the length of prior wakefulness before the start of the ultrashort cycle, by the sleep-to-wake ratio, by the starting time of the experiment, by the length of the testing period, and by the specific instructions to the subjects whether to fall asleep or to try and resist sleep.

Investigating the 24-h pattern of sleep propensity this way has revealed a consistent picture. The basic features of the 24-h pattern of sleep propensity are a prominent nocturnal crest in sleepiness, an evening nadir in sleepiness and in some of the subjects, a secondary sleepiness peak during the afternoon. This basic structure was little changed by sleep deprivation before the start of the 7/13 paradigm, or by instructing sleep-deprived subjects to "resist sleep" instead of "attempt sleep" (Lavie 1986). Impressively, in spite of the accumulated sleep deprivation during the 24 h preceding the study and during the progression of the 7/13 sleep-wake paradigm itself, subjects found it more difficult to fall asleep during the evening period than at earlier times. Because of its remarkable consistency and prominence, this period has been termed the forbidden zone for sleep (Lavie 1986). Its timing was identical to the "wake maintenance zone" identified by Strogatz (1986) in desynchronized, free-running subjects and to the period of nadir in sleep time observed in the short sleep-wake cycles (Weitzman et al 1974, Carskadon & Dement 1977, Moses et al 1975). Another feature of the temporal structure of sleep propensity that has become most prominent under sleep deprivation conditions, is the abrupt transition from the low sleep propensity during the evening period to the high sleep-propensity nocturnal period. For many subjects, this appeared as an all or none phenomenon. Following a period of 2–3 h during which subjects had low sleep propensity, in one trial they fell asleep within 30–60 s and continued to do so on every subsequent trial. The timing of this nocturnal sleep "gate" was found to be a stable individual characteristic (Lavie & Zvuluni 1992) that could reliably distinguish between subjectively assessed "morning" and "evening" persons (Lavie & Segal 1989). The sleep gate was found to be phase-locked to the circadian rhythm in melatonin, appearing approximately 2 h after the nocturnal increase in melatonin secretion (see Figure 3) (Tzischinsky et al 1993, Shochat et al 1997, Liu et al 2000). Evening administration of exogenous melatonin advanced the nocturnal sleep gate by about an hour (Tzischinsky & Lavie 1994), whereas evening exposure to bright light delayed it (Tzischinsky & Lavie 1997).

Lack & Lushington (1996) utilized a 10/20 ultrashort sleep-wake cycle preceded by a constant routine, and investigated the phase relationship between the sleep propensity rhythm and the rhythm in core body temperature. They confirmed the existence of a well-defined 24-h sleep propensity rhythm, and reported on the existence of a secondary 12-h sleep propensity component in 8 of their 14 subjects. They also confirmed the early evening drop in sleep propensity and

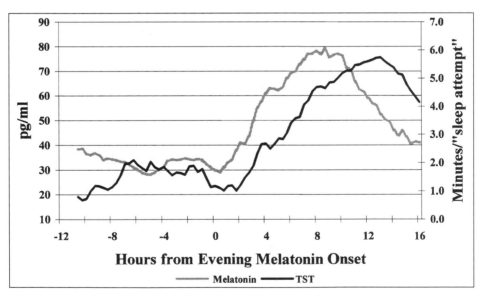

Figure 3 Phase relationship between the 24-h sleep propensity and the melatonin rhythms was determined by the 7/13 paradigm. TST, total sleep in each 7 min sleep "attempt." The individual data were synchronized to the time of onset of melatonin seceretion (0), and then averaged across all subjects (N = 5). The 1.5–2 h lag between the onset of melatonin secretion and the opening of the sleep gate was replicated in 3 independent experiments (reproduced by permission from Shochat et al 1997).

the abrupt nocturnal increase in sleepiness. These phase markers of the sleep propensity rhythm had a consistent phase relationship with the body temperature minimum, suggesting that they are under the control of the circadian pacemaker.

THE WAKE-PROCESS

The most surprising yet most consistent finding in all studies investigating the circadian rhythms in sleep propensity as to whether they used forced desynchrony or short and ultrashort sleep-wake cycles, is that during the evening period, just before the "opening" of the sleep gate, sleep propensity is at its minimum level. The existence of an evening nadir in sleepiness also emerged from prolonged sleep deprivation studies. Studying the dynamics of the EEG variations during prolonged wakefulness, Aeschbach et al (1997) reported that delta, theta, and lower alpha EEG activities, which indicate increased sleep pressure, showed an evening trough. Thus, in all protocols the pressure for sleep paradoxically declines just before habitual bedtime under the entrained conditions.

This remarkable convergence of experimental findings from such diverse experimental methodologies points to the existence of a powerful drive for wakefulness at the end of the "wakeful" day just before the opening of the sleep gate. Such an active drive for wakefulness has never been considered in any of the models or theories proposed to explain sleep-wake regulation. Studies performed in squirrel monkeys (Edgar et al 1993) provided an interpretation for these observations and allowed their incorporation within a framework of a new conceptual approach to sleep-wake regulation. Edgar et al (1993) demonstrated that suprachiasmatic nuclei (SCN)-lesioned squirrel monkeys maintained in constant light lost their circadian rhythms in sleep-wakefulness, in sleep stages, in brain temperature, and in drinking. Unexpectedly, however, the lesioned animals had significantly increased total sleep time, which was associated with a 15-fold reduction in the length of wake bouts during the subjective day. There was no change in the length of the wake bouts during the subjective night. This led the investigators to suggest that in contrast to the classical sleep models postulating an interaction between a homeostatic sleep process and a circadian oscillating rhythm that essentially gates the wake and sleep thresholds (Daan et al 1984), the SCN appeared to be actively involved in the promotion of wakefulness, thus opposing the homeostatic accumulated drive for sleep. Therefore, sleep propensity at a particular time of the day is determined by the sum of the accumulated homeostatic drive for sleep and the SCN drive for wakefulness. Based on these observations, Dijk & Czeisler (1994) proposed that the paradoxical positioning of the peak of alertness just before habitual sleep time, and peak sleep propensity just before habitual waking up, help to consolidate sleep time during the night and wakefulness during the day. These findings still await incorporation into a formal model of sleep-wake regulation.

It is yet unclear if the evening peak in the drive for wakefulness is the crest of a well-defined circadian cycle in wake propensity, or the result of a specific interaction at that time between the wake and sleep drives. Based on the forced desynchrony protocol, it was suggested that the signal that promotes wakefulness increases gradually along the rising limb of the temperature cycle, starting some hours after the temperature minimum (Dijk & Czeisler 1995). However, the findings of two preferred zones for sleep and two preferred "wake maintenance" zones (Strogatz et al 1987), and the possibility of short term variations in sleep propensity during the daytime hours (Lavie 1986) raise the possibility that the interaction between sleep- and wake-driven processes results in more complex variations in sleep pressure. These may also include short-term as well as circadian variations in sleep pressure.

MAJOR AGENTS OF ENTRAINMENT

Light

There is evidence that humans' circadian rhythms can be entrained by both photic and nonphotic stimuli (Klerman et al 1998). Both social contact and physical exercise may have an effect on the phase of the circadian pacemaker (Buxton et al 1997). However, as in all other organisms, light plays the primary role in the entrainment of the human circadian pacemaker to the environment. This was not immediately recognized. Aschoff et al (1975), based on the Andechs isolation studies, concluded that "an artificial light-dark cycle seems to be of little importance for the entrainment of human circadian rhythms in otherwise constant conditions" (p. 64). Likewise, Wever (1979) concluded that "light does not have the capacity to affect parameters of autonomous rhythms regularly when operating continuously" (p. 93). The observation that the length of the free-running sleep-wake rhythm in isolation was longer when subjects had control over the lighting condition than when lighting was continuous, was interpreted by Wever to indicate that the changes in light intensity indirectly affected the rhythm by exerting behavioral effects. An example of such an indirect effect was the case when a subject turned off the light and changed his behavior from reading to listening to music, or vice-versa. The finding that subjects isolated in total darkness throughout the study period, and that blind subjects isolated for a few weeks had significantly shorter free-running rhythms than subjects isolated under a variety of lighting conditions, did not change Wever's conclusion.

The first evidence that circadian rhythms in humans can be entrained by a cycle of ordinary indoor room light alternating with total darkness was provided by Czeisler (1978) in his doctoral dissertation. Later, he and his associates played the leading role in delineating the effects of light on the circadian system. In two seminal papers, Czeisler and his colleagues (Czeisler et al 1986, 1989) demonstrated that bright light induced powerful resetting effects on the human circadian system. In the first, they investigated an elderly woman by the constant routine paradigm, before and after 4 h of bright light exposure for 7 consecutive evenings, and before and after a control study in ordinary room light, while her sleep-wake cycle and social contacts remained unchanged. The evening bright light induced a rapid 6-h phase delay in both the temperature and cortisol rhythms. In their second study, using 3 cycles of exposure to a daily illuminance pattern that included bright light (5 h), ordinary indoor light, and darkness, applied at different phases of the circadian temperature rhythm, a strong resetting of the circadian cycle was found. The magnitude and direction of the phase shifts were dependent on the initial circadian phase at which the bright light was applied. Using core temperature as the circadian marker, shifts in the advance direction were seen when subjects were exposed to light in the early morning hours, just after the minimum of core body temperature. Shifts in the delay direction occurred when the light was applied early in the subjective night, before the temperature minimum. Only small shifts were observed when light was applied during the subjective day. Later, another report from the same group (Jewett et al 1997) demonstrated that the circadian pacemaker in humans is sensitive to light at all circadian phases, which implies that the entire 24-h pattern of light exposure contributes to entrainment. Minors et al (1991) showed that a single 3-h bright light exposure was sufficient to delay or advance the circadian system when applied before or after the minimum of core body temperature. The resultant curve describing the relationship between the timing of the light stimulus and the phase shift it provokes is termed the phase response curve. This was first described by DeCoursey in the flying squirrel in 1960. Czeisler et al's (1986, 1989) data have demonstrated that human's phase response curve to light was consistent with the phase response curve properties described in all other diurnal species.

In contrast to earlier beliefs that ordinary indoor light has no effect on the circadian pacemaker, it was shown to have phase-advancing and phase-delaying effects, albeit of less potency than bright light stimuli. Boivin et al (1994) demonstrated that 3 cycles of relatively moderate light stimulus (1260 Lux) produced a robust phase advance of the circadian pacemaker when applied 1.5 h after the minimum core body temperature. Later, these findings were enlarged and generalized in the form of a dose-response relationship between light intensity and its resetting properties (Boivin et al 1996). Using 3 light intensities, 180, 1260, and 9500 Lux, and a darkness control condition (0.03 Lux), Boivin et al showed that even exposure to low light intensities such as those produced by artificial lamps can synchronize the human circadian system. The phase-shifting effects of light stimulus were linearly related to the cubic root of light intensity, as predicted by Kronauer's mathematical model (1990). These results were later confirmed by Waterhouse et al (1998).

When light stimulus was precisely centered around the minimum of the circadian rhythm in temperature, the time at which the circadian pacemaker is most sensitive to light-induced phase shifts (Jewett et al 1991), it significantly suppressed the endogenous circadian amplitude. In some cases, this resulted in apparent loss of circadian rhythmicity.

The studies of phase shifting by light stimuli provided further evidence that the circadian system in humans comprises a single pacemaker that affects multiple physiological and behavioral systems. This was shown by demonstrating simultaneous shifts in several variables. Thus, Czeisler et al (1989) reported that the circadian cycles in urine production and plasma cortisol maintained a stable temporal relationship with the core temperature rhythm after the light-induced phase shifts. Shanahan & Czeisler (1991) reported that bright light induced equivalent phase shifts of the melatonin and temperature rhythms. Boivin et al (1994) enlarged these findings to subjective alertness and cognitive performance.

Melatonin

Melatonin, which is a small molecule produced in the pineal gland in the depth of the brain, appears to play a critical role in the entrainment of the sleep-wake cycle by the circadian pacemaker. In all organisms, melatonin synthesis is limited to the dark period and is acutely inhibited by light. Although it can be entrained by the external light-dark cycle, melatonin production is under the control of the circadian pacemaker and it continues to oscillate under constant darkness conditions (Arendt 1995). Being responsive to light, the level of circulating melatonin provides an internal signal that is proportional to the length of the solar day. Lewy et al (1980), in a paper published back-to-back with Czeisler et al's (1980a) paper on free-running rhythms in isolated subjects, was the first to demonstrate that exposing humans during the night to bright light suppresses melatonin production. Later it was demonstrated that illuminance well below typical indoor light can also suppress melatonin production (Brainard et al 1988). The effects of light on the circadian pacemaker and on melatonin production are mediated through a specific neural pathway, the retinohypothalamic tract that projects from the retina directly to the hypothalamus, near the suprachiasmatic nuclei. This pathway is distinctly different from the neural pathways subservient to vision. There is a wealth of evidence that the paired SCN function as the circadian pacemaker that regulates circadian rhythms (see review in Weaver 1998). Their dense linkage with numerous parts of the central nervous system allows circadian regulation of physiologic and behavioral systems (LeSauter & Silver 1998). The SCN relays neural signals to the pineal via the intermediolateral cell column in the thoracic spinal cord, and via the superior cervical ganglion (Moore 1996). Thus, the retina detects photic information and sends neural signals along the retinohypothalamic pathway to the SCN, and from there to the pineal gland where it entrains the circadian cycles in melatonin production. Timed exposure of bright light can induce large phase-advance and phase-delay shifts in the melatonin rhythm, equivalent to the shifts in other endogenous circadian rhythms (see review in Shanahan et al 1997).

In addition to light, exogenous melatonin also exerts phase-shifting effects on the endogenous melatonin production in humans (Lewy et al 1992). Administration of exogenous melatonin, close to the endogenous offset of its own production in the morning hours, causes phase delay of the endogenous rhythm and, conversely it phase advances the rhythm when administered before the onset of the endogenous production. These phase-shifting effects are a mirror image of the phase-response curve of melatonin to light (see recent review in Lewy & Sack 1997).

Several lines of evidence link melatonin with the circadian regulation of sleep. First, in normal individuals, under entrained conditions, nocturnal onset of melatonin secretion is phase-locked with the opening of the sleep gate as determined by the ultra-short sleep-wake paradigm. This is demonstrated in Figure 3. Nocturnal increase in melatonin anticipated the sleep gate by 1.5–2 h (Tzischinsky et al 1993, Shochat et al 1997).

Daytime administration of melatonin modified the temporal pattern of sleep propensity in a time-dependent manner. When administered at 1200, it delayed the appearance of the sleep gate, whereas administration at 1700, 1900, and 2100 significantly advanced it. These changes resemble the phase-response curve of endogenous melatonin secretion to exogenous melatonin (Lewy et al 1992), and may be mediated by changes in the pattern of endogenous melatonin secretion. Possibly, the phase shifting effects of bright light on the sleep gate (Tzischinsky & Lavie 1997) may be also mediated by the delay in melatonin rhythm. Exogenous melatonin was also shown to be able to facilitate phase shifts of the sleep-wake rhythms. Facilitation of phase shifts has been reported both in field studies in vestigating adaptation to time zone changes, and in phase shifts induced under controlled laboratory conditions (see review in Arendt et al 1997). The soporific effects of exogenous melatonin were convincingly demonstrated when melatonin was administered during the daytime (Lavie 1997). Minimal effects, or none at all, were reported for nighttime administrations. The association between increased sleep propensity and endogenous rise in melatonin was also reported for blind individuals whose melatonin rhythm free-ran (Lockley et al 1997). Daytime naps in these blind individuals occurred within 5 h of the peak melatonin secretion. Furthermore, exposing subjects to a photoperiod of 10 h light and 14 h darkness for 4 weeks increased the duration of both melatonin secretion and sleep time (Wehr 1991).

These accumulated findings linking melatonin secretion with increased sleep propensity have led to the suggestion that the endogenous cycle of melatonin is involved in the regulation of the sleep-wake cycle not by actively promoting sleep, but by inhibiting the SCN wakefulness-producing mechanism (Lavie 1997). Thus, the evening onset of melatonin secretion, which coincides with the crest of the SCN-driven arousal cycle, inhibits the wakefulness-generating mechanisms, thereby enabling the brain's sleep-related structures to be activated unopposed by the drive for wakefulness. Recent evidence demonstrating that in addition to its well-known phase-shifting effects on SCN neuronal activity, melatonin also exerts acute inhibition of SCN neurons, provides support for this hypothesis (Liu et al 2000). Melatonin, therefore, may play a major role in the mediation between the circadian pacemaker and sleep-wake behavior. Being sensitive to light, melatonin also helps to entrain the sleep-wake cycles to the environmental light-dark cycles.

SUMMARY

Our understanding of the regulation of the sleep-wake cycle has come a long way since the pioneering studies in Andechs demonstrating free-running rhythms in subjects isolated from environmental time cues. Summarizing the wealth of data amassed since, it is apparent that the specific conditions of experimental paradigm employed to investigate the determinants of sleep-wake regulation, as well as the prevailing conceptions about the function of sleep and its evolutionary significance, have had a major impact on the evolving theories and models. Isolating subjects from the environment without stringently controlling their behavior was not sufficient to unmask the activity of the endogenous circadian pacemaker. Subjects' behavior during isolation, particularly their control over the lighting schedule, combined with the then unrecognized effects of ordinary room lights, introduced a systematic bias into the results. This resulted in overestimation of the period of the circadian pacemaker by about an hour, and in great instability of the free-running, sleep-wake rhythm. The demonstration that the human circadian pacemaker, as in all other organisms, is relatively stable and only deviates slightly from 24 h, was essential to resolve several of the long-lasting controversies in the field, such as the existence of a single or multiple circadian pacemakers, or whether the circadian pacemaker is altered with aging. Likewise, it is most probable that the traditional views on sleep as a restorative process that is under a powerful homeostatic-regulating control, have diverted attention from the importance of the experimental results pointing so clearly to the paradoxical positioning of the evening nadir in sleepiness. Only the seminal discovery by Edgar et al (1993) of the existence of a drive for wakefulness, and the confirmation of these observations in the forced desynchrony protocol, have led to a revision of the prevailing views on sleep-wake regulation. Now it is not only a homeostatic sleep principle that has to be taken into account but also a powerful drive for wakefulness.

Visit the Annual Reviews home page at www.AnnualReviews.org

LITERATURE CITED

Aeschbach D, Matthews JR, Postolache TT, Jackson MA, Giesen HA, Wehr TA. 1997. Dynamics of the human EEG during prolonged wakefulness: evidence for frequency-specific circadian and homeostatic influences *Neurosci. Lett.* 239:121–24

Åkerstedt T. 1977. Inversion of the sleep wakefulness pattern: effects on circadian variations in psychophysiological activation. *Ergonomics* 20:459–64

Åkerstedt T. 1988. Sleepiness as a consequence of shift work. *Sleep* 11:17–34

Åkerstedt T, Fröberg J, Friberg Y, Wetterberg L. 1979. Melatonin excretion, body temperature, and subjective arousal during 64 hours of sleep deprivation. *Psychoneuroendocrinology* 4:219–25

Arendt J. 1995. *Melatonin and the Mammalian Pineal Gland.* London: Chapman-Hall

Arendt J, Skene DJ, Middleton B, Lockley SW,

Deacon S. 1997. Efficacy of melatonin treatment in jet lag, shift work, and blindness. *J. Biol. Rhythms* 12:604–17

Aschoff J. 1965. Circadian rhythms in man. *Science* 148:1427–32

Aschoff J. 1990. Interdependence between locomotor activity and duration of wakefulness in humans during isolation. *Experientia* 46:870–71

Aschoff J. 1994. Naps as integral parts of the wake time within the human sleep-wake cycle. *J. Biol. Rhythms* 9:145–55

Aschoff J, Fatranska M, Giedke H, Doerr P, Stamm D, et al. 1971. Human circadian rhythms in continuous darkness: entrainment by social cues. *Science* 171:213–15

Aschoff J, Gerecke U, Wever R. 1967. Desynchronization of human circadian rhythms. *Jpn. J. Physiol.* 17:450–57

Aschoff J, Hoffman K, Pohl H, Wever R. 1975. Re-entrainment of circadian rhythms after phase-shifts of the zeitgeber. *Chronobiologia* 11:23–78

Aschoff J, Wever R. 1962. Spotanperiodik des Menschen bei Ausschluss aller Zeitgeber. *Naturwissenschaften* 49:337–42

Aschoff J, Wever R. 1976. Human circadian rhythms: a multioscillatory system. *Fed. Proc.* 35:2326–32

Aserinsky E, Kleitman N. 1953. Regularly occurring periods of eye motility, and concomitant phenomena during sleep. *Science* 118:273–74

Bjerner B, Holm Å, Swansson Å. 1955. Diurnal variation in mental performance. *Br. J. Ind. Med.* 12:103–10

Blake MJF. 1967. Time of day effects on performance in a range of tasks. *Psychonom. Sci.* 9:349–50

Boivin DB, Duffy J, Kronauer RE, Czeisler CA. 1994. Sensitivity of the human circadian pacemaker to moderately bright light. *J. Biol. Rhythms* 9:315–31

Boivin DB, Duffy JF, Kronauer RE, Czeisler CA. 1996. Dose-response relationships for resetting of human circadian clock by light. *Nature* 379:540–42

Brainard GC, Lewy AJ, Menaker M, Fredrickson RH, Miller LS. 1988. Dose-response relationship between light irradiance and the suppression of plasma melatonin in human volunteers. *Brain Res.* 454:212–18

Broughton JR. 1975. Biorhythmic variations in consciousness and psychological functions. *Can. Psychol. Rev.* 16:217–39

Broughton JR. 1998. SCN controlled circadian arousal and the afternoon "nap zone". *Sleep Res. Online* 1:166–78

Bünning E, ed. 1964. *The Physiological Clock.* Berlin: Springer-Verlag

Buxton OM, Frank SA, L'hermite-Baleriax M, Leproult R, Turek F, et al. 1997. Roles of intensity and duration of nocturnal exercise in causing phase delays of human circadian rhythms. *Am. J. Physiol.* 36:E536–42

Campbell SS, Zulley J. 1989. Napping in time free environments. In *Sleep and Alertness: Chronobiological, Behavioral, and Medical Aspects of Napping*, ed. DF Dinges, RJ Broughton, pp. 121–38. New York: Raven

Carskadon MA, Dement WC. 1977. Sleepiness and sleep state on a 90-min schedule. *Psychophysiology* 14:127–33

Carskadon MA, Dement WC. 1982. The multiple sleep latency test: What does it measure? *Sleep* 5:S67–72

Clodoré M, Benoit O, Foret J, Bouard G. 1990. The multiple sleep latency test: individual variability and time of day effect in normal young adults. *Sleep* 13:385–94

Colquoun WP, ed. 1971a. *Biological Rhythms and Human Performance.* London: Academic

Colquoun WP. 1971b. Circadian variations in mental efficiency. See Colquoun 1971a, pp. 39–107

Conroy RTWL, Mills JN. 1970. *Human Circadian Rhythms.* London: Churchill

Czeisler CA. 1978. *Human circadian physiology: internal organization of temperature, sleep-wake, and neuroendocrine rhythms monitored in an environment free of time cues.* PhD thesis. Stanford Univ., Stanford, CA

Czeisler CA, Allan JS, Strogatz SH, Ronda JM, Sanchez R, et al. 1986. Bright light resets the human circadian pacemaker independent of the timing of the sleep-wake cycle. *Science* 233:667–71

Czeisler CA, Duffy JF, Shanahan TL, Brown EN, Mitchell RE, et al. 1999. Stability, precision, and near-24-hour period of the human circadian pacemaker. *Science* 284:2177–81

Czeisler CA, Kronauer RE, Allan JS, Duffy JF, Jewett ME, et al. 1989. Bright light induction of strong (type 0) resetting of the human circadian pacemaker. *Science* 244:1328–33

Czeisler CA, Weitzman ED, Moore-Ede MC, Zimmerman JC, Knauer RS. 1980a. Human sleep: Its duration and organization depend on its circadian phase. *Science* 210:1264–67

Czeisler CA, Zimmerman JC, Ronda JM, Moore-Ede MC, Weitzman ED. 1980b. Timing of REM sleep is coupled to the circadian rhythm of body temperature in man. *Sleep* 2:329–46

Daan S, Beersma DG, Borbély AA. 1984. Timing of human sleep recovery process gated by a circadian pacemaker. *Am. J. Physiol.* 246:R161–83

DeCoursey PJ. 1960. Daily light sensitivity rhythm in a rodent. *Science* 131:33–35

Dijk DJ, Czeisler CA. 1994. Paradoxical timing of the circadian rhythm of sleep propensity serves to consolidate sleep and wakefulness in humans. *Neurosci. Lett.* 166:63–68

Dijk DJ, Czeisler CA. 1995. Contribution of the circadian pacemaker and the sleep homeostat to sleep propensity, sleep structure, electroencephalographic slow waves, and sleep spindle activity. *J. Neurosci.* 15:3526–38

Dijk DJ, Shanahan TL, Duffy JF, Ronda JM, Czeisler CA. 1997. Variation of electroencephalographic activity during non-rapid eye movement and rapid eye movement sleep with phase of circadian melatonin rhythm in humans. *J. Physiol.* 505:851–58

Edgar DM, Dement WC, Fuller CA. 1993. Effect of SCN lesions on sleep in squirrel monkeys: evidence for opponent processes in sleep-wake regulation. *J. Neurosci.* 13:1065–79

Endo S, Yamamoto T, Sasaki M. 1978. Effects of time zone changes on sleep—west-east flight and east-west flight. *Jikeikai Med. J.* 25:249–68

Evans JI, Christie GA, Lewis SA, Daly J, Moore-Robinson M. 1972. Sleep and time-zone changes. *Arch. Neurol.* 26:36–48

Folkard S. 1975. Diurnal variation in logical reasoning. *Br. J. Psychol.* 66:1–8

Fröberg J. 1977. Twenty-four-hour patterns in human performance, subjective and physiological variables and differences between morning and evening types. *Biol. Psychol.* 5:119–34

Globus GG, Phoebus EV, Boyd R. 1972. Temporal organization of night workers' sleep. *Aerosp. Med.* 43:266–68

Halberg F. 1969. Chronobiology. *Annu. Rev. Physiol.* 31:675–725

Hume KI. 1980. Sleep adaptation after phase shifts of the sleep-wakefulness rhythm in man. *Sleep* 2:417–35

Hume KI, Mills JN. 1977. Rhythms of REM and slow-wave sleep in subjects living on abnormal time schedules. *Waking Sleep.* 1:291–96

Jewett ME, Kronauer RE, Czeisler CA. 1991. Light-induced suppression of endogenous circadian amplitude in humans. *Nature* 350:59–62

Jewett ME, Rimmer DW, Duffy JF, Klerman EB, Kronauer RE, Czeisler CA. 1997. The human circadian pacemaker is sensitive to light throughout subjective day without evidence of transients. *Am. J. Physiol.* 273:R800–9

Klein KE, Bruner H, Holtmann H, Rehme H, Stolze J, et al. 1970. Circadian rhythm of pilots' efficiency and effects of multiple time zone travel. *Aerosp. Med.* 41:125–13

Kleitman N. 1939. *Sleep and Wakefulness as Alternating Phases in the Cycle of Existence.* Chicago: Univ. Chicago Press

Kleitman N. 1963. *Sleep and Wakefulness.* Chicago: Univ. Chicago Press. 2nd ed.

Klerman EB, Rimmer DW, Jan-Dijk D, Kronauer RE, Rizzo FJ III, et al. 1998. Nonphotic entrainment of the human circadian pacemaker. *Am. J. Physiol.* 274:R991–96

Kripke DF, Cook B, Lewis OF. 1971. Sleep of night workers, EEG recordings. *Psychophysiology* 7:377–84

Kronauer RE. 1990. A quantitative model for the effects of light on the amplitude and phase of the deep circadian pacemaker, based on human data. In *Sleep '90, Proc. 10th Eur. Congr. Sleep Res.*, Strasbourg, France, pp. 306–9. Bochem: Pontenagel Press

Lack LC, Lushington K. 1996. The rhythms of human sleep propensity and core body temperature. *J. Sleep Res.* 5:1–11

Lavie P. 1986. Ultrashort sleep-waking schedule: III. 'Gates' and 'forbidden zones' for sleep. *Electroencephalogr. Clin. Neurophysiol.* 63:414–25

Lavie P. 1993. The sleep theory of Constantin von Economo. *J. Sleep Res.* 2:175–78

Lavie P. 1997. Melatonin: role in gating nocturnal rise in sleep propensity. *J. Biol. Rhythms* 12:657–65

Lavie P, Scherson A. 1981. Ultrashort sleep-waking schedule. I. Evidence of ultradian rhythmicity in "sleepability." *Electroencephalogr. Clin. Neurophysiol.* 52:163–74

Lavie P, Segal S. 1989. Twenty-four-hour structure of sleepiness in morning and evening persons investigated by ultrashort sleep-wake cycle. *Sleep* 12:522–28

Lavie P, Zvuluni A. 1992. The 24-hour sleep propensity function: experimental bases for somnotypology. *Psychophysiology* 29:566–75

LeSauter J, Silver R. 1998. Output signals of the SCN. *Chronobiol. Int.* 15:535–50

Lewy AJ, Ahmed S, Jackson JM, Sack RL. 1992. Melatonin shifts human circadian rhythms according to a phase-response curve. *Chronobiol. Int.* 9:380–92

Lewy AJ, Sack RL. 1997. Exogenous melatonin's phase-shifting effects on the endogenous melatonin profile in sighted humans: a brief review and critique of the literature. *J. Biol. Rhythms* 12:588–94

Lewy AJ, Wehr TA, Goodwin FK, Newsome DA, Markey SP. 1980. Light suppresses melatonin secretion in humans. *Science* 210:1267–69

Liu X, Uchiyama M, Shibui K, Kim K, Kudo Y, et al. 2000. Diurnal preference, sleep habits, circadian sleep propensity and melatonin rhythm in healthy human subjects. *Neurosci. Lett.* 280:199–202

Lockley SW, Skene DJ, Arendt J, Tabandeh H, Bird AC, Defrance R. 1997. Relationship between melatonin rhythms and visual loss in the blind. *J. Clin. Endocrinol. Metab.* 82:3763–70

Mills JN. 1964. Circadian rhythms during and after three months in solitude underground. *J. Physiol.* 174.217–31

Mills JN, ed. 1973. *Biological Aspects of Circadian Rhythms.* London: Plenum

Mills JN, Minors DS, Waterhouse JM. 1978. Adaptation to abrupt time shifts of the oscillators controlling human circadian rhythms. *J. Physiol.* 285:455–70

Minors DS, Waterhouse JM, Wirz-Justice A. 1991. A human phase response curve to light. *Neurosci. Lett.* 133:36–40

Moore RY. 1996. Neural control of the pineal gland. *Behav. Brain Res.* 73:125–30

Monk TH, Buysse DJ, Reynolds CF III. 1996. Circadian determinants of the postlunch dip in performance. *Chronobiol. Int.* 13:123 33

Monk TH, Buysse DJ, Reynolds CF III, Kupfer DJ. 1995. Inducing jet lag in an older person: directional asymmetry. *Exp. Gerontol.* 30:137–45

Monk TH, Moline ML, Graeber RC. 1988. Inducing jet lag in the laboratory: patterns of adjustment to an acute shift in routine. *Aviat. Space Environ. Med.* 59:703–10

Moruzzi G. 1964. The historical development of the deafferentation hypothesis of sleep. *Proc. Am. Philos. Soc.* 108:19–28

Moses JM, Hord DJ, Lubin A, Johnson LC,

Naitoh P. 1975. Dynamics of nap sleep during a 40-hour period. *Electroencephalogr. Clin. Neurophysiol.* 39:627–33

Moses J, Lubin A, Naitoh P, Johnson LC. 1978. Circadian variation in performance, subjective sleepiness, sleep and oral temperature during an altered sleep-wake schedule. *Biol. Psychol.* 6:301–8

Nicholson AN, Pascoe PA, Spencer MB, Stone BM, Roehrs T, et al. 1986. Sleep after transmeridian flights. *Lancet* 2:1205–8

Piéron H. 1913. *Le Probléme Physiologique du Sommeil.* Paris: Masson

Richardson G, Carskadon MA, Flagg W, Van Den Hoed J, Dement WC, et al. 1978. Excessive daytime sleepiness in man: multiple sleep latency measurement in narcoleptic and control subjects. *Electroencephalogr. Clin. Neurophysiol.* 45:621–27

Shanahan TL, Czeisler CA. 1991. Light exposure induces equivalent phase shifts of the endogenous circadian rhythms of circulating plasma melatonin and core body temperature in men. *J. Clin. Endocrinol. Metab.* 73:227–35

Shanahan TL, Zeitzer JM, Czeisler CA. 1997. Resetting the melatonin rhythm with light in humans. *J. Biol. Rhythms* 12:556–67

Shochat T, Luboshitzky R, Lavie P. 1997. Nocturnal melatonin onset is phase locked to the primary sleep gate. *Am. J. Physiol.* 273:R364–70

Siffre M. 1963. *Hors du Temps.* Paris: Tuillard

Sollberger A. 1965. *Biological Rhythm Research.* Amsterdam: Elsevier

Steel GD, Callaway M, Suedfeld P, Palinkas L. 1995. Human sleep-wake cycles in High Arctic: effects of unusual photoperiodicity in a natural setting. *Biol. Rhythm Res.* 26:582–92

Strogatz SH. 1986. *The Mathematical Structure of the Human Sleep Wake Cycle.* New York: Springer-Verlag

Strogatz SH, Kronauer RE, Czeisler CA. 1987. Circadian pacemaker interferes with sleep onset at specific times each day: role in insomnia. *Am. J. Physiol.* 253:R172–78

Tayer RE. 1970. Activation states as assessed by verbal report and four psychophysiological variables. *Psychophysiology* 7:86–94

Tzischinsky O, Lavie P. 1994. Melatonin possesses time-dependent hypnotic effects. *Sleep* 17:638–45

Tzischinsky O, Lavie P. 1997. The effects of evening bright light on next-day sleep propensity. *J. Biol. Rhythms* 12:259–65

Tzischinsky O, Shlitner A, Lavie P. 1993. The association between the nocturnal sleep gate and nocturnal onset of urinary 6-sulfatoxymelatonin. *J. Biol. Rhythms* 8:199–209

Waterhouse J, Minors D, Folkard S, Owens D, Atkinson G, et al. 1998. Light of domestic intensity produces phase shifts of the circadian oscillator in humans. *Neurosci. Lett.* 245:97–100

Weaver DR. 1998. The suprachiasmatic nucleus: a 25-year retrospective. *J. Biol. Rhythms* 13:100–12

Webb WB, Agnew HW. 1971. Stage 4 sleep: influence of time course variables. *Science* 174:1354–56

Webb WB, Agnew HW, Williams RL. 1971. Effect on sleep of a sleep period time displacement. *Aerosp. Med.* 42:152–55

Webb WB, Dinges DF. 1989. Cultural perspectives on napping and siesta. In *Sleep and Alertness: Chronobiological, Behavioral, and Medical Aspects of Napping*, ed. DF Dinges, RJ Broughton. pp. 121–38. New York: Raven

Wehr T. 1991. The duration of human melatonin secretion and sleep respond to changes in daylength (photoperiod). *J. Clin. Endocrinol. Metab.* 73:1276–80

Weitzman ED, Czeisler CA, Zimmerman JC, Ronda JM. 1980. Timing of REM and stages 3+4 sleep during temporal isolation in man. *Sleep* 2:391–407

Weitzman ED, Kripke DF, Goldmacher D, McGregor P, Nogeire CH. 1970. Acute reversal of the sleep-waking cycle in man. *Arch. Neurol.* 22:483–89

Weitzman ED, Nogeire CH, Perlow M, Fukushima D, Sassin J, et al. 1974. Effects of a prolonged 3-hour sleep-wake cycle on sleep stages, plasma cortisol, growth hormone and body temperature in man. *J. Clin. Endocrinol. Metab.* 38:1018–30

Wever RA. 1979. *The Circadian System of Man: Results of Experiments Under Temporal Isolation.* New-York: Springer

Wyatt JK, Cecco AR, Czeisler CA, Dijk DJ. 1999. Circadian temperature and melatonin rhythms, sleep, and neurobehavioral function in humans living on a 20-h day. *Am. J. Physiol.* 277:R1152–63

Zulley J. 1980. Distribution of REM sleep in entrained 24 hour and free-running sleep-wake cycles. *Sleep* 2:377–89

Zulley J, Campbell SS. 1985. Napping behavior during "spontaneous internal desynchronization": Sleep remains in synchrony with body temperature. *Hum. Neurobiol.* 4:123–26

Zulley J, Schulz H. 1980. Sleep and body temperature in free-running sleep-wake cycles. In *Sleep '78. Proc. 4th Eur. Congr. Sleep Res.,* Tirgu-Mures, Romania, pp. 341–44. Basel: Karger

Zulley J, Wever R, Aschoff J. 1981. The dependence of onset and duration of sleep on the circadian rhythm of rectal temperature. *Pflugers. Arch.* 391:314–18

Annu. Rev. Psychol. 2001. 52:305–35

STATISTICAL GRAPHICS: Mapping the Pathways of Science

Howard Wainer
Educational Testing Service, Princeton, New Jersey 08541; e-mail: hwainer@ets.org

Paul F. Velleman
Cornell University, Ithaca, NY 14853; e-mail: pfv2@cornell.edu

Key Words   linking, slicing, brushing, EDA, rotating plots, dynamic display, interactive displays, multivariate analysis

■ **Abstract**   This chapter traces the evolution of statistical graphics starting with its departure from the common noun structure of Cartesian determinism, through William Playfair's revolutionary grammatical shift to graphs as proper nouns, and alights on the modern conception of graph as an active participant in the scientific process of discovery. The ubiquitous availability of data, software, and cheap, high-powered, computing when coupled with the broad acceptance of the ideas in Tukey's 1977 treatise on exploratory data analysis has yielded a fundamental change in the way that the role of statistical graphics is thought of within science—as a dynamic partner and guide to the future rather than as a static monument to the discoveries of the past. We commemorate and illustrate this development while pointing readers to the new tools available and providing some indications of their potential.

CONTENTS

0066-4308/01/0201-0305$14.00

305

INTRODUCTION: Graphs as Nouns, from Common to Proper

Graphic displays abounded in ancient times. For example, a primitive coordinate system of intersecting horizontal and vertical lines that enabled a precise placement of data points was used by Nilotic surveyors as early as 1400 BC. A more refined coordinate system was used by Hipparchus (ca. 140 BC), whose terms for the coordinate axes translates into Latin as *longitudo* and *latitudo*, to locate points in the heavens. Somewhat later, Roman surveyors used a coordinate grid to lay out their towns on a plane that was defined by two axes. The *decimanus* were lines running from east to west, and the *cardo* ran north to south (Smith 1925). There are many other examples of special-purpose coordinate systems in wide use before the end of the first millennium; musical notation placed on horizontal running lines was in use as early as the ninth century (Apel 1944); the chessboard was invented in seventh century India.

Costigan-Eaves & Macdonald-Ross (in preparation) found what appears to be one of the earliest examples of printed graph paper dating from about 1680. Large sheets of paper engraved with a grid were apparently printed to aid in designing and communicating the shapes of the hulls of ships.[1] Both Beniger & Robyn (1978) and Funkhouser (1937) describe Descartes' 1637 development of a coordinate system as an important intellectual milestone in the path toward statistical graphics. We join Biderman (1978) in interpreting this in exactly the opposite way—that it was an intellectual impediment that took a century and a half and William Playfair's (1759–1823) eclectic mind to overcome.

Because natural science originated within natural philosophy, it favored a rational rather than empirical approach to scientific inquiry. Such an outlook was antithetical to the more empirical modern approach to science that does not disdain the atheoretical plotting of data points with the goal of investigating suggestive patterns. Graphs in existence before Playfair (with some notable exceptions discussed below) grew out of the same rationalist tradition that yielded Descartes' coordinate geometry—that is, the plotting of curves on the basis of an a priori mathematical expression (e.g. Oresme's "pipes" on the first page of the Padua edition of his 1486 *Tractatus de latitudunibus formarum*[2] is often cited as an early example; see Figure 1).

This notion is supported by statements like that of Luke Howard, a prolific grapher of data in the late eighteenth and early nineteenth century who, as late as

---

[1] This material is classed in the "collection" category of the British Library with the entry, "A collection of engraved sheets of squared paper, whereon are traced in pencil or ink the curves or sweeps of the hulls of sundry men-of-war."

[2] Clagett (1968) argued convincingly that this work was not written by Oresme, but probably by Jacobus de Sancto Martino, one of his followers, in about 1390—yet another instance of how surprisingly often eponymous referencing is an indication only of who did not do it (Stigler 1980).

difform's vniformiter variatio reddit vniſoꝛ ſcͣꝑ.ꞇ ſiaſ ad iiȝ
mter diffoꝛmꝛer difformej. ☙ Latum? vni
foꝛm c̃ dmoꝛis c̃ illa q̃ Ꝯ inꞇ excellus graduuȝ
eq̃ diſtâuuȝ buat eidé ꝓportioȝ aia iii a ꝓ
portõe eq̃ltatis. Ná ſi uiꞇ excellus graduuꝫ
inter ſe eq̃ diſtauuū buarent ꝓportioȝ eq̃uta
tis .uc ẽꞇ .auuu? vnuformiꞇ dinꞇfis uꞇ pȝ ex
diffunuomibus membroꝛum ſeciide diuuiois
Rurſus ſi nulla proporcio ſeruaꞇ tuic nulla
poſſeꞇ attendi vnuformitas in laumdine tali ꞇ
ſic non eſſeꞇ vnuformiꞇer difioꝛm c̃ difformis
☙ Latuu? difformiter difformiter difformis
ẽ illa q̃ inter excellus graduú eque diſtantiuȝ
non ſeruaꞇ candem propoꝛtionem ſicu.ᷤin ſe
cunda parꞇe patebiꞇ. Notandum tamen eſt
ꝙ ſicuꞇ in ſupꝛadictis diffiniꞇõibᵘ ubi loqtur
de exceſſu graduum inter ſe eque diſtantium
debȝ accipi diſtancia ſcóm parꞇes latitudinis
extélise ꞇ nõ intélisue ꞇita uꞇ loquunꞇ d.ciᷤe dif
funiꞇões ð diſtáꞇia ȝ duú ſimuali ſi auꞇ graduali

Equiꞇ.ſcða ps in qua uꞇ
ſupradicta intelligauꞇur ad
ſenluȝ per figuras gccme
tricas oſtenduntur.Et uꞇ
omnem ſpeciem latitudis
in preſcnti materia via oc
currat apparentior latitudics ad figuras gco
mefcaȝ explicanꞇ. Iſta ps diuidiꞇ p tria ca
piꞇula q̃ꝰ pᵐ ꝓtinet d.óꞇiõcs.ȝᵐ ſuppoſitiõ.s

Figure 1　Oresme's graphical illustration of functions taken from the first page of the Padua edition of his 1486 *Tractatus de latitudunibus formarum*. (British Library IA. 3Q024)

1847, apologized for his methodology and referred to it as an "autograph of the curve ... confessedly adapted rather to the use of the *dilettanti* in natural philosophy than that of regular students" (Howard 1847, p. 21).

It is not inaccurate to think of early graphic displays as nouns, indeed common nouns, that were used to depict some theoretical relationship. Thus, we can conceive of the first major revolution in the use of graphic display in science as a shift from its use as a common noun (e.g. the theoretical relationship between supply and demand) to that of a proper noun (e.g. England's imports and exports from 1700 to 1800). This revolution seems to have begun in 1665 with the invention of the barometer. This inspired Robert Plot to record the barometric pressure in Oxford every day of 1684 and summarize his findings in a remarkably contemporary graph (Figure 2) that he called a "History of the Weather." He sent a copy of this graph with a letter to Martin Lister[3] in 1685 with a prophetic insight on the eventual use:

> For when once we have procured fit persons enough to make the same Observations in many foreign and remote parts, how the winds stood in each, at the same time, we shall then be enabled with some grounds to examine, not only the coastings, breadth, and bounds of the winds themselves, but of the weather they bring with them; and probably in time thereby learn, to be forewarned certainly, of divers emergencies (such as heats, colds, dearths, plague, and other epidemical distempers) which are not unaccountable to us; and by their causes be instructed for prevention, or remedies: thence too in time we may hope to be informed how far the positions of the planets in relation to one another, and to the fixed stars, are concerned in the alterations of the weather, and in bringing and preventing diseases and other calamities...we shall certainly obtain more real and useful knowledge in matters in a few years, than we have yet arrived to, in many centuries. (Plot 1685)

Plot and Lister's use of graphic display was scooped by the seventeenth century polymath Christiaan Huygens (1629–1693). On October 30, 1669, Christiaan's brother Lodewijk sent him a letter containing some interpolations of life expectancy data taken from John Graunt's 1662 book *Natural and Political Observations on the London Bills of Mortality*. Christiaan's responded in letters dated November 21 and 28, 1669, with graphs of those interpolations (Huygens, 1895). Figure 3 shows one of those graphs, with age on the horizontal axis and number of survivors of the original birth cohort on the vertical axis. The curve was fitted to his brother's

---

[3]The origin of the graphic depiction of weather data sadly, for the obvious eponymous glory, rests not with Plot but rather with Lister, who presented various versions of graphical summaries of weather data before the Oxford Philosophical Society on March 10, 1683 and later in the same year a modified version to the Royal Society. Plot was not the only one enthusiastic about Lister's graphical methods. William Molyneux was so taken that he had an engraving made of the grid and he would faithfully send a "weather diary" monthly to William Musgrave. One of Molyneux's charts was reproduced in Gunther (1968).

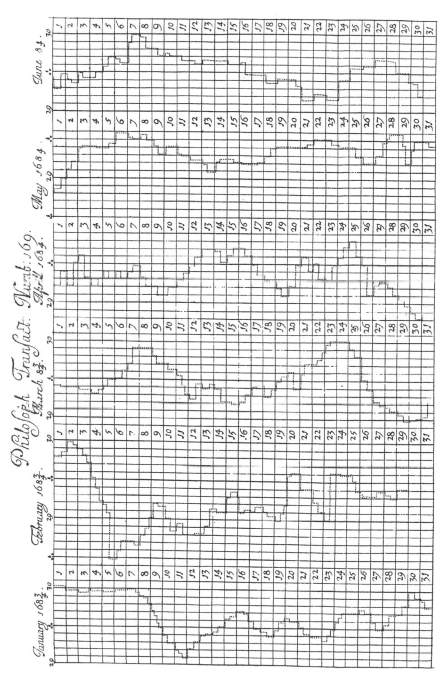

Figure 2 Robert Plot's (1685) "History of the Weather" recording of the daily barometric pressure in Oxford for the year 1684 (based on the original work of Martin Lister).

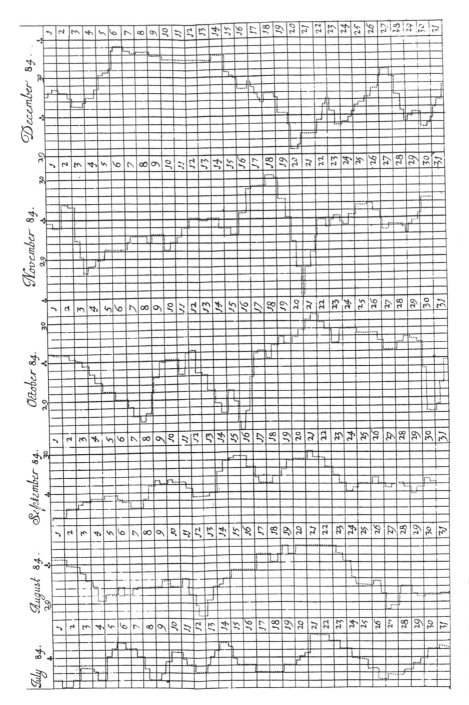

Figure 2 (*Continued*)

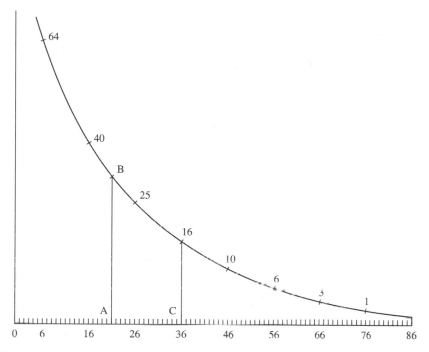

Figure 3   A redrafting of Christiaan Huygens' 1669 curve showing how many people out of a hundred survive between the ages of infancy to 86. [Data from John Graunt's (1662) *Natural and Political Observations on the Bills of Mortality*].

interpolations.[4] The letters on the chart are related to an associated discussion on how to construct a life expectancy chart from this one—that is, analyzing a set of data to yield deeper insights into the subject. Christiaan's constructed such a chart and indicated that it was more interesting from a scientific point of view; Figure 3, he felt, was more helpful in wagering.

There was a smattering of other examples of empirically based graphs that appeared in the century between Huygens' letter and the publication of Playfair's *Commercial and Political Atlas* (1786), for although some graphic forms were available before Playfair, they were rarely used to plot empirical information. Biderman (1978) argued that this was because there was an antipathy toward such a use as a scientific approach. This suggestion was supported by such statements as that made by Luke Howard. However, at least sometimes when data were available (e.g. Pliny's astronomical data, Graunt's survival data, Plot's weather

---

[4]There are many other graphical devices contained in the 22 volume *Oeuvres Complètes* (1888–1950) to be explored by anyone with fluency in ancient Dutch, Latin, and French. Incidentally, Huygen's graphical work on the pendulum proved to him that a pendulum's oscillations would be isochronic regardless of its amplitude. This discovery led him to actually build the first clock based on this principle.

data, and several other admirable uses) they were plotted. Perhaps part of the exponential increase in the use of graphics since the beginning of the nineteenth century is merely concomitant to the exponential growth in the availability of data. Of course, there might also be a symbiosis, in that the availability of graphic devices for analyzing data encouraged data gathering. For whatever the reasons, Playfair was at the cusp of an explosion in data gathering, and his graphic efforts appear causal. He played an important role in that explosion.

The consensus of scholars, well phrased by P Costigan-Eaves & M Macdonald-Ross (in preparation), is that until Playfair "many of the graphic devices used were the result of a formal and highly deductive science.... This world view was more comfortable with an arm-chair, rationalistic approach to problem-solving which usually culminated in elegant mathematical principles" often associated with elegant geometrical diagrams. The empirical approach to problem solving, a critical driving force for data collection, was slow to get started. However, the empirical approach began to demonstrate remarkable success in solving problems, and with improved communications,[5] the news of these successes, and hence the popularity of the associated graphic tools, began to spread quickly.

We are accustomed to intellectual diffusion taking place from the natural and physical sciences into the social sciences; certainly that is the direction taken for both calculus and the scientific method. However, statistical graphics in particular, and statistics in general, went the reverse route. Although, as we have seen, there were applications of data-based graphics in the natural sciences, it was only after Playfair applied them within the social sciences that their popularity began to accelerate. Playfair should be credited with producing the first chartbook of social statistics; indeed publishing an atlas that contained not a single map is one indication of his belief in the methodology (to say nothing of his chutzpah). Playfair's work was immediately admired, but emulation, at least in Britain, took a little longer (graphic use started up on the continent a bit sooner). Interestingly, one of Playfair's earliest emulators was the banker S Tertius Galton (the father of Francis Galton, and hence the biological grandfather of modern statistics) who, in 1813, published a multiline time series chart of the money in circulation, rates of foreign exchange, and prices of bullion and wheat.[6] The relatively slower diffusion of the graphical method back into the natural sciences provides additional support for the hypothesized bias against empiricism there. The newer social sciences, having no such tradition and faced with both problems to solve and relevant data, were quicker to see the potential of Playfair's methods.

Playfair's graphical inventions and adaptations look contemporary. He invented the statistical bar chart out of desperation because he lacked the time series data required to draw a line showing the trade with Scotland, and so used bars to symbolize

---

[5]The first encyclopedia in English appeared in 1704. The number of scientific periodicals began a rapid expansion at the end of the eighteenth century; between 1780 and 1789 20 new journals appeared, between 1790 and 1800 25 more (McKie 1972).

[6]Biderman (1978, 1990) pointed out that ironically, Galton's chart predicted the financial crisis of 1831 that created a ruinous run on his own bank.

the cross-sectional character of the data he did have. Playfair acknowledged Priestley's (1769) priority in this form, although Priestly used bars to symbolize the life spans of historical figures in a time line.[7]

Playfair's role was crucial for several reasons, but not for his development of the graphic recording of data; others preceded him in that. Indeed, in 1805 he pointed out that as a child his brother John had him keep a graphic record of temperature readings. However, Playfair was in a remarkable position. Because of his close relationship with his brother and his connections with James Watt he was on the periphery of science. He was close enough to know the value of the graphical methods, but sufficiently detached in his own interests to apply them in a very different arena—that of economics and finance. These areas, then as now, tend to attract a larger audience than matters of science, and Playfair was adept at self-promotion. [For more about the remarkable life and accomplishments of William Playfair (including the fascinating story of his attempted blackmail of Lord Archibald Douglas) the interested reader is referred to Spence & Wainer (1997, 2000), Wainer (1996) and Wainer & Spence (1997).]

In a review of Playfair's 1786 *Atlas*, which appeared in *The Political Herald*, Dr. Gilbert Stuart wrote, "The new method in which accounts are stated in this work, has attracted very general notice. The propriety and expediency of all men, who have any interest in the nation, being acquainted with the general outlines, and the great facts relating to our commerce are unquestionable; and this is the most commodious, as well as accurate mode of effecting this object, that has hitherto been thought of ... To each of his charts the author has added observations (which) ... in general are just and shrewd; and sometimes profound ... Very considerable applause is certainly due to this invention; as a new, distinct, and easy mode of conveying information to statesmen and merchants ..." Such wholehearted approval rarely greets any scientific development. Playfair's adaptation of graphic methods to matters of general interest provided an enormous boost to the popularity of statistical graphics.

THE NEXT GRAPHICAL REVOLUTION: Graphs as Dynamic Colleagues

"Eppur si muove!"[8]
Galileo (c. 1622)

For almost 200 years, from 1786 and the publication of Playfair's *Atlas* until 1977 and the publication of Tukey's *Exploratory Data Analysis*, the use

---

[7]Priestley's use of the bar as a metaphor is somewhat different then Playfair's in that the data were not really statistical. Moreover, Priestly was not the first to construct a graphical time-line; in 1753 the French physician Jacques Barbeu-Dubourg produced a graphic in the form of a 54 foot long scroll, configured in a way not unlike a torah, that contains thumbnail sketches of famous people from The Creation to 1750 (see Wainer 1998 for a fuller story).
[8]"And yet it moves!"

of graphics within science remained static. Statistical graphics became widely used to communicate information, to decorate and enliven scientific presentations, and to store information. Their use as the principal tool in the exploration of quantitative phenomena also grew in fits and starts, but sentiments, analogous to Luke Howard's were still voiced. Tukey's *Exploratory Data Analysis* changed things. Suddenly terms like data snooping, data dredging, and the currently trendy "data mining" were no longer pejorative.[9]

Coupled with the scientific acceptability, even desirability, of the clever plotting of data points in the search for suggestive patterns, was the ubiquitous appearance of cheap powerful computing. This manuscript is being prepared on a $2000 computer more powerful than any institutional mainframe available when Tukey's book was published. Although most of its MIPS are wastefully idle, they can be called upon whenever needed. However, the computer revolution does not stop with machinery (although it is surely powered by it). Enormous data sets, on varied topics, are readily available. A CD-ROM or two can provide you with the results of the decenniel census or the entire National Assessment of Educational Progress. Through the Cochrane Collaboration the results of 250,000 different random assignment medical experiments are immediately accessible for scrutiny and meta-analysis. Soon all three billion pieces of the human genome will be available to serve as biology's analog to the periodic table. And then there is "the web," overflowing with data (and nondata).

Software for data analysis and visualization when added to the assets of powerful computing and extensive data completes the scientific triumvirate. Studies that were either too expensive, too tedious, or too difficult can now be done with the click of a mouse. It is this ease of manipulation that characterizes the latest transformation of graphics in scientific inquiry. The graph is no longer a static object to be carefully constructed and enshrined for further study. It is a dynamic partner in the investigation.

The rest of this chapter focuses on some of the new dynamic tools that are available for examining data. We ignore the set of useful tools for data exposition that were described 20 years ago in an earlier incarnation of this chapter (Wainer & Thissen 1981) and instead refer interested readers to that review.

There are many more ways to display data badly (Wainer 1997, Chapt. 1), than there are to display data well—that is, to say what you mean about the data clearly and grammatically. Whereas the earlier chapter on graphical data analysis discussed clear, grammatical presentation of data, including methods that are resistant to influence by outliers, the balance of this chapter discusses how to hold a conversation about your data with a data display.

---

[9]Data mining, which usually implies fitting a very complex general model to an enormous data set, still seems to deserve critical scrutiny. Bert Green (personal communication) characterizes data mining as being akin to the Ganzwelt of the nineteenth century psychophysicists; sooner or later you begin to see things, whether or not anything is really there.

The key to conversational graphics is the recognition of a graph as dynamic and malleable. During the course of a good conversation, each party changes, learns, and grows. A good conversation about data is much the same: We may see something new in the data that leads us to want to view it in a new way. By viewing the data in many different but consistent ways, we have a greater chance of noting patterns, relationships, and exceptions. As the conversation leads us to a new point of view, we understand the data differently.

Conversational Graphics

Data graphics have evolved from depicting numbers, to depicting variables (e.g. distributions), to depicting relationships among variables. At each stage, however, the communication has been in only one direction: from the graph (or graph maker) to the viewer. But, as computers have taken over almost all graph drawing for data, we have come to realize the possibility of interacting with graphs, of holding a conversation with a graph in an attempt to mutually achieve greater insight. We have come to realize the extraordinary enhancement that such interaction brings to the understanding of data through graphs. There is good experimental evidence that we learn better through interaction. Such "active learning" is almost a fad among educators, but the principle that interacting with something new aids in understanding is sound.

Graphs that interact with the viewer first appeared in the early 1970s with projects such as PRIM-9 (Fisherkeller et al 1974), the first multidimensional rotating scatterplot and early experiments with plot brushing at AT&T Bell Labs (Becker & Cleveland 1984). It is only with the wide availability of powerful desktop computers, however, that they have become widely available. Various kinds of real-time interaction can be found in many statistics programs, although few offer all of the methods we discuss here. However, each method has usually been discussed on its own. We attempt here to bring together discussions of interactive graphics and provide unifying principles and insights.

The Absurdity of Graphing Data

The Nobel Laureate Eugene P Wigner (1960), in his address commemorating the opening of the Courant Institute, remarked on the unusual effectiveness of mathematics in science. He pointed out that "mathematics works so often in science that it is disquieting. It is like a man with a large key ring and a sequence of doors to open who finds that after choosing a key at random each door opens on the first or second try. Sooner or later you begin to doubt the relationship between the keys and the locks. So it is with mathematics and science." Why should the universe operate in such a way that human mathematics accurately describes it?

It is with the same sense of wonder that we ask the identical question about graphical display, for graphs of data are based on the somewhat absurd notion that we can usefully represent data values whose meaning relates to units of measurement in the real world by arbitrarily assigning them a position in space, a color, a symbol, or a behavior. Moreover, although the data values themselves have no position, color, symbol, or behavior, an appropriate assignment will not only allow us to perceive patterns and relationships that might not otherwise be evident, but will meaningfully relate to the original measurement units.

Just as the unusual effectiveness of mathematics in science suggests something about the universal truth of mathematics, the unusual effectiveness of graphs for communication with humans suggests fundamental truths about human perception. In his Silliman Lectures, Jacob Bronowski (1978) notes that human perceptual abilities evolved along with our species and are thus optimized for certain survival-enhancing perceptions. We see edges well. We see straight lines and understand their relative slopes easily. We can compare areas and sizes visually unless distracted by an illusion of depth and volume. We are well-equipped to see smooth, physically-appropriate motion and we implicitly understand trajectories.

As a result, Bronowski points out, we see the world the way *we* look rather than the way *it* looks, which constrains what we perceive. Data graphics, however, must take account of how we look and what we will see. Properly designed graphics use human perception abilities wisely. Thus, well-planned layouts, straight lines, starkly different colors, areas of simple shapes, and smooth motion facilitate understanding and perception in graphs.

More generally, modern graphics take advantage of human perception by constraining the points and symbols representing the data to behave with a "cartoon reality" that obeys reasonable laws. These laws include the principle that elements in a graph move smoothly (not jumping from place to place), that they have a consistent color, shape, and selection state, and that the mapping of numeric value to physical plot attribute is consistent and shows an appropriate association (e.g. the well-established "area principle," which holds that the perceived size of a plot element should correspond to the magnitude of the value displayed).

In fact, the wise use of these principles makes it possible for modern statistical graphics to display greater complexity than humans can easily understand otherwise. Well-designed statistical displays enable analysts to understand relationships among four, five, or even more variables—certainly more than three-dimensional (3-D) creatures are usually comfortable manipulating in Cartesian coordinates.

Multiple Dimensions

Traditional graphics are limited by the two-dimensional page or screen on which they appear. It is difficult to display more than two variables, and nearly impossible to display more than three clearly. [The now famous Minard graph depicting Napoleon's disastrous invasion of Russia (see Wainer 1997, p. 64) is remarkable precisely because it surpasses these limits so gracefully.]

The world is not bivariate. The challenges of understanding multivariate relationships makes graphs that can help in this understanding particularly useful.

Time as a Dimension

Because the human eye tracks smooth motion well, motion can be an effective display dimension. Physicists have told us for a century that time should be regarded as a dimension along with the three spatial dimensions. Designers of data graphics have now taken this admonition to heart, although not in the sense that Einstein had in mind. Rather, it is possible to use motion to show how a relationship that has been graphed changes as some other term is modified. The ability of a graph to change in real time, in response to viewer action, can display relationships among variables in ways that are perceived by most viewers as naturally as the mapping of value to physical location on a bivariate plot.

One use of this capability that has become relatively common is the display of three variables in a three dimensional scatterplot, whose structure is displayed by rotating it smoothly on the computer screen. Even though the display in fact shows successive projections of the point cloud on the screen, the illusion of a three dimensional display seen in rotation is compelling.

Another use of such animation is to show a display changing as a parameter is altered. For example, the analyst might control the value of an exponent used in the reexpression of one variable by sliding an on-screen control with the mouse. Simultaneously, a display of the residuals from a regression analysis can be updated, smoothly changing as the reexpression changes. Some animations of this sort show residuals becoming more homoskedastic as an appropriate reexpression is found. Others might show a single data value drifting away from the others and becoming an outlier, vividly revealing the sensitivity of that particular value to the parameter change.

Yet another use of animation shows the relationship among two variables as a third variable is added smoothly to the model or otherwise modified. Such methods display an interaction effect—an aspect of statistical modeling that is notoriously difficult to understand and display, but that nevertheless is of great importance in discerning the truth about multivariate relationships.

To achieve this perceptually comfortable mapping, changes over time must follow their own rules of consistency. Displays must change smoothly and must keep up with mouse-based controls. (A delay of as little as 0.1 second can make the display appear to lag behind the mouse and destroy the illusion of physical reality.) Other rules usually lean toward simplification. For example, despite a number of attempts to simulate three dimensions accurately on a computer screen with perspective and shadow, most viewers are more comfortable with a flat projection of a three dimensional pseudoreality onto the screen, which then moves to show the third dimension. Such a view of the data is much like the view through a telescope at some distance, in which the depth of field is lost. It also corresponds to the mathematical operation of projecting from higher dimensions onto lower dimensions—an operation fundamental to most multivariate statistics.

Such a display sacrifices all cues about the direction of rotation. Some viewers can reverse the illusion, switching the perception that the frontmost points are moving to the left (and the rearward points to the right) with the perception that the motions are reversed. Interestingly, the two displays are equivalent in data analysis content, so the ambiguity has no important consequences.

Kinds of Interaction

Modern data-display software provides several kinds of interaction with data graphics and some underlying principles that support them. All of these methods assume that what we are seeing shows the data from many points of view and in many different ways but continues to preserve the data's central reality and consistency. The displays observe the principle of "linking," in which multiple arrays of related data are consistent in how the data are displayed, in particular in the use of color, symbol, and highlighting of points. Changes in one view of the data alter all other views simultaneously, preserving the illusion that, for example, the color of a datapoint is the same regardless of how it is viewed.

Selecting is a fundamental operation because selected points stand out from the background of other points. Selected points and regions are usually highlighted by becoming brighter, by becoming slightly larger, by changing color, or by filling in open spaces. The unselected points are displayed as well, providing a context for the selected points. It is thus easy to see whether, for example, the selected points cluster together consistently or show a trend that differs from the background trend.

Linking shows each case consistently across several displays. When a case is selected in one plot, all views of that case are selected immediately and highlighted so that the selection can be seen. The selected case stands out from the other cases in each window, so its relationship to them becomes clearer, making it easy to see conditional relationships. Clusters of points in one display can be selected to see whether they appear as a group in other views of the data or whether the observed clustering is a local feature.

Linking makes it easy to answer questions such as

1. Is this extreme point also extreme in any other view of the data?
2. Do the points in this part of the histogram cluster on other variables?
3. Is the relationship between these two variables the same for each of the groups in this pie chart?
4. Does the pattern shown in this rotating plot correspond to any patterns shown in other views of the data?

These questions require sophisticated and complex statistical calculations to answer numerically but are easy to investigate with linked plots.

More fundamentally, linking treats each case as an object with a graphic reality. Just as real world objects have a shape, location, and color, graphic representations of data values benefit from having a consistent existence. Thus, graphing programs can also link plot symbols and colors. Each case is drawn in all of the plots with the same symbol (where symbols are appropriate) and in the same color (where colors are possible).

Linking also makes possible the interactive actions *brush* and *slice*. These actions have emerged as fundamental parts of the conversation that data analysts can hold with graphic displays of their data.

Brushing and *slicing* can reveal joint patterns and relationships among many variables. Thus, they are actions appropriate for multivariate analysis.

Plot brushing was developed initially by statisticians at AT&T Bell Labs (Becker & Cleveland 1984) as a way to work with scatterplot matrices and is still offered in that specialized form by some statistics programs. Other programs generalize brushing beyond that isolated framework, making the plot brush a tool that works in any appropriate display.

Brushing focuses attention on a selected subset of points while showing them against the background of the rest of the points. Each kind of display can offer an appropriate way to define the selected subset. The simplest case is brushing a scatterplot in which a rectangle (whose size and shape can be controlled by the analyst) is dragged over a scatterplot controlled by mouse movements. Points covered by the rectangle are highlighted in the scatterplot and in all other displays simultaneously. One can usually define brushes of different sizes and shapes; a tall, thin brush, for example, selects small, local parts of an x-axis variable. The highlighted points in other plots show the patterns and distributions conditional on the selected slice of points.

By contrast, selecting points in a dotplot focuses attention on a subrange of the plotted brushed variable and shows where those points reside in other displays. Such a strip of values in effect, conditions on the selected subrange of the brushed variable, and shows the effects of changing the conditioning.

One can even brush bars in a histogram, watching the corresponding selection in other displays. More subtly, the effects of brushing can link into a histogram. Experience has shown that the best display for this is a highlighted "subset histogram" shown against the background of the full data histogram. By selecting points in a rotating plot, you can orient the rotation to identify a key dimension or to isolate a subgroup.

A *slicing tool* selects points in vertical or horizontal slices of a plot. The tool slices right to left, left to right, top to bottom, or bottom to top, according to its initial direction. In contrast to a plot brush, in which points leaving the brush lose their highlighting, points selected by a slicing tool are selected as the tool passes their position and remain selected unless you reverse direction and drag back over them.

Brushing and slicing help to answer questions such as

1. Do the same cases seem to be in roughly the same places in each plot?
2. Is there any trend in sales from east to west?
3. Which variables change systematically as I move along this principal dimension in a rotating plot?

4. How does the relationship between the gas mileage and weight of cars change as drive ratio increases?

Brushing and slicing are based on the principle that by emphasizing the common identity of cases in multiple displays, we can help analysts relate several displays to one another. They do not add information that is not already in the displays; rather, they provide easier access to that information.

80 Companies Slicing Example   As an example of how slicing can help, consider the scatter plot of Log(Assets) versus Log(Market Value) from 80 companies drawn randomly from the *Forbes* 500 (Figure 4, in which original data were in millions of dollars). We see three interesting features:

1. There is surely a trend of companies with greater market value to have greater assets (see the regression line in Figure 4);

2. There are about seven companies with a market value of about a billion dollars that have lower than expected assets; and

3. There seems to be a string of companies, of varying market values, that have unusually large assets.

It seems sensible to look at the residuals from the overall trend (item 1). These are shown, as a function of predicted value, in Figure 5. We next use our slicing

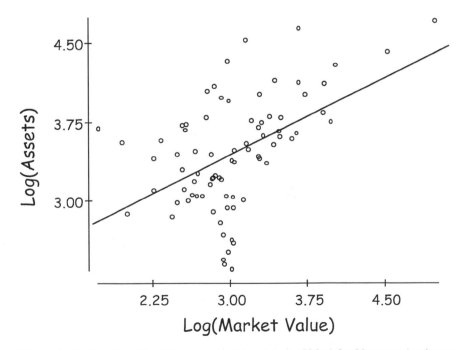

Figure 4   Scatter plot of Log(Assets) against Log(Market Value) for 80 companies drawn at random from the *Forbes* 500. A least squares regression line is drawn in.

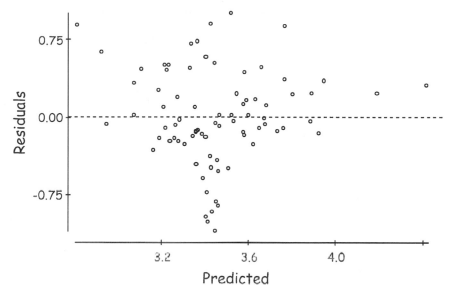

Figure 5   Residuals from the regression depicted in Figure 8 are plotted against their predicted values.

tool to select companies with large positive residuals (Figure 6*A*). The selection tool is indicated by the two horizontal lines and the selected companies are now shaded. As we select these companies a linked bar chart, which shows the number of companies within the sample that are drawn from each of nine industrial sectors, reacts. The reaction is in real time, but a snapshot of it is shown in Figure 6*B*. It shows us that most of the companies with large assets relative to their market value are finance companies (banks).

The linking of the scatter plot with the bar chart provided the environment within which the explanatory power of slicing can be effectively utilized. Slicing from the bottom up would show us that companies of less than expected assets seem to be distributed more or less uniformly across all of the industrial sectors.

Identification   Often simply identifying cases on a display proves to be a powerful way to add information to the display. It aids understanding by going beyond displaying general patterns and relationships in the data. Usually interpreting such patterns or trends requires that we know which cases make up each of the groups, which cases form the heart of the trend, and which cases fail to follow the pattern established by the others. For this, we need to be able to identify data points on a plot. The most common method of identifying points interactively on a display is to click on the points in question and have identifying text appear—usually near the mouse cursor, but occasionally in a related table.

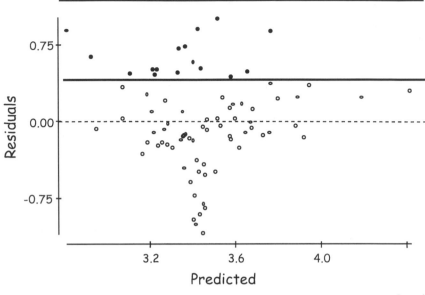

Panel A

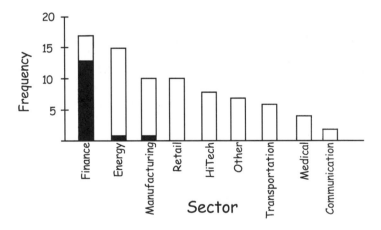

Panel B

Figure 6   (*Panel A*) The residual plot from Figure 9 is sliced downward from the top of the vertical axis. Those items selected by the slicer are shown darkened. (*Panel B*) A barchart showing the number of companies in each of nine industrial sectors. As a company is selected by the slicer in *Panel A*, the sector that it belongs to is shaded. This display shows that most of the companies with positive residuals are in the finance sector.

Subset Selection   Selection and linking can also work between graphics and quantitative statistical analyses, providing a powerful way to condition analyses. A quantitative analysis such as a regression, ANOVA, or contingency table can be constrained to be computed only for the selected cases. The data analyst can then select cases in an appropriate display and immediately see the quantitative analysis conditional on the selected cases. The lesson here is that graphics and quantitative analyses are part of the larger whole of data analysis and understanding, and are not two separate enterprises related only by their common database.

Subset selection is a first step from univariate and bivariate displays into analyses that depend on several variables. However, the most common subset conditioning selects levels in a categorical variable rather than ranges of a quantitative variable. Multivariate analyses of quantitative variables often turn to rotation for initial display.

Rotation   Rotating plots provide appropriate displays for many of the standard multivariate methods and can provide an intuitive way to learn about relationships among several variables without the need for advanced mathematics. The first program for rotating data was the PRIM-9 system developed by Fisherkeller, Friedman, and Tukey in 1972. It required several million dollars' worth of computer and display hardware so it remained a prototype system "proof-of-concept" implementation. PRIM stood for projection, rotation, isolation, and masking—the elementary operations that were found to be a basis for using plot rotations in data analysis. PRIM is a nice acronym, but the elements are more usefully discussed in "RIMP" order.

1. Rotation is an excellent, effective, general-purpose way to create the illusion of three dimensions. It provides both an immediate three-dimensional view of the point cloud and the ability to orient the point cloud in interesting ways. Early, special-purpose plot rotating programs restricted rotation to motion around one of the three standard axes, but modern software lets you rotate the points around any axis in the projection plane, often by "grabbing" the point cloud with a mouse and pushing it in any direction, much as you might rotate a globe mounted on gimbals by pushing lightly on its surface.

2. Isolation is the identification of subsets of points on the plot and the use of those subsets in further analyses, what we have called selection above. Often, rotated point clouds consist of several differently structured subgroups. Isolation makes it easy to focus attention on one at a time without viewing the others.

3. Masking is the ability to hide some part of the plot conditional on some other variable and concentrate on the remaining points. For example, one might want to know which part of the point cloud corresponds to points at one end of the range of some other variable or in some levels of a

categorical variable. Much of the masking principle is served in modern implementations by brushing and slicing.

4. Projection is the most subtle of the elementary operations. Rotating plots always show a projection of the point cloud on the screen. This projection establishes a relationship between the original variables (shown by the plotted data axis lines) and the plotting axes that point up-down, right-left, and in-out. Projection is especially powerful when the rotating plot accommodates more than three variables—a capability found in only a few of the current rotation implementations (see, for example, *Data Desk*, Velleman 1998). Often data originally recorded in several variables can be simplified to a few projected dimensions. A complete implementation of plot rotation should offer to record the linear combination of the original variables that results in the currently viewed projection, but this feature is often absent.

The Illusion of Three Dimensions

In the real world, we see three-dimensional objects in perspective. Objects farther away appear smaller; those closer appear larger. When we look at a real-world object we also have the benefit of stereo vision; each eye sees a slightly different view of the object, and our brain puts these views together to see the object at its true position in space. Rotating plots usually offer neither stereo views nor true perspective. Instead, the perception of depth comes from the animated rotation. In fact, the plotted points are just moving back and forth or up and down on the screen, but the viewer perceives this movement as a rotating three-dimensional cloud of points.

Because rotating plots show only a flat projection of the point cloud, true perspective plotting would be confusing. For data analysis, the initial view of the data (in which the y- and x-axes are in their ordinary orientation) is identical to a scatterplot. If a rotating plot showed true perspective, data points that were farther away (along the z-axis in-and-out of the screen) would shrink nearer to the center of the plot and data points that were closer to the viewer would spread away from the center of the plot, producing a distorted scatterplot.

To avoid this problem, rotating plots are usually drawn without any adjustment for perspective, much the way the world looks through a telescope or powerful telephoto lens. In this way, three-dimensional data analysis displays are different from representational three-dimensional drawings or computer-aided design displays. Such direct projection corresponds to the mathematical operation of projecting higher dimensional data into lower dimensional spaces that is fundamental to many multivariate analyses.

What Is an Interesting View?

Often we rotate a plot in search of interesting views of the data. Interesting views do not necessarily align with the data axes. If they did we could just plot simple scatterplots and would have little need for plot rotation. Of course, the definition of "interesting" is deliberately vague. Sometimes an interesting view is a direction along which the data stretch out. Sometimes it is a view that shows distinct separated clusters. Often "interestingness" depends on the nature of your data or on your goals.

Fisherkeller et al (1974) discovered that many interesting orientations of the point cloud had the property that points seemed to clump together in separated clusters, which might then be isolated for further analysis. One might phrase this as groups with small within-group variance but large between-group variance, except that this phrasing suggests analysis of variance, which in turn suggests regularities such as homoskedasticity, which are definitely not restrictions on these patterns.

Instead, the pattern reflects the more general observation that one of the most important concerns of data exploration is with the homogeneity of the data. If our data do not describe a consistent, homogeneous population, it is difficult to imagine what it would mean to describe patterns with a statistical model or draw formal inferences from the data to the population. Thus, the discovery that a data set holds separate subgroups is often an important first step in understanding the data. We can then isolate each of the subgroups and analyze it separately, comparing the analyses along the way to understand how the subgroups resemble or differ from each other.

Projection is fundamental to many multivariate analyses. The combination of graphic techniques is often more effective than traditional multivariate computations at finding and clarifying multivariate structure in data. Principal components analysis and cluster analysis are among the methods that can be approximated by finding appropriate orientations of the point cloud and then using other statistical methods.

Seeing Patterns in Rotating Plots

Some statisticians have proposed that the best way to understand interesting patterns is to consider the least interesting pattern possible. For example, the normal distribution, useful though it may be in formal statistics, is fundamentally uninteresting in terms of real data. It is the deviations from normality that often prove interesting. A rotating plot of three random normal variables is basically uninteresting. It might then be argued that the more distant rotating plot data are from the multivariate normal, the more interesting they are in prospect. Unfortunately for this definition (and, of course, for all who would like to test their residuals to see whether they satisfy a multivariate normal assumption) there are many ways to deviate from normality. Fortunately, real data usually are interesting, although interesting patterns may be hidden from view at first. Several kinds of patterns are common and meaningful in data displays.

Orientations that show clusters of points separated from one another are often useful. Rather than showing most of the structure, a view of clusters often comes about by looking at an interesting structure from the side. For example, if a point cloud consists of two separate stripes or "pencils" of points, rotating to look at the points of the pencils shows their separation but hides information about whether they are parallel or not. If you find an orientation with separated groups, consider assigning different plot symbols to the groups, or even hiding one temporarily and continuing the analysis with the other.

Uncovering* Randu's *Flaws: An Example of Discovery Through Rotation   A well-known illustration of the value of a mobile display comes from IBM's ill-fated random number generator *Randu*. *Randu* is of a linear congruential type that yields numbers that depart from randomness in an interesting way. Suppose we generate 1200 numbers between 0 and 1 with this generator and consider each succeeding triple a point in three-dimensional space. We should end up with a uniform distribution of points on the unit cube. A two-dimensional projection of that cube is shown in Figure 7. Nothing in this display looks out of the ordinary. If we rotate the three-dimensional cube we find that most views support the conclusion that *Randu* has yielded a set of 400 points uniform in this space, yet suddenly we discover that (Figure 8) all the points line up on 15 planes in 3-space—a most decidedly nonrandom configuration. We note that this pattern of 15 stripes disappears quickly as we rotate away from this viewpoint by even a few degrees. This phenomenon is familiar to anyone who has ever driven past a cornfield and noticed how the corn rows sometimes line up and at other times look as if they are planted helter-skelter.

This flaw in *Randu* was described first by Marsaglia (1968), but is trivially uncovered with a rotation engine. The story might be more dramatically told if it was done dynamically, but the value of the outcome is fully appreciated with the static view of the end result.

In some displays, points cluster into isolated groups, but only in particular orientations of the display. It is often interesting to know whether the same cases cluster together in other displays of related variables. Assign a different plot symbol or color to each group, highlight clusters, or brush the plots to look for clustering across plots. Single variables with two clusters show up as two-humped, bimodal histograms. Slicing across one hump selects those cases so you can consider them in other plots.

Uncovering Differences Among Iris Species: An Example of the Power of Adding Identification   As an example consider the 150 data points in Figure 9 [measurements made by the botanist Edgar Anderson, but first published by RA Fisher (1936)]. There were four measurements (in centimeters) made on each of three varieties of iris: sepal length, sepal width, petal length, and petal width. Originally there were only two varieties, *Iris Setosa* and *I. versicolor*, but Fisher added data [also gathered by Anderson (1928)] on *I. Virginica* to test Randolph's (1934) hypothesis that *I. versicolor* is a polyploid hybrid of the other two species.

Unrotated Randu Data

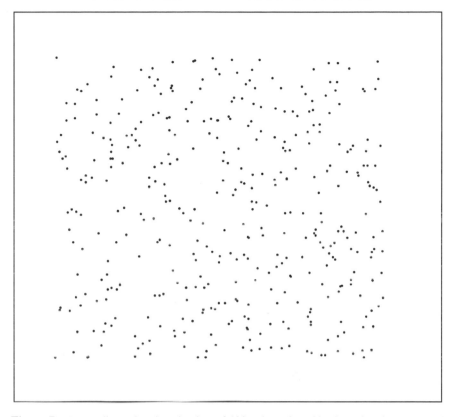

Figure 7   A two-dimensional projection of 400 points plotted in the unit cube generated by the congruential random number generator, *Randu*.

We combine the four variables into two, sepal area (sepal width x sepal length) and petal area (petal width x petal length), and plot them (Figure 9). There seem to be two obvious groupings, but what are they? By assigning a different plotting symbol to each species we see that there are three, almost nonoverlapping distributions (Figure 10). This not only demonstrates the power of identification, but provides evidence about the relative power of graphical and analytic methods for scientific discovery. The graphic provides the primary evidence, and the analytic method (in this case discriminant analysis) is merely backup.

As we noted earlier, recognizing subgroups in data is an important exploratory step. When you find that your data can be split into subgroups, you may first want to find ways to characterize them. Often the best way to characterize clusters is to identify some of the cases in each cluster. For example, you may find that males and females form separate groups in your data (even though gender was not one of the

Rotated Randu data

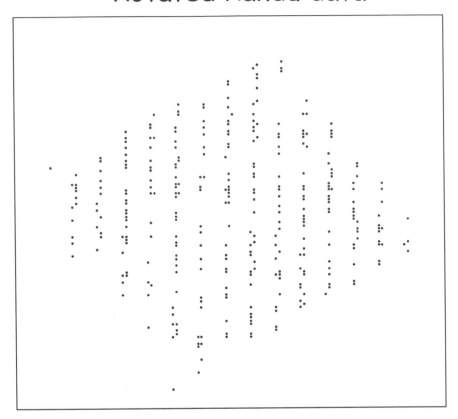

Figure 8   A different two-dimensional projection of the cube shown in Figure 7 showing the striped pattern that is evidence for the conclusion that *Randu* does not yield entirely random numbers.

variables displayed), or that region, age, or season define subgroups. If the characterization is one that you did not anticipate, you have discovered a lurking variable.

Whether you can characterize the subgroups or not, it is often worthwhile to pursue analyses of the subgroups separately. Although it is rarely stated explicitly, a fundamental assumption of virtually every statistical analysis—even when no inference is planned—is that the data come from a single homogeneous population. If, in fact, the data come from two or more different subpopulations, it is usually more effective and more appropriate to analyze the groups separately.

Another interesting orientation is one in which the points are as spread out as possible along a particular axis (although in this case we must choose our scaling carefully; a common default scaling method, dividing each variable by its standard deviation, corresponds to a standard practice in multivariate statistics).

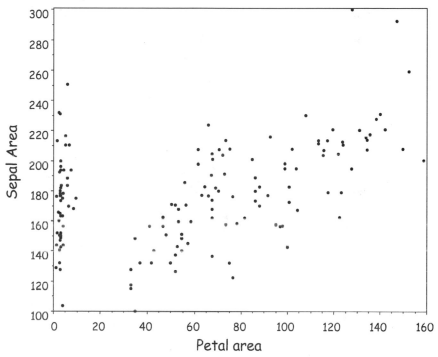

Sepal Area vs. Petal Area for 150 Irises

Figure 9   A scatter plot of sepal areas versus petal areas for 150 iris plants. These measurements were drawn from 50 of each of 3 varieties of iris; *Iris Setosa, I. versicolor*, and *I. Virginica.*

The direction of greatest variance, if we scale by standard deviation, is the first principal component of the data. One advantage of rotating plots is that it is relatively easy to ignore an outlier when positioning the display, even when the outlier might otherwise affect a multivariate calculation.

Many multivariate plots actually have only two or three directions of substantial variance, but these may not be aligned with the original variables. By identifying these principal axes we can simplify the analysis, reducing the number of dimensions to consider. An axis of great variance can also be a good axis to relate to other variables. For example, brushing along the axis while watching other plots can tell you much about its relationship to other variables.

Whether you can characterize the subgroups or not, it is often worthwhile to pursue analyses of the subgroups separately.

Some Rotating Plot Orientations Show a Clear Trend   Trends that are straight lines can be described with regression analyses or assessed with a correlation

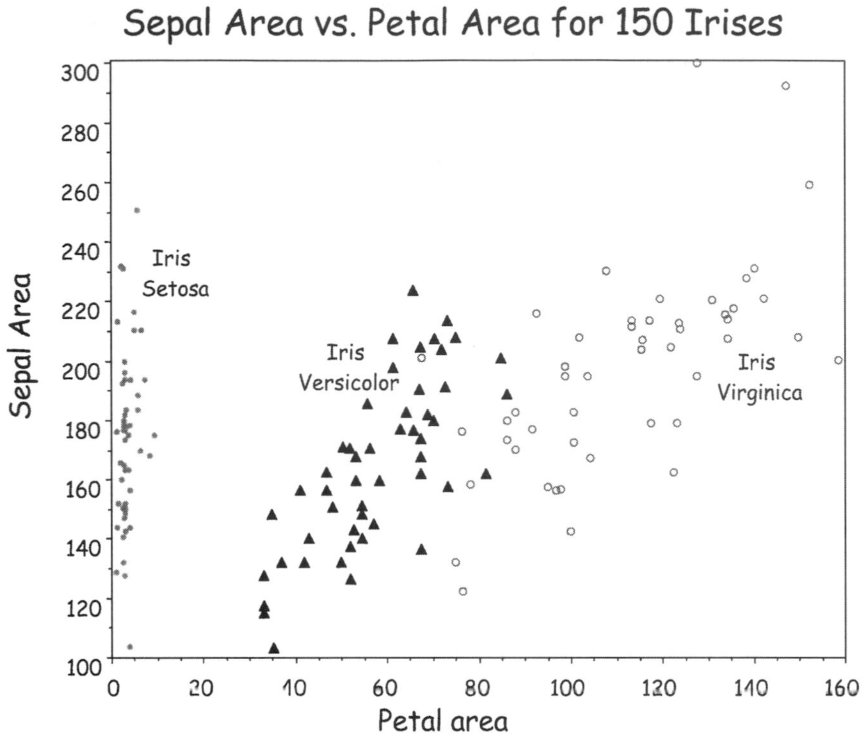

Sepal Area vs. Petal Area for 150 Irises

Figure 10   The scatter plot shown in Figure 9 with members of the three varieties of iris identified. The key aspect of this plot, which makes it different from similar plots done in earlier times, is how easily the identification was accomplished.

coefficient (although, of course, the relationship is probably more concisely described in terms of the projected variables). Trends that are not straight can be assessed with a nonlinear regression analysis or a nonparametric correlation coefficient such as the Spearman or Kendall correlations. Alternatively, they might become both clearer and more useful by transforming one or more of the variables.

Some Rotating Plots Show a Flat Surface   Flat surfaces can be described statistically with a multiple regression analysis. They tell us there is a combination of the variables that varies little, suggesting that we do not really need three dimensions to describe the data.

One of the Most Common and Useful Patterns Is the Simple Extraordinary Point or Outlier   Points can be extraordinary by being very far from the rest of the data or by failing to conform to a pattern, even though they are not particularly far from the data. An extraordinary point may be a sign of errors in the data such as a misplaced decimal point or swapped digits. It may be a point that should not be a part of the data (for example, a motorcycle or truck included with cars).

An extraordinary point may be a perfectly correct and valid point that simply does not fit. These are often the most interesting points because we can learn a great deal by discovering why the point does not fit with the rest. Sometimes it may be better to remove or suppress an extraordinary point during part of the analysis so it does not dominate the calculations.

Occasionally a Rotating Plot Reveals a Complex Pattern Examples of such patterns are planes that twist into a helical shape, parallel or intersecting lines or planes, and patterns with multiple extraordinary points. These represent patterns beyond the reach of any static statistics computation. The only really good way to describe such patterns is with several pictures or with a rotating plot. Unfortunately, rotating plots pasted into text documents and printed no longer rotate, so you may find that you must spend the traditional 1000 words to describe the picture.

Rotation and Color as an Additional Dimension

Used wisely, color can be a valuable addition to a rotating plot. You can use color to identify different groups or to represent values on another variable. When color represents a continuous variable it provides another dimension of information in addition to the three dimensions seen in the rotation. This can be an effective way to see four variables together, especially if the colored dimension is well ordered relative to the spatial dimensions. Sadly, combining the words color and well-ordered in the same sentence is typically an oxymoron, at least as it concerns human perception (Bertin 1973). The only aspect of color that is well ordered is saturation, and hence if we wish to represent an ordered variable with color we ought to do it by varying the saturation. Of course, using color for purposes of identification (e.g. "note the red points") can work very well indeed.

Four Variables and More

Some rotating plot implementations can handle more than 3 spatial dimensions (PRIM-9 could work with nine, *Data Desk* can work with twelve or more). Although most people find it hard to visualize four or more dimensions, virtually every multivariate statistical method searches for patterns or structure in a multidimensional array of points. Multidimensional rotating plots let you see the patterns and relationships that multivariate methods describe with numbers. Along with linking, symbols, color, and brushing, multidimensional plots make concrete what could only be imagined before. When a rotating plot has more than three dimensions, the viewer must select three dimensions to rotate. All other dimensions are held perpendicular to the chosen dimensions and do not rotate.

Practical Multivariate Graphics

Multivariate analyses are a constant struggle to reduce high-dimensional patterns to fewer dimensions to facilitate our understanding. Interactive displays can play a valuable role in this quest. For that to happen, displays must be integrated with analyses so that the data analyst can move smoothly from looking at aspects of the data to quantitative descriptions and tests and then back again to examine residuals or look for additional patterns. For multivariate analyses the investment in learning to use interactive graphics pays great dividends.

CONCLUSIONS AND LIMITATIONS

In the early part of the last century the poet Edna St. Vincent Millay wrote,

> Upon this gifted age in its dark hour
> Falls from the sky a meteoric shower
> Of facts. They lie, unquestioned, uncombined.
> Wisdom enough to leach us of our ills is daily spun,
> But there exists no loom to weave it into fabric.

This chapter is our attempt to chronicle the progress that has been made toward the construction of a glorious loom.

Space limitations have precluded more detailed discussions, and the obvious practical limitations of a print medium have forced us too often to tell rather than show. We hope we have been able to convey a sense of the exciting developments that widely available, powerful computers have made possible. Simultaneously, we would like to emphasize that the same perceptual system that led to the design of efficacious static displays remains with us for dynamic displays. Multicolored pseudo-three-dimensional pie charts that communicated data structures poorly when they were static, are not likely to improve if they spin through space in real time. The popularity of flashy (and often expensive) data-mining software demonstrates how easy it is to be seduced by the sizzle. In the assessment of new display technology we must ask first what can we learn using it that we would have missed without it. Or, more weakly, how much easier is it to have learned it this way?

Psychology, because of its long history and expertise in the measurement of perceptual phenomena, ought to take a lead role in such an assessment. We would like to encourage psychologists' involvement.

Penultimately, although there is an enormous amount of graphical software commercially available, very little of it thoughtfully melds the analytic side of the data analysis with the visual. *Data Desk* (Velleman 1998) is one such realization.[10]

---

[10]The reader must forgive the apparent self-serving nature of this recommendation. It is made defensible by two facts–the recommendation was written by the first author and it is true.

Details on programming graphics, and more importantly, how to think about programming graphics are now available in Wilkinson (2000).

Readers interested in pursuing the last two decades of developments toward a graphical loom should consult the marvelous work of Edward Tufte (1983, 1990, 1997), Bill Cleveland (1994a,b; Cleveland & McGill 1984, 1988), and of course, John Tukey (Tukey 1990, Basford & Tukey 1999).

ACKNOWLEDGMENTS

Howard Wainer's time on this research was partially supported by the research allocation of the Educational Testing Service as well as the Senior Scientist Award he received from the Trustees of the Educational Testing Service. He is delighted to have the opportunity to acknowledge this support. In addition, we are grateful to John Tukey (1915–2000) for the wisdom gained from many discussions with him on effective data display. This chapter is dedicated to his memory.

Visit the Annual Reviews home page at www.AnnualReviews.org

LITERATURE CITED

Anderson E. 1928. The problem of species in the northern blue flags, *Iris versicolor L.* and *Iris virginica L. Ann. Bot. Gard.* 15:241–332

Apel W. 1944. *The Notation of Polyphonic Music.* Cambridge, MA: Mediaeval Acad. Am.

Basford KE, Tukey JW. 1999. *Graphical Analysis of Multiresponse Data.* New York: Chapman & Hall

Becker RA, Cleveland WS. 1984. *Brushing a Scatterplot Matrix: High-Interaction Graphical Methods for Analyzing Multidimensional Data.* AT&T Bell Lab. Tech. Memo.

Beniger JR, Robyn DL. 1978. Quantitative graphics in statistics: a brief history. *Am. Stat.* 32:1–10

Bertin J. 1973. *Semiologie Graphique.* The Hague: Mouton-Gautier. (In French) 2nd ed. (W Berg, H Wainer. 1983. *Semiology of Graphics.* Madison: Univ. Wisc. Press)

Biderman AD. 1978. *Intellectual Impediments to the Development and Diffusion of Statistical Graphics, 1637–1980.* Presented at 1st Gen. Conf. Soc. Graph., Leesburg, VA

Biderman AD. 1990. The Playfair enigma: toward understanding the development of schematic representation of statistics from origins to the present day. *Inf. Des. J.* 6(1):3–25

Bronowski J, 1978. *The Origins of Knowledge and Imagination.* Binghamton, NY: Vail-Ballou

Clagett M. 1968. *Nicole Oresme and the Medieval Geometry of Qualities and Motions.* Madison: Univ. Wis. Press

Cleveland WS. 1994a. *The Elements of Graphing Data.* Summit, NJ: Hobart

Cleveland WS. 1994b. *Visualizing Data.* Summit, NJ: Hobart

Cleveland WS, McGill ME, eds. 1988. *Dynamic Graphics for Statistics.* Belmont, CA: Wadsworth

Cleveland WS, McGill R. 1984. Graphical perception: theory, experimentation, and application to the development of graphical methods. *J. Am. Stat. Assoc.* 79:531–54

Fisher RA. 1936. The use of multiple measurements in taxonomic problems. *Ann. Eugen.* 7:179–88

Fisherkeller MA, Friedman JH, Tukey JW. 1974. PRIM-9: An interactive multidimensional data display and analysis system. A.E.C. Sci. Comp. Inf. Exchange Meet. (Movie available from the Am. Stat. Assoc. An allied technical report same title, available from the Stanford Linear Accelerator Cent., SLAC-PUBL-1408)

Funkhouser HG. 1937. Historical development of the graphic representation of statistical data. *Osiris* 3:269–404

Galilei Galileo 1622. The assayer. In *The Controversy on the Comets of 1618*, Galileo Galilei, Horatio Grassi, Mario Guiducci, and Johannes Kepler. Transl. S Drake, CD O'Malley, 1960. Philadelphia: Univ. Penn. Press

Graunt J. 1662. *Natural and Political Observations on the London Bills of Mortality*. London: Martyn

Gunther RT. 1968. *Early Science in Oxford*, Vol. XIII. *Dr. Plot and the Correspondence of the Philosophical Society of Oxford*. London: Dawsons of Pall Mall

Howard L. 1847. *Barometrigraphia: Twenty Years' Variation of the Barometer in the Climate of Britain, Exhibited in Autographic Curves, With the Attendant Winds and Weather, and Copious Notes Illustrative of the Subject*. London: Richard & John E. Taylor

Huygens C. 1895. *Oeuvres Completes, Tome Sixieme Correspondance*, pp. 515–18, 526–39. The Hague: Nijhoff

Marsaglia G. 1968. Random numbers fall mainly in the planes. *Proc. Natl. Acad. Sci. USA* 61:25–28

McKie D. 1972. Scientific societies to the end of the eighteenth century. In *Natural Philosophy Through the 18th Century and Allied Topics*, ed. A Ferguson, pp. 133–43. London: Taylor & Francis

Playfair W. 1786. *The Commercial and Political Atlas*. London: Corry

Plot R. 1685. A letter from Dr. Robert Plot of Oxford to Dr. Martin Lister of the Royal Society concerning the use which may be made of the following history of the weather made by him at Oxford through out the year 1684. *Philos. Trans.* 169:930–31

Priestley J. 1769. *A New Chart of History*. London. (Reprinted 1792. New Haven: Amos Doolittle)

Randolph LF. 1934. Chromosome numbers in native American and introduced species and cultivated varieties of Iris. *Bull. Am. Iris Soc.* 52:61–66

Smith DE. 1925. *History of Mathematics*, Vol. 2. Boston: Ginn & Co.

Spence I, Wainer H. 1997. William Playfair: A Daring Worthless Fellow. *Chance* 10(1):31–34

Spence I, Wainer H. 2000. William Playfair (1759–1823): an inventor and ardent advocate of statistical graphics. In *Statisticians of the Centuries*, ed. CC Heyde. Voorburg, The Netherlands: Int. Stat. Inst. In press

Stigler SM. 1980. Stigler's Law of Eponymy. *Trans. NY Acad. Sci.* 239:147–57

Tufte ER. 1983. *The Visual Display of Quantitative Information*. Cheshire, CT: Graphics Press

Tufte ER. 1990. *Envisioning Information*. Cheshire, CT: Graphics Press

Tufte ER. 1997. *Visual Explanations*. Cheshire, CT: Graphics Press

Tukey JW. 1977. *Exploratory Data Analysis*. Reading, MA: Addison-Wesley

Tukey JW. 1990. Data based graphics: visual display in the decades to come. *Stat. Sci.* 5:327–29

Velleman PF. 1998. *Data Desk*. Ithaca, NY: Data Description, Inc.

Wainer H, Spence I. 1997. Who was Playfair? *Chance* 10(1):35–37

Wainer H, Thissen D. 1981. Graphical data analysis. *Annu. Rev. Psychol.* 32:191–241

Wainer H. 1996. Why Playfair? *Chance* 9(2):43–52

Wainer H. 1997. *Visual Revelations: Graphical Tales of Fate and Deception from Napoleon Bonaparte to Ross Perot*. New York: Copernicus/Hillsdale, NJ: Erlbaum. 2nd print. 2000

Wainer H. 1998. The graphical inventions of Dubourg and Ferguson: two precursors to William Playfair. *Chance* 11(4):39–41

Wigner EP. 1960. The unreasonable effectiveness of mathematics in the natural science. *Commun. Pure Appl. Math.* 13:1–14

Wilkinson L. 2000. *The Grammar of Graphics*. New York: Springer-Verlag

Annu. Rev. Psychol. 2001. 52:337–67

THE DEVELOPMENT OF VISUAL ATTENTION IN INFANCY

John Colombo

Department of Human Development, University of Kansas, Lawrence, Kansas 66045-2133; e-mail: colombo@ukans.edu

Key Words   infancy, attention, development, cognitive neuroscience, orienting, alertness

■ **Abstract**   Over the past decade, the study of attention in infancy has seen dramatic progress. This review delineates four attentional functions (alertness, spatial orienting, attention to object features, and endogenous attention) that are relevant to infancy and uses these functions as a framework for summarizing the developmental course of attention in infancy. Rudimentary forms of various attentional functions are present at birth, but each of the functions exhibits different and apparently dissociable periods of postnatal change during the first years of life. The role of attention in development should therefore be considered in the context of interaction among different systems at different levels of maturity during the first years of life.

CONTENTS

0066-4308/01/0201-0337$14.00

INTRODUCTION

Attention and Infant Cognition

The study of cognitive development has seen great change and progress over the past three decades, and in many ways the research effort on cognition during human infancy has made significant and considerable contributions to this progress. Such progress is represented within a number of core areas of inquiry, such as sensory (Simons 1993, Werner & Gray 1998) and perceptual (e.g. Quinn & Eimas 1996) development, category acquisition (e.g. Madole & Oakes 1999), memory (e.g. Hartshorn et al 1998), multimodal/cross-modal perception (e.g. Bahrick & Lickliter 2000), and higher-order reasoning about the properties of objects and space (Baillargeon 1999, Spelke & Van de Walle 1993).

Such progress represents an impressive record of achievement. It is worth noting, however, that progress in each of these areas is attributable to research paradigms that involve the measurement of infants' visual attention to displays or events. Over the past decade, the topic of visual attention per se in infancy has attracted increasing interest and exposition within the cognitive-developmental literatures (e.g. Burack & Enns 1997, Atkinson & Hood 1997, Richards 1998, Ruff & Rothbart 1996). This proliferation of interest and activity may be attributable to at least two developments in the past decade.

One reason is that interest has grown in the measurement of attention during infancy either as a means to assess of the efficacy of early interventions on cognitive development (e.g. Colombo 1997), or as a means to predict cognitive status in childhood (Colombo & Mitchell 1990, Rose & Feldman 1990, Ruff 1990). The observation that early measures of attention were correlated with both concurrent and future indices of cognitive status sparked interest in determining which particular attentional functions were responsible for such continuity from infancy (e.g. Colombo & Janowsky 1998, Colombo & Frick 1999, Rose & Feldman 1995).

A second and perhaps more important influence on the growing interest in infant visual attention has been the emerging influence of cognitive neuroscience on developmental psychology. Visual attention has been one of the primary topics in the area of human cognitive neuroscience (e.g. Parasuraman 1998), and progress in that area has readily spilled over into the developmental literatures. Nowhere in the developmental literatures has the influence of cognitive neuroscience been greater than in the study of early development, and nowhere within early development has this approach been more apparent than in the investigation of early attentional processes.

Purpose and Plan of the Review

The fundamental aim of this paper is to provide an overview and summary of recent advances in the area of visual attention in infancy. Other reviews (Johnson 1995a, 1998; Ruff & Rothbart 1996) or edited compilations (Richards 1998) on the topic have appeared within the past decade. Some have addressed a limited set of attentional functions; the more comprehensive reviews have been quite lengthy. This review was designed to encompass a breadth of attentional functions and a developmental perspective within a more concise format.

Four Attentional Functions   The review begins by drawing a conceptual framework for visual attention that has been guided by recent advances in the field of cognitive neuroscience. In *The Principles of Psychology*, William James (1890) wrote that "every one knows what attention is." James' confidence notwithstanding, psychologists have since the inception of the field struggled for a satisfactory definition (Moray 1969, 1993). A perusal of the most recent collections of reviews of attention by the foremost scientists in the field (see especially recent collections in Gazzaniga 1995, Parasuraman 1998) finds the definition of attention still elusive. James also referred to the existence of "varieties of attention," and although a century has passed since this characterization, a strong argument can still be made for its validity (see Parasuraman & Davies 1984). Among the major differences between the turn of the last century and the turn of this one, however, is that the mechanisms and substrates of visual attention are far better understood. Indeed, it is possible to derive a working framework for attentional functions, based on knowledge from studies that have been accumulating on the topic for the past 25 years.

For this review, four particular functions appear to be particularly relevant (see Figure 1). These functions are drawn from several existing theoretical models of visual attention (see Webster & Ungerleider 1998 for a summary), as well as from aspects of attentional function that appear to be uniquely relevant to early development. In the following sections, each of these functions is explicated with the putative neural substrate that has been identified in the adult.[1] This is followed

---

[1] There are reasonable indications to support the notion that the neural substrate that mediates a particular behavioral function in adults may be the same neural substrate that mediates the same behavioral function in infancy. However, it is clear that some degree of caution is in order on this point (e.g. Colombo & Janowsky 1998).

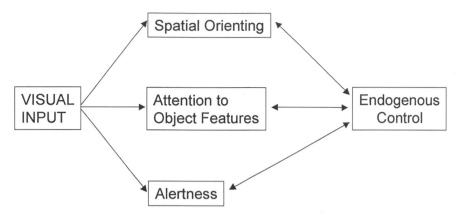

Figure 1 Proposed conceptual framework for the development of visual attention in infancy. Basic components of visual attention considered in the review, along with a fundamental organizational scheme, are considered.

by a review of the available data on the development of that function during infancy.

ALERTNESS

Background

In everyday terms, attention may be referred to as a state of preparedness or readiness also known as "alertness." In the adult, psychologists have been mostly interested in the ability to maintain alertness in "sustained attention" or "vigilance" tasks. In such tasks, the maintenance of alertness is presumed to reflect the control of lower-order attentional functions by higher-order attentional structures (e.g. the influence of cortical areas on subcortical structures). As such, the concepts of sustained attention or vigilance fit with the section on endogenous attention below.

However, for the consideration of the development of alertness in infancy, the ability to attain (rather than maintain) the alert state is the more fundamental issue. This is because the attainment of the alert state is not possible until very late in gestation, and is a relatively uncommon event, even at term. Furthermore, it appears that in very young infants (e.g. prior to 2 or 3 months postnatal), an argument can be made that alertness is more readily initiated by exogenous events (e.g. Wolff 1965) or by lower-level mechanisms of arousal (Karmel et al 1991) than by more endogenous ("volitional") sources. As such, it may be that the emergence of the alert state in very young infants (e.g. prior to 3 months postnatal) may be more accurately conceptualized in terms of the ascending influence of subcortical pathways on cortical targets. Because of this particular conceptualization, the development of alertness in infancy is addressed separately in this section rather than with issues of vigilance and sustained attention.

Ascending Brainstem Pathways and Functions Related to Alertness

If the attainment of the alert state is a function of subcortical influence on higher-order structures, it makes most sense to start with the brainstem, as brainstem reticular activating systems have been linked to arousal and attention since Morruzzi & Magoun (1949). Furthermore, it also makes sense to look for ascending pathways from brainstem loci that have been linked with attentional function. Indeed, four pathways ascend from the brainstem to neocortical areas and have been consistently associated with attentional function (Doty 1995, Parasuraman et al 1998, Robbins 1998, Robbins & Everitt 1995). These ascending pathways are generally characterized as independent entities and identified by their predominant neurotransmitter (noradrenergic, cholinergic, serotonergic, and dopaminergic), although in reality the situation is somewhat more complicated (Doty 1995). The pathways share several common limbic and cortical targets, including frontal areas (Robbins & Everitt 1995). Although all four pathways may have some role in mediating cognitive function, two of the four ascending pathways appear to be especially involved in this function.

The function of the ascending noradrenergic system may be most closely linked to the notion of anticipatory readiness, or "alertness" for stimulus input. The primary brainstem locus for this system is the locus coeruleus, which is highly active during episodes of behavioral alertness or vigilance (Aston-Jones et al 1994, Rajkowski, Kubiak, & Aston-Jones 1994, Usher et al 1999), and such activity is correlated with increases in norepinephrine in the cortex (Aston-Jones et al 1991). Marrocco & Davidson (1998) suggested that locus coeruleus activity is increased during periods when attention is in a state of anticipation of exogenous input, and decreased during periods of high arousal (see Carli et al 1983).

The cholinergic pathway has been implicated in a wide range of cognitive tasks, including sustained attention tasks (Robbins et al 1989, Sahakian et al 1993, Sarter 1994, Warburton 1977). Porges (1976, 1992) has suggested that this pathway may mediate the psychophysiological responses associated with sustained attention that have been observed across the life span.

The role of the other two ascending pathways in attention is less clear. The dopaminergic systems appears to be more closely allied with the activation of behavior (Brown & Robbins 1991, Koob 1992, Phillips et al 1991, Robbins et al 1989). The function of the serotonergic pathway is not well understood (Robbins 1998), although one working hypothesis is that it mediates aspects of behavioral inhibition (Gray 1982; Harrison et al 1997a,b, 1992).

The Development of Alertness

The best source of data on the development of alertness comes from the research on infant state (Korner 1972, Thoman 1990).

The Alert State in Young Infants   It has been commonly noted that the emergence of well-defined behavioral states is a distinguishing characteristic of gestational age. For example, in premature infants under 30 weeks conceptional age, even the basic sleep-wake states are not particularly distinct; from 30 weeks to term, the sleep and wake states become clearly differentiated, and the waking states themselves become reliably distinguishable (Aylward 1981, Berg & Berg 1979, Wolff 1965). Indeed, the neonate has been characterized as having six distinct states, including two states of alertness (e.g. Wolff 1965, 1966).

Of particular note is that only a minority of the newborn's time is spent in alert states. It is commonly noted that the newborn spends three-quarters of its time in sleep states, and less than 20% in alert states (Colombo & Horowitz 1987). Dramatic changes occur in the distribution and quality of waking and sleeping across the first 3 months of age (Berg & Berg 1979), and among those changes is a dramatic increase in the amount of time spent in alert states over the first 10–12 postnatal weeks (Gerson 1969, Tronick & Brazelton 1975, Wolff 1955). By the twelfth postnatal week, periods of alertness have become consolidated, are fairly well entrained with the dark-light cycle, and the infant is commonly observed being able to attain, and perhaps maintain, more and more extended periods of alertness (Berg & Berg 1979).

Some evidence supports the involvement of the ascending brainstem pathways in alertness. For example, vestibular and tactile stimulation typically induces visual alertness in human newborns (Becker et al 1993, Korner & Grobstein 1966, Korner & Thoman 1970). Structures in the ascending noradrenergic pathway are involved in the processing of vestibular input (Nishiike et al 1997, Pompeiano et al 1991, Schuerger & Balaban 1999), and so it seems possible that stimulation involved in common caregiving activities (picking up or rocking the infant) may produce changes in norepinephrine in any number of higher-order brain areas. Furthermore, it is also the case that newborns' and 1-month-old infants' visual responses to stimuli of different levels of complexity, motion, or novelty are strongly affected by manipulations of arousal, such as feeding or swaddling (Gardner & Karmel 1981, 1984; Gardner et al 1992; Gardner & Turkewitz 1982; Geva et al 1999), or by prior stimulation in modalities other than vision (Gardner et al 1986). This is not the case with older infants, however. Such findings fit well with animal work showing that brainstem-mediated functions can modulate transmission of signals in the primary visual pathway (see Doty 1995).

Summary

The attainment of the alert state is possible in the newborn, but is not a frequent or extended occurrence during the first month. During the first month, alertness is readily elicited by exogenous stimulation and its quality is affected by manipulations that presumably increase or decrease levels of arousal. During the interval from 4 to 8 or 10 weeks postnatal, alertness is attained more frequently and for longer periods, which are increasingly consolidated and entrained with the dark-light cycle. It is of some note that early state organization has been shown to relate to later cognitive function within infancy (Colombo et al 1989, Moss et al 1988), and that early state disorganization is a powerful indicant of systemic risk (see Colombo & Horowitz 1987 for a review).

SPATIAL ORIENTING

Background

The concept of selection is an integral component of the classic definitions of attention (e.g. James 1890). Research over the past two decades has clearly indicated that one distinct type of selection involved in human attention involves selection on the basis of the spatial coordinates in the visual field (e.g. Desimone & Ungerleider 1989). That is, the function of one brain system concerned with attention involves the orienting and shifting of attention to a particular spatial locus.

In reality, it is a matter of some current debate whether visual attention is shifted to a locus, or to a stimulus located at a particular spatial coordinate. Based on the results of several experiments (Egly et al 1994, He & Nakayama 1995), Driver & Baylis (1999) have suggested that the posterior system orients visual attention to some "segmented" regions of space rather than to a spatial locus per se. Such a region may be described as a crudely defined "blob" or "patch," although Pylyshyn et al (1994) suggested that more than one region may be involved. It is possible that identification of and orienting to this crudely defined segmented region of the visual field may relate to the kind of "preattentive" search that is observed in feature-positive "pop-out" effects in vision (see Nakayama & Joseph 1998). In such tasks, visual attention is automatically drawn to particular discrepant elements within a visual display, and detection of such discrepancies is generally unaffected by the number of other elements within the display (Treisman & Souther 1985).

The Components of Spatial Orienting and Their Neural Substrates

In any case, spatial orienting can be decomposed into three subfunctions: the engagement of visual attention at a particular stimulus/locus, the disengagement of visual attention from a stimulus/locus, and the shifting of visual attention from one stimulus/locus to another. A "posterior attention system" (e.g. Posner & Petersen 1990) has been identified as the neural substrate that presumably mediates these functions. The system (sometimes called the "where" system) is composed of three core structures, each of which has been identified with one of the functions listed above. The pulvinar (a nucleus of cells in the thalamus) has been hypothesized to mediate engagement of visual attention to stimuli in particular spatial locations. The posterior parietal lobe mediates disengagement of visual attention from stimuli in such locations (see also Csibra et al 1997). Finally, the superior colliculus mediates the shifting of visual attention from one locus to another.

Of note is the fact that spatial orienting can be either overt or covert (see, e.g. Posner & Rothbart 1998). In covert orienting, the effects of an attentional shift can be noted prior to the initiation of an ocular movement to a location. In adults, such covert orienting is thought to be a function of the posterior system. In contrast, overt orienting involves an actual eye movement, and the execution of this response is thought to bring in other (likely frontal) systems that are related to saccade planning and execution.

Spatial-orienting has been indexed by a number of measures. One measure is smooth pursuit, which is a class of continuous, slow, smooth, and automatic eye movements that can only be elicited by the tracking of a target moving across the visual field. Such eye movements are distinct from the class of discontinuous and rapid saccadic movements that are generated either reflexively in response to the appearance of peripheral targets, or endogenously in the course of foveal visual inspection.

Another set of measures is provided by assessments of covert attentional shifts and rapid saccadic eye movements. Reflexive or "express" saccades are made in response to a target that appears abruptly in the peripheral visual field. Such saccades are mediated by some combination of structures and pathways within the posterior, or "where," attentional system described by Posner and others (Posner & Petersen 1990, Schiller 1998, Webster & Ungerleider 1998; see also Richards & Hunter 1998). Covert attentional shifts are typically assessed in paradigms in which a subject's visual attention is "cued" to a spatial location by some visual signal prior to the appearance of a target in that location (Posner 1980). After such cueing, the target usually appears at the cued location (i.e. the cue is valid), but may appear elsewhere (i.e. the cue is invalid). Reaction time is facilitated with valid cues (evidence of a covert attentional shift to the cued location), and slowed by invalid cues (evidence of the need to disengage visual attention from the cued location before moving it to the locus in which the target actually appears).

Furthermore, if the time interval between the target and cue is extended, the response to the appearance of the target is slower to the cued location than it is to a contralateral location. This slowed response is known as inhibition-of-return (Posner et al 1985). It is hypothesized that visual attention is shifted to the cued locus, but during the long interval between cue and target, visual attention is shifted back to midline. When the target eventually appears, the response time to it is believed to be slower because the posterior system tends to resist shifting visual attention back to locations that have been previously attended (e.g. Johnson 1995a).

Finally, disengagement has also been assessed with the gap or competition paradigm. Here, a central visual target is presented prior to the appearance of a target in the periphery. The central target may remain after the peripheral target is presented (overlap/competition condition), may disappear coincident with the appearance of the peripheral target (no-overlap/noncompetition condition), or may be turned off some brief interval prior to the presentation of the peripheral target (gap condition). Time to respond to the peripheral target is slowest under overlap conditions (where disengagement is most difficult) and fastest under gap conditions (where disengagement is not necessary).

The Development of Spatial Orienting

The development of functions involved in orienting to spatial loci is generally revealed through studies of infants' performance on particular marker tasks. These include smooth pursuit, the shifting of visual attention with reflexive or "express" saccadic eye movements, disengagement of attention, and inhibition of return.

Smooth Pursuit   Smooth pursuit has been elicited in newborns (Kreminitzer et al 1979, Shea & Aslin 1990) under conditions in which target speeds are moderately slow and velocity is constant (see Hainline 1998). A rapid improvement in smooth pursuit performance apparently occurs between birth and 3–4 months of age (Aslin 1981, Phillips et al 1997, Von Hofsten & Rosander 1997). Older infants show more smooth pursuit, fixate moving targets more accurately, and track faster-moving targets more readily (Richards & Holley 1999) than younger infants. As such, it is likely that the mechanisms mediating smooth pursuit per se are intact and functional early on (Hainline 1998), but that the development of the prevalence and accuracy of smooth pursuit may also be affected by immaturity elsewhere in the visual system (Richards & Hunter 1998). Especially relevant in this regard is that visual input to the superior colliculus is generally based on the magnocellular pathway of the primary visual system. This pathway, which largely mediates visual sensitivity to motion, develops quite slowly relative to the other (parvocellular) visual pathway (Hickey 1977, Hickey & Peduzzi 1987). In addition, Richards & Hunter (1998) suggested that the accuracy of smooth pursuit is affected by interactions with other attentional functions mediated by frontal areas.

Shifting Attention to Visuospatial Loci   In addition to smooth pursuit, a number of measures that involve overt and covert shifts of visual attention to particular locations in the visual field are generally part of the spatial orienting functions.

Reflexive Saccades to Peripheral Targets   Exogenously driven saccades (presumably controlled by the superior colliculus) are present very early in life (see Bronson 1974; Johnson 1990, 1995a; Johnson et al 1991b). Richards & Hunter (1998) suggested that they are present from birth. In adults, such saccades involve one long movement to the approximate location of the target, followed by one or two very small saccades that localize the target exactly (e.g. Prablanc & Jennerod 1975). In infants less than 2 months old, a few studies have reported such saccadic movements to be executed in a series of small, equivalent steps from midline to the target (Aslin & Salapatek 1975, Salapatek et al 1980). These are called hypometric saccades, and they have the same properties as the main sequence saccades used by adults to move the eyes to within a degree or two of the peripheral target (Ashmead 1984). Such saccades may reflect the degree to which overt shifts of visual attention by infants are initiated without a guiding covert shift in young infants. However, it should be noted that there is considerable disagreement over the prevalence of such hypometric saccades in young infants (see Hainline 1998, Hainline et al 1985); the resolution of this controversy will need to precede any speculation about what such saccades may reflect.

Targets of Spatial-Orienting in Infancy   As noted above, spatial orienting may be directed toward a crudely defined visual object at a particular spatial location. If such spatial orienting is related to the automatic shift of eye movements to particular types of discrepant elements within visual arrays, then a discussion of the small volume of literature on pop-out effects in infancy is warranted here. This issue has been addressed with infants in both attentional (Catherwood et al 1996a, Colombo et al 1995, Quinn & Bhatt 1998, Salapatek 1975, Van Giffen & Haith 1984) and memory (e.g. Gerhardstein et al 1999; Rovee-Collier et al 1996, 1992; see Bhatt 1997, for a review) paradigms.

All of these studies suggest the presence of pop-out-like effects (e.g. asymmetry of feature-positive versus feature-negative effects) by 3 months of age, although Catherwood et al (1996a) did find a decrement in performance as a function of increasing distractors. It should be noted that, even at these ages, the pop-out effects are not particularly strong (e.g. Colombo et al 1995). Two studies report the results of infants' visual attention to obvious discrepancies in visual arrays with infants younger than 3 months, and these results are equivocal. Salapatek (1975) did find that 2-month-old infants' saccades were drawn to discrepant areas within visual arrays, although the nature of the response was affected by the stimulus properties of both the discrepant elements and the distractors (see also Colombo et al 1984). Van Giffen & Haith (1984) observed that 1-month-olds failed to attend to violations of form continuity in hierarchically constructed forms. In some ways, it is surprising that these effects do not appear in very young infants. However, it should be noted that this trend is consistent with other reports, suggesting that some Gestalt visual effects are not present during the neonatal period (Bertenthal et al 1980, Ghim 1990, Spelke et al 1992, Treiber & Wilcox 1980) and even in older infants may not be demonstrable except under specific stimulus conditions (e.g. Kellman & Spelke 1983). If such effects are mediated by low–spatial frequency vision (as intimated by Posner 1995), then this may be due to the relatively slower maturation of the magnocellular visual pathway in infancy (Colombo 1995).

In addition to this work on orienting to static objects or object forms, research has been conducted on the infants' spatial orienting to small moving elements in the peripheral visual field (Dannemiller & Freedland 1993). This work indicates that there is substantial improvement in such orienting from 6 to 14 weeks of age (Dannemiller 1994). Furthermore, within these ages, the stimulus properties of other elements in the visual field have been shown to affect the probability of such orienting (Dannemiller & Nagata 1995, Nagata & Dannemiller 1996). The latter finding suggests the viability of a model for visual orienting based on competition among perceptual entities distributed across the entire visual field

(Dannemiller 1998, 2000). Although the former finding may simply reflect an age-related improvement in sensitivity to visual motion, this may also be attributable to deficits in the very young infant's ability to distribute visual attention globally across the entire visual field.

Spatial Cueing of Infants' Attention   Several studies have examined the effect of spatial cueing on visual attention in 2- through 6-month-old infants. The facilitation of infants' eye movements to a target by a cue prior to the appearance of the target can be taken as evidence of one type of covert attentional shift. Studies of such cueing (Johnson et al 1994; Johnson & Tucker 1996; Richards 2000a,b) report evidence for covert shifting in infants 4 months or older, whereas Hood et al (1998) have observed facilitation as early as 3 months. Johnson & Tucker (1996), however, have reported that 2-month-olds' performance in such a task was not strongly facilitated by a cue.

Disengagement of Attention   An important component of the spatial orienting system is the ability to disengage attention. Disengagement is a function that has been linked directly to the parietal lobe and/or tempo-parietal junction, based on studies of visual neglect (e.g. Rafal & Robertson 1995). Data on the development of disengagement in infancy comes from two sources.

Obligatory Looking   Through the 1960s and 1970s, researchers on occasion made reference to a pattern of prolonged visual fixation in infants from birth to 2 months old. The essential characteristics of this pattern included the idea that the infant was not truly in control of the fixation, but rather that the looking was held by the stimulus in an "obligatory" (Johnson et al 1991a, Stechler & Latz 1966) or "tropistic" (Caron et al 1977) fashion, and that the looking was in some way dissociated from actual stimulus processing (Greenberg & Weizmann 1971, Hopkins & Van Wulfften-Palthe 1985). Hood (1995) recently recast this fixation pattern as simply a deficiency in disengagement, and has coined the term sticky fixation. Evidence reviewed below bears on the relationship of look/fixation duration and disengagement.

Performance in Overlap/Gap Tasks   Attentional disengagement has been measured more directly in a number of published studies with human infants. As described above, such studies use tasks in which a central target is used in conjunction with a peripheral target under overlap, nonoverlap, or gap conditions. The dependent measure is generally the latency of the first saccade to the peripheral target.

As with adults, the latencies of infants' saccades are slowest in overlap conditions and fastest in gap conditions (Csibra et al 1998, Hood & Atkinson 1993, Matsuzawa & Shimojo 1997). Young infants tested in these studies are clearly capable of disengaging visual attention from a central stimulus, so the presence of the function is not at issue. At issue, however, is the facility with which disengagement occurs, and how this facility changes over the next few months. Most studies have reported that disengagement is more readily observed in older infants than in younger infants (Atkinson et al 1992, Hood & Atkinson 1993, Matsuzawa & Shimojo 1997; but see Goldberg et al 1997). Several studies in particular report that a major change in the facility of disengagement occurs sometime between 2 and 4 months of age (Frick et al 1999, Johnson et al 1991b, Hood & Atkinson 1993). An additional study (Hood et al 1998) observed that 3-month-olds had considerable difficulty with disengagement of attention in overlap conditions.

Inhibition of Return   As noted above, if visual attention is cued to a peripheral spatial location and allowed to return to midline, saccades to the previously cued location are slower than to peripheral locations on the opposite side (Posner & Cohen 1980). This inhibition of return (Posner et al 1985) has been posited to be a manifestation of the posterior system's predisposition to orient to novel loci. Inhibition of return is not seen in patients with lesions to the superior colliculus (Posner & Cohen 1984), so it is considered to be a function aligned with the posterior system.

All studies on the development of inhibition of return in infancy agree that it is present by 6 months of age (Hood 1993), but at issue are its onset and developmental course. Clohessy et al (1991) reported that it was absent in 3- and 4-month-olds, but inhibition of return has recently been documented in 4-month-olds (Johnson & Tucker 1996, Richards 2000b), 3-month-olds (Harman et al 1994, Richards 2000a) and in newborns (Valenza et al 1994, Simion et al 1995). Again, stimulus and procedural considerations may be important in resolving the differences here (Ruff & Rothbart 1996). Valenza et al suggested that the phenomenon may be seen in younger infants only when visual attention is truly shifted to or engaged at the initially cued position, and Harman et al (1994) found it only at smaller eccentricities.

The basic function therefore appears to be present very early, but the developmental course is again at issue. Clohessy et al's (1991) data likely reflect an improvement in inhibition of return after 3 or 4 months of age. In support of this contention, Richards (2000a) recently reported an increase in inhibition of return from 3 to 6 months.

Summary

The various components within the spatial orienting system appear to have somewhat different developmental courses, but all seem fairly well established by 6 months. Smooth pursuit, which is probably mediated by an interaction of subcortical and cortical systems, can be elicited in neonates. However, it is generally not a robust response during the first months, and progresses readily across the first half-year. Functions related specifically to the subcortical structures of the system (i.e. the superior colliculus), such as reflexive saccades and inhibition of return, have been reported in neonates, but also show sizeable changes from 2 or

3 months to 6 months of age. Indeed, the coarse parsing of objects involved in the shifting of visual attention does not appear to have a particularly early emergence. Finally, disengagement of attention (which has been linked to posterior parietal cortex) is also present in a rudimentary form very early in life, but appears to show considerable improvement particularly from 2 to 4 months.

ATTENTION TO OBJECT FEATURES

Background

The where system (described above) selects and moves visual attention to a spatial locus for foveal inspection. The complementary "what" system involves attentional mechanisms that are involved in the analysis of foveal input and the processing of fundamental visual properties that eventually lead to the identification of patterns and objects (Webster & Ungerleider 1998).

The Neural Substrate of Object Attention

This pathway extends from occipital cortex through higher visual areas in the posterior inferior temporal cortex and to inferior temporal cortex. Along this pathway, basic visual properties of the pattern or object at hand are processed independently of one another (e.g. Livingstone & Hubel 1987). At some point, these features of the patterns or objects are reintegrated. As such, this pathway presumably mediates stimulus discrimination and recognition (Ungerleider & Mishkin 1982).

It is clear that visual attention to object features cannot be sharply dissociated from visual attention to the location of that object in the visual field (Posner 1995). A current debate in the literature concerns the degree to which object features (form and color are those usually put forth as examples, although size and texture are also sometimes mentioned; Robertson 1998) that are apparently processed independently are re-integrated or "bound" together to form a coherent percept (Treisman & Gelade 1980; but see Duncan & Humphreys 1989). It can be argued that the "what" pathways extract the visual properties of the stimulus (e.g. Corbetta et al 1995), whereas the "where" system provides common spatial coordinates through which these properties may be bound. Indeed, bilateral parietal damage spares the ability to identify object features, but impairs visual search for such features in conjunction (Friedman-Hill et al 1995, Robertson et al 1997).

The Development of Attention to Object Features

In the discussion of the development of object attention (i.e. those processes that lead to object recognition and perception) in infancy, several lines of evidence are considered. One concerns infants' attention and processing of visual features and stimulus compounds. Another concerns infants' visual attention to features and elements that are present within defined stimulus boundaries. Finally, there is a small amount of literature that speaks to the independence of the processing of visual features from spatial orienting during infancy, which is considered below.

Infant Processing of Visual Features and Compounds   Perhaps the first issue addressed by the empirical field of perceptual development was whether the human newborn was capable of perceiving visual patterns (Fantz 1963). Indeed, studies conducted since that time have documented very early sensitivity to the essential properties of visual stimuli (see, e.g. Slater 1997). Studies of the processing of stimulus compounds during infancy are somewhat less clear. Although infants clearly attend to both color and form (Cohen et al 1971), early reports (Cohen 1973, Cornell & Strauss 1973) suggested that 4-month-olds process color and form as separable components and not as compounds. More recent reports, however, agree that multidimensional visual stimuli can be perceived in a compound (conjunctive) manner by infants 4 or 5 months old (Bushnell & Roder 1985, Dannemiller & Braun 1988, Mundy 1985).

Intrastimulus Attentional Shifts and Whole-Part Processing   A sizeable literature on young infants' scanning of visual stimuli exists that dates back to the 1970s (see Ruff & Rothbart 1996). Because such behavior surely involves multiple attentional systems, it is difficult to justify its inclusion in this review. However, some general points are worth considering. First, infants under the age of 2 months scan visual stimuli less extensively than infants older than 2 months (Leahy 1976, Salapatek 1975; but see Hainline & Lemerise 1982). Second, it has also been reported that young infants are biased toward scanning the external contours of stimuli (Bronson 1990, Maurer 1983, Maurer & Salapatek 1976, Milewski 1976), although this external bias is subject to stimulus size (Hainline 1981), motion (Girton 1979), or other aspects of stimulus salience (Ganon & Swartz 1980).

In any case, much evidence suggests that such scanning patterns (and the distribution of attention that such scanning patterns presumably reflect) affect stimulus identification/recognition performance. For example, infants who scan less extensively perform less well on stimulus recognition probes (Bronson 1991, Jankowsky & Rose 1997). In addition, it appears that patterns of prolonged look duration from 3 to 6 months are related to less extensive visual scanning; infants who look for longer durations have been shown to rely on local elements or features in visual stimuli for recognition (Colombo et al 1991, 1996; Freeseman et al 1993, Frick & Colombo 1996).

Object Features and Spatial Mapping in Infancy   The final pieces of evidence considered here concern studies that have examined the interaction of spatial and object cues in infancy. In an operant stimulus discrimination paradigm, Colombo et al (1990) trained 3-, 6-, and 9-month-olds to attend to (i.e. look at) color-form compounds (e.g. red circle, green square). The compounds were presented to the right and left of midline, and looking to a "correct" dimension (color, form, or spatial position) produced synchronous auditory reinforcement. Six- and nine-month-olds learned to attend to both object and spatial dimensions in immediate tests, and retained them over 5-minute delays. Three-month-olds did not show long-term retention of the object-based cues, however. In a subsequent experiment, object and spatial cues were confounded during training and then dissociated during a test. On the test trial, the two older age groups clearly chose to attend to the object cues over the spatial cue, whereas 3-month-olds showed a strong bias for attending to the spatial cue. Harman et al (1994) have recently interpreted that pattern of results as reflecting the independence (if not differences in the developmental course) of attentional systems that code spatial versus object cues. In support of this, Harman et al (1994) conducted a similar set of studies in which 3-, 6-, and 9-month-old infants were observed orienting to novel objects at novel spatial locations. Location and object novelty were equally attractive to 3-month-olds, but 6- and 9-month-olds responded more strongly to novel visual stimuli than to novel locations.

Finally, Catherwood et al (1996a) manipulated exposure time in an effort to determine the time course of the processing of visual features and their joining as compounds in 5- to 6-month-old infants. They found that primary visual features were encoded after very brief exposures (e.g. 250 msec), but that the mapping of color to particular spatial locations (i.e. coding of a space/color compound) was observed only after exposure was increased to 2500 msec.

Summary

The fundamental functions that relate to object perception (detection of color and form) are probably present in some rudimentary form at birth. However, as with spatial orienting, it also appears that substantial changes occur in object attention during the interval from 2 months of age to 5 or 6 months of age. During that time, positive evidence for feature binding is observed, and the dominance of object cues/features over spatial cues emerges. The development of intrastimulus shifts may be considered to reflect an interaction between the object and spatial attention systems, and may bear on issues of binding and perception of compound stimuli.

ENDOGENOUS ATTENTION

Background

To this point, the systems described have allowed for a visual stimulus to be detected, localized, brought to the fovea, and integrated into a unitary "object." Two critical aspects of attentional function remain to be discussed. One involves the apparently volitional direction of attention as a function of the tasks in which the individual is engaged. Another aspect is the ability to inhibit attention, or "hold" one's attention to the stimulus, event, or task at hand. In some ways, this latter function represents the classic vernacular definition of attention, in that it would seem to relate to commonplace attentional constructs such as attention span, perseverance, and distractibility. These functions together can be characterized broadly as endogenous attention in that they conform to the concept of endogenous, or internally directed, attentional functions.[2]

The Substrates of Endogenous Visual Attention

The evidence strongly suggests that these functions are mediated by frontal areas such as the anterior cingulate (Posner 1995, Posner & Petersen 1990), the frontal eye fields, and dorsolateral prefrontal cortex (Funahashi et al 1989, 1990; Guitton et al 1985). Directed or voluntary attentional saccadic movements (sometimes labeled executive control) (Parasuraman et al 1998) have been associated with cingulate cortex in the medial frontal areas (Posner 1995, Posner & Petersen 1990). The maintenance of attention and the inhibition of shifting have also been associated with frontal areas such as the frontal eye fields (e.g. Johnson 1998).

The frontal cortex is among the targets of the four brainstem systems discussed previously (Robbins & Everitt 1995). As such, the frontal areas can be affected by (for example) lower-level inputs that stimulate the locus coeruleus and in turn result in manifestations of alertness. Furthermore, frontal areas are anatomically linked with the substrates that mediate both spatial orienting and object recognition (Webster & Ungerleider 1998); as such, the frontal areas presumably exert influence on the functions of either of these systems based on input received from the other systems. Finally, it also appears that the frontal systems project to brainstem structures (Watson et al 1981) and may thus initiate or maintain states of arousal that are endemic to vigilant or sustained attentional states.

The Development of Endogenous Attention

Evidence from three particular areas of infant cognitive function can be brought to bear on endogenous attentional functions in infancy.

Interstimulus Attentional Shifts and Spontaneous Alternation   The first of these areas come from shifts in visual attention in which two simultaneously presented stimuli are alternately inspected. The novelty-familiarization paired-comparison paradigm is a fundamental technique for the study of infant cognition (e.g. Fagan 1971). Here, the infant is exposed ("familiarized") to a stimulus, and then presented with a choice between fixating the familiarized stimulus or a novel one. Most often, such paired stimuli are presented to either side of midline, and infants will alternately fixate the two stimuli. Such interstimulus shifting occurs at a relatively

---

[2]Statements like these are risky because invoking a "voluntary" process without accounting for it in strictly monist (and perhaps mechanistic) terms can be taken to imply the existence of a homunculus (see Posner 1995, p. 620). I acknowledge this difficulty and can merely note that this is a problem yet to be solved, although I also note that it has begun to be addressed conceptually by both cognitive neuroscientists (Posner & Rothbart 1991) and by progress in the connectionist modeling of metacognitive processes (e.g. Elman et al 1996).

rapid rate (Colombo et al 1990), and the rate is affected by stimulus similarity (Ruff 1975). As a result, intrastimulus shifting has been taken to reflect an active and purposeful comparison of the paired stimuli (Ruff & Rothbart 1996), and thus fits with the endogenous nature of these forms of attention. Interstimulus shifting is more common and faster in older infants than in younger infants (Bronson 1972, Colombo et al 1988, Harris 1973, Ruff 1975). For example, in paired-comparison tests, lack of interstimulus shifting is four times more likely to be observed in 3-month-olds (Frick et al 2000) than it is at 4 months (e.g. Colombo et al 1991). In addition to changes in the frequency of shifting with age, there is evidence that the quality or nature of shifting may also change. That is, in older infants, shifting may reflect a particular attentional style or strategy. Colombo et al (1988) reported that shift rate was reliable across a one-week test-retest period at 7 months of age, but not at 4 months, where intrastimulus shifting may be more to stimulus or task factors.

Shifting has also been considered within an operant discrimination learning paradigm, in which infants were reinforced for fixating one of two paired stimuli (Colombo et al 1990). As described above, in this study, 3-, 6-, and 9-month-old infants learned to fixate the reinforced dimension. The finding that infants showed a "burst" of alternate fixations on the trial just prior to the attainment of a criterion for learning the discrimination (Colombo et al 1990) is relevant.

A special form of interstimulus shifting is spontaneous alternation, which is a pattern in which the subject systematically alternates the position to which motor responses (reaching or searching) are made across trials. This pattern of responding depends on location memory for the previous choice in guiding the next choice, and on the subject's ability to resist repeating a response to a spatial location when the response to that location has just been previously rewarded. As a result, spontaneous alternation has been taken as a measure of response inhibition in children (Reed et al 1984). Such alternation has traditionally been attributed to the function of higher brain areas, including the hippocampus, thalamus, and the frontal lobes (e.g. Divac et al 1975). Vecera et al (1991) observed that 18-month-olds readily showed spontaneous alternation on a reaching task, but 6-month-olds showed virtually none.

Attentional Inhibition and Sustained Attention   The second area of research relevant to the development of endogenous visual attention in infancy concerns the ability to inhibit attentional shifts. This has been studied in two ways.

Suppression of Saccadic Eye Movements   One means of studying the development of this function has been to use modifications of cueing paradigms and have infants inhibit or suppress saccades to the appearance of peripheral targets. As noted above, frontal cortex is involved in the inhibition of saccades to peripherally appearing stimuli (e.g. Guitton et al 1985). Voluntary suppression of such saccades may be taken as evidence of endogenous attentional function. Such suppression has been demonstrated by having the appearance of the peripheral stimulus serve as a cue to the infant that an attractive display will appear at some locus other than the cued one. Four-month-old infants can learn to inhibit orienting to the peripheral target under such conditions (Johnson 1995b, Johnson et al 1994). Furthermore, Gilmore & Johnson (1995) have presented evidence suggesting that 6-month-olds can delay orienting for up to 5 sec after being cued to look to a particular location. Thus, it seems possible for infants to inhibit a saccadic response to a cue by 4 to 6 months of age.

Assessment of Distraction in Infants   Another means of studying this is to use a psychophysiological or behavioral marker of the infant's attentional engagement (e.g. Ruff 1986). This strategy has been used predominantly by Richards (e.g. Richards & Casey 1991, 1992) in his research program. Infants show robust heart rate deceleration during cognitive tasks. Richards (e.g. 1985a,b) has delineated several distinct phases of attention based on the time course of the deceleration. One of these phases is called sustained attention, and is demarcated by a substantial and maintained heart rate deceleration. It has been argued that this phase is the result of frontal-brainstem interactions that have various autonomic (e.g. cardiac and respiratory) effects (see Richards 1985b, 1987, 1989a, 1994; Richards & Casey 1991).

Furthermore, sustained attention is thought to represent a period of voluntary attentional engagement, where most (if not all) of infants' information processing takes place (e.g. Richards & Gibson 1997). This is strongly supported by findings with infants from 3 through 6 months tested under conditions involving dynamic and multimodal stimuli. Infants are far less distractible during periods of sustained attention in both experimental laboratory settings (Richards 1985a, 1987, 1988, 1989b, 1997b; Casey & Richards 1988) as well as in more naturalistic settings during object manipulation and examination (Lansink & Richards 1997, Oakes & Tellinghuisen 1994, Ruff et al 1996, Tellinghuisen & Oakes 1997). Infants show improved recognition performance if either familiarization or the recognition test is conducted during sustained attention (Richards 1997a; see also Linnemayer & Porges 1986). Finally, smooth pursuit performance is enhanced under conditions of sustained attention (Richards & Holley 1999).

The developmental course of sustained attention has not been completely established. Heart rate deceleration has not been definitively established in newborns (Jackson et al 1971), and may not emerge until 6 weeks postnatal (Graham et al 1970; see also Berg & Berg 1979). Functional assessments of sustained attention have been obtained in infants only as young as 8 weeks (Richards 1989b), and there is considerable evidence that there are significant changes in the amount, depth, and frequency of sustained attention from 3 to 6 months (Richards 1989a, Richards & Casey 1992). However, changes in sustained attention also occur across the latter half of the first year (Lansink et al 2000, Ruff et al 1992b, 1998), and well into the second and third years (Ruff & Lawson 1990).

A Vigilance Task for Infants   Finally, the construct of sustained attention in the adult is usually synonymous with the construct of vigilance. Ruff et al (1990) devised a paradigm for measuring vigilance in infants. Infants viewed an interesting event at a particular place that is repeated after brief but variable (5–25 sec) time intervals. The main measure of vigilance was the maintenance of looking during the inter-event interval. Apparently, the ability to sustain a vigilant state was present in the youngest age group tested (5 months), but the paradigm has not been applied to infants below this age.

Summary

As with the other attentional systems reviewed, measures that presumably reflect endogenous visual attention show change across infancy. Arguments can be made for the presence of some rudimentary form of endogenous visual attention at birth, but the strong evidence for the emergence of such functions and for considerable postnatal change is present during the latter parts of the first year and beyond. Many of these functions have been successfully documented from about the period starting at 3–6 months and extending into the rest of the first year. Thus, the limited data that exist on the development of endogenous attentional functions in infancy suggest that they have a somewhat later and slower developmental course than other attentional systems reviewed here.

GENERAL DISCUSSION

The Developmental Courses of Attentional Functions in Infancy

Figure 2 presents a summary schematic for the development of the attentional functions presented here. Figure 2 suggests that there are at least three important postnatal periods of development with respect to visual attention in infancy. One is a period from term to 2 months, when the development of the alert state takes place. Another takes place from 2 or 3 to about 6 months, during which there are rapid changes in both the spatial orienting and object attention functions. The third is from 5 or 6 months and beyond, during which significant change in endogenous attentional function is observed. It is worth noting that Colombo et al (1999) recently conducted a meta-analysis of look duration from infant habituation and fixation paradigms, and concluded that the look duration follows a "triphasic," or cubic, developmental course. That is, look duration increases from birth to 8–10 weeks postnatal, drops from 3 to about 6 months, and then begins a gradual increase that extends from about 6 months through the second and third years.

Varieties of Attention in Infancy: Conclusions and Implications for Future Research

The first and perhaps most important conclusion to be drawn from this review is that, in keeping with James' (1890) traditional characterization of attention,

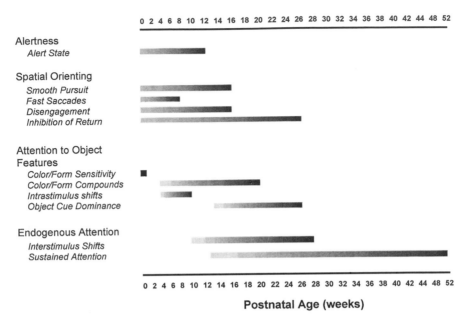

Figure 2 Summary table of the developmental course of visual attentional functions in infancy. The relative darkness of the line indicates the relative degree of maturity at each age for each function as indicated in the literature review.

a variety of attentional forms can be observed and dissociated during infancy. Forms of the attentional functions that have been clearly and reliably documented in the adult appear to exist during the first year of life. Furthermore, the fact that these functions exhibit somewhat different developmental courses adds to the evidence that they are dissociable in infancy as they are in adulthood. In turn, this lends further credence to the possibility that they are subserved by different neural substrates.

Such apparent modularity of visual attention in infancy (see also Colombo & Janowsky 1998) has important implications for characterizing early attention and for the future of applied research in this area. First, Figure 2 suggests that the assessment of infants' attentional responses to visual stimuli at any one point during the first year will necessarily be the result of an interaction of various systems, with each system at different levels of maturity. Thus, at 8 weeks of age, the infant may have considerable skills in spatial orienting and object attention, but bringing the infant to the alert state will be the primary obstacle in demonstrating those skills. At 16 weeks, attainment of the alert state is generally not such an obstacle, but both spatial and object attention are undergoing rapid developmental change, and endogenous or "controlled" functions might only just be emerging.

The presence of multiple and modular attentional functions also has clear implications for research that seeks to use attentional measures for characterizing current or future cognitive outcome. The existence of such varieties of visual attention in infancy clearly implies that no one attentional task or measurement in infancy will account for large amounts of variance in the cognitive status. For research purposes, such modularity implies two alternatives with respect to the choice of attentional measures. First, investigators' choices of specific assessments of infant attention in such studies will need to (a) be guided by a firm theoretical grasp of the type of visual attention that such experiences are expected to affect, or (b) build a wide range of attentional measures into the design of the intervention (e.g. Colombo 1997).

Furthermore, the repeated observation that many (if not all) of these varieties of attention are present in some rudimentary form at birth but develop at different times during infancy suggests that the simple psychometrically based model that has been applied to infant cognition in the past (e.g. Colombo 1993) may no longer be adequate (Colombo & Saxon 2000). Thus, measurements designed to indicate the presence or absence of attentional functions, or measurement of continuous parameters of attentional functions at a single age point will not serve as the best indicators of early cognitive function. Instead, the optimal assessment of cognitive development in infancy will be more accurately achieved through the measurement and/or modeling of change across periods of rapid development during the first years.

ACKNOWLEDGMENTS

I am grateful to Steve Fowler for helpful discussions, and to Andrea Greenhoot, Allen Richman, Jill Shaddy, Julie Maikranz, Dale Walker, and especially Janet Frick for comments on an earlier draft. Preparation of this review was supported by NIH grant HD35903.

Visit the Annual Reviews home page at www.AnnualReviews.org

LITERATURE CITED

Ashmead D. 1984. Parameters of infant saccadic eye movements. *Infant Behav. Dev.* 7:16 (Abstr.)

Aslin RN. 1981. Development of smooth pursuit in human infants. See Fisher & Monty 1981, pp. 31–51

Aslin RN, Salapatek P. 1975. Saccadic localization of visual targets by the very young human infant. *Percept. Psychophys.* 17:293–302

Aston-Jones G, Chiang C, Alexinsky T. 1991. Discharge of noradrenergic locus coeruleus

neurons in behaving rats and monkeys suggests a role of vigilance. *Progr. Brain Res.* 88:501–20

Aston-Jones G, Rajkowski J, Kubiak P, Alexinsky T. 1994. Locus coeruleus neurons in monkey are selectively activated by attended cues in a vigilance task. *J. Neurosci.* 14:4467–80

Atkinson J, Hood B. 1997. Development of visual attention: bridging disciplines. See Burack & Enns 1997, pp. 31–54

Atkinson J, Hood B, Wattam-Bell J, Braddick

O. 1992. Changes in infants' ability to switch visual attention in the first three years of life. *Perception* 21:643–53

Aylward G. 1981. The development course of behavioral states in preterm infants: a descriptive study. *Child Dev.* 52:564–68

Bahrick LE, Lickliter R. 2000. Intersensory redundancy guides attentional selectivity and perceptual learning in infancy. *Dev. Psychol.* 36:190–201

Baillargeon R. 1999. Infants' understanding of the physical world. In *Advances in Psychological Science. Vol. 2. Biological and Cognitive Aspects*, ed. M Sabourin, F Craik, pp. 503–29. Hove, UK: Psychol. Press

Becker PT, Grunwald PC, Moorman J, Struhr S. 1993. Effects of developmental care on behavioral organization in very-low-birth-weight infants. *Nurs. Res.* 42:214–20

Berg WK, Berg KM. 1979. Psychophysiological development in infancy: state, sensory function, and attention. In *Handbook of Infant Development*, ed. JD Osofsky, pp. 283–43. New York: Wiley

Bertenthal BI, Campos JJ, Haith MM. 1980. Development of visual organization: the perception of subjective contours. *Child Dev.* 51:1072–80

Bhatt RS. 1997. The interface between perception and cognition: feature detection, visual pop-out effects, feature integration, and long-term memory in infancy. *Adv. Infancy Res.* 11:143–91

Bronson GW. 1972. Infants' reactions to unfamiliar persons and novel objects. *Monogr. Soc. Res. Child Dev.* 373(148): whole issue

Bronson G. 1974. The postnatal growth of visual capacity. *Child Dev.* 45:873–90

Bronson GW. 1990. Changes in infants' visual scanning across the 2- to 14-week age period. *J. Exp. Child Psychol.* 49:101–25

Bronson GW. 1991. Infant differences in rate of visual encoding. *Child Dev.* 62:44–54

Brown VJ, Robbins TW. 1991. Simple and choice reaction time performance following unilateral striatal dopamine depletion. *J. Neurosci.* 9:983–89

Burack JA, Enns JT, eds. 1997. *Attention, Development, and Psychopathology.* New York: Guilford

Bushnell EW, Roder BJ. 1985. Recognition of color-form compounds by 4-month-old infants. *Infant Behav. Dev.* 8:255–68

Campbell BA, Hayne H, eds. 1992. *Attention and Information Processing in Infants and Adults: Perspectives from Human and Animal Research.* Hillsdale, NJ: Erlbaum

Carli M, Robbins TW, Evenden JL, Everitt BJ. 1983. Effects of lesions to ascending noradrenergic neurons on performance of a 5-choice serial reaction task in rats: implications for theories of dorsal noradrenergic bundle function based on selective attention and arousal. *Behav. Brain Res.* 9:361–80

Caron AJ, Caron RJ, Minichiello MD, Weiss SJ, Friedman SL. 1977. Constraints on the use of the familiarization-novelty method in the assessment of infant discrimination. *Child Dev.* 48:747–62

Casey BJ, Richards JE. 1988. Sustained visual attention in young infants measured with an adapted version of the visual preference paradigm. *Child Dev.* 59:1514–21

Catherwood D, Skoien P, Green V, Holt C. 1996a. Assessing the primary moments in infant encoding of compound visual stimuli. *Infant Behav. Dev.* 19:1–11

Catherwood D, Skoien P, Holt C. 1996b. Colour pop-out in infant response to visual arrays. *Br. J. Dev. Psychol.* 14:315–26

Clohessy AB, Posner MI, Rothbart MK, Vecera SP. 1991. The development of inhibition of return in infancy. *J. Cogn. Neurosci.* 3:345–50

Cohen LB. 1973. A two-process model of infant attention. *Merrill-Palmer Q.* 19:157–80

Cohen LB, Gelber E, Lazar M. 1971. Infant habituation and generalization to repeated visual stimulation. *J. Exp. Child Psychol.* 11:379–89

Colombo J. 1993. *Infant Cognition: Predicting Later Intellectual Functioning.* Newbury Park, CA: Sage

Colombo J. 1995. On the neural mechanisms underlying individual differences in infant fixation duration: two hypotheses. *Dev. Rev.* 15:97–135

Colombo J. 1997. Individual differences in infant cognition: methods, measures and models. In *Developing Brain and Behavior: The Role of Lipids in Infant Formulas*, ed. J Dobbing, pp. 339–72. London: Academic

Colombo J, Fagen JW, eds. 1990. *Individual Differences in Infancy: Reliability, Stability, Prediction.* Hillsdale, NJ: Erlbaum

Colombo J, Frick JE. 1999. Recent advances and issues in the study of preverbal intelligence. In *Development of Intelligence*, ed. M Anderson, pp. 43–71. London: Univ. Coll. London Press

Colombo J, Frick JE, Ryther JS, Gifford JJ. 1996. Individual differences in infant visual attention: four month-olds' recognition of forms connoted by complementary contour. *Infant Behav. Dev.* 19:113–19

Colombo J, Harlan JE, Mitchell DW. 1999. *Look Duration in Infancy: Evidence for a Triphasic Developmental Course.* Presented at Soc. Res. Child Dev., Albuquerque, NM

Colombo J, Horowitz FD. 1987. Behavioral state as a lead variable in neonatal research. *Merrill-Palmer Q.* 33:423–38

Colombo J, Janowsky J. 1998. A cognitive neuroscience approach to individual differences in infant cognition. See Richards 1998, pp. 363–91

Colombo J, Laurie C, Martelli T, Hartig B. 1984. Stimulus context and infant orientation discrimination. *J. Exp. Child Psychol.* 37: 576–86

Colombo J, Mitchell DW. 1990. Individual and developmental differences in infant visual attention. See Colombo & Fagen 1990, pp. 193–227

Colombo J, Mitchell DW, Coldren JT, Atwater JD. 1990. Discrimination learning during the first year of life: stimulus and positional cues. *J. Exp. Psychol.: Learn. Mem. Cogn.* 16:98–109

Colombo J, Mitchell DW, Coldren JT, Freeseman LJ. 1991. Individual differences in infant attention: are short lookers faster processors or feature processors? *Child Dev.* 62:1247–57

Colombo J, Mitchell DW, Horowitz FD. 1988. Infant visual attention in the paired-comparison paradigm: test-retest and attention-performance relations. *Child Dev.* 59:1198–210

Colombo J, Moss MM, Horowitz FD. 1989. Neonatal state profiles: reliability and short-term prediction of neurobehavioral status. *Child Dev.* 60:1102–10

Colombo J, Ryther JS, Frick JE, Gifford JJ. 1995. Visual pop-out in infants: evidence for preattentive search in 3- and 4-month-olds. *Psychonom. Bull. Rev.* 2:266–68

Colombo J, Saxon T. 2000. Infant attention and the development of cognition: Does the environment moderate continuity? In *Infant Development: Ecological Perspectives*, ed. H Fitzgerald, K Karraker, T Luster. Washington, DC: Garland. In press

Corbetta M, Shulman GL, Miezin FM, Petersen SE. 1995. Superior parietal activation during spatial attention shifts and visual feature conjunction. *Science* 270: 802–5

Cornell LB, Strauss MS. 1973. Infants' responsiveness to compounds of habituated visual stimuli. *Dev. Psychol.* 9:73–78

Csibra G, Johnson MH, Tucker LA. 1997. Attention and oculomotor control: a high-density ERP study of the gap effect. *Neuropsychologia* 35:855–65

Csibra G, Tucker LA, Johnson MH. 1998. Neural correlates of saccade planning in infants: a high-density ERP study. *Int. J. Psychophys.* 29:201–15

Dannemiller JL. 1994. Reliability of motion detection by young infants measured with a new signal detection paradigm. *Infant Behav. Dev.* 17:101–5

Dannemiller JL. 1998. A competition model of exogenous orienting in 3.5-month-old infants. *J. Exp. Child Psychol.* 68:169–201

Dannemiller JL. 2000. Competition in early exogenous orienting between 7 and 21 weeks. *J. Exp. Child Psychol.* 76:253–74

Dannemiller JL, Braun A. 1988. The perception of chromatic figure-ground relationships in 5-month-olds. *Infant Behav. Dev.* 11:31–42

Dannemiller JL, Freedland RL. 1993. Motion-based detection by 14-week-old infants. *Vis. Res.* 33:657–64

Dannemiller JL, Nagata Y. 1995. The robustness of infants' detection of visual motion. *Infant Behav. Dev.* 18:371–89

Desimone RJ, Ungerleider LG. 1989. Neural mechanisms of visual processing in monkeys. In *Handbook of Neuropsychology*, Vol. 2, ed. F Boller, J Grafman, pp. 267–99. New York: Elsevier

Divac I, Wikmark R, Gade A. 1975. Spontaneous alternation in rats with lesions in the frontal lobes: an extension of the frontal lobe syndrome. *Physiol. Psychol.* 3:39–42

Doty RW. 1995. Brainstem influences on forebrain processes, including memory. In *Neurobehavioral Plasticity: Learning, Development, and the Response to Brain Insults*, ed. NE Spear, LP Spear, ML Woodruff, pp. 349–70. Hillsdale, NJ: Erlbaum

Driver J, Baylis GC. 1998b. Attention and visual object segmentation. See Parasuraman 1998b, pp. 299–326

Duncan J, Humphreys GW. 1989. Visual search and stimulus similarity. *Psychol. Rev.* 96:433–58

Egly R, Driver J, Rafal R. 1994. Shifting attention between objects and locations: evidence from normal and parietal lesion subjects. *J. Exp. Psychol.: Gen.* 123:161–77

Elman JL, Bates EA, Johnson MH, Karmiloff-Smith A, Parisi D, Plunkett K. 1996. *Rethinking Innateness: A Connectionist Perspective on Development.* Cambridge, MA: MIT Press

Fagan JF. 1971. Infants' recognition memory for a series of visual stimuli. *J. Exp. Child Psychol.* 11:244–50

Fantz RL. 1963. Pattern vision in newborn infants. *Science* 140:296–97

Fisher DF, Monty JW. 1981. *Eye Movements: Cognition and Visual Perception.* Hillsdale, NJ: Erlbaum

Freeseman LJ, Colombo J, Coldren JT. 1993. Individual differences in infant visual attention: discrimination and generalization of global and local stimulus properties. *Child Dev.* 64:1191–203

Frick JE, Colombo J. 1996. Individual differences in infant visual attention: recognition of degraded visual forms by 4-month-olds. *Child Dev.* 67:188–204

Frick JE, Colombo J, Allen JSR. 2000. The temporal sequence of global-to-local processing in 3-month-olds. *Infancy* 1:375–86

Frick JE, Colombo J, Saxon TF. 1999. Individual and developmental differences in disengagement of fixation in early infancy. *Child Dev.* 70:537–48

Friedman-Hill S, Robertson LC, Triesman A. 1995. Parietal contributions to visual feature binding: evidence from a patient with bilateral lesions. *Science* 269:853–55

Funahashi S, Bruce CJ, Goldman-Rakic PS. 1989. Mnemonic coding of visual space in the monkey's dorsolateral prefrontal cortex. *J. Neurophysiol.* 61:331–49

Funahashi S, Bruce CJ, Goldman-Rakic PS. 1990. Visuospatial coding in primate prefrontal neurons revealed by oculomotor paradigms. *J. Neurophysiol.* 63:814–31

Ganon EC, Swartz KB. 1980. Perception of internal elements of compound figures by one-month-old infants. *J. Exp. Child Psychol.* 30:159–70

Gardner JM, Karmel BZ. 1981. Preferential looking at temporal frequencies by preterm infants. *Child Dev.* 52:1299–302

Gardner JM, Karmel BZ. 1984. Arousal effects on visual preferences in neonates. *Dev. Psychol.* 20:374–77

Gardner JM, Karmel BZ, Magnano CL. 1992. Arousal/visual preference interactions in high-risk neonates. *Dev. Psychol.* 28:821–30

Gardner JM, Lewkowicz DJ, Rose SA, Karmel BZ. 1986. Effects of visual and auditory stimulation on subsequent visual preferences in neonates. *Int. J. Behav. Dev.* 9:251–63

Gardner JM, Turkewitz G. 1982. The effect of arousal level on visual preferences in preterm infants. *Infant Behav. Dev.* 5:369–85

Gazzaniga MS, ed. 1995. *The Cognitive Neurosciences.* Cambridge, MA: MIT Press

Gerhardstein P, Renner P, Rovee-Collier C. 1999. The roles of perceptual and categorical similarity in colour pop-out in infants. *Br. J. Dev. Psychol.* 17:403–20

Gerson EF. 1969. Dimensions of infant behavior in the first six months of life. *Proc. Annu. Conv. Am. Psychol. Assoc.* 4:269–70 (Abstr.)

Geva R, Gardner JM, Karmel BZ. 1999. Feeding-based arousal effects on visual recognition memory in early infancy. *Dev. Psychol.* 35:640–50

Ghim H-R. 1990. Evidence for perceptual organization in infants: perception of subjective contours by young infants. *Infant Behav. Dev.* 13:221–48

Gilmore RO, Johnson MH. 1995. Working memory in infancy: six-month-olds' performance on two versions of the oculomotor delayed response task. *J. Exp. Child Psychol.* 59:397–418

Girton MR. 1979. Infants' attention to intrastimulus motion. *J. Exp. Child Psychol.* 28:416–23

Goldberg MC, Maurer D, Lewis TL. 1997. Influence of a central visual stimulus on infants' visual fields. *Infant Behav. Dev.* 20:359–70

Graham FK, Berg KM, Berg WK, Jackson JC, Hatton HM, Kantowitz SR. 1970. Cardiac orienting response as a function of age. *Psychonom. Sci.* 19:363–65

Gray J. 1982. *The Neuropsychology of Anxiety.* Oxford, UK: Clarendon

Greenberg DJ, Weizmann F. 1971. The measurement of visual attention in infants: a comparison of two methodologies. *J. Exp. Child Psychol.* 11:234–43

Guitton HA, Buchtel HA, Douglas RM. 1985. Frontal lobe lesions in man cause difficulties in suppressing reflexive glances and in generating goal-directed saccades. *Exp. Brain Res.* 58:455–72

Hainline L. 1981. Eye movements and form perception in human infants. See Fisher & Monty 1981, pp. 3–19

Hainline L. 1998. Summary and commentary: Eye movements, attention, and development. See Richards 1998, pp. 163–78

Hainline L, Lemerise E. 1982. Infants' scanning of geometric forms varying in size. *J. Exp. Child Psychol.* 33:235–56

Hainline L, Turkel J, Abramov I, Lemerise E, Harris C. 1985. Characteristics of saccades in human infants. *Vis. Res.* 24:1771–80

Harman C, Posner MI, Rothbart MK, Thomas-Thrapp L. 1994. Development of orienting to locations and objects in human infants. *Can. J. Exp. Psychol.* 48:301–18

Harris PL. 1973. Eye movements between adjacent stimuli: an age change in infancy. *Br. J. Psychol.* 64:215–18

Harrison AA, Everitt BJ, Robbins TW. 1997a. Central 5-HT depletion enhances impulsive responding without affecting the accuracy of attentional performance: interactions with dopaminergic mechanisms. *Psychopharmacology* 133:329–42

Harrison AA, Everitt BJ, Robbins TW. 1997b. Doubly dissociable effects of selective median raphé lesions on performance on the five-choice serial reaction time test of attention in rats. *Brain Behav. Res.* 89:135–49

Harrison AA, Muir JL, Robbins TW, Everitt BJ. 1992. The effect of forebrain 5-HT depletion on visual attentional performance in the rat. *J. Psychopharmacol.* 236:A59 (Abstr.)

Hartshorn K, Rovee-Collier C, Gerhardstein P, Bhatt RS, Wondoloski TL, et al. 1998. The ontogeny of long-term memory over the first year-and-a-half of life. *Dev. Psychobiol.* 32:69–89

He ZJ, Nakayama K. 1995. Visual attention to surfaces in 3-D space. *Proc. Natl. Acad. Sci. USA* 92:11155–59

Hickey TL. 1977. Postnatal development of the human lateral geniculate nucleus: relationship to a critical period for the visual system. *Science* 198:836–38

Hickey TL, Peduzzi JD. 1987. Structure and development of the visual system. In *Handbook of Infant Perception*, ed. L Cohen, P Salapatek, pp. 1–42. New York: Academic

Hood BM. 1993. Inhibition of return produced by covert shifts of visual attention in 6-month-olds. *Infant Behav. Dev.* 16:245–54

Hood BM. 1995. Shifts of visual attention in the infant: a neuroscientific approach. In *Advances in Infancy Research*, ed. C Rovee-Collier, L Lipsitt, 9:163–216. Norwood, NJ: Ablex

Hood BM, Atkinson J. 1993. Disengaging visual attention in the infant and adult. *Infant Behav. Dev.* 16:405–22

Hood BM, Willen JD, Driver J. 1998. Adult's eyes trigger shifts of visual attention in human infants. *Psychol. Sci.* 9:131–34

Hopkins B, Van Wulfften-Palthe T. 1985. Staring in infancy. *Early Hum. Dev.* 12:261–67

Jackson JC, Kantowitz SR, Graham FK. 1971. Can newborns show cardiac orienting? *Child Dev.* 42:107–21

James W. 1890. *The Principles of Psychology.* New York: Dover

Jankowsky JJ, Rose SA. 1997. The distribution of attention in infants. *J. Exp. Child Psychol.* 65:127–40

Johnson MH. 1990. Cortical maturation and the development of visual attention in early infancy. *J. Cogn. Neurosci.* 16:405–22

Johnson MH. 1995a. The development of visual attention: A cognitive neuroscience perspective. See Gazzaniga 1995, pp. 735–47

Johnson MH. 1995b. The inhibition of automatic saccades in early infancy. *Dev. Psychobiol.* 28:281–91

Johnson MH. 1998. Developing an attentive brain. See Parasuraman 1998b, pp. 427–44

Johnson MH, Dziurawiec S, Ellis HD, Morton J. 1991a. Newborns' preferential tracking of face-like stimuli and its subsequent decline. *Cognition* 40:1–19

Johnson MH, Posner MI, Rothbart MK. 1991b. Components of visual orienting in early infancy: contingency learning, anticipatory

looking, and disengaging. *J. Cogn. Neurosci.* 3:335–44

Johnson MH, Posner MI, Rothbart MK. 1994. Facilitation of saccades toward a covertly attended location in early infancy. *Psychol. Sci.* 5:90–93

Johnson MH, Tucker LA. 1996. The development and temporal dynamics of spatial orienting in infants. *J. Exp. Child Psychol.* 63:171–88

Karmel BZ, Gardner JM, Magnano CL. 1991. Attention and arousal in early infancy. In *Newborn Attention: Biological Constraints and the Influence of Experience*, ed. MJS Weiss, PR Zelazo, pp. 339–76. Norwood, NJ: Ablex

Kellman PJ, Spelke ES. 1983. Perception of partly occluded objects in infancy. *Cogn. Psychol.* 15:483–524

Koob GF. 1992. Dopamine, addiction, and reward. *Semin. Neurosci.* 4:139–48

Korner AF. 1972. State as variable, as obstacle, and as mediator of stimulation in infant research. *Merrill-Palmer Q.* 18:77–94

Korner AF, Grobstein R. 1966. Visual alertness as related to soothing in neonates: implications for maternal stimulation and early deprivation. *Child Dev.* 37:867–76

Korner AF, Thoman EB. 1970. Visual alertness in neonates as evoked by maternal care. *J. Exp. Child Psychol.* 10:67–78

Kreminitzer JP, Vaughan HG, Kurtzberg D, Dowling K. 1979. Smooth pursuit eye movements in the newborn infant. *Child Dev.* 50:442–48

Lansink JM, Mintz S, Richards JE. 2000. The distribution of infant attention during object examination. *Dev. Sci.* 3:163–70

Lansink JM, Richards JE. 1997. Heart rate and behavioral measures of attention in 6-, 9-, and 12-month-old infants during toy play. *Child Dev.* 68:610–20

Leahy RL. 1976. Development of preferences and processes of visual scanning in the human infant. *Dev. Psychol.* 12:250–54

Linnemayer SA, Porges SW. 1986. Recognition memory and cardiac vagal tone in

6-month-old infants. *Infant Behav. Dev.* 9: 43–56

Livingstone MS, Hubel DL. 1987. Psychophysical evidence for separate channels for the perception of form, color, movement, and depth. *J. Neurosci.* 7:3416–68

Madole KL, Oakes LM. 1999. Making sense of infant categorization: stable processes and changing representations. *Dev. Rev.* 19:263–96

Marrocco RT, Davidson MC. 1998. Neurochemistry of attention. See Parasuraman 1998b, pp. 35–50

Matsuzawa M, Shimojo S. 1997. Infants' fast saccades in the gap paradigm and development of visual attention. *Infant Behav. Dev.* 20:449–55

Maurer D. 1983. The scanning of compound figures by young infants. *J. Exp. Child Psychol.* 15:437–48

Maurer D, Salapatek P. 1976. Developmental changes in the scanning of faces by young infants. *Child Dev.* 47:523–27

Milewski A. 1976. Infants' discrimination of internal and external pattern elements. *J. Exp. Child Psychol.* 22:229–46

Moray N. 1969. *Attention: Selective Processes in Vision and Hearing.* London: Hutchinson Educational

Moray N. 1993. Designing for attention. In *Attention: Selection, Awareness, and Control,* ed. AD Baddeley, L Weiskrantz, pp. 111–34. New York: Oxford Univ. Press

Morruzzi G, Magoun HH. 1949. Brain stem reticular formation and activation of the EEG. *Electroencephalogr. Clin. Neurophysiol.* 1:455–73

Moss MM, Colombo J, Mitchell DW, Horowitz FD. 1988. Neonatal behavioral organization and 3-month visual discrimination. *Child Dev.* 59:1211–20

Mundy PC. 1985. Compound-stimulus information processing by 3-month-old infants. *J. Genet. Psychol.* 146:357–65

Nagata Y, Dannemiller JL. 1996. The selectivity of motion-driven visual attention in infants. *Child Dev.* 67:2608–20

Nakayama K, Joseph J. 1998. Attention, pattern recognition, and pop-out in visual search. See Parasuraman 1998b, pp. 279–326

Nishiike S, Takeda N, Kubo T, Nakamura S. 1997. Neurons in rostral ventrolateral medulla mediate vestibular inhibition of locus coeruleus in rats. *Neuroscience* 77:219–32

Oakes LM, Tellinghuisen DJ. 1994. Examining in infancy: Does it reflect active processing? *Dev. Psychol.* 30:748–56

Parasuraman R. 1998a. The attentive brain: issues and prospects. See Parasuraman 1998b, pp. 3–15

Parasuraman R. 1998b. *The Attentive Brain.* Cambridge, MA: MIT Press

Parasuraman R, Davies DR, eds. 1984. *Varieties of Attention.* San Diego: Academic

Parasuraman R, Warm JS, See JE. 1998. Brain systems of vigilance. See Parasuraman 1998b, pp. 221–56

Phillips AG, Pfaus JG, Blaha CD. 1991. Dopamine and motivated behavior. In *The Mesolimbic Dopamine System: From Motivation to Action,* ed. P Willner, J Scheel-Kruger, pp. 199–224. Chichester, UK: Wiley

Phillips JO, Finocchio DV, Ong L, Fuchs AF. 1997. Smooth pursuit in 1- to 4-month-old human infants. *Vis. Res.* 37:3009–20

Pompeiano O, Manzoni D, Barnes CD. 1991. Responses of locus coeruleus neurons to labyrinth and neck stimulation. *Progr. Brain Res.* 88:411–34

Porges SW. 1976. Peripheral and neurochemical parallels of psychopathology: a psychophysiological model relating autonomic imbalance in hyperactivity, psychopathology, and autism. In *Advances in Child Development and Behavior,* ed. HW Reese, 11:35–65. New York: Academic

Porges SW. 1992. Autonomic regulation and attention. See Campbell & Hayne 1992, pp. 201–26

Posner MI. 1980. Orienting of attention. *Q. J. Exp. Psychol.* 32:3–25

Posner MI. 1995. Attention in cognitive neuroscience: an overview. See Gazzaniga 1995, pp. 615–24

Posner MI, Cohen Y. 1980. Attention and the control of movements. In *Tutorials in Motor Behavior*, ed. GE Stelmach, J Requin, pp. 243–58. Amsterdam: North Holland

Posner MI, Cohen Y. 1984. Components of visual orienting. In *Attention and Performance X*, ed. H Bouma, DG Bowhuis, pp. 531–56. Hillsdale, NJ: Erlbaum

Posner MI, Petersen S. 1990. The attention system of the human brain. *Annu. Rev. Neurosci.* 13:25–42

Posner MI, Rafal RD, Choate LS, Vaughan J. 1985. Inhibition of return: neural basis and function. *Cogn. Neuropsychol.* 2:211–28

Posner MI, Rothbart MK. 1991. Attentional mechanisms in conscious experience. In *The Neuropsychology of Consciousness*, ed. AD Milner, MD Rugg, pp. 91–112. London: Academic

Posner MI, Rothbart MK. 1998. Summary and commentary: developing attentional skills. See Richards 1998, pp. 317–23

Prablanc C, Jennerod M. 1975. Corrective saccades: dependence on retinal reafferent signals. *Vis. Res.* 18:557–60

Pylyshyn Z, Burkell J, Fisher B, Sears C, Schmidt W, Trick L. 1994. Multiple parallel access in visual attention. *Can. J. Exp. Psychol.* 48:60–83

Quinn PC, Bhatt RS. 1998. Visual pop-out in young infants: convergent evidence and an extension. *Infant Behav. Dev.* 21:273–88

Quinn PC, Eimas PD. 1996. Perceptual organization and categorization in young infants. In *Advances in Infancy Research*, ed. CK Rovee-Collier, LP Lipsitt, 10:1–36. Norwood, NJ: Ablex

Rafal R, Robertson LC. 1995. The neurology of visual attention. See Gazzaniga 1995, pp. 625–48

Rajkowski J, Kubiak P, Aston-Jones G. 1994. Locus coeruleus activity in monkey: phasic and tonic changes are associated with altered vigilance. *Brain Res. Bull.* 35:607–16

Reed MA, Pien DL, Rothbart MK. 1984. Inhibitory self-control in preschool children. *Merrill-Palmer Q.* 30:131–47

Richards JE. 1985a. The development of sustained attention in infants from 14 to 26 weeks of age. *Psychophysiology* 22:409–16

Richards JE. 1985b. Respiratory sinus arrhythmia predicts heart rate and visual responses. *Psychophysiology* 22:101–9

Richards JE. 1987. Infant visual sustained attention and respiratory sinus arrhythmia. *Child Dev.* 58:488–96

Richards JE. 1988. Heart rate offset responses to visual stimuli in infants from 14 to 26 weeks of age. *Psychophysiology* 25:278–91

Richards JE. 1989a. Development and stability in visual sustained attention in 14-, 20-, and 26-week-old infants. *Psychophysiology* 26:422–30

Richards JE. 1989b. Sustained visual attention in 8-week-old infants. *Infant Behav. Dev.* 12: 425–36

Richards JE. 1994. Baseline respiratory sinus arrhythmia and heart rate responses during sustained visual attention in preterm infants from 3 to 6 months of age. *Psychophysiology* 31:235–43

Richards JE. 1997a. Effects of attention on infants' preference for briefly exposed visual stimuli in the paired-comparison recognition-memory paradigm. *Dev. Psychol.* 33:22–31

Richards JE. 1997b. Peripheral stimulus localization by infants: attention, age, and individual differences in heart rate variability. *J. Exp. Psychol.: Hum. Percept. Perform.* 23: 667–80

Richards JE, ed. 1998. *Cognitive Neuroscience of Attention: A Developmental Perspective.* Mahwah, NJ: Erlbaum

Richards JE. 2000a. Localizing the development of covert attention in infants with scalp event-related potentials. *Dev. Psychol.* 36: 91–108

Richards JE. 2000b. Cortical indices of saccade planning following covert orienting in 20-week-old infants. *Infancy.* In press

Richards JE, Casey BJ. 1991. Heart rate variability during attention phases in young infants. *Psychophysiology* 28:43–53

Richards JE, Casey BJ. 1992. Development of sustained visual attention in the human infant. See Campbell & Hayne 1992, pp. 30–60

Richards JE, Gibson TL. 1997. Extended visual fixation in young infants: look distributions, heart rate changes, and attention. *Child Dev.* 68:1041–56

Richards JE, Holley FB. 1999. Infant attention and the development of smooth pursuit tracking. *Dev. Psychol.* 35:856–67

Richards JE, Hunter SK. 1998. Attention and eye movement in young infants: neural control and development. See Richards 1998, pp. 131–62

Robbins TW. 1998. Arousal and attention: psychopharmacological and neuropsychological studies in experimental animals. See Parasuraman 1998b, pp. 189–220

Robbins TW, Everitt BJ. 1995. Arousal systems and attention. See Gazzaniga, 1995, pp. 703–20

Robbins TW, Everitt BJ, Marston HM, Wilkinson J, Jones GH, Page KJ. 1989. Comparative effects of ibotenic acid- and quisqualic acid-induced lesions of the substantia nigra nominata on attentional function in the rat: further implications for the role of the cholinergic neurons of the nucleus basalis in cognitive processes. *Behav. Brain Res.* 35:221–40

Robertson LC. 1998. Visuospatial attention and parietal function: their role in object perception. See Parasuraman 1998b, pp. 257–78

Robertson LC, Triesman A, Friedman-Hill S, Grabowecky M. 1997. A possible connection between spatial deficits and feature binding in a patient with parietal damage. *J. Cogn. Neurosci.* 9:295–317

Rose SA, Feldman J. 1990. Infant cognition: individual differences and developmental continuities. See Colombo & Fagen 1990, pp. 229–45

Rose SA, Feldman JF. 1995. *Cognitive Continuity from Infancy: A Single Thread or a Twisted Skein?* Presented at Soc. Res. Child Dev., Indianapolis, IN

Rovee-Collier C, Bhatt RS, Chazin S. 1996. Set size, novelty, and visual pop-out in infancy. *J. Exp. Psychol.: Hum. Percept. Perform.* 22:1178–87

Rovee-Collier C, Hankins E, Bhatt R. 1992. Textons, visual pop-out effects, and object recognition in infancy. *J. Exp. Psychol.: Gen.* 121:435–45

Ruff HA. 1975. The function of shifting fixations in the visual perception of infants. *Child Dev.* 46:857–65

Ruff HA. 1986. Components of attention during infants' manipulative exploration. *Child Dev.* 57:105–14

Ruff HA. 1990. Individual differences in sustained attention during infancy. See Colombo & Fagen 1990, pp. 247–70

Ruff HA, Capozzoli M, Dubiner K, Parrinello R. 1990. A measure of vigilance in infancy. *Infant Behav. Dev.* 13:1–20

Ruff HA, Capozzoli M, Saltarelli LM. 1996. Focused visual attention and distractibility in 10-month-old infants. *Infant Behav. Dev.* 19:281–93

Ruff HA, Capozzoli M, Saltarelli LM, Dubiner K. 1992a. The differentiation of activity in infants' exploration of objects. *Dev. Psychol.* 28:851–61

Ruff HA, Capozzoli M, Weissberg R. 1998. Age, individuality, and context as factors in sustained visual attention during the preschool years. *Dev. Psychol.* 34:454–64

Ruff HA, Lawson KR. 1990. Development of sustained, focused attention in young children during free play. *Dev. Psychol.* 26:85–93

Ruff HA, Rothbart MK. 1996. *Attention in Early Development: Themes and Variations.* New York: Oxford Univ. Press

Ruff HA, Saltarelli LM, Capozzoli M, Dubiner K. 1992b. The differentiation of activity in infants' exploration of objects. *Dev. Psychol.* 28:851–61

Sahakian BJ, Owen AM, Morantz NJ, Eagger

SA, Boddington S, et al. 1993. Further analysis of the cognitive effects of tetrahydroaminoacridine THA in Alzheimer's disease: assessment of attentional and mnemonic function using CANTAB. *Psychopharmacology* 110:395–401

Salapatek P. 1975. Pattern perception and early infancy. In *Infant Perception: From Sensation to Cognition*, ed. L Cohen, P Salapatek, 2:133–248. New York: Academic

Salapatek P, Aslin RN, Simonson J, Pulos E. 1980. Infant saccadic eye movements to visible and previously visible targets. *Child Dev.* 51:1090–94

Sarter M. 1994. Neuronal mechanisms of the attentional dysfunctions in senile dementia and schizophrenia: two sides of the same coin? *Psychopharmacology* 114:539–50

Schiller PH. 1998. The neural control of visually guided eye movements. See Richards 1998, pp. 3–50

Schuerger RJ, Balaban CD. 1999. Organization of the coeruleo-vestibular pathway in rats, rabbits, and monkeys. *Brain Res. Brain Res. Rev.* 30:189–217

Shea SL, Aslin RN. 1990. Oculomotor responses to step-ramp targets by young human infants. *Vis. Res.* 30:1077–92

Simion F, Valenza E, Umiltà C, Dalla-Barba B. 1995. Inhibition of return in newborns is temporo-nasal asymmetrical. *Infant Behav. Dev.* 18:189–94

Simons K, ed. 1993. *Early Visual Development, Normal and Abnormal*. Oxford: Oxford Univ. Press

Slater A. 1997. Visual perception and its organisation in early infancy. In *Infant Development: Recent Advances*, ed. G Bremner, A Slater, pp. 31–53. Hove, UK: Psychol. Press

Spelke ES, Breinlinger K, Macomber J, Jacobson K. 1992. Origins of knowledge. *Psychol. Rev.* 99:605–32

Spelke ES, Van de Walle G. 1993. Perceiving and reasoning about objects: insights from infants. In *Spatial Representation: Problems in Philosophy and Psychology*, ed. N Eilan, R McCarthy, pp. 132–61. Oxford: Blackwell

Stechler G, Latz E. 1966. Some observations on attention and arousal in the human infant. *J. Am. Acad. Child Psychiatry* 5:517–25

Tellinghuisen DJ, Oakes LM. 1997. Distractibility in infancy: the effects of distractor characteristics and type of attention. *J. Exp. Child Psychol.* 64:232–54

Thoman EB. 1990. Sleeping and waking states in infants: a functional perspective. *Neurosci. Biobehav. Rev.* 14:93–107

Treiber F, Wilcox S. 1980. Perception of a "subjective" contour by infants. *Child Dev.* 51:915–17

Treisman AM, Gelade G. 1980. A feature integration theory of attention. *Cogn. Psychol.* 12:97–136

Treisman AM, Souther J. 1985. Search asymmetry: a diagnostic for preattentive processing of separable features. *J. Exp. Psychol.: Gen.* 114:285–310

Tronick E, Brazelton TB. 1975. Clinical uses of the Brazelton Neonatal Behavioral Assessment. In *Exceptional Infant*, Vol. 3. *Assessment and Intervention*, ed. BZ Friedlander, GM Sterritt, GE Kirk, pp. 137–56. New York: Brunner/Mazel

Ungerleider LG, Mishkin MM. 1982. Two cortical visual systems. In *Analysis of Visual Behavior*, ed. DJ Ingle, MA Goodale, RJW Mansfield, pp. 549–86. Cambridge, MA: MIT Press

Usher M, Cohen JD, Servan-Schreiber D, Rajkowski J, Aston-Jones G. 1999. The role of locus coeruleus in the regulation of cognitive performance. *Science* 283:549–54

Valenza E, Simion F, Umiltà C. 1994. Inhibition of return in newborn infants. *Infant Behav. Dev.* 17:293–302

Van Giffen K, Haith MM. 1984. Infant response to Gestalt geometric forms. *Infant Behav. Dev.* 7:335–46

Vecera SP, Rothbart MK, Posner MI. 1991. Development of spontaneous alternation in infancy. *J. Cogn. Neurosci.* 3:351–54

Von Hofsten C, Rosander K. 1997. Development of smooth pursuit tracking in young infants. *Vis. Res.* 37:1799–810

Warburton DM. 1977. Stimulus selection and behavioral inhibition. In *Handbook of Psychopharmacology*, ed. LL Iversen, SD Iversen, SH Snyder, pp. 385–431. New York: Plenum

Watson RT, Valenstein E, Heilman KM. 1981. Thalamic neglect: possible role of the medial thalamus and nucleus reticularis in behavior. *Arch. Neurol.* 38:501–6

Webster MJ, Ungerleider LG. 1998. Neuroanatomy of visual attention. See Parasuraman 1998b, pp. 19–34

Werner LA, Gray L. 1998. Behavioral studies of hearing development. In *Development of the Auditory System: Springer Handbook of Auditory Research*, ed. EW Rubel, A Popper, R Fay, 5:12–79. New York: Springer-Verlag

Wolff PH. 1965. The development of attention in young infants. *Ann. NY Acad. Sci.* 118:815–30

Wolff PH. 1966. The causes, controls, and organization of behavior in the neonate. *Psychol. Issue* 5:7–11

Annu. Rev. Psychol. 2001. 52:369–96

PSYCHOLINGUISTICS: A Cross-Language Perspective

Elizabeth Bates, Antonella Devescovi, and Beverly Wulfeck
Center For Research in Language, University of California at San Diego, La Jolla, California 92093; e-mail: bates@crl.ucsd.edu, antonella.devescovi@uniroma1.it, wulfeck@crl.ucsd.edu

Key Words cross-linguistic, aphasia, language development

■ **Abstract** Cross-linguistic studies are essential to the identification of universal processes in language development, language use, and language breakdown. Comparative studies in all three areas are reviewed, demonstrating powerful differences across languages in the order in which specific structures are acquired by children, the sparing and impairment of those structures in aphasic patients, and the structures that normal adults rely upon most heavily in real-time word and sentence processing. It is proposed that these differences reflect a cost-benefit trade-off among universal mechanisms for learning and processing (perception, attention, motor planning, memory) that are critical for language, but are not unique to language.

CONTENTS

INTRODUCTION

The purpose of psycholinguistic research is to uncover universal processes that govern the development, use, and breakdown of language. However, to the extent that research in a given subfield of psycholinguistics is dominated by English, we cannot distinguish between universal mechanisms and English-specific facts. Below we present a brief, selective review of cross-linguistic research on language development in children, language symptoms in brain-injured adults (i.e. aphasia), and language processing in normal adults, in an order that reflects the impact that cross-language variations have had on theoretical frameworks within each field.

Cross-linguistic studies of monolinguals come in two varieties.[1] One approach treats language as a between-subjects variable, applying the same experimental design in two or more languages to determine how theoretically relevant linguistic differences affect performance. Examples from child language include cross-linguistic comparisons of tense and aspect in narratives (Berman & Slobin 1994), the use of "path verbs" (e.g. "ascended") versus "manner verbs" (e.g. "wiggled") to describe an action-packed cartoon (Slobin 1996), the acquisition of terms for spatial location (Bowerman & Choi 1994), and differential use to word order, semantics, and grammatical morphology to assign agent-object relations in a "Who did the action?" task (Bates et al 1999, Devescovi et al 1997, Slobin & Bever 1982, MacWhinney & Bates 1989). Studies of aphasia from this perspective are summarized in Bates et al (1991b). Studies of word and sentence processing in normal adults that treat language as a between-subjects variable are reviewed in MacWhinney & Bates (1989) and Hillert (1998).

The second approach treats languages as experiments of nature, exploiting particular properties of a single target language to ask questions that could not be answered in (for example) English. A host of child language studies from this point of view are summarized in Slobin's five-volume work, *The Cross-Linguistic Study of Language Acquisition* (Slobin 1985–1997), most of them emphasizing the analysis of free speech (see also Sokolov & Snow 1994, and virtually any volume of the *Journal of Child Language*). Case studies of grammatical deficits in speech production by Broca's aphasics in many different languages can be found in Menn & Obler (1990). An increasing number of descriptive and/or experimental studies of aphasia in various languages can be found in the journal *Brain and Language*. Finally, studies of word and sentence processing in healthy adult native speakers of languages other than English have increased in frequency in the past few years, including special issues devoted to the processing of morphology (Sandra & Taft 1994) and grammatical gender (Friederici et al 1999).

Studies from both points of view will be considered here. First, however, let us consider some concrete examples of structural contrasts with powerful implications for psycholinguistic theory, and use them to illustrate how cross-linguistic research can be used in the search for universal mechanisms.

---

[1] Because of length limitations, this review is restricted entirely to research on monolinguals. However, the literatures on bilingual development, bilingual aphasia, and processing in bilingual adults are certainly relevant to basic science in psycholinguistics, especially those studies that treat the contrast between a bilingual's two languages as a within-subjects variable.

CROSS-LANGUAGE CONTRASTS AND THEIR RELEVANCE FOR PROCESSING

We assume that psycholinguistic universals do exist. Languages such as English, Italian, and Chinese draw on the same mental/neural machinery. They do not "live" in different parts of the brain, and children do not differ in the mechanisms required to learn each one. However, languages can differ (sometimes quite dramatically) in the way this mental/neural substrate is taxed or configured, making differential use of the same basic mechanisms for perceptual processing, encoding and retrieval, working memory, and planning. It is of course well known that languages can vary qualitatively, in the presence/absence of specific linguistic features (e.g. Chinese has lexical tone, Russian has nominal case markers, English has neither). In addition, languages can vary quantitatively, in the challenge posed by equivalent structures (lexical, phonological, grammatical) for learning and/or real-time use. For example, passives are rare in English but extremely common in Sesotho, and relative clause constructions are more common in Italian than in English. To the extent that frequency and recency facilitate structural access, these differences should result in earlier acquisition and/or a processing advantage. As shown below, this seems to be the case for passives in Sesotho and for relative clauses in Italian.

Holding frequency constant, equivalent lexical, phonological and/or grammatical structures can also vary in their reliability ("cue validity") and processibility ("cue cost"). These two constructs figure prominently in the competition model (Bates & MacWhinney 1989, MacWhinney 1987), a theoretical framework developed explicitly for cross-linguistic research on acquisition, processing, and aphasia. Like other interactive-activation or constraint-based theories, the competition model assumes parallel processing, across different information sources, with detailed and bidirectional interactions among different information types. Within this framework, cue validity refers to the information value of a given phonological, lexical, morphological, or syntactic form within a particular language, whereas cue cost refers to the amount and type of processing associated with the activation and deployment of that form (e.g. perceivability, salience, neighborhood density versus structural uniqueness, demands on memory, demands on speech planning, and articulation). These two principles codetermine the nature of linguistic representations in a particular language and the nature of the dynamic processes by which form and meaning are activated and mapped onto each other in real time. Linguistic information is represented as a broadly distributed network of probabilistic connections among linguistic forms and the meanings they typically express, as in other connectionist theories of language. Linguistic rules are treated as form-meaning and form-form mappings that can vary in strength, in that the "same" rule may be stronger in one language than it is in another. Within a given language, structures that are high in cue validity should be the ones that normal adults attend to and rely upon most in real-time language processing, and they should also be acquired earlier by children and retained under stress by aphasic patients. However, effects of cue validity may be reduced or amplified by variations in cue cost, especially in young children and/or brain-injured patients whose processing costs are already very high.

To illustrate contrasts in cue validity, consider some of the factors that influence sentence interpretation (especially agent-object relations, or "who did what to whom") in English, Italian, and Chinese. In English, subjects are obligatory in free-standing declarative sentences (including dummy subjects like "it" in "It is raining"), and word order is preserved with a rigidity that is unusual among the world's languages. By contrast, Italian is a "pro-drop" language in which it is possible to omit the subject if it can be inferred from the context or from markings on the verb (e.g. the best translation of "It is raining" in Italian, is "*Piove*," or "Rains"). Italian also permits extensive variation in word order for pragmatic purposes (e.g. it is possible to say "*La lasagna (la) mangia Giovanni*," or "The lasagna (it) eats Giovanni," with the normal reading in which people eat pasta, not the other way around). Because of these contrasts, word order (e.g. noun-verb-noun) is a highly reliable cue to agent-object relations in English but a relatively poor cue in Italian.

In direct contrast with the situation for word order, subject-verb agreement is a weak cue to agent-object relations in English, but a powerful cue in Italian. For example, English has only two contrasting inflected forms in the present indicative paradigm (singular: I eat, you eat, he eats; plural: we eat, you-all eat, they eat), compared with six in Italian (singular: *io mangio, tu mangi, lui mangia*; plural: *noi mangiamo, voi mangiate, loro mangiano*). Looking at the full verb paradigm, Italian verbs can take up to 47 different forms, compared with only 5 in English (e.g. eat, eating, eats, ate, eaten). Such extensive verb marking provides the listener with a rich source of information about "who did what to whom" that is not available in English.

In contrast with both English and Italian, Chinese has no inflectional paradigms at all (e.g. no plural inflections on nouns or tense inflections on verbs). It does have function words and particles to convey some of the functions carried out by inflections in other languages. However, these particles come in a single unalterable form and are optional in all but a handful of contexts, and most are homophones or near-homophones of the content words from which they were historically derived (e.g. past-tense particle *wan* also means to finish). Despite the absence of case or agreement markers to indicate agent-object relations, word order is flexible in Chinese, and both subject and object can be omitted. As a result, a sentence literally translated as "Chicken eat" could mean "The chicken is eating" or "Someone is eating the chicken." Because of all these factors, Chinese listeners have to make flexible and rapid use of many different sources of information in sentence processing, including aspects of prosody, semantics, and pragmatics that are less important in English or Italian.

These contrasts have clear implications for sentence-level processing (with effects that are discussed below), but they also interact with cross-linguistic differences in word structure to affect lexical access. This includes cross-language differences in lexical ambiguity, and differences in lexical structure that challenge the oft-cited distinction between words and rules (Pinker 1999).

With regard to lexical ambiguity, the rich inflectional morphology of Italian makes it relatively easy to distinguish between nouns, verbs, and other grammatical classes. In contrast, the sparse grammatical morphology of English means that nouns, verbs, and other word classes often sound alike and must be disambiguated by context (the comb versus to comb), or by prosodic cues (to re<u>cord</u> versus the <u>re</u>cord). In Chinese, the absence of inflectional morphology means the potential for lexical ambiguity is even greater than it is in English. Some of this ambiguity is reduced in Chinese by lexical tone in the auditory modality (Cutler & Chen 1997) and by the one-to-many mapping between syllables and the nonalphabetic characters that represent them in the written modality (Chen & Tzeng 1992, Chen & Zhou 1999). However, ambiguity is also affected by the rich sublexical structure of Chinese, owing to the dominance and productivity of compounding. More than 80% of Chinese words are compounds (65% disyllabic), and the syllables that comprise them occur in many other words. Hence, most words are highly ambiguous on the first syllable, and many are not resolved until the end of the final syllable. A further complication lies in the fact that Chinese compounds and the morphemes inside them can belong to different form classes, including verb-noun compounds that can either be nouns (zipper = *la-lian*, literally pull-chain) or verbs (to forge = *da-tie*, literally strike-iron). As a result, it is not always clear in Chinese whether we are dealing with a compound word (stored in the lexicon) or a novel noun or verb phrase (compiled on-line) (for a discussion, see Bates et al 1991a, 1993; Zhou et al 1993).

With regard to the distinction between words and rules, English morphology and orthography are both highly irregular, a fact that has shaped theories of processing in both domains. To deal with the regular-irregular contrast, "dual route" or "dual mechanism" theories propose that regular forms are handled by a rule-based system, including grammatical rules in morphology (Pinker 1999, Ullman et al 1997), and phonological rules in reading (i.e. grapheme-phoneme correspondence rules) (Coltheart et al 1980). In these theories, irregular or exception forms are handled by rote memory (lexical look-up in morphology; whole-word access in reading) or by a limited neural network that is capable of generated new forms by analogy (Pinker 1999). Evidence cited in favor of dual-route models includes differential patterns of acquisition in children, dissociations in brain-injured patients, and differential processing of regulars and irregulars in normal adults. An alternative account is provided by connectionist or interactive-activation theories, in which the same differential patterns for regulars and irregulars are explained by domain-general dimensions such as frequency, similarity, and set size (Rumelhart & McClelland 1986). Evidence for this alternative view is provided by neural network models in which regular-irregular contrasts (including double dissociations) are simulated within a single architecture (e.g. Hinton & Shallice 1991, Joanisse & Seidenberg 1999, Juola & Plunkett 1998, Marchman 1993, McClelland & Seidenberg 1989, Plaut et al 1996).

The dual-mechanism debate takes a different form when we move outside the boundaries of English. For example, Italian orthography is extremely transparent (i.e. direct grapheme-phoneme correspondence), but its morphology involves many irregular inflections. This irregularity is often a matter of degree, with multiple subregularities and partially productive patterns that pose an interesting challenge for dual-mechanism theories (Orsolini & Marslen-Wilson 1997). Applying the dual-mechanism view to Italian, some proponents of the modular view (Say & Clahsen 1999) have proposed that the *-are* conjugation class in Italian is regular (handled by the grammar), but the other two classes (*-ire, -ere*) are irregular. However, this also means the lexicon contains many highly productive conjugation patterns, an intellectual move that blurs the word-rule dichotomy. Such in-between cases would be easier to handle if regularity were the product of continuous dimensions such as frequency and similarity, as proposed by some connectionist accounts.

Chinese poses an even greater challenge to dual-mechanism theories because the regular-irregular distinction simply does not apply (at least in its original form) to reading in a language without an alphabet or to grammar in a language with no inflectional paradigms. However, there may be analogues to regularity within the lexicon itself, ranging from "regular" compound patterns (many members, low in frequency and similarity) to irregular or idiosyncratic compound patterns (few members, high in frequency and similarity). To the extent that this kind of regular-irregular distinction can be demonstrated within the lexicon itself, we have to question the English-based assumption that regulars are handled by rules (grammatical and/or phonological) whereas irregulars are handled in the lexicon (Ullman et al 1997).

We are not suggesting that some languages are inherently harder to learn, process, or retain under brain damage than others. All languages must have achieved a roughly comparable degree of learnability and processibility across the course of history, or they would not still be around. However, overall processibility is the product of cost-benefit tradeoffs, a constraint satisfaction problem that must be solved across multiple dimensions of the language system. As a result, we may obtain powerful differences between languages in the relative difficulty of specific linguistic structures, with differential effects on performance by children, aphasic patients, and healthy normal adults. We will also contend that this kind of cross-language variation in structural difficulty reflects universal facts about perception, learning, and processing that are not specific to language at all.

CROSS-LINGUISTIC VARIATIONS IN LANGUAGE DEVELOPMENT

Speech Perception

Human newborns are "citizens of the world" (Kuhl 1985), able to discriminate virtually all of the sound contrasts (phonetics) that are used systematically by the world's languages (for a detailed review, see Aslin et al 1998). Nevertheless, preferential-listening studies have shown that newborn infants have already acquired a weak preference for the sounds of their native language in utero (Jusczyk et al 1993, Mehler et al 1988), although the basis for this preference is still unknown. By 3 months of age, infants show selective preference for their own names, with discrimination of many detailed and language-specific phonotactic features following soon thereafter (Jusczyk 1997), including a clear preference for the prototypic vowels of their native language by 6 months (Kuhl et al 1992). Although such evidence for rapid learning of speech-specific structure was initially cited as evidence for the existence of a domain-specific "speech acquisition device" (Mehler et al 1988), recent demonstrations of rapid statistical induction in 7–8-month-old infants (e.g. Marcus et al 1999, Saffran et al 1996), including results with nonspeech stimuli (Haith 1994, Saffran et al 1997), have led some theorists to conclude that the infant brain is a powerful learning device that is capable of rapid learning from arbitrarily sequenced materials in any modality (e.g. Bates & Elman 1996, Elman & Bates 1997). Hence, the acquisition of speech contrasts in the first year of life may be a language-specific manifestation of domain-general learning mechanisms (Kuhl 1985).

As a result of these findings, recent research in the development of speech perception has focused not only on the continued acquisition of language-specific preferences (Kuhl 1994), but also on the corresponding suppression of phonetic contrasts that are not used systematically in the child's linguistic input (e.g. the process by which Japanese infants lose the ability to hear "ra" versus "la") (Polka & Werker 1994, Werker & Tees 1984). "Tuning in" to language-specific speech contrasts appears to be related systematically (and perhaps causally) to "tuning out" of phoneme contrasts outside child's language, a process that begins around 8–10 months of age. The timing of this "linguistic xenophobia" is probably no accident because it co-occurs with the onset of systematic evidence for word comprehension. Indeed, such "learned inhibition" (which continues unabated for many years in a monolingual environment) may be at least partially responsible for the oft-cited observation that adults find it difficult to acquire a second language without an accent (McClelland et al 1999).

Speech Production   Despite ample evidence for the early acquisition of language-specific contrasts in speech perception, we know relatively little about the emergence of corresponding contrasts in speech production. For most children, canonical or reduplicative babbling begins between 6–8 months, with short segments or longer strings that are punctuated by consonants (e.g. "dadada"). Boysson-Bardies and colleagues (1984) have reported that babbling "drifts" toward the particular sound patterns of the child's native language between 6–10 months (i.e. native speakers can discriminate at above-chance levels between babble by Chinese, Arabic, English, or French infants). However, the phonetic basis of these adult judgments is still unknown. Critics of this research have argued that there are hard maturational limits on the infant's ability to control the detailed gestures required for speech production, suggesting that babbling and early words are relatively immune to language-specific effects until the second year of life (Eilers et al 1993).

At first glance, the absence of language-specific effects on early speech production looks like evidence in favor of Jakobson's classic proposal that speech development is governed by a universal markedness hierarchy (Jakobson 1968), with all children everywhere displaying the same passage from unmarked ("easy," universal) to marked ("hard," language-specific) speech contrasts. However, careful descriptive studies of early phonological development suggest instead that there are large individual differences among children (even within a single language) in the sounds they prefer for babble and early words (Vihman 1986). Studies of the relationship between word comprehension and phonological production in the first two years of life suggest that children may start with "favorite phonemes" that are at least partially derived from the sounds that are present in their first and favorite words (Leonard et al 1980).

Word Comprehension and Production   We have learned a great deal in the past few years regarding cross-linguistic similarities and differences in early lexical development, due in part to the development and proliferation of new parent report instruments that are low in cost but high in reliability and validity (Fenson et al 1994, 2000). By tapping into parental knowledge, researchers have charted means and variations in word comprehension and production in children between 8–30 months of age, with instruments that are now available in more than a dozen languages [Afrikaans, American Sign Language, Catalan, Chinese, Croatian, Danish, Dutch, English (British and New Zealand), Finnish, French (Canadian), Greek, Hebrew, Icelandic, Italian, Japanese, Korean, Malawian, Polish, Sign Language of the Netherlands, Spanish (Mexican and Spain), Swedish]. These parental inventories rely on recognition memory rather than recall (using checklists of words that are among the first 600–700 to be acquired in that language), and they are used only within the age ranges in which parents can give reliable reports of newly emerging behaviors (e.g. word comprehension can only be assessed with these methods between 8–18 months; word production can be assessed reliably between 8–30 months). Briefly summarized, two universal conclusions have emerged from this multinational effort: (*a*) Average onset times appear to be the same across languages for word comprehension (8–10 months) and word production (11–13 months); (*b*) huge variation in lexical growth is found in every language and appears to be equivalent across languages in shape and magnitude (e.g. a range from no word production at all to production of more than 500 words at 24 months).

Although cross-language similarities outweigh differences in these studies, a few cross-language variations have emerged (Caselli et al 1995, 1999). For example, Italian children appear to have larger repertoires of social words (including proper nouns and social routines) than their American counterparts. These differences reflect cultural contrasts, including the fact that Italian infants tend to live in closer proximity to an extended family (e.g. on average, grandma is the thirtieth word produced in the US norms but the fifth word produced in the Italian norms). There are also small but significant differences in the order and shape of function word production between 16–30 months (slow and constant linear growth in Italian; a flat function followed by a nonlinear spurt in English), which may be related to structural contrasts between the two languages (including differences in the perceptual salience of grammatical function words).

A lively debate is currently underway regarding cross-linguistic differences in the order of emergence of nouns versus verbs. In a classic paper, Gentner (1982) argued that nouns must always precede verbs in development because early verbs refer to evanescent events, whereas early nouns refer to solid and bounded objects, and because verbs tend to carve up reality in more variable ways from one language to another. This view has been challenged by Gopnik & Choi for Korean (1995) and by Tardif for Chinese (1996). Based primarily on analyses of free speech, these authors report that verbs are acquired early in these languages (often before nouns) because verbs are more salient: They appear in sentence-final position in Korean, a subject-object-verb (SOV) language, and both languages permit extensive subject and object omission, so that a sentence is often composed of a single naked verb. Gopnik & Choi also suggested that these differences feed into nonlinguistic cognition, resulting in better performance by Korean children on means-end tasks (which are related to verbs) and better performance by English children on object permanence tasks (which are related to nouns). This interesting proposal has been challenged by studies using diaries and/or parental report (Pae 1993; for a review, see Caselli et al 1999) and by studies in which novel verbs and nouns are taught to American and Korean children (Au et al 1994). In those studies, the same familiar noun-before-verb pattern is observed in English, Italian, and Korean, despite sharp contrasts in linguistic structure and in the verb-noun ratios to which children are exposed. Caselli et al (1999) suggest that free-speech records may yield differences because they are sensitive language-specific constructions that are high in frequency (i.e. what children like to do), whereas parent report yields a more representative estimate of the child's full lexical repertoire (i.e. what children know).

Choi & Bowerman (1991) have built on another difference between English and Korean: Both languages use prepositions to convey the concepts of in and out, but Korean also makes a contrast between in-close fitting and in-loose fitting. Young Korean children seem to pick this up quite easily, and show differential response to terms for containment and support by 18 months of age (McDonough et al 1997). It may be that children are sensitive to "small-scale" contrasts in lexical frequency and salience that draw their attention to specific social and contextual facts (e.g. to grandmothers, or to the close fit between objects and containers), but these are not sufficient to move large-scale contrasts like the cognitive and linguistic factors that differentiate nouns from verbs.

Development of Grammar   The most compelling evidence for cross-language variation begins between 18–20 months (on average), when grammatical development is finally underway. Ironically, early cross-linguistic work on language acquisition was based on the assumption that grammar (as opposed to phonology or the lexicon) would prove to be the bastion of language universals. Some secondary sources still claim that all children acquire language on the same schedule, in the same way, and this putative fact has led to further claims about a universal bioprogram that governs language acquisition in children as well as the emergence of new languages from pidgin codes (i.e. creolization) (Bickerton 1984). In this scenario, all children (and all creoles) begin their linguistic careers with single uninflected words, followed by telegraphic combinations of uninflected words in ordered strings, with inflections and function words acquired only after this syntactic base has been established. None of these proposed universals have held up in cross-linguistic research.

Grammatical development does begin with something like a one-word stage in every language, but there are cross-language variations in the form of one-word speech. For example, infant speakers of Western Greenlandic start out by producing little pieces of the large and complex words of their language (in which a sentence may consist of a single word with 10–12 inflections). In other richly inflected languages (e.g. Turkish), children often produce inflected nouns and verbs late in the one-word stage, before they have produced any word combinations at all. Some of these inflected forms may be accomplished by rote, but when there are multiple examples in which the same word appears with several contrasting inflections, it seems reasonable to infer that some kind of productive process is underway.

When word combinations are unequivocally established (between 20–24 months, on average), the evidence suggests that all children everywhere are trying to convey the same basic stock of meanings (e.g. possession, location, volition, disappearance and reappearance, and basic aspects of transitivity). Table 1 illustrates the similar meanings expressed by infants in English and Italian, similarities reported not only for these two languages but for every language that has ever been studied. However, as Martin Braine was the first to report (1976), there are striking differences across languages in the linguistic forms that 2-year-olds use to convey these meanings. Word order is rigidly preserved in some languages (especially English), but it varies markedly in others (Bates 1976). English children produce a relatively high proportion of sentence subjects, compared with Italian children at the same stage (Valian 1991). Telegraphic speech is typical of some children, but even in English there are individual children who use a high ratio of pronouns and function words in their first word combinations (albeit with limited productivity) (Bates et al 1988). The entire system of case morphology appears to be mastered by Turkish children by 2 years of age, reflecting the exceptional regularity and phonological salience of Turkish inflections (Slobin 1985). Finally, many so-called complex forms appear quite early if they are very frequent and used for common pragmatic purposes [e.g. relative clauses in Italian, which are 5 times as common in Italian 3-year-olds than they are in their English counterparts) (Bates & Devescovi 1989) and passives in Sesotho, used very

TABLE 1   Semantic relations underlying first word combinations in English and Italian (adapted from Braine 1976)

Semantic Functions	English Examples	Italian Examples
Attention to X	See doggie!	*Gadda bau*
Property of X	Big doggie	*Gande bau*
Possession	My truck	*Mia brum-brum*
Plurality or iteration	Two shoe	*Due pappe*
Recurrence	Other cookie	*Atto bototto*
Disappearance	Daddy bye bye	*Papà via*
Negation or refusal	No bath	*Bagno no*
Actor-action	Mommy do it	*Fa mamma*
Location	Baby car	*Bimbo casa*
Request	Have dat	*Dà chetto*

frequently by adults and acquired by 3 years of age by Sesotho children (Demuth 1989)].

To some extent, this had to be true. For example, adult Italians have to produce approximately three times more morphological contrasts than English speakers to convey the same idea. This leaves us with at least two logical possibilities for early grammatical development: (*a*) Italian children take three times as long to acquire their grammar or (*b*) Italian and English children acquire their respective languages at the same rate, but along the way Italian children produce roughly three times as much morphology as their English counterparts. Evidence to date provides support for the latter view. In fact, if anything, children exposed to richly and systematically inflected languages may get off the ground faster, suggesting that the contrasting forms in their input force earlier learning of inflectional options—a result that has also been seen in connectionist simulations of grammatical learning (Harris 1991, MacWhinney & Leinbach 1991).

In fact, grammatical errors are surprisingly rare in early child grammars (Slobin 1985–1997), despite the many opportunities for error that are present in richly inflected languages. Tomasello (1992, 1998) has argued that this low incidence of error reflects a highly conservative approach to learning and generalization, a verb-by-verb and construction-by-construction approach in which undergeneralization (use of a new inflection or ordering principle with a small subset of legal options) is far more common than the oft-cited phenomenon of overgeneralization (use of a new inflection outside of its domain). The theoretical literature on grammatical development has focused on overgeneralization (e.g. overextension of the regular past tense, as in goed and comed), owing in part to the belief (now under challenge)

TABLE 2 Examples of speech by two-year-olds in different languages

English (30 months):

I	*wanna*	*help*	*wash*	*car*
1st pers. singular	modal indicative	infinitive	infinitive	

Italian (24 months):

Lavo	*mani,*	*sporche,*	*apri*	*acqua.*
Wash	hands	dirty	open	water
1st pers. singular indicative	3rd pers. feminine plural	feminine plural	2nd pers. singular imperative	3rd pers. singular

I wash hands, dirty, turn on water

Western Greenlandic (26 months):

anner-	*punga.............*	*anni-*	*ler-*	*punga*
hurt-	1st singular indicative	hurt-	about-to	1st singular indicative

I've hurt myself ... I'm about to hurt myself ...

Mandarin (28 months):

Bu	*yao*	*ba*	*ta*	*cai-*	*diao*	*zhege*	*ou*
not	want	object-marker	it	tear-	down	this	warning-marker

Don't tear apart it! Oh!

Sesotho (32 months):

o-		*tla-*	*hlaj-*	*uw-*	*a*	*ke*	*tshehlo*
class 2 singular subject marker		future	stab-	passive marker	mood	by	thorn class 9

You'll get stabbed by a thorn.

Japanese (25 months):

Okashi	*tabe-*	*ru*	*tte*	*yut-*	*ta*
Sweets	eat	non-past	quote-marker	say	past

She said that she'll eat sweets.

that such cases constitute evidence for the maturation of a rule system and/or the mastery of individual rules (compare Elman et al 1996 and Juola & Plunkett 1998 with Marcus 1999 and Pinker 1999). However, such cases are far less common that one might infer from the space they occupy in textbooks (Maratsos 2000, Marcus et al 1992), and it is no longer clear that they require a maturational or a rule-based account. To underscore the extraordinary richness, diversity, and language specificity that is observed in the speech of 2-year-olds, a series of examples from Slobin and other sources is presented in Table 2.

As a final point, recent evidence suggests that the single best predictor of early grammatical development comes from outside the grammar. That is, grammatical

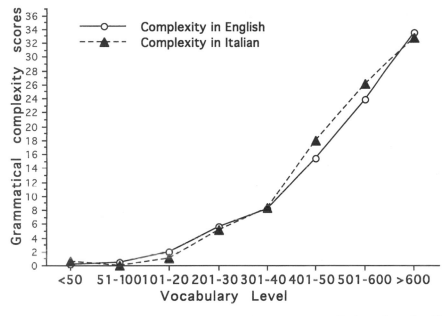

Figure 1 Grammatical complexity as a function of vocabulary size. (Redrawn from Caselli et al 1999)

changes are tied in both rate and shape to vocabulary expansion (Bates & Goodman 1997, Marchman et al 1991). Figure 1 illustrates a powerful nonlinear relationship between vocabulary expansion and grammatical growth in large samples of English- and Italian-speaking children. These results are based on parental report, but they have been validated repeatedly against samples of free speech. Given large differences in the number of inflections that must be acquired by English and Italian children, these similarities are striking. However, they are based on instruments that were constructed to be comparable in numbers of vocabulary items (between 670–690) and grammatical items (37 pairs of sentence contrasts in each language, tapping into the structures that emerge for each language between 16–30 months). Hence, they do not show us rich cross-language differences in amount of morphology. We have a large study in progress in which Italian and English children are matched for vocabulary size (from parental report), permitting us to compare free-speech samples together with parent reports of the three longest utterances they have heard their children produce in the past two weeks. Evidence to date provides further support for a powerful link between grammatical development and vocabulary size in both languages, but it also unleashes the structural differences masked in Figure 1. Some examples of the sentences produced by a subset of Italian versus English children at the same vocabulary level are presented in Table 3.

TABLE 3   Utterances reported for English and Italian children matched for vocabulary[a]

ITALIAN	ENGLISH
Female, 24 months, 231 words	Female, 24 months, 235 words
Chicca e mamma mangiamo la stessa cosa	Daddy work boat
Chicca and mamma eat (1st pl) the(fs) same(fs)	
thing(fs)	
Dal dottore no Chicca	Baby go night-night
To the(ms) doctor(ms) no Chicca	
Nonna Silvia cade, bua ginocco, naso, denti	Mommy in there?
Grandma Silvia falls(3rd s), booboo knee,(ms)	
nose(ms), teeth(mpl)	
Male, 24 months, 364 words	Male, 24 months, 352 words
Il papa porta il gelato a Davide	Daddy go work
The(ms) daddy(ms) brings(3rd. s) the(ms)	
ice cream(ms) to Davide	
Mamma andiamo dalla nonna in campagna	Happy day to you
con la macchina	
Mommy, go(1st, pl) to the(fs) grandma(fs)	
in country with the(fs) car(fs)	
Mamma fa il bagno a Davide	Wanna talk to Grandma phone
Mommy makes(3rd. s) the(ms) bath(ms) to Davide	
Male, 24 months, 479 words	Male, 24 months, 494 words
Prendiamo l'autobus e andiamo dalla zia	Mamma, Megan touched TV
Take (1st. pl. the(el) bus(ms) and go(1st. pl.)	
to the(fs) aunt(fs)	
Non c'e il sole oggi, mamma?	Go bye-bye see grandma, grandpa
Not there-is(3rd. s) the(ms) sun(ms) today, Mommy?	
La ruspa fa un buco grande grande, e poi se ne	I want milk please
va a casa	
The(fs) bulldozer(fs) makes(3rd. s) a(ms) hole (ms)	
big(uns) big(uns), and then (ref) (part)	
go(3rd. s) to home	
Male, 30 months, 590 words	Male, 30 months, 595 words
Metti l'acqua in questo bicchiere, l'altro e sporco	Daddy see lights on the ground,
	out the window
put(2nd. s. imp.) the(el) water(fs) in this(ms)	
glass(ms), the(el) other(ms) is(3rd s) dirty(ms)	
Prendo il mio orso e gli do la pappa	Alan wants pizza from the pizza store
Take(1st. s) the(ms) my(ms) bear(ms) and it(dat)	
give(1st s) the(fs) food(fs).	
Voglio lavarmi i denti con lo spazzolino nuovo	I got curly hair too
Want(1st. s) to-wash-myself(1st. s ref) the(mpl)	
teeth(mpl) with the(ms) toothbrush(ms) new(ms)	

[a]s, singular; p, plural; m, masc.; f, fem.; el, elided; un, gender unmarked; 1st-3rd, person; imp, imperative; dat, dative; ref, reflexive; part, partitive.

CROSS-LINGUISTIC VARIATIONS IN APHASIA

In contrast with child language and adult psycholinguistics (relatively modern fields that blossomed in the 1960s), the study of acquired speech and language disorders in adults (i.e. aphasia) has been underway for literally thousands of years (Goodglass 1993). However, the English language has dominated research on aphasia since World War II, with the establishment of Veteran's Administration hospitals in conjunction with academic research centers, and the development of modern diagnostic batteries. Although considerable progress has been made, the hegemony of English in aphasia research has led to some historical errors that have only been corrected in the past few years, as a result of new cross-linguistic studies of grammatical and lexical symptoms.

The term agrammatism is attributable to Arnold Pick (1913), whose own research was based on aphasic speakers of German and Czech. Pick clearly noted that there are two forms of agrammatism: nonfluent (associated with frontal damage) and fluent (associated with temporal-lobe damage). The frontal form is a symptom of Broca's aphasia and is characterized by omissions and reductions in complexity, coupled with occasional errors of substitution. The temporal form is associated with Wernicke's aphasia, and "is characterized by erroneous grammatical constructions (paragrammatisms), in contrast to the frontal type with its telegraphic style" (Pick 1913, p. 76). In other words, Broca's aphasics err by omission, Wernicke's aphasics err by substitution. In both cases, Pick believed that patients retain *Sprachgefuehl* or feeling for language, a deep knowledge of their grammar despite these contrasting symptoms of grammatical expression. He noted, however, that the two forms of agrammatism might look very different in English, "an essentially formless language of high standing" (p. 80). Pick was prophetic: From the 1960s until today, based primarily on studies of English, receptive and expressive agrammatism have been identified primarily with Broca's aphasia, and by extension, grammatical processing has been ascribed to regions of left frontal cortex (Caplan & Waters 1999a,b; Dick & Bates 2000; see papers in Kean 1985, Kim et al 1997).

Detailed reviews of this historical anomaly are provided by Bates & Wulfeck (1989), Bates et al (1991b), and Bates & Goodman (1997). The punchline is straightforward: The equation of grammatical deficits with damage to Broca's area derives from a peculiarity of English. Because English has relatively sparse grammatical morphology, errors of substitution are difficult to detect, but errors of omission (especially omission of function words) are very evident. It is therefore easy to discount the severity of grammatical deficits in English-speaking Wernicke's aphasics because their speech is otherwise relatively fluent, preserving melodic line, with function words included in appropriate positions. Consider an analogy: There is a genetic deficit that results in the inability to trill r's; this deficit is very apparent in Italian (where it is known to run in families), but entirely undetectable in English. Fluent paragrammatism has a similar status.

The equation of agrammatism with damage to Broca's area was supported by well-controlled studies of sentence comprehension in English-speaking patients who revealed deficits in the use of grammar by Broca's aphasics that are not evident in everyday conversations (Grodzinsky 2000, Heilman & Scholes 1976, Kean 1985, Zurif & Caramazza 1976). Unfortunately, as Goodglass (1993) noted in his review of this literature, many of the original studies compared Broca's aphasics to elderly controls but did not investigate receptive agrammatism in other patient groups. More recently, specific deficits in the receptive processing of inflections, function words, and complex syntax have been reported for virtually every form of aphasia, and for many other disorders as well (for reviews, see Bates & Goodman 1997, Dick et al 1999). Furthermore, these receptive deficits have also been demonstrated in normal college students forced to process sentence stimuli under perceptual degradation (Dick et al 1999, Kilborn 1991) or cognitive overload (Blackwell & Bates 1995, Miyake et al 1994). Indeed, now that psycholinguistic techniques have been applied to a wide variety of patient groups, similarities in profiles of deficit greatly outweigh differences, a conclusion summarized as follows by Sheila Blumstein and William Milberg:

"What we have learned are two complementary findings: (1) that structural analyses reveal similar patterns of breakdown (qualitatively, if not quantitatively) across patients. In particular, those properties of language that are more "complex" are more vulnerable and a hierarchy of impairment can be established within each linguistic domain, and (2) that patients rarely have a selective impairment affecting only a single linguistic component. Most patients evidence a constellation of impairments implicating deficits that affect phonology, the lexicon, as well as syntax." (Blumstein & Milberg 2000, p. 27).

Our own cross-linguistic results and those of other investigators are in accord with this conclusion (Bates et al 1991b, Menn & Obler 1990), but they add an extra dimension: The hierarchy of difficulty that patient groups share can vary over languages, and cross-linguistic studies can help us develop a better theory of just what "hard" and "easy" mean. At the same time, cross-linguistic studies also reveal just how much detailed language-specific knowledge (*Sprachgefuehl*) is retained by aphasic patients, despite their lexical and grammatical errors, forcing a rethinking of aphasic syndromes in terms of processing deficits rather than loss of linguistic content. This conclusion is supported by studies of sentence comprehension, production, and grammaticality judgment, all showing significant differences between patient groups that correspond directly to cross-linguistic differences in normals. Across studies of both comprehension and production, both Broca's and Wernicke's aphasics retain the basic word order biases of their native language [e.g. subject-verb-object (SVO), as in "the girl eats the apple" in English, Italian, and German; subject-object-verb (SOV) as in "the girl the apple eats" in Turkish and Japanese; both in Hungarian, depending on the definiteness of the object]. In the same studies, use of grammatical morphology proves to be especially vulnerable in receptive processing, but the degree of loss is directly correlated with strength of morphology in the premorbid language. In studies of

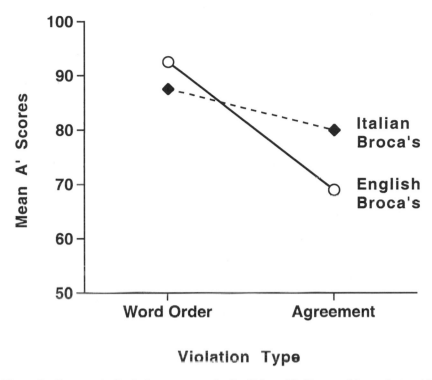

Figure 2   Grammaticality judgment scores for English- and Italian-speaking patients with "agrammatic" Broca's aphasia. (redrawn from Wulfeck et al 1991)

grammaticality judgment, fluent and nonfluent patients show above-chance abilities (at equivalent levels) to detect subtle grammatical errors, often in constructions that they themselves can no longer produce without error (Devescovi et al 1997 for Italian; Linebarger et al 1983, Lu et al 2000 for Chinese; Shankweiler et al 1989 for Serbo-Croatian; Wulfeck 1988).

Because of length limitations, we use only one concrete empirical example to illustrate this very general point. Figure 2 compares A' scores (a nonparametric variant of d', a signal detection statistic that corrects for response bias) in Italian and American Broca's aphasics in a grammaticality judgment task. Patients were asked to push one of two buttons to indicate whether a sentence was "bad" (has a mistake) or "good" (has no mistakes). Two types of errors were derived from the same well-formed sentence materials: word order errors (e.g. "The girl is selling books..." became "The girl selling is books...") and agreement errors (e.g. "The girl are selling books...."). Figure 2 displays a significant language by patient group interaction, and illustrates three conclusions: (a) agrammatic Broca's aphasics are above chance in their judgments of grammaticality in both languages (although they do perform below normal controls); (b) for both groups, agreement errors are harder to detect than word order errors (also true for normals under cognitive overload—Blackwell & Bates 1995); (*c*) however, Italian Broca's are significantly better at detecting agreement errors than their American counterparts, whereas Americans are significantly better at detecting word order errors. We also looked at reaction time data for the same patients compared with college-age controls, using z-scores to equate for the overall difference in reaction times between groups. This analysis showed that Broca's aphasics also retain the characteristic reaction time profile for their language: Italians are faster at detecting agreement errors, and Americans are faster at detecting word order errors.

The general picture that has emerged so far is one in which cross-language differences are robust under brain damage, but patient group differences are few and far between. This does not hold, however, for all linguistic symptoms. For example, the fluency differences that distinguish Broca's and Wernicke's aphasics are attested in every language, although the omission-based profile of Broca's and the substitution-based profile of Wernicke's take different forms depending on the opportunities presented by the language. There are also some very puzzling differences in lexical access that show up in every language tested to date, including a peculiar double dissociation between nouns and verbs: Nouns are better preserved in Broca's aphasics, but verbs are better preserved in Wernicke's aphasics. This dissociation has now been reported in English (Goodglass 1993), Italian (Miceli et al 1984), Hungarian (Osmán-Sági 1987) and Chinese (Bates et al 1991a, 1993; Chen & Bates 1998). The Chinese version of this dissociation is particularly interesting, for two reasons: (*a*) It demonstrates that the verb-finding difficulty of Broca's aphasics cannot be attributed to the heavy morphological load that verbs bear in Indo-European languages, because verbs (like nouns) are uninflected in Chinese; (*b*) it occurs at the whole-word level (regardless of sublexical structure), but it also occurs at the sublexical level in compound words (e.g. given a verb-noun verb like *da-tie*, literally strike-iron, Broca's have more difficulty lexicalizing the verb element *da-*, whereas Wernicke's have more trouble with the nominal element *-tie*). Hence, the noun-verb dissociation is not a byproduct of grammatical processing, nor is it a simple product of two separate lexicons (verbs in the front, nouns in the back). Instead, the processes responsible for this double dissociation must be tied to the meanings (lexical and sublexical) that underlie nouns versus verbs (Damasio & Tranel 1993, Perani et al 1999). These results illustrate the value of the second cross-linguistic strategy described earlier, where the special opportunities offered by a given language are exploited to learn more about the nature of (in this case) word-finding deficits in aphasia.

CROSS-LINGUISTIC VARIATIONS IN WORD AND SENTENCE PROCESSING

Cross-linguistic studies of word and sentence processing in normal adults are relatively rare, compared with the rich comparative data base that is now available for child language and adult aphasia. In surveying several major textbooks in psycholinguistics (which we do not cite), one finds many statements about "the speaker" or "the listener" in reference to studies that were carried out almost exclusively in English. In none of these textbooks have we been able to find any mention of the possibility that results might look a bit different in another language. At the sentence level, some exceptions to this general trend include Cuetos & Mitchell (1988), Cuetos et al (1996), Hillert (1998), MacWhinney & Bates (1989), and Thornton et al (1998). In addition, there has been a marked increase in research on aspects of inflectional and derivational morphology that are underrepresented in English (Friederici et al 1999, Sandra & Taft 1994). Although these trends are promising, few other basic works in adult psycholinguists take into account the problem of generalizing from English-specific results to universal mechanisms.

One of the largest bodies of comparative research on sentence comprehension and production can be found in MacWhinney & Bates (1989), with chapters on the hierarchy of cues to sentence processing displayed by native speakers of English, Italian, German, Spanish, French, Dutch, Hebrew, Hungarian, Serbo-Croatian, Turkish, Chinese, Japanese, and Warlpiri. Table 4 summarizes the order of importance of cues to actor assignment across all these languages, in adults and (where available) in children. All of these studies rely on a single method. a "Who did it?" task in which listeners are presented (on-line or off-line) with some factorial combination of word order [noun-verb-noun (NVN), noun-noun-verb (NNV), verb-noun-noun (VNN)], morphology (agreement or case marking on the first noun, second noun, or both), semantics (animate-animate, animate-inanimate, inanimate-animate), contrastive stress (on the first noun, second noun, or neither), and/or topicalization. The factorial design permits an assessment of cue strength (a correlate of cue validity) by determining which cues "win" (and to what extent) in various competing and converging combinations of information. The cue hierarchies in Table 4 reflect the winners in a competition design. For example, given a sentence like "The rock is kissing the cow," English listeners (from ages 2 to 92) chose the first noun (slavishly following SVO), whereas speakers of most other languages chose the second noun (animacy defeats basic word order). Given a sentence like "The cows is chasing the horse," English listeners also chose the first noun (SVO defeats agreement), whereas speakers of more richly inflected languages tended to choose the second noun (agreement trumps canonical word order). These "victories" and "defeats" are not absolute, within or across subjects; they are probabilistic in nature, directly corresponding to levels of cue validity within each language.

In some languages, this competition design results in a mix of grammatical and ungrammatical sentences, a fact that has led some critics (Gibson 1992) to conclude that results cannot be generalized to normal language processing. However, the same probabilistic results have been observed in languages in which all combinations are grammatical, and similar results are obtained in Hungarian when semigrammatical forms are allowed (using common nouns) or disallowed (using possessive markers like "Your red one is chasing my blue one," which do not carry case). For these reasons, MacWhinney & Bates (1989) concluded that it is

TABLE 4   Order of importance of cues to actor assignment across language (from Bates & MacWhinney 1989)

English	
Adults:	SVO > VOS, OSV > animacy, agreement > stress, topic
5–7:	SVO > animacy > agreement > NNV, VNN, stress
Under 5:	SVO > animacy > stress, SOV, VSO > agreement
Italian	
Adults:	SV agreement > clitic agreement > animacy > SVO > stress, topic (NNV, VNN interpretable only in combination with stress, clitics)
Under 7:	Animacy > SVO > SV agreement > clitic agreement > SOV, VSO (no interactions of NNV, VNN with stress, clitics)
French	
Adults:	SV agreement > clitic agreement > animacy > SVO > stress
Under 6:	SVO > animacy > VSO, SOV (agreement not tested)
Spanish	
Adults:	Accusative preposition > SV agreement > clitic agreement > word order (animacy not tested)
German	
Adults:	Case > agreement > animacy > SOV, VSO, SVO
Dutch	
Adults:	Case > SVO > animacy
Under 10:	SVO > case > animacy
Serbo-Croatian	
Adults:	Case > agreement > animacy > SVO, VSO, SOV
Under 5:	Animacy > case > SVO, VSO, SOV > agreement
Hungarian	
Adults:	Case > SV > agreement > SVO, SOV > animacy > V – O agreement
Under 3:	Animacy > case > SVO > stress (agreement not tested)
Turkish	
Adults:	Case > animacy > word order
Under 2:	Case > word order (animacy not tested)
Hebrew	
Adults:	Case > agreement > order
Under 10:	Case > order > agreement
Warlpiri	
Adults:	Case > animacy > order
Under 5:	Animacy > case > order
Chinese	
Adults:	Animacy > SVO
Japanese	
Adults:	Case > animacy > SVO

possible to derive generalizable principles from stimuli that include semigrammatical forms (similar to the visual illusions used by perceptual psychologists to obtain insight into the principles that govern visual perception). However, these results do not respond to another criticism of this cross-linguistic design: Results for simple sentences may reflect heuristics or "short-cuts" that do not generalize to processing of more complex sentence forms.

To investigate this last possibility, Bates et al (1999) examined sentence comprehension in English and Italian, comparing reliance on word order versus agreement in complex two-clause sentences. All sentences contained three noun participants, with one "criminal verb" and one "verb of witness" either in the main clause or the relative clause (e.g. "The secretaries who the journalist sees shoot the cowboy" or "The waitress hears the policeman who the ballerinas stab"). Subjects were asked to "identify the one who does the bad action, as fast as you can" so that we could direct the subject's attention either to the main or relative clause, within random lists varying word order and agreement conditions at both levels of the sentence. Sentences were presented visually, and reading times were recorded up to a button press, at which point subjects reported orally (off-line) the name of the criminal. We found the same massive cross-language differences uncovered in previous studies: overwhelming reliance on word order in English, in both the main clause and the relative clause; overwhelming reliance on agreement in Italian, at both levels of the sentence. We also uncovered new information about the costs associated with these contrasting strategies. First, reaction times were more affected by center embedding in English than Italian, suggesting that the reaction time costs associated with center embedding are greater with a strong reliance on word order. Second, reaction times were slower for morphologically ambiguous sentences in Italian but not in English, suggesting that Italian subjects are frustrated by the absence of their favorite cue. These differences in processing costs may reflect a fundamental contrast between "geometric strategies" (track word order) and "algebraic strategies" (match agreement endings), with implications for the profiles of vulnerability observed in each language for complex sentences, in aphasic patients and in normals under stress.

Cross-linguistic studies within the competition model constitute one of the largest and oldest research programs using language differences as a between-subjects variable. However, there is a growing body of cross-language research from other points of view as well. For example, studies based on English had led some investigators to conclude that listeners have universal parsing biases (e.g. minimal attachment, late closure) that lead them to prefer one interpretation of ambiguous phrases over another, sometimes resulting in garden path phenomena. Thus, given a phrase like "The daughter of the colonel who had the accident," English listeners typically conclude that the accident happened to the colonel, which means they prefer to attach the relative clause to the nearest (local) noun phrase. However, Cuetos & Mitchell (1988) showed that Spanish listeners have a different bias, preferring a reading in which the accident happened to the daughter, which means they prefer to attach the relative clause to the highest noun phrase. This pioneering study set off a flurry of cross-language studies investigating putative universal constraints on sentence processing, resulting in the general conclusion that listeners behave as they should, with processing biases that are appropriate for the structural options and statistical distributions in their language (Mitchell & Brysbaert 1998, Thornton et al 1998; but see Frazier & Clifton 1996).

Other recent studies have focused on grammatical cues to lexical access, including phenomena such as grammatical gender agreement or noun classifiers that simply are not available in English. Significant gender and/or classifier priming has now been reported for Serbo-Croatian (Gurjanov et al 1985), French (Grosjean et al 1994), Italian (Bates et al 1996), German (Hillert & Bates 1996, Jacobsen 1999), Russian (Akhutina et al 1999), Chinese (Lu et al 2000), and Swahili (Alcock & Ngorosho 2000). In most of these studies, results include facilitation relative to neutral baseline, indicating the presence of automatic, top-down effects (but see Friederici & Jacobsen 1999 for a different view). In addition, studies of Spanish (N Wicha, E Bates, A Hernandez, I Reyes, L Gavaldón de Barreto, submitted), and Italian (Bentrovato et al 1999) have shown that grammatical gender interacts significantly with sentential meaning when pictures are named within a sentence context, with the two sources of information together producing massive facilitation (around 100 ms) relative to several different neutral baselines. The emerging picture is one in which language-specific cues to lexical access are used as soon as they are available, alone or in combination with other sources of information. In this respect, language processing is similar to many other complex perceptual-motor skills, suggesting that language use follows domain-general principles.

CONCLUSION

The dominance of English in twentieth-century psycholinguistics was a historical accident, more socio-political than scientific. However, it has had particularly unfortunate consequences for those fields that try to study the universal psychological and neural underpinnings of language. Psycholinguistics has finally broken away from the hegemony of English, and the field is better for it. There is, however, an immense amount of work that needs to be done to verify whether English-based findings can be generalized and to explore the opportunities afforded by the dramatic structural contrasts that characterize human language.

ACKNOWLEDGMENTS

Support was provided by Cross-Linguistic Studies of Aphasia (DC00216), Center for the Study of the Neural Bases of Language & Learning (NS22343), and Origins of Communication Disorders (DC01289). Thanks to Meiti Opie for assistance in manuscript preparation.

Visit the Annual Reviews home page at www.AnnualReviews.org

LITERATURE CITED

Akhutina T, Kurgansky A, Polinsky M, Bates E. 1999. Processing of grammatical gender in a three-gender system: experimental evidence from Russian. *J. Psycholinguist. Res.* 28:695–713

Alcock KJ, Ngorosho D. 2000. *Grammatical Noun Class Agreement Processing in Kiswahili.* Tech. Rep. CRL-0003. La Jolla: Univ. Calif., San Diego, Cent. Res. Lang.

Aslin RN, Jusczyk PW, Pisoni DB. 1998. Speech and auditory processing during infancy: constraints on and precursors to language. In *Handbook of Child Psychology*, Vol. 2. *Cognition, Perception & Language*, ser. ed. W Damon, vol. ed. D Kuhn, R Siegler, pp. 147–98. New York: Wiley. 5th ed.

Au T, Dapretto M, Song Y-K. 1994. Input vs. constraints: early word acquisition in Korean and English. *J. Mem. Lang.* 33:567–82

Bates E. 1976. *Language and Context: Studies in the Acquisition of Pragmatics.* New York: Academic

Bates E, Bretherton I, Snyder L. 1988. *From First Words to Grammar: Individual Differences and Dissociable Mechanisms.* New York: Cambridge Univ. Press

Bates E, Chen S, Tzeng O, Li P, Opie M. 1991a. The noun-verb problem in Chinese aphasia. *Brain Lang.* 41:203–33

Bates E, Chen S, Li P, Opie M, Tzeng O. 1993. Where is the boundary between compounds and phrases in Chinese? A reply to Zhou et al. *Brain Lang.* 45:4–107

Bates E, Devescovi A. 1989. Crosslinguistic studies of sentence production. See MacWhinney & Bates 1989, pp. 225–53

Bates E, Devescovi A, D'Amico S. 1999. Processing complex sentences: a cross-linguistic study. *Lang. Cogn. Process* 14:69–123

Bates E, Devescovi A, Hernandez A, Pizzamiglio L. 1996. Gender priming in Italian. *Percept. Psychophys.* 85:992–1004

Bates E, Elman J. 1996. Learning rediscovered. *Science* 274:1849–50

Bates E, Goodman J. 1997. On the inseparability of grammar and the lexicon: evidence from acquisition, aphasia and real-time processing. *Lang. Cogn. Process.* 12:507–86 (special issue on the lexicon)

Bates E, MacWhinney B. 1989. Functionalism and the competition model. See MacWhinney & Bates 1989, pp. 3–76

Bates E, Wulfeck B. 1989. Crosslinguistic studies of aphasia. See MacWhinney & Bates 1989, pp. 328–74

Bates E, Wulfeck B, MacWhinney B. 1991b. Crosslinguistic research in aphasia: an overview. *Brain Lang.* 41:123–48

Bentrovato S, Devescovi A, D'Amico S, Bates E. 1999. The effect of grammatical gender and semantic context on lexical access in Italian. *J. Psycholinguist. Res.* 28:677–93

Berman RA, Slobin DI. 1994. *Relating Events in Narrative: A Cross-Linguistic Developmental Study.* Hillsdale, NJ: Erlbaum

Bickerton D. 1984. The language bioprogram hypothesis. *Behav. Brain Sci.* 7:173–87

Blackwell A, Bates E. 1995. Inducing agrammatic profiles in normals: evidence for the selective vulnerability of morphology under cognitive resource limitation. *J. Cogn. Neurosci.* 7:228–57

Blumstein SE, Milberg WP. 2000. Neural systems and language processing: toward a synthetic approach. *Brain Lang.* 71:26–29

Bowerman M, Choi S. 1994. *Linguistic and Nonlinguistic Determinants of Spatial Semantic Development: A Crosslinguistic Study of English, Korean, and Dutch.* Presented at Boston Univ. Conf. Lang. Dev.

Boysson-Bardies B, Sagart L, Durand C. 1984. Discernible differences in the babbling of infants according to target language. *J. Child Lang.* 11:1–15

Braine MDS. 1976. Children's first word

combinations. With commentary by Melissa Bowerman. *Monogr. Soc. Res. Child Dev.* 41(1):whole issue

Caplan D, Waters GS. 1999a. Verbal working memory and sentence comprehension. *Behav. Brain Sci.* 22:77–94

Caplan D, Waters GS. 1999b. Issues regarding general and domain-specific resources. *Behav. Brain Sci.* 22:114–26

Caselli MC, Bates E, Casadio P, Fenson J, Fenson L, et al. 1995. A cross-linguistic study of early lexical development. *Cogn. Dev.* 10:159–99

Caselli MC, Casadio P, Bates E. 1999. A comparison of the transition from first words to grammar in English and Italian. *J. Child Lang.* 26:69–111

Chen H-C, Tzeng O, eds. 1992. *Language Processing in Chinese.* Amsterdam: North-Holland

Chen H-C, Zhou X, eds. 1999. *Lang. Cogn. Process.* 14:425–748 (Special Issue on processing East Asian languages)

Chen S, Bates E. 1998. The dissociation between nouns and verbs in Broca's and Wernicke's aphasia: findings from Chinese. *Aphasiology* 12:5–36 (Special issue on Chinese aphasia)

Choi S, Bowerman M. 1991. Learning to express motion events in English and Korean: the influence of language-specific lexicalization patterns. *Cognition* 41:83–121

Coltheart M, Patterson KE, Marshall JC. 1980. *Deep Dyslexia.* London: Routledge & Keagan Paul

Cuetos F, Mitchell DC. 1988. Cross-linguistic differences in parsing: restrictions on the use of the Late Closure Strategy in Spanish. *Cognition* 30:73–105

Cuetos F, Mitchell DC, Corley MMB. 1996. Parsing in different languages. In *Language Processing in Spanish*, ed. M Carreiras, J Garcia-Albea, N Sebastian-Galles, pp. 145–87. Mahwah, NJ: Erlbaum

Cutler A, Chen H-C. 1997. Lexical tone in Cantonese spoken-word processing. *Percept. Psychophys.* 59:265–79

Damasio A, Tranel D. 1993. Nouns and verbs are retrieved with differently distributed neural systems. *Proc. Natl. Acad. Sci. USA* 90:4957–60

Demuth K. 1989. Subject, topic and Sesotho passive. *J. Child Lang.* 17:67–84

Devescovi A, Bates E, D'Amico S, Hernandez A, Marangolo P, et al. 1997. An on-line study of grammaticality judgments in normal and aphasic speakers of Italian. *Aphasiology* 11:543–79 (Special issue on cross-linguistic aphasia)

Dick F, Bates E. 2000. Grodzinsky's latest stand—or, just how specific are "lesion-specific" deficits? *Behav. Brain Sci.* 23:29

Dick E, Bates E, Wulfeck B, Utman J, Dronkers N. 1999. *Language Deficits, Localization, and Grammar: Evidence for a Distributive Model of Language Breakdown in Aphasics and Normals.* Tech. Rep. No. 9906. La Jolla: Univ. Calif., San Diego, Cent. Res. Lang.

Eilers R, Oller DK, Levine S, Basinger O, Lynch M, Urbano R. 1993. The role of prematurity and socioeconomic status in the onset of canonical babbling in infants. *Infant Behav. Dev.* 16:297–316

Elman J, Bates E. 1997. Acquiring language: response. *Science* 276:1180

Elman J, Bates E, Johnson M, Karmiloff-Smith A, Parisi D, et al. 1996. *Rethinking Innateness: A Connectionist Perspective on Development.* Cambridge, MA: MIT Press/Bradford Books

Fenson L, Bates E, Dale P, Goodman J, Reznick JS, Thal D. 2000. Measuring variability in early child language: Don't shoot the messenger. Comment on Feldman et al. *Child Dev.* 71:323–28

Fenson L, Dale PA, Reznick JS, Bates E, Thal D, Pethick SJ. 1994. Variability in early communicative development. *Monogr. Soc. Res. Child Dev.* Ser. No. 242, 59(5): whole issue

Frazier L, Clifton C. 1996. *Construal.* Cambridge, MA: MIT Press

Friederici A, Garrett MF, Jacobsen T, eds. 1999. *J. Psycholinguist. Res.* 28(5, 6) (special issue on processing grammatical gender)

Friederici A, Jacobsen T. 1999. Processing grammatical gender during language comprehension. *J. Psycholinguist. Res.* 28(5): 467–84

Gentner D. 1982. Why are nouns learned before verbs: linguistic relativity versus natural partitioning. *In Language Development*, Vol. 2: *Language, Thought and Culture*, ed. SA Kuczaj II. Hillsdale, NJ: Erlbaum

Gibson E. 1992. On the adequacy of the competition model. (review of the crosslinguistic study of sentence processing). *Language* 68:812–30

Goodglass H. 1993. *Understanding Aphasia.* San Diego: Academic

Gopnik A, Choi S. 1995. Names, relational words, and cognitive development in English- and Korean-speakers: Nouns are not always learned before verbs. In *Beyond Names for Things: Young Children's Acquisition of Verbs*, ed. M Tomasello, W Merriman, pp. 63–80. Hillsdale, NJ: Erlbaum

Grodzinsky Y. 2000. The neurology of syntax: language use without Broca's area. *Behav. Brain Sci.* 23:1–71

Grosjean F, Dommergues J-Y, Cornu E, Guillelmon D, Besson C. 1994. The gender-marking effect in spoken word recognition. *Percept. Psychophys.* 56:590–98

Gurjanov M, Lukatela G, Lukatela K, Savic M, Turvey M. 1985. Grammatical priming of inflected nouns by the gender of possessive adjectives. *J. Exp. Psychol.: Learn. Mem. Cogn.* 11:692–701

Haith MM. 1994. Visual expectations as the first step toward the development of future-oriented processes. In *The Development of Future-Oriented Processes*, ed. MM Haith, JB Benson, RJ Rogers Jr, BF Pennington, pp. 11–38. Chicago: Univ. Chicago Press

Harris CL. 1991. *Parallel distributed processing models and metaphors for language and development*. PhD thesis. Univ. Calif., San Diego

Heilman KM, Scholes RJ. 1976. The nature of comprehension errors in Broca's, conduction and Wernicke's aphasics. *Cortex* 12:258–65

Hillert D, ed. 1998. *Sentence Processing: A Cross-Linguistic Perspective.* San Diego: Academic

Hillert D, Bates E. 1996. *Morphological Constraints on Lexical Access: Gender Priming in German*. Tech. Rep. No. 9601. La Jolla: Univ. Calif., San Diego, Cent. Res. Lang.

Hinton GE, Shallice T. 1991. Lesioning an attractor network: investigations of acquired dyslexia. *Psychol. Rev.* 98:74–95

Jacobsen T. 1999. Effects of grammatical gender on picture and word naming: evidence from German. *J. Psycholinguist. Res.* 28:499–514

Jakobson R. 1968. *Child Language. Aphasia and Phonological Universals.* The Hague/Paris: Mouton

Joanisse MF, Seidenberg MS. 1999. Impairments in verb morphology after brain injury: A connectionist model. *Proc. Natl. Acad. Sci USA* 96:7592–97

Juola P, Plunkett K. 1998. Why double dissociations don't mean much. In *Proc. 20th Annu. Conf. Cogn. Sci. Soc.*, ed. MA Gernsbacher, SJ Derry, pp. 561–66. Mahwah, NJ: Erlbaum

Jusczyk PW. 1997. Finding and remembering words: some beginnings by English-learning infants. *Curr. Dir. Psychol. Sci.* 6:170–74

Jusczyk PW, Friederici AD, Wessels JMI, Svenkerud V, Jusczyk AM. 1993. Infants' sensitivity to the sound pattern of native-language words. *J. Mem. Lang.* 32:402–20

Kean M-L, ed. 1985. *Agrammatism.* Orlando, FL: Academic

Kilborn K. 1991. Selective impairment of grammatical morphology due to induced stress in normal listeners: implications for aphasia. *Brain Lang.* 41:275–88

Kim KHS, Relkin NR, Lee KY-M, Hirsch J. 1997. Distinct cortical areas associated with native and second languages. *Nature* 388:171–74

Kuhl PK. 1994. Learning and representation in speech and language. *Curr. Opin. Neurobiol.* 4:812–22

Kuhl PK. 1985. Categorization of speech by infants. In *Neonate Cognition: Beyond the*

Blooming Buzzing Confusion, ed. J Mehler, R Fox. Hillsdale, NJ: Erlbaum

Kuhl PK, Williams KA, Lacerda F, Stevens KN, Lindblom B. 1992. Linguistic experiences alter phonetic perception in infants by 6 months of age. *Science* 255:606–8

Leonard LB, Newhoff M, Mesulam L. 1980. Individual differences in early child phonology. *Appl. Psycholinguist.* 1:7–30

Linebarger M, Schwartz M, Saffran E. 1983. Sensitivity to grammatical structure in so-called agrammatic aphasics. *Cognition* 13:361–92

Lu C-C, Bates E, Li P, Tzeng O, Hung D, et al. 2000. Judgments of grammaticality in aphasia: the special case of Chinese. *Aphasiology.* In press

MacWhinney B. 1987. The competition model. In *Mechanisms of Language Acquisition*, ed. B MacWhinney, pp. 249–308. Hillsdale, NJ: Erlbaum

MacWhinney B, Bates E, eds. 1989. *The Crosslinguistic Study of Sentence Processing*. New York: Cambridge Univ. Press

MacWhinney B, Leinbach J. 1991. Implementations are not conceptualizations—revising the verb-learning model. *Cognition* 40:121–57

Maratsos M. 2000. More overregularizations after all: new data and discussion on Marcus, Pinker, Ullman, Hollander, Rosen & Xu. *J. Child Lang.* 27:183–212

Marchman V. 1993. Constraints on plasticity in a connectionist model of the English past tense. *J. Cogn. Neurosci.* 5:215–34

Marchman V, Bates E, Burkhardt A, Good A. 1991. Functional constraints on the acquisition of the passive: toward a model of the competence to perform. *First Lang.* 11:65–92

Marcus G. 1999. Do infants learn grammar with algebra or statistics? Response. *Science* 284:436–37

Marcus G, Pinker S, Ullman M, Hollander M, Rosen TJ, Xu F. 1992. Overregularization in language acquisition. *Monogr. Soc. Res. Child Dev.* 7(4): whole issue

Marcus G, Vijayan S, Rao SB, Vishton PM. 1999. Rule learning by seven-month-old infants. *Science* 283:77–80

McClelland JL, Thomas AG, McCandliss BD, Fiez JA. 1999. Understanding failures of learning: Hebbian learning, competition for representational space, and some preliminary experimental data. In *Progress in Brain Research*, Vol. 121, ed. JA Reggia, E Ruppin, D Glanzman. Amsterdam: Elsevier

McClelland M, Seidenberg M. 1989. A distributed developmental model of visual word recognition and naming. *Psychol. Rev.* 98:523–68

McDonough L, Choi S, Bowerman M, Mandler JM. 1997. The use of preferential looking as a measure of semantic development. In *Advances in Infancy Research*, ed. EL Bavin, D Burnham, pp. 336–54. Norwood, NJ: Ablex

Mehler J, Jusczyk PW, Lambertz G, Halsted N, Bertoncini J, Amiel-Tison C. 1988. A precursor of language acquisition in young infants. *Cognition* 29:143–78

Menn L, Obler LK, eds. 1990. *Agrammatic Aphasia: Cross-Language Narrative Sourcebook*. Amsterdam/Philadelphia: Benjamins

Miceli G, Silveri M, Villa G, Caramazza A. 1984. On the basis for the agrammatic's difficulty in producing main verbs. *Cortex* 20:207–20

Mitchell D, Brysbaert M. 1998. Challenges to recent theories of language differences in parsing: evidence from Dutch. In *Syntax and Semantics*, Vol. 31. *Sentence Processing: A Cross-Linguistic Perspective*, ser. ed. BD Joseph, C Pollard, vol. ed. D Hillert, pp. 313–36. San Diego: Academic

Miyake A, Carpenter PA, Just MA. 1994. A capacity approach to syntactic comprehension disorders: making normal adults perform like aphasic patients. *Cogn. Neuropsychol.* 11:671–717

Orsolini M, Marslen-Wilson M. 1997. Universals in morphological representation: evidence from Italian. *Lang. Cogn. Process.* 12:1–47

Osmán-Sági J. 1987. Action naming in Hungarian aphasic patients. Abstracts of the Second World Congress of Neuroscience IBRO. *Neurosci.* (Suppl.) 22:S509

Pae S. 1993. *Early vocabulary in Korean: Are nouns easier to learn than verbs?* PhD thesis. Univ. Kansas, Lawrence

Perani D, Cappa S, Schnur T, Tettamanti M, Collina S, et al. 1999. The neural correlates of verb and noun processing: a PET study. *Brain* 122:2337–44

Pick A. 1913. *Aphasia.* Transl./ed. J Brown, 1973. Springfield, IL: Thomas. (From German)

Pinker S. 1999. *Words and Rules: The Ingredients of Language.* New York: Basic Books

Plaut D, McClelland J, Seidenberg M, Patterson K. 1996. Understanding normal and impaired word reading: computational principles in quasiregular domains. *Psychol. Rev.* 103:56 115

Polka L, Werker JF. 1994. Developmental changes in perception of nonnative vowel contrasts. *J. Exp. Psychol. Hum. Percept. Perform.* 20:421–35

Rumelhart D, McClelland JL, eds. 1986. *Parallel Distributed Processing: Explorations in the Microstructure of Cognition,* Vol. 1. *Foundations.* Cambridge, MA: MIT Press

Saffran JR, Aslin RN, Newport EL. 1996. Statistical learning by 8-month-old infants. *Science* 274:1926–28

Saffran JR, Aslin RN, Newport EL. 1997. Acquiring language (letter to the editor). *Science* 276:1180, 1276

Sandra D, Taft M, eds. 1994. *Lang. Cogn. Process.* 9(3) (special issue on morphological structure, lexical representation and lexical access)

Say T, Clahsen H. 1999. *Words, rules and stems in the Italian Mental Lexicon.* Essex Res. Rep. Linguist., Univ. Essex

Shankweiler D, Crain S, Gorrell P, Tuller B. 1989. Reception of language in Broca's aphasia. *Lang. Cogn. Process.* 4:1–33

Slobin D. 1985. Crosslinguistic evidence for the language-making capacity. See Slobin 1985, 2:1157–256

Slobin D, ed. 1985–1997. *The Crosslinguistic Study of Language Acquisition,* Vols. 1–5. Hillsdale, NJ: Erlbaum

Slobin D. 1996. Two ways to travel: verbs of motion in English and Spanish. In *Grammatical Constructions: Their Form and Meaning,* ed. M Shibatani, SA Thompson, pp. 195–219. Oxford: Oxford Univ. Press

Slobin D, Bever TG. 1982. Children use canonical sentence schemas: a crosslinguistic study of word order and inflections. *Cognition* 58:265–89

Sokolov J, Snow C, eds. 1994. *Handbook of Research in Language Development Using CHILDES.* Hillsdale, NJ: Erlbaum

Tardif T. 1996. Nouns are not always learned before verbs: evidence from Mandarin speakers' early vocabularies. *Dev. Psychol.* 32:492–504

Thornton R, Gil M, MacDonald MC. 1998. Accounting for crosslinguistic variation: a constraint-based perspective. In *Syntax and Semantics,* Vol. 31. *Sentence Processing: A Cross-Linguistic Perspective,* ser. ed. BD Joseph, C Pollard, vol. ed. D Hillert, pp. 211–25. San Diego: Academic

Tomasello M. 1992. *First Verbs: A Case Study of Early Grammatical Development.* Cambridge/New York: Cambridge Univ. Press

Tomasello M. 1998. The return of constructions (book review).). *J. Child Lang.* 25:431–42

Ullman M, Corkin S, Coppola M, Hickok G, Growdon JH, et al. 1997. A neural dissociation within language: evidence that the mental dictionary is part of declarative memory, and that grammatical rules are processed by the procedural system. *J. Cogn. Neurosci.* 9:266–76

Valian V. 1991. Syntactic subjects in the early speech of American and Italian children. *Cognition* 40:21–81

Vihman M. 1986. Individual differences in babbling and early speech: predicting to age three. In *Precursors of Early Speech,* ed. B Lindblom, R Zetterstrom. Basingstoke, UK: MacMillan

Werker J, Tees R. 1984. Cross-language speech perception: evidence for perceptual reorganization during the first year of life. *Infant Behav. Dev.* 7:49–63

Wulfeck B. 1988. Grammaticality judgments and sentence comprehension in agrammatic aphasia. *J. Speech Hear. Res.* 31:72–81

Wulfeck B, Bates E, Capasso R. 1991. A crosslinguistic study of grammaticality judg-ments in Broca's aphasia. *Brain Lang.* 41:311–36

Zhou X, Ostrin RK, Tyler LK. 1993. The noun-verb problem and Chinese aphasia: comments on Bates et al 1991. *Brain Lang.* 45:86–93

Zurif E, Caramazza A. 1976. Psycholinguistic structures in aphasia: studies in syntax and semantics. In *Studies in Neurolinguistics*, Vol. I, ed. H Whitaker, HA Whitaker, pp. 260–92. New York: Academic

Annu. Rev. Psychol. 2001. 52:397–422

JOB BURNOUT

Christina Maslach[1], Wilmar B. Schaufeli[2],
Michael P. Leiter[3]

[1]*Psychology Department, University of California, Berkeley, California 94720-1650;*
e-mail: maslach@socrates.berkeley.edu
[2]*Psychology Department, Utrecht University, 3508 TC Utrecht, The Netherlands;*
e-mail: w.schaufeli@fss.uu.nl
[3]*Psychology Department, Acadia University Wolfville, NS BOP 1X0 Canada;*
e-mail: leiter@acadiau.ca

Key Words   work stress, organizational behavior, job engagement, stress
management, job-person fit

■ **Abstract**   Burnout is a prolonged response to chronic emotional and interpersonal
stressors on the job, and is defined by the three dimensions of exhaustion, cynicism,
and inefficacy. The past 25 years of research has established the complexity of the
construct, and places the individual stress experience within a larger organizational
context of people's relation to their work. Recently, the work on burnout has expanded
internationally and has led to new conceptual models. The focus on engagement, the
positive antithesis of burnout, promises to yield new perspectives on interventions to
alleviate burnout. The social focus of burnout, the solid research basis concerning
the syndrome, and its specific ties to the work domain make a distinct and valuable
contribution to people's health and well-being.

CONTENTS

0066-4308/01/0201-0397$14.00

INTRODUCTION

The relationship that people have with their work, and the difficulties that can arise when that relationship goes awry, have been long recognized as a significant phenomenon of the modern age. The use of the term burnout for this phenomenon began to appear with some regularity in the 1970s in the United States, especially among people working in the human services. This popular usage was presaged by Greene's 1961 novel, *A Burn-Out Case*, in which a spiritually tormented and disillusioned architect quits his job and withdraws into the African jungle. Even earlier writing, both fictional and nonfictional, described similar phenomena, including extreme fatigue and the loss of idealism and passion for one's job. What is noteworthy is that the importance of burnout as a social problem was identified by both practitioners and social commentators long before it became a focus of systematic study by researchers.

The evocative power of the burnout term to capture the realities of people's experiences in the workplace is what has made it both important and controversial in the research field. As the "language of the people," burnout was more grounded in the complexities of people's relationship to work and gave new attention to some aspects of it. However, burnout was also derided at first as nonscholarly "pop psychology." Unlike other research on the workplace, which used a top-down approach derived from a scholarly theory, burnout research initially utilized a bottom-up or "grass-roots" approach derived from people's workplace experiences. At first, the popular, nonacademic origins of burnout were more of a liability than an advantage. However, given the subsequent development of theoretical models and numerous empirical studies, the issue of research scholarship has now been laid to rest.

What has emerged from all of this research is a conceptualization of job burnout as a psychological syndrome in response to chronic interpersonal stressors on the job. The three key dimensions of this response are an overwhelming exhaustion, feelings of cynicism and detachment from the job, and a sense of ineffectiveness and lack of accomplishment. The exhaustion component represents the basic individual stress dimension of burnout. It refers to feelings of being overextended and depleted of one's emotional and physical resources. The cynicism (or depersonalization) component represents the interpersonal context dimension of burnout. It refers to a negative, callous, or excessively detached response to various aspects of the job. The component of reduced efficacy or accomplishment represents the self-evaluation dimension of burnout. It refers to feelings of incompetence and a lack of achievement and productivity at work.

The goal of this chapter is to provide a critical analysis of what has been learned from the past 25 years of work on job burnout. We frame each of the sections in terms of key research questions that have been raised and then summarize the theoretical and empirical responses to them. A comprehensive citation of the research literature is available elsewhere (Cordes & Dougherty 1993, Schaufeli & Enzmann 1998); our focus here is on what we see as the major issues in the field.

HISTORY OF BURNOUT RESEARCH

These major issues and themes have been shaped in important ways by the history of the research on burnout. This research has gone through distinct phases of development.

The Pioneering Phase

In the first phase, the work was exploratory and had the goal of articulating the phenomenon of burnout. The initial articles appeared in the mid-1970s in the United States and their primary contribution was to describe the basic phenomenon, give it a name, and show that it was not an uncommon response. This early writing was based on the experience of people working in human services and health care—occupations in which the goal is to provide aid and service to people in need, and which can therefore be characterized by emotional and interpersonal stressors. The initial articles were written by Freudenberger (1975), a psychiatrist working in an alternative health care agency, and by Maslach (1976), a social psychologist who was studying emotions in the workplace. Freudenberger provided direct accounts of the process by which he and others experienced emotional depletion and a loss of motivation and commitment, and he labeled it with a term being used colloquially to refer to the effects of chronic drug abuse: burnout. Maslach interviewed a wide range of human services workers about the emotional stress of their jobs and discovered that the coping strategies had important implications for people's professional identity and job behavior.

Thus, burnout research had its roots in care-giving and service occupations, in which the core of the job was the relationship between provider and recipient. This interpersonal context of the job meant that, from the beginning, burnout was studied not so much as an individual stress response, but in terms of an individual's relational transactions in the workplace. Moreover, this interpersonal context focused attention on the individual's emotions, and on the motives and values underlying his or her work with recipients.

The clinical and social psychological perspectives of the initial articles influenced the nature of the first phase of burnout research. On the clinical side, the focus was on symptoms of burnout and on issues of mental health. On the social side, the focus was on the relationship between provider and recipient and on the situational context of service occupations. Most of this initial research was descriptive and qualitative in nature, utilizing such techniques as interviews, case studies, and on-site observations.

Several themes emerged from these early interviews in the human services, suggesting that the burnout phenomenon had some identifiable regularities. First, it was clear that the provision of service or care can be a very demanding and involving occupation and that emotional exhaustion is not an uncommon response to such job overload. The second component of depersonalization (cynicism) also emerged from these interviews, as people described how they tried to cope with the emotional stresses of their work. Moderating one's compassion for clients by emotional distance from them ("detached concern") was viewed as a way of protecting oneself from intense emotional arousal that could interfere with functioning effectively on the job. However, an imbalance of excessive detachment and little concern seemed to lead staff to respond to clients in negative, callous, and dehumanized ways.

A better feel for the situational context of the provider-recipient relationship came from field observations, in addition to the interviews. It was possible to see first-hand some of the job factors that had been described in earlier interviews, such as the high number of clients (caseload), prevalence of negative client feedback, and scarcity of resources. It was also possible to observe other, unreported aspects of the interaction between provider and client, such as nonverbal "distancing" behaviors.

Interwoven throughout this early work was a central focus on relationships—usually between provider and recipient, but also between provider and coworkers or family members. These relationships were the source of both emotional strains and rewards and sometimes they functioned as a resource for coping with stress. The centrality of these interactions for the experiences that were being described made it clear that a contextual analysis of the overall phenomenon would be the most appropriate way to gain insight into it.

In addition, this first phase was characterized by a strong applied orientation, which reflected the particular set of social, economic, historical, and cultural factors

of the 1970s. These factors influenced the professionalization of the human services in the United States and had made it more difficult for people to find fulfillment and satisfaction in these careers (see Cherniss 1980, Farber 1983). The
strong concern in these occupations about the problem of burnout led to calls for
immediate solutions, despite the lack of much solid knowledge of burnout's causes
and correlates. Burnout workshops became a primary mode of intervention, and
were also used as sources of data by some researchers (e.g. Pines et al 1981).

The Empirical Phase

In the 1980s the work on burnout shifted to more systematic empirical research.
This work was more quantitative in nature, utilizing questionnaire and survey
methodology and studying larger subject populations. A particular focus of this
research was the assessment of burnout, and several different measures were developed. The scale that has had the strongest psychometric properties and continues
to be used most widely by researchers is the Maslach Burnout Inventory (MBI)
developed by Maslach & Jackson (1981). The MBI was originally designed for use
in human service occupations. However, in response to the interest in burnout by
teachers, a second version of the MBI was soon developed for use by educational
occupations. With the growing body of empirical research, alternative proposals
began to be generated about the developmental course of burnout over time.

The shift to greater empiricism was accompanied by theoretical and methodological contributions from the field of industrial-organizational psychology.
Burnout was viewed as a form of job stress, with links to such concepts as job satisfaction, organizational commitment, and turnover. The industrial-organizational
approach, when combined with the prior work based in clinical and social psychology, generated a richer diversity of perspectives on burnout and strengthened
the scholarly base via the use of standardized tools and research designs.

In the 1990s this empirical phase continued, but with several new directions.
First, the concept of burnout was extended to occupations beyond the human
services and education (e.g. clerical, computer technology, military, managers).
Second, burnout research was enhanced by more sophisticated methodology and
statistical tools. The complex relationships among organizational factors and the
three components of burnout led to the use of structural models in much burnout
research. This approach permits researchers to examine the contribution of many
potential influences and consequences simultaneously, separating unique contrib-
utors to the development of burnout from those that are redundant. Third, a few
longitudinal studies began to assess the links between the work environment at
one time and the individual's thoughts and feelings at a later time. In addition to
addressing the fundamental premise that burnout is a consequence of the interaction of an individual with a worksetting, longitudinal studies are important for
assessing the impact of interventions to alleviate burnout.

In the following sections, we summarize the key themes and issues that have
emerged from this body of work. We first consider the concept of burnout, in

terms of both theory and assessment. Next we review the findings for situational factors and individual factors. We then review three areas in which there has been a recent expansion of work on burnout: an international expansion of research, a theoretical expansion to a model of person-job fit, and an expansion of the basic construct to include the positive state of job engagement. Finally, we consider implications of all this work for intervention.

DEFINING THE CONSTRUCT: What Is Burnout?

Burnout was initially a very slippery concept—there was no standard definition of it, although there was a wide variety of opinions about what it was and what could be done about it. Different people used the term to mean very different things, so there was not always a basis for constructive communication about the problem and solutions for it. However, there was actually an underlying consensus about three core dimensions of the burnout experience, and subsequent research on this issue led to the development of a multidimensional theory of burnout (Maslach 1982, 1998). This theoretical framework continues to be the predominant one in the burnout field.

Assessment

The only measure that assesses all three of the core dimensions is the MBI (see Maslach et al 1996 for the most recent edition). The MBI-Human Services Survey (MBI-HSS) was designed for use with people working in the human services and health care. A second version was developed for use by people working in educational settings (the MBI-Educators Survey, or MBI-ES). In both the HSS and ES forms, the labels for the three dimensions reflected the focus on occupations where workers interacted extensively with other people (clients, patients, students, etc): emotional exhaustion, depersonalization, and reduced personal accomplishment.

Given the increasing interest in burnout within occupations that are not so clearly people-oriented, a third, general version of the MBI was developed (the MBI-General Survey, or MBI-GS). Here, the three components of the burnout construct are conceptualized in slightly broader terms, with respect to the job, and not just to the personal relationships that may be a part of that job. Thus, the labels for the three components are: exhaustion, cynicism (a distant attitude toward the job), and reduced professional efficacy. The MBI-GS assesses the same three dimensions as the original measure, using slightly revised items, and maintains a consistent factor structure across a variety of occupations.

Three Dimensions of Burnout

Exhaustion is the central quality of burnout and the most obvious manifestation of this complex syndrome. When people describe themselves or others as experiencing burnout, they are most often referring to the experience of exhaustion.

Of the three aspects of burnout, exhaustion is the most widely reported and the most thoroughly analyzed. The strong identification of exhaustion with burnout has led some to argue that the other two aspects of the syndrome are incidental or unnecessary (Shirom 1989). However, the fact that exhaustion is a necessary criterion for burnout does not mean it is sufficient. If one were to look at burnout out of context, and simply focus on the individual exhaustion component, one would lose sight of the phenomenon entirely.

Although exhaustion reflects the stress dimension of burnout, it fails to capture the critical aspects of the relationship people have with their work. Exhaustion is not something that is simply experienced—rather, it prompts actions to distance oneself emotionally and cognitively from one's work, presumably as a way to cope with the work overload. Within the human services, the emotional demands of the work can exhaust a service provider's capacity to be involved with, and responsive to, the needs of service recipients. Depersonalization is an attempt to put distance between oneself and service recipients by actively ignoring the qualities that make them unique and engaging people. Their demands are more manageable when they are considered impersonal objects of one's work. Outside of the human services, people use cognitive distancing by developing an indifference or cynical attitude when they are exhausted and discouraged. Distancing is such an immediate reaction to exhaustion that a strong relationship from exhaustion to cynicism (depersonalization) is found consistently in burnout research, across a wide range of organizational and occupational settings.

The relationship of inefficacy (reduced personal accomplishment) to the other two aspects of burnout is somewhat more complex. In some instances it appears to be a function, to some degree, of either exhaustion, cynicism, or a combination of the two (Byrne 1994, Lee & Ashforth 1996). A work situation with chronic, overwhelming demands that contribute to exhaustion or cynicism is likely to erode one's sense of effectiveness. Further, exhaustion or depersonalization interfere with effectiveness: It is difficult to gain a sense of accomplishment when feeling exhausted or when helping people toward whom one is indifferent. However, in other job contexts, inefficacy appears to develop in parallel with the other two burnout aspects, rather than sequentially (Leiter 1993). The lack of efficacy seems to arise more clearly from a lack of relevant resources, whereas exhaustion and cynicism emerge from the presence of work overload and social conflict.

Discriminant Validity

Some of the early discussion about burnout focused on issues of discriminant validity—that is, was burnout truly a distinctly different phenomenon from other established constructs? A variety of such constructs were considered, but the primary focus was on two: depression and job satisfaction. Speculation on these issues was often more frequent than empirical data.

Research conducted during the development of the MBI found burnout to be related to anxiety and depression. Subsequently, the distinction between burnout and depression was established empirically in several studies using the MBI and various measures of depression (Bakker et al 2000, Glass & McKnight 1996, Leiter & Durup 1994). This research established that burnout is a problem that is specific to the work context, in contrast to depression, which tends to pervade every domain of a person's life. These findings lent empirical support to earlier claims that burnout is more job-related and situation-specific than general depression (Freudenberger 1983, Warr 1987). However, as noted later, individuals who are more depression-prone (as indicated by higher scores on neuroticism) are more vulnerable to burnout.

Further support for this distinction comes from an analysis of various conceptualizations of burnout, which notes five common elements of the burnout phenomenon (Maslach & Schaufeli 1993). (*a*) There is a predominance of dysphoric symptoms such as mental or emotional exhaustion, fatigue, and depression. (*b*) The emphasis is on mental and behavioral symptoms more than physical ones. (*c*) Burnout symptoms are work-related. (*d*) The symptoms manifest themselves in "normal" persons who did not suffer from psychopathology before. (*e*) Decreased effectiveness and work performance occur because of negative attitudes and behaviors. Most of these elements are represented in the diagnosis for job-related neurasthenia (WHO 1992), so recent research has been utilizing this diagnosis as the psychiatric equivalent of burnout. A new study has found that burnout scores on the MBI can distinguish psychiatric outpatients diagnosed with job-related neurasthenia from outpatients diagnosed with other mental disorders, and that the former group shows a less pathological profile than the latter (Schaufeli et al 2000).

In the case of the distinction between job satisfaction and burnout, the issue concerns the interpretation of the commonly found negative correlation between these two constructs (ranging from .40 to .52). Although the correlation is not large enough to conclude that the constructs are actually identical, they are clearly linked. However, the specific nature of that link is still a matter of speculation. Does burnout cause people to be dissatisfied with their job? Or does a drop in satisfaction serve as the precursor to burnout? Alternatively, both burnout and job dissatisfaction may be caused by another factor, such as poor working conditions.

Developmental Models

There has been a great deal of theorizing about the developmental trajectory of burnout over time. However, there has been scant research to actually test any of these hypotheses, primarily because of the inherent difficulties of doing the requisite longitudinal research. Most of the relevant data have come from either cross-sectional studies or studies utilizing statistical causal models. The few studies that have used repeated measures have usually used a timeframe ranging from a few months to one year; the one notable exception is the set of case study interviews done as a 12-year follow-up by Cherniss (1995). The most recent longitudinal research has developed more sophisticated analyses for identifying how changes in work stressors can predict changes in burnout (Peiro et al 2001).

Several folk theories about the development of burnout emerged from the interviews of the earliest pioneering phase of research. One theory is that it is the best and most idealistic workers who experience burnout—as captured in the common phrase, "You have to have been on fire in order to burn out." The notion here is that such dedicated people end up doing too much in support of their ideals, thus leading to exhaustion and eventual cynicism when their sacrifice has not been sufficient to achieve their goals. A second theory is that burnout is the end result of long exposure to chronic job stressors. Consequently, burnout ought to occur later in people's careers, rather than earlier, and it should be relatively stable over time if people stay in the same job. There has also been debate about whether burnout results from overload (i.e. too many demands with too few resources) or from underload (i.e. tedium and monotony).

Once the three dimensions of the burnout syndrome had been identified, several developmental models were presented in these dimensional terms. The phase model proposed that each of the three dimensions be split into high and low scores, so that all possible combinations of the three dimensions resulted in eight patterns, or phases, of burnout (Golembiewski & Munzenrider 1988). In terms of development, one alternative was that depersonalization (cynicism) is the first phase of burnout, followed by inefficacy, and finally exhaustion. Another alternative was that the different dimensions developed simultaneously but independently, and thus could result in the eight different patterns. Research based on the phase model has established that the progression of phases from low to high burnout is correlated with worsening indices of both work and personal well-being.

Another model of the three dimensions hypothesized a different sequential progression over time, in which the occurrence of one dimension precipitates the development of another. According to this model, exhaustion occurs first, leading to the development of cynicism, which leads subsequently to inefficacy. For example, a study of hospital nurses yielded the following sequence: (*a*) Stressful interactions with supervisors increase the workers' feelings of exhaustion; (*b*) high levels of exhaustion lead to cynicism, especially if workers lack supportive contact with their coworkers; (*c*) as cynicism persists, the workers' feelings of efficacy diminish, although supportive contact with coworkers may help to decelerate this process (Leiter & Maslach 1988).

In general, the research on burnout has established the sequential link from exhaustion to cynicism. However, as mentioned earlier, the subsequent link to inefficacy is less clear, with the current data supporting a simultaneous development of this third dimension rather than a sequential one. It is also the case that burnout scores are fairly stable over time, which supports the notion that burnout is a prolonged response to chronic job stressors.

Outcomes

The significance of burnout, both for the individual and the workplace, lies in its links to important outcomes. Most of the outcomes that have been studied have been ones related to job performance. There has also been some attention paid to health outcomes, given that burnout is considered a stress phenomenon. However, the research findings have to be interpreted with some caution because of the reliance on self-report measures (rather than other indices of performance or health) and the relative absence of methodological designs that permit causal inferences.

Job Performance   Burnout has been associated with various forms of job withdrawal—absenteeism, intention to leave the job, and actual turnover. However, for people who stay on the job, burnout leads to lower productivity and effectiveness at work. Consequently, it is associated with decreased job satisfaction and a reduced commitment to the job or the organization.

People who are experiencing burnout can have a negative impact on their colleagues, both by causing greater personal conflict and by disrupting job tasks. Thus, burnout can be "contagious" and perpetuate itself through informal interactions on the job. There is also some evidence that burnout has a negative "spillover" effect on people's home life (Burke & Greenglass 2001).

Health   The exhaustion component of burnout is more predictive of stress-related health outcomes than the other two components. These physiological correlates mirror those found with other indices of prolonged stress. Parallel findings have been found for the link between burnout and various forms of substance abuse.

In terms of mental health, the link with burnout is more complex. As mentioned earlier, burnout has been linked to the personality dimension of neuroticism and the psychiatric profile of job-related neurasthenia. Such data might support the argument that burnout is itself a form of mental illness. However, a more common assumption has been that burnout causes mental dysfunction—that is, it precipitates negative effects in terms of mental health, such as anxiety, depression, drops in self-esteem, and so forth. An alternative argument is that people who are mentally healthy are better able to cope with chronic stressors and thus less likely to experience burnout. Although not assessing burnout directly, one study addressed this question by analyzing archival longitudinal data of people who worked in interpersonally demanding jobs (i.e. emotionally demanding "helper" roles, or jobs that deal with people in stressful situations). The results showed that people who were psychologically healthier in adolescence and early adulthood were more likely to enter, and remain in, such jobs, and they showed greater involvement and satisfaction with their work (Jenkins & Maslach 1994). Given this longitudinal data set, this study was better able to establish possible causal relationships than typical correlational studies can.

SITUATIONAL FACTORS: Where Does Burnout Occur?

Burnout is an individual experience that is specific to the work context. Thus, the research over the past 25 years has maintained a consistent focus on the situational factors that are the prime correlates of this phenomenon. The results of this research paint a clear picture of the impact of the work situation on individual burnout.

Job Characteristics

Quantitative job demands (e.g. too much work for the available time) have been studied by many burnout researchers, and the findings support the general notion that burnout is a response to overload. Experienced workload and time pressure are strongly and consistently related to burnout, particularly the exhaustion dimension. This pattern is found with both self-reports of experienced strain and more objective measures of demands (such as number of hours worked and number of clients).

Studies of qualitative job demands have focused primarily on role conflict and role ambiguity, both of which consistently show a moderate to high correlation with burnout. Role conflict occurs when conflicting demands at the job have to be met, whereas role ambiguity occurs when there is a lack of adequate information to do the job well. Other qualitative job demands (such as the severity of clients' problems) have only been studied occasionally, but the correlations are in the same direction.

In addition to studying the presence of job demands, burnout researchers have investigated the absence of job resources. The resource that has been studied most extensively has been social support, and there is now a consistent and strong body of evidence that a lack of social support is linked to burnout. Lack of support from supervisors is especially important, even more so than support from coworkers. Within the social support literature, there is also a "buffering" hypothesis that suggests that social support should moderate the relationship between job stressors and burnout (i.e. the relationship will be strong when social support is low, but weak when support is high). However, studies of this hypothesis have met with mixed success, and it is not clear whether this outcome is due to methodological or theoretical issues.

Another set of job resources has to do with information and control. A lack of feedback is consistently related to all three dimensions of burnout. Burnout is also higher for people who have little participation in decision making. Similarly, a lack of autonomy is correlated with burnout, although the strength of the relationship is weaker.

Occupational Characteristics

The initial work on burnout developed out of the occupational sector of human services and education (which continues to be the primary focus of burnout studies). Of particular concern in these occupations were the emotional challenges of working intensively with other people in either a caregiving or teaching role. Later research expanded the focus to occupations that included contact with people, but for which the contact fell short of the demands of this more extensive relationship (e.g. managers), and eventually some studies utilized occupations for which contact with people was a lesser consideration (e.g. computer programmers). Although the burnout concept seems to pertain to this wider range of occupations, there was still the hypothesis that the emotional stressors of people-work were something uniquely related to burnout. Earlier research did not find much evidence to support such a hypothesis; instead, common job-related stressors (such as workload, time pressure, or role conflicts) correlated more highly with burnout than client-related stressors (such as problems in interacting with clients, frequency of contact with chronically or terminally ill patients, or confrontation with death and dying). However, new research has focused explicitly on emotion-work variables (e.g. requirement to display or suppress emotions on the job, requirement to be emotionally empathic) and has found that these emotion factors do account for additional variance in burnout scores over and above job stressors (Zapf et al 2001).

Another approach has been to look at the prevalence of burnout for different occupations, as defined by their profiles on the three dimensions. A recent comparison was made of burnout profiles for five occupational sectors (teaching, social services, medicine, mental health, and law enforcement) in two countries (the United States and Holland), and the results revealed similar occupational profiles in both nations (Schaufeli & Enzmann 1998). Profiles of law enforcement (i.e. police officers and prison guards) were characterized by comparatively high levels of cynicism and inefficacy and low levels of exhaustion. Teaching was characterized by the highest level of exhaustion, with both other dimensions close to the nation's average. Medicine in both countries was characterized by somewhat lower levels of exhaustion and cynicism, and by slightly higher levels of inefficacy. However, the profiles of workers in social services and mental health care differed by nation. In the United States, levels of cynicism in the social services were relatively high, whereas they were about average in Holland. Mental health workers in the United States experienced lower levels of exhaustion and cynicism, but in Holland these levels were higher.

Such profiles suggest that there are important characteristics of these occupations that affect workers' experience of burnout. However, these findings need to be viewed with some caution, as there are other factors that could be involved. For example, there is a greater heterogeneity of specific occupations within some sectors than in others, so the overall profiles might be masking important differences. Furthermore, there are confounding variables with some occupations, which need to be taken into account. For example, men predominate in law enforcement occupations, and cynicism is usually higher for males. It is not clear at this point whether the latter findings reflect methodological variations (e.g. in sampling) or substantive national differences (e.g. in nature of job demands or personal selection). Despite these differences in average level, the more noteworthy point is that the basic patterns of burnout are fairly similar across both countries.

Organizational Characteristics

The increasing breadth of occupational sectors has required a rethinking of the situational context for burnout. Prior research has tended to focus on the immediate context in which work occurs, whether that be a nurse's work with patients in a hospital or a teacher's work with students in a school. However, this work often takes place within a larger organization that includes hierarchies, operating rules, resources, and space distribution. All of these factors can have a far-reaching and persistent influence, particularly when they violate basic expectations of fairness and equity. Consequently, the contextual focus has been broadened to include the organizational and management environment in which work occurs. This focus has highlighted the importance of the values implicit in organizational processes and structures, and how these values shape the emotional and cognitive relationship that people develop with their work. This research has important implications for burnout, but because it is still fairly new, a summary of major patterns in the data is not yet warranted.

The organizational context is also shaped by larger social, cultural, and economic forces. Recently, this has meant that organizations have undergone a lot of changes, such as downsizing and mergers, that have had significant effects on the lives of their employees. This is perhaps most evident in changes in the psychological contract—i.e. the belief in what the employer is obliged to provide based on perceived promises of reciprocal exchange (Rousseau 1995). Now employees are expected to give more in terms of time, effort, skills, and flexibility, whereas they receive less in terms of career opportunities, lifetime employment, job security, and so on. Violation of the psychological contract is likely to produce burnout because it erodes the notion of reciprocity, which is crucial in maintaining well being.

INDIVIDUAL FACTORS: Who Experiences Burnout?

People do not simply respond to the work setting; rather, they bring unique qualities to the relationship. These personal factors include demographic variables (such as age or formal education), enduring personality characteristics, and work-related attitudes. Several of these individual characteristics have been found to be related to burnout. However, these relationships are not as great in size as those for burnout and situational factors, which suggests that burnout is more of a social phenomenon than an individual one.

Demographic Characteristics

Of all the demographic variables that have been studied, age is the one that has been most consistently related to burnout. Among younger employees the level of burnout is reported to be higher than it is among those over 30 or 40 years old. Age is confounded with work experience, so burnout appears to be more of a risk earlier in one's career. The reasons for such an interpretation have not been studied very thoroughly. However, these findings should be viewed with caution because of the problem of survival bias—i.e. those who burn out early in their careers are likely to quit their jobs, leaving behind the survivors who consequently exhibit lower levels of burnout.

The demographic variable of sex has not been a strong predictor of burnout (despite some arguments that burnout is more of a female experience). Some studies show higher burnout for women, some show higher scores for men, and others find no overall differences. The one small but consistent sex difference is that males often score higher on cynicism. There is also a tendency in some studies for women to score slightly higher on exhaustion. These results could be related to gender role stereotypes, but they may also reflect the confounding of sex with occupation (e.g. police officers are more likely to be male, nurses are more likely to be female).

With regard to marital status, those who are unmarried (especially men) seem to be more prone to burnout compared with those who are married. Singles seem to experience even higher burnout levels than those who are divorced. As for ethnicity, very few studies have assessed this demographic variable, so it is not possible to summarize any empirical trends.

Some studies have found that those with a higher level of education report higher levels of burnout than less educated employees. It is not clear how to interpret this finding, given that education is confounded with other variables, such as occupation and status. It is possible that people with higher education have jobs with greater responsibilities and higher stress. Or it may be that more highly educated people have higher expectations for their jobs, and are thus more distressed if these expectations are not realized.

Personality Characteristics

Several personality traits have been studied in an attempt to discover which types of people may be at greater risk for experiencing burnout. People who display low levels of hardiness (involvement in daily activities, a sense of control over events, and openness to change) have higher burnout scores, particularly on the exhaustion dimension. Burnout is higher among people who have an external locus of control (attributing events and achievements to powerful others or to chance) rather than an internal locus of control (attributions to one's own ability and effort). Similar results have been reported on coping styles and burnout. Those who are burned-out cope with stressful events in a rather passive, defensive way, whereas active and confrontive coping is associated with less burnout. In particular, confrontive coping is associated with the dimension of efficacy. In other research, all three burnout dimensions have been related to lower self-esteem.

It has been argued that low levels of hardiness, poor self-esteem, an external locus of control, and an avoidant coping style typically constitute the profile of a stress-prone individual (Semmer 1996). Obviously, the results from the burnout research confirm this personality profile.

Research on the Big Five personality dimensions has found that burnout is linked to the dimension of neuroticism. Neuroticism includes trait anxiety, hostility, depression, self-consciousness, and vulnerability; neurotic individuals are emotionally unstable and prone to psychological distress. The exhaustion dimension of burnout also appears to be linked to Type-A behavior (competition, time-pressured lifestyle, hostility, and an excessive need for control). There are also indications that individuals who are "feeling types" rather than "thinking types" (in terms of a Jungian analysis) are more prone to burnout, especially to cynicism.

Job Attitudes

People vary in the expectations they bring to their job. In some cases these expectations are very high, both in terms of the nature of the work (e.g. exciting, challenging, fun) and the likelihood of achieving success (e.g. curing patients, getting promoted). Whether such high expectations are considered to be idealistic or unrealistic, one hypothesis has been that they are a risk factor for burnout. Presumably, high expectations lead people to work too hard and do too much, thus leading to exhaustion and eventual cynicism when the high effort does not yield the expected results. This hypothesis has received mixed empirical support—about half of the studies find the hypothesized correlation, whereas the rest do not. Once again, however, this is an instance where a correlation does not actually test the causal relationship inherent in the hypothesis. Longitudinal studies with repeated measures will be necessary to shed light on this issue.

EXPANDING THE RESEARCH: International Studies

One of the key domains in which burnout research has expanded is in extending beyond its original American borders. At first, the phenomenon drew attention in English-speaking countries, such as Canada and Great Britain. Soon articles, books, and research measures were translated into numerous languages, and subsequently research on burnout emerged in many European countries, as well as Israel.

Because burnout research in these countries started after the concept and measures had been established in the United States, that work built on an already established theoretical and methodological base. Hence, the initial conceptual debate on burnout was less broad, and alternative measures were rarely developed. Given that the MBI had become the instrument of choice to measure burnout in North America, the concept of burnout as operationalized in terms of the MBI was exported to other countries. However, by the 1990s, the intellectual contributions of non-Anglo-Saxon authors in terms of theory, research, and intervention were considerable.

To date, burnout has been studied in many countries around the globe. Interestingly, the term burnout is left untranslated in almost all countries, although literal translations in many cases do exist: *ausgebrannt* (German), *opgebrand* (Dutch), *utbränd* (Swedish), and *utbranthet* (Norwegian), just to name a few.

In most countries, the MBI has simply been translated and its psychometric properties taken for granted. However, some versions, most notably the French (Dion & Tessier 1994), German (Büssing & Perrar 1992), and Dutch (Schaufeli & van Dierendonck 2000) have been extensively studied psychometrically. Generally speaking, foreign language versions of the MBI have similar internal consistencies and show similar factorial and construct validity as the original American version. Moreover, the three-factor structure of the MBI appears to be invariant across different countries.

Despite these similarities in psychometric properties of the MBI measure, there are national differences in the average levels of burnout. For instance, several studies of various European workers have found lower average levels of exhaustion and cynicism, compared with similar North American samples. It is not clear what the explanation might be for these differences, but it might involve different cultural values. Perhaps Europeans are less likely than Americans to respond extremely to self-report questionnaires. Public expression of some aspects of burnout—notably cynicism—may be more socially acceptable in the strongly individualized North American society than it is in Europe, where sentiments of group solidarity play a more significant role. Or it may be that the greater achievement orientation of North American society would cause people to feel more stress about their jobs. An alternative explanation might be that jobs are actually more stressful in North America than in Western Europe. Interestingly, the only European country where burnout levels have been reported to be as high as in North America is Poland, where working conditions are relatively poor compared to Western European standards. It is unlikely that the translation of the MBI can be held responsible for the differences in levels of burnout between North America and Europe, because lower burnout scores were found among nurses in English-speaking European countries (Britain and Ireland) and higher scores were found among nurses in French-Canada (see Schaufeli & Janczur 1994).

Considerable differences within and between countries have also been found in research using the scoring methodology of the phase model of burnout (Golembiewski et al 1996). In 62 samples including over 25,000 North American employees, over 20% of them were judged to be in the most advanced burnout phase. However, the incidence across these samples varied greatly from 1% to 25%. In comparison, data were also collected within 12 countries that were almost exclusively Asian or East European (21 samples of almost 7000 employees). The results indicated that slightly more of these non-Americans were classified in the most advanced burnout phase (28%; range 12%–69%). The highest incidences were found in Japan and Taiwan (between 48% and 69%). Hence, it appears that the lower average burnout scores for Western Europe are not typical for countries in other parts of the world. However, given the variation in sample selection (i.e. the samples were not random and representative), it would be premature to propose strong conclusions about national differences and the possible underlying reasons for them.

EXPANDING THE THEORETICAL FRAMEWORK:
The Person Within Context

Recent work on burnout has begun to develop new theoretical frameworks that more explicitly integrate both individual and situational factors, rather than considering them in separate either-or terms. This call for such an integration is certainly not new. Indeed, there is a long history within psychology of trying to explain behavior in terms of the interaction of person and environment. Many of these interactional models view person and environment as independent entities, but characterize them along commensurate dimensions so that the degree of fit, or congruence, between person and environment can be assessed. This approach is evident in some of the earliest models of job-person fit (e.g. French et al 1974), in which better fit was assumed to predict better adjustment and less stress.

Thus, a model of job-person fit would seem to be an appropriate framework for understanding burnout. However, prior conceptualizations of job-person fit are limited in terms of their direct application to this phenomenon. For example, the person is usually framed in terms of personality or an accurate understanding of the job, rather than in terms of emotions, motivations, or stress responses. Similarly, the job is often defined in terms of specific tasks, and not the larger situation or organizational context. The notion of fit is often presumed to predict such outcomes as choice of job/occupation or of organization (entry issues), or adjustment to the job (newcomer issues). In contrast, burnout involves a later point in the process, when the person has been working for a while and is experiencing a more chronic misfit between self and the job. Thus, the challenge is to extend the job-person paradigm to a broader and more complex conceptualization of the person situated in the job context.

Maslach & Leiter (1997) have begun to address this challenge by formulating a model that focuses on the degree of match, or mismatch, between the person and six domains of his or her job environment. The greater the gap, or mismatch, between the person and the job, the greater the likelihood of burnout; conversely, the greater the match (or fit), the greater the likelihood of engagement with work. One new aspect of this approach is that the mismatch focus is on the enduring working relationship people have with their job. This relationship is similar to the notion of a psychological contract (Rousseau 1995). Mismatches arise when the process of establishing a psychological contract leaves critical issues unresolved, or when the working relationship changes to something that a worker finds unacceptable. Secondly, whereas prior models of job-person fit predict that such fit produces certain outcomes (such as commitment, satisfaction, performance, and job tenure), this new model hypothesizes that burnout is an important mediator of this causal link. In other words, the mismatches lead to burnout, which in turn leads to various outcomes.

This model has brought order to the wide variety of situational correlates by proposing six areas of worklife that encompass the central relationships with burnout: workload, control, reward, community, fairness, and values. Burnout arises from chronic mismatches between people and their work setting in terms of some or all of these six areas. This is a comprehensive model that includes the full range of organizational factors found in research related to burnout. Despite their close interrelationships, each area brings a distinct perspective to the interactions of people with their work settings. These six areas of worklife come together in a framework that encompasses the major organizational antecedents of burnout.

Workload

A mismatch in workload is generally found as excessive overload, through the simple formula that too many demands exhaust an individual's energy to the extent that recovery becomes impossible. A workload mismatch may also result from the wrong kind of work, as when people lack the skills or inclination for a certain type of work, even when it is required in reasonable quantities. Emotional work is especially draining when the job requires people to display emotions inconsistent with their feelings. Generally, workload is most directly related to the exhaustion aspect of burnout.

Control

A mismatch in control is generally related to the inefficacy or reduced personal accomplishment aspect of burnout. Mismatches in control most often indicate that individuals have insufficient control over the resources needed to do their work or have insufficient authority to pursue the work in what they believe is the most effective manner. Individuals who are overwhelmed by their level of responsibility may experience a crisis in control as well as in workload. This mismatch is reflected as one of responsibility exceeding one's authority. It is distressing for people to feel responsible for producing results to which they are deeply committed while lacking the capacity to deliver on that mandate.

Reward

A third type of mismatch involves a lack of appropriate rewards for the work people do. Sometimes these may be insufficient financial rewards, as when people are not receiving the salary or benefits commensurate with their achievements. Even more important at times is the lack of social rewards, as when one's hard work is ignored and not appreciated by others. This lack of recognition devalues both the work and the workers. In addition, the lack of intrinsic rewards (such as pride in doing something of importance and doing it well) can also be a critical part of this mismatch. Lack of reward is closely associated with feelings of inefficacy.

Community

The fourth mismatch occurs when people lose a sense of positive connection with others in the workplace. People thrive in community and function best when they share praise, comfort, happiness, and humor with people they like and respect. In addition to emotional exchange and instrumental assistance, this kind of social support reaffirms a person's membership in a group with a shared sense of values. Unfortunately, some jobs isolate people from each other, or make social contact impersonal. However, what is most destructive of community is chronic and un-resolved conflict with others on the job. Such conflict produces constant negative feelings of frustration and hostility, and reduces the likelihood of social support.

Fairness

A serious mismatch between the person and the job occurs when there is not perceived fairness in the workplace. Fairness communicates respect and confirms people's self-worth. Mutual respect between people is central to a shared sense of community. Unfairness can occur when there is inequity of workload or pay, when there is cheating, or when evaluations and promotions are handled inappropriately. If procedures for grievance or dispute resolution do not allow for both parties to have a voice, then those will be judged as unfair. A lack of fairness exacerbates burnout in at least two ways. First, the experience of unfair treatment is emotionally upsetting and exhausting. Second, unfairness fuels a deep sense of cynicism about the workplace.

Values

The sixth area of mismatch occurs when there is a conflict between values. In some cases, people might feel constrained by the job to do things that are unethical and not in accord with their own values. For example, in order to make a sale or to obtain a necessary authorization, they might have to tell a lie or be otherwise deceptive or not forthcoming with the truth. In other instances, there may be a mismatch between their personal aspirations for their career and the values of the organization. People can also be caught between conflicting values of the organization, as when there is a discrepancy between the lofty mission statement and actual practice, or when the values are in conflict (e.g. high quality service and cost containment do not always co-exist).

Interaction of the Six Areas

Research on this model is beginning to elucidate the relationship between these six areas, as well as their relation to the three dimensions of burnout. Preliminary evidence suggests that the area of values may play a central mediating role for the other areas. Another possibility is that the weighting of the importance of the six areas may reflect an important individual difference. For example, some people might place a higher weight on rewards than on values, and thus might be more distressed by insufficient rewards than by value conflicts. It is not clear how much of a mismatch people are willing to tolerate, and this may depend on both the particular area of mismatch and the pattern of the other five areas. For example, people may be willing to tolerate a mismatch in workload if they receive praise and good pay, work well with their colleagues, feel their work is valuable and important, and so on.

Thus, the mismatches in these six critical areas of organizational life are not simply a list summarizing research findings from burnout studies. Rather, they provide a conceptual framework for the crises that disrupt the relationships people develop with their work. This approach emphasizes the importance of looking at the person in context, in terms of his or her fit with the key domains of worklife.

EXPANDING THE CONSTRUCT: Job Engagement

Traditionally, the focus of psychology has been on negative states rather than on positive ones. In fact, the number of articles examining negative states outnumbers the positive states by a ratio of 17 to 1 (Diener et al 1999). However, more attention is now being paid to the study of human strengths and optimal functioning. This "positive psychology" is seen as an alternative to the predominant focus on pathology and deficits. Viewed from this perspective, it is not surprising that the concept of burnout (which represents a negative psychological state) is being supplemented and enlarged by its positive antithesis of job engagement. Our current work on this concept has taken two different, but related, paths.

Maslach & Leiter (1997) rephrased burnout as an erosion of engagement with the job. What started out as important, meaningful, and challenging work becomes unpleasant, unfulfilling, and meaningless. Energy turns into exhaustion, involvement turns into cynicism, and efficacy turns into ineffectiveness. Accordingly, engagement is characterized by energy, involvement, and efficacy—the direct opposites of the three burnout dimensions. By implication, engagement is assessed by the opposite pattern of scores on the three MBI dimensions.

According to this analysis, engagement is distinct from established constructs in organizational psychology, such as organizational commitment, job satisfaction, or job involvement. Organizational commitment refers to an employee's allegiance to the organization that provides employment. The focus is on the organization, whereas engagement focuses on the work itself. Job satisfaction is the extent to which work is a source of need fulfillment and contentment, or a means of freeing employees from hassles or dissatisfiers; it does not encompass the person's relationship with the work itself. Job involvement is similar to the involvement aspect of engagement with work, but does not include the energy and effectiveness dimensions. Thus, engagement provides a more complex and thorough perspective on an individual's relationship with work.

If engagement is indeed the opposite of burnout, then a profile of engagement scores on the MBI should be associated with a profile of better matches in the six areas of job-person fit. Such a "matched" profile would include a sustainable workload, feelings of choice and control, appropriate recognition and reward, a supportive work community, fairness and justice, and meaningful and valued work. Some empirical support for this conceptualization of engagement is provided by case studies of two hospital units (Maslach & Leiter 1997). The employees in one unit displayed a typical burnout profile (i.e. high scores on exhaustion and cynicism and low scores on efficacy), whereas employees in the other unit had an opposite profile of engagement (i.e. low scores on exhaustion and cynicism and high scores on efficacy). Indeed, and as expected, the former unit showed unfavorable scores on most of the six areas—particularly on reward and values—whereas the latter unit showed predominantly favorable scores—particularly on workload, control, fairness, and values. Thus, it seems that burnout and engagement—operationalized as favorable and unfavorable scores on the MBI, respectively—are inversely related to the six domains of worklife outlined in the previous model.

Schaufeli has taken a different approach to the concept of engagement. Here, engagement is defined and operationalized in its own right. Even though engagement is still conceptualized as the positive antithesis of burnout, there is not the presumption that it is assessed by the opposite profile of MBI scores. Furthermore, burnout and engagement may be considered two prototypes of employee well-being that are part of a more comprehensive taxonomy constituted by the two independent dimensions of pleasure and activation (Watson & Tellegen 1985). According to this framework, burnout is characterized by low levels of activation and pleasure, whereas engagement is characterized by high levels of activation and pleasure.

Based on this theoretical reasoning and on interviews with engaged employees, Schaufeli and his colleagues have defined engagement as a persistent, positive affective-motivational state of fulfillment in employees that is characterized by vigor, dedication, and absorption. Vigor refers to high levels of energy and resilience, the willingness to invest effort in one's job, the ability to not be easily fatigued, and persistence in the face of difficulties. Dedication refers to a strong involvement in one's work, accompanied by feelings of enthusiasm and significance, and by a sense of pride and inspiration. Finally, absorption refers to a pleasant state of total immersion in one's work, which is characterized by time passing quickly and being unable to detach oneself from the job. A self-report questionnaire has been developed to assess engagement that includes items such as: "I feel strong and vigorous in my job" (vigor); "I'm enthusiastic about my job" (dedication); "I feel happy when I'm engrossed in my work" (absorption). Preliminary, unpublished results based on Spanish and Dutch samples show that the three engagement scales have sufficient internal consistencies; they are moderately to strongly related; the fit of the hypothesized three-factor model to the data is superior to a one-factor solution; and all correlations with the MBI burnout scales are negative, with the correlations between engagement and efficacy being the strongest. It is interesting to note that burnout is particularly related to job demands (e.g. work overload, emotional demands), but engagement is particularly related to job resources (e.g. job control, availability of feedback, learning opportunities).

In sum, it seems that broadening the scope by including engagement as the positive antithesis of burnout, either by using the full range of the MBI scores instead of concentrating only on the negative pole, or by using an alternative engagement questionnaire, is a promising avenue that contributes to our understanding of employees' well-being.

IMPLICATIONS FOR INTERVENTION: How Do We Deal with Burnout?

The applied nature of burnout research has prompted calls for effective intervention throughout the research literature. This perspective has encouraged considerable effort, but relatively little systematic research. Various intervention strategies have been proposed—some try to treat burnout after it has occurred, whereas others focus on how to prevent burnout.

Interestingly, most discussions of burnout interventions focus primarily on individual-centered solutions, such as removing the worker from the job, or individual strategies for the worker, in which one either strengthens one's internal resources or changes one's work behaviors. This is particularly paradoxical given that research has found that situational and organizational factors play a bigger role in burnout than individual ones. Individual-oriented approaches (e.g. developing effective coping skills or learning deep relaxation) may help individuals to alleviate exhaustion, but they do not really deal with the other two components of burnout. Also, individual strategies are relatively ineffective in the workplace, where a person has much less control over stressors than in other domains of his or her life. There are both philosophical and pragmatic reasons underlying the predominant focus on the individual, including notions of individual causality and responsibility, and the assumption that it is easier and cheaper to change people than organizations (Maslach & Goldberg 1998).

Changing the Individual

The primary focus of studies of burnout reduction has been educational interventions to enhance the capacity of individuals to cope with the workplace. The goal of these studies is to alleviate burnout (as measured by reductions in MBI scores). Intervention groups generally comprise a relatively small number of participants—usually less than 100. Often, the training has focused on the participants' capacity to cope with challenges as individuals, but some have addressed team-based coping strategies. At the root of this approach are three questions: Can people learn coping skills? Can they apply this learning at work? Do new ways of coping affect burnout?

With respect to the first question, both the stress literature and a burgeoning self-help literature in the popular press have demonstrated that people can indeed learn new ways of coping. The similar conclusion to be drawn from the burnout research is that educational sessions can enhance the capacity of human service professionals to cope with the demands of their jobs.

However, the second question does not receive such a positive answer. Applying new knowledge at work can be a challenge because people are operating under various constraints. Their roles at work require that they behave in specified ways, and organizational procedures stipulate the time and place in which much work occurs. Coworkers are designated according to their job functions, not their personal compatibility. Thus, if there is going to be significant change in the way work is done, it will require a degree of autonomy and an understanding of the organizational consequences of such change.

Assuming that it is indeed possible for people to apply new coping skills at work, does this lead to reductions in burnout? The research findings are mixed. A wide variety of intervention strategies have been tried, including stress inoculation training, relaxation, time management, assertiveness training, rational emotive therapy, training in interpersonal and social skills, teambuilding, management of professional demands, and meditation. In some cases, a reduction in exhaustion has been reported, but in other cases it has not. Rarely do any programs report a change in cynicism or inefficacy. Limitations in study design, especially difficulties in access to appropriate control groups and a lack of longitudinal assessment, have constrained the interpretation of the existing research.

Changing the Organization

In line with the findings from the research literature, a focus on the job environment, as well as the person in it, is essential for interventions to deal with burnout. This suggests that the most effective mode of intervention is to combine changes in managerial practice with the educational interventions described above. Managerial interventions are necessary to change any of the six areas of worklife but are insufficient unless educational interventions convey the requisite individual skills and attitudes. Neither changing the setting nor changing the individuals is enough; effective change occurs when both develop in an integrated fashion.

The recognition of six areas of worklife expands the range of options for organizational intervention. For example, rather than concentrating on the area of work overload for an intervention (such as teaching people how to cope with overload, how to cut back on work, or how to relax), a focus on some of the other mismatches may be more effective. People may be able to tolerate greater workload if they value the work and feel they are doing something important, or if they feel well-rewarded for their efforts, and so an intervention could target these areas of value and reward.

Initial work in this area is encouraging but incomplete. One promising approach focused on the area of fairness and equity. Employees participated in weekly group sessions designed to identify ways of reducing the perceived inequities in their job situation. In comparison with control groups, participants reported a significant decrease in emotional exhaustion at six months and one year after the intervention. These changes were accompanied by increases in perceived equity. Again, however, the other two aspects of burnout did not change relative to baseline levels (van Dierendonck et al 1998).

One advantage of a combined managerial and educational approach to intervention is that it tends to emphasize building engagement with work. The focus on engagement permits a closer alliance with the organizational mission, especially those aspects that pertain to the quality of worklife in the organization. A worksetting that is designed to support the positive development of energy, vigor, involvement, dedication, absorption, and effectiveness among its employees should be successful in promoting their well-being and productivity. Moreover, the statement of a positive goal for intervention—building engagement (rather than reducing burnout)—enhances the accountability of the intervention. Assessing the presence of something is more definite than assessing the absence of its opposite.

Although the potential value of organizational interventions is great, they are not easy to implement. They are often complex in the level of collaboration that is necessary and they require a considerable investment of time, effort, and money. A new approach to such interventions has been designed on the basis of past research and consultation on burnout, and may provide better guidance to organizations for dealing with these issues (Leiter & Maslach 2000).

CONCLUSION

Our goal in this chapter has been to look at both the past and the future of burnout research. With regard to the past, we have tried to provide an overview of how the field has grown and developed over the past 25 years. It is a field that was born out of a social problem, and that has grown towards a more coherent set of theoretical models and empirical studies. It has yet, however, to achieve solutions to the original problem itself, and it is here that the future of burnout research may be most promising. The expanded directions that we outlined in the latter part of the chapter have the potential to make a major breakthrough in our understanding of what burnout is, what causes it, and what we can do about it.

Visit the Annual Reviews home page at www.AnnualReviews.org

LITERATURE CITED

Bakker AB, Schaufeli WB, Demerouti E, Janssen PMP, Van der Hulst R, Brouwer J. 2000. Using equity theory to examine the difference between burnout and depression. *Anxiety Stress Coping* 13:247–68

Burke RJ, Greenglass ER. 2001. Hospital restructuring, work-family conflict and psychological burnout among nursing staff. *Psychol. Health.* In press

Büssing A, Perrar KM. 1992. Die Messung von Burnout. Untersuchung einer deustchen Fassung des Maslach Burnout Inventory

(MBI-D) (The measurement of burnout: investigation on the German version of the MBI). *Diagnostica* 38:328–53

Byrne BM. 1994. Burnout: testing for the validity, replication, and invariance of causal structure across elementary, intermediate, and secondary teachers. *Am. Educ. Res. J.* 31:645–73

Cherniss C. 1980. *Professional Burnout in Human Service Organizations.* New York: Praeger

Cherniss C. 1995. *Beyond Burnout.* New York: Routledge

Cordes CL, Dougherty TW. 1993. A review and an integration of research on job burnout. *Acad. Manage. Rev.* 18:621–56

Diener E, Suh EM, Lucas RE, Smith HI. 1999. Subjective well-being: three decades of progress. *Psychol. Bull.* 125:267–302

Dion G, Tessier R. 1994. Validation de la traduction de l'Inventaire d'épuisement professionnel de Maslach et Jackson (Validation and translation of the burnout inventory of Maslach and Jackson). *Can. J. Behav. Sci.* 26:210–27

Farber BA, ed. 1983. *Stress and Burnout in the Human Services.* New York: Pergamon

Farber BA. 1983. A critical perspective on burnout. See Farber 1983, pp. 1–20

French JRP Jr, Rodgers W, Cobb S. 1974. Adjustment as person-environment fit. In *Coping and Adaptation*, ed. GV Coelho, DA Hamburg, JE Adams, pp. 316–33. New York: Basic Books

Freudenberger HJ. 1975. The staff burnout syndrome in alternative institutions. *Psychother. Theory Res. Pract.* 12:72–83

Freudenberger HJ. 1983. Burnout: contemporary issues, trends, and concerns. See Farber 1983, pp. 23–28

Glass DC, McKnight JD. 1996. Perceived control, depressive symptomatology, and professional burnout: a review of the evidence. *Psychol. Health* 11:23–48

Golembiewski RT, Boudreau RA, Munzenrider RF, Luo H. 1996. *Global Burnout: A World-wide Pandemic Explored by the Phase Model.* Greenwich, CT: JAI Press

Golembiewski RT, Munzenrider R. 1988. *Phases of Burnout: Developments in Concepts and Applications.* New York: Praeger

Greene G. 1961. *A Burnt-out Case.* New York: Viking Press

Jenkins SR, Maslach C. 1994. Psychological health and involvement in interpersonally demanding occupations: a longitudinal perspective. *J. Organ. Behav.* 15:101–27

Lee RT, Ashforth BE. 1996. A meta-analytic examination of the correlates of the three dimensions of job burnout. *J. Appl. Psychol.* 81:123–33

Leiter MP. 1993. Burnout as a developmental process: Consideration of models. See Schaufeli et al 1993, pp. 237–50

Leiter MP, Durup J. 1994. The discriminant validity of burnout and depression: a confirmatory factor analytic study. *Anxiety Stress Coping* 7:357–73

Leiter MP, Maslach C. 1988. The impact of interpersonal environment on burnout and organizational commitment. *J. Organ. Behav.* 9:297–308

Leiter MP, Maslach C. 2000. *Preventing Burnout and Building Engagement: A Complete Program for Organizational Renewal.* San Francisco: Jossey-Bass

Maslach C. 1976. Burned-out. *Hum. Behav.* 5:16–22

Maslach C. 1982. *Burnout: The Cost of Caring.* Englewood Cliffs, NJ: Prentice-Hall

Maslach C. 1998. A multidimensional theory of burnout. In *Theories of Organizational Stress*, ed. CL Cooper, pp. 68–85. Oxford, UK: Oxford Univ. Press

Maslach C, Goldberg J. 1998. Prevention of burnout: new perspectives. *Appl. Prev. Psychol.* 7:63–74

Maslach C, Jackson SE. 1981. The measurement of experienced burnout. *J. Occup. Behav.* 2:99–113

Maslach C, Jackson SE, Leiter MP. 1996. *Maslach Burnout Inventory Manual.* Palo Alto, CA: Consult. Psychol. Press. 3rd ed.

Maslach C, Leiter MP. 1997. *The Truth About Burnout*. San Francisco: Jossey-Bass

Maslach C, Schaufeli WB. 1993. Historical and conceptual development of burnout. See Schaufeli et al 1993, pp. 1–16

Peiro JM, Gonzalez-Roma V, Tordera N, Manas MA. 2001. Does role stress predict burnout over time among health care professionals? *Psychol. Health*. In press

Pines A, Aronson E, Kafry D. 1981. *Burnout: From Tedium to Personal Growth*. New York: Free Press

Rousseau D. 1995. *Psychological Contracts in Organizations: Understanding Written and Unwritten Agreements*. Thousand Oaks, CA: Sage

Schaufeli WB, Bakker AB, Hoogduin K, Schaap C, Kladler A. 2001. The clinical validity of the Maslach Burnout Inventory and the Burnout Measure. *Psychol. Health*. In press

Schaufeli WB, Enzmann D. 1998. *The Burnout Companion to Study & Practice: A Critical Analysis*. Philadelphia: Taylor & Francis

Schaufeli WB, Janczur B. 1994. Burnout among nurses. A Polish-Dutch comparison. *J. Cross-Cult. Psychol.* 25:95–113

Schaufeli WB, Maslach C, Marek T, eds. 1993. *Professional Burnout: Recent Developments in Theory and Research*. Washington, DC: Taylor & Francis

Schaufeli WB, van Dierendonck D. 2000. *Utrechtse Burnout Schaal–UBOS: Handleiding (Utrecht Burnout Scale–UBOS: Testmanual)*. Lisse, Neth.: Swets & Zeitlinger

Semmer N. 1996. Individual differences, work stress, and health. In *Handbook of Work and Health Psychology*, ed. MJ Schabracq, JAM Winnubst, CL Cooper, pp. 51–86. Chichester, UK: Wiley

Shirom A. 1989. Burnout in work organizations. In *International Review of Industrial and Organizational Psychology*, ed. CL Cooper, I Robertson, pp. 25–48. New York: Wiley

van Dierendonck D, Schaufeli WB, Buunk BP. 1998. The evaluation of an individual burnout intervention program: the role of inequity and social support. *J. Appl. Psychol.* 83:392–407

Warr PB. 1987. *Work, Unemployment and Mental Health*. Oxford, UK: Clarendon

Watson D, Tellegen A. 1985. Toward a consensual structure of mood. *Psychol. Bull.* 98:219–35

World Health Organ. 1992. *The ICD-10 Classification of Mental and Behavioral Disorders*. Geneva: WHO

Zapf D, Seifert C, Schmutte B, Mertini H. 2001. Emotion work and job stressors and their effects on burnout. *Psychol. Health*. In press

Annu. Rev. Psychol. 2001. 52:423–52

OLFACTION

Richard L. Doty

*Smell and Taste Center, University of Pennsylvania Medical Center, Philadelphia,
Pennsylvania 19104; e-mail: doty@mail.med.upenn.edu*

Key Words aging, diseases, functional imaging, molecular biology,
pheromones, psychophysics, vomeronasal organ

■ **Abstract** The main and accessory olfactory systems have received considerable attention on the part of scientists and clinicians during the last decade, largely
because of (*a*) quantum advances in understanding their genetically expressed receptor mechanisms, (*b*) evidence that their receptor cells undergo neurogenesis and both
programmed and induced cell death, and (*c*) important technical and practical developments in psychophysical measurement. The latter developments have led to the
proliferation of standardized olfactory testing in laboratories and clinics, and to the
discovery that smell loss is among the first signs of a number of neurodegenerative
diseases, including Alzheimer's disease and Idiopathic Parkinson's disease. Recent
controversial claims that humans possess a functioning vomeronasal system responsive to "pheromones" has added further interest in intranasal chemoreception. This
review focuses on recent progress made in understanding olfactory function, emphasizing transduction, measurement, and clinical findings.

CONTENTS

INTRODUCTION

Most land mammals possess, within their left and right nasal chambers, receptors or elements of five specialized neural systems: (*a*) the main olfactory system (cranial nerve I or CN I), (*b*) the vomeronasal or accessory olfactory system, (*c*) the trigeminal somatosensory system (CN V), (*d*) the septal organ of Masera, and (*e*) the nervus terminalis or terminal nerve (CN O). CN I mediates what we commonly term odor sensations (e.g. rose, chocolate, strawberry, apple, etc) and is responsible, in large part, for the flavor of foods and beverages, as well as numerous other chemically mediated aesthetic perceptions. Additionally, this system serves as an early warning system for spoiled food and noxious or dangerous environmental chemicals. CN V mediates, via both chemical and nonchemical stimuli, somatosensory sensations (e.g. irritation, burning, cooling, and tickling), and induces reflexive responses, such as secretion of mucus and halting of inhalation, that prevent or minimize chemically or thermally induced injury to the nasal and pulmonary passages. The nature of vomeronasal and CN O sensations, if any, are unknown to humans, whereas those of the septal organ—a small patch of neuroepithelial tissue on the anterior ventral nasal septum—are presumably the sensations of CN I in those species that possess this structure. The latter organ, whose histology is similar to that of the main olfactory epithelium, sends its axons to a relatively circumscribed region of the main olfactory bulb (Astic & Saucier 1988) and is electrophysiologically responsive, at least in the rat, to the same sets of stimuli as CN I (Marshall & Maruniak 1986). Although this organ has been well described in rodents, lagomorphs, and marsupials (e.g. the bandicoot, house mouse, deer mouse, Norway rat, hamster, rabbit, and guinea pig), its existence in other mammals has not been established.

CN 0 was discovered after the other cranial nerves had been named and is highly conserved, with remarkably constant anatomy across all vertebrate species, including humans (Schwanzel-Fukuda & Pfaff 1995). Its peripheral component is a loose plexus distinguished by the presence of ganglia at nodal points. This nerve, notable for its high gonadotropin-releasing hormone (GnRH) content, ramifies throughout the nasal epithelium before crossing the nasal mucosa and coursing through the foramina of the cribriform plate medial to the olfactory nerves. In rodents, it converges centrally into three or four rootlets that enter the forebrain caudal to the medial sides of the olfactory bulbs (Schwanzel-Fukuda & Pfaff 1995). It has been suggested that CN O may help modulate the vascular pump that brings stimuli into the accessory olfactory system's vomeronasal organ (VNO), an elongated tubelike structure located at the base of the nasal septum (Wirsig-Wiechmann & Lepri 1991). However, it is consistently present in animals lacking functional main and accessory olfactory systems, such as porpoises (Schwanzel-Fukuda & Pfaff 1995). Despite the possibility that CN O may play a sensory role in some species (Demski 1993), evidence for a chemosensory role is generally lacking. An endocrine role is supported by the fact that deficits in mating behavior occur in male hamsters after its central rootlets are severed, whereas tactile-induced lordosis in female hamsters is facilitated after such lesions (Wirsig-Wiechmann 1997). The GnRH content of the nervus terminalis is regulated, at least in part, by estrogen (Wirsig-Wiechmann & Lee 1999).

This review focuses on the primary and accessory olfactory systems because these are the most salient and widely studied nasal chemosensory systems of vertebrates. These systems employ different projection pathways to different regions of the amygdala and hypothalamus (Scalia & Winans 1975). Advances in practical psychophysical measurement of CN I and attendant findings in humans are presented, along with advances in functional imaging techniques destined to increase our understanding of central olfactory coding. The question of whether humans possess a functioning vomeronasal organ is addressed, and recent studies that further elucidate the function of the vomeronasal organ in nonhuman forms are described.

THE MAIN OLFACTORY SYSTEM (CN I)

General Anatomy

In humans, the sensory receptors of the main olfactory system are located in the upper recesses of the nasal chambers within a neuroepithelium lining the cribriform plate and sectors of the superior turbinate, middle turbinate, and septum. In amphibia, the neuroepithelium is flat and planar, whereas in rodents, carnivores, and many other mammals, it is distributed over a very convoluted surface dictated by the complexity of the turbinal folds arising from the ethmoid bone. The number of ethmoidal turbinates varies among species, extending from one to three in primates to over a dozen in the spiny anteater (*Echidna*). Although only a single row of turbinates—termed ectoturbinates—is found in primates, in many other forms, including most rodent and carnivores, two rows of turbinates are present, the more central row being termed endoturbinates (Negus 1958).

The olfactory epithelium is comprised of at least six morphologically and biochemically distinct cell types (Huard et al 1998), although additional classes of less well-defined microvilli-containing cells have been noted prenatally (Menco & Jackson 1997b) and postnatally (Carr et al 1991). The first cell type—the bipolar sensory receptor neuron—extends odorant receptor–containing cilia into the mucus. The axons of these cells, in aggregate, constitute CN I. In most vertebrates, including humans, the number of receptor cells exceeds that of any other sensory system except vision. Collectively, the surface area of the cilia is quite large, being estimated as exceeding, for example, 22 cm^2 in the human (Doty 1998) and 7 m^2 (not cm!) in the German shepherd dog (Moulton 1977). The second cell type is the supporting or sustentacular cell. These cells, which have microvilli rather than cilia, insulate the bipolar receptor cells from one another and may help regulate the composition of the mucus. They also likely deactivate odorants, as well as help to protect the epithelium from damage from foreign agents. The supporting cells contain xenobiotic-metabolizing enzymes (e.g. cytochrome P-450), a feature shared with the acinar and duct cells of Bowman's glands, the major source of mucus in the olfactory epithelium. The third cell type is the poorly understood microvillar cell located at the surface of the epithelium. Microvillar cells, which look similar to the so-called brush cells found throughout the upper and lower airways of many species, extend axon-like processes to the olfactory bulb and, like the supporting cells, have microvillae at their apical surfaces. In the human, microvillar cells occur in about a 1:10 ratio with the bipolar receptor cells. A chemosensory function of these cells has yet to be demonstrated, and preliminary in vitro patch clamp studies of dissociated microvillar cells have failed to find them responsive to odorants (N Rawson, personal communication). The fourth cell type is the cell that lines the Bowman's glands and ducts, whereas the fifth and sixth cell types are the globose (light) basal cell and horizontal (dark) basal cell—cells located near the basement membrane from which most of the other cell types arise. Recent data suggest that, under conditions of marked damage to the olfactory epithelium, the same type of basal cell, most likely a globose cell, seems to have the potential for giving rise to neurons and nonneural cells, including the horizontal basal cells, implying a multipotency in stem cells not previously recognized (Huard et al 1998).

The cilia of the bipolar receptor cells, which differ from the cilia of the cells making up the respiratory epithelium in being much longer and lacking dynein arms (hence, intrinsic motility), contain the seven domain transmembrane receptors that interact with incoming odorants. In some cases, the transport of odorants through the mucus to the cilia is aided by transporting molecules termed odorant binding proteins. In situ hybridization studies with probes to putative odor receptors of rats and mice suggest the receptors are topographically organized, in these species, into four striplike zones within the olfactory epithelium that roughly parallel the dorsal-vental axis of the cribriform plate (Vassar et al 1993). Approximately 1000 putative odorant receptors are believed to exist, reflecting the expression of the largest known vertebrate gene family—a gene family that accounts for ~1% of all expressed genes (Buck & Axel 1991). In general, putative receptors of a given type are confined to one of the four zones. Menco & Jackson (1997a), employing scanning electron microscopy, have recently shown a possible morphological correlate to these zones—by embryonic day 16, the posterior regions (roughly corresponding to zones 1 and 2) have much higher receptor cell knob densities than the more anterior regions (corresponding to zones 3 and 4). Furthermore, the supporting cell microvilli are longer in region 1 than in region 2, and the tops of cells adjacent to the receptor cells are flatter in regions 1 and 2 than in regions 3 and 4. Regions 3 and 4 also have glandular openings and scattered microvillous cells that resemble hair cells of the inner ear.

In the human, the axons of the ~6 million bipolar receptor cells coalesce into 30–40 fascicles, termed the olfactory fila, which are formed by ensheating glia. The fila traverse the cribriform plate and pia matter, and the axons make connections within the olfactory bulb. It is now believed that the neurotransmitter of the receptor cells is glutamate (Trombley & Shepherd 1993), although the olfactory bulb itself contains a remarkable number of neurotransmitters. In situ hyridization studies have shown that, in the rat and mouse, neurons expressing a given receptor type typically project their axons to one or, at most, two glomeruli—spherical structures within the outer margins of the olfactory bulb (Mombaerts et al 1996). This implies that a given odorant activates a spatially defined or restricted set of glomeruli and that the olfactory code is reflected, at this early stage, not only as different patterns across the mucosa (Kent et al 1995), but across the glomeruli as well (Vassar et al 1994).

The axons of the major second-order neurons—the mitral and tufted cells—come under considerable modulation via inhibitory processes within the bulb, resulting in the sharpening or altering of the neural information at this level. The mitral and tufted cells project directly to the primary olfactory cortex without synapsing with the thalamus. Although commonly divided into "lateral" and "medial" olfactory tracts in textbooks of anatomy, there is no medial tract in primates (Price 1990). The olfactory cortex is comprised of (a) the anterior olfactory nucleus, (b) the prepiriform cortex, (c) the lateral entorhinal cortex, (d) the periamygdaloid cortex (a region contiguous with the underlying amygdala), and (e) the cortical nucleus of the amygdala. Major connections between the primary olfactory cortex and the secondary olfactory cortex in the orbitofrontal region occur via the mediodorsal nucleus of the thalamus, as well as via direct cortico-cortical projections from prorhinal cortex to the posterolateral orbitofrontal region.

Transduction Mechanisms

During the past decade there have been monumental strides in understanding the initial events of olfactory transduction, beginning with the identification of a large gene family that likely encodes olfactory receptors (Buck & Axel 1991). Although a given receptor cell seems to express only one type of receptor derived from a single allele (Chess et al 1994), each cell is electrophysiologically responsive to a wide, but circumscribed, range of stimuli (Holley et al 1974). This implies that a single receptor accepts a range of molecular entities, and that coding occurs via a complex cross-fiber patterning of responses. Odorant binding leads to an inwardly depolarizing current within the cilia of the bipolar receptor cells that ultimately triggers the action potentials that collectively provide the neural code that is deciphered by higher brain centers.

Most, if not all, of the olfactory receptor proteins are linked to the stimulatory guanine nucleotide-binding protein G_{olf} (Jones & Reed 1989). When stimulated, they activate the enzyme adenylate cyclase to produce the second messenger adenosine monophosphate (cAMP) (Lowe et al 1989). G_{olf}-induced cAMP diffuses through the cell and activates cellular depolarization via the opening of cyclic-nucleotide-gated ionic channels and Ca^{2+}-dependent Cl^- or K^+ channels (Restrepo et al 1993, Firestein et al 1991). The amount of adenylate cyclase activity produced by various odorants in a frog ciliary preparation (Sklar et al 1986) is positively correlated with the magnitude of the frog's electro-olfactogram (a surface potential associated with the number of receptors activated; Lowe et al 1989), as well as with the perceived intensity of these same odorants to humans (Doty et al 1990). Some odorants also activate cyclic guanosine monophosphate (cGMP), which is believed to play a role in the modulation of the sensitivity of olfactory receptor neurons, such as during adaptation (Leinders-Zufall et al 1996). Although G proteins other than G_{olf} (e.g. G_{i2} and G_o) have been identified in olfactory receptor cells, they appear not to be involved in early transduction events, likely assisting in such processes as axonal signal propagation, axon sorting, and target innervation (Wekesa & Anholt 1999).

Prior to the discovery of G_{olf}, support for the hypothesis that another G protein, $G_s\alpha$, plays a major role in the initial phases of olfactory transduction in humans came from findings of variably decreased olfactory ability in type Ia pseudohypoparathyroidism (PHP). PHP is a syndrome in which generalized hormone resistance is associated with a deficiency of $G_s\alpha$, as measured in red blood cells (Weinstock et al 1986). However, these patients have other problems that might cause or contribute to their olfactory dysfunction, including an unusual constellation of skeletal and developmental deficits termed Albright hereditary osteodystrophy (AHO). Whereas a more recent study has confirmed that PHP type Ia patients have defective olfaction, patients with type Ib PHP, who have no AHO, no generalized hormone resistance, and normal $G_s\alpha$ activity, also exhibited olfactory dysfunction relative to matched controls (Doty et al 1997a). Furthermore, patients with pseudopseudohypoparathyroidism, who have AHO, no generalized hormone resistance, and deficient $G_s\alpha$ protein activity, were found to have relatively normal olfactory function. These observations do not support the hypothesis that the olfactory dysfunction associated with PHP is the result of generalized $G_s\alpha$ protein deficiency and imply that other mechanisms are responsible for the olfactory deficits of this disorder. Whether G_{olf} is deficient in the olfactory epithelia of PHP patients has not been determined.

Although it is generally thought that some odorants activate a second transduction pathway in vertebrates (namely, that associated with the activation of the enzyme phospholipase C to produce the second messenger inositol triphosphate or IP_3) (Breer & Boekhoff 1991), recent data suggest this may not be the case, at least in mice (Gold 1999). The discordant studies have employed knockout mice in which genes responsible for both the cyclic-nucleotide-gated ion channel and for G_{olf} have been deleted. In the channel knockout mouse, electro-olfactogram responses to all odors tested were eliminated, including those previously believed to be mediated by the IP_3 system (Brunet et al 1996). To date, IP_3-gated channels have not been demonstrated in mammalian olfactory nerve cells using patch clamp techniques (Firestein et al 1991, Lowe & Gold 1993).

A significant development in understanding the nature of olfactory transduction is the functional characterization of odorant receptors themselves. Several approaches have been employed. Zhao et al (1998) used an adenovirus-mediated gene transfer procedure to increase the expression of a specific receptor gene in an increased number of receptor neurons in the rat olfactory epithelium, demonstrating ligand-specific increases in electro-olfactogram amplitude. Krautwurst et al (1998) employed a polymerase chain reaction strategy to generate an olfactory receptor library from which cloned receptors were screened for odorant-induced responsiveness to a panel of odorants, as measured by an assay sensitive to intracellular Ca^{2+} changes. Several receptor types with ligand specificity were found, including one differentially sensitive to the $(-)$ and $(+)$ stereoisomers of citronella.

Olfactory Receptor Cell Regeneration

An important ongoing revolution in the field of olfaction is the elucidation of the nature of degeneration and regeneration within the olfactory neuroepithelium. Unlike the sensory neurons of other major systems, those of the olfactory epithelium have a propensity to replace themselves after injury. Although it was long thought—largely on the basis of [^{3}H]thymidine studies—that the olfactory neuroepithelium undergoes complete cell turnover every 30 or so days (Graziadei & Monti Graziadei 1979), recent data suggest that the situation is much more complex. Thus, many receptor cells are relatively long-lived despite continuous neurogenesis within the olfactory epithelium (Hinds et al 1984), and both endogenous and exogenous factors promote receptor cell death or replenishment from progenitor stem cells (Mackay-Sim & Kittel 1990). Interestingly, the receptor cells of older animals appear to live longer than those of younger animals (Weiler & Farbman 1999b).

Biochemical or mechanical stress appears to induce subgroups of stem cells to differentiate into mature olfactory receptor cells (Feron et al 1999), and differentiated neurons send back regulatory signals that inform the neuronal progenitor cells as to the numbers of new neurons that need to be produced to maintain equilibrium in the cell population (Calof et al 1998b). Importantly, apoptotic cell death has been observed in cells representing all stages of regeneration (e.g. in proliferating neuronal precursors, immature olfactory receptor neurons, and mature olfactory receptor neurons), implying that apoptotic regulation of neuronal numbers may occur at multiple stages of the neuronal lineage (Holcomb et al 1995). Recently, it has been shown that the mitral cells of the bulb may contain a trophic substance that helps to maintain the survival of olfactory receptor neurons (Weiler & Farbman 1999a). Chemical factors that inhibit (e.g. fibroblast growth factor-2, bone morphogenetic proteins, dopamine) or promote (e.g. transforming growth factor-alpha, olfactory marker protein) neurogenesis or differentiation, or actively produce apoptotic cascades (e.g. tumor necrosis factor-alpha, Fas ligand), are currently under active investigation (Calof et al 1998a, Goldstein et al 1997, Shou et al 1999, Farbman et al 1999, MacDonald et al 1996).

It is noteworthy that the olfactory ensheathing cells, which form the bundles of axons that make up the fila containing the olfactory receptor cell axons that traverse the cribriform plate and constitute the outermost layer of the olfactory bulb, have been found to have unique properties useful in repair or regeneration of both central and peripheral nerves. They exhibit, for example, both Schwann cell–like and astrocyte-like properties, and have been shown to enhance remyelination and axonal conduction in demyelinated spinal tract nerves, as well as in the joining of severed rat sciatic nerves (Verdú et al 1999, Imaizumi et al 1998).

Functional Imaging Studies of the Human Olfactory System

The advent of functional imaging procedures such as positron emission tomography, single photon emission computed tomography, and functional magnetic resonance imaging (fMRI) now makes it possible to establish, in vivo, brain regions activated by odors, as well as by the act of sniffing. Although the spatial resolution of these imaging techniques limits the degree to which activity in some structures can be visualized (e.g. the olfactory bulbs), odor-induced activation of most of the major olfactory-related cortical structures has been observed, albeit in some cases sporadically. This includes the piriform cortex, the orbitofrontal cortex, and the inferior frontal lobe (Koizuka et al 1994, Zatorre et al 1992, Dade et al 1998, Yousem et al 1997). Recently, Sobel et al (2000) demonstrated that inconsistent activation of primary olfactory cortex in fMRI studies likely reflects sampling factors and the time course of activation in these regions. Their data, along with those from animal studies, suggest that rapid habituation occurs in the primary olfactory cortex despite continued odorant presentation and detection. By employing statistical procedures sensitive to temporal changes in signal variability and magnitude, these authors have demonstrated that consistent fMRI-related activation of primary olfactory cortex structures can be obtained.

fMRI studies demonstrating decreased relative activation with age and less activation in men than in women are in accord with psychophysical findings (Yousem et al 1999b,c). Interestingly, an early positron emission tomography study found that the right orbitofrontal cortex was more activated by odorants than the contralateral homologous orbitalfrontal cortex, whereas the medial temporal lobes were symmetrically activated (Zatorre et al 1992). This suggested the hypothesis that some right hemisphere structures may be more specialized than corresponding structures in the left hemisphere in encoding olfactory information. Greater right-than left-side activation has been observed in subsequent studies, including those employing single photon emission computed tomography (Malaspina et al 1998) and fMRI (Yousem et al 1997, Terashima 1988), although reports of greater left than right activation for aversive stimuli, as well as equal activation for other stimuli, have also appeared (Koizuka et al 1994, Zald & Pardo 1997). Interestingly, psychophysical findings of better right than left performance on tests of odor discrimination and memory (but not detection-threshold sensitivity) have also been reported (Zatorre & Jones-Gotman 1991; RL Doty, unpublished).

Recently, Royet et al (2000) performed a positron emission tomography study to establish whether different odor-related cognitive tasks activated different central olfactory structures. Regional cerebral blood flow was determined in 15 normal participants under 3 yes/no conditions in which they reported whether an odor was (a) present (control detection task), (b) familiar, or (c) edible. The authors hypothesized that the detection task required a superficial judgment that did not involve stored representations of odors, whereas the other two tasks, respectively, required the activation of perceptual and perceptual plus semantic neural representations of odors. Thus, a hierarchy of complexity (and thus breadth of activation) was hypothesized: detection task > familiarity task > edibility task. In some analyses, the detection task activation was subtracted from the activation of the other two conditions, whereas in one the familiarity task activation was subtracted from that of the edibility task. These subtractions were done to better define the unique activation of each of the two presumed higher-order conditions. Although their general hierarchy theory was not supported, these investigators found that the familiarity judgments were mainly associated with increased regional cerebral blood flow in the right orbitofrontal area, the subcallosal gyrus, the left inferior and superior frontal gyri, and the anterior cingulate cortices. Edibility judgments selectively activated the primary visual areas, suggesting that visual imagery was evoked by this task. In contrast, decreased regional cerebral blood flow occurred in the visual regions under the familiarity judgment task, and in the orbitofrontal regions under the edibility task. This pioneering study suggests that orbital regions are involved in judgments of odor quality, and that orbitofrontal and visual cortices may interact with one another in some types of odor-related tasks.

An intriguing discovery from several functional imaging studies is that odors reliably and significantly activate regions of the human cerebellum, a structure classically considered to be involved mainly in motor learning (Sobel et al 1998a,b; Yousem et al 1997). Whereas there are early clinical reports of olfactory dysfunction in patients with tumors near the cerebellum (Tucker 1911, Peregud 1931), the cerebellar activity was unexpected and serendipitous in light of current knowledge of the olfactory projection pathways and views of the cerebellum. Interestingly, other functional imaging studies have now implicated the cerebellum in a broad range of sensory and cognitive processing tasks (Kim et al 1994, Gao et al 1996, Hanamori et al 1986). In a detailed assessment of the influences of odor on fMRI-determined cerebellar activity, Sobel et al (1998b) found that odorants activated, in a concentration-dependent manner, largely posterior lateral areas of the cerebellum. On the other hand, sniffing blank air activated mainly anterior central cerebellar regions. Generalizing a model proposed by Bower et al (1981) to explain tactile activation of the cerebellum, Sobel et al (1998b, p. 8998) suggested the hypothesis that "the cerebellum is monitoring incoming data (odorant concentration) and adjusting the position of the stimulus (odorant air stream) relative to the sensory surface (olfactory epithelium) by controlling the motor behavior (sniff), in real time."

Development of Standardized Psychophysical Tests of Human Olfactory Function

Advances in the technology of psychophysical measurement and the proliferation of easy-to-use tests of olfactory function have significantly increased our understanding of the sense of smell in humans, including the functional influences of such factors as age, gender, exposure to toxic agents, and various disease states. During the past decade, standardized and practical psychophysical tests have become widely employed, with several becoming commercially available. Such tests include the 40-odor University of Pennsylvania Smell Identification Test (UPSIT; known commercially as the Smell Identification Test™ or SIT) (Doty et al 1984b, Doty 1995), the 12-odor Brief-Smell Identification Test™ (also known as the Cross-Cultural Smell Identification Test™) (Doty et al 1996), the 3-odor Pocket Smell Test™ (Doty et al 1995), the 12-item Odor Memory Test™ (Doty et al 1995b, Bromley & Doty 1995b), the Odor Confusion Matrix Test (Wright 1987), the San Diego Odor Identification Test (Anderson et al 1992), the Scandinavian Odor Identification Test (Nordin et al 1999), the "Sniff 'n Sticks" test (Hummel et al 1997), the Viennese Olfactory Test Battery (Lehrner & Deecke 1999), an 8-odor identification test (Simmen et al 1999), and several tests of odor threshold, including the T&T olfactometer test (Takagi 1989) and the Smell Threshold Test™ (Doty 2000).

Of these tests, the UPSIT has proved to be the most popular, having been administered to ∼180,000 people in Europe and North America. This highly reliable (test-retest $r = 0.94$) (Doty et al 1989), self-administered microencapsulated odorant test employs norms based upon nearly 4000 persons, and is available in English, Spanish, French, and German versions (Doty et al 1984b, Doty 1995). The UPSIT was the impetus for a massive smell function survey sent to nearly 11 million subscribers of *National Geographic* in 1986 (Gibbons 1986, Gilbert & Wysocki 1987).

Application of Standardized Psychophysical Tests to Normal and Clinical Populations

Major nonclinical findings of the past decade and a half that have been derived from such tests, primarily the UPSIT, include the following: (*a*) women, on average, have a better sense of smell than men—superiority that spans cultures and is noticable as early as four years of age (Doty 1986; Doty et al 1984a, 1985; Liu et al 1995); (*b*) there is a substantial genetic influence on the ability of humans to identify odors (Segal et al 1992, 1995); (*c*) major loss of olfactory function occurs after age 65, with over half of those between 65 and 80, and over three quarters of those 80 years of age and older, having such loss (Doty et al 1984a, Ship & Weiffenbach 1993, Liu et al 1995); (*d*) women, on average, retain the ability to smell longer than men (Doty et al 1984a); (*e*) the decrement in olfactory function associated with smoking is present in former smokers and recovery to presmoking levels, while possible, can take years, depending upon the duration and amount of past smoking (Frye et al 1990); and (*e*) olfactory function is compromised in urban residents and workers in some industries, including the paper and chemical manufacturing industries (Schwartz et al 1989, 1990, 1991; Ahman et al 1996; Hirsch & Zavala 1999).

Clinical studies employing such methodology during this period have found—to one degree or another—decreased smell function, relative to matched controls, in a wide variety of diseases and conditions, as listed in Table 1. It is noteworthy that such tests have also found that a number of disorders are not associated with meaningful smell losses, including corticobasal degeneration (Wenning et al 1995), depression (Amsterdam et al 1987), panic disorder (Kopala & Good 1996), progressive supranuclear palsy (Wenning et al 1995, Doty et al 1993), 1-methyl-4-phenyl-1,2,3,6-tetrahydropyridine (MPTP)-induced parkinsonism (Doty et al 1992a), essential tremor (Busenbark 1991), and multiple chemical hypersensitivity (Doty et al 1988a). Such findings suggest that smell dysfunction can aid in differential diagnosis among several neurodegenerative disorders, especially those that present with clinical signs similar to those of Alzheimer's disease, Parkinson's disease, and schizophrenia. McCaffrey et al (2000) have recently shown that even the 3-item Pocket Smell Test[TM] discriminates better between patients with Alzheimer's disease and major affective disorder (i.e. depression) than the widely used 30-item Mini-Mental State Examination.

The ability to quantify olfactory function using the aforementioned tests, along with advances in in vivo medical imaging, has allowed for a better understanding of the underlying reasons for olfactory loss in some patients. We now know, for example, that congenitally anosmic individuals typically lack, or have markedly deformed, olfactory bulbs and stalks, as determined from MRI studies (Yousem et al 1996a). Furthermore, patients who have head trauma–related smell loss typically exhibit contusions of the frontal and temporal poles of the brain, as well as a decrease in the size of their olfactory bulbs and tracts (Doty et al 1997c, Yousem et al 1996b). The latter finding may reflect mitigation of trophic factors from the olfactory receptor neurons, which are often sheared off or otherwise damaged in head trauma cases. The olfactory dysfunction associated with chronic alcoholism has been found to be correlated with MRI-determined (*a*) increased cortical and ventricular cerebral spinal fluid volumes and (*b*) reduced volumes of the thalamus and of cortical and subcortical gray matter (Shear et al 1992). In multiple sclerosis, a strong inverse correlation ($r = -0.94$) has been observed between UPSIT scores and the number of MRI-determined plaques within central brain structures associated with olfactory processing (inferior frontal and temporal lobes)—a correlation not present when plaque numbers in other brain regions were similarly examined (Doty et al 1997b, 1998). A 1:1 association was recently observed, longitudinally, between UPSIT scores and the remission and exacerbation of such plaque numbers in each of 5 multiple sclerosis patients tested over an 18- to 20-month period, with greater numbers of plaques reflecting lower UPSIT scores (Doty et al 1999). Hence, discrepant findings among studies evaluating olfactory function in multiple sclerosis patients likely reflects the waxing and waning, over time, of plaques in central olfactory structures.

TABLE 1   Examples of medical conditions or disorders associated with olfactory dysfunction, as measured by modern quantitative tests of olfactory function, particularly the UPSIT

Medical condition	References
Alcoholism and drug abuse	DiTraglia et al 1991, Kesslak et al 1991,
Amyotrophic lateral sclerosis (ALS)	Sajjadian et al 1994, Hawkes et al 1998
Attention deficit/hyperactivity disorders	Gansler et al 1998
Alzheimer's disease	Corwin & Serby 1985, Doty et al 1987, Murphy et al 1990, Kesslak et al 1988, Mesholam et al 1998, Graves et al 1999
Anorexia nervosa—severe stage	Fedoroff et al 1995
Breast cancer-estrogen receptor positive	Lehrer et al 1985
Chemical exposure	Schwartz et al 1989, 1990, Hirsch & Zavala 1999
Chronic obstructive pulmonary disease	Dewan et al 1990
Cystic fibrosis	Weiffenbach & McCarthy 1984
Down's syndrome	Warner et al 1988, McKeown et al 1996, Murphy & Jinich 1996
Epilepsy and temporal lobe resection	Martinez et al 1993, West et al 1993
Guam ALS/PD/dementia	Doty et al 1991, Ahlskog et al 1998
Head trauma	Deems et al 1991, Duncan & Seiden 1995, Doty et al 1997c, Yousem et al 1999a
Human immunodeficiency virus (HIV)	Brody et al 1991, Razani et al 1996, Hornung et al 1999
Huntington's disease	Bylsma et al 1997, Moberg & Doty 1997
Kallmann's syndrome	Yousem et al 1993
Korsakoff's psychosis	Mair et al 1986
Multiple sclerosis (MS)	Doty et al 1997b, 1998, 1999; Hawkes et al 1997b
Multiple system atrophy	Wenning et al 1995
Nasopharyngeal carcinoma	Hua et al 1999
Parkinson's disease	Doty et al 1988b, 1992b, 1995a; Hawkes et al 1997a Mesholam et al 1998
Pseudoparahypothyroidism	Doty et al 1997b
Psychopathy	Lapierre et al 1995

TABLE 1   *(Continued)*

Medical condition	References
Restless leg syndrome	Adler et al 1998
Rhinosinusitis	Akerlaud et al 1995, Apter et al 1995, Cowart et al 1993, Deems et al 1991, Downey et al 1996, Golding-Wood et al 1996, Lane et al 1996
Schizophrenia	Moberg et al 1997; Purdon 1998; Striebel et al 1999; Kopala et al 1995, 1998; Seidman et al 1991; Stedman & Clair 1998
Schizophrenia-like affective disorders	Striebel et al 1999
Schizotypy	Park & Schoppe 1997
Seasonal affective disorder	Postolache et al 1999
Sjögren's syndrome	Weiffenbach et al 1995
Surgical/radiological interventions	Friedman et al 1999, Hua et al 1999, Golding-Wood et al 1996, el Naggar et al 1995

Several studies suggest that smell loss —particularly in conjunction with other risk factors such as the APOE-$\epsilon4$ allele— may be a predictor of subsequent development of Alzheimer's disease, or at least of cognitive dysfunction, in older persons. Furthermore, there is circumstantial evidence that estrogen therapy in later life may protect against or decrease such loss in a manner perhaps analogous to its effects on some measures of cognitive function (Deems et al 1991, Dhong et al 1999, Henderson 1997). In a recent epidemiological study of 1604 nondemented, community-dwelling senior citizens 65 years of age or older, scores on the 12-item Brief-Smell Identification Test^{TM} were a better predictor of cognitive decline over a subsequent 2-year period than scores on a global cognitive test (Graves et al 1999). Persons who were anosmic and possessed at least one APOE-$\epsilon4$ allele had 4.9 times the risk of having cognitive decline than normosmic persons not possessing this allele (i.e. an odds ratio of 4.9). This is in contrast to the 1.23 times greater risk for cognitive decline in normosmic individuals possessing at least one such APOE allele. When the data were stratified by sex, women who were anosmic and possessed at least one APOE-$\epsilon4$ allele had an odds ratio of 9.71, compared to an odds ratio of 1.90 for women who were normosmic and possessed at least one allele. The corresponding odds ratios for men were 3.18 and 0.67, respectively. The authors noted, "Therefore, a simple test of olfaction may be more useful in clinical practice to predict cognitive decline than a test of global cognition."

THE ACCESSORY/VOMERONASAL OLFACTORY SYSTEM

Largely as a result of a series of provocative anatomical and electrophysiological studies (for review, see Monti-Bloch et al 1998), there has been considerable recent speculation as to whether humans possess a functional accessory olfactory system. Indeed, one study has suggested that human "pheromones" modulate menstrual cycle length via this system (Stern & McClintock 1998). As is discussed below, however, the weight of the evidence is against the notion that humans have a functioning accessory olfactory system, despite the fact that most individuals possess a ventrally-located rudimentary vomeronasal tube near the nasal septum.

General Anatomy

Receptors for the accessory olfactory system are found within the vomeronasal organ (VNO), a tube-like structure surrounded by cartilage at the base of each nasal chamber that is present in most amphibia, reptiles, and mammals (Keverne 1999). It is absent in birds, fishes, and Old World Monkeys. The accessory olfactory system, termed the vomeronasal organ complex by Cooper & Bhatnagar (1976), consists of not only the epithelial tubular VNO, but the vomeronasal duct that opens into the VNO, seromucous glands that secrete into the lumen of the organ, paravomeronasal ganglia lying adjacent to the VNO neuroepithelium, blood vessels adjacent to the epithelium, vomeronasal nerve bundles, the vomeronasal cartilage, the accessory olfactory bulbs, and central connections of the bulbs. The underdevelopment or lack of development of any of these structures results in a nonfunctional VNO (Bhatnagar & Meisami 1998). Based on numerous comparative studies, Bhatnagar & Meisami (1998, p. 467) noted that

> No entire class of vertebrates exists in which the VNO is consistently and invariably found in all species within that group in a structurally well-developed and presumably fully functional manner. The mere presence of one or the other vomeronasal structures, almost always the vomeronasal epithelial tubular organ . . . does not qualify for a functionally sound sensory organ. In order for the vomeronasal system to be functional, a vomeronasal nerve and accessory olfactory bulb must also be present. It thus appears that variability from complete lack to full development of the vomeronasal organ complex is an inherent evolutionary characteristic of the accessory olfactory system in tetrapods.

In most species that have been examined, the VNO is sexually dimorphic in the adult (larger in males than in females), reflecting the organizational action of sex steroids during the early postnatal period (Segovia & Guillamón 1982). The left and right VNOs are filled with fluid from vomeronasal glands and are separated from one another by the nasal septum. The VNO neuroepithelium, like that of the main olfactory system, is comprised of neural, supporting, microvillar, and basal cells. As in the case of the main olfactory epithelium, chemicals are sensed by bipolar receptor cells embedded in the epithelium lining the medial concave side of the organ. Unlike the olfactory receptor cells, however, the VNO receptor cells of adult organisms lack cilia, instead containing microvillae upon which seven-transmembrane chemoreceptors are located. The large blood vessels and sinuses along the lateral wall of the VNO, whose engorgement is controlled largely by the autonomic nervous system, can induce a pumplike action for bringing materials into the organ (Meredith et al 1980). Depending upon the species, entrance of chemicals into the VNO occurs via ducts from the anterior nasal or oral cavities. Stimulus access to the VNO is enhanced in some forms by distinct behaviors, such as the flehmen response—a characteristic lip-curling and snorting behavior in which the external nares are closed. This behavior is frequently seen in cows, horses, deer, and sheep as the male samples the female's urine stream prior to estrus (Crump et al 1984).

The axons from the VNO's sensory neurons project through the vomeronasal nerve, which typically runs along the base of the olfactory bulbs to the accessory olfactory bulb (AOB), the first relay of the system. Recent data suggest that this system, unlike the main olfactory system, may be active only postnatally, at least in mice, because transneuronal tracers do not label mitral cells within the AOB prior to that time (Horowitz et al 1999). Like the VNO proper, the AOB is sexually dimorphic, being larger in males than in females (Segovia & Guillamón 1993). Dendritic processes of mitral cells within the AOB communicate, via glomeruli, with the axonal terminals of the bipolar receptor cells. Axons of a given class of receptors converge onto numerous glomeruli with the AOB (Rodriguez et al 1999). The axons of the mitral cells project via a fiber bundle to the "vomeronasal amygdala," consisting of the medial and posteromedial cortical amygdaloid nuclei and the nucleus of the accessory olfactory tract (Kevetter & Winans 1981). The terminations within the medial nuclei are adjacent, but separate, from those from CN I projections, and this nucleus connects through the stria terminalis to the medial preoptic region of the hypothalamus.

Even though, as mentioned above, nearly all adult humans possess paired VNO-like structures at the base of the septum and paired VNO ducts ~15–20 mm from the posterior aspect of the external nares, the human VNO appears to be a "simple epithelial tube" relative to the well-developed VNO of other species (Smith & Bhatnagar 2000). Recent research indicates that the human VNO appears to develop a pseudo-stratified epithelium and to lose receptor cells and their associated neural elements in the second trimester of pregnancy (Smith & Bhatnagar 2000). The adult human VNO has a comparatively homogeneous epithelium along both its medial and lateral aspects, in contrast to the receptor-rich medial and receptor-free (but vascular-rich) lateral elements of the VNOs of other organisms. Adult human VNOs contain cilia (which are present only in the early embryonic stages of VNO development in most species) and short microvillae, unlike the elongated microvillae typical of other VNOs.

Although the epithelia of human VNOs express immunoreactivity to molecular markers characteristic of neurons [i.e. neuron-specific enolase and protein gene product 9.5], the density of such neurons is comparatively sparse (Takami et al 1993), and antibodies against olfactory marker protein—a marker for functional bipolar receptor cells—have failed to reveal olfactory marker protein–expressing cells in the human VNO. Whereas Takami et al (1993) suggested that the neuron-specific enolase and protein gene product–labeled epithelial cells were vomeronasal receptor neurons, Johnson (1998) has suggested that the immuno-labeled cells are likely neuroendocrine cells. The observation that the human VNO is spatially separated from the paraseptal cartilages has led some to question whether it is, in fact, homologous with the VNO of other mammals (Smith & Bhatnagar 2000). Although there is a suggestion of local electrophysiological responsiveness within the human VNO (Monti-Bloch et al 1998), attempts to trace neural connections from this organ to the brain have been uniformly unsuccessful (Bhatnagar et al 1987, Meisami & Bhatnagar 1998). The lack of a VNO nerve and associated accessory olfactory bulb in postnatal humans is in stark contrast to the clearly delineated VNO nerves and accessory olfactory bulbs present in other mammals with functioning VNOs. Because the postnatal human VNO appears to lack basic elements necessary for a functioning VNO (e.g. the elements of the "vomeronasal organ complex" delineated by Cooper & Bhatnagar (1976), it is most likely a nonfunctional entity (Bhatnagar & Meisami 1998).

Transduction Mechanisms

Two large multigene families of G-protein-linked receptors have been identified within the mouse VNO that are only distally related to the multigene family involved in CN I odor receptors (Dulac & Axel 1995, Ryba & Tirindelli 1997), implying that the VNO responds to somewhat different classes of stimuli. The two VNO gene families—V1R and V2R—are also considerably smaller than the gene family involved in CN I odor receptor induction, implying less diversity in the types of stimuli that can be detected. The first of the VNO gene families has $G_{i\alpha 2}$ protein–linked receptors located in the apical regions of the VNO, whose cells project to glomeruli within the anterior region of the accessory olfactory bulb (Jia & Halpern 1996). Exposure of male mice to bedding soiled by female mice appears to selectively activate this region of the accessory olfactory bulb (Dudley & Moss 1999). The receptors of the second VNO gene family express $G_{o\alpha}$ and are located in the basal region of the VNO. The cells containing these receptors project to glomeruli in the posterior accessory olfactory bulb. Like olfactory receptor neurons, each bipolar receptor cell appears to express only one type of receptor (Dulac & Axel 1995). Recent data suggest that the two classes of receptors may differentially respond to volatile and non-volatile agents (Krieger et al 1999). Thus, upon stimulation with lipophilic volatile agents from mouse urine, only G_i proteins were activated. Upon stimulation with a major urinary protein of the lipocalin superfamily, only G_o proteins were activated.

Electrophysiologically, the cells within the VNO tend to fire in a sustained manner, in contrast to the cells within the main olfactory epithelium, which fire in single pulses or bursts (Døving & Trotier 1998). The sustained firing may maximize the summed neural activity induced on central structures from even brief exposures to biologically active chemicals, allowing for the induction of endocrine effects (Keverne 1999).

Vomeronasal Organ Cell Regeneration

Considerably less is known about the regenerative properties of the VNO than those of the primary olfactory mucosa. After unilateral transection of the vomeronasal nerves in the adult hamster, the receptor cells degenerate, reaching 16% of the original number 6 days after the transection. Although cell numbers return to normal after 40 to 60 days, thickness of the epithelium never recovers beyond 70% of the control thickness (Ichikawa et al 1998). From 12 to 32 weeks after transection, less than a third of projection fibers appear to make synaptic contacts within the anterior olfactory nucleus, implying that full recovery from total transection does not occur (Ichikawa 1999).

Recent Studies of Vomeronasal Organ Function

It has been known for some time that the VNO plays a role, either exclusively or in combination with CN I, in a number of reproduction-related phenomena. Data, primarily from rodents, suggests VNO participation in a variety of endocrine responses and social related behaviors, including (a) estrous synchrony or regulation (Johns et al 1978), (b) blockage of ova implantation following exposure to "strange" (i.e. nonstud) male odor (Lloyd-Thomas & Keverne 1982), (c) activation of reproduction and male-induced sexual receptivity (Wysocki et al 1991, Rajendren et al 1990), (d) acceleration of puberty (Lomas & Keverne 1982), (e) male copulatory behavior (Wekesa & Lepri 1994, Winans & Powers 1974), (f) nursing behavior (Saito et al 1990), (g) attraction to odors of the opposite sex (Romero et al 1990), and (h) various forms of male agonistic behavior (Wekesa & Lepri 1994).

Knowledge of VNO activity across a wide range of species is still limited. Recent data suggest that the VNO does not mediate a widely touted "pheromonal" effect in pigs and that, even within the same genus of vole, the VNO may have opposite effects on reproductive behaviors. Thus, Dorries et al (1997) have demonstrated that inactivating the VNO has no influence on either the female pig's attraction to androstenone, one of the few mammalian secretions that has been widely described as a pheromone, or the facilitative effects of this steriod on receptive standing behavior (lordosis). If one accepts the notion that, in fact, mammalian pheromones exist (which is debatable), and that androstenone is a pheromone, then this observation would throw into question the concept that the VNO can be considered, in a general sense, as "the" pheromone detector in mammals (Belluscio et al 1999). Although the VNO appears to mediate the induction of behavioral estrus in prairie voles (*Microtus ochrogaster*) by male odors (Wysocki et al 1991), this is not the case in meadow voles (*M. pennsylvanicus*), a species believed to be a spontaneous ovulator. Meek et al (1994) removed the VNO from nulliparous female meadow voles maintained under long photoperiods simulating summer (14 h light: 10 h dark) and short photoperiods simulating winter (10 h light: 14 h dark). Under the winter lighting condition, the VNO removal had no influence on either the percentage of animals mating or the latency to copulation. Under the summer lighting condition, removal of the organ actually increased the percentage of the females mating and decreased the latency to mating after pairing.

Re-establishment of mating behavior in the male hamster whose VNO has been removed occurs following injection of gonadotropin-releasing hormone (GnRH), implying that stimulation of the VNO is needed to produce GnRH at levels high enough to allow for the activation of sexual behavior (Meredith & Howard 1992). GnRH's influences may be mediated independently of the pituitary, however, since the GnRH analog, AcLHRH5-10, which does not induce luteinizing hormone release, facilitates mating behavior in hamsters whose VNOs have been removed (Fernandez-Fewell & Meredith 1995). Bilateral lesions within the corticomedial nucleus of the amygdala (a major projection center of the VNO) eliminates or greatly attenuates male mating behavior, and mitigates investigatory sniffing and licking behavior directed toward the female hamster's anogenital region (Lehman et al 1980). This result is not secondary to decreases in testosterone, as testosterone injections do not restore normal mating behavior (Lehman et al 1980). Whether GnRH restores mating behavior in rats with such lesions is apparently not known but would seem probable.

CONCLUSIONS

Remarkable progress has been made in the past decade in understanding the function of both the main and accessory olfactory systems. The development of proliferation of practical and reliable olfactory tests has spurned an awakening on the part of the medical community as to the important role of olfaction in a wide range of clinical disorders, and has led to the realization that olfactory loss is likely the first clinical sign of some neurodegenerative diseases. The application of new technologies, including those of molecular biology and functional imaging, are beginning to unravel the mysteries of both peripheral and central coding, and should lead, within the next decade, to a rather complete understanding of olfactory system function. Studies of vomeronasal function are continuing in a wide range of species, and the complexity of behaviors influenced by the accessory olfactory system is now beginning to be realized.

ACKNOWLEDGMENTS

This paper was supported, in part, by Research Grants PO1 DC 00161, RO1 DC 04278, and RO1 DC 02974 from the National Institute on Deafness and Other Communication Disorders, and RO1 AG17496 from the National Institute on Aging, National Institutes of Health, Bethesda, MD, USA. I thank Lloyd Hastings, David Kareken, Igor Kratskin, Paul Moberg, Noam Sobel, and Greg Smutzer for their comments on a previous version of the manuscript.

GLOSSARY OF BASIC ANATOMICAL TERMS

Accessory olfactory system: The chemosensory system that includes the paired vomeronasal organs located on each side of the ventral nasal septum, the vomeronasal nerve, the accessory olfactory bulb, and central connections. In mammals, this system has been implicated in numerous reproduction-related processes. Although humans exhibit a rudimentary set of vomeronasal organs, they lack the other neural components of the system.

Basal cells: Cells located at the base of the olfactory and vomeronasal organ epithelia from which the other cell types of the epithelia arise. In the olfactory epithelium, such cells are divided into globose (light) and horizontal (dark) basal cells, the former of which appear to give rise to both neural and nonneural elements of the epithelium.

Bowman's glands: Secretory glands within the olfactory epithelum that produce most of the mucus of this region. These glands contain xenobiotic metabolizing enzymes that protect the region from toxic and other insults and may aid in deactivating odorants.

Cribriform plate: A thin section of the ethmoid bone that separates the upper nasal cavity from the brain cavity. The olfactory nerve fibers project through this bone from the nasal cavity to the brain.

Main olfactory system: The chemosensory system that is most commonly associated, in vertebrates, with the sense of smell. This system is comprised of the olfactory receptor cells, the paired olfactory bulbs and tracts at the base of the brain, and central processing structures, including regions of the piriform, entorhinal, and orbitofrontal cortices.

Microvillar cells: Bell-shaped cells located at the surface of the olfactory epithelium that project microvillae into the mucus. Although these cells appear to possess axons that extend through the cribriform plate into the olfactory bulb, it is not known whether they are chemoreceptive.

Nasal turbinates: The projections of thin bone from the lateral wall of the nasal cavity that are covered by highly vascularized mucous membrane and, in the human, are designated as superior, middle, or inferior. Also termed nasal conchae. The engorgement of these structures, which aid in the cleansing, warming, and humidification of the nasal airstream, is altered by environmental (e.g. air temperature) and organismal (e.g. hormones) factors. In humans, much of the olfactory epithelium is located on the superior and middle nasal turbinates.

Nervus terminalis: A plexus of nerves and ganglia that ramify throughout the nasal epithelum before crossing the olfactory mucosa and coursing through the cribriform plate medial to the olfactory and vomeronasal nerves. Also known as the terminal nerve or cranial nerve 0. Noted for its high content of GnRH (a hormone that has major influences on the reproductive organs), the nervus terminalis plays a significant role in reproduction in some species.

Olfactory bulbs: Paired oval structures at the base of the brain from which the olfactory tracts arise and that serve as the first relay station of the olfactory system. These structures, which have distinct layers of neurons and related cells, are involved in the initial processing of olfactory information.

Olfactory cortex: Regions of the cerebral cortex that interpret and transmit information coming in from lower centers. The olfactory cortex is divided into the primary olfactory cortex (i.e. brain regions receiving information from the olfactory bulb, such as the entorhinal, piriform, and periamygdala cortices) and secondary olfactory cortex, most notably the orbitofrontal cortex.

Olfactory epithelium: The sensory neuroepithelium that contains the olfactory receptor cells and that lines the upper recesses of the nasal cavity, including, in humans, sectors of the superior and middle turbinates.

Olfactory receptor cells: Ciliated bipolar neurons within the olfactory neuroepithelium that possess the olfactory receptors where initial odor reception takes place. These cells are both the receptor cell and the first-order neuron of the olfactory system, and project their axons from the nasal cavity into the brain. Humans have ~six million olfactory receptor cells that, in aggregate, comprise cranial nerve I.

Septal organ: A small region of neuroepithelial tissue found on the anterior ventral nasal septum in some species, also known as the organ of Masera. This structure, whose epithelium is similar to that of the main olfactory system, sends axons to a small sector of the olfactory bulb and is believed by some to be the first chemosensory structure to be activated by incoming molecules.

Trigeminal chemosensory system: Those branches of cranial nerve V whose free nerve endings, largely located in mucosal tissue within the nose and sinuses, oral cavity, eyelids, and cornea, can be activated by chemicals. Somatosensory sensations, such as burning, stinging, sharpness, and coolness, are produced by chemical activation of fibers within this system.

Vomeronasal Organ: A tubelike structure located adjacent to the anterior ventral nasal septum of most vertebrates (also termed Jacobson's organ). This organ contains the receptors that activate the other components of the accessory olfactory system. Depending upon the species, the vomeronasal organ typically has openings into either the nasal cavity or the oral cavity, and is responsive to both liquid-borne and airborne chemical stimuli.

Visit the Annual Reviews home page at www.AnnualReviews.org

LITERATURE CITED

Adler CH, Gwinn KA, Newman S. 1998. Olfactory function in restless legs syndrome. *Mov. Disord.* 13:563–65

Ahlskog JE, Waring SC, Petersen RC, Estenban-Santillan C, Craig UK, et al. 1998. Olfactory dysfunction in Guamanian ALS, parkinsonism, and dementia. *Neurology* 51:1672–77

Ahman M, Holmstrom M, Cynkier I, Soderman E. 1996. Work related impairment of nasal function in Swedish woodwork teachers. *Occup. Environ. Med.* 53:112–17

Akerlund A, Bende M, Murphy C. 1995. Olfactory threshold and nasal mucosal changes in experimentally induced common cold. *Acta Oto-Laryngol.* 115:88–92

Amsterdam JD, Settle RG, Doty RL, Abelman E, Winokur A. 1987. Taste and smell perception in depression. *Biol. Psychiatry* 22:1481–85

Anderson J, Maxwell L, Murphy C. 1992. Odorant identification testing in the young child. *Chem. Senses* 17:590

Apter AJ, Mott AE, Frank ME, Clive JM. 1995. Allergic rhinitis and olfactory loss. *Ann. Allergy Asthma Immunol.* 75:311–16

Astic L, Saucier D. 1988. Topographical projection of the septal organ to the main olfactory bulb in rats: ontogenetic study. *Dev. Brain Res.* 42:297–303

Belluscio L, Koentges G, Axel R, Dulac C. 1999. A map of pheromone receptor activation in the mammalian brain. *Cell* 97:209–20

Bhatnagar KP, Kennedy RC, Baron G, Greenberg RA. 1987. Number of mitral cells and the bulb volume in the aging human olfactory bulb: a quantitative morphological study. *Anat. Rec.* 218:73–87

Bhatnagar KP, Meisami E. 1998. Vomeronasal organ in bats and primates: extremes of structural variability and its phylogenetic implications. *Microsc. Res. Tech.* 43:465–75

Bower JM, Beermann DH, Giberson JM, Shambes GM, Welker W. 1981. Principles of organization of a cerebro-cerebellar circuit: micromapping the projections from the cerebral (SI) to cerebellar (granule cell layer) tactile areas of rats. *Brain Behav. Evol.* 18:1–18

Breer H, Boekhoff I. 1991. Odorants of the same odor class activate different second messenger pathways. *Chem. Senses* 16:19–29

Brody D, Serby M, Etienne N, Kalkstein DS. 1991. Olfactory identification deficits in HIV infection. *Am. J. Psychiatry* 148:248–50

Bromley SM, Doty RL. 1995. Odor recognition memory is better under bilateral than unilateral test conditions. *Cortex* 31:25–40

Brunet LJ, Gold GH, Ngai J. 1996. General anosmia caused by a targeted disruption of the mouse olfactory cyclic nucleotide-gated cation channel. *Neuron* 17:681–93

Buck L, Axel R. 1991. A novel multigene family may encode odorant receptors: a molecular basis for odor recognition. *Cell* 65:175–87

Busenbark KL, Huber SI, Greer G, Pahwa R, Koller WC. 1991. Olfactory function in essential tremor. *Neurology* 42:1631–32

Bylsma FW, Moberg PJ, Doty RL, Brandt J. 1997. Odor identification in Huntington's disease patients and asymptomatic gene carriers. *J. Neuropsychiatr. Clin. Neurosci.* 9:598–600

Calof AL, Mumm JS, Rim PC, Shou J. 1998a. The neuronal stem cell of the olfactory epithelium. *J. Neurobiol.* 36:190–205

Calof AL, Rim PC, Askins KJ, Mumm JS, Gordon MK, et al. 1998b. Factors regulating neurogenesis and programmed cell death in mouse olfactory epithelium. *Ann. NY Acad. Sci.* 30:226–29

Carr VM, Farbman AI, Colletti LM, Morgan JI. 1991. Identification of a new non-neuronal cell type in rat olfactory epithelium. *Neuroscience* 45:433–49

Chess A, Simon I, Cedar H, Axel R. 1994. Allelic inactivation regulates olfactory receptor gene expression. *Cell* 78:823–34

Cooper JG, Bhatnagar KP. 1976. Comparative anatomy of the vomeronasal organ complex in bats. *J. Anat.* 122:571–601

Corwin J, Serby M. 1985. Olfactory recognition deficit in Alzheimer's and Parkinsonian dementias. *IRCS Med. Sci.* 13:260

Cowart BJ, Flynn-Rodden K, McGready SJ, Lowry LD. 1993. Hyposmia in allergic rhinitis. *J. Allergy Clin. Immunol.* 91:747–51

Crump D, Swigar AA, West JR, Silverstein RM, Muller-Schwarze D, Altieri R. 1984. Urine fractions that release flehmen in black-tailed deer, *Odocoileus hemionus columbianus. J. Chem. Ecol.* 10:203–15

Dade LA, Jones-Gotman M, Zatorre RJ, Evans AC. 1998. Human brain function during odor encoding and recognition. A PET activation study. *Ann. NY Acad. Sci.* 855:572–74

Deems DA, Doty RL, Settle RG, Moore-Gillon V, Shaman P, et al. 1991. Smell and taste disorders, a study of 750 patients from the University of Pennsylvania Smell and Taste Center. *Arch. Otolaryngol. Head Neck Surg.* 117:519–28

Demski LS. 1993. Terminal nerve complex. *Acta Anat.* 148:81–95

Dewan NA, Bell CW, Moore J, Anderson B, Kirchain W, O'Donohue WJ Jr. 1990. Smell and taste function in subjects with chronic obstructive pulmonary disease. Effect of long-term oxygen via nasal cannulas. *Chest* 97:595–97

Dhong HJ, Chung SK, Doty RL. 1999. Estrogen protects against 3-methylindole-induced olfactory loss. *Brain Res.* 824:312–15

DiTraglia GM, Press DS, Butters N, Jernigan TL, Cermak LS, et al. 1991. Assessment of olfactory deficits in detoxified alcoholics. *Alcohol* 8:109–15

Dorries KM, Adkins-Regan E, Halpern BP. 1997. Sensitivity and behavioral responses to the pheromone androstenone are not mediated by the vomeronasal organ in domestic pigs. *Brain Behav. Evol.* 49:53–62

Doty RL. 1986. Gender and endocrine-related influences upon olfactory sensitivity. In *Clinical Measurement of Taste and Smell*, ed. HL Meiselman, RS Rivlin, pp. 377–413. New York: Macmillan

Doty RL. 1995. *The Smell Identification Test^{TM} Administration Manual.* Haddon Heights, NJ: Sensonics

Doty RL. 1998. Cranial nerve I: olfaction. In *Textbook of Clinical Neurology*, ed. CG Goltz, EJ Pappert, pp. 90–101. Philadelphia: Saunders

Doty RL. 2000. *Odor Threshold Test^{TM} Administration Manual.* Haddon Heights, NJ: Sensonics

Doty RL, Applebaum S, Zusho H, Settle RG. 1985. Sex differences in odor identification ability: a cross-cultural analysis. *Neuropsychologia* 23:667–72

Doty RL, Bromley SM, Stern MB. 1995a. Olfactory testing as an aid in the diagnosis of Parkinson's disease: development of optimal discrimination criteria. *Neurodegeneration* 4:93–97

Doty RL, Deems DA, Frye RE, Pelberg R, Shapiro A. 1988a. Olfactory sensitivity, nasal resistance, and autonomic function in patients with multiple chemical sensitivities. *Arch. Otolaryngol. Head Neck Surg.* 114:1422–27

Doty RL, Deems DA, Stellar S. 1988b. Olfactory dysfunction in parkinsonism: a general deficit unrelated to neurologic signs, disease stage, or disease duration. *Neurology* 38:1237–44

Doty RL, Fernandez AD, Levine MA, Moses A, McKeown DA. 1997a. Olfactory dysfunction in type I pseudohypoparathyroidism: dissociation from $G_s\alpha$ protein deficiency. *J. Clin. Endocrinol. Metabol.* 82:247–50

Doty RL, Frye RE, Agrawal U. 1989. Internal consistency reliability of the fractionated and whole University of Pennsylvania Smell

Identification Test. *Percept. Psychophys.* 45:381–84

Doty RL, Golbe LI, McKeown DA, Stern MB, Lehrach CM, Crawford D. 1993. Olfactory testing differentiates between progressive supranuclear palsy and idiopathic Parkinson's disease. *Neurology* 43:962–65

Doty RL, Kreiss DS, Frye RE. 1990. Human odor intensity perception: correlation with frog epithelial adenylate cyclase activity and transepithelial voltage response. *Brain Res.* 527:130–34

Doty RL, Li C, Mannon LJ, Yousem DM. 1997b. Olfactory dysfunction in multiple sclerosis. *N. Engl. J. Med.* 336:1918–19

Doty RL, Li C, Mannon LJ, Yousem DM. 1998. Olfactory dysfunction in multiple sclerosis: relation to plaque load in inferior frontal and temporal lobes. *Ann. NY Acad. Sci.* 855:781–86

Doty RL, Li C, Mannon LJ, Yousem DM. 1999. Olfactory dysfunction in multiple sclerosis: relation to longitudinal changes in plaque numbers in central olfactory structures. *Neurology* 53:880–82

Doty RL, Marcus A, Lee WW. 1996. Development of the 12-item cross-cultural smell identification test (CC-SIT). *Laryngoscope* 106:353–56

Doty RL, McKeown DA, Lee WW, Shaman P. 1995b. A study of the test-retest reliability of ten olfactory tests. *Chem. Senses* 20:645–56

Doty RL, Perl DP, Steele JC, Chen KM, Pierce JD Jr, et al. 1991. Odor identification deficit of the parkinsonism-dementia complex of Guam: equivalence to that of Alzheimer's and idiopathic Parkinson's disease. *Neurology* 41:77–80

Doty RL, Reyes PF, Gregor T. 1987. Presence of both odor identification and detection deficits in Alzheimer's disease. *Brain Res. Bull.* 18:597–600

Doty RL, Shaman P, Applebaum SL, Giberson R, Siksorski L, Rosenberg L. 1984a. Smell identification ability: changes with age. *Science* 226:1441–43

Doty RL, Shaman P, Dann M. 1984b. Development of the University of Pennsylvania Smell Identification Test: a standardized microencapsulated test of olfactory function. *Physiol. Behav.* 32:489–502 (Monogr.)

Doty RL, Singh A, Tetrude J, Langston JW. 1992a. Lack of olfactory dysfunction in MPTP-induced parkinsonism. *Ann. Neurol.* 32:97–100

Doty RL, Stern MB, Pfeiffer C, Gollomp SM, Hurtig HI. 1992b. Bilateral olfactory dysfunction in early stage treated and untreated idiopathic Parkinson's disease. *J. Neurol. Neurosurg. Psychiatry* 55:138–42

Doty RL, Yousem DM, Pham LT, Kreshak AA, Geckle R, Lee WW. 1997c. Olfactory dysfunction in patients with head trauma. *Arch. Neurol.* 54:1131–40

Døving KB, Trotier D. 1998. Structure and function of the vomeronasal organ. *J. Exp. Biol.* 201:2913–25

Downey LL, Jacobs JB, Lebowitz RA. 1996. Anosmia and chronic sinus disease. *Arch. Otolaryngol. Head Neck Surg.* 115:24–28

Dudley CA, Moss RL. 1999. Activation of an anatomically distinct subpopulation of accessory olfactory bulb neurons by chemosensory stimulation. *Neuroscience* 91:1549–56

Dulac C, Axel R. 1995. A novel family of genes encoding putative pheromone receptors in mammals. *Cell* 83:195–206

Duncan HJ, Seiden AM. 1995. Long-term follow-up of olfactory loss secondary to head trauma and upper respiratory tract infection. *Arch. Otolaryngol. Head Neck Surg.* 121:1183–87

el Naggar M, Kale S, Aldren C, Martin F. 1995. Effect of Beconase nasal spray on olfactory function in post-nasal polypectomy patients: a prospective controlled trial. *J. Laryngol. Otol.* 109:941–44

Farbman AI, Bucholtz JA, Suzuki Y, Coines A, Speert D. 1999. A molecular basis of cell death in olfactory epithelium. *J. Comp. Neurol.* 414:306–14

Fedoroff IC, Stoner SA, Andersen AE, Doty RL, Rolls BJ. 1995. Olfactory dysfunction in anorexia and bulimia nervosa. *Int. J. Eating Dis.* 18:71–77

Fernandez-Fewell GD, Meredith M. 1995. Facilitation of mating behavior in male hamsters by LHRH and AcLHRH5-10: interaction with the vomeronasal system. *Physiol. Behav.* 57:213–21

Feron F, Mackay-Sim A, Andrieu JL, Matthaei KI, Holley A, Sicard G. 1999. Stress induces neurogenesis in non-neuronal cell cultures of adult olfactory epithelium. *Neuroscience* 88:571–83

Firestein S, Darrow B, Shepherd GM. 1991. Activation of the sensory current in salamander olfactory receptor neurons depends on a G protein-mediated cAMP second messenger system. *Neuron* 6:825–35

Friedman M, Tanyeri H, Landsberg R, Caldarelli D. 1999. Effects of middle turbinate medialization on olfaction. *Laryngoscope* 109:1442–45

Frye RE, Schwartz BS, Doty RL. 1990. Dose-related effects of cigarette smoking on olfactory function. *JAMA* 263:1233–36

Gansler DA, Fucetola R, Krengel M, Stetson S, Zimering R, Makary C. 1998. Are there cognitive subtypes in adult attention deficit/hyperactivity disorder? *J. Nerv. Ment. Dis.* 186:776–81

Gao JH, Parsons LM, Bower JM, Xiong J, Li J, Fox PT. 1996. Cerebellum implicated in sensory acquisition and discrimination rather than motor control. *Science* 272:545–47

Gilbert AN, Wysocki CJ. 1987. The smell survey results. *Natl. Geogr.* 172:514–25

Gold GH. 1999. Controversial issues in vertebrate olfactory transduction. *Annu. Rev. Physiol.* 61:857–71

Golding-Wood DG, Holmstrom M, Darby Y, Scadding GK, Lund VJ. 1996. The treatment of hyposmia with intranasal steroids. *J. Laryngol. Otol.* 110:132–35

Goldstein BJ, Wolozin BL, Schwob JE. 1997. FGF2 suppresses neuronogenesis of a cell line derived from rat olfactory epithelium. *J. Neurobiol.* 33:411–28

Graves AB, Bowen JD, Rajaram L, McCormick

WC, McCurry SM, et al. 1999. Impaired olfaction as a marker for cognitive decline: interaction with apolipoprotein E epsilon4 status. *Neurology* 53:1480–87

Graziadei PPC, Monti Graziadei AG. 1979. Neurogenesis and neuron regeneration in the olfactory system of mammals: I. Morphological aspects of differentiation and structural organization of the olfactory sensory neurons. *J. Neurocytol.* 8:1–18

Hanamori T, Nakashima M, Ishiko N. 1986. Responses of cerebellar cortex to electrical stimulation of the glossopharyngeal nerve in the frog. *Neurosci. Lett.* 68:345–50

Hawkes CH, Shephard BC, Daniel SE. 1997a. Olfactory dysfunction in Parkinson's disease. *J. Neurol. Neurosurg. Psychiatry* 62:436–46

Hawkes CH, Shephard BC, Geddes JF, Body GD, Martin JE. 1998. Olfactory disorder in motor neuron disease. *Exp. Neurol.* 150:248–53

Hawkes CH, Shephard BC, Kobal G. 1997b. Assessment of olfaction in multiple sclerosis: evidence of dysfunction by olfactory evoked response and identification tests. *J. Neurol. Neurosurg. Psychiatry* 63:145–51

Henderson VW. 1997. The epidemiology of estrogen replacement therapy and Alzheimer's disease. *Neurology* 48:S27–S35

Hinds JW, Hinds PL, McNelly NA. 1984. An autoradiographic study of the mouse olfactory epithelium: evidence for long-lived receptors. *Anat. Rec.* 210:375–83

Hirsch AR, Zavala G. 1999. Long-term effects on the olfactory system of exposure to hydrogen sulphide. *Occup. Environ. Med.* 56:284–87

Holcomb JD, Mumm JS, Calof AL. 1995. Apoptosis in the neuronal lineage of the mouse olfactory epithelium: regulation in vivo and in vitro. *Dev. Biol.* 172:307–23

Holley A, Duchamp A, Revial MF, Juge A. 1974. Qualitative and quantitative discrimination in the frog olfactory receptors: analysis from electrophysiological data. *Ann. NY Acad. Sci.* 237:102–14

Hornung DE, Kurtz DB, Bradshaw CB, Seipel

DM, Kent PF, et al. 1999. The olfactory loss that accompanies HIV infection. *Physiol. Behav.* 64:549–56

Horowitz LF, Montmayeur JP, Echelard Y, Buck LB. 1999. A genetic approach to trace neural circuits. *Proc. Natl. Acad. Sci. USA* 96:3194–99

Hua MS, Chen ST, Tang LM, Leung WM. 1999. Olfactory function in patients with nasopharyngeal carcinoma following radiotherapy. *Brain Injury* 13:905–15

Huard JMT, Youngentob SL, Goldstein BJ, Luskin MB, Schwob JE. 1998. Adult olfactory epithelium contains multipotent progenitors that give rise to neurons and non-neural cells. *J. Comp. Neurol.* 400:469–86

Hummel T, Sekinger B, Wolfe SR, Pauli F, Kobal G. 1997. 'Sniffin' Sticks': olfactory performance assessed by the combined testing of odor identification, odor discrimination and olfactory threshold. *Chem. Senses* 22:39–52

Ichikawa M. 1999. Axonal growth of newly formed vomeronasal receptor neurons after nerve transection. *Anat. Embryol.* 200:413–17

Ichikawa M, Osada T, Costanzo RM. 1998. Replacement of receptor cells in the hamster vomeronasal epithelium after nerve transection. *Chem. Senses* 23:171–79

Imaizumi T, Lankford KL, Waxman SG, Greer CA, Kocsis JD. 1998. Transplanted olfactory ensheathing cells remyelinate and enhance axonal condition in the demyelinated dorsal columns of the rat spinal cord. *J. Neurosci.* 18:6176–85

Jia C, Halpern M. 1996. Subclasses of vomeronasal receptor neurons: differential expression of G proteins ($G_{i\alpha2}$ and G $_{(o\alpha2)}$) and segregated projections to the accessory olfactory bulb. *Brain Res.* 719:117–28

Johns MA, Feder HH, Komisaruk BR, Mayer AD. 1978. Urine-induced reflex ovulation in anovulatory rats may be a vomeronasal effect. *Nature* 272:446–48

Johnson EW. 1998. CaBPs and other immunohistochemical markers of the

human vomeronasal system: a comparison with other mammals. *Microsc. Res. Tech.* 41:530–41

Jones DT, Reed RR. 1989. G_{olf}: an olfactory neuron specific-G protein involved in odorant signal transduction. *Science* 244:790–95

Kent PF, Youngentob SL, Sheehe PR. 1995. Odorant-specific spatial patterns in mucosal activity predict perceptual differences among odorants. *J. Neurophysiol.* 74:1777–81

Kesslak JP, Cotman CW, Chui HC, van den Noort S, Fang H, et al. 1988. Olfactory tests as possible probes for detecting and monitoring Alzheimer's disease. *Neurobiol. Aging* 9:399–403

Kesslak JP, Profitt BF, Criswell P. 1991. Olfactory function in chronic alcoholics. *Percept. Motor Skills* 73:551–54

Keverne EB. 1999. The vomeronasal organ. *Science* 286:716–20

Kevetter GA, Winans SS. 1981. Connections of the corticomedial amygdala in the golden hamster: I. Efferents of the "vomeronasal amygdala." *J. Comp. Neurol.* 197:81–98

Kim SG, Ugurbil K, Strick PL. 1994. Activation of a cerebellar output nucleus during cognitive processing. *Science* 265:949–51

Koizuka I, Yano H, Nagahara M, Mochizuki R, Seo R, et al. 1994. Functional imaging of the human olfactory cortex by magnetic resonance imaging. *J. Oto-Rhino-Laryngol. Relat. Spec.* 56:273–75

Kopala LC, Good K, Honer WG. 1995. Olfactory identification ability in pre- and postmenopausal women with schizophrenia. *Biol. Psychiatry* 38:57–63

Kopala LC, Good KP. 1996. Olfactory identification ability in patients with panic disorder. *J. Psychiatry Neurosci.* 21:340–42

Kopala LC, Good KP, Koczapski AB, Honer WG. 1998. Olfactory deficits in patients with schizophrenia and severe polydipsia. *Biol. Psychiatry* 43:497–502

Krautwurst D, Yau KW, Reed RR. 1998. Identification of ligands for olfactory receptors by functional expression of a receptor library. *Cell* 95:917–26

Krieger J, Schmitt A, Lobel D, Gudermann T, Schultz G, et al. 1999. Selective activation of G protein subtypes in the vomeronasal organ upon stimulation with urine-derived compounds. *J. Biol. Chem.* 274:4655–62

Lane AP, Zweiman B, Lanza DC, Swift D, Doty RL, et al. 1996. Acoustic rhinometry in the study of the acute nasal allergic response. *Ann. Otol. Rhinol. Laryngol.* 105:811–18

Lapierre D, Braun CM, Hodgins S. 1995. Ventral frontal deficits in psychopathy: neuropsychological test findings. *Neuropsychologia* 33:139–51

Lehman MN, Winans SS, Powers JB. 1980. Medial nucleus of the amygdala mediates chemosensory control of male hamster sexual behavior. *Science* 210:557–60

Lehrer S, Levine E, Bloomer WD. 1985. Abnormally diminished sense of smell in women with oestrogen receptor positive breast cancer. *Lancet* 2:333

Lehrner J, Deecke L. 1999. Die Wiener Olfaktorische Testbatterie (WOTB). *Akt. Neurol.* 26:1–8

Leinders-Zufall T, Shepherd GM, Zufall F. 1996. Modulation by cyclic GMP of the odour sensitivity of vertebrate olfactory receptor cells. *Proc. R. Soc. London Ser. B* 263:803–11

Liu HC, Wang SJ, Lin KP, Lin KN, Fuh JL, Teng EL. 1995. Performance on a smell screening test (the MODSIT): a study of 510 predominantly illiterate Chinese subjects. *Physiol. Behav.* 58:1251–55

Lloyd-Thomas A, Keverne EB. 1982. Role of the brain and accessory olfactory system in the block to pregnancy in mice. *Neuroscience* 7:907–13

Lomas DE, Keverne EB. 1982. Role of the vomeronasal organ and prolactin in the acceleration of puberty in female mice. *J. Reprod. Fertil.* 66:101–7

Lowe G, Gold GH. 1993. Contribution of the ciliary cyclic nucleotide-gated conductance to olfactory transduction in the salamander. *J. Physiol.* 462:175–96

Lowe G, Nakamura T, Gold GH. 1989. Adeny-late cyclase mediates olfactory transduction for a wide variety of odorants. *Proc. Natl. Acad. Sci. USA* 86:5641–45

MacDonald KP, Murrell WG, Bartlett PF, Bushell GR, Mackay-Sim A. 1996. FGF2 promotes neuronal differentiation in explant cultures of adult and embryonic mouse olfactory epithelium. *J. Neurosci. Res.* 44:27–39

Mackay-Sim A, Kittel PW. 1990. On the life span of olfactory receptor neurons. *Eur. J. Neurosci.* 3:209–15

Mair RG, Doty RL, Kelly KM, Wilson CS, Langlais PJ, et al. 1986. Multimodal sensory discrimination deficits in Korsakoff's psychosis. *Neuropsychologia* 24:831–39

Malaspina D, Perera GM, Lignelli A, Marshall RS, Esser PD, et al. 1998. SPECT imaging of odor identification in schizophrenia. *Psychiatr. Res.* 82:53–61

Marshall DA, Maruniak JA. 1986. Masera's organ responds to odorants. *Brain Res.* 366:329–32

Martinez BA, Cain WS, de Wijk RA, Spencer DD, et al. 1993. Olfactory function before and after temporal lobe resection for intractable seizures. *Neuropsychology* 7:351–63

McCaffrey RJ, Duff K, Solomon GS. 2000. Olfactory dysfunction discriminates probable Alzheimer's dementia from major depression: a cross validation and extension. *J. Neuropsychiatry Clin. Neurosci.* 12:29–33

McKeown DA, Doty RL, Perl DP, Frye RE, Simms I, Mester AF. 1996. Olfactory function in young adolescents with Down's syndrome. *J. Neurol. Neurosurg. Psychiatry* 61:412–14

Meek LR, Lee TM, Rogers EA, Hernandez RG. 1994. Effect of vomeronasal organ removal on behavioral estrus and mating latency in female meadow voles (*Microtus pennsylvanicus*). *Biol. Reprod.* 51:400–4

Meisami E, Bhatnagar KP. 1998. Structure and diversity in mammalian accessory olfactory bulb. *Microsc. Res. Tech.* 43:476–99

Menco BP, Jackson JE. 1997a. A banded topography in the developing rat's olfactory epithelial surface. *J. Comp. Neurol.* 388:293–306

Menco BP, Jackson JE. 1997b. Cells resembling hair cells in developing rat olfactory and nasal respiratory epithelia. *Tissue Cell* 29:707–13

Meredith M, Howard G. 1992. Intracerebroventricular LHRH relieves behavioral deficits due to vomeronasal organ removal. *Brain Res. Bull.* 29:75–79

Meredith M, Marques DM, O'Connell RO, Stern FL. 1980. Vomeronasal pump: significance for male hamster sexual behavior. *Science* 207:1224–26

Mesholam RI, Moberg PJ, Mahr RN, Doty RL. 1998. Olfaction in neurodegenerative disease: a meta-analysis of olfactory functioning in Alzheimer's and Parkinson's diseases. *Arch. Neurol.* 55:84–90

Moberg PJ, Doty RL. 1997. Olfactory function in Huntington's disease patients and at-risk offspring. *Int. J. Neurosci.* 89:133–39

Moberg PJ, Doty RL, Turetsky BI, Arnold SE, Mahr RN, et al. 1997. Olfactory identification deficits in schizophrenia: correlation with duration of illness. *Am. J. Psychiatry* 154:1016–18

Mombaerts P, Wang F, Dulac C, Chao SK, Nemes A, et al. 1996. Visualizing an olfactory sensory map. *Cell* 87:675–86

Monti-Bloch L, Jennings-White C, Berliner DL. 1998. The human vomeronasal system. A review. *Ann. NY Acad. Sci.* 855:373–89

Moulton DG. 1977. Minimum odorant concentrations detectable by the dog and their implications for olfactory receptor sensitivity. In *Chemical Signals in Vertebrates*, ed. D Müller-Schwarze, MM Mozell, pp. 455–64. New York: Plenum

Murphy C, Gilmore MM, Seery CS, Salmon DP, Lasker BR. 1990. Olfactory thresholds are associated with degree of dementia in Alzheimer's disease. *Neurobiol. Aging* 11:465–69

Murphy C, Jinich S. 1996. Olfactory dysfunction in Down's syndrome. *Neurobiol. Aging* 7:631–37

Negus V. 1958. *The Comparative Anatomy and Physiology of the Nose and Paranasal Sinuses*. Edinburgh: Livingstone

Nordin S, Bramerson A, Liden E, Bende M. 1999. The Scandinavian Odor-Identification Test: development, reliability, validity and normative data. *Acta Otolaryngol.* 118:226–34

Park S, Schoppe S. 1997. Olfactory identification deficit in relation to schizotypy. *Schizophr. Res.* 26:191–97

Peregud GM. 1931. Anosmia in tumors of the fourth ventricle. *Rus. Oto-laringol.* 24:101–5

Postolache TT, Doty RL, Wehr TA, Jimma LA, Han L, et al. 1999. Monorhinal odor identification and depression scores in patients with seasonal affective disorder. *J. Affect. Dis.* 56:27–35

Price JL. 1990. Olfactory system. In *The Human Nervous System*, ed. G Paxinos, pp. 979–98. San Diego: Academic

Purdon SE. 1998. Olfactory identification and Stroop interference converge in schizophrenia. *J. Psychiatr. Neurosci.* 23:163–71

Rajendren G, Dudley CA, Moss RL. 1990. Role of the vomeronasal organ in the male-induced enhancement of sexual receptivity in female rats. *Neuroendocrinology* 52:368–72

Razani J, Murphy C, Davidson TM, Grant I, McCutchan A. 1996. Odor sensitivity is impaired in HIV-positive cognitively impaired patients. *Physiol. Behav.* 59:877–81

Restrepo D, Okada Y, Teeter JH, Lowry LD, Cowart B, Brand JG. 1993. Human olfactory neurons respond to odor stimuli with an increase in cytoplasmic Ca2+. *Biophys. J.* 64:1961–66

Rodriguez I, Feinstein P, Mombaerts P. 1999. Variable patterns of axonal projections of sensory neurons in the mouse vomeronasal system. *Cell* 97:199–208

Romero PR, Beltramino CA, Carrer HF. 1990. Participation of the olfactory system in the control of approach behavior of the female rat to the male. *Physiol. Behav.* 47:685–90

Royet J-P, Koenig O, Gregoire M-C, Cinotti L, Lavenne F, et al. 2000. Functional anatomy of perceptual and semantic processing of odors. *J. Cogn. Neurosci.* 11:94–109

Ryba NJ, Tirindelli R. 1997. A new multigene family of putative pheromone receptors. *Neuron* 19:371–79

Saito TR, Igarashi N, Hokao R, Wakafuji Y, Takahashi KW. 1990. Nursing behavior in lactating rats—the role of the vomeronasal organ. *Jikken Dobutsu* 39:109–11

Sajjadian A, Doty RL, Gutnick DN, Chirurgi RJ, Sivak M, Perl D. 1994. Olfactory dysfunction in amyotrophic lateral sclerosis. *Neurodegeneration* 3:153–57

Scalia F, Winans SS. 1975. The differential projections of the olfactory bulb and accessory olfactory bulb in mammals. *J. Comp. Neurol.* 161:31–55

Schwanzel-Fukuda M, Pfaff DW. 1995. Structure and function of the nervus terminalis. In *Handbook of Olfaction and Gustation*, ed. RL Doty, pp. 835–64. New York: Marcel Dekker

Schwartz BS, Doty RL, Monroe C, Frye R, Barker S. 1989. Olfactory function in chemical workers exposed to acrylate and methacrylate vapors. *Am. J. Public Health* 79:613–18

Schwartz BS, Ford DP, Bolla KI, Agnew J, Bleecker ML. 1991. Solvent-associated olfactory dysfunction: not a predictor of deficits in learning and memory. *Am. J Psychiatry* 148:751–56

Schwartz BS, Ford DP, Bolla KI, Agnew J, Rothman N, Bleecker ML. 1990. Solvent-associated decrements in olfactory function in paint manufacturing workers. *Am. J. Ind. Med.* 18:697–706

Segal NL, Brown KW, Topolski TD. 1992. A twin study of odor identification and olfactory sensitivity. *Acta Genet. Med. Gemellol.* 41:113–21

Segal NL, Topolski TD, Wilson SM, Brown KW, Araki L. 1995. Twin analysis of odor identification and perception. *Physiol. Behav.* 57:605–9

Segovia S, Guillamón A. 1993. Sexual dimorphism in the vomeronasal pathway and sex differences in reproductive behaviors. *Brain Res. Rev.* 18:51–74

Segovia S, Guillamón A. 1982. Effects of sex steroids on the development of the vomeronasal organ in the rat. *Dev. Brain Res.* 14:209–91

Seidman LJ, Talbot NL, Kalinowski AG, McCarley RW, Faraone SV, et al. 1991. Neuropsychological probes of fronto-limbic system dysfunction in schizophrenia. Olfactory identification and Wisconsin card sorting performance. *Schizophicula Res.* 6:55–65

Shear PK, Butters N, Jernigan TL, DiTraglia GM, Irwin M, et al. 1992. Olfactory loss in alcoholics: correlations with cortical and subcortical MRI indices. *Alcohol* 9:247–55

Ship JA, Weiffenbach JM. 1993. Age, gender, medical treatment, and medication effects on smell identification. *J. Gerontol.* 48:M26–M32

Shou J, Rim PC, Calof AL. 1999. BMPs inhibit neurogenesis by a mechanism involving degradation of a transcription factor. *Nat. Neurosci.* 2:339–45

Simmen D, Briner HR, Hess K. 1999. Screeningtest des Geruchssinnes mit Riechdisketten. *Laryngo-Rhino-Otol.* 78:125–30

Sklar PB, Anholt RRH, Snyder SH. 1986. The odorant-sensitive adenylate cyclase of olfactory receptor cells. *J. Biol. Chem.* 261:15538–41

Smith TD, Bhatnagar KP. 2000. The human vomeronasal organ: II. Prenatal development. *J. Anat.* In press

Sobel N, Prabhakaran V, Desmond JE, Glover GH, Goode RL, et al. 1998a. Sniffing and smelling: separate subsystems in the human olfactory cortex. *Nature* 392:282–86

Sobel N, Prabhakaran V, Hartley CA, Desmond JE, Zhao Z, et al. 1998b. Odorant-induced and sniff-induced activation in the cerebellum of the human. *J. Neurosci.* 18:8990–9001

Sobel N, Prabhakaran V, Zhao Z, Desmond JE, Glover GH, et al. 2000. Time course of odorant-induced activation in the human primary olfactory cortex. *J. Neurophysiol.* 83:537–51

Stedman TJ, Clair AL. 1998. Neuropsychological, neurological and symptom correlates of impaired olfactory identification in schizophrenia. *Schizophr. Res.* 32:23–30

Stern K, McClintock MK. 1998. Regulation of ovulation by human pheromones. *Nature* 392:177–79

Striebel KM, Beyerstein B, Remick RA, Kopala L, Honer WG. 1999. Olfactory identification and psychosis. *Biol. Psychiatry* 45:1419–25

Takagi SF. 1989. *Human Olfaction.* Tokyo: Univ. Tokyo Press

Takami S, Getchell ML, Chen Y, Monti-Bloch L, Berliner DL, et al. 1993. Vomeronasal epithelial cells of the adult human express neuron-specific molecules. *NeuroReport* 4:375–78

Terashima K. 1988. Reduction of musty odor substances in drinking water—a pilot plant study. *Water Sci. Technol.* 20:275–81

Trombley PQ, Shepherd GM. 1993. Synaptic transmission and modulation in the olfactory bulb. *Curr. Opin. Neurobiol.* 3:540–47

Tucker BR. 1911. Report of a case of tumor of the ponto-cerebella angle on the left side of the brain with bilateral loss of smell and disturbance of taste. *Old Dominion J. Med. Surg.* XIII:327–34

Vassar R, Chao SK, Sitcheran R, Nunez JM, Vosshall LB, Axel R. 1994. Topographic organization of sensory projections to the olfactory bulb. *Cell* 79:981–91

Vassar R, Ngai J, Axel R. 1993. Spatial segregation of odorant receptor expression in the mammalian olfactory epithelium. *Cell* 74:309–18

Verdú E, Navarro X, Gudiño-Cabrera G, Rodríguez FJ, Ceballos D, et al. 1999. Olfactory bulb ensheathing cells enhance peripheral nerve regeneration. *NeuroReport* 10:1097–101

Warner MD, Peabody CA, Berger PA. 1988. Olfactory deficits in Down's syndrome. *Biol. Psychiatry* 23:836–39

Weiffenbach JM, McCarthy VP. 1984. Olfactory deficits in cystic fibrosis: distribution and severity. *Chem. Senses* 9:193–99

Weiffenbach JM, Schwartz LK, Atkinson JC, Fox PC. 1995. Taste performance in Sjogren's syndrome. *Physiol. Behav.* 57:89–96

Weiler E, Farbman AI. 1999a. Mitral cell loss following lateral olfactory tract transection increases proliferation density in rat olfactory epithelium. *Eur. J. Neurosci.* 11:3265–75

Weiler E, Farbman AI. 1999b. Proliferation decrease in the olfactory epithelium during postnatal development. *Ann. NY Acad. Sci.* 855:230–34

Weinstock RS, Wright HN, Spiegel AM, Levine MA, Moses AM. 1986. Olfactory dysfunction in humans with deficient guanine nucleotide-binding protein. *Nature* 322:635–36

Wekesa KS, Anholt RRH. 1999. Differential expression of G proteins in the mouse olfactory system. *Brain Res.* 837:117–26

Wekesa KS, Lepri JJ. 1994. Removal of the vomeronasal organ reduces reproductive performance and aggression in male prairie voles. *Chem. Senses* 19:35–45

Wenning GK, Shephard B, Hawkes C, Petruckevitch A, Lees A, Quinn N. 1995. Olfactory function in atypical parkinsonian syndromes. *Acta Neurol. Scand.* 91:247–50

West SE, Doty RL, O'Connor MJ, Sperling MA. 1993. Pre- and post-operative studies of olfactory function in patients with anterior temporal lobectomy. *Chem. Senses* 18:649

Winans SS, Powers JB. 1974. Neonatal and two-stage olfactory bulbectomy: effects on male hamster sexual behavior. *Behav. Biol.* 10:461–71

Wirsig-Wiechmann CR. 1997. Nervus terminalis lesions: II. Enhancement of lordosis induced by tactile stimulation in the hamster. *Physiol. Behav.* 61:867–71

Wirsig-Wiechmann CR, Lee CE. 1999. Estrogen regulates gonadotropin-releasing hormone in the nervus terminalis of *Xenopus laevis*. *Gen. Comp. Endocrinol.* 115:301–8

Wirsig-Wiechmann CR, Lepri JJ. 1991. LHRH-immunoreactive neurons in the pterygopalatine ganglia of voles: a component of the nervus terminalis? *Brain Res.* 568:289–93

Wright HN. 1987. Characterization of olfactory dysfunction. *Arch. Otolaryngol. Head Neck Surg.* 113:163–68

Wysocki CJ, Kruczek M, Wysocki LM, Lepri JJ. 1991. Activation of reproduction in nulliparous and primiparous voles is blocked by vomeronasal organ removal. *Biol. Reprod.* 45:611–16

Yousem DM, Geckle RJ, Bilker W, McKeown DA, Doty RL. 1996a. MR evaluation of patients with congenital hyposmia or anosmia. *Am. J. Roentgenol.* 166:439–43

Yousem DM, Geckle RJ, Bilker WB, McKeown DA, Doty RL. 1996b. Posttraumatic olfactory dysfunction: MR and clinical evaluation. *Am. J. Neuroradiol.* 17:1171–79

Yousem DM, Geckle RJ, Bilker WB, Kroger H, Doty RL. 1999a. Posttraumatic smell loss: relationship of pyschophysical tests and volumes of the olfactory bulbs and tracts and the temporal lobes. *Acad. Radiol.* 6:264–72

Yousem DM, Maldjian JA, Hummel T, Alsop DC, Geckle RJ, et al. 1999b. The effect of age on odor-stimulated functional MR imaging. *Am. J. Neuroradiol.* 20:600–8

Yousem DM, Maldjian JA, Siddiqi F, Hummel T, Alsop DC, et al. 1999c. Gender effects on odor-stimulated functional magnetic resonance imaging. *Brain Res.* 818:480–87

Yousem DM, Turner WJ, Li C, Snyder PJ, Doty RL. 1993. Kallmann syndrome: MR evaluation of olfactory system. *Am. J. Neuroradiol.* 14:839–43

Yousem DM, Williams SC, Howard RO, Andrew C, Simmons A, et al. 1997. Functional MR imaging during odor stimulation: preliminary data. *Radiology* 204:833–38

Zald DH, Pardo JV. 1997. Emotion, olfaction, and the human amygdala: amygdala activation during aversive olfactory stimulation. *Proc. Natl. Acad. Sci. USA* 94:4119–24

Zatorre RJ, Jones-Gotman M. 1991. Human olfactory discrimination after unilateral frontal or temporal lobectomy. *Brain* 114:71–84

Zatorre RJ, Jones-Gotman M, Evans AC, Meyer E. 1992. Functional localization and lateralization of human olfactory cortex. *Nature* 360:339–40

Zhao H, Ivic L, Otaki JM, Hashimoto M, Mikoshiba K, Firestein S. 1998. Functional expression of a mammalian odorant receptor. *Science* 279:237–42

Annu. Rev. Psychol. 2001. 52:453–70

ACQUISITION OF INTELLECTUAL AND PERCEPTUAL-MOTOR SKILLS

David A. Rosenbaum, Richard A. Carlson, and Rick O. Gilmore

Department of Psychology, Pennsylvania State University, University Park, Pennsylvania 16802; e-mail: dar12@psu.edu, cvy@psu.edu, rog1@psu.edu

Key Words brain mechanisms, imagery, individual differences, memory, skill learning

■ **Abstract** Recent evidence indicates that intellectual and perceptual-motor skills are acquired in fundamentally similar ways. Transfer specificity, generativity, and the use of abstract rules and reflexlike productions are similar in the two skill domains; brain sites subserving thought processes and perceptual-motor processes are not as distinct as once thought; explicit and implicit knowledge characterize both kinds of skill; learning rates, training effects, and learning stages are remarkably similar for the two skill classes; and imagery, long thought to play a distinctive role in high-level thought, also plays a role in perceptual-motor learning and control. The conclusion that intellectual skills and perceptual-motor skills are psychologically more alike than different accords with the view that all knowledge is performatory.

CONTENTS

0066-4308/01/0201-0453$14.00

INTRODUCTION

This review is concerned with the similarities and differences between the acquisition of intellectual skills and the acquisition of perceptual-motor skills. The main question is whether the psychological mechanisms underlying the two forms of skills differ. If they do, the important question is why and how they differ. If they do not, the equally important question is why two such seemingly disparate skill domains are more alike than their surface features suggest.

The review is organized into three major sections. First, we define the terms in the title and review claims that acquisition of intellectual skills and perceptual-motor skills rely on different psychological mechanisms. Then we review evidence favoring the opposite viewpoint. Finally, we ask why the evidence supports the no-difference view so consistently.

Before proceeding, we wish to establish the limits of what is covered. Because of space limitations, the review must be selective. The discussion is restricted to one principal question: How "intellectual" are perceptual-motor skills? This question reflects our expertise (or lack of expertise in other areas) as well as our sense that recent work across a wide range of disciplines now provides evidence for the view that "skills of mind" and "skills of eye, ear, and muscle" are fundamentally similar.

A second limitation is that the tasks we discuss under the perceptual-motor heading and under the intellectual heading are diverse. More microscopic comparisons of tasks within these domains might reveal more subtle differences between them, but because the two classes of skill turn out to be fundamentally similar, this outcome obviates concern with more microscopic differences.

DEFINITIONS AND DISTINCTIONS

Definitions help. When we speak of a "skill" we mean an ability that allows a goal to be achieved within some domain with increasing likelihood as a result of practice. When we speak of "acquisition of skill" we refer to the attainment of those practice-related capabilities that contribute to the increased likelihood of goal achievement. By an "intellectual skill" we mean a skill whose goal is symbolic. By a "perceptual-motor skill" we mean a skill whose goal is nonsymbolic. Examples of intellectual skills are solving or making significant headway toward solving mathematics problems, and winning or at least competing respectably in chess. Examples of perceptual-motor skills are playing the violin so as to attract rather than repel one's listeners, and boxing so as to repel rather than attract one's opponents.

Intuitively, intellectual skills and perceptual-motor skills seem very different. Perceptual-motor skills seem more primitive than intellectual skills. Ontogenetically, perceptual-motor skills develop before intellectual skills, or at least before most intellectual skills are manifested. Phylogenetically, creatures "high on the evolutionary ladder" are more obviously capable of intellectual skills than are creatures "lower down."

Perceptual-motor skills also seem more tied to specific forms of expression. Being a chess player does not mean one can only play with pieces of a certain size, that one can only move pieces with one's right hand, and so on. By contrast, being a violinist means one can play an instrument whose size occupies a fairly narrow range and that one must play with a rather rigid assignment of functions to effectors (bowing with the right hand, and fingering with the left). The seeming narrowness of perceptual-motor skill expression, contrasted with the seeming openness of intellectual skill expression, seems to follow from intellectual skills having symbolic outcomes and perceptual-motor skills having nonsymbolic outcomes. Symbolic outcomes need not be realized in specific ways and can rely on abstract rules. Nonsymbolic outcomes, by contrast, need more specific forms of realization and seem to depend on restricted associations between stimuli and responses.

Another difference between intellectual and perceptual-motor skills is that the two kinds of skill seem to be represented in different parts of the brain. For example, structures homologous to the optic tectum, a nucleus located on the dorsal surface of the midbrain, have a common function in all vertebrates—coordinating visual, auditory, and somatosensory information relevant to the control of orienting movements of the eyes, ears, and head (Stein & Meredith 1993). Similarities in structure and function between these and other brain areas associated with perceptual-motor behavior suggest that mechanisms for control of perceptual-motor skills are both highly specialized and conserved across species. In contrast, what distinguishes the human brain from the brains of other species (even closely related ones) is the differential growth of brain regions most strongly associated with intellectual skills, such as the association areas of the cerebral cortex (Allman 1999). That these areas serve intellectual functions is supported by a large clinical and experimental literature (Gazzaniga et al 1998). Together, these diverse sources of information suggest that perceptual-motor and intellectual skills depend on distinct brain circuits.

Another way in which intellectual and perceptual-motor skills seem to differ is that it is usually easier to articulate the knowledge that allows for performance of intellectual skill than to articulate the knowledge that allows for performance of perceptual-motor skills. Thus, one can write the steps needed to solve a mathematics or chess problem and expect others to solve the same or similar problems by consulting those instructions. By contrast, no one has ever managed to write the instructions for riding a bicycle or bouncing on a trampoline and then find the reader successfully engaging in these tasks based on reading alone. The only way to learn perceptual-motor skills, it is said, is to do them.

A final way in which intellectual and perceptual-motor skills are said to differ is that individual differences seem faithfully to reflect the division between the two skill types. Some gifted gymnasts are inarticulate, and some gifted orators are clumsy. Specialization of talent seems to reflect specialization of acquisition mechanisms. The fact that talents seem to divide so easily between intellectual and perceptual-motor domains provides more fuel for the argument that the two kinds of skills are functionally far apart—as far apart, one might say, as gym lockers and libraries in a typical university.

QUESTIONING THE DISTINCTION

Having offered arguments for the proposition that there is a psychologically meaningful basis for the view that intellectual skills and perceptual-motor skills are fundamentally different, we consider arguments for the opposite view. We begin by re-examining some of the claims made in the previous section and then turn to other lines of evidence. This section is longer and more replete with references than the last, which hints at where we think most of the evidence lies.

Transfer Specificity

As mentioned above, one putative difference between intellectual and perceptual-motor skills is that perceptual-motor skills seem more specific than intellectual skills. There are two reasons to question this proposal. One pertains to transfer specificity. The other pertains to perceptual-motor generativity.

Both perceptual-motor and intellectual skills are typically characterized by specificity of transfer. Practiced skills generally carry over only narrowly to similar contents and contexts. This phenomenon forms the basis for the identical elements theory of Thorndike (1903; see Hilgard and Bower 1975 for discussion). The main idea in identical elements theory is that transfer depends on having shared elements in acquisition and transfer; the larger the number of such shared elements, the greater the likelihood that transfer will occur. Singley & Anderson (1989) updated Thorndike's identical elements theory by suggesting that the relevant elements are production rules that apply both in acquisition and in new situations. Other versions of identical elements theory have been discussed by MacKay (1982), Kramer et al (1990), and Rickard & Bourne (1996). None of these theorists emphasizes a split between symbolic and nonsymbolic elements. Rather, all of them allow elements to be abstract in the sense that they pertain to whatever declarative or procedural knowledge is relevant for the task at hand. From the perspective of identical elements theory, there is no reason to expect transfer to be more limited for perceptual-motor skills than for intellectual skills, or vice versa, and the literature supports this expectation.

A particularly striking phenomenon is transfer asymmetry—the failure of transfer between different uses of what appears to be the same underlying knowledge. For example, McKendree & Anderson (1987) demonstrated failure of transfer between practice in generating and evaluating functions of the LISP programming language. Similarly, Fendrich et al (1993) found only partial transfer between items as similar as reversed multiplication facts (e.g. 3 × 4 and 4 × 3). Transfer asymmetry has also been demonstrated in the perceptual-motor domain (for review, see

Schmidt & Lee 1999, pp. 318–21). For example, Proteau et al (1992) showed that performance in a manual aiming task (hitting a target as quickly and accurately as possible) was impaired by letting participants see what they were doing if they had previously practiced the task without visual feedback. Usually manual aiming is aided by visual feedback, which makes it remarkable that supplying visual feedback late in training hurts performance. The fact that specificity of transfer is not markedly different within intellectual or perceptual-motor skill domains has been underscored in a volume edited by Healy & Bourne (1995).

Perceptual-Motor Generativity

Another reason to question the claim that perceptual-motor skills are more specific than intellectual skills is that perceptual-motor skills are more generative than often assumed. The hallmark of generativity in intellectual performance is, of course, the endless novelty of language. Perceptual-motor skills may seem, by contrast, to be less creative, but as more research has been done on perceptual-motor skill acquisition, a richer appreciation has developed of the endless novelty of physical action.

Consider the fact that any healthy person who can write with the preferred hand can also write with the nonpreferred hand. Written output from the nonpreferred hand preserves most of the spatial characteristics of written output from the preferred hand, and though writing with the nonpreferred hand is less fluent at first, with practice it becomes more so (Newell & van Emmerick, 1989). A challenge for motor control research has been to explain how it is possible to generate what is essentially the same written output with virtually any part of one's body—for example, even when the pen is held between one's toes or teeth.

Recent computer simulations have shown that writing with any part of the body can be achieved by guiding the pentip through series of spatial and postural positions specified by a visuo-spatial representation of desired written output (Meulenbroek et al 1996). This method allows the same written output to be generated with different body parts. Other perceptual-motor achievements that may be taken for granted, such as reaching around obstacles to take hold of desired objects, rely on equally sophisticated computational and representational capabilities (Rosenbaum et al 1999).

Abstract Rules Versus Reflexlike Productions

As stated above, intellectual skills seem to rely on abstract rules more than do perceptual-motor skills. How well does this contrast stand up to scrutiny?

Contrary to the hypothesis, some intellectual skills seem to be represented by highly specific associations. Logan (1988), for instance, in his instance theory of automaticity, argued that intellectual skills such as arithmetic may be acquired as specific episodes involving particular answers to particular problems. Artificial grammar learning may likewise depend on the learning of specific features or chunks of grammatical strings rather than abstract rules (Dulany et al 1984). There is debate about the extent to which intellectual skills depend on instances rather than rules, but it is almost certainly incorrect to say that intellectual skills rely only on abstract rules.

Similarly, it is almost certainly incorrect to say that perceptual-motor skills rely only on learned instances (i.e. simple reflexlike productions). This is illustrated by Koh & Meyer's (1991) finding that subjects can induce functions relating continuous stimulus dimensions (e.g. the length of a seen line) to continuous response dimensions (e.g. the duration of a button press). When subjects in Koh & Meyer's experiment were presented with new line lengths, their response durations indicated that they had induced the function relating line length to duration.

Other perceptual-motor skills seem to manifest function learning as well. Examples are prism adaptation (see Redding & Wallace 1997, for review), haptic exploration (Turvey 1996), and adaptation of limb movements to force perturbations (Conditt et al 1997).

Neural Substrates

As noted above, another supposed difference between intellectual and perceptual-motor skills is that the two kinds of skill are subserved by different brain areas. However, this view has been challenged by recent findings concerning the motor cortex and cerebellum.

The traditional view of the cerebellum is that it contributes primarily to the coordination and control of movement. Damage to the cerebellum often results in distinctive motor symptoms, such as reduced muscle tone, delayed movement initiation, motor planning errors, and tremor (Holmes 1939). However, since the mid-1980s substantial evidence has also accumulated that the cerebellum serves a number of cognitive functions (Fiez 1996, Leiner et al 1995). Clinical studies have suggested that cerebellar damage is associated with deficits in conditioning (Bracke-Tolkmitt et al 1989) as well as the analysis of temporal duration (Ivry & Keele 1989). Neurological studies of children with developmental disorders have linked disturbances in the cerebellum to autism (Courchesne et al 1987) and Williams' syndrome (Rae et al 1998). Brain imaging research has shown that the cerebellum is active during performance of tasks as varied as word generation (Petersen et al 1989), sequence learning (Jenkins et al 1994), tactile discrimination (Gao et al 1996), and maintenance of information in working memory (Desmond et al 1997). Thus, an emerging view of the cerebellum is that it plays a role in intellectual as well as perceptual-motor performance (Leiner et al 1995). A general hypothesis about the cerebellum that may provide a unified account of its role is that it contributes to the prediction and preparation of sequences (Courchesne & Allen 1997). Insofar as sequences can consist of symbols (the sine qua non of intellectual skills) or stimuli and response (the sine qua non of perceptual-motor skills), the cerebellum need not be viewed as a purely perceptual-motor organ nor as a purely intellectual organ. The distinction between intellectual and perceptual-motor skills is not one that the cerebellum respects.

With regard to the motor cortex, the classical view is that this site is little more than a "launch pad" for movements (see Evarts 1981, for review). However, this view has undergone considerable revision. In one well-known study, Georgopoulos et al (1989), recorded from cells in the motor cortex of a monkey that saw a light and then had to direct its hand to a target 45° away. The composite activity of the cells could be represented as a "population vector" with a magnitude and direction closely related to the monkey's hand movement. Georgopoulos et al found that the direction of the motor cortical population vector "rotated" between the time the monkey first saw the light and the time it began directing its hand to the angularly displaced target. This outcome suggests that the motor cortex is involved in a higher level of planning than would be expected if it merely received and relayed signals from higher centers at the moment movement is due.

Explicit Versus Implicit Knowledge

Another difference between intellectual and perceptual-motor skills mentioned above is that perceptual-motor skills are generally harder to articulate than intellectual skills. Implicit knowledge seems more naturally linked to perceptual-motor skills than to intellectual skills, whereas explicit knowledge seems more naturally linked to intellectual skills than to perceptual-motor skills.

How meaningful are these links? Not very, in our opinion. Certainly, perceptual-motor skills are often acquired without an accompanying ability to articulate rules governing performance. For example, Pew (1974) reported that participants learning to track a moving spot on a computer screen got better and better on the middle portion if it was repeated, though they indicated that they did not notice the repetition. Similarly, nonverbal creatures (animals and preverbal children) can acquire perceptual-motor skills without the symbolic skills to represent and report the corresponding rules. Thus, perceptual-motor skills can be learned implicitly, as suggested earlier.

But can intellectual skills also be learned implicitly, contrary to what was said before? There is evidence that they can be. Repeated sequences of stimuli (lights) and responses (keypresses) in reaction time tasks can be learned without easily verbalizable knowledge of the repetitions (Nissen & Bullemer 1987; but see Shanks & Johnstone 1999). As in the study of Pew (1974), performance improves on repeated sequences even when subjects do not report explicit knowledge of the repetitions (see Goschke 1998, for review).

One might say that serial reaction-time tasks are not "intellectual enough" to shed light on tasks that are unambiguously intellectual. There is evidence, however, that both mathematical problem solving and artificial grammars are learnable on the basis of rules or regularities that are not verbally represented as such. Acquisition of arithmetic problem-solving skills with complex goal structures shows a benefit of consistent goal structures even though subjects are poor at reporting those goal structures (Wenger & Carlson 1996). Similarly, learning of artificial verbal grammars does not depend on the ability to articulate the rules defining the grammars (see Reber 1992, for review). Finally, speakers of natural languages cannot articulate rules for generating or comprehending grammatical sentences; if they could, theoretical linguistics would be easier. In general, the available evidence indicates that intellectual skills need not depend on the deliberate application of rules in verbal or other symbolic formats.

A caveat is in order here. It must be admitted that the empirical and theoretical status of implicit learning of intellectual skills remains controversial (e.g. Carlson 1997, Dienes & Perner 1999, Shanks & St. John 1994). Assessing explicit knowledge poses methodological difficulties (Perruchet et al 1990, Shanks & Johnstone 1999), and for many tasks competing accounts suggest alternative ways in which the knowledge underlying intellectual skill might be divided between declarative and procedural components (Redington & Chater 1996, Servan-Schreiber & Anderson 1990). Explicit declarative knowledge of facts is often, though not always, accompanied by awareness of what has been learned as well as the circumstances of learning, in contrast to typical instances of perceptual-motor learning. Still, intellectual and perceptual-motor skill acquisition cannot be generally distinguished on the basis that one is explicit and the other is implicit. Neither category of skill learning is necessarily accompanied by the ability to articulate the rules governing observed performance.

Individual Differences

The previous list of putative differences between perceptual-motor skills and intellectual skills included individual differences. The fact that some people are talented in perceptual-motor domains or in intellectual domains suggests a rift between the two skill areas.

Two responses can be given to this argument. The first is that individual differences in the expression of a skill do not necessarily bear on the capacity for acquisition of the skill. An actor with a beautiful speaking voice, for example, may not necessarily be able to learn his or her lines more easily than an actor with a raspy voice. Second, the question of how and whether skill competencies should be partitioned is an old but still unresolved issue (see, for example, Gardner 1983).

Regarding the partitioning of intellectual and perceptual-motor skills, it is striking that correlations between performance levels within some domains are as low, or nearly as low, as the correlations one would expect for wholly unrelated realms of performance. For example, the correlation between the time to maintain balance on a seesaw or on a freely standing ladder is less than 0.25 (Bachman 1961). Obtaining such a small value violates what one would expect if one thought there were a general "balancing ability." In general, correlations over participants between different perceptual-motor tasks rarely exceed 0.40 (see Schmidt & Lee 1999, for review). The low correlations between perceptual-motor tasks weaken the hypothesis that perceptual-motor skills comprise some set of abilities that can be isolated from intellectual skills on the basis of high inter-correlations.

Learning Rates

If perceptual-motor skills and intellectual skills were acquired in fundamentally different ways, one would not necessarily expect the time course of their acquisition to be the same. In fact, charts of progress over time in the two skill domains are remarkably similar. As observed by Crossman (1959), the time to complete a task diminishes with practice at a lower and lower rate as practice continues. One way to capture this relation is with a power function, $T = aP^{-b}$, relating the time, T, to complete the task to the number of trials, P, that the task has been practiced; where a and b are nonnegative constants. Debate has arisen about whether the power function is the best formula for relating T to P (Heathcote et al 2000), but the tendency for performance time to decrease at ever lower rates is well established.

The feature of practice-related speeding of performance that is of greatest importance for present purposes is that the way performance speeds with practice is the same in perceptual-motor domains and in intellectual domains. Thus, in addition to the task studied by Crossman (1959)—cigar rolling—the relation holds for the time to draw figures with sight of the drawing hand restricted to a mirror (Snoddy 1926), the time to edit text with a computerized word processor (Singley & Anderson 1989), the time to prove theorems in a geometrylike system (Neves & Anderson 1981), and even for the time for the prolific author Isaac Asimov to write books (Ohlsson 1992).

What mechanisms allow the time on a task to decrease with practice by smaller and smaller amounts as practice continues? One answer can be based on Bryan & Harter's (1897) classic model of chunking. Skill acquisition entails formation of procedures at successively higher levels. The higher the level of the procedure, the longer it takes to learn it, so the longer it takes to see a corresponding reduction in the task completion time. Consistent with this explanation, and consistent with the view that intellectual and perceptual-motor skills are formed through similar means, the timing of successive responses in perceptual-motor tasks as well as intellectual tasks both reveal hierarchical "unpacking" of chunks of knowledge. Thus, skilled chess players returning pieces from a game onto a board return the pieces in bursts separated by longer lags. The long and short time intervals are related, respectively, to inter- and intrachunk boundaries (Chase & Simon 1973). Similar timing results are found in recall of semantically organized word lists (Reitman & Rueter 1980) and production of rapid finger-tapping sequences (Povel & Collard 1982, Rosenbaum et al 1983).

Training Effects

Many similarities have been observed between the effects of different training regimens on the learning of perceptual-motor and intellectual skills (Schmidt & Bjork 1992). Massed practice produces better immediate performance than spaced practice, both in verbal learning (e.g. Glenberg 1977a) and in motor learning (e.g. Shea & Morgan 1979), and random or spaced practice leads to better long-term retention than does blocked or massed practice in both domains. Relevant evidence is reviewed for perceptual-motor skill in Magill & Hall (1990), and for intellectual skill in Melton (1970), Landauer & Bjork (1978), and Rea & Modigliani (1985).

Perceptual-motor and intellectual learning are also affected in similar ways by variations in feedback frequency. As reviewed by Schmidt & Bjork (1992), providing frequent feedback to subjects learning a motor task such as rapid serial arm positioning leads to good short-term retention but poor long-term retention, whereas providing infrequent feedback leads to good long-term retention but poor short-term retention (Schmidt et al 1989, Winstein & Schmidt 1990, Wulf & Schmidt 1989). Comparable results have been obtained for acquisition of verbal paired associates (Krumboltz & Weisman 1962, Schulz & Runquist 1960) and computer languages (Schooler & Anderson 1990).

Yet another way in which motor and verbal learning show similar training-related effects pertains to the consequences of exposing subjects to the same or different materials during training. Using the same materials (constant training) leads to better performance just after training but worse performance in later tests. By contrast, exposing learners to different materials (variable training) leads to worse performance just after training but better performance in later tests. The long-term benefit of variable training is observed with perceptual-motor tasks such as pressing a button when a moving object reaches a target or tossing a bean bag into a bin (see Shapiro & Schmidt 1982, for review). The long-term benefit of variable training is also observed with intellectual tasks such as learning new words for familiar concepts (see Bransford et al 1977).

Learning Stages

As might be expected from the foregoing, long-term learning of intellectual and perceptual-motor skills appears to go through similar stages. The classical view of skill acquisition proposed by Fitts (1964) to account for perceptual-motor skill acquisition has been extended to the acquisition of intellectual skills, most notably by Anderson and colleagues (Anderson 1982). Fitts proposed that there is a declarative stage in which the basic rules of a task are learned and, if necessary, articulated. Then there is an associative stage in which the procedures of the task become more fluent. Finally, there is an autonomous stage in which the procedures become more automatic, being performed more rapidly and with greater immunity to disruption from outside events. Anderson (1982) showed that this stage description applies to intellectual skills as well as perceptual-motor skills.

Imagery

A hallmark of intellectual skill is the capacity for imagery. Albert Einstein claimed that images came to him before equations, and others have also reported that imagery played a major role in their thinking. Insofar as imagery plays such a prominent role in thinking, one might expect it to play little or no role in perceptual-motor skill and to be scarcely influenced by ongoing perceptual-motor activity. Neither of these expectations is borne out, however.

That imagery plays a role in perceptual-motor skill has been shown in many studies (see Crammond 1997, Jeannerod 1994, for review). Imaging one's own body movements "lights up" many of the same brain areas as actual performance of those movements (Roland 1993). Mental simulation of perceptual-motor tasks also takes about as long as actual performance of those tasks, and this is true for tasks as varied as walking (Decety & Jeannerod 1995), writing (Decety et al 1989), pointing (Sirigu et al 1996), speaking (MacKay 1982), and grasping (Johnson 2000). When people are asked to imagine performing movements in time with a metronome, the pace at which they report imagined breakdowns of performance corresponds to the frequencies at which the same tasks break down when they are actually performed (Sirigu et al 1996).

Whereas the studies just mentioned concern imagery of one's own movements, other studies have explored the possibility that imagery for events in the external environment is affected by ongoing perceptual-motor activity. Wohlschläger & Wohlschläger (1998) and Wexler et al (1998) found that mental rotation is affected by manual rotation. If the hand turns in the same direction as a mentally rotated object, the mental rotation speed is higher than if the mental and manual rotations go in opposite directions. This outcome suggests that visual imagery and the control of perceptual-motor tasks rely on common mechanisms. Direct physiological support for this conclusion was mentioned above in connection with the monkey mental rotation study of Georgopoulos et al (1989).

CONCLUDING REMARKS

In this review we have asked whether the acquisition of intellectual skills and the acquisition of perceptual-motor skills rely on similar or different psychological mechanisms. Our conclusion is that though the two kinds of skills may be distinct in their forms of expression, their means of acquisition are strikingly similar. In the remainder of this article we ask why the evidence leads to this conclusion.

Possible Reasons for the Similarities

One reason may be rooted in development. Perceptual-motor skills and intellectual skills have closely related developmental origins, as observed by Piaget (1954). Piaget's description of early development associates the development of thought with the emergence of skilled action. For example, the achievement of object permanence is based, according to Piaget, on the infant's realization that the identity and persistence of objects is independent of one's own behavior.

This view has been amplified and extended by others. For example, Diamond (1990) argued that the achievement of object permanence requires both the development of memory and the emergence of mechanisms for inhibiting inappropriate responses, such as reaching to a location where an object recently was but no longer is. Diamond associated the development of object permanence with the maturation of circuits in prefrontal regions of the cerebral cortex. Diamond's neurological perspective illustrates the close, perhaps inseparable, links between intellectual and perceptual-motor substrates of a wide range of concepts.

In a similar vein, Smith et al (1999) argued that puzzling aspects of infants' behavior in a classic object permanence task (the A-not-B task) may reflect infants' inabilities to successfully coordinate looking and manual reaching motions and memories of past actions. Smith et al's (1999) argument challenges the notion that during development intellectual skills can be usefully separated from their perceptual-motor realizations.

Another reason to believe in the fundamental similarity of the acquisition of intellectual and perceptual-motor skills is the growing popularity of the hypothesis that all intellectual skills are performatory—that is, that all skills are grounded in and supported by perceptual-motor activity, even at high levels. Piaget (1954), as noted earlier, suggested that mental operations and the intellectual achievements they support originate in interiorized action (see Chapman 1988); Bartlett (1932, 1958) argued that thinking is a skill (see Johnson-Laird 1982 for discussion); Weimer (1977) advocated a motor theory of mind, emphasizing the role of perceptual-motor activity in cognition; Kolers (Kolers & Roediger 1984) promoted a "proceduralist" view of memory and cognition, and Neisser (1983) endorsed a similar view, motivated by ecological considerations. Glenberg (1997b) discussed the role of perceptual-motor activity in memory processes, and Barsalou (1999) argued that all symbolic representation may be based in perception. One of the present authors offered a similar argument in the context of a theory of consciousness and cognitive skill (Carlson 1997). A class of findings that supports the view that intellectual skills are performatory is that coordination and timing seem to be required for intellectual as well as perceptual-motor skills. Mental skills in a number of domains depend on the use of the external environment to maintain information for immediate performance, requiring real-time coordination of mental activity with externally available information (Ballard et al 1995, Cary & Carlson 1999, Larkin 1989, Zhang & Norman 1994). Similarly, performatory properties of speech affect the capacity and other properties of short-term memory for verbal materials (Cowan et al 1997; Zhang & Simon 1985). Finally, as with perceptual-motor skills, practicing intellectual skills results in establishing appropriate timing and coordination of component subskills (Cary & Carlson 1999, Wenger & Carlson 1995, Yee et al 1991). Thus, coordination, which has long been viewed as crucial for skills of perception and movement, turns out to be needed as well for skills of the intellect (Neisser 1983).

A final reason why the evidence points to a basic similarity of intellectual and perceptual-motor skill acquisition is that across animal species, the complexity of observed perceptual-motor skills is correlated with the complexity of intellectual skills. Complex nonverbal skills, such as manufacture of multi-component tools, only occur in humans. Recognition of this relation has prompted the hypothesis that the evolution of brain areas credited with the development of language (e.g. Broca's area) may have paved the way for complex behavioral sequencing (Greenfield 1991, Calvin 1994; Keele, interviewed in Gazzaniga et al 1998, pp. 398–99).

What's the Difference?

Having argued for the view that intellectual and perceptual-motor skills are acquired in similar ways, we need to dispel the impression that we think there is no difference between the two kinds of skill. Clearly, there is something special about intellectual function. But what is the difference?

Intellectual skills, as indicated in our definition of the term, have symbolic outcomes. They consist of actions that relate not just to the here and now but also to events that may be remote in time or space. Perceptual-motor skills, by contrast, have nonsymbolic outcomes and consist (or seem to consist) of actions that relate only to the immediate time and place in which they occur. What distinguishes intellectual skills from perceptual-motor skills then is the remoteness of the events to which they relate. This suggests that intellectual and perceptual-motor skills differ in degree rather than in kind, which may be why their means of acquisition seem so similar.

How remote are the events to which perceptual-motor activities relate? Granting that intellectual skills, expressed in such forms as writing science fiction, can relate to events infinitely far away in time and location, are perceptual-motor skills exclusively related to the place and time in which they are situated? Addressing this question provides a final clue about the similarities between perceptual-motor and intellectual skill acquisition. A great deal of research in the area of perceptual-motor control has shown that the genesis of voluntary action is accompanied by anticipation of future events. The time to initiate a sequence of motor responses increases with the length of the forthcoming sequence (Rosenbaum 1987, Sternberg et al 1978); errors in performance suggest that behavioral plans contain considerable structure (Dell 1986, Lashley 1951, Norman 1981); latencies of different types of responses to different types of stimuli suggest that perceptual consequences of forthcoming acts are represented in advance (Greenwald 1970, Hommel 1996); and action choices made early in behavioral sequences reflect anticipation of later behavioral states (Rosenbaum et al 1993). These findings indicate that action plans project into the future. This body of research has also shown that low-level features of performance have relatively short spans, whereas high-level features have longer spans, some extending to months (e.g. animal migration).

Considering the long time scales over which purposeful action can occur, one must again question the meaningfulness of the distinction between perceptual-motor skills and intellectual skills. If bees can communicate the whereabouts of recently visited flowers, it is unclear why, except for the fact that bees aren't human, this behavior should not be viewed as an intellectual skill.

What this leads to is the realization that perceptual-motor skills are no less intelligent than intellectual skills. The fact that modern technology has enabled computers to beat the world's greatest chess master (*Newsweek* May 5, 1997), but has not yet enabled robots to climb trees as well as five-year-olds or pick strawberries as well as farm workers attests to the fact that our understanding of the psychological substrates of perceptual-motor skill is still primitive compared to what we know about intellectual skills. We have verbal intelligence that makes it easier for us to describe verbal intelligence than to describe nonverbal intelligence, but we must be careful not to conclude from this that perceptual-motor skills are inferior to their intellectual counterparts.

ACKNOWLEDGMENTS

Preparation of this chapter was aided by grants from the National Science Foundation, a grant from the Research and Graduate Studies Office of Penn State University, a Research Scientist Development Award from the National Institutes of Health, and grants from the Royal Netherlands Academy of Arts and Sciences and the Dutch Organization for Scientific Research (NWO Stimulans Premie). The work benefited from comments by Daniel Schacter and Wouter Hulstijn.

Visit the Annual Reviews home page at www.AnnualReviews.org

LITERATURE CITED

Allman JM. 1999. *Evolving Brains*. New York: Freeman

Anderson JR. 1982. Acquisition of cognitive skill. *Psychol Rev.* 89:369–406

Bachman JC. 1961. Specificity vs. generality in learning and performing two large muscle motor tasks. *Res. Q.* 32:3–11

Ballard DH, Hayhoe MM, Pelz JB. 1995. Memory representations in natural tasks. *J. Cogn. Neurosci.* 7:66–80

Barsalou LW. 1999. Perceptual symbol systems. *Behav. Brain Sci.* 22:577–660

Bartlett FC. 1932. *Remembering*. Cambridge, UK: Cambridge Univ. Press

Bartlett FC. 1958. *Thinking: An Experimental and Social Study*. New York: Basic Books

Bracke-Tolkmitt R, Linden A, Canavan AGM, Diener HC. 1989. The cerebellum contributes to mental skills. *Behav. Neurosci.* 103:442–46

Bransford JD, Franks JJ, Morris CD, Stein BS. 1977. Some general constraints on learning and memory research. In *Levels of Process-*ing in Human Memory, ed. LS Cermak, FIM Craik, pp. 331–54. Hillsdale, NJ: Erlbaum

Bryan WL, Harter N. 1897. Studies in the physiology and psychology of the telegraphic language. *Psychol. Rev.* 4:27–53

Calvin WH. 1994. The emergence of intelligence. *Sci. Am.* 271(4):101–7

Carlson RA. 1997. *Experienced Cognition*. Mahwah, NJ: Erlbaum

Cary M, Carlson RA. 1999. External support and the development of problem-solving routines. *J. Exp. Psychol.: Learn. Mem. Cogn.* 25:1053–70

Chapman M. 1988. *Constructive Evolution: Origins and Development of Piaget's Thought*. Cambridge: Cambridge Univ. Press

Chase WG, Simon HA. 1973. The mind's eye in chess. In *Visual Information Processing*, ed. WG Chase, pp. 215–81. New York: Academic

Conditt MA, Gandolfo F, Mussa-Ivaldi FA. 1997. The motor system does not learn the dynamics of the arm by rote memorization of past experience. *J. Neurophys.* 78:554–60

Courchesne E, Allen G. 1997. Prediction and preparation fundamental functions of the cerebellum. *Learn. Mem.* 4:1–35

Courchesne E, Hesselink JR, Jernigan TL, Yeung-Courchesne X. 1987. Abnormal neuroanatomy in a nonretarded person with autism: unusual findings with magnetic resonance imaging. *Arch. Neurol.* 44:335–441

Cowan N, Wood NL, Nugent LD, Treisman M. 1997. There are two word length effects in verbal short-term memory: opposed effects of duration and complexity. *Psychol. Sci.* 8:290–95

Crammond DJ. 1997. Motor imagery: never in your wildest dreams. *Trends Neurosci.* 20:54–57

Crossman ERFW. 1959. A theory of the acquisition of speed skill. *Ergonomics* 2:153–66

Decety J, Jeannerod M, Prablanc C. 1989. The timing of mentally represented actions. *Behav. Brain Res.* 34:35–42

Decety J, Jeannerod M. 1995. Mentally simulated movements in virtual reality: Does Fitts's law hold in motor imagery? *Behav. Brain Res.* 72:127–34

Dell GS. 1986. A spreading activation theory of retrieval in sentence production. *Psychol. Rev.* 93:283–321

Desmond JE, Gabrielli JD, Wagner AD, Binier BL, Glover GH. 1997. Lobular patterns of cerebellar activation of verbal working-memory and finger-tapping tasks as revealed by functional MRI. *J. Neurosci.* 17:9675–85

Diamond A. 1990. The development and neural bases of memory functions, as indexed by AB and delayed response tasks, in human infants and infant monkeys. *Ann. NY Acad. Sci.* 608:637–76

Dienes Z, Perner J. 1999. A theory of implicit and explicit knowledge. *Behav. Brain Sci.* 22:735–808

Dulany DE, Carlson RA, Dewey GI. 1984. A case of syntactical learning and judgment: how conscious and how abstract? *J. Exp. Psychol.: Gen.* 113:541–55

Evarts EV. 1981. Role of motor cortex in voluntary movements in primates. In *Handbook of Physiology*, Section 1: *The Nervous System*, Vol II. *Motor Control*, ed. VB Brooks, pp. 1083–120. Bethesda, MD: Am. Physiol. Soc.

Fendrich DW, Healy AF, Bourne LE Jr. 1993. Mental arithmetic: training and retention of multiplication skill. In *Cognitive Psychology Applied*, ed. C Izawa, pp. 111–33. Hillsdale, NJ: Erlbaum

Fiez JA. 1996. Cerebellar contributions to cognition. *Neuron* 16:13–15

Fitts PM. 1964. Perceptual-motor skill learning. In *Categories of Human Learning*, ed. AW Melton, pp. 243–85. New York: Academic

Gao JH, Parsons LM, Bower JM, Xiong J. 1996. Cerebellum implicated in sensory acquistion and discrimination rather than motor control. *Science* 272:545–47

Gardner H. 1983. *Frames of Mind—The Theory of Multiple Intelligences*. New York: Basic Books

Gazzaniga MS, Ivry RB, Mangun GR. 1998. *Cognitive Neuroscience: The Biology of The Mind*. New York: Norton

Georgopoulos AP, Lurito JT, Petrides M, Schwartz AB, Massey JT. 1989. Mental rotation of the neuronal population vector. *Science* 243:234–36

Glenberg AM. 1977a. Influences of retrieval processes on the spacing effect in free recall. *J. Exp. Psychol.: Learn. Mem. Cogn.* 3:282–94

Glenberg AM. 1997b. What memory is for? *Behav. Brain Sci.* 201:1–55

Goschke T. 1998. Implicit learning of perceptual and motor sequences: evidence for independent learning systems. In *Handbook of Implicit Learning*, ed. MA Stadler, PA Frensch, pp. 401–44. Thousand Oaks, CA: Sage

Greenfield P. 1991. Language, tools, and brain: the ontogeny and phylogeny of hierarchically organized sequential behavior. *Behav. Brain Sci.* 14:531–95

Greenwald AG. 1970. Sensory feedback mechanisms in performance control: with special reference to the ideo-motor mechanism. *Psychol. Rev.* 77:73–99

Healy AF, Bourne LE Jr, eds. 1995. *Learning and Memory of Knowledge and Skills: Durability and Specificity.* Thousand Oaks, CA: Sage

Heathcote A, Brown S, Mewhort DJK. 2000. The Power Law repealed: the case for an Exponential Law of Practice. *Psychonom. Bull. Rev.* 7:185–207

Hilgard ER, Bower GH. 1975. *Theories of Learning.* Englewood Cliffs, NJ: Prentice Hall. 4th ed.

Holmes G. 1939. The cerebellum of man. *Brain* 62:1–30

Hommel B. 1996. The cognitive representation of action: automatic integration of perceived action effects. *Psychol. Res.* 59:176–86

Ivry RB, Keele SW. 1989. Timing functions of the cerebellum. *J. Cogn. Neurosci.* 1:136–52

Jeannerod M. 1994. The representing brain: neural correlates of motor intention and imagery. *Brain Behav. Sci.* 17:187–245

Jenkins I, Brooks D, Nixon P, Frackowiack R, Passignham R. 1994. Motor sequence learning: a study with positron emission tomography. *J. Neurosci.* 14:3775–90

Johnson SH. 2000. Thinking ahead: the case for motor imagery in prospective judgements of prehension. *Cognition* 74:33–70

Johnson-Laird PN. 1982. Thinking as a skill. *Q. J. Exp. Psychol. A* 34:1–29

Koh K, Meyer DE. 1991. Induction of continuous stimulus-response associations for perceptual-motor performance. *J. Exp. Psychol.: Learn. Mem. Cogn.* 17:811–36

Kolers PA, Roediger HLI. 1984. Procedures of mind. *J. Verbal Learn. Verbal Behav.* 23:425–49

Kramer AF, Strayer DL, Buckley J. 1990. Development and transfer of automatic processing. *J. Exp. Psychol.: Hum. Percept. Perform.* 16:505–22

Krumboltz JD, Weisman RG. 1962. The effect of intermittent confirmation in programmed instruction. *J. Educ. Psychol.* 53:250–53

Landauer TK, Bjork RA. 1978. Optimal rehearsal patterns and name learning. In *Practical Aspects of Memory,* ed. MM Gruneberg,

PE Morris, RN Sykes, pp. 625–32. London: Academic

Larkin JH. 1989. Display-based problem solving. In *Complex Information Processing: The Impact of Herbert A. Simon,* ed. D Klahr, K Kotovsky, pp. 319–41. Hillsdale, NJ, Erlbaum

Lashley KS. 1951. The problem of serial order in behavior. In *Cerebral Mechanisms in Behavior,* ed. LA Jeffress, pp. 112–31. New York: Wiley

Leiner HC, Leiner AL, Dow RS. 1995. The underestimated cerebellum. *Hum. Brain Mapp.* 2:244–54

Logan GD. 1988. Toward an instance theory of automatization. *Psychol. Rev.* 95:492–527

MacKay DG. 1982. The problem of flexibility, fluency, and speed-accuracy trade-off in skilled behavior. *Psychol. Rev.* 89:483–506

Magill RA, Hall KG. 1990. A review of the contextual interference effect in motor skill acquisition. *Hum. Mov. Sci.* 9:241–89

McKendree J, Anderson JR. 1987. Effect of practice on knowledge and use of basic LISP. In *Interfacing Thought: Cognitive Aspects of Human Computer Interaction,* ed. JM Carroll, pp. 236–59. Cambridge, MA: Bradford

Melton AW. 1970. The situation with respect to the spacing of repetitions and memory. *J. Verbal Learn. Verbal Behav.* 9:596–606

Meulenbroek RGJ, Rosenbaum DA, Thomassen AJWM, Loukopoulos LD, Vaughan J. 1996. Adaptation of a reaching model to handwriting: how different effectors can produce the same written output, and other results. *Psychol. Res.* 59:64–74

Neisser U. 1983. Toward a skillful psychology. In *Acquisition of Symbolic Skill,* ed. DR Rogers, JA Sloboda, pp. 1–17. New York: Plenum

Neves DM, Anderson JR. 1981. Knowledge compilation: mechanisms for the automatization of cognitive skills. In *Cognitive Skills and Their Acquisition,* ed. JR Anderson, pp. 57–84. Hillsdale, NJ: Elbaum

Newell KM, van Emerick REA. 1989. The acquisition of coordination: preliminary analysis of learning to write. *Hum. Mov. Sci.* 8:17–32

Nissen MJ, Bullemer P. 1987. Attentional requirements of learning: evidence from performance measures. *Cogn. Psychol.* 19:1–32

Norman DA. 1981. Categorization of action slips. *Psychol. Rev.* 88:1–15

Ohlsson S. 1992. The learning curve for writing books: evidence from Professor Asimov. *Psychol. Sci.* 3:380–82

Perruchet P, Gallego J, Savy I. 1990. A critical reappraisal of the evidence for unconscious abstraction of deterministic rules in complex experimental situations. *Cogn. Psychol.* 22:493–516

Petersen SE, Fox PT, Posner MI, Mintun M, Raichle ME. 1989. Positron emission tomographic studies of the processing of single words. *J. Cogn. Neurosci.* 1:153–70

Pew RW. 1974. Levels of analysis in motor control. *Brain Res.* 71:393–400

Piaget J. 1954. *The Construction of Reality in the Child.* New York: Basic Books

Povel DJ, Collard R. 1982. Structural factors in patterned finger tapping. *Acta Psychol.* 52:107–24

Proteau L, Marteniuk RG, Lévesque L. 1992. A sensorimotor basis for motor learning: evidence indicating specificity of practice. *Q. J. Exp. Psychol. A* 44:557–75

Rae C, Karmiloff-Smith A, Lee MA, Dixon RM, Grant J, et al. 1998. Brain biochemistry in Williams syndrome: evidence for a role of the cerebellum in cognition? *Neurology* 51:33–40

Rea CP, Modigliani V. 1985. The effect of expanded versus massed practice on the retention of multiplication facts and spelling lists. *Hum. Learn.* 4:11–18

Reber AS. 1992. *Implicit Learning And Tacit Knowledge—An Essay On The Cognitive Unconscious.* New York: Oxford Univ. Press

Redding GM, Wallace B. 1997. *Adaptive Spatial Alignment.* Mahwah, NJ: Erlbaum

Redington M, Chater N. 1996. Transfer in artificial grammar learning: a reevaluation. *J. Exp. Psychol.: Gen.* 125:123–38

Reitman JS, Rueter HH. 1980. Organization revealed by recall orders and confirmed by pauses. *Cogn. Psychol.* 12:554–81

Rickard TC, Bourne LE Jr. 1996. Some tests of an identical elements model of basic arithmetic skill. *J. Exp. Psychol.: Learn., Mem. Cogn.* 22:1281–95

Roland PE. 1993. *Brain Activation.* New York: Wiley

Rosenbaum DA. 1987. Successive approximations to a model of human motor programming. In *Psychology of Learning and Motivation,* ed. GH Bower, 21:153–82. Orlando, FL: Academic

Rosenbaum DA, Kenny S, Derr MA. 1983. Hierarchical control of rapid movement sequences. *J. Exp. Psychol.: Hum. Percept Perform.* 9:86–102

Rosenbaum DA, Meulenbroek R, Vaughan J, Jansen C. 1999. Coordination of reaching and grasping by capitalizing on obstacle avoidance and other constraints. *Exp. Brain Res.* 128:92–100

Rosenbaum DA, Vaughan J, Jorgensen MJ, Barnes HJ, Stewart E. 1993. Plans for object manipulation. In *Attention and Performance XIV—A Silver Jubilee: Synergies in Experimental Psychology, Artificial Intelligence and Cognitive Neuroscience,* ed. DE Meyer, S Kornblum, pp. 803–20. Cambridge, MA: MIT Press

Schmidt RA, Bjork RA. 1992. New conceptualizations of practice: common principles in three paradigms suggest new concepts for training. *Psychol. Sci.* 3:207–14

Schmidt RA, Lee TD. 1999. *Motor Control and Learning—A Behavioral Emphasis.* Champaign, IL: Hum. Kinetics. 3rd ed.

Schmidt RA, Young DE, Swinnen W, Shapiro DC. 1989. Summary knowledge of results for skill acquisition: support for the guidance hypothesis. *J. Exp. Psychol.: Learn. Mem. Cogn.* 15:352–59

Schooler LJ, Anderson JR. 1990. The disruptive potential of immediate feedback. In *Proc. Cogn. Sci. Soc.,* 702–8. Hillsdale, NJ: Erlbaum

Schulz RW, Runquist WN. 1960. Learning and retention of paired adjectives as a function of percentage occurrence of response members. *J. Exp. Psychol.* 59:409–13

Servan-Schreiber E, Anderson JR. 1990. Learning artificial grammars with competitive chunking. *J. Exp. Psychol.: Learn. Mem. Cogn.* 16:592–608

Shanks DR, Johnstone T. 1999. Evaluating the relationship between explicit and implicit knowledge in a sequential reaction time task. *J. Exp. Psychol.: Learn. Mem. Cogn.* 25:1435–51

Shanks DR, St. John MF. 1994. Characteristics of dissociable human learning systems. *Behav. Brain Sci.* 17:367–447

Shapiro DC, Schmidt RA. 1982. The schema theory: recent evidence and developmental implications. In *The Development of Movement Control and Coordination*, ed. JAS Kelso, JE Clark, pp. 113–50. New York: Wiley

Shea JB, Morgan RL. 1979. Contextual interference effects on acquisition, retention, and transfer of a motor skill. *J. Exp. Psychol.: Learn. Mem. Cogn.* 5:179–87

Singley K, Anderson JR. 1989. *The Transfer of Cognitive Skill.* Cambridge, MA: Harvard Univ. Press

Sirigu A, Duhamel JR, Cohen L, Pillon B, Dubois B, Agid Y. 1996. The mental representation of hand movements after parietal cortex damage. *Science* 273:1564–68

Smith LB, Thelen E, Titzer R, McLin D. 1999. Knowing in the context of acting: the task dynamics of the A-not-B error. *Psychol. Rev.* 106:235–60

Snoddy GS. 1926. Learning and stability: a psychophysical analysis of a case of motor learning with clinical applications. *J. Appl. Psychol.* 10:1–36

Stein BE, Meredith MA. 1993. *The Merging of the Senses.* Cambridge, MA: MIT Press

Sternberg S, Monsell S, Knoll RL, Wright CE. 1978. The latency and duration of rapid movement sequences: comparisons of speech and typewriting. In *Information Processing in Motor Control and Learning*, ed. GE Stelmach, pp. 117–52. New York: Academic

Thorndike EL. 1903. *Educational Psychology.* New York: Lemcke & Buechner

Turvey MT. 1996. Dynamic touch. *Am. Psychol.* 51:1134–52

Weimer WB. 1977. A conceptual framework for cognitive psychology: motor theories of the mind. In *Perceiving, Acting, and Knowing: Toward an Ecological Psychology*, ed. R Shaw, J Bransford, pp. 267–311. Hillsdale, NJ: Erlbaum

Wenger JL, Carlson RA. 1996. Cognitive sequence knowledge: what is learned? *J. Exp. Psychol.: Learn. Mem. Cogn.* 22:599–619

Wenger JL, Carlson RA. 1995. Learning and the coordination of sequential information. *J. Exp. Psychol.: Hum. Percept. Perform.* 21: 170–82

Wexler M, Kosslyn SM, Berthoz A. 1998. Motor processes in mental rotation. *Cognition* 68:7–94

Winstein CJ, Schmidt RA. 1990. Reduced knowledge of results enhances motor skill learning. *J. Exp. Psychol.: Learn. Mem. Cogn.* 16:677–91

Wohlschläger A, Wohlschläger A. 1998. Mental and manual rotation. *J. Exp. Psychol.: Hum. Percept. Perform.* 24:397–412

Wulf G, Schmidt RA. 1989. The learning of generalized motor programs: reducing the relative frequence of knowledge of results enhances memory. *J. Exp. Psychol.: Learn. Mem. Cogn.* 15:748–57

Yee PL, Hunt E, Pellegrino JW. 1991. Coordinating cognitive information: task effects and individual differences in integrating information from several sources. *Cogn. Psychol.* 23:615–80

Zhang G, Simon HA. 1985. STM capacity for Chinese words and idioms: chunking and the acoustical loop hypothesis. *Mem. Cogn.* 13:193–201

Zhang J, Norman DA. 1994. Representations in distributed cognitive tasks. *Cogn. Sci.* 18:87–122

Annu. Rev. Psychol. 2001. 52:471–99

THE SCIENCE OF TRAINING: A Decade of Progress

Eduardo Salas[1] and Janis A. Cannon-Bowers[2]

[1]Department of Psychology and Institute for Simulation & Training,
University of Central Florida, Orlando, Florida 32816-1390;
e-mail: esalas@pegasus.cc.ucf.edu
[2]Naval Air Warfare Center Training Systems Division, Orlando,
Florida 32826-3224; e-mail: Cannon-BowJA@navair.navy.mil

Key Words   training design, training evaluation, distance training, team training, transfer of training

■ **Abstract**   This chapter reviews the training research literature reported over the past decade. We describe the progress in five areas of research including training theory, training needs analysis, antecedent training conditions, training methods and strategies, and posttraining conditions. Our review suggests that advancements have been made that help us understand better the design and delivery of training in organizations, with respect to theory development as well as the quality and quantity of empirical research. We have new tools for analyzing requisite knowledge and skills, and for evaluating training. We know more about factors that influence training effectiveness and transfer of training. Finally, we challenge researchers to find better ways to translate the results of training research into practice.

CONTENTS

0066-4308/01/0201-0471$14.00

INTRODUCTION

In the 30 years since the first review of training in the *Annual Review of Psychology*, things have progressed dramatically in terms of both the science and practice of training. On the practice side, socio-cultural, technological, economic, and political pressures have all combined to force modern organizations to take a closer look at their human capital in general, and training in particular (Thayer 1997, Howard 1995). In fact, now more than ever, organizations must rely on workplace learning and continuous improvement in order to remain competitive (London & Moore 1999). In addition, organizations have shifted their views about training from a separate, stand-alone event to a fully integrated, strategic component of the organization. New training-related approaches, including action learning, just-in-time training, mentoring, coaching, organizational learning, and managing skill portfolios are all currently being explored. Finally, modern organizations must cope with training needs associated with the changing demographics of the population—both an older and more diverse workforce can be expected as we move into the new millennium.

It is important to note that improved training comes at a cost. Recent estimates suggest that the investment in training activities in organizations ranges from $55.3 billion to $200 billion annually (Bassi & Van Buren 1999, McKenna 1990), an investment that has not only created a growing interest in training, but also in learning technologies and performance-improvement processes, practices, and services. In fact, there is an increasing concern in organizations that the investment made in training must be justified in terms of improved organizational performance—increased productivity, profit, or safety; reduced error, enhanced market share (e.g. Huselid 1995, Martocchio & Baldwin 1997, Salas et al 2000).

The past 30 years have also witnessed tremendous growth in training research. This trend has been so pronounced that we are led to conclude that there has been nothing less than an explosion in training-related research in the past 10 years. More theories, models, empirical results, reviews, and meta-analyses are available today than ever before. Whether this research is having an effect on training practice—that is, a meaningful impact on how organizations actually train—is a matter of some debate. We return to this issue after documenting the many advances in training research over the past decade.

This is the sixth review of training and development to appear in the *Annual Review of Psychology* (see Campbell 1971, Goldstein 1980, Wexley 1984, Latham 1988, Tannenbaum & Yukl 1992). In this review, we focus on research published from 1992 to January 2000. Similar to Tannenbaum & Yukl's (1992), our review is selective and descriptive. We focus primarily on the research that is concerned with the design, delivery, and evaluation of training in work organizations. Our review is organized as follows. We first discuss the recent theoretical advancements in training over the past decade. Then we address the relevant research on training needs analysis, including organization, job/task, and person analysis. Following this, we address antecedent training conditions (i.e. pretraining variables) that may enhance or disrupt learning. Next we turn our discussion to research on training methods and instructional strategies. In this section we discuss recent developments in simulation-based training, learning approaches, team training, and the influence of technology on training research and practice. Finally we review the research on post-training conditions. This includes a discussion of training evaluation and transfer of training. Wherever appropriate we point out the research needs and gaps. We conclude with a few observations and trends and a word about the future. Consistent with previous reviews, this review does not cover basic issues involved in skill acquisition and learning, organizational development, socialization in organizations, or educational psychology. We also do not synthesize the large literature in practitioner-oriented publications.

Initial Observations

Our first observation is that in 30 years of documenting the progress of training research, it is clear that the field, by any measure, has changed dramatically—for the better. Now, as recent reviews have documented, training-related theories abound. As noted earlier, there is also more empirical training-related research going on—in the field as well as in the lab—than ever before. Researchers are adopting a systems view of training and are more concerned with the organizational context. There are new models, constructs (e.g. opportunity to perform), and influences (e.g. technology) in the reported research. The traditional training evaluation paradigm has been expanded, and there are more evaluations being conducted and reported. There are better tools with which to conduct training evaluations, and better (and more practical) experimental designs have emerged. The field can now offer sound, pedagogically based principles and guidelines to practitioners and instructional developers. Furthermore, the impact of training on performance and organizational effectiveness is being felt (Bassi & Van Buren 1999), although clearly more documentation is needed here. Finally, there are more books and textbooks related to training (e.g. Ford et al 1997, Quinones & Ehrestein 1997, Noe 1999, Wexley & Latham 2000, Goldstein 1993; plus over 20 more that have been reviewed in *Personnel Psychology*). The science of training has progressed and matured—it is now truly an exciting and dynamic field. As evidence for this assertion, we summarize some of the latest theoretical advances in the next section.

Theoretical Developments

There have been some influential theories developed about training since 1992. In fact, the past decade has offered us myriad new and expanded theoretical frameworks, as well as concepts and constructs. This thinking is deeper, richer, more comprehensive, and more focused. More importantly, the field has been energized by these developments so that empirical work has followed. Some of these frameworks and concepts are broad, general, and integrating. For example, Tannenbaum and colleagues provided an integrative framework for all the variables that influence the design and delivery of training (see Tannenbaum et al 1993, Cannon-Bowers et al 1995). The framework outlines in detail the pretraining and during-training conditions that may influence learning, as well as the factors that may facilitate the transfer of skills after training. Kozlowski & Salas (1997), drawing from organizational theory, discussed the importance of characterizing the factors and processes in which training interventions are implemented and transferred in organizations. Moreover, Kozlowski and colleagues (Kozlowski et al 2000) consider organizational system factors and training design issues that influence the effectiveness of vertical transfer processes. Vertical transfer refers to the upward propagation of individual-level training outcomes that emerge as team- and organizational-level outcomes. This issue has been largely neglected by researchers yet is suggested to be crucial to training effectiveness. Similarly, researchers have begun to understand and outline the barriers and myths that exist in organizations as they implement training (Dipboye 1997, Salas et al 1999). In other work, Kraiger et al (1993) provided new conceptualizations of learning and evaluation theory, approaches, and measurement. These authors expanded Kirkpatrick's (1976) evaluation typology by incorporating recent notions in cognitive psychology.

Other conceptual developments are more focused. For example, Ford et al (1997) invoked "the opportunity to perform" construct as a way to understand the transfer of training process. Colquitt et al (2000) summarized (qualitatively and quantitatively) the literature on training motivation and offered a new, integrative model. Cannon-Bowers & Salas (1997) proposed a framework for how to conceptualize performance measurement in training. Thayer & Teachout (1995) developed a model to understand the climate for transfer in organizations, as well as in-training conditions that enhance transfer. Cannon-Bowers et al (1998) advanced a number of conditions, concepts, and interventions that may enhance practice. Ford and colleagues have looked at individual differences and learner control strategies (e.g. Ford et al 1998). Training researchers have also examined variables such as the pretraining context (e.g. Baldwin & Magjuka 1997, Quinones 1995), conscientiousness and training outcomes (e.g. Colquitt & Simmering 1998, Martocchio & Judge 1997), individual and situational characteristics that influence training motivation (e.g. Facteau et al 1995, Mathieu & Martineau 1997), and participation in developmental activities (e.g. Noe & Wilk 1993, Baldwin & Magjuka 1997), just to name a few.

In sum, these theoretical advancements have provided a much needed forum in which to discuss, debate, analyze, and understand better the design and delivery of training in organizations. Moreover, they have provided an organized framework in which systematic research could be couched. Our conclusion is that training research is no longer atheoretical as charged by our predecessors. We believe the field is healthier because of these influences and all the empirical work that has followed.

TRAINING NEEDS ANALYSIS

It is well acknowledged that one of the most important steps in training development is conducting a training needs analysis. This first step in training development focuses on the process of deciding who and what should be trained. A training needs analysis is primarily conducted to determine where training is needed, what needs to be taught, and who needs to be trained (Goldstein 1993). This phase has several outcomes. One is the specification of learning objectives, which in turn shape the design and delivery of training, as well as the process of criterion development. Consistent with Tannenbaum & Yukl (1992), we found a limited amount of empirical work on training needs analysis. In this section we discuss two components: organizational analysis and job/task analysis. We briefly address the third phase—person analysis.

Organizational Analysis

The purpose of an organizational analysis is to outline the systemwide components of the organization that may affect the delivery of a training program (Goldstein 1993). That is, it focuses on the congruence between training objectives with such factors as organizational goals, available resources, constraints, and support for transfer. Unfortunately, many training programs fail to reach their goals because of organizational constraints and conflicts, which could have been identified and ameliorated before training was implemented. Hence, conducting an organizational analysis is an important first-step training design. The best treatment of this topic can be found in Goldstein (1993).

Only recently have training researchers begun to pay attention to organizational analysis. One study, conducted by Rouiller & Goldstein (1993) in a chain of fast food restaurants, demonstrated that organizational climate (e.g. situational cues, consequences) was a powerful predictor of whether trainees transferred the learned skills. A second study conducted in a chain of supermarkets by Tracey et al (1995) showed that organizational climate and culture were directly related to posttraining behaviors. Clearly, these two studies illustrate how powerful an effect the organizational environment can have on whether newly acquired knowledge, skills, and attitudes (KSAs) are applied on the job (see also the transfer of training section).

As job requirements change, so does the need to help organizations plan their human resources activities. A number of issues have emerged that are related to organizational analysis. For example, authors have expressed the need to understand how the organizational context influences human resources strategies (e.g. Tannenbaum & Dupuree-Bruno 1994) to enhance continuous learning environments (e.g. London & Moore 1999), to manage knowledge effectively (e.g. Tannenbaum 1997), and to determine the best organizational strategy (e.g. who is responsible for training?) for learning and training (e.g. Martocchio & Baldwin 1997). Obviously, organizational analysis is crucial for ensuring the success of a training program. However, more research is needed to develop practical and diagnostic tools to determine the organizational context relative to training.

Job/Task Analysis

Historically, job/task analysis has been used to identify the information necessary to create the learning objectives (Goldstein 1993). A job/task analysis results in a detailed description of the work functions to be performed on the job, the conditions under which the job is to be performed, and the KSAs needed to perform those tasks.

In the past decade, new research aimed at developing solid methods, approaches, and knowledge elicitation techniques for determining training needs and requirements have emerged. For example, Arvey et al (1992) explored the use of task inventories to forecast skills and abilities necessary for a future job. The results indicated that such forecasting predictions could represent useful information to training analysis. Wilson & Zalewski (1994) tested an expert system program as a way to estimate the amount of 11 abilities required for performing a job. The results indicated that most incumbents preferred the expert system method to the traditional ability rating scales.

Some attention has been given to better understanding the job/task analysis process for training purposes. For example, Ford et al (1993) examined the impact of task experience and individual factors on task ratings of training emphasis. Results indicated that as experience (and self-efficacy) increased over time, it tended to cause trainees to increase their ratings of training emphasis. Also, a few researchers have focused on outlining a task analysis procedure for teams (e.g. Baker et al 1998, Bowers et al 1993, Blickensderfer et al 2000). Much more research is needed, however. Specifically, we need to design and develop a methodology that helps instructional designers and analysts uncover the team-based tasks and their related KSAs.

Cognitive Task Analysis   Cognitive task analysis refers to a set of procedures for understanding the mental processing and mental requirements for job performance. It has received much attention recently (see Dubois et al 1997/1998, Schraagen et al 2000), fueled primarily by interest in understanding how trainees acquire and develop knowledge, and how they organize rules, concepts, and associations (see Zsambok & Klein 1997). In addition, research aimed at uncovering the nature of expertise and how experts make decisions in complex natural environments has led to the development of tools such as cognitive task analysis (see Salas & Klein 2000, Schraagen et al 2000).

Cognitive task analysis is based on techniques (e.g. verbal protocols) used by cognitive scientists to elicit knowledge from subject matter experts. Products of a cognitive task analysis include information-generating templates for mental model development, cues for fostering complex decision-making skills, cues for developing simulation and scenarios used during training, and information for designing performance measurement and feedback protocols. For example, Neerincx & Griffoen (1996) applied a cognitive task analysis to assess the task load of jobs and to provide indicators for the redesign of jobs. This new application showed its benefits over the "old" task load analysis.

A cognitive task analysis can complement existing (behavioral) forms of training-need analysis. For example, research on meta-cognition suggests that through continued practice or experience, individuals automatize complex behaviors, thus freeing up cognitive resources for monitoring and evaluating behavior (Rogers et al 1997). By determining trainees' current complex cognitive skills, instructional designers can gain insight into trainees' capacity for proficiency and diagnose performance deficiencies. Thus, training needs analysis should identify not only the requisite knowledge and skills to perform tasks, but also the cues and cognitions that enable trainees to know when to apply those skills. By incorporating the development of these skills into training, instructional designers can provide trainees with valuable self-help tools. Cognitive task analysis is becoming a useful tool but needs more development. Specifically, a theoretically driven methodology that clearly outlines the steps to take and how to analyze the data is needed.

We found no empirical work regarding the third phase of training-needs analysis—person analysis. However, the emerging literature of 360° feedback may be relevant. This approach identifies individual strengths and weaknesses, but perhaps more importantly, provides suggestions for improvement that often revolve around training and development activities.

In summary, it is interesting to note that whereas most training researchers believe and espouse that training-needs analysis is the most important phase in training, this phase remains largely an art rather than a science. We need more research that would enable us to develop a systematic methodology to determine the training needs of organizations.

ANTECEDENT TRAINING CONDITIONS

Events that occur before training can be as important as (and in some cases more important than) those that occur during and after training. Research has shown that activities that occur prior to training have an impact on how effective training turns out to be (Tannenbaum et al 1993). These factors fall into three general categories: (*a*) what trainees bring to the training setting, (*b*) variables that engage the trainee to learn and participate in developmental activities, and (*c*) how the training can be prepared so as to maximize the learning experience. Each of these is described in more detail below.

Individual Characteristics

Cognitive Ability   Research aimed at understanding how characteristics the trainee brings to the training environment influence learning has proliferated in the past decade. For example, Ree et al (1995) developed a causal model showing the role of general cognitive ability and prior job knowledge in subsequent job-knowledge attainment and work-sample performance during training. The resulting model showed that ability influenced the attainment of job knowledge directly, and that general cognitive ability influenced work samples through job knowledge. Similar findings have been obtained by Ree & Earles (1991), Colquitt et al (2000), Randel et al (1992), Quick et al (1996), Kaemar et al (1997), Warr & Bunce (1995), and many others. Therefore, it is safe to conclude, based on this body of evidence (and others as well, e.g. Hunter 1986), that g (general intelligence) is good—it promotes self-efficacy and performance, and it helps a great deal with skill acquisition. Clearly, those who have high cognitive ability (all other things being equal) will likely learn more and succeed in training.

At this point, we probably need to look more closely at low-ability trainees and conduct research on how to optimize learning for them. Also, it might be worthwhile to examine in more depth concepts such as tacit knowledge and practical intelligence (Sternberg 1997) and their relation to on-the-job learning. Finally, it is worth noting that cognitive ability is a viable predictor of training performance (i.e. learning), but not necessarily performance on the job. Many jobs have requirements that go beyond cognitive ability (e.g. psychomotor demands), and/or depend on other factors (e.g. motivation) for success. Therefore, it is important to understand the nature of the job to determine whether cognitive ability will be a valid predictor of training transfer.

Self-efficacy   This construct has been widely studied in this past decade. The findings are consistent: Self-efficacy, whether one has it before or acquires it during training, leads to better learning and performance. Self-efficacy (the belief that one can perform specific tasks and behaviors) is a powerful predictor of performance, as has been shown time and time again (e.g. Cole & Latham 1997 Eden & Aviram 1993, Ford et al 1998, Mathieu et al 1993, Martocchio 1994, Martocchio & Webster 1992, Mathieu et al 1992, Quinones 1995, Mitchell et al 1994, Phillips & Gully 1997, Stevens & Gist 1997, Stajkovic & Luthans 1998). Self-efficacy also mediates a number of personal variables including job satisfaction, organizational commitment, intention to quit the job, the relationship between training and adjustment in newcomers (Saks 1995), and the relationship between conscientiousness and learning (Martocchio & Judge 1997). Self-efficacy has also been shown to have motivational effects (e.g. Quinones 1995), to influence training reactions (Mathieu et al 1992), and to dictate whether trainees will use training technology (Christoph et al 1998).

In sum, it is well established that self-efficacy enhances leaning outcomes and performance. A research need that still remains is to expand what we know about self-efficacy at the team level. Whereas a few studies have investigated collective efficacy in training (e.g. Guzzo et al 1993, Smith-Jentsch et al 2000), considerably more work is needed to better understand the mechanisms of collective efficacy in learning as a means to raise team performance. In addition, it might be useful to consider the use of self-efficacy as a deliberate training intervention (i.e. developing training targeted at raising self-efficacy), as well as a desirable outcome of training (i.e. as an indicator of training success).

Goal Orientation   Goal orientation has received considerable attention in recent years (e.g. Brett & VandeWalle 1999, Ford et al 1998, Phillips & Gully 1997). This construct is broadly conceptualized as the mental framework used by individuals to interpret and behave in learning- or achievement-oriented activities. Two classes of goal orientation have been identified (Dweck 1986, Dweck & Leggett 1988): (*a*) mastery (or learning) goal orientation, whereby individuals seek to develop competence by acquiring new skills and mastering novel situations, and (*b*) performance goal orientation, whereby individuals pursue assurances of their own competence by seeking good performance evaluations and avoiding negative ones. There is a debate in the literature as to whether goal orientation is a disposition, a state, or both (e.g. Stevens & Gist 1997), whether it is a multidimensional construct (e.g. Elliot & Church 1997, VandeValle 1997), or whether these two goal strategies are mutually exclusive (Button et al 1996). Although continued research will bring more conceptual clarity, recent studies have shown, in general, that goal orientation influences learning outcomes and performance. For example, Fisher & Ford (1998) found that a mastery orientation was a strong predictor of a knowledge-based learning outcome. Ford et al (1998) showed that mastery orientation was positively related to the meta-cognitive activity of the trainee. Phillips & Gully (1997) demonstrated that mastery goal orientation was positively related to self-efficacy. All these results are promising. More research is needed to determine how goal orientation is developed. Specifically, it must be determined whether goal orientation is a relatively stable trait, or if it can be modified prior to training. Should the latter be true, then efforts to move trainees toward a mastery orientation should be developed.

Training Motivation

Training motivation can be conceptualized as the direction, effort, intensity, and persistence that trainees apply to learning-oriented activities before, during, and after training (Kanfer 1991, Tannenbaum & Yukl 1992). Recently, several studies have found (and confirmed) that trainees' motivation to learn and attend training has an effect on their skill acquisition, retention, and willingness to apply the newly acquired KSAs on the job (e.g. Martocchio & Webster 1992, Mathieu et al 1992, Quinones 1995, Tannenbaum & Yukl 1992). Whereas the literature is, in general, clear about the influence of training motivation on learning outcomes, it has lacked some conceptual precision and specificity, and has been somewhat piecemeal. An exception is a recent effort by Colquitt et al (2000) that has shed light on the underlying processes and variables involved in understanding training motivation throughout the training process. Their integrative narrative and meta-analytic review suggest that training motivation is multifaceted and influenced by a set of individual (e.g. cognitive ability, self-efficacy, anxiety, age, conscientiousness) and situational (e.g. climate) characteristics. This effort provides the beginnings of an integrative theory of training motivation—a much needed synthesis and organization.

A number of important implications for research and practice can be drawn from Colquitt et al's review. For example, they point out the need to assess trainee's personality during training-needs analysis, a much neglected or ignored assessment during person analysis. In fact, Colquitt et al also called for the need to expand the kind of personality variables we have examined in recent years to include emotions, adaptability, trait goal orientation, and other Big Five variables. Another important implication is the link they found between age and motivation to learn—older workers showed lower motivation, learning, and post-training efficacy. However, it may be prudent to consider this conclusion carefully because a host of other issues must be considered when discussing the training needs of older workers (including the design of training itself). Clearly, in an era of technology-driven instruction and an aging workforce, a challenge for instructional developers will be to design learning environments where older trainees can be trained (and retrained) with ease.

In the future, we also need to continue gaining a deeper understanding of training motivation because it is crucial for learning and has direct implications for the design and delivery of training. Future work should consider those factors that influence training motivation for job development activities and for situations in which workers acquire new skills through informal learning mechanisms. Longitudinal studies are also needed.

Training Induction and Pretraining Environment

Considerable research has gone into understanding which factors help trainees to optimize the benefits of training. These are usually interventions employed before training to ensure that the trainee gets the most out of the learning experience.

Prepractice Conditions   It is well documented that practice is a necessary condition for skill acquisition. However, all practice is not equal. In fact, the precise nature of practice and its relationship to learning outcomes has been largely ignored or misunderstood. Recent thinking and research is beginning to suggest that practice may be a complex process, not simply task repetition (e.g. Ehrenstein et al 1997, Shute & Gawlick 1995, Schmidt & Bjork 1992); we address this issue further in Specific Learning Approaches. For example, Cannon-Bowers et al (1998) provided a framework for delineating the conditions that might enhance the utility and efficacy of practice in training. They drew from the literature a number of interventions (e.g. meta-cognitive strategies, advanced organizers, and preparatory information) that can be applied before actual practice as a way to prepare the trainee for training. Empirical verification of these interventions needs to be conducted.

The Pretraining Environment and Climate   Can pretraining contextual factors also affect learning outcomes? Recent research suggests that the manner in which the organization frames the training and the nature of trainees' previous experiences in training do influence learning outcomes. For example, Quinones (1995) demonstrated that the manner in which training was framed (i.e. as advanced or remedial) influenced training motivation and learning (see also Quinones 1997). Martocchio (1992), who labeled the training assignment as an "opportunity," showed similar findings. Smith-Jentsch et al (1996a) demonstrated that trainees' previous experiences with training (e.g. prior negative events) affected learning and retention. Baldwin & Magjuka (1997) explored the notion of training as an organizational episode and laid out a framework of other pretraining contextual factors (e.g. voluntary versus mandatory attendance) that may influence motivation to learn. These studies suggest that experience with training (both task-based and event-based) is important to subsequent training outcomes. This is certainly a neglected area, and one in which much more work is needed. Specifically, we need to know how these experiences shape self-efficacy, expectations about the training, motivation to learn and apply skills on the job, and learning.

TRAINING METHODS AND INSTRUCTIONAL STRATEGIES

Instructional strategies are defined as a set of tools (e.g. task analysis), methods (e.g. simulation), and content (i.e. required competencies) that, when combined, create an instructional approach (Salas & Cannon-Bowers 1997). Most effective strategies are created around four basic principles: (*a*) They present relevant information or concepts to be learned; (*b*) they demonstrate the KSAs to be learned; (*c*) they create opportunities for trainees to practice the skills; and (*d*) they provide feedback to trainees during and after practice. Because there is no single method to deliver training, researchers continue to address how to best present targeted information to trainees. Specifically, researchers are seeking cost-effective, content-valid, easy-to-use, engaging, and technology-based methods (e.g. Baker et al 1993, Bretz & Thompsett 1992, Steele-Johnson & Hyde 1997). In the next section, we review research related to instructional strategies in several major categories. First, we review specific learning approaches and learning technologies and distance training. Next, we cover simulation-based training and games, followed by a review of recent work in team training.

Specific Learning Approaches

Traditionally, training researchers have investigated how to optimize learning and retention by manipulating feedback, practice intervals, reinforcement schedules, and other conditions within the learning process itself. In this regard, Fisk, Kurlik, and colleagues (Kirlik et al 1998) improved performance in a complex decision-making task by training consistently mapped components of the task to automaticity (i.e. so that they could be performed with little or no active cognitive control). Along these same lines, Driskell et al (1992) conducted a meta-analysis of the effects of overlearning on retention. The results of their analysis showed that overlearning produces a significant effect on retention which, in turn, is moderated by the degree of overlearning, length of retention period, and type of task.

Attention has also been focused on developing collaborative training protocols. This is distinguished from team training (see below) by the fact that team training applies to training competencies that are required for performance of a team task. Collaborative learning, on the other hand, refers to situations where trainees are trained in groups, but not necessarily to perform a team task. The idea is that there are features of group interaction that benefit the learning process (e.g. the opportunity for vicarious learning or interaction with peers). For example, Arthur et al (1997) provided strong support and justification for the ongoing use of innovative dyadic protocols (i.e. training two trainees at once) for the training of pilots and navigators in both military and nonmilitary settings. However, Arthur et al (1996) showed that the comparative effectiveness of dyadic versus individual protocols for computer-based training is moderated by trainees' level of interaction anxiety, with only low interaction anxiety trainees benefiting from dyadic protocols (see also Arthur et al 1997). Collaborative protocols have also been shown to reduce required instructor time and resources by half (Shebilske et al 1992), and to provide observational learning opportunities that compensate for hands-on practice efficiently and effectively, as predicted by social learning theory (Shebilske et al 1998).

Researchers have also studied the conditions of practice as they relate to learning. For example, Goettl et al (1996) compared an alternating task module protocol, which alternated sessions on video game–like tasks and algebra word problems, with a massed protocol, which blocked sessions on the tasks. The findings showed that alternating task modules provided an advantage in learning and retention in both the video games and algebra word problems.

Along these lines, Bjork and colleagues (Schmidt & Bjork 1992, Ghodsian et al 1997) have provided an interesting reconsideration of findings regarding practice schedules. These authors argued that introducing difficulties for the learner during practice will enhance transfer (but not necessarily immediate posttraining performance). By reconceptualizing interpretation of data from several studies, Schmidt & Bjork (1992) provided a compelling case for a new approach to arranging practice. This approach includes introducing variation in the way tasks are ordered for practice, in the nature and scheduling of feedback, and in the versions of the task to be practiced, and also by providing less frequent feedback. In all cases, the authors argue that even though acquisition (i.e. immediate) performance may be decreased, retention and generalization are enhanced owing to additional—and most likely deeper—information processing requirements during practice. Shute & Gawlick (1995) supported this conclusion in an investigation of computer-based training for flight engineering knowledge and skill.

In other work, Driskell and colleagues (Driskell & Johnston 1998, Johnston & Cannon-Bowers 1996; JE Driskell, E Salas, JH Johnston, submitted) have investigated the use of stress-exposure training (SET) as a means to prepare trainees to work in high stress environments. SET, which is based on clinical research into stress inoculation, has several phases. In the first phase, trainees are provided with preparatory information that includes a description of which stressors are likely to be encountered in the environment and what the likely impact of those stressors on the trainee will be. The second phase—skill acquisition—focuses on behavioral- and cognitive-skills training designed to help trainees cope with the stress. In the final phase, application and practice of learned skills is conducted under conditions that gradually approximate the stress environment. Results of investigations of this protocol have indicated that SET is successful in reducing trainees' subjective perception of stress, while improving performance. Moreover, the effects of SET generalized to novel stressors and tasks.

Learning Technologies and Distance Training

There is no doubt that technology is shaping how training is delivered in organizations. While still relying heavily on classroom training, organizations have begun to explore technologies such as video conferencing, electronic performance support systems, video discs, and on-line Internet /Intranet courses. Indeed, Web-based training may make "going-to" training obsolete. It is being applied in education, industry, and the military at an alarming rate (these days, one can get a PhD through the Web). What is probably more alarming is that this implementation is happening without much reliance on the science of training. Many issues about how to design distance learning systems remain open. Theoretically-based research is needed to uncover principles and guidelines that can aid instructional designers in building sound distance training. A few have begun to scratch the surface (e.g. Schreiber & Berge 1998) of this topic, but a science of distance learning and training needs to evolve. Specifically, it must be determined what level of interaction is needed between trainees and instructors. Moreover, the nature of such interaction must be specified. For example, do instructors need to see trainees in order to conduct effective instruction? Do trainees need to see instructors or is it better for them to view other material? What is the best mechanism for addressing trainee questions (e.g. through chat rooms or e-mail)? Should learners have control over the pace and nature of instruction [some evidence from studies of computer-based training support the use of learner control (see Shute et al 1998), but the extent of its benefits for distance learning is not known]? These and other questions must be addressed as a basis to develop sound distance-training systems.

Advances in technology are also enabling the development of intelligent tutoring systems that have the potential to reduce or eliminate the need for human instructors for certain types of learning tasks. Early indications are that intelligent software can be programmed to successfully monitor, assess, diagnose, and remediate performance in tasks such as computer programming and solving algebra problems (e.g. see Anderson et al 1995). As this technology becomes more widely available (and less costly to develop), it may provide organizations with a viable alternative to traditional computer-based or classroom training.

Simulation-Based Training and Games

Simulation continues to be a popular method for delivery training. Simulators are widely used in business, education, and the military (Jacobs & Dempsey 1993). In fact, the military and the commercial aviation industry are probably the biggest investors in simulation-based training. These simulations range in cost, fidelity, and functionality. Many simulation systems (including simulators and virtual environments) have the ability to mimic detailed terrain, equipment failures, motion, vibration, and visual cues about a situation. Others are less sophisticated and have less physical fidelity, but represent well the KSAs to be trained (e.g. Jentsch & Bowers 1998). A recent trend is to use more of these low-fidelity devices to train complex skills. There is also more evidence that skills transfer after training that uses these simulations (e.g. MT Brannick, C Prince, E Salas, unpublished manuscript; Gopher et al 1994). For example, some researchers are studying the viability of computer games for training complex tasks. Gopher et al (1994) tested the transfer of skills from a complex computer game to the flight performance of cadets in the Israeli Air Force flight school. They argued that the context relevance of the game to flight was based on a skill-oriented task analysis, which used information provided by contemporary models of the human processing system as the framework. Flight performance scores of two groups of cadets who received 10 hours of training in the computer game were compared with a matched group with no game experience. Results showed that the groups with game experience performed much better in subsequent test flights than did those with no game experience. Jentsch & Bowers (1998) and Goettl et al (1996) have reported similar findings.

Precisely why simulation and simulators work is not well known. A few studies have provided preliminary data (e.g. Bell & Waag 1998, Jentsch & Bowers 1998, Ortiz 1994), but there is a somewhat misleading conclusion that simulation (in and of itself) leads to learning. Unfortunately, most of the evaluations rely on trainee reaction data and not on performance or learning data (see Salas et al 1998). More systematic and rigorous evaluations of large-scale simulations and simulators are needed. Nonetheless, the use of simulation continues at a rapid pace in medicine, maintenance, law enforcement, and emergency management settings. However, some have noted (e.g. Salas et al 1998) that simulation and simulators are being used without much consideration of what has been learned about cognition, training design, or effectiveness. There is a growing need to incorporate the recent advances in training research into simulation design and practice. Along these lines, some have argued for an event-based approach to training with simulations (Cannon-Bowers et al 1998, Oser et al 1999, Fowlkes et al 1998). According to this perspective, simulation-based training should be developed with training objectives in mind, and allow for the measurement of training process and outcomes, and provisions for feedback (both during the exercise and for debriefing purposes).

In related work, Ricci et al (1995) investigated the use of a computer-based game to train chemical, biological, and radiological defense procedures. In this case, the game was not a simulation (as discussed above), but a computer-based slot machine that presented trainees with questions about the material. Trainees earned points for correct answers, and received corrective feedback for incorrect ones. The authors argued that motivation to engage in this type of presentation (over text-based material) would result in higher learning. Results indicated that reactions and retention (but not immediate training performance) were higher for the game condition.

Behavior role modeling is another type of simulation-based training that has received attention over the years. Recently, Skarlicki & Latham (1997) found that a training approach that included role-playing, and other elements of behavior modeling, was successful in training organizational citizenship behavior in a labor union setting. Similarly, Smith-Jentsch et al (1996b) found that a behavior modeling approach emphasizing practice (i.e. role playing) and performance feedback was superior to a lecture only or lecture with demonstration format for training assertiveness skills. Also studying assertiveness, Baldwin (1992) found that behavioral reproduction (i.e. demonstrating assertiveness in a situation that was similar to the training environment) was best achieved by exposing trainees only to positive model displays. Conversely, the combination of both positive and negative model displays was most effective in achieving behavioral generalization (i.e. applying the skill outside of the training simulation) four weeks later.

Team Training

As noted by Guzzo & Dickson (1996) and Tannenbaum & Yukl (1992), teams are heavily used in industry, government, and the military. Therefore, these organizations have invested some resources in developing teams (Tannenbaum 1997). A number of theoretically-driven team training strategies has emerged. These include cross-training (Blickensderfer et al 1998), team coordination training (Prince & Salas 1993), team leadership training (Tannenbaum et al 1998), team self-correction (Smith-Jentsch et al 1998), and distributed team training (Dwyer et al 1999). All of these have been tested and evaluated with positive results (see Cannon-Bowers & Salas 1998a).

The aviation community has arguably been the biggest advocate and user of team training (see Helmreich et al 1993). The airlines and the military have extensively applied a strategy labeled crew resource management (CRM) training. This strategy has a 20-year history in the aviation environment. It is used as a tool to improve teamwork in the cockpit but, more importantly, to reduce human error, accidents, and mishaps (Helmreich & Foushee 1993). CRM training has gone through several evolutions (Helmreich et al 1999) and is maturing. Systematic procedures for designing and developing CRM training have been developed (Salas et al 1999), and the evaluation data are encouraging (see Leedom & Simon 1995, Salas et al 1999, Stout et al 1997). CRM training seems to work by changing the crew's attitudes toward teamwork, and by imparting the relevant team competencies. Crew that have received CRM training exhibit more teamwork behaviors in the cockpit (Salas et al 1999, Stout et al 1997). However, more and better evaluations are needed. Most of the evaluations conducted have been in simulation environments. Only recently have evaluations begun to determine the transfer of this training to the actual cockpit.

Other research in team training has focused on developing strategies to train specific competencies (see also Cannon-Bowers & Salas 1998b). For example, Smith-Jentsch et al (1996b) examined determinants of team performance–related assertiveness in three studies. These studies concluded that, whereas both attitudinally focused and skill-based training improved attitudes toward team member assertiveness, practice and feedback were essential to producing behavioral effects. In addition, Volpe et al (1996) used shared mental model theory (Cannon-Bowers et al 1993) as a basis to examine the effects of cross-training and workload on performance. The results indicated that those who received cross-training were more effective in teamwork processes, communication, and overall team performance.

In sum, the literature has begun to provide evidence that team training works. It works when the training is theoretically driven, focused on required competencies, and designed to provide trainees with realistic opportunities to practice and receive feedback. Also, guidelines for practitioners have emerged (e.g. Swezey & Salas 1992, Salas & Cannon-Bowers 2000), tools for designing team training strategies have surfaced (e.g. Bowers et al 1993), and a number of strategies are now available for team training (e.g. Cannon-Bowers & Salas 1997). In the future, we need to know more about how to diagnose team cognitions during training. We also need better and more rigorous measurement protocols to assess shared knowledge. In addition, we need to understand better the mechanisms by which to conduct effective distributed team training.

POST-TRAINING CONDITIONS

Events that occur after training are as important as those that occur before and during training. Therefore, recent research has focused on improving the methods and procedures we use to evaluate training, and on examining the events that ensure transfer and application of newly acquired KSAs. In examining this body of work, we get a clear sense that it is in these two areas where we probably have made the most significant progress. There are theoretical, methodological, empirical, and practical advances. All the issues have not been solved, but meaningful advances have been made in the last decade. This is very encouraging. We first look at training evaluation and then at transfer of training.

Training Evaluation

Kirkpatrick's Typology and Beyond   Kirkpatrick's typology (Kirkpatrick 1976) continues to be the most popular framework for guiding evaluations. However, recent work has either expanded it or pointed out weaknesses, such as the need to develop more diagnostic measures. For example, Kraiger et al (1993) proposed a multi-dimensional view of learning, implying that learning refers to changes in cognitive, affective, and/or skill-based outcomes. The proposed taxonomy can be used to assess and document learning outcomes. In a meta-analysis of studies employing Kirkpatrick's model, Alliger et al (1997) noted that utility-type reaction measures were more strongly related to learning and performance (transfer) than affective-type reaction measures. Surprisingly, they also found that utility-type reaction measures are more predictive of transfer than learning measures. Kraiger & Jung (1997) suggested several processes by which learning outcomes can be derived from instructional objectives of training. Goldsmith & Kraiger (1997) proposed a method for structural assessment of an individual learner's knowledge and skill in a specific domain. This model has been used with some success in several domains (e.g. Kraiger et al 1995, Stout et al 1997).

Clearly, Kirkpatrick's typology has served as a good foundation for training evaluation for many decades (Kirkpatrick 1976). It has been used, criticized, misused, expanded, refined, adapted, and extended. It has served the training research community well—but a richer, more sophisticated typology is needed. Research needs to continue finding better, more diagnostic and rigorous assessments of learning outcomes. The next frontier and greatest challenge in this area is in designing, developing, and testing on-line assessments of learning and performance. As we rely more on technology for training delivery, we need better and more protocols to access learning not only after but also during training (e.g. Ghodsian et al 1997).

Evaluation Design Issues   Training evaluation is one of those activities that is easier said than done. Training evaluation is labor intensive, costly, political, and many times is the bearer of bad news. We also know that it is very difficult to conduct credible and defensible evaluations in the field. Fortunately, training researchers have derived and tested thoughtful, innovative and practical approaches to aid the evaluation process. For example, Sackett & Mullen (1993) proposed other alternatives (e.g. posttesting-only, no control group) to formal experimental designs when answering evaluation questions. They suggested that those questions (e.g. How much change has occurred? What target performance has been reached?) should drive the evaluation mechanisms needed, and that each requires different designs. Haccoun & Hamtiaux (1994) proposed a simple procedure for estimating effectiveness of training in improving trainee knowledge—the internal referencing strategy. This situation tests the implicit training evaluation notion that training-relevant content should show more change (pre-post) than training-irrelevant content. An empirical evaluation using internal referencing strategy versus a more traditional experimental evaluation indicated that the internal referencing strategy approach might permit inferences that mirror those obtained by the more complex designs.

The costs of training evaluation have also been addressed recently. Yang et al (1996) examined two ways to reduce costs. The first method is by assigning different numbers of subjects into training and control groups. An unequal group size design with a larger total sample size may achieve the same level of statistical power at lower cost. In a second method, the authors examined substituting a less expensive proxy criterion measure in place of the target criterion when evaluating the training effectiveness. Using a proxy increases the sample size needed to achieve a given level of statistical power. The authors described procedures for examining the tradeoff between the costs saved by using the less expensive proxy criterion and the costs incurred by the larger sample size. Similar suggestions have been made by Arvey et al (1992).

Evaluations   It is refreshing to see that more evaluations are being reported in the literature; we hope this trend continues. It is only by drawing lessons learned from past evaluations that the design and delivery of training will continue to progress. Several field training evaluations have been reported in team training settings (e.g. Leedom & Simon 1995, Salas et al 1999), sales training (e.g. Morrow et al 1997), stress training (e.g. Friedland & Keinan 1992), cross-cultural management training (e.g. Harrison 1992), transformational leadership training (e.g. Barling et al 1996), career self-management training (e.g. Kossek et al 1998), workforce diversity training (e.g. Hanover & Cellar 1998) and approaches to computer training (e.g. Simon & Werner 1996). All suggest that training works. However, an examination of evaluations where training did not work is also needed (and we suspect there are many). Some important lessons can be learned from these types of evaluations as well.

Transfer of Training

Transfer of training is conceptualized as the extent to which KSAs acquired in a training program are applied, generalized, and maintained over some time in the job environment (Baldwin & Ford 1988). There has been a plethora of research and thinking in the transfer of training area (see Ford & Weissbein 1997). This emerging body of knowledge suggests a number of important propositions and conclusions. For example, (*a*) the organizational learning environment can be reliably measured and varies in meaningful ways across organizations (Tannenbaum

1997); (*b*) the context matters (Quinones 1997)—it sets motivations, expectations, and attitudes for transfer; (*c*) the transfer "climate" can have a powerful impact on the extent to which newly acquired KSAs are used back on the job (e.g. Tracey et al 1995, Thayer & Teachout 1995); (*d*) trainees need an opportunity to perform (Ford et al 1992, Quinones et al 1995); (*e*) delays between training and actual use on the job create significant skill decay (Arthur et al 1998); (*f*) situational cues and consequences predict the extent to which transfer occurs (Rouiller & Goldstein 1993); (*g*) social, peer, subordinate, and supervisor support all play a central role in transfer (e.g. Facteau et al 1995, Tracey et al 1995); (*h*) training can generalize from one context to another (e.g. Tesluk et al 1995); (*i*) intervention strategies can be designed to improve the probability of transfer (e.g. Brinkerhoff & Montesino 1995, Kraiger et al 1995); (*j*) team leaders can shape the degree of transfer through informal reinforcement (or punishment) of transfer activities (Smith-Jentsch et al 2000); (*k*) training transfer needs to be conceptualized as a multidimensional construct—it differs depending on the type of training and closeness of supervision on the job (Yelon & Ford 1999).

As noted by Ford & Weissbein (1997), much progress has been made in this area. There are more studies using complex tasks with diverse samples that actually measure transfer over time. However, much more is needed. Specifically, we need more studies that actually manipulate the transfer climate (e.g. Smith-Jentsch et al 2000). The measurement problems remain. Most studies still use surveys as the preferred method for measuring transfer. Other methods need to be developed and used. Finally, we need to assume that learning outcomes at the individual level will emerge to influence higher level outcomes. Vertical transfer of training is the next frontier. Vertical transfer may be a leverage point for strengthening the links between learning outcomes and organizational effectiveness (see Kozlowski et al 2000).

Taken together, these studies validate the importance of the organizational environment in training. In the future we need to continue to determine which factors affect transfer so that we can maximize it.

FINAL OBSERVATIONS, CONCLUSIONS, AND THE FUTURE

In closing, we draw on the extensive literature just reviewed to offer the following observations:

1. As Tannenbaum & Yukl (1992) predicted, the quality and quantity of research has increased. We truly have seen an explosion of theoretical, methodological, and empirical work in training research, and we do not see an end to this trend. This is very encouraging, and we believe this body of work will pay off as we learn more about how to design and deliver training systems. Therefore, we contend that training research is here to stay and prosper.

2. The progress in theoretical development, especially the attention given to cognitive and organizational concepts, is revolutionizing the field. These new developments promise to change how we conceptualize, design, implement, and institutionalize learning and training in organizations. In the future, we will need a deeper understanding of these concepts, we must strive for more precision and clarity of constructs, and our methods must be more rigorous.

3. The body of literature generated over the past decade suggests that the field does not belong to any single discipline anymore. In the past, industrial/organizational and educational psychologists primarily conducted training research. A closer look at the literature now suggests that cognitive, military, engineering, human factors, and instructional psychologists are involved in training research to an equal degree. In fact, computer scientists and industrial engineers are also researching learning, training technology, and training systems. As many others have observed, we need more cross-fertilization, collaboration, and dialogue among disciplines. To start, we need to read each other's work, and leverage each other's findings, ideas, and principles.

4. Technology has influenced—and will continue to do so for the foreseeable future—the design and delivery of training systems. Whether we like it or not, technology has been embraced in industrial, educational, and military institutions as a way to educate and train their workforces. Technology may, or may not, have instructional features because it is often employed without the benefit of findings from the science of training. However, as we learn more about intelligent tutoring systems, modeling and simulation, multimedia systems, learning agents, Web-based training, distance learning, and virtual environments, this state of affairs may change. It is encouraging that basic and applied research is currently going on to uncover how these technologies enhance learning and human performance (e.g. Cannon-Bowers et al 1998). More research is needed, and the prospects of it happening are very promising. Specifically we need to know more about how to best present knowledge over the Internet, how and when to provide feedback, which instructional strategies are best for Web-based applications, what role instructors and trainees play in these modern systems, and how effectiveness can best be evaluated.

5. The distinction between training effectiveness and training evaluation is much clearer. Kraiger et al (1993) provided the seed for this important distinction. Training effectiveness is concerned with why training works and it is much more "macro" in nature. That is, training effectiveness research looks at the training intervention from a systems perspective—where the success of training depends not only on the method used but on how training (and learning) is positioned, supported, and reinforced by the organization; the motivation and focus of trainees; and

what mechanisms are in place to ensure the transfer of the newly acquired KSAs to the job. Training evaluation on the other hand, examines what works and is much more "micro" (i.e. focused on measurement). It looks at what was learned at different levels and is the basis for determining the training effectiveness of a particular intervention. This distinction has made some significant contributions to practice possible and, more importantly, is helping avoid the simplistic view of training (i.e. that training is just a program or curriculum rather than the complex interaction of many organizational factors). More research aimed at uncovering why training works is, of course, desirable.

6. Much more attention has been given to discussing training as a system embedded in an organizational context (e.g. Dipboye 1997, Kozlowski & Salas 1997, Kozlowski et al 2000, Tannenbaum & Yukl 1992). This is refreshing and welcome. For many decades, training researchers have ignored the fact that training cannot be isolated from the system it supports. In fact, the organizational context matters (e.g. Quiñones 1997, Rouillier & Goldstein 1993) and matters in a significant way. Research aimed at studying how organizations implement training and why even the best-designed training systems can fail is encouraged.

7. Research has begun to impact practice in a more meaningful, and it is to be hoped, quantifiable way. We can offer principles and guidelines to organizations regarding how to analyze, design, develop, implement, and evaluate training functions. Much needs to be done, but it is only through mutual reciprocity—science and practice—that real progress will be made (see Salas et al 1997). As already stated, we have seen more evaluations conducted, there are more guidelines for designers and practitioners, and viable strategies that seem to impact organizational outcomes and the link between learning and performance are more tangible today (Bassi & Van Buren 1999).

A number of training issues need considerable attention in the next few years (in addition to the ones we have noted throughout this chapter). In particular, we need research that helps us get a better understanding of what, how, and when on-the-job training works. On-the-job training is a common practice in organizations, but few principles and guidelines exist on how to optimize this strategy. We need a deeper understanding of how to build expertise and adaptability through training. Although some work has started (e.g. Kozlowski 1998, Smith et al 1997), longitudinal studies in the field are desirable. How learning environments are created and maintained in organizations needs to be researched and better understood. A related issue is how, and under what circumstances, individuals and teams learn from informal organizational activities. In addition, as organizations become older and more diverse, more attention must be paid to the special training needs of nontraditional workers (especially given the anticipated reliance on high-tech systems). Moreover, as organizations allow more flexibility in how work is accomplished (e.g. telecommuting), training practices must keep pace. In fact, organizations will increasingly depend on workers who can develop, maintain, and manage their own skills, requiring attention to the challenge of how to develop and attract self-directed learners. Finally, as noted, training researchers need to embrace and investigate new technologies. We know that organizations will; we hope that new developments in training are driven by scientific findings rather than the band wagon.

In conclusion, we are happy to report that, contrary to charges made by our predecessors over the years, training research is no longer atheoretical, irrelevant, or dull. Exciting advances in all areas of the training enterprise have been realized. Training research has also been called faddish, a characteristic we hope is beginning to fade as well. However, we wonder whether there is compelling evidence to suggest that training practitioners in organizations are actually applying what has been learned from the research. This brings us back to a question we raised at the beginning of this chapter; namely, to what degree does the science of training affect organizational training practices? In other words, can we find evidence that organizations are implementing the lessons being learned from training research (especially the work reviewed here), or are practitioners still prone to latch on to the latest training craze? The answer is, quite simply, that we just do not know. This is due, at least in part, to the fact that detailed records documenting training practices (and more importantly, the rationale that went into developing them) are not typically available. However, one thing seems clear: The stage for the application of training research is set. We say this because, as noted, organizations are beginning to question the value-added of human resource activities (including training), and to pay more attention to human capital. Simply put, organizations want to know what the return is on their training investment.

Assuming this trend continues, it should force training professionals to turn to the science of training for empirically verified guidelines regarding how to optimize training outcomes (including transfer), and how to evaluate whether training has been effective in reaching organizational goals. As the pressure grows to show an impact on the bottom line, training practitioners will do well to employ sound principles, guidelines, specifications, and lessons learned from the literature, rather than relying on a trial-and-error approach. For this reason, we believe a new era of training has begun—one in which a truly reciprocal relationship between training research and practice will be realized.

ACKNOWLEDGMENTS

We thank Clint Bowers, Ken Brown, Irv Goldstein, Steve Kozlowski, Kevin Ford, John Mathieu, Ray Noe, Paul Thayer, Scott Tannenbaum, and Will Wooten for their valuable comments and suggestions on earlier drafts of this chapter. We were aided in the literature review by two doctoral students in the Human Factors program from the University of Central Florida: Katherine Wilson and Shatha Samman.

Visit the Annual Reviews home page at www.AnnualReviews.org

LITERATURE CITED

Alliger GM, Tannenbaum SI, Bennett W, Traver H, Shotland A. 1997. A meta-analysis of the relations among training criteria. *Pers. Psychol.* 50:341–58

Anderson JR, Corbett AT, Koedinger KR, Pelletier R. 1995. Cognitive tutors: lessons learned. *J. Learn. Sci.* 4:167–207

Arthur W, Bennett W, Stanush PL, McNelly TL. 1998. Factors that influence skill decay and retention: a quantitative review and analysis. *Hum. Perform.* 11:79–86

Arthur W, Day EA, Bennett W, McNelly TL, Jordan JA. 1997. Dyadic versus individual training protocols: loss and reacquisition of a complex skill. *J. Appl. Psychol.* 82:783–91

Arthur W, Young B, Jordan JA, Shebilske WL. 1996. Effectiveness of individual and dyadic training protocols: the influence of trainee interaction anxiety. *Hum. Factors* 38:79–86

Arvey RD, Salas E, Gialluca KA. 1992. Using task inventories to forecast skills and abilities. *Hum. Perform.* 5:171–90

Baker D, Prince C, Shrestha L, Oser R, Salas E. 1993. Aviation computer games for crew resource management training. *Int. J. Aviat. Psychol.* 3:143–56

Baker D, Salas E, Cannon-Bowers J. 1998. Team task analysis: lost but hopefully not forgotten. *Ind. Organ. Psychol.* 35:79–83

Baldwin TT. 1992. Effects of alternative modeling strategies on outcomes of interpersonal-skills training. *J. Appl. Psychol.* 77:147–54

Baldwin TT, Ford JK. 1988. Transfer of training: a review and directions for future research. *Personnel Psychol.* 41:63–105

Baldwin TT, Magjuka RJ. 1997. Training as an organizational episode: pretraining influences on trainee motivation. See Ford et al 1997, pp. 99–127

Barling J, Weber T, Kelloway EK. 1996. Effects of transformational leadership training on attitudinal and financial outcomes: a field experiment. *J. Appl. Psychol.* 81:827–32

Bassi LJ, Van Buren ME. 1999. *The 1999 ASTD State of the Industry Report.* Alexandria, VA: Am. Soc. Train. Dev.

Bell H, Waag W. 1998. Evaluating the effectiveness of flight simulators for training combat skills: a review. *Int. J. Aviat. Psychol.* 8:223–42

Blickensderfer E, Cannon-Bowers JA, Salas E. 1998. Cross training and team performance See Cannon-Bowers & Salas 1998b, pp. 299–311

Blickensderfer E, Cannon-Bowers JA, Salas E, Baker DP. 2000. Analyzing knowledge requirements in team tasks. In *Cognitive Task Analysis*, ed. JM Schraagen, SF Chipman, VJ Shalin. Mahwah, NJ: Erlbaum

Bowers CA, Morgan BB Jr, Salas E, Prince C. 1993. Assessment of coordination demand for aircrew coordination training. *Mil. Psychol.* 5:95–112

Brett JF, VandeValle D. 1999. Goal orientation and goal content as predictors of performance in a training program. *J. Appl. Psychol.* 84:863–73

Bretz RD Jr, Thompsett RE. 1992. Comparing traditional and integrative learning methods in organizational training programs. *J. Appl. Psychol.* 77:941–51

Brinkerhoff RO, Montesino MU. 1995. Partnership for training transfer: lessons from a corporate study. *Hum. Res. Dev. Q.* 6:263–74

Buttom SB, Mathieu JE, Zajac DM. 1996. Goal orientation in organizational research: a conceptual and empirical foundation. *Organ. Behav. Hum. Decis. Process.* 67:26–48

Campbell JP. 1971. Personnel training and development. *Annu. Rev. Psychol.* 22:565–602

Cannon-Bowers J, Burns J, Salas E, Pruitt J. 1998. Advanced technology in decision-making training. See Cannon-Bowers & Salas 1998b, pp. 365–74

Cannon-Bowers JA, Salas E. 1997. Teamwork competencies: the interaction of team member knowledge, skills, and attitudes. In *Workforce Readiness: Competencies and Assessment*, ed. HF O'Niel, pp. 151–74. Mahwah, NJ: Erlbaum

Cannon-Bowers JA, Salas E. 1998a. Individual and team decision making under stress: theoretical underpinnings. See Cannon-Bowers & Salas 1998b, pp. 17–38

Cannon-Bowers JA, Salas E, eds. 1998b. *Making Decisions Under Stress: Implications for Individual and Team Training*. Washington, DC: Am. Psychol. Assoc.

Cannon-Bowers J, Salas E, Converse S. 1993. Shared mental models in expert team decision making. In *Individual and Group Decision Making: Current Issues*, ed. NJ Castellan Jr, pp. 221–46. Hillsdale, NJ: Erlbaum

Cannon-Bowers JA, Salas E, Tannenbaum SI, Mathieu JE. 1995. Toward theoretically-based principles of trainee effectiveness: a model and initial empirical investigation. *Mil. Psychol.* 7:141–64

Christoph RT, Schoenfeld GA Jr, Tansky JW. 1998. Overcoming barriers to training utilizing technology: the influence of self-efficacy factors on multimedia-based training receptiveness. *Hum. Res. Dev. Q.* 9:25–38

Cole ND, Latham GP. 1997. Effects of training in procedural justice on perceptions of disciplinary fairness by unionized employees and disciplinary subject matter experts. *J. Appl. Psychol.* 82:699–705

Colquitt JA, LePine JA, Noe RA. 2000. Toward an integrative theory of training motivation: a meta-analytic path analysis of 20 years of research. *J. Appl. Psychol.* In press

Colquitt JA, Simmering MS. 1998. Consciousness, goal orientation, and motivation to learn during the learning process: a longitudinal study. *J. Appl. Psychol.* 83:654–65

Dipboye RL. 1997. Organizational barriers to implementing a rational model of training. See Quinones & Ehrenstein 1997, pp. 119–48

Driskell JE, Johnston JH. 1998. Stress exposure training. See Cannon-Bowers & Salas 1998b, pp. 191–217

Driskell JE, Willis RP, Copper C. 1992. Effect of overlearning on retention. *J. Appl. Psychol.* 77:615–22

Dubois DA, Shalin VL, Levi KR, Borman WC. 1997/1998. A cognitively-oriented approach to task analysis. *Train. Res. J.* 3:103–41

Dweck CS. 1986. Motivational processes affecting learning. *Am. Psychol.* 41:1040–48

Dweck CS, Leggett EL. 1988. A social-cognitive approach to motivation and personality. *Psychol. Rev.* 95:256–73

Dwyer DJ, Oser RL, Salas E, Fowlkes JE. 1999. Performance measurement in distributed environments: initial results and implications for training. *Mil. Psychol.* 11:189–215

Eden D, Aviram A. 1993. Self-efficacy training to speed reemployment: helping people to help themselves. *J. Appl. Psychol.* 78:352–60

Ehrenstein A, Walker B, Czerwinski M, Feldman E. 1997. Some fundamentals of training and transfer: Practice benefits are not automatic. See Quinones & Ehrenstein 1997, pp. 31–60

Elliot AJ, Church MA. 1997. A hierarchical model of approach and avoidance achievement motivation. *J. Pers. Soc. Psychol.* 72:218–32

Facteau JD, Dobbins GH, Russel JEA, Ladd RT, Kudisch JD. 1995. The influence of general perceptions for the training environment on pretraining motivation and perceived training transfer. *J. Manage.* 21:1–25

Fisher SL, Ford JK. 1998. Differential effects of learner efforts and goal orientation on two learning outcomes. *Pers. Psychol.* 51:397–420

Ford JK, Kozlowski S, Kraiger K, Salas E, Teachout M, eds. 1997. *Improving Training Effectiveness in Work Organizations*. Mahwah, NJ: Erlbaum. 393 pp.

Ford JK, Quinones MA, Sego DJ, Sorra JS.

THE SCIENCE OF TRAINING **495**

1992. Factors affecting the opportunity to perform trained tasks on the job. *Pers. Psychol.* 45:511–27

Ford JK, Smith EM, Sego DJ, Quinones MA. 1993. Impact of task experience and individual factors on training-emphasis ratings. *J. Appl. Psychol.* 78:218–33

Ford JK, Smith EM, Weissbein DA, Gully SM, Salas E. 1998. Relationships of goal-orientation, metacognitive activity, and practice strategies with learning outcomes and transfer. *J. Appl. Psychol.* 83:218–33

Ford JK, Weissbein DA. 1997. Transfer of training: an updated review and analysis. *Perform. Improv. Q.* 10:22–41

Fowlkes J, Dwyer D, Oser R, Salas E. 1998. Event-based approach to training. *Int. J. Aviat. Psychol.* 8:209–22

Friedland N, Keinan G. 1992. Training effective performance in stressful situations: three approaches and implications for combat training. *Mil. Psychol.* 4:157–74

Ghodsian D, Bjork R, Benjamin A. 1997. Evaluating training during training: obstacles and opportunities. See Quinones & Ehrenstein 1997, pp. 63–88

Goettl BP, Yadrick RM, Connolly-Gomez C, Regian WJ, Shebilske WL. 1996. Alternating task modules in isochronal distributed training of complex tasks. *Hum. Factors* 38:330–46

Goldsmith T, Kraiger K. 1997. Structural knowledge assessment and training evaluation. See Ford et al 1997, pp. 19–46

Goldstein IL. 1980. Training in work organizations. *Annu. Rev. Psychol.* 31:229–72

Goldstein IL. 1993. *Training in Organizations: Needs Assessment, Development and Evaluation.* Monterey, CA: Brooks/Cole. 3rd ed.

Gopher D, Weil M, Bareket T. 1994. Transfer of skill from a computer game trainer to flight. *Hum. Factors* 36:387–405

Guzzo RA, Dickson MW. 1996. Teams in organizations: recent research on performance and effectiveness. *Annu. Rev. Psychol.* 47:307–38

Guzzo RA, Yost PR, Campbell RJ, Shea GP.

1993. Potency in groups: articulating a construct. *Br. J. Soc. Psychol.* 32:87–106

Haccoun RR, Hamtiaux T. 1994. Optimizing knowledge tests for inferring learning acquisition levels in single group training evaluation designs: the internal referencing strategy. *Pers. Psychol.* 47:593–604

Hanover JMB, Cellar DF. 1998. Environmental factors and the effectiveness of workforce diversity training *Hum. Res. Dev. Q.* 9:105–24

Harrison JK. 1992. Individual and combined effects of behavior modeling and the cultural assimilator in cross-cultural management training. *J. Appl. Psychol.* 77:952–62

Helmreich RL, Foushee HS. 1993. Why crew resource management? Empirical and theoretical bases of human factors training in avaiation. See Wiener et al 1993, pp. 3–45

Helmreich RL, Merritt AC, Wilhelm JA. 1999. The evolution of crew resource management training in commercial aviation. *Int. J. Aviat. Psychol.* 9:19–32

Helmreich RL, Wiener EL, Kanki BG. 1993. The future of crew resource management in the cockpit and elsewhere. See Wiener & Kanki 1993, pp. 479–501

Howard A, ed 1995. *The Changing Nature of Work.* San Francisco: Jossey-Bass

Hunter JE. 1986. Cognitive ability, cognitive aptitudes, job knowledge, and job performance. *J. Vocat. Behav.* 29:340–62

Huselid MA. 1995. The impact of human resource management practices on turnover, productivity, and corporate financial performance. *Acad. Manage. J.* 38:635–72

Jacobs JW, Dempsey JV. 1993. Simulation and gaming: fidelity, feedback, and motivation. In *Interactive Instruction and Feedback*, ed. JV Dempsey, GC Sales, pp. 197–229. Englewood Cliffs, NJ: Educ. Technol.

Jentsch F, Bowers C. 1998. Evidence for the validity of PC-based simulations in studying aircrew coordination. *Int. J. Aviat. Psychol.* 8:243–60

Johnston JH, Cannon-Bowers JA. 1996. Training for stress exposure. In *Stress and Human*

Performance, ed. JE Driskell, E Salas, pp. 223–56. Mahweh, NJ: Erlbaum

Kaemar KM, Wright PM, McMahan GC. 1997. The effects of individual differences on technological training. *J. Manage. Issues.* 9:104–20

Kanfer R. 1991. Motivational theory and industrial and organizational psychology. In *Handbook of Industrial and Organizational Psychology*, ed. MD Dunnette, LM Hough, M Leaetta, 2:75–170. Palo Alto, CA: Consult. Psychol. 2nd ed.

Kirkpatrick DL. 1976. Evaluation of training. In *Training and Development Handbook*, ed. RL Craig, Ch. 18. New York: McGraw-Hill. 2nd ed.

Kirlik A, Fisk AD, Walker N, Rothrock L. 1998. Feedback augmentation and part-task practice in training dynamic decision-making skills. See Cannon-Bowers & Salas 1998b, pp. 247–70

Kossek EE, Roberts K, Fisher S, Demarr B. 1998. Career self-management: a quasi-experimental assessment of the effects of a training intervention. *Pers. Psychol.* 51:935–62

Kozlowski SW. 1998. Training and developing adaptive teams: theory, principles, and research. See Cannon-Bowers & Salas 1998b, pp. 247–70

Kozlowski SWJ, Brown K, Weissbein D, Cannon-Bowers J, Salas E. 2000. A multilevel approach to training effectiveness: enhancing horizontal and vertical transfer. In *Multilevel Theory, Research and Methods in Organization*, ed. K Klein, SWJ Kozlowski. San Francisco: Jossey-Bass

Kozlowski SWJ, Salas E. 1997. A multilevel organizational systems approach for the implementation and transfer of training. See Ford et al 1997, pp. 247–87

Kraiger K, Ford JK, Salas E. 1993. Application of cognitive, skill-based, and affective theories of learning outcomes to new methods of training evaluation. *J. Appl. Psychol.* 78:311–28

Kraiger K, Jung K. 1997. Linking training objectives to evaluation criteria. See Quinones & Ehrenstein 1997, pp. 151–76

Kraiger K, Salas E, Cannon-Bowers JA. 1995. Measuring knowledge organization as a method for assessing learning during training. *Hum. Perform.* 37:804–16

Latham GP. 1988. Human resource training and development. *Annu. Rev. Psychol.* 39:545–82

Leedom DK, Simon R. 1995. Improving team coordination: a case for behavior-based training. *Mil. Psychol.* 7:109–22

London M, Moore EM. 1999. Continuous learning. In *The Changing Nature of Performance*, ed. DR Ilgen, ED Pulakos, pp. 119–53. San Francisco: Jossey-Bass

Martocchio JJ. 1992. Microcomputer usage as an opportunity: the influence of context in employee training. *Pers. Psychol.* 45:529–51

Martocchio JJ. 1994. Effects of conceptions of ability on anxiety, self-efficacy and learning in training. *J. Appl. Psychol.* 79:819–25

Martocchio JJ, Baldwin TT. 1997. The evolution of strategic organizational training. In *Research in Personnel and Human Resource Management*, ed. RG Ferris, 15:1–46. Greenwich, CT: JAI

Martocchio JJ, Judge TA. 1997. Relationship between conscientiousness and learning in employee training: mediating influences of self-deception and self-efficacy. *J. Appl. Psychol.* 82:764–73

Martocchio JJ, Webster J. 1992. Effects of feedback and cognitive playfulness on performance in microcomputer software training. *Pers. Psychol.* 45:553–78

Mathieu JE, Martineau JW. 1997. Individual and situational influences in training motivation. See Ford et al 1997, pp. 193–222

Mathieu JE, Martineau JW, Tannenbaum SI. 1993. Individual and situational influences on the development of self-efficacy: implication for training effectiveness. *Pers. Psychol.* 46:125–47

Mathieu JE, Tannenbaum SI, Salas E. 1992. Influences of individual and situational characteristics on measures of training effectiveness. *Acad. Manage. J.* 35:828–47

McKenna JA. 1990. Take the "A" training: Facing world-class challenges, leading-edge companies use progressive training techniques to stay competitive. *Ind. Week* 239:22–26

Mitchell TR, Hopper H, Daniels D, George-Falvy J, James LR. 1994. Predicting self-efficacy and performance during skill acquisition. *J. Appl. Psychol.* 79:506–17

Morrow CC, Jarrett MQ, Rupinski MT. 1997. An investigation of the effect and economic utility of corporate-wide training. *Pers. Psychol.* 50:91–119

Neerincx MA, Griffoen E. 1996. Cognitive task analysis: harmonizing tasks to human capacities. *Ergonomics* 39:543–61

Noe RA, ed. 1999. *Employee Training and Development.* Boston: Irwin/McGraw-Hill

Noe RA, Wilk SL. 1993. Investigation of the factors that influence employees' participation in development activities. *J. Appl. Psychol.* 78:291–302

Ortiz GA. 1994. Effectiveness of PC-based flight simulation. *Int. J. Aviat. Psychol.* 4:285–91

Oser RL, Cannon-Bowers JA, Salas E, Dwyer DJ. 1999. Enhancing human performance in technology-rich environments: guidelines for scenario-based training. In *Human/Technology Interaction in Complex Systems*, ed. E Salas, 9:175–202. Greenwich, CT: JAI

Phillips JM, Gully SM. 1997. Role of goal orientation, ability, need for achievement, and locus of control in the self-efficacy and goal-setting process. *J. Appl. Psychol.* 82:792–802

Prince C, Salas E. 1993. Training and research for teamwork in the military aircrew. See Wiener et al 1993, pp. 337–66

Quick JC, Joplin JR, Nelson DL, Mangelsdorff AD, Fiedler E. 1996. Self-reliance and military service training outcomes. *Mil. Psychol.* 8:279–93

Quinones MA. 1995. Pretraining context effects: training assignment as feedback. *J. Appl. Psychol.* 80:226–38

Quinones MA. 1997. Contextual influencing on training effectiveness. See Quinones & Ehrenstein 1997, pp. 177–200

Quinones MA, Ehrenstein A. 1997. *Training for a Rapidly Changing Workplace: Applications of Psychological Research.* Washington, DC: Am. Psychol. Assoc.

Quinones MA, Ford JK, Sego DJ, Smith EM. 1995. The effects of individual and transfer environment characteristics on the opportunity to perform trained tasks. *Train. Res. J.* 1:29–48

Randel JM, Main RE, Seymour GE, Morris BA. 1992. Relation of study factors to performance in Navy technical schools. *Mil. Psychol.* 4:75–86

Ree MJ, Carretta TR, Teachout MS. 1995. Role of ability and prior job knowledge in complex training performance. *J. Appl. Psychol.* 80:721–30

Ree MJ, Earles JA. 1991. Predicting training success: not much more than G. *Pers. Psychol.* 44:321–32

Ricci KE, Salas E, Cannon-Bowers JA. 1995. Do computer based games facilitate knowledge acquisition and retention? *Mil. Psychol.* 8:295–307

Rogers W, Maurer T, Salas E, Fisk A. 1997. Task analysis and cognitive theory: controlled and automatic processing task analytic methodology. See Ford et al 1997, pp. 19–46

Rouillier JZ, Goldstein IL. 1993. The relationship between organizational transfer climate and positive transfer of training. *Hum. Res. Dev. Q.* 4:377–90

Sackett PR, Mullen EJ. 1993. Beyond formal experimental design: towards an expanded view of the training evaluation process. *Pers. Psychol.* 46:613–27

Saks AM. 1995. Longitudinal field investigation of the moderating and mediating effects of self-efficacy on the relationship between training and newcomer adjustment. *J. Appl. Psychol.* 80:221–25

Salas E, Bowers CA, Blickensderfer E. 1997. Enhancing reciprocity between training theory and training practice: principles, guidelines, and specifications. See Ford et al 1997, pp. 19–46

Salas E, Bowers CA, Rhodenizer L. 1998. It is not how much you have but how you use it: toward a rational use of simulation to support aviation training. *Int. J. Aviat. Psychol.* 8:197–208

Salas E, Cannon-Bowers JA. 1997. Methods, tools, and strategies for team training. See Quinones & Ehrenstein 1997, pp. 249–80

Salas E, Cannon-Bowers JA. 2000. The anatomy of team training. In *Training and Retraining: A Handbook for Business, Industry, Government and the Military*, ed. S Tobias, D Fletcher. Farmington Hills, MI: Macmillan. In press

Salas E, Fowlkes J, Stout RJ, Milanovich DM, Prince C. 1999. Does CRM training improve teamwork skills in the cockpit?: two evaluation studies. *Hum. Factors* 41:326–43

Salas E, Klein G, eds. 2000. *Linking Expertise and Naturalistic Decision Making*. Mahwah, NJ: Erlbaum. In press

Salas E, Rhodenizer L, Bowers CA. 2000. The design and delivery of CRM training: exploring the available resources. *Hum. Factors*. In press

Schmidt RA, Bjork RA. 1992. New conceptualizations of practice: Common principles in three paradigms suggest new concepts for training. *Psychol. Sci.* 3:207–17

Schraagen JM, Chipman SF, Shalin VL, eds. 2000. *Cognitive Task Analysis*. Mahwah, NJ: Erlbaum. 392 pp.

Schreiber D, Berge Z, eds. 1998. *Distance Training: How Innovative Organizations Are Using Technology to Maximize Learning and Meet Business Objectives*. San Francisco: Jossey-Bass

Shebilske WL, Jordan JA, Goettl BP, Paulus LE. 1998. Observation versus hands-on practice of complex skills in dyadic, triadic, and tetradic training-teams. *Hum. Factors* 40:525–40

Shebilske WL, Regian JW, Arthur W Jr, Jordan JA. 1992. A dyadic protocol for training complex skills. *Hum. Factors* 34:369–74

Shute VJ, Gawlick LA. 1995. Practice effects on skill acquisition, learning outcome, retention, and sensitivity to relearning. *Hum. Factors* 37:781–803

Shute VJ, Gawlick LA, Gluck KA. 1998. Effects of practice and learner control on short- and long-term gain. *Hum. Factors* 40:296–310

Simon SJ, Werner JM. 1996. Computer training through behavior modeling, self-paced, and instructional approaches: a field experiment. *J. Appl. Psychol.* 81:648–59

Skarlicki DP, Latham GP. 1997. Leadership training in organizational justice to increase citizenship behavior within a labor union: a replication. *Pers. Psychol.* 50:617–33

Smith E, Ford K, Kozlowski S. 1997. Building adaptive expertise: implications for training design strategies. See Quinones & Ehrenstein 1997, pp. 89–118

Smith-Jentsch KA, Jentsch FG, Payne SC, Salas E. 1996a. Can pretraining experiences explain individual differences in learning? *J. Appl. Psychol.* 81:909–36

Smith-Jentsch KA, Salas E, Baker DP. 1996b. Training team performance-related assertiveness. *Pers. Psychol.* 49:110–16

Smith-Jentsch KA, Salas E, Brannick M. 2000. To transfer or not to transfer? An investigation of the combined effects of trainee characteristics and team transfer environments. *J. Appl. Psychol.* In press

Smith-Jentsch KA, Zeisig RL, Acton B, McPherson JA. 1998. Team dimensional training: a strategy for guided team self-correction. See Cannon-Bowers & Salas 1998b, pp. 247–70

Stajkovic AD, Luthans F. 1998. Self efficacy and work-related performance. A meta-analysis. *Psychol. Bull.* 124:240–61

Steele-Johnson D, Hyde BG. 1997. Advanced technologies in training: intelligent tutoring systems and virtual reality. See Quinones & Ehrenstein 1997, pp. 225–48

Sternberg RJ. 1997. Managerial intelligence: Why IQ isn't enough. *J. Manage.* 23:475–93

Stevens CK, Gist ME. 1997. Effects of self-efficacy and goal-orientation training on negotiation skill maintenance: what are the mechanisms? *Personnel Psychol.* 50:955–78

Stout RJ, Salas E, Fowlkes J. 1997. Enhancing teamwork in complex invironments through team training. *Group Dyn.: Theory Res. Pract.* 1:169–82

Swezey RW, Salas E, eds. 1992. *Teams: Their Training and Performance.* Norwood, NJ: Ablex

Tannenbaum SI. 1997. Enhancing continuous learning: diagnostic findings from multiple companies. *Hum. Res. Manage.* 36:437–52

Tannenbaum SI, Cannon-Bowers JA, Mathieu JE. 1993. *Factors That Influence Training Effectiveness: A Conceptual Model and Longitudinal Analysis.* Rep. 93-011, Naval Train. Syst. Cent., Orlando, FL

Tannenbaum SI, Dupuree-Bruno LM. 1994. The relationship between organizational and evironmental factors and the use of innovative human resource practices. *Group Organ. Manage.* 19:171–202

Tannenbaum SI, Smith-Jentsch KA, Behson SJ. 1998. Training team leaders to facilitate team learning and performance. See Cannon-Bowers & Salas 1998b, pp. 247–70

Tannenbaum SI, Yukl G. 1992. Training and development in work organizations. *Annu. Rev. Psychol.* 43:399–441

Tesluk PE, Farr JL, Mathieu JE, Vance RJ. 1995. Generalization of employee involvement training to the job setting: individual and situational effects. *Pers. Psychol.* 48:607–32

Thayer PW. 1997. A rapidly changing world: some implications for training systems in the year 2001 and beyond. See Quinones & Ehrenstein 1997, pp. 15–30

Thayer PW, Teachout MS. 1995. *A Climate for Transfer Model.* Rep. AL/HR-TP-1995-0035, Air Force Mat. Command, Brooks Air Force Base, Tex.

Tracey JB, Tannenbaum SI, Kavanagh MJ. 1995. Applying trained skills on the job: the importance of the work environment. *J. Appl. Psychol.* 80:239–52

VandeValle D. 1997. Development and validation of a work domain goal orientation instrument. *Educ. Psychol. Meas.* 57:995–1015

Volpe CE, Cannon-Bowers JA, Salas E, Spector PE. 1996. The impact of cross-training on team functioning: an empirical investigation. *Hum. Factors* 38:87–100

Warr P, Bunce D. 1995. Trainee characteristics and the outcomes of open learning. *Pers. Psychol.* 48:347–75

Wexley KN. 1984. Personnel training. *Annu. Rev. Psychol.* 35:519–51

Wexley KN, Latham GP. 2000. *Developing and Training Human Resources in Organizations*, Vol. 3. Englewood Cliffs, NJ: Prentice-Hall. In press

Wiener EL, Kanki BG, Helmreich RL, eds. 1993. *Cockpit Resource Management.* San Diego, CA: Academic

Wilson MA, Zalewski MA. 1994. An expert system for abilities-oriented job analysis. *Comp. Hum. Behav.* 10:199–207

Yang H, Sackett PR, Arvey RD. 1996. Statistical power and cost in training evaluation: some new considerations. *Pers. Psychol.* 49:651–68

Yelon SL, Ford JK. 1999. Pursuing a multi-dimensional model of transfer. *Perform. Improv. Q.* 12:58–78

Zsambok C, Klein G, eds. 1997. *Naturalistic Decision Making.* Mahweh, NJ: Erlbaum

Annu. Rev. Psychol. 2001. 52:501–25

COMPARING PERSONAL TRAJECTORIES AND DRAWING CAUSAL INFERENCES FROM LONGITUDINAL DATA

Stephen W. Raudenbush

School of Education and Institute for Social Research, University of Michigan,
610 East University Avenue, Ann Arbor, Michigan 48109; e-mail: rauden@umich.edu

■ **Abstract** This review considers statistical analysis of data from studies that obtain repeated measures on each of many participants. Such studies aim to describe the average change in populations and to illuminate individual differences in trajectories of change. A person-specific model for the trajectory of each participant is viewed as the foundation of any analysis having these aims. A second, between-person model describes how persons very in their trajectories. This two-stage modeling framework is common to a variety of popular analytic approaches variously labeled hierarchical models, multilevel models, latent growth models, and random coefficient models. Selected published examples reveal how the approach can be flexibly adapted to represent development in domains as diverse as vocabulary growth in early childhood, academic learning, and antisocial propensity during adolescence. The review then considers the problem of drawing causal inferences from repeated measures data.

CONTENTS

INTRODUCTION

Longitudinal studies serve many purposes in psychology. They trace the course of normal growth, identify risk factors for mental illness, and assess the effects

0066-4308/01/0201-0501$14.00

of interventions. They identify the timing of onset of new abilities, the duration of disorders, and desistance from self-destructive behavior. What these purposes share in common is a focus on individual change and thus a need for repeated assessment of each participant. The time series for a person creates a basis for sketching that person's history. Whereas a person's history can capture many domains of change—for example, changes in cognitive skill, emotional self-regulation, mood, and social behavior—a trajectory describes a person's development in one well-defined domain. In this article, I view longitudinal analysis as beginning with the development of a model for individual trajectory. Only if the trajectory is clearly defined does it become possible quantitatively to summarize evidence across trajectories. The logical foundation for all longitudinal analysis is thus a statistical model defining parameters of change for the trajectory of a single participant. The task of comparing people then becomes the task of comparing the parameters of these personal trajectories. A model is thus needed for the population distribution of the parameters of personal change.

Within this framework, I review current methodological developments that have dramatically expanded the analytic choices available to psychologists. The explosive growth of new methodology enables astonishing flexibility for studying change and comparing trajectories of change in the presence of missing data and varied timing and spacing of time points. This growth in new methods can also cause seemingly terminal confusion. Part of the confusion emanates from a proliferation of jargon often associated with new software packages. So part of my task is to clarify the new vocabulary and connect it to key logical issues in the analysis.

A brief article cannot comprehensively review a topic as vast as methods of longitudinal analysis. Therefore, the first section of this article, while outlining a variety of conceptions of "trajectory," selects a subset of these for more intensive discussion. By choosing to focus on just a part of the terrain, it becomes possible to portray quite vividly what is meant quantitatively by a trajectory and how such trajectories can be compared.

Researchers have often criticized cross-sectional research designs as inadequate for identifying causal effects and have advocated longitudinal data collection as a solution. The second half of this article therefore considers the assumptions required to justify causal inferences in longitudinal studies.

Trajectories of Change

Longitudinal studies use quite varied conceptions of a trajectory of change. Let us briefly sketch three of these before moving to a fourth conception that provides the basis for the remainder of the paper.

Models for Time as an Outcome   Many important research questions concern the timing of an event, for example, the age of onset of menarche, time until recovery from depression, and the time until a student receives a degree. The probability that the event of interest will occur at time t, given that it has not already occurred, is called the "hazard" of the event. The hazard changes over time. A participant's changing hazard is then that person's trajectory. The trajectory may depend on time-invariant covariates, including gender, social background, and personality characteristics, and also on time-varying covariates, that is, events and experiences that unfold over time. The key methodological challenge arises from the fact that the study will typically end before some members of the sample experience the event. Of those not experiencing the event, many or all will ultimately experience it after the termination of the study. For these people, the time of the event is "censored," that is, unobservable. Survival analysis involves an important class of longitudinal models that are tailored to deal with duration time as an outcome when outcomes for some participants are censored. This important class of models, reviewed, for example, by Cox & Oakes (1984), Kalbfleisch & Prentice (1980), and Singer & Willett (1991) will not be considered further in this article.

Transitions Between States   It is often of interest to develop theories that predict transitions between states, for example, whether a recovering alcoholic will be actively drinking at any time t (yes or no) given that this participant was (or was not) drinking at time $t - 1$. In this kind of study, a person's trajectory is the sequence of such transitions. The probability of a given state (e.g. drinking at time t) given the prior state (e.g. not drinking at time $t - 1$) is called a transition probability. A model for a person's trajectory begins with a theory about what determines a sequence of transition probabilities for a given person. Covariates describing personal background and experience may determine these probabilities and thus strongly influence a person's trajectory. The current article will not consider these models in further detail. We refer the interested reader to Diggle et al (1994, Chapter 10), Collins (2001), and Collins & Wugalter (1992).

Sequences of Age-Appropriate Markers   Developmental psychologists are interested in whether early impulsivity predicts conduct disorder in elementary school and juvenile crime later (Moffitt 1993). Status attainment researchers consider how parental social status predicts a person's educational attainment and how these, together, predict that person's adult occupation and income (Duncan et al 1972, Sewell & Hauser 1975). In these cases, the focus is on associations among variables, each of which marks a person's status at a given stage of life. A trajectory in such studies is the sequence of values on the variables of interest. Common methods of analysis include structural equation models or path models, as introduced by Blau & Duncan (1967), Blalock (1969), and Duncan (1966) and refined considerably since (cf Joreskog & Sorbom 1979). Although longitudinal data are essential to studying these important relationships, the analytic methods are not different from multivariate methods commonly used in cross-sectional research, so we shall not consider them further.

Smooth Curves to Describe Trajectories of Growth or Change   Perhaps the most common analytic goal in current longitudinal psychological research is to describe and compare growth curves or other smooth functions that describe a person's changing status. For this purpose, analysts have recommended approaches with the labels "covariance component models," "hierarchical linear models," "latent curve analysis," "mixed models," "multilevel models," "random-coefficient models," and "random-effect models." Much of the remainder of this article aims to clarify the logic of these models while giving some meaning to these labels. Researchers interested in these approaches generally collect repeated measures of a given outcome variable for each participant with the aim of describing how people grow or change over some fairly broad interval of time.

Other Studies of Repeated Measures   This review is confined to studies performed over some significant segment of the life course. Such a focus omits other important types of repeated-measure studies. Studies of repeated measures over the short term, for example, can assess sequences of social interaction in detail, model reaction times in a series of cognitive tasks, or predict biophysical changes in response to a series of stimuli. We refer the interested reader to Gottman (1995, Part II), for reviews of methods for such data.

Describing and Comparing Growth and Change Curves

We begin with a simple and easily understandable example and then extend this logic to more complex cases.

Defining the Trajectory for Person i   Suppose that each person's status with respect to cognitive outcome, Y, grows with age at a constant rate and that these rates vary randomly over a population of persons. More specifically, we have an outcome Y_{ti} for person i at time t, with T_i time points ($t = 1, \ldots, T_i$) observed for person i. We can formulate a simple linear model such as the following for individual change:

$$Y_{ti} = \pi_{0i} + \pi_{1i}a_{ti} + e_{ti}, \quad e_{ti} \sim N(0, \sigma^2) \tag{1}$$

where a_{ti} is the age of person i at time t. Here person i's trajectory is the straight line $\pi_{0i} + \pi_{1i}a_{ti}$. The parameters of individual i's trajectory are two: π_{0i}, the status of that person at $a_{ti} = 0$, and π_{1i}, that person's linear rate of change per unit increase in age. The discrepancy between the actual score Y_{ti} and the trajectory is e_{ti}, assumed for simplicity here to be distributed normally with a mean of zero and constant variance, σ^2.

The simple model of Equation 1 has found varied application in psychology. Francis et al (1991) defined π_{1i} as the rate of recovery of patient i's cognitive functioning after suffering a head injury. For Raudenbush and Chan (1993), π_{1i} was adolescent i's rate of increase in antisocial thinking. For Seltzer et al 1994, π_{1i} was the rate of growth of i's reading comprehension. Having defined the parameters of personal change, the next stage of the model expresses a theory about individual differences: differences, for example, in the rate of recovery from head injury, in the rate of increase of antisocial thinking, or the rate of growth in reading.

Describing the Population Distribution of Personal Trajectories   Next we consider how the personal trajectories of change are distributed in the population. A very simple model states that person-specific parameters (π_{0i}, π_{1i}) vary around their grand means (β_{00}, β_{01}), with variance (τ_{00}, τ_{11}) and covariance (τ_{01}), according to a bivariate normal distribution:

$$\pi_{0i} = \beta_{00} + u_{0i}$$

$$\pi_{1i} = \beta_{10} + u_{1i} \tag{2}$$

$$with \quad \begin{pmatrix} u_{0i} \\ u_{1i} \end{pmatrix} \sim N\left[\begin{pmatrix} 0 \\ 0 \end{pmatrix}, \begin{pmatrix} \tau_{00} & \tau_{01} \\ \tau_{10} & \tau_{11} \end{pmatrix} \right].$$

Unpacking the Terminology

The model described by Equations 1 and 2 is a "hierarchical" model because it specifies a model for Y_{ti} given first-level parameters (π_{0i}, π_{1i}), while these parameters, in turn, depend on second-level parameters (the β_s and τs). Levels could be added; the second-level parameters could depend on third-level parameters, and so on. Thus, it is the hierarchical dependence among the parameters that is decisive in making the model "hierarchical," not necessarily the hierarchical structure of the data, although the two often go together.

This idea is central to the current article. All of the models considered in this paper are hierarchical. The essence of the decision framework I propose is to ensure that specification of the model at each level fits the research question, design, and data.

The model described by Equations 1 and 2 is a hierarchical linear model (Bryk & Raudenbush 1992) because, at the first stage, Y is a linear function of π_{0i}, π_{1i}, whereas at the second stage, each π is a linear function of β_{00}, β_{10}. Note that all polynomial models at the first stage are linear. The model is "multilevel" (Goldstein 1995) because it describes data that vary at two levels: within persons and between persons. The model is a "random-coefficients" model (Longford 1993) because the level-1 model defines coefficients π_{0i}, π_{1i}, that vary randomly over participants at level 2. It is a "latent-curve" model (Meredith & Tisak 1990) because the trajectory or curve $\pi_{0i} + \pi_{1i}a_{it}$ is unobservable, depending, that is, on unobserved latent variables π_{0i} and π_{1i}. It may also be a "latent-growth" model, although the use of the term "growth" implies a monotonic increasing trajectory which may or may not be the case.

The model is also a "mixed" model (Diggle et al 1994). To see this, substitute Equation 1 into Equation 2, yielding the combined model

$$Y_{ti} = \beta_{00} + \beta_{01}a_{ti} + \varepsilon_{ti} \tag{3}$$

where

$$\varepsilon_{ti} = u_{0i} + u_{1i}a_{ti} + e_{ti}. \tag{4}$$

Thus, the model has fixed effects (β_{00}, β_{01}) and random effects (u_{0i}, u_{1i}) as well as the elemental residual e_{ti}. Models that incorporate both fixed and random effects have historically been labeled "mixed models." This is a random-effects model (Laird & Ware 1982) because individual differences are characterized by random effects u_{0i}, u_{1i}. It is a covariance components model because it allows the random effects to covary.

The model is also a "structural-equation" model (SEM) (Joreskog & Sorbom 1979). The first-stage model can be viewed as a measurement model with observed variable Y, latent variables π, and factor loadings 1 (for π_{0i}) and a_{ti}, (for π_{1i}). The second-level model is an exceedingly simple structural equation model for the πs.

A Framework for Analytic Choices

The essence of the framework I propose is as follows.

1. In light of the developmental theory at hand, the design, and the data, choose a model for individual development over time. The model has a structural part that specifies a trajectory in terms of person-specific parameters (the πs). It may be a linear trajectory (including polynomials) as in Equation 1 or nonlinear. The model also includes a probabilistic part that describes the random behavior of Y around the person-specific trajectory. The probability model may be normal, as in Equation 1, or it may not.

2. In light of key research questions and data, define a model for the distribution of trajectories in the population. It will also have a structural part, which describes the expected trajectory given the measured characteristics of persons, and a probabilistic part, which describes the random behavior of the trajectories in the population.

3. From this point, we continue to higher levels as necessary. For example, the model might have a three-level structure with level 1 describing individual change, level 2 describing interindividual variation within clusters such as schools (Bryk & Raudenbush 1992, Chapter 8), and level 3 describing variation between clusters.

4. Assess alternative estimation methods, algorithms, and (hopefully) available software for making inferences about all unknowns.

Unfortunately, constraints in estimation theory, algorithms, and software often distort model choices. In particular, the convenience of linear models and normal distribution theory at each level, contrasted with the relative difficulty of constructing efficient computational algorithms for nonlinear models and non-normal assumptions, has encouraged an unhealthy reliance on linearity and normality.

Below we consider two classes of models. In the first, both the data Y (and the πs) are normal with a linear structure. In the second class, either Y (given the πs) or the πs or both are non-normal (and possibly nonlinear). The first class of models is most familiar to psychology, and, although it has many useful applications, it is often chosen more out of convenience than conviction. The second class is enormously broad and offers vast untapped potential for the modeling of developmental phenomena.

Normal Data and Normal Trajectories

We consider the examples in which assumptions of normality and linearity are benign in this section, while urging analysts to consider the broader range of models described in the subsequent section.

Vocabulary Growth During the Second Year of Life Following the tradition of Bryk & Weisberg (1977) and Rogosa et al (1982), this article asserts that the appropriate foundation for longitudinal analysis is a model for the individual trajectory. To illustrate, we review the study by Huttenlocher et al (1991) of expressive vocabulary during the second year of life. These researchers visited the home of each child in their study every 2 months, each time counting the number of unique words uttered by the child. Figure 1 displays the scatter plot of vocabulary (vertical

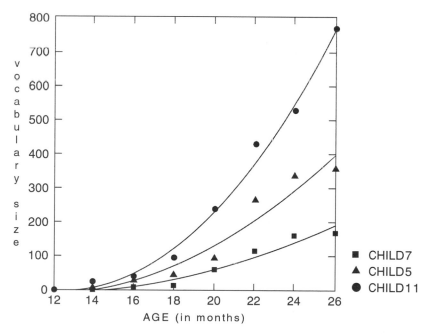

Figure 1 A sample of individual vocabulary growth trajectories. The symbols □, ○, and △ represent the actual observations. The smooth curves result from fitting a separate quadratic polynomial to each child's vocabulary data.

axis) as a function of age in months (horizontal axis) for three randomly selected children. An accelerating curve nicely summarizes the growth pattern for each child. Such a quadratic curve can be described by the level-1 model for the growth of individual i:

$$Y_{ti} = \pi_{0i} + \pi_{1i}a_{it} + \pi_{2i}a_{it}^2 + e_{ti}, \tag{5}$$

where age a_{ti} is expressed as a deviation from some meaningful constant. For example, if $a_{ti} = $ age $- 18$, months for child i at time t, π_{0i} is the size of child i's vocabulary at 18 months, π_{1i} is the rate of growth of child i at that same age, and π_{2i} captures that child's rate of acceleration. In Huttenlocher's study, π_{2i} turned out to be the key growth parameter because acceleration was the single feature of growth that strongly differentiated the growth curves. By using all of the data to strengthen inference about correlates of acceleration, the researchers were able to discover reliable associations between key predictors (e.g. gender and maternal speech) and vocabulary growth.

Growth of Reading and Math Achievement During the Elementary Years   A key feature of Huttenlocher's study was the construction of an outcome variable (vocabulary) measured on the same scale at every age of interest. Without such an invariant outcome metric, discussion of quantitative change or growth is meaningless. Standardized tests often fail to provide such a metric; different forms of a test are constructed with age-appropriate items for different age groups, and no effort is made to equate the forms. However, by calibrating the items across alternate forms, it is possible to construct a common measure for studies of cognitive growth. The Sustaining Effects Study (Carter 1984) used such a measure to characterize growth in early-elementary reading and math.

Two features of individual growth were apparent. First, academic-year growth was essentially linear. Second, growth rates during the summer were much smaller than growth rates during the academic year. Figure 2 plots the average trajectory for reading and math during the elementary years. Notice that assessments twice annually (fall and spring) enable one to distinguish academic-year and summer growth. On average, there is no growth during the summer in math, but the academic-year growth rate is substantially positive. For reading, the summer rate is modestly positive, with faster academic-year growth. To capture key features of growth, a sensible model for the individual trajectory for either math or reading is

$$Y_{ti} + \pi_{0i} + \pi_{1i}(grade_{ti} - 1) + \pi_{2i}(fall_{ti}) + e_{ti} \tag{6}$$

where $grade_{ti} - 1$ takes a value of 0 for first grade, 1 for second grade, etc, and "*fall*" is an indicator for the fall time point (*fall* $= 1$ if the first occurred in the fall, 0 if spring). Under this specification, π_{1i} is the calendar-year growth rate, and $\pi_{1i} + \pi_{2i}$ is the summer growth rate. Bryk & Raudenbush (1992, Chapter 8) were able to discern the following features of early elementary growth by using such an approach: (*a*) much greater academic-year than summer growth in math

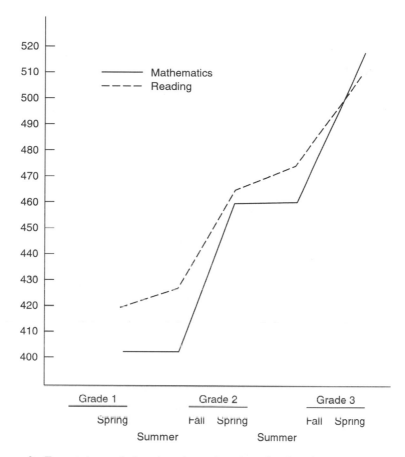

Figure 2 Expected growth functions in math and reading based on three-level model analysis of data from the sustaining effects study.

and reading on average; (*b*) modest summer growth in reading with no summer growth on average in math; (*c*) subject matter differences in school effects such that most of the variation in academic-year rates in math was between schools while most of the variation in academic-year growth in reading lay between children within schools; (*d*) a stronger dependence of growth rates on social background for reading than for math.

Summary   The two examples illustrate the centrality of the model of the individual trajectory for studying longitudinal data on growth or change. For the first example, representing the accelerating nature of vocabulary growth during the second year of life was essential not only in describing individual growth and mean growth but also in discovering correlates of growth. In the second example, distinguishing between the summer growth rate and the academic-year growth rate for a given child was essential in illuminating school effects and clarifying differences between the growth processes for reading and math.

Expanding the Class of Level-1 Models

So far we have considered only linear models to characterize a person's trajectory in the level-1 model. The level-1 model also assumes a normally distributed random error e_{ti}. The generalized linear model of McCullagh & Nelder (1989) provides a far more general class of level-1 models.

Consider Horney et al's (1995) longitudinal study of high-rate offenders. Their interest focused on how changing life circumstances such as getting a job or moving in with a spouse are related to the propensity to commit crime. They therefore conceived each participant's propensity as having a trajectory over time that could be deflected by such changes in life circumstances. However, the data, collected by means of a life history calendar over 36 months, involved binary Y_{ti}; that is, $Y_{ti} = 1$ if person i committed a crime during time $t, t = 1, \ldots, 36$. The binary character of the data strongly suggests that a Bernoulli probability model

$$E(Y_{ti} \mid \mu_{ti}) = Prob\,(Y_{ti} = 1 \mid \mu_{ti}) = \mu_{ti}$$
$$Var\,(Y_{ti} \mid \mu_{ti}) = \mu_{ti}(1 - \mu_{ti}). \tag{7}$$

Note that, unlike the normal model, the conditional variance at level 1 is intrinsically heteroscedastic, depending on μ_{ti} and therefore varying over i at time t.

A linear structural model for μ_{ti} would make little sense in this case. A linear model would be inconsistent with the bounds ($0 < \mu_{ti} < 1$) because a linear model could easily generate predicted values less than zero or greater than one. Thus, any effect sizes associated with such a model would be suspect. A more natural model and that used by Horney et al is the logit-linear structural model

$$\eta_{ti} = \log\left(\frac{\mu_{ti}}{1 - \mu_{ti}}\right) = \pi_{0i} + \sum_{p=1}^{P}\pi_{pti}a_{pti}. \tag{8}$$

Here a_{pti}, $p = 1, \ldots, P$, are time-varying predictors, measured aspects of life circumstances; and μ_{pi} can be thought of as a deflection in the propensity to commit crime associated with a change in a_{pti}. At level 2, the πs can be viewed as having the same kind of model as before (Equation 2), that is, a linear structural model and a multivariate normal-probability model.

In sum, the two-level model of Horney et al (1995) is similar conceptually to Equations 1 and 2, conceiving each participant to have a trajectory of development characterized by certain parameters π that, in turn, vary over a population of persons. However, the nature of the data calls for a nonlinear structural model at level 1 and a non-normal sampling model.

In the language of the generalized linear model (McCullagh & Nelder 1989), the logit transformation η_{ti} of the mean μ_{ti} is called the link function for the binomial mean. Other standard link functions are the log-link for count data and the identity

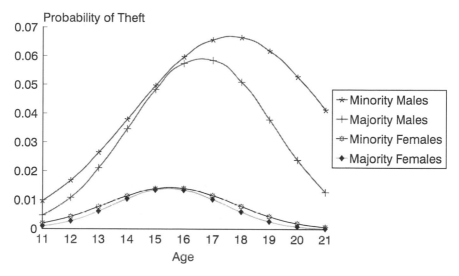

Figure 3   Probability of theft during adolescence.

link for normal data. Typically, the link function is set equal to a linear model as in Equation 8; that is, η_{ti} is a linear function of the πs. Diggle et al (1994) review applications of hierarchical generalized linear models.

However, it will not always be the case that a linear model for the link function captures the interesting features of development. Consider now the "age-crime" curve, described by Gottfredson & Hirschi (1990) as one of the "brute facts" of criminology. Researchers have found that, for many societies and many subgroups, the probability of committing a serious crime tends to be very small during pread-olescence. However, this probability tends to increase at an accelerating rate early in adolescence, typically reaching a peak around ages 16–17 and then diminishing rapidly during late adolescence and early adulthood. This curve thus takes on a bell shape as a function of age, as displayed in Figure 3, based on an analysis of data from all seven cohorts of the National Youth Survey (Raudenbush 2001).

These curves describe the fitted values based on a two-level hierarchical model. At level 1, the outcome Y_{ti} takes on a value of 1 if participant i commits serious theft during time interval t, and the value is 0 if not. We thus adopt a Bernoulli probability model as in Horney et al (1995) and, provisionally, a logit linear structural model in

$$\eta_{ti} = \pi_{0i} + \pi_{1i}a_{ti} + \pi_{2i}a_{ti}^2, \qquad (9)$$

which the log odds of committing serious theft are a quadratic function of age: where a_{ti} is the age of person i at time t minus 16 (the median age of the sample during the 5 years of data collection). Ages range from 11 to 21 across the seven cohorts during the 5 years of the study. At level 2, each of the three πs depends on gender (an indicator for female status), family income, and ethnicity (an indicator for minority status, with $1 =$ African American or Hispanic American; $0 =$ other):[1]

$$\pi_{pi} = \beta_{p0} + \beta_{p1}(female)_i + \beta_{p2}(minority)_i + u_{pi}, \qquad (10)$$

for $p = 0, 1$, and 2. The level-2 probability model assumes the random effects u_{pi} to be normal in distribution with coefficients for linear and quadratic age fixed. The curves in Figure 3 apply the results to the inverse logit transform

$$\hat{\mu}_{ti} = \frac{1}{1 + \exp\{-\hat{\eta}_{ti}\}} \qquad (11)$$

that is, the predicted probability of committing serious theft for each of four groups (majority males, majority females, minority males, and minority females).

While Figure 3 is interesting, it is difficult to interpret the polynomial coefficients. More interesting would be parameters that map onto a developmental theory linked to literature from the age-crime curve. SW Raudenbush (2001) transformed the polynomial model for the individual trajectory into a model with three parameters: (*a*) the peak age of offending, that is, the age at which the expected probability of offending is at a maximum; (*b*) the peak probability of offending, that is, the probability of offending at the peak age; and (*c*) the persistence of offending, that is, the extent to which a person continues to offend rather than to desist from offending during the transition to young adulthood. The graph suggests, for example, that females "peak" earlier than males and that, when they do, their offending rate is much lower than that of males. It also suggests that minority and majority youth have quite similar curves except that minority males tend to peak later and to persist. Consistent with the results of Horney et al (1995), we might expect that this persistence reflects the fact that minority males are having a harder time getting jobs and are more likely to remain single than are majority males, although we cannot test this hypothesis with the current data.

The example shows that the level-1 structural model can be recast such that the parameters capture theoretically interesting properties of development. At the same time, the probabilistic part of the model is consistent with the binary nature of the data. A parallel analysis using the frequency of crime reached similar results. In this case, μ_{ti} was the event rate for person *i* at time *t*, the link function was the log link, that is $\eta_{ti} = \log(\mu_{ti})$, and the structural model for η_{ti} is the same as in Equation 9.

Expanding the Class of Level-2 Models

Thus far I have emphasized the importance of "getting the model for individual development right." It is equally important to make sound choices about the model for individual variation in development.

---

[1] The vast majority of those sampled in the National Youth Survey were either European American or African American. Sample sizes of other subgroups were too small for analysis, especially in light of the low frequency of serious theft.

Simultaneous Equation Models   Applications of hierarchical models to date have nearly always specified multivariate regression models at level 2. In terms of our paradigm example of Equations 1 and 2, this means expanding the level-2 model, that is, in an especially simple case,

$$\pi_{0i} = \beta_{00} + \beta_{01}X_i + u_{0i}$$

$$\pi_{1i} = \beta_{10} + \beta_{11}X_i + u_{1i} \tag{12}$$

$$with \quad \begin{pmatrix} u_{0i} \\ u_{1i} \end{pmatrix} \sim N\left[\begin{pmatrix} 0 \\ 0 \end{pmatrix}, \begin{pmatrix} \tau_{00} & \tau_{01} \\ \tau_{10} & \tau_{11} \end{pmatrix} \right].$$

Here the level-1 parameters of individual change, π_{0i} and π_{1i}, become correlated outcomes predicted by person characteristic X_i. Raudenbush & Sampson (1999) show, however, how to specify and estimate simultaneous equation models in which the random coefficient, say π_{0i}, becomes a mediating variable. In the model below, X_i has both a direct effect on the rate of change π_{1i}, given the intercept π_{0i}, and an indirect effect operating through the intercept. The model simple moves π_{0i} in Equation 13 to the right side of the equation for π_{1i}:

$$E(\pi_{1i} \mid \pi_{0i}) = \alpha_{10} + \alpha_{11}X_i + \alpha_{12}\pi_{0i}$$

$$= \beta_{10} - \alpha_{12}\beta_{00} + (\beta_{11} - \alpha_{12}\beta_{01})X_i + \alpha_{12}u_{0i}. \tag{13}$$

Here $\alpha_{11} = \beta_{11} - \alpha_{12}\beta_{01}$ is the direct effect of X on π_1; $\alpha_{12}\beta_{01}$ is the indirect effect of X on π_1 operating through π_0 and $\alpha_{12} = \tau_{10}/\tau_{00}$.

A Multinomial Prior Assumption   In many studies of growth, it is reasonable to assume that all participants are growing according to some common function but that the growth parameters vary in magnitude. For example, vocabulary growth curves for a normative sample of children invariably show upward curvature (acceleration) during the second year of life, and the interesting question about individual differences is the rate of acceleration (Huttenlocher et al 1991). For many other repeated-measures studies, however, the situation is quite different.

Consider a study of changes in depression. It makes no sense to assume that everyone is increasing (or decreasing) with respect to depression. In a normative sample, many persons will never be high in depression, whereas others will always be high; some persons will be recovering from serious depression, but others will become increasingly depressed, and perhaps another group will oscillate between high and low levels of depression. Such "depression curves" can certainly be represented by a polynomial of sufficiently high degree, say three (i.e. the cubic degree) in the level-1 model. However, linear models for the polynomial coefficients, π, at level 2 may not capture the qualitatively different types of trajectories found in the population.

To model these kinds of data, Nagin (1999) has developed a two-level model in which the first level is similar to those discussed in this paper (see also Muthen

2001). However, the second level of the model is reconceptualized such that the population is viewed as (approximately) falling into a fixed number of groups, where each group's development is characterized by a common set of change parameters (πs). The summary of evidence from this model is a set of conditional probabilities for each person: the probability that a person is in group 1, the probability that the person is in group 2, etc. In the example of a study of depression, group 1 might be the "always depressed" group while group 2 might be those who are "becoming depressed." A multinomial regression model then can predict the probabilities of group membership. It may be, for example, that the predictors of being in the "always depressed" group are quite different from the predictors of being in the "becoming depressed" group. This model thus seems especially useful when trajectories of change involve sets of parameters that mark qualitatively different kinds of development. Nagin shows how to test the appropriateness of the assumed number of groups and thus to test alternative models for types of change.

Alternative Probabilistic Models   The vast majority of level-2 models assume that departures of the change parameters (the πs) from their predicted values are multivariate normal. This is certainly a convenient assumption, as mentioned, but it may poorly fit the data, and results may not be robust for departures from it. In particular, outlier values of the growth parameters may be far more influential than one would desire, particularly in small-sample settings.

To develop more robust estimation, Seltzer (1993) adopted a multivariate t-prior distribution for the random effects (e.g. u_{0i}, u_{1i} in Equation 2). The t-prior anticipates more outliers than does the normal prior, and, as a result, model estimates are more resistant to the influence of such outliers. Seltzer embedded this approach within a Bayesian framework—a three-level hierarchical model with the first two levels of the type given by Equations 1 and 2 and a third level specifying a prior for the level-2 parameters. Thum (1997) also adopted a t-prior in his multilevel-multivariate model with estimation via maximum likelihood. This model allows covariance structure analysis at each of two levels based on incomplete data.

Causal Inference

Let us consider the problem of causal inference in studies in which the "outcome" is an entire trajectory of change. However, I first review some basic ideas about causation in cross-sectional studies.

Causal Effects in Cross-Sectional Studies   What is a causal effect? Many discussions of causal inference and research design neglect to confront this issue. However, a theory that has come to dominate modern thinking in statistics about cause begins with this fundamental question. Pioneered by Rubin (1974) and Rosenbaum & Rubin (1983) and elaborated by Holland (1986), this theory has come to be known as the "Rubin-Rosenbaum-Holland" (RRH). To describe this theory, the simplest case will suffice; given a causal variable ("the treatment") with two possible values ("experimental" and "control"), for clarity, consider a case in which a child receives either the new experimental approach to daycare (E) or the currently available approach (C) and the outcome, Y, is a measure of self-regulation. If the child receives E, we observe $Y_i(E)$, the outcome of child i under E. However, if that same child receives C, we observe $Y_i(C)$, the outcome of child i under C. The causal effect of the experimental treatment (relative to the control) is defined as the difference between these two potential outcomes,

$$\Delta_i = Y_i(E) - Y_i(C). \tag{14}$$

Several conclusions follow from this definition.

First, the causal effect Δ_i is defined uniquely for each child. The impact of the treatment can thus vary from child to child. Modern thinking about cause thus rejects the conventional assumption that a new treatment adds a constant effect for every child. This assumption, never realistic to scientists or practitioners, was imposed historically to simplify statistical analysis.

Second, the causal effect cannot be observed. If a given child is assigned to E, we will observe $Y_i(E)$, but not $Y_i(C)$. On the other hand, if the child is assigned to C, we will observe $Y_i(C)$ but not $Y_i(E)$. The outcome that cannot be observed is the counter-factual outcome.

Third, it must be reasonable at least to imagine a scenario in which that child could have received either E or C. If it is not possible to conceive of each child's response under each treatment, it is not possible to define a causal effect. Therefore, in current thinking about cause in statistical science, a fixed attribute of a child (say sex or ethnic background) cannot typically be a cause. We cannot realistically imagine how a girl would have responded if she had been a boy or how a black child would have responded if that child had been white. Epidemiologists have referred to such attributes as fixed markers (Kraemer et al 1996), unchangeable attributes that may be statistically related to an outcome but cannot be causes.

Randomized Studies   According to RRH, the problem of causal inference is a problem of missing data. If both potential outcomes $Y_i(E)$ and $Y_i(C)$ were observed, the causal effect could simply be calculated for each participant. However, one of the potential outcomes (the counterfactual) is always missing. Randomized studies ensure that the missing counterfactual is missing completely at random. In effect, the mechanism of random assignment ensures that the decision about which outcome is observed [$Y_i(E)$ or $Y_i(C)$] is decided by chance alone. While it is not possible to estimate the causal effect for each participant, a randomized experiment enables unbiased estimation of the average causal effect, that is

$$\Delta = E[Y_i(E) - Y_i(C)], \tag{15}$$

the population average difference between potential outcomes. The estimator is simply the difference between sample means of the experimental and control groups.

Nonrandomized Studies   Without random assignment, we cannot assume that the counterfactual is missing at random. First, those selected into the experimental group may be more (or less) disadvantaged than those selected into the control group. If so, the potential outcomes of those assigned to the experimental group would be higher (or lower), on average, than of those assigned to the control group in the absence of a treatment effect. Researchers often attempt to control for confounding variables—preexisting variables that predict treatment group membership and are related to the potential outcomes—by means of matching or statistical adjustments such as the analysis of covariance (Cook & Campbell 1979). However, one can never be sure that the relevant confounding variables have been identified or that the method of adjustment has been completely effective. Second, participants may have information about the likely benefit of choosing to participate in the treatment, information not available to the researcher. For example, a person choosing not to participate in a job-training program may know that she is about to be offered a good-paying job, better than can be expected to result from participating in the program. Such biases cannot be controlled because, by definition, the information needed to adjust for bias is unknown to the researcher. However, certain "natural experiments" can be exploited to avoid such bias. For example, a job-training program may be available only in certain states, ensuring that the choice to participate is not entirely under the control of the participants. Instrumental variable methods (cf Angrist et al 1996, Little & Yau 1998) can be used to exploit such natural experiments in order to minimize bias in nonexperimental studies.

It has often been argued that collecting longitudinal data can also increase the credibility of causal inferences when randomization is impossible. We consider this issue, among others, in the following sections.

Causal Inference in Longitudinal Studies: Between-Subject Causes

Consider a case in which participants are assigned to one of two treatments to assess how the treatment affects an entire trajectory. Now we have a trajectory characterized by change parameters $\pi_i(E)$ if person i is assigned to E and $\pi_i(C)$ if person i is assigned to C. Only one of the two trajectories will be observed, leaving the counterfactual trajectory missing.

Randomized Experiments   Under random assignment, the counterfactual trajectory is missing completely at random, making it easy to calculate an unbiased estimate of the average treatment effect as the mean trajectory in the experimental group minus the mean trajectory in the control group—assuming no attrition. If data are missing through attrition, for example, because some participants miss some appointments to be assessed or some drop out of the study, there are three possibilities (Little & Rubin 1987, Schafer 1997).

1. The attrition may lead to data that are missing completely at random (MCAR). Data that are MCAR result when the missing time points are a random sample of all time points or the dropouts are a random sample of all participants. In this case unbiased estimation follows easily using conventional methods, for example analyzing only those cases with complete data. However, to assume that data are MCAR is generally implausible, impossible to verify, and risky.

2. The data may be missing at random (MAR). MAR occurs when the probability of missing a time point is independent of the missing data, given the observed data. This assumption is reasonable when the observed data capture key confounding influences, for example, variables that predict both attrition and the outcome of interest. Under the MAR case, estimation of the treatment effect will be unbiased if (*a*) all of the data are used in the analysis and (*b*) a fully efficient estimation procedure is used. For example, maximum likelihood estimation of hierarchical models (also termed multilevel models or mixed models—see earlier discussion) will efficiently use all of the available time points to estimate the model, assuring unbiased estimation of treatment effects under the MAR case. Under these conditions, the mechanism that produces the "missingness" is "ignorable." Use of multiple, model-based imputation (Little & Rubin 1987, Schafer 1997) will also ensure ignorable missingness when data are MAR.

3. "Nonignorable" missingness arises when the data are neither MCAR or MAR. In this case, the probability of attrition does depend on the missing value, even after controlling for all observed data. Results will be robust to nonignorable missingness to the extent that (*a*) all of the data are efficiently used and (*b*) the fraction of missing information is small.[2] Little (1995) and Hedekker & Gibbons (1997) describe methods for nonignorably missing longitudinal data under the rubric of pattern-mixture models.

Nonrandomized Studies   Without random assignment, estimation of treatment effects will, in general, be biased even if there is no attrition. We therefore consider only the "no-attrition case," keeping in mind that the concerns about attrition that apply in randomized experiments will also apply in nonrandomized experiments.

Below I consider how longitudinal studies can overcome or reduce bias when it is impossible to randomly assign participants to treatments. I consider studies with two time points, three time points, and more than three time points.

---

[2]The fraction of missing information is not the fraction of missing data points. It is, rather, related to the amount of variation in missing data that is not explained or accounted for by observed data. If the associations between the observed and missing data are strong, the fraction of missing data will be small even if the fraction of missing cases appears quite large.

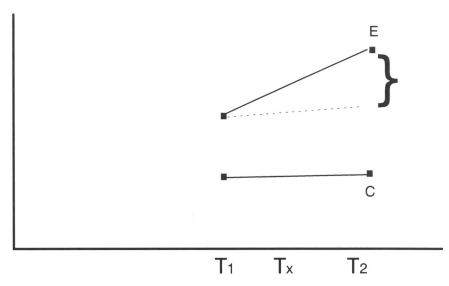

E

C

T₁   Tₓ   T₂

Figure 4 Causal inference when children are growing: pre-post design.

Causal Comparative Studies with Two Time Points   Consider a nonrandom-ized cross-sectional study. As mentioned above, the mean difference between out-comes of experimental and control groups is not, in general, an unbiased estimate of the treatment effect. One strategy to cope with bias is to add a pretest. As-suming Y is measured on a common scale at each time point, the difference in gain scores is arguably less biased than the difference in post-test scores. Con-sider, for example, Figure 4. The figure shows the average pre-post trajectory for experimental groups and for controls. The length of the interval in curly braces is presumably the treatment effect. Using Equation 12 as a model, this estimate is

$$\hat{\beta}_{11}\,(T_2 - T_1),\tag{16}$$

that is, the difference in mean growth rates between the two groups (β_{11}) multiplied by the time elapsed between the pre- and post-test.

The problem is that such an estimate assumes that the two groups would have experienced identical growth rates in the absence of the treatment. Given nonran-dom assignment, this seems improbable. A design having two time points gives no information about the rate of growth of the experimental group in the absence of a treatment. This fact is illustrated in Figures 5A and 5B. Figure 5A shows parallel growth of the two groups before the treatment, making the interval in curly braces plausible as a measure of treatment impact. However, Figure 5B shows nonparallel growth before the implementation of the treatment, undermin-ing any case for that estimate. Two time points provide no basis for adjudicating

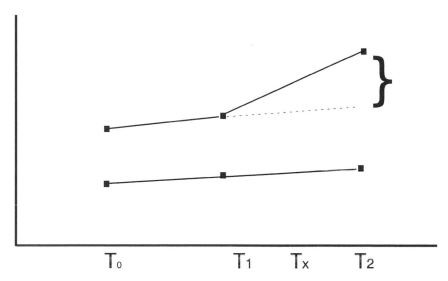

Figure 5A   Scenario 1: parallel growth in absence of treatment.

between Figures 5*A* and 5*B* or any other pretreatment growth configuration. The problem does not follow from the use of gain scores. Bryk & Weisberg (1977) showed that all strategies of linear adjustment (including not only the gain score adjustment but also the analysis of covariance) are subject to biases that cannot be investigated with only two time points.

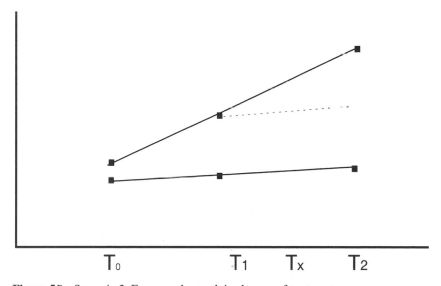

Figure 5B   Scenario 2: Fan spread growth in absence of treatment.

Three Time Points   Adding a third time point, in particular, a "pre-pre-test," adds substantially to the information available in estimating the treatment effect. When we elaborate Equations 1 and 2 to incorporate this information, our level-1 model becomes

$$Y_{ti} = \pi_{0i} + \pi_{1i}a_{ti} + \delta_i Z_{ti} + e_{ti}. \tag{17}$$

Here Z_{ti} is a dummy variable taking on a value of 1 at the third time point and 0 otherwise, so that δ_i is the deflection experienced by participant i between times 2 and 3, that is, when the treatment is implemented. The other terms in Equation 4 are defined as in Equation 1. We now elaborate the level-2 model to allow the deflection to depend on group membership:

$$\pi_{0i} = \beta_{00} + \beta_{01}X_i + u_{0i}$$

$$\pi_{1i} = \beta_{10} + \beta_{11}X_i + u_{1i} \tag{18}$$

$$\delta_i = \Delta_c + \Delta X_i.$$

As displayed in Figure 6, this model allows estimation of (*a*) different mean initial status for C and E; (*b*) different pretreatment growth rates for C and E; and (*c*) different nonlinear deflections for C and E at time of treatment. The difference between these nonlinear deflections is the presumptive treatment effect. Clearly, adding a single time point has added a substantial amount of information relevant to estimating the treatment effect.

More Than Two Time Points   The quasi experimental design with three points, while much stronger than the design with two points, may be criticized for assuming that both groups would have the same nonlinear deflection in the absence of a treatment. Adding a fourth time point can distinguish nonlinear deflections and a treatment effect. Adding a fourth time point (a second post-test) can also enable the estimation of a randomly varying effect of treatment. This brings the model into closer alignment with the notion of participant-specific effects that is central to the potential-outcomes framework.

Time-Varying Treatments

We have limited the discussion so far to the case in which participants experience one and only one treatment. Yet many interesting causal questions involve time-varying treatments. Every time a child speaks, a caregiver's response can be conceived as a treatment. A time series unfolds in which each speech event triggers such a "treatment," which affects the next speech event, and so on. Other examples include the use of medical treatment: a physician will assess a child and prescribe (or not prescribe) a drug; the physician will then follow up later with another assessment and another decision to prescribe or not, etc. In school, children are assigned to special education (or not) based on assessments of academic progress

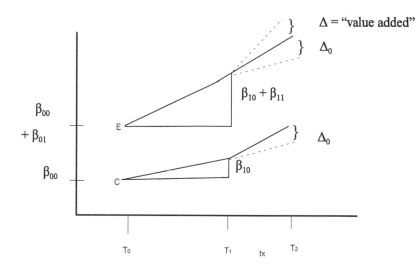

Model for individual growth

$$Y_{it} = \pi_{0i} + \pi_{1i}\alpha_{ti} + \delta_i D_{2i} + e_{ti}$$

Model for population variation in growth curve

$$\pi_{0i} = \beta_{00} + \beta_{01}X_i + U_{0i}$$

$$\pi_{1i} = \beta_{10} + \beta_{11}X_i + U_{1i}$$

$$\delta_i = \Delta_0 + \Delta X_i$$

$$X_i = \{1 \text{ if } E, 0 \text{ if } C\}$$

Figure 6   Estimating the treatment effect based on three time points.

and behavior and are then "mainstreamed" (or not) based on subsequent behavior, which has arisen, in part, as a result of the first placement decision.

In all of these examples, the assessment, treatment, later assessment, and later treatment are interconnected. There is a serious risk in these examples that the analyst will estimate the effect of treatment on the outcome with bias. Children who are assigned medication will do worse than those who are not, making the medication look harmful; children assigned to special education will look worse than those who are not, making special-education placement look harmful; and the mainstreamed will look better than those who are not, making mainstreaming look helpful—even if the medication, placement, and mainstreaming have no effect.

A dynamic-treatment regime arises when a time-varying treatment or "dose" is calibrated to the current status of the participant. It is normally true that "the worse the current status, the larger the dose." The "regime" is the set of rules that assign doses to children by their statuses. Methodological research shows that one can make sound inferences about regimes, for example, by assigning participants at random to the regime (Robins et al 2000). However, if a regime is strictly adhered to, it is not possible, within regimes, to assess the causal effect of a dose. Only if the dose can vary, given current status, is it possible to make a causal inference about the dose.

The problem of causal inference for time-varying treatments, assuming no randomization, is extraordinarily challenging. It is a cutting-edge issue on which progress is being made, but methodological workers in this area have not yet achieved a consensus on the best ways to proceed.

Summary and Conclusions

A statistical model is essential in precisely defining each participant's trajectory and facilitating comparisons of persons by comparing their trajectories. Based on such a model, one can define and estimate the reliability of measures of change. One can also define effect sizes and, with supplementary data at hand, compute the power of alternative designs (Hedeker & Gibbons 1997; Muthen & Curran 1997). Alternative models posit alternative views of confounding variables and alternative ways in which attrition might affect the precision and bias of inferences.

An important new line of research considers how to extend modern thinking about causal effects to longitudinal data. According to this modern theory, a causal effect is person specific; it is the difference between how a person would respond under one condition and how that same person would respond under a different condition. The causal effect can thus vary among people. However, it cannot be directly computed, because invariably, a person will experience one condition but not the other at any given time. The set of responses that might occur for a person under the varied conditions possible is called the set of potential outcomes. A confounder is a pretreatment characteristic of a participant that is related to both the propensity to receive the treatments and to the potential outcomes. Valid causal inferences require that the propensity to receive treatments is independent of the potential outcomes, given the potential confounders on which the investigator has collected data. Randomized experiments ensure independence. In nonrandomized experiments, knowledge of predictors of propensity to receive the various treatments is essential in seeking valid causal inferences. In the nonrandomized setting, the burden of proof is on the shoulders of the investigator to show that the relevant confounders have been taken into account, and it will be difficult to avoid lingering disagreement about the success of the attempt to take these into account.

It is often essential in developmental research to recognize that participants are naturally growing or changing even in the absence of a treatment. A model for individual growth in the absence of treatments can be extremely useful in identifying causal effects, especially in the challenging nonrandomized setting. Multiple time points can lay a basis for interrupted time series designs with improved validity of causal inference in nonrandomized studies.

When the growth of interest is psychological, it is challenging to define clearly the dimensions in which children are growing, to devise assessments that are sensitive to growth, and to evaluate the capacity of alternative designs to reliably gauge individual differences in growth. Given that repeated measures are required to assess growth, the problem of attrition cannot be ignored. Attrition can not only weaken statistical precision but also introduce bias, even in randomized experiments. In these settings, it is incumbent on the investigator to study the predictors of attrition and to devise ways to control attrition in assessing effects.

Finally, time-varying treatments pose special challenges because a treatment will often be tailored to the past behavior of the participants. Valid causal inference in this setting constitutes an area of intense interest in methodological research.

ACKNOWLEDGMENTS

Research reported here was supported by grants to the Project on Human Development in Chicago Neighborhoods by the MacArthur Foundation, the National Institute of Justice, and the National Institute of Mental Health.

Visit the Annual Reviews home page at www.AnnualReviews.org

LITERATURE CITED

Angrist JD, Imbens GW, Rubin DB. 1996. Identification of causal effects using instrumental variables. *J. Am. Stat. Assoc.* 91(434):444–72

Blalock H. 1969. *Theory Construction*. Englewood Cliffs, NJ: Prentice-Hall

Blau P, Duncan O. 1967. *The American Occupational Structure*. New York: Wiley & Sons

Bryk A, Raudenbush S. 1992. *Hierarchical Linear Models for Social and Behavioral Research: Applications and Data Analysis Methods*. Newbury Park, CA: Sage

Bryk A, Weisberg H. 1977. Use of the nonequivalent control gorup design when subjects are growing. *Psychol. Bull.* 84(5):950–62

Carter L. 1984. The sustaining effects study of compensatory and elementary education. *Educ. Res.* 13(7):4–13

Collins L. 2001. Measurement reliability for static and dynamic categorical latent variables. In *New Methods for the Analysis of Change*, ed. L Collins A Sayer. Washington, DC: Am. Psychol. Assoc. In press

Collins L, Wugalter S. 1992. Latent class models for stage-sequential dynamic latent variables. *Multivar. Behav. Res.* 27:131–57

Cook T, Campbell D. 1979. *Quasi-Experimentation*. New York: Rand McNally

Cox D, Oakes D. 1984. *Analysis of Survival Data*. London: Chapman & Hall

Diggle P, Liang K, Zeger S. 1994. *Analysis of*

Longitudinal Data. New York: Oxford Univ. Press

Duncan O. 1966. Path analysis: sociological examples. *Am. J. Sociol.* 72(1):1–16

Duncan O, Featherman D, Duncan B. 1972. *Socioeconomic Background Achievement.* New York: Seminar Press

Francis DJ, Fletcher JM, Stubting KK, Davidson KC, Thompson NM. 1991. Analysis of change: modeling individual growth. *J. Consult. Clin. Psychol.* 39(1):27–37

Goldstein H. 1995. *Multilevel Statistical Models.* New York: Wiley & Sons. 2nd ed.

Gottfredson M, Hirschi T. 1990. *A General Theory of Crime.* Stanford, CA: Stanford Univ. Press

Gottman J. 1995. *The Analysis of Change.* Hillsdale, NJ: Erlbaum

Hedeker D, Gibbons R. 1997. Application of random effects pattern mixture models for missing data in social sciences. *Psychol. Methods* 2(1):64–78

Holland P. 1986. Statistics and causal inference. *J. Am. Stat. Assoc.* 81(396):945–60

Horney J, Osgood D, Marshall I. 1995. Criminal careers in the short-term: intra-individual variability in crime and its relation to local life circumstances. *Am. Sociol. Rev.* 60: 655–73

Huttenlocher J, Haight W, Bryk A, Seltzer M. 1991. Early vocabulary growth: relation to language input and gender. *Dev. Psychol.* 27(2):236–49

Joreskog K, Sorbom D. 1979. *Advance in Factor Analysis and Structural Equation Models.* Cambridge, MA: ABT Assoc.

Kalbfleisch J, Prentice R. 1980. *The Statistical Analysis of Failure Time Data.* New York: Wiley & Sons

Kraemer HC, Kazdin AE, Offord DR, Kessler RC, Jensen PS, Kupfer DJ. 1996. Coming to terms with the terms of risk. *Arch. Gen. Psychiatry*

Laird N, Ware J. 1982. Random-effects models for longitudinal data. *Biometrika* 65(1):581–90

Little R, Rubin D. 1987. *Statistical Analysis with Missing Data.* New York: Wiley & Sons

Little R, Yau L. 1998. Statistical techniques for analyzing data from prevention trials: treatment of no-shows using Rubin's causal model. *Psychol. Methods* 3(2):147–59

Little R. 1995. Modeling the drop-out mechanism in repeated measures studies. *J. Am. Stat. Assoc.* 90:1112–21

Longford N. 1993. *Random Coefficient Models.* Oxford, UK: Clarendon

McCullagh P, Nelder J. 1989. *Generalized Linear Models.* London: Chapman & Hall. 2nd ed.

Meredith W, Tisak J. 1990. Latent curve analysis. *Psychometrika* 55:107–22

Moffitt T. 1993. Adolescence-limited and life-course persistent antisocial behavior: a developmental taxonomy. *Psychol. Rev.* 100:674–701

Muthen B. 2001. Second generation structural equation modeling with a combination of categorical and continuous latent variables: new opportunities for latent class-latent growth modeling. In *New Methods of the Analysis of Change*, ed. L Collins, A Sayer. Washington, DC: Am. Psychol. Assoc. In press

Muthen BO, Curran PJ. 1997. General longitudinal modeling of individual differences in experimental designs: a latent variable framework for analysis and power estimation. *Psychol. Methods* 2(4):371–402

Nagin DS. 1999. Analyzing developmental trajectories: a semi-parametric, group-based approach. *Psychol. Methods* 4(2):139–57

Raudenbush SW. 2001. Toward a coherent framework for comparing trajectories of individual change. In *Best Methods for Studying Change*, ed. L Collins, A Sayer. Washington, DC: Am. Psychol. Assoc. In press

Raudenbush SW, Chan WS. 1993. Application of a hierarchical linear model to the study of deviance in an overlapping cohort design. *J. Consult. Clin. Psychol.* 61(6):941–51

Raudenbush SW, Sampson R. 1999. Assessing direct and indirect associations in multilevel designs with latent variables. *Sociol. Methods Res.* 28(2):123–53

Robins JM, Greenland S, Hu F-C. 2000. Estimation of the causal effect of a time-varying exposure on the marginal mean of a repeated binary outcomes. *J. Am. Stat. Assoc.* In press

Rogosa D, Brandt D, Zimowski M. 1982. A growth curve approach to the measurement of change. *Psychol. Bull.* 90:726–48

Rosenbaum P, Rubin D. 1983. The central role of the propensity score in observational studies for causal effects. *Biometrika* 17:41–55

Rubin D. 1974. Estimating causal effects of treatments in randomized and non-randomized studies. *J. Educ. Psychol.* 66:688–701

Schafer J. 1997. *Analysis of Incomplete Multivariate Data.* London: Chapman & Hall

Seltzer M. 1993. Sensitivity analysis for fixed effects in the hierarchical model: a Gibbs sampling approach. 18(3):207–35

Seltzer MH, Frank KA, Bryk AS. 1994. The metric matters: the sensitivity of conclusions concerning growth in student achievement to choice of metric. *Educ. Eval. Policy Anal.* 16(1):41–49

Sewell W, Hauser R. 1975. *Education, Occupations, and Earnings: Achievement in the Early Career.* New York: Academic

Singer J, Willett J. 1991. Modeling the days of our lives: using survival analysis when designing and analyzing longitudinal studies of duration and the time of events. *Psychol. Bull.* 110(2):268–90

Thum Y. 1997. Hierarchical linear models for multivariate outcomes. *J. Educ. Behav. Stat.* 22:77–108

Annu. Rev. Psychol. 2001. 52:527–53

DISRESPECT AND THE EXPERIENCE OF INJUSTICE

Dale T. Miller

*Department of Psychology, Princeton University, Princeton, New Jersey 08540;
e-mail: dmiller@princeton.edu*

Key Words   justice, fairness, procedural justice, retribution, distributive justice

■ **Abstract** This review analyzes research and theory pertaining to the psychology
of injustice, using as its organizing theme the role that the perception of disrespect
plays in the experience of injustice. The analysis focuses primarily on the links between
disrespect and anger, disrespect and injustice, and anger and injustice. Determinants of
the intensity of people's reactions to injustices are also reviewed. In addition, the review
examines the goals of retaliation as well as the forms that retaliation can take. Parallels
between justice reactions to those acts of disrespect directed toward the self and those
directed toward others are noted. Finally, the review discusses the implications of
justice research for understanding the specific and general entitlements that people
believe are their due.

CONTENTS

0066-4308/01/0201-0527$14.00

INTRODUCTION

Of fascination to philosophers since Aristotle, the topic of justice has only recently engaged the interest of psychologists. The fourth edition of the *Handbook of Social Psychology* (Gilbert et al 1998) devotes a chapter to justice (Tyler & Smith 1998), but the third edition (Lindzey & Aronson 1985) does not even have an entry for justice in the subject index. To some extent, this neglect is more apparent than real, because a number of research traditions with long-standing interest in justice have only recently started to sail under the flag of "justice research." Research on relative deprivation (Crosby 1976, Merton & Kitt 1950, Olson et al 1986, Stouffer et al 1949) and prosocial behavior (Batson 1998, Krebs & Miller 1985, Lerner 1980) are two cases in point. Not even these latter research traditions, however, can boast a long history of direct investigation of justice reactions. Relative deprivation and equity researchers, for example, traditionally have not asked participants how just their outcomes or circumstances are, but rather how satisfied the participants are with them (Adams 1965, Crosby 1976). What qualifies such research as justice research is the assumption that outcome satisfaction is mediated by perceptions of outcome fairness. The tendency to view perceived justice primarily as a mediating or moderating variable rather than as a dependent variable continues to the present, although contemporary justice researchers are much more likely to probe people's perceptions of fairness and justice directly.

Strongly influenced by exchange theorists (e.g. Blau 1964, Homans 1961, Thibaut & Kelley 1959), early justice researchers focused primarily on distributive justice. In particular, they focused on people's relative preference for three different principles of resource distribution: need, equity, and equality. The two most common means of assessing this preference were by examining the rules people followed when allocating resources to others and by examining people's reactions to the resources they received from others (see Adams 1965, Deutsch 1985, Walster et al 1978). Distributive justice as a topic has diminished in popularity in recent years (Tyler & Smith 1998); perhaps more significantly, the topic has been appropriated to a considerable extent by researchers in the judgment- and decision-making tradition (Elster 1992, Mellers & Baron 1993, Mitchell et al 1993). From the decision-analytic perspective (Mellers et al 1998), questions about distributive justice are viewed most appropriately as judgment- and decision-making tasks.

Without question, the most popular topic in justice research over the past 2 decades has been "procedural justice." Procedural justice refers to the fairness of the methods, mechanisms, and processes used to determine outcomes as opposed to the fairness of the outcomes themselves (Lind & Tyler 1988). Initial work on this topic focused on the formal, structural aspects of fair procedure (Leventhal 1976,

Thibaut & Walker 1975), whereas more recent work has focused on the less formal, interpersonal aspects of fair procedure (Bies 1987, Greenberg 1990, Folger & Cropanzo 1998, Tyler 1990).

The shift in the focus of procedural justice research is illustrated best by the history of the variable of "voice" (Folger & Cropanzo 1998, Tyler 1987). Thibaut & Walker (1975) introduced the concept they termed "process control," later renamed voice (Folger 1977), to describe the extent to which the formal structure of a legal proceeding provided the disputants with the opportunity to have a say in how their case was presented. Legal disputants are said to have this type of voice to the extent that the formal structure of the proceedings permits them to convey their interests to the judge or decision maker. Legal disputants, however, also may or may not be afforded a second, more informal type of voice. Specifically, they may or may not be listened to when they choose to exercise the voice option that the formal structure affords them. The presence of both types of voice, sometimes referred to as "instrumental" and "value expressive" voice, respectively (Tyler & Bies 1990), enhances the perception of procedural fairness (Lind et al 1990).

The shift in focus from formal to informal aspects of procedural justice (Tyler et al 1997) reflected a more fundamental transformation in the way justice was perceived, or at least experimentally assessed, by researchers. Early procedural justice theorists (Leventhal 1976, Thibaut & Walker 1975) characterized people's concern with fair procedures as instrumental in nature. Pursuit of principles of procedural justice was assumed to maximize the individual's outcomes in the same way as pursuit of the principles of distributive justice (Homans 1961, Walster et al 1978). From this perspective, the main challenge for researchers was not explanations of why people care about procedural justice (self-interest was the assumed motivation) but identification of the criteria that people use in deciding whether a procedure is just (Leventhal 1976).

By the late 1980s the tenor of procedural justice research had changed. Procedural concerns were no longer viewed as important simply because their effects were independent from those of distributive concerns. Procedural concerns were now seen as important because they revealed the human actor to be less utility-maximizing and more justice-seeking than was assumed by the dominant neoclassical economic model. People care about procedural justice, it was now asserted, not as a means to an end (better outcomes) but as an end in itself. With this assertion, procedural justice researchers joined a growing chorus of social scientists who expressed dissatisfaction with the rational-actor model (Etzioni 1988, Lerner 1977, Mansbridge 1990, Miller 1999).

Procedural justice researchers, turning increasingly from laboratory to field settings, also sought to show that concerns with procedure were often more powerful than—and not simply independent from—concerns with outcomes (Tyler 1990). Furthermore, in light of the mounting evidence that people's concern with fair treatment was independent of its effects on outcomes, theories of procedural justice began to propose noninstrumental accounts of procedural justice motivation. The most influential of these theories was Lind & Tyler's (1988) group value theory.

According to this theory, people care whether their treatment (and not simply their outcomes) is fair because fair treatment indicates something critically important to them—their status within their social group.

The Right to Respect

The shift in empirical and theoretical attention from distributive to procedural justice signified a more general shift in justice research from a concern with abstract rules of resource distribution to a concern with interpersonal rules of conduct (Hogan & Emler 1981, Tyler et al 1997, Vidmar 2000). This change paralleled the increasing attention that moral philosophers were devoting to humanitarian standards of justice (Furby 1986, Moore 1978, Rawls 1971). An especially relevant example of the latter is the claim by Rawls (1971) that one of the entitlements that individuals are due by virtue of their humanity is the right to be treated in a way that fosters positive self-regard.

Respect, it should be noted, also can play an important role in the perception of distributive justice. As many have noted, the indignation with which people respond to unfavorable outcomes (e.g. lower than expected salary offers) often reflects the fact that their prestige or status has been threatened more than the fact that their purchasing power has been diminished (Berger et al 1972, Homans 1976). Status and prestige, therefore, are conveyed both by the resources people receive and by the procedures used to determine and administer those resources. The fact that the perception of distributive fairness often has less to do with an outcome's exchange value than with its symbolic or status value is one reason it has proven so difficult to draw a sharp distinction between procedural and distributive injustice (Folger & Cropanzo 1998, Van den Bos et al 1997).

Injustice in Everyday Life

The growing importance that formal justice theories accord to respectful treatment comports with findings from investigations of the layperson's understanding of everyday injustices. The most commonly reported experiences of everyday injustice involve some form of disrespectful treatment (Lupfer et al 2000, Messick et al 1985, Mikula 1986, Mikula et al 1990). For example, consider the responses Mikula (1986) elicited from college students when he asked them to describe the unjust experiences they experienced in daily life. The three events most frequently mentioned by students were (a) unjustified accusation and blaming, (b) unfair grading or lack of recognition for performance or effort, and (c) violations of promises and agreements. Less frequently mentioned events included failure to admit an error, giving orders in an inappropriate tone, meddling in one's business, and ruthless or illegal misuses of one's status and power. Violations of interpersonal codes of conduct are also a common source of feelings of injustice in organizations. Instances of injustices reported by workers include the violation of codes of conduct (Aram & Salipante 1981), betrayal by coworkers (Bies 1993), and humiliation and wrongful accusation by superiors (Bies & Tripp 1996).

ENTITLEMENTS

In the case of research on retributive and distributive justice, the nature of the offending action traditionally has been some blatant form of physical, economic, or psychological maltreatment and, as such, tends not to be a big part of the study's story. The situation is very different in the case of procedural justice research. Procedural justice researchers typically are as interested in providing demonstrations of what constitutes just procedures as they are in demonstrating that procedural justice matters. For this reason, procedural justice research has contributed greatly to our knowledge of the range and nature of the actions that give offense and arouse feelings of injustice in informal as well as formal relationships.

Specific Entitlements

To ask people what acts they consider disrespectful and unjust is, basically, to ask them what they consider people to be entitled to from others. The entitlement that has received the most attention, as noted earlier, is voice. People believe they are entitled to have their say and to be listened to in their dealings with others, whether these dealings are formal or informal (see Lind & Tyler 1988 for a review). An illustration of the importance of voice is provided by studies of perceptions by fathers of the fairness of custody court cases. Fathers virtually always lose such cases, but if they believe they were permitted to make their case to the judge and that the judge listened to them, they often leave the court thinking they were treated fairly (Emery et al 1994). Tyler (1987, 1990; Tyler et al 1985) has found that voice considerations similarly affect the perceived fairness of dealings with police officers and other participants in the legal system. In fact, voice has been shown to affect perceptions of fairness even when there is little possibility that it could affect outcomes—for instance, if the opportunity to express oneself comes after the outcome has been decided (Lind et al 1990).

No other entitlement has received the degree of empirical attention that has been accorded voice, but various theorists have sought to identify the different components of the respect people think that they are due from others. Tyler & Lind (1992), for example, have attempted to specify the types of considerations that people believe they are entitled to from those in positions of authority. Recent work on what has been termed "interactional justice" (Bies & Moag 1986, Cropanzo & Greenberg 1997, Skarlicki & Folger 1997) has shown particular interest in identification of the forms of consideration that people believe they are due from others. On the basis of this work, it appears that people's sense of entitlement comes down to two broad requirements. The first requirement is interpersonal sensitivity (Greenberg 1994). People believe they are entitled to polite and respectful treatment from others (Baron 1993, Bies & Moag 1986). The second requirement is accountability. People think they are entitled to explanations and accounts for any actions that have personal consequences for them (Bies & Shapiro 1987, Bobocel et al 1998, Shapiro et al 1994).

Psychological Contracts

As various researchers have noted (e.g. Folger & Cropanzo 1998), it is often difficult, even for the those involved, to specify precisely what constitutes respectful treatment in a given situation. People may express the belief that they are entitled to respectful treatment from someone (e.g. a romantic partner, a police officer, or a government bureaucrat), but what precisely do they mean? Because of the difficulty in defining what constitutes procedural justice, many justice researchers have concluded that people in relationships do not operate under explicit agreements of entitlement but under something more informal and implicit. The most common term for this type of informal agreement, the content of which will vary from context to context and relationship to relationship, is "psychological contract" (Robinson et al 1994, Rousseau 1995). A psychological contract is an implicit understanding of what is and is not acceptable in a relationship (Robinson 1996, Taylor et al 1995). People may not always be able to articulate what their entitlements are in any particular relationship, but they know when a sense of rightness has been violated (Cropanzo & Byrne 2000) or when someone has "crossed the line" (Folger & Skarlicki 1998). In essence, a psychological contract constitutes a code of conduct or, to use Folger & Skarlicki's (1998) term, a "human covenant." The violation of a psychological contract, like that of any contract, constitutes an injustice in people's eyes. Disrespectful treatment, therefore, can both compound the injustice created by an undeserved outcome and constitute an injustice of its own.

THE EXPERIENCE OF INJUSTICE

To understand better how disrespectful treatment produces feelings of injustice, it is useful to examine the phenomenology of injustice. The experience of injustice can be analyzed from the perspective of three conceptual relationships, that between disrespect and anger, disrespect and injustice, and anger and injustice.

The Link Between Disrespect and Anger

The relationship between disrespect and anger has been theorized about and empirically investigated extensively. Indeed, the perception that one has been treated disrespectfully is widely recognized as a common, perhaps the most common, source of anger. Aristotle emphasized this link in his definition of anger as ". . .an impulse, accompanied by pain, to a conspicuous revenge for a conscious slight directed without justification towards what concerns oneself. . . ." (1945, p. 173). Bacon (1909, cited in Heider 1958) similarly traced the origin of anger to insult. In his words, ". . .contempt is that which putteth an edge upon anger, as much or more than the harm itself." Many contemporary authorities are no less insistent on the role of insult in anger. Lazarus (1991), for example, asserts that insult is the primary component in the arousal of anger.

Whether the perception of disrespect is a necessary condition for the arousal of anger is difficult to establish, but a considerable amount of research supports the claim that disrespectful treatment is a common determinant of both anger and aggression (Bettencourt & Miller 1996, Cohen et al 1996). Furthermore, research shows that a common characteristic of those who exhibit especially high levels of anger and aggression is a low threshold for inferring disrespect from the actions of others (Dodge et al 1990, Dodge & Somberg 1987, Graham & Hudley 1994). Disrespectful treatment does not inevitably arouse anger, however. Sometimes people do not think they deserve respect (Heuer et al 1999), and insults that are perceived to be deserved or justified rarely arouse anger, however they may diminish the target of the insult (Donnerstein & Walster 1982).

Additional evidence of the link between insult and anger comes from its prominence in people's naïve theories of interpersonal relations. People routinely assume that the presence of anger in another person indicates that he or she feels insulted and, perhaps because of this, people routinely respond to the anger of another with an apology (Gergen & Gergen 1988, Riordan et al 1983). Anger has a similarly important cue value to the individual who experiences it; it is a powerful signal to a person that he or she has been insulted. As Averill (1983, p. 184) asserts, if you "convince people that they are angry... you have gone a long way toward convincing them, rightfully or wrongfully, that action is appropriate and necessary." This fact is one of the reasons anger has been termed an "empowering emotion" (Ellsworth & Gross 1994).

The Link Between Disrespect and Injustice

Requests to describe unjust events, as noted earlier, generally elicit references to circumstances in which the participants felt that they were insulted or were otherwise treated disrespectfully. That people consider disrespectful treatment unpleasant, even painful, is not surprising, but why do they consider it unjust? Bourdieu's (1965) analysis of insults offers one possible explanation. In his words, "An insult sullies both the picture of himself that the individual intends to project, and that which he imagines to be his" (Bourdieu 1965, p. 211). According to Bourdieu, therefore, an insult, and presumably any disrespectful act, is experienced as unjust because it deprives people of something that they believe is rightfully theirs. When they are denied the respect to which they believe they are entitled, people feel as unjustly treated as when they are denied the material resources to which they believe they are entitled. Miller (1993) offers a somewhat different explanation of why insults give rise to feelings of injustice. He argues that insults produce feelings of injustice because they create a social imbalance. In his words, "insults and injuries are understood as gifts, of negative moral value to be sure, but as gifts nonetheless and as such demand repayment" (p. 16). An act of disrespect, then, is unjust for Bourdieu because it deprives people of something to which they are entitled and, for Miller, because it subjects people to something they do not deserve.

Additional evidence for the claim that acts of disrespect are viewed as unjust comes from studies of audience reactions to people who retaliate against disrespectful acts. This research shows that people are much less critical of a person's hostile actions against another when they view these actions as retaliation for a previous slight or injury (Carpenter & Darley 1978, Harvey & Enzle 1978, Robinson & Darley 1995). The greater tolerance of retaliatory aggression may derive partially from the belief that this type of aggression is more comprehensible but it probably also derives from the belief that this type of aggression is more justifiable (Tedeschi et al 1974). Retaliation, seen as necessary to preserve one's image and honor, represents a form of self-defense.

The Link Between Anger and Injustice

The perception of injustice is frequently tied to the emotion of anger (Keltner et al 1993, Scher 1997). However, positing an invariant causal relationship between the experience of anger and the perception of injustice is problematic. On the one hand, the perception of injustice can lead to anger. For example, people report that their most common response to injustice is anger (Clayton 1992, Mikula 1986). On the other hand, the arousal of anger can lead to the perception of injustice. One reason for the latter is that people rely on anger to cue them to the occurrence of injustices. As Solomon (1990) notes, anger serves as "an alarm system" that triggers the perception of injustice.

A second reason anger can produce the perception of injustice stems from the fact that it is normatively problematic for people to act upon their anger without the belief that their action is in the service of justice. However angry people are made by the treatment they receive at the hands of another, the likelihood that they will retaliate against the other will be greater if they also perceive this treatment to be unjust (Bies & Tripp 1996, Solomon 1990). In this vein, Lind (2000) contends that strong feelings of injustice are necessary for people to feel justified in taking aggressive action against members of their own group. Similarly, Martin et al (1984) contend that perceiving inequality between their group and another is a necessary condition for people to initiate collective violence. The claim has also been made that labeling a harmful action an injustice is necessary for its recipient to feel comfortable proceeding toward litigation. At least, it is rare that a lawsuit is pursued without the plaintiff thinking that he or she has suffered an injustice (Lind 1997). The dependence of retaliation on the perception of injustice raises the prospect that the perception of injustice is often simply a rationalization. As Nietzsche (1967) observed, often the urge to punish comes first; the reason, later.

Injustices have a transcendent quality, which is one reason that it is more legitimate to respond to an injustice than to that which is merely an insult, even when both offenses provoke equivalent anger. To label an insult an injustice transforms it from a personal matter to an impersonal matter of principle (Frankena 1963, Gamson 1968, Kelsen 1943). Put differently, the cry of injustice transforms the private into the public (Pitkin 1981). It also implies a strategy for action (Capek 1993).

In short, a personal insult that is labeled an injustice becomes a collective injustice, and avenging the injustice becomes a defense of the honor and integrity of the entire moral community.

The power of justice rhetoric extends beyond its capacity to justify retaliatory actions. It also has the capacity to compel support for retaliatory actions. Cries of injustice from one's peers are difficult to resist (Lind et al 2000). At the very least, people perceive a greater obligation to rally around someone who claims to have suffered an injustice than around someone who merely claims to have suffered a deprivation (Steil et al 1978).

Respect For Group Values and Rules

The arousal of moralistic anger is not confined to injustices perpetrated against one's self. Witnessing the harming of a third party can also arouse strong feelings of anger and injustice (Vidmar 2000). Even so-called "victimless" crimes, such as prostitution or pornography, can arouse strong moralistic and punitive impulses (Vidmar & Miller 1980). These "disinterested" feelings of injustice (Ranulf 1964) are not necessarily identical to those that arise in response to a direct offense against one's self, but they also depend greatly on the perception of disrespect. Individuals are committed to the "ought forces" of their moral community, as Heider (1958) termed them, and people believe that these forces deserve respect from all members of the community. The violation of these forces represents an insult to the integrity of the community and provokes both moralistic anger and the urge to punish the offender in its members (Durkheim 1964, Vidmar 2000). Viewed from this perspective, disinterested justice reactions are not disinterested at all, because everyone has a stake in seeing that the rules and values of the authority structure under which they live are respected (Vidmar 2000).

For example, consider a norm violation that provokes considerable moralistic anger—line intrusion or queue jumping—a phenomenon described at some length by Cooley (1902). As Cooley observed, and subsequent research shows (Milgram et al 1986, Schmitt et al 1992), people are much more likely to confront and express indignation toward a line intruder if that person intrudes in front of them rather than behind them. It is also true, however, that people feel indignation even toward those who intrude behind them. Moreover, the indignation aroused in the latter case does not derive solely, or perhaps even primarily, from feelings of empathy with those behind the intruder. Rather, it arises from the perceived disrespect the intruder has shown the system of social rules under which all members of the moral community are expected to live. In fact, however great the empathy is that people have for victims of injustices, their anger toward the perpetrator is generally greater. At least, research shows that people are more strongly motivated to punish perpetrators than to compensate victims (Hogan & Emler 1981, Miller & McCann 1979).

If people believe that an in-group member disrespects the group's values (as opposed to specific laws or rules), these people will also experience moralistic anger (Durkheim 1964). The same is true if they believe that valuable resources were distributed to in-group members in a manner that violates shared conceptions of fairness (Crosby & Gonzalez-Intel 1984; Feather 1996, 1999; Skitka & Tetlock 1992). The expression of indignation will often be indirect when the offending action pertains to group values. After all, it is difficult socially, and often psychologically, to punish someone simply because he or she rejects one's values. It is much less difficult to support policies and political causes that disadvantage or otherwise control those perceived to repudiate the group's values (Gusfield 1963, Herek & Glunt 1988, Sears & Funk 1991, Tyler & Boeckmann 1997).

DETERMINANTS OF THE REACTION TO THE INJUSTICE

Most authorities agree that moralistic anger depends greatly on the degree of disrespect implicit in the offending act. As Greenwell & Dengerink (1973) stated, "While attack is an important instigator of aggressive behavior, it appears that the physical discomfort experienced by a person may be subordinate to the symbolic elements that are incorporated into that attack" (p. 70). Of the factors that affect how disrespectful a harmful act is perceived to be, two of the most important are the perpetrator's responsibility for the act and his or her reaction to it.

The Offender's Responsibility

Foremost among the factors that affect reactions to a harm-doer are the motives, or state of mind, attributed to the offender (Heider 1958). The less responsibility the instigator of a harmful action bears for that action, the less disrespectful it will seem and the less anger it will provoke (Averill 1983, Ferguson & Rule 1981, Zillmann 1979).

Intentionality   A key component of responsibility is intentionality (Heider 1958). People bear more responsibility for those actions and consequences they intended than those that they did not intend. Most of the relevant research on the variable of harm-doer intentionality is found in the literature on aggression (see Geen 1998 for a review). In fact, there may be no more well-established finding in the aggression literature than the finding that unintentional acts of harm provoke less anger and less retaliation than do intentional acts of harm (Dyck & Rule 1978, Epstein & Taylor 1967, Greenwell & Dengerink 1973). The importance of the perpetrator's state of mind is further underscored by the fact that even actions that do not actually produce harm can arouse moralistic anger in their intended victim if he or she believes that harm was the intended goal of the perpetrator's actions (Batson et al 2000, Horai 1977). Research that has focused more directly on justice reactions than does the typical aggression study also indicates that the degree of intentionality attributed to the perpetrator is inversely related to the intensity of the victim's reaction to that harm (Bies & Tripp 1996, Torestad 1990).

The factors that influence the attribution of malevolent intent are less well understood than the consequences of such an attribution. To citizens of ancient Greece there was no such thing as accidental harm (Miller 1993). Any harm received at the hands of another was assumed intentional and hence deserved retaliation. The intentionality of harm is certainly no longer taken for granted, at least in Western cultures. As Kramer (1994) notes, however, even members of contemporary western cultures exhibit a low threshold for inferring intentionality, a tendency he terms the "sinister attribution error."

Forseeability   When the victim does not think that the perpetrator intended to give offense, he or she may still hold the perpetrator responsible for the offending act. People also bear responsibility for harmful consequences that were foreseeable, whether or not they were intended. A harm-doer's claim, "I meant no disrespect," even if believed, will not exempt the harm-doer from responsibility if the victim believes that the harm was foreseeable. Showing due respect to others requires that a person scrupulously avoid giving even inadvertent offense to others (Goffman 1971). In fact, harm-doers are sometimes blamed more for foreseeable but unintended consequences of actions than for intended consequences of actions made without malevolent intentions (Ferguson & Rule 1980).

The Offender's Reaction

Accounts and Justifications   The reaction of the perpetrator to his or her act and its consequences also affects the victim's response. For one thing, the perpetrator's reaction can provide information about his or her state of mind. In general, harm-doers who communicate to their victims that their actions were inadvertent or uncontrollable, or that they occurred under mitigating circumstances, typically provoke less anger (Folger & Martin 1986, Folger et al 1983, Greenberg 1993, Sitkin & Bies 1993).

However, the perpetrator's reaction does more than neutralize the offense by characterizing it as nonintentional, unforeseeable, or unavoidable. It can also convey respect for the victim and affirm his or her status. The very fact that the perpetrator thinks that the victim is due an explanation signals respect for the victim and tends to diminish the victim's anger (Bies 1987, Bies et al 1988, Greenberg 1990, Johnson & Rule 1986).

Apologies   When the offender's response goes beyond mere explanation and includes an apology, this action is likely to diminish the victim's anger even more (Bobocel & Farrell 1996). As Heider (1958) notes, the expression of remorse takes the sting out of an offense because it affirms the status of the victim and acknowledges that he or she has been treated unjustly. Tedeschi & Nesler (1993) propose that successful apologies contain three components: (*a*) an acceptance of responsibility and blame for the negative event; (*b*) an expression of remorse, indicating an acceptance of the norm that was violated and a promise not to violate the norm again; and (c) an expression of unhappiness about the harm that was done and an offer to engage in some form of restitution.

According to Tedeschi & Nesler's analysis, it would seem that a person can learn a considerable amount about his or her status by viewing the way that others react to acts that diminish that status. In fact, in cases where the profuseness of an apology exceeds that expected or deemed necessary by the victim, he or she might even be left feeling more socially valued than before the injury. Of course, only if the apologies are perceived as sincere will they have the effects just described. When victims perceive apologies to be insincere and designed simply to "cool them out," they often react with more rather than less indignation (Baron 1988, Cohen 1986, Goffman 1952).

Third-Party Reactions   The perpetrator's state of mind and response to the harm that has been caused also influences the reactions of those not directly affected by the perpetrator's actions. For example, unintentional acts that hurt a third party are punished less severely than acts that are intentional (Fincham & Jaspars 1980, Robinson & Darley 1995, Shaw & Reitan 1969). Furthermore, offering a reason for harming a third party reduces the punishment given the harm-doer (Felson & Ribner 1981) and so too does the offering of an apology or an expression of remorse (Ohbuchi et al 1989, Rumsey 1976, Schlenker & Darby 1981). Here also, however, the belief that the expression of remorse is insincere will lead to an increase rather than a decrease in punishment (Pepitone 1975).

Expressions of remorse reduce the punishment that is assigned rule violators because these actions lower people's estimates of likelihood of subsequent violations (Sykes & Matza 1957). This reason is not the only one, however. As many authorities have noted, expressions of contrition by rule violators also reduce the urge to punish because such expressions reaffirm the validity and status of the rule (Erikson 1966, Sykes & Matza 1957, Vidmar 2000). This fact would appear to be the reason that the Japanese legal system actually seeks apologies from lawbreakers (Hamilton & Sanders 1992). In some cases rules are affirmed more strongly by the existence of rule violators who express remorse than when there are only rule followers (Alexander & Staub 1956). As Miller & Vidmar (1981) observed, "Sometimes the act of full contrition may serve to affirm the validity of the rule so completely that punitive reactions against the offender totally dissipate and may even be replaced by positive responses" (p. 162). In contrast, a rule violator who is unapologetic provokes especially severe punishment (Schwartz et al 1978). What invokes such punishment is the idea that a nonpenitent perpetrator seems especially likely to commit further violations and that the perpetrator's apparent challenge to the validity of the rule compounds the offense (Heider 1958, Toch 1969).

Social Factors

The perception of what constitutes disrespectful behavior obviously will depend to some extent on the social context. The two contextual factors in this domain that have been most extensively investigated are the nature of the relationship between the offender and the victim and the public visibility of the offense.

The Relationship Between the Harm-Doer and the Victim   How disrespectful an individual finds another's action depends upon his or her relationship to the offender. One important consideration is whether or not the individuals involved belong to the same group. People typically believe they are entitled to more respect from in-group members than from out-group members (Tyler 1994). Furthermore, the indignation produced by disrespectful acts by out-group members tends to be different than that aroused by disrespectful acts by in-group members (Bond & Venus 1991). An insult from an out-group member is more likely to be perceived as insolent and to provoke a "How dare they?" response, whereas an insult from an in-group member is more likely to seem like a betrayal and to provoke a "How could they?" response. The action of an out-group member is most likely to seem disrespectful when it violates a norm that pertains to intergroup relations (DeRidder et al 1992). Thus, although an out-group member who rejects the in-group's values will not necessarily seem disrespectful (at least compared with an in-group member who behaves similarly), this is not true of an out-group member who violates the in-group's right to respect its own values and customs.

The power relationship existing between the two parties also affects what will be perceived as an insult (Heider 1958). An insult from a lower-status person will arouse a different form of indignation than an insult from a higher-status person. In the case of a lower-status person, the source of the indignation will generally be the belief that the offender does not know his or her place, whereas in the case of a higher-status person the source of the indignation will generally be the belief that the offender has abused his or her position.

The Public's Knowledge of the Offense   Whether or not an audience is present and who that audience is can powerfully affect the pain of an insult as well as the reaction to it. Generally, insults delivered in front of others produce more anger (Ferguson & Rule 1981). One reason for this reaction is that a public insult seems more unjust. Whereas all insults threaten a person's "face" and status, this is especially true of those insults that are delivered in public (Pitt-Rivers 1965). In some cases, an insult becomes an injustice only because it was delivered in public. For example, criticism that seems legitimate and appropriate when delivered in private can appear offensive and unjust if delivered in public (Bies & Moag 1986).

A second reason public insults produce more moralistic anger is that they hurt more. To be insulted in public compounds the victim's feelings of disrespect with public humiliation. It should come as no surprise, therefore, that evidence from both experimental and natural settings shows that people were more likely to retaliate against an insult when it was delivered in front of an audience (Felson 1982). The nature of the audience who witnesses an insult also affects the intensity of the victim's feelings of injustice. For example, a worker criticized in front of coworkers will experience stronger feelings of injustice than when the worker is criticized either in private or in front of others whose good opinion the worker cares less about.

In addition to affecting the intensity of the moralistic anger that is produced by an insult, the nature of the audience also affects the likelihood and intensity of retaliation. The reason for this reaction is that a person's image in the eyes of others is affected by the manner in which he or she responds to insults. Concern about the good opinion of others often leads to a greater likelihood of retaliation, especially when there is pressure to retaliate from a third party (Kim et al 1998). On the other hand, if the audience disapproves of retaliation, a strong bond between the target of the insult and the audience may actually reduce the likelihood of retaliation (Borden 1975).

Public vs Private Responses

The matter of audience impact raises a more general question: Namely, to what extent can people's public reactions to acts of disrespect be taken as evidence of their private reactions to it? For instance, is it reasonable to assume that because a person's likelihood of retaliating against an insult is lower when the insult was unintentional that the level of moralistic anger is also lower? The main reason to question the assumption of isomorphism between public and private reactions is that powerful social norms exist that stipulate when retaliation is and is not appropriate. To the extent that the victim has internalized these norms, they can be expected to affect his or her public and private reactions similarly (Miller & Prentice 1996). When these norms have not been internalized, however, the victim's public and private reaction may diverge. Consider the finding that people are less likely to retaliate against unintended harm. One interpretation of this finding is that the level of responsibility that the victim attributes to the harm-doer determines the amount of anger that the victim experiences and, in turn, the likelihood that victim will retaliate. A second possibility is that a social norm exists that proscribes retaliation against unintentional harm-doers, however much anger their harm arouses (Zillmann 1979). In general, then, the existence of retaliation-governing social norms means that people, irrespective of their level of moralistic anger, will be less likely to retaliate under some circumstances than others (e.g. the harm was unintended, an apology was offered). Therefore, caution is in order when drawing inferences about private reactions from public reactions.

GOALS OF RETALIATION

Of the various goals that guide people's responses to acts of disrespect, two are especially powerful. The first is the restoration of the victim's self-esteem; the second, the education of the offender.

Restoring Self-Esteem

Much of the sting of being insulted or exploited derives from the identity implications of the act (Greenberg 1993). To be taken advantage of is resented because it implies to oneself, and others, that one is the sort of person who can be taken advantage of (Lind 2000). Retaliation against the offender, by challenging the threats to identity posed by his or her action, serves to restore the victim's self-image (Westermarck 1932). In fact, the failure to respond to a perceived injustice can actually further diminish the victim, both in the victim's eyes (Vidmar 2000) and the eyes of others (Felson 1982, Pitt-Rivers 1965).

In some cases the mere expression of moralistic anger, unaccompanied by action, can help restore one's private and public image, because anger constitutes not simply a response to demeaning treatment but also a challenge to it (Lazarus 1991). In this way, anger serves a self-presentational function. It establishes one's identity as a strong and determined person who demands respect and does not tolerate unjust treatment by others (Averill 1983, Novaco 1976, Tedeschi & Nesler 1993).

Educating the Offender

Many commentators on the nature of revenge have noted its educational mission. For example, Heider (1958) regarded one of the primary goals of revenge to be changing the perpetrator's "...ideas about the relative power, importance, and value of the two persons, as well as his ethical evaluation of these relations" (pp. 267–68). Adam Smith (1869) described the goal of revenge similarly: "To bring him back to a more just sense of what he owes us, and of the wrong that he has done to us, is frequently the principal end posed in our revenge, which is always imperfect when it cannot accomplish this" (p. 139). De Waal (1996) reports that even in the animal world there is a tendency "to teach a lesson to those who act negatively" (p. 159). In many cases the lesson that retaliators seek to teach pertains to the relative status or moral worth of the offender. By retaliating, recipients of disrespectful treatment seek to communicate that it is the offender who deserves contempt, not them (Novaco 1976). In other cases, retaliation aims to educate the perpetrator about the more general unacceptability of his or her behavior, not merely its unacceptability vis-a-vis the victim. For example, Folger & Pugh (2001) claim that people often will retaliate against someone behaving rudely simply because they believe the offender needs to be reminded that it costs nothing to be polite.

The fact that the education of the offender is a strong motivation behind retaliation has important implications for whether retaliation will or will not be satisfying. To the extent that (re)education of the perpetrator is its goal, retaliation will be satisfying only to the extent that perpetrator shows evidence of being educated; minimally, this objective will require that the perpetrator knows why he or she is being punished (Durkheim 1964, Vidmar 2000).

Disinterested Reactions   The goals of status affirmation and offender education also guide people's reactions to those who have harmed a third party or violated a group norm or rule. In other words, along with controlling the rule violator's future behavior and punishing his or her past behavior, disinterested punishment reactions seek to reaffirm the group's norms and values and to educate the perpetrator (Vidmar 2000, Vidmar & Miller 1980). Punishment is the principal means by which group members degrade the status of the rule offender and affirm the status of the group's rules and values (Braithwaite 1989, Garfinkel 1956). On the one hand, punishment serves to disavow the disrespectful act as well as the offender. The failure to punish, on the other hand, further diminishes the status of the group and its rules. As the Israeli court stated in sentencing Eichmann, "...punishment is necessary to defend the honor of the authority of him who was hurt by the offense so that the failure to punish may not cause his degradation" (Arendt 1964, p. 287).

TYPES OF JUSTICE REACTIONS

Recent justice research has greatly expanded our knowledge of the forms that reactions to perceived injustices can take. The growing preference of researchers for the field rather than the laboratory is the main reason for this expansion. Early justice researchers, as is often the case when the research venue is the laboratory, appeared more interested in independent variables than dependent measures. That is, they were more interested in identifying the range of variables that affect the perception of injustice than in identifying the ways in which feelings of injustice manifest themselves, with relative deprivation researchers being somewhat, but only somewhat, of an exception (e.g. Hafer & Olson 1993).

By and large, dependent measures in traditional justice research tended to be straightforward questions about the participants' perceptions of the fairness of outcomes—sometimes, only the participant's satisfaction with the outcomes. In some cases, the simplicity and directness of the dependent measure reflected the researcher's desire to approximate a particular real world context. In research that examines justice in the legal system, for example, feelings of injustice were, and continue to be, assessed primarily through questions about recommended criminal sentences or civil awards (Hamilton & Sanders 1992, Robinson & Darley 1995). Even when justice studies (e.g. distributive justice studies) included behavioral measures (e.g. resource allocations), these measures tended to be standard and highly uniform across studies. The same situation is true in research on the causes and consequences of moralistic aggression. Investigations of the insult-aggression relationship, for example, have been primarily laboratory-based and have used a much broader range of insult manipulations than aggression measures.

The situation is very different with more recent justice research, especially that on procedural justice. Whereas early procedural justice research focused primarily on reported satisfaction (Thibaut & Walker 1975), recent work places an increasingly high premium on discovering the range of people's reactions to being treated unfairly (Giacalone & Greenberg 1997, Tyler & Lind 2000). By and large, justice reactions in procedural justice research fall into two broad categories: withdrawal reactions and attack reactions. Reactions of the former type occur when the aggrieved person omits actions that he or she previously performed; reactions of the latter type occur when the aggrieved person commits actions that he or she has not previously performed.

Retaliation by Withdrawal

Voluntary Withdrawal   Much procedural justice research focuses on the effects of disrespectful treatment by authorities (Lind 2000, Tyler & Blader 2001). Two effects have proven especially robust. The first effect pertains to people's willingness to comply with authorities. As has been demonstrated across an impressive array of contexts and research domains, people show a marked disinclination to comply with authorities when they think those authorities have treated them disrespectfully (Huo et al 1996, Lind et al 1993). It is as though authorities, by their disrespectful treatment, forfeit the right to continued compliance from those under them (Greenberg 1994, Huo et al 1996).

The second robust effect of disrespectful treatment by authorities pertains to the willingness of individuals to subordinate their personal goals and concerns to group goals and concerns. In organizational contexts, for example, retaliation against unjust procedures commonly results in diminished levels of helpfulness, courtesy, and sportsmanship (Jeremier et al 1994, Moorman 1991, Niehoff & Moorman 1993). Reductions in levels of work performance are also common (Lind et al 1990). Although most of the research on retaliation by withdrawal has been conducted in organizational contexts, such reactions are by no means restricted to these contexts. Disrespectful and unjust treatment can lead to withdrawal reactions even in romantic relationships (Reichle & Montada 1994). For example, giving one's partner the "silent treatment" is a common withdrawal reaction to the perception that he or she has been unjust. (Mikula et al 1998, Sommer et al 2000).

Involuntary Withdrawal   In many cases the withdrawal of commitment to an organization, group, or personal relationship will be a voluntary and deliberate response to the indignation aroused by the perception of injustice, but in other cases it will be an involuntary reaction to one or more of the other psychological states that the perception of injustice elicits. In this respect it is important to note that perception of injustice, in addition to moralistic anger, can produce lowered self-esteem (Koper et al 1993, Smith et al 1998), depression (Hafer & Olson 1993, Tennen & Affleck 1991), and self-derogation (Heilman et al 1990). These reactions are all capable of producing an involuntary decrease in commitment to the relationship in which the injustice occurred.

Consider the link between organizational injustice and worker absenteeism, which illustrates the distinction between voluntary and involuntary withdrawal reactions. One means by which the perception of organizational injustice can increase absenteeism is by affecting the conscious decision-making process of workers. They simply may have a lower threshold for deciding to stay home when they feel they have been treated unjustly (Gellatly 1995, Guerts et al 1994).

However, the perception of organizational injustice could also increase absenteeism more indirectly, and less consciously, by affecting workers' physical and psychological health (Markovsky 1991).

Retaliation by Attack

Feelings of injustice may also lead the aggrieved person to seek justice through acts of commission. Again, much of the relevant research takes place in organizational contexts where the motive to "even the score" (Greenberg & Scott 1996) following a perceived injustice has been linked to increases in worker protest (Folger 1977, Leung et al 1993, Vermunt et al 1997), theft (Greenberg 1993, Greenberg & Scott 1996), sabotage (Giacalone et al 1997), and violence (Folger & Skarlicki 1998, Neuman & Baron 1997).

Disrespectful treatment can also increase people's willingness to avail themselves of more formal and legitimate avenues of justice restoration. For example, workers who think that organizational procedures are unfair are both more likely to bad-mouth and publicly embarrass their employers (Bies & Tripp 1996) and more likely to sue them (Bies & Tyler 1993) and to pursue wrongful termination claims against them (Lind et al 2000). Similar effects have been observed in non-organizational contexts. For example, research shows that the desire for retribution is a common motivation for lawsuits across a wide range of situations (Keeva 1999, Merry & Silbey 1984, Shuman 2000, Vidmar 2000).

The Dominance of Justice Motivation   The finding that the perception of disrespect motivates people to pursue formal grievance avenues is interesting. More interesting, however, is that the perception of disrespect is often a better predictor of the likelihood of a person pursuing a claim than more objective features of the situation, such as the probability of winning or even the very factors that the procedures were put in place to address, such as the degree of material or physical harm (Lind 1997, Lind et al 1993). The decision to pursue medical malpractice claims, for example, often depends less upon the merits of the claim than the claimant's perception of the degree of respect and caring shown by the medical staff (Imershine & Brents 1992). Ironically, then, procedures that are put in place as instrumental mechanisms to restore distributive injustice tend to be utilized primarily as expressive mechanisms to avenge procedural and interactional injustice.

The fact that people see grievance and compensation mechanisms in expressive terms has another consequence. Namely, it renders people reluctant to avail themselves of these procedures when they think that the agent of harm, despite having legal or technical responsibility for the harm, has basically treated them respectfully (Merry & Silbey 1984). People act as though it would be an injustice to sue someone who has treated them respectfully, however much legal merit their claim might have. More generally, fair procedures serve to mute the impact of unfavorable outcomes (Brockner & Wiesenfeld 1996, Cropanzo & Greenberg 1997). Furthermore, the power of perceived respect to diminish the impact of negative outcomes is not restricted to organizational contexts. For example, one reason women give for tolerating unjust distributions in their relationships—of household responsibilities, for example—is the belief that their partner respects them (Mikula et al 1998, Thompson 1991).

CONCLUSIONS

The pursuit of justice is a fundamental aspect of social life. In explaining why he and other philosophers have devoted so much attention to the normative question of what is just, Rawls (1971) claimed that justice was "the first virtue of social institutions." As this review indicates, justice is also a central concern in people's everyday life (see also Lerner & Lerner 1981, Ross & Miller 2001). For 50 years, psychologists have known that people's satisfaction with their material outcomes depends highly, and often primarily, on their perception of the fairness of those outcomes. For just this reason, social exchange theorists (e.g. Blau 1964, Homans 1961, Walster et al 1978) traditionally have accorded considerations of justice (equity) a prominent place in their theories. Economists, at least those calling themselves behavioral economists, have also come to acknowledge the importance of perceptions of fairness in economic decision making (Frank 1988, Kahneman et al 1986, Mellers & Baron 1993).

The quest for justice is not confined to the market place, however. As this review indicates, justice pervades virtually all aspects of social and personal life. However, this is not because every interaction represents a social exchange and every form of social behavior represents a resource. Conceptions of justice are important because they are central to defining the way in which people think of themselves (Lerner 1987). The question of what people are entitled to is fundamentally a question about what it means to be a person (Furby 1986). Concern for justice and respect for personhood are powerfully and inseparably linked (Sampson 1983). By discovering what people believe to be the entitlements and responsibilities of the members of a moral community, we glimpse what it means to be a member of that community (Opotow 1990). By discovering how conceptions of justice vary across cultures, we discover how conceptions of the person vary across cultures (Shweder & Bourne 1984). Understanding the psychology of justice is central to understanding both human psychology and social life.

Visit the Annual Reviews home page at www.AnnualReviews.org

LITERATURE CITED

Adams JS. 1965. Inequity in social exchange. In *Advances in Experimental Social Psychology*, ed. L Berkowitz, 2:267–99. New York: Academic

Alexander F, Staub H. 1956. *The Criminal, the Judge, and the Public.* Glencoe, IL: Free Press

Aram JD, Salipante PF. 1981. An evaluation

of organizational due process in the resolution of employee/employer conflict. *Acad. Manage. Rev.* 6:197–204

Arendt H. 1964. *Eichmann in Jerusalem.* New York: Viking

Aristotle. 1945. *The Nicomachean Ethics.* Cambridge, MA: Harvard Univ. Press

Averill JR. 1983. Studies on anger and aggression: implications for theories of emotion. *Am. Psychol.* 28:1145–60

Bacon F. 1909 (1597). *Essays.* In *Harvard Classics,* Vol. 3, pp. 129–46. New York: Collier

Baron RA. 1988. Attributions and organizational conflict: the mediating role of apparent sincerity. *Organ. Behav. Hum. Decis. Process.* 69:272–79

Baron RA. 1993. Criticism (informal negative feedback) as a source of perceived unfairness in organizations: effects, mechanisms, and countermeasures. In *Justice in the Workplace: Approaching Fairness in Human Resource Management,* ed. R Cropanzo, pp. 155–70. Hillsdale, NJ: Erlbaum

Batson CD. 1998. Altruism and prosocial behavior. See Gilbert et al 1998, pp. 282–316

Batson CD, Bowers MJ, Leonard EA, Smith EC. 2000. Does personal morality exacerbate or restrain retaliation after being harmed? *Pers. Soc. Psychol. Bull.* 26:35–45

Berger J, Zelditch M, Anderson B, Cohen BP. 1972. Structural aspects of distributive justice: a status value formulation. In *Sociological Theories in Progress,* ed. J Berger, M Zelditch, B Anderson, 2:119–46. Boston, MA: Houghton Mifflin

Bettencourt BA, Miller N. 1996. Sex differences in aggression as a function of provocation: a meta-analysis. *Psychol. Bull.* 119:422–47

Bies RJ. 1987. The predicament of injustice: the management of moral outrage. In *Research in Organizational Behavior,* ed. LL Cummings, BM Staw, 9:289–319. Greenwich, CT: JAI

Bies RJ. 1993. Privacy and procedural justice in organizations. *Soc. Justice Res.* 6:69–81

Bies RJ, Moag JS. 1986. Interactional justice: communication criteria for fairness. In *Research on Negotiation in Organizations,* ed. B Sheppard, 1:43–55. Greenwich, CT: JAI

Bies RJ, Shapiro DL. 1987. Interactional fairness judgments: the influence of causal accounts. *Soc. Justice Res.* 1:199–218

Bies RJ, Shapiro DL, Cummings LL. 1988. Causal accounts and managing organizational conflict: Is it enough to say it is not my fault? *Commun. Res.* 15:381–99

Bies RJ, Tripp TM. 1996. Beyond distrust: getting even and the need for revenge. In *Trust in Organization,* ed. RM Kramer, TR Tyler, pp. 246–60. Thousand Oaks, CA: Sage

Bies RJ, Tyler TR. 1993. The "litigation explosion" in organizations: a test of alternative psychological explanations. *Organ. Sci.* 4:352–66

Blau P. 1964. Justice in social exchange. *Sociol. Inq.* 34:193–246

Bobocel DR, Agar SE, Meyer JP, Irving PG. 1998. Managerial accounts and fairness perceptions in conflict resolution: differentiating the effects of minimizing responsibility and providing justification. *Basic Appl. Soc. Psychol.* 20:133–43

Bobocel DR, Farrell AC. 1996. Sex-based promotion decisions and interactional fairness: investigating the influence of managerial accounts. *J. Appl. Psychol.* 81:22–35

Bond M, Venus C. 1991. Resistance to group or personal insults in an in-group or out-group context. *Int. J. Psychol.* 26:83–94

Borden RJ. 1975. Witnessed aggression: influence of an observer's sex and values on aggressive responding. *J. Pers. Soc. Psychol.* 31:567–73

Bourdieu P. 1965. The sentiment of honour in the Kabyle Society. In *The Nature of Human Society: Honor and Shame,* ed. JG Peristiany, pp. 191–242. London: Weidenfeld & Nicolson

Braithwaite J. 1989. *Crime, Shame, and Reintegration.* Cambridge, UK: Cambridge Univ. Press

Brockner J, Wiesenfeld BM. 1996. An integrative framework for explaining reactions to decisions: the interactive effects of outcomes and procedures. *Psychol. Bull.* 120:189–208

Capek SM. 1993. The "environmental justice" frame: a conceptual discussion and application. *Soc. Probl.* 1:5–24

Carpenter B, Darley JM. 1978. A naïve psychological analysis of counter-aggression. *Pers. Soc. Psychol. Bull.* 4:68–72

Clayton SD. 1992. The experience of injustice: some characteristics and correlates. *Soc. Justice Res.* 5:71–91

Cohen D, Nisbett RE, Bowdle BF, Schwarz N. 1996. Insult, aggression, and the Southern culture of honor: an "experimental ethnography." *J. Pers. Soc. Psychol.* 70:945–60

Cohen RL. 1986. Power and justice in intergroup relations. In *Justice in Social Relations*, ed. HW Bierhoff, RL Cohen, J Greenberg, pp. 65–84. New York: Plenum

Cooley CH. 1902. *Human Nature and the Social Order.* New York: Scribners

Cropanzo R, Byrne ZS. 2000. How workers manage relationships in a complex social world: a multi-foci approach to procedural and interactional justice. In *Cooperation in Modern Society: Dilemmas and Solutions*, ed. M Van Vugt, M Snyder, T Tyler, A Biels. London: Routledge. In press

Cropanzo R, Greenberg J. 1997. Progress in organizational justice: tunneling through the maze. In *International Review of Industrial and Organizational Psychology*, ed. CL Cooper, IT Robertson, pp. 317–72. New York: Wiley & Sons

Crosby F. 1976. A model of egoistical relative deprivation. *Psychol. Rev.* 83:85–113

Crosby F, Gonzalez-Intel A. 1984. Relative deprivation and equity theories: felt injustice and the undeserved benefits of others. In *The Sense of Injustice: Social Psychological Perspectives*, ed. R Folger, pp. 141–66. New York: Plenum

DeRidder R, Schruijer SG, Tripathi RC. 1992. Norm violation as a precipitating factor of negative intergroup relations. In *Norm Violations and Intergroup Relations*, ed. R De-Ridder RC, Tripathi, pp. 3–37. Oxford, UK: Oxford Univ. Press

Deutsch M. 1985. *Distributive Justice: A Social Psychological Perspective.* New Haven, CT: Yale Univ. Press

De Waal F. 1996. *Good Natured: The Origins of Right and Wrong in Humans and Other Animals.* Cambridge, MA: Harvard Univ. Press

Dodge KA, Price JM, Bachorowski JA, Newman JP. 1990. Hostile attribution biases in severely aggressive adolescents. *J. Abnorm. Psychol.* 99:385–92

Dodge KA, Somberg DR. 1987. Hostile attribution biases among aggressive boys are exacerbated under conditions of threats to the self. *Child Dev.* 58:213–24

Donnerstein E, Walster E. 1982. Aggression and inequity. In *Equity and Justice in Social Behavior*, ed. J Greenberg, R Cohen, pp. 309–36. New York: Academic

Durkheim E. 1858. *The Division of Labor in Society.* Transl. G. Simpson, 1964. Toronto: Collier-Macmillan

Dyck RJ, Rule BG. 1978. Effect on retaliation of causal attributions concerning attack. *J. Pers. Soc. Psychol.* 36:521–29

Elster J. 1992. *Local Justice: How Institutions Allocate Scarce Goods and Necessary Burdens.* New York: Russell Sage

Ellsworth P, Gross SR. 1994. Hardening of the attitudes: Americans' views on the death penalty. *J. Soc. Issues* 50:19–52

Emery RE, Mathews SG, Kitzmann KM. 1994. Child custody mediation and litigation: parents' satisfaction and functioning one year after settlement. *J. Consult. Clin. Psychol.* 62:124–29

Epstein S, Taylor SP. 1967. Instigation to aggression as a function of degree of defeat and perceived aggressive intent of the opponent. *J. Pers.* 35:265–89

Erikson K. 1966. *Wayward Puritans: A Study in the Sociology of Deviance.* New York: Wiley & Sons

Etzioni A. 1988. *The Moral Dimension: Toward a New Economics.* New York: Free Press

Feather NT. 1996. Reactions to penalties for an offense in relation to authoritarianism, values, perceived responsibility, perceived seriousness and deservingness. *J. Pers. Soc. Psychol.* 71:571–87

Feather NT. 1999. *Values, Achievement, and Justice: Studies in the Psychology of Deservingness.* New York: Kluwer Acad.

Felson RB. 1982. Impression management and the escalation of aggression and violence. *Soc. Psychol. Q.* 45:245–54

Felson RB, Ribner SA. 1981. An attributional approach to accounts and sanctions for criminal violence. *Soc. Psychol. Q.* 44:137–42

Ferguson TJ, Rule BG. 1980. Effects of inferential set, outcome severity, and basis for responsibility in children's evaluation of aggressive acts. *Dev. Psychol.* 16:141–46

Ferguson TJ, Rule BG. 1981. An attributional perspective on anger and aggression. In *Perspectives on Aggression: Theoretical and Empirical Review,* ed. R Geen, RE Donnerstein, pp. 41–74. San Diego, CA: Academic

Fincham FD, Jaspars JM. 1980. Attribution of responsibility: From man the scientist to man as lawyer. In *Advances in Experimental Social Psychology,* ed. L Berkowitz, 13:81–138 New York: Academic

Folger R. 1977. Distributive and procedural justice: combined impact of "voice" and improvement on experienced inequity. *J. Pers. Soc. Psychol.* 35:108–19

Folger R, Cropanzo R. 1998. *Organizational Justice and Human Resource Management.* Thousand Oaks, CA: Sage

Folger R, Martin C. 1986. Relative deprivation and referent cognitions: distributive and procedural justice effects. *J. Exp. Soc. Psychol.* 22:532–46

Folger R, Pugh SD. 2001. The just world and Winston Churchill: an approach/avoid conflict about psychological distance when harming victims. See Ross & Miller 2001. In press

Folger R, Rosenfield D, Robinson T. 1983. Relative deprivation and referent cognitions. *J. Pers. Soc. Psychol.* 45:172–84

Folger R, Skarlicki DP. 1998. A popcorn metaphor for employee aggression. In *Dysfunctional Behavior in Organizations: Violent and Deviant Behavior. Monographs in Organizational Behavior and Industrial Relations,* ed. R Griffin, A O'Leary-Kelly, J Collins, pp. 43–81. Stamford, CT: JAI

Frank RH. 1988. *Passions Within Reasons: The Strategic Role of Emotions.* New York: Norton

Frankena WK. 1963. *Ethics.* Englewood Cliffs, NJ: Prentice-Hall

Furby L. 1986. Psychology and justice. In *Justice: Views from the Social Sciences,* ed. R Cohen, pp. 153–204. New York: Plenum

Gamson WA. 1968. *Power and Discontent.* Homewood, IL: Dorsey

Garfinkel H. 1956. Conditions of successful degradation ceremonies. *Am. J. Sociol.* 61:420–35

Geen RG. 1998. Aggression and antisocial behavior. See Gilbert et al 1998, pp. 317–56

Gellatly IR. 1995. Individual and group determinants of employee absenteeism: test of a causal model. *J. Organ. Behav.* 16:469–85

Gergen KJ, Gergen M. 1988. Narrative and the self as relationship. In *Advances in Experimental Social Psychology,* ed. L Berkowitz, 21:17–56. San Diego, CA: Academic

Giacalone RA, Greenberg J. 1997. *Anti-Social Behavior in Organizations.* Thousand Oaks, CA: Sage

Giacalone RA, Riordan CA, Rosenfeld P. 1997. Employee sabotage: toward a practitioner-scholar understanding. See Giacalone & Greenberg 1997, pp. 109–29

Gilbert DT, Fiske ST, Lindzey G, eds. 1998. *Handbook of Social Psychology,* Vol. 2. New York: McGraw-Hill. 4th ed.

Goffman E. 1952. On cooling the mark out. *Psychiatry* 15:451–63

Goffman E. 1971. *Relations in Public.* New York: Harper & Row

Graham S, Hudley C. 1994. Attributions of aggressive and nonaggressive African-American male early adolescents. *Dev. Psychol.* 30:365–73

Greenberg J. 1990. Employee theft as a reaction to underpayment inequity: the hidden costs of pay cuts. *J. Appl. Psychol.* 75:561–68

Greenberg J. 1993. Stealing in the name of justice. *Organ. Behav. Hum. Decis. Process.* 54:81–103

Greenberg J. 1994. Using socially fair treatment to promote acceptance of a worksite smoking ban. *J. Appl. Psychol.* 79:288–97

Greenberg J, Scott KS. 1996. Why do workers bite the hands that feed them? Employee theft as a social exchange process. In *Research in Organizational Behavior*, ed. BM Staw, LL Cummings, 8:111–56. Greenwich, CT: JAI

Greenwell J, Dengerink HA. 1973. The role of perceived versus actual attack in human physical aggression. *J. Pers. Soc. Psychol.* 26:66–71

Guerts S, Buunk BP, Schaufeli WB. 1994. Social comparisons and absenteeism: a structural modeling approach. *J. Appl. Soc. Psychol.* 54:81–103

Gusfield J. 1963. *Symbolic Crusade: Status Politics and the American Temperance Movement.* Urbana: Univ. Ill. Press

Hafer CL, Olson JM. 1993. Beliefs in a just world, discontent, and assertive actions by working women. *Pers. Soc. Psychol. Bull.* 19:30–38

Hamilton VL, Sanders J. 1992. *Everyday Justice: Responsibility and the Individual in Japan and the United States.* New Haven, CT: Yale Univ. Press

Harvey MD, Enzle ME. 1978. Effects of retaliation latency and provocation level on judged blameworthiness for retaliatory aggression. *Pers. Soc. Psychol. Bull.* 4:579–82

Heider F. 1958. *The Psychology of Interpersonal Relations.* New York: Wiley & Sons

Heilman ME, Lucas JA, Kaplow SR. 1990. Self-derogating consequences of sex-based preferential selection: the moderating effect of initial confidence. *Organ. Behav. Hum. Decis. Process.* 46:202–16

Herek GM, Glunt EK. 1988. An epidemic of stigma: public reactions to AIDS. *Am. Psychol.* 43:886–91

Heuer L, Blumenthal E, Douglas A, Weinblatt T. 1999. A deservingness approach to respect as a relationally based fairness judgements. *Pers. Soc. Psychol. Bull.* 1279–92

Hogan R, Emler NP. 1981. Retributive justice. See Lerner & Lerner 1981, pp. 125–44

Homans GC. 1961. *Social Behavior: Its Elementary Forms.* New York: Harcourt, Brace & World

Homans GC. 1976. Commentary. In *Advances in Experimental Social Psychology*, ed. L Berkowitz, E Walster, 9:231–44. Orlando, FL: Academic

Horai J. 1977. Attributional conflict. *J. Soc. Issues* 33:88–100

Huo YJ, Smith HJ, Tyler TR, Lind EA. 1996. Superordinate identification, subgroup identification, and justice concerns. *Psychol. Sci.* 7:40–45

Imershine A, Brents A. 1992. The impact of large medical malpractice awards on malpractice awardees. *J. Legal Med.* 13:33–49

Jeremier J, Knights D, Nord WR. 1994. *Resistance and Power in Organizations.* London: Routledge

Johnson TE, Rule BG. 1986. Mitigating circumstances information, censure, and aggression. *J. Pers. Soc. Psychol.* 50:537–42

Kahneman D, Knetsch JL, Thaler RH. 1986. Fairness and the assumptions of economics. *J. Bus.* 59:285–300

Keeva S. 1999. Does law mean never having to say you are sorry? *Am. Bar J.* 85:64–68

Kelsen HJ. 1943. *Society and Nature.* Chicago, IL: Univ. Chicago Press

Keltner D, Ellsworth PC, Edwards K. 1993. Beyond simple pessimism: effects of sadness and anger on social perception. *J. Pers. Soc. Psychol.* 64:740–52

Kim SH, Smith RH, Brigham NL. 1998. Effects of power imbalance and the presence of third parties on reactions to harm: upward and downward revenge. *Pers. Soc. Psychol. Bull.* 24:353–61

Koper G, Van Knippenberg D, Bouhuijs F,

Vermunt R, Wilke H. 1993. Procedural fairness and self-esteem. *Eur. J. Soc. Psychol.* 23:313–25

Kramer RM. 1994. The sinister attribution error. *Motiv. Emot.* 18:199–231

Krebs D, Miller DT. 1985. Altruism and aggression. In *Handbook of Social Psychology,* ed. G Lindzey, E Aronson, 2:1–71. New York: Random House. 3rd ed.

Lazarus RS. 1991. Progress on a cognitive-motivational-relational theory of emotion. *Am. Psychol.* 46:819–34

Lerner MJ. 1977. The justice motive: some hypotheses as to its origins and forms. *J. Pers.* 45:1–52

Lerner MJ. 1980. *The Belief in a Just World.* New York: Plenum

Lerner MJ. 1987. Integrating societal and psychological rules of entitlement: the basic task of each social actor and a fundamental task for the social sciences. *Soc. Justice Res.* 1:107–25

Lerner MJ, Lerner S. 1981. *The Justice Motive in Soc. Behav.* New York: Plenum

Leung K, Chiu WH, Au YF. 1993. Sympathy and support for industrial actions: a justice analysis. *J. Appl. Psychol.* 78:781–87

Leventhal GS. 1976. Fairness in social relationships. In *Contemporary Topics in Social Psychology,* ed. JW Thibaut, JT Spence, RC Carson, pp. 212–39. Morristown, NJ: Gen. Learn.

Lind EA. 1997. Litigation and claiming in organizations: anti-social behavior or quest for justice? See Giacalone & Greenberg 1997, pp. 150–71

Lind EA. 2000. Fairness heuristic theory: justice judgments as pivotal cognitions in organizational relations. In *Advances in Organizational Justice,* ed. J Greenberg, R Cropanzo. Lexington, MA: New Lexington. In press

Lind EA, Greenberg J, Scott KS, Welchans TD. 2000. The winding road from employee to complaint: situational and psychological determinants of wrongful termination claims. *Admin. Sci. Q.* In press

Lind EA, Kanfer R, Earley PC. 1990. Voice, control, and procedural justice: instrumental and noninstrumental concerns in fairness judgements. *J. Pers. Soc. Psychol.* 59:952–59

Lind EA, Kulik CT, Ambrose M, de Vera-Park MW. 1993. Individual and corporate dispute resolution: using procedural fairness as a decision heuristic. *Admin. Sci. Q.* 38:224–51

Lind EA, Tyler TR. 1988. *The Social Psychology of Procedural Justice.* New York: Plenum

Lindzey G, Aronson E. 1985. *Handbook of Social Psychology,* Vols. 1 & 2. New York: Random House. 3rd ed.

Lupfer MB, Weeks KP, Doan KA, Houston DA. 2000. Folk conceptions of fairness and unfairness. *Eur. J. Soc. Psychol.* 30:299–346

Mansbridge JJ. 1990. *Beyond Self-interest.* Chicago, IL: Univ. Chicago Press

Markovsky B. 1991. Prospects for a cognitive-structural justice theory. In *Social Justice in Human Relations,* ed. R Vermunt, H Steensma, 1:33–58. New York: Plenum

Martin J, Brickman P, Murray A. 1984. Moral outrage and pragmatism: explanations for collective action. *J. Exp. Soc. Psychol.* 20:484–96

Mellers BA, Baron J. 1993. *Perspectives in Justice: Theory and Applications.* Cambridge, UK: Cambridge Univ. Press

Mellers BA, Schwartz A, Cooke AD. 1998. Judgment and decision making. *Annu. Rev. Psychol.* 49:447–77

Merry SE, Silbey SS. 1984. What do plaintiffs want? Reexamining the concept of dispute. *Just. Sys. J.* 9:151–78

Merton RK, Kitt AS. 1950. Contributions to the theory of reference group behavior. In *Continuities in Social Research: Studies in the Scope and Method of "The American Soldier,"* ed. RK Merton, PF Lazarsfeld, pp. 40–105. Glencoe, IL: Free Press

Messick DM, Bloom S, Boldizar JP, Samuelson CD. 1985. Why we are fairer than others. *J. Exp. Soc. Psychol.* 21:480–500

Mikula G. 1986. The experience of injustice:

toward a better understanding of its phenomenology. In *Justice in Social Relations*, ed. HW Bierhoff, RL Cohen, J Greenberg, pp. 103–24. New York: Plenum

Mikula G. 1993. On the experience of injustice. In *European Review of Social Psychology*, ed. W Stroebe, M Hewstone, vol. 4, pp. 223–44. Chichester, UK: Wiley

Mikula G, Petri B, Tanzer N. 1990. What people regard as unjust: types and structures of everyday experiences of injustice. *Eur. J. Soc. Psychol.* 20:133–49

Mikula G, Scherer KR, Athenstaedt V. 1998. The role of injustice in the elicitation of different emotional reactions. *Pers. Soc. Psychol. Bull.* 24:769–83

Milgram S, Liberty HJ, Toledo R, Wackenhut J. 1986. Response to intrusion into waiting lines. *J. Pers. Soc. Psychol.* 51:683–89

Miller DT. 1999. The norm of self-interest. *Am. Psychol.* 54:1–8

Miller DT, McCann DC. 1979. Children's reactions to the victims and perpetrators of injustices. *Child Dev.* 50:861–68

Miller DT, Prentice DA. 1996. The construction of social norms and standards. In *Social Psychology: Handbook of Basic Principles*, ed. ET Higgins, AW Kruglanski, pp. 799–829. New York: Guilford

Miller DT, Vidmar N. 1981. The social psychology of punishment reactions. See Lerner & Lerner 1981, pp. 145–72

Miller WI. 1993. *Humiliation and Other Essays on Honor, Social Discomfort, and Violence.* Ithaca, NY: Cornell Univ. Press

Mitchell G, Tetlock PE, Mellers BA, Ordonez LD. 1993. Judgments of social justice: compromises between equality and efficiency. *J. Pers. Soc. Psychol.* 65:629–39

Moore B. 1978. *Injustice: The Social Basis of Obedience and Revolt.* White Plains, NY: Sharpe

Moorman RH. 1991. Relationship between organizational justice and organizational citizenship: Do fairness perceptions influence employee citizenship? *J. Appl. Psychol.* 76:845–55

Neuman JH, Baron RA. 1997. Aggression in the workplace. See Giacalone & Greenberg 1997, pp. 37–67

Niehoff BP, Moorman RH. 1993. Justice as a mediator of the relationship between methods of monitoring and organizational citizenship behavior. *Acad. Manage. J.* 36:527–56

Nietzsche F. 1967 (1887). *On the Genealogy of Morals.* New York: Vintage

Novaco RW. 1976. The functions and regulation of the arousal of anger. *Am. J. Psychiatry* 133:1124–28

Ohbuchi K, Kameda M, Agarie N. 1989. Apology as aggression control: its role in mediating appraisal of and response to harm. *J. Pers. Soc. Psychol.* 56:219–27

Olson JM, Herman CP, Zanna MP. 1986. *Relative Deprivation and Social Comparison: The Ontario Symposium.* Hillsdale, NJ: Erlbaum

Opotow S. 1990. Moral exclusion and injustice: an introduction. *J. Soc. Issues* 46(1):1–20

Pepitone A. 1975. Social psychological perspectives on crime and punishment. *J. Soc. Issues* 31(4):197–216

Pitkin HF. 1981. Justice: on relating private and public. *Polit. Theory* 9:327–52

Pitt-Rivers J. 1965. Honour and social status. In *The Nature of Human Society: Honour and Shame*, ed. JG Peristiany, pp. 19–78. London: Weidenfeld & Nicolson

Ranulf S. 1964. *Moral Indignation and Middle-Class Psychology.* New York: Schocken

Rawls J. 1971. *A Theory of Justice.* Cambridge, MA: Harvard Univ. Press

Reichle B, Montada L. 1994. Problems with the transition to parenthood: perceived responsibility for restrictions and losses and the experience of injustice. In *Justice in Close Relationships: Entitlement and the Affectional Bond*, ed. MJ Lerner, G Mikula, pp. 205–28. New York: Plenum

Riordan CA, Marlin NA, Kellogg RT. 1983. The effectiveness of accounts following transgression. *Soc. Psychol. Q.* 46:213–19

Robinson PH, Darley JM. 1995. *Justice,*

Liability, and Blame: Community Views and the Criminal Law. San Francisco: Westview

Robinson SL. 1996. Trust and breach of the psychological contract. *Admin. Sci. Q.* 41:574–99

Robinson SL, Kraatz MS, Rousseau DM. 1994. Changing obligations and the psychological contract: a longitudinal study. *Acad. Manage. J.* 37:137–52

Ross M, Miller DT. 2001. *The Justice Motive in Social Life: Essays in Honor of Melvin Lerner.* New York: Cambridge Univ. Press. In press

Rousseau DM. 1995. *Psychological Contracts in Organizations: Understanding Written and Unwritten Agreements.* Thousand Oaks, CA: Sage

Rumsey MG. 1976. Effects of defendant background and remorse on sentencing judgments. *J. Appl. Soc. Psychol.* 6:64–68

Sampson EE. 1983. *Justice and the Critique of Pure Psychology.* New York: Plenum

Scher SJ. 1997. Measuring the consequences of injustice. *Pers. Soc. Psychol. Bull.* 23:482–97

Schlenker BR, Darby BW. 1981. The use of apologies in social predicaments. *Soc. Psychol. Q.* 44:271–78

Schmitt BH, Dube L, Leclerc F. 1992. Intrusions into waiting lines: Does the queue constitute a social system? *J. Pers. Soc. Psychol.* 63:806–15

Schwartz GS, Kane T, Joseph J, Tedeschi JT. 1978. The effects of post-transgression remorse on perceived aggression, attributions of intent, and level of punishment. *Br. J. Soc. Clin. Psychol.* 17:293–97

Sears DO, Funk CL. 1991. The role of self-interest in social and political attitudes. In *Advances in Experimental Social Psychology*, ed. MP Zanna, 24:2–92. Orlando, FL: Academic

Shapiro DL, Buttner EH, Barry B. 1994. Explanations for rejection decisions: What factors enhance their perceived adequacy and moderate their enhancement of justice perceptions. *Organ. Behav. Hum. Decis. Process.* 58:346–68

Shaw M, Reitan H. 1969. Attribution of responsibility as a basis for sanctioning behavior. *Br. J. Soc. Clin. Psychol.* 8:217–25

Shuman D. 2000. The role of apology in tort law. *Judicature* 83:180–89

Shweder RA, Bourne EJ. 1984. Does the concept of person vary cross-culturally? In *Culture Theory: Essays on Mind, Self, and Emotion*, ed. RA Shweder, R Levine, pp. 158–99. Cambridge, UK: Cambridge Univ. Press

Sitkin SB, Bies RJ. 1993. Social accounts in conflict situations: using explanations to manage conflict. *Hum. Relat.* 46:349–70

Skarlicki DP, Folger R. 1997. Retaliation for perceived unfair treatment: examining the roles of procedural and interactional justice. *J. Appl. Psychol.* 82:434–43

Skitka LJ, Tetlock PE. 1992. Allocating scarce resources: a contingency model of distributive justice. *J. Exp. Soc. Psychol.* 28:491–522

Smith A. 1869 (1759). *A Theory of Moral Sentiments.* London: Ball & Daldy

Smith HJ, Tyler TR, Huo YJ, Ortiz D, Lind AE. 1998. Group membership, self-esteem, and procedural justice. *J. Exp. Soc. Psychol.* 34:470–93

Solomon RC. 1990. *A Passion for Justice: Emotions and the Origins of the Social Contract.* Reading, MA: Addison-Wesley

Sommer KL, Williams KD, Ciarocco NJ, Baumeister RF. 2000. Explorations into the intrapsychic and interpersonal consequences of social ostracism. *Basic Appl. Soc. Psychol.* In press

Steil JM, Tuchman B, Deutsch M. 1978. An exploratory study of the meanings of injustice and frustration. *Pers. Soc. Psychol. Bull.* 4:393–98

Stouffer S, Lumsdaine M, Williams R, Smith M, Janis I, et al. 1949. *The American Soldier.* Princeton, NJ: Princeton Univ. Press

Sykes GM, Matza D. 1957. Techniques of neutralization: a theory of delinquency. *Am. J. Sociol.* 22:664–70

Taylor MS, Tracy KB, Renard MK, Harrison JK, Carroll SJ. 1995. Due process in performance appraisal: a quasi-experiment in procedural justice. *Admin. Sci. Q.* 40:495–502

Tedeschi JT, Nesler MS. 1993. Grievances: development and reactions. In *Aggression and Violence: Social Interactionist Perspectives*, ed. RB Felson, JT Tedeschi, pp. 13–46. Washington, DC: Am. Psychol. Assoc.

Tedeschi JT, Smith RB, Brown RC. 1974. A reinterpretation of research on aggression. *Psychol. Bull.* 81:540–62

Tennen H, Affleck G. 1991. Blaming others for threatening events. *Psychol. Bull.* 108:209–32

Thibaut JT, Kelley HH. 1959. *The Social Psychology of Groups*. New York: Wiley & Sons

Thibaut JT, Walker L. 1975. *Procedural Justice: A Psychological Perspective.* Hillsdale, NJ: Erlbaum

Thompson L. 1991. Family work: women's sense of fairness. *J. Fam. Issues* 12:181–96

Toch H. 1969. *Violent Men: An Inquiry into the Psychology of Violence.* Chicago, IL: Aldine

Torestad B. 1990. When is anger provoking? A psychophysical study of perceived causes of anger. *Aggress. Behav.* 16:9–26

Tyler TR. 1987. Conditions leading to value expressive affect in judgments of procedural justice: a test of four models. *J. Pers. Soc. Psychol.* 52:333–44

Tyler TR. 1990. *Why People Obey the law: Procedural Justice, Legitimacy, and Compliance.* New Haven, CT: Yale Univ. Press

Tyler TR. 1994. Psychological models of the justice motive: antecedents of distributive and procedural justice. *J. Pers. Soc. Psychol.* 67:850–63

Tyler TR, Bies RJ. 1990. Beyond formal procedures: the interpersonal context of procedural justice. In *Applied Social Psychology and Organizational Contexts*, ed. JS Carroll, pp. 77–98. Hillsdale, NJ: Erlbaum

Tyler TR, Blader S. 2001. *Cooperation in Groups: Procedural Justice, Social Identity, and Behavioral Engagement.* Philadelphia, PA: Psychology Press. In press

Tyler TR, Boeckmann RJ. 1997. Three strikes and you are out, but why? *Law Soc. Rev.* 31:237–65

Tyler TR, Boeckmann RJ, Smith HJ, Huo YJ. 1997. *Social Justice in a Diverse Society* Boulder, CO: Westview

Tyler TR, Lind EA. 1992. A relational model of authority in groups. In *Advances in Experimental Social Psychology*, ed. L Berkowitz, 25:115–92. Orlando, FL: Academic

Tyler TR, Lind EA. 2000. Procedural justice. In *Handbook of Justice Research in Law*, ed. J Sanders, VL Hamilton. New York: Kluwer Acad. In press

Tyler TR, Rasinski K, Spodick N. 1985. Influence of voice and satisfaction with leaders: exploring the meaning of process control. *J. Pers. Soc. Psychol.* 42:333–44

Tyler TR, Smith HJ. 1998. Social justice and social movements. See Gilbert et al 1998, pp. 595–662

Van den Bos K, Lind EA, Vermunt R, Wilke HAM. 1997. How do I judge my outcome when I do not know the outcome of others? The psychology of the fair process effect. *J. Pers. Soc. Psychol.* 72:1034–46

Vermunt R, Wit A, Van den Bos K, Lind EA. 1997. The effect of inaccurate procedure on protest: the mediating role of perceived unfairness and situational self-esteem. *Soc. Justice Res.* 9:109–20

Vidmar N. 2000. Retribution and revenge. In *Handbook of Justice Research in Law*, ed. J Sanders, VL Hamilton. New York: Kluwer Acad. In press

Vidmar N, Miller DT. 1980. Social psychological processes underlying attitudes toward legal punishment. *Law Soc. Rev.* 14:401–39

Walster E, Walster GW, Berscheid E. 1978. *Equity: Theory and Research.* Boston, MA: Allyn & Bacon

Westermarck E. 1932. *Ethical Relativity.* New York: Harcourt Brace

Zillmann D. 1979. *Hostility and Aggression.* Hillsdale, NJ: Erlbaum

Annu. Rev. Psychol. 2001. 52:555–80

HEALTH PSYCHOLOGY: Psychosocial and Biobehavioral Aspects of Chronic Disease Management

Neil Schneiderman, Michael H. Antoni, Patrice G. Saab, and Gail Ironson

Department of Psychology, University of Miami, Coral Gables, Florida 33124-2070; e-mail: nschneid@miami.edu, mantoni@miami.edu, psaab@umiami.ir.miami.edu, gironson@aol.com

Key Words cancer, coronary heart disease, HIV/AIDS, psychosocial interventions

■ **Abstract** Psychosocial factors appear to impact upon the development and progression of such chronic diseases as coronary heart disease, cancer, and HIV/AIDS. Similarly, psychosocial interventions have been shown to improve the quality of life of patients with established disease and seem to influence biological processes thought to ameliorate disease progression. Small-scale studies are useful for specifying the conditions under which psychosocial factors may or may not impact quality of life, biological factors, and disease progression. They are also useful for informing us about the conditions under which psychosocial interventions can serve as adjuvants (e.g. adherence training) to medical treatments. Only large-scale clinical trials, however, can determine the extent to which these psychosocial interventions may impact morbidity and mortality.

CONTENTS

0066-4308/01/0201-0555$14.00

INTRODUCTION

Behavioral scientists have developed a number of psychosocial interventions based upon research showing how psychosocial and biobehavioral factors impact quality of life and disease processes in relationship to the management of chronic diseases. This chapter reviews some of the psychosocial and biobehavioral factors that appear to moderate and/or mediate the outcomes of such management, with particular reference to coronary heart disease (CHD), cancer, and HIV/AIDS. These specific diseases provide a focus for discussion because they are major causes of morbidity and mortality, have caught the attention of both scientists and the public alike, and have given rise to considerable research that is relevant to the development of psychosocial interventions. This review represents a selective rather than a comprehensive survey of the research literature and attempts to provide an analysis of the present state of research.

CORONARY HEART DISEASE

Risk Factors

The clinical manifestations of CHD occur in adulthood and include angina pectoris, myocardial infarction, heart failure, and sudden death. Grundy (1999) classified risk factors for CHD as causal, conditional, and predisposing. Major cardiovascular causal risk factors are those that independently influence the development of atherosclerosis. The Framingham Heart Study identified cigarette smoking, elevated serum cholesterol, hypertension, and advancing age (Dawber et al 1951). Age is regarded as a proxy for plaque burden (Grundy 1999). The causal roles for additional risk factors such as low high-density lipoprotein and elevated low-density lipoprotein cholesterol as well as elevated plasma glucose have also been acknowledged (Wilson et al 1998). Examination of over 400,000 participants with baseline assessments from the Multiple Risk Factor Intervention Trial and the Chicago Heart Association Detection Project in Industry showed that risk factor stratum is related to mortality (Stamler et al 1999).

Although there is a positive association for serum triglycerides, coagulation factors, certain lipoproteins, and homocysteine with increased CHD, unequivocal evidence is lacking as to whether these factors are causally related to CHD. As such, these variables constitute conditional risk factors. Other factors commonly associated with CHD, including obesity, sedentary lifestyle, family history of CHD, being a male, insulin resistance, and various psychosocial variables are considered predisposing risk factors. Predisposing factors may impact cardiovascular risk by influencing causal and conditional risk factors (Grundy 1999).

The results of two recent reviews (Hemingway & Marmot 1999, Rozanski et al 1999) concur that considerable evidence implicates depression, anxiety, social isolation and low perceived emotional support, hostility, Type A behavior, and work-related stress in the development of heart disease. Furthermore, there is strong evidence supporting prognostic associations with social isolation and low perceived emotional support (Hemingway & Marmot 1999, Rozanski et al 1999) and depression (Hemingway & Marmot 1999). As a group, these psychosocial risk factors for CHD are associated with unhealthy lifestyle behaviors. When psychosocial risk factors co-occur, cardiovascular risk further increases (Rozanski et al 1999).

Schneiderman & Skyler (1996) hypothesize that the frequently found positive associations among dyslipidemia and elevations in blood pressure, obesity, and glucose metabolism, are attributable to relationships involving insulin metabolism and sympathetic nervous system functioning. They suggest that a positive feedback loop involving increases in sympathetic nervous system activity, insulin resistance, and hyperinsulinemia may provide a particularly pernicious mechanism underlying the development of CHD. Schneiderman & Skyler contend that sedentary lifestyle and a diet high in sugars and fats, as well as psychosocial and psychological factors, affect the positive feedback loop.

Rozanski and colleagues (Rozanski et al 1999) have outlined the potential pathophysiological mechanisms underlying the association of psychological risk factors and heart disease. Abnormal hypothalamic-pituitary-adrenocortical functioning is implicated in depression, hostility, and social isolation as predictors of CHD. Impaired vagal control characterizes depression and hostility, and elevated sympathetic nervous system activation accompanies hostility, social isolation, anxiety, and work stress. Depression and hostility are also associated with impaired platelet function. This information provides insight into how psychological factors may influence disease progression and suggests how interventions designed to improve psychological functioning may alter physiological functioning and lessen cardiac events.

Psychosocial and Psychoeducational Interventions with Post–Myocardial Infarction Patients

A variety of behavioral and psychosocial interventions have been conducted with post–myocardial infarction patients. In addition to maximizing the return to pre-morbid physical functioning, the purview of traditional cardiac rehabilitation efforts, rehabilitation efforts now address patients' psychosocial needs (Cardiac Rehabilitation Guideline Panel 1995). Interventions are presented in inpatient and outpatient settings and conducted by individuals from various training backgrounds including psychology, medicine, social work, and nursing. A definitive case cannot be made for the appropriateness of one discipline over another (Dusseldorp et al 1999). Rather, what is essential is that those delivering the intervention possess the requisite skills and training to present the intervention expertly and as intended.

The majority of controlled group-outcome studies published in the past 20 years have involved comparison of a psychosocial and/or psychoeducational intervention with usual standard medical care. The intent of this design is to determine whether the addition of such an intervention improves upon the benefits conferred by usual care alone. As a body of literature, this research has examined the influence of interventions on physical as well as psychological functioning. The psychosocial intervention usually involves health education, counseling and/or cognitive-behavioral stress management (CBSM).

Psychosocial and psychological interventions have been delivered in individual as well as group formats. The major benefits associated with individual interventions are the opportunity to specifically tailor interventions to the needs of the individual patient and to intervene intensively with that patient. The group format provides a context to normalize patient experiences and to derive benefit not only from interaction with a designated group leader but also from the experience of other cardiac patients. In addition, patients are likely to benefit from the social support provided by the group members (Bracke & Thoresen 1996).

The publication of meta-analyses examining the efficacy of exercise, health education, and counseling/stress management interventions has synthesized a vast literature and permitted conclusions to be drawn about their efficacy compared with usual care. Meta-analyses conducted by O'Connor et al (1989) and Oldridge et al (1988) demonstrated that besides having beneficial effects on various cardiovascular risk factors, submaximal aerobic exercise is associated with decreased reinfarction and approximately a 25% reduction in cardiovascular and all cause mortality relative to usual care. It should be noted that the exercise studies analyzed by Oldridge and collaborators included risk factor counseling. The contribution of the nonexercise components to the outcomes in those studies was not determined and cannot be ruled out.

The efficacy of health education and counseling/stress management interventions on psychosocial and biological risk factors, morbidity, and mortality, however, has been evaluated (Dusseldorp et al 1999, Linden et al 1996, Mullen et al 1992). Conclusions have been mixed for smoking and negative affect with regard to the effectiveness of the interventions. The mixed meta-analytic findings for negative affect, supported by Linden et al (1996) but not Dusseldorp et al (1999), are surprising in light of the plethora of research implicating psychosocial factors in the development and exacerbation of CHD. In fact, Dusseldorp attributed her observed lack of positive findings to: (*a*) two large-scale studies (i.e. Frasure-Smith et al 1997, Jones & West 1996) that reported negative results and (*b*) possible floor effects suggesting that highly distressed patients might benefit, whereas those mildly distressed may not (Hill et al 1992). Linden's results are consistent with the findings of the Cardiac Rehabilitation Guideline Panel (1995). Upon a careful review of the literature, the Cardiac Rehabilitation Guideline Panel concluded that there is strong scientific evidence supporting the efficacy of psychosocial and psychoeducational interventions to attenuate stress (i.e. anxiety, depression, distress, and Type A behavior) and enhance quality of life.

Compared to usual care, psychosocial and psychoeducational interventions have desirable effects on risk factors, reducing cholesterol levels (Dusseldorp et al 1999, Linden et al 1996), systolic blood pressure (Dusseldorp et al 1999, Linden et al 1996, Mullen et al 1992), weight (Dusseldorp et al 1999), and resting heart rate (Linden et al 1996). The improvements in biological risk factors are likely to have accounted for the findings obtained for the outcomes of critical interest, morbidity, and mortality. Both Linden et al (1996) and Dusseldorp et al (1999) reported significant reductions in cardiac morbidity (ranging from approximately 20% to 40%) as a function of participating in the psychoeducational and psychosocial interventions, whereas Mullen et al (1992) did not. More importantly, despite differences in methodology, the types and quality of studies included, and the limitations associated with meta-analytic strategies, the results of the meta-analyses are consistent with respect to mortality. Psychosocial and psychoeducational interventions decrease mortality above and beyond decreases associated with usual care (Dusseldorp et al 1999, Linden et al 1996, Mullen et al 1992). With respect to follow-up periods less than or equal to 2 years, Linden reported a 41% reduction in all cause mortality. For periods greater than 2 years Dusseldorp found a 34% reduction in cardiac mortality. When, as in Dusseldorp's report, Linden included the results of the Recurrent Coronary Prevention Project (Friedman et al 1986), the effects for long-term mortality improved.

The Recurrent Coronary Prevention Project (Friedman et al 1986) enrolled over 900 participants and was the first large-scale clinical trial to examine whether Type A behavior was modifiable in post–myocardial infarction patients. This study also followed patients for several years to determine the effects of the intervention on morbidity and mortality. Participants were randomized to either a cardiology (health education) plus Type A treatment group or to cardiology counseling only. Both groups were compared with a nonrandomized no-treatment control. Though there were no overall differences in mortality, the cardiology plus Type A treatment group had substantially lower total coronary recurrence (fatal and nonfatal) rates. To date, the Recurrent Coronary Prevention Project constitutes the most convincing demonstration that CBSM favorably impacts CHD morbidity in high risk individuals.

Findings from the Lifestyle Heart Trial (Ornish et al 1990) were not included in the aforementioned meta-analyses. It is worthy of comment since its findings suggest that it may be possible to reverse disease progression in patients willing to adhere to an extremely demanding lifestyle (e.g. very low fat diet) intervention. At one year, treated patients relative to the usual care group displayed a small though significant regression in coronary artery stenosis (Ornish et al 1990) maintained at five years after study onset (Ornish et al 1998). Despite these improvements, 25 cardiac events occurred to the 20 remaining lifestyle patients, suggesting that aggressive lifestyle change may be necessary but not sufficient to reverse disease.

Although the Lifestyle Heart Trial (Ornish et al 1990, 1998) reported good adherence rates, the nature of the lifestyle intervention prompts consideration of what constitutes a realistic intervention with which patients will comply. Clearly, adherence to recommended treatments influences treatment efficacy. The literature suggests that nonadherence to these interventions is significant; 79% of smokers relapse and 50% of cardiac rehabilitation participants drop out within one year (Burke et al 1997). Although contradictory evidence is available (Mullen et al 1992), as an adjunct to drug treatment and as a component of behavioral treatment, psychological interventions improve compliance and contribute to better outcomes. Thus, a comprehensive review of the literature supports the efficacy of adherence-enhancing strategies incorporating self-management principles such as behavioral and contingency contracting, skills training, self-monitoring, prompts and reminders, self-efficacy enhancement, social support, and convenient work- or school-based services. Although it is known that psychosocial factors, such as negative affective states, social isolation, and low socioeconomic status, contribute to nonadherence (e.g. Brezinka & Kittel 1996, Carney et al 1995, Rozanski et al 1999), such factors do not receive adequate attention in research addressing adherence and require further study.

Future Considerations

Although the conclusions derived from the literature reviewed above are generally positive with respect to outcomes, a number of factors need to be clarified in future research. The pathophysiological mechanisms by which psychological interventions decrease morbidity and mortality need to be determined (Rozanski et al 1999). Most research has been conducted with samples composed predominantly of white, middle-aged men. As such, it is unclear whether commonly used interventions are equally effective with women, minorities, and the elderly. In addition, what is known about the efficacy of psychological treatments on outcomes is derived from small-scale studies varying with respect to design, methodology, and rigor. Although the results of small-scale studies have been informative and have suggested promising avenues to pursue, a need exists to conduct well-designed, randomized, controlled clinical trials with long-term follow-up. Only large-scale clinical trials that recruit demographically diverse patients can fully determine the extent to which psychological interventions impact morbidity and mortality.

CANCER

Risk Behaviors and Preventive Screening Behaviors

A considerable amount of behavioral research has helped identify psychosocial variables associated with the adoption and maintenance of cancer risk behaviors such as smoking, excessive exposure to ultraviolet rays, unprotected sexual behaviors, and obesity (e.g. Glanz et al 1999b). There is also a growing recognition of the importance of studying how psychosocial factors (e.g. depression) may interact with a genetic predisposition to engage in risk behaviors (Lerman et al 1998). A similarly large literature has identified psychosocial factors that may facilitate or act as obstacles to the use of cancer risk screening tests such as regular Pap smears (cervical cancer), mammography (breast cancer), prostate-specific antigen (prostate cancer), occult fecal blood (colorectal cancer), and skin cancer (melanoma) screening (Lerman et al 1993). Behavioral research has also focused on factors associated with adjustment to positive cancer or cancer risk test results (Pap smears). Psychological reactions to such results may predict critical follow-up visits, in which early interventions may be implemented (Baum & Posluszny 1999). Psychosocial factors also affect decisions to engage in genetic testing that has the capacity to identify genes associated with elevated risk for specific cancers long before the first signs of cellular dedifferentiation or neoplastic changes (Lerman et al 1997). This work has helped to identify demographic (e.g. socioeconomic status), cognitive (e.g. perceived risk) (Glanz et al 1999a), and emotional (e.g. depressive symptoms) (Lerman et al 1999b) factors that identify subpopulations in greatest need of efforts to increase participation in genetic counseling.

Cancer Initiation and Promotion

One recently conducted meta-analysis of 46 retrospective or quasi-prospective studies revealed significant effect sizes for denial/repression, separation/loss, stressful life events, and to a lesser extent, conflict avoidance, in association with breast cancer development (McKenna et al 1999). This meta analysis did not measure other potentially important psychosocial factors such as lack of social support, which has been associated with cancer development in some studies but not others (Helgeson et al 1998). Inconsistencies in this literature may be due to these studies not focusing on cancers whose development is tied to psychosocial-related phenomena such as immune system decrements.

One set of human cancers that is believed to be detected by the immune system during development and is, therefore, possibly more likely to be influenced by immunomodulatory psychosocial factors, includes virally initiated cancers such as cervical carcinoma, certain lymphomas, liver cancers, and nasopharyngeal carcinomas and possibly rare opportunistic virally related cancers such as Kaposi's sarcoma (Bovbjerg & Valdimarsdottir 1998). One such cancer is cervical carcinoma and preclinical neoplastic processes denoted as squamous intraepithelial lesions, both now well linked to infection with certain types of human papillomavirus (HPV) (Antoni & Goodkin 1996). Elevations in stressful life events, pessimism, emotional nonexpression, and the use of passive and disengaging coping strategies are associated with greater promotion of squamous intraepithelial lesions (Antoni & Goodkin 1988, 1989). Depressive symptoms have also been associated with immune measures such as lower T-cytotoxic/suppressor (CD3+CD8+) cells in women at risk for cervical cancer (Savard et al 1999). These associations may be even stronger in women, who as a group are more immunosuppressed (e.g. women with HIV infection). In fact, among HIV+HPV+Black women, greater pessimism was associated with poorer natural killer cell cytotoxicity (NKCC) and lower T-suppressor/cytotoxic cell percent (Byrnes et al 1998).

Another set of cancers whose initiation processes may be related to psychosocial factors includes those associated with faulty DNA repair. Psychosocial stressors have also been associated with decreased methyltransferase synthesis (Glaser et al 1985)—an important process for DNA repair in certain tumors. Also, once a cell is beyond the point of repair, apoptosis, or programmed cell death, is initiated. Interestingly, the course of one form of cancer related to faulty repair or cell death—malignant melanoma—has also been related to psychosocial factors (Fawzy et al 1993). Many other cancers may develop under conditions of disturbed DNA repair or apoptotic mechanisms.

Psychosocial factors such as stress may influence certain hormonally controlled cancers (e.g. prostate cancer) independent of immune pathways. The chief reproductive or hypothalamic-pituitary gonadal–related hormones that have been associated with human cancers are testosterone and estrogen (for both prostate and breast cancer) (Key 1995, van der Pompe et al 1994). Focusing on populations with certain types of precancerous processes such as women with HPV infection or cervical neoplasia, men with elevated prostate-specific antigen levels, or men and women at risk for developing melanoma may be fruitful.

Cancer Progression and Recurrence

A wide range of psychosocial factors have been associated with the course of established cancer, though this literature is replete with inconsistencies (Fox 1998). For instance, some studies suggested that breast cancer patients' reactions to the stress of diagnosis characterized by a "fighting spirit" predicted the course of disease (e.g. Greer et al 1990). One recent study, however, reported that among 578 women with breast cancer, an increased risk of relapse or death over a 5-year period was associated with greater helplessness/hopelessness but was unrelated to stoicism, denial or fighting spirit (Watson et al 1999). These inconsistencies may be due to the heterogeneity in the samples of patients studied (e.g. mixed cancer types and stages), psychosocial variables assessed, psychosocial interventions tested, and the study designs, control variables, and analytic procedures used (Antoni & Goodkin 1996, Andersen et al 1994).

Psychosocial variables have been associated with immune measures on the one hand and disease progression of cancer on the other. Early-stage breast cancer patients with greater distress after surgery had lower NKCC by 15 months after surgery, and lower NKCC at this time point predicted a shorter time to recurrence over the 5–8 year follow-up (Levy et al 1990). Malignant melanoma patients with greater increases in active coping over a 6-week structured stress reduction intervention showed the greatest reductions in anxiety and depression; greater reductions in anxiety and depression were related to greater increases in NK cell counts and NKCC, and greater increases in active coping during the intervention were in turn related to a greater likelihood of survival at 5–6 year follow-up (Fawzy et al 1993). The association between psychosocial factors and disease course may have been mediated by stress-related mechanisms or changes in health behaviors. Because psychosocial interventions may act in cancer patients by modulating perceived stressors, stress responsivity, and/or emotional expressivity, understanding the role of stress-associated neuroendocrine substances and their regulation is important. Thus, stress hormones such as catecholamines or cortisol may affect disease course in cancer through their suppressive effects on T-lymphocytes and immune system functions such as NKCC (Maier et al 1994, McEwen 1998). To the extent that changes in these hormones are associated directly with tumor initiation, or with recurrence via impairments in immune surveillance, they are important to study as possible mediators of psychosocial influences on cancer course.

Interventions to Reduce Cancer Risk

Health psychologists have demonstrated the effectiveness of workplace cancer prevention programs for reducing exposure to excessive sunlight (Glanz et al 1998), smoking cessation (Westmaas et al 2000), and changing cancer-related dietary elements (Glanz 1997). Recent decreases in mortality rates for prostate cancer and breast cancer through the use of regular prostate-specific antigen testing and early and regular mammography, respectively, suggest the potential value of using psychosocial interventions to promote the use of early detection tests. Recent work suggests the importance of tailoring such interventions in a culturally sensitive fashion (Lerman et al 1999a).

Psychosocial Interventions to Facilitate Adjustment and Improve Quality of Life

There is growing awareness of the need to create clear guidelines for the management of cancer-related distress (Payne et al 1999, Roth et al 1998). Beyond affecting quality of life, cancer-related distress may increase visits to physicians offices and hospitals, interfere with treatment decision making, and disrupt ongoing curative and adjuvant treatments as well as increase caregiver burden and burnout. Psychosocial interventions available during different phases of the cancer experience usually fall into one or more of four common forms, including education, behavioral training, group supportive therapy, and individual supportive therapy (Fawzy et al 1997). The majority of these studies have been conducted with women dealing with breast cancer or mixed disease groups. Far fewer randomized studies have evaluated the efficacy of psychosocial interventions in men with prostate cancer, but those that have been used appear effective (Johnson et al (1997).

Reviews of studies of psychosocial interventions with cancer patients (Andersen 1992, Trijsburg et al 1992) have revealed mostly positive effects on indices of psychosocial adjustment using procedures that involve CBSM. These CBSM interventions appear to be the most widely used psychosocial intervention in comprehensive cancer centers in the United States (Coluzzi et al 1995) and have had a major impact in the areas of pain relief, controlling aversive reactions to chemotherapy (e.g. nausea), lowering distress, and enhancing well-being and quality of life (Jacobsen & Hann 1998). The CBSM interventions show promise in addressing the issues of personal control, coping, and hopelessness that are central to the phenomenology of cancer patients. For example, in one study, 132 Stage I and II breast cancer patients receiving a 10-week CBSM intervention using a group format showed lower prevalence of moderate depression as well as positive changes such as increased optimism and finding meaning in life as compared with controls receiving a one-day educational seminar; these positive changes remained significantly greater than those experienced by controls up to 9 months after the intervention (Antoni et al 2000c). These intervention-associated improvements in adjustment may have been brought about by cognitive (e.g. cognitive restructuring and positive reframing) and/or social elements (e.g. supportive group environment and teaching assertive communications). In addition, increases in benefit-finding mediated the effects of this intervention in decreasing serum cortisol levels during the 10-week treatment period (Cruess et al 2000b).

Another type of psychosocial intervention, known as existential/experiential group therapy or supportive expressive therapy (SET), is designed to help individuals express and work through anxieties (e.g. death anxieties) (Spiegel et al 1981) and ventilate negative feelings. SET also provides emotional support and the encouragement to pursue positive goals and activities. The interventions offer the opportunity for group participants to share their strategies for dealing with stressors common to cancer patients, the chance for members to help one another, and a sense of universality and a buffer to the sense of isolation that many of them face (Spiegel et al 1981). It is plausible that patients with early-stage disease (and a good prognosis) might benefit more from a CBSM intervention, whereas those with advanced metastatic disease might benefit more from SET group support programs that focus on pain management and existential issues (Fawzy & Fawzy 1998). Educational groups may be more beneficial for early-stage breast cancer patients, especially those with adequate social support, whereas groups focusing on providing social support may be more efficacious for women at later stages of breast cancer or earlier stage breast cancer patients lacking social support (Helgeson et al 2000). Some key methodological issues that remain for studies evaluating the efficacy of psychosocial interventions for improving adjustment in cancer patients include the need to utilize information on genetic factors, disease type/stage, treatment type and duration, demographic, sociocultural and spiritual factors, and personality and contextual characteristics that could moderate intervention effects on adjustment.

Optimizing Health Outcomes and Increasing Survival

Preventing Complications After Treatment Many of the medical treatments that cancer patients undergo may promote opportunistic infections and possibly disease progression. Surgical stress can cause immunological changes, including decreases in T, B, and NK cells, NKCC, and T and B-lymphocyte proliferative responses to mitogens, some of which may be relevant for eradicating those tumor cells spread into the circulatory system during surgery (Pollock et al 1992, van der Pompe et al 1998). There is also a body of work indicating that adjuvant therapy for cancers (including chemotherapy, radiation, and endocrine therapy) can have significant immunomodulatory effects including reductions in NKCC (Brenner & Margolese 1991). A large number of chemotherapeutic agents available today have potentially different effects on immune status and quality of life. It is arguable that in conducting psychosocial intervention research, participants should be recruited and assessed either before the onset or after the completion of any adjuvant treatment for cancer in order to minimize potential confounds.

Because stressors and surgery have both been associated with decrements in immune functioning (van der Pompe et al 1998), it would be of interest to explore whether stress-reducing psychosocial interventions administered just before surgery can affect post-surgical immune status. One study showed that breast cancer patients receiving two 90-minute sessions of information, problem-solving, relaxation, and psychosocial support showed a tendency toward lower declines in gamma-interferon production by peripheral blood mononuclear cells stimulated with anti-CD3 antibody after surgery as compared with those receiving standard care (Larson et al 2000). An intriguing target for future psychosocial intervention research involves the proposed link between stress and susceptibility to infectious disease (Bovbjerg & Valdimarsdottir 1996). Bovbjerg & Valdimarsdottier (1998) have suggested that because stress is associated with increased susceptibility to upper respiratory infections (Cohen et al 1991) and bacterial infections, cancer patients, especially those who are emotionally distressed and receiving chemotherapy or other immunosuppressive adjuvant therapies, may be quite vulnerable to stress-associated opportunistic infections. Although infectious disease is the leading cause of death in cancer patients (White 1993), little work has examined the effects of stressors or stress management interventions on the incidence of infectious disease in cancer patients receiving adjuvant therapy. Because many curative treatments for cancer involve some form of surgery, recent work implicating stress in delayed wound healing may also be relevant in further research with cancer patients (Kiecolt-Glaser et al 1995). Conversely, stress reduction interventions capable of modulating wound healing and related immunologic processes (e.g. cytokine production) may contribute to optimal health outcomes by preventing secondary infections among cancer patients undergoing procedures such as mastectomy or prostatectomy.

Reducing Recurrence and Extending Survival   The question of whether psychosocial interventions can affect survival of cancer patients and patients with other life-threatening diseases has been the subject of reviews (e.g. Classen et al 1998). As Classen and collaborators point out, there have been at least six studies using either random assignment or matched controls that have tested the effects of psychosocial interventions on survival in cancer patients. Among these, three appeared to produce beneficial effects on survival (Speigel et al 1989, Richardson et al 1990, Fawzy et al 1993), whereas three did not (Linn et al 1982, Gellert et al 1993, Ilnyckyj et al 1994). In one of these studies significant improvements in mood, phobic symptoms, maladaptive coping strategies, and pain were observed among metastatic breast cancer patients participating in a 1-year existential-based SET intervention (Spiegel et al 1981). Moreover, the 50 women assigned to this intervention appeared to live, on average, twice as long as the 36 assigned to the standard of care condition (Spiegel et al 1989). Richardson and colleagues found that among 94 patients with hematologic malignancies, those assigned to any of 3 possible psychosocial conditions (each involving education about treatment side effects and the importance of compliance and self-care) showed greater survival time over a 2–5-year follow-up (Richardson et al 1990). Finally, one study showed that among 68 patients diagnosed with early stage malignant melanoma, those assigned to a 6-week CBSM group showed significantly longer survival and longer time to recurrence over a 5–6-year follow-up compared with those receiving standard care (Fawzy et al 1993). Two of the studies showing no survival effects were randomized trials using patients with cancers at various sites (Linn et al 1982, Ilnyckyj et al 1994). The third study used breast cancer patients and matched (nonrandomized) controls (Gellert et al 1993).

Classen et al (1998) summarized common factors that existed across the interventions producing significant effects on survival and that are relatively absent in those failing to show survival effects. These include: (*a*) the inclusion of patients with the same type and stage of cancer within each group, (*b*) the creation of a supportive environment, (*c*) the inclusion of an educational component, and (*d*) the provision of stress management and coping skills training. Some emerging studies focus on possible biobehavioral mechanisms. Fawzy et al (1993) showed that melanoma patients receiving a 6-week group psychosocial intervention shortly after surgery showed increased active coping and increased NKCC compared with those who received surgery plus standard care only. Studies in breast cancer patients have been based on smaller samples but have shown evidence that time-limited stress management interventions ranging from 9–13 weeks in duration, can modulate endocrine levels (e.g. cortisol) and immune system indices such as lymphocyte number, lymphocyte proliferative responses to mitogens, and NKCC in early-stage breast cancer patients (Schedlowski et al 1994, Gruber et al 1993, van der Pompe et al 1997). One recent report noted significant distress reductions and quality of life increases, in parallel with increases in NKCC among 100 Stage II and III patients in a CBSM intervention (Andersen et al 1998).

Future Directions

At present, several research programs are investigating the effects of psychosocial interventions on quality of life and survival in breast cancer patients. Future work studying the effects of psychosocial intervention on disease recurrence and survival in patients dealing with other cancers such as virally or hormonally related cancers may show similar effects. Investigators should control for factors such as sample homogeneity and include supportive, educational, and skill-building elements to their intervention protocols. This will facilitate comparisons of treatment efficacy across research centers.

HIV/AIDS

The human immunodeficiency virus, type 1 (HIV-1) is the causative agent of acquired immunodeficiency syndrome (AIDS). HIV belongs to a subgroup of viruses known as lentiviruses or "slow viruses" (Levy et al 1985). The course of infection of lentiviruses is characterized by a long interval between initial infection and the onset of serious symptoms. During this interval CD4+ cells, whose receptors provide a portal for the virus, become disabled and die. Healthy CD4 (T-helper) cells normally signal other cells such as cytotoxic T and B cells to mount an immune response. When the CD4 count in blood falls below 500/mm^3, approximately half of the immune system reserve has been destroyed. At this point minor infections such as cold sores (herpes simplex) and fungal infections such as vaginal candidiasis may begin to appear. Once the CD4 count falls below 200/mm^3, life threatening opportunistic infections and cancers typically occur. AIDS, the end stage of HIV disease, is defined by a CD4 count of less than 200/mm^3 or the presence of a serious life-threatening infection such as pneumocystic carinii pneumonia or a cancer such as Kaposi's sarcoma (Pantaleo et al 1993) in an HIV seropositive individual.

Psychosocial Factors and the Course of HIV Infection

Individuals infected with HIV show a wide variation in physical disease course. Some HIV infected individuals develop symptoms rapidly, whereas others remain free of AIDS symptoms for 10 to 15 years even in the absence of combination therapy (Rutherford et al 1990). The sources of individual variability in HIV progression remain unknown but may be due to some combination of biological (Harrer et al 1996) and psychosocial factors (Leserman et al 1999).

Findings relating psychosocial factors to immune system changes and disease progression have been interesting and provocative, but somewhat inconsistent. A meta-analysis found that depressive symptoms, but not stressors, were observed to be longitudinally related to symptoms of HIV infection (Zorrilla et al 1996). Neither stress nor depressive symptoms were related to changes in CD4 count. Stress, however, was associated with declines in NK number and NKCC. Leserman et al (1999) suggested that the negative findings may be explained by the inclusion of studies having short follow-up periods, which measured depressive symptoms only at baseline rather than making repeated assessments more proximal to disease changes. Thus, for instance, Burack et al (1993) found a relationship between depression and decline in CD4 count, but no relationship between baseline depression and development of AIDS at 5 years. In contrast, a 9-year longitudinal study conducted on the same cohort found that higher levels of depression at study entry were associated with faster progression to AIDS (Page-Shafer et al 1996). An even more recent report on this cohort found that those who had elevated depression symptoms at every visit had a 1.7 times greater risk of mortality compared with those who never showed elevated depression scores (Mayne et al 1996).

Another study followed HIV-infected men over a 5-year period and reported that depressive symptoms predicted shorter survival time after controlling for initial HIV-associated symptoms and CD4 cell number (Patterson et al 1996). In contrast, Lyketsos et al (1993) found no relationship between depressive symptoms and declines in CD4 count or clinical disease progression. There was a tendency, however, for the men in the Lyketsos study to be at a more advanced stage of CD4 cell loss at the start of their study than was reported in the studies that reported a relationship between depressive symptoms and disease progression.

In a study of HIV-infected gay men who were asymptomatic at baseline, Leserman et al (1999) found that faster progression to AIDS was associated with more cumulative stressful life events, more cumulative depressive symptoms, and less cumulative social support. When these three variables were concomitantly analyzed, stress and social support remained significant in a regression model. Further analyses on this cohort confirmed the findings for stressful life events and lack of social support, but also related faster disease progression to denial coping and elevated serum cortisol (Leserman et al 2000).

One stressful event associated with disease progression in HIV-infected people is bereavement. Coates et al (1989b) found that both the number of losses and accompanying distress levels were significantly related to faster HIV progression during a 2-year follow-up period. Similarly, Kemeny et al (1994) found that a bereaved group of HIV-infected men who had lost a partner had significantly higher serum neopterin levels and lower proliferative responses to the plant mitogen, phytohemagglutinin. In summary, although a number of studies have failed to show a relationship between psychosocial factors and either immune system changes or disease progression, a reasonable number of well-controlled studies have now documented such relationships. The resolution of inconsistencies will require further research.

Psychosocial Interventions

During the past decade a number of studies examined the effects of psychosocial interventions on HIV-infected persons. One study used an individual psychotherapy format for HIV+ individuals presenting with depressive symptoms and compared interpersonal therapy, cognitive behavioral therapy, supportive psychotherapy (SP), and SP with imipramine (Markowitz et al 1998). The interpersonal therapy intervention defined depression as a medical illness and helped participants relate changes in their mood to environmental events that altered social roles. The cognitive behavioral therapy intervention focused upon cognitive restructuring and rational thought replacement. Finally, the SP condition involved client-centered therapy with a psychoeducational portion about depression and HIV. At the end of the 16-week period individuals assigned to interpersonal therapy and SP with imipramine revealed significantly greater reductions in depressive symptoms than people assigned to cognitive behavioral therapy or SP. There were no changes in CD4 cell counts over time in any condition.

One of the few studies that tested the effects of supportive group therapy in a randomized trial was conducted by Goodkin et al (1996). This study enrolled HIV+ and HIV− gay men who had recently experienced the loss of a loved one. The intervention focused on three bereavement-related areas—making contact, ventilation, and moving on with one's life. Those in the intervention as opposed to the usual care control condition showed significantly greater reductions in distress and grief. Further examination of this cohort by Goodkin et al (1998) found that the intervention decreased cortisol levels in HIV+ and HIV− intervention participants and buffered the decline of CD4 cells in HIV+ men. Both the HIV+ and HIV− participants reported fewer health care visits over the 6-month follow-up period than the control groups.

The first study to report the effects of a CBSM intervention in HIV-infected individuals was conducted by Coates et al (1989a). They randomized HIV+ gay men to either stress management training or a control group. Although the intervention appeared to change sexual behavior (i.e. self-report of significantly fewer sexual partners), there were no apparent effects on CD4 cell counts or lymphocyte proliferative responses to challenge.

More recently, Chesney et al (1996) reported the effects of a 3-month coping effectiveness training (CET) intervention for HIV+ gay men who had some symptoms of depression. Participants were randomly assigned to CET, an HIV education group, or a wait list control group. The CET approach taught participants to match appropriately their coping strategies to particular stressors. Both problem-focused (communication and negotiating skills) and emotion-focused (relaxation, distancing) approaches were taught in the intervention groups. Those in the CET condition showed significant increases in self-efficacy and decreases in perceived stress as compared with either the HIV information or wait list control group. There were no differences among conditions in changes in CD4 count or symptoms.

Comparisons have been made between separate group-based psychosocial interventions in HIV+ gay men. Kelly et al (1993) compared the effects of group-based CBSM, socially supportive (SS) group therapy, and a standard of care control condition in depressed (Center for Epidemiologic Survey-Depression [CES-D] defined) HIV/AIDS men. In comparison with the control condition, both the CBSM and SS groups reduced depressed mood, hostility, and somatization. The SS group also reduced overall psychiatric symptomatology and anxiety, and the CBSM group reduced illicit drug use. Overall, the SS group was superior to the CBSM group in reducing psychological distress at the 3-month follow-up, which the investigators attributed to the greater opportunity for emotional expression and social support available in the SS group.

Mulder et al (1994) compared asymptomatic HIV+ men in group-based CBSM, group-based experiential therapy or a wait list control condition. Both interventions were matched in terms of size, contact time, and session duration and frequency. Despite the differences in theoretical orientation, both CBSM and experiential therapy decreased Profile of Mood States–defined total mood disturbance and Beck Depression Inventory scores in comparison with the control condition.

Several other studies have used group-based CBSM in studies conducted separately on asymptomatic or symptomatic HIV+ men (e.g. Antoni et al 1991, Esterling et al 1992, Lutgendorf et al 1997, Cruess et al 2000c). The intervention, which uses a group format to encourage interpersonal interaction and the sharing of interpersonal experiences, also includes relaxation skills training and practice, cognitive restructuring, instruction in self-monitoring of environmental stressors, and social skills training. In the 10-week Antoni et al (1991) study, the objective was to examine the stress-buffering effects of the intervention upon anxiety, depressed affect, and immune system status in asymptomatic gay and bisexual men learning of their HIV antibody test results. Participants were enrolled at study entry into either a CBSM group or to an assessment-only control condition. HIV antibody testing, notification of serostatus, and postnotification counseling occurred between weeks 5 and 6 for both intervention and control participants. In the intervention groups, however, participants worked on the anticipation of test results for the first 5 weeks, and on adjusting to their HIV status and life-style needs during the next 5 weeks.

Men in the control group who learned that they were HIV+ reported significant increases in anxiety and depressed affect after serostatus notification. In contrast, men in the CBSM intervention group showed significantly less Profile of Mood States anxiety or depression postnotification. The immunological results mirrored the psychological findings. Thus, the HIV+ men in the control group revealed significant decreases in CD4 and NK cell counts as well as lymphocyte proliferative response to phytohemagglutinin in response to the HIV+ diagnosis. These effects were buffered among the HIV+ men in the intervention group.

In a subsequent study on the same asymptomatic HIV+ cohort, Esterling et al (1992) examined the effects of CBSM on cellular control over latent herpesvirus activation, particularly Epstein-Barr virus (EBV), as a function of serostatus notification. The study focused on EBV because HIV can infect and multiply in EBV-infected B lymphocytes (Montagnier et al 1984), and these cells may represent a potentially important reservoir for HIV (Rosenberg & Fauci 1991). The goal was to determine whether CBSM could help shrink the reservoir.

Briefly, Esterling et al (1992) examined the effects of CBSM on EBV on viral capsid antigen and human herpesvirus type-6 (HHV-6) antibody modulation in the 5 weeks preceding and following notification of HIV serostatus. Among both HIV+ and HIV− participants, those randomized to the CBSM condition had significant decreases in both EBV and HHV-6 antibody titers after serostatus notification as compared with the assessment-only HIV+ and HIV− controls. It therefore appears that CBSM can help to normalize immunological surveillance over certain herpesviruses in both healthy individuals and in asymptomatic persons infected with HIV.

In a subsequent experiment Lutgendorf et al (1997) examined the effects of a weekly 10-week group-based CBSM intervention upon mood and immunological parameters in HIV+ gay men who did not yet have AIDS, but whose disease had progressed to a symptomatic stage. In this study symptomatic HIV+ men were randomized to either CBSM or a modified wait-list control group. The control group consisted of an optional one-day didactic and experiential stress management seminar given after the 10-week assessment session and wait-list period. Lutgendorf and colleagues observed that the CBSM intervention significantly decreased self-reported dysphoria, anxiety, and total distress. The intervention group also showed decreases in HSV-2 antibody titers (i.e. genital herpes), whereas the control group showed changes in neither mood nor antibody titers. Neither group showed changes in CD4 count over the intervention period. More recently, Cruess et al (2000d) found that an increase in social support partially mediated the intervention effects on HSV-2. Also, lower mean levels of stress achieved after home relaxation practice were associated with greater decreases in antibody titers to HSV-2 among CBSM participants.

The lack of a change in CD4 count in the Lutgendorf et al (1997) study is interesting, because an effect on CD4 count was observed in the Antoni et al (1991) investigation. It is conceivable that the differences in CD4 changes across studies were due either to the use of a profound stressor (i.e. serostatus notification) in the first study or to the possibility that CD4 count and various measures of CD4 status (e.g. lymphocyte proliferation) may become less influenced by psychosocial factors once the immune system is compromised (i.e. the population of CD4 cells is reduced).

In a subsequent study conducted on the Lutgendorf et al (1997) cohort, Lutgendorf et al (1998) examined the relative contributions of changes in coping skills and social support during the intervention period to reductions in dysphoria, anxiety, and distress-related symptoms. The study found that the CBSM, but not the control group, showed significant improvement in cognitive coping strategies involving positive reframing and acceptance, and in social support involving attachment and alliance formation. Further analyses indicated that changes in social support and coping skills each mediated the decreases in distress observed during the intervention.

Several CBSM studies have now shown close relationships between psychosocial changes induced in symptomatic HIV+ men and concomitant changes occurring in neuroendocrines. Thus, for example, Antoni et al (2000b) found that the CBSM intervention led to decreases in depressed mood that were closely paralleled by reductions in urinary free cortisol. In another study Cruess et al (2000a) examined mood and salivary cortisol before and after weekly relaxation training sessions in a 10-week group-based CBSM intervention study. Decreases in Profile of Mood States total mood disturbance and anxiety scores were significantly and positively related to reductions in pre-session salivary cortisol levels. Pre- to post-session cortisol levels also decreased, with the largest changes taking place earlier in training. Greater reductions in cortisol during early sessions were associated with more frequent relaxation practice at home.

The group-based CBSM intervention on HIV+ symptomatic gay men also appears to impact on relationships among anxiety, 24-hour urinary norepinephrine output, and changes in CD8 count over time (Antoni et al 2000a). Men randomly assigned to the CBSM condition showed significantly lower post-treatment levels of self-reported anxiety, anger, total mood disturbance, and perceived stress than men in the wait-list control condition. The men in the CBSM condition also revealed greater decreases in urinary norepinephrine across the intervention period. At the individual level, decreases in anxiety were significantly correlated with decreases in norepinephrine; greater decreases in norepinephrine predicted a slower decline in CD8 count at 6–12-month follow-up. Thus, it appears that the long-term immunological effects of CBSM were mediated in part by decreases in norepinephrine that were associated with intervention-induced reductions in tension and anxiety.

Alterations in endocrine functions occurring during the course of HIV-infection include a progressive decrease in free testosterone, which can ultimately lead to decreased muscle mass or wasting (Coodley et al 1994). Interestingly, symptomatic HIV+ gay men randomized into the group-based CBSM condition showed significant increases in urinary free testosterone that were associated with reduction in distress (Cruess et al 2000c). In contrast, participants in the modified wait-list control condition showed significant decreases in testosterone. Follow-up data suggest that the CBSM intervention helped maintain free testosterone within the normal clinical range.

In summary, it would appear that a variety of individual and group-based psychological interventions can ameliorate distress in HIV+ individuals. Interventions that focus upon social support and experiential factors appear to be particularly effective in reducing distress, whereas CBSM appears to be especially useful in changing behaviors (e.g. decreasing number of sexual partners or illicit drug use). This may have particular significance for contemporary issues because the advent of combination therapy with protease inhibitors is likely to make skills learning for medication adherence a major priority. Although the exact relationships among psychosocial factors, neuroendocrine changes, immune status, and the effectiveness of psychosocial factors in slowing HIV disease are unknown, the research literature in this area is promising. However, only a large-scale clinical trial with well-defined end-points (e.g. viral load, mortality) can establish whether psychosocial interventions not only improve quality of life but also slow disease progression. It should be noted, however, that because of the manner in which the HIV/AIDS epidemic evolved, most studies have been conducted upon men. Future intervention studies and large clinical trials need to be conducted upon women and minorities as well as upon white gay men.

CONCLUSIONS

Psychosocial factors including depressed affect, low perceived emotional support, and stressful life events appear to contribute to disease progression in CHD (Hemingway & Marmot 1999) and HIV/AIDS (Leserman et al 1999); separation/loss experiences, lack of social support, stressful life events and denial/repression coping have also been associated with the development of some cancers (Helgeson et al 1998, McKenna et al 1999). Numerous studies have also shown relationships between psychosocial factors and pathophysiological mechanisms associated with CHD (Rozanski et al 1999), cancer (Levy et al 1990), and HIV/AIDS (Zorrilla et al 1996). Thus, the link between psychosocial factors and the development or progression of several diverse chronic diseases seems to be established.

Numerous psychosocial interventions have also been shown to have a positive impact on the quality of life of CHD (Dusseldorp et al 1999, Linden et al 1996), cancer (Andersen 1992), and HIV/AIDS (Lutgendorf et al 1997) patients. Of considerable interest is the positive impact that psychosocial interventions have been shown to have on mortality, disease progression, and biological factors associated with improved health. Thus, psychosocial interventions have been reported to increase survival for CHD (Linden et al 1996) and cancer (Fawzy et al 1993) and to improve immune status in HIV/AIDS (Esterling et al 1992).

Although psychosocial intervention studies with chronically ill patients have as their goal improvement in quality of life and decreased morbidity and mortality, they also can provide useful information about relationships between psychosocial factors and putative disease processes. Thus, unlike descriptive epidemiological investigations, intervention studies offer the opportunity to manipulate variables. Studies in breast cancer patients, for instance, have shown that CBSM can modulate neuroenedocrine levels (e.g. cortisol) and immune system indices such as NKCC in early-stage breast cancer patients (Schedlowski et al 1994). Also, studies conducted on HIV-infected individuals have shown that long-term immunological effects of CBSM can be mediated in part by decreases in norepinephrine that are associated with intervention-induced reductions in tension and anxiety (Antoni et al 2000a).

During the past decade major improvements have been made in the medical management of patients with CHD, cancer, and HIV/AIDS. Whereas these advances have improved the quality and duration of life of patients with established disease, they have brought about a need for adherence training to improve the efficacy of medical treatments. HIV infected patients, for example, may be prescribed 18 or more pills per day. For patients on combination therapy including protease inhibitors, missing even a few doses of medication can lead to the production of HIV strains that are resistant to medication. In addition, the patient may still feel well and engage in activities such as unprotected sex that could lead to the infection of either HIV+ or HIV− partners with drug-resistant strains of the virus (Schneiderman 1999). In the face of such obvious needs for adherence training, the good news is that the literature suggests that many adherence enhancing strategies have already been developed (Burke et al 1997). A major need now is to tailor intervention strategies to specific diseases.

The research literature just described indicates that psychosocial variables impact upon CHD, cancer, and HIV/AIDS. Furthermore, this literature indicates that psychosocial interventions can impact positively on quality of life and disease processes and possibly on morbidity and mortality. However, only large-scale clinical trials can determine the extent to which psychosocial interventions can impact on such endpoints as death and disease recurrence. Before such trials can be undertaken a suitable knowledge base needs to be developed. This now seems to be in place for at least some specific chronic diseases.

Visit the Annual Reviews home page at www.AnnualReviews.org

LITERATURE CITED

Andersen BL. 1992. Psychological interventions for cancer patients to enhance the quality of life. *J. Consult. Clin. Psychol.* 60:552–68

Andersen BL, Farrar WB, Golden-Kreutz D, Kutz LA, MacCallum R, et al. 1998. Stress and immune responses after surgical treatment for regional breast cancer. *J. Natl. Cancer Inst.* 90:30–36

Andersen BL, Kiecolt-Glaser JK, Glaser R. 1994. A biobehavioral model of cancer stress and disease course. *Am. Psychol.* 49:389–404

Antoni MH, Baggett L, Ironson G, August S, LaPerriere A, et al. 1991. Cognitive behavioral stress management intervention buffers distress responses and immunologic changes following notification of HIV-1 seropositivity. *J. Consult. Clin. Psychol.* 59:906–15

Antoni MH, Cruess DG, Cruess S, Lutgendorf S, Kumar M, et al. 2000a. Cognitive behavioral stress management intervention effects on anxiety, 24-hour urinary catecholamine output, and T-cytotoxic/suppressor cells over time among symptomatic HIV-infected gay men. *J. Consult. Clin. Psychol.* 68:31–46

Antoni MH, Cruess S, Cruess D, Kumar M, Lutgendorf S, et al. 2000b. Cognitive behavioral stress management reduces distress and 24-hour urinary free cortisol among symptomatic HIV-infected gay men. *Ann. Behav. Med.* 22:1–11

Antoni MH, Goodkin K. 1988. Life stress and moderator variables in the promotion of cervical neoplasia. I: Personality facets. *J. Psychosom. Res.* 32:327–38

Antoni MH, Goodkin K. 1989. Life stress and moderator variables in the promotion of cervical neoplasia. II: Life event dimensions. *J. Psychosom. Res.* 33:457–67

Antoni MH, Goodkin K. 1996. Cervical neoplasia, human papillomavirus and psychoneuroimmunology. In *Psychoneuroimmunology and Infectious Disease*, ed. H Friedman, T Klein, A Friedman, pp. 243–62. Boca Raton, FL: CRC Press

Antoni MH, Lehman J, Kilbourn K, Boyers A, Yount S, Culver J. 2000c. Cognitive-behavioral stress management intervention enhances optimism and the sense of positive contributions among women under treatment for early-stage breast cancer. *Health Psychol.* In press

Baum A, Posluszny DM. 1999. Health psychology: Mapping biobehavioral contributions to health and illness. *Annu. Rev. Psychol.* 50:137–63

Bovbjerg D, Valdimardottir H. 1996. Stress, immune modulation, and infectious disease during chemotherapy for breast cancer. *Ann. Behav. Med.* 18:S63 (Abstr.)

Bovbjerg DH, Valdimarsdottir HB. 1998. Psychoneuroimmunology: implications for psycho-oncology. See Holland 1998, pp. 125–34

Bracke PE, Thoresen CE. 1996. Reducing type A behavior patterns: a structured-group approach. In *Heart & Mind. The Practice of Cardiac Psychology*, ed. R Allan, S Scheidt, pp. 255–90. Washington, DC: Am. Psychol. Assoc.

Brenner B, Margolese R. 1991. The relationship of chemotherapeutic and endocrine intervention on natural killer cell activity in human breast cancer. *Cancer* 68:482–88

Brezinka V, Kittel F. 1996. Psychosocial factors of coronary heart disease in women: a review. *Soc. Sci. Med.* 42:1351–65

Burack JH, Barrett DC, Stall RD, Chesney MA, Ekstrand ML, Coates TJ. 1993. Depressive symptoms and CD4 lymphocyte decline among HIV-infected men. *JAMA* 270:2567–73

Burke LE, Dunbar-Jacob JM, Hill MN. 1997. Compliance with cardiovascular disease prevention strategies: a review of the research. *Ann. Behav. Med.* 19:239–63

Byrnes D, Antoni MH, Goodkin K, Efantis-Potter J, Simon T, et al. 1998. Stressful events, pessimism, natural killer cell cytotoxicity, and cytotoxic/suppressor T-cells in HIV+ Black women at risk for cervical cancer. *Psychosom. Med.* 60:714–22

Cardiac Rehabil. Guideline Panel. 1995. Cardiac rehabilitation. *Clin. Pract. Guideline,* Vol. 17. US Dep. Health Hum. Serv., Natl. Heart, Lung, Blood Inst., Publ. No. 96–0672

Carney RM, Saunders RD, Freedland KE, Stein P, Rich MW, Jaffe AS. 1995. Association of depression with reduced heart rate variability in coronary artery disease. *Am. J. Cardiol.* 76:562–64

Chesney MA, Folkman S, Chambers D. 1996. Coping effectiveness training for men living with HIV: preliminary findings. *Int. J. STDs AIDS* 7(Suppl. 2):75–82

Classen C, Sephton SE, Diamond S, Spiegel D. 1998. Studies of life-extending psychosocial interventions. See Holland 1998, pp. 730–42

Coates TJ, McKusick L, Kuno R, Stites DP.

1989a. Stress management training reduced number of sexual partners but did not improve immune function in men infected with HIV. *Am. J. Public Health* 79:885–87

Coates TJ, Stall R, Ekstrand M, Solomon G. 1989b. *Psychological predictors as cofactors for disease progression in men infected with HIV: the San Francisco men's health study.* Presented at 5th Int. AIDS Conf., Montreal, Can.

Cohen S, Tyrrell DA, Smith AP. 1991. Psychological stress in humans and susceptibility to the common cold. *N. Engl. J. Med.* 325:606–12

Coluzzi PH, Grant M, Doroshow JH, Rhiner M, Ferrell B, et al. 1995. Survey of the provision of supportive care services at National Cancer Institute-designated cancer centers. *J. Clin. Oncol.* 13:756–64

Coodley GO, Coodley MK. 1997. A trial of testosterone therapy for HIV-associated weight loss. *AIDS* 11:1347–52

Coodley GO, Loveless MO, Nelson HD, Coodley MK. 1994. Endocrine function in the HIV wasting function. *J. AIDS* 7:46–51

Cruess D, Antoni MH, Kumar M, Schneiderman N. 2000a. Reductions in salivary cortisol are associated with mood improvement during relaxation training among HIV-1 seropositive men. *J. Behav. Med.* 23:107–22

Cruess DG, Antoni MH, McGregor BA, Boyers A, Kumar M, et al. 2000b. Cognitive-behavioral stress management reduces serum cortisol by enhancing positive contributions among women being treated for early stage breast cancer. *Psychosom. Med.* 62:304–8

Cruess DG, Antoni MH, Schneiderman N, Ironson G, McCabe P, et al. 2000c. Cognitive-behavioral stress management increases free testosterone and decreases psychological distress in HIV-seropositive men. *Health Psychol.* 19:12–20

Cruess S, Antoni M, Cruess D, Fletcher MA, Ironson G, Kumar M. 2000d. Reductions in HSV-2 antibody titers after cognitive behavioral stress management and relationships with neuroendocrine function, relaxation skills and social support in HIV+ men. *Psychosom. Med.* In press

Dawber TR, Meadors CF, Moore FE. 1951. Epidemiological approaches to heart disease: the Framingham Study. *Am. J. Public Health* 41:279–90

Dusseldorp E, van Elderen T, Maes S, Meulman J, Kraaij V. 1999. A meta-analysis of psychoeducational programs for coronary heart disease patients. *Health Psychol.* 18:506–19

Esterling B, Antoni M, Schneiderman N, Ironson G, Carver CS, et al. 1992. Psychosocial modulation of antibody to Epstein-Barr viral capsid antigen and herpes virus type-6 in HIV-1 infected and at-risk gay men. *Psychosom. Med.* 54:354–71

Fawzy FI, Fawzy NW, Hyun CS, Elashoff R, Guthrie D, et al. 1993. Malignant melanoma. Effects of an early structured psychiatric intervention, coping, and affective state on recurrence and survival 6 years later. *Arch. Gen. Psychol.* 50:681–89

Fawzy FI, Fawzy N, Hyun C, Wheeler J. 1997. Brief, coping-oriented therapy for patients with malignant melanoma. In *Group Therapy for Medically Ill Patients*, ed. J Spria, pp. 133–64. New York: Guilford

Fawzy FI, Fawzy NW. 1998. Psychoeducational interventions. In *Textbook of Psycho-Oncology*, ed. J Holland, pp. 676–93. New York: Oxford Univ. Press

Fox BH. 1998. Psychosocial factors in cancer incidence and prognosis. See Holland 1998, pp. 110–24

Frasure-Smith N, Lesperance F, Prince R, Verrier P, Garber RA, et al. 1997. Randomised trial of home-based psychosocial nursing intervention for patients recovering from myocardial infarction. *Lancet* 350:473–79

Friedman M, Thoresen CE, Gill J, Ulmer D, Powell LH, et al. 1986. Alteration of Type A behavior and its effect on cardiac recurrences in postmyocardial infarction patients: summary results of the Recurrent Coronary Prevention Project. *Am. Heart J.* 112:653–65

Gellert G, Maxwell R, Siegel B. 1993. Survival of breast cancer patients receiving adjunctive psychosocociai support therapy: a 10-year follow-up study. *J. Clin. Oncol.* 11:66–69

Glanz K. 1997. Behavioral research contributions and needs in cancer prevention and control: dietary change. *Prev. Med.* 26:S43–S55

Glanz K, Chang L, Song V, Silverio R, Muneoka L. 1998. Skin cancer prevention for children, parents, and caregivers: a field test of Hawaii's SunSmart program. *J. Am. Acad. Dermatol.* 38:413–17

Glanz K, Grove J, Lerman C, Gotay C, Le Marchand L. 1999a. Correlates of intentions to obtain genetic counseling and colorectal cancer gene testing among at-risk relatives from three ethnic groups. *Cancer Epidemiol. Biomark. Prev.* 8:329–36

Glanz K, Lew R, Song V, Cook VA. 1999b. Factors associated with skin cancer prevention practices in a multiethnic population. *Health Educ. Behav.* 26:344–59

Glaser R, Thorn B, Tarr K, Kiecolt-Glaser J, D'Ambrosio S. 1985. Effects of stress on methyltransferase synthesis: an important DNA repair enzyme. *Health Psychol.* 4:403–12

Goodkin K, Feaster D, Asthana D, Blaney N, Kumar M, et al. 1998. A bereavement support group intervention is longitudinally associated with salutary effects on the CD4 cell count and number of physician visits. *Clin. Diagn. Immunol.* 5:382–91

Goodkin K, Tuttle R, Blaney N, Feaster D, Shapshak P, et al. 1996. A bereavement support group intervention is associated with immunological changes in HIV-1+ and HIV-1− homosexual men. *Psychosom. Med.* 58:83–84

Greer S, Morris T, Pettingale K, Haybittle J. 1990. Psychological response to breast cancer and 15-year outcome. *Lancet* 1:49–50

Gruber B, Hersh S, Hall N, Waletzky L, Kunz J, et al. 1993. Immunologic responses of breast cancer patients to behavioral interventions. *Biofeedback Self-Regul.* 18:1–22

Grundy SM. 1999. Primary prevention of coronary heart disease. Integrating risk assessment with intervention. *Circulation* 100:988–98

Harrer T, Harrer E, Kalams SA, Elbeik T, Staprans SI, et al. 1996. Strong cytotoxic T cell and weak neutralizing antibody responses in a subset of persons with stable non-progressing HIV type 1 infection. *AIDS Res. Hum. Retrovir.* 1:585–92

Helgeson VS, Cohen S, Fritz HL. 1998. Social ties and cancer. See Holland 1998, pp. 99–109

Helgeson V, Cohen S, Schultz R, Yasko J. 2000. Group support interventions for women with breast cancer: Who benefits from what? *Health Psychol.* 19:107–14

Hemingway H, Marmot M. 1999. Psychosocial factors in the aetiology and prognosis of coronary heart disease: systematic review of prospective cohort studies. *Br. Med. J.* 318:1460–67

Hill DR, Kelleher K, Shumaker SA. 1992. Psychosocial interventions in adult patients with coronary artery disease and cancer. A literature review. *Gen. Hosp. Psychiatry* 30:S28–S42

Holland J, ed. 1998. *Textbook of Psycho-Oncology.* New York: Oxford Univ. Press

Ilnyckyj A, Farber J, Cheang M, Weinerman B. 1994. A randomized controlled trial of psychotherapeutic intervention in cancer patients. *Ann. R. Coll. Phys. Surg. Can.* 27:93–96

Jacobsen PB, Hann DM. 1998. Cognitive-behavioral interventions. In *Textbook of Psycho-Oncology,* ed. J Holland, pp. 717–29. New York: Oxford Press

Johnson J, Fieler V, Wlasowicz G, Mitchell M, Jones L. 1997. The effects of nursing care guided by self-regulation theory on coping with radiation therapy. *Oncol. Nurs.* 24:1041–50

Jones DA, West RR. 1996. Psychological rehabilitation after myocardial infarction: multicentre randomised controlled trial. *Br. Med. J.* 313:1517–21

Kelly J, Murphy D, Bahr G, Kalichman S, Morgan M, et al. 1993. Outcome of cognitive-behavioral and support group brief therapies for depressed HIV-infected persons. *Am. J. Psychol.* 150:1679–86

Kemeny ME, Weiner H, Taylor SE, Schneider S, Visscher B, Fahey JL. 1994. Repeated bereavement, depressed mood, and immune parameters in HIV seropositive and seronegative gay men. *Health Psychol.* 13:14–24

Key T. 1995. Hormones and cancer in humans. *Mutat. Res.* 333:59–67

Kiecolt-Glaser JK, Marucha PT, Malarkey WB, Mercado AM, Glaser R. 1995. Slowing of wound healing by psychological stress. *Lancet* 346:1194–96

Larson MR, Duberstein PR, Talbot N, Caldwell C, Moynihan JA. 2000. A pre-surgical psychosocial intervention for breast cancer patients: psychological distress and the immune response. *Psychosom. Med.* In press

Lerman C, Caporaso N, Main D, Audrain J, Boyd NR, Bowman ED. 1998. Depression and self-medication with nicotine: the modifying influence of the dopamine D4 receptor gene. *Health Psychol.* 17:56–62

Lerman C, Daly M, Sands C, Balshem A, Lauftbader E, et al. 1993. Mammography adherence and psychological distress among women at risk for breast cancer. *J. Natl. Cancer Inst.* 85:1074–80

Lerman C, Hughes C, Benkendorf JL, Biefecker B, Kerner J, et al. 1999a. Racial differences in testing motivation and psychological distress following pretest education for BRCA1 gene testing. *Cancer Epidemiol. Biomark. Prev.* 8:361–67

Lerman C, Hughes C, Trock B, Myers R, Main D, Bonney A. 1999b. Genetic testing in families with hereditary nonpolyposis colon cancer. *JAMA* 281:1618–22

Lerman C, Rimer B, Glynn T. 1997. Priorities in behavioral research in cancer prevention and control. *Prev. Med.* 26:S3–S9

Leserman J, Jackson ED, Petitto JM, Golden RN, Silva SG, Perkins DO. 1999. Progression to AIDS: the effects of stress, depressive symptoms, and social support. *Psychosom. Med.* 61:397–406

Leserman J, Petitto JM, Golden RN, Gaynes BN, Gu H, Perkins DO. 2000. The impact of stressful life events, depression, social support, coping and cortisol on progression to AIDS. *Am. J. Psychol.* 57:1221–28

Levy JA, Kaminsky LS, Morrow WJW, Steimer K, Luciw P, Dina D. 1985. Infection by the retrovirus associated with the acquired immunodeficiency syndrome. *Ann. Intern. Med.* 103:694–99

Levy SM, Herberman RB, Whiteside T, Sanzo K, Lee J, Kirkwood J. 1990. Perceived social support and tumor estrogen/progesterone receptor status as predictors of natural killer cell activity in breast cancer patients. *Psychosom. Med.* 52:73–85

Linden W, Stossel C, Maurice J. 1996. Psychosocial interventions for patients with coronary artery disease. *Arch. Intern. Med.* 156:745–52

Linn MW, Linn BS, Harris R. 1982. Effects of counseling for late stage cancer patients. *Cancer* 49:1048–55

Lutgendorf S, Antoni M, Ironson G, Klimas N, Kumar M, Starr K. 1997. Cognitive behavioral stress management decreases dysphoric mood and Herpes Simplex Virus Type-2 antibody titers in symptomatic HIV seropositive gay men. *J. Consult. Clin. Psychol.* 65:31–43

Lutgendorf S, Antoni MH, Ironson G, Starr K, Costello N, Zuckerman M. 1998. Changes in cognitive coping skills and social support mediate distress outcomes in symptomatic HIV-seropositive gay men during a cognitive behavioral stress management intervention. *Psychosom. Med.* 60:204–14

Lyketsos CG, Hoover DR, Guccione M, Senterfitt W, Dew MA, Wesch J. 1993. Depressive symptoms as predictors of medical outcomes in HIV infection. *JAMA* 270:2563–67

Maier SF, Watkins L, Fleshner M. 1994. Psychoneuroimmunology; the interface between behavior, brain, and immunity. *Am. Psychol.* 49:1004–17

Markowitz J, Kocsis J, Fishman B, Spielman L, Jacobsberg L, Frances A. 1998. Treatment of depressive symptoms in Human Immunodeficiency Virus—positive patients. *Arch. Gen. Psychiatry* 55:452–57

Mayne TJ, Vittinghoff E, Chesney MA, Barrett DC, Coates TJ. 1996. Depressive affect and survival among gay and bisexual men infected with HIV. *Arch. Intern. Med.* 156:2233–38

McEwen BS. 1998. Protective and damaging effects of stress mediators. *N. Engl. J. Med.* 338:171–79

McKenna MC, Zevon MA, Corn B, Rounds J. 1999. Psychosocial factors and the development of breast cancer: a meta-analysis. *Health Psychol.* 18:520–31

Montaganier L, Gruest S, Chamaret C, Douguet C, Axler D, Guetard D. 1984. Adaptation of lymphoadenopathy associated virus (LAV) to replication in EBV-transformed B-lymphoblastoid cell lines. *Science* 226:63–66

Mulder CL, Emmelkamp MG, Antoni MH, Mulder JW, Sandfort TGM, de Vries MJ. 1994. Cognitive-behavioral and experiential group psychotherapy for HIV-infected homosexual men: a comparative study. *Psychosom. Med.* 56:423–31

Mullen PD, Mains DA, Velez R. 1992. A meta-analysis of controlled trials of cardiac patient education. *Patient Educ. Couns.* 19:143–62

O'Connor GT, Buring JE, Yusuf S, Goldhaber SZ, Olmstead EM, Paffenbarger RS. 1989. An overview of randomized trials of rehabilitation with exercise after myocardial infarction. *Circulation* 80:234–44

Oldridge NB, Guyatt GH, Fischer ME, Rimm AA. 1988. Cardiac rehabilitation after myocardial infarction: combined experience of randomized clinical trials. *JAMA* 260:945–50

Ornish D, Brown SE, Scherwitz LW, Billings JH, Armstrong WT, et al. 1990. Can lifestyle changes reverse coronary heart disease? *Lancet* 336:129–33

Ornish D, Scherwitz LW, Billings JH, Gould L, Merritt TA, Sparler S. 1998. Intensive lifestyle changes for reversal of coronary heart disease. *JAMA* 280:2001–7

Page-Shafer K, Delorenze GN, Satariano W, Winkelstein W Jr. 1996. Comorbidity and survival in HIV-infected men in the San Francisco Men's Health Survey. *Ann. Epidemiol.* 6:420–30

Pantaleo G, Graziosi C, Fauci AS. 1993. The immunopathogenesis of human immunodeficiency virus infection. *N. Engl. J. Med.* 328:327–35

Patterson T, Shaw W, Semple S, Cherner M, McCutchan J, Atkinson J. 1996. Relationship of psychosocial factors to HIV disease progression. *Ann. Behav. Med.* 18:30–39

Payne DK, Hoffman RG, Theodoulou M, Dosik M, Massie MJ. 1999. Screening for anxiety and depression in women with breast cancer. *Psychosomatics* 40:64–69

Pollock RE, Lotzova E, Stanford SD. 1992. Surgical stress impairs natural killer cell programming of tumor for lysis in patients with sarcomas and other solid tumors. *Cancer* 70:2192–2202

Richardson J, Shelton D, Krailo M, Levine A. 1990. The effect of compliance with treatment on survival among patients with hematologic malignancies. *J. Clin. Oncol.* 8:356–64

Rosenberg ZF, Fauci AS. 1991. Activation of latent HIV infection. *J. Natl. Inst. Health Res.* 2:41–45

Roth AJ, Kornblith AB, Batel-Copel L, Peabody E, Scher HI, Holland JC. 1998. Rapid screening for psychologic distress in men with prostate carcinoma: a pilot study. *Cancer* 82:1904–8

Rozanski A, Blumenthal JA, Kaplan J. 1999. Impact of psychological factors on the pathogenesis of cardiovascular disease and implications for therapy. *Circulation* 99:2192–2217

Rutherford GW, Lifson AR, Hesso NA. 1990. Course of HIV-1 infection in a cohort of homosexual and bisexual men: an 11 year follow up study. *Br. Med. J.* 301:1183–88

Savard M, Miller S, Mills M, O'Leary A, Harding H, et al. 1999. Association between subjective sleep quality and depression on immunocompetence in low-income women at risk for cervical cancer. *Psychosom. Med.* 61:496–507

Schedlowski M, Jungk C, Schimanski G, Tewes U, Schmoll HJ. 1994. Effects of behavioral intervention on plasma cortisol and lymphocytes in breast cancer patients: an exploratory study. *Psycho-Oncology* 3:181–87

Schneiderman N. 1999. Behavioral medicine and the management of HIV/AIDS. *Int. J. Behav. Med.* 6:3–12

Schneiderman N, Skyler J. 1996. Insulin metabolism, sympathetic nervous system regulation, and coronary heart disease prevention. In *Behavioral Medicine Approaches to Cardiovascular Disease Prevention*, ed. K Orth-Gomer, N Schneiderman, pp. 105–34. Mahwah, NJ: Erlbaum

Spiegel D, Kraemer HC, Bloom JR, Gottheil E. 1989. Effect of psychosocial treatment on survival of patients with metastatic breast cancer. *Lancet* 2:888–91

Spiegel D, Bloom J, Yalom I. 1981. Group support for patients with metastatic cancer: a randomized prospective outcome study. *Arch. Gen. Psychol.* 38:527–33

Stamler J, Stamler R, Neaton JD, Wentworth D, Daviglus ML, et al. 1999. Low risk-factor profile and long-term cardiovascular and noncardiovascular mortality and life expectancy. *JAMA* 282:2012–18

Trijsburg RW, van Knippenberg FCE, Rijpma SE. 1992. Effects of psychological treatment on cancer patients: a critical review. *Psychosom. Med.* 54:489–517

van der Pompe G, Antoni MH, Heijnen C. 1998. The effects of surgical stress and psychological stress on the immune function of operative cancer patients. *Psychol. Health* 13:1015–26

van der Pompe G, Antoni MH, Mulder N, Heijnen C, Goodkin K, et al. 1994. Psychoneuroimmunology and the course of breast cancer, an overview: the impact of psychosocial factors on progression of breast cancer through immune and endocrine mechanisms. *Psycho-Oncology* 3:271–88

van der Pompe G, Duivenvoorden H, Antoni MH, Visser A, Heijnen C. 1997. Effectiveness of a short-term group psychotherapy program on endocrine and immune function in breast cancer patients: an exploratory study. *J. Psychosom. Res.* 42:453–66

Watson M, Haviland JS, Greer S, Davidson J, Bliss JM. 1999. Influence of psychological response on survival in breast cancer: a population-based cohort study. *Lancet* 354:1331–36

Westmaas JL, Nath V, Brandon TH. 2000. Contemporary smoking cessation. *Cancer Control* 7:56–62

White MH. 1993. Prevention of infection in patients with neoplastic disease: use of a historical model for developmental strategies. *Clin. Infect. Dis.* 17:S355–58

Wilson PWF, D'Agostino RB, Levy D, Belanger AM, Silbershatz H, Kannel WB. 1998. Prediction of coronary heart disease using risk factor categories. *Circulation* 97:1837–47

Zorrilla EP, McKay JR, Luborsky L, Schmidt K. 1996. Relation of stressors and depressive symptoms to clinical progression of viral illness. *Am. J. Psychiatry* 153:626–35

Annu. Rev. Psychol. 2001. 52:581–606

DECISION TECHNOLOGY

W. Edwards
Wise Decisions, Inc., Studio City, California, 91604; e-mail: wedwards@mizar.usc.edu

B. Fasolo
*Psychology Department, University of Colorado, Boulder, Colorado 80309;
e-mail: barbara.fasolo@colorado.edu*

Key Words decision theory, utility, probability, subjectively expected utility, World Wide Web

■ **Abstract** This review is about decision technology—the rules and tools that help us make wiser decisions. First, we review the three rules that are at the heart of most traditional decision technology—multi-attribute utility, Bayes' theorem, and subjective expected utility maximization. Since the inception of decision research, these rules have prescribed how we should infer values and probabilities and how we should combine them to make better decisions. We suggest how to make best use of all three rules in a comprehensive 19-step model. The remainder of the review explores recently developed tools of decision technology. It examines the characteristics and problems of decision-facilitating sites on the World Wide Web. Such sites now provide anyone who can use a personal computer with access to very sophisticated decision-aiding tools structured mainly to facilitate consumer decision making. It seems likely that the Web will be the mode by means of which decision tools will be distributed to lay users. But methods for doing such apparently simple things as winnowing 3000 options down to a more reasonable number, like 10, contain traps for unwary decision technologists. The review briefly examines Bayes nets and influence diagrams—judgment and decision-making tools that are available as computer programs. It very briefly summarizes the state of the art of eliciting probabilities from experts. It concludes that decision tools will be as important in the 21st century as spreadsheets were in the 20th.

CONTENTS

0066-4308/01/0201-0581$14.00

THE TWO QUESTIONS OF DECISION RESEARCH

Research on decision making, whether performed by psychologists or by people from other disciplines, has for the most part focused on two questions about decisions. The first question is how people go about making decisions. This question is the main topic of the nine chapters about decision making that appeared during the period from 1960 to 1999 in the *Annual Review of Psychology* (Edwards 1961, Becker & McClintock 1967, Rapoport & Wallsten 1972, Slovic et al 1977, Einhorn & Hogarth 1981, Pitz & Sachs 1984, Payne et al 1992, Lopes 1994, and Mellers et al 1998). However, this question is not the topic of this review.

Decision research has, from its inception in the late 1940s and early 1950s, drawn much of its intellectual content from a different question: How should decisions be made? What is the best decision, and how can the decision maker (DM) find, recognize, and implement it? Questions of this kind are asked about the content of almost any human performance that requires skill or knowledge. What should the person do? How can he or she produce appropriate behavior? How can the appropriateness of various alternative behaviors be measured and turned into a score? How can an individual's score be improved?

Such questions about quality of performance, although ubiquitous in research on human performance, seem more central to research on human decisions than to research on any other kind of behavior. A "decision" implies actions that the DM considers sufficiently important to justify an investment of effort and thought. The goal of that investment is to do what, in retrospect, the DM will consider to have been the right thing. In short, a decision is an irrevocable choice of an action that has value-relevant consequences. Both the impact on values and irrevocability encourage care and thought. Decisions are defined by their stakes, not by the processes used to make them, by the nature of the task at hand, nor by the kind of human capability (other than for making decisions) required to perform well.

Normative and Descriptive Theories About Decision Making

Theories about how people do in fact make decisions are called "descriptive"; theories about how decisions should be made are called "normative.." Because decisions are made by a DM, with or without the aid of physical and intellectual tools, normative theories of decision making, like descriptive theories, attempt to describe the behavior (or hoped for behavior) of a human DM. The distinction is that normative theories are concerned with a human DM who wishes to use intellectual tools to make decisions. They specify how to go about choosing and using those tools. Descriptive theories are not directly linked to tools, but they obviously cannot omit the possibility that the DM may use them. Thus, normative theories are special cases of descriptive theories of decision making. Every normative theory may also be descriptive; however, not all descriptive theories are normative.

Three Normative Rules and a Preliminary Step

The tools used in normative theories of decision making are mathematical in nature. They grow out of a fundamental underlying premise: that the goal of a decision is to choose the best option available, and that "best" is a quantitative idea. The three formal tools of decision theory around which this chapter is organized are extremely simple and all of them can be understood in the context of the following simple example: Someone offers you a bet. You will toss a coin three times. If it comes up heads on all three tosses, you win $1.00. Otherwise, you lose $0.15. For you, the value of money is the same as its amount in this range and under these circumstances. Gambling, at least for these stakes, doesn't thrill or upset you. (These two statements are together called Assumption 1 below. Assumption 1 permits the utility or subjective value of each outcome to be taken as equal to its objective monetary value). You know that each of the coins available, when tossed, is equally likely to land heads or tails and that all tosses are independent of one another.

You should base this trivial decision on a trivial calculation. You will either win $1.00 or lose $0.15. You believe that the probability of winning $1 is 1/2 raised to the 3rd power, or 1/8. So you calculate the expected value (EV) of the bet as follows:

$$EV = 1/8(\$1.00) + 7/8(-\$0.15) = \$(1.00/8 - 1.05/8) = -\$(0.05/8) \quad (1)$$

This calculation shows that the EV of the gamble is $-5/8$ of $0.01 per play. The EV of rejecting the gamble is $0. A familiar piece of advice about gambling is take the best bet available. Applying that advice, you should reject the gamble.

Formally, four different processes lie behind this example. They correspond to the three rules that jointly comprise normative decision theory at its most abstract, preceded by a preliminary step that will be called "understanding the situation." These three rules—multi-attribute utility (MAU) measurement, Bayes' theorem of probability theory (Bayes), and maximization of subjectively expected utility (Max SEU)—are the ideas that the good DM needs to apply. This review and decision technology as a topic deal with how to apply these ideas.

To understand a situation, you need to think first about the following questions: What can I do? What are my options? You need to think hard about the choice in its context. Having a list of at least two options is the first step toward understanding any situation in which a decision must be made. Often the task of generating a list

TABLE 1   An example of a payoff matrix

Options	States of the world	
	Three heads	Not three heads
Accept gamble	$1	−$0.15
Reject gamble	$0	$0

of available options is very demanding. Sometimes a list of options fully specifies what can happen in a decision situation. More commonly, events not under
the DM's control combine with the DM's choice among the available options to
determine what happens; that is, what the "outcome" of the decision is. The list of
options is often called a list of "acts." The events not under the DM's control, which
are defined so as to be mutually exclusive and exhaustive, are called "states" or
"states of the world." The coin may or may not produce three heads in three flips.
Therefore, in this example, three heads is one state, and not three heads is the other.
A very common and useful display of decision situations shows the options available to a DM as the rows of a table, and the states as columns of that table. Each cell
of the table is a possible outcome of the decision. If the entry in each cell shows, in
dollars or some similar objective unit, the value of each outcome, the table is called
a "payoff matrix." If the DM can specify in detail a payoff matrix appropriate to the
decision, including the probabilities of the states and the values of the outcomes,
the DM understands the situation to a substantial degree. Table 1 shows the payoff
matrix appropriate to our example. Note that the various ways in which you can
fail to get three heads in three tosses are lumped together into a single column.
This is appropriate because they all have the same consequences for the DM.

Evaluation of Outcomes   The values of the outcomes relative to one another are
necessary inputs to decisions. These values must all be measured on the same
scale. Except in special cases in which the best act can be identified from less
information, that scale must be at least an interval scale; that is, all quantities
measured on it must be defined up to a positive linear transformation. In general,
although not in our example, these assessments of value are subjective and vary
from one DM to another. (Our example does not need any transformations on
its objective payoffs because the differences between payoff values are so small
and because we made Assumption 1.) Such subjective values are called "utilities,"
a name borrowed from economics and philosophy. The process of finding those
subjective numbers, MAU measurement, is the first of the three normative rules
that are the three themes of this chapter.

Assessment of Probabilities   When we asserted that the probability of three heads
in three tosses is one in eight, we made two strong assumptions: that the probability of one head in one toss of any relevant coin is exactly one in two and that

the outcomes of all relevant tosses are independent of one another. Real contexts seldom permit such precise knowledge about probabilities. Perhaps in a dull but easy-to-live-in world, there might be no uncertainty. Every action would lead inevitably and predictably to its foreordained outcome, and no one would need to think about how easy or hard it would be to get three heads in three flips. In the real world, most decisions are made under conditions of uncertainty, which means that at least some acts have more than one possible outcome, and the DM cannot fully control which outcome will occur. However, a DM usually has information bearing on the possible outcomes of available acts—information that permits the DM to judge the probabilities of those outcomes. The tools used to assess these probabilities can all be seen as applications of Bayes' theorem of probability theory. For that rather inadequate reason, decision theory, as presented and advocated in many places, including this review, is usually called Bayesian, even when the aspect of it that bears on the task at hand has nothing to do with measurement of uncertainty.[1]

One often gathers evidence to help in assessing probabilities. The process of using that evidence for making inferences usually "fallible inference" or "inference under uncertainty"—stems from the Bayes' theorem of probability theory and is the second normative rule described in this review.

Combination of Values and Probabilities   If you know the relevant utilities and, if needed, the relevant probabilities, you have the quantitative basis for decision making. But you must aggregate the numbers to extract from them an answer to the question: Which is the best act? We illustrated one version of that aggregation in the EV calculation presented as Equation (1) Maximization of expected utility (EU), not EV, is by far the most common and most useful decision rule. Because the probabilities that enter into EUs are judgments, as are all probabilities, the psychological literature on decision making often calls the numbers to be maximized subjectively expected utilities (SEUs). The equation for any EV, EU, or SEU is simply that of a weighted average; the probabilities are the weights. It will become clear later in this review that the utility of any single outcome is itself a weighted average taken over scores on each attribute for that outcome. Users of these ideas must be aware of the difference between these two averaging processes.

This third normative rule for making decisions is as simple to state as it is hard to apply without some kind of mechanical help:

1. In the rare situation in which you have no uncertainty about the outcome of any available act, choose the act with the highest utility.

2. In decisions under uncertainty, choose the act with the highest SEU.

---

[1]A distinction can be found in older decision literature between risk and uncertainty. Uncertainty is the general term; risk refers to situations in which probabilities of the relevant events are known. This old-fashioned distinction is vanishing because one can never have either perfect knowledge or no knowledge at all bearing on those probabilities. All real contexts fall in between.

Figure 1 Bayes and multi-attribute utility (MAU) measurement provide the inputs for maximizing subjectively expected utility (Max SEU).

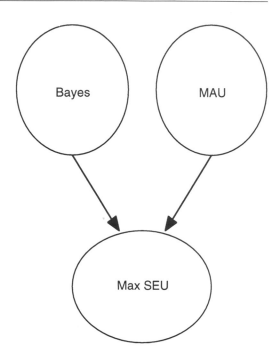

As Figure 1 implies, MAU and Bayes' theorem each separately produces inputs to Max SEU. In real decision contexts in which the stakes are high, these three normative principles often operate separately, and their outcomes can be used as inputs to many different kinds of decisions.

NINETEEN STEPS TO A DECISION

It would be a severe oversimplification to suppose that only three intellectual processes are involved in decision making, whether from a normative or a descriptive point of view. A necessary early step in any decision is to recognize that one must choose among options. The list of options available to the DM is a necessary input to any utility measurement and to any decision. Nonetheless, option invention is not and cannot be done by means of any of the three normative models listed above. It is a task that must be performed judgmentally by the DM, and is part of the preliminary process that we have called understanding the situation.

The three normative rules imply a total of 19 tasks, 8 of which can be done using an algorithm specified by one of the three rules. That leaves 11 to be done by the DM, or his or her helpers. Those 11 tasks include much of what is interesting and important about decision making.

TABLE 2   Nineteen steps to a decision

Step	Task
1	Identify options
2	Identify possible outcomes of each option
3	Identify attributes with which to evalute outcomes
4	Score each outcome on each attribute
5	Weight attributes
6	Aggregate scores and weights into utilities (MAU)
7	Identify events that determine which outcome will follow choice of an option
8	For each event, specify a prior distribution
9	Identify information that might modify the probabilities specified in step 8
10	If information is free or cheap, buy it (Max SEU)
11	If information costs, find out how much
12	Determine the conditional gain from information purchase
13	Aggregate cost of information and gain from having it (Max SEU)
14	Decide whether to buy the information (Max SEU + Bayes)
15	If information is bought, update prior probabilities (Bayes)
16	Back to Step 11. Iterate till no new information is bought (Max SEU)
17	Assemble the numbers output at steps 6 and 15.
18	Calculate expected utilities (Max SEU)
19	Choose the option with the highest expected utility (Max SEU)

MAU, multi attribute utility; Max SEU, maximum subjectively expected utility, Bayes, Bayes' theorem of probability theory.

The three normative rules have different purposes and come from different historical roots. However, if we want a complete list of the intellectual tasks that are collectively called decision making, we should ignore their different origins and purposes and treat them as the elements of one model. Table 2 lists the 19 steps to a decision.

Table 2 does not list the elementary tasks involved in decision making in final form. Still, it is enough to suggest some important questions. Are the 19 steps (*a*) necessary, and (*b*) sufficient for decision making? The formulation of the steps involved in decisions to purchase information is technically unsatisfactory. In addition, it omits the predecisional steps required to recognize that a decision problem exists. So the list is not sufficient—although it comes close.

In its present form, Table 2 is also not a list of necessary steps. Gigerenzer et al (1999) have written a book to argue that human beings can and sometimes should base their decisions on one cue, not many. Such a procedure would eliminate step 5 and much change step 6.

However, this review is about how decisions should be made, not about how they are made. Failure to consider relevant information about values will generally reduce the quality of choices (for an exploration of when that reduction is unimportant, see Gigerenzer et al 1999). A more important way in which normal human decision-making methods differ from those listed in Table 2 is that the processes specified in the table are designed to attach a numerical value to each option and then to choose the option with the highest value. People don't explicitly do that for most of their decisions.

Our crucial contention about Table 2 is that each subtask specified in it must be performed in such a way that its major objective is met, in order to make a careful, good decision. People do not need to apply explicit weights to value dimensions to perform evaluations, for example. However, they must compare the importance of value dimensions and recognize that good performance of an option on an important dimension more than compensates for the poor performance of that option on a less important one. A similar comment applies to each subtask in Table 2. Human beings have developed a great deal of skill in performing the kinds of transformations implicit in Table 2 in nonnumerical ways. However, the fact that they are skilled at nonnumerical versions of these tasks does not change the essential nature of the tasks themselves. Single-cue decision making is not a counterexample; if more than one possible cue exists, the cues must be compared in order to choose which one to use.

Inspection of Table 2, considered as a set of steps necessary for a normative approach to decision making, suggests a useful question. Which steps can be automated? Steps 1 through 5, 7 through 9, and 11 clearly cannot be. Each depends in some fundamental, essential way on human judgment and understanding. Thus, this normative approach to decisions still depends in many and essential ways on the judgments of a human DM. Except for steps 12 and 17, each of the nonjudgmental steps has listed with it the model from which the algorithm required to execute the step is derived. Steps 12 and 17 can be automated, but their automation does not depend on any specific normative model. Steps 6, 15, and 19 are the three output-generating steps: one per normative model. All of the other steps are required to provide inputs on which those outputs depend.

MAN-MACHINE SYSTEMS FOR MAKING DECISIONS

Given the abundance of human judgments required in Table 2, the idea of a procedure for making important decisions that does not depend heavily on human inputs seems unlikely as well as unattractive. Selection, training, and elicitation of responses from the person (or, more often, people) whom we have so lightly called the DM become crucial. Decision theorists rather casually say that the function of any decision is to implement the values of the DM. The opinions that, in systematic form, become the probabilities needed for SEUs should either be those of the DM or those of a domain expert in whose judgment the DM has confidence.

Such statements are helpful as ways of dividing difficulties and responsibilities in system design. However, the selection and training of the DM and the design of the DM's tasks and work environments are essential parts of the design of every man-machine system.

THE SCOPE OF THIS REVIEW

The literature of decision making using normative principles is vast. Inclusion within it of literature bearing on selection, training, and job design for DMs makes it much bulkier than it would be otherwise. We have neither the time, the courage, nor the space to review it. Instead, in the remainder of this review we shall try to highlight some recent work that seems to us both very well done and very likely to influence future work concerned with making, not decisions in general, but wise decisions.

NORMATIVE USE OF MULTI-ATTRIBUTE UTILITY MEASUREMENT

MAU, sometimes also called "MAUT" (T for theory or technology) or "MAUM" (M for measurement), implements an obvious, important principle. Virtually never is the value system that a DM brings to bear on any decision composed of just one value. Price is typically important to purchasing decisions, but so is quality—and quality itself has multiple attributes. The powerful sports car that catches your eye in the dealer's showroom is attractive and fast but it is also expensive, uncomfortable to ride in, noisy, and a gas guzzler. The point that the values of most outcomes have multiple attributes was first seen as a core issue of decision analysis by Raiffa (1968), and the processes that can be used to aggregate single-dimension utilities into the aggregate utilities needed for decisions were spelled out by Keeney & Raiffa (1976). A textbook treatment is available in von Winterfeldt & Edwards (1986).

Step 6 of Table 2—the task of aggregating the value-laden attributes of an option or of one of its possible outcomes—is the core of MAU. Choice of an aggregation rule depends on the issues having to do with the size of interactions among attributes. Speed and maneuverability both contribute to the aggregate value of a sports car. The two dimensions may interact; you might be unwilling to use the speed unless you feel that you can rely on maneuverability. Most manufacturers of sports cars make sure that their sports cars are both speedy and maneuverable. If you will never encounter a speedy but hard-to-maneuver sports car, you will not need to evaluate it. Perhaps these attributes, although they interact in an important way at low values of maneuverability, do not interact so much at the levels of both attributes that exist in sports cars. You can ignore the possible levels of each value that do not exist within the available option set. Thus, even if the attributes interact, as in this example, it may be a good approximation to use an additive aggregation rule that treats aggregate utility as the weighted average of the single-attribute utilities. Consider a set of sports cars named $X_1, X_2, X_j, \ldots, X_J$. Each sports car has value on each of a set of K attributes, in which the generic attribute is called k. The aggregate MAU of car j is then:

$$\text{SEU}(X_\text{j}) = \sum_{k=1}^{K} [w_k u_k(X_\text{j})] \qquad (2)$$

The quantity $u_k(X_j)$ is the single-dimension utility of car X_j on the kth attribute. The quantity w_k is the weight of the kth attribute. The sum of the w_k over the K different attributes is taken to be 1. Equation (2) is simply the equation for a weighted average of the single-dimension utilities for car j. To work with the interactions of attributes, one would need product terms for interacting attributes in pairs, triples, etc, each with its own weight. Such a procedure adds enormously to the elicitation burden, but often makes little difference to the result. Recently, users of these tools have come to believe that the absence of value interaction among attributes is a sign that the attribute set is appropriate. Interacting attributes are often redundant or in some other way ill chosen to describe the values relevant to a particular decision (Keeney 1992).

MAU is a very simple, powerful tool. The following true story illustrates both its simplicity and its power.

Personal Decisions: Choosing Which Course to Take

The decision scientist at the telephone had never met the caller.

"Professor Edwards, I must choose between two courses and am having great difficulty deciding which to take. Can you help me? I got your name from the USC public relations office. They say you are an expert on how to make decisions."

Over lunch, more details emerged. The DM was a foreign-born graduate student seeking a Masters in Performing Arts. (She is a dancer.) Her choice was between two advanced courses, one in international relations and one in political science; they were both to be taught this semester, and the times they were offered conflicted. The semester had already started; she had sampled both. Either course would meet a degree requirement. The choice was difficult because the political science course was easy but emotionally disturbing (details of its subject matter and its mode of presentation reminded her of her unhappy European childhood). The international relations course was more conventional, harder, and she found its professor and students far less congenial. After some probing to make sure that this decision was the one to work on, I concluded that so narrow an analysis would indeed be sensible and worthwhile, even though the decision between the two courses in part reflected a far larger issue having to do with what her long-term career goals were.

I began by eliciting attributes. (Options were already well defined.) Table 3 lists the six attributes she identified—in order of decreasing weight, not of elicitation. Attribute 1 refers to the course materials and the instructor's style more than to her

TABLE 3 The student's decision problem

		Courses			
		International relations		Political science	
Number	Attribute (wt.[a])	Score	Score × wt.	Score	Score × wt.
1	Feel safe and comfortable (0.4567)	18	8.2206	62	28.3154
2	Learn something (0.2567)	70	17.9690	25	8.9845
3	Not too much work (0.1567)	25	3.9175	68	10.6556
4	Relevant to career (not used)				
5	Course materials not too disturbing (0.0900)	66	5.9400	38	3.4200
6	Interpersonal interactions (with professor, other students) (0.0400)	42	1.6800	80	3.2000
	MAUs		37.7271		54.5755

[a]These are rank order centroid weights—transformations of the rank of the attribute. The weight of the kth attribute, out of a total of K attributes whose weights must sum to 1, is $w_k = (1/K) \sum_{i=k}^{K} (1/i)$. For explanatory details and tables of rank order centroid weights, see Edwards & Barron (1994).

interactions with instructor and students, which are the topic of attribute 6. I felt some hesitation about including both attributes 1 and 5, because both reflected her judgment that the Political Science course materials and teaching style disturbed her. However, after exploring the question of whether courses could be imagined that would score high on both or low on both (yes, easily), I accepted these as two attributes.

The next step in elicitation was weighting. We used swing weights and the SMARTER (Edwards & Barron 1994) method of approximating attribute weights from judgments of their rank order. She understood the concept of swing weights with an ease that surprised me, because I have often found this idea difficult to get across in class settings. I explained it in terms of the contribution of each attribute to final MAU, not in terms of indifferences among artificial stimuli. The idea that doubling a weight doubles the contribution of that attribute to the final score seemed to be easy to understand.

The basic idea of the SMARTER method (Edwards & Barron 1994) is that of eliciting the rank order of the weights and then using the ranks as a basis for approximating them. This made good sense to her, and she had no trouble ordering the weights by thinking about the relative merits of adding 10 points to the scores on each attribute. She liked the "rank order centroid" weights that resulted, and she was quite willing to accept them as embodying her values.

Scoring each of the two courses on a 0–100 scale for each attribute was the final elicitation step. Larger numbers were preferable to smaller numbers for all scores. She had no trouble with the judgments except for those concerning attribute 4, relevance to her career. She did not feel sure enough about what her career would be to make those two judgments. Therefore, attribute 4 was not used. I did not revise the weights to be appropriate for five attributes rather than six, because she had already accepted the six attributes and weights. (It would have made no difference to the conclusion if I had.)

I made the obvious recommendation, the political science course. She told me that she intended to choose that option. The amount of time required to explain MAU, swing weights, and SMARTER, to collect the judgments, and to do the arithmetic was less than 3 h.

WEB-BASED DECISION TECHNOLOGY

In an exciting and promising recent development, some almost recognizable aspects of decision technology are now available on the World Wide Web. Exploring them is a good way to understand issues that might not arise otherwise, simply because so few analyses of real decisions about such familiar questions as which car to buy have been published.

Consider a clever DM who wants to buy a digital camera but knows nothing about them. She might look at a catalog or a store window, which tells her little more than that she has many options, all of which are costly, and that she needs to know something about the features (or attributes) that matter to her (e.g. resolution or the camera's ability to zoom). Advertising may not help much, because many ads try to limit the option set and to focus on one or two features rather than giving a broad survey of both options and features. In addition to browsing catalogs and camera stores, our clever DM could consult experts, read *Consumer Reports*, record the information gathered, and aggregate it all in some convenient way. A full afternoon might not be enough to complete these initial steps of her decision process.

Alternatively, our clever DM now has the possibility of browsing the Web, where the same information (probably even better organized and more up to date) can instead be quickly found using any of the easily available search engines.

The first reason why the Web matters to DMs is that it improves information input, making it more current, easier to obtain, and cheaper. Reexamination of Table 2 shows that such information enters into decision processes in various ways, but especially in step 1: identify options. For a purchasing decision, such gathering and organizing of information may be the most time-consuming part of the decision process. Having it done for you is clearly likely to be helpful.

Are such decisions based on the Web now always faster and better as a result of improved information input? No. Often the Web provides too much information. A search for a mountain bike can produce more than 3000 options from which to choose. In an effort to make each bike brand distinctive, design details may vary from one to the next in ways that do not matter to a DM. Recognizing the irrelevance of irrelevant attributes is hard for a DM to do quickly, and it may be impossible for the vendor or website developer to do at all. The color of a car may be virtually irrelevant to one shopper, but it may be crucial to another shopper. The site developer can find out about the relevance of different attributes to choice only by asking the DM or by inferring attribute preference for this shopper from records of real or hypothetical choices made by this or previous shoppers.

The Web is of interest to DMs and researchers alike for another reason. Recently, an increasing number of Web sites, recognizing that information overload does not facilitate wise decisions, have started to provide tools to deal with the excess of information. Such "decision-facilitating sites" (hereafter DS) do not overwhelm users with long shopping lists of options, and/or attributes; they elicit preferences and values and structure the information in ways that respond to the users' needs and values. This Web-based decision technology is increasingly used worldwide every day. The remainder of this section attempts to describe some tools that are currently being made available.

First, it is important to point out that our statements about the forms of decision technology available on the Web are based only on time we have spent looking at some of those sites. The intellectual characteristics of these tools are as nearly invisible as the site designer can make them. So far as we know, every site that presents such tools focuses its materials on the options being described and the attributes on which the options can be compared, not on how the comparisons and final choice should be made. The proprietary nature of DS means that the hidden algorithms used in them are just that—hidden. Often one can make a good guess about the logic and arithmetic behind the sequence of Web pages that constitutes any DS. However, such guesses are insecure. It is sometimes possible to recognize technical errors, but it is rarely possible to learn why the errors exist or who made them.

Winnowing and Winnowed-Out Winners

The minimum service that a DS could offer is a list of options. To be relevant that list would have to make clear what attributes characterize each option. Such options-by-attributes matrices, familiar to us all, appear in sources like *Consumer Reports*. Until recently, such matrices were the only form of decision aid available on the Web. Nowadays, the format is still used, but because in situations like purchasing decisions the number of available options (N) is typically very large, the task "Choose 1 from N" is often divided into two separate stages. The first is "choose n (a number smaller than N) winnowed options from the initial set of N options." The second is "choose 1 (or perhaps 2 or 3, but not $n - 1$) from the n winnowed options." We call the first stage "winnowing," and the second "comparison." (One could imagine a process with any number of stages between 2 and $N - 1$, but we know of no DS that uses more than two.)

Plausible values of N can be 50 or more. Plausible values of n are rarely larger than 10. Five is a good number of options to have in the final comparison set from which a choice is to be made. By coincidence, that is something like the maximum number of columns that one can conveniently display on a computer screen at one time, leaving space for feature names and brief explanations. Thus the output of the winnowing stage is typically a display in which each row represents an option, and each column represents a feature. (Order can be reversed).

Many DS now distinguish the winnowing from the comparison stage. Most provide different kinds of aids for each stage, supporting winnowing in a fast, noncompensatory way and comparison in a more thorough, compensatory way—"compensatory" meaning that a good score on one attribute can make up for a bad score on another. The idea of using a fast and coarse screening procedure for initial winnowing and a less coarse and more time-consuming procedure for final comparison and choice is sensible; it saves time and effort. However, any two-stage process in which the first stage discards options and the second chooses among the survivors has a serious intellectual flaw. Should the decision procedures for the two stages be different? If the answer is no, little is gained by having two stages; they should be combined into one. If the answer is yes, the possibility exists that an option excluded from further consideration during winnowing might, if it had survived, have been the ultimate winner. Such "winnowed-out winners" can occur whenever the two stages use any two of the following five decision rules (Payne et al 1993):

1. Satisficing (SAT). Choose the first option acceptable on all attributes; if none are acceptable, then choose the first option acceptable on all but one attribute, etc.

2. Most confirming dimensions (MCD). Choose the option that is acceptable on the largest number of dimensions.

3. Lexicographic (LEX). Select the option that is best on the most important attribute.

4. Elimination by aspects (EBA). Eliminate options that are not acceptable for any given attribute, one attribute at a time. (Order of consideration is random, not linked to importance).

5. Weighted averaging (WAV). Use Equation 2.

Of these decision rules, only WAV requires scores (measured on at least an interval scale) reflecting option performance on every attribute and weights (on an identity scale) reflecting the potential contribution of each attribute to the final score. WAV can be used at both stages, excluding all possibility of winnowed-out winners. However, WAV is cumbersome in terms of judgmental effort, time, and complexity—the reason why only a few DS, which we will call compensatory, are daring to implement WAV at the winnowing stage. Most DS instead facilitate noncompensatory winnowing by simplifying the judgmental basis required for weighted averaging in two ways. The first simplification is the introduction of two-level attribute scores: acceptable vs not acceptable[2] (as in all the decision

---

[2]This discussion treats the dividing line between "acceptable" and "not acceptable" as fixed for each attribute. In use, such dividing lines may turn out to be flexible, which fits human intuition better but enormously complicates DM's judgmental task and the DS' ability to support it.

rules listed above, except WAV and LEX). The second simplification is to treat all attributes as of equal weight (as in SAT, MCD, and EBA).

Compensatory Decision Sites

The distinction between the winnowing and comparison stages is artificial when compensatory procedures are used for winnowing. Therefore, compensatory DS make N multi-attribute calculations. The four following examples, available today on the Web,[3] illustrate how they work.

Example 1: The Overall Winnowing Process (City Decision)   Need to choose which city to move to? Go to "City Finder" (now at http://www.personalogic.com), and in few clicks you are presented with: (*a*) an initial option set ($N = 353$, a huge number), and (*b*) a list of attributes preselected by Personalogic and assumed to be relevant to your city decision (geography, climate, people, jobs/costs, school/commute, crime, and leisure). The attributes are then presented one by one, decomposed into two to four subattributes. For each subattribute, you are asked to indicate on a five-point scale how important that subattribute is to you. For instance, the "people" attribute is decomposed into "age" ("Do you prefer to live in an area where the residents tend to be younger or older?") and "ethnicity" ("How important to you is living in an ethnically diverse metropolitan area?"). Each subattribute is explained in detail (e.g. for ethnicity you read that "An ethnically diverse city is one in which its residents come from a wide variety of ethnic backgrounds. Living in such an area will expose you to an array of different cultures and foods"). (*d*) Last, you are asked to judge how important each attribute is relative to one another. (*e*) Now the DS has your unique preferences and weights and uses them to compute an overall score for each of the 353 cities. A score of 100% means that that city perfectly meets your preferences. All cities will be rank-ordered by score, from best to worst.

These procedures differ from those of typical individual MAU elicitations in two important ways.

1. The value-tree structure used for the elicitation is supplied rather than elicited. Moreover, the supplied structure is intended for general use, which almost guarantees that any individual user will find in it a number of irrelevant attributes.

2. Weights are elicited by means of judgments of "importance." People find such judgments natural and easy to make. However, no effort is made to explain such judgments as comparisons among the contributions of ranges of single-attribute scores to total score. This is a classic problem of MAU

---

[3]DS are constantly being updated on an almost daily basis. We therefore expect that most of the URLs we list here will change, evolve, or disappear very soon. Nonetheless, these are useful snapshots of the kind of decision technology that is available on-line as of May 2000, and we believe that the suggestions for improvements that end this discussion may also be of some use to future DS developers.

elicitation. For an extensive discussion, see any discussion of swing weights (e.g., chap. 8 in von Winterfeldt & Edwards 1986).

Example 2: User Profiles Help Express Preferences (Dog Decision)   In the previous city decision example, steps *c* and *d* (weights and preferences elicitation) were fairly straightforward. Most of us have an idea of the kind of people we like to live close to, the crime level we are comfortable with, the level of leisure activity we enjoy, etc. However, how well can users know their preferences and weights if faced with a decision on a topic about which they know little? For example, take the case of a person who wants a dog, but has never had one—a dog novice. She goes to "Dog Match" (again at http://www.personalogic.com), where she finds that (*a*) there are 178 breeds of dogs among which to choose, (*b*) the attributes supplied are: size, activity, temperament, dog groups, and coat. Because she is inexperienced, the DM feels knowledgeable enough to have preferences related to the first three attributes, but not the last two. What to do? A possibility is to learn what the preferences of people like her are for dog groups and coats. Some compensatory DS, in fact, store profiles of "typical" decision makers with preselected weights and preferences. Dog Match stores profiles for apartment dwellers, dog novices, mature adults, and working mothers. The DM can ask herself, "What kind of person am I?" and her answer will lead her to a template of weights and values that she can then edit at her convenience.

Example 3: Weights Sensitive to Attribute Range (Computer Decision)   Most DS assess users' preferences and weights via five- to eight-point importance ratings (Remember Example 1). On the basis of decision theory, we know that paying attention to attribute importance alone might lead to inaccurate weights because weights need to be adjusted for the range of the attribute. Frictionless (http://www.frictionless.com) is the first DS to have incorporated this "range-adjustment" as part of step *d* of the winnowing process. Let's consider a graduate student who needs a new computer. He goes through the usual steps: (*a*) options set ($N = 614$ computers), (*b*) externally supplied list of attributes (hard drive capacity, manufacturer, memory, operating system, price, and processor), (*c*) preference ratings on each single attribute. In step *d* he needs to rank the six attributes in importance. Price is the most important attribute for him. In addition to the usual importance-rating scale, he is also asked to specify the preferred range of variation for each attribute (editing a default range, which—for price—is $400–$7,000). If the graduate student cannot afford computers more expensive than $1,000, the DS will have a better perception of his heavy weighting on price if he narrows the price range based on his preferences ($400–$1,000), than if the range were kept at $400–$7,000. This example illustrates the problem with two-level scoring rules. It makes sense to treat all computers above some specified price as too expensive to be worth considering. However, computers costing less than that cutoff price are not all equal on this dimension.

Example 4: Weights Elicited via Tradeoff Procedures (Digital Camera Decision)
Tradeoffs are the most uncomfortable step in any decision. As a DM, we prefer to
avoid them. Most compensatory DS calculate them, but in a hidden way. Tradeoffs
are, in fact, usually done out of the user's sight, between steps *d* and *e* of the
decision process. However, tradeoff decisions are the essence of evaluation. The
user, not the Web, should make them.

Activebuyersguide (http://www.activebuyersguide.com) is the first DS that elicits tradeoffs explicitly. As an example, let us invite our clever DM in need of a digital
camera to use the activebuyersguide. She will be guided through the usual steps
of the winnowing stage [steps *a–d*], until she is asked to make explicit tradeoffs
among features that she has rated as important. For instance, she will be presented
with two fictitious cameras. Camera A costs $500 and has a 1-s delay between
shots, Camera B costs $300 and has a 3-s delay between shots, all other features
being equal. She is asked to rate—on an eight-point scale—how much she prefers
camera A over camera B. (We do not know how this quantitative information is
used.) Tradeoffs are presented, with several different combinations of features,
and the sophistication of this tool is such that it even counterbalances the order of
presentation of the features!

Noncompensatory Decision Systems

Noncompensatory DS focus the users' attention on attributes, helping a DM select
the most important attributes for his or her decisions, and set aspiration levels or
cutoff values. Attribute-based strategies simplify the decision task, reducing the
option set from *N* to some smaller number, but they also make winnowed-out
winners possible.

A common method for reducing the option set from *N* to *n* is elimination by
aspects (other methods are SAT, MCD, and LEX). Suppose you decide that digital
cameras without zoom capability are unacceptable, as are cameras that cost over
$1000. A way of winnowing down the candidate set is therefore to eliminate from
it all cameras that do not meet these two criteria. If this process reduces the set
of choices too far, you can work with one requirement instead of two. If there are
too many survivors (the more common experience), then one can either tighten
the requirements in use, usually by redefining the standard of acceptability, or add
other requirements that refer to other features.

Another example from the Web: To date more than 10 different DS support
cell phone plans. Consider the available cell phone service plans for the Denver-
Boulder area (http://www.point.com). For the entire choice set, $N = 95$. Five clicks
(checking the desired monthly access fee, minutes per month, technology, free first
minute of incoming calls, and no contract period) reduce the choice set to $n = 4$.
However, there is no guarantee that the best cell phone plan overall is among these
four choices.

In summary, the main problem with noncompensatory DS is the possibility of
winnowed-out winners. The need to make winnowed-out winners stand out has

been faced very recently by Activebuyersguide. Exploiting the interactivity of the Web, this DS alerts users to the consequences of setting an absolutely binding cutoff (Click OK if you are SURE you would never buy a product that didn't satisfy this requirement) as opposed to a "nonbinding" cutoff (This requirement would not automatically exclude options from your consideration—usually for price). When attributes have nonbinding cutoffs, winnowed-out winners are still presented in the options-by-attributes matrices and are highlighted in red. This action is a promising move but unfortunately it seems to offer a solution where the problem in fact does not exist. These alerting devices are for the moment only available on compensatory DS and not on noncompensatory ones where the likelihood of winnowed-out winners is much higher.

If noncompensatory DS have these flaws, why do Web developers develop them, and why does a DM use them at all? The answer comes from research on information-processing models of decision making (e.g. Payne et al 1993), which shows that attribute-based strategies (i.e. EBA, SAT, MCD, LEX) are preferred by normally unaided and pressured DMs. On the Web, people are in fact normally unaided (nobody expects to find a compensatory DS to help choose what dog to get) and act fast, as though they were under pressure (even when no objective reason for feeling under pressure exists. Morkes & Nielsen 1997). Noncompensatory DS seem to fit well with user needs and tastes about decision processes.

Knowing that DMs want to act fast on the Web has very important implications for decision technology: (a) DMs tend to prefer time-saving to time-consuming guides; (b) compensatory guides are currently time-consuming and noncompensatory guides are time-saving; (c) users tend to prefer noncompensatory DS to compensatory ones, even if they would (probably) make better decisions otherwise.

Comparison Stage

So far, we have dealt with sites that support the winnowing stage. In the comparison stage, aids are generally less sophisticated and less helpful than those offered in the winnowing stage. All DS support comparisons in the same, rudimentary, *Consumer Reports*-like way: surviving options along one dimension and attributes (usually all attributes, even the ones not relevant to the DM) along the other dimension of comparison tables. Some tables let users rearrange the options along one attribute; others let users remove unsatisfactory options.

No devices have yet been introduced to assist users in making normatively useful comparisons. Normative models suggest that DMs should process most— if not all—of the information available, aggregating to produce a single number that represents the attractiveness of each option, and then should choose the most attractive option.

A recent experiment using Web-based information display boards (Fasolo & McClelland 1999) has shown that users can be partially normative. Participants in that experiment tended to look at all available information, even when presented with a demanding choice among eight computers varying on eight attributes.

However, users did not aggregate the items of information in such a way as to produce a number representing the aggregate value of each option. When the attributes were positively related, participants processed by attribute (a nonnormative strategy, but still helpful, because the relative ordering of the options along positively related attributes tends to be the same for all attributes). When the attributes were instead mainly negatively correlated, users were more likely to aggregate information about attributes into information about options. These preliminary results point to the need for providing assistance to users, especially when the attributes are negatively related. All of the college student subjects in Fasolo & McClelland's study were, of course, familiar with aggregating numbers by adding or averaging. What they were (and Web users are) unfamiliar with, we believe, is how to produce numbers that can be aggregated and used appropriately in making the right choice.

Can We Improve Compensatory Decision Sites Further?

We are impressed with the decision technology available on the Web. Compensatory DS are quite appealing decision-analysis tools and improve every day. (Noncompensatory tools seem to us to be about as good as they will get. The way to improve these tools is to turn them into compensatory tools.) The problem is, however, that compensatory tools are hard to use and are often time consuming.

We have some very minor suggestions for DS designers who want to improve compensatory sites.

Suggestion 1: Check For and Remove Dominated Options   We discussed above techniques for winnowing that depend on human judgment. However, one formally appropriate method of reducing the size of the option set has not been used in any DS with which we are familiar. Option A dominates option B if it is at least as good as option B on every attribute and definitely better on at least one attribute. Because a DM, confronted with a choice set including both options A and B, should never choose B, should not it be eliminated from the choice set?

The technically correct answer is yes. A guess is that DS designers might prefer not to implement that answer. The fact that an option available on the market disappears from the winnowed choice set for all site users is easy to discover and constitutes unfortunate advertising for that option—and for its seller. Such dominance does not depend on weights and depends only on the ordinal properties of scores. A site that specifies attributes and their ordinal properties in the process, as most do, also specifies dominance. Few DS can afford to adopt unpopular processing rules such as "B is inherently inferior to A, therefore remove it."

Still, dominance is an important and uncontroversial decision rule. Checking for it (not a trivial task!) can be automated. Elimination of all dominated options is a sensible first step in winnowing. For some contexts dominance may exist or not, depending on, for example, the direction of preference on an attribute. An apartment dweller who wants a dog as a companion but wants to keep his rug reasonably free of dog hair may prefer less shagginess to more. A shepherd shopping for a dog to work outside in all kinds of inclement weather may have the reverse preference. Clearly, in such contexts option A may dominate option B for one DM and option B may dominate option A for another. Automated dominance checkers would be useful in such contexts. To have an option removed because another dominates it should not be so disturbing to the loser in such a context.

Suggestion 2: Use Rank (Preferably Rank Order Centroid) Weights   Weight assessment is perhaps the most difficult judgmental task required for MAU measurement. However, the rank ordering of attribute weights is quite easy to elicit. Simply ask the DM to imagine an option that scores at least 10 points below the maximum on all attributes, and then to order the attributes according to their rank by asking the following questions: Which attribute score would you most prefer to increase by 10 points? Which next? Which after that? Formally, that does it. Informally, it is a good idea to make sure that DMs are not concerned about strengthening the strongest (or the weakest) attribute first. A set of ranks can easily be converted into weights in any of a number of ways (see Edwards & Barron 1994 for details and for a full presentation of one such conversion, rank order centroid weights, which have some particularly attractive properties as approximations to swing weights).

So far as we know, no DS has yet discovered any version of rank weights.

Suggestion 3: Use Sensitivity Analysis Tools   Sensitivity analyses, standard elements of well-done decision analyses, can be used for a variety of purposes:

1. To determine whether an option is a big winner or whether it was almost tied with one or more others. One likes to think of any winner as having won decisively by a large margin. However, quite often the differences in attractiveness between, say, five quite different options may be so small that any one of them could have won.

2. To identify the sensitive judgments or measurements—the ones that should be revisited carefully if the DM is uncertain whether or not to accept the final choice.

3. To understand the final choice—especially the attributes on which the final choice depended. For instance, we might wonder what role ethnicity played in our city decision (Example 1). What if we cared much more/less about it?

4. To explore individual differences in preferences.

There are almost as many different ways of doing and presenting the result of a sensitivity analysis as there are sensitivity analysts. It seems likely that, as DS designers come to use such tools, a new generation of tools that are tailor-made for Web applications will emerge. At the moment, a few DS display hints of sensitivity analysis tools (e.g. Frictionless.com).

HOW TO ELICIT IMPORTANT PROBABILITIES
FROM EXPERTS

Probabilities, and related quantities such as odds, are far less important than single-dimension utilities, but they are more often elicited and are more controversial. The formal mathematical rules of probability theory constrain probabilities more than their equivalents in utility theory constrain values. For example, probabilities must lie between 0 and 1, and the sum of the probabilities of an exhaustive set (a list of events of which one and only one must happen) must be 1. Probabilities are more often elicited because the probability scale is universally used by scientists to measure uncertainty, whereas the most common value measure, money, is often objectively known.

The Bayesian view of probability denies the possibility of an objective, non-judgmental scale that measures uncertainty. Many important and useful probabilities are obtainable only by means of judgments about which experts can easily disagree. The following example illustrates this point.

In 1989, the US Nuclear Regulatory Commission (1989) published NUREG 1150, intended to be the definitive analysis of the safety of US nuclear reactors. Unfortunately, the study was quickly and severely criticized for not following state-of-the-art expert elicitation techniques, among other things (Keeney & von Winterfeldt 1991, p. 191). The Nuclear Regulatory Commission decided to fund a re-elicitation of crucial probabilities in NUREG 1150. Keeney & von Winterfeldt (1991) report the process used; they designed the study in collaboration with S Hora.

The crux of the process used in the re-elicitation consisted of a disciplined and consistent use of seven successive steps:

1. Identification and selection of the experts;
2. Training in probability judgments;
3. Presentation and discussion of the uncertain events and quantities;
4. Analysis and data collection;
5. Presentation and discussion of the results of step 4;
6. Elicitation;
7. Analysis, aggregation, and documentation.

Experts were chosen for diversity as well as expertise. For each issue, the study tried to have three experts, chosen from differing contexts. Steps 2 and 3, conducted in face-to-face meetings, included quite a lot of didactic training, not only on how probabilities should be elicited, but also on the kinds of errors (e.g. overconfidence) to be found in the research literature.

Step 4 was the second day of the first meeting. The goal was to help the experts become sufficiently familiar both with probability assessment as a process and with the specifics of the contexts at hand so that they could proceed without further help from the study staff. Experts conducted their own analyses, computer runs, literature reviews, and other data collection efforts that they regarded as relevant to their problem. This took 2–3 months.

Steps 5 and 6 occurred at another face-to-face meeting. Experts first presented and discussed (with project staff and with one another) their own analyses and judgments. After that, each expert was separately elicited by a project staff member. These sessions, typically lasting 1–3 hours, required each expert to provide an organized, coherent way of decomposing the uncertain event, assessing probabilities for the pieces, and then putting the pieces together to calculate the final probability of interest.

The product was a set of cumulative probability distributions for all of the sequences of events that could lead to catastrophic failure of containment at each of five nuclear power plants. This product was expected to be, and was, different for each expert. Results were combined across experts in such a way as to preserve the underlying differences of opinion, thus leading to quite broad cumulative distributions.

This study is an example of a sophisticated probabilistic risk assessment. Such assessments permit decision and action in contexts in which expert disagreements about the probabilities of uncertain events are large and inevitable. At present, this study is state-of-the-art with respect to probability elicitation. Other decision technologists would disagree about details of the procedures (see e.g. Phillips 1999 and other references cited therein). The most lively disagreements are not about procedures for elicitation, but rather about what to do when several sources, all expert by whatever criteria the study is using, nevertheless produce numbers or functions that differ from one another in substantial ways. Options include: (*a*) pick one expert, (*b*) average functions or parameters across experts, (*c*) discuss and then re-elicit, or (*d*) elicit a single agreed-on estimate from the experts working together as a face-to-face group. Neither theory nor experimentation nor extensive experience (e.g. in the National Oceanic and Atmospheric Administration, which produces probabilistic weather forecasts every day) has given us unambiguous guidance about what to do when experts disagree about probabilities.

BAYES NETS AND INFLUENCE DIAGRAMS

Anything said that bears on the calculation or use of a SEU can be said in a straightforward and unambiguous manner in the language of mathematics. Symbols such as $+$, $-$, Σ, and even $\prod$ refer to well-defined and explicit sets of operations; equally, symbols like x_i and y_j clearly specify quantities on which these operations are to be performed. The language of mathematics, although clear, is extremely condensed and is silent about sequencing of operations. Such sequencing and stashing is the essence of what computers and computer programs do.

Computer scientists have developed graphic languages for tasks for which the procedural requirements are quite complex. Bayes nets (BNs) and influence

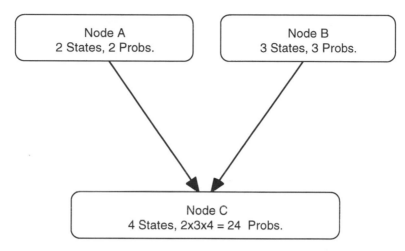

Figure 2   A very simple Bayes net.

diagrams (IDs) are examples of graphical languages for judgmental and decision-making tasks.

BNs are judgmental devices for performing applications of Bayes' theorem (to finite sets of data only) that can respect and work with very complicated probabilistic linkages among the data. Figure 2 contains an example. A BN is composed of chance nodes, linked with other nodes by arcs. These arcs are directed: the arc runs from a parent node to a child node. Which of its states a parent node is in is not affected by which states its children are in. But the probability of each of the states that a child node can be in depends on the Cartesian product of the current states of all of its parent nodes. Each chance node can be thought of as a four-level structure. The topmost layer contains the node name and the identities of its parents, if any. The second layer contains the names of the different states in which the node can exist (that is, the possible outcomes of the uncertain event that the node represents). The third layer contains conditional probability tables. If the node has no parents, it contains a table that shows the probability that the node will be in each of its possible states. If the node has one or more parents, the third layer has a table of probabilities for each element of the Cartesian product of the possible states of all its parent nodes. In Figure 2, for example, node C contains six ($= 2 \times 3$) conditional probability tables, each containing four probabilities that total to 1–24 probabilities in all. The fourth layer of each chance node, inaccessible to users, contains the computational machinery that makes the BN work. A BN can also contain deterministic nodes, in which housekeeping arithmetic such as conversion of units of measurement is performed.

An ID can be thought of as a BN with decision-making capabilities added. In addition to the chance nodes, an ID contains one or more "decision nodes." One decision node represents the options available to a DM with respect to his or her ultimate decision. Other decision nodes, if present, represent what might be called incidental decisions (e.g. decisions about whether or not to buy information before making the ultimate decision). An ID also contains exactly one value node, which links the values the DM wishes to maximize to the options. An ID, like a BN, can also contain deterministic nodes.

Computer programs that implement these ideas are now readily available. They run on personal computers and can accommodate problems of considerable complexity. Some such computer programs are available to students at little or no cost; such student programs may have restrictions that affect usability, but they are excellent tools for hands-on learning. A particularly attractive example is the program called Netica. Much more complex and harder to use, as well as more expensive, is one called DPL. However, DPL exploits a very important property of ID. Every ID is equivalent to a traditional decision tree. One can enter either the ID or the decision tree into DPL, push a button, and DPL will display the equivalent other representation. This can be very useful, especially to individuals who have been trained on decision trees and who now wish to learn how to represent decision problems as ID. No program now available combines ID with an explicit representation of MAU.

Learning the technology of BN and ID is not easy. Most students trying to learn how to work with BN and ID do so by reading articles, obtaining appropriate free software via the Web, and then spending day after day representing problems, ranging from the simple to the complex. It is time consuming, but very much worth it. One textbook is available (Jensen 1996). It deals with these technically demanding topics in a technically demanding way. Other textbooks are now in preparation.

Neither BN nor ID contains or represents anything intellectually new or different from the two normative rules (Bayes and Max SEU) discussed above. Nonetheless, in our opinion they represent one of the most important new developments in decision technology in the last 30 years. Why?

BN and ID provide convenient graphical forms in which to represent inference and decision problems of great complexity. For example, the BN with which we are most familiar, Hailfinder (see Edwards 1998), has 56 nodes and requires judgmental assessment of over 3700 highly conditional probabilities. Real inference and decision problems can be and sometimes are considerably more complicated (requiring more nodes and more probabilities) than that. Indeed, the advantages of BN and ID to their users do not begin to be apparent until a problem grows sufficiently complex that it becomes difficult or impossible to think about in more conventional mathematical notation.

One feature of BN that we consider especially useful is that BNs naturally break into reusable fragments. We speculate that in contexts in which use of a BN will become routine, such as intelligence analysis and medical diagnosis, they will come to be constructed, not out of single nodes, but out of multinode fragments. Systematic collection and use of data to support and improve performance of each fragment can then be a background activity that supports use of the fragments in a new BN appropriate to new problems.

The record keeping that characterizes most businesses and governments means that enormous amounts of little-used data, typically well enough organized to be searched by computer, is available on almost any topic imaginable. The technology of BN permits what is called data mining—an automated search through vast databases for useful probabilistic linkages (see Heckerman 1995 for a review). One context in which decision technologists at Microsoft Corporation have extensively applied such tools is in the management of telephone inquiries to Help Desks. Breese & Heckerman (1999) have reported on the results of such mining. They rediscovered a long-known principle concerning trial replacements of defective parts and extended it in various ways that look to be very useful in the design of Help-Desk systems.

CONCLUSIONS

The ubiquity of personal computers and the increasing access to the World Wide Web provide greater availability of decision technology for all levels of problems. Even 10 years ago, sophisticated decision analysis would have required an expensive consultant. Now, on-line decision aids and personal computer programs are making inexpensive, yet sophisticated, decision technology available to everyone. However, much work remains to be done to make these tools more theoretically sound and more responsive to decision makers' needs.

Visit the Annual Reviews home page at www.AnnualReviews.org

LITERATURE CITED

Becker GM, McClintock CG. 1967. Value: behavioral decision theory. *Annu. Rev. Psychol.* 18:239–86

Breese JS, Heckerman D. 1999. Decision theoretic troubleshooting: a framework for repair and experiment. See Shanteau et al 1999, pp. 271–87

Edwards W. 1961. Behavioral decision theory. *Annu. Rev. Psychol.* 12:473–98

Edwards W. 1998. Hailfinder: tools for and experiences with Bayesian normative modeling. *Am. Psychol.* 53:416–28

Edwards W, Barron FH. 1994. SMARTS and SMARTER: improved simple methods for multiattribute utility measurement. *Organ. Behav. Hum. Decis. Process.* 60:306–25

Einhorn HJ, Hogarth RM. 1981. Behavioral decision theory: processes of judgment and choice. *Annu. Rev. Psychol.* 32:53–88

Fasolo B, McClelland GH. 1999. *Tracing decision processes on the Web.* Presented at Annu. Meet. Soc. Judgm. Decis. Mak., Los Angeles

Gigerenzer G, Todd PM, the ABC Res. Group. 1999. *Simple Heuristics That Make Us Smart.* New York: Oxford Univ. Press

Heckerman D. 1995. *A Tutorial on Learning Bayesian Networks. Tech. Rep. MSR-TR-95-06*, Microsoft Corp., Redmond, WA

Jensen FV. 1996. *An Introduction to Bayesian Networks.* New York: Springer-Verlag

Keeney RL. 1992. *Value-Focused Thinking.* Cambridge, MA: Harvard Univ. Press

Keeney RL, Raiffa H. 1976. *Decisions with Multiple Objectives.* New York: Wiley & Sons

Keeney RL, von Winterfeldt D. 1991. Eliciting probabilities from experts in complex technical problems. *Trans. Eng. Manage.* 38:191–201

Lopes LL. 1994. Psychology and economics: perspectives on risk, cooperation and the marketplace. *Annu. Rev. Psychol.* 45:197–227

Mellers BA, Schwartz A, Cooke ADJ. 1998. Judgment and decision-making. *Annu. Rev. Psychol.* 49:447–77

Morkes J, Nielsen J. 1997. *Concise, SCANNABLE and Objective: How to Write for the Web.* http:/www.useit.com/alertbox/9710a.html

Nucl. Regul. Comm. 1989. *Severe Accident Risks: An Assessment of Five U. S. Nuclear Power Plants. Summ. Rep. NUREG 1150,* Nucl. Regul. Comm., Washington, DC

Payne JW, Bettman JR, Johnson EJ. 1992. Behavioral decision research: a constructive processing perspective. *Annu. Rev. Psychol.* 43:87–131

Payne JW, Bettman JR, Johnson EJ. 1993. *The Adaptive Decision Maker.* Cambridge, UK: Cambridge Univ. Press

Phillips LD. 1999. Group elicitation of probability distributions: Are many heads better than one? See Shanteau et al. 1999, pp. 313–30

Pitz GF, Sachs NJ. 1984. Judgment and decision: theory and application. *Annu. Rev. Psychol.* 35:139–63

Raiffa H. 1968. *Decision Analysis.* Reading, MA: Addison-Wesley

Rapoport A, Wallsten TS. 1972. Individual decision behavior. *Annu. Rev. Psychol.* 23:131–76

Shanteau J, Mellers BA, Schum DA, eds. 1999. *Decision Science and Technology: Reflections on the Contributions of Ward Edwards.* Boston, MA: Kluwer Acad.

Slovic P, Fischhoff B, Lichtenstein S. 1977. Behavioral decision theory. *Annu. Rev. Psychol.* 28:1–39

von Winterfeldt D, Edwards W. 1986. *Decision Analysis and Behavioral Research.* New York: Cambridge Univ. Press

Annu. Rev. Psychol. 2001. 52:607–28

EVOLUTIONARY PSYCHOLOGY: Toward a Unifying Theory and a Hybrid Science

Linnda R. Caporael

Department of Science and Technology Studies, Rensselaer Polytechnic Institute, Troy, New York 12180; e-mail: caporl@rpi.edu

Key Words social behavior, inclusive fitness theory, systems, cultural evolution, concilience, science and society

■ **Abstract** Although evolutionary psychology is typically associated with "selfish gene theory," numerous other approaches to the study of mind and behavior provide a wealth of concepts for theorizing about psychology, culture, and development. These include general evolutionary approaches and theories focused on sociality, dual inheritance, multilevel selection, and developmental systems. Most evolutionary accounts use the same methods as Darwin—the "fit among facts"—to use natural selection as an explanation for behavior. Scientific standards for constraining and evaluating such accounts, research into the mutual influence of science and society on the understanding of evolution, and computational technologies for modeling species-typical processes are important considerations. Coevolutionary theories and developmental systems theories may eventually give rise to unification in a broad and general sense. Such a unification would be interdisciplinary and problem centered rather than discipline centered.

CONTENTS

0066-4308/01/0201-0607$14.00

INTRODUCTION: What's in a Name?

Evolutionary psychology is a broad and eclectic topic. The evolutionary study of mind and behavior includes work on animal behavior (Boesch & Tomasello 1998, Heyes 1998, Waal & Lanting 1997), paleoanthropological studies of cognition (Mellars & Gibson 1996), neuropsychology (Deacon 1997, Edelman 1992), neurobehavioral genetics (Wahlsten 1999), and evolutionary theory (Depew & Weber 1996). If the fruitful alliance between cognitive science and philosophy (e.g. Bechtel 1998, Fodor 1983) is any indication, evolutionary psychology would also include the theoretical and conceptual contributions of philosophers of biology (e.g. Callebaut 1993, Sober 1994, Wimsatt 1980).

Recently, the term evolutionary psychology has become associated with a specific interpretation of evolution represented, for example, by the work of Buss (1999a), Symons (1979, 1992), and Tooby & Cosmides (1992), which is based on influential sociobiological theories from the 1970s (EO Wilson 1975). Sociobiology and evolutionary psychology are based on inclusive fitness theory and the "selfish gene." As this perspective is but one of many, the term evolutionary psychology is used here to accommodate a variety of theoretical approaches and research traditions from animal studies to neurobehavioral genetics. The term inclusive fitness evolutionary psychology is used to refer to studies of human nature drawing from the sociobiological tradition (see Jones 1999 for a review). This article focuses primarily on human social behavior and takes inclusive fitness evolutionary psychology as a starting point to discuss a common aim among evolutionary psychologists: the search for a unifying theory of behavior. It concludes that such a theory would be broadly conceived and include culture and development in its portfolio. Evolutionary psychology by necessity is an interdisciplinary hybrid science informed by a postmodern reflexivity; that is, a keen awareness of the ongoing interchanges between science and society.

INCLUSIVE FITNESS EVOLUTIONARY PSYCHOLOGY

Theory and Research

Theoretical population biologists define evolution as changes in population gene frequencies. The primary factors of interest are genes and their transmission generation-to-generation. Environment and development are secondary factors, subsumed in coefficients of selection, which with various population parameters are manipulated in mathematical models. The dependent variables in such models are changes in frequencies (or fitness, loosely speaking) of alternative alleles (versions of a gene, e.g. "altruistic" or "selfish" alleles). Hamilton (1964) showed that the average fitness of a gene could be influenced by interactions among organisms. In particular, benefiting kin, even at the cost of individual reproduction, could cause the increase of altruistic genes because related individuals share genes. The inclusive fitness of a gene refers to the number of copies of it passed on to the next generation by an individual plus the number of genes passed on by relatives as a result of behavior toward them. Trivers (1971, 1972, 1974) built on Hamilton's insight, showing how other types of social interactions such as reciprocal altruism, parent-offspring and sibling conflict, sexual selection, and parental investment could influence changes in gene frequencies. Hamilton's and Trivers' work, widely disseminated by EO Wilson (1975) and Dawkins (1976), became the foundation for sociobiology and introduced the "gene's eye view" of quantitative population biology to the human sciences. The gene's eye view is an anthropomorphic metaphor or heuristic device: What decisions would a gene make to facilitate its survival and reproduction (Buss 1999a)?

Cosmides & Tooby (1987) adapted sociobiology, arguing that evolved psychological mechanisms were the missing links between inclusive fitness theory and the evolutionary analysis of behavior. These views were elaborated by Tooby & Cosmides (1992), who also emphasized the designed features of evolved psychological mechanisms or modules and the environment of evolutionary adaptedness (Bowlby 1969) in which such mechanisms evolved. Buss (1995) organized the foundation work on inclusive fitness into a level-of-analysis framework, in which he equates Hamilton's (1964) inclusive fitness theory with "general evolutionary theory." Trivers' work (1971, 1972, 1974) is identified as middle-level or motivating theories, which provide the basis for general hypotheses and specific predictions about behavior.

Inclusive fitness evolutionary psychologists have conducted research on a range of topics (Crawford & Krebs 1998; see also Crawford et al 1987, Simpson & Kenrick 1997). These include mating preferences (Buss & Schmitt 1993, Buss 1990), rape (Thornhill & Palmer 2000), Judaism as an evolutionary group strategy (MacDonald 1994), cheater detection mechanisms (Cosmides 1989), mind (Pinker 1997), "killer sperm" (Baker & Bellis 1995), female inhibition mechanisms (Bjorklund & Kipp 1996), judgments of attractiveness (Singh 1993), and effects of family on pubertal timing (Ellis et al 1999). Inclusive fitness evolutionary psychologists have been charged with proposing untestable hypotheses (Kenrick 1995), but in fact, several hypotheses have been disconfirmed. For example, there is no evidence of human killer sperm (Moore et al 1999); hip-to-waist ratio judgments of attractiveness have been shown to be artifacts of a limited range of stimuli (Tassinary & Hansen 1998), and judgments of attractiveness do not predict health status (Kalick et al 1998).

Alternative explanations have been proposed for other findings. For example, Miller & Fishkin (1997) argue that large mean differences in number of desired mates reported by Buss & Schmitt (1993) were an artifact of highly skewed data (i.e. a few outliers desiring a large number of mates). Using median measures, Miller & Fishkin (1997) found that both men and women reported wanting a relatively small number of long-term partnerships. Sex differences predicted for males by Buss and Schmitt, such as jealousy and desiring a large number of partners, were reported by anxious-ambivalent males as predicted by attachment fertility theory. Eagly & Wood (1999), in a reanalysis of data reported in Buss et al (1990), correlated social structural conditions with mate preferences. They found that males' preference for younger females and a good cook and housekeeper (found to be significant sex differences in the original study) and females' preference for older males with good earning potential was associated with gender equality as provided by United Nations indices. Differences in preferences were greatest in cultures with the least gender equality. These results indicate that social structural variables can account for sex differences in mating preferences.

Limitations: Psychological Mechanisms or Interpretive Lens

Inclusive fitness evolutionary psychology has produced large numbers of empirical studies; however, there are concerns about their relationship to evolutionary theory and what they actually contribute to psychological understanding (Lloyd 1999, Smith 2000). The scientific critiques of sociobiology are well known, extensive, and apply directly to evolutionary psychology (Gould & Lewontin 1979, Kitcher 1985, Lloyd 1999, Rose & Rose 2000; see also Commentary on Buss 1995). These concern the inability to demonstrate a correlation between phenotypic variation and reproductive variation (a *sine qua non* for evolutionary biology research), the difficulty of identifying a history of adaptation, and the lack of detail (analogous to the detail available for artificial selection in plants and animals) that would enable understanding of possible sources of variation. Without a theoretical vocabulary for development and culture, genetic determinism is an almost inevitable consequence of inclusive fitness theory.

For example, the most common concept of gene-environment interaction requires that all possible phenotypic possibilities be preformed in the genes, to be triggered by appropriate environmental stimuli. The environment fills in gaps in "open programs," "shapes" innate proclivities, or "shunts" behavior from one option to another (e.g. Buss 1999b, Crawford & Anderson 1989, Tooby & Cosmides 1992). Genetic determinism is also part of inclusive fitness evolutionary psychology's cultural theory, which assumes that cultural differences are "evoked" from a panhuman genome. Different environmental conditions shared within groups evoke the same individual psychological mechanisms differentially across groups (Buss 1999a). Thus, interaction in inclusive fitness evolutionary psychology usually refers to selection among pre-existing genetic possibilities, all of which are coded in all humans (the panhuman genome). An alternative view sees gene-environment interaction as chains of contingent events composed of reciprocal influences at multiple levels of organization, including genes and various features of the environment (Gottlieb 1992, Wimsatt 1999).

Many constructs in inclusive fitness evolutionary psychology present challenges to the boundaries between culture and science (Caporael & Brewer 1991, Maynard Smith 1987; cf Buss 1994). For example, kinship, neighborliness, divorce, and sibling rivalry are familiar features of everyday life. It is not clear in the absence of genetic data that theories of inclusive fitness, reciprocal altruism, parental investment, and parent-offspring conflict explain their corresponding everyday categories or redescribe them. Other topics parallel old and familiar aphorisms: women as gold diggers and men sowing their wild oats (Buss 1987) or the madonna-whore dichotomy (Gangestad & Simpson 1990). Thiessen (1996) argues that everyday life makes sense when viewed through an evolutionary lens. However, it can be just as well argued that selfish gene theory was created in the image of common beliefs about everyday life (Caporael 1994). The influence of culture on theory, problem choice, methods, and interpretation is a scientific issue—not a political or ideological one. First, science is a human practice well worth understanding, and second, to the extent that culture holds science on a leash (e.g. through media attention, needs to appeal to mass markets, and funding opportunities), traditional canons of scientific objectivity can be undermined.

Although evolutionary theory, broadly conceived, still holds promise for the study of mind and behavior, it seems likely that inclusive fitness theory is too narrow to serve a unifying theoretical role. The heuristic device of a selfish gene may have simplified the work of theoretical population biologists (Dawkins 1976). However, imbuing genes with fictional psychological characteristics (e.g. preferences, intentionality, agency) eliminated the complexities of development and environment, including social interaction and culture. These complexities are recognized to be important by evolutionary biologists (Endler 1986) and central to the concerns of psychologists generally.

OTHER EVOLUTIONARY PSYCHOLOGIES

This section illustrates some approaches to evolutionary psychology at other levels of analysis than that offered by inclusive fitness evolutionary psychology. These other approaches also focus more on culture or development. The categorization below is neither mutually exclusive nor the only one possible.

General Selection Theories

Natural selection is a powerful general principle in the world of living things. What makes a theory "evolutionary" or "Darwinian" is not that it is based in biology, but rather the integration of three interacting principles of change: variation, selection and retention. What varies, what are the conditions for selection, and what are the mechanisms for retention may differ: neuronal selection, selection in the immune system, and learning are all examples of selection (Cziko 1995). Cultural artifacts, practices, and even scientific theories may be selected (Campbell 1997). Most evolutionary psychologies can be classified as general selection theories in at least a minimal sense of invoking natural selection to explain change over time. They may take the form of a unifying theory of the evolution of mind and behavior, or they may focus on a specific feature. Implicitly, there is at least one alternative variant (the absence of the focal trait), and an account is derived showing how the focal trait could have been an adaptive advantage.

Donald (1991) is a fine example of the unifying theory approach. He proposes three major phases in the evolution of human cognition. The first is *episodic culture*, where memory is dependent on environmental cues; second is *mimetic culture*, which enabled using the body for representation and memory, and the third is *mythic culture*, where lexical invention becomes the basis for language and narrative. Donald (1991) argues that a fourth phase, based on the external symbolic storage and symbol manipulation as in print and computers, is beginning. Examples of special-focus theories address the evolution of landscape preferences (Orians & Heerwagen 1992), egalitarianism, (Boehm 2000), and handedness (Corballis 1997). Studies on the evolution of language (Bickerton 1990, Deacon 1997, Pinker 1997) illustrate just how diverse special-focus theories can be.

Following Darwin (1965), ethologists traced the evolution of a trait such as smiling through its primate antecedents, developmental sequence, cross-cultural communicative competence and cultural specific contexts in which smiling could take on different meanings (Eibl-Eibesfeldt 1971, 1989). The emphasis in these studies is on progression, from a simpler to a more complex expression. Recent research on emotional expression follows similar trajectories, but with greater methodological and conceptual sophistication including a more complex selection account (Ekman & Rosenberg 1997, Griffiths 1997). Research has also addressed how evolved characteristics also may be exapted for use in other contexts. (In contrast to an adaptation, defined in terms of a history of use for a particular function, an exaptation evolved for one use and is used, or exapted, for another; feathers were adaptations for thermal control and then exapted for flight.) For example, expressions of disgust have different communicative values, and through processes of development and cultural evolution, may be co-opted for use in a broader system of cultural meanings including expression of moral responses (Rozin et al 1994). As Rozin et al (1994) point out, disgust may be an excellent system for studying the connections between evolution, cultural evolution and development because the facial markers are reliably observable and communicative.

An area where more research is needed concerns artifacts in the study of mind and behavior. The earliest stone tools, associated with *Homo habilis* ("handy man"), are about 2.4 million years old, indicating that artifacts are as much a part of the evolution of human mind and behavior as group living. Tools mediate the reciprocal exchange between organisms and environment; today, satisfying the human fascination with the artifactual world threatens ecological disaster. Artifacts function in the coordination of behavior by entraining human activity and accumulating knowledge over generations (Caporael & Baron 1997, Hutchins 1996). Yet surprisingly few psychological studies focus on tools (Kipnis 1997).

An exception has been in the important area of tools and language (Calvin & Bickerton 2000, Gibson & Ingold 1993, Greenfield 1991), largely because speech and the manipulation of objects appear to share common developmental, cognitive and neural substrates.

Roughly speaking, general selection theories are the most common form of evolutionary psychology. They vary in quality from informal adaptive story-telling drawing on common knowledge to well-done theorizing unifying research results in two or more scientific areas.

Sociality Theories

Sociality theories are midway between inclusive fitness evolutionary psychology and multilevel evolutionary theories (below). They center on the evolution of "social intelligence" or "Machiavellian intelligence" (Byrne & Whiten 1988). For decades, the standard assumption has been that animal and human intelligence evolved for interacting with concrete nonsocial objects for subsistence. Social intelligence theorists (Humphrey 1976, Jolly 1966) proposed that social objects offered a different order of complexity compared to physical ones. Physical objects are more or less stable compared to conspecifics, which are much more labile and unpredictable. Consequently, the requirements for intelligence as members of group-living animals would have been much higher than what would have been required to simply find food or make tools. Machiavellian theorists, such as Byrne and Whiten (1988), married social intelligence to inclusive fitness theory. They proposed a model for an actor (human as well as non-human) with highly developed faculties to manipulate other individuals by tactical deception so as to serve the actor's inclusive-fitness interests. Apparent cooperation among individuals is interpreted as behavior in the service of genetic self-interest or an expression of competition within and between groups (Alexander 1989).

Dunbar (1993) built on the Machiavellian hypothesis in his proposition that language evolved as part of increasing group size and neocortical expansion. Maintaining and manipulating social relationships in large groups required an ability that could fulfill the same functions as social grooming, but service a larger number of relationships. Time budgets limit the number of relationships that can be serviced by grooming; however, language—and specifically gossip—allows a much larger number of relationships to be maintained as well as a corresponding increase in group size. Dunbar's hypothesis reverses a conventional wisdom. He sees language as having evolved for social relationships, and abilities for referring to objects and coordinating activities such as hunting as emerging as a by-product, or exaptation, from the social function of language.

Although Machiavellian theorists locate their origins in Humphrey (1976), his paper suggests a radically different view of human intelligence. Humphrey rejected the common view that human intelligence evolved for surviving on the savannah by developing tools. Rather, creative intellect evolved for holding society together so that subsistence skills and knowledge of the habitat could be passed on in a protective environment. Although there were benefits to group living, it posed a challenge because each individual's priority would be the survival of his own genes. Escalating within-group competition would result in a high level of social intelligence. However, this social intelligence was not just deceptive and manipulative. It was "truly social" (Caporael 1997) in the sense that "technical intelligence" was not just a different kind of intelligence, but rather an application of social intelligence to other objects. The result could be a "mistaken" proto-social exchange; that is, humans would anthropomorphize non-living systems and from these misapplications of social intelligence, scientific and technological discoveries would emerge—or cognitive limitations would be apparent (Caporael 1986, Cheney et al 1986). In other words, Humphrey proposed a "general purpose" mind, but its purpose was social transactions with conspecifics.

Sociality theories opened new possibilities for conceptions of mind and behavior although these remain insufficiently developed. Where inclusive fitness evolutionary psychology drew on a familiar model of "economic man" or exchange theory using the currency of genetic success, sociality theories suggested a framework that was neither economic nor folk psychological. Instead, they focused on the social origins of human nature and the attributes necessary for group living (Brewer 1997). Unfortunately, the idea of "selection by the group" seemed too close to group selection, which is re-emerging as part of multilevel evolutionary theory.

Multilevel Evolutionary Theories

A persistent debate among evolutionary theorists has been whether the gene was the sole level of selection or whether selection operated at multiple levels. With the publication of Leo Buss' book, *The Evolution of Individuality* (1987), scientists have begun exploring alternatives to selfish gene theory (Jablonka 1994, Maynard Smith & Szathmáry 1995). Unlike inclusive fitness theories, which identify genes as the level of selection, multievolutionary theories incorporate other levels where selection can occur (e.g. chromosomes, individuals, groups). Different levels of selection provide opportunities for conflict and synergisms between levels. For example, in the evolution of multicellularity, some cells "gave up" reproductive autonomy to become body cells as others eventually became reproducing gametes (Buss 1987). Similar conflicts and opportunities obtain for humans in the relationship between the individual and the group. Individual advantage may be curtailed at the level of the group, sometimes resulting in cooperative groups better adapted to the habitat than are other groups (Caporael et al 1989).

The question of how group structure can influence the evolution of altruistic genes has received much attention from group selection theorists (Sober & Wilson 1998, DS Wilson 1975, 1997). This interest has been driven by the observation that altruistic behavior should be self-limiting; the reproductive advantage afforded non-altruistic genes should drive out altruistic variants. In Wilson's (1983) models, subgroups ("trait groups") of a larger group vary in the proportion of altruists and non-altruists. Some groups will have low ratios of altruists to non-altruists; other groups will have high ratios. Within all the groups, the nonaltruists increase relative to the altruists. However, if groups with higher proportions of altruists also produce more offspring, then the total number of altruists in the global population will increase. In other words, within-group selection favors the evolution of self-interest whereas between-group selection favors the evolution of cooperation (because altruists benefit themselves as well as others).

Multilevel selection has always been implicit in theories incorporating culture as part of human evolution. In coevolutionary theories, genes and culture are two distinct modes of inheritance that nevertheless influence the distribution of each other (Janicki 1998). For example, lactose tolerance is believed to be a trait that has probably coevolved with dairy practices, including food-processing techniques such as cheese and yogurt manufacture, which reduce lactose concentrations and thereby increase digestibility. There are several approaches to coevolutionary theory.

Research in evolutionary ecology assumes culture is an adaptive behavioral system and actors behave "as if" they are rational decision makers with respect to a genetic currency (e.g. Smith & Winterhalder 1992). Evolutionary ecologists (once called sociobiologists, now also called "Darwinian anthropologists") do not invoke specific psychological mechanisms. They assume that behavior is fitness-maximizing and study differences in reproductive output as a result of variations in ecological and cultural factors such as marriage system, hunting prowess, or status.

Boyd and Richerson (1985) propose a dual inheritance of culture and genes. They are distinctive in their effort to bridge research in psychology with group-level cultural processes. Boyd and Richerson propose a theory of forces to describe the Darwinian evolution of cultural creatures. Some of the forces are random, analogs of genetic drift and mutation; others are the outcome of individual decision making and choice, and finally, there is natural selection of cultural variation. They do not assume the rational decision maker of neoclassical economics or of evolutionary ecology. Instead, they assume that human decision making is imperfect, and trial and-error learning expensive. One of the advantages of culture, then, is to attenuate the inherent limitations of fallible human cognition, and at the individual level, the advantage is realized through social learning—copying the behavior of other people. Boyd and Richerson provide one of the few theories about human sociality that is explicitly developmental, concerned with variations in socialization patterns (e.g., "lateral" transmission from peers or "vertical" transmission from parents).

Durham (1991) emphasizes the ideational aspects of culture, drawing on Dawkins' (1976) term, memes, for units of culture. Genes specify primary values, sensations experienced as intrinsically pleasurable or unpleasant. Memes provide "secondary values," or rules-of-thumb, scripts, or other guides to behavior. Cultural selection, guided by secondary values, is a function of choices made by individuals or groups and/or imposed by individuals or groups on others (e.g. marital forms).

Durham (1991) proposes that there are at least five modes of gene-culture interaction. In two modes, genes and culture act as the selection environment for each other. In the other three modes, secondary value selection favor cultural variants that can reduce, improve, or have no effect at all on individual reproductive fitness. By affecting the phenotype, culture influences the genotypic distribution in the population.

In contrast, Fiske's complementarity theory (2000) assumes that genes specify particular and highly structured social proclivities that become functional when combined with different features of cultural paradigms. The results are rituals, institutions, artifacts, etc that enable people to use four basic models of relationships. Fiske (1991) calls these communal sharing, authority ranking, equality matching, and market pricing. These are not strictly cognitive models; rather, they are relational models that span the public-private and external-internal dichotomies generally used to differentiate culture and cognition.

Multilevel evolutionary theories provide a conceptual embarrassment of riches, although connecting these to current scientific knowledge about human psychology is a formidable task. An important difference from selfish gene theory is the recognition that organisms shape their own niches, which in turn affect the evolution of "organism-in-system" (Levins & Lewontin 1985). Work such as that by Laland et al (2000) suggests that coevolutionary theories could eventually combine with systems approaches like those in the next section.

Systems Theories

Systems theories are a different breed of evolutionary psychology altogether (Gottlieb 1992, 1998; Griffiths & Gray 1994, Hejl et al 1997, Ho 1991, Lewontin 1982, Wimsatt 1999). The gene is not viewed as a privileged source of information containing blueprints or programs for phenotypic formation. Rather, the information emerges through the reliable recurrence of components (including the products of development itself) that in the past have produced a viable system in a specific environment (Oyama 1989, Oyama et al 2000). The concept of inheritance is also expanded to include not only genes but also items from cellular components to language environments to atmospheric constancies. Organisms are not designed to solve problems presented by an independent environment. Instead, organism and environment are coevolving and mutually defining (Brandon & Antonovics 1996, Levins & Lewontin 1985, Thelen 1992). The anthropomorphic metaphor of natural selection favoring or selecting some variants over others is de-emphasized because organism and environment are viewed as an interrelated, self-organizing system. One common metaphor for the organism, which is always undergoing development, is ecological succession: Activity at one phase alters conditions that become the basis for the next stage without any need for a priori specification. This "ontogeny of information" (Oyama 1985)—the recurrent developmental system itself–is the product and process of evolution. From the perspective of systems theorists, species-typical behavior is repeatedly constructed or emergent (rather than transmitted) in the history of the lineage, in ontogeny, and in the situated activity of organism-in-setting.

Systems approaches can be illustrated by infant walking, which is commonly considered to be a genetically programmed trait. From a more or less global view, walking demonstrates a sequence of irreversible stages that reliably recur in infants (Thelen & Smith 1994). The first stage in walking is marked by the loss, at about two months, of the coordinated steplike movements newborns make when held erect. Stepping movements appear again about nine months later, and at about one year, the final stage, intentional walking begins. But the sequence hardly seems programmed or designed when it is closely examined. For example, although newborn stepping disappears, the same kinematics and muscle activation continue when infants are in supine, prone, or sitting positions. Infants who "practice" stepping (e.g. are held on a slow-moving treadmill) retain the movement throughout the first year. Seemingly extraneous factors such as weight and arousal influence stepping. Infants who do not normally perform stepping movements may do so when they are held with their legs submerged in water.

From the closer view, the appearance of a unified and coherent progression vanishes. Thelan & Smith (1994) observed that walking is composed of multiple subcomponents such as responsiveness to backward leg-extension (which occurs when an infant is held on a treadmill), intentionality, the ability to support body weight on the legs, the ability to move the legs in alternating patterns of swing and stance, and so on. These capacities are modular: They develop over time at different rates and depend on context during the first year. The local variation is not just noise in the system; it is the process that engenders developmental change and provides the variation that potentiates evolutionary change (Slobodkin & Rapoport 1974).

Thelan & Smith's (1994) research suggests another important point. The linguistic/perceptual categories we used to describe behavior, for example, walking, mating, or parenting, are not likely to be at the level of analysis or granularity that results in natural selection. As in the case of walking, observational research indicates that human courtship initiation consists of a surprisingly consistent sequence of behavior that also suggests modular components (Perper 1985). Such findings are to be expected because evolution is a mosaic, jury-rigging process. Different features of an organism may evolve independently of others (within constraints) as products of "adaptively relevant environments" (Irons 1998). These are features of the organism-environment system with which the components making up the trait interact and contribute to reproduction and survival to reproductive age.

Caporael (1995, 1997) combines elements of multilevel selection theory and systems approaches (Caporael & Baron 1997). She suggests that the observation that psychologists attempt to explain by resorting to genes is recurrence. Rather than using genes in a metaphoric sense, she proposes a vocabulary based on the "repeated assembly" of reliably recurrent resources. Organisms, their settings, artifacts, and practices may be repeatedly assembled. The objective of evolutionary psychology would then be to understand the system dynamics that result in variation, retention, and selection of the component parts of repeated assemblies

(Caporael 1999). Taking a developmental-evolutionary approach, Caporael (1995, 1997) proposes a model of group structure with core subgroup configurations based on considerations of group size and modal tasks. For example, a dyad is a core configuration with a size of two and modal tasks that include interaction with an infant. A core configuration is an environment where certain capacities, such as finely tuned microcoordination (as used in interactional synchrony) can evolve. The other configurations are teams, demes, and macrodemes, analogous to the foraging parties, bands, and macrobands in anthropology. The basic hypothesis is that aspects of mental systems should correspond to features of modal tasks characteristic to configurations, which in turn are grounded in morphology and ecology.

Core configurations are repeatedly assembled from generation to generation, in an expanding circle of other actors during ontogeny, and in the day-to-day interaction of humans (cf Hendriks-Jansen 1996). The configurations both maintain and are maintained by cognitive specializations for small group living.

Limitations

Perhaps the greatest shortcoming of the evolutionary psychologies presented in this section is the difficulty of getting from theory to testable hypotheses. Co-evolutionary theory (Boyd & Richerson 1985) and developmental systems theory (Oyama 1985) are both over 15 years old and have yet to generate a body of research results. Conversely, one could argue that they are only 15 years old—quite a deal younger than the nature-nurture dualism inspired by Francis Galton's work in the mid-nineteenth century—and more time is needed to see what they can produce. General evolutionary theories have a longer history than multilevel evolutionary or systems theories. However, they may be too diverse in their range of topics for a research community to form around them—an advantage amply illustrated by the success of inclusive fitness evolutionary psychology in creating an identifiable group of researchers, problem areas, and journals.

WORK TO BE DONE

Concepts and Methods

Evolutionary biologists use a number of methods and have several requirements for demonstrating adaptation, almost always including measures of fitness (Boake 1994, Endler 1986). They have demonstrated natural selection for human physiological traits (e.g. sickle cell anemia), but biologists' typical methods for studying evolution (Endler 1986) do not lend themselves to research on psychological constructs. The problem is not specific to the human sciences: Various disciplines such as ecology, paleontology, and developmental biology have begun reconstructing Darwinism to accommodate their research questions and subject matter (Boucher 1985, Eldredge & Grene 1992, Kauffman 1993). Signs of such reconstruction are showing in evolutionary psychology, for example, in the notion of repeated assembly (Caporael 1999) or "virtual genes" (Dennett 1995) to indicate recurrence without making unwarranted causal assumptions.

Almost all evolutionary psychology relies on the same method Darwin used in his work, William Whewell's "consilience of inductions" (Forster & Wolfe 1999, Ruse 1989). (Whewell's consilience should not be confused with EO Wilson's 1998 use as a reduction to biology.) Darwin reasoned that whereas no single example could prove natural selection, it would be implausible to dismiss the fit among so many pieces of evidence. Experiments, archival data, animal observation, computer modeling, and narrative argument can provide a network of research findings for consilient arguments. The quality of a consilient argument depends on its plausibility given sets of constraints, which come from a variety of sources. The most familiar constraints come from existing research.

For example, hypotheses about the environment of evolutionary adaptedness are constrained by evidence from several fields. Fossils provide evidence about changes in hard tissues over time and provide the basis for inferences about diet, sexual dimorphism, and phylogenetic relationships (Johanson & Edgar 1996, Lewin 1998, Tattersall 1995). Comparative studies of primates (Boesch & Tomasello 1998, Cheney et al 1986, Cheney & Seyfarth 1990) are useful for understanding continuities and discontinuities among primate characteristics distinct from human characteristics. Ethnoarcheologists examine the material residue of modern hunter-gatherers so as to better interpret findings of ancient origins (Binford 1983), and behavioral archeologists attempt to recreate the performance characteristics of particular objects such as the wear pattern on stone tools (Schick & Toth 1994). Hunter-gatherers (Gowdy 1998) suggest a range of variation for theorizing about human evolution. Constraints are also introduced by conceptual analyses about the environment of evolutionary adaptedness (Foley 1996, Irons 1998).

Psychology, Society and Science

The evolutionary study of mind and behavior goes back to Charles Darwin and his contemporary Herbert Spencer (Richards 1987). In the twentieth century, the subject went through cycles of rejection and reprise that were influenced by the controversial politics of eugenics, the rise of behaviorism, and most recently, Nazism (Deichmann 1996). Although references to evolution continued in animal and infant research, a "tacit consensus" (Kaye 1986) against biological explanation of the adult human mind led to a hiatus in human evolutionary studies, which was broken only in the past 25 years. Nevertheless, the application of evolutionary theory to human behavior continues to be criticized on conceptual grounds for foreclosing or "sewing up" research on the human mind (Smith 2000) or for ideological implications not justified by the science (Lewontin et al 1984). These criticisms are significant for scientific practice.

In the human sciences, scientists are both subjects who study and objects being studied, which can complicate evolutionary psychological research. These complications could also be considered constraints against which scenarios and hypotheses require testing. For example, evolutionary theorizing should be tempered by current psychological research on heuristics and biases, including resemblance, confirmatory biases, theory-driven data perception, overconfidence in judgment, and the relationship between the amount of detail in scenarios and their believability (cf Caporael et al 1989, Kahneman et al 1982). Conceptual history is another source of constraints because new ideas do not pre-exist; they emerge from their predecessors. Anthropologists have been more circumspect in their constructions of the evolutionary past since Landau (1984, 1991) demonstrated that many of their reconstructions had the narrative structure of hero-myths. Similarly, certain aspects of selfish gene theory share a conceptual deep structure with religion: Like the soul, the immortal genes are the essence of the individual, whereas the body, vessel of the soul or vehicle of the genes, is transitory and ephemeral (Caporael 1994; cf Dawkins 1976). Certain conventions used in reconstructions (Kuper 1988, Landau 1991), such as projection from the present to the past and narrative conventions, should also be considered as constraints contributing to the evaluation of scenarios.

Evolutionary psychology is vulnerable to a number of meta-scientific influences from the political, social, and psychological contexts of science (Brewer & Caporael 1990, Caporael & Brewer 1991). Increasingly, researchers are studying the exchange between science and its context. For example, Weingart et al (1997) concluded that evolutionary psychologists influence and are influenced by the ideological contexts of their work, although the direction of influences vary. More study is needed to understand how these mutual influences operate for three reasons. First, they need to be understood and treated as any confounding variable in the design and interpretation of research. Second, such "confounds" are scientifically interesting as data in the study of mind and associated ecologies of knowledge (Star 1995) and evolutionary epistemology (Campbell 1988). Third, such work may play an important role in understanding and improving theory construction. For example, deconstructing metaphors of "transmission" and "construction" imply two theoretically different notions of heritability in evolutionary psychology.

TOWARD A UNIFYING THEORY AND A HYBRID SCIENCE

Why Do We Want a Unifying Theory and What Would It Look Like?

The appeal of evolutionary theory is its potential to serve as a unifying theory in the human sciences (Alexander 1975, Buss 1999a), although there are numerous reasons to be pessimistic about this goal (Dupré 1993, Rosenberg 1994). Human cognition may impose a limit on understanding the complexity of the natural world; the natural world may be far more random and disordered than scientists expect it to be, and/or the linguistic conventions for describing the world at any particular level of analysis cannot be mapped onto other levels. Nevertheless, there are many ways to have a unifying theory, aside from the usual convention of reduction to lower and lower levels, passing through culture, to psychology, to genes (Wilson 1998).

Thirty years ago, Campbell (1969) proposed replacing the disciplinary tribal model of science with a fish-scale model of omniscience. Instead of disciplines aggregating as clusters of specialties, they would be distributed in overlapping areas, much as the scales of a fish overlap. (The chapter by Weingart et al 1997 is the product of one such effort.) There are several forces that erode such attempts, including institutional and disciplinary structures that operate against an interdisciplinary field and promote ingroup-outgroup competition. However, other forces do promote a fish-scale-type of unification. Consilience as a research method imposes interdependence among scholars because constraints on theorizing come from other disciplines. For example, hypotheses about male jealousy as a universal adaptation (Buss 1999a) or reconstructions assuming that prehistoric women engaging in extramarital affairs suffered murder, physical abuse, or abandonment (Bjorklund & Kipp 1996) are constrained by anthropological research such as that in cultures where children are believed to made from the accumulation of semen and several men can share in their paternity (Beckerman et al 1998, Conklin & Morgan 1996). Unifying overlap would be produced by a problem-centered rather than disciplinary-centered overlap. Excellent examples include work on the study of language and artifacts (Gibson & Ingold 1993) and comparative female life histories (Morbeck et al 1997).

New Methodologies Such as Complex Adaptive Systems Research, Artificial Life, Simulations, and Situated Robotics

Most research concerned with human evolution concerns phenomena described at the perceptual/linguistic level. This level of analysis is easily communicable and makes possible cross-species and cross-cultural comparisons. However, it does not stand up well to close observation. As in the example of walking, early ethologists found that a purportedly evolved behavior like "parenting" in ducks breaks down into a number of distinct activities. The only common element is that they are centered on the duckling through the changing interactions between it and the mother duck. Information technology may represent new avenues for understanding the dynamic interactions between the micro- and macro-processes in development and evolution. Computer simulations have a relatively long history in understanding topics such as cooperation and are becoming increasingly sophisticated (Harms 1999). Advances in computation technologies have opened new possibilities by creating artificial models of living systems (Flake 1998). One of the most ambitious attempts to make these methods relevant for understanding human evolution is by Hendriks-Jansen (1996), who develops his arguments from ethology, developmental psychology, and artificial life research. Hendriks-Jansen observes that species-typical activity patterns arise through interactive emergence in three different senses: They emerge through an evolutionary history of selection, through developmental processes, and through the execution of low-level activities in interaction with a species-typical environment. Hendriks-Jansen claims that robotic models can be used as existence proofs to confirm hypotheses about emergent interaction. For example, Maja Mataric (1992, cited in Hendriks-Jansen 1996) has created a robot that follows walls as if it had representations of landmarks and maps. However, there are no programs for wall-following; it is an emergent activity of some simple "reflexes" (e.g. STROLL, AVOID) and sensors in interaction with a stable environment. If the robot were an evolved creature, the evidence that wall-following was a stable component of its evolutionary history would come from the landmark detectors and maps. These are crucially dependent on the lower-level structured organism-in-setting that enables the situated activity of wall-following; if the structured activity was disrupted, the detectors and maps would fail.

Computational approaches and artificial models have a long way to go in proving themselves for understanding the evolution of mind and behavior. The most immediate problem is oversimplification. Nevertheless, they can suggest new concepts, and among the most important of these are notions of iteration, replication, recursion, and repeated assembly.

CONCLUSION: Interdisciplinarity and Reflexivity

It has been almost 150 years since Darwin published his theory of natural selection. It has been hotly debated in public life as few scientific theories have ever been. It has influenced the lives of millions of people, yet with little scientific understanding of how that influence occurs. The future of evolutionary psychology requires problem-centered, interdisciplinary research, both to solve problems within the discipline and to negotiate the boundaries of practice where subject and object and science and society are unavoidably intertwined.

This article suggests a continuum between what evolutionary psychology is and what it could become. At one extreme is inclusive fitness evolutionary psychology, which attempts to show how patterns of everyday life can be explained by adaptations to life in the past. Closer to the center are general selection and coevolutionary theories that rely on consilient methodology and interdisciplinary research. At the other extreme are systems theories that involve humans and robots and are struggling to find the levels of analysis and the language to ground a theory of mind and action in natural selection. It would be fair to say that the current state of evolutionary psychology is a working out of possible theories, languages, concepts, and methods. The evolutionary study of mind and behavior has more of the appearance of an adaptive radiation of species after the appearance of a major evolutionary novelty than it does the unifying look of a theory after all its competitors have become extinct. For those who hoped for a quick unification of the social sciences, some consolation can be taken from the Copernican Revolution; it took 150 years for people to believe that the sun, and not the earth, was the center of the universe. It should be no surprise if it takes that long for the Darwinian Revolution.

Visit the Annual Reviews home page at www.AnnualReviews.org

LITERATURE CITED

Alexander RD. 1989. Evolution of the human psyche. In *The Human Revolution*, ed. P Mellars, C Stringer, pp. 455–513. Princeton: Princeton University Press

Alexander RD. 1975. The search for a general theory of behavior. *Behav. Sci.* 20:77–100

Baker RR, Bellis MA. 1995. *Human Sperm Competition*. London: Chapman & Hall

Barkow JH, Cosmides L, Tooby J, eds. 1992. *The Adapted Mind*. New York: Oxford Univ. Press

Bechtel W. 1998. Representations and cognitive explanations: assessing the dynamicist challenge in cognitive science. *Cogn. Sci.* 22:295–318

Beckerman S, Lizarralde R, Ballew C, Schroeder S, Fingelton C, et al. 1998. The Bari partible paternity project: preliminary results. *Curr. Anthropol.* 39:164–67

Bickerton D. 1990. *Language and Species*. Chicago: Univ. Chicago Press

Binford LR. 1983. *In Pursuit of the Past*. New York: Thames & Hudson

Bjorklund DF, Kipp K. 1996. Parental investment theory and gender differences in the evolution of inhibition mechanisms. *Psychol. Bull.* 120:163–88

Boake CRB, ed. 1994. *Quantitative Genetic Studies of Behavioral Evolution*. Chicago: Univ. Chicago Press

Boehm C. 2000. *Hierarchy in the Forest: The Evolution of Egalitarian Behavior*. Cambridge, MA: Harvard University Press

Boesch C, Tomasello M. 1998. Chimpanzees and human culture. *Curr. Anthropol.* 39: 591–614

Boucher DH. 1985. The idea of mutualism, past and future. In *The Biology of Mutualism*, ed. DH Boucher, pp. 1–28. New York: Oxford Univ. Press

Bowlby J. 1969. *Attachment and Loss*, Vols. 1–2. New York: Basic Books

Boyd R, Richerson PJ. 1985. *Culture and the Evolutionary Process*. Chicago: Univ. Chicago Press

Brandon R, Antonovics J. 1996. The coevolution of organism and environment. In *Concepts and Methods in Evolutionary Biology*, ed. R Brandon. New York: Cambridge Univ. Press

Brewer MB. 1997. On the social origins of human nature. In *The Message of Social Psychology*, ed. C McGarty, A Haslam, pp. 54–62. Oxford: Blackwell

Brewer MB, Caporael LR. 1990. Selfish genes versus selfish people: sociobiology as origin myth. *Motiv. Emot.* 14:237–42

Buss DM, Abbott M, Angleitner A, Biaggio A, Blanco-Villasenor A, et al. 1990. International preferences in selecting mates: a study of 37 cultures. *J. Cross-Cult. Psychol.* 21:5–47

Buss DM. 1994. The strategies of human mating. *Am. Sci.* 82:238–49

Buss DM. 1995. Evolutionary psychology: A new paradigm for psychological science. *Psychol. Inq.* 6:1–30

Buss DM. 1999a. *Evolutionary Psychology*. Boston: Allyn & Bacon

Buss DM. 1999b. Interactionism, flexibility, and inferences about the past. *Am. Psychol.* 54:443–45

Buss DM, Schmitt DP. 1993. Sexual strategies theory: a contextual evolutionary analysis of human mating. *Psychol. Rev.* 100:204–32

Buss LW. 1987. *The Evolution of Individuality*. Princeton, NJ: Princeton Univ. Press

Byrne RW, Whiten A, eds. 1988. *Machiavellian Intelligence*. Oxford: Clarendon Press

Callebaut W. 1993. *Taking the Naturalistic Turn, or, How Real Philosophy of Science is Done*. Chicago: Chicago Univ. Press

Calvin WH, Bickerton D. 2000. *Lingua ex Machina: Reconciling Darwin and Chomsky with the Human Brain*. Cambridge, MA: MIT Press

Campbell DT. 1969. Ethnocentrism of disciplines and the fish-scale model of omniscience. In *Interdisciplinary Relationships in the Social Sciences*, ed. M Sherif, CW Sherif, pp. 328–48. Chicago: Aldine

Campbell DT. 1988. *Methodology and Epistemology for Social Sciences*. Chicago: Univ. Chicago Press

Campbell DT. 1997. From evolutionary epistemology via selection theory to a sociology of scientific validity. *Evol. Cogn.* 3:5–38

Caporael LR. 1986. Anthropomorphism and mechanomorphism: Two faces of the human machine. *Comput. Hum. Behav.* 2:215–34

Caporael LR. 1994. Of myth and science: origin stories and evolutionary scenarios. *Soc. Sci. Inf.* 33:9–23

Caporael LR. 1995. Sociality: coordinating bodies, minds and groups. *Psycoloquy* 6:http://www.cogsci.soton.ac.uk/cgi/psyc/newpsy?6.01

Caporael LR. 1997. The evolution of truly social cognition: the core configurations model. *Pers. Soc. Psychol. Rev.* 1:276–98

Caporael LR. 1999. *From Selfish Genes to Repeated Assembly*. Presented at Annu. Meet. Am. Psychol. Assoc., Boston

Caporael LR, Baron RM. 1997. Groups as the mind's natural environment. See Simpson & Kenrick 1997, pp. 317–43

Caporael LR, Brewer MB. 1991. The quest for human nature. *J. Soc. Issues* 47:1–9

Caporael LR, Dawes RM, Orbell JM, van de Kragt AJC. 1989. Selfishness examined: cooperation in the absence of egoistic incentives. *Behav. Brain Sci.* 12:683–739

Cheney D, Seyfarth R, Smuts B. 1986. Social relationships and social cognition in nonhuman primates. *Science* 234:1361–66

Cheney DL, Seyfarth RM. 1990. *How Monkeys See the World*. Chicago: Univ. Chicago Press

Conklin BA, Morgan LM. 1996. Babies, bodies and the production of personhood in North America and a Native Amazonian society. *Ethos* 24:657–94

Corballis MC. 1997. The genetics and evolution of handedness. *Psychol. Rev.* 104:714–27

Cosmides L. 1989. The logic of social exchange: Has selection shaped how humans reason? Studies with the Wason selection task. *Cognition* 31:187–276

Cosmides L, Tooby J. 1987. From evolution to behavior: evolutionary psychology as the missing link. In *The Latest on the Best: Essays on Evolution and Optimality*, ed. J Dupré, pp. 277–306. Cambridge, MA: MIT Press

Crawford C, Krebs DL, eds. 1998. *Handbook of Evolutionary Psychology*. Mawah, NJ: Erlbaum

Crawford C, Smith M, Krebs D, eds. 1987. *Sociobiology and Psychology*. Hillsdale, NJ: Erlbaum

Crawford CB, Anderson JL. 1989. Sociobiology: an environmentalist discipline? *Am. Psychol.* 44:1449–59

Cziko G. 1995. *Without Miracles: Universal Selection Theory and the Second Darwinian Revolution*. Cambridge, MA: MIT Press

Darwin C. 1965 (1872). *The Expression of the Emotions in Man and Animals*. Chicago: Chicago Univ. Press

Dawkins R. 1976. *The Selfish Gene*. New York: Oxford Univ. Press

Deacon TW. 1997. *The Symbolic Species: The Co-evolution of Language and the Brain*. New York: Norton

Deichmann U. 1996. *Biologists Under Hitler*. Cambridge, MA: Harvard Univ. Press

Dennett DC. 1995. *Darwin's Dangerous Idea*. New York: Simon & Schuster

Depew DJ, Weber BH. 1996. *Darwinism Evolving*. Cambridge, MA: MIT Press

Donald M. 1991. *Origins of the Modern Mind*. Cambridge, MA: Harvard Univ. Press

Dunbar RIM. 1993. Coevolution of neocortical size, group size and language in humans. *Behav. Brain Sci.* 16:681–735

Dupré J. 1993. *The Disorder of Things*. Cambridge, MA: Harvard Univ. Press

Durham WH. 1991. *Coevolution: Genes, Culture and Human Diversity*. Stanford, CA: Stanford Univ. Press

Eagly AH, Wood W. 1999. The origins of

sex differences in human behavior: evolved dispositions versus social roles. *Am. Psychol.* 54:408–23

Edelman GM. 1992. *Bright Air, Brilliant Fire.* New York: Basic Books

Eibl-Eibesfeldt I. 1971. *Love and Hate.* London: Methuen

Eibl-Eibesfeldt I. 1989. *Human Ethology.* New York: Aldine

Ekman P, Rosenberg EL, eds. 1997. *What the Face Reveals: Basic and Applied Studies of Spontaneous Expression Using the Facial Action Coding System (FACS).* New York: Oxford Univ. Press

Eldredge N, Grene M. 1992. *Interactions: The Biological Context of Social Systems.* New York: Columbia Univ. Press

Ellis BJ, McFadyen-Ketchum S, Dodge KA, Pettit GS, Bates JE. 1999. Quality of early family relationships and individual differences in the timing of pubertal maturation in girls: a longitudinal test of an evolutionary model. *J. Pers. Soc. Psychol.* 77:387–401

Endler J. 1986. *Natural Selection in the Wild.* Princeton, NJ: Princeton Univ. Press

Fiske AP. 1991. *Structures of Social Life: The Four Elementary Forms of Human Relations.* New York: Free Press

Fiske AP. 2000. Complementarity theory: why human social capacities evolved to require cultural complements. *Pers. Soc. Psychol. Rev.* 4:76–94

Flake GW. 1998. *The Computational Beauty of Nature: Computer Explorations of Fractals, Chaos, Complex Systems and Adaptation.* Cambridge, MA: MIT Press

Fodor JA. 1983. *The Modularity of Mind.* Cambridge, MA: MIT Press

Foley R. 1996. The adaptive legacy of human evolution: a search for the environment of evolutionary adaptedness. *Evol. Anthropol.* 4:194–203

Forster MR, Wolfe A. 1999. *Conceptual Innovation and the Relational Nature of Evidence: The Whewell-Mill Debate.* http://philosophy.wisc.edu/forster/papers/Whewell1.pdf

Gangestad SW, Simpson JA. 1990. Toward an evolutionary history of female sociosexual variation. *J. Pers.* 58:69–96

Gibson KR, Ingold T, eds. 1993. *Tools, Language and Cognition in Human Evolution.* New York: Cambridge Univ. Press

Gottlieb G. 1992. *Individual Development and Evolution.* New York: Oxford Univ. Press

Gottlieb G. 1998. Normally occurring environmental and behavioral influences on gene activity: from central dogma to probabilistic epigenesis. *Psychol. Rev.* 105:792–802

Gould SJ, Lewontin RC. 1979. The spandrels of San Marco and the Panglossian paradigm. *Proc. R. Soc. London Ser. B* 205:581–98

Gowdy J, ed. 1998. *Limited Wants, Unlimited Means: A Reader on Hunter-Gather Economics and the Environment.* Washington, DC: Island

Greenfield PM. 1991. Language, tools and brain: the ontogeny and phylogeny of hierarchically organized sequential behavior. *Behav. Brain Sci.* 14:531–95

Griffiths PE. 1997. *What Emotions Really Are: The Problem of Psychological Categories.* Chicago: Chicago Univ. Press

Griffiths PE, Gray RD. 1994. Developmental systems and evolutionary explanation. *J. Philos.* 91:277–304

Hamilton WD. 1964. The genetical evolution of social behavior, I & II. *J. Theor. Biol.* 7:1–52

Harms W. 1999. *The Evolution of Cooperation on Hostility Gradients.* http://eame.ethics.ubc.ca/Hostility/index.html

Hejl PM, Falk R, Hendrichs H, Jablonka E. 1997. Complex systems: multilevel and multiprocess approaches. In *Human by Nature: Between Biology and the Social Sciences,* ed. P Weingart, SD Mitchell, PJ Richerson, S Maasen, pp. 387–425. Mahwah, NJ: Erlbaum

Hendriks-Jansen H. 1996. *Catching Ourselves in the Act.* Cambridge, MA: MIT Press

Heyes CM. 1998. Theory of mind in nonhuman primates. *Behav. Brain Sci.* 21:101–48

Ho M-W. 1991. The role of action in evolution: evolution by process and the ecological approach to perception. *Cult. Dyn.* 4:336–54

Humphrey NK. 1976. The social function of intellect. In *Growing Points in Ethology*, ed. PPG Bateson, RA Hinde, pp. 303–21. Cambridge: Cambridge Univ. Press

Hutchins E. 1996. *Cognition in the Wild*. Cambridge, MA: MIT Press

Irons W. 1998. Adaptively relevant environments versus the environment of evolutionary adaptedness. *Evol. Anthropol.* 6:194–204

Jablonka E. 1994. Inheritance systems and the evolution of new levels of individuality. *J. Theor. Biol.* 170:301–9

Janicki MG. 1998. Evolutionary approaches to culture. See Crawford & Krebs 1998, pp. 163–207

Johanson D, Edgar B. 1996. *From Lucy to Language*. New York: Simon & Schuster

Jolly A. 1966. Lemur social behavior and primate intelligence. *Science* 153:501–6

Jones D. 1999. Evolutionary psychology. *Annu. Rev. Anthropol.* 28:553–75

Kahneman D, Slovic P, Tversky A, eds. 1982. *Judgment Under Uncertainty: Heuristics and Biases*. New York: Cambridge Univ. Press

Kalick SM, Zebrowitz LA, Langlois JH, Johnson RM. 1998. Does human facial attractiveness honestly advertise health? Longitudinal data on an evolutionary question. *Psychol. Sci.* 9:8–13

Kauffman SA. 1993. *The Origins of Order*. New York: Oxford Univ. Press

Kaye HL. 1986. *The Social Meaning of Modern Biology: From Social Darwinism to Sociobiology*. New Haven, CT: Yale Univ. Press

Kenrick DT. 1995. Evolutionary theory versus the confederacy of dunces. *Psychol. Inq.* 6:56–62

Kipnis D. 1997. Ghosts, taxonomies, and social psychology. *Am. Psychol.* 52:205–11

Kitcher P. 1985. *Vaulting Ambition: Sociobiology and the Quest for Human Nature*. Cambridge, MA: MIT Press

Kuper A. 1988. *The Invention of Primitive Society: Transformations of an Illusion*. New York: Routledge

Laland KN, Odling-Smee J, Feldman MW. 2000. Niche construction, biological evolution, and cultural change. *Behav. Brain Sci.* 23:131–75

Landau M. 1984. Human evolution as narrative. *Am. Sci.* 72:262–68

Landau M. 1991. *Narratives of Human Evolution*. New Haven, CT: Yale Univ. Press

Levins R, Lewontin R. 1985. *The Dialectical Biologist*. Cambridge, MA: Harvard Univ. Press

Lewin R. 1998. *Principles of Human Evolution*. Malden, MA: Blackwell Sci.

Lewontin RC. 1982. Organism and environment. In *Learning, Development and Culture*, ed. HC Plotkin, pp. 17–38. New York: Wiley & Sons

Lewontin RC, Rose S, Kamin LJ. 1984. *Not in Our Genes*. New York: Pantheon

Lloyd EA. 1999. Evolutionary psychology: the burdens of proof. *Biol. Philos.* 14:211–33

MacDonald K. 1994. *A People that Shall Dwell Alone: Judaism as a Group Evolutionary Strategy*. Westport, CT: Praeger

Maynard Smith J. 1987. Science and myth. In *The Natural History Reader in Evolution*, ed. N Eldredge, pp. 222–29. New York: Columbia Univ. Press

Maynard Smith J, Szathmáry E. 1995. *The Major Transitions in Evolution*. New York: Freeman

Mellars P, Gibson K, eds. 1996. *Modelling the Early Human Mind*. Oxford: McDonald Inst. Archaeol. Res.

Miller LC, Fishkin SA. 1997. On the dynamics of human bonding and reproductive success: seeking windows on the adapted-for-human-environmental interface. See Simpson & Kenrick 1997, pp. 197–235

Moore HDM, Martin M, Birkhead TR. 1999. No evidence for killer sperm or other selective interactions between human spermatozoa in ejaculates of different males in vitro. *Proc. R. Soc. London* 266:2343–50

Morbeck ME, Galloway A, Zihlman AL, eds. 1997. *The Evolving Female*. Princeton, NJ: Univ. Princeton Press

Orians GH, Heerwagen JH. 1992. Evolved responses to landscapes. See Barkow et al 1992, pp. 555–79

Oyama S. 1985. *The Ontogeny of Information*. New York: Cambridge Univ. Press

Oyama S. 1989. Ontogeny and the central dogma: Do we need the concept of genetic programming in order to have an evolutionary perspective? In *Systems and Development. The Minnesota Symposia on Child Psychology*, ed. MR Gunnar, E Thelen, 22:1–34. Hillsdale, NJ: Erlbaum

Oyama S, Griffiths PE, Gray RD, eds. 2000. *Cycles of Contingency: Developmental Systems and Evolution*. Cambridge, MA: MIT Press

Perper T. 1985. *Sex Signals: The Biology of Love*. Philadelphia: ISI Press

Pinker S. 1997. *How the Mind Works*. New York: Norton

Richards RJ. 1987. *Darwin and the Emergence of Evolutionary Theories of Mind and Behavior*. Chicago: Univ. Chicago Press

Rose H, Rose S. 2000. *Alas, Poor Darwin: Arguments Against Evolutionary Psychology*. New York: Harmony Books

Rosenberg A. 1994. *Instrumental Biology or the Disunity of Science*. Chicago: Univ. Chicago Press

Rozin P, Lowery L, Ebert R. 1994. Varieties of disgust faces and the structure of disgust. *J. Pers. Soc. Psychol.* 66:870–81

Ruse M. 1989. *The Darwinian Paradigm*. New York: Routledge

Schick KD, Toth N. 1994. *Making Silent Stones Speak: Human Evolution and the Dawn of Technology*. New York: Simon & Schuster

Simpson JA, Kenrick DT, eds. 1997. *Evolutionary Social Psychology*. Mahwah, NJ: Erlbaum

Singh D. 1993. Adaptive significance of waist-to-hip ratio on judgments of women's attractiveness. *J. Pers. Soc. Psychol.* 65:293–307

Slobodkin L, Rapoport A. 1974. An optimal strategy of evolution. *Q. Rev. Biol.* 49:181–200

Smith BH. 2000. Sewing up the mind: the claims of evolutionary psychology. See Rose & Rose 2000, pp. 129–43

Smith EA, Winterhalder B, eds. 1992. *Evolutionary Ecology and Human Behavior*. New York: Aldine

Sober E, ed. 1994. *Conceptual Issues in Evolutionary Biology*. Cambridge, MA: MIT Press

Sober E, Wilson DS. 1998. *Unto Others: The Evolution and Psychology of Unselfish Behavior*. Cambridge, MA: Harvard Univ. Press

Star SL, ed. 1995. *Ecologies of Knowledge: Work and Politics in Science and Technology*. Albany, NY: SUNY Press

Symons D. 1979. *The Evolution of Human Sexuality*. New York: Oxford Univ. Press

Symons D. 1992. On the use and misuse of Darwinism in the study of human behavior. See Barkow et al. 1992, pp. 137–59

Tassinary LG, Hansen KA. 1998. A critical test of the waist-to-hip-ratio hypothesis of female physical attractiveness. *Psychol. Sci.* 9:150–55

Tattersall I. 1995. *The Fossil Trail*. New York: Oxford Univ. Press

Thelen E. 1992. Development as a dynamic system. *Curr. Dir. Psychol. Sci.* 1:189–93

Thelen E, Smith LB. 1994. *A Dynamic Systems Approach to the Development of Cognition and Action*. Cambridge, MA: MIT Press

Thiessen D. 1996. *Bittersweet Destiny: The Stormy Evolution of Human Behavior*. New Brunswick, NJ: Transaction

Thornhill R, Palmer CT. 2000. *A Natural History of Rape*. Cambridge, MA: MIT Press

Tooby J, Cosmides L. 1992. The psychological foundations of culture. See Barkow et al 1992, pp. 19–136

Trivers RL. 1971. The evolution of reciprocal altruism. *Q. Rev. Biol.* 46:35–57

Trivers RL. 1972. Parental investment and sexual selection. In *Sexual Selection and the Descent of Man*, ed. B Campbell, pp. 136–79. Chicago: Aldine

Trivers RL. 1974. Parent-offspring conflict. *Am. Zool.* 14:249–64

Waal FBM de, Lanting F. 1997. *Bonobo: The Forgotten Ape*. Berkeley: Univ. Calif. Press

Wahlsten D. 1999. Single-gene influences on brain and behavior. *Annu. Rev. Psychol.* 50:599–624

Weingart P, Maasen S, Segerstråle U. 1997. Shifting boundaries between the biological and the social: the social and political contexts. In *Human by Nature: Between Biology and the Social Sciences*, ed. P Weingart, SD Mitchell, PJ Richerson, S Maasen, pp. 65–102. Mahwah, NJ: Erlbaum

Wilson DS. 1975. A theory of group selection. *Proc. Natl. Acad. Sci. USA* 72:143–46

Wilson DS. 1983. The group selection controversy: history and current status. *Annu. Rev. Ecol. Syst.* 14:157–87

Wilson DS. 1997. Altruism and organism: disentangling the themes of multilevel selection theory. *Am. Nat.* 150:S122–34

Wilson EO. 1975. *Sociobiology*. Cambridge, MA: Harvard Univ. Press

Wilson EO. 1998. *Consilience: The Unity of Knowledge*. New York: Knopf

Wimsatt WC. 1999. Generativity, entrenchment, evolution and innateness. In *Biology Meets Psychology: Constraints, Connections and Conjectures*, ed. V Hardcastle. Cambridge, MA: MIT Press

Wimsatt WC. 1980. Reductionistic research strategies and their biases in the units of selection controvery. In *Scientific Discovery: Case Studies*, ed. T Nickles, pp. 213–59. Dordrecht, The Netherlands: Reidel

Annu. Rev. Psychol. 2001. 52:629–51

ATTENTION AND PERFORMANCE

Harold Pashler,[1] James C. Johnston,[2] and Eric Ruthruff[2]

[1]Department of Psychology, University of California, San Diego, La Jolla, California 92093; e-mail: hpashler@ucsd.edu
[2]NASA Ames Research Center, Moffett Field, California 94035; e-mail: jcjohnston@mail.arc.nasa.gov, eruthruff@mail.arc.nasa.gov

Key Words dual-task interference, psychological refractory effect, task switching, attentional control, reflexive orienting

■ **Abstract** Recent progress in the study of attention and performance is discussed, focusing on the nature of attentional control and the effects of practice. Generally speaking, the effects of mental set are proving more pervasive than was previously suspected, whereas automaticity is proving less robust. Stimulus attributes (e.g. onsets, transients) thought to have a "wired-in" ability to capture attention automatically have been shown to capture attention only as a consequence of voluntarily adopted task sets. Recent research suggests that practice does not have as dramatic effects as is commonly believed. While it may turn out that some mental operations are automatized in the strongest sense, this may be uncommon. Recent work on task switching is also described; optimal engagement in a task set is proving to be intimately tied to learning operations triggered by the actual performance of a new task, not merely the anticipation of such performance.

CONTENTS

0066-4308/01/0201-0629$14.00

INTRODUCTION

The phrase "attention and performance" has come to refer to a venerable research tradition that began during World War II in the United Kingdom. Research within this tradition has sought to illuminate basic questions about the architecture of the human mind by examining the human performance in relatively simple tasks. Although some of the topics that once occupied attention and performance researchers are no longer studied very intensively (e.g. choice reaction time and matching), the core issues of attentional mechanisms, limits, and control have probably undergone more intensive study within the past five years than in any comparable period of time in the past. There has also been a great increase in efforts to relate attentional mechanisms characterized at a functional level to brain activity and neural circuits (Parasuraman 1998).

It is not possible, given space limitations, to do justice to all of the important results and ideas that have emerged from this research. This review has a much more modest aim: to review recent work as it bears on two important themes around which some notable progress has occurred recently. These themes would seem to have broad implications for psychologists beyond those primarily focusing on attention and performance. The two themes that will be discussed in this chapter are, first, new evidence painting a very different view of attentional control from what has previously been assumed, and second, new analyses of the effects of practice.

Both themes involve issues often discussed with reference to the concept of automaticity, which was widely discussed in the late 1970s and early 1980s. However, the new findings emerging in the past 5 or 10 years suggest quite a different picture from early formulations of automaticity (such as Schneider & Shiffrin 1977, Posner & Snyder 1975).

TOP-DOWN CONTROL AND BOTTOM-UP PROCESSING

Human behavior emerges from the interaction of the goals that people have and the stimuli that impinge on them. Behaviors are commonly viewed as lying along a continuum reflecting the relative influence of these two factors in their causation. At one extreme are reflexes, which occur in direct response to certain classes of stimuli unless actively inhibited (e.g. very hot temperatures on the fingers cause retraction of the hand). At the other extreme are voluntary behaviors such as speaking a certain word at a capricious moment of one's own choosing, which are not directly and reliably triggered by any particular incoming stimulus, as far as can be discerned. Most human behavior would seem to lie in between these two extremes, reflecting the joint impact of high-level goals (so-called top-down influences) and recent stimuli (so-called bottom-up influences). Teasing apart the principles that govern the interaction of top-down and bottom-up forces is critical to understanding any type of human behavior.

In the area of selective attention, the issue of top-down versus bottom-up control has played an important role in many influential theoretical formulations. Several theorists have hypothesized separate modes of attention control that correspond closely to the general categories of reflexive and voluntary behavior discussed above. Two influential examples are Posner's (1980) distinction between exogenous and endogenous attention control, and Jonides's (1981) distinction between automatic and nonautomatic attention control. Note that Posner's concept of exogenous control (explicitly modeled on the neurological concept of a reflex) and Jonides's concept of automatic control both suggest that attention control lies outside of the organism, namely in the stimuli impinging on the organism. If the appropriate stimulus arises, the response of attending to that stimulus will occur. Because of the key role attributed to the stimulus, exogenous control has often been characterized as stimulus-driven or bottom-up control.

In the other hypothesized mode of attention control (endogenous/nonautomatic/voluntary), control is thought to reflect the same sort of decisions that we make to initiate any other (overt) voluntary action. Just as I can decide to reach out with my hand to grasp a coffee cup, I can decide to move my spatial attention to the location of the coffee cup. Note that whereas a cognitive decision is hypothesized to be necessary for an endogenous attention shift, no particular stimulus event is necessary. Thus, whereas exogenous attention control is characterized as stimulus driven, endogenous control is typically characterized as cognitively driven. These suggestions echo those of early writers on attention. Titchener (1908), for example, remarked that any sudden change or movement, including a change in pitch, could distract a person who was trying to concentrate on something else (p. 192), and James (1890) made similar suggestions.

In order to empirically test predictions about voluntary attention, it is usually assumed that subjects will make voluntary decisions in accord with systematic rewards and punishments imposed by the experimenter. Thus, in practice it is expected that voluntary attention allocation will follow experimenter-imposed incentives. If, on the other hand, attention is systematically drawn[1] to objects when there is no incentive for such an allocation, that allocation of attention is involuntary (and hence by exclusion must be accomplished by the automatic/exogenous/reflexive control mode).

Although, in principle both hypothesized modes of attention control would appear equally deserving of study, in practice most research has focused on reflexive control of attention.[2] We review two recent lines of research. The first has attempted to characterize what critical stimulus properties allow an object to

---

[1] The use of the term drawn should not suggest that visual attention is a single spotlight which, when allocated to one stimulus, must depart from another (cf. Bichot et al 1999, Kramer & Hahn 1995).

[2] Why this should be so is not clear. Perhaps the category of reflexive control is more readily investigated because it emphasizes the role of the stimuli, whose nature and timing are readily manipulated by researchers.

capture attention reflexively. The second has examined whether reflexive attention is indeed involuntary in the way that is traditionally claimed.

What Stimulus Properties Reflexively Attract Attention?

Various theorists have offered related but somewhat different suggestions about what critical stimulus properties might reflexively draw attention. A number of researchers have hypothesized that changes in stimuli over time ("transients") are prone to capture visual attention, especially when these occur rapidly. Yantis & Jonides (1984, 1990) theorized that stimuli with abrupt onsets have a special propensity to attract attention. Their visual search experiments showed that abrupt onset targets were found unusually rapidly, as if attention were preferentially drawn to those items. Yantis & Hillstrom (1994) later refined this view, suggesting that what should be ecologically most useful is for attention to be drawn to new objects in the field because these may well present either an important threat to be avoided (like a predator) or an important opportunity to be sought out (like prey). Yantis & Hillstrom noted that in the earlier experiments of Yantis & Jonides the stimuli shown to especially attract attention not only had abrupt luminance onsets but also marked the appearance of new objects. To unconfound these properties, they created special stimuli that constituted new objects but did not appear abruptly (the stimuli were made visible by manipulation of texture, motion, or binocular disparity). Visual search was unusually fast for these new object items. In another experiment, Yantis & Hillstrom showed that stimulus objects that did not generate the percept of a new object, but did contain a strong luminance burst, yielded no significant speedup in search. Thus, they concluded that the key stimulus feature that captures attention is not an abrupt luminance change, as previously hypothesized, but rather the appearance of a new object.

Whereas Yantis and colleagues have emphasized the importance of temporal discontinuities in stimulus properties or objects present in a scene, others have emphasized the importance of discontinuities in the spatial distribution of stimulus properties. Some researchers have argued that attention is strongly attracted to "singletons," stimuli whose properties differ strongly from all of their immediate neighbors (Wolfe 1992, Wolfe et al 1989, Theeuwes 1991; but see Pashler 1988, Bacon & Egeth 1994). Other researchers have hypothesized that all stimuli have at least some tendency to attract attention. Stimuli differ in the strength of this tendency (usually dubbed salience), and those stimuli having the highest relative salience are most likely to attract attention (cf. Lee et al 1999, Theeuwes 1992, Braun 1999).

In spite of the heterogeneity of these hypotheses, they share an emphasis on the properties of stimuli (whether individually or in relation to other stimuli) that attract attention, without reference to any cognitive goals of the observer. These goals are presumed to play a role in the control of attention, but only when attention is controlled voluntarily rather than involuntarily (reflexively).

Is Reflexive Attention Control Involuntary?

One of the key properties attributed to the exogenous or reflexive mode of attention control is that it is involuntary. That is, attention capture depends only on the occurrence of the proper stimulus, not on the goals of the observer. Visual search times decrease with abrupt-onset targets and increase with abrupt-onset distractors even when, across trials, the location of abrupt onset stimuli is uncorrelated with the location of the target (e.g. Yantis & Jonides 1990, Mueller & Rabbitt 1989). Thus, it was argued that abrupt-onset stimuli can capture attention independently of the will of the subject. Remington et al (1992) pushed the argument for involuntary capture of attention further by using abrupt-onset distractors that were guaranteed to be in nontarget locations on all trials. With this arrangement, allocating attention to abrupt onsets could only hurt performance (rather than merely failing to help, on average, as with the uncorrelated-locations design[3]); hence, subjects should have had the strongest possible motivation to prevent attention from being captured by these distractors. Nevertheless, abrupt-onset distractors still impaired performance. This result provides strong support for involuntary attention capture by abrupt-onset stimuli.

By the early 1990s there appeared to be a broad consensus that the reflexive mode of attention control is free of influence from top-down cognitive processes. According to this view, attentional control is at the mercy of the appearance of certain classes of stimuli (be they transients, abrupt-onset stimuli, new objects, or more generally, relatively salient stimuli). Such stimuli would draw attention in a completely bottom-up manner, overriding or at least delaying the cognitively driven, top-down control of attention.

Yantis & Jonides (1990), however, noted one special case in which voluntary processes could prevent capture. If subjects know with certainty the location of a target and are given sufficient time to focus attention on that target, then distractor stimuli are at least momentarily unable to capture attention (see also Theeuwes 1991). This finding suggests that if an observer's attention is already locked onto one location, the power of other stimuli to draw attention is nullified. (It is unclear whether this nullification occurs because perceptual processing of the distractors is prevented, or due to a "lock-up" of the attention-shifting mechanism, which prevents a new shift.) In any event, this exception appears restricted to situations in which attention is tightly focussed on a object.

New View of Involuntary Attention Capture

To summarize, the allocation of spatial attention has commonly been claimed to operate through two modes. In the voluntary mode, high-level cognitive processes determine where attention is needed and shift attention accordingly in a

---

[3]Phenomena such as probability matching suggest that people may fail to optimize whenever consequences have some random variation from trial to trial.

top-down, cognitively driven manner. In the reflexive mode, stimuli that are high in absolute or relative attention-attracting properties cause an involuntary shift of attention. The reflexive mode, unlike the voluntary mode, was hypothesized to operate independently of the goals of the observer.

This consensus was challenged by Folk et al (1992), who argued that, paradoxically, even the involuntary capture of attention is subject to top-down cognitive control. Folk et al noted that previous studies of involuntary attention capture always used distractor stimuli sharing properties that defined the class of targets subjects were searching for. In particular, studies such as Remington et al (1992) that documented attention capture by abrupt-onset distractors had always used abrupt onset targets (inadvertently, one might say). Under the display conditions tested, it is thus conceivable that subjects were relying on the abrupt-onset property to help find targets. If so, the ability of abrupt-onset distractor stimuli to capture attention might have derived not from their stimulus properties per se, but from the match between their stimulus properties and the subject's voluntary set. What had not been studied were conditions in which distractor properties clearly failed to match the properties subjects used to find targets.

Folk et al (1992) set out to study attention capture with careful control of the relation between distractor properties and the properties used to find targets. They tested two unique distractor properties (color or abrupt onset) against each of two unique target-finding properties (again, color or abrupt onset). Confirming previous results, they found that when subjects are looking for abrupt onset targets, abrupt-onset distractors capture attention and color distractors do not. However, when subjects are looking for color targets (e.g. a red object in a background of green objects), abrupt-onset distractors do not capture attention, and color distractors (e.g. red distractors in a green background) do. Folk et al (1992) concluded that it is not the stimulus properties of distractors per se that determine whether attention capture will occur, but rather the relationship of distractor properties to the target-finding properties. They hypothesized that involuntary attention capture occurs if and only if distractors have a property that subjects are using to find targets.

To explain these results Folk et al (1992) proposed a new theory of attention capture. The theory describes the workings of attention as being analogous in some respects to that of a thermostat. Once set, a thermostat automatically activates the furnace when the temperature falls below a certain temperature without requiring further intervention by the person who set the thermostat. The person does, in one sense, control the thermostat, but in computer parlance the control is exercised off-line. That is, the person presets the critical temperature but has no role in the (on-line) events that trigger the furnace to turn on when the temperature falls below the preset value. Similarly, in the case of involuntary attention capture, Folk et al proposed that cognitive goals determine attentional control settings in advance (off-line); given the attention control settings in place at any particular time, the appearance of stimuli matching that setting will (on-line) capture attention with no further involvement of cognitive processes. Folk et al dubbed their hypothesis contingent orienting because the reflexive allocation of attention is contingent on the match between the stimulus properties of distractors and the attentional control settings.

Recent Findings on Contingent Orienting

Folk et al (1994) confirmed the generality of the claim that distractors draw attention involuntarily if and only if their distinctive property matches the property subjects are looking for. They tested various pairwise combinations of the three properties of apparent motion (present or absent), color, and abrupt onsets (present or absent). In each case, the principle was upheld. From the same perspective, Folk & Remington (1998) recently examined the claim by Yantis & Hillstrom (1994), described above, that attentional capture is triggered by the appearance of a new object (not necessarily marked by an abrupt onset). Folk & Remington found that the power of new-object distractors to capture attention was modified by the attentional control setting of the subject in the same manner as previously shown for abrupt onsets. Most importantly, they found that when observers were set for color targets, new-object distractors did not involuntarily capture attention.

The studies described thus far involve small effects of a single precue and relatively uncrowded displays. H Pashler (2000, submitted) attempted to magnify any effects of irrelevant transient distractors by presenting a very large number of them and presenting them concurrently with the target display. Pashler's task required observers to search for a particular red digit (e.g. "3") in a crowded display of 30 stationary red digits plus an additional 30 green distractors. To avoid introducing an incentive to search for onsets, observers previewed displays for a short while until a voice told them which digit to look for. The question asked was how performance would be affected if all of the green distractors were made to flash, twinkle, or "shimmy" rather than remaining stationary. One might expect the presence of all these potentially distracting stimulus changes to drastically increase search times, but the data showed that performance was little affected or actually improved. These results show a striking ability of top-down processes to tune selective attention so effectively that even large numbers of changing distractors will not capture attention, provided that their properties do not fit what the subject is looking for.

Recent research has shown that the "cognitive penetration" of involuntary attention capture by top-down processes is subtle and wide-reaching. Folk et al (1992) were able to experimentally demonstrate how the properties required to distinguish targets from distractors could alter control settings and thereby alter attention capture. They conjectured that control settings might also be tuned for other properties of targets, even those properties shared by distractors. For example, if the target display consists of an abrupt onset of targets (red) and abrupt-onset distractors (green), the most efficient strategy might be to first locate abrupt-onset stimuli and then search among them for red objects. Gibson & Kelso (1998) have since elegantly confirmed this conjecture. They showed that manipulations of the property used to signal the onset of the target field (shared by all stimuli in that field) did in fact produce corresponding changes in which properties showed attentional capture. For instance, when color as well as onsets signaled the target display, attentional capture was found for color stimuli as well as onset stimuli. This line of research has served to clarify several conflicting results regarding the relative ability of onsets and offsets to capture attention (e.g. Miller 1989, Martin-Emerson & Kramer 1997). Atchley et al (2000) found that they could produce attention capture by onsets, by offsets, or by either, simply by manipulating whether subjects needed to use onsets, offsets, or either to find candidate objects that might be targets.

We referred above to the common suggestion that objects that differed strongly from a relatively homogenous field of neighbors—so-called singletons—sometimes draw attention even when this is disadvantageous to performance of the task (Pashler 1988, Theeuwes 1992). These results, too, have also been shown to require re-interpretation. It is critical that in most experiments with distractor singletons, the subject is looking for unique targets that also constitute singletons in some different stimulus dimension (isolated elements different from surrounding stimuli). Hence, even when, for example, a color singleton captures attention when subjects are looking for a form singleton (Pashler 1988), it may be that subjects have a very general set for singletons. Bacon & Egeth (1994) confirmed this conjecture, showing that the ability of singletons to capture attention is dependent upon whether observers are or are not looking for target singletons. Gibson & Jiang (1998) have also reported that color singletons do not attract attention unless their relevance has become clear to the observer. An experiment by Jonides & Yantis (1988), using a different methodology (visual search), also supports this conclusion: Search was not slowed by the presence of certain properties in distractors that made them singletons, so long as the distribution of those properties was not correlated with the target location (ensuring subjects had no incentive to look for the distractor property at issue).

Yantis & Egeth (1999) have succeeded in closing an apparent "loophole" in the case for top-down control of involuntary attention capture. Is it not possible, they asked, that certain stimuli (e.g. feature singletons) do capture attention in a completely bottom-up, stimulus-driven fashion, but that this mechanism can be inhibited by top-down control? This hypothesis would still leave a core of attention-capture behavior that was not actually caused by top-down control. Yantis & Egeth (1999) set up an ingenious test of this hypothesis. If the key stimuli (e.g. feature singletons) that might capture attention were presented only rarely, it seems unlikely that capture would come to be inhibited. What Yantis & Egeth (1999) found, however, is that if feature singletons were presented only rarely, little or no capture occurred. The inhibition hypothesis is therefore wrong. In the absence of any top-down influence, feature singletons simply do not capture attention. Overall, as the consequences of the contingent capture hypothesis have been explored, further successes have been achieved and the generality of the model has been extended considerably.

In recent years there has also been progress clarifying what is actually happening when attention is captured by distractor stimuli. Much of our evidence comes from a cueing paradigm in which the distractors are presented for a short period (e.g. 50 ms), followed by a brief interval (e.g. 100 ms), followed by the target field (which might remain on until the response). The usual evidence for capture by a distractor is a delay—typically 40–50 ms or so—in the response to the target. This distractor-induced delay provides strong evidence that as a result of processing the distractor *something* happens to delay processing of the target. Because the distractor-induced delay only occurs if the distractor is in a different location than the target, it is natural to hypothesize that attention has been temporarily drawn to the distractor location. However, it is plausible that attention might only have been drawn *toward* the target without dwelling there; it is even possible that attention to the target was in some way impaired without the focus of attention being drawn in any particular direction. Remington et al (2000) showed that attention really *is* allocated to the cued location. They hypothesized that if attention capture really does involve a shift of attention to the distractor object, then that object should be processed to a deeper level. As a measure of distractor processing depth, they tested whether response-compatibility of the distractor would influence response time (RT) to the target. Whenever they found the traditional evidence for capture (a distractor-induced delay) they also found evidence for deep processing of distractors (a response compatibility effect); when traditional evidence for capture was lacking, there was no evidence for deep processing of distractors. Hence it appears likely that what we have been calling attention capture does indeed involve a brief allocation of attention to the distractor.

This research has—rather long after the introduction of the concept of attention capture—finally placed the metaphor on strong ground. Spatial attention is indeed allocated to distractor stimuli to which the subjects are not voluntarily trying to pay attention. What now seems fairly clear, however, is that though the ability of the distractor stimuli themselves to draw attention is unwanted in a local sense, it is properly understood as an inevitable by-product of what the subject *is* voluntarily trying to attend.

CONTROL OF PROCESSING: Task Switching and Cueing

Task Switching Effects

In the previous section we saw that the phenomenon of involuntary attention capture, often presumed to be entirely bottom-up and stimulus driven, turns out to be subtly influenced by top-down goals. We turn now to another area within the field of attention and performance that has undergone a remarkable resurgence of research in the past few years: task switching. Here, by contrast to attention capture, we will be discussing a phenomenon that appears at first glance to be entirely under top-down cognitive control, but that turns out to be heavily influenced by bottom-up, stimulus-driven processing.

In most studies of basic information-processing mechanisms, people are instructed to perform a particular task, and the focus of the researcher is on the events occurring between the presentation of an imperative stimulus and the occurrence of the response. The actions that a person undertakes in order to prepare to perform a task are not illuminated in such studies. Research on task switching, by contrast, sheds light on these preparatory activities.

The study of executive control of task-set was pioneered by the educational psychologist Arthur Jersild (1927). To measure the cost of switching task sets, Jersild had subjects perform various speeded tasks involving lists of items. Some lists ("pure lists") required the subject to perform the same task on each item in turn. Other lists ("alternating lists") required the subject to alternate tasks, e.g. performing task A on the first item, task B on the second, task A on the third, and so forth. Jersild found that when the two tasks involved a common stimulus set (e.g. addition versus subtraction of digits), subjects responded much more slowly on the alternating lists. The extra time required, often referred to as the switch cost, was very large by the standards of research on simple tasks (sometimes exceeding 500 msec/item). In the alternating-list condition, subjects not only had to keep close track of which task was due to be performed next (the stimulus itself was no help in this regard), but also needed to avoid any tendency to perform the (irrelevant) task-set used on the previous trial. In contrast, when the two tasks had distinct stimulus sets (e.g. adding digit pairs versus naming an antonym of a word) Jersild found no switch cost (or even a small switch benefit). In this condition the stimulus typically provides a strong task cue, and there is little tendency to perform the wrong task. This basic pattern of results has since been replicated using modern methods of timing individual responses (e.g. Allport et al 1994, Fagot 1994, Spector & Biederman 1976).

One question left unanswered by Jersild's work is whether the slower RTs sometimes observed in the alternating-task blocks are caused by task-switching per se, or rather by the "overhead" involved in keeping two task sets active at the same time. To address this question, Rogers & Monsell (1995) recently added a new twist to the task-switching paradigm. Instead of presenting the switch and nonswitch conditions in separate blocks of trials, they mixed these two conditions together within the same block of trials. In their "alternating-runs" paradigm, subjects performed tasks A and B in runs of two or more trials (e.g. AABBAABB). By comparing switch and nonswitch trials within the same block of trials, Rogers & Monsell were able to measure switch costs uncontaminated by unwanted differences between conditions in executive overhead, arousal, etc.

Using the alternating-runs paradigm, Rogers & Monsell (1995) verified Jersild's finding that switching between cognitive tasks (even very simple ones) can result in a substantial time cost (300 msec or more). However, the results differed from those of Jersild (1927) in that reliable switch costs were found even with distinct stimulus sets (~50 msec). This empirical discrepancy might be partly due to the fact that Rogers & Monsell presented individual stimuli, whereas Jersild presented lists of stimuli; Jersild's lists allowed for preview of upcoming items, which might have been more useful in the mixed list condition (see Spector & Biederman 1976).

What causes the switch cost? The most obvious explanation is that task switch trials require an active, top-down process that changes the current task set (also known as task-set reconfiguration). There are at least two lines of evidence in favor of this hypothesis. First, Rogers & Monsell (1995) found that switch costs can be reduced by allowing the subjects extra time to prepare for the upcoming task switch (see also Biederman 1973, Fagot 1994, Sudevan & Taylor 1987). Interestingly, preparation time reduced the switch cost only when this variable was manipulated between blocks rather than within blocks; it appears that subjects failed to reconfigure their task set when not guaranteed sufficient time to complete the process. This finding suggests that switch-cost reduction reflects an active (top-down) process, rather than a passive decay of interfering representations from the previous task (see Allport et al 1994). Further evidence for an active top-down reconfiguration process comes from Meiran (1996). By presenting subjects with a task cue either early or late within a fixed inter-trial interval, he was able to vary the available preparation time while holding constant the time elapsed since the previous trial (and hence the opportunity for passive decay). The results showed that the switch cost was indeed much smaller when subjects had more time to prepare for the upcoming task. This result confirms that the switch cost is reduced by an active top-down preparatory process (e.g. a task-set reconfiguration) during the inter-trial interval, rather than by a passive decay of interfering representations from the previous trial. If the top-down task-set reconfiguration were the only source of the switch cost, then providing a very long inter-trial interval should allow subjects to finish the reconfiguration in advance, completely eliminating the switch cost. This prediction, however, has been disconfirmed in several studies (Allport et al 1994, Fagot 1994, Rogers & Monsell 1995) that found residual switch costs at long inter-trial intervals. Responses to a task switch are especially slow when that response is incompatible with the response suggested by the irrelevant task (Meiran 1996, Rogers & Monsell 1995, Sudevan & Taylor 1987). Hence, the task set from the previous trial remains somewhat active even when subjects know it will not be needed on the upcoming trial and have plenty of time to suppress it.

In order to answer the question of why task switching hurts performance, it is helpful to reverse the question and ask why task repetition helps performance. From this perspective, residual switch costs occur because no amount of top-down task preparation can provide benefits as strong as the bottom-up effect of having just performed the task on the previous trial.

Explaining Residual Switch Cost

To explain the residual switch cost, Rogers & Monsell (1995) conjectured that top-down attempts at reconfiguring the task set are inherently incomplete. Specifically, they hypothesized that completion of the task-set reconfiguration on switch trials can only be triggered exogenously, by the appearance of the actual stimulus. Thus, no amount of preparation can eliminate the residual switch cost. According to this hypothesis, performing a task once leaves the system optimally prepared to perform that task again on the next trial. Therefore, when subjects are presented with alternating runs of four trials (e.g. AAAABBBB) the switch cost will be borne entirely by the first trial within a run of four. Rogers & Monsell have confirmed this prediction (however, see Salthouse et al 1998).

Rogers & Monsell's explanation of the residual cost offers one plausible analysis, but other alternatives deserve consideration. One attractive possibility is that certain critical mental processes (e.g. response selection) are performed more slowly on task switch trials than on task repetition trials. Allport et al (1994), for instance, proposed that performance on task switch trials is slowed owing to interference from the task set implemented on the previous trial. According to their "task-set inertia" model, switch costs are reduced over time (on the order of minutes) owing to passive decay. This hypothesis is difficult to reconcile with the evidence discussed above that the reduction in the switch cost during the inter-trial interval is due to an active (top-down) process (see Meiran 1996, Rogers & Monsell 1995). In addition, this hypothesis seems to predict that performance within a run of trials of one task should show gradual improvement over a period of several minutes. However, as noted above, Rogers & Monsell found that the switch cost was borne entirely by the first trial within the run.

Ruthruff et al (2000c) have also attempted to explain the residual switch cost in terms of a processing slowdown. These authors used a variant of the Rogers & Monsell (1995) alternating-runs paradigm, with long inter-trial intervals in which the presented task was not always the expected task. Thus, subjects usually received task sequences such as AABBAA, but occasionally received sequences such as AABBAB. This allowed Ruthruff et al to examine the interaction between the effects of task expectancy and the effects of task recency (i.e. the residual switch cost). These authors found additive effects between task expectancy and task recency in several experiments involving single-affordance conditions. Furthermore, two experimental factors thought to influence the duration of response selection (namely, stimulus repetition and the complexity of the stimulus-repetition mapping) had effects that were generally additive with task expectancy but overadditive[4] with task recency. This pattern of data is most easily reconciled with a model in which task recency influences the stage of response selection, whereas task expectancy influences some earlier stage (see Sternberg 1969). The inference that task recency influences response selection is incompatible with Rogers & Monsell's suggestion that the task-recency effect is caused by a task-set reconfiguration stage inserted on task switch trials. [One caveat, however, is that Ruthruff et al (2000c) studied only conditions in which the two tasks had distinct

[4]Two factors, A and B, are said to interact when the effects of factor A depend on the level of factor B (and vice versa). When the effects of factor A tend to be larger in the "difficult" levels of factor B than in the "easy" levels of factor B, the interaction is said to be overadditve.

stimulus sets, so it is not clear whether their conclusions apply equally well to conditions in which the two tasks share the same stimulus set.] Ruthruff et al did argue for the existence of a task-set reconfiguration stage, but they proposed that this stage is needed only when the task is unexpected, not when it is merely a task switch. Ruthruff et al went on to speculate that the role of top-down, goal-driven processes is to ensure that the proper task set is in place, but that these top-down processes have little or no direct, on-line influence over elementary cognitive processes.

Further work will be needed to determine which of the competing models of the residual switch cost are correct. In any case, the data at least permit us to draw several conclusions regarding executive control. First, switch costs clearly are much greater when the tasks being studied involve overlapping stimulus sets, so that the stimulus itself does not unambiguously indicate which task needs to be performed upon it. Second, deliberate (top-down) mechanisms can be successfully employed to ready critical mental machinery to carry out a particular task in the near future, substantially reducing reaction times to that task. Third, it appears that these top-down mechanisms alone cannot always achieve the full state of task readiness that can be achieved by actually having performed the task on the previous trial. Thus, there is a lingering bottom-up component to the switch cost, the exact cause of which is not yet known.

Taken together, this section and the previous section on attention capture show that recent research is making some progress toward unraveling the complex and subtle interplay of top-down, goal-directed and bottom-up, stimulus-driven processes in human performance. In retrospect, perhaps it should have been expected that the interplay would be rather complicated. The distinction between bottom-up and top-down control closely parallels the distinction in development between learned behaviors (controlled by the demands of the environment) and innate behaviors (controlled by an internal genetic program). Several decades ago it became clear that the development process typically involves an intricate and subtle interaction over time of environmental influences and genetic programming; few processes can be neatly classified as either learned or innate. An analogous picture is emerging from the areas of recent research reviewed here. It is possible that few, if any, classes of human behavior will turn out to be neatly classified as purely top-down or purely bottom-up.

EFFECTS OF PRACTICE

A number of influential theories proposed in the late 1970s suggested that tasks become "automatized" after they have enjoyed sufficient consistent practice (e.g. Schneider & Shiffrin 1977). Automatization is normally understood to mean that a task or operation acquires several properties. One feature is a lack of voluntary control—that the operation proceeds more or less reflexively given the appropriate stimulus input. Another is the lack of interference with other ongoing mental operations. Highly practiced tasks, it was said, can be performed simultaneously with other tasks without interference (except for structural conflicts such as common reliance on the same effectors, requiring foveation, etc.).

Effects of Practice on Discrete Dual-Task Performance

The psychological refractory period (PRP) effect refers to a ubiquitous and often large slowing effect observed when people try to perform two speeded tasks close together in time (each task involving a choice of responses based on a distinct stimulus). While responses to the first-presented stimulus are often little affected by temporal proximity to the second task, responses to the second stimulus are usually slowed as the interval between stimuli is reduced. The increase in second-task RTs as the interval between stimuli is reduced is the most commonly used measure of the magnitude of the PRP effect. Several decades of work have provided strong support for the view that the PRP effect arises from postponement of central processing stages in the second task—a processing bottleneck. On this account, central stages in task 2 cannot commence until corresponding stages of the first task have been completed, whereas perceptual and motoric stages in the two tasks can overlap without constraint. This "central bottleneck" theory (Welford 1967) is supported by a variety of evidence, including the existence of PRP slowing in tasks that do not share input or output modalities, and the results of chronometric studies in which different stages of the two tasks are manipulated (see Pashler 1994, for a review).

The PRP effect is a particularly clearcut example of true dual-task interference, and according to the central bottleneck theory, the interference is severe, in the sense that mental operations in one task are said completely to displace mental operations in the other task. Thus, the PRP effect provides a natural experimental design with which to ask whether practice produces automatization.

Does practice dramatically reduce the size of the PRP effect, and if so, does it completely circumvent the central bottleneck? Many early studies of practice in PRP designs concluded that although practice substantially reduces RTs, it has only a modest effect on the amount of PRP interference (e.g. Bertelson & Tisseyre 1969, Borger 1963, Dutta & Walker 1995, Karlin & Kestenbaum 1968). From these results it would appear that the cognitive limitations responsible for the PRP effect are robust across practice. There is reason to question the generality of these findings, however, owing to the specific task combinations employed in these experiments. Most used pairs of tasks that both required a manual response (perhaps due to the technical difficulties involved in automatically detecting and scoring vocal responses). Recent research suggests that it is difficult or even impossible to control the two hands independently (De Jong 1993; McLeod 1977, 1978). Hence, it is possible that subjects in these early practice studies did not have a fair chance to learn to perform both tasks at the same time.

To see if a dramatic reduction in the PRP effect is possible with distinct responses, Van Selst et al (1999) recently studied the effects of 36 practice sessions in a PRP design combining an auditory-vocal task (saying aloud whether a tone is high or low in pitch) with a visual-manual task (pressing a button to indicate the identity of a letter on the computer screen). Van Selst et al observed a rather dramatic reduction in the magnitude of dual-task interference with practice. The initial PRP effect (increase in second-task RT as the interval between the tone and the letter was reduced) was 353 msec—typical of PRP studies with unpracticed tasks—but after extensive practice the effect had shrunk to a mere 50 msec. (When the experiment was repeated with manual responses on both tasks, a much larger residual PRP effect remained after practice, confirming that the choice of response modalities can be important.)

Although practice dramatically reduced the PRP effect when input and output conflicts were minimized in this way, the effect had not entirely disappeared. Based on the effects of manipulating variables targeted to slow particular stages in the two tasks, Van Selst et al (1999) were able to show that a central bottleneck was still present after extensive practice. Thus, although practice reduced stage durations (as one would have expected), it did not allow stages that previously operated in series to begin operating in parallel. If the central bottleneck model holds both before and after practice, then the reduction in the PRP effect with practice reflects the speedup in the perceptual and central stages of task 1. Speedups in later stages of task 1, or in any stages of task 2, should not modulate the effect. To test this prediction, Ruthruff et al (2000a) had the highly trained subjects of Van Selst et al complete two additional transfer experiments. The first transfer experiment paired a new task 1 judgment with the old (highly practiced) task 2 judgment. The second transfer experiment paired the old (highly practiced) task 1 judgment with a new task 2. As predicted by the bottleneck model with stage-shortening, the PRP effect was relatively large in the first experiment (with a new task 1) but relatively small in the second experiment (with a new task 2).

The results of these transfer experiments argue against other interpretations of the effects of practice on PRP interference. For instance, it has often been supposed that when subjects practice doing two tasks at the same time, what they really learn is how to efficiently integrate this particular pair of tasks (e.g. Neisser 1976). If this account holds true in the present context, subjects should have produced relatively large PRP effects in both transfer experiments because they involved new pairs of tasks. Alternatively, if subjects had completely automatized the two tasks, so that they no longer required any limited resources, then subjects should produce small or nonexistent PRP effects in any transfer experiment involving either one of these highly practiced tasks. Contrary to this prediction, Van Selst et al (1999) found that the PRP effect shrunk if and only if the previously practiced task 1 was retained.

It should be noted, however, that while most of the results of Van Selst et al (1999) and Ruthruff et al (2000a) suggested that practice merely shortened the time required for central processing stages, there were persistent hints that practice may also have produced some small degree of true automatization on some trials, at least for some subjects.

Practice in Continuous Dual-Task Performance

So far we have discussed practice in the context of the discrete dual-task (PRP) design because this procedure allows one to test hypotheses about the effects of practice with exceptional clarity. However, the best known studies of practice effects have used continuous tasks and aggregate performance measures. A number of these studies have yielded extraordinary improvements in dual-task processing with practice. One commonly used approach has been to study the effects of practice in dual-task designs in which accuracy is the primary dependent measure. For example, Hirst et al (1980) found striking improvements in people's ability to read while taking dictation (though dual-task interference never completely disappeared). These results are sometimes taken to mean that even difficult mental operations (seemingly more sophisticated than any involved in the typical PRP task) became able to operate simultaneously and without interference. This conclusion is unwarranted, however, because such designs may be quite insensitive to processing delays. It is quite possible that critical mental operations on the two tasks never proceed at the same time, but subjects are nonetheless able to smoothly switch back and forth between the two tasks (see Broadbent 1982; McCann & Johnston 1992; Pashler 1990, 1998; Pashler & Johnston 1998). As an analogy, from the point of view of a user, time-sharing computers appear capable of performing two tasks at once without loss, even though the central processing unit never performs more than one operation at a time. In order to reliably detect capacity limitations, it is necessary to measure RT on individual tasks (as in the PRP design). Many other studies commonly cited as demonstrating that practice causes automatization (e.g. Schneider & Shiffrin 1977) involved tasks such as holding memory loads and visual search, which are not necessarily prone to queuing, even at the onset of practice.

Other investigators have studied the effects of practice on dual-task designs in which RT was the dependent measure, but all dual-task trials used the same stimulus-onset asynchrony (SOA) (as opposed to the typical PRP design, in which SOA is systematically varied within blocks). Schumacher et al (1997), for instance, trained subjects for 5 sessions in a dual-task design to compare single-task performance to dual-task performance at a 0 msec SOA (i.e. simultaneous stimulus presentation). One task was to say "one," "two," or "three," to low-, medium-, and high-pitched tones, respectively. The other task was to press one of three response keys that corresponded to the position of a disk on the computer screen. By the fifth session, subjects were able to perform these tasks together with no significant impairment in either RT or accuracy on the two tasks.

Schumacher et al's (1997) data, like that of Van Selst et al (1999) and Ruthruff et al (2000a), indicate that dual-task interference effects can be greatly reduced with extensive practice. Their data might also appear to indicate that practice in their design allowed subjects to bypass the central bottleneck. This might or might not be the case. One feature of their design (specifically, the use of simultaneous stimulus presentations) might have encouraged subjects to conjoin the two tasks into one. For instance, subjects may have learned to map each stimulus pair {S1, S2} onto the appropriate response pair {R1, R2}. A second limitation is that their visual-manual task involved a highly compatible mapping of stimuli onto responses, and thus might not require any central operations. It has been known for a long time that certain highly compatible tasks produce little or no PRP interference, perhaps because they do not require response selection or any other central processes (Greenwald 1972, Greenwald & Shulman 1973, Halliday et al 1959, Johnston & Delgado 1993, Pashler et al 1993). It will be interesting to see whether the results extend to more difficult tasks with neutral or incompatible response mappings.

Several recent studies using similar designs but less compatible response mappings have found sizable dual-task interference effects (e.g. Levy & Pashler 2000, Ruthruff et al 2000b). It is also not clear whether Schumacher et al's (1997) subjects had bypassed the bottleneck (i.e. central operations can operate in parallel with no interference) or whether there was what Van Selst et al (1999) call a latent bottleneck. A latent bottleneck occurs when the central operations on the two tasks cannot overlap, in principle, but due to the timing of the stimulus presentations they rarely "need to" occur simultaneously (i.e. central operations on one task generally finish before central operations on the other task are set to begin).

Hazeltine et al (2000) have found ways to address several of the concerns with Schumacher et al's (1997) study. They first replicated the basic finding of no-interference after practice. To evaluate the possibility that subjects converted the two tasks into a single conjoint task, Hazeltine et al trained subjects on only six of the nine possible stimulus pairs created by combining the three task 1 stimuli with the three task 2 stimuli. Then, in a subsequent testing phase, they presented the three stimulus combinations that had never appeared during the training phase, along with the six combinations that were trained. Subjects responded just as quickly to the new stimulus pairs as to the old stimulus pairs. This finding argues against the possibility that the learning gained in the training phase was specific to the particular stimulus combinations presented. However, this finding does not rule out the possibility that subjects learned a more abstract integration of the two tasks that was generalizable to all stimulus pairs, even those not yet experienced. To test this more general hypothesis, Hazeltine et al conducted a follow-up study in which they included −50 and +50 msec SOA conditions, in addition to the usual 0 msec SOA condition. The asynchronous presentations should force subjects to first wait (approximately 50 msec) for both stimuli to arrive before beginning the conjoint response selection. However, RTs were not slowed substantially in any of the SOA conditions. To address the concern that the visual-manual task was ideo-motor compatible, Hazeltine et al transferred subjects to a condition with an incompatible mapping of screen positions to fingers. This manipulation increased RTs to the visual-manual task, as expected, but had very little effect on the amount of dual-task interference.

The results of Hazeltine et al (2000) and Schumacher et al (1997), therefore, provide tantalizing evidence that practice allows subjects to bypass the central bottleneck under certain conditions. It remains to be seen whether this finding will generalize to other pairs of tasks and to conditions with large variations in SOA (as is the case in many real-world tasks).

CONCLUSION

Recent studies show that practice can dramatically reduce dual-task interference (Hazeltine et al 2000, Ruthruff et al 2000a, Schumacher et al 1997, Van Selst et al 1999). Thus, the very large interference effects observed with novel tasks (300–400 msec) might overestimate the amount of interference observed between pairs of highly practiced tasks in the real world. In many cases, however, it appears that practice merely reduces stage-durations, without allowing subjects to bypass the processing bottleneck (Ruthruff et al 2000a, Van Selst et al 1999). At the same time, some new evidence suggests that under some conditions practice can eliminate the processing bottleneck entirely (Hazeltine et al 2000, Schumacher et al 1997). Further work is needed to better define the boundary conditions for these two outcomes.

Locus of Practice Effects in Skill Learning

In the previous section, we discussed recent research on how practice affects the PRP. The key question was whether practice merely reduced the duration of component stages of the central bottleneck or allowed subjects to carry out more central operations in parallel on two tasks. Recent evidence suggests that the great bulk of the improvement with practice comes from reducing the duration of central stages, whereas relatively little of the improvement reflects being able to perform central operations on both tasks in parallel.

The question of how practice reduces RTs has been intensively studied in a separate but closely related research area, that of skill learning. Over the past two decades much interest has focussed on the so-called power law of learning. Rosenbloom & Newell (1987) proposed this law after observing that in a wide variety of RT tasks the shortening of RT with practice closely followed a power function. Numerous theories have been proposed to account for this empirical relation; one of the best known is the instance theory of Logan (1988). Logan theorized that reductions in RT with practice do not come about from improvements in the speed of executing a basic algorithm used by subjects at low practice levels. Rather, the reduction in RT with practice occurs because subjects employ an alternative strategy of retrieving memory traces left by previous performances ("instances") and directly choosing the retrieved solution without need for calculation. Logan theorized that the algorithmic process and instance retrieval process operate in parallel in accordance with a "race" model—the first process to finish determines the RT. Because both of the processes (algorithm-based retrieval and instance retrieval) hypothesized to operate in parallel would seem to be examples of central processes in the sense discussed in the previous section, this theory appears inconsistent with the conclusions of PRP research (cf. Pashler & Johnston 1998). Thus, assessing the validity of this race model is relevant to the goal of providing a unified theory of information processing limitations.

An empirical challenge to Logan's race model of improvement with practice has emerged from studies of numerosity judgments about dot patterns. Palmeri (1997) reported that judgments in this paradigm improved rapidly with practice, closely following the power law, and data collected using this design initially appeared to be consistent with Logan's model. Rickard (1999), however, reanalyzed this data set and argued that although the data showed the usual pattern of a decline in RT over time with a positive second derivative (i.e. practice had diminishing returns over sessions of practice), careful examination showed systematic deviations from a perfect power law fit. Rickard argued that the data more closely fit predictions from his component power law theory. According to this theory, performance during the course of practice reflects a mixture of instance-based and rule-based performance. The essence of Rickard's model is that on any given trial, subjects perform only the rule-based or the exemplar-based strategy—but not both—and that, over practice, the mixture ratio becomes increasingly shifted toward the exemplar-based strategy. If Rickard's mixture model is correct, contrary to Palmeri's race model, the data can be explained without assuming that subjects can execute both strategies in parallel. Rickard's analysis would be entirely congenial to the findings of the PRP literature suggesting that only one central process can operate at a time.

Palmeri (1999), in a reply to Rickard, argued that more complex versions of the race model can fit the data, but the complexities needed to achieve such fits seem rather uninviting. They include an assumption that the algorithmic process can speed up with practice; it was an important motivation for the Logan model to avoid this assumption. The matter is presently not resolved, and it will be very intriguing if results from future skill-learning studies support or overturn the idea that multiple memory retrieval processes generally cannot, or at least do not, operate in parallel.

CONCLUDING COMMENTS

We have surveyed several particularly active research areas within the scope of the attention and performance tradition, focusing on studies of attention capture and studies of the limits of practice effect. One cannot examine this literature without being struck that the traditional focus on distinguishing parallel and serial processing remains very much a focus of research, despite skepticism expressed from time to time (e.g. Newell 1973). It is certainly the case that serial and parallel models may mimic each other in certain contexts, particularly with respect to patterns of mean response times (Townsend 1974). However, a variety of techniques now exist for successfully distinguishing these types of processes, and the question of whether different sorts of mental events can or cannot operate simultaneously is so fundamental that it simply cannot be evaded. Indeed, it may turn out that behavioral data can provide us with better answers to questions about the time course of processing than it can on questions of mental representation or underlying computational architecture.

At a more substantive level, one of the main themes to emerge from the research surveyed above is the idea that the effects of mental set are more pervasive than had previously been thought. As described in the first sections of this chapter, a variety of proposals for "wired-in" attention capture by particular stimulus attributes have been effectively challenged; attention, it turns out, is subject to a far greater degree of top-down control than was suspected 10 years ago. A second broad conclusion is that the effects of practice appear much more circumscribed than was previously appreciated. Although it may turn out that some mental operations are truly subject to automatization in the strongest sense, it appears quite unlikely that this holds nearly as broadly as was once suspected.

Visit the Annual Reviews home page at www.AnnualReviews.org

LITERATURE CITED

Allport A, Styles EA, Hsieh S. 1994. Shifting intentional set: exploring the dynamic control of tasks. In *Attention and Performance XV: Conscious and Nonconscious Information Processing*, ed. C Umilta, M Moscovitch, pp. 421–52. Cambridge: MIT Press

Atchley P, Kramer AF, Hollstrom AP. 2000. Contingent capture for onsets and offsets: attentional set for perceptual transients. *J. Exp. Psychol.: Hum. Percept. Perform.* 26:594–606

Bacon WF, Egeth HE. 1994. Overriding stimulus-driven attentional capture. *Percept. Psychophys.* 55:485–96

Bertelson P, Tisseyre F. 1969. Refractory period of c-reactions. *J. Exp. Psychol.* 79:122–28

Bichot N, Cave K, Pashler H. 1999. Visual selection mediated by location: feature-based selection of noncontiguous locations. *Percept. Psychophys.* 61:403–23

Biederman I. 1973. Mental set and mental arithmetic. *Mem. Cogn.* 1:383–86

Borger R. 1963. The refractory period and serial choice reactions. *Q. J. Exp. Psychol.* 15:1–12

Braun J. 1999. On the detection of salient contours. *Spat. Vis.* 12:211–25

Broadbent DE. 1982. Task combination and the selective intake of information. *Acta Psychol.* 50:253–90

De Jong R. 1993. Multiple bottlenecks in overlapping task performance. *J. Exp. Psychol.: Hum. Percept. Perform.* 19:965–89

Dutta A, Walker BN. 1995. *Persistence of the PRP effect: evaluating the response-selection bottleneck.* Presented at 36th Annu. Meet. Psychonom. Soc., Los Angeles

Fagot C. 1994. *Chronometric investigations of task switching.* PhD thesis. Univ. Calif., San Diego

Folk CL, Remington RW. 1998. Selectivity in distraction by irrelevant featural singletons: evidence for two forms of attentional capture. *J. Exp. Psychol.: Hum. Percept. Perform.* 24:847–58

Folk CL, Remington RW, Johnston JC. 1992. Involuntary covert orienting is contingent on attentional control settings. *J. Exp. Psychol.: Hum. Percept. Perform.* 18:1030–44

Folk CL, Remington RW, Wright JH. 1994. The structure of attentional control: contingent attentional capture by apparent motion, abrupt onset, and color. *J. Exp. Psychol.: Hum. Percept. Perform.* 20:317–29

Gibson BS, Jiang Y. 1998. Surprise! An unexpected color singleton does not capture attention in visual search. *Psychol. Sci.* 9:176–82

Gibson BS, Kelsey EM. 1998. Stimulus-driven attentional capture is contingent on attentional set for displaywide visual features. *J. Exp. Psychol.: Hum. Percept. Perform.* 24:699–706

Greenwald A. 1972. On doing two things at once: time sharing as a function of ideomotor compatibility. *J. Exp. Psychol.* 94:52–57

Greenwald A, Shulman HG. 1973. On doing two things at once: II. Elimination of the psychological refractory period effect. *J. Exp. Psychol.* 101:70–76

Halliday AM, Kerr M, Elithorn A. 1959. Grouping of stimuli and apparent exceptions to the psychological refractory period. *Q. J. Exp. Psychol.* 11:72–89

Hazeltine E, Teague D, Ivry R. 2000. *Dual-task performance during simultaneous execution: evidence for concurrent response selection processes.* Presented at Annu. Meet. Cogn. Neurosci. Soc., San Francisco

Hirst W, Spelke ES, Reaves CC, Caharack G, Neisser U. 1980. Dividing attention without alternation or automaticity. *J. Exp. Psychol. Gen.* 109:98–117

James W. 1890/1950. *The Principles of Psychology*, Vol. 1. New York: Dover

Jersild AT. 1927. Mental set and shift. *Arch. Psychol.* 89:whole issue

Johnston JC, Delgado DF. 1993. *Bypassing the single-channel bottleneck in dual-task performance.* Presented at 34th Annu. Meet. Psychonom. Soc., Washington, DC

Jonides J. 1981. Voluntary versus automatic movements of the mind's eye. In *Attention and Performance IX*, ed. J Long, A Baddeley pp. 197–203. Hillsdale, NJ: Lawrence Erlbaum

Jonides J, Yantis S. 1988. Uniqueness of abrupt visual onset in capturing attention. *Percept. Psychophys.* 43:346–54

Karlin L, Kestenbaum R. 1968. Effect of number of alternative on the psychological

refractory period. *Q. J. Exp. Psychol.* 20:167–78

Kramer AF, Hahn S. 1995. Splitting the beam: distribution of attention over noncontiguous regions of the visual field. *Psychol. Sci.* 6:381–86

Lee DK, Itti L, Koch C, Braun J. 1999. Attention activates winner-take-all competition among visual filters. *Nat. Neurosci.* 2:375–81

Levy J, Pashler HE. 2000. Is dual task slowing instruction dependent? Accepted pending revision. *J. Exp. Psychol.: Hum. Percept. Perform.* In press

Logan GD. 1988. Toward an instance theory of automatization. *Psychol. Rev.* 95:492–527

Martin-Emerson R, Kramer AF. 1997. Offset transients modulate attentional capture by sudden onsets. *Percept. Psychophys.* 59:739–51

McCann RS, Johnston JC. 1992. Locus of the single-channel bottleneck in dual-task interference. *J. Exp. Psychol.: Hum. Percept. Perform.* 18:471–84

McLeod P. 1977. A dual task response modality effect: support for multiprocessor models of attention. *Q. J. Exp. Psychol.* 29:651–67

McLeod P. 1978. Does probe RT measure central processing demand? *Q. J. Exp. Psychol.* 30:83–89

Meiran N. 1996. Reconfiguration of processing mode prior to task performance. *J. Exp. Psychol.: Learn. Mem. Cogn.* 22:1423–42

Miller JO. 1989. The control of attention by abrupt visual onsets and offsets. *Percept. Psychophys.* 45:567–71

Mueller HJ, Rabbitt PM. 1989. Reflexive and voluntary orienting of visual attention: Time course of activation and resistance to interruption. *J. Exp. Psychol.: Hum. Percept. Perform.* 15:315–30

Neisser U. 1976. Cognition and reality: principles and implications of cognitive psychology. San Francisco: Freeman

Newell A. 1973. You can't play twenty questions with nature and win: projective comments on the papers of this symposium. In *Visual Information Processing*, ed. WG Chase, pp. 283–308. New York: Academic

Palmeri TJ. 1997. Exemplar similarity and the development of automaticity. *J. Exp. Psychol.: Learn. Mem. Cogn.* 23:324–54

Palmeri TJ. 1999. Learning categories at different hierarchical levels: a comparison of category learning models. *Psychonom. Bull. Rev.* 6:495–503

Parasuraman R. 1998. *The Attentive Brain.* Cambridge, MA: MIT Press

Pashler H. 1988. Cross-dimensional interaction and texture segregation. *Percept. Psychophys.* 43:307–18

Pashler H. 1990. Do response modality effects support multiprocessor models of divided attention. *J. Exp. Psychol.: Hum. Percept. Perform.* 16:826–42

Pashler H. 1994. Dual-task interference in simple tasks: data and theory. *Psychol. Bull.* 16: 220–44

Pashler H. 1998. *The Psychology of Attention.* Cambridge, MA: MIT Press

Pashler H, Carrier M, Hoffman J. 1993. Saccadic eye movements and dual-task interference. *Q. J. Exp. Psychol. A* 46:51–82

Pashler H, Johnston J. 1998. Attentional limitations in dual-task performance. In *Attention*, ed. HE Pashler, pp. 155–89. Hove, UK: Psychology Press/Erlbaum

Posner MI. 1980. Orienting of attention. *Q. J. Exp. Psychol.* 32:3–25

Posner MI, Snyder CRR. 1975. Facilitation and inhibition in the processing of signals. See Rabbitt & Dornic 1975, pp. 669–81

Rabbitt PMA, Dornic S, eds. 1975. *Attention and Performance V.* London: Academic

Remington RW, Folk CL, McLean JP. 2000. Contingent attentional capture or delayed allocation of attention? *Percept. Psychophys.* In press

Remington RW, Johnston JC, Yantis S. 1992. Involuntary attentional capture by abrupt onsets. *Percept. Psychophys.* 51:279–90

Rickard T. 1999. A CMPL alternative account of practice effects in numerosity judgment

tasks. *J. Exp. Psychol.: Learn. Mem. Cogn.* 25:532–42

Rogers RD, Monsell S. 1995. Costs of a predictable switch between simple cognitive tasks. *J. Exp. Psychol.: Gen.* 124:207–31

Rosenbloom P, Newell A. 1987. Learning by chunking: a production system model of practice. In *Production System Models of Learning and Development*, ed. D Klahr, P Langley, pp. 221–86. Cambridge, MA: MIT Press

Ruthruff E, Johnston JC, Van Selst MV. 2000a. Why practice reduces dual-task interference. *J. Exp. Psychol.: Hum. Percept. Perform.* In press

Ruthruff E, Pashler HE, Klaassen A. 2000b. Processing bottlenecks in dual-task performance: structural limitation or voluntary postponement? *Psychonom. Bul. Rev.* In press

Ruthruff E, Remington RW, Johnston JC. 2000c. Switching between simple cognitive tasks: the interaction between top-down and bottom-up factors. *J. Exp. Psychol.: Hum. Percept. Perform.* In press

Salthouse TA, Fristoe N, McGuthry KE, Hambrick DZ. 1998. Relation of task switching to speed, age, and fluid intelligence. *Psychol. Aging* 13:445–61

Schneider W, Shiffrin RM. 1977. Controlled and automatic human information processing: I. Detection, search and attention. *Psychol. Rev.* 84:1–66

Schumacher EH, Seymour T, Glass JM, Lauber EJ, Kieras DE, Meyer DE. 1997. *Virtually perfect time sharing in dual-task performance.* Presented at 38th Annu. Meet. Psychonom. Soc., Philadelphia

Spector A, Biederman I. 1976. Mental set and mental shift revisited. *Am. J. Psychol.* 89:669–79

Sternberg S. 1969. The discovery of processing stages: extensions of Donders' method. In *Attention and Performance II*, ed. WG Koster, pp. 276–315. Amsterdam: North Holland

Sudevan P, Taylor DA. 1987. The cueing and

priming of cognitive operations. *J. Exp. Psychol.: Hum. Percept. Perform.* 13:89–103

Theeuwes J. 1991. Exogenous and endogenous control of attention: the effect of visual onsets and offsets. *Percept. Psychophys.* 49:83–90

Theeuwes J. 1992. Perceptual selectivity for color and form. *Percept. Psychophys.* 51:599–606

Titchener EB. 1908. *Lectures on the Elementary Psychology of Feeling and Attention.* New York: Macmillan

Townsend JT. 1974. Issues and models concerning the processing of a finite number of inputs. In *Human Information Processing: Tutorials in Performance and Cognition*, ed. BH Kantowitz, pp. 133–68. Hillsdale, NJ: Erlbaum

Van Selst MV, Ruthruff E, Johnston JC. 1999. Can practice eliminate the Psychological Refractory Period effect? *J. Exp. Psychol.: Hum. Percept. Perform.* 25:1268–83

Welford AT. 1967. Single-channel operation in the brain. *Acta Psychol.* 27:5–22

Wolfe JM. 1992. The parallel guidance of visual attention. *Curr. Dir. Psychol. Sci.* 1:124–28

Wolfe JM, Cave KR, Franzel SL. 1989. Guided search: an alternative to the feature integration model of visual search. *J. Exp. Psychol.: Hum. Percept. Perform.* 15:419–33

Yantis S, Egeth HE. 1999. On the distinction between visual salience and stimulus-driven attentional capture. *J. Exp. Psychol.: Hum. Percept. Perform.* 25:661–76

Yantis S, Hillstrom A. 1994. Stimulus-driven attentional capture: evidence from equiluminant visual objects. *J. Exp. Psychol.: Hum. Percept. Perform.* 20:95–107

Yantis S, Jonides J. 1984. Abrupt visual onsets and selective attention: evidence from visual search. *J. Exp. Psychol.: Hum. Percept. Perform.* 10:601–21

Yantis S, Jonides J. 1990. Abrupt visual onsets and selective attention: evidence from visual search. *J. Exp. Psychol.: Hum. Percept. Perform.* 16:121–34

Annu. Rev. Psychol. 2001. 52:653–83

PROBLEMS FOR JUDGMENT
AND DECISION MAKING

R. Hastie

*Psychology Department, University of Colorado, Boulder, Colorado 80309-0345;
e-mail: reid.hastie@colorado.edu*

Key Words   values, utilities, preferences, expectations, uncertainty, decision
weights, probabilities reference point, emotions

■ **Abstract** This review examines recent developments during the past 5 years in
the field of judgment and decision making, written in the form of a list of 16 research
problems. Many of the problems involve natural extensions of traditional, originally
rational, theories of decision making. Others are derived from descriptive algebraic
modeling approaches or from recent developments in cognitive psychology and cognitive neuroscience.

"Wir müssen wissen. Wir werden wissen." (We must know. We will know.)
David Hilbert, *Mathematische Probleme* (1900)

CONTENTS

INTRODUCTION

"Who of us would not be glad to lift the veil behind which the future lies hidden
and direct our thoughts towards the unknown future . . . (Hilbert 1900, p. 437)." In
1900, Hilbert began a paper presented at the International Congress of Mathematicians in Paris with these words. (*Mathematical Problems*, an English translation

by Newson, was published in 1902). In this paper, Hilbert proposed 22 problems as the focus of mathematical research in the immediate future. His judgment was impeccable, and many of his problems turned out to be the most studied and productive in the next century. The present review attempts a modest version of Hilbert's feat for the field of judgment and decision making. First, I briefly consider what makes a good research problem; this is followed by an introduction to the field of judgment and decision making; and finally, a list of 16[1] problems designed to promote productive research on judgment and decision making in the next decade or two.

GOOD PROBLEMS

The two primary motives for research in the behavioral sciences are to develop scientific theories and to solve problems that occur in everyday life. In the case of research on judgment and decision making, there are three theoretical frameworks that provide the motivation for current and future research: (*a*) traditional expected and nonexpected utility theories, most prominently represented by von Neumann and Morgenstern's expected utility theory and Kahneman and Tversky's (cumulative) prospect theory, which focus on choice and decision-making behaviors; (*b*) cognitive algebraic theories, primarily concerned with judgment and estimation; and (*c*) cognitive computational theories of the mind's perceptual, inferential, and mnemonic functions. Each of these three theoretical frameworks provides a general image of the human mind, although sometimes, when research is focused on a specific issue within any one of the frameworks, it is unclear exactly what larger question about the nature of human nature is being addressed.

Most academic researchers seek solutions, usually in controlled laboratory experiments, that reveal basic behavioral and cognitive processes. The biggest rewards go to researchers who appear to have discovered something fundamental and general about human nature—for example, the general diminishing marginal utility tendency for rewards and punishments to have decreasing impacts on evaluations and behavior as the overall amount of reward or punishment increases; the loss aversion tendency, in which losses have a greater impact than gains of equal magnitude; the general habit of integrating separate items of information according to an averaging (linear, weight and add, or anchor and adjust) combination rule when estimating magnitudes of all kinds; the properties of capacity limits on working memory and selective attention; etc.

---

[1]My original list had 22 problems to be consistent with Hilbert's example. However, length constraints and lack of energy whittled the total down to the present 16. Anyone interested in reading the material excluded from this review should contact the author (e-mail: reid.hastie@colorado.edu); anyone who wishes to contribute additional problems to a master list of problems should send a suggestion to the author. I will maintain a current list and make it available to anyone who requests it.

The second strategy is to start with a phenomenon that is important in everyday life and independent of any scholarly tradition and then to study it with the primary motive of contributing to general social welfare. This is sometimes called the Pasteur heuristic, after the great French biologist's habit of starting with a phenomenon of practical importance, subjecting it to rigorous empirical analysis, and presenting solutions to major social and theoretical problems. On the practical side, the major "real world" problems that have been the subject of extensive study would include medical diagnosis and decisions by both health care professionals and their patients (especially relating to psychotherapy); financial and economic forecasting; legal, policy, and diplomatic judgments; and weather forecasting. The contributions of researchers in judgment and decision making to improved social welfare are more difficult to identify than the constantly increasing numbers of archived scientific papers, but I submit that many instances of applied decision analysis and aiding have had their origins in research by behavioral scientists (see Cooksey 1996 and Swets et al 2000 for many examples).

In the present review, I attempt to identify research problems that are justified with reference to either or both motives. Some of the attributes of good, productive research problems identified by Hilbert and others that apply to either theory- or practice-motivated research include the following:

1. The statement of the problem is clear, comprehensible, and succinct.
2. The statement of the problem is expressed in intuitively sensible and meaningful symbols.
3. The problem is difficult but accessible—it is challenging but not apparently impossible.
4. It is possible to evaluate the correctness (or at least the relative-correctness) of a candidate solution.
5. The answer to the problem connects to current knowledge; it has an important location in a chain of problems. A solution to the problem will have ramifications in many other theoretical and practical domains.

I have attempted to state problems that exemplify these attributes; although, unlike mathematical problems that can be proved or derived, most behavioral science problems have many answers, or at least answers with multiple, interrelated parts. As the adage states, almost any problem, however complicated, becomes still more complicated when looked at in the right way. However, that is not necessarily a bad quality for a scientific problem to possess.

THE PSYCHOLOGY OF JUDGMENT AND DECISION MAKING

What is the field of judgment and decision making about? The focus of research is on how people (and other organisms and machines) combine desires (utilities, personal values, goals, ends, etc) and beliefs (expectations, knowledge, means, etc) to choose a course of action. The conceptual (perhaps defining) template for a decision includes three components: (*a*) courses of action (choice options and alternatives); (*b*) beliefs about objective states, processes, and events in the world (including outcome states and means to achieve them); and (*c*) desires, values, or utilities that describe the consequences associated with the outcomes of each action-event combination. Good decisions are those that effectively choose means that are available in the given circumstances to achieve the decision-maker's goals.

The most common image of a decision problem is in the form of a decision tree, analogous to a map of forking roads (Figure 1). The diagram in Figure 1 highlights the three major components: alternative courses of action, consequences, and uncertain conditioning events. For the sake of clarity, I will state a few basic definitions. Decisions are situation-behavior combinations, like the one

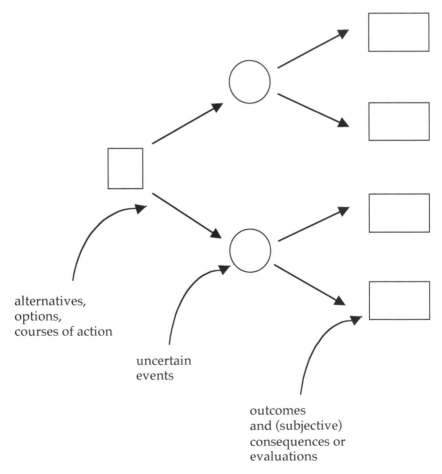

alternatives,
options,
courses of action

uncertain
events

outcomes
and (subjective)
consequences or
evaluations

Figure 1   Definitional template for a decision.

summarized in Figure 1, which can be described in terms of three essential components: alternative actions, consequences, and uncertain events. Outcomes are the publicly describable situations that occur at the end of each path in the decision tree (of course, outcomes may become mere events if the horizon of the tree is extended further into the future). Consequences are the subjective evaluative reactions (measurable on a good-bad, gain-loss scale) associated with each outcome. Uncertainty refers to the decision-maker's judgments of the propensity for each of the conditioning events to occur. Uncertainty is described with several, sometimes competing, measures in various decision theories, including probabilities, confidences, and likelihoods (there are several prescriptions for precise usage of these terms, but for present purposes I lump together all measures of judgment of the propensity for events and outcomes to occur under the rubric "uncertainty;" see Luce & Raiffa 1957 for an introduction to traditional distinctions). Preferences are behavioral expressions of choosing (or intentions to choose) one course of action over others. Decision making refers to the entire process of choosing a course of action. Judgment refers to the components of the larger decision-making process that are concerned with assessing, estimating, and inferring what events will occur and what the decision-maker's evaluative reactions to those outcomes will be.

Historically, behavioral research has been divided into two separate streams: judgment and decision making (see Goldstein & Hogarth 1997 for an excellent history of recent research in the field). Research on judgment has been inspired by analogies between perception and prediction. For judgment researchers, the central empirical questions concern the processes by which as-yet obscure events, outcomes, and consequences could be inferred (or, speaking metaphorically, "perceived"): How do people integrate multiple, fallible, incomplete, and sometimes conflicting cues to infer what is happening in the external world? The most popular models have been derived from statistical algebraic principles developed originally to predict uncertain events [especially linear or averaging models, fitted to behavioral data using multiple regression techniques; (Anderson 1982, Cooksey 1996)]. The primary standards for the quality of judgment are based on accuracy the correspondence between a judgment, and the criterion condition that was the target of the judgment (Hammond 1996, Hastie & Rasinski 1987). This approach has also been applied to study judgments of internal events, such as personal evaluations of consequences or predictions of evaluative reactions to possible future outcomes.

The second stream of research was inspired by theories concerned with decision making that were originally developed by philosophers, mathematicians, and economists. These theorists were most interested in understanding preferential choice and action: How do people choose what action to take to achieve labile, sometimes conflicting goals in an uncertain world? These models are often expressed axiomatically and algebraically, in the tradition established for measurement theories in physics and economics. Here the standards used to evaluate the quality of decisions usually involve comparisons between behavior and the prescriptions of rational, normative models, which often take the form of tests for the coherence of expectations, values, and preferences or the achievement of ideal optimal outcomes.

Although the field is becoming more behavioral, more psychological, and more descriptive, its boundaries and major theoretical concerns are all related to the historically dominant expected utility family of theories. These theories (and there are many flavors) are exemplified by the subjective expected utility theory made popular by von Neumann & Morgenstern (1947) and Savage (1954; Friedman & Savage 1948). Several good recent introductions to expected and closely related nonexpected utility frameworks are available [e.g. Camerer 1995, Dawes 1998, the papers cited in Edwards 1992; and Luce 2000; see Miyamoto (1988) for a distillation of the formal essence of these theories]. At the center of all these frameworks is a basic distinction between information about what the decision maker wants (often referred to as utilities) and what the decision maker believes is true about the situation (often called expectations). The heart of the theory, sometimes called the rational expectations principle, proposes that each alternative course of action or choice option should be evaluated by weighting its global expected satisfaction-dissatisfaction with the probabilities that the component consequences will occur and be experienced.

The subjective expected utility framework was first applied analytically—if the preferences of a decision maker (human or other) satisfied the axioms, then the decision process could be summarized with a numerical (interval-scale) expected utility function relating concrete outcomes to behavioral preferences: first the choice behavior, then an application of the theory to infer what utilities and beliefs are consistent with those preferences. However, more recently, the theory has often been used synthetically to predict decisions: If a person has certain utilities and expectations, how will he or she choose to maximize utility? This second perspective on the theory seems more natural, at least to a psychologist; intuitively, it seems that we first judge what we want and think about ways to get it, and then we choose an action.

There are two important limits on the expected utility framework. First, it is incomplete. Many aspects of the decision process lie outside of its analysis. For example, the framework says nothing about how the decision situation is comprehended or constructed by the decision maker: Which courses of action are under consideration in the choice set? In addition, the theory says nothing about the sources of inputs into the decision process: What should the trade-off be between adaptive flexibility and the precise estimation of optimal choices by a realistic computational system (the human brain) in a representatively complex, nonstationary environment? Where does information about alternatives, consequences, and events come from in the first place, and how is it used to construct the representation on which the expected values/expected utilities are computed? Finally, how are personal values, utilities, and satisfactions inferred, predicted, and known?

The second limit on the expected utility framework is that it does not provide a valid description of the details of human decision-making processes. Today a myriad of qualifications is applied to the basic expected utility model when it is used to describe everyday decision-making behavior. As the saying goes, Compared to the assumptions of the rational model, people are boundedly rational and moderately selfish, and they exercise limited self-control (Jolls et al 1998).

However, even with its limitations,[2] subjective expected utility has been the dominant conceptual framework for rational and empirical studies of decision making for the past 2 or 3 centuries. Therefore, many research problems concerning judgment and decision making are best conceptualized and stated in the context of this overarching theoretical framework. Furthermore, there is some sensible reason for most behaviors (Anderson 1990, March 1978, Newell 1982; see Oaksford & Chater 1998 for a sample of applications of rational models to cognitive achievements). Even when people appear to be making systematically biased judgments or irrational decisions, it is likely that they are trying to solve some problem or achieve some goal to the best of their abilities. The behavioral researcher is well advised to look carefully at his or her research participant's behavior, beliefs, and goals to discern "the method in the apparent madness" (Becker 1976, Miller & Cantor 1982).

The following problems are all concerned with aspects of the distinctive focus of research on decision making the manner in which organisms integrate what they believe is true and what they expect will happen with what they want. Most of the problems can be interpreted as extensions of the enduring research program that produced the subjective expected utility framework, although the new directions are often more cognitive, more neural, and more descriptive than anticipated by that seminal framework. For each problem I attempt to provide an introduction to interest the reader in the subject matter and to initiate further scholarly and empirical research on the topic.

THE PROBLEMS

Overarching and Foundational Questions

Problem 1 (CK Hsee, RH Thaler[3]) What makes a decision good? The origins of the field of decision making lie in efforts to prescribe good, winning decisions in gambling and insurance situations. The original answers to the question of

---

[2]Many behavioral scientists would say that these limitations are advantages: At least there has been some agreement on the nature of the rational man that underlies traditional theories (see Problem 1), although there is, even today, no clear conception of and little consensus on the nature of the irrational person. At least at present, there are few clear theoretical ideas about how people comprehend and mentally represent decision situations (see Problem 5). What kind of a more psychologically realistic theory could be framed without answers to those questions?

[3]I have received too much constructive advice from too many sources to provide full acknowledgments. I have listed the names of those individuals I remember as being most influential on my selection or formulation of a problem in parentheses with each problem statement. I beg forgiveness from the many people whom I must have forgotten to thank.

what makes a decision a good one involved identifying the actions that would maximize desirable (and minimize undesirable) outcomes under idealized conditions. These rational solutions proved to be remarkably general and led to the enterprise of representing complex everyday situations as well-formed, regular gambles to allow the direct application of decision analysis (e.g. Clemen 1996, Hammond et al 1999). Recent analyses have shifted the emphasis to the robustness and generality of decision-making methods, especially when information is unreliable and incomplete, the environment is complex and changing, and mental computations are limited (in quantity and quality). Thus, there is a historical shift from criteria based on internal coherence [e.g. did the person's decisions satisfy the principles of rational thinking (usually the formal axioms of the probability theory or rational choice theories)?] to criteria based on measures of accuracy or success with reference to conditions in the decision-maker's external environment (correspondence) in the operational evaluation of decision goodness (cf Hammond 1996, Hastie & Rasinski 1987, Kahneman 1994). There are many conceptions of the nature of rationality. A useful introduction to modern views is provided by Harman (1995), who emphasizes the distinctions between theoretical (belief and judgment) and practical rationality (intentions, plans, and action) and between inference (psychological processes) and logical implication (relationships among ideal propositions). A common approach to identify rationality is to use simple, indubitable rules to detect irrationality; for example, if a logical contradiction is established within a set of beliefs, the beliefs and corresponding behavior must be irrational (Dawes 2000, Tversky & Kahneman 1974). Another solution is to rely on people's intuitions: If someone thinks hard about a decision (more often two or more decisions) and wishes that he or she had not made the decision, there is at least a hint of irrationality (especially if the thinker is someone whose credentials establish that he or she is an expert). Of course, the ability to recognize irrationality in decisions may not be directly related to the ability to reason rationally when making those decisions.

A second approach is to assess the success of various decision rules, algorithms, or heuristics in complex simulated choice environments. A precursor to this approach is the analytic study of the long-term survival of decision makers over a long sequence of decisions (Dubins & Savage 1965, Lopes 1982). The recent simulation methods have been pioneered by Axelrod (1984), Payne et al (1993), and Gigerenzer et al (1999). All have used simulation to evaluate the relative adaptive success of decision rules in abstractions of social and distributed-resource environments. An important property of robust computational systems is that they degrade gracefully, rather than fail catastrophically, when challenged. One of the surprises from these research programs has been the discovery that, under some representative conditions, "less is better." That is, more limited processing is actually more adaptive (Gigerenzer & Goldstein 1996, Kareev et al 1997).

A third approach is to study the adaptive success of decision habits in natural environments. This approach has been neglected by psychologists, although there are instructive examples in studies of optimal foraging by humans and animals (Kaplan & Hill 1985, Krebs & Davies 1993, Real 1991, Stanford 1995), in studies of the success of economic strategies in naturally occurring markets (e.g. Camerer 1997), and in studies of global individual differences in everyday decision-making habits (Larrick et al 1993). Thus, the very definition of rationality, adaptive rationality, or ecologically fit rationality is under construction. One of the most interesting recent directions is an effort to reduce traditional definitions and precepts to a more fundamental, biological-evolutionary level—for example, Cooper's (1987) attempt to derive Savage's axioms from the concept of an evolutionarily stable strategy (an approach that assumes the bounded forms of rationality may still be adaptively optimal). Of course, additional work remains to be done on operational methods to measure the concept(s) of adaptive rationality, when it has stabilized.

Problem 2   (B Fasolo, JM Greenberg, JW Payne) What makes a decision difficult? There is no consensus on a comprehensive principle that predicts decision difficulty, provides measures of difficulty, or even provides a definition of difficulty. For example, consider an idealized choice set (the kind of stimulus display that would be presented to readers of a product review in *Consumer Reports* or to participants in a study of consumer choice on a MouseLab® information display board). What characteristics of the alternatives, their attributes, and their relationships to the choice maker's goals make the decision difficult? If the two decision problems are clearly described, how can we predict which will be more difficult? Are the choice sets that make us look smart in the Gigerenzer et al (1999) research program easy decisions, at least compared to market-driven consumer choice sets, in which the attribute values are often negatively correlated and where we are challenged by difficult attribute-value tradeoffs?

One answer is a very general "it depends"; most theorists presume that the number of elementary information processes executed to make a typical choice is a good index of difficulty, so that difficulty is defined on the basis of the relationship between the choice set and the decision-maker's capacities and strategy (e.g. Bettman et al 1990).

However, at least two aspects of cognitive load have been ignored in previous measures: the effort required to infer attribute values and to align attributes in the choice process (Medin et al 1995) and the demands on working memory imposed by choice strategies (Miyake & Shah 1999). Surely we can say more about the effects on difficulty of the number of alternatives, similarity of alternatives, number of important, goal relevant attributes, and, perhaps most importantly, the intercorrelations of the attribute values across alternatives.

A second approach to defining and measuring difficulty is to rely on choice makers' subjective evaluations of difficulty, effort, strain, or anxiety (e.g. Chatterjee & Heath 1996, Luce et al 1999). A third approach is to identify correct choice alternatives and to work backward from situations and conditions in which decision makers make many or few errors. These later approaches do not seem as fundamental as the proactive development of a theory of the causes of cognitive and emotional difficulty. However, any progress toward a theory of decision difficulty will be a major contribution.

Problem 3   (KR Hammond, JM Greenberg, WM Goldstein) What are the roles of intuitive vs analytic modes of thinking in judgment and decision making? What are the relative roles of intuitive (e.g. implicit, associative, or automatic) vs analytic (e.g. explicit, rule-based, or controlled) cognitive processes in a decision? Both kinds of cognitive process are involved in any deliberate, goal-directed decision. Implicit processes seem to be fundamental, more likely to involve emotional reactions, and likely to be modified by slow, incremental learning processes. Explicit processes seem to be optional, more likely to involve context-independent abstractions, and likely to be modifiable by brief, even one-trial, learning episodes. If there is a signature distinction between the two kinds of processes, it is based on conscious awareness. If a process occurs outside of awareness, it is probably implicit; and any process that can be inspected and modified consciously is explicit. I suspect that it is useful to describe some fundamental cognitive functions as being performed by procedures that are essentially implicit: memory retrieval (including emotional reactions), familiarity and similarity judgments, registration and estimation of experienced frequencies, and probably some form of causal or contingency judgment. Obviously, these fundamental cognitive procedures will be employed in higher-order explicit, analytic, goal-directed strategies.

There are many neuroscientific findings that imply a distinction between implicit, intuitive processes and explicit, analytic processes (e.g. Alvarez & Squire 1994, McClelland et al 1995, papers in Schacter & Tulving 1994). In addition, some decision processes are deeply ingrained in the nervous system at a level at which they are unlikely to be consciously penetrable (e.g. Knowlton et al 1994, Lieberman 2000, Nichols & Newsome 1999, Platt & Glimcher 1999). However, there is little consensus in cognitive and social psychology on the relationship between implicit and explicit processes or on standard operations to separate implicit from explicit aspects of responding [Smith & DeCoster (2000) provide a nice summary of diverging views]. The most popular methods in empirical studies of implicit vs explicit processes study the unconscious effects of prior experience on the perception or comprehension of a stimulus (i.e. priming; e.g. Bargh & Chartrand 2000, Leeper 1935).

An interactive model that assumes a constant mixture of intuitive-analytic modes (e.g. Anderson 1983, Jacoby 1991) seems more plausible than an independent channel model (e.g. Bargh & Chartrand 1999, Schacter 1994, Sloman 1996). I suspect that many phenomena that have been described as a race between an implicit and an explicit process, both of which finish, [sometimes these processes promote competing responses (e.g. Sloman's S-criterion)], are actually examples of sequential processing. However, I have little confidence in this speculation, and a good answer awaits advances in the methods to identify the existence and outputs of different process types. I agree with the common assumption that implicit processes rely less, if at all, on immediate, working memory capacities than do explicit processes, and this assumption does imply that the cognitive resources for simultaneous processes are available.

I strongly endorse Hammond's cognitive continuum framework, which proposes that pure intuition and pure analysis anchor a descriptive scale in which most cognitive performances are quasi-rational mixtures of the two ingredient modes of processing (Hammond 1996) and also describe the characteristics of the different modes of judgment and the task conditions that promote one process rather than the other. I suggest that the cognitive continuum framework should be further developed in terms of a successful cognitive architecture [e.g. JR Anderson's ACT family of information processing models (1983); NH Anderson's information integration theory (1996); or perhaps a connectionist formulation, e.g. Rumelhart et al (1988)]. In my view, one weakness of research on the differences between implicit and explicit processes has been the tendency to settle for empirical demonstrations of the mere existence of implicit processes followed by piecemeal theoretical assertions. What is sorely needed now are comprehensive process models for the overall cognitive performance in the experimental tasks under study that assign relative roles to implicit and explicit processing modes. Only within the framework of a comprehensive process model can we achieve conceptual clarity about the nature and interrelations between the two or more types of processes and also develop useful empirical methods to study the relationships between the processes.

For example, the roles of implicit and explicit processes are going to change in relation to the following events: an emotional reaction to one or more of the choices affecting the larger decision strategy, the retrieval of remembered cases and analogical reasoning, the matching of the current situation to an abstract prototype or narrative schema, or the deliberate enumeration of reasons for and reasons against each imagined course of action. I would speculate that the role of intuition would be more dominant in the first two strategies and the least dominant in the last strategy; but again, I have little confidence in any hypothesis without empirical research and theories that identify the roles of implicit and explicit processes within the context of a comprehensive model of the larger decision-making process.

Problem 4 (WM Goldstein, T Kameda, TK Landauer, R Tourangeau) What are the alternatives to consequentialist models of decision processes? Many apparent decisions are not conceptualized as such by the decision maker; for example, "I'm tailgating because I want to get to work as fast as I can" (not "I made a choice between driving at a reasonable speed and hurrying."), "I'm having sex because I can," "I'm taking the drug because the doctor told me to," "I'm signing the contract because I can't stand any more of this irritation," etc. Many such decisions are the result of applying a plan, a policy, or a self-concept formed in the past to the current situation; for example, "I didn't decide whether or not to vote by considering means and consequences; I voted because I am a good citizen,"

"I didn't decide whether or not to recycle; it's just an expression of my attitude about protecting the environment," "I didn't decide whether or not to overfish the stream; I just acted the way a Native American would act," "I didn't marry Donald because I reasoned through the means and ends; he's just the right kind of husband for me."

March & Simon have discussed the reliance on social roles and personal identity in decision making (i.e. decision making as rule following; March & Heath 1994, March & Simon 1993), and Baron (1994), and Baron & Spranca (1997) demonstrated the impact of protected, obligatory values on behavior. However, clear models of nonconsequential decision processes are still needed (see also Goldstein & Weber 1995). Cognitive and production system models would seem to be natural candidates to describe these processes, and similarity is likely to play a key role (cf Medin et al 1995). Furthermore, many decisions are made by imitation of the behavior of others; for example, important financial decisions appear to be well described by herd instincts. We know of almost no discussion or research on the role of social imitation in decision making.

Problem 5 (B Fischhoff, EJ Mulligan, DA Rettinger) How are deliberate decision-making problems represented cognitively (e.g. causal explanations and naïve conceptualizations of random processes), and what are the major determinants of the representation of situations? How do people comprehend the decision situation; in other words, how do they perceive, retrieve, or create alternative courses of action; represent the events that will condition which outcomes occur; and evaluate the consequences they might experience? If they do create a mental representation of actions and consequences that is something like the decision tree from traditional decision theory (Figure 1), what determines which branches, contingencies, and components are included; the temporal extent or horizon of the tree; and the point at which a person stops looking ahead and begins to reason backward about what will happen and what he or she will receive as a consequence? What little we know about the generation and representation of alternative courses of action suggests that decision makers are myopic and do not consider many options (Fischhoff 1996, Keller & Ho 1988), although obviously this habit may not be a handicap if the focal options are good ones (Klein et al 1995).

Far more is known about the consequences of alternative decision problem representations (e.g. gain vs loss frames and summary vs unpacked event descriptions) than is known about the determinants of the representations. Thus, one key problem is understanding the determinants of decision frames (Levin et al 1998) and event descriptions (Johnson-Laird et al 1999, Macchi et al 1999, Rottenstreich & Tversky 1997, Tversky & Koehler 1994) and the impact of these differences on evaluations and judgments when a person is uncertain.

This is a problem that seems to invite applications of the cognitive theories and methods to describe knowledge representations (Markman 1998).

Recent work applying graphical plus algebraic representations to evidence evaluation and causal reasoning points the direction to useful hybrid structure-process representations (Pearl 2000, Schum 1994). Some applications of this approach have been attempted in studies of judgment and decision making (e.g. Hastie & Pennington 2000, Klayman & Schoemaker 1993, Weber et al 1991), although almost all of the psychological research on decision problems with which we are familiar is concerned with the representation of evidence but not of alternative courses of action, consequences, and evaluations (some example exceptions might include Fischhoff et al 1999, Kintsch 1998, and Rettinger & Hastie 2000). For ideas about how to proceed, there are suggestions from economists, game theorists, and management scientists (e.g. Ho & Weigelt 1996, Manski 1999). One reason that research on decision making has been so closely connected to normative theories in economics and statistics and so little influenced by research on problem solving, reasoning, language, and other higher cognitive functions is because the cognitive methods are less developed and much more labor-intensive than the methods used to test algebraic process models. A major challenge for cognitive approaches is to standardize and simplify methods for the measurement of knowledge structures involved in decision processes.

Problem 6   (RD Luce, MC Mozer) It would be useful to develop a theory that provides an integrated account of one-shot, well-defined decisions (current theories) and sequences of linked decisions in a dynamic, temporally extended future. Most current decision theories are designed to account for the choice of one action at one point in time. The image of a decision maker standing at a choice point like a fork in a road and choosing one direction or the other is probably much less appropriate for major everyday decisions than the image of a boat navigating a rough sea with a sequence of many embedded choices and decisions to maintain a meandering course toward the ultimate goal (Hogarth 1981). This is exactly the image that has dominated analysis in research by psychologists and computer scientists concerned with problem solving and planning: a problem space composed of a series of problem states with connecting paths, with the problem solver navigating from start to goal and relying on evaluation functions for guidance (Newell & Simon 1972). Each move from one state to the next can be treated as a decision, with the evaluation function serving to define expected utilities for the alternative moves to each available next state.

The temporal dimension enters the decision process in many ways. The decision process takes time, and some theories describe the dynamics of the temporally localized decision process (e.g. Busemeyer & Townsend 1993). Sometimes the anticipated outcomes are distributed over a future epoch or located at a distant point in time; if so, the decision maker has to project his or her goals into the future to evaluate courses of action in the present (Loewenstein & Elster 1992). Sometimes the theory attempts to incorporate the future via a temporal horizon by supposing that the decision maker anticipates some possible consequences by constructing scenarios or decision trees as extensions of his or her mental situation model (although almost nothing is known about the psychology of these constructive planning processes). Sometimes choice in the current situation involves a sequence of decisions that are dependent on each other and on changing future circumstances.

This issue of projection and, especially, controllability of the anticipated sequence of decisions is frequently mentioned in strategic managerial contexts; however, we do not have much factual knowledge about these decisions or a clearly specified theoretical framework to account for empirical findings (Brehmer 1999, March & Shapira 1992, papers in Shapira 1997). Some recent developments in behavioral game theory include an especially promising source of research paradigms and theoretical concepts to study people's reasoning about choices and contingencies in an extended temporal frame (e.g. Camerer 1997, Ho & Weigelt 1996).

Problem 7   What is the nature of value-expectation (payoff-probability) interactions, and where do they occur? The existence of wishful thinking (the valence of an event has an impact on expectations of its probability of occurrence) or Pollyanna effects (the probability of an event's occurrence has an impact on judgments of its valence) is assumed in many discussions of judgment and decision-making phenomena. However, there is little hard evidence for the reliable occurrence of these phenomena, and there are contrary hypotheses with some support (e.g. simple pessimism and defensive pessimism). Nonetheless, research literature exists, mostly concerned with judgments of health and medical risks, that assumes that optimistic thinking is the norm and is adaptive (Taylor & Brown 1988; Weinstein 1980, 1989; but see Colvin & Block 1994).

An instructive recent example comes from research on physicians' estimates of patients' longevity. Initial results suggested that the estimates were much too optimistic; it appeared that the physicians overestimated the patients' longevity by a factor of 5, but careful follow-up studies revealed that in most cases the physicians' overestimates were deliberate errors and that their true estimates were much more accurate (Lamont & Christakis 2000). Similar effects are prevalent in many apparent demonstrations of optimistic and overconfident judgment: When incentives are increased for accuracy or when disincentives are increased for errors, wishful thinking decreases or disappears.

My reading of this literature suggests that there are only two situations in which unrealistic optimism has been reliably established: judgments of cost and time to complete future multicomponent projects (e.g. Griffin & Buehler 1999) and early judgments of the longevity of personal relationships, such as in dating and marriage (MacDonald & Ross 1999). Results in gambling situations and results that require responses on well-defined probability-of-occurrence scales have been mixed over the past 50 years [Slovic's 1966 dissertation summary (p. 22) still seems apt: "Desirability was found to bias probability estimates in a complex manner which varied systematically between subjects and between estimation trials ... some subjects were consistently optimistic. Some were quite pessimistic."] Nonetheless, I believe that the quest for reliable value-expectation interactions is a productive problem for research. The results of careful research on this problem will be useful in practice and will illuminate the relationships between value and belief that lie at the center of the decision-making process.

Questions About Values, Utilities, and Goals

Problem 8   (D Kahneman, GF Loewenstein, RD Luce, B Fischhoff, JW Payne) If people don't have preferences like those postulated by expected utility theories, what do they have instead? Economists postulate the existence of preferences, and psychologists interpret some data as evidence of unstable or nonexistent preferences. In psychology, the most popular conception of values and preferences supposes that they are like attitudes. This analogy between values and (other) attitudes is useful, but it needs further development: What kind of attitudes? It would be interesting to apply the general belief-sampling model of attitudes that has been developed by researchers concerned with the quality of survey responses (Tourangeau & Rasiniski 1988); this seems close to what Kahneman and others have in mind in the context of contingent valuation processes (Kahneman et al 1999b). This belief-sampling model assumes, with some empirical support, that a person carries around a store of relevant ideas in his or her long-term memory that can be retrieved in response to an attitude question or object. The attitude (evaluation) on any one occasion is a function of the number and affective-evaluative qualities of the ideas retrieved at the time when a question, object, or situation is encountered. Because the memory retrieval system is variable, attitudes (evaluations) will be labile. The degree of lability can be predicted by the statistical properties of the long-term memory store, the sampling-retrieval process, and the response scale characteristics (Tourangeau et al 2000).

What are the implications of constructed, and highly contingent, preferences (values) for such important applied problems as the measurement of consumer preferences for new products and for the design of future decisions [e.g. helping a person make a decision about medical treatment or assessing preferences as inputs into public policy decisions (Payne et al 1999)]? Research on the construction of preferences had some of its origins in practical applications such as the design of methods to elicit reliable preferences for nonmarket goods (e.g. Fischhoff 1991 and Slovic 1995). The original embedding, framing, and other context effects (oversensitivity and undersensitivity) are now well documented, and sophisticated theories of their sources have been proposed (Hsee et al 1999, Tversky et al 1988). However, the normative implications remain to be explored: Can we make a distinction between better-constructed and more poorly constructed preferences? What advice can we give people to help them construct better preferences? What are the implications of differences in quality of preferences for the practices of social choice?

Another important aspect of preferences and values concerns the construction of summary evaluations from memory and the prediction of future values and evaluative reactions to anticipated outcomes (see many of the papers cited in Kahneman et al 1999a, 1997). In addition, there is always the need to verify that alternative expressions of preferences and values agree and, more importantly, to understand why they do not (e.g. Bernstein & Michael 1990).

Problem 9   (RD Luce, CF Camerer) What is the form of the function(s) that relate decision outcomes to personal values, satisfactions, and utilities? The best-known models of choice among uncertain alternatives have assumed (and have been tested to a degree) properties that, when suitably combined, imply a utility representation. Specifically, behavior can be represented in terms of a utility function over consequences and a weighting function over events. The utility function of a gamble (i.e. an uncertain alternative) is some sort of weighted sum of the utilities of the individual consequences. A common proposal is that the utility function is linear in utilities and linear in some function of the weights (i.e. bilinear, a multiplicative relationship), although there is contradicting evidence from some empirical studies (see Birnbaum 1999, Chechile & Butler 2000, and Luce 2000 for entry points into this literature). Theorists must confront this challenge to their hypotheses and try to understand what is going on. A major distinction is whether the consequences are treated as homogeneous or are sharply partitioned into gains and losses. Most current proposals assume the dual bilinear form: two bilinear functional systems with different forms in gains and in losses (Luce 2000) [This general algebraic model was probably first introduced in psychology under the label "configural weight model," (e.g. Birnbaum & Stegner 1979)].

Problem 10   (CF Camerer, A Chakravarti) How are reference points chosen and changed when expected values are inferred (within the context of a two-value function, mixed gains/losses theory)? To a psychologist, the traditional economic assumption that choices are among states of wealth, not increments or decrements of it, is counterintuitive. Some of the earliest psychological contributions to decision making commented on this unrealistic interpretation (Edwards 1954). The major break with that tradition occurred with the prospect theory's many demonstrations of the failure of the absolute gains and losses assumption, accompanied by the proposal of a labile reference point (Kahneman & Tversky 1979).

Many economists are hesitant to use the prospect theory (and other psychological models) because the central framing process forces the theorist to specify a reference point, usually the 0,0 point in an objective outcome by subjective value space. However, psychological principles about plausible reference points provide little guidance; as Heath et al (1999, pp. 105–106) noted: "We are proposing that whenever a specific point of comparison is psychologically salient, it will serve as a reference point." An open question remains: When is a reference point set and then reset? This freedom may be liberating to an empirical psychologist, but it is off-putting to a theoretical economist.

There have been many follow-up demonstrations of the lability of reference points via framing manipulations. The most common values hypothesized to be reference points are related to current, status quo conditions. However, various authors have proposed that norms, expectations, levels of aspiration, foregone alternatives, and social comparisons also function as reference points (locations in a value function where the slope changes suddenly; Heath et al 1999, Kahneman 1992, Luce et al 1993, Thaler 1999). In addition, if multiple reference points are chosen, is their selection motivated by hedonic considerations? Do people pick the point of comparison that makes the decision maker happiest? This seems unlikely, because then we would all compare ourselves to the worst status or to the most pathetic people we could imagine to make ourselves feel good.

A closely related problem is partly solved by considering the contextual, comparative, and referential properties of the judgment of well-being or satisfaction: Many studies show that people in dramatically different life circumstances (e.g. paraplegics vs people in normal health or rich vs poor, etc) report similar levels of well-being. In many cases, however, poor people exert considerable efforts to become rich, paraplegics would pay a lot to regain use of their limbs, and those who are rich and in good health make strenuous efforts to remain in these conditions. How can these observations be reconciled (GF Loewenstein)? The answer to this question seems to be partly related to the solution of the reference point problem: Because a person's sense of well-being is heavily determined by their frames of reference, what are the comparisons they make to evaluate how well they are doing?

Questions About Uncertainty, Expectations, Strength of Belief, and Decision Weights

Problem 11 (JW Payne, AG Sanfey) What are the sources of the primitive uncertainties and strengths of beliefs that apply to our estimates, predictions, and judgments? Uncertainty is an essential element of our relationship with the external world; members of very different species also perceive and forage in an uncertain subjective world (i.e. their brains are "wired" to encode and manage uncertainty). Most research by psychologists (and others) has been directed at the updating and integration of several primitive strengths of belief, after they have been inferred (e.g. Anderson 1996, Schum 1994, Tversky & Koehler 1994, papers in Shafer & Pearl 1990). However, another challenging problem is concerned with the sources of primitive uncertainty—or, more basically, how does primitive uncertainty moderate or mediate our behavior?

One possibility is to address the cognition of uncertainty as a secondary impression associated with a primary judgment. We can be very confident of a judgment or estimate [e.g. "I'm sure that my answer, 'Hamburg has a greater population than Bonn,' is correct"; "I'm certain (in my belief that) my leg is broken"; or "I'm confident about my estimate that it will take me about 4 h to drive to Aspen today."] or not so confident. Under this interpretation, uncertainty is derived from aspects of the primary judgment (e.g. evaluations of the completeness, coherence, diversity, and credibility of evidence for the primary judgment or perhaps from the feelings associated with the judgment process: Did it feel fluent, fast, and effortless or not?). This approach implies that several subtheories of uncertainty are needed because the secondary evaluation of certainty will differ for different primary judgment processes (see discussions of certainty conditions in Collins & Michaelski 1989 and Pennington & Hastie 1991).

A related theoretical proposal is that there are alternative modes or strategies for representing uncertainty: singular (episodic, intensional, or inside) vs distributional (aleatory, extensional, or outside). These representations are hypothesized to occur with different reasoning strategies or heuristics. For example, the representativeness and simulation heuristics seem distinctively singular, whereas the availability and anchor-and-adjust heuristics are possibly more distributional, as evidenced by their associated biases. There are also many interesting connections and (possibly misleading) relationships among different situations in which uncertainty is apparent: Is it just a coincidence that uncertainty about whether an event will occur has a similar impact on behavior as does uncertainty about when an event will occur (e.g. Mazur 1993)? Is uncertainty a fundamental metacognitive realization that our mental models of the world must be poor analogies to reality because they are models? Will a comprehensive psychological theory of inductive strength be the answer to our questions about primitive uncertainties, or is there something more involved in the psychology of uncertainty (Osherson et al 1990)?

Problem 12   (RD Luce) In the context of decisions, what are the determinants and the common forms of the decision-weighting function that allow probabilities and propensities to moderate the impact of consequences on decisions? The most common forms of expected and unexpected utility models assume that the central process in decision making is the combination of scaled value and expectation information via a multiplicative rule: for example, utility = probability × value. In the most popular kinds of utility theory, fairly natural properties place severe constraints on the form of the utility function (for values). Specifically, the functions are from the one- or two-parameter family over (usually monetary) gains, and the same holds true for losses, with one parameter linking the two domains. Basically, these are exponential functions, linearly transformed so Utility(0) = 0, of a positive power of money. If the exponent of the power is taken to be 1, as it often is, then they are one-parameter functions; otherwise, they are two parameter functions.

The situation for decision weights, derived from expectations of occurrence or probabilities, in non-expected utility theories is much more poorly defined. One can deduce from a rationality assumption that the weights should be powers of probability (Luce 2000). In early studies, the results are reasonably consistent with power functions, but later studies, since Kahneman & Tversky (1979), suggest an asymmetric, inverse S-shaped function. We need to concentrate on finding out more about what limits the form of these weighting functions. Prelec (1998) has suggested plausible constraints on the function form, and one of his candidate functions is consistent with the best relevant empirical data (Gonzalez & Wu 1999).

However, there are still many open questions concerning the stability of these functions within individuals and across decision-making domains and even the range of alternative permissible functions (cf Weber 1994). It is important to note that the family of permissible functions should at least include power functions as a special case, because our theories should not preclude the possibility of some people behaving rationally.

As an aside, I am particularly enthusiastic about the theoretical justifications for the weighting functions and aspiration levels in the security-potential/aspiration theory (Lopes & Oden 1999). This theory neatly combines individual differences (security vs potential orientations) and situational attention factors (aspiration criteria) to yield psychologically plausible hypotheses. It has fared well in competitive tests against other rank- and sign-dependent models, at least in the domain of multioutcome lotteries.

Questions About Emotions and Neural Substrates

Problem 13   (F Loewenstein, E Peters, P Slovic, EU Weber) What is the role of emotions in the evaluation of experienced outcomes (consequences) and in the evaluation of expected outcomes? A major obstacle to the study of the role of emotions in decision making is that there is little consensus on a definition of emotion. A recent survey volume, *The Nature of Emotion: Fundamental Questions* (Ekman & Davidson 1994), does not provide a definition and notes that there was disagreement on virtually every fundamental question addressed. [In a summary section, "What Most Students of Emotion Agree About," the authors comment: "We originally did not include the word 'most' in the title of this section..." (p. 412); see discussion in Larsen & Fredrickson 1999.] For present purposes, I think three concepts will be useful: emotion, mood, and evaluation. I would propose the following definition of emotion: reactions to motivationally significant stimuli and situations, including three components: a cognitive appraisal, a signature physiological response, and phenomenal experiences. I would add that emotions usually occur in reaction to perceptions of changes in the current situation that have hedonic or valenced consequences. Furthermore, I propose that the term "mood" be reserved for longer-duration background states of the physiological (autonomic) system and the accompanying feelings. Finally, I suggest that the expression evaluation be applied to hedonic, pleasure-pain and good-bad judgments of consequences.

There seems to be agreement that an early, primitive reaction to almost any personally relevant object or event is a good-bad evaluative assessment. Many behavioral scientists have concluded that the reaction occurs very quickly and includes emotional feelings and distinctive somatic and physiological events (Bechara et al 2000, Loewenstein 1996, Zajonc 1980). Neuroscientists have attempted to describe the properties of the underlying neurophysiological response (Damasio 1994, LeDoux 1996, Rolls 1999), addressing such issues as: Is the reaction located on a unitary, bipolar, good-bad dimension; or are there two neurally independent reactions, one (dopamine mediated) assessing positivity and one (acetycholine mediated) assessing negativity [the so-called "bivariate evaluative response system" (Ashby et al 1999, Cacioppo & Berntson 1994, Coombs & Avrunin 1977, Gray 1971, Ito & Cacioppo 1999, Lieberman 2000, Russell & Carroll 1999)]? There must be a discernable physiological difference at some point before the responses diverge into an approach or avoid reaction; but is it a deep, central difference or is it peripheral, at either the stimulus-processing or response-generation ends of the system?

The primary function usually attributed to the fast good-bad reaction is to guide adaptive approach-avoidance actions and, collaterally, to winnow down large choice sets into smaller numbers of options for a more thoughtful evaluation (e.g. Damasio's somatic marker hypothesis). The alternative functional interpretation in the decision-making literature is that emotions serve a crucial override function that operates when it is necessary to interrupt the course of an ongoing plan or behavior sequence in order to respond quickly to a sudden emergency or opportunity (Simon 1967; see also LeDoux 1996 on learned triggers).

The analysis so far is vague on the role(s) of the traditionally designated palette of emotions in the decision process (Ekman & Davidson 1994, Roseman et al 1996, Yik et al 1999). An important distinction is between emotions that are experienced at the time the decision is being made (decision-process emotions or just process emotions) and emotions that are anticipated or predicted to occur as reactions to consequences of a decision (consequence emotions) (GF Loewenstein, EU Weber, CK Hsee, ES Welch, unpublished manuscript). Thus, studies of mood or emotional state at the time a decision is being made fall into the first category [e.g. research on the effects of mood on estimates and judgments (DeSteno et al 2000, Forgas 1995, Johnson & Tversky 1983, Mayer et al 1992, Wright & Bower 1992) and research on stress or the effects of difficulty with trade-offs involved in the decision process (e.g. Luce et al 1999)], and studies of the effects of anticipated consequence-related emotions on choices fit into the second category (e.g. Loewenstein & Schkade 1999, Gilbert & Wilson 2000, Mellers et al 1999).

Problem 14   Are there different basic decision processes in different domains of behavior, or is there one evolutionarily selected fundamental decision module? To what extent are various habits or behavioral tendencies that are relevant to decision making context independent and general across behavioral contexts? Is there a central neural module or organ that computes decisions across different domains of activity, perhaps a neural unexpected utility calculator? Do people who are risky in recreational situations (e.g. rock climbing or skiing under extreme conditions) also take more risks in sexual, financial, or other domains? Is there an underlying evolutionary implication such that decision domains that pose related reproductive survival problems (e.g. mate selection, parental investment, health, shelter, social exchange, and within-species combat) elicit similar risk attitudes and decision strategies?

The evolutionary psychology research program pursued by Cosmides, Tooby, and colleagues is suggestive of domain-specific reasoning and decision modules (Barkow et al 1992, Cosmides & Tooby 1996). However, the question of how to define and evaluate claims about the generality vs context specificity of decision processes is still open. It would not be as interesting to discover that the peripheral perceptual or response aspects of the decision process are different in different domains as it would be to discover that that central information integration principle was different. Would it surprise anyone to learn that we attend to different attributes of potential mates and of potential shelters? However, it would be very important to learn that the unexpected utility principle applies in some domains (e.g. mate selection and competition) but not in others (e.g. health and social exchange).

Questions About Methods

Problem 15   (CF Camerer, B Fischhoff, KR Hammond, BA Mellers) What methods will allow us to best apply results from one situation to another, especially in generalizing from a simplified, controlled situation to a complex, uncontrolled nonlaboratory situation? How can we gain an understanding of the relationship between the conditions in our experiments and the situations in which decisions are actually made? The questions of generality of results and the scope of theoretical principles are, of course, critical for any experimental science. In the behavioral sciences, the usual argument for the generality of a finding begins with the interpretation of the existence of a phenomenon (e.g. a cause-effect relationship) as a prima facie case for its generality. Then the projectability of the result is systematically evaluated by examining each conceptual dimension along which variation occurs from one setting to the other target settings of interest (Hastie et al 1983). Thus, typically, progress on the problem of generalizability, projectability, or scope is made by discovering interesting empirical limits and testing feelings of skepticism in order to control the tendency to overgeneralize. This tactic identifies boundary conditions, the manipulation of which changes the prevalence of a response pattern. However, such an incremental process leaves us vulnerable when asked (by ourselves or others) to make summary statements about, say, the quality of human judgment or how people usually behave. Those statements are meaningless without specifying a universe of observations. However, all we usually have is a biased sample of anecdotal or experimental evidence. The laboratory should be a place to complement field studies and dissect theory, but it should not be a substitute for looking at other types of data (Fischhoff 1996).

There are two common methodological strategies used to address the generality problem: First, sample phenomena (subjects, tasks, stimuli, etc) as representatively as possible in research, and only generalize (from the original study) with confidence when you are replicating the previous situation (e.g. Gigerenzer et al 1999, Hammond et al 1986). Of course, there is still a crucial open question: What are the attributes or dimensions of situations that afford projection from a past finding to a future result? Second, identify fundamental causal mechanisms and forces that will support inductive generalization. Under this imperative, research should focus on the identification of generative causal mechanisms—perhaps by studying unrepresentative situations, preparations, or samples—and then generalize based on deeper causal theoretical principles (Dawes 1996). Psychologists might well heed the thoughtful commentaries on the experimental method from practitioners who do not take it for granted [Lopes (1994); experimental economists Friedman & Shyam (1994), Kagel & Roth (1995); and experimental political scientists Kinder & Palfrey (1993)].

At present, the largest mutual enterprise in the field of judgment and decision making is the development of measurement-theoretical extensions of traditional utility theory and associated empirical research on evaluations of monetary gambles and lotteries [Luce (2000) provides a summary of this endeavor]. Many of the present problems are best understood within the context of that research program. The measurement-theoretical approach looks like a model scientific research program that is making visible progress on both theoretical and empirical fronts. However, this research program has one major weakness: How much can one generalize from the results of gambling studies in a laboratory and the resultant theoretical principles to important nonlaboratory decisions? Ironically, the primary research problem for this approach may be the methodological generalizability problem. Perhaps the enormous impact of prospect theory owes more to its strong case for the generalizability of its theoretical principles to real decisions in everyday social, economic, and political life than to its theoretical elegance and originality.

Problem 16   (NH Anderson) How can useful methods be developed to measure variables such as psychological uncertainty and personal value on true linear, equal interval scales? Linear, equal interval measurement is fundamental because of the multiple determinants of behavior: Virtually all perceptions, thoughts, and actions result from the integration of multiple determinants. Prediction and understanding both require linear scales. With even three competing response tendencies, monotone (ordinal) scales cannot generally predict even the direction of a response. This problem has been around for over a century, and it is central to the study of judgment and decision making because the measurement of values is central. However, measurement has been neglected in empirical work. Makeshift measurement is a common practice, notably in applied multiattribute analysis, research on social judgment, and in many studies of cognitive processes. Makeshift measurement is not necessarily wrong, and it is sometimes useful, especially in early research, to identify the major environmental and individual difference causes of behavior. Current conceptual frameworks have become successful by focusing on issues that can be attacked without true measurement. This was reasonable at first, but it is an inadequate foundation for general theory. Anderson (e.g. 1982, 1996) and Michell (1990, 1999) provide introductions to this profound and daunting problem.

AFTERTHOUGHTS AND CONCLUSIONS

There have been a few dramatic intellectual events in the recent history of the field of judgment and decision making. One is the sudden acceptance of non-expected utility theories with labile reference (inflection) points, separate value functions for gains and losses, and nonadditive probability weighting functions (e.g. see Luce 2000 and Birnbaum 1999 for overviews of these developments; and see Tversky & Kahneman 1992 for the best-known formulation). Another is the sudden popularity of cognitive heuristics models for judgment (Tversky & Kahneman 1974) and choice (summarized in Payne et al 1993). As an aside, the most notable historical event to occur during the years covered by this review was the untimely death in 1996 of Tversky, the greatest researcher of judgment and decision making of the twentieth century. (See Laibson & Zeckhauser 1998, McFadden 1999, and Rabin et al 1996 for assessments of Tversky's impact.) However, reactions to these important events have not been as dramatic as, for example, the response would be to a major mathematical proof or to a breakthrough discovery of the genetic code structure.

In 1995, when Andrew Wiles publicly presented his proof of Fermat's last theorem, it is likely that every major mathematician in the world knew of his achievement within 24 h. Is there any plausible analogous scenario in the scientific field of judgment and decision making? Would the solution of any of the problems we have posed result in the same kind of immediate, worldwide reaction? The sole possibility might be a genetic or neuroscience result (problems 13 and 14). For example, the identification of a specific genetic source of cross-situational general risk taking habits or the localization of a neural circuit that computes probability-weighting or evaluation functions such as those proposed in expected utility theories might elicit a dramatic reaction. However, empirical and theoretical results in the decision sciences tend to disperse gradually, more like the conclusions of a Newton or an Einstein than like those of Watson and Crick, or a Wiles.

There are some aspects of the proposed 16 problems that are worth noting. First, some of the problems are already "on the table" and under investigation. The purpose of this review of these problems is to introduce them to readers who are not knowledgeable and to provide some recent context for those to whom these problems are already familiar. For the most part, these are the problems that I predict will be solved sooner," such as problems 1, 3, 8, 9, and 12–14. Other problems are my personal picks; they have received some attention but, in my view, not enough. My goal in mentioning these neglected problems is more exhortatory; my hope is that the present review will focus more attention on these issues in the future, especially problems 2, 4–7, and 11.

One of the most persistent metatheoretical issues for the field of judgment and decision making concerns the relationships among theoretical approaches. What are the relationships among the alternative theoretical descriptions, including connectionist-neural computational processing (e.g. Grossberg & Gutowski 1987,

Leven & Levine 1996), information processing (symbolic production systems; e.g. Lovett 1998, Payne et al 1993), traditional cognitive algebra (Anderson 1981, Birnbaum 1999), and measurement-theoretical algebra (Luce 2000, Tversky & Kahneman 1992)?

Are these actually different descriptions of different phenomena, or are they simply alternative notations to describe the same phenomena? One popular answer is that the cognitive process descriptions of phenomena are at a finer resolution than the algebraic models; that the cognitive descriptions actually capture individual thought processes at a causal level, whereas the smoother, continuous, quantitative, algebraic representations describe averages of those cognitive processes (e.g. Lopes 1996 and Oden & Lopes 1997; but see Anderson 1996 for a different view). I believe that further consideration of the relationships among theoretical frameworks is a worthy metaproblem and would not be merely an exercise in academic hairsplitting. In addition, an even greater issue concerns the selection of a behavioral theoretical representation that will effectively guide and incorporate developments in cognitive neuroscience.

"As long as a branch of science offers an abundance of good problems, so long is it alive..." (Hilbert 1900, p. 444). By Hilbert's abundance of problems criterion, the field of judgment and decision making is in excellent health. The fundamental obstacle in preparing this review was the difficulty of choosing the problems to exclude from among the diversity of inviting prospects. The review is organized around problems for future research because I believe that research in our young scientific field will be improved by thinking harder about the nature of the problems we should be attacking. Perhaps the most important step in successful research (as in writing a good review) is the selection and definition of the research problem. I believe that the wise fictional detective Father Brown could have been describing many scientists when he commented: "It isn't that they can't see the solution. It's that they can't see the problem" (Chesterton 1951, p. 949). Researchers on decision making, of all people, need to be reminded that they are placing a bet when they choose their research direction.[4]

Moreover, there is evidence from research that evaluations of uncertain prospects are better when they are made in the context of alternative courses of action than when made in isolation (Hsee et al 1999, Read et al 1999).

ACKNOWLEDGMENTS

Preparation of this manuscript was supported by funds from the National Science Foundation (SBR-9816458) and the National Institute of Mental Health (R01 MH58362).

---

[4]It is interesting (and humbling) to remind ourselves that although David Hilbert had a wonderful eye for good problems, his own bet on the development of a general, uniform method for mathematical proof was a loser, but perhaps it was still a good bet in 1900 (cf Gödel 1934).

Visit the Annual Reviews home page at www.AnnualReviews.org

LITERATURE CITED

Alvarez P, Squire LR. 1994. Memory consolidation and the medial temporal lobe: a simple network model. *Proc. Natl. Acad. Sci. USA* 91:7041–45

Anderson JR. 1983. *The Architecture of Cognition.* Cambridge, MA: Harvard Univ. Press

Anderson JR. 1990. *The Adaptive Character of Thought.* Hillsdale, NJ: Erlbaum

Anderson NH. 1981. *Foundations of Information Integration Theory.* New York: Academic

Anderson NH. 1982. *Methods of Information Integration Theory.* New York: Academic

Anderson NH. 1996. *A Functional Theory of Cognition.* Mahwah, NJ: Erlbaum

Ashby FG, Isen AM, Turken AU. 1999. A neuropsychological theory of positive affect and its influence on cognition. *Psychol. Rev.* 106:529–50

Axelrod R. 1984. *The Evolution of Cooperation.* New York: Basic Books

Bargh JA, Chartrand TL. 1999. The unbearable automaticity of being. *Am. Psychol.* 54:462–79

Bargh JA, Chartrand TL. 2000. The mind in the middle: a practical guide to priming and automaticity research. In *Handbook of Research Methods in Social and Personality Psychology*, ed. HT Reis, CM Judd, pp. 253–85. Cambridge, UK: Cambridge Univ. Press

Barkow JH, Cosmides L, Tooby J, eds. 1992. *The Adapted Mind: Evolutionary Psychology and the Generation of Culture.* New York: Oxford Univ. Press

Baron J. 1994. Nonconsequentialist decisions. *Behav. Brain Sci.* 17:1–10

Baron J, Spranca M. 1997. Protected values. *Organ. Behav. Hum. Decis. Process.* 70:1–16

Bechara A, Damasio H, Damasio AR. 2000. Emotion, decision making and the orbitofrontal cortex. *Cereb. Cortex* 10:295–307

Becker GS. 1976. *The Economic Approach to Human Behavior.* Chicago, IL: Univ. Chicago Press

Bernstein DJ, Michael RL. 1990. The utility of verbal and behavioral assessments of value. *J. Exp. Anal. Behav.* 54:173–84

Bettman JR, Johnson EJ, Payne JW. 1990. A componential analysis of cognitive effort in choice. *Organ. Behav. Hum. Decis. Process.* 45:111–39

Birnbaum MH. 1999. The paradoxes of Allais, stochastic dominance, and decision weights. In *Decision Science and Technology*, ed. J Shanteau, BA Mellers, DA Schum, pp. 27–52. Boston: Kluwer Acad.

Birnbaum MH, Stegner SE. 1979. Source credibility in social judgment: bias, expertise, and the judge's point of view. *J. Pers. Soc. Psychol.* 37:48–74

Brehmer B. 1999. Man as a stabiliser of systems: from static snapshots of judgment processes to dynamic decision making. *Think. Reason.* 2:225–38

Busemeyer JR, Townsend JT. 1993. Decision field theory: a dynamic-cognitive approach to decision making in an uncertain environment. *Psychol. Rev.* 100:432–59

Cacioppo JT, Berntson GG. 1994. Relationship between attitudes and evaluative space: a critical review, with emphasis on the separability of positive and negative substrates. *Psychol. Bull.* 115:401–23

Camerer CF. 1995. Individual decision making. In *The Handbook of Experimental Economics*, ed. JH Kagel, AE Roth, pp. 587–703. Princeton, NJ: Princeton Univ. Press

Camerer CF. 1997. Progress in behavioral game theory. *J. Econ. Perspect.* 11:167–88

Chatterjee S, Heath TB. 1996. Conflict and loss aversion in multi-attribute choice: the effects of tradeoff size and reference dependence on decision difficulty. *Organ. Behav. Hum. Decis. Process.* 67:144–55

Chechile RA, Butler SF. 2000. Is "Generic Utility Theory" a suitable theory of choice behavior for gambles with mixed gains and losses? *J. Risk Uncertain.* 20:189–211

Chesterton GK. 1951. The point of the pin. In *The Father Brown Omnibus.* New York: Dodd, Mead & Co.

Clemen RT. 1996. *Making Hard Decisions: An Introduction to Decision Analysis.* Pacific Grove, CA: Duxbury. 2nd ed.

Collins A, Michaelski R. 1989. The logic of plausible reasoning: a core theory. *Cogn. Sci.* 13:1–49

Colvin CR, Block J. 1994. Do positive illusions foster mental health? An examination of the Taylor and Brown formulation. *Psychol. Bull.* 116:3–20

Cooksey RW. 1996. *Judgment Analysis: Theory, Methods, and Applications.* San Diego, CA: Academic

Coombs CH, Avrunin GS. 1977. Single-peaked functions and the theory of preference. *Psychol. Rev.* 84:216–30

Cooper WS. 1987. Decision theory as a branch of evolutionary theory: a biological derivation of the Savage axioms. *Psychol. Rev.* 94:395–411

Cosmides L, Tooby J. 1996. Are humans good intuitive statisticians after all? Rethinking some conclusions from the literature on judgment under uncertainty. *Cognition* 58:1–73

Damasio AR. 1994. *Descartes' Error: Emotion, Reason, and the Human Brain.* New York: Putnam & Sons

Dawes RM. 1996. The purpose of experiments: ecological validity versus comparing hypotheses. *Behav. Brain Sci.* 19:20

Dawes RM. 1998. Behavioral decision making and judgment. In *The Handbook of Social Psychology,* ed. DT Gilbert, ST Fiske, G Lindzey, pp. 497–548. New York: McGraw-Hill. 4th ed.

Dawes RM. 2000. *Irrationality: Theory and Practice.* Boulder, CO: Westview

DeSteno D, Petty RE, Wegener DT, Rucker DD. 2000. Beyond valence in the perception of

likelihood: the role of emotional specificity. *J. Pers. Soc. Psychol.* 78:397–416

Dubins LE, Savage LJ. 1965. *How to Gamble if You Must.* New York: McGraw-Hill

Edwards W. 1954. The theory of decision making. *Psychol. Bull.* 51:380–417

Edwards W, ed. 1992. *Utility Theories: Measurements and Applications.* Boston, MA: Kluwer Acad.

Ekman P, Davidson RJ, eds. 1994. *The Nature of Emotion: Fundamental Questions.* Oxford, UK: Oxford Univ. Press

Fischhoff B. 1991. Value elicitation: Is there anything in there? *Am. Psychol.* 46:835–47

Fischhoff B. 1996. The real world: What good is it? *Organ. Behav. Hum. Decis. Process.* 65:232–48

Fischhoff B, Welch N, Frederick S. 1999. Contrual processes in preference assessment. *J. Risk Uncertain.* 19:139–64

Forgas JP. 1995. Emotion in social judgments: review and a new affect infusion model (AIM). *Psychol. Bull.* 117:39–66

Friedman D, Shyam S. 1994. *Experimental Methods: A Primer for Economists.* Cambridge, UK: Cambridge Univ. Press

Friedman M, Savage LJ. 1948. The utility analysis of choices involving risk. *J. Polit. Econ.* 56:279–304

Gigerenzer G, Goldstein DG. 1996. Reasoning the fast and frugal way: models of bounded rationality. *Psychol. Rev.* 103:650–69

Gigerenzer G, Todd PM, ABC Res. Group, eds. 1999. *Simple Heuristics That Make Us Smart.* Oxford, UK: Oxford Univ. Press

Gilbert DT, Wilson TD. 2000. Miswanting: some problems in the forecasting of future affective states. In *Feeling and Thinking: The Role of Affect in Social Cognition,* ed. JP Forgas, pp. 178–97. Cambridge, UK: Cambridge Univ. Press

Gödel K. 1934. On undecidable propositions of formal mathematics: the Princeton Lectures. In *Collected Works,* ed. K Gödel, 1:346–69. Oxford, UK: Oxford Univ. Press

Goldstein WM, Hogarth RM. 1997. Judgment and decision research: some historical context. In *Research on Judgment and Decision Making: Currents, Connections, and Controversies*, ed. WM Goldstein, RM Hogarth, pp. 3–68. Cambridge, UK: Cambridge Univ. Press

Goldstein WM, Weber EU. 1995. Content and discontent: indications and implications of domain specificity in preferential decision making. In *Decision Making from a Cognitive Perspective*, ed. J Busemeyer, R Hastie, DL Medin, pp. 83–136. San Diego, CA: Academic

Gonzalez R, Wu G. 1999. On the shape of the probability weighting function. *Cogn. Psychol.* 38:129–66

Gray JA. 1971. *The Psychology of Fear and Stress*. London: Weidenfeld & Nicholson

Griffin D, Buehler R. 1999. Frequency, probability, and prediction: easy solutions to cognitive illusions? *Cogn. Psychol.* 38:48–78

Grossberg S, Gutowski WE. 1987. Neural dynamics of decision making under risk: affective balance and cognitive-emotional interactions. *Psychol. Rev.* 94:300–18

Hammond JS, Keeney RL, Raiffa H. 1999. *Smart Choices: A Practical Guide to Making Better Decisions*. Boston, MA: Harvard Bus. Sch. Press

Hammond KR. 1996. *Human Judgment and Social Policy: Irreducible Uncertainty, Inevitable Error, Unavoidable Injustice*. Oxford, UK: Oxford Univ. Press

Hammond KR, Hamm RM, Grassia J. 1986. Generalizing over conditions by combining the multitrait-multimethod matrix and the representative design of experiments. *Psychol. Bull.* 100:257–69

Harman G. 1995. Rationality. In *An Invitation to Cognitive Science: Thinking*, ed. DN Osherson, 3:175–211. Cambridge, MA: MIT. 2nd ed.

Hastie R, Pennington N. 2000. Explanation-based decision making. *Judgment and Decision Making: An Interdisciplinary Reader*, ed. T Connolly, HR Arkes, KR Hammond, pp. 212–28. Cambridge, UK: Cambridge Univ. Press

Hastie R, Penrod SD, Pennington N. 1983. *Inside the Jury*. Cambridge, MA: Harvard Univ. Press

Hastie R, Rasinski K. 1987. The concept of accuracy in social judgment. In *The Social Psychology of Knowledge*, ed. D Bar-Tal, A Kruglanski, pp. 193–208. Cambridge, UK: Cambridge Univ. Press

Heath C, Larrick RP, Wu G. 1999. Goals as reference points. *Cogn. Psychol.* 38:79–109

Hilbert D. 1900. *Mathematical Problems*. Transl. MW Newson, 1902, in *Bull. Am. Math. Soc.* 8:437–79 (From German)

Ho T-H, Weigelt K. 1996. Task complexity, equilibrium selection, and learning: an experimental study. *Manage. Sci.* 42:659–79

Hogarth RM. 1981. Beyond discrete biases: functional and dysfunctional aspects of judgmental heuristics. *Psychol. Bull.* 90:197–217

Hsee CK, Loewenstein GF, Blount S, Bazerman MH. 1999. Preference reversals between joint and separate evaluations of options: a review and theoretical analysis. *Psychol. Bull.* 125:576–90

Ito TA, Cacioppo JT. 1999. The psychophysiology of utility appraisals. See Kahneman et al 1999a, pp. 470–88

Jacoby LL. 1991. A process dissociation framework: separating automatic from intentional uses of memory. *J. Mem. Lang.* 30:513–41

Johnson EJ, Tversky A. 1983. Affect, generalization, and the perception of risk. *J. Pers. Soc. Psychol.* 45:20–31

Johnson-Laird PN, Legrenzi P, Girotto V, Legrenzi MS, Caverni J-P. 1999. Naïve probability: a mental model theory of extensional reasoning. *Psychol. Rev.* 106:62–88

Jolls C, Sunstein CR, Thaler R. 1998. A behavioral approach to law and economics. *Stanford Law Rev.* 50:1471–550

Kagel JH, Roth AE, eds. 1995. *Handbook of Experimental Economics*. Princeton, NJ: Princeton Univ. Press

Kahneman D. 1992. Reference points, norms, and mixed feelings. *Org. Behav. Hum. Decis. Process.* 51:296–312

Kahneman D. 1994. New challenges to the rationality assumption. *J. Inst. Theor. Econ.* 150:18–36

Kahneman D, Diener E, Schwarz N, eds. 1999a. *Well-Being: The Foundations of Hedonic Psychology.* New York: Russell Sage Found.

Kahneman D, Ritov I, Schkade DA. 1999b. Economic preferences or attitude expressions? An analysis of dollar responses to public issues. *J. Risk Uncertain.* 19:203–35

Kahneman D, Tversky A. 1979. Prospect theory: an analysis of decision under risk. *Econometrica* 47:263–91

Kahneman D, Wakker PP, Sarin R. 1997. Back to Bentham? Explorations of experienced utility. *Q. J. Econ.* 112:375–405

Kaplan H, Hill K. 1985. Food sharing among Ache foragers: tests of explanatory hypotheses. *Curr. Anthropol.* 26:223–46

Kareev Y, Lieberman I, Lev M. 1997. Through a narrow window: sample size and the perception of correlation. *J. Exp. Psychol.: Gen.* 126:278–87

Keller LR, Ho JL. 1988. Decision problem structuring: generating options. *IEEE Trans. Syst. Man. Cybern.* 18:715–28

Kinder DR, Palfrey TR, eds. 1993. *Experimental Foundations of Political Science.* Ann Arbor: Univ. Mich. Press

Kintsch W. 1998. *Comprehension: A Paradigm for Cognition.* Cambridge, UK: Cambridge Univ. Press

Klayman J, Schoemaker PJH. 1993. Thinking about the future: a cognitive perspective. *J. Forecast.* 12:161–86

Klein G, Wolf S, Militello L, Zsambok C. 1995. Characteristics of skilled option generation in chess. *Organ. Behav. Hum. Decis. Process.* 62:63–69

Knowlton BJ, Squire LR, Gluck MA. 1994. Probabilistic classification learning in amnesia. *Learn. Mem.* 1:106–20

Krebs JR, Davies NB. 1993. *An Introduction to Behavioural Ecology.* Oxford, UK: Blackwell Sci. 3rd ed.

Laibson D, Zeckhauser R. 1998. Amos Tversky and the ascent of behavioral economics. *J. Risk Uncertain.* 16:7–47

Lamont EB, Christakis NA. 2000. *Physician's preferences for prognostic disclosure to cancer patients near the end of life.* Presented at 19th Annu. Meet. Am. Soc. Clin. Oncol., New Orleans (Abstr. 1704)

Larrick RP, Nisbett RE, Morgan JN. 1993. Who uses the cost-benefit rules of choice? Implications for the normative status of microeconomic theory. *Organ. Behav. Hum. Decis. Process.* 56:331–47

Larsen RJ, Fredrickson BL. 1999. Measurement issues in emotion research. See Kahneman et al 1999a, pp. 40–60

LeDoux JE. 1996. *The Emotional Brain: The Mysterious Underpinnings of Emotional Life.* New York: Simon & Schuster

Leeper R. 1935. A study of a neglected portion of the field of learning: the development of perceptual organization. *J. Genet. Psychol.* 46:41–75

Leven SJ, Levine DS. 1996. Multiattribute decision making in context: a dynamic neural network methodology. *Cogn. Sci.* 20:271–99

Levin IP, Schneider SL, Gaeth GJ. 1998. All frames are not created equal: a typology and critical analysis of framing effects. *Organ. Behav. Hum. Decis. Process.* 76:149–88

Lieberman MD. 2000. Intuition: a social cognitive neuroscience approach. *Psychol. Bull.* 126:109–37

Loewenstein GF. 1996. Out of control: visceral influences on behavior. *Organ. Behav. Hum. Decis. Process.* 65:272–92

Loewenstein GF, Elster J, eds. 1992. *Choice Over Time.* New York: Russell Sage Found.

Loewenstein GF, Schkade DA. 1999. Wouldn't it be nice? Predicting future feelings. See Kahneman et al 1999a, pp. 85–108

Lopes LL. 1982. Decision making in the short run. *J Exp. Psychol.: Learn. Mem. Cogn.* 7:377–85

Lopes LL. 1994. Psychology and economics: perspectives on risk, cooperation, and the marketplace. *Annu. Rev. Psychol.* 45:197–227

Lopes LL. 1996. Algebra and process in the modeling of risky choice. In *Decision Making from a Cognitive Perspective*, ed. J Busemeyer, R Hastie, DL Medin, pp. 177–220. San Diego, CA: Academic

Lopes LL, Oden GC. 1999. The role of aspiration level in risky choice: a comparison of cumulative prospect theory and SP/A theory. *J. Math. Psychol.* 43:286–313

Lovett M. 1998. Choice. In *The Atomic Components of Thought*, ed. JR Anderson, C Lebiere, pp. 255–96. Mahwah, NJ: Erlbaum

Luce MF, Payne JW, Bettman JR. 1999. Emotional trade-off difficulty and choice. *J. Mark. Res.* 36:143–59

Luce RD. 2000. *Utility of Gains and Losses: Measurement-Theoretical and Experimental Approaches*. Mahwah, NJ: Erlbaum

Luce RD, Mellers B, Chang S-J. 1993. Is choice the correct primitive? On using certainty equivalents and reference levels to predict choices among gambles. *J. Risk Uncertain* 6:115–43

Luce RD, Raiffa H. 1957. *Games and Decisions: Introduction and Critical Survey*. New York: Wiley & Sons

Macchi L, Osherson D, Krantz DH. 1999. A note on superadditive probability judgment. *Psychol. Rev.* 106:210–14

MacDonald TK, Ross M. 1999. Assessing the accuracy of predictions about dating relationships: How and why do lovers' predictions differ from those made by observers? *Pers. Soc. Psychol. Bull.* 25:1417–29

Manski CF. 1999. Analysis of choice expectations in incomplete scenarios. *J. Risk Uncertain.* 19:49–65

March JG. 1978. Bounded rationality, ambiguity, and the engineering of choice. *Bell J. Econ.* 9:587–608

March JG, Heath C. 1994. *A Primer on Decision Making: How Decisions Happen*. New York: Free Press

March JG, Shapira Z. 1992. Variable risk preferences and the focus of attention. *Psychol. Rev.* 99:172–83

March JG, Simon HA. 1993. *Organizations*. Oxford, UK: Blackwell. 2nd ed.

Markman AB. 1998. *Knowledge Representation*. Mahwah, NJ: Erlbaum

Mayer JD, Gaschke YN, Braverman DL, Evans TW. 1992. Mood congruent judgment is a general effect. *J. Pers. Soc. Psychol.* 63:119–32

Mazur JE. 1993. Predicting the strength of a conditioned reinforcer: effects of delay and uncertainty. *Curr. Dir. Psychol. Sci.* 2:70–74

McClelland JL, McNaughton BL, O'Reilly RC. 1995. Why there are complementary learning systems in the hippocampus and neocortex: insights from successes and failures of connectionist models of learning and memory. *Psychol. Rev.* 102:419–57

McFadden D. 1999. Rationality for economists? *J. Risk Uncertain.* 19:73–105

Medin DL, Goldstone RL, Markman AB. 1995. Comparison and choice: relations between similarity processes and decision processes. *Psychon. Bull. Rev.* 2:1–19

Mellers B, Schwartz A, Ritov I. 1999. Emotion-based choice. *J. Exp. Psychol.: Gen.* 128:332–45

Michell J. 1990. *An Introduction to the Logic of Psychological Measurement*. Hillsdale, NJ: Erlbaum

Michell J. 1999. *Measurement in Psychology: Critical History of a Methodological Concept*. Cambridge, UK: Cambridge Univ. Press

Miller GA, Cantor N. 1982. Review of the book *Human Inference: Strategies and Shortcomings of Social Judgment*. *Soc. Cogn.* 1:83–93

Miyake A, Shah P, eds. 1999. *Models of Working Memory: Mechanisms of Active Maintenance and Executive Control*. Cambridge, UK: Cambridge Univ. Press

Miyamoto JM. 1988. Generic utility theory: measurement foundations and applications. *J. Math. Psychol.* 32:357–404

Newell A. 1982. The knowledge level. *Artif. Intel.* 18:87–127

Newell A, Simon HA. 1972. *Human Problem Solving*. Englewood Cliffs, NJ: Prentice-Hall

Nichols MJ, Newsome WT. 1999. Monkeys play the odds. *Nature* 400:217–18

Oaksford M, Chater N, eds. 1998. *Rational Models of Cognition*. Oxford, UK: Oxford Univ. Press

Oden GC, Lopes LL. 1997. Risky choice with fuzzy criteria. In *Qualitative Aspects of Decision Making*, ed. RW Scholz, AC Zimmer, pp. 56–82. Lengerich, Ger: Pabst Sci.

Osherson DN, Smith EE, Wilkie O, Lopez A, Shafir E. 1990. Category-based induction. *Psychol. Rev.* 97:185–200

Payne JW, Bettman JR, Johnson EJ. 1993. *The Adaptive Decision Maker*. Cambridge, UK: Cambridge Univ. Press

Payne JW, Bettman JR, Schkade DA. 1999. Measuring constructed preferences: towards a building code. *J. Risk Uncertain.* 19:243–70

Pearl J. 2000. *Causality: Models, Reasoning, and Inference*. Cambridge, UK: Cambridge Univ. Press

Pennington N, Hastie R. 1991. A cognitive theory of juror decision making: the Story model. *Cardozo Law Rev.* 13:519–57

Platt ML, Glimcher PW. 1999. Neural correlates of decision variables in parietal cortex. *Nature* 400:233–38

Prelec D. 1998. The probability weighting function. *Econometrica* 66:497–527

Rabin M, Kahneman D, Tversky A. 1996. In *American Economists of the Late Twentieth Century*, ed. WJ Samuels, pp. 111–37. Cheltenham, UK: Elgar

Read D, Loewenstein GF, Rabin M. 1999. Choice bracketing. *J. Risk Uncertain.* 19:171–97

Real LA. 1991. Animal choice behavior and the evolution of cognitive architecture. *Science* 253:980–86

Rettinger DA, Hastie R. 2000. Comprehension and decision making. In *Emerging Perspectives in Judgment and Decision Making*, ed. S Schneider, J Shanteau. Cambridge, UK: Cambridge Univ. Press. In press

Rolls ET. 1999. *The Brain and Emotion*. Oxford, UK: Oxford Univ. Press

Roseman IJ, Antoniou AA, Jose PE. 1996. Appraisal determinants of emotions: constructing a more accurate and comprehensive theory. *Cogn. Emot.* 10:241–77

Rottenstreich Y, Tversky A. 1997. Unpacking, repacking, and anchoring: advances in support theory. *Psychol. Rev.* 104:408–15

Rumelhart DE, McClelland JL, PDP Res. Group. 1988. *Parallel Distributed Processing: Explorations in the Microstructure of Cognition*, Vols. 1, 2. Cambridge, MA: MIT

Russell JA, Carroll JM. 1999. On the bipolarity of positive and negative affect. *Psychol. Bull.* 125:3–30

Savage LJ. 1954. *The Foundations of Statistics*. New York: Wiley & Sons

Schacter DL. 1994. Priming and multiple memory systems: perceptual mechanisms of implicit memory. See Schacter & Tulving, pp. 233–68

Schacter DL, Tulving E, eds. 1994. *Memory Systems*. Cambridge, MA: MIT

Schum DA. 1994. *The Evidential Foundations of Probabilistic Reasoning*. New York: Wiley & Sons

Shafer G, Pearl J, eds. 1990. *Readings in Uncertain Reasoning*. Palo Alto, CA: Morgan Kaufmann

Shapira Z, ed. 1997. *Organizational Decision Making*. Cambridge, UK: Cambridge Univ. Press

Simon HA. 1967. Motivation and emotional controls of cognition. *Psychol. Rev.* 74:29–39

Sloman SA. 1996. The empirical case for two systems of reasoning. *Psychol. Bull.* 119:3–22

Slovic P. 1995. The construction of preference. *Am. Psychol.* 50:364–71

Slovic P. 1966. Value as a determiner of subjective probability. *IEEE Trans. Hum. Factors Electron.* 7:22–28

Smith ER, DeCoster J. 2000. Dual-process models in social and cognitive psychology:

conceptual integration and links to underlying memory systems. *Pers. Soc. Psychol. Rev.* 4:108–31

Stanford CB. 1995. Chimpanzees hunting behavior and human evolution. *Am. Sci.* 83:256–61

Swets JA, Dawes RM, Monahan J. 2000. Psychological science can improve diagnostic decisions. *Psychol. Sci. Public Interest* 1:1–26

Taylor SE, Brown JD. 1988. Illusion and well-being: a social psychological perspective on mental health. *Psychol. Bull.* 103:193–210

Thaler RH. 1999. Mental accounting matters. *J. Behav. Decis. Mak.* 12:183–206

Tourangeau R, Rasinski KA. 1988. Cognitive processes underlying context effects in attitude measurement. *Psychol. Bull.* 103:299–314

Tourangeau R, Rips LJ, Rasinski K. 2000. *The Psychology of Survey Response.* Cambridge, UK: Cambridge Univ. Press

Tversky A, Kahneman D. 1974. Judgment under uncertainty: heuristics and biases. *Science* 185:1124–31

Tversky A, Kahneman D. 1992. Advances in prospect theory: cumulative representation of uncertainty. *J. Risk Uncertain.* 5:297–323

Tversky A, Koehler DJ. 1994. Support theory: a nonextensional representation of subjective probability. *Psychol. Rev.* 101:547–67

Tversky A, Sattah S, Slovic P. 1988. Contingent weighting in judgment and choice. *Psychol. Rev.* 95:371–84

von Neumann J, Morgenstern O. 1947. *Theory of Games and Economic Behavior.* Princeton, NJ: Princeton Univ. Press. 2nd ed.

Weber EU. 1994. From subjective probabilities to decision weights: the effect of asymmetric loss functions on the evaluation of uncertain outcomes and events. *Psychol. Bull.* 115:228–42

Weber EU, Goldstein WM, Busemeyer JR. 1991. Beyond strategies: implications of memory representation and memory processes for models of judgment and decision making. In *Relating Theory and Data: Essays on Human Memory in Honor of Bennet B. Murdock,* ed. WE Hockley, S Lewandowsky, pp. 75–100. Hillsdale, NJ: Erlbaum

Weinstein ND. 1980. Unrealistic optimism about future life events. *J. Pers. Soc. Psychol.* 39:806–20

Weinstein ND. 1989. Optimistic biases about personal risks. *Science* 246:1232–33

Wright WF, Bower GH. 1992. Mood effects on subjective probability assessment. *Organ. Behav. Hum. Decis. Process.* 52:276–91

Yik MSM, Russell JA, Barrett LF. 1999. Structure of self-reported current affect: integration and beyond. *J. Pers. Soc. Psychol.* 77:600–19

Zajonc RB. 1980. Feeling and thinking: preferences need no inferences. *Am. Psychol.* 35:151–75

Annu. Rev. Psychol. 2001. 52:685–716

EMPIRICALLY SUPPORTED PSYCHOLOGICAL INTERVENTIONS: Controversies and Evidence

Dianne L. Chambless

Department of Psychology, University of North Carolina at Chapel Hill, Chapel Hill, North Carolina 27599-3270; e-mail: chambles@email.unc.edu

Thomas H. Ollendick

Child Study Center, Department of Psychology, Virginia Polytechnic Institute and State University, Blacksburg, Virginia 24061-0355; e-mail: tho@vt.edu

Key Words empirically supported therapies, empirically validated treatments, psychotherapy efficacy, psychotherapy effectiveness

■ **Abstract** Efforts to increase the practice of evidence-based psychotherapy in the United States have led to the formation of task forces to define, identify, and disseminate information about empirically supported psychological interventions. The work of several such task forces and other groups reviewing empirically supported treatments (ESTs) in the United States, United Kingdom, and elsewhere is summarized here, along with the lists of treatments that have been identified as ESTs. Also reviewed is the controversy surrounding EST identification and dissemination, including concerns about research methodology, external validity, and utility of EST research, as well as the reliability and transparency of the EST review process.

CONTENTS

0066-4308/01/0201-0685$14.00

INTRODUCTION

In 1995, the Task Force on Promotion and Dissemination of Psychological Procedures (henceforth, referred to as Task Force) of Division 12 (Clinical Psychology) of the American Psychological Association (APA) issued the first of three reports [Task Force 1995; Chambless et al 1996, 1998; also available on the Division 12 web page (http://www.apa.org/divisions/div12/est/est.html)] in which it identified a number of psychological interventions as empirically validated treatments [later called empirically supported treatments (ESTs)]. Reaping both praise and opprobrium, these reports have been the subject of conference presentations, newsletter articles, and special sections of journals (e.g. Kendall & Chambless 1998, Elliott 1998b, Kazdin 1996, *Can. Psychol.* 1999). In this review we consider the history of this effort, the evidence amassed by the Task Force and like bodies, and issues that give rise to the controversy over ESTs.

Appointed in 1993, the Task Force was charged with considering issues in the dissemination of psychological treatments of known efficacy. After acceptance by the Division 12 Board of Directors in October of that year, the Task Force's report was circulated to a number of groups for discussion, including the APA Boards of Educational Affairs, Scientific Affairs, and Professional Affairs; the APA Continuing Education Committee, Committee for Approval of Continuing Education Sponsors, and Committee on Accreditation; the Council of University Directors of Clinical Psychology; and the Association of Psychology Postdoctoral and Internship Centers. Individuals were informed of the report and its contents through a symposium at the APA convention, summaries published in *The Clinical Psychologist* and the *APA Monitor* with full copies available upon request (>1000 requests have been filled), and electronic mailings to list servers in clinical psychology. Copies of the full report or of pertinent sections were mailed to the APA Board of Directors, state psychological associations, directors of APA-approved clinical doctoral and internship programs, and those in attendance at an APA conference on postdoctoral education. The report was then published early in 1995, along with responses to comments.

Division 12's interest in promoting the awareness and use of ESTs is part of a broader movement that arose in the United Kingdom and was initially known as evidence-based medicine (Sackett et al 1997). The premises of this movement are that (*a*) patient care can be enhanced by acquisition and use of up-to-date empirical knowledge and (*b*) it is difficult for clinicians to keep up with newly emerging information pertinent to their practice but (*c*), if they do not, their knowledge and clinical performance will deteriorate over the years after their training; consequently, (*d*) clinicians need summaries of evidence provided by expert reviews and instructions on how to access this information during their routine practice. Although developed independently, the Task Force's recommendations are clearly consistent with these tenets. Among the more controversial of its recommendations are that APA engage in an ongoing effort to develop and maintain a list of ESTs for distribution and that training programs in clinical psychology include some didactic and applied training in ESTs. The latter recommendation followed a survey by task force members (Crits-Christoph et al 1995) of directors of APA-approved clinical-training programs. Respondents (83% of all directors) were asked to indicate which ESTs of a preliminary list assembled by the Task Force were included in students' didactic coursework or practicum training. The authors defined minimal coverage as some inclusion of 25% of ESTs in didactic courses and some clinical training in at least two ESTs. By these criteria, about one-fifth of the programs failed to include minimal coverage of ESTs. More recently, the successor committee to the Task Force has established a web page to disseminate information about ESTs to the public through Division 12's web site (http://www.apa.org/divisions/div12/rev_est/index.shtml).

Efforts to identify psychological ESTs have not been limited to the initial Task Force. Because the first task force was focused largely on ESTs for adults, Division 12 appointed a second task force with an emphasis on ESTs and prevention programs for children, the Task Force on Effective Psychosocial Interventions: A Lifespan Perspective. Reports from this task force have also been published (Spirito 1999, *J. Clin. Child Psychol.* 1998). Division 12 also commissioned a book entitled *A Guide to Treatments That Work*, spearheaded by yet another task force. Edited by Nathan & Gorman (1998), this mammoth book contains reviews of the psychotherapy and pharmacology outcome literature by experts in various psychological disorders. Apart from Division 12, a number of other authors have undertaken reviews of ESTs [e.g. Kendall & Chambless (1998), including publications identifying ESTs in adult, child, marital, and family therapy, Wilson & Gil's review of ESTs for chronic pain (1996), and Gatz et al's review of ESTs for the elderly (1998)]. Psychologists in the United Kingdom have been leaders in this area, including publication of *What Works for Whom?* by Roth & Fonagy (1996), who conducted a review of psychotherapy efficacy for the British National Health Service (Parry 1996). The Canadian Psychological Association's Clinical Psychology Section appointed its own EST task force (see Hunsley et al 1999). Strauss & Kaechele (1998) have described somewhat different but related efforts in Germany.

In the 1995 report, the Task Force published criteria for selection of ESTs and a very preliminary list of 25 treatments that met these criteria. This list was quickly constructed to allow the survey of clinical directors described above and to demonstrate that treatments meeting these criteria could be identified. In subsequent reports, the Task Force expanded the list of ESTs (Chambless et al 1996, 1998) and also collected and published information concerning training opportunities and materials for therapists (Sanderson & Woody 1995, Woody & Sanderson 1998). As of 1998, the list included 71 treatments. The decision by the Committee on Accreditation (American Psychological Association 1996) to include some training in ESTs as part of the guidelines for accreditation of doctoral- and internship-training programs in applied psychology no doubt heightened the already intense interest in the delineation of ESTs. As it became clear that APA would not itself pick up the work of the EST list, Division 12 committed itself to continuing these efforts by transforming the Task Force into a standing committee charged with evaluating the efficacy and effectiveness of psychological interventions. By a vote of the membership, this transition was approved and took effect in January 1999.

IDENTIFICATION OF EMPIRICALLY SUPPORTED THERAPIES

In Table 1, we summarize the criteria used by the various work groups to define ESTs and, in Tables 2 and 3, their findings to date. The groups are identified by letters: A for the original task force (Chambless et al 1998), B for the special section of *Journal of Pediatric Psychology* (Spirito 1999), C for the special section of *Journal of Child Clinical Psychology* (1998), D for the special section of *Journal of Consulting and Clinical Psychology* (Kendall & Chambless 1998), E for the British review *What Works for Whom?* (Roth & Fonagy 1996), F for Nathan & Gorman's (1998) *A Guide to Treatments that Work*, G for Gatz et al's (1998) review of treatments for the elderly, and H for Wilson & Gil's (1996) review of treatments for chronic pain. For purposes of comparison, we created three rough categories indicating level of support, based on the criteria listed in Table 1. These take into account the number of studies available and their experimental rigor. The following points need to be kept in mind for interpretation of these tables. First, because the different work groups did not use the exact same definitions, the distinction between categories I and II for work groups not following the task force criteria (Chambless et al 1998) completely is not precise. Moreover, Roth & Fonagy (1996) did not distinguish between category-I and -II treatments; thus, their ESTs are listed in the tables under both these categories with a question mark. Second, not all work groups listed promising treatments; those doing so were groups B, E, and F. Third, Nathan & Gorman (1998) eschewed categories. Accordingly, we imposed the category scheme on the reviews in their book, requiring two type-1 studies for inclusion in category I and one type-1 study for inclusion in category II, and relegating treatments supported by only type-2 or -3 studies to category III.

Treatments in category I are supported by at least two rigorous randomized controlled trials (RCTs) showing their superiority to placebo control conditions or another bona fide treatment. Alternatively, work groups following task force criteria (Chambless et al 1998) accepted a large series of rigorous single case experiments as meeting this definition, and authors in the Nathan & Gorman volume (1998) may have accepted the use of a waiting list control group for comparison. Treatments in category II were typically supported by at least one RCT in which the treatment proved superior to a control condition or alternative bona fide treatment. Also, most groups followed the task force criteria in relegating treatments demonstrated to be efficacious only by comparison to waiting list control groups to this category, regardless of the number of supporting studies, and accepted a small series of rigorous single case experiments as meeting threshold for this level

TABLE 1 Workgroup criteria for identification of empirically supported therapies

Division 12 Task Force criteria (Chambless et al 1998), group A
Well-established treatments
    I. At least two good between-group design experiments must demonstrate efficacy in one or more of the following ways:
        A. Superiority to pill or psychotherapy placebo, or to other treatment
        B. Equivalence to already established treatment with adequate sample sizes
OR
    II. A large series of single-case design experiments must demonstrate efficacy with
        A. Use of good experimental design and
        B. Comparison of intervention to another treatment
    III. Experiments must be conducted with treatment manuals or equivalent clear description of treatment
    IV. Characteristics of samples must be specified
    V. Effects must be demonstrated by at least two different investigators or teams
Probably efficacious treatments
    I. Two experiments must show that the treatment is superior to waiting-list control group
OR
    II. One or more experiments must meet well-established criteria IA or IB, III, and IV above but V is not met
OR
    III. A small series of single-case design experiments must meet well-established-treatment criteria
Experimental treatments
    Treatment not yet tested in trials meeting task force criteria for methodology

Special section of *Journal of Pediatric Psychology* (Spirito 1999) criteria, group B
Well-established treatments
    Same as Chambless et al (1998)
Probably efficacious treatments
    Same as Chambless et al (1998)
Promising interventions
    I. There must be positive support from one well-controlled study and at least one other less-well-controlled study
OR
    II. There must be positive support from a small number of single-case design experiments
OR
    III. There must be positive support from two or more well controlled studies by the same investigator

Special section of *Journal of Clinical Child Psychology* (1998, vol. 27, no. 2) criteria, group C
Well-established treatments
    Same as Chambless et al (1998)
Probably efficacious treatments
    Same as Chambless et al (1998) except:
        There must be at least two, rather than one, group design studies meeting criteria for well-established treatments if conducted by the same investigator

Special section of *Journal of Consulting and Clinical Psychology* (Kendall & Chambless 1998) criteria, group D

(Continued)

TABLE 1   (*Continued*)

Efficacious and specific
   Same as Chambless et al (1998) for well-established treatments
Possibly efficacious and specific treatments
   Same as efficacious and specific above except:
      Treatment only required to be found superior to rival treatment in one study
Efficacious and possibly specific treatments
   Same as efficacious and specific criteria above except:
      Treatment was found superior to wait-list group in one study and superior to rival
      treatment in another study by a different team
Efficacious treatments
   Same as Chambless et al (1998) for well-established treatments except:
      Treatment must be demonstrated to be better than no treatment but not been shown to be
      better than nonspecific intervention, placebo, or rival intervention
Possibly Efficacious Treatments
   Same as Chambless et al (1998) for probably efficacious treatments

What Works for Whom? (Roth & Fonagy 1996) criteria, group E
Clearly effective treatments
   I. There must be a replicated demonstration of superiority to a control condition or another
     treatment condition
OR
   II. There must be a single high-quality randomized control trial in which:
     A. Therapists followed a clearly described therapeutic method useable as the basis for
       training
     B. There is a clearly described patient group
Promising limited-support treatments
   Treatment must be innovative and a promising line of intervention
OR
   Treatment is a widely practiced method with only limited support for effectiveness

A Guide to Treatments That Work (Nathan & Gorman 1998) criteria, group F
Type 1 studies
   I. Study must include a randomized prospective clinical trial
   II. Study must include comparison groups with random assignment, blind assessments,
     clear inclusion and exclusion criteria, state-of-the-art diagnostic methods, and
     adequate sample size for power
   III. There must be clearly described statistical methods
Type 2 studies
   Clinical trials must be performed, but some traits of type-1 study were missing (e.g. trial
     with no double blind or group assignment not randomized)
Type 3 studies
   I. These are open treatment studies that are aimed at obtaining pilot data
OR
   II. These are case control studies in which treatment information was obtained
     retrospectively

Treatments for older adults (Gatz et al 1998) criteria, group G
   Same as Chambless et al (1998) criteria

Treatments for chronic pain (Wilson & Gil 1996) criteria, group H
   Same as Chambless et al (1998) criteria

of support. Category III is quite heterogeneous, in that groups E and F accepted a low level of evidence (e.g. a case series) as sufficient evidence to label a treatment as promising, whereas group B demanded more rigorously collected data, such as two or more well-controlled studies conducted by the same investigator.

When ESTs involved the addition of psychological procedures to pharmacological or other medical interventions (e.g. treatment for pain), the control group had to receive the same medical treatments. Work groups varied in their requirements for assessment. For example, those following the task force's criteria (Chambless et al 1998) required only that some reliable and valid method for determination of outcome was employed. Others imposed specific criteria pertinent to a given EST, such as requiring chemical verification of smoking cessation or behavioral observation measures of a child's hyperactive behavior. Given the difficulty in collecting follow-up data unconfounded by additional treatment and extensive attrition, efficacy was typically determined immediately posttreatment.

Table 2 lists ESTs identified for adults, and Table 3 lists those for children. Review of these tables permits some determination of the degrees to which different groups have identified the same treatments in their reviews. When review groups did not use precisely the same label to describe an EST, some judgment was required on our part to determine whether the same treatment was meant. In this case we were guided by the citations authors used to support their categorization of the treatment, as well as our own review of the articles in question.

A number of caveats pertain to the contents of the tables. First, on the whole, review groups have not attempted to determine which treatments are not efficacious. Second, no group essayed a complete review of the psychotherapy literature. For example, the Task Force reports explicitly note that their lists are works in progress. Thus, that a treatment does not appear on any one or all of the lists could have several meanings: (*a*) the treatment in question has fared poorly in research trials, (*b*) the treatment has not been examined in research trials, or (*c*) the treatment was not reviewed. Finally, all groups did not review all treatments. Thus, that one group listed a treatment as an EST and another did not cannot be taken to mean that the groups were in disagreement about a treatment's status. Disagreements may be indicated when one group assigned a treatment to a different category than another. However, because the groups published their work at different times, even then the discrepancy might be due to the publication of new studies.

Despite the number of individuals involved in the various independent review groups and the different approaches taken to evaluation, a review of these tables makes it apparent that, when two or more groups reported a review of the same treatment, the results were generally consistent. This should provide some reassurance to those who have expressed concern about unreliability or biases of individual reviewers for the various work groups. At the time of this review 108 category-I and -II ESTs had been identified for adults and 37 for children, reflecting considerable progress in discernment of ESTs since the first Task Force report with its list of 25 treatments. Nonetheless, that one can identify and disseminate information about ESTs does not address the arguments that it is ill advised to do so. We turn now to a consideration of critiques of the EST work.

TABLE 2 Empirically supported treatments for adults: a summary across workgroups

Condition and Treatment[a]	Category of Empirical Support[b, c]		
	I	II	III
Anxiety and stress			
Agoraphobia/panic disorder with agoraphobia			
CBT	A, E?, F	E?	
Couples communication training as adjunct to exposure		A, D	
Exposure	A, D, E?, F	E?	
Partner-assisted CBT		D, F	
Blood injury phobia			
Applied tension		F	E
Exposure			E
Generalized anxiety disorder			
Applied relaxation	F	A, D, E	
CBT	A, D, E?, F	E?	
Geriatric anxiety			
CBT			F, G
Relaxation		F	
Obsessive-compulsive disorder			
ERP	A, D, E?, F	E?	
Cognitive therapy		A, D	E
RET + exposure			E
Family-assisted ERP + relaxation		D	
Relapse prevention		A	
Panic disorder			
Applied relaxation	F	A, D, E	
CBT	A, D, E?, F	E?	
Emotion-focused therapy			F
Exposure	E?	D, E?	
Post-traumatic stress disorder			
EMDR		A (civilian only), D	
Exposure	F	A, D	
Stress inoculation	F	A, D	
Stress inoculation in combination with CT + exposure	E?	E?, F	
Structured psychodynamic treatment			E
Public-speaking anxiety			
Systematic desensitization		A	
Social anxiety/phobia			
CBT	E?, F	A, D, E?	
Exposure	E?,	A, D, E?, F	
Systematic desensitization		A	

TABLE 2   (*Continued*)

Condition and Treatment[a]	Category of Empirical Support[b, c]		
	I	**II**	**III**
Specific phobia			
Exposure	A, E?, F	E?	
Systematic desensitization		A	
Stress			
Stress inoculation	A		
Chemical abuse and dependence			
Alcohol abuse and dependence			
Community reinforcement	E?, F?	A, D, E?, F?	
Cue exposure therapy		A, D	
Cue exposure therapy + urge-coping skills		D	
Cue exposure with inpatient treatment		A	
Motivational interviewing	E?	E?	
BMT + disulfiram	E?, F?	A, D, E?, F?	
Social skills training with inpatient treatment	E?, F?	A, D, E?, F?	
Benzodiazepine withdrawal for panic disorder			
CBT		A	
Cocaine abuse			
Behavior therapy		A	
CBT relapse prevention		A, D	
Opiate dependence			
Behavior therapy (reinforcement)		D	
Brief dynamic therapy		A, D	
CT		A, D	
Depression			
Bipolar Disorder			
Psychoeducation		F	
CBT for medication adherence		F	
Family Therapy			F
Geriatric depression			
Behavior therapy	E?, F	E?, G	
Brief psychodynamic therapy	E?, F	E?, G	
CBT	E?, F	A, E?, G	
Interpersonal therapy		F	
Problem-solving therapy		F, G	
Psychoeducation	F		
Reminiscence therapy (mild-moderate)	F	A, G	
Major depression			
Behavior therapy	A, F	D	
BMT (for those with marital discord)	F	D	
Brief dynamic therapy		A	E

(Continued)

TABLE 2   (*Continued*)

Condition and Treatment[a]	Category of Empirical Support[b, c]		
	I	**II**	**III**
CBT	A, D, E?, F	E?	
Interpersonal therapy	A, E?, F	D, E?	
Self-control therapy		A, F	
Social problem solving		A, D	
Health problems			
Anorexia			
Behavior therapy	E?	E?	
BFST		F	
CT	E?	E?	
Family therapy			F
Binge-eating disorder			
Behavioral weight control		F	
CBT	F	A	
Interpersonal therapy		A, F	
Bulimia			
CBT	A, E?, F	D, E?	
Interpersonal therapy	E?	A, D, E?, F	
Cancer pain			
CBT			H
Chemotherapy side effects (for cancer patients)			
Progressive muscle relaxation with or without guided imagery		D	
Chronic pain (heterogeneous)			
CBT with physical therapy		A, D, H	
EMG biofeedback		A	
Operant behavior therapy		A, D	
Chronic pain (back)			
CBT	H	A, D	
Operant behavior therapy		D	
Headache			
Behavior therapy	A		
Idiopathic pain			
CBT			H
Irritable-bowel syndrome			
CT		A, D	
Hypnotherapy		D	
Multicomponent CBT		A, D	
Migraine			
EMG biofeedback + relaxation		D	
Thermal biofeedback + relaxation training		A, D	

TABLE 2   (*Continued*)

Condition and Treatment[a]	Category of Empirical Support[b, c]		
	I	**II**	**III**
Obesity			
Hypnosis with CBT		A	
Raynaud's			
Thermal biofeedback		A	
Rheumatic disease pain			
Multicomponent CBT	A, D, H		
Sickle cell disease pain			
Multicomponent CT		A	
Smoking cessation			
Group CBT		D	
Multicomponent CBT with relapse prevention	A, D		
Scheduled reduced smoking with multicomponent behavior therapy		A, D	
Somatoform pain disorders			
CBT		F	
Marital discord			
BMT	A, D		
CBT		D	
CT		D	
Emotion-focused couples therapy		A (no more than moderately distressed), D	
Insight-oriented marital therapy		A, D	
Systemic therapy		D	
Sexual dysfunction			
Erectile dysfunction			
Behavior therapy aimed at reducing sexual anxiety and improving communication	E?	E?	
CBT aimed at reducing sexual anxiety and improving communication	E?	E?	
Female hypoactive sexual desire			
Hurlbert's combined therapy		A, D	
Zimmer's combined sex and marital therapy		A, D	
Female orgasmic disorder/dysfunction			
BMT with Masters & Johnson's therapy		D	
Masters & Johnson's sex therapy		A, D	
Sexual-skills training		D	

(*Continued*)

TABLE 2   (*Continued*)

Condition and Treatment[a]	Category of Empirical Support[b, c]		
	I	**II**	**III**
Premature ejaculation			
Behavior therapy			E
Vaginismus			
Exposure-based behavior therapy	E?	E?	
Other			
Avoidant personality disorder			
Exposure		F	
Social skills training	E?	E?, F	
Body dysmorphic disorder			
CBT		F	
Borderline personality disorder			
Dialectical behavior therapy	E?	A, E?, F	
Psychodynamic therapy			F
Dementia			
Behavioral interventions applied at environmental level for behavior problems	G		
Memory and cognitive retraining for slowing cognitive decline		G	
Reality orientation		G	E
Geriatric care givers' distress			
Psychoeducation		G	
Psychosocial interventions	E?	E?	
Hypochondriasis			
CBT			F
Paraphilias/Sex Offenders			
Behavior therapy		A	
CBT			F
Schizophrenia			
Assertive case management			F
Behavior therapy and social learning/ token economy programs	F		
Clinical case management			F
CT (for delusions)			E, F
Behavioral family therapy	D, E?, F	A, E?	
Family systems therapy		D	
Social-learning programs	F		
Social-skills training	F	A, D	
Supportive group therapy		F	
Supportive long-term family therapy	D		

TABLE 2   (*Continued*)

Condition and Treatment[a]	Category of Empirical Support[b, c]		
	I	II	III
Training in community living program	F		
Severely mentally ill			
Supported employment		A, F	
Sleep disorders			
Behavior therapy			F
CBT (for geriatric sleep disorders)		G	
Unwanted habits			
Habit reversal and control techniques		A	

[a]CBT, cognitive behavior therapy; BMT, behavioral marital therapy; ERP, exposure plus ritual prevention; BFST, behavioral family systems therapy; EMDR, eye movement desensitization and reprocessing; CT, cognitive therapy; EMG, electromyographic.

[b]Category I, well-established/efficacious and specific/two type-1 studies; Category II, probably efficacious/efficacious/or possibly efficacious/one type-1 study; Category III, promising/type-2 or -3 studies. Only Groups B, E, and F listed Category III treatments.

[c]*Work groups:* A, Task Force (Chambless et al 1998); B, Special section of *Journal of Pediatric Psychology* (Spirito 1999); C, Special section of *Journal of Clinical Child Psychology* (1998); D, Special section of *Journal of Consulting and Clinical Psychology* (Kendall & Chambless 1998); E, *What Works for Whom?* (Roth & Fonagy 1996); F, *A Guide to Treatments That Work* (Nathan & Gorman 1998); G, Gatz et al (1998); H, Wilson & Gil (1996). ?, unclear from author's description whether treatment belongs in Category I or II.

CONTROVERSY

In this section we review a number of the criticisms leveled at the work on ESTs, some of which are particular to the publications of the Task Force and others of which are general to the very concept of identification of ESTs. Much contention stems from guild or economic concerns that the EST findings (*a*) will be misused by managed care companies to disenfranchise practitioners of psychotherapies that are not so designated (e.g. Silverman 1996), (*b*) will make these same practitioners more vulnerable to malpractice suits (Kovacs 1996), or (*c*) will restrict practice to a limited number of treatments, thus precluding flexibility and clinical innovation (see Elliott 1998a). We do not focus on these concerns, which although important, are outside the scientific arena. Rather, in the space permitted, we consider the empirical evidence for and against assertions that the EST list, criteria, and premises are flawed.

Treatment Selection

The Task Force and all other groups listed in Table 1 have adopted a similar approach to their reviews. They have defined ESTs as being specific treatments for specific issues, for example, cognitive-behavior therapy (CBT) for chronic back

TABLE 3   Empirically validated treatments for children and adolescents: a summary across workgroups[a]

Condition and Treatment[b]	Category of Empirical Support		
	I	II	III
ADHD			
Behavioral parent training	C		
Behavior modification in classroom	C		F
Long-term multimodal therapy			E
Anxiety disorders (separation anxiety, avoidant disorder, overanxious disorder)			
CBT		A, C	E
CBT + family AMT		A, C	
Psychodynamic psychotherapy			E
Chronic pain (musculoskeletal disorders)			
CBT			B
Conduct disorder (oppositional defiant disorder)			
Anger control training with stress inoculation (adolescents)		C	
Anger-coping therapy (children)		C	
Assertiveness training		C	
CBT	E?	E?	
Cognitive problem-solving skills	F		
Delinquency prevention program		C	
Functional family therapy	F		
Multisystemic therapy	F	C	
Parent-child interaction therapy		C	
Parent training based on living with children (children)	A, E?, F	C, E?	
Parent training based on living with children (adolescents)	C		
Problem-solving skills training		C	
Rational emotive therapy		C	
Time out plus signal seat treatment		C	
Videotape-modeling parent training	C		
Depression			
Coping with depression course with skills training (adolescents)		C	
CBT (children)		C	
Disruptive disorders			
Structural family therapies			E
Distress due to medical procedures (mainly for cancer)			
CBT	B		
Encopresis			
Behavior modification	E?	A, E?	

TABLE 3   (*Continued*)

Condition and Treatment[b]	Category of Empirical Support		
	I	**II**	**III**
Enuresis			
Behavior modification	A, E?	E	
Obesity			
Behavior therapy		A	
Obsessive-compulsive disorder			
ERP			E
Phobias			
CBT		C	
Filmed modeling		C	
Imaginal desensitization		C	
In vivo desensitization		C	
Live modeling		C	
Participant modeling	C		
Rapid exposure (school phobia)	E?	E?	
Reinforced practice	C	A	
Psychophysiological disorder			
Family therapy	E?	E?	
Psychodynamic psychotherapy			E
Pervasive developmental disorders, undesirable behavior in			
Contingency management	E?	E?	
Recurrent abdominal pain			
CBT		D, F	
Recurrent headache			
Biofeedback with self-hypnosis			B
Relaxation/self-hypnosis	B		
Thermal biofeedback		B	

[a]See footnotes in Table 2 for explanation of categories and listing of workgroups.

[b]ADHD, attention deficit/hyperactivity disorder; AMT, anxiety management training.

pain, multisystemic family therapy for conduct disorder, or brief psychodynamic therapy for depression. Copious evidence already exists for the proposition that psychotherapy in general is effective for clients in general [see, e.g., the meta-analyses by Shapiro & Shapiro (1982) and Weisz et al (1995)]. Thus, the various task forces and independent groups have sought to take the next step, to identify more precisely which treatments practitioners of evidence-based psychological interventions might consider for particular clients. This decision in and of itself has proved controversial (e.g. Garfield 1996).

Sample Description

Arguing that it is unwise to conclude that all treatments are beneficial for all types of clients, the Task Force required that tests of ESTs be conducted on a sample identified with some specificity. This might be and often was a diagnosis based on some system such as the *Diagnostic and Statistical Manual of Mental Disorders* (American Psychiatric Association 1994) but could include any reliable and valid approach to defining the sample of interest, for example, a cutoff score on a questionnaire indicating martial distress for couples seeking marital therapy. A number of critics have objected to this decision for two reasons: (*a*) they dispute that there are meaningful differences in the efficacy of different forms of psychological interventions (e.g. Wampold et al 1997), and (*b*) they decry the acceptance of the medical model implied in frequent use of *Diagnostic and Statistical Manual of Mental Disorders* diagnoses to describe samples (e.g. Henry 1998). We consider the first of these objections in a later section (see "Treatment Specificity" below). Regarding the second objection, critics have argued that no system of describing clients is needed, that groupings of clients are impossible because each case is unique, or that diagnosis is dehumanizing (e.g. Bohart et al 1998). Others have called for a different sort of organizing principle, perhaps one based on important personality factors that may affect response to psychotherapy, such as reactance (e.g. Beutler et al 1996), or on functional relationships (i.e. the cause of the dysfunctional behavior; e.g. Scotti et al 1996). In response, task force members (Task Force 1995) have noted that some method for describing clients is necessary to enable clinicians to evaluate the likelihood of generalization from research samples for their own practice and to organize data. Without some categorization, synthesis of evidence is extremely difficult, if not impossible. Fonagy & Target (1996) noted that, whatever the limitations of diagnostic systems such as the DSM, critics have yet to suggest a better feasible alternative.

Research Design

A second criticism of the criteria concerns the Task Force's reliance on RCTs (or comparable single-case design approaches) to test the outcome of research on psychological interventions. This criterion has been attacked from three perspectives. First, it has been rejected as a poor approach to gaining knowledge by those who suggest that qualitative research would be more appropriate (e.g. Bohart et al 1998). Second, because cognitive and behavioral approaches have been more often the subject of RCTs than have other forms of psychotherapy, some fear that the criteria lend unfair advantage to CBT over other therapies (e.g. Bohart et al 1998). Third, Seligman (1995), among others, has argued that, because clients in treatment in the community are not randomly assigned to treatment, ESTs based on RCTs are unlikely to generalize to clinical practice. Only the last of these points can be addressed through empirical findings, and we devote a separate section to these later (see "Effectiveness" below).

The Task Force's decision to require careful definition of the independent variable (the therapy or therapies), most often, although not necessarily, in the form of a treatment manual, has resulted in heated controversy. A treatment manual is a statement of the principles and procedures of a psychological intervention, including both prescribed and proscribed interventions. Manuals may be in the detailed form of session-by-session guidelines or may provide extensive flexibility within the general framework provided by the authors (Kendall et al 1998). The better manuals are richly elaborated with examples of dialogue illustrating application of the procedures and with descriptions of courses of action to take when problems arise in treatment. The Task Force concluded that treatment manuals or their equivalent in the form of a clear description of the treatment are necessary to provide an operational definition of the intervention under study, because very different procedures may fall under the general rubric of, for example, psychodynamic psychotherapy or CBT. Failing such a description, clinicians are unable to determine the similarity of their own practices to ESTs, and educators are ignorant of how they might train their students in ESTs. That is, in terms of generalizable knowledge, it is meaningless to say that a treatment works without being able to say what that treatment is.

In part, the negative reaction to the requirement that EST research include manuals or other clear descriptions of the treatment appears to be an emotional one (see Fonagy 1999), with some clinicians reacting to a perceived threat to their independence of practice. For example, some have viewed manuals as "promoting a cookbook mentality" (Smith 1995, p. 40), "paint[ing] by numbers" (Silverman 1996, p. 207), or even as "a hangman of life" (Lambert 1998, p. 391). This reaction is captured nicely by Bohart et al (1998), who wrote, "[the therapist is]. . .a disciplined improvisational artist, not a manual-driven technician" (p. 145). Others have viewed manualization (as it has come to be called) in more positive terms. For example, Wilson (1998, p. 363) has asserted that ". . . use of standardized, manual based treatments in clinical practice represents a new and evolving development with far-reaching implications for the field of psychotherapy." Indeed, in a survey of licensed psychologists, Addis & Krasnow (2000) found that practitioners were equally likely to be positively vs negatively inclined toward treatment manuals.

Seligman (1995) and Garfield (1996), among others, have objected to the use of manuals on another basis—that therapists in the community do not follow manuals and, thus, their use in efficacy research limits generalization. Indeed, according to Addis & Krasnow's (2000) survey, 47% of licensed psychologists in practice had never used manuals in their clinical work. However, that therapists may not, on the whole, use manualized treatments now does not address the question of whether it would be desirable for them to do so. At present, 23% of psychologists in practice report that they have never heard of treatment manuals, and of those aware of their existence, 38% are unclear as to what manuals are (Addis & Krasnow 2000). For a further review of the controversy surrounding manualization, see Addis et al (1999).

Some authors (e.g. Elliott 1998a) have complained that the task force criteria are too lenient, because they are focused solely on the efficacy of the treatments in RCTs and not on their effectiveness, that is, on whether these treatments work in what the authors term real clinical practice. This issue, in our judgment, is far more important than whether therapists are currently using ESTs as described in treatment manuals in their practice. We consider this topic at some length below (see "Effectiveness"). Finally, there are general complaints about the clarity of the criteria and the methods for reaching decisions (e.g. Elliott 1998a); for example, when are two versions of CBT for depression similar enough to lump together and when should they be considered separate treatments? The Task Force required that experiments have been conducted with "good" methodology, but what defines good? Chambless & Hollon (1998) have provided considerable detail on evaluation of the methodology of psychotherapy research as used by the Task Force and others (Kendall & Chambless 1998). Despite this detail, these authors did not draw hard and fast decision rules, leaving room for potential bias on the reviewers' part. In our view, this is one of the more telling criticisms of the Task Force's work. The group provided no evidence of the reliability of its decisions and no detailed explanation of the process involved in reaching those decisions. Nonetheless, as previously noted, a review of Table 2 indicates that multiple review groups have generally arrived at the same conclusions about the efficacy of treatments evaluated. (Treatments in Table 3 are less likely to have been reviewed by more than one group.)

Cognizant of the importance that the reviews should be viewed as reasoned and impartial, the Division 12 Committee on Science and Practice, which succeeded the Task Force, has postponed the EST review process for several years in favor of developing an elaborate manual for members to use in evaluating treatments. The twelfth draft of this manual was recently completed (JR Weisz & KM Hawley, unpublished manuscript) and is under review by committee members. The present plan is for this manual to be used by two other groups identifying ESTs, the Committee for Empirically Supported Practice of APA Division 53 (Clinical Child Psychology) and the Interdisciplinary Committee on Evidence-Based Youth Mental Health Care. These groups provided feedback on the development of the manual. It is likely that treatments already on the EST list will be reevaluated according to the criteria set forth in this new manual. Because the Committee has yet to vote on final approval of the manual, we do not summarize it in detail here. However, from our own review we conclude that adoption and use of this manual will address most complaints about clarity of process, as well as many of the technical concerns.

Standardization of Treatment

The use of treatment manuals in EST research and in training of psychotherapists has been criticized not only on emotional grounds but also on the grounds that use of treatment manuals will lead to a degradation in the quality of treatment that clients receive (e.g. Garfield 1996, Henry 1998). The assumptions are (*a*) that therapists trained in a standardized treatment will not be able to deviate flexibly from such protocols when necessary to treat a particular case and (*b*) that a standardized treatment approach will be less beneficial than a treatment program designed specifically for an individual case. Concerning the first point, Garfield, Henry, and others have pointed to research on adherence to protocol in psychotherapy research to buttress their arguments that manual-based training will be detrimental to the efficacy of psychotherapy. The empirical findings on this point are inconsistent, with some authors finding that, at least under some circumstances (e.g. rupture of the therapeutic alliance), greater adherence is related to poorer outcome (e.g. Castonguay et al 1996), whereas others have found greater adherence to be related to better outcome (e.g. Frank et al 1991). However, such arguments miss the point, in that such research tells us nothing about the success of manual-trained therapists in their unstructured clinical practice. We know of no research on this first point, and other authors (e.g. Moras 1993) have argued that students grasp the general principles of treatment and acquire skills more quickly when they are presented in the organized form of a manual rather than solely relying on the informal teaching that occurs during supervision. Thus, research directed at this question would be highly desirable.

For now, this leaves us to question the second point: Is standardized treatment less efficacious than an individualized treatment program? We located only three studies addressing this issue: (*a*) Jacobson et al's (1989) comparison of standardized behavioral marital therapy to the same form of therapy delivered flexibly with regard to the total length of treatment and the amount of time spent on any one component; (*b*) Schulte et al's (1992) comparison of treatment of phobias (mostly agoraphobia) by standardized treatment with prolonged exposure vs individually designed treatment in which the therapist was given total flexibility in designing the treatment for each client; and (*c*) Emmelkamp et al's comparison (1994) of self directed exposure plus ritual prevention for obsessive-compulsive disorder to a program of various cognitive and behavioral treatments based on an individual behavioral analysis. In all of these studies, the same therapists administered treatments in the standardized vs individualized conditions, ruling out the possibility that therapist main effects contributed to the outcome, and clients were randomly assigned to treatments.

In none of the studies was flexible treatment statistically superior to standardized treatment. Indeed, Schulte et al (1992) found the standardized treatment for phobia to be significantly better than that based on the therapist's discretion, largely because some therapists failed to use exposure treatment in this condition, even though exposure is the best validated treatment for phobia. On the other hand, in the marital-therapy study, there was a trend at 6-month follow-up in favor of the flexible treatment group, and effect sizes were higher in the flexible group. Unfortunately, because length of treatment was confounded with flexibility of treatment procedures (treatment was, on average, longer in the flexible condition), these data are difficult to interpret. In addition, in this study therapists were constrained to use the same treatment components regardless of condition. Thus, this study is less a test of manualization than of a more vs less flexible manual. Additional research of this nature with a wider variety of problems and including children and adolescents should be conducted. For now, the data do not support the assertion that manualizing treatments will be detrimental to clients.

Treatment Specificity

Obviously, if all forms of psychotherapy were equally efficacious for all problems, the identification of ESTs would be a much less important exercise. Many would claim that reviews of psychotherapy research have demonstrated this to be the case. For example, Wampold et al (1997) conducted a meta-analysis in which they tested the hypothesis that the effect size for comparisons between different types of psychotherapy is zero. Their results were consistent with this hypothesis and are typical of findings from similar meta-analyses. A common interpretation of such findings is that nonspecific factors (e.g. the quality of the therapist-client relationship) are responsible for all of the meaningful variance in treatment outcome. Nonspecific factors are clearly of great importance in psychotherapy, with, for example, the therapeutic relationship accounting for about 9% of the outcome variance [see meta-analysis by Horvath & Symonds (1991)]. Nonetheless, we would argue that it is hasty to conclude that there are no meaningful differences in the effects of psychotherapies, for several reasons.

First, meta-analyses such as those conducted by Wampold et al (1997) are generally focused on a somewhat restricted sample of clients, including college students and outpatients with problems with anxiety, depression, eating disorders, and the like. Comparisons among different theoretical schools are not available for treatment of the chronically mentally ill and the developmentally disabled. We doubt that such comparisons will be conducted because of the strength of the belief, right or wrong, that behavioral methods are the treatments of choice for these clients.

Second, meta-analyses demonstrating lack of specificity often include little research on children or adolescents. For example, Wampold et al (1997) did not search journals in the child area such as the *Journal of Clinical Child Psychology*, the *Journal of Abnormal Child Psychology*, or the *Journal of the American Academy of Child and Adolescent Psychiatry*. Meta-analyses of treatment research on children and adolescents have yielded different conclusions. In their meta-analysis of treatment outcome studies conducted between 1967 and 1993 with children and adolescents, Weisz et al (1995) concluded that behavioral treatments (e.g. behavioral contracting, parent management training, modeling, and CBT) were more effective than nonbehavioral treatments (e.g. insight-oriented therapy or client-centered counseling). Casey & Berman (1985) reached a similar conclusion in their early meta-analysis of psychotherapy research with children, conducted between 1952 and 1982.

Third, it is often suggested that some problems such as depression are benefited by a wide range of treatments (Beutler et al 2000), whereas others, such as obsessive-compulsive disorder and phobias, respond better to specific behavioral treatments or CBTs than to other treatments. To evaluate these arguments, we now examine evidence for the specificity of psychotherapy effects, taken from studies meeting criteria for EST research. This body of literature is very large. Owing to space considerations, we include only a sampling of studies for two problems for which specificity research is available—anxiety disorders and depression. Within these categories we focus, whenever possible, on particularly well-designed studies in which authors have ruled out alternative explanations for differences between treatments, such as uncontrolled therapists' effects and differences in the quality of the therapeutic relationship and in the credibility of treatment.

Anxiety Disorders   Research on treatment of adult obsessive-compulsive disorder has demonstrated a high degree of specificity, in that different forms of behavior therapy have significantly different effects. Fals-Stewart et al (1993), Lindsay et al (1997), Hodgson et al (1972), and Marks et al (1975) all compared exposure plus response prevention, a well-established EST, to progressive muscle relaxation, either alone or elaborated as anxiety management training. Designs in the 1970s were quasi-experimental, but the more recent two studies were RCTs. In all four studies, exposure plus response prevention was significantly superior to the alternative treatment. Lindsay et al (1997) tested whether differences in the therapeutic relationship might account for these findings. This proved not to be the case. When interviewed by an independent assessor, clients rated therapists as highly and comparably supportive and understanding, regardless of treatment condition. Unfortunately, these authors did not assess clients' expectancies for change or credibility of treatment. This oversight was corrected in a study of a different anxiety disorder.

Studying generalized anxiety disorder among adults, Borkovec & Costello (1993) found that CBT was significantly superior to nondirective therapy at posttest and 1-year follow-up. This study represents one of the most sophisticated comparisons available in the specificity literature. The authors demonstrated that clients in CBT and nondirective therapy were comparable in their ratings of expectancy of change and their therapists. Furthermore, in both conditions therapists were guided by detailed treatment manuals, and the authors verified that treatment effects were consistent across therapists. Consistent with the theory of nondirective therapy, observers rated clients in that condition as having greater depth of experiencing than clients in the other conditions. Nonetheless, these clients failed to improve as much as those in CBT.

Research on treatments for children's and adolescent's anxiety disorders also demonstrates specificity. Using a controlled, single-case design, Ollendick (1995) showed that a developmental adaptation of Barlow & Craske's (1994) CBT for panic disorder with agoraphobia was beneficial for adolescents, whereas education and support alone were not. Treatment gains persisted at 6-month follow-up. In the specific phobia domain, specificity is also evident (Ollendick & King 1998, 2000). For example, participant modeling (in which the therapist models, prompts, and assists the child in approaching the phobic stimulus) has been shown to be more effective than nondirective, supportive therapy as well as other variants of behavioral and cognitive therapies, including systematic desensitization and filmed modeling. Furthermore, reinforced practice (based on principles of shaping, positive reinforcement, and extinction) has been shown to be more effective than verbal coping skills and therapist modeling alone.

Depression   Specificity is also evident in psychotherapy effects for depression among children and adolescents. For example, Stark et al (1991) compared CBT to nondirective, supportive therapy in the treatment of children who reported high levels of depressive symptoms on the Children's Depression Inventory. At postintervention and at 7-month follow-up, children in the CBT group reported fewer depressive symptoms on a semistructured interview and indicated fewer depressive symptoms on the Children's Depression Inventory than children in the supportive condition. Brent et al (1997) obtained consistent results, showing that CBT was more effective than supportive, nondirective therapy with adolescents who have major depressive disorders. Moreover, CBT was marginally more effective than a family intervention utilizing techniques of functional family therapy.

Specificity breaks down where treatment of depressed adults is concerned. For example, in the large-scale National Institute of Mental Health (NIMH) study comparing CBT to interpersonal therapy (Elkin et al 1989), no significant differences between treatments were observed. Similarly, Thompson et al (1987) found no evidence of treatment specificity in their comparison of behavioral, cognitive, and brief dynamic therapies for depressed elders, and Jacobson et al (1996) found that the full CBT package was no more efficacious than one of its components, behavioral activation (i.e. assignment of activities to build mastery and positive mood), alone.

It is not entirely clear why the patterns of findings differ between depressed children and adults. This may be the result of developmental differences. It is also possible that the difference between the findings for adults and children has to do with the therapies with which CBT is contrasted. In the child studies, the comparison group received supportive, nondirective therapy, whereas, in the adult studies, comparison treatments were behavior therapy and psychodynamic therapy.

Effectiveness

One of the strongest arguments posed against the dissemination of ESTs is the dearth of evidence that research treatments are beneficial when applied (*a*) in ordinary clinical settings such as private practices and community mental health and medical centers and (*b*) to ordinary clients, that is, those who are not selected according to an extensive list of exclusion criteria and those who have not agreed to be randomly assigned to treatments as part of a research enterprise. In the psychotherapy literature, this distinction is known as the difference between evidence of efficacy vs effectiveness [see Hoagwood et al (1995) or Moras (1998) for a concise presentation of these concepts]; almost always this distinction overlaps highly with the contrast between experiments with high internal vs high external validity. It is true that, until recently, psychotherapy researchers concentrated almost exclusively on efficacy research, but effectiveness data are beginning to emerge. Here we describe samples of effectiveness research on a number of well-established treatments, including, for adults, CBT for depression and panic disorder and, for children, two parent training programs for conduct/oppositional defiant disorder.

Panic Disorder   In a study notable for its external validity, Wade et al (1998) reported the effectiveness of Barlow & Craske's (1994) CBT for panic disorder with or without agoraphobia for 110 clients of a community mental health center. Therapists were staff members trained to administer a standard 15-session protocol. Minimal exclusion criteria were employed. Clients showed significant pretest-posttest changes on all major outcome measures, and improvements were comparable in effect size to changes observed with the same treatment program in efficacy studies. However, the authors reported that the dropout rate was higher than that in efficacy studies, although still considerably lower than the dropout rate usually observed in community mental health center samples.

A significant challenge to the external validity of efficacy studies is the limited range of ethnic groups included in research samples. It is typical for the large majority of subjects to be white or for the ethnic characteristics of samples to go unreported. Sanderson et al (1998) reported the results of 12 sessions of Barlow & Craske's (1994) CBT for panic disorder when applied to a medical center outpatient clinic sample of 30 low income, urban clients, the majority of whom were Latino. Statistically significant improvement was observed, although clients remained more impaired than those in the benchmark study. The authors noted that the level of disorder in their population was initially more severe but also suggested that the high rate of stress in this sample may have limited the success of treatment.

Depression   We located five studies of the effectiveness of CBT for depression, all with positive results. Peterson & Halstead (1998) examined the outcome of an abbreviated form of standardized CBT (6 sessions vs the typical 20) administered in a group format. Clients were 210 patients referred to a depression management program in military clinics. Minimal exclusion criteria were applied. Significant pretest-posttest reductions on the Beck Depression Inventory were observed, regardless of the initial level of severity of depression. The authors noted that the average reduction in depressive symptoms (37%) was less than that usually reported in efficacy studies (57%), but they also pointed out that their treatment was considerably briefer for practical reasons—cost reduction and prevention of attrition.

Persons and colleagues have published the results of two investigations of CBT for depression in private-practice samples (Persons et al 1988, 1999). Treatment was applied in a flexible manner according to individual case formulations to clients with a variety of depressive disorders regardless of their comorbidity. Significant improvement was observed, and outcomes for intention-to-treat samples (including all clients, regardless of whether they completed treatment) were comparable to those in benchmark efficacy studies. However, private-practice clients received, on average, more sessions than those in efficacy studies. Whether improvement would have been comparable had this not been the case couldn't be determined from these data.

In two separate samples, Organista et al (1994) and Miranda et al (J Miranda, F Azocar, K Organista, E Dwyer, P Arean, manuscript under review) tested the benefits of standardized group CBT for depression in low-income medical outpatients treated at a hospital depression clinic. The majority were members of ethnic minority groups (Latino or African-American) and had significant medical problems. Significant improvement was observed in both studies, and Miranda et al reported that 62%–80% (depending on ethnicity) no longer met diagnostic criteria for depression after treatment. Nonetheless, on average clients remained in the depressed range, according to questionnaire scores. The dropout rate was higher with this disadvantaged population (40%–60%) than in efficacy studies [e.g. 32% (Elkin et al 1989)], but change was significant for the intention-to-treat sample (i.e. the sample of all clients who began treatment, including dropouts). Miranda et al found that adding case management services reduced dropouts significantly.

Oppositional-Defiant Disorder   Two effectiveness studies have been conducted with children presenting with oppositional problems. In the first study, Taylor et al (1998) examined the effectiveness of Webster-Stratton's Parents and Children Series (PACS) at a community-based children's mental health center. Parents seeking help in managing their 3- to 8-year-old-children's behaviors were randomly assigned to one of three conditions: PACS, treatment as usual (TAU), or a waiting-list control group. TAU was defined by each therapist and included ecological, solution-focused, family systems, and popular-press parenting approaches. Therapists were affiliated with the center; 7 were trained in Webster-Stratton's approach, and 11 were not. Both active treatments were superior to the waiting list, but mothers in the PACs program reported significantly fewer behavior problems and greater satisfaction with treatment than mothers in the TAU program. Outcomes were similar to those obtained in the efficacy trials. Thus, this trial provides evidence of PACS's specificity as well as effectiveness. However, because therapists were not crossed with treatment conditions or randomly assigned to conditions, it is also possible that PACS's superiority to TAU was due to some superiority of PACS therapists unrelated to the treatment.

A second, uncontrolled effectiveness trial with oppositional children was recently reported. Using parent management training and child social skills training, Tynan et al (1999) treated 55 consecutive admissions to a hospital-affiliated child psychiatry clinic. The children, ranging in age from 5 to 11 years, all presented with oppositional problems, and most were comorbid with other disorders including attention deficit/hyperactivity disorder. Therapists were trained in the implementation of the manualized treatment. Pre-post changes were large, significant, and comparable to benchmark efficacy studies.

Focus of Treatment

A further criticism leveled at the external validity of EST research is the charge that, in such studies, the researchers focus only on so-called symptoms. Depending on theoretical orientation, clinicians may reject the importance of symptoms in favor of goals such as self-transcendence (Kovacs 1996) or improvement in overall life adjustment. To call problems such as depression or panic "symptoms" is consistent with approaches such as psychodynamic theory, in which it is assumed that these conditions reflect some more central underlying problems. In behavioral or cognitive approaches, these conditions are generally not viewed as symptoms but as valid problems in their own right. Be that as it may, it is legitimate to question whether ESTs lead to improvement in quality of life or overall adjustment.

In response to calls for data on quality of life, EST researchers are now including measures for this construct in their assessment battery, but these studies are mostly in progress, with findings not yet available (Gladis et al 1999). In the adult arena, we located two studies, including three different ESTs. No such studies were found in the child and adolescent arena. Indeed, Gladis et al pointed out that adequate instruments for assessing quality of life in children have yet to be developed. For the adult studies, we examined findings at both posttest and follow-up, because changes in overall adjustment may be slow to emerge, typically lagging after changes in presenting problems even in non-symptom-focused treatment, such as psychodynamic psychotherapy (e.g. Howard et al 1993).

Cognitive Therapy for Depression   Blatt et al (2000) analyzed data from the NIMH Treatment for Depression Collaborative Research Program, in which two ESTs—cognitive and interpersonal therapies—were compared to treatments with an antidepressant plus clinical management and with a placebo plus clinical management. Analyses controlled for overall symptom severity and level of functioning at pretest, as well as other variables that had proved predictive of treatment outcome. There were no differences among treatments at posttest, but by an 18 month follow up, clients in both psychotherapy groups rated their life adjustment significantly more positively than clients in the placebo or medication group. Findings were not due to differences in expectancy.

Cognitive Behavioral Therapy for Panic Disorder   Telch et al (1995) compared the effects of 12 sessions of CBT to a delayed-treatment control group. Quality of life measures included assessment of global impairment in work, social and leisure activities, and family life. At posttest, the treated clients showed significantly more improvement than waiting-list clients on both measures of global adjustment, as well as on most of the measures' subscales. Because the control group participants entered treatment after posttest, follow-up data are uncontrolled. Six months after treatment, client scores continued to be significantly improved compared with pretest scores, with no significant change from posttest to follow-up.

CONCLUSION

In conclusion, we summarize the arguments for and against identification and dissemination of ESTs and our responses:

1. Argument: ESTs should be ignored because this effort has been the work of a small group of biased individuals in Division 12 (Society for Clinical Psychology of the American Psychological Association).

Response: Tables 2 and 3 summarize the results of searches by eight different review groups. Because the groups had different foci (e.g. geriatric vs child clients), their review areas often did not overlap. When they did, there is evidence of considerable agreement in the judgment of different groups. This suggests that, once decisions are based on common assumptions (e.g. use of RCTs, specifically defined samples, and treatments), EST designations can and have been made reliably. This assertion needs to be tempered by the presence of some overlap in the membership of the Task Force and the authors of the *Journal of Consulting and Clinical Psychology* special section on this subject (Groups A & D) (Kendall & Chambless 1998).

2. Argument: Quantitative research is not an appropriate paradigm for psychotherapy research. Qualitative research or clinical observation should be the evidence source.

    Response: Evidence reviewed in this chapter cannot address this question, which results from a schism in paradigms. No matter how large or consistent the body of evidence found for identified ESTs, findings will be dismissed as irrelevant by those with fundamentally different views, and such views characterize a number of practitioners and theorists in the psychotherapy area.

3. Argument: EST research is based on treatment manuals or their equivalent, and use of manuals to train therapists will lead to decrements in the quality of psychotherapy.

    Response: We found no studies addressing the concern that, when working outside a restricted treatment protocol, manual-trained therapists would be less effective than therapists trained without manuals. Such research would be valuable in addressing these concerns. We did locate two studies in which the results from therapists trained in ESTs were compared under two conditions: one in which therapists were free to design individually tailored treatments (all within a general cognitive-behavioral framework) and one in which therapists operated under the standard EST guidelines. Standardized treatment proved equivalent or superior to individually tailored treatment. Unfortunately, both of these studies involved treatments of anxiety disorders. Additional research in this area with a broader range of treatments and problems is clearly needed.

4. Argument: There is no difference in efficacy among various forms of psychotherapy; hence, identification of ESTs is unnecessary.

    Response: In our abbreviated review of anxiety disorders and childhood depression, we found considerable evidence of specificity, even within cognitive and behavioral methods. Authors were not consistent in the care they took to rule out alternative explanations for differences among treatments, such as possible confounding discrepancies in expectancy and the therapeutic relationship. However, in studies in which such confounds could be discounted, treatment differences were still obtained.

Nonetheless, evidence of specificity is not uniform, in that, for adult depression, no treatment has been clearly demonstrated to be superior to another. These data and those from meta-analyses indicate that the question of specificity is a complex one and may depend on the target problem and clients' age (child vs adult).

5. Argument: EST research should be ignored because it will not generalize to clinical practice, defined as typical settings, clients, therapists, and treatment goals.

   Response: Thus far, the evidence reviewed indicates that ESTs are effective in clinical settings and with a diverse group of clients. Nonetheless, this conclusion needs to be tempered by the following considerations. (*a*) As would be expected in effectiveness research, these studies were high in external validity but low on internal validity, typically relying on uncontrolled pretest-posttest designs and evaluation by comparison with standard outcomes in the efficacy literature. (*b*) Clients in effectiveness studies often did not improve as much as those in efficacy studies or did not achieve as positive a level of functioning at the end of treatment. (*c*) Clients in some effectiveness studies received more treatment than is typical in RCTs, in the form of a longer course of treatment or adjunctive treatments such as concomitant pharmacotherapy or case management services. (*d*) The body of effectiveness research is small.

Hence, although we found no evidence that ESTs could not be beneficially applied in real clinical settings by those trained or supervised in their use, depending on the population served, treatments may need to be modified or included as part of a broader course of treatment. More research on effectiveness is clearly a priority if clinicians are to give credence to the value of ESTs. The NIMH is currently making such studies a priority in its mission for treatment research; this should ensure that effectiveness studies rapidly multiply.

Where treatment goals are concerned, we found very little research on whether ESTs affect quality of life. The two studies we found yielded positive results. To the degree that ESTs focus on clients with significant psychological disturbance, researchers are likely to find that improvements in presenting problems will be associated with enhanced quality of life. This follows from the substantial correlations of measures of disorder with quality of life measures. These effect sizes are typically moderate to large (Gladis et al 1999, Telch et al 1995). Should EST researchers focus on healthy but dissatisfied clients, we would expect quality-of-life measures to play a more unique role and, indeed, to become the central outcome measures in such research. More research on improved quality of life as an effect of ESTs is clearly needed, and such data should be available soon from studies presently under way.

The drive to identify and disseminate ESTs is less than a decade old. From the review above, it is clear that there is much to be learned about the application of ESTs and their benefits in clinical practice. Whatever the reluctance of some to embrace ESTs, we expect that the economic and societal pressures on practitioners for accountability will encourage continued attention to these treatments (cf Beutler 1998). At the same time, it is important to note that the effective practice of evidence-based psychotherapy involves more than the mastery of specific procedures outlined in EST manuals. Almost all ESTs rely on therapists' having good nonspecific therapy skills. For example, in the NIMH Treatment of Depression Collaborative Research Program of two ESTs (interpersonal therapy and cognitive therapy) for depression, in which therapists followed elaborate treatment manuals, treatment effects varied according to therapists' competence (Shaw et al 1999). Client characteristics such as ability to form an alliance with the therapist (Krupnick et al 1996) and initial functioning (e.g. Elkin et al 1995) also proved to be important in predicting treatment outcome. Research on the interaction of client characteristics (e.g. personality) with treatment approaches is in its early stages (e.g. Beutler et al 1991). Such research is difficult to conduct because of the large sample sizes required for sufficient power. Yet such research has great potential for addressing practitioners' questions about which among several ESTs might be best for a particular client. Thus, the practice of evidence-based psychotherapy is a complex one, and ESTs are only one piece of the puzzle.

ACKNOWLEDGMENTS

We are very grateful to Steffany Fredman and Carol Woods for their invaluable assistance in the construction of Tables 1 through 3.

Visit the Annual Reviews home page at www.AnnualReviews.org

LITERATURE CITED

Addis ME, Krasnow AD. 2000. A national survey of practicing psychologists' attitudes toward psychotherapy treatment manuals. *J. Consult. Clin. Psychol.* 68:331–39

Addis ME, Wade WA, Hatgis C. 1999. Barriers to dissemination of evidence-based practices: addressing practitioners' concerns about manual-based psychotherapies. *Clin. Psychol. Sci. Pract.* 4:430–41

Am. Psychiatr. Assoc. 1994. *Diagnostic and Statistical Manual of Mental Disorders.* Washington, DC: Am. Psychiatr. Assoc. 886 pp. 4th ed.

Am. Psychol. Assoc. 1996. *Guidelines and Principles for Accreditation of Programs in Professional Psychology.* Washington, DC: Am. Psychol. Assoc.

Barlow DH, Craske MG. 1994. *Mastery of Your Anxiety and Panic*, Vol. II. Albany, NY: Graywind. 150 pp.

Beutler LE. 1998. Identifying empirically supported treatments: What if we didn't? *J. Consult. Clin. Psychol.* 66:113–20

Beutler LE, Clarkin J, Bongar B. 2000. *Guidelines for the Systematic Treatment of the Depressed Patient.* Oxford, UK: Oxford Univ. Press. 455 pp.

Beutler LE, Engle D, Mohr D, Daldrup RJ, Bergan J, et al. 1991. Predictors of differential response to cognitive, experiential, and self-directed psychotherapeutic procedures. *J. Consult. Clin. Psychol.* 59:333–40

Beutler LE, Kim JE, Davison E, Karno M,

Fisher D. 1996. Research contributions to improving managed health care outcomes. *Psychotherapy* 33:197–206

Blatt SJ, Zuroff DC, Bondi CM, Sanisolow CA III. 2000. Short and long-term effects of medication and psychotherapy in the brief treatment of depression: further analyses of data from the NIMH TDCRP. *Psychother. Res.* 10:215–34

Bohart AD, O'Hara M, Leitner LM. 1998. Empirically violated treatments: disenfranchisement of humanistic and other psychotherapies. *Psychother. Res.* 8:141–57

Borkovec TD, Costello E. 1993. Efficacy of applied relaxation and cognitive behavioral therapy in the treatment of generalized anxiety disorder. *J. Consult. Clin. Psychol.* 61:611–19

Brent DA, Holder D, Kolko D, Birmaher B, Baugher M, et al. 1997. A clinical psychotherapy trial for adolescent depression comparing cognitive, family, and supportive therapy. *Arch. Gen. Psychiatry* 54:877–85

Can. Psychol. 1999. Symposium: empirically supported treatments in psychology. 40:289–327

Casey RJ, Berman JS. 1985. The outcome of psychotherapy with children. *Psychol. Bull.* 98:388–400

Castonguay LG, Goldfried MR, Wiser S, Raue PJ, Hayes AM. 1996. Predicting the effect of cognitive therapy for depression: a study of unique and common factors. *J. Consult. Clin. Psychol.* 64:497–504

Chambless DL, Baker M, Baucom DH, Beutler LE, Calhoun KS, et al. 1998. Update on empirically validated therapies, II. *Clin. Psychol.* 51(1):3–16

Chambless DL, Hollon SD. 1998. Defining empirically supported therapies. *J. Consult. Clin. Psychol.* 66:7–18

Chambless DL, Sanderson WC, Shoham V, Bennett Johnson S, Pope KS, et al. 1996. An update on empirically validated therapies. *Clin. Psychol.* 49(2):5–18

Crits-Christoph P, Frank E, Chambless DL, Brody C, Karp JF. 1995. Training in empirically-validated treatments: What are clinical psychology students learning? *Prof. Psychol. Res. Pract.* 26:514–22

Elkin I, Gibbons RD, Shea MT, Sotsky SM, Watkins JT, Pilkonis PA. 1995. Initial severity and differential treatment outcome in the National Institute of Mental Health Treatment of Depression Collaborative Research Program. *J. Consult. Clin. Psychol.* 63:841–47

Elkin I, Shea T, Watkins JT, Imber SD, Sotsky SM, et al. 1989. National Institute of Mental Health Treatment of Depression Collaborative Research Program: general effectiveness of treatments. *Arch. Gen. Psychiatry* 46:971–82

Elliott RE. 1998a. Editor's introduction: a guide to the empirically supported treatments controversy. *Psychother. Res.* 8:115–25

Elliott RE, ed. 1998b. The empirically supported treatments controversy. *Psychother. Res.* 8:115–70 (special issue)

Emmelkamp PMG, Bouman T, Blaauw E. 1994. Individualized versus standardized therapy: a comparative evaluation with obsessive-compulsive patients. *Clin. Psychol. Psychother.* 1:95–100

Fals-Stewart W, Marks AP, Schafer J. 1993. A comparison of behavioral group therapy and individual behavior therapy in treating obsessive-compulsive disorder. *J. Nerv. Ment. Dis.* 181:189–93

Fonagy P. 1999. Achieving evidence-based psychotherapy practice: a psychodynamic perspective on the general acceptance of treatment manuals. *Clin. Psychol. Sci. Pract.* 6:442–44

Fonagy P, Target M. 1996. Should we allow psychotherapy research to determine clinical practice? *Clin. Psychol. Sci. Pract.* 3:245–50

Frank E, Kupfer DJ, Wagner EF, McEachran AB, Cornes C. 1991. Efficacy of interpersonal psychotherapy as a maintenance treatment of recurrent depression: contributing factors. *Arch. Gen. Psychiatry* 48:1053–59

Garfield SL. 1996. Some problems with "validated" forms of psychotherapy. *Clin. Psychol. Sci. Pract.* 3:218–29

Gatz M, Fiske A, Fox LS, Kaskie B, Kasl-Godley JE, et al. 1998. Empirically validated psychological treatments for older adults. *J. Ment. Health Aging* 41:9–46

Gladis MM, Gosch EA, Dishuk NM, Crits-Christoph P. 1999. Quality of life: expanding the scope of clinical significance. *J. Consult. Clin. Psychol.* 67:320–31

Henry WP. 1998. Science, politics, and the politics of science: the use and misuse of empirically validated treatments. *Psychother. Res.* 8:126–40

Hoagwood K, Hibbs E, Brent D, Jensen P. 1995. Introduction to the special section: efficacy and effectiveness in studies of child and adolescent psychotherapy. *J. Consult. Clin. Psychol.* 63:683–87

Hodgson R, Rachman S, Marks IM. 1972. The treatment of chronic obsessive-compulsive neurosis: follow-up and further findings. *Behav. Res. Ther.* 10:181–89

Horvarth AO, Symonds DB. 1991. Relationship between working alliance and outcome in psychotherapy: a meta-analysis. *J. Couns. Psychol.* 38:139–49

Howard KI, Lueger RJ, Maling MS, Martinovich Z. 1993. A phase model of psychotherapy outcome: causal mediation of change. *J. Consult. Clin. Psychol.* 61:678–85

Hunsley J, Dobson KS, Johnston C, Mikail SF. 1999. Empirically supported treatments in psychology: implications for Canadian professional psychology. *Can. Psychol.* 40:289–302

Jacobson NS, Dobson KS, Truax PA, Addis ME, Koerner K, et al. 1996. A component analysis of cognitive-behavioral treatment for depression. *J. Consult. Clin. Psychol.* 64:295–304

Jacobson NS, Schmaling KB, Holtzworth-Munroe A, Katt JL, Wood LF, et al. 1989. Research-structured vs. clinically flexible versions of social learning-based marital therapy. *Behav. Res. Ther.* 27:173–80

J. Clin. Child Psychol. 1998. Special issue: empirically supported psychosocial interventions for children. 27:138–226

Kazdin AE, ed. 1996. Validated treatments: multiple perspectives and issues. *Clin. Psychol. Sci. Pract.* 3:216–67 (special issue)

Kendall PC, Chambless DL, eds. 1998. Empirically supported psychological therapies. *J. Consult. Clin. Psychol.* 66:3–167 (special issue)

Kendall PC, Chu B, Gifford A, Hayes C, Nauta M. 1998. Breathing life into a manual: flexibility and creativity with manual-based treatments. *Cogn. Behav. Pract.* 5:177–98

Kovacs AL. 1996. Winter: "We have met the enemy and he is us!" *AAP Adv.*, pp. 6, 19, 20, 22

Krupnick JL, Sotsky SM, Simmens S, Moyer I, Elkin I, et al. 1996. The role of the therapeutic alliance in psychotherapy and pharmacotherapy outcome: findings in the NIMH Treatment of Depression Collaborative Research Program. *J. Consult. Clin. Psychol.* 64:532–39

Lambert MJ. 1998. Manual-based treatment and clinical practice: hangman of life or promising development? *Clin. Psychol. Sci. Pract.* 5:391–95

Lindsay M, Crino R, Andrews G. 1997. Controlled trial of exposure and response prevention in obsessive-compulsive disorder. *Br. J. Psychiatry* 171:135–39

Marks IM, Hodgson R, Rachman S. 1975. Treatment of chronic obsessive-compulsive neurosis by in-vivo exposure: a two-year follow-up and issues in treatment. *Br. J. Psychiatry* 127:349–64

Moras K. 1993. The use of treatment manuals to train psychotherapists: observations and recommendations. *Psychotherapy* 30:581–86

Moras K. 1998. Internal and external validity of intervention studies. In *Comprehensive Clinical Psychology*, ed. AS Bellack, M Hersen, 3:201–24. Oxford, UK: Elsevier. 380 pp.

Nathan PE, Gorman JM, eds. 1998. *A Guide to Treatments That Work*. New York: Oxford Univ. Press. 594 pp.

Ollendick TH. 1995. Cognitive-behavioral treatment of panic disorder with agoraphobia in adolescents: a multiple baseline design analysis. *Behav. Ther.* 26:517–31

Ollendick TH, King NJ. 1998. Empirically supported treatments for children with phobic and anxiety disorders: current status. *J. Clin. Child Psychol.* 27:156–67

Ollendick TH, King NJ. 2000. Empirically supported treatments for children and adolescents. In *Child and Adolescent Therapy*, ed. PC Kendall, pp. 386–425. New York: Guilford. 436 pp. 2nd ed.

Organista KC, Munoz RF, Gonzalez G. 1994. Cognitive-behavioral therapy for depression in low-income and minority medial outpatients: description of a program and exploratory analyses. *Cogn. Ther. Res.* 18:241–59

Parry G. 1996. *NHS Psychotherapy Services in England, Rep. 96PP0043.* London: Dep. Health. 112 pp.

Persons JB, Bostrom A, Bertagnolli A. 1999. Results of randomized controlled trials of cognitive therapy for depression generalize to private practice. *Cogn. Ther. Res.* 23:535–48

Persons JB, Burns DB, Perloff JM. 1988. Predictors of dropout and outcome in cognitive therapy for depression in a private practice setting. *Cogn. Ther. Res.* 12:557–75

Peterson AL, Halstead TS. 1998. Group cognitive behavior therapy for depression in a community setting: a clinical replication series. *Behav. Ther.* 29:3–18

Roth AD, Fonagy P. 1996. *What Works for Whom? A Critical Review of Psychotherapy Research.* New York: Guilford. 484 pp.

Sackett DL, Richardson WS, Rosenberg W, Haynes RB. 1997. *Evidence-Based Medicine.* New York: Churchill Livingstone. 250 pp.

Sanderson WC, Raue PJ, Wetzler S. 1998. The generalizability of cognitive behavior therapy for panic disorder. *J. Cogn. Psychother.* 12:323–30

Sanderson WC, Woody SR. 1995. Manuals for empirically validated treatments: a project

of the Task Force on Psychological Interventions. *Clin. Psychol.* 48(4):7–11

Schulte D, Kunzel R, Pepping G, Schulte-Bahrenberg T. 1992. Tailor-made versus standardized therapy of phobic patients. *Adv. Behav. Res. Ther.* 14:67–92

Scotti JR, Morris TL, McNeil CB, Hawkins RP. 1996. DSM-IV and disorders of childhood and adolescents: Can structural criteria be functional? *J. Consult. Clin. Psychol.* 64:1177–91

Seligman MEP. 1995. The effectiveness of psychotherapy: the Consumer Reports study. *Am. Psychol.* 50:965–74

Shapiro DA, Shapiro D. 1982. Meta-analysis of comparative therapy outcome studies: a replication and refinement. *Psychol. Bull.* 92:581–604

Shaw BF, Elkin I, Yamaguchi J, Olmsted M, Vallis TM, et al. 1999. Therapist competence ratings in relation to clinical outcome in cognitive therapy of depression. *J. Consult. Clin. Psychol.* 67:837–46

Silverman WH. 1996. Cookbooks, manuals, and paint-by-numbers: psychotherapy in the 90's. *Psychotherapy* 33:207–15

Smith EWL. 1995. A passionate, rational response to the "manualization" of psychotherapy. *Psychother. Bull.* 30:36–40

Spirito A, ed. 1999. Empirically supported treatments in pediatric psychology. *J. Pediatr. Psychol.* 24:87–174 (special issue)

Stark K, Rouse L, Livingston R. 1991. Treatment of depression during childhood and adolescence: cognitive-behavioral procedures for the individual and family. In *Child and Adolescent Therapy*, ed. PC Kendall, pp. 165–206. New York: Guilford. 436 pp.

Strauss BM, Kaechele H. 1998. The writing on the wall: comments on the current discussion about empirically validated treatments in Germany. *Psychother. Res.* 8:158–77

Task Force Promot. Dissem. Psychol. Procedures. 1995. Training in and dissemination of empirically-validated psychological treatments: report and recommendations. *Clin. Psychol.* 48(1):3–23

Taylor TK, Schmidt F, Pepler D, Hodgins C. 1998. A comparison of eclectic treatment with Webster-Stratton's parents and children series in a children's mental health setting: a randomized controlled trial. *Behav. Ther.* 29:221–40

Telch MJ, Schmidt NB, Jaimez L, Jacquin KM, Harrington PJ. 1995. Impact of cognitive-behavioral treatment on quality of life in panic disorder patients. *J. Consult. Clin. Psychol.* 63:823–30

Thompson LW, Gallagher E, Steinmetz Breckenridge J. 1987. Comparative effectiveness of psychotherapies for depressed elders. *J. Consult. Clin. Psychol.* 55:385–90

Tynan WD, Schuman W, Lampert N. 1999. Concurrent parent and child therapy groups for externalizing disorders: from the laboratory to the world of managed care. *Cogn. Behav. Pract.* 6:3–9

Wade WA, Treat TA, Stuart GL. 1998. Transporting an empirically supported treatment for panic disorder to a service clinic setting: a benchmarking strategy. *J. Consult. Clin. Psychol.* 66:231–39

Wampold BE, Mondin GW, Moody M, Stich F, Benson K, et al. 1997. A meta-analysis of outcome studies comparing bona fide psychotherapies: empirically, "All must have prizes." *Psychol. Bull.* 122:203–15

Weisz JR, Weiss B, Han SS, Granger DA, Morton T. 1995. Effects of psychotherapy with children and adolescents revisited: a meta-analysis of treatment outcome studies. *Psychol. Bull.* 117:450–68

Wilson GT. 1998. Manual-based treatment and clinical practice. *Clin. Psychol. Sci. Pract.* 5:363–75

Wilson JJ, Gil KM. 1996. The efficacy of psychological and pharmacological interventions for the treatment of chronic disease-related and non-disease-related pain. *Clin. Psychol. Rev.* 16:573–97

Woody SR, Sanderson WC. 1998. Manuals for empirically supported treatments: 1998 update. *Clin. Psychol.* 51(1):17–21

AUTHOR INDEX

Subject Index

longitudinal analysis and,
501, 505
Latent inhibition
associative learning in
animals and, 114–17
Lateral transmission
evolutionary psychology
and, 615
Latinos
adolescent development
and, 92
Learning
associative learning in
animals and, 111–32
longitudinal analysis and,
501, 507–10
performance and attention,
629–48
psycholinguistics and,
369–90
reasoning and, 223, 228
science of training and,
482–84
skill acquisition and, 453,
461–62
statistical graphics and, 315
Lentiviruses
health psychology and, 567
Level-1/level-2 models
longitudinal analysis and,
510–14
Lexical heads
sentence and text
comprehension, 177
Lexical structure
sentence and text
comprehension, 167,
173–77
Life-course persistent
problems
adolescent development
and, 86–87
Life pursuits
agentic perspective on
social cognitive theory
and, 1–23
Lifespan perspectives

hedonic and eudaimonic
well-being, 157–58
Lifestyle Heart Trial
health psychology and, 560
Light-dark cycle
environmental
sleep-wake rhythm and,
277–98
"Lighting up"
skill acquisition and, 463
Linguistics
evolutionary psychology
and, 620
psycholinguistics and,
369–90
sentence and text
comprehension, 167–90
Linguistic xenophobia
psycholinguistics and, 375
Link function
longitudinal analysis and,
510–12
Linking
disrespect and injustice,
527, 532–35
statistical graphics and,
305, 318, 321, 323
LISP programming language
skill acquisition and, 456
Listeners
sentence and text
comprehension, 167
Lister, Martin
weather data depiction by
statistical graphics and,
308
Literature reviews
quantitative methods for
meta-analysis and, 59–80
Local coherence
sentence and text
comprehension, 182–85,
188
Lock-up
performance and attention,
633
Logical Form

sentence and text
comprehension, 180
Logical mental models
thinking and, 229
Logit-linear structural model
longitudinal analysis and,
510
Log-link
longitudinal analysis and,
510–12
Long-term memory
sentence and text
comprehension, 167,
185–86
thinking and, 229
Longitudinal analysis
alternative probabilistic
models, 514
between-subject causes,
516–20
causal effects in
cross-sectional studies,
514–15
causal inference, 514–20
conclusions, 522–23
defining trajectory for
person i, 504–5
describing and comparing
growth and change
curves, 504–5
describing population
distribution of personal
trajectories, 505
framework for analytic
choices, 506–7
introduction, 501–2
level-1 models, 510–12
level-2 models, 512–14
models for time as
outcome, 502–3
more than two time points,
520
multinomial prior
assumption, 513–14
nonrandomized studies,
516–17
normal data and normal

statistical graphics and, 316
Multiply self-embedded
sentences
sentence and text
comprehension, 172–73
Multivariate analysis
longitudinal analysis and,
513–14
statistical graphics and,
305, 316–17, 319, 325,
328–29, 331–32
Mutability
thinking and, 239
Mutual immobilization
agentic perspective on
social cognitive theory
and, 17
Myocardial infarction
health psychology and,
557–60
Mythic culture
evolutionary psychology
and, 612, 620

N
Naive theories
thinking and, 230, 233–35
Napping
sleep-wake rhythm and,
285–86
Narrative methods
meta-analysis and, 62
National life
exercising control over
agentic perspective on
social cognitive theory
and, 1–23
Native Americans
adolescent development
and, 92, 96
"Natural experiments"
longitudinal analysis and,
516
Natural selection
evolutionary psychology
and, 607, 612, 615–16,
619, 622

Nature-nurture dualism
evolutionary psychology
and, 618
Nazis
agentic perspective on
social cognitive theory
and, 20
Needs analysis
science of training and,
471, 475–77
Negativity
adolescent development
and, 89, 91
hedonic and eudaimonic
well-being, 149, 156
job burnout and, 404
Negativity bias
attitudes and, 35
Neighborhood
adolescent development
and, 98
Nested settings
adolescent development
and, 98
The Netherlands
job burnout and, 408, 412,
417
Neural substrates
judgement and decision
making, 671–73
skill acquisition and,
458–59
visual attention in infancy
and, 343–45, 349–51,
352–53
Neurasthenia
job burnout and, 404
Neurogenesis
olfaction and, 423
Neurophysiological systems
agentic perspective on
social cognitive theory
and, 22
Neuroticism
hedonic and eudaimonic
well-being, 149, 156
job burnout and, 411

Neurotransmitters
personality and, 206
New Zealand
personality and, 214
psycholinguistics and,
376
19-step model
decision technology and,
581, 586–88
Noncompensatory decision
systems
decision technology and,
597–98
"Nonignorable" missingness
longitudinal analysis and,
517
Nonindependence of effects
meta-analysis and, 67
Nonrandomized trials
health psychology and, 566
longitudinal analysis and,
516–17
Nonreliance
hedonic and eudaimonic
well-being, 160
Normally-unpreferred
analysis
sentence and text
comprehension, 175
Normative disturbance
adolescent development
and, 85
Normative theories
attitudes and, 44–45
decision technology and,
582–86, 589–92
North America
adolescent development
and, 95
job burnout and, 411–12
Norway
job burnout and, 412
Noun phrases
sentence and text
comprehension, 170–78,
181
Nouns

science of training and, 471, 488, 490

Transfer specificity
skill acquisition and, 453, 456–57

Transients
performance and attention, 629–48

Transmission
evolutionary psychology and, 620

Transnational embeddedness/ interdependence
agentic perspective on social cognitive theory and, 1, 16–17

Treatment specificity
empirically-supported therapies and, 704–6

Truancy
adolescent development and, 90

Trying
hedonic and eudaimonic well being, 156–57

t-test
meta-analysis and, 65

Tukey's graphics
statistical graphics and, 314

"Tuning in"
psycholinguistics and, 375

Turkish language
psycholinguistics and, 378, 384

25-hour sleep-wake rhythm
sleep-wake rhythm and, 277, 281–82

Two-stage modeling framework
longitudinal analysis and, 501, 513–14

Two time points
longitudinal analysis and, 518–20

Typeshifting

sentence and text comprehension, 180

U

Ultrashort sleep-wake cycles
sleep-wake rhythm and, 291–93

Uncertainty
judgement and decision making, 653, 669–71

Uncontrollability
agentic perspective on social cognitive theory and, 12

Unheralded pronouns
sentence and text comprehension, 186

Unifying theory
evolutionary psychology and, 607–22

United Kingdom
empirically-supported therapies and, 685–712
performance and attention, 630

United States
agentic perspective on social cognitive theory and, 21
attitudes and, 34
empirically-supported therapies and, 685–712
hedonic and eudaimonic well-being, 153, 160
job burnout and, 408, 411
longitudinal analysis and, 512
psycholinguistics and, 376
thinking and, 241

Universality
hedonic and eudaimonic well-being, 159–60
psycholinguistics and, 369–90

User profiles
decision technology and, 596

Utbränd
job burnout and, 412

Utbranthet
job burnout and, 412

Utility
decision technology and, 581
judgement and decision making, 653, 667–69

Uxoricide
personality and, 209

V

Valences
attitudes and, 32–33, 42

Validation
consumer research and, 265
empirically-supported therapies and, 685

Values
attitudes and, 27, 42
decision technology and, 581, 585–86
disrespect and injustice, 535–36
hedonic and eudaimonic well-being, 159
job burnout and, 415–16
judgement and decision making, 653, 667–69

Variability
meta-analysis and, 69

Vatican guards
agentic perspective on social cognitive theory and, 21

Vertical transfer
science of training and, 489

Vertical transmission
evolutionary psychology and, 615

Victimization
peer
adolescent development

Cumulative Indexes

CONTRIBUTING AUTHORS, VOLUMES 42–52

CHAPTER TITLES, VOLUMES 42–52

793

Clinical and Counseling Psychology: Specialized Modes of Therapy

Cognitive Processes

Consumer Behavior

Counseling (See also Education and Counseling; Clinical and Counseling Psychology)

Developmental Psychology

Personnel-Organizational Psychology

Personnel Development and Training

Personnel Psychology

Psycholinguistics

See Cognitive Processes

Psychopharmacology
See Biological Psychology

Research Methodology

Data Analysis

Design and Analysis Research Natural Settings